economics

sixth edition

economics
sixth edition

david begg
**Professor of Economics
Birkbeck College
University of London**

stanley fischer
**First Deputy Director
International Monetary Fund**

rudiger dornbusch
**Ford Professor of Economics and Internaional Managment
Massachusetts Institute of Technology**

THE McGRAW-HILL COMPANIES

London · Burr Ridge IL · New York · St Louis · San Francisco

Auckland · Bogotá · Caracas · Lisbon · Madrid · Mexico

Milan · Montreal · New Delhi · Panama · Paris · San Juan

São Paulo · Singapore · Sydney · Tokyo · Toronto

for
Honora, Mary, and Robin

Published by
McGraw-Hill Publishing Company
Shoppenhangers Road, Maidenhead, Berkshire, SL6 2QL, England
Telephone +44 (0)1628 502569
Facsimile +44 (0)1628 770224

British Library Cataloguing in Publication Data
A catalogue record for this book is available from the British Library

ISBN 0 07 709615 0

Created for McGraw-Hill by the independent production company
Steven Gardiner Ltd TEL +44 (0)1223 364868 FAX +44 (0)1223 364875

McGraw-Hill

A Division of The **McGraw·Hill** *Companies*

We wish to thank the following organizations for permission to publish tables and figures
in the text: in each case the source is given.
American Economic Association; Bank of England; Blackwell Publishers; Cambridge University Press; Centre for Economic Research; EBRD; Economic Journal; Financial Times; Harvard University Press; HM Treasury; HMSO; IMF; Institute of Economics Budapest; Institute of Economics and Statistics; International Trade Centre; OECD; Office for National Statistics; Oxford University Press; Times Newspapers Limited; The Economist; The United Nations; University of Munich.

1 2 3 4 5 VB 4 3 2 1 0

Printed and bound in Italy by Vincenzo Bona, Turin

Contents

Suggested outlines for a shortened course

First option   A short introduction to economics

1 Economics and the economy
2 The tools of economic analysis
3 Demand, supply, and the market
4 Government in the mixed economy
5 The effect of price and income on demand quantities
7 Business organization and behaviour
8 Developing the theory of supply: costs and production
9 Perfect competition and pure monopoly: the limiting cases of market structure
10 Market structure and imperfect competition
12 The analysis of factor markets: labour
14 Capital and land: completing the analysis of factor markets
16 Introduction to welfare economics
20 Introduction to macroeconomics and national income accounting
21 The determination of national income
22 Aggregate demand, fiscal policy, and foreign trade
23 Money and modern banking
24 Central banking and the monetary system
25 Monetary and fiscal policy in a closed economy
32 Macroeconomics: where do we stand?
33 International trade and commercial policy

Second option An introduction to microeconomics

1 Economics and the economy
2 The tools of economic analysis
3 Demand, supply, and the market
4 Government in the mixed economy
5 The effect of price and income on demand quantities
6 The theory of consumer choice
7 Business organization and behaviour
8 Developing the theory of supply: costs and production
9 Perfect competition and pure monopoly: the limiting cases of market structure
10 Market structure and imperfect competition
12 The analysis of factor markets: labour
14 Capital and land: completing the analysis of factor markets
16 Introduction to welfare economics
17 Taxes and government spending

Third option   An introduction to macroeconomics

Getting the most out
of this book

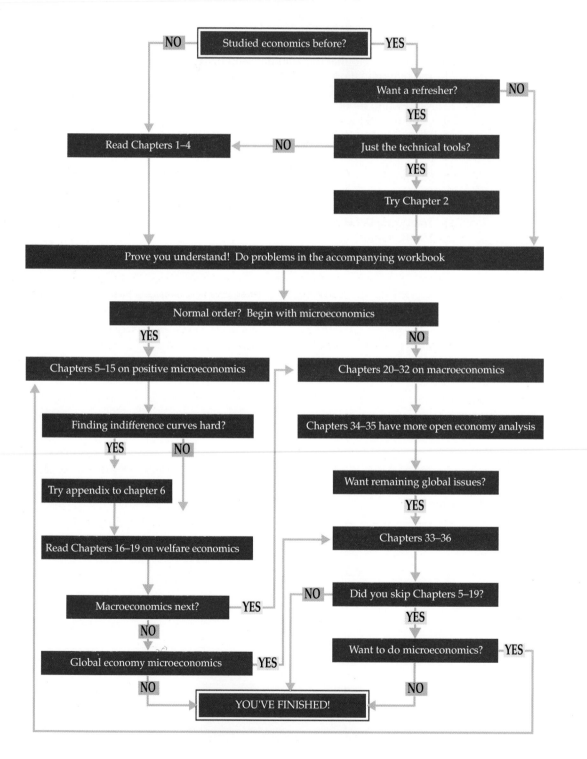

Preface

Economics is much too interesting to be left to professional economists. It affects almost everything we do, not merely at work or at the shops but also in the home and the voting booth. It influences how well we look after our planet, the future we leave for our children, the extent to which we can care for the poor and the disadvantaged, and the resources we have for enjoying ourselves.

These issues are discussed daily, in bars and buses, as well as in cabinet meetings and boardrooms. The formal study of economics is exciting because it introduces a toolkit that allows a better understanding of the problems we face. Everyone knows a smoky engine is a bad sign, but sometimes only a trained mechanic can give the right advice on how to fix it.

This book is designed to teach you the toolkit and give you practice in using it. Nobody carries an enormous toolbox very far. Useful toolkits are small enough to be portable but contain enough proven tools to deal both with routine problems and unforeseen circumstances. With practice, you will be surprised at how much light this analysis can shed on daily living. This book is designed to make economics seem as useful as it really is.

How much do economists disagree?

There is an old complaint that economists never agree about anything. This is simply wrong. The media, taxi drivers, and politicians love to talk about topics on which there is disagreement; it would be boring TV if all participants in a panel discussion held identical views. But economics is not a subject in which there is always an argument for everything. There *are* answers to many questions. We aim to show where economists agree – on what and for what reason – and why they sometimes disagree.

Economics for the new millennium

Our aim is to allow students to understand today's economic environment. This requires mastering the theory and practising its application. Just as the theory of genetics or information technology is steadily progressing, so the theory of economics continues to make progress, sometimes in dramatic and exciting ways.

We believe in introducing students immediately to the latest ideas in economics. If these can be conveyed simply, why force students to use older approaches that work less well? Two recent developments in economics underlie much of what we do. One is the role of information, the other is globalization.

How information is transmitted and manipulated is central to many issues in incentives and competition, including the recent boom in e-commerce. Ease of information, coupled with lower transport costs, also explains trends towards globalization, and associated reductions in national sovereignty, especially in smaller countries. Modern economics helps us make sense of our changing world, think about where it may go next, and evaluate choices that we currently face. We back up this claim with a whole new chapter showing that the information economy in general, and the internet in particular, are merely following standard economic principles.

Learning by doing

Few people practise for a driving test just by reading a book. Even when you think you understand how to do a hill start, it takes a lot of practice to master the finer points. We give you lots of examples and real-world applications not just to emphasize the relevance of economics but also to help you master it for yourself. We start at square one and take you slowly through the tools of theoretical reasoning and how to apply them. We do not use algebra and there are very few equations in the book. The best ideas are simple and robust, and can usually be explained quite easily.

How to study

Don't just read about economics, try to do it! It is easy, but mistaken, to read on cruise control, highlighting the odd sentence and gliding through paragraphs we have worked hard to simplify. Active learning needs to be interactive. When the text says 'clearly', ask yourself 'why' is it clear? See if you can construct the diagram before you look at it. As soon as you don't follow something, go back and read it again. Try to think of *other* examples to which the theory could be applied. The only way to check you are really understanding things is to try problems and see if you got the right answer. The best way to do this is to use the *Workbook*.

Workbook

The main text is accompanied by a sixth edition of the *Workbook* written by Peter Smith. This takes you step by step through the analysis of each chapter, and provides many questions, exercises and solutions that enable you to master the material of each chapter.

For lecturers and teachers

Freely available to lecturers and teachers who adopt the main text as their course textbook, the online *Instructor's Manual*, written by David Begg, discusses key ideas in each chapter and how to put them across. It also provides answers to questions at the end of each chapter of the main text. The *Computer Test Bank*, available on floppy disk, provides multiple choice questions (and answers) which can be used for class teaching, individual study, or setting of exams.

Changes and additions to the sixth edition

We are always trying to improve the quality of this text and the supplements that accompany it. In this edition we have worked hard to improve the online support for the text as well as the range of materials available to lecturers and students. Please visit our online learning centre at www.begg6.com to gain access to a continuously up-dated range of supporting materials.

As always, recent events are reflected in the pages of this book. Here is a brief summary of the **key content additions** for this edition:

- The information economy (a new chapter on the economics of e-commerce)
- Analysing the New Deal
- The Private Finance Initiative
- Reassessing UK Competition policy
- The Monetary Policy Committee
- The Code for Fiscal Stability
- The economics of EMU
- Speculative attacks on exchange rates

David Begg
Stanley Fischer
Rudiger Dornbusch

Acknowledgements to sixth edition

We thank the team at McGraw Hill for their support, advice, and enthusiasm, and the many readers of previous editions who have taken the trouble to write with suggestions for improvements and ideas for the new edition.

David Begg

Test quiz

Before you even look at this book, try the quiz below. Tick the answers you think are correct. When you have worked through the book, try the quiz again and compare your answers.

1 Economics is the study of:
   (a) how to produce the most goods for the most people;
   (b) how society decides what, how, and for whom to produce;
   (c) how to avoid waste and inefficiency.

2 (a) By encouraging customers, lower food prices raise revenues of farmers.
   (b) By discouraging customers, higher oil prices reduce revenues to oil producers.
   (c) Neither of the above.

3 (a) Higher income tax rates are a disincentive to work.
   (b) Higher income tax rates are an incentive to work.
   (c) Income tax rates have only a small effect on the incentive to work.

4 Public goods are:
   (a) those provided by the public sector;
   (b) those government believes people should consume;
   (c) those which everyone must consume in the same quantity.

5 An increase in the proportion of income saved:
   (a) tends to increase output since investment rises;
   (b) tends to reduce output since consumer spending falls;
   (c) tends to increase inflation since the money supply rises.

6 (a) Inflation makes people worse off because goods become more expensive.
   (b) Inflation makes a country uncompetitive in international markets.
   (c) A high but constant rate of inflation need not be a major problem.

7 An exchange rate devaluation improves a country's international competitiveness:
   (a) only after a few years;
   (b) only for a few years;
   (c) only if interest rates are simultaneously reduced.

8 It is well known that economists cannot forecast changes in stock market prices. This shows:
   (a) that economics works;
   (b) that economics pays insufficient attention to real world problems;
   (c) neither of the above.

Guided tour

Part Openings set the scene for each general topic of study, giving you an introductory overview of the subjects to be covered and a brief chapter listing.

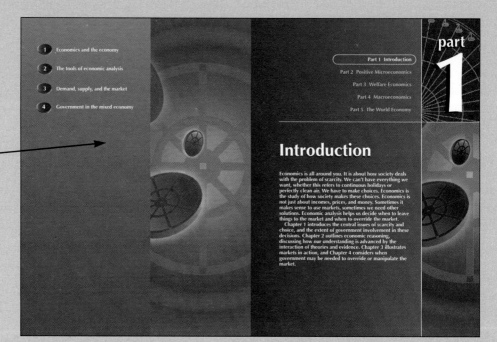

Learning Outcomes: bullet-points identify the primary topics in terms of the learning outcomes you should acquire after studying each chapter.

Definitions: key terms are highlighted in the text so that you have a handy on-page reference for new concepts as they appear in the text. These are particularly useful for revision.

URLs (Internet addresses) point you towards useful Internet sights. If you want more useful Internet addresses to help you study economics, go to www.begg6.com and have a look at the links sections.

Graphs and tables: simple design and clear use of colour throughout tables and graphs helps you understand key economic data and concepts

Boxes provide additional illustrative examples to highlight the practical application of concepts, and to encourage you to analyse and discuss current issues.

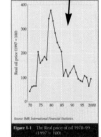

Review Questions: these questions encourage you to review and apply your knowledge. The review questions can be used either individually or as a focus for group discussion.

Chapter Summary: this section briefly reviews and reinforces the main topics you will have covered in each chapter.

Key Terms: all key terms that have been defined throughout the text are grouped together here so that you can easily review your understanding of new concepts at the end of each chapter.

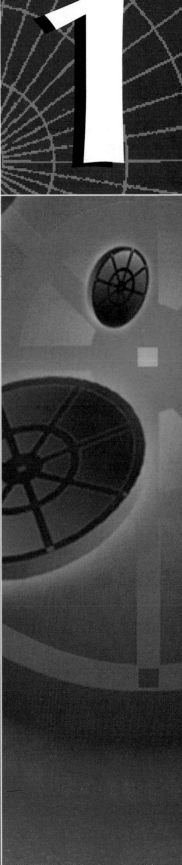

part

1

Introduction

Economics is all around you. It is about how society deals with the problem of scarcity. We can't have everything we want, whether this refers to continuous holidays or perfectly clean air. We have to make choices. Economics is the study of how society makes these choices. Economics is not just about incomes, prices, and money. Sometimes it makes sense to use markets, sometimes we need other solutions. Economic analysis helps us decide when to leave things to the market and when to override the market.

Chapter 1 introduces the central issues of scarcity and choice, and the extent of government involvement in these decisions. Chapter 2 outlines economic reasoning, discussing how our understanding is advanced by the interaction of theories and evidence. Chapter 3 illustrates markets in action, and Chapter 4 considers when government may be needed to override or manipulate the market.

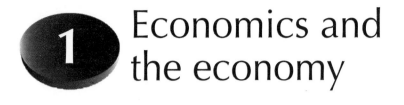

1 Economics and the economy

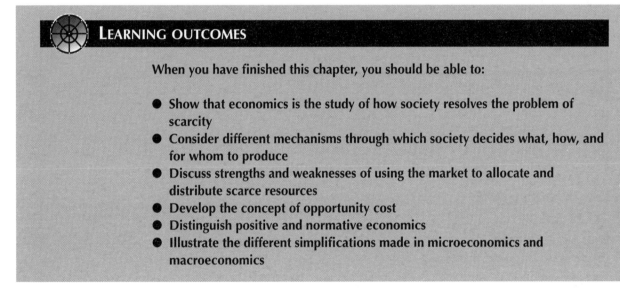

LEARNING OUTCOMES

When you have finished this chapter, you should be able to:

- Show that economics is the study of how society resolves the problem of scarcity
- Consider different mechanisms through which society decides what, how, and for whom to produce
- Discuss strengths and weaknesses of using the market to allocate and distribute scarce resources
- Develop the concept of opportunity cost
- Distinguish positive and normative economics
- Illustrate the different simplifications made in microeconomics and macroeconomics

Every group of people must solve three basic problems of daily living: *what* goods and services to produce, *how* to produce them, and *for whom* to produce them.

Economics is the study of how society decides what, how, and for whom to produce.

Goods are physical commodities such as steel and strawberries. Services are activities such as massages or live concerts, consumed or enjoyed only at the instant they are produced. In rare cases some of the questions about what, how, and for whom to produce have already been answered; until the arrival of Man Friday, Robinson Crusoe can ignore the 'for whom' question. In general, however, society must answer all three questions.

By emphasizing the role of society, our definition places economics within the social sciences, the sciences that study and explain human behaviour. The subject matter of economics is human behaviour in the production, exchange, and use of goods and services. The central economic problem for society is how to reconcile the conflict between people's virtually limitless desires for goods and services, and the scarcity of resources (labour, machinery, and raw materials) with which these goods and services can be produced. In answering the questions what, how, and for whom to produce, economics explains how scarce resources are allocated between competing claims on their use.

Economics is about human behaviour, yet we describe it as a science rather than a subject within the arts or humanities. This reflects the way economists analyse problems, not the subject matter of economics. Economists develop theories of human behaviour and test them against the facts. Chapter 2 discusses the tools economists use and explains the sense in which this approach is scientific. This does not mean that economics ignores people as individuals. Moreover, good economics retains an element of art, for it is only by having a feel for how people actually

BOX 1-1   Web sights

Industry dominated the nineteenth century, services the latter half of the twentieth century. Information will dominate the twenty-first century. The table shows the UK's top 10 websites in mid-1999.

Internet transactions are free or paid by credit card. The Bank of England is already wondering about the effect of its ability to control interest rates via its monopoly of cash supply; and the Treasury is examining how to stop VAT revenue being affected.

The information economy is so important – and such a nice illustration that the laws of economics are very robust – that we devote the whole of Chapter 11 to studying it. First, you need to learn what we mean by the laws of economics.

Million hits per month		
America on Line	(subscriber only)	141
CompuServe	(subscriber only)	102
Yahoo!	www.yahoo.co.uk	62
Excite	www.excite.co.uk	50
LineOne	www.lineone.net	50
CricInfo	www.cricket.org	48
Microsoft Network	www.msn.co.uk	40
BBC News	www.news.bbc.co.uk	39
Freeserve	www.freeserve.net	38
SoccerNet	www.soccernet.com	17

Source: London Evening Standard, 2 June 1999.

behave that economists can focus their analysis on the right issues.

1-1 Economic issues

Trying to understand what economics is about by studying definitions is like trying to learn to swim by reading an instruction manual. Formal analysis makes sense only once you have some practical experience. In this section we discuss two examples of how society allocates scarce resources between competing uses. In each case we see the importance of the questions what, how, and for whom to produce.

The oil price shocks

Oil provides fuel for heating, transport, and machinery, and is a basic input for petrochemicals and many household products ranging from plastic utensils to polyester clothing. From 1900 until 1973 the use of oil increased steadily. Economic activity was organized on the assumption of cheap and abundant oil.

In 1973–74 there was an abrupt change. The main oil-producing nations belong to OPEC – the Organization of Petroleum Exporting Countries (www.opec.org). OPEC decided in 1973 to raise the price for which their oil was sold. OPEC correctly anticipated that a substantial price increase would lead to only a small reduction in sales volume. It would be very profitable for OPEC members.

Figure 1-1 shows the real (or inflation-adjusted) price of oil from 1970–99. The price tripled in 1973–74 and doubled again in 1979–80. These dramatic movements are known as the *oil price shocks*. Figure 1-1 also shows that markets found ways to overcome the oil shortage that OPEC had created. High oil prices did not last indefinitely.

Much of this book teaches you that people respond to prices. When the price of some commodity increases, consumers try to use less but producers want to sell more. These responses, guided by prices, are part of the process by which many societies determine what, how, and for whom to produce.

Consider first *how* the economy produces goods and services. When the price of oil increases sixfold, every firm tries to reduce its use of oil-based products. Chemical firms develop artificial substitutes for petroleum inputs; airlines look for more fuel-efficient aircraft; electricity is produced from more coal-fired generators. Higher oil prices make the economy produce in a way that uses less oil.

How does the oil price increase affect *what* is being produced? Firms and households reduce use of oil products which are now more expensive. Households switch to gas-fired central heating and buy smaller cars. Commuters form car-pools or move closer to the city. High prices not only choke off the demand for oil-related commodities; they also encourage consumers to purchase substitute commodities. Higher demand for these commodities bids up their price and encourages their production. Designers produce smaller cars, architects use solar energy, and research laboratories develop alternatives to petroleum in chemical production.

The *for whom* question in this example has a clear answer. OPEC revenues from oil sales increased from $35 billion in 1973 to nearly $300 billion in 1980. Much of their increased revenue was spent on goods produced in the industrialized Western nations. In contrast, oil-importing nations had to give up more of their own production in exchange for oil imports. In terms of goods as a whole, the rise in oil prices raised the buying power of OPEC and reduced the buying power of oil-importing countries such as Germany and Japan. The world economy was producing more for OPEC and less for Germany and Japan.

In 1986 there was a sharp fall in world oil prices. Try working out for yourself what effect this should have had on what goods the world economy produces, how they are produced, and for whom they are produced.

The OPEC oil price shocks illustrate how society allocates scarce resources between competing uses.

A **scarce resource** is one for which the demand at a zero price would exceed the available supply.

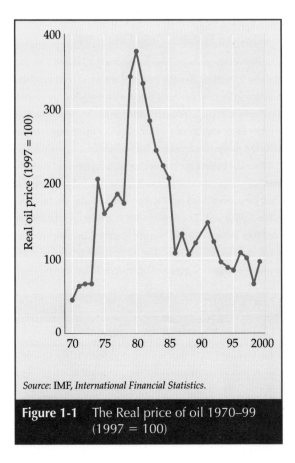

Source: IMF, International Financial Statistics.

Figure 1-1   The Real price of oil 1970–99 (1997 = 100)

We can think of oil as having become more scarce in economic terms when its price rose.

Income distribution

You and your family have an annual income which allows you to enjoy various goods and services and live in a particular place. Your standard of living will include what you think of as the necessities of life – food, shelter, health, education – but also something beyond, such as recreation. Your income will be less than some of your neighbours but more than that of some other people, both in this country and abroad.

Nations also have different levels of income. A nation's income, or national income, is the sum of the incomes of all its citizens. World income is the sum of all countries' incomes or the sum of the incomes earned by all the people in the world.

The **income distribution** (in a country or in the world) tells us how income is divided between different groups or individuals.

Income distribution is closely linked to the what, how, and for whom questions.

Table 1-1 reports the percentage of world population that lives in different groups of countries. 35 per cent of the world's population live in poor countries, the three largest of which are India, China, and Indonesia. 49 per cent live in middle-income countries, a group including Thailand, Brazil, Mexico, and Hungary. The rich countries, including the United States, Western Europe, Canada, and Japan, account for 16 per cent of world population.

Income per person provides an approximate indication of the standard of living within each group of countries. The first row of Table 1-1 shows income per person for each group. In poor countries the average income per person is only £213 *per year*, or just 58p *per day*. In the rich industrial countries income is £15 690 *per person per year*, over *seventy* times larger. These are striking differences.

Table 1-1   World population and income

	Poor countries	Middle-income countries	Rich countries
Income per head (£)	213	1154	15 690
% of world population	35	49	16
% of world income	2	18	80

Source: World Bank, World Development Report, 1998–99.

The last row in Table 1-1 makes the same point in a different way. More than a third of the world's population, living in the poor countries, receive only 2 per cent of total world income. The 16 per cent of world population living in the industrial countries, including the UK, receives 80 per cent of the world income. These income differences raise a number of questions both for society and for economists.

For whom does the world economy produce? Essentially, for the 16 per cent of its population living in the rich industrial countries. This answer about for whom the goods and services are produced also suggests the answer to *what* is produced. World production is directed chiefly to the goods and services consumed in the rich countries.

Why are there huge differences in incomes between groups? This relates to the question of *how* goods are produced. In poor countries there is little machinery, and few people have professional and technical training. In an industrialized country a worker may use power-driven earth-moving equipment to accomplish a task undertaken in a poor country by many more workers equipped only with shovels. Workers in poor countries are less productive because they work under less favourable conditions.

Income is unequally distributed within each country as well as between countries. In Brazil, the richest 20 per cent of families receive 64 per cent of Brazil's national income. In countries such as Denmark, the richest 20 per cent of families receive 35 per cent of national income. In the UK, the top 20 per cent of families receive 40 per cent of national income.

In part, these differences can be attributed to factors we have already discussed. The provision of state education reduces the disparity in training and education that workers receive compared with countries in which expensive education must be privately purchased. However, when examining the income distribution *within* a country we must take account of two additional factors, which can largely be neglected when discussing differences in income per person *between* countries.

First, individual incomes come not just from working but also from ownership of assets (land, buildings, corporate equity) which earn rent, interest payments, and dividends. In comparing national incomes (in total or per person) it does not matter which members of the population own these assets and earn this income; in assessing the distribution of incomes within a country, it does matter. In Brazil, ownership of land and factories is concentrated in the hands of a small group.

Second, societies can decide whether or not to take steps to change the distribution of income. A state-owned economy aims to produce a fair degree of equality of income and wealth. In an economy of private ownership, wealth and power may become concentrated in the hands of a few rich families. Between these extremes, the government may levy taxes to alter the income distribution that would otherwise have emerged in a private ownership economy. One reason why Denmark has a more equal income distribution than Brazil is that Denmark levies high taxes on high incomes to reduce the buying power of the rich, and levies high taxes on inheritances to reduce the concentration of wealth in the hands of a few families.

The degree to which income is unequally distributed within a country will directly affect the question of for whom goods and services are produced, but it will also affect what goods are produced. In Brazil, where income is unequally distributed, many people work as domestic servants, chauffeurs, and maids. In Holland, where income is much more evenly distributed, few people can afford to hire servants.

1-2　Scarcity and the competing use of resources

Consider an economy with four workers who can produce either food or films.

Table 1-2 shows how much of each good can be produced. The answer depends on how workers are allocated between the two industries. In each industry, the more workers there are, the greater is the total output of the good produced. Production in each industry satisfies the *law of diminishing returns*. Each additional worker adds less to industry output than the previous additional worker added.

What lies behind the law of diminishing returns? We have implicitly assumed that workers in the film industry have at their disposal a fixed total amount of cameras, studios, and other equipment. The first worker has sole use of all these facilities. When a second worker is added, the two workers must share these facilities. The addition of further workers reduces equipment per worker to even lower levels. Thus,

Table 1-2　Production possibilities

Food		Films	
Employment	Output	Employment	Output
4	25	0	0
3	22	1	9
2	17	2	17
1	10	3	24
0	0	4	30

BOX 1-2

Service with a smile: the changing composition of what is produced

Production is divided into three sectors: agriculture, services, and industry. Which sector accounts for the largest share of national output? Which sector's share has fallen most in the last 25 years?

The table below provides some answers that you may find surprising. First, agriculture is really quite a small part of national output. The TV news may show French farmers protesting about cuts in farm subsidies, but even French agriculture is only 2 per cent of national output. The table shows this is typical of other industrial countries. Second, industrial output is usually around 30 per cent of national output; in some countries it is even less. Third, services are over two-thirds of national output in the advanced countries. Fourth, it is in services that the big growth has come in the last 25 years.

What exactly are these services? The most important are financial services (banking and insurance), transport (road, sea and air), communications (mail, phone,

satellite), tourism, and leisure and entertainment. There is a popular myth that countries need agriculture and industry because they can never export services in sufficient quantities to pay for all the imports they want. Yet exports of services are frequently the fastest growing component of total exports. Cool Britannia's success in exporting fashion, film and pop music helped make the UK the second largest exporter of services in the world in 1998.

% of national output		Japan	France	UK
1965	Agriculture	10	8	3
	Industry	44	39	46
	Services	46	53	51
1997	Agriculture	2	2	2
	Industry	38	27	30
	Services	60	71	68

Source: World Bank, *World Development Report*, 1998/99.

output per worker in the film industry falls as employment in the film industry rises. A similar story applies in the food industry. Both industries exhibit diminishing returns as additional workers are added.

Table 1-2 shows the combinations of food and films produced if all workers are employed. By transferring workers from one industry to the other, the economy can produce more of one good, but only at the expense of producing less of the other good. There is a *trade-off* between food production and film production.

Figure 1-2 illustrates the maximum combinations of food and film output that the economy can produce. The point *A* corresponds to the first row in Table 1-2, where food output is 25 units and film output is zero. The points *B, C, D,* and *E* correspond to the other rows of Table 1-2. The curve joining points *A* to *E* in Figure 1-2 is the 'production possibility frontier'.

The **production possibility frontier** shows, for each level of the output of one good, the maximum amount of the other good that can be produced.

Notice the way the frontier curves around the point given by zero production of both goods. This is because of the law

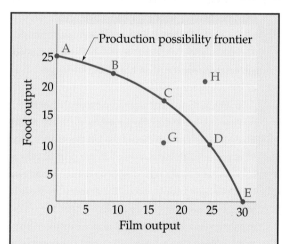

The frontier shows the maximum combinations of output that the economy can produce using all available resources. The frontier displays a trade-off; more of one commodity implies less of the other. Points above the frontier need more inputs than the economy has available. Points inside the frontier are inefficient. By fully using available inputs the economy could expand output to the frontier.

Figure 1-2   The production possibility frontier

BOX 1-3   Developing a healthy scepticism

Many people rely on newspapers and TV to do their thinking for them. We hope in this book to give you the tools to think for yourself. Here is a typical example.

A TV presenter is interviewing two politicians about health services. The opposition politician is angry about cuts in government support for hospitals: fewer beds, fewer nurses, longer waiting lists. The government minister is patiently explaining that the government is spending more than ever before on health.

Your first instinct is probably that one of the politicians must be lying. Perhaps you automatically believe the politician from the party you normally support. Alternatively, you could try to think for yourself about the arguments. What are they saying? What evidence would be needed to check them out? Let's see how we could think more clearly about government policy on health services. We illustrate for the UK, although health spending is a major public policy issue in every country.

UK opinion polls confirm widespread concern about cutbacks in services; people noticed (and minded) the changes. In that sense, the opposition politician was telling the truth. But so was the government minister. The table below shows that real (inflation-adjusted) government spending on health increased more than 27 per cent during 1990–98.

So why is there a widespread perception that health services are being cut? Two reasons. First, we are all living longer. The fraction of the UK population over 65 is projected to increase from 23 per cent in 1980 to 31 per cent by 2030. Older people need more health care than younger people. Second, advances in medical technology not merely keep us alive longer, they make available some very sophisticated and expensive treatments. Naturally, patients want any treatment that might help.

The bottom row of the table shows that health spending has increased at about the same rate as the rest of national output. Its share has remained pretty constant. However, with an ageing population, health spending has to increase faster than national output if needy old people are to get the same standard of care as

in the past. And if everyone is allowed unlimited access to every new treatment, however expensive, health spending would have to rise *much* faster still.

Both the politicians in the TV interview are really ducking the issue. They are quibbling about who is fiddling the figures: whether, properly measured, real health spending has risen or fallen. This is not the right question. Health spending could rise a lot without coming close to meeting all the needs of the new elderly and all the requests for new treatments.

The real issue is *scarcity*. Our resources are limited, and we have to choose on what to spend them. If we want to maintain past standards across a population now comprising many more older people, and if we want all medical break-throughs to be widely available, we shall have to spend so much more on health that we shall have to spend *much less* on something else. This cutback could be in the public sector (defence cuts) or in the private sector (fewer consumer goods, allowing us to pay more income in taxes to finance health).

Alternatively, as a society we can decide that we cannot cut back much on peacekeeping troops and consumer electronics, in which case we had better face the consequences for health. Somehow, we shall have to ration people's access to health services in order to prevent total spending on health rising to such an extent that it crowds out everything else. This rationing can be done through markets (making people pay for some health services) or through rules (restricting entitlement to treatment). How society resolves this issue will affect what health services and other output is produced, how it is produced, and, dramatically in this example, for whom it is produced. This, of course, is a hard debate to instigate. Politicians face huge temptations to leave difficult issues to their successors.

UK government spending on health, 1990–98			
	1990	1995	1998
Real spending (£bn, 1998 prices)	36	44	46
Spending as % of national output	5.0	5.6	5.5

Source: ONS, *UK National Accounts*.

of diminishing returns. Movements from A to B to C each involve the transfer of one worker from the food industry to the film industry, and each transfer reduces output per person in the film industry but increases output per person in the food industry. With each transfer we get less additional film output and have to give up increasing amounts of food output.

The **opportunity cost** of a good is the quantity of other goods which must be sacrificed to obtain another unit of that good.

In Figure 1-2 suppose we begin at point A with 25 units of food but no films. Moving from A to B, we gain 9 films but give up 3 units of food. Thus, 3 units of food is the opportunity cost of producing the first 9 films. The slope of the production possibility frontier tells us the opportunity cost: how much of one good we have to sacrifice to make more of another.

To explain why the curve is called a 'frontier', think about the point G in Figure 1-2. Society is producing 10 units of food and 17 units of films. This is a *feasible* combination. From Table 1-2, it requires one person in the food industry and two in the film industry. But with only three people working, society has spare resources because the fourth person is not being employed. G is *not* a point on the production possibility frontier because one can produce more of one good without sacrificing output of the other good. Putting the extra person to work in the food industry would take us to the point C, yielding 7 extra units of food for the same film output. Putting the extra person to work in the film industry would take us to the point D, with 7 extra units of films but no loss of food output.

The production possibility frontier shows the points at which society is producing *efficiently*.

Production efficiency means more output of one good can be obtained only by sacrificing output of other goods.

Points such as G, which lie inside the frontier, are *inefficient* because society is wasting resources. More output of one good would not require less output of the other.

Points outside the production possibility frontier, such as H in Figure 1-2, are *unattainable*. It would be nice to have even more food and films but, given the amount of labour available, it is impossible to produce this output combination. Scarcity of resources limits society to a choice of points that lie inside or on the production possibility frontier. Society has to accept that its resources are scarce and make choices about how to allocate these scarce resources between competing uses.

Given that people like food and films, society should want to produce efficiently. A point inside the production possibility frontier sacrifices output unnecessarily. Society must therefore choose between the different points that lie on the production possibility frontier. In so doing, it decides *what* to produce. However, in choosing a particular point, society will also be choosing *how* to produce. Table 1-2 shows how many workers must be allocated to each of the industries to produce the desired output combination. As yet, our example is too simple to show *for whom* society produces. To answer that question, we need more information than the position on the production possibility frontier.

How does society decide where to produce on the production possibility frontier? One possibility is that the government decides. That is one way of allocating scarce resources. But in most Western economies, the most important process that determines what, how, and for whom goods are produced is the operation of *markets*.

1-3 The role of the market

Markets bring together buyers and sellers of goods and services. In some cases, such as a local fruit stall, buyers and sellers meet physically. In other cases, such as the stock market, business can be transacted by computer. We need not go into details. Instead, we use a general definition of markets.

A **market** is a shorthand expression for the process by which households' decisions about consumption of alternative goods, firms' decisions about what and how to produce, and workers' decisions about how much and for whom to work are all reconciled by adjustment of *prices*.

Prices of goods, and of resources, such as labour, machinery, and land, adjust to ensure that scarce resources are used to produce the goods and services that society demands.

Much of economics is devoted to the study of how markets and prices enable society to solve the problems of what, how, and for whom to produce. Suppose you bought a hamburger for lunch. What does this have to do with markets and prices? You chose the café because it was fast, convenient and cheap. Given your desire to eat, and your limited resources, the low hamburger price told you that this was a good way to satisfy your appetite. You may prefer steak but that is more expensive. The price of steak is high enough to ensure that society answers the 'for whom' question about lunchtime steaks in favour of someone else.

Now think about the seller's viewpoint. The café owner is

BOX 1-4

Poor marks for central planners

During 1989–91, countries of the Soviet bloc abandoned Marxist central planning and began making the difficult transition to being market economies. The Soviet bloc had grown rapidly until the 1960s, but then stagnated. The Berlin Wall fell because their economies were getting left behind by market economies in the West. Key difficulties that emerged were

● **Information Overload** Planners simply could not keep track of the details of economic activity. Machinery would be left to rust because nobody came to pick it up, new houses would be left exposed to the elements because nobody ordered the roofer to come, crops would rot because storage and distribution was not co-ordinated.

● **Bad Incentives** Complete job security undermined the incentive to work. Factory managers ordered excess raw materials, merely to ensure they were allocated enough materials in the next year's plan. Since planners could monitor quantity more easily than quality, there was a systematic incentive to meet plan targets by skimping on quality. Consumers had no mechanism through which to register discontent with quality. Similarly, since

planners kept no record of environmental quality, producers engaged in massive pollution whenever it made production easier. Central planning led to low-quality goods and an environmental disaster.

● **Insufficient Competition** Planners generally believed that big was beautiful. A single tractor factory served the Soviet bloc from the Urals to Vladivostok. Large-scale created some potential for greater efficiency. However, it also deprived the planners of information from competing firms, making it difficult to assess how efficiently a factory was being run. Managers could then get away with inefficiencies. Insufficient competition extended to government itself. Without electoral competition, it was impossible to get rid of governments that were making economic mistakes.

Markets are devices for economizing on information, for providing incentives, and for introducing competition. However, the countries of the former Soviet bloc have not found it easy to make the transition to a market economy. This reminds us that like icebergs, markets have quite a lot of important infrastructure beneath the surface.

in the business because, given the price of hamburger meat, the rent, and the wages that must be paid, it is still possible to sell hamburgers at a profit. If rents were higher, it might be more profitable to sell hamburgers in a cheaper area or to switch to luxury lunches for rich executives. The student behind the counter is working there because it is a suitable part-time job which pays a bit of money. If the wage were much lower, it would hardly be worth working at all. Conversely, the job is unskilled and there are plenty of students looking for such work, so owners of cafés do not have to offer very high wages.

Prices are guiding your decision to buy a hamburger, the owner's decision to sell hamburgers, and the student's decision to take the job. Society is allocating resources – meat, buildings, and labour – into hamburger production through the price system. If nobody liked hamburgers, the owner could not sell enough at a price that covered the cost of running the café and society would devote no resources to hamburger production. People's desire to eat hamburgers

guides resources into hamburger production. However, if cattle contracted a disease, leading consumers to abandon hamburgers in favour of bacon sandwiches, the price of BLTs would rise. As the fast food industry scrambled to get enough pork, the price of pigs would rise but the price of beef, now unpopular, would fall. Adjustments in prices would thus encourage society to reallocate land from beef to pig farming. During the British beef crisis caused by fears about mad cow disease, in the year to June 1996 pork prices rose 30 per cent while beef prices fell. Quite an incentive to reallocate!

The command economy

To highlight the role of markets and prices, we now ask how resources might be allocated if markets did not exist. One example is a command economy.

In a **command economy** a government planning office decides what will be produced, how it will be produced, and for whom it will be produced. Detailed instructions are then issued to households, firms, and workers.

Such planning is a very complicated task, and there is no complete command economy where all allocation decisions are undertaken in this way. However, in many countries, for example China, Cuba, and those formerly in the Soviet bloc, there was a large measure of central direction and planning. The state owned factories and land, and made the most important decisions about what people should consume, how goods should be produced, and how much people should work.

To appreciate the immensity of this task, imagine that you had to run by command the city in which you live. Think of the food, clothing, and housing allocation decisions you would have to make. How would you decide who should get what and the process by which these goods and services would be produced? Of course these decisions are being made every day in your own city, but chiefly through the allocative mechanism of markets and prices.

The invisible hand

Markets in which governments do not intervene are called **free markets**.

Individuals in free markets pursue their own interests, trying to do as well for themselves as they can without any government direction or interference. The idea that such a system could solve the what, how, and for whom problems is one of the oldest themes in economics, dating back to Adam Smith, the famous Scottish economist whose book *The Wealth of Nations* (1776) remains a classic. Smith argued that individuals pursuing their self-interest would be led 'as by an invisible hand' to do things that are in the interests of society as a whole.

Suppose you wish to become a millionaire. You play around with new ideas and invent a new good, perhaps the CD ROM. Although motivated by self-interest, you make society better off by creating new jobs and opportunities. You move society's production possibility frontier outwards – the same resources now make more or better goods – and become a millionaire in the process. Smith argued that the pursuit of self-interest, *without any central direction*, could produce a coherent society making sensible allocative decisions.

This remarkable insight has been studied at length by modern economists. In later chapters, we discuss in detail the circumstances in which the invisible hand works well. We also show that sometimes it works badly. Some government intervention may then be justified.

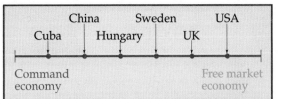

The role of the market in allocating resources differs vastly between countries. In the command economy resources are allocated by central government planning. In the free market economy there is virtually no government regulation of the consumption, production, and exchange of goods. In between lies the mixed economy, where market forces play a large role but the government intervenes extensively.

Figure 1-3 Market orientation

The mixed economy

The free market allows individuals to pursue their self-interest without any government restrictions. The command economy allows little scope for individual economic freedom since most decisions are taken centrally by the government. Between these two extremes lies the mixed economy.

In a **mixed economy** the government and private sector interact in solving economic problems. The government controls a significant share of output through taxation, transfer payments, and the provision of services such as defence and the police force. It also regulates the extent to which individuals may pursue their own self-interest.

Most countries are mixed economies, though some are close to command economies and others are much nearer the free market economy. Figure 1-3 illustrates this point. Even Cuba allows consumers some choice over the goods they buy. Conversely, even countries such as the United States, which espouse more enthusiastically the free market approach, still have substantial levels of government activity in the provision of public goods and services, the redistribution of income through taxes and transfer payments, and the regulation of markets.

1.4 Positive and normative

In studying economics it is important to distinguish 'positive' and 'normative' economics.

Positive economics deals with objective or scientific explanations of the working of the economy.

The aim of positive economics is to explain how society makes decisions about consumption, production, and

BOX 1-5   Green piece

Many people are worried that our planet is running out of natural resources such as rain forests, fish stocks, and clean air. Why do we manage the environment so badly? An economist's automatic response is to say 'because we do not price it like other commodities'. Figure 1-1 showed how the market 'solved' the problem of scarcity when OPEC tried to restrict oil supplies. High prices were the incentive to increase supply and reduce demand. Why don't we simply price the environment, encouraging people to look after it and penalizing its degradation?

Historically, much of the answer has been technological. We have not had the means to exclude people who refuse to pay. Anyone can walk in a field, dump rubbish after dark, pump chemicals into a river, or drive down a public street. Turnstiles every 50 metres would not be feasible. Gradually, however, electronic monitoring of usage is becoming easier and cheaper. At some point, it may become possible to treat aspects of the environment as just another commodity to be marketed. Of course this will immediately give rise to a vigorous debate about how the what, how, and for whom questions should then be answered.

For example, it is already feasible to charge cars for using a particular street at a particular time. A smart card in the car would pick up signals as the car passed various charge points. The driver would get a monthly bill like a credit card bill. Rush-hour city traffic could be made to pay more than drivers in places or times where congestion was not a problem. The for whom question could be addressed. Residents could get a 'poll subsidy', a flat rate annual payment, in exchange for agreeing to support a government introducing road pricing. Pricing the environment has one big advantage. It introduces a feedback mechanism, however crude, so that when society does stupid things an alarm bell rings *automatically*.

exchange of goods. The purpose of this investigation is twofold: to satisfy our curiosity about why the economy works as it does, and to have some basis for predicting how the economy will respond to changes in circumstances. Normative economics is very different.

Normative economics offers recommendations based on personal value judgements.

In positive economics, we hope to act as detached scientists. Whatever our political persuasion, whatever our view about what we would regard as 'a good thing', in the first instance we have to be concerned with how the world actually works. At this stage, there is no scope for personal value judgements. We are concerned with propositions of the form: if *this* is changed then *that* will happen. In this regard, positive economics is similar to the natural sciences such as physics, geology, or astronomy.

Here are some examples of positive economics in action. Economists of widely differing political persuasions would agree that, when the government imposes a tax on a good, the price of that good will rise. The normative question of whether this price rise is desirable is entirely distinct. Many propositions in positive economics command widespread agreement among professional economists.

Of course, as in any other science, there are unresolved questions where disagreement remains. These disagreements are at the frontiers of economics. Research in progress will resolve some of these issues but new issues will arise and provide scope for further research.

Although competent and comprehensive research can in principle resolve many of the outstanding issues in positive economics, no corresponding claim can be made about the resolution of disagreement in normative economics. Normative economics is based on subjective value judgements, not on the search for any objective truth. The following statement combines positive and normative economics: 'The elderly have very high medical expenses, and the government should subsidize their health bills.' The first part of the proposition – the claim that the aged have relatively high medical bills – is a statement in positive economics. It is a statement about how the world works, and we can imagine a research programme that could determine whether or not it is correct. Broadly speaking, this assertion happens to be correct. The second part of the proposition – the recommendation about what the government should do – could never be 'proved' to be correct or false by any scientific research investigation. It is simply a subjective value judgement based on the feelings of the person making the statement. Many people might share this subjective judgement. But other people might reasonably disagree. You might believe that it is more important to devote society's scarce resources to improving the environment.

There is no way that economics can be used to show that one of these normative judgements is correct and the other is wrong. It all depends on the preferences or priorities of the individual or the society that has to make this choice. But we can use positive economics to spell out the detailed implications of making the choice one way or the other. Positive economics can be used to clarify the menu of options from which society must eventually make its normative choice.

Most economists have normative views and some economists are vociferous champions of particular normative recommendations. However, this *advocacy role* about what society should do must be distinguished from the role of the economist as an expert about the likely consequences of pursuing any course of action. In the latter case, the professional economist is offering expert advice on positive economics. However, in a democracy economists have no monopoly on pure value judgements merely because they happen to be economists. Scrupulous economists clearly distinguish their role as an expert adviser on positive economics from their status merely as involved private citizens in arguing for particular normative choices.

1-5 Micro and macro

Many economists specialize in a particular branch of the subject. Labour economics deals with problems of the labour market. Urban economics deals with city problems: land use, transport, congestion, and housing. However, we need not classify branches of economics according to the area of economic life in which we ask the standard questions what, how, and for whom. We can also classify branches of economics according to the approach that is used. The very broad division of approaches into microeconomic and macroeconomic cuts across the large number of subject groupings cited above.

Microeconomic analysis offers a detailed treatment of individual decisions about particular commodities.

For example, we might study why individual households prefer cars to bicycles and how producers decide whether to produce cars or bicycles. We can then aggregate the behaviour of all households and all firms to discuss total car purchases and total car production. Within a market economy we can discuss the market for cars. Comparing

this with the market for bicycles, we may be able to explain the relative price of cars and bicycles and the relative output of these two goods. The sophisticated branch of microeconomics known as *general equilibrium* theory extends this approach to its logical conclusion. It studies simultaneously every market for every commodity. From this it is hoped that we can understand the complete pattern of consumption, production, and exchange in the whole economy at a point in time.

If you think this sounds very complicated you are correct. It is. For many purposes, the analysis becomes so complicated that we lose track of the phenomena in which we were interested. The interesting task for economics, a task that retains an element of art in economic science, is to devise judicious simplifications which keep the analysis manageable without distorting reality too much. It is here that microeconomists and macroeconomists proceed down different avenues. Microeconomists tend to offer a detailed treatment of one aspect of economic behaviour but ignore interactions with the rest of the economy in order to preserve the simplicity of the analysis. A microeconomic analysis of miners' wages would emphasize the characteristics of miners and the ability of mine owners to pay. It would largely neglect the chain of indirect effects to which a rise in miners' wages might give rise. For example, car workers might use the precedent of the miners' pay increase to secure higher wages in the car industry, thus being able to afford larger houses which burned more coal in heating systems. When microeconomic analysis ignores such indirectly induced effects it is said to be *partial analysis*.

In some instances, indirect effects may not be too important and it will make sense for economists to devote their efforts to very detailed analyses of particular industries or activities. In other circumstances, the indirect effects are too important to be swept under the carpet and an alternative simplification must be found.

Macroeconomics emphasizes the interactions in the economy as a whole. It deliberately simplifies the individual building blocks of the analysis in order to retain a manageable analysis of the complete interaction of the economy.

For example, macroeconomists typically do not worry about the breakdown of consumer goods into cars, bicycles, televisions, and calculators. They prefer to treat them all as a single bundle called 'consumer goods' because they are more interested in studying the interaction between households' purchases of consumer goods and firms' decisions about purchases of machinery and buildings.

Because these macroeconomic concepts refer to the economy as a whole, they receive more coverage on television and in the newspapers than microeconomic concepts, which are chiefly of interest to those who belong to the specific group in question. To give an idea of the building blocks of macroeconomics, we introduce three concepts which you have probably come across in the media.

Gross domestic product (GDP) is the value of all goods and services produced in the economy in a given period such as a year.

GDP is the basic measure of the total output of goods and services in the economy.

The **aggregate price level** is a measure of the average level of prices of goods and services in the economy.

There is no reason why the prices of different goods should always move in line with one another. The aggregate price level tells us what is happening to prices on average. When the price level is rising, we say that the economy is experiencing *inflation*.

The **unemployment rate** is the percentage of the labour force without a job.

By the labour force we mean those people of working age who in principle would like to work if a suitable job were available. Some of the landed gentry are of working age but have no intention of looking for work. They are not in the labour force and not counted as unemployed.

Already we can see two themes of modern macroeconomic analysis. Society reveals, both through statements by individuals and by the policy pronouncements of politicians who must submit themselves for re-election by the people, that it does not like inflation and unemployment. During the 1970s, economic interactions within and between national economies led to substantial inflation rates. Since then, inflation has fallen in most Western economies, but the unemployment rate has increased. Macroeconomists wish to understand how interactions within the economy can lead to these outcomes and whether government policy can make any difference.

Getting the most out of each chapter

At the end of each chapter in the book you will find a summary of the main points of the chapter. There are problems for you to work through to check that you have understood the chapter. Do the problems. The last problem in each chapter lists a number of fallacies. Use the material in the chapter to show why these statements are incorrect. The accompanying *Workbook* offers many more problems and a complete set of answers.

SUMMARY

● Economics analyses what, how, and for whom society produces. The central economic problem is to reconcile the conflict between people's virtually unlimited demands with society's limited ability to produce goods and services to fulfil these demands.

● The production possibility frontier shows the maximum amount of one good that can be produced given the level of output of the other good. It depicts the trade-off or menu of choices for society in deciding what to produce. Resources are scarce and points outside the frontier are unattainable. It is inefficient to produce within the frontier.

● Industrial countries rely extensively on markets to allocate resources. The market is the process by which production and consumption decisions are co-ordinated through adjustments in prices.

● In a command economy, decisions on what, how, and for whom are made in a central planning office. No economy relies entirely on command.

● A free market economy has no government intervention. Resources are allocated entirely through markets in which individuals pursue their own self-interest. Adam Smith argued that an invisible hand would nevertheless allocate resources efficiently.

● Modern economies are mixed, relying mainly on the market but with a large dose of government intervention. The optimal level of intervention remains a subject of controversy.

● Positive economics studies how the economy actually behaves. Normative economics makes prescriptions about what should be done. The two should be kept separate as far as possible. Given sufficient research, economists should eventually agree on issues in positive economics. Normative economics involves subjective value judgements. There is no reason why economists should agree about normative statements.

● Microeconomics offers a detailed analysis of particular activities in the economy. For simplicity, it may neglect some interactions with the rest of the economy. Macroeconomics emphasizes these interactions at the cost of simplifying the individual building blocks.

KEY TERMS

- Scarce resource 5
- Income distribution 5
- Production possibility frontier 7
- Opportunity cost 9
- Production efficiency 9
- Market 9
- Command economy 10
- Free market 11
- Mixed economy 11
- Positive and normative economics 11–12
- Microeconomics and macroeconomics 13
- Gross domestic product 14
- Aggregate price level 14
- Unemployment rate 14

REVIEW QUESTIONS

1 How are the problems, what, how, and for whom settled within your own family?

2 There are five workers in an economy. Each worker can make either four cakes or three shirts. Output per worker is independent of the number of other workers in the same industry. (a) Draw society's production possibility frontier. (b) How many cakes could society produce if it was willing to do without shirts? (c) Indicate the points in your diagram that show inefficient organization of production.

3 Communist Russia relied on prices to allocate production among different consumers. Central planners determined production targets but then put output in shops, fixed prices, and gave workers a certain amount of money to spend. Why not plan everything including the allocation of particular goods to particular people?

4 Suppose society abolishes higher education. Students have to find jobs immediately. If there are no jobs available, how should wages and prices adjust so that the invisible hand will ensure that those who want jobs can find them?

5 Which of the following statements are positive and which are normative? Explain: (a) The rate of inflation has fallen below 2 per cent per annum. (b) Because inflation has fallen the government should now expand its activity. (c) The level of income is higher in the UK than in Poland. (d) People in the UK are happier than people in Poland. (e) People should not be encouraged to drink and taxes must be kept high on alcoholic beverages.

6 Which of the following statements refer to microeconomics and which refer to macroeconomics? (a) The inflation rate is lower than in the 1980s. (b) Food prices fell this month. (c) Sunny weather will mean a good harvest this year. (d) Unemployment in the capital is lower than the national average.

7 *Common fallacies* Show why the following statements are incorrect: (a) Since some economists are right-wing and others left-wing, economics can be used to justify anything we like. (b) There is no such thing as a free lunch. To get more of one thing you always have to give up something else. (c) Economics is all about money and greed. It has no relevance in discussing a true socialist state.

2 The tools of economic analysis

It is more fun to play tennis if you know how to serve, and felling trees is much easier with a chain saw. Every activity or academic discipline involves a basic set of tools. The tools may be tangible, like the dentist's drill, or intangible, like the ability to serve in tennis. In this chapter the emphasis is on mastering the tools of the trade. To analyse economic issues we use both *models* and *data*.

A **model** or theory makes a series of simplifying assumptions from which it deduces how people will behave. It is a deliberate simplification of reality.

Models are frameworks for organizing the way we think about a problem. They simplify by omitting some details of the real world to concentrate on the essentials. From this manageable picture of reality we develop our analysis of how the economy works.

An economist uses a model in the way a traveller uses a map. A map of London misses out many features of the real world – traffic lights, roundabouts, the exact width of streets – but if you study it carefully you can get a good picture of how the traffic is likely to flow and what will be the best route to take. This simplified picture is easy to follow, yet helps you understand real-world behaviour when you must drive through the city in the rush hour.

Data are pieces of evidence about economic behaviour.

The data or facts interact with models in two ways. First, the data help us quantify the relationships to which our theoretical models draw attention. It may be insufficient to work out that all bridges across the Thames are likely to be congested. To choose the best route we need to know how long we would have to queue at each bridge. We need some facts. The model is useful because it tells us which facts are likely to be the most important. Bridges are more likely to be congested than six-lane motorways.

Second, the data help us to test our models. Like all careful scientists, economists must check that their theories square with the relevant facts. Here the crucial word is *relevant*. For example, the number of Scottish dysentery deaths was closely related to the actual inflation rate in the

UK over many decades. Is this a factual coincidence or the key to a theory of inflation? The facts alert us to the need to ponder this question, but we can make a decision only by recourse to logical reasoning.

In this instance, since we can find no theoretical connection, we regard the close factual relationship between Scottish dysentery deaths and UK inflation as a coincidence that should be ignored. Without any logical underpinning, the empirical connection will break down sooner or later. Paying attention to a freak relationship in the data increases neither our understanding of the economy nor our confidence in predicting the future.

The blend of models and data is thus a subtle one. The data may alert us to logical relationships we had overlooked. And whatever theory we wish to maintain should certainly be checked against the facts. But only theoretical reasoning can guide an intelligent assessment of what evidence is of reasonable relevance.

To introduce the tools of the trade we begin with the representation of the economic data. Then we show how an economist might develop a theoretical model of an economic relationship. Finally, we discuss how actual data might be used to test the theory that has been developed.

2-1 Economic data

Initially we focus on the data or facts. How might we present them to help us think about an economic problem?

Time series data

Table 2-1 reports a time series of monthly silver prices.

Time series is a sequence of measurements of a variable at different points in time.

It shows how a variable changes over time. This information may be presented in tables or charts.

Figure 2-1 *plots*, or *graphs*, the data shown in Table 2-1. Each point in the figure corresponds to an entry in the table. Point A shows graphically that in January 1999 the price of silver was 555 cents per troy ounce. The series of points or dots in Figure 2-1, in whichever colour, contains exactly the same information as Table 2-1.

However, charts or diagrams must be interpreted with care. The eye is easily misled by simple changes in the presentation of the data. In Figure 2-1 the top graph corresponds to the left-hand scale but the bottom graph corresponds to the enlarged scale on the right-hand side. Even though both graphs plot the same data, the bottom graph seems to show much more movement. Diagrams can

Table 2-1	The price of silver in 1999 (US cents/troy ounce)		
Jan.	Feb.	Mar.	Apr.
555	520	509	508

Source: IMF, *International Financial Statistics*.

Table 2-2	The price of silver in 1998–99 (US cents/troy ounce)			
98 I	98 II	98 III	98 IV	99 I
625	571	522	496	528

Source: IMF, *International Financial Statistics*.

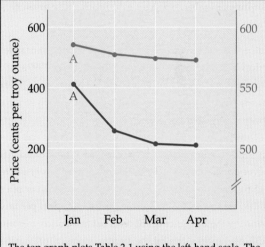

The top graph plots Table 2-1 using the left-hand scale. The bottom one uses the right-hand scale. Prices seem now to vary more.

Figure 2-1 The price of silver in 1999

be manipulated in suggestive ways even to the point of being misleading, a point well understood in advertising and politics. For most purposes daily data contain too much detail. It would be tedious to work with a table of daily prices over 10 or 20 years. Averages over a month, over a quarter (three months), or over a whole year may then be the best way to present data.

Table 2-2 presents quarterly averages for silver prices in 1998–99. By the four quarters of the year we mean the four three-month periods January–March, April–June, July–September, and October–December. For the first quarter of 1999 the data in Tables 2-1 and 2-2 overlap. The quarterly average of 528 for the 1999 I in Table 2-2 is simply one-third of the sum of the monthly numbers for January, February, and March in Table 2-1.

Cross-section data

Time series data record the way a particular variable changes over time. Economists also use cross-section data.

Cross-section data record at a point in time the way an economic variable differs across different individuals or groups of individuals.

Table 2-3 shows a cross-section of unemployment rates in different countries in 1999.

2-2 Index numbers

To compare numbers without emphasizing the units to which they refer, we can present data as index numbers.

An **index number** expresses data relative to a given base value.

Table 2-4 shows annual averages for copper and silver prices in selected years. Suppose that we choose 1990 as the base year and assign the value 100 to the copper price index in this year. We assign the same value to the silver price index in this base year.

Now consider 1998. The silver price of 553 cents per troy ounce is 1.15 times the silver price in 1990. If we pretend that silver prices were 100 in 1990, this index must have risen to 115 by 1998. To calculate the 1970 value of the silver price index, we divide the 1970 silver price of 177 cents per troy ounce by the 1990 price of 482 cents per troy ounce to obtain 0.37. Multiplying this by the starting value of 100 for the index in 1990, we obtain 37, as in Table 2-4. The price index

for copper is calculated in the same way, dividing each price by the 1990 price and multiplying the answer by 100.

Now check that you understand this procedure. In 1975 average silver prices were 442 cents per troy ounce and average copper prices 93 cents per pound. What were the values of the silver and copper price indices? (Answer: 92 and 77.)

Index number as averages

Suppose we now wish to know about movements in the price of metals as a whole. The prices of individual metals do not necessarily change in the same way. To derive a single measure of metals prices we have to *average* different metal prices.

Suppose copper and silver are the only two metals. To construct an index of all metal prices, we must make a single time series out of the two time series shown in the bottom two rows of Table 2-4. We give the price index of each metal a weight or share in the new index for metals as a whole. The weight should reflect the purpose for which the index is being constructed. If it is to be used to summarize what firms must pay for metal inputs, the weights should reflect the relative use of silver and copper as industrial inputs. Since copper is much more widely used than silver, we might decide to assign a weight of 0.8 to copper and 0.2 to silver. The weights are always chosen to add up to unity.

Table 2-5 shows how the metal price index, the *weighted average* of the indices for silver and copper, changes over time. In the base year 1990, the metals index is 100, being $(0.2 \times 100) + (0.8 \times 100)$. By 1998 the index has fallen to 73, since this equals $(0.8 \times 62) + (0.2 \times 115)$. In 1970 the index was 50.

The metals index is a weighted average of silver and copper prices and must lie between the indices for the two separate metals. The weights determine whether the metals index more closely resembles the behaviour of copper prices or of silver prices.

Table 2-3 Unemployment by country, 1998 (% of labour force)

USA	Japan	Germany	France	UK
4.5	4.1	11.2	11.8	6.2

Source: OECD, *Economic Outlook*.

Table 2-4 Prices of silver (cents/troy ounce) and of copper (cents/pound)

	1970	1990	1998
Silver price	177	482	553
Copper price	64	121	75
Silver index (1990 = 100)	37	100	115
Copper index (1990 = 100)	53	100	62

Source: IMF, *International Financial Statistics*.

Table 2-5 Price indices for silver, copper, and metals (1990 = 100)

	1970	1990	1998
Silver	37	100	115
Copper	53	100	62
Metals	50	100	73

Source: Calculated from Table 2-4.

The RPI and other indices

Most countries keep track of the prices faced by consumers. They construct a *consumer price index*. In the UK this is called the *retail price index* (RPI). Announced monthly, and closely watched by the news media and economic commentators, the RPI is an index of the prices of consumer goods purchased by a typical household. It includes everything from food and housing to entertainment. The RPI is used to measure changes in the cost of living, the money that must be spent to purchase the typical bundle of goods consumed by a representative household.

The **inflation rate** is the annual rate of change of the price index.

The RPI is constructed in two stages. First, index numbers are calculated for each category of commodity purchased by households. Then the RPI is constructed by taking a weighted average of the different commodity groupings. Table 2-6 shows the weights used and the main commodity groupings. A 10 per cent rise in food prices will change the RPI more than a 10 per cent rise in tobacco prices because food has a much larger weight than tobacco.

Other examples of indices are the index of wages in manufacturing, a weighted average of wages in different manufacturing industries, and the 'footsie', or FTSE, the *Financial Times–Stock Exchange* index of share prices quoted on the London stock exchange. Nor need the use of index numbers be confined to the prices of goods, labour, or corporate shares. The *index of industrial production* is a weighted average of the *quantity* of goods produced by industry. However, the procedure by which index numbers are calculated is always the same. We choose a base date and set the index equal to 100 at that date. Where the index refers to more than one commodity, we have to choose weights by which to average across the different commodities that the index describes.

2-3 Nominal and real variables

The first row of Table 2-7 shows the average price of a new house, which increased from £2500 in 1960 to £96 700 in 1998. Are houses really 40 times as expensive as in 1960? Not when we allow for inflation, which has also raised incomes and the ability to buy houses.

Nominal values are measured in the prices ruling at the time of measurement. **Real values** adjust nominal values for changes in the price level.

The second row of Table 2-7 shows the retail price index,

Table 2-6 RPI weights in the UK	
Item	Weight
Housing	0.193
Food	0.128
Motoring	0.139
Household goods	0.074
Alcohol	0.069
Leisure services	0.061
Clothing and footwear	0.055
Household services	0.057
Leisure goods	0.047
Fuel and light	0.034
Catering	0.051
Personal goods and services	0.040
Tobacco	0.031
Travel costs and fares	0.021

Source: ONS, *Monthly Digest of Statistics*.

Table 2-7 UK house prices (average price of a new house)			
	1960	1980	1998
House price (£'000s)	2.5	27.2	96.7
RPI (1998 = 100)	7.7	41.1	100.0
Real price of houses (1998 £'000s)	32.5	66.2	96.7

Source: ONS, *Economic Trends*.

using 1998 as the base year. Inflation led to substantial increases in the price level, and hence the RPI, during 1960–98. The third row of Table 2.7 calculates an index of real house prices, expressed in 1998 prices. The value of house prices is the same in 1998 in the top and bottom row.

To calculate the real price of houses in 1960, by expressing them also at 1998 prices, we take the nominal price of £2500 and multiply by (100/7.7) to allow for subsequent inflation, yielding £32 500. Real prices have roughly tripled since 1960. Most of the increase in nominal house prices in the top row of Table 2-7 was actually due to inflation.

Real or relative prices

The distinction between nominal and real variables applies to all variables whose unit of measurement is so many pounds per unit. It does not apply to units of output, such as 4000 washing machines per annum, which relate to physical quantities. Whatever the inflation rate, 4000 washing

---

BOX 2-1	Millionaire: not the tag it once was

One in every 550 adults in Britain is now a millionaire (*London Evening Standard*, 11 February 1997). A triumph for the National Lottery? Not really: the lottery has created only a handful of Britain's 81 000 millionaires. It's mainly just the effect of inflation. The table below shows how much an old-fashioned millionaire would be worth at today's prices: a million pounds in 1999 was worth only 1/43rd of a million pounds in 1938. Being a millionaire is getting easier all the time.

£1 million in prices of year:	1988	1978	1968	1948	1938
Value in 1999 prices (£ million)	1.6	3.4	10.1	21.0	43

Sources: ONS, *Economic Trends*; United Nations, *Economic Surveys of Europe*.

---

machines is 4000 washing machines. However, we do not know whether £100 is a large or a small number until we know the general price level for goods.

The argument carries over to prices themselves. The nominal price of silver has risen considerably since 1970. We can calculate an index of the *real price of silver* by dividing an index of nominal silver prices by the retail price index and multiplying by 100.

Real prices provide an indicator of economic scarcity. They show whether the price of some commodity is rising more rapidly than prices of goods in general. For this reason real prices are sometimes called *relative prices*.

Consider the price of televisions over the last 20 years. Television prices, measured in pounds, have risen very slowly. The RPI has risen much more quickly. Thus, the real price of televisions has actually fallen. Advances in technology have reduced the cost of producing televisions. The real price, measuring economic scarcity, has fallen. Because the real price has fallen, many more households are now able to afford a television. It is misleading to base our analysis on nominal values of variables.

The purchasing power of money

When the price of goods rises, we say that the purchasing power of money falls because £1 buys fewer goods.

The **purchasing power of money** is an index of the quantity of goods that can be bought for £1.

The distinction between real and nominal variables is sometimes expressed by saying that real variables measure nominal variables as if the purchasing power of money had been constant. Another way to express this idea is to say that we distinguish between measurements of nominal variables in *current* pounds and real variables in *constant* pounds.

Table 2-7 described the trend in real prices of houses by measuring house prices in 1998 pounds. We could of course have used 1960 pounds instead. Although the level of the real price index for houses would have been different, it would have grown at exactly the same rate as the final row of Table 2-7.

2-4 Measuring changes in economic variables

During the BSE crisis in 1996, UK beef production fell from 90 000 tonnes in January to 50 000 tonnes in April. The *absolute change* was −40 000. The minus sign tells us output fell.

The **percentage change** is the absolute change divided by the original number, then multiplied by 100.

Thus, the percentage change in UK beef output was (100) × (−40 000)/(90 000) = −44 per cent. Whereas absolute changes specify units (e.g. tonnes) percentage changes are *unit-free*. It is often convenient to display data in this way.

When we study time series data over long periods such as a decade, we do not want to know just the percentage or absolute change between the initial date and the final date.

The **growth rate** is the percentage change per period (typically per year).

Negative growth rates simply show percentage falls. Economists usually take *economic growth* to mean the percentage annual change in the national income of a country or a group of countries.

2-5 Economic models

Now for an example of economics in action. The London Underground is losing money. Some people think it cannot survive without government subsidies. Others think that if it was run differently it could break even. You are called in to advise on the level of fares that would raise most revenue. How would you analyse the problem?

To organize our thinking, or – as economists describe it – to build a model, we require a simplified picture of reality which picks out the most important elements of the problem. We begin with the simple equation

$$\text{Revenue} = \text{fare} \times \text{number of passengers} \qquad (1)$$

Equation (1) emphasizes, and thus organizes our thoughts around, two factors: the fare and the number of passengers. London Transport directly controls the fare, but can influence the number of passengers only through the fare that is set. (Cleaner stations and better service might also matter, but we neglect these for the moment.)

The number of passengers may be determined by habit, convenience, and tradition, and be completely unresponsive to changes in fares. This is *not* the view of traveller behaviour that an economist would initially adopt. It is possible to travel by car, bus, taxi, or tube, and decisions about the mode of transport are likely to be sensitive to the relative costs of the competing alternatives. Thus equation (1) must not view the number of passengers as fixed. We need a 'theory' or 'model' (we use these terms interchangeably) of what determines the number of passengers. We must model the *demand* for tube journeys.

First, the fare itself matters. Other things equal, higher tube fares reduce the quantity of tube journeys demanded. Of course what matters is the price of the tube relative to the price of other means of transport – cars, buses, and taxis. If their prices remain constant, lower tube fares will encourage tube passengers. Rises in the price of these other means of transport will also encourage tube passengers even though tube fares remain unaltered. Finally, if passengers have larger incomes, they can afford more tube journeys.

We now have a bare-bones model of the demand for tube journeys.

$$\text{Quantity of tube journeys demanded}$$
$$= f \text{ (tube fare, taxi fare, petrol price,}$$
$$\text{bus fare, passenger incomes, . . .)} \qquad (2)$$

The quantity of tube journeys 'depends on', or 'is a function of', the tube fare, the taxi fare, petrol prices, bus fares, incomes, and some other things. The notation f ( ) is just a shorthand for 'depends on all the things listed inside the brackets'. In equation (2) we name the most important determinants of the demand for tube journeys. The row of dots reminds us that we have omitted some possible determinants of demand to simplify our analysis. For example, tube demand probably depends on the temperature. It gets uncomfortable in the underground when it is very hot. Since the purpose of our model is to study *changes* in the number of tube passengers, it will probably be all right to neglect the weather provided weather conditions are broadly the same every year.

To answer our original question, it is not sufficient to know the factors on which the demand for tube journeys depends. We shall somehow have to quantify each of these separate effects.

Writing down a model is a safe way of forcing ourselves to look for all the relevant effects, to worry about which effects must be taken into account and which are minor and can probably be ignored in answering the question we have set ourselves. Without writing down a model, we might have forgotten about the influence of incomes on tube journeys, an omission that might have led to serious errors in trying to understand and forecast revenue raised from tube fares.

We can summarize our model of total revenue collected by London Transport from tube fares as

$$\text{tube revenue}$$
$$= \text{tube fare} \times \text{number of passengers}$$
$$= \text{tube fare} \times f \text{ (tube fare, taxi fare,}$$
$$\text{petrol price, bus fare, incomes, . . .)} \qquad (3)$$

Your natural reaction may be to ask what all the fuss is about. Given five minutes thought, you would probably have organized your approach along similar lines. That is the correct reaction. Models are simply devices for ensuring that we think clearly about a particular problem. Clear thinking requires some simplification. The real world is too complicated for us to think about everything at once. Nor can we offer any precise guidelines about how far a model should deliberately simplify reality. Learning to use models is more of an art than a science. Too much simplicity will lead to the omission of a crucial factor in the analysis. Too much complexity and we lose any feel for why the answer is turning out as it is.

Sometimes we can use data to guide us about which factors are crucial and which are not. At other times, as in our example with tube fares, it is not enough to understand the forces at work. We need to quantify them. For both these reasons, we turn now to the interaction of economic models and economic data.

2-6 Models and data

Equation (3) is our model of the factors determining revenue from tube fares. In organizing our thinking, we have concluded that, other things equal, higher tube fares will be accompanied by fewer passengers. Theory alone cannot answer our question. Whether or not higher tube fares raise or lower total revenue depends entirely on the *empirical* or factual issue of how many passengers are discouraged by higher fares.

Nevertheless, our model has been of some use. It tells us that the key fact we have to discover is how many passengers are put off by higher fares alone, holding constant the price of all other means of transport. Knowing this, we can calculate whether higher or lower fares are better for revenue.

Empirical evidence

We need some empirical research to establish the facts. *Experimental* sciences, including many branches of physics and chemistry, can conduct controlled experiments in a laboratory, varying one factor at a time while holding constant all the other relevant factors. Like astronomy, economics is primarily a *non-experimental* science. Astronomers cannot suspend planetary motion to examine the relation between the earth and the sun in isolation;

economists can rarely suspend the laws of economic activity to conduct controlled experiments.

Thus most empirical research in economics must deal with data collected over periods in which many of the relevant factors were simultaneously changing. The problem is how to disentangle the separate influences on observed behaviour. We approach this in two stages. First, we proceed by examining the relationship of interest – the dependence of journeys on fares – neglecting the possibility that other relevant factors were changing. Then we indicate how economists deal with the harder problem in which variations in other factors are also included in the analysis.

Table 2-8 presents data on tube fares and passengers collected by the Department of Environment, Transport and the Regions (www.detr.gov.uk). Column (1) shows the real tube fare per passenger kilometre.

Column (2) shows tube demand, measured in passenger usage in billions of passenger kilometres per annum. However, it is hard to tell by looking at Table 2-8 whether there is any clear relationship between real fares (column 1) and real revenue (column 3).

Scatter diagrams

It is often convenient to present evidence such as that given in Table 2-8 in a *scatter diagram* such as Figure 2-2. A scatter diagram shows how two variables are related. Along the vertical axis we measure the units of column (1), 1994 pence per passenger kilometre. Along the horizontal axis we measure the units of column (3), real revenue in billions of 1998 pounds. Real revenue is simply the real fare per

Table 2-8	The Tube 1979–98		
Year	(1) Real fare (1998 £)	(2) Pass. km (bn)	(3) Real revenue (1998 £ m.)
1979	0.128	4.5	576
1980	0.141	4.3	607
1981	0.131	4.1	540
1982	0.149	3.7	550
1983	0.123	4.4	543
1984	0.102	5.2	535
1985	0.097	5.9	572
1986	0.104	6.2	649
1987	0.105	6.2	619
1988	0.103	6.2	643
1989	0.106	6.0	638
1990	0.110	6.1	669
1991	0.116	5.8	672
1992	0.121	5.7	687
1993	0.126	5.8	730
1994	0.133	6.0	801
1995	0.131	6.3	827
1996	0.136	6.2	841
1997	0.141	6.5	918
1998	0.146	6.7	977

Source: Department of Environment, Transport and the Regions.

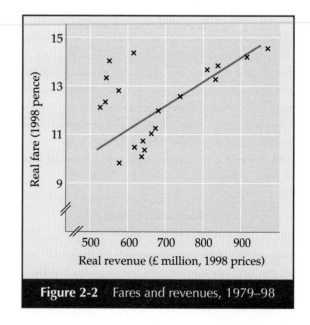

Figure 2-2 Fares and revenues, 1979–98

passenger kilometre multiplied by the number of passenger kilometres travelled.

The years of lowest real revenue coincides with the years in which the real tube fare was lowest. Yet Figure 2-2 offers no clear answer to our original question. Revenue is not closely related to real fares. A fuller analysis will also have to examine other determinants of passenger use, such as the real income of passengers.

2-7 Diagrams, lines, and equations

We now give a formal definition of scatter diagrams.

A **scatter diagram** plots pairs of values simultaneously observed for two different variables.

If it is possible to draw a line or curve through all the points or crosses, this suggests, but does not prove, that there is an underlying relationship between the two variables. If, when the points are plotted, they lie all over the place, this suggests, but does not prove, that there is no strong underlying relationship between the two variables. Only if economics were an experimental science, in which we could conduct controlled experiments guaranteeing that all other relevant factors had been held constant, could we interpret scatter diagrams unambiguously. Nevertheless, they often provide helpful clues.

Fitting lines through scatter diagrams

In Figure 2-2 we could draw a line through the collection or scatter of points we had plotted. The line would show the average relation between fares and revenue during the period 1979–98. We could use the line to make more precise statements than we have offered so far. By looking at the *slope* of the line, how much usage changes each time we raise the fare 0.1 pence, we could quantify the average relation between fares and usage.

Given a particular scatter of points, how do we decide where to draw the line, given that it cannot fit all the points exactly?

Econometrics is the branch of economics devoted to measuring relationships using economic data.

The details need not concern us here, but the idea is simple enough. Having plotted the points describing the data, a computer works out where to draw the line to minimize the dispersion of points around the line.

After some practice, most people get used to working with two-dimensional diagrams such as Figure 2-2. A few gifted souls can even draw diagrams in three dimensions.

Fortunately, computers can work in 10 or 20 dimensions at once, even though we cannot imagine what this looks like.

And therein lies the answer to the problem of trying to hold other things constant. The computer can measure the tube fare on one axis, the bus fare on another, petrol prices on a third, passenger incomes on a fourth, and tube revenue on a fifth, plot all these variables at the same time, and fit or work out the average relation between tube revenue and each of these influences when they are simultaneously considered. Although this is technically quite difficult, conceptually it is simply an extension of fitting lines through scatter diagrams. By disentangling separate influences from data where many different factors are all moving at once, econometricians can conduct empirical economic research even though economics is not an experimental science like physics. In later chapters we report the results of some econometric research, but we never use anything more complicated than two-dimensional diagrams in the text.

Reading diagrams

It is important to make sure you know how to read a diagram or understand what it says. In Figure 2-3 we show a hypothetical relationship between two variables labelled P for price and Q for quantity. The diagram plots $Q = f(P)$ which in words means that quantity Q is a function of price

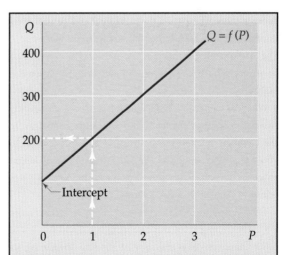

The diagram shows a straight line or linear relation between the two variables P and Q. The schedule $Q = f(P)$ describes the relation between P and Q. The statement $Q = f(P)$ says that to every value of P, say $P = 1$, there corresponds a particular value of Q that can be read off the schedule. For example, with $P = 1$ we can read off the value $Q = 200$.

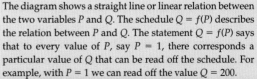

Figure 2-3   A positive linear relationship

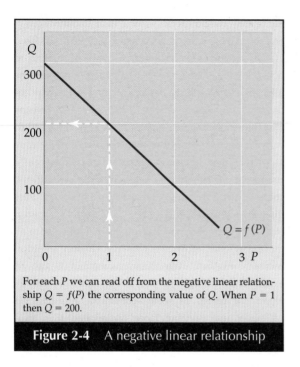

For each P we can read off from the negative linear relationship $Q = f(P)$ the corresponding value of Q. When $P = 1$ then $Q = 200$.

Figure 2-4 A negative linear relationship

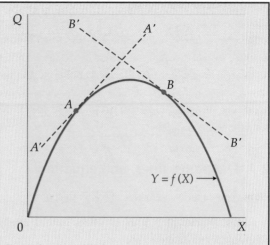

For each value of X the nonlinear function $Y = f(X)$ still allows us to determine the corresponding value of Y. The slope of a nonlinear function is not constant. At A the function $Y = f(X)$ has the same positive slope as the line $A'A'$, but at B the function $Y = f(X)$ has the same negative slope as the line $B'B'$.

Figure 2-5   A nonlinear relationship

P. Knowing the value of P allows us to work out the corresponding value of Q. The notation $f(P)$ merely tells us that we need to know values of P to make statements about Q. The diagram is a special case of this general idea. In Figure 2-3 Q is a *positive* function of P. By this we mean that higher values of P are associated with higher values of Q. Because there are units on the horizontal and vertical axes, the diagram also implies that Q is a particular function of P. The diagram tells us exactly what value of Q is implied by a particular value of P, not merely that Q is higher when P is higher.

When, as in Figure 2-3, the function is a straight line, only two pieces of information are needed to allow us to draw in the complete relationship between Q and P. We need to know the *intercept* and the *slope*. The intercept is the height at which the line crosses the vertical axis. In Figure 2-3 this occurs at $Q = 100$. It is the value of Q when $P = 0$.

There are many lines that we might have drawn in Figure 2-3, all beginning at the same point, $Q = 100$ and $P = 0$. The other characteristic is the *slope* of the line, measuring its steepness. The slope tells us how much Q (the variable on the vertical axis) changes each time we increase P (the variable on the horizontal axis) by one unit. In Figure 2-3, the slope is 100. By definition, a straight line has a constant slope. Q increases by 100 whether we move from a price of 1 to 2 or from 2 to 3 or from 3 to 4.

Figure 2-3 displays a *positive* relation between Q and P. In

a diagram, the fact that higher P values are associated with higher Q values is shown by a line that slopes *up* as we move to the right. We say the line has a positive slope. Figure 2-4 shows a case where Q is a *negative* function of P. Higher P values now imply smaller Q values. The line has a negative slope.

Relationships in economics need not be straight lines, or what we call linear relationships. Figure 2-5 shows a nonlinear relationship between two variables Y and X. Notice that the slope keeps changing. Each time we increase X by one unit we obtain a different increase (or decrease) in Y. Such a relationship might characterize the relationship between the rate of income tax X and total revenue from income tax Y. When the tax rate is zero, no revenue is raised. When the tax rate is 100 per cent nobody bothers to work and revenue is again zero. Beginning from a zero tax rate, increases in tax rates first raise then lower total tax revenue. Diagrams are useful in economics because they can display in a simple way the essence of real-life problems.

2-8 A final look at the problem of 'other things equal'

Diagrams are especially useful for thinking about the relationship between two variables when it is known that other things can be held constant. A diagram might help

BOX 2-2

Get a Becker view: use an economist's spectacles

Most people accept that the economic analysis of markets – thinking about how incentives affect resource allocation – helps us understand trends in things like inflation or unemployment. Can the same tools be applied to other social behaviour less immediately identifiable as 'economic'? Should economic analysis be applied to crime? To marriage? To drug use?

Since many of our tools embody the assumption that individual behaviour is driven by self-interest, rather than, say, by an altruistic concern for others, some economists are doubtful of the ability of economics to shed useful light on highly interactive 'social' situations. Other economists have no such fears. In 1992 Chicago economist Gary Becker was awarded the Nobel Prize for Economics for his pioneering efforts to apply the logic of economic incentives to almost every facet of human behaviour. Some examples of Becker in action . . .

Drugs: Prohibition of alcohol gave the US Al Capone but failed to stop drinking. The end of Prohibition 'was a confession that the US experiment in banning drinking had failed dismally. It was not an expression of support for heavy drinking or alcoholism'. Becker's solution for drugs is the same – legalize, boost government tax revenue, protect minors, and cut out organized crime's monopoly on supply.

Marriage and divorce: 'The courtroom is not a good place to make judgements about the unique circumstances of each marriage or relationship. We should replace judicial determination with marriage contracts that specify, among other things, the financial and child custodial terms of a divorce. Marriage contracts would become much more common if we set aside the legal tradition that they are not unenforceable.'

Do such views shed new light on old problems or merely reveal the limitations of traditional economic analysis? You must make up your own mind. But, even if you are unconvinced, it is helpful to ask what feature of a particular social situation you think renders it immune to economic analysis.

Source: G. S. Becker and G. N. Becker, *The Economics of Life*, McGraw-Hill, 1997.

London Transport think about the effects of changing tube fares.

Between 1979 and 1998 Britain's national income, in constant 1995 prices, increased from £516 billion to £773 billion. People had a lot more spending power by 1998. They could afford more tube journeys even if (real) prices remained unchanged. Unless we take account of this, we omit a key determinant of demand and misinterpret what was going on. Figure 2-6 replots Figure 2-2 but divides it into two periods: 1979–83, when national income averaged £510 billion a year, and 1984–98 during which national income averaged nearly £658 billion a year. Once we allow for the fact that higher incomes tend to increase demand for tube journeys, the underlying positive relationship between fares and revenue becomes much clearer. Figure 2-6 makes more sense of the data than Figure 2-2.

Other things equal is a device for looking at the relation between two variables, but remembering other variables also matter.

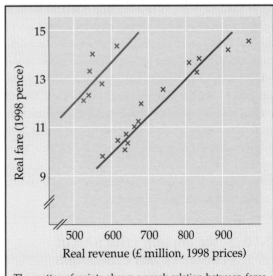

The scatter of points shows a weak relation between fares and revenue. However, incomes of passengers were much lower before 1984. Allowing for changes in income, the relation between fares and revenue is clear.

Figure 2-6   Other things equal

2-9 Theories and evidence

We can now summarize the way in which economists approach the analysis of a particular problem. There are three distinct stages. First, a phenomenon is observed or contemplated and the problem is formulated. By armchair reasoning or a cursory inspection of the data, we see that tube fares have something to do with tube revenues. We want to understand what this relationship is and why it exists.

The second stage is to develop a theory or model that captures the essence of the phenomenon. By thinking about the decision about which type of transport to use, we identify the factors relevant to tube usage and hence tube revenue.

The third stage is to *test* the predictions of the theory by confronting it with economic data. An econometric examination of the data can be used to quantify the factors the model emphasizes. In particular, we can see if on average these factors work in the direction our model suggests. Indeed, we can go further. By including in our econometric investigation some additional factors that we deliberately left out of our model in the quest for simplicity, we can check that these additional influences were of sufficiently small quantitative importance that it was legitimate to leave them out of the analysis.

Suppose we confront our theory with the data and conclude that the two seem compatible. We then say that we *do not reject* our theory. When our model is rejected we have to start again. However, when our model is not rejected by the data, this does not guarantee that we have found the correct model. There may be a completely different model which has escaped our attention and which would also be compatible with our particular collection of data. As time elapses, we will acquire new data. We can also use data from other countries. The more we confront our model with different collections of data and find that it is still not rejected, the more confidence we shall have that we have discovered the correct explanation of the economic behaviour in which we are interested.

2-10 Some popular criticisms of economics and economists

In this chapter we have introduced the toolkit used by economists. You may have some nagging doubts about some of these techniques or about the whole approach. We conclude this chapter by discussing some of the popular criticisms of economics and economists.

Economics is a non-subject. No two economists ever agree It is important to distinguish positive economics and normative economics. In Chapter 1 we pointed out that, even if all economists agreed on a positive economic analysis of how the world works, there would be enormous scope for disagreement on normative recommendations based on differing value judgements. A great deal of the disagreements between economists fall under this heading.

Nor is it surprising that there are important and persistent disagreements in positive economics. Economics can only rarely be an experimental science. It would be prohibitively expensive to induce half of the population to become unemployed merely to find out how the economy then works. Since we cannot typically undertake such experiments, we have to try to disentangle different factors from past data to overcome the problem of other things equal. Using data from a large number of years makes it easier to do this unravelling but introduces a new problem. Since attitudes and institutions are slowly changing, data from many years ago may no longer be relevant to current behaviour. The problems we confront are difficult ones and we simply have to do the best we can.

Finally, it would be a mistake to suppose that there are not serious disagreements between physicists or doctors or engineers. These may be less apparent than disagreements between economists. Most ordinary citizens do not pretend to know much about physics; everybody thinks he or she knows a bit about the problems that economists study.

Models in economics are hopelessly simple. They have nothing to do with reality A model is a deliberate simplification to help us think more clearly. A good model simplifies a lot but does not distort reality too much. It is successful in capturing the main features of the problem. The test of a good model is not how simple it is, but how much of observed behaviour it is capable of explaining.

Sometimes we can get a long way with a very simple model. You will see examples of such models in later chapters. On other occasions, the behaviour we wish to describe is genuinely complex and a simple model may be insufficient. Where a more realistic model would take us beyond the scope of this book, we will nevertheless introduce a simple model to allow us to begin to understand the elements of the problem.

People are not as mercenary as economists make out. Prices, incomes, and profit are not the main determinants of behaviour We can certainly think of decisions where this is a fair comment. Marriage is typically though not exclusively determined by non-economic considerations. Economists believe that most of the phenomena they study, such as the decision about whether to travel by bus or tube, are determined primarily by economic incentives. This is very different from asserting that only economic incentives matter.

A successful advertising campaign by tube operators would change the relation between tube fares and revenue. So would a change in social attitudes as, for example, if it became the 'done thing' to take the tube. Economists recognize that knowledge of politics, sociology, and psychology would be necessary to provide a more complete description of human behaviour. These are all factors that economists subsume under the heading of 'other things equal'. Economics emphasizes the effect of economic incentives. Social attitudes change only slowly and for many purposes may be treated as being held constant. However, if an economist were told, or discovered, that there had been an important change in social attitudes, it would be straightforward to include this in the analysis.

People are human beings. You cannot reduce their actions to scientific laws Physicists accept that molecules behave randomly but that it is possible to construct and test theories based on average or systematic behaviour. Economists take the same view about people. We shall never explain actions based on whim or because you got out of bed on the wrong side. However, random differences in behaviour tend to cancel out on average. We may be able to describe average behaviour with a lot more certainty.

If behaviour shows no systematic tendencies – tendencies to do the same thing when confronted by the same situation – there is really nothing to discuss. The past will be no guide to the future and every decision is a one-off decision. Not only is this view unconstructive, but it is not usually supported by the data. In the last resort the economic theories that survive are those that are consistently compatible with the data. The more random is human behaviour, the less will be the systematic element about which we can form theories and use to make predictions. Nevertheless, we must always do the best we can. It is better to be able to say something about behaviour than nothing at all. Sometimes, as you will shortly discover, we can say rather a lot about behaviour.

SUMMARY

● There is a continuing interplay between models and facts in the study of economic relationships and problems. A model is a simplified framework for organizing the way we think about a problem.

● Data or facts are essential for two reasons. They suggest relationships which we should aim to explain. Having formulated our theories, we can also use data to test our hypotheses and to quantify the effects that they imply.

● Tables present data in a form that is easily understood. Time series data are values of a given variable at different points in time. Cross-section data refer to the same point in time but to different values of the same variable across different people.

● Index numbers express data relative to some given base value.

● Many index numbers refer to averages of many variables. The retail price index summarizes changes in the prices of all goods bought by households. It weights the price of each good by its importance in the budget of a typical household.

● The annual percentage change in the retail price index is the usual measure of inflation, the rate at which prices in general are changing.

● Nominal or current price variables refer to values at the prices ruling when the variable was measured. Real or constant price variables adjust nominal variables for changes in the general level of prices. They are inflation-adjusted measures.

● Scatter diagrams show the relationship between two variables plotted in the diagram. It is possible to fit a line through these points to summarize the average relationship between the two variables. Econometricians use computers to fit average relationships between many variables simultaneously. In principle, this allows us to get round the other-things-equal problem which always applies in two dimensions.

● Analytical diagrams are often useful in building a model. They show relationships between two variables holding other things equal. If we wish to change one of these other things, we have to shift the line or curve we have shown in our diagram.

● To understand how the economy works we need both theory and facts. We need theory to know what facts to look for: there are too many facts for the facts alone to tell us the correct answer. Facts without theory are useless, but theory without facts remains an unsupported assertion. We need both.

KEY TERMS

REVIEW QUESTIONS

1 Use the data of Table 2-7 to plot a scatter diagram of the relation between nominal house prices and the retail price index.

2 The accompanying table shows total consumption (spending by households) and total income received by households in the UK, both in £ billion at 1995 prices.

(a) Plot the scatter diagram showing consumption on the vertical axis and income on the horizontal axis. (b) Sketch in a fitted line through these points. (c) Can you use this to suggest a relation between consumption and income of households? Does this make sense?

	Income	Consumption
1992	462	421
1993	476	434
1994	482	447
1995	495	454
1996	505	471
1997	525	489
1998	525	505

3 Draw a diagram showing the variable X measured in pounds on the vertical axis and the variable Y measured in tons on the horizontal axis. (a) Plot the scatter diagram. (b) Is the relation between the two variables positive or negative? (c) Would it be better to fit a straight line or a curve through these points?

Year							
	1	2	3	4	5	6	7
Y	40	33	29	56	81	19	20
X	5	7	9	3	1	11	10

4 You have been employed by the police research department to study whether the level of crime is affected by the percentage of people unemployed. (a) How would you test this idea? What data would you want? (b) What other-things-equal problems would you want to bear in mind?

5 *Common fallacies* Show why the following statements are incorrect: (a) The purpose of a theory is to allow you to ignore the facts. (b) Economics cannot claim to be a science since it is incapable of controlled laboratory experiments. (c) If you look hard enough at the facts you will inevitably discover the correct theory. (d) People are people not machines. They have feelings and act haphazardly. It is misguided and even insulting to reduce their actions to scientific laws.

3 Demand, supply, and the market

Society has to find *some* way of deciding what, how, and for whom to produce. Western economies rely heavily on markets and prices to allocate resources between competing uses.

The framework of analysis is very general. It can be applied to the market for cars, haircuts, or even footballers. In each case, the interplay of *demand* (the behaviour of buyers) and *supply* (the behaviour of sellers) determines the quantity of the good produced and the price at which it is bought and sold.

3-1 The market

A **market** is a set of arrangements by which buyers and sellers are in contact to exchange goods or services.

Some markets (shops and fruit stalls) physically bring together the buyer and seller. Other markets (the Stock Exchange) operate through intermediaries (stockbrokers) who transact business on behalf of clients. E-commerce is now conducted via the Internet. In supermarkets, sellers choose the price, and leave customers to choose whether or not to buy. Antique auctions force buyers to bid against each other with the seller taking a passive role.

Although superficially different, these markets perform the same economic function. They determine prices that ensure that the quantity people wish to buy equals the quantity people wish to sell. Price and quantity cannot be considered separately. In fixing the price of a Rolls-Royce at 20 times the price of a small Ford, the market for motor cars ensures that production and sales of small Fords will greatly exceed the production and sale of Rolls-Royces. These prices guide society in choosing what, how, and for whom to produce.

To understand this process more fully, we require a model of a typical market. The essential features are demand, the behaviour of buyers, and supply, the behaviour of sellers. We can study the interaction of these forces to see how a market works in practice.

3-2 Demand, supply, and equilibrium

Demand is the quantity of a good buyers wish to purchase at each conceivable price.

Thus demand is not a particular quantity, such as six bars of chocolate, but rather a full description of the quantity of chocolate the buyer would purchase at each and every price which might be charged. The first column of Table 3-1 shows a range of prices for bars of chocolate. The second column shows the quantities demanded at these prices. Even when chocolate is free, only a finite amount is wanted. People get sick from eating too much chocolate. As the price of chocolate rises, the quantity demanded falls, other things equal. We have assumed that nobody will buy any chocolate when the price is more than £0.40 per bar. Taken together, columns (1) and (2) describe the demand for chocolate as a function of its price.

Supply is the quantity of a good sellers wish to sell at each conceivable price.

Supply is not a particular quantity but a complete description of the quantity that sellers would like to sell at each possible price. The third column of Table 3-1 shows how much sellers wish to sell at each price. Chocolate cannot be produced for nothing. Nobody would wish to supply if they receive a zero price. In our example, it takes a price of £0.20 before there is any incentive to supply chocolate. At higher prices it is increasingly lucrative to supply chocolate bars and there is a corresponding increase in the quantity supplied. Together, columns (1) and (3) describe the supply of chocolate bars as a function of their price.

Notice the distinction between *demand* and the *quantity demanded*. Demand describes the behaviour of buyers at every price. At a particular price there is a particular quantity demanded. The term 'quantity demanded' makes sense only in relation to a particular price. The same applies to *supply* and *quantity supplied*.

In everyday language, we say that when the demand for football tickets exceeds their supply some people will not get into the ground. Economists must be more precise. At the price charged for tickets, the quantity demanded exceeded the quantity supplied. A higher ticket price would have reduced the quantity demanded, perhaps leaving empty space in the ground. Yet there has been no change in demand, the schedule describing how many people want admission at each possible ticket price. The quantity demanded has changed because the price has changed.

The demand schedule relating price and quantity demanded and the supply schedule relating price and quantity supplied are each constructed on the assumption of 'other things equal'. In the demand for football tickets, one of the 'other things' is whether or not the game is being shown on television. If it is, the quantity of tickets

Table 3-1	Demand and supply of chocolate	
(1) Price (£/bar)	(2) Demand (number of boxes)	(3) Supply (number of bars)
0.00	200	0
0.10	160	0
0.20	120	40
0.30	80	80
0.40	40	120
0.50	0	160

demanded at each and every price will be lower than if the game is not televised. To understand how a market works, we must first explain why demand and supply are what they are. (Is the game on television? Has the ground capacity been extended by building a new stand?) Then we examine how the price adjusts to balance the quantities supplied and demanded, given the underlying supply and demand schedules relating quantity to price.

Let us think again about the market for chocolate described in Table 3-1. Other things equal, *the lower the price of chocolate, the higher the quantity demanded*. Other things equal, *the higher the price of chocolate, the higher the quantity supplied*. A campaign by dentists warning of the effect of chocolate on tooth decay, or a fall in household incomes, would change the 'other things' relevant to the demand for chocolate. Either of these changes would reduce the demand for chocolate, reducing the quantities demanded at each price. Cheaper cocoa beans, or technical advances in packaging chocolate bars, would change the 'other things' relevant to the supply of chocolate bars. They would tend to increase the supply of chocolate bars, increasing the quantity supplied at each possible price.

The market and the equilibrium price

For the moment, we assume that all these other things remain constant. We combine the behaviour of buyers and sellers to model how the market for chocolate bars would actually work. At low prices, the quantity demanded exceeds the quantity supplied but the reverse is true at high prices. At some intermediate price, which we call the 'equilibrium price', the quantity demanded just equals the quantity supplied.

The **equilibrium price** clears the market for chocolate. It is the price at which the quantity supplied equals the quantity demanded.

Table 3-1 shows that the equilibrium price is £0.30: 80 bars is the quantity buyers wish to buy and sellers wish to sell at this price. We call 80 bars the *equilibrium quantity*. At prices below £0.30, the quantity demanded exceeds the quantity supplied and some buyers will be frustrated. There is a shortage, what we call *excess demand*. You will realize that when economists say there is excess demand they are using a convenient shorthand for the more complicated expression: the quantity demanded exceeds the quantity supplied *at this price*.

Conversely, at any price above £0.30, the quantity supplied exceeds the quantity demanded. Sellers will be left with unsold stock. To describe this surplus, economists use the shorthand *excess supply*, it being understood that this means excess in the quantity supplied *at this price*. Only at £0.30, the equilibrium price, does the quantity demanded equal the quantity supplied. The market clears and people can buy or sell as much as they want at the equilibrium price.

Is the market automatically in equilibrium? If so, what brings this about? Suppose the price of chocolate is initially £0.50, higher than the equilibrium price. Producers wish to sell 160 bars but nobody wishes to buy at this price. Sellers have to cut the price to clear their stock. Cutting the price to £0.40 has two effects. It increases the quantity demanded to 40 bars and it reduces the quantity producers wish to supply to 120 bars. Both effects reduce the excess supply. The process of price-cutting will continue until the equilibrium price of £0.30 is reached and excess supply has been eliminated. At this price the market clears.

When the price lies below the equilibrium price the process works in reverse. At a price of £0.20, the quantity demanded is 120 bars but the quantity supplied is only 40 bars. Sellers run out of stock and realize they can charge higher prices. This incentive to raise prices continues until the equilibrium price is reached, excess demand is eliminated, and the market clears.

At any particular instant, the market price may not be the equilibrium price. If not, there will be either excess supply or excess demand, depending on whether the price lies above or below the equilibrium price. But these forces themselves provide the incentive to change prices towards the equilibrium price. In this sense, markets are self-correcting.

Later in this book, we shall see that some key issues in economics turn on how quickly prices adjust to restore equilibrium in particular markets.

3-3 Demand and supply curves

Table 3-1 shows demand and supply conditions in the chocolate market and allows us to find the equilibrium price

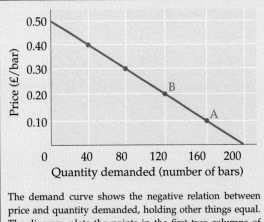

The demand curve shows the negative relation between price and quantity demanded, holding other things equal. The diagram plots the points in the first two columns of Table 3-1. Plotting all the points and joining them up, we obtain the demand curve.

Figure 3-1   The demand curve for chocolate

and quantity. It is convenient to approach the same problem diagrammatically.

The *demand curve* shows the relation between price and quantity demanded, holding other things constant. In Figure 3-1 we measure on the vertical axis prices of chocolate bars. Corresponding quantities demanded are measured on the horizontal axis. The demand curve plots the data in the first two columns of Table 3-1. The point *A* shows that 160 bars are demanded at a price of £0.10. The point *B* shows that 120 bars are demanded at a price of £0.20. Plotting all the points and joining them up, we obtain the demand curve. In our example, this curve happens to be a straight line. It has a negative slope. Larger quantities are demanded at lower prices.

The *supply curve* shows the relation between price and quantity supplied, holding other things constant. In Figure 3-2 we plot columns (1) and (3) of Table 3-1. Again we join up the different data points.

In Figure 3-3, we show the demand curve, labelled *DD*, and the supply curve, labelled *SS*, in the same diagram. We can now re-examine our analysis of excess supply, excess demand, and equilibrium. Consider a particular price as represented by a height on the vertical axis. At a price below the equilibrium price, the horizontal distance between the supply curve and the demand curve at this height shows the excess demand at this price. For example, at £0.20 the quantity supplied is 40 bars, the quantity demanded 120 bars, and the distance *AB* represents the excess demand of 80 bars. Conversely, at a price above the equilibrium price there is excess supply. At £0.40, 40 bars are demanded, 120

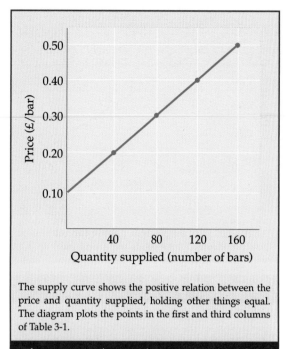

The supply curve shows the positive relation between the price and quantity supplied, holding other things equal. The diagram plots the points in the first and third columns of Table 3-1.

Figure 3-2   The supply curve for chocolate

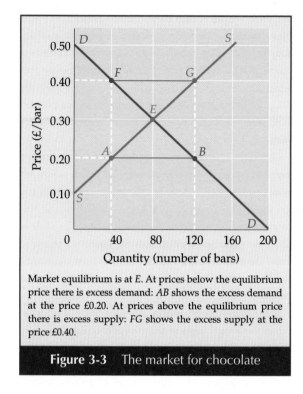

Market equilibrium is at E. At prices below the equilibrium price there is excess demand: AB shows the excess demand at the price £0.20. At prices above the equilibrium price there is excess supply: FG shows the excess supply at the price £0.40.

Figure 3-3   The market for chocolate

bars are supplied and the horizontal distance FG measures the excess supply of 80 bars at this price.

Suppose the price is £0.40. Only 40 bars are sold even though sellers would like to sell 120 bars. How do we know that it is sellers not buyers who are frustrated when their wishes differ? Participation in a market is voluntary. Buyers are not *forced* to buy nor sellers forced to sell. When markets are not in equilibrium, the quantity transacted must be the *smaller* of the quantity supplied and the quantity demanded. Any quantity larger than 40 bars at a price of £0.40 would involve buyers in forced purchases. Similarly, when the price is £0.20, any quantity larger than 40 bars would involve sellers in forced sales.

Market equilibrium is shown by the intersection of the demand curve DD and the supply curve SS, at a price of £0.30, at which 80 bars are transacted. At any other price, the quantity traded is the smaller of the quantity demanded and the quantity supplied. We can now reconsider *price determination* in the chocolate market. Figure 3-3 implies that there is excess supply at all prices above the equilibrium price of £0.30. Sellers react to unsold stocks by cutting prices. Only when prices have been reduced to the equilibrium price will excess supply be eliminated. The equilibrium position is shown by the point E. Conversely, at prices below £0.30 there is excess demand, which bids up the price of chocolate, gradually eliminating excess demand until the equilibrium point E is reached. In equilibrium

buyers and sellers can trade as much as they wish at the equilibrium price and there is no incentive for any further price changes.

3-4 Behind the demand curve

The demand curve depicts the relation between price and quantity demanded *holding other things constant*. What are those 'other things'? The other things relevant to demand curves can usually be grouped under three headings: the price of related goods, the income of consumers (buyers), and consumer tastes or preferences. We look at each of these in turn.

The price of related goods

In Chapter 2 we discussed the demand for tube travel. A rise in bus fares or petrol prices would increase the quantity of tube travel demanded at each possible price. In everyday language, buses and cars are *substitutes* for the tube. A journey may be made by bus or car instead of by tube. Similarly, petrol and cars are *complements* because you cannot use a car without also using fuel. A rise in the price of petrol tends to reduce the demand for cars.

A price increase for one good raises the demand for **substitutes** for this good, but reduces the demand for **complements** to the good.

BOX 3-1 — One little piggy went to market

The 1996 BSE crisis led to a collapse of the demand for British beef. With a lower demand curve, the equilibrium price of beef fell. Consumers switched to chicken and pork, bidding up the price of pig meat by almost 40 per cent. Many farmers switched from rearing cows to pigs, but it took nearly two years before these new ventures could get pigs to market. Unfortunately there was a surge of pig supply and prices collapsed again!

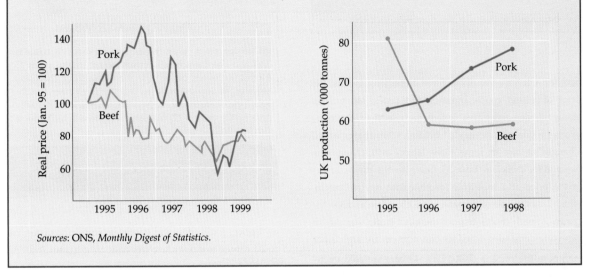

Sources: ONS, *Monthly Digest of Statistics*.

How do these ideas about substitutes and complements relate to the demand for chocolate bars? Clearly, other sweets (jelly babies) are substitutes for chocolate. An increase in the price of other sweets increases the quantity of chocolate demanded at each possible chocolate price, as people substitute away from other sweets towards chocolate. If people buy chocolate to eat at the cinema, films would be a complement for bars of chocolate. A rise in the price of cinema tickets would reduce the demand for chocolate since fewer people will go to the cinema. Nevertheless, it is difficult to think of a lot of goods that are complements for chocolate. This suggests, correctly, that most of the time goods are substitutes for each other. Complementarity is usually a more specific feature (CD players and CDs, coffee and milk, shoes and shoelaces).

Consumer incomes

The second category of 'other things equal' when we draw a particular demand curve is consumer income. When incomes rise, the demand for most goods increases. Typically, consumers buy more of everything. However, there are exceptions.

For a **normal good** demand increases when incomes rise. For an **inferior good** demand falls when incomes rise.

As their name suggests, most goods are normal goods. Inferior goods are typically cheap but low-quality goods which people would prefer not to buy if they could afford to spend a little more.

Tastes

The third category of things held constant along a particular demand curve is consumer tastes or preferences. In part, these are shaped by convenience, custom, and social attitudes. The fashion for the mini-skirt reduced the demand for textile material. The emphasis on health and fitness has increased the demand for jogging equipment, health foods, and sports facilities while reducing the demand for cream cakes, butter, and cigarettes.

3-5 Shifts in the demand curve

We are now in a position to distinguish between movements along a given demand curve and shifts in the demand curve itself. In Figure 3-1 we drew the demand curve for chocolate

Table 3-2	Ice cream prices and chocolate demand	
Price of chocolate (£/bar)	Demand for chocolate (number of bars)	
	Low ice cream price	High ice cream price
0.00	200	280
0.10	160	240
0.20	120	200
0.30	80	160
0.40	40	120
0.50	0	80

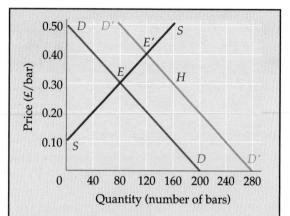

At low ice cream prices, the demand curve for chocolate is *DD* and the market equilibrium occurs at the point *E*. Higher ice cream prices raise the demand for chocolate, shifting the demand curve to *D'D'*. At the former equilibrium price there is now excess demand *EH*, which gradually bids up the price of chocolate until the new equilibrium is reached at *E'*.

Figure 3-4 Ice cream prices and chocolate demand

bars for a given level of the three underlying factors: the price of related goods, incomes, and tastes. Movements along the demand curve isolate the effects of chocolate prices on quantity demanded holding other things equal. Changes in any of these three factors will change the demand for chocolate. Table 3-2 illustrates the effect of a rise in the price of a substitute for chocolate, say ice cream, which leads people to demand more chocolate and less ice cream. At each chocolate price there is a larger quantity of chocolate demanded when ice cream prices are high, since people substitute chocolate for ice cream. In Figure 3-4 we show the change in ice cream prices leading to a *shift* in the demand curve from *DD* to *D'D'*. The entire demand curve shifts to the right.

Changes in the price of ice cream have no effect on the incentives to supply chocolate bars: at each price suppliers wish to supply the same quantity of chocolate as before. The increase in demand, or rightward shift in the demand curve, changes the equilibrium price and quantity in the chocolate market. Equilibrium has changed from *E* to *E'*. The new equilibrium price is £0.40 and the new equilibrium quantity is 120 bars. A glance back at Table 3-1 will confirm this.

We can even sketch the transition from the old equilibrium at *E* to the new equilibrium at *E'*. Consider the instant when ice cream prices rise. The demand curve for chocolate shifts from *DD* to *D'D'*. Until the price changes from £0.30 there is an excess demand *EH* at this price: 160 bars are now demanded but only 80 bars are supplied. This excess demand puts upward pressure on prices which gradually rise to the new equilibrium price of £0.40, choking the quantity demanded back from 160 bars to 120 bars and providing the incentive to increase the quantity supplied from 80 bars to 120 bars.

We draw two general lessons from this example. First, the quantity of chocolate demanded depends on four things: its

own price, prices of related goods, incomes, and tastes. We could choose to draw a two-dimensional diagram showing the relation between quantity of chocolate demanded and any one of these four factors. The other three factors would then become the 'other things equal' for this particular diagram. In drawing demand curves, we single out the price of the commodity itself (here the price of chocolate bars) to put in the diagram with quantity demanded. The other three factors become the 'other things equal' for drawing a particular demand curve, and changes in any of these other three factors will shift the position of demand curves.

Why do we single out the price of the commodity itself to plot against quantity demanded? Chiefly because we are interested in how the market for chocolate works. Prices of related goods, incomes, and tastes are all determined elsewhere in the economy. In particular, by focusing on the price of chocolate, we have been able to show the self-correcting mechanism by which the market reacts to excess demand or excess supply, inducing changes in chocolate prices within the chocolate market to restore equilibrium.

Second, our example shows the method of analysis by *comparative statics*.

In **comparative static analysis** we change one of the 'other things equal' and examine the effect on equilibrium price and quantity.

The analysis is comparative because it compares the old and new equilibrium positions, and it is static because it compares only the two equilibrium positions. In each equilibrium, prices and quantities are unchanging. Comparative static analysis is not interested in the dynamic path by which the economy moves from one equilibrium to the other, only in the point from which it began and the point at which it ends up.

Figure 3-4 may also be used to analyse the effect of a change in one of the 'other things equal' which reduces the demand for chocolate. Suppose the demand curve is initially $D'D'$ and the market begins in equilibrium at the point E'. Let there be a change that reduces the demand for chocolate to DD. This change might be a fall in the price of a chocolate substitute such as ice cream, a fall in consumer incomes, or a change in tastes away from liking chocolate. When the demand curve shifts left to DD, showing less chocolate demanded at each price, the new equilibrium will be given at the point E. At the original price of £0.40 there will be excess supply, which will gradually bid prices down to the new equilibrium price of £0.30. When the demand curve shifts to the left, there is a fall in both the equilibrium price and the equilibrium quantity.

3-6 Behind the supply curve

Before discussing changes that shift supply curves, we discuss in greater detail why increases in price increase the quantity supplied, hold constant all other factors. At low prices, only the most efficient chocolate producers will be able to make any profits. As prices rise, producers who could not previously compete can now make a profit in the chocolate business and will wish to supply. Moreover, previously existing firms may be able to expand output by working overtime, or buying fancy equipment not justified when selling chocolate at lower prices. In general, higher prices are needed to provide an incentive for firms to produce more chocolate. Other things equal, supply curves slope upwards as we move to the right.

Just as we investigated the 'other things equal' along a demand curve, we now examine three categories of 'other things equal' along a supply curve. These categories are: technology available to producers, the cost of inputs (labour, machines, fuel, and raw materials), and government regulation. Along any particular supply curve, all of these are held constant. A change in any of these categories will shift the supply curve by changing the amount producers wish to supply at each price.

Technology

A supply curve is drawn for a given technology. Better technology will shift the supply curve to the right since producers will supply a larger quantity than previously at each price. An improvement in cocoa refining makes it possible to produce more chocolate for any given total cost. Faster shipping and better refrigeration lead to less wastage in spoiled cocoa beans. Technological advance enables firms to supply more at each price.

As a determinant of supply, technology must be interpreted very broadly. It embraces all know-how about production methods, not merely the state of available machinery. In agriculture, the development of disease-resistant seeds is a technological advance. Improved weather forecasting might enable better timing of planting and harvesting. A technological advance is any idea that allows more output from the same inputs as before. Using the terminology of Chapter 1, a technological advance shifts the production possibility frontier outwards.

Input costs

A particular supply curve is drawn for a given level of input prices. A reduction in input prices (lower wages, lower fuel costs) will induce firms to supply more output at each price, shifting the supply curve to the right. Higher input prices make production less attractive and shift the supply curve to the left. For example, if a late frost destroys much of the cocoa crop, the ensuing scarcity will bid up the price of cocoa beans. Chocolate producers supply less chocolate at each price than previously.

Government regulation

In discussing technology we spoke only of technological advances. Once people have discovered a better production method they are unlikely subsequently to forget it. Government regulations can sometimes be viewed as imposing a technological change that is *adverse* for producers. If so, the effect of regulations will be to shift the supply curve to the left, reducing quantity supplied at each price.

More stringent safety regulations prevent chocolate producers using the most productive process because it is quite dangerous to workers. Anti-pollution devices may raise the cost of making cars, and regulations to protect the environment may make it unprofitable for firms to extract surface mineral deposits which could have been cheaply quarried but whose extraction now requires expensive landscaping. Whenever regulations prevent producers from selecting the production methods they would otherwise

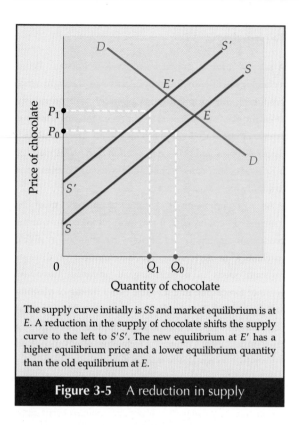

The supply curve initially is SS and market equilibrium is at E. A reduction in the supply of chocolate shifts the supply curve to the left to $S'S'$. The new equilibrium at E' has a higher equilibrium price and a lower equilibrium quantity than the old equilibrium at E.

Figure 3-5 A reduction in supply

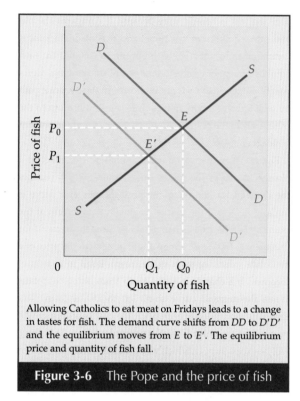

Allowing Catholics to eat meat on Fridays leads to a change in tastes for fish. The demand curve shifts from DD to $D'D'$ and the equilibrium moves from E to E'. The equilibrium price and quantity of fish fall.

Figure 3-6 The Pope and the price of fish

have chosen, the effect of regulations is to shift the supply curve to the left.

3-7 Shifts in the supply curve

Along a given supply curve we hold constant technology, the prices of inputs, and the extent of government regulation. We now undertake a comparative static analysis of what happens when a change in one of these 'other things equal' categories leads to a reduction in supply. Suppose, for example, that an increase in the stringency of safety legislation makes it more expensive to produce chocolate bars in highly mechanized factories. In Figure 3-5 we show a shift to the left in the supply curve from SS to $S'S'$. If we wish to know only the direction, but not the magnitude, of the change in equilibrium price and quantity, it is not necessary to put scale units on the horizontal and vertical axis. Equilibrium shifts from the point E to the point E'. Thus equilibrium price rises but equilibrium quantity falls when the supply curve shifts to the left. Conversely, a supply curve shift to the right can be analysed by supposing the supply curve is initially $S'S'$ and the market is in equilibrium at the point E'. A change that increases supply will shift the supply curve to the right, say to the position shown by the supply curve SS. The new equilibrium will be

at the point E. Thus an increase in supply leads to a higher equilibrium quantity and lower equilibrium price.

3-8 The Pope and the price of fish

Hypothetical examples are all very well, but it is reassuring to learn that demand and supply analysis works in practice. We report an interesting example based on research by Frederick Bell.[1] Until 1966 Roman Catholics were not allowed to eat meat on Fridays and tended to eat fish instead. In 1966 the Pope said that henceforth Catholics could eat meat on Friday. What do you think happened to the average weekly price of fish and average weekly quantity of fish consumed?

In 1966 we should expect the demand curve for fish to shift to the left as in Figure 3-6. Some Catholics who had previously been forced to eat fish no doubt preferred to eat meat and would substitute meat for Friday fish when allowed to do so. This is a simple example of the effect of a change in tastes on the demand curve. Our model predicts that the demand curve should shift from DD to $D'D'$, leading to a fall in the equilibrium price and quantity of fish

---

[1] Frederick W. Bell, 'The Pope and the price of Fish', *American Economic Review*, December 1968.

as equilibrium shifts from the point E to the point E'. Using data on fish prices and fish sales in the United States before and after 1966, Bell showed that this was precisely what happened.

3-9 Free markets and price controls

Free markets allow prices to be determined purely by the forces of supply and demand.

Government actions may shift demand and supply curves, as when changes in safety legislation shift the supply curve, but the government makes no attempt to regulate prices directly. If prices are sufficiently flexible, the pressure of excess supply or excess demand will quickly bid prices in a free market to their equilibrium level. Markets will not be free when effective price controls exist.

Price controls are government rules or laws that forbid the adjustment of prices to clear markets.

Price controls may be *floor* prices (minimum prices) or *ceiling* prices (maximum prices).

Price ceilings make it illegal for sellers to charge more than a specific maximum price and are typically introduced when a shortage of a commodity threatens to raise its price by a substantial amount. High prices are the device by which a free market rations goods in scarce supply. Although high prices are one way to solve the allocation problem, ensuring that only a small quantity of the scarce commodity will be demanded, they may lead to a solution that society believes to be unfair, a normative value judgement. For example, high food prices mean considerable hardship for the poor. Faced with a national food shortage, a government might prefer to impose a price ceiling on food so that poor people can continue to buy adequate quantities of food.

In Figure 3-7 we show the market for food. Perhaps war has disrupted imports of food. The supply curve lies far to the left and the free market equilibrium price P_0 is very high. Instead of allowing free market equilibrium at the point E, the government imposes a price ceiling at P_1. The quantity sold is then Q_1 and excess demand is given by the distance AB. The price ceiling creates a shortage of supply relative to demand by holding food prices below their equilibrium level.[2]

---

[2] Notice that a price ceiling imposed at P_2 above the equilibrium price would simply be irrelevant. The free market equilibrium at E could still be attained and the price control would make no difference.

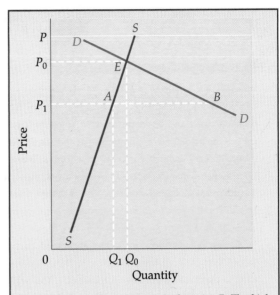

Free market equilibrium occurs at the point E. The high price P_0 chokes off quantity demanded to ration scarce supply. A price ceiling at P_1 succeeds in holding down the price but leads to excess demand AB. It also reduces quantity supplied from Q_0 to Q_1. A price ceiling at P_2 is irrelevant since the free market equilibrium at E can still be attained.

Figure 3-7   The effect of a price ceiling

The ceiling price P_1 allows some of the poor to buy food they could not otherwise have afforded. However, it has reduced total food supplied from Q_0 to Q_1. Furthermore, since there is excess demand AB at the ceiling price, some form of rationing must be used to decide which potential buyers are actually supplied. This rationing system could be highly arbitrary. Food suppliers may reserve supplies for their friends, not necessarily the poor. Indeed, suppliers may even accept bribes from those who can afford to pay to jump the queue: a 'black market'. Holding down the price of food might not help the poor after all. For this reason, the imposition of ceiling prices may be accompanied by government-organized rationing by quota, to ensure that available supply is shared out fairly, independently of ability to pay.

Where price controls are maintained for many years they may have further repercussions. Many countries have imposed rent controls limiting the rent a landlord can charge tenants for accommodation. Intended to provide cheap housing for the poor, such legislation may have perverse effects, as Figure 3-8 illustrates. Initially, the supply curve SS may be very steep. Existing landlords cannot quickly put their accommodation to other uses. Hence a

BOX 3-2 — An important distinction: movements along a curve and shifts of the curve itself

In everyday language we refer to an increase in demand without distinguishing between *shifts* in the demand curve and *movements along* a given demand curve. The accompanying figure shows that, from the point A on the demand curve DD two quite different 'increases in demand' are possible. One is an increase in the quantity demanded, moving along the curve from A to B. This increase results from consumer adjustment to a reduction in price.

The second is a shift in the entire demand curve from DD to D'D'. At the going price P_0 the consumer used to purchase Q_0 but now purchases Q_1. This shift in demand is the response to an increase in the price of a substitute good (decrease in the price of a complement good), an increase in income, or a change of tastes.

The distinction between the two kinds of demand change is very important. Movement along the demand curve represents consumer adjustment to changes in the market price. Shifts in demand, by contrast, represent adjustment to outside factors (other prices, income, tastes) and lead in turn to changes in the equilibrium price and quantity.

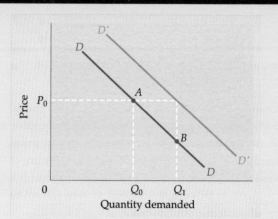

The same distinction between movements along a schedule and shifts in the schedule applies on the supply side. Sellers adjust to higher prices by moving along the supply curve. But changes in input prices, technology, or regulation shift the supply curve.

Other things equal, changes in price move us along demand and supply curves. 'Other things equal' is an important reminder that the price of a good is only one determinant of demand and supply. When other determinants change, they shift the schedules.

---

reduction in rents may scarcely diminish the quantity of rental housing supplied. In the short run the total quantity supplied at the ceiling rent R_1 is only a little less than the free market equilibrium quantity Q_0. As time elapses, however, some landlords respond to lower rents by converting their property for their own use or for sale to purchasers who wish to own their own home. After some time, the supply curve will become flatter, reaching the position $S'S'$. The rent control R_1 now leads to a large reduction to Q_2 in the quantity of rental accommodation supplied. Shortages increase, and less and less housing is available for the poor who cannot afford to buy their own houses.

Whereas the aim of a ceiling price is to reduce the price for consumers, the aim of a floor price is to raise the price for suppliers. One example of a floor price is a national minimum wage. Figure 3-9 shows the demand curve and supply curve for labour. The free market equilibrium is at the point E, where the wage is W_0. A minimum wage below W_0 will be irrelevant since the free market equilibrium can

still be attained. Suppose, in an effort to help workers, the government imposes a minimum wage at W_1. Firms will demand the quantity Q_1 and there will be excess supply AB. The lucky workers who manage to sell as much labour as they wish will be better off than before, but some workers may be worse off since total number of hours worked has fallen from Q_0 to Q_1.

Many countries set floor prices for agricultural products. Figure 3-10 shows a floor price P_1 for butter. In previous examples we have assumed that the quantity traded would be the smaller of quantity supplied and quantity demanded at the controlled price since private individuals cannot be forced to participate in a market. There is, however, another possibility: the government may intervene not only to set the control price but also to buy or sell quantities of the good to supplement private purchases and sales.

At the floor price P_1 private individuals demand Q_1 but supply Q_2. In the absence of government sales or purchases the quantity traded will be Q_1, the smaller of Q_1 and Q_2.

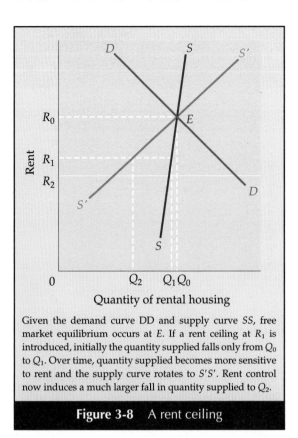

Given the demand curve DD and supply curve SS, free market equilibrium occurs at E. If a rent ceiling at R_1 is introduced, initially the quantity supplied falls only from Q_0 to Q_1. Over time, quantity supplied becomes more sensitive to rent and the supply curve rotates to $S'S'$. Rent control now induces a much larger fall in quantity supplied to Q_2.

Figure 3-8   A rent ceiling

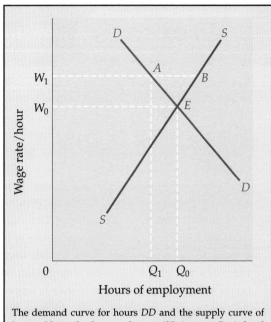

The demand curve for hours DD and the supply curve of hours SS imply free market equilibrium at E. A legal minimum wage at W_1 raises hourly wages for those who remain employed but reduces the quantity of hours of employment available from Q_0 to Q_1.

Figure 3-9   A minimum wage

However, the government may agree to purchase the excess supply AB so that neither private suppliers nor private demanders need be frustrated. Because European butter prices are set above the free market equilibrium price as part of the Common Agricultural Policy, European governments have been forced to purchase massive stocks of butter which would otherwise have been unsold at the controlled price. Hence the famous 'butter mountain'.

3-10 What, how, and for whom

The free market is one way for society to solve the basic economic questions what, how, and for whom to produce. In this chapter we have begun to see how the market allocates scarce resources among competing uses.

The market decides how much of a good should be produced by finding the price at which the quantity demanded equals the quantity supplied. Other things being equal, more of a good is produced in market equilibrium the higher is the quantity demanded at each price (the further the demand curve lies to the right) and the higher the quantity supplied at each price (the further the supply curve lies to the right).

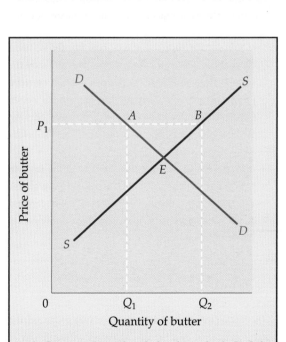

At the floor price P_1 supply is Q_2, but demand only Q_1. Only Q_1 will be traded. By buying up the excess supply AB, the government can satisfy both suppliers and consumers at the price P_1.

Figure 3-10   A floor price for butter

BOX 3-3 — Anatomy of price and quantity changes

The accompanying figure shows data for the UK construction industry. Economists are frequently asked to interpret such data. What was happening in the construction market? Was it a shift in demand, in supply, or in both that caused this pattern during 1985–98?

The construction market is a free market. It is reasonable to suppose that all the observations represent *equilibrium* prices and quantities. Thus each observation can be viewed as the intersection of a demand and a supply curve. Next, we ask what changes in the 'other things equal' determinants of supply and demand may have led to shifts in supply and demand curves and hence to changes in equilibrium price and quantity. Is it possible that all shifts are supply curve shifts? Try drawing a diagram with a given demand curve and a shifting supply curve. The equilibrium points you will trace out all lie on the given demand curve. If only supply shifts we expect a negative relation between price and quantity. We must rule out this explanation. In our data low prices tend to be associated with low quantities.

Suppose the supply curve is fixed but the demand curve shifts. The equilibrium points then all lie on the supply curve and exhibit a positive relation between price and quantity. That fits the data much better. Construction demand increased steadily during 1985–89 and then fell back during 1990–93, before recovering again.

Of course, in practice there will be shifts in both demand and supply curves. The points in the scatter diagram suggest large fluctuations in the demand curve but relatively small shifts in the supply curve. Try drawing this for yourself.

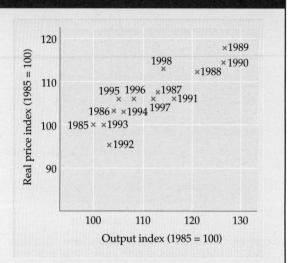

Having made a diagnosis, we now attempt to gather corroborating evidence. Economy-wide activity is an important determinant of the demand for construction. UK real GDP grew strongly during 1985–89, fell sharply during 1990–92, and grew again during 1993–98.

Examining price and quantity data, it is sometimes difficult to disentangle supply shifts and demand shifts. Given only the data from 1989–90, it would have been much harder to be confident that we could interpret the data correctly. Our example really has two lessons. By plotting a scatter diagram it may become evident that the points essentially lie along either a supply curve or a demand curve, suggesting it was the other curve that was shifting. However, we should then bring our economic theory to bear in the search for corroborating evidence. Supply and demand have determinants that differ.

The market tells us for whom the goods are produced: the good is purchased by all those consumers willing to pay at least the equilibrium price for the good. The market also tells us who is producing: all those willing to supply at the equilibrium price. Later in this book we shall see that the market also tells us how goods are produced.

Finally, the market determines what goods are being produced. Nature supplies goods free of charge. People engage in costly production activities only if they are paid. The supply curve tells us how much has to be paid to bring supply. Figure 3-11 shows an example of a good that will not be produced. The highest price, P_1, that consumers are prepared to pay is still insufficient to persuade producers to produce.

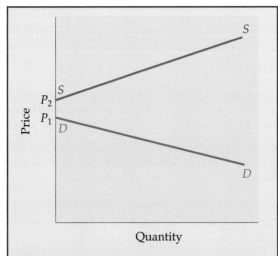

Even P_1, the highest price consumers will pay, is lower than P_2, the minimum price producers require to produce any of this good.

Figure 3-11   A good not produced

We have seen too that society may not like the answers the market provides. Free markets *do not* provide enough food for everyone to go without hunger, or enough medical care to treat all the sick. They provide food and medical care for those willing and *able to pay* the equilibrium price. Society may adopt the normative judgement that the poor should be able to enjoy more food and medical care than the free market provides them with. Society may also adopt the normative judgement that, although people are willing and able to pay for pornography, it would be socially better if this activity were banned. Few societies allow completely unrestricted free markets for all commodities. Governments intervene widely to alter the market outcome through direct regulation, taxation, and transfer payments such as unemployment benefit.

SUMMARY

● Demand is the quantity that buyers wish to buy at each price. Other things equal, the lower the price, the higher the quantity demanded. Demand curves slope downwards.

● Supply is the quantity of a good sellers wish to sell at each price. Other things equal, the higher the price, the higher the quantity. Supply curves slope upwards.

● The market clears, or is in equilibrium, when the price equates the quantity supplied and the quantity demanded. At this point supply and demand curves intersect or cross. At prices below the equilibrium price there is excess demand (shortage), which itself tends to raise the price. At prices above the equilibrium price there is excess supply (surplus), which itself tends to reduce the price. In a free market, deviations from the equilibrium price tend to be self-correcting.

● Along a given demand curve, the other things assumed equal are the prices of related goods, consumer incomes, and tastes or habits.

● An increase in the price of a substitute good (or decrease in the price of a complement good) will raise the quantity demanded at each price. An increase in consumer income will increase demand for the good if the good is a normal good but decrease demand for the good if it is an inferior good.

● Along a given supply curve the other things assumed constant are technology, the price of inputs, and the degree of government regulation. An improvement in technology, or a reduction in input prices, will increase the quantity supplied at each price.

● Any factor inducing an increase in demand shifts the demand curve to the right, increasing equilibrium price and equilibrium quantity. A decrease in demand (leftward shift of the demand curve) reduces both equilibrium price and equilibrium quantity. Any factor increasing supply shifts the supply curve to the right, increasing equilibrium quantity but reducing equilibrium price. Reductions in supply (leftward shift of the supply curve) reduce equilibrium quantity but increase equilibrium price.

● To be effective, a price ceiling must be imposed below the free market equilibrium price. It will then reduce the quantity supplied and lead to excess demand unless the government itself provides the extra quantity required. An effective price floor must be imposed above the free market equilibrium price. It will then reduce the quantity demanded unless the government adds its own demand to that of the private sector.

KEY TERMS

REVIEW QUESTIONS

1 Supply and demand data for toasters are shown below. Plot the supply curve and demand curve and find the equilibrium price and quantity.

Supply and demand for toasters

Price (£)	Quantity demanded	Quantity supplied
10	10	3
12	9	4
14	8	5
16	7	6
18	6	7
20	5	8

2 In the sample example, what is the excess supply or demand when price is (a) £12? (b) £20?

3 Describe the price movements induced by the positions described in parts (a) and (b) of the previous question. Be as precise as you can.

4 What happens to the demand curve for toasters when the price of bread rises? Show in a supply–demand diagram how the equilibrium price and quantity of toasters change.

5 How is the demand curve for toasters affected by the invention of the toaster oven, which to many people seems like a new and better way of toasting? What effect would this have on the equilibrium quantity of toasters bought and sold, and on the price of toasters? Why?

6 Goods with snob value, such as Rolex watches, may be demanded only because they are expensive. Does the demand curve for such goods slope downwards?

7 (a) Suppose that cold weather makes it more difficult to catch fish. What happens to the supply curve for fish? What happens to price and quantity? (b) Suppose that the cold weather also reduces the demand for fish, because people do not go shopping. Show what happens to the demand curve for fish. (c) What happens to the quantity of fish bought and sold when the cold weather sets in? (d) Can you say what happens to the price of fish?

8 (A much harder question. If you can do this you have really understood this chapter.) Using the toaster data, suppose a tax of £1 per toaster is now imposed directly on firms supplying toasters. Thus if a seller charges £16, the seller gets £15 and the government £1. What happens to the quantity of toasters sold when the tax is imposed? What happens to the price that consumers pay? (*Hint*: There is now a gap between the price consumers pay and the net price sellers receive. If you measure the price to the consumer on the vertical axis, does either the demand curve or the supply curve shift? If so, by how much?)

9 *Common fallacies* (a) Manchester United is a more famous football club than Sunderland. United will always have greater success in filling their stadium. (b) The European 'butter mountain' illustrates the success of the Common Agricultural Policy. It shows how productivity can be improved when farmers are inspired by the European ideal. (c) Holding down rents ensures plenty of cheap housing for the poor.

4 Government in the mixed economy

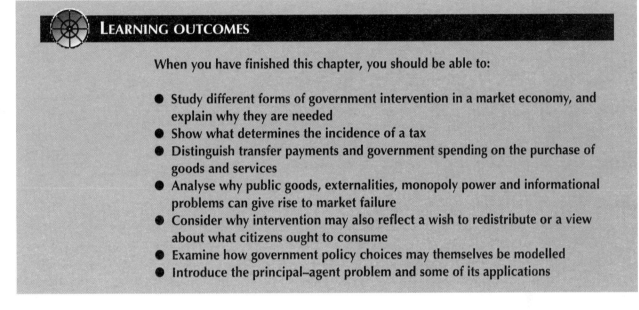

LEARNING OUTCOMES

When you have finished this chapter, you should be able to:

- Study different forms of government intervention in a market economy, and explain why they are needed
- Show what determines the incidence of a tax
- Distinguish transfer payments and government spending on the purchase of goods and services
- Analyse why public goods, externalities, monopoly power and informational problems can give rise to market failure
- Consider why intervention may also reflect a wish to redistribute or a view about what citizens ought to consume
- Examine how government policy choices may themselves be modelled
- Introduce the principal–agent problem and some of its applications

Most resources in Western economies are allocated through markets in which individuals and private firms trade with other individuals or firms. However, governments play a major role. They set the legal rules; they buy goods and services, from paper clips to aircraft carriers; they produce services, such as defence; and they make payments such as pensions. Through taxation and borrowing, governments exert a major influence on prices, interest rates, and production.

This chapter addresses three basic questions about the government's role in economic life. What do governments *actually do*? How can governments *in principle* improve the allocation of resources in the economy? How do governments *decide* what to do?

4-1 What governments do

Table 4-1 shows how the scale of government activity has grown steadily over the last century. It now ranges from a third of national income in the United States to nearly two-thirds in Sweden. What do governments actually do?

Table 4-1 Government spending as percentage of national income

	1880	1929	1960	2000
Japan	11	19	18	40
USA	8	10	28	32
Germany	10	31	32	47
UK	10	24	32	41
France	15	19	35	54
Sweden	6	8	31	59

Sources: World Bank, *World Development Report*; OECD, *Economic Outlook*.

BOX 4-1   Provision of market infrastructure: lessons from transition economies

One way to think about the role of government in underpinning markets is to examine what governments have had to do (or have failed to to do!) in economies now making the transition from Soviet planning to market economies. When economies are poor, resources are scarce – and that includes resources for government itself. As a Czech minister remarked in 1990, 'to start with, the best we are going to achieve is wild west capitalism'. This vivid phrase reminds us that even the United States took a while to establish fully the rule of law, clear cut property rights, and state regulation of many private activities. Without confidence in contracts, and credible procedures for resolving disputes, it is hard to imagine markets allocating resources efficiently.

The former Soviet bloc embarked on transition to market economies because central planning was patently failing. But lacking the initial infrastructure to make markets operate reliably, the early years of transition were universally difficult. The table shows substantial falls in real output, although most transition economies in central and eastern Europe have now turned the corner. The data confirm the key role of government in supporting successful market economies.

		Central Europe	Baltics and Balkans	Ex-Soviet Republics
Annual real output change (%):	1989–94	−1.6	−4.2	−8.1
	1994–98	4.0	4.9	−5.0

Source: World Bank, World Development Report.
Note: Official statistics tend to underestimate growth – the new private sector is usually under recorded.

Create laws, rules, and regulations

Governments determine the legal framework that sets the basic rules for ownership of property and the operation of markets. If the legal framework outlaws private ownership of businesses, the economy is socialist; if businesses are owned by individuals and operated for private profit, the economy is capitalist.[1] Even in the most capitalist economies, there are limits to the rights of ownership. Not everyone can own a gun. Nor are people entirely free to use their property as they please; it is usually illegal to build a factory in a residential area.

In addition, governments at all levels *regulate* economic behaviour, setting detailed rules for the operation of businesses. Regulations include planning permission (how land can be used and where businesses can locate), health and safety regulations, and attempts to prevent some types of business, such as the sale of heroin. Some regulations apply to all businesses; examples include laws against fraud and laws that prohibit competitors from agreeing to fix prices. Some regulations apply only to certain industries, such as requirements that doctors have appropriate training.

Buy and sell goods and services

Governments buy and produce many goods and services, such as defence, education, parks, and roads, which they provide to firms and households. Most of these goods, such as defence and education, are provided to users free of direct charge. Some, such as local bus rides and government publications, are paid for directly by the user.

Governments, like private firms, must decide what to buy and what to produce themselves. For instance, governments typically buy computers but write the programs they need to operate them. In order to do this, governments must act as buyers in the markets for the services of computer programmers.

Governments also produce and sell goods. In some countries, the phone company is government-owned; in most countries, the government owns and operates urban transport such as buses and the underground.

Make transfer payments

Governments also make transfer payments, such as social security and unemployment benefits, to individuals.

Transfer payments are payments for which no current direct economic service is provided in return.

A fireman's salary is not a transfer payment; a social security

[1] The extent of private ownership is always a matter of degree, however. Governments own some businesses even in the most capitalist economies; some farms are private in even the most socialist economies.

Table 4-2 Government activity in 2000 (% of GDP)

	UK	USA	France	Germany
Spending:				
Goods & services	21	17	22	20
Transfer payments	20	16	32	27
Tax revenue	41	34	51	45
Budget deficit	0	−1	3	2

Source: OECD, *Economic Outlook*.

Table 4-3 Government debt as a percentage of national income, 1980–99

	1980	1989	1999
USA	37	54	54
Japan	52	63	107
Germany	32	41	63
France	37	41	67
Italy	58	96	119
UK	54	43	55
Sweden	44	48	68
Netherlands	45	79	67
Ireland	78	104	49

Source: OECD, *Economic Outlook*.

cheque is, as are unemployment benefits and interest payments on government borrowing.

Government spending is the sum of government purchases of goods and services and transfer payments. Table 4-2 gives a breakdown of government activity for several countries. It is much bigger in a country such as Germany than in a country such as the United States (for more data, see www.oecd.org).

Impose taxes

Governments pay for the goods they buy and for the transfer payments they make by levying taxes or by borrowing. Taxes raised at national level, such as income tax or VAT, are usually supplemented by local taxes assessed on property values or household size.

Spending, taxes, and deficits Table 4-1 shows that the scale of government activity has risen over a long period. For much of this time, governments have been reluctant to meet this extra cost in full by raising taxes. They have run *budget deficits* financed by borrowing. Budget deficits add to the government's debt. Table 4-3 shows how government debt has changed since 1980. In countries such as Italy it has now grown to very high levels indeed. In later chapters we shall address several questions. Will government spending continue to increase? Should it? Can government debt be allowed to increase indefinitely?

Try to stabilize the economy

Every market economy suffers from business cycles.

The **business cycle** consists of fluctuations of total production, or GDP, accompanied by fluctuations in the level of unemployment and the rate of inflation.

Governments often attempt to modify fluctuations in the business cycle. The government may reduce taxes in a recession in the hope that people will increase spending and

thus raise the GDP. The central bank [in the UK the Bank of England (www.bankofengland.co)], which controls the interest rates, may cut interest rates to help bring the economy out of the recession. When inflation is high, the central bank may raise the rate with the aim of reducing inflation.

These are macroeconomic policies through which the government attempts to *stabilize* the economy, keeping it close to full employment but with low inflation. We study macroeconomics in Part 4.

Affect the allocation of resources

By spending and taxing, the government plays a major part in allocating resources in the economy. In terms of what, how, and for whom, government chooses much of *what* gets produced, from defence expenditures to education to its support for the arts. It affects *how* goods are produced through regulation and through the legal system. It affects *for whom* goods are produced through its taxes and transfers, which take income away from some people and give it to others.

Beyond these direct effects, the government also affects the allocation of resources indirectly through taxes (and subsidies, which are negative taxes) on the price and level of production in individual markets. When government taxes a good, such as cigarettes, it generally reduces the quantity of that good produced; when it subsidizes a good, such as milk, it generally increases the quantity of the good produced.

The power to tax is thus the power to affect the allocation of the economy's resources, or to change what gets produced. By taxing cigarettes, the government can reduce the amount of cigarettes smoked and thereby improve health. By taxing income earned from work, the government affects the amount of time people want to work. Because

BOX 4-2   Who really pays the tax?

Suppose cigarettes cost £1 a packet. Then the government imposes a tax of 50p per packet. Do smokers end up paying the tax, or is it borne by manufacturers of cigarettes? How much of the tax can producers pass on to the consumer? We now show that this depends on the slopes of the supply and demand curve.

In the figure we plot the (after-tax) price to the consumer on the vertical axis. DD' shows the demand curve, which depends on the price to smokers (consumers). Since the price received by the producer is the consumer price minus the 50p tax per packet, the effect of the tax is to *shift* the supply curve from SS to SS' in both diagrams. Each possible quantity supplied depends on the price received by the producer, which will be the same as before only if consumer prices are 50p higher; that is why we must shift the supply curve up by 50p.

In part (a), with a flat supply curve and steep demand curve, the tax is borne mainly by cigarette consumers. Point B is nearly 50p higher than point A. Since demand is inelastic, producers can pass on most of the tax in higher prices. Supply is elastic, so the price received by producers cannot fall much. Consumers pay £1.45 and producers get £0.95 a packet. In part (b), with a flat demand curve and a steep supply curve, most of the tax is borne by cigarette producers. Demand is elastic, so attempts to pass on the tax in higher prices quickly lead to a drop in sales. Supply is inelastic, and producers hardly cut back even though the price they receive has fallen nearly 50p. Consumers pay £1.05 and producers get £0.55 a packet.

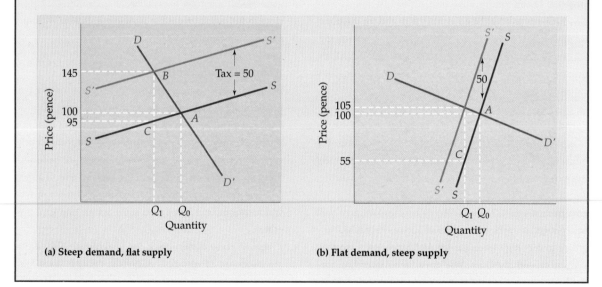

(a) Steep demand, flat supply   (b) Flat demand, steep supply

they affect the allocation of resources indirectly, through their effects on relative prices, as well as directly, taxes loom large in the workings of the market system and have a profound effect on the way society allocates its scarce resources.

4-2 What should governments do?

Why should governments intervene in a market economy? Adam Smith, the father of economics, argued in his 1776

classic, *The Wealth of Nations*, that people pursuing their own interests are led as if by 'an invisible hand' to promote the interests of society.

In this section we discuss theoretical justifications for government intervention in a market economy. The general argument for government intervention is *market failure*. Sometimes markets do not allocate resources efficiently, and government intervention may improve economic performance. Economic theory identifies six broad types of market failure, which we describe below.

Very few economists dispute the idea that the government could in theory improve the allocation of resources by correcting market failures, but many dispute the idea that government in fact improves the allocation of resources. Conservative economists, including Nobel Prize winners Milton Friedman and James Buchanan, argue that in practice the government is even more likely to fail to allocate resources efficiently than are markets. We take up their arguments in Part 3, but first we discuss the six reasons why government intervention may, at least in principle, improve the allocation of resources.

The business cycle

The business cycle has many external causes, from wars or oil price changes to bursts of new inventions. Government policies also affect it. Increases in taxes and reductions in government spending generally reduce GNP; cuts in interest rates increase GNP and prices. Government policy can make the business cycle worse, lengthening recessions and creating inflation, or it can reduce economic fluctuations.

There are major controversies in macroeconomics over whether and to what extent the government can stabilize the economy. Obviously, the government cannot control the economy perfectly or we would not have severe recessions and inflation. But since the government does control a large share of total spending, it must make its decisions with their effect on the business cycle in mind. Sometimes, the government may choose to delegate some of these decisions to an agency operating on its behalf. In 1997 the Labour government made the Bank of England 'operationally independent'. In part 4 we discuss the reasons behind this decision.

Public goods

Most goods are private goods.

A **private good**, if consumed by one person, cannot be consumed by another.

Ice cream is a private good. When you eat your ice cream, your friend can't consume it. Your clothes are also private goods. When you wear them, everyone else is precluded from wearing them at the same time.

But there are goods we can all consume simultaneously. These are called public goods.

A **public good** is a good that, even if it is consumed by one person, is still available for consumption by others.

Clean air is a public good. So is national defence, or public safety. If the armed forces protect the country, your being safe in no way prevents anyone else from being safe.

It is no coincidence that most public goods are not provided in private markets. Because of the *free-rider* problem, private markets have trouble ensuring that the right amount of a public good will be produced. A free-rider is someone who gets to consume a good that is costly to produce without paying for it. The free-rider problem applies particularly to public goods because, if anyone were to buy the good, it would then be available for everyone else to consume.

Suppose a market were set up for national defence. Even if each of us felt that we needed defence, we would not have the right incentives to buy our share of defence. Since the amount of national defence I will have is the same as the amount everyone else has, I have a strong incentive to wait for someone else to buy it rather than contribute my fair share. I free-ride on everyone else's purchases. But, of course, if everyone is waiting for someone else to buy national defence, there will be no defence.

To get around the free-rider problem, the country has to find some way of deciding *together* how much to spend on defence. Governments are set up to make such *collective* decisions. Many of the goods provided by the government are in fact public goods. National defence and police services are certainly public goods. National parks are a mixed case, since the views in the parks are a public good, at least until congestion sets in, but use of the eating facilities is not.

It may seem from this discussion that the government *should* produce public goods and *should not* produce any other goods. Neither conclusion is correct. The government does not have to produce public goods; it only has to specify how much of each should be produced. It may rely on private contractors to do the actual production, as with defence equipment. Indeed, it used to be common for countries to have private contractors provide armies on a commercial basis. It is increasingly common for municipalities to hire private contractors to remove rubbish.

On the other hand, there is no general economic reason why governments should not produce private goods. There are government-owned firms or nationalized industries in most countries. Some government enterprises appear successful and efficient. None the less, experience suggests that in many circumstances the government is less likely to produce efficiently than is the private sector.

Externalities

Markets work well when the price of a good equals society's cost of producing that good and when the value of the good to the buyer is equal to the benefit of the good to society. However, the costs and benefits are sometimes not fully reflected in market prices.

Consider the problem of pollution. A firm produces chemicals and discharges the waste into a lake. The discharge pollutes the local water supply, kills fish and birds, and creates an offensive smell. These adverse side-effects represent costs to society of producing the chemical, and should accordingly be reflected in its market price – but they may not be. Unless the chemical company is charged for the damages caused by its pollution, the market price of its output will understate the true cost of production to society. There is an externality in the production of the chemical.

An **externality** exists when the production or consumption of a good directly affects businesses or consumers not involved in buying and selling it and when those spillover effects are not fully reflected in market prices.

Externalities are not all negative. The homeowner who repaints her house provides spillover benefits for the neighbours; they no longer have to look at a dilapidated house. In all externalities, there exists something that affects firms' costs or consumers' welfare (such as pollution or views of newly painted houses) but is not traded in a market. Economists often say that externalities are caused by 'missing markets'.

When externalities are present, market prices do not reflect all the social costs and benefits of the production of a good. Government intervention may improve the functioning of the economy, for example by requiring firms to treat their waste products in certain ways before dumping them. Since externalities involve missing markets, they can also be handled in principle by market-type solutions. The government might charge firms (an estimate of) the damages their pollution causes, or might permit a certain amount of total pollution and allow firms to buy and sell rights to pollute.

Externalities can provide the justification for a number of government activities besides pollution control. Examples range from control of broadcasting (interference is an externality) to various restrictions on land use.

Information-related problems

Unless firms and consumers are well informed, they may take actions that are not in their own interests. Unless decisions are based on good information, markets will not work well. But in a modern, complex free market economy, firms and consumers are unlikely to be well informed about the consequences of all their decisions.

Private markets may not produce the right kinds and amounts of information. Firms have little incentive to study the long-term health hazards to which their workers are exposed. Without penalties for fraud, producers of unsafe goods have every incentive to conceal the flaws in their products. Furthermore, modern economies are so complex that few individuals can digest and evaluate all the information necessary to make fully informed decisions all the time. It may be efficient to have the government process some complex information on behalf of its citizens.

Governments have long recognized a need to protect poorly informed consumers from actions they would regret. Laws against fraud have been around for centuries. Modern governments regulate working conditions, grade foods, regulate the safety of consumer products, and require that certain products (such as foods and dangerous chemicals) have informative labels.

Monopoly and market power

Competitive markets generally work well, but markets where either buyers or sellers can manipulate prices generally do not. In particular, too little output will be produced and price will be too high in a market where a single seller controls supply.

A **monopolist** is the single seller of a good or service.

Monopolists can earn high profits by restricting the quantity sold and raising the price. Because they are the only sellers, they have no fear of being undercut by competitors – and consumers end up paying more than they should.

Some monopolies are almost unavoidable. Most public utilities (gas, for example) are potential monopolies. The government can regulate such companies by controlling the prices they are allowed to charge, or it may elect to supply the products itself. Other monopolies may be artificial, brought about through manipulation by firms. Here governments intervene with competition laws, seeking to make competition more vigorous and to prevent monopolies or other attempts to control supply.

Any buyer or seller who has the ability to affect market price significantly is described as having *market power* or *monopoly power*. Government intervention to limit market power, for instance by preventing firms with market power from charging high prices, can improve the allocation of resources.

Income redistribution and merit goods

The distribution of income generated by free markets has no ethical claim to being fair. Depending on who starts out with what resources, private markets can produce many different final distributions – different 'for whoms' – of resources and welfare. Government may want to intervene to affect the distribution of income, by taxing some and giving to others.

In practice, modern governments engage in large-scale redistribution of income. The share of transfers in government spending has increased all over the world in the period since 1960. Government spending on transfer payments, shown in Table 4-2, represents government redistribution of income – towards the elderly (through social security), the unemployed (through unemployment benefits), farmers (through price supports), and other beneficiaries. The rapid growth of transfer spending has been a source of controversy, with critics arguing that many government welfare programmes have harmed the people they were designed to help.

There is a difference between government intervention to affect the distribution of income and intervention to ensure the right level of production of public goods or to make market prices reflect externalities. In the latter cases the government is taking actions that at least in principle can make everyone in society better off. But when the government intervenes to affect the income distribution, it makes some people better off by making others worse off.

Governments are concerned not just with the distribution of income, but also with the consumption of particular goods and services.

Merit goods are goods that society thinks people should consume or receive, no matter what their incomes are.

Merit goods typically include health, education, shelter, and food. We – society – might think that everyone should have adequate housing. Is there an economic justification for government intervention in regard to merit goods? In a sense there always is, because the sight of someone who is homeless creates an externality, making everyone else unhappy. By providing housing or shelter for those who would otherwise be on the streets, the government make the rest of us feel better.

Society's concern over merit goods is closely related to its concern over the distribution of income. The difference in the case of merit goods is that society wants to ensure an individual's consumption of *particular* goods rather than goods in general. Some of the goods provided by the government (such as health and education) are merit goods.

With merit goods, as with public goods, government concern with consumption does not justify government production. Economic theory justifies policies that ensure that individuals consume the specified amounts of merit goods. It does *not* say that the government should produce these goods itself.

The most difficult issue in discussing both merit goods and the distribution of income is how society or the government decides who should get what. Any one person can have a perfectly sensible viewpoint on these issues – for instance, that the more even the distribution of income the better, that the distribution of income we have is best, that people who work harder should be rewarded, that people who need more should get more, or that everyone should have decent housing and no one should starve. Translating these different opinions into a consistent view that is taken by the government and implemented in taxation and transfer policy is the impossible task of politics.

Recap

The discussion in this section provides some theoretical justification for government intervention in a market economy. However, governments do not make their tax and spending decisions on the basis of what economists say their role should be. We now discuss the mechanisms that democratic societies use to make their actual decisions about taxation and government spending.

4-3 How do governments decide?

The motivations economists ascribe to individuals and firms are simple. Firms are in business to make profits for their owners. Individuals are assumed to choose those combinations of goods that make them best off. These simple assumptions permit economists to explain most consumer and business decision-making.

Government decision-making cannot be explained so simply. Voters express their preferences by electing governments to make the basic decisions on spending and taxing, pass new laws, and establish new regulatory programmes. By voting, the electorate gets to express its preferences among alternative policy packages, though not on each issue.

The people who run the government – elected officials and civil servants – are not mere robots who simply do the bidding of society. They have their own objectives, trying like everyone else to maximize their own well-being. They may maximize their own well-being by doing what they believe is good for the public, or they may have much narrower goals, such as getting re-elected or advancing up the hierarchy. In a well-designed system the government are led to pursue the interests of society as they pursue their own goals.

Voting

If everyone were identical and of one mind, public decision-making would be easy. The problem that society solves through the political process is how to reconcile different views and different interests. In this section we discuss two features of majority voting. The first is the *paradox of voting*, which concerns cases where majority voting will lead to inconsistent decision-making. The second is the *median voter result*, which shows how public choice will tend to avoid extreme outcomes.

The paradox of voting Table 4-4 shows how voters 1, 2, and 3 rank three possible outcomes A, B, and C. For example, voter 1 likes A best, then B, then C. Voter 2 likes B best, then C, then A. Let the group choose by *majority vote* between outcomes A and B. Voters 1 and 3 prefer A to B so the group will prefer A to B by two votes to one. Similarly, the group will vote two to one for outcome B rather than C. Since A is preferred to B, and B preferred to C, you might expect the group to prefer A to C. But the first and third columns of Table 4-4 imply that the group would choose C rather than A by two votes to one. When individual preferences are as depicted in Table 4-4 majority voting will choose A over B, B over C, and C over A. *Consistent* decision-making will not be possible under majority voting.

The **paradox of voting** is that majority voting may lead to inconsistent decision making.

This is a serious problem. Society cannot necessarily rely on majority voting to lead to consistent decision-making. It also means that the decisions taken by society may well depend on the order in which it votes on them.

The median voter Majority voting does not always lead to inconsistent public choice. Figure 4-1 shows for 17 voters how much between £0 and £1000 each would like to spend

on the police. Each dot represents an individual voter's preferred amount.

We assume each voter will vote for a spending level close to his own preferred amount. A voter who wants to spend £250 will prefer £300 to £400 and will prefer £200 to £100. Each person has *single-peaked* preferences, being happier with an outcome the closer it is to his peak or preferred level.

Now suppose there is a vote on how much to spend on the police. A proposal to spend £0 would be defeated by 16 votes to 1. Only the voter represented by the left-hand dot in Figure 4-1 would vote for £0 rather than £100. As we move to the right we get more people voting for any particular proposal. Figure 4-1 emphasizes the special position of the median voter. With 17 voters, the median voter is the person who wants to spend the ninth-highest amount on the police. There are 8 voters wanting to spend more and 8 wanting to spend less.

The **median voter** is the person in the middle on this particular issue.

What is special about the median voter? Suppose the vote is between the amount the median voter wants to spend and some higher amount. The 8 people wanting less than either will vote for the median voter's proposal, and so will the median voter. There will be a majority against higher expenditure. By an identical argument there will be a 9–8 majority against lower expenditure when the alternative is the amount wanted by the median voter. Hence the median voter's preferred outcome will be chosen by majority voting.

Thus, majority voting works when each individual has single-peaked preferences. The paradox of voting arises in Table 4-4 precisely because preferences are not single-peaked. Suppose outcome A is low expenditure, B is moderate expenditure, and C is high expenditure on the

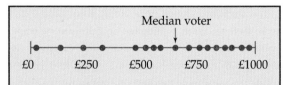

Each dot represents the preferred expenditure of each of 17 voters. The outcome under majority voting will be the level preferred by the median voter. Everybody to the left will prefer the median voter's position to any higher spending level. Everybody to the right will prefer it to any lower spending level. The median voter's position is the only position that cannot be outvoted against some alternative. Hence it will be chosen.

Figure 4-1 The median voter

Table 4-4	The paradox of voting		
	Outcomes		
Voter	A	B	C
1	1	2	3
2	3	1	2
3	2	3	1

police. Voter 1 prefers low to moderate and moderate to high. Voter 1 has single-peaked preferences. So does voter 2, whose peak is at moderate expenditure. But voter 3 prefers high to low and low to moderate expenditure, even though moderate expenditure is closer than low expenditure to the best outcome of high expenditure. Voter 3 does not have single-peaked preferences.

This is why majority voting is likely to get into trouble when individual preferences are not single-peaked. In contrast, with single-peaked preferences the outcome is likely to be that most preferred by the median voter. Consistent public choice under majority voting on particular issues is more likely the more each voter feels that the next best thing is an outcome close to that voter's preferred outcome. On issues where voters feel they must make an all-or-nothing choice between very different alternatives, intermediate positions are a complete waste of time. The failure of preferences to be single-peaked may result in inconsistent public choices.

Legislators

When preferences are single-peaked the median voter models helps us to understand how society makes decisions on particular issues, especially if there is a referendum on the issue. But the process of making decisions through legislative compromises is much more complicated. Decisions are not made issue by issue. There may be a trading of votes between different issues. *Logrolling* is one example.

Table 4-5 shows two issues, A and B, and three legislators, 1, 2, and 3. The value in pounds of each outcome to each individual is shown. These values are merely illustrative measures of how much each individual stands to gain or lose under each outcome. Suppose each person votes for a proposal only if the outcome is positive. Person 1 votes against A and B, person 2 against A but for B, and person 3 for A but against B. Both issues would be defeated on a majority vote.

Now suppose persons 2 and 3 do a deal and vote together. Suppose they decide to vote for A, which person 3 wants,

and for B, which person 2 wants. Person 2 will make a net gain of +£1, gaining £4 since B passes, and losing only £3 when A passes. Person 3 gains a total of £5, gaining £6 since A passes and only losing £1 when B passes. By forming a coalition they do better than they would have done under independent majority voting, when neither A nor B would have passed.

Logrolling is the trading of votes on different issues.

This kind of model helps us understand some behaviour by politicians, but they are subject to many other forces. They want to do good, to be powerful, to be popular, and above all to be re-relected. Even if society as a whole has consistent goals, it does not follow that politicians will act so as to reflect those goals as faithfully as possible.

Civil servants

Civil servants influence public decision-making and its execution in two ways. They offer advice and expertise, which influence the government in deciding how laws and policies should be framed. They are also responsible for carrying out the enacted laws and stated policies and may have some discretion in how far and how fast to put into practice the directives with which they have been issued.

Civil servants also have vested interests. Those at the defence ministry are likely to try to persuade the government to expand defence activities. Those in education will press for higher spending on education. Civil servants are quite skilled in obstructing policies that the civil servants do not like.

The main point of this section is that governments do not magically and automatically translate society's wishes into the appropriate action. Indeed, as the paradox of voting shows, it may be impossible for society always to express consistent aims. The simple view that the government acts to maximize the public good is a convenient one on which we frequently fall back. But a complete understanding of how public choices are made requires an extension of the ideas we have briefly examined in this section.

The principal–agent problem

Several of the issues discussed above are examples of the *principal–agent problem*, which is found in many areas of economics. In each case, one person (the principal) finds it convenient to delegate decision-making to another person (the agent) to act on behalf of the principal. The problem arises because of the self-interest of the agent may not be the same as the self-interest of the principal. When information is hard to come by, it is difficult for the principal to monitor

Table 4-5	Logrolling	
Person	A	B
1	−4	−1
2	−3	4
3	6	−1

the agent, checking that the agent is acting in the best interest of the principal.

A **principal–agent problem** arises when the principal cannot fully observe the information available to the agent to whom decisions have been delegated.

Thus, we can think of voters as the principals, delegating day-to-day decisions to elected governments. Similarly, governments act as principals, delegating some decisions to public officials who act as their agents. It is also helpful to view large companies in the same way: the management is the agent appointed by the principal (shareholders if the company is private, the government if it is state-owned). We can also think about workers as agents of the management.

Of course, principals are not stupid. It is obvious that imperfectly monitored agents face temptations to pursue their own agenda. Governments may reward their own supporters rather than voters as a whole; civil servants may think they know better than their political masters ('Yes, minister!'); managers may opt for the easy life rather than strive to create profits for shareholders; workers may shirk on the job. What can the principals, who employ agents, do to fight back?

The general solution offered by principal–agent theory is for the principal to design a contract for the agent that best suits the interests of the principal. It tries to offer the agent incentives to behave as the principal wishes. And, since information is not automatically available to the principal, the performance-related contract has to be specified in terms of results that the principal can easily observe.

Thus, the electorate and the government may both believe there is an implicit contract: voters are unsure of the day-to-day possibilities open to the government, but a major disaster on unemployment, inflation, or the budget may be punished by defeat at the next election. Sometimes the contract is much more explicit. For example, in New Zealand control of monetary policy and inflation has now been completely delegated to the Reserve Bank of New Zealand, whose governor has to agree an annual inflation target with the government; if inflation is much off target, the governor gets fired!

SUMMARY

● Governments play a major role in modern mixed economies purchasing goods and services, raising taxes, and making transfer payments. Governments also set the legal framework, regulate economic activity, and attempt to stabilize the business cycle.

● Taxes affect the allocation of resources. Taxing a good raises the price to the buyers and lowers the price to the seller, thereby reducing the output of the good.

● Government intervention can be justified by market failure. Stabilizing the business cycle, deciding on the amount of public goods, responding to externalities, correcting informational problems, preventing the exercise of market power, and creating a socially desirable distribution of income and merit goods are all economic grounds for a government role in the economy.

● Government decisions should represent the interests of society, but society's true preferences may be hard to ascertain. A democratic society votes for legislators who make decisions that are carried out by civil servants under the supervision of the government.

● Unless individual preferences are single-peaked, majority voting can lead to inconsistent public choices. With single-peaked preferences, majority voting will lead to consistent results. Society will choose according to the median voter on any issue. Legislative decisions may reflect complex deals and vote-trading on different issues. There is no simple relation between the final choices of public servants and the underlying preferences of the voters who make up society.

KEY TERMS

REVIEW QUESTIONS

1 Which of the following items of government spending reflect (a) provision of public goods, (b) concern with merit goods, (c) concern with income distribution: (i) police patrols, (ii) old age pensions, (iii) unemployment benefit, (iv) free state primary schools?

2 Which of the following are public goods: (a) clean streets, (b) ambulance services, (c) the postal service? Discuss alternative ways of providing these services.

3 Give an example of a good where the tax is mainly passed on to the consumer, and a good where it is largely borne by the producer. Why is this?

4 Name the two goods or services you buy from a monopolist. Should the government regulate the price? Does it?

5 Why should the European Commission seek to enforce tough standards reducing pollution of rivers by nitrates used as fertilizers in farming?

6 An individual usually manages to make consistent choices. Why is it harder for governments?

7 *Common fallacies* Show why the following statements are incorrect: (a) My tax bill is £100; that is how much worse off the tax has made me. (b) Public goods are whatever the public sector provides. (c) Free markets always allocate resources efficiently. (d) Majority voting makes public decisions reflect society's wishes.

part 2

Positive Microeconomics

Positive economics looks at how the economy functions. Microeconomics takes a detailed look at particular decisions without worrying about all the induced effects elsewhere. Part 2 studies in detail the demand behaviour of consumers and the supply decisions of producers, showing how markets work and why different markets can exhibit very different forms of competitive behaviour. By applying similar tools to the analysis of input markets, we can understand why some people earn so much more than others.

Chapter 5 measures the responsiveness of demand behaviour. Chapter 6 develops a theory of how consumers behave in pursuit of their self-interest. Chapter 7 introduces different types of firm, and considers motives behind production decisions. Chapter 8 analyses how costs of production influence the output that firms choose to supply. Chapters 9 and 10 explore how differences in market structure affect competition and the output decisions of firms. Chapter 11 shows these ideas help us make sense of what is happening in the new information economy. Chapters 12–14 analyse input markets for labour, capital and land, and derive the implications for the distribution of income. Chapter 15 explains why people dislike risk and how institutions develop to shift risk on to those who can bear it more cheaply.

5 The effect of price and income on demand quantities

LEARNING OUTCOMES

When you have finished this chapter, you should be able to:

- Develop the concepts of own price and cross price elasticity of demand
- Analyse how (own) price elasticity relates to the revenue effect of a price change
- Show why bad harvests can help farmers
- Explain the fallacy of composition
- Relate cross price elasticity to the concepts of complements and substitutes
- Define the income elasticity of demand, and relate it to inferior, normal, and luxury goods

In Chapter 3 we learned to use demand curves to show the effect of the price of a good on the quantity demanded. We saw also that changes in income, or in the price of related goods, would shift demand curves, altering the quantity demanded at each price. In this chapter we examine these effects in more detail.

We introduce the concept of the *price elasticity of demand*, a measure of the sensitivity of the quantity demanded to the price. The price elasticity of demand is a key piece of information in many economic problems such as the pricing decision about tube fares that we studied in Chapter 2.

Suppose you own a football club. Before the season begins you have to set the price of football tickets for the season. Your sole aim is to maximize revenue from ticket sales so you can afford to buy some better players next season. Should you set a ticket price to ensure that the ground is full? It depends on the sensitivity of ticket sales to ticket prices. If the quantity demanded is insensitive to the price, it will require a low price to fill the ground and total revenue will collapse. If, however, small reductions in ticket prices

lead to large increases in the quantity sold, it makes more sense to charge a price that will fill the ground. Higher sales volume will more than compensate for the lower ticket price. Without empirical research to find out the price elasticity of demand for football tickets, you cannot make a sensible pricing decision.

The demand for football tickets depends also on the price of related goods. Lower prices for race courses, cinemas, and other ways of spending Saturday afternoon reduce the demand for football tickets. The *cross price elasticity of demand* measures the sensitivity of the quantity demanded of one good to changes in the price of a related good.

The demand curve for football tickets will also be shifted by changes in consumer incomes. If people become richer they can afford more football tickets whatever the price. The *income elasticity of demand* measures the sensitivity of the quantity demanded to changes in consumer incomes. Goods for which demand grows quickly as incomes rise will have better growth prospects in an expanding economy than goods for which demand increases more slowly with income. Investors and businesses will be interested in differences in the income elasticity of demand for different goods.

5-1 The price responsiveness of demand

The downward slope of the demand curve shows that quantity demanded increases as the price of a good falls. Frequently we need to know by how much the quantity demanded will increase. Table 5-1 presents some hypothetical numbers for the relation between ticket price and quantity demanded, other things equal. Figure 5-1 plots the demand curve, which happens to be a straight line in this example.

How should we measure the responsiveness of the quantity of tickets demanded to the price of tickets? One obvious measure is the slope of the demand curve. Each price cut of £1 leads to 8000 extra ticket sales per game. Suppose, however, that we wish to compare the price responsiveness of football ticket sales with the price responsiveness of the quantity of cars demanded: clearly, £1 is a trivial cut in the price of a car and will have a negligible effect on the quantity of cars demanded.

In Chapter 2 we argued that when commodities are measured in different units it is often best to examine the percentage change, which is unit-free.

The **price elasticity of demand** is the percentage change in the quantity demanded divided by the corresponding percentage change in its price.

Although we shall introduce other demand elasticities – the cross price elasticity and the income elasticity – the (own) price elasticity is the most frequently used of the three. Whenever economists speak of *the demand elasticity* they mean the price elasticity of demand, as defined above.

If a 1 per cent increase reduces the quantity demanded by 2 per cent, the demand elasticity is −2. Because the quantity *falls* 2 per cent, this is a change of −2 per cent. Dividing by the price change of 1 per cent (a price rise) we obtain −2. If a price fall of 4 per cent increases the quantity demanded by 2 per cent, the demand elasticity is −½ since the quantity change of 2 per cent is divided by the price change of −4 per cent. Since demand curves slope down, we are either dividing a positive percentage change in quantity (a quantity rise) by a negative percentage change in price (a price fall), or dividing a negative percentage change in quantity (a quantity fall) by a positive percentage change in price (a price rise). The price elasticity of demand tells us

Table 5-1	The demand for football tickets
Price (£/ticket)	Quantity of tickets demanded ('000s)
12.50	0
10.00	20
7.50	40
5.00	60
2.50	80
0	100

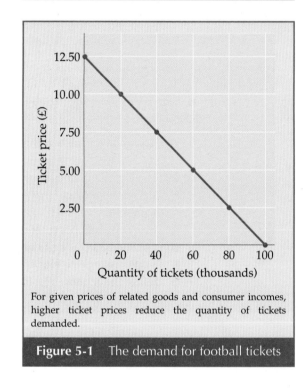

For given prices of related goods and consumer incomes, higher ticket prices reduce the quantity of tickets demanded.

Figure 5-1   The demand for football tickets

about movements along a demand curve and the demand elasticity must be a negative number.[1]

We now investigate the price elasticity of demand for football tickets. Table 5-2 reproduces in columns (1) and (2) the demand data from Table 5-1. By considering the effect of price cuts of £2.50, we then calculate the price elasticity of demand at each price, shown in column (3). Beginning at the price of £10 and a corresponding quantity of 20 000 tickets demanded, consider a price cut to £7.50. There is a price change of −25 per cent, from £10 to £7.50, and a corre-

---

[1] For further brevity, economists sometimes omit the minus sign. It is easier to say the demand elasticity is 2 than to say it is −2. Whenever the price elasticity of demand is expressed as a positive number, it should be understood (unless there is an explicit warning to the contrary) that a minus sign should be added. Otherwise, we should be implying that demand curves slope upwards, a rare but not unknown phenomenon.

sponding change in quantity demanded of 100 per cent, from 20 000 to 40 000 tickets. The demand elasticity at £10 is thus $(100/-25) = -4$. Other elasticities are calculated in the same way, dividing the percentage change in quantity by the corresponding percentage change in price. When we begin from the price of £12.50 the demand elasticity is minus infinity. This is because the percentage change in quantity demanded is $(20 - 0)/0$. Any positive number divided by zero yields plus infinity. Dividing by the -20 per cent change in price, from £12.50 to £10.00, we obtain minus infinity as the demand elasticity at this price.

We say that the demand elasticity is *high* when it is a large negative number. The quantity demanded is then very sensitive to the price. We say the demand elasticity is *low* when it is a small negative number and the quantity demanded is relatively insensitive to the price. 'High' or 'low' thus refer to the magnitude of the elasticity ignoring the minus sign. The demand elasticity falls when it becomes a smaller negative number and quantity demanded becomes less sensitive to the price.

Although the demand curve for football tickets is a straight line with constant slope – along its entire length a £1 cut in price always leads to 8000 extra ticket sales – Table 5-2 shows that the demand elasticity falls as we move down the demand curve from higher prices to lower prices. At high prices, £1 is a small percentage change in the price but 8000 tickets is a large percentage change in the quantity demanded. Conversely, at low prices £1 is a large percentage change in the price but 8000 is a small percentage change in the quantity. When the demand curve is a straight line, the price elasticity falls steadily as we move down the demand curve.[2]

It is possible to construct curved demand schedules (still, of course, sloping downwards all the time) along which the price elasticity of demand remains constant. Generally, however, the price elasticity changes as we move along demand curves, and we expect the elasticity to be high at high prices and low at low prices.[3]

Because the demand curve is a straight line in this example, we get the same size of quantity response (20 000

Table 5-2   The price elasticity of demand

(1) Price (£/ticket)	(2) Thousands of tickets demanded	(3) Price elasticity of demand
12.50	0	$-\infty$
10.00	20	-4
7.50	40	-1.5
5.00	60	-0.67
2.50	80	-0.25
0	100	0

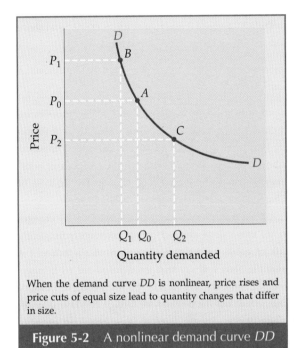

When the demand curve *DD* is nonlinear, price rises and price cuts of equal size lead to quantity changes that differ in size.

Figure 5-2   A nonlinear demand curve *DD*

---

tickets) whether we raise or lower the price by £2.50. That is why it does not matter whether we use price rises or price cuts to calculate the demand elasticity. When, as in Figure 5-2, the demand curve is not a straight line we encounter a minor difficulty. Beginning at point *A* where the price is P_0, moves to points *B* and *C* represent percentage price changes of equal magnitude but opposite sign. Figure 5-2 makes clear that the size of quantity response (from Q_0 to either Q_1 or Q_2) differs for price rises and price falls when the demand curve is not a straight line.

When dealing with nonlinear demand curves, economists resolve this ambiguity about the definition of price elasticity of demand by defining it with respect to *very small* changes in price. If we move only a short distance to either side of the point *A*, the demand curve hardly has time to bend round. Over the very short distance corresponding to a small

---

[2] There are two special cases of linear demand curves where this is not true. A horizontal or infinitely elastic demand curve has an elasticity of $-\infty$ at all points since the price never changes. A vertical or completely inelastic demand curve has an elasticity of zero at all points since the *quantity* never changes.

[3] You may be puzzled about the elasticity at a zero price. Raising the price of £2.50 induces a change in quantity of -20 per cent. The change in price is $(2.50 - 0)/0$ per cent, which is ∞ per cent. However, any number divided by infinity yields zero. Hence the demand elasticity is $(-20/\infty) = 0$ at this price.

percentage price rise or fall, the demand curve is as near a straight line as makes no difference. With this amendment we can continue to use the old definition.

Elastic and inelastic demand

Although elasticity typically falls as we move down the demand curve, an important dividing line occurs at the demand elasticity of −1.

Demand is **elastic** if the price elasticity is more negative than −1. Demand is **inelastic** if the price elasticity lies between −1 and 0.

In Table 5-2 demand is elastic at all prices of £7.50 and above and inelastic at all prices of £5.00 and below.

If the demand elasticity is exactly −1, we say that demand is **unit-elastic**.

Later in this section we show that a cut in prices raises revenue from football ticket sales if demand for football tickets is elastic but lowers revenue if demand is inelastic. Whether or not demand is elastic is the key piece of information required in setting tube fares in the example of Chapter 2, or in setting the price of football tickets.

Although the price elasticity of demand typically changes as we move along demand curves, economists frequently talk of goods with high or low demand elasticities. For example, they will say that the demand for oil is price-inelastic (price changes have only a small effect on quantity demanded) but the demand for foreign holidays is price-elastic (price changes have a large effect on quantity demanded). Such statements implicitly refer to parts of the demand curve corresponding to prices that are typically charged for these goods or services.

The determinants of price elasticity

What determines whether the price elasticity of demand for a good is high (say, −5) or low (say, −0.5)? Ultimately the answer must be sought in consumer tastes. If it is socially essential to own a television, higher television prices may have little effect on quantity demanded. If televisions are considered a frivolous luxury, the demand elasticity will be much higher. Psychologists and sociologists may be able to explain more fully than economists why tastes are as they are. Nevertheless, as economists, we can identify some considerations likely to affect consumer responses to changes in the price of a good. *The most important consideration is the ease with which consumers can substitute another good that fulfils approximately the same function.*

Consider two extreme cases. Suppose first that the price

of all cigarettes is raised 1 per cent. Do you expect the quantity of cigarettes demanded to fall by 5 per cent or by 0.5 per cent? Probably the latter. People who can easily quit smoking have already done so. In contrast, suppose the price of one particular brand of cigarettes is increased by 1 per cent, all other brand prices remaining unchanged. We should now expect a much larger quantity response from buyers. Consumers will switch away from the more expensive brand to other brands that basically fulfil the same function of nicotine provision. For a particular cigarette brand the demand elasticity could be quite high.

Ease of substitution implies a high demand elasticity for a particular good. Our example suggests a general rule. The more narrowly we define a commodity (a particular brand of cigarette rather than cigarettes in general), the larger will be the price elasticity of demand.

Measuring price elasticities

To illustrate these general principles we report estimates of price elasticities of demand in Table 5-3. The table confirms that the demand for general categories of basic commodities, such as fuel, food, or even household durable goods, is inelastic. As a category, only services such as haircuts, the theatre, and sauna baths, have an elastic demand. Households simply do not have much scope to alter the broad pattern of their purchases.

In contrast, there is a much wider variation in the demand elasticities for narrower definitions of commodities. Even then, the demand for some commodities, such as dairy produce, is very inelastic. However, particular kinds of services such as entertainment and catering have a much more elastic demand.

Table 5-3 Estimates of price elasticities of demand in the UK

Good (general category)	Demand elasticity	Good (narrower category)	Demand elasticity
Fuel and light	−0.47	Dairy produce	−0.05
Food	−0.52	Bread and cereals	−0.22
Alcohol	−0.83	Entertainment	−1.40
Durables	−0.89	Expenditure abroad	−1.63
Services	−1.02	Catering	−2.61

Source: The left-hand column is taken from John Muellbauer, 'Testing the Barten Model of Household Composition Effects and the Cost of Children', *Economic Journal*, September, 1977, Table 7. The right-hand column is taken from Angus Deaton, 'The Measurement of Income and Price Elasticities', *European Economic Review*, Volume 6, 1975.

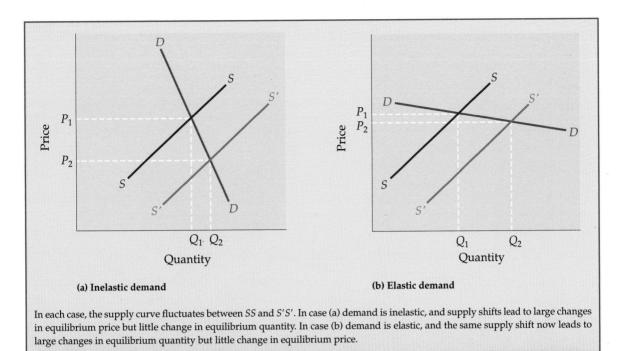

(a) Inelastic demand   (b) Elastic demand

In each case, the supply curve fluctuates between SS and $S'S'$. In case (a) demand is inelastic, and supply shifts lead to large changes in equilibrium price but little change in equilibrium quantity. In case (b) demand is elastic, and the same supply shift now leads to large changes in equilibrium quantity but little change in equilibrium price.

Figure 5-3   The effect of demand elasticity on equilibrium price and quantity fluctuations

Using price elasticities

Price elasticities of demand are useful in calculating the price rise required to eliminate a shortage (excess demand) or the price fall required to eliminate a surplus (excess supply). One important source of surpluses and shortages is shifts in the supply curve. Harvest failures (and bumper crops) are a feature of agricultural markets. Because the demand elasticity for many agricultural products is very low, harvest failures produce large increases in the price of food. Conversely, bumper crops induce very large falls in food prices. When demand is very inelastic, shifts in the supply curve lead to large fluctuations in price but have little effect on equilibrium quantities.

Figure 5-3(a) illustrates this point. SS is the supply curve in an agricultural market when there is a harvest failure and $S'S'$ the supply curve when there is a bumper crop. The equilibrium price fluctuates between P_1 (harvest failure) and P_2 (bumper crop) but induces little fluctuation in the corresponding equilibrium quantities. Contrast this with Figure 5-3(b), which shows the effect of similar supply shifts in a market with very elastic demand. Price fluctuations are much smaller but quantity fluctuations are now much larger. Knowing the demand elasticity helps us understand why some markets exhibit volatile quantities but stable prices, while other markets exhibit volatile prices but stable quantities.

5.2 Price, quantity demanded, and total expenditure

Other things equal, the demand curve shows how much consumers of a good wish to purchase at each price. At each price, total spending by consumers is the price multiplied by the quantity demanded. We now discuss the relation between total spending and price and show the relevance of the price elasticity of demand.

Figure 5-4 shows how total spending changes as price changes. In case A, we begin at the point A with price P_A and quantity demanded Q_A. Total spending is given by $P_A \times Q_A$ or the area of the rectangle $OP_A AQ_A$. We then examine a price cut to P_B at which consumers demand Q_B. Total spending is now $P_B \times Q_B$ or the area of the rectangle $OP_B BQ_B$. What is the change in total spending when prices are reduced from P_A to P_B? Spending falls by the area marked $(-)$ but rises by the area marked $(+)$. In case A the $(+)$ area exceeds the $(-)$ area and total spending increases. In the elastic range of the demand curve (towards the upper end) a cut in price raises the quantity demanded by more than sufficient to offset the lower price. Total spending increases.

Case B examines the lower end of the demand curve where demand is inelastic. Although the price cut raises the quantity demanded, the increase in quantity is insufficient

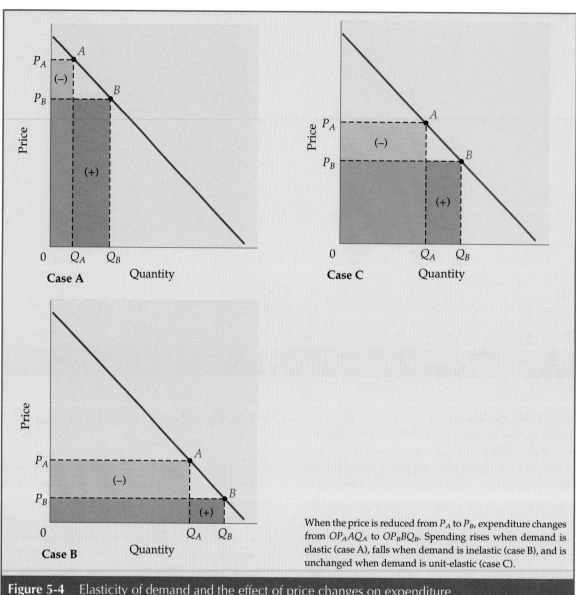

When the price is reduced from P_A to P_B, expenditure changes from $OP_A AQ_A$ to $OP_B BQ_B$. Spending rises when demand is elastic (case A), falls when demand is inelastic (case B), and is unchanged when demand is unit-elastic (case C).

Figure 5-4 Elasticity of demand and the effect of price changes on expenditure

to compensate for the lower price. The (+) area is smaller than the (−) area. Total spending falls. If price cuts increase total spend at high prices where the demand elasticity is high and reduce total spending at low prices where the demand elasticity is low, you might guess that at some intermediate price a price cut will leave total spending unaltered. Case C shows this possibility. The higher quantity demanded exactly compensates for the lower price.

If quantity demanded rises 1 per cent when the price falls 1 per cent, total spending will remain unaltered. In fact, case C depicts the point on the demand curve at which the price elasticity of demand is −1 (a 1 per cent change in quantity divided by a −1 per cent change in price). If demand is

elastic, a demand elasticity that is more negative than −1, as in case A, a 1 per cent price cut leads to an increase in quantity by *more* than 1 per cent. Hence total spending rises. Conversely, when demand is inelastic, a demand elasticity lying between 0 and −1, as in case B, a 1 per cent price cut leads to an increase in quantity by *less* than 1 per cent. Hence total spending falls. These results are summarized in Table 5-4.

The price of football tickets

We are now required to advise the owner of the football club on the ticket price that maximizes spending on football tickets and the owner's revenue. Table 5-5 shows the demand data of Tables 5-1 and 5-2. We also show the

Table 5-4   Demand elasticities and changes in spending

Changes in total spending induced by	Price elasticity of demand		
	Elastic (e.g. −3)	Unit-elastic (−1)	Inelastic (e.g. −0.3)
Price increase	Fall	Unchanged	Rise
Price reduction	Rise	Unchanged	Fall

Table 5-6   Brazilian coffee exports 1993–95

	1993	1994	1995
Price (US $/lb)	0.9	2.0	2.1
Export quantity (1990 = 100)	113	102	85
Price × quantity	102	204	179

Prices are in 1995 US$.
Source: IMF, *International Financial Statistics*.

Table 5-5   Ticket demand and revenue

(1) Price per ticket (£)	(2) Quantity demanded ('000s)	(3) Price elasticity of demand	(4) Total spending (£'000s)
12.50	0	−∞	0
10.00	20	−4	200
7.50	40	−1.5	300
6.25	50	−1	312.5
5.00	60	−0.67	300
2.50	80	−0.25	200
0	100	0	0

quantity of tickets demanded at a price of £6.25 per ticket. At this price the demand elasticity is −1. A 20 per cent price change (of £1.25) induces a 20 per cent change in the quantity demanded (of −10 000 tickets per game). Column (4) shows total spending on football tickets at each price.

Beginning from the highest price of £12.50, successive price cuts first increase total spending on tickets then reduce it. Table 5-4 explains why. When the price is high, demand is elastic: price reductions increase total spending. When demand is unit-elastic, at the price of £6.25, we reach a turning point. Above this price, price cuts have steadily increased total spending. Below this price, further price cuts reduce total spending. We can thus draw two conclusions. First, as we imagine moving down the demand curve, total spending is instantaneously unchanging as we move through the price £6.25 at which demand is unit-elastic. Second, *spending and revenue reach a maximum at the point of unit-elastic demand*. This idea, and the empirical knowledge that this occurs at the price of £6.25 per ticket, are the pieces of information the football club owner needs to know.

5-3   Further applications of the price elasticity of demand

The first oil price shock

Perhaps the most dramatic illustration of the relation between demand elasticity and total spending is the oil price shock of 1973–74. By collectively restricting oil supplies, OPEC induced a quadrupling of the equilibrium price of oil in 1973–74.

Increases in price raise consumer spending and seller revenues when demand is inelastic. And demand for oil was *very* inelastic. Estimates of the demand elasticity for oil in the mid-1970s were around −0.1. Oil users had little immediate prospects of substituting other commodities for oil in its many uses: fuel for cars and aeroplanes, fuel for heating and for oil-fired power stations generating electricity, inputs for petrochemical processes. A small restriction in total supply produced a large rise in the equilibrium price and vast revenue gains for OPEC members.

The coffee frost

There's an awful lot of coffee in Brazil – it supplies a large share of the world market. In 1994, people first began to realize that a frost in Brazil would cause havoc with the 1995 harvest. *The Economist* magazine [30 July 1994 (www.economist.co.uk)] reported estimates that the 1995 crop would not be the 26.5 million bags previously thought, but perhaps only 15.7 million bags. Obviously, coffee was going to be scarce in 1995. Anticipating this, speculators bought coffee in 1994, bidding up its price even before the supply fell.

Table 5-6 shows the effect on Brazilian exports during 1993–95. The first row shows that, even after adjusting for general inflation, coffee prices more than doubled in US dollars. The second row shows an index of the volume of Brazilian coffee exports. The final row shows Brazilian export revenue from coffee. Real revenue, of course, went up sharply in 1994: prices had risen *before* production had fallen too much. The interesting comparison is between 1993 and 1995. Brazilian export revenue from coffee *increased* despite the 'bad' harvest.

The demand for coffee is inelastic, although armchair reasoning might suggest an abundance of substitutes – tea, soft drinks, and beer. This example emphasizes the

---

BOX 5-1   Overegging the pudding

Egg, the direct-banking arm of the Prudential (www.egg.com) won 500 000 new customers during its first six months of operation but traded at a loss. An Egg savings account offered generous interest rates, sometimes a few tenths of a per cent above its rivals. To cut its costs, in April 1999 Egg closed its doors to telephone customers, accepting new savings only via the Internet. The example confirms that each lender faces a very elastic demand. However, there is no point offering customers a good deal if the firm's costs are not covered.

---

importance of consumer tastes. If buyers refuse to abandon coffee drinking it is useless to point out that a blend of tea and Coca-Cola contains as much caffeine as the average cup of coffee.

Farmers and bad harvests

The example of coffee illustrates a general result. When demand is inelastic farmers may earn more revenue from a bad harvest than from a good one. When the supply curve shifts to the left it requires a large increase in price to eliminate excess demand if demand is inelastic. And price increases *raise* consumer spending and producer revenues when demand is inelastic. Nor is it surprising that the demand elasticity is low for many commodities such as coffee, milk, and wheat. These are part of the staple diet of most households and eating habits are slow to change, even when prices of these commodities change.

If bad harvests raise farmers' revenues and good harvests lead to a collapse in agricultural prices and hence farmers' revenue, you may now be wondering why farmers do not get together like OPEC to restrict their supply to increase revenues in the face of inelastic demand. If so, you are beginning to think like an economist. If it were easy to organize such collusion between farmers, it would occur more frequently. Later we discuss the difficulties that arise in trying to maintain a co-operative policy to restrict supply.

When demand is inelastic, suppliers *taken together* will be better off if supply can be reduced. However, if one farmer has a fire that destroys part of the crop but all other farmers' crops are unaffected, the unlucky farmer will definitely be worse off (unless fully insured). The reduction in a single farmer's output, unlike the reduction of all farmer's outputs simultaneously, will have only a negligible effect on supply. Market price will be unaffected and the unlucky farmer will simply be selling less output at the price that would have prevailed in any case. This illustrates an important lesson in economics.

The **fallacy of composition** means that what is true for the individual is not necessarily true for everyone together, and what is true for everyone together does not necessarily hold for the individual.

The individual producer faces a demand that is very elastic – consumers can easily switch to the output of similar farmers – even if the demand for the crop as a whole is very inelastic.

5-4 Short run and long run

The price elasticity of demand varies with the length of time that consumers have to adjust their spending patterns when prices change. The dramatic oil price rise of 1973–74 caught many households owning a new but fuel-inefficient car. The immediate response to higher oil prices may have been to *plan* to buy a smaller car with greater fuel economy, but some households were unable to buy smaller cars immediately. In the *short-run*, they were stuck. Unless they could rearrange their life-styles to make less use of a car, these households had to pay the higher petrol prices. That is why the demand for petrol was so inelastic.

Over a longer period, consumers had time to sell their cars and buy cars with better fuel economy, or to move from the distant suburbs closer to their place of work. Over this longer period, they could reduce the quantity of petrol demanded much more than they could initially.

The price elasticity of demand is lower in the short run than in the long run when there is more scope for substitution of other goods. This result is very general. Even if addicted smokers cannot adjust to a rise in the price of cigarettes, fewer young people will start smoking if the price rises and gradually the number of smokers will fall.

How long is the long run?

The *short run* refers to the period immediately after prices change and before long-term adjustment can occur. The *long run* is the period necessary for complete adjustments to a price change. Its length depends on the type of adjustments consumers wish to make. Demand responses to a change in the price of chocolate should be completed within a few months, but full adjustment to changes in the price of oil or cigarettes may take several years.

5-5 The cross price elasticity of demand

The price elasticity of demand tells us about movements along a given demand curve holding constant all determinants of demand except the price of the good itself. We now hold constant the own price of the good and examine the effect of variations in the prices of related goods. In the next section we examine the effect of changes in consumer income.

The cross price elasticity tells us the effect on the quantity demanded of the good *i* when the price of good *j* is changed. As before, we use percentage changes.

The **cross price elasticity of demand** for good *i* with respect to changes in the price of good *j* is the percentage change in the quantity of good *i* demanded, divided by the corresponding percentage change in the price of good *j*.

The cross price elasticity may be positive or negative. It is positive if a rise in the price of good *j* increases the quantity demanded of good *i*. Suppose good *i* is tea and good *j* is coffee. An increase in the price of coffee raises the demand for tea. The cross price elasticity of tea with respect to coffee is positive. Cross price elasticities tend to be positive when two goods are substitutes and negatives when two goods are complements. We expect a rise in the price of petrol to reduce the demand for cars because petrol and cars are complements.

Table 5-7 shows estimates for the UK. Own price elasticities for food, clothing and footwear, and travel and communication are given down the diagonal of the table, from top left (the own price elasticity of demand for food) to bottom right (the price elasticity of demand for travel and communication). Off-diagonal entries in the table show cross price elasticities of demand. Thus, 0.1 is the cross price elasticity of demand for food with respect to transport. A

Table 5-7	Cross price and own price elasticities of demand in the UK		
	With respect to a 1% price change in		
Percentage change in quantity demanded of	Food	Clothing	Transport
Food	−0.4	0	0.1
Clothing and footwear	0.1	−0.5	−0.1
Travel and communication	0.3	−0.1	−0.5

Source: R. Blundell *et al.*, 'What do we learn about consumer demand patterns from micro data?', *American Economic Review*, 1993.

1 per cent increase in the price of transport increases the quantity of food demanded by 0.1 per cent.

The own price elasticities for the three goods lie between −0.4 (clothing and footwear) and −0.5. For all three goods the quantity demanded is more sensitive to changes in the own price of the good than to changes in the price of any other good.

5-6 The effect of income on demand

Finally, holding constant the own price of a good and the prices of related goods, we examine the response of the quantity demanded to changes in consumer incomes. For the moment we neglect the possibility of saving. Thus a rise in the income of consumers will typically be matched by an equivalent increase in total consumer spending.

Chapter 3 pointed out that higher consumer incomes tend to increase the quantity demanded. However, demand quantities typically increase by different amounts as incomes rise. Thus the pattern of consumer spending on different goods depends on the level of consumer incomes. We define the budget share of a good as the fraction of total consumer spending for which it accounts.

The **budget share** of a good is its price multiplied by the quantity demanded, divided by total consumer spending or income.

Table 5-8 reports the share of consumer spending in the UK devoted to food and to services (personal and leisure activities such as eating out and going to the theatre) between 1990 and 1998. The first column shows that real consumer spending (and incomes) have risen over the period. Column (2) shows that the budget share of food has fallen over the period, whereas column (3) shows that the budget share of services has risen. Since the real price of both food and services has remained fairly constant over the

Table 5-8	Budget shares 1990–98		
	(1) Real consumer spending (1998 £ bn)	(2) % budget share:	(3)
		Food	Services
1990	430	12.4	43
1998	523	10.3	47

Source: ONS, UK National Accounts.

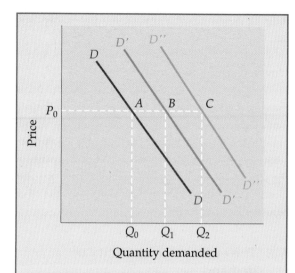

Beginning at A on the demand curve DD, the income elasticity measures the horizontal shift in the demand curve when income rises 1 per cent. At the given price P_0, a shift to B on the demand curve $D'D'$ reflects a lower income elasticity than a shift to C on the demand curve $D''D''$. Leftward shifts in the demand curve when income rises indicate a negative income elasticity.

Figure 5-5   Income elasticity and shifts in the demand curve

period, these changes in budget share mainly reflect changes in real consumer incomes.

The **income elasticity of demand** for a good is the percentage change in quantity demanded divided by the corresponding percentage change in income.

Since our strategy for analysing demand has been to consider varying one determinant at a time, the income elasticity of demand measures the effect on quantity demanded when incomes are changed but the own price of the good and the prices of related goods are held constant.

Normal, inferior, and luxury goods

The income elasticity of demand measures how far the demand curve shifts horizontally when incomes change. Figure 5-5 shows two possible shifts caused by a given percentage increase in income. The income elasticity is larger if the given rise in income shifts the demand curve from DD to $D''D''$ than if the same income rise shifts the demand curve only from DD to $D'D'$. When an income rise shifts the demand curve to the left, the income elasticity of demand is a negative number, indicating that higher incomes are associated with smaller quantities demanded at any given prices.

In Chapter 3 we distinguished *normal* goods, for which demand increases as income rises, and *inferior* goods, for which demand falls as income rises.

A **normal good** has a positive income elasticity of demand. An **inferior good** has a negative income elasticity of demand.

We also distinguish luxury goods and necessities.

A **luxury good** has an income elasticity larger than one. A **necessity** has an income elasticity less than one.

All inferior goods are necessities, since their income elasticities of demand are negative. However, necessities also include normal goods whose income elasticity of demand lies between zero and one.

These definitions also tell us what will happen to budget shares when incomes are changed but prices remain unaltered. The budget share of inferior goods must fall as incomes rise. Higher incomes (budgets) are associated with lower quantities demanded at constant prices. Conversely, the budget share of luxuries must rise when income rises. Because the income elasticity of demand for luxuries exceeds one, a 1 per cent rise in income increases quantity demanded (and hence total spending on luxury goods) by more than 1 per cent. Rises in income *reduce* the budget share of normal goods that are necessities. A 1 per cent income rise leads to a rise in quantity demanded by less than 1 per cent, so the budget share must fall.

Inferior goods tend to be low-quality goods for which there exist higher-quality, but more expensive, substitutes. Poor people satisfy their needs for meat and clothing by buying low-quality cuts of meat and nylon shirts. As their incomes rise, they switch to better cuts of meat (steak) and more comfortable shirts (cotton). Rising incomes lead to an absolute decline in the demand for cheap cuts of meat and nylon shirts.

Luxury goods tend to be high-quality goods for which there exist lower-quality, but quite adequate, substitutes: Mercedes cars rather than small Fords, foreign rather than

Table 5-9   Summary of demand responses to a 1 per cent increase in income

Type of good	Income elasticity	Change in quantity demanded	Change in budget share	Example
Normal	Positive	Increases		
Luxury	Larger than 1	Increases by more than 1%	Increases	Yachts
Necessity	Between 0 and 1	Increases by less than 1%	Falls	Food
Inferior	Negative	Falls	Falls	Bread

Table 5-10   Estimates of income elasticities of demand in the UK

Broad categories of goods	Income elasticity of demand	Narrower categories of goods	Income elasticity of demand
Tobacco	−0.50	Coal	−2.02
Fuel and light	0.30	Bread and cereals	−0.50
Food	0.45	Dairy produce	0.53
Alcohol	1.14	Vegetables	0.87
Clothing	1.23	Travel abroad	1.14
Durables	1.47	Recreational goods	1.99
Services	1.75	Wines and spirits	2.60

Sources: as in Table 5-3.

domestic holidays. Necessities that are normal goods lie between these two extremes. As incomes rise, the quantity of food demanded will rise but only a little. Most people still enjoy fairly simple home cooking even when their incomes rise. Looking back at Table 5-8, we see that services are luxuries whose budget share increased as UK incomes rose after 1990. Food cannot be a luxury, since its budget share fell as incomes rose, but it is not an inferior good either. At constant (1998) prices which adjust for the effects of inflation, real food spending *increased* from £53 billion in 1990 to £55 billion in 1998.

Table 5-9 summarizes the demand responses to changes in incomes holding constant the prices of all goods. The table shows the effect of income increases. Reductions in income have the opposite effect on quantity demanded and budget share.

Table 5-10 reports income elasticities of demand in the UK. As in the estimates of own price elasticity presented in Table 5-3, we show broad categories of goods in the left-hand column and narrower definitions of commodities in the right-hand column. Again we notice that the variation in elasticities is larger for narrower definitions of goods. Higher incomes have much more effect on the way in which households eat (more prawns, less bread) than on the amount they eat in total. As we suggested earlier, food is a normal good but not a luxury. The income elasticity of 0.45 confirms this. The right-hand column indicates that, within the food budget, increases in income lead to a switch towards vegetables (whose income elasticity is higher than that for food as a whole) and away from bread, for which the quantity demanded declines. Richer households can afford to eat lots of salads in order to avoid getting fat. Poorer people need large quantities of bread to ward off the pangs of hunger. Notice that tobacco (chiefly cigarettes) is not only a necessity but an inferior good. Although inessential for physical survival, tobacco has the largest budget share among poor people. Richer people get their kicks in other (more expensive) ways.

Using income elasticities of demand

Income elasticities are key pieces of information in forecasting the pattern of consumer demand as the economy grows and people become richer. Suppose we think that incomes will grow at 3 per cent per annum for the next five years. Given the estimates of Table 5-10, a 15 per cent change in incomes will reduce the demand for tobacco by 7.5 per cent (even if tobacco taxes are not raised) but will increase the demand for wines and spirits by 39 per cent. The growth prospects for these two industries are very different. These forecasts will affect decisions by firms about whether or not to build new factories and projections by governments of tax revenue from cigarettes and alcohol (the former will fall if tax rates per packet remain unchanged but the latter will rise sharply if taxes per bottle remain unchanged).

These considerations apply not only within national economies but in trade between nations. As Third World countries become richer, their demand for luxuries such as the familiar household durables, televisions, washing machines, and cars will rise rapidly.

5-7 Inflation and demand

Elasticities measure the response of quantity demanded to separate variations in three factors – the own price, the price of related goods, and income. In Chapter 2 we distinguished *nominal* variables, measured in the prices of the day, and *real* variables, which make adjustments for inflation when comparing measurements at different dates. You may have noticed that the examples in this chapter that discuss actual numbers for the UK and other economies refer to real prices and real incomes. We conclude this chapter by examining the effect of inflation on demand behaviour.

Suppose all nominal variables double. Every good costs twice as much, wage rates are twice as high, rents charged by landlords and dividends paid by firms double in money terms. Whatever bundle of goods could previously be bought out of income can still be bought. Goods cost twice as much but incomes are twice as high. If meat costs twice as much as bread it still costs twice as much. In fact, nothing has really changed. Demand behaviour will be unaltered by a doubling of the nominal value of *all* prices and *all* forms of income.

How do we reconcile this with the idea that demand elasticities measure changes in quantity demanded as prices change? Remember that each of the elasticities (own price, cross price, and income) measured the effect of changing that variable holding constant all other determinants of demand. When all prices and all incomes are simultaneously changing, the definitions of elasticities warn us that it is incorrect simply to examine the effect of one variable, such as the own price, on quantity demanded. We

can decompose the change in quantity demanded into three components: the effect of changes in the own price alone, plus the effect of changes in price of other goods alone, plus the effect of changing incomes. When all nominal variables change by the same proportion, the sum of these three effects is exactly zero.

In examining economic data we can pursue one of two strategies. The first is to undertake an econometric analysis capable of simultaneously capturing the three distinct effects. However, a simpler strategy will sometimes suffice. Let us think again about the definition of elasticities. If we hold income and the price of all other goods constant, the own price elasticity tells us the effect of changes in the price of a good that affect its real or relative price compared with other goods. Similarly, holding constant the prices of all goods, the income elasticity tells us the effect of changes in money income that affect its real purchasing power, the quantity of goods that it will purchase. The definitions of elasticities make sense not because they refer to nominal variables but because their 'other things equal' assumptions make nominal and real changes coincide. Own price and cross price elasticities tell us about the effects of changes in real or relative prices. Income elasticities tell us about the effects of changes in real income.

We can amend our analysis to handle economies that are experiencing inflation, where the nominal values of most prices and incomes are rising over time. We can see now why doubling all prices has no effect on demand: it affects neither real income nor relative prices. We can also see how it may be possible to examine data in a simple way without resorting to econometric analysis. If an economy is experiencing inflation, prices are changing. We may be able to get round the 'other things equal' problem simply by measuring all variables in real terms.

SUMMARY

● Unless otherwise specified, the elasticity of demand refers to the own price elasticity. It measures the sensitivity of quantity demanded to changes in the own price of a good, holding constant the prices of other goods and income. Demand elasticities are negative since demand curves slope down. In general, the demand elasticity changes as we move along a given demand curve. Along a straight line demand curve, elasticity falls as price falls.

● Demand is elastic if the price elasticity is more negative than −1 (for example −2). Price cuts then increase total spending on the good. Demand is inelastic if the demand elasticity lies between −1 and 0. Price cuts then reduce total spending on the good. When demand is unit-elastic the demand elasticity is −1 and price changes have no effect on total spending on the good.

● The demand elasticity depends on how long customers have to make adjustments to a price change. In the short run the substitution possibilities may be limited. Demand elasticities will typically rise (become more negative) with the length of time allowed for adjustment. The time required for complete adjustment will vary from good to good.

● The cross price elasticity of demand measures the sensitivity of quantity demanded of one good to changes in the price of a related good. Positive cross elasticities tend to imply that goods are substitutes. Negative cross elasticities tend to imply that goods are complements.

● The income elasticity of demand measures the sensitivity of quantity demanded to changes in income, holding constant the prices of all goods.

● Inferior goods have negative income elasticities of demand. Higher incomes reduce the quantity demanded and the budget share of such goods. Luxury goods have income elasticities larger than 1. Higher incomes raise the quantity demanded and the budget share of such goods.

● Goods that are not inferior are called normal goods and have positive income elasticities of demand. Goods that are not luxuries are called necessities and have income elasticities less than 1. All inferior goods are necessities, but normal goods are necessities only if they are not luxuries.

● Doubling all nominal variables should have no effect on demand since it alters neither the real value (purchasing power) of incomes nor the relative prices of goods. In examining data from economies experiencing inflation it is often best to look at real prices and real incomes which measure prices and incomes adjusted for the rate of inflation.

KEY TERMS

◆ Price elasticity of demand   58

◆ Elastic, inelastic, and unit-elastic demand   60

◆ Fallacy of composition   64

◆ Cross price elasticity of demand   65

◆ Budget share   65

◆ Income elasticity of demand   66

◆ Normal and inferior goods   66

◆ Luxuries and necessities   66

REVIEW QUESTIONS

1 You own a fruit stall, and have 100 baskets of strawberries that must be sold immediately, regardless of the price. Your supply curve of strawberries is vertical. From past experience you know that the demand curve for strawberries slopes down and that you can sell 100 baskets if you charge £1 per basket. (a) Draw a supply and demand diagram showing market equilibrium. (b) You believe that the elasticity of demand for strawberries at £1 per basket is −0.5. You suddenly discover that 10 of your baskets are rotten and cannot be sold. Draw the new supply curve. What is the new equilibrium price?

2 Consider the following goods: (a) milk, dental services, beer; (b) chocolate, chickens, train journeys; (c) theatre trips, tennis clubs, films. For each of the three categories, state whether you expect demand to be elastic or inelastic. Then rank the elasticities within each category. Explain your answer.

3 Where along a straight line demand curve does consumer spending reach a maximum? Explain why. What use is this information to the owner of a football club?

4 The following table shows price and income elasticities for vegetables and catering services. For each good, explain whether it is a luxury or a necessity, and whether demand is elastic or inelastic.

	Price elasticity	Income elasticity
Vegetables	−0.17	0.87
Catering services	−2.61	1.64

5 In 1974 UK households spent £1.3 million on bread and cereals and in 1999 they spent over £5 million on bread and cereals, yet bread is supposed to be an inferior good. How do you account for this?

6 (Harder question) Suppose the price of oil falls. Think about the market for coal. How will the oil price fall affect the demand curve for coal (a) in the short run? (b) in the long run? What will happen to the price of each substitute for oil as a result of the fall in oil prices?

7 Common fallacies Show why the following statements are incorrect: (a) Because cigarettes are a necessity the government can raise the tax on cigarettes (and hence cigarette prices) as much as it likes. Tax revenues from cigarettes will always increase when the tax rate is raised. (b) Farming is a risky business. Farmers should take out insurance against bad weather which could lead to a huge reduction in all their crops. (c) Higher levels of consumer income must be good news for producers.

6 The theory of consumer choice

LEARNING OUTCOMES

When you have finished this chapter, you should be able to:

- **Explain how a budget constraint is derived from consumer income and market prices**
- **Define consumer tastes, diminishing marginal utility and a diminishing marginal rate of substitution**
- **Show how to represent tastes as indifference curves**
- **Use indifference curves and budget lines to show what a consumer will do in order to maximize utility**
- **Analyse the effect of giving a consumer more income**
- **Explain income and substitution effects, and use them to analyse the effect of a price change**
- **Relate the market demand curve to individual demand curves**

In previous chapters we have learned to use demand curves to represent consumer behaviour. In this chapter we go behind demand curves by building a model of consumer choice. It explains how buyers reconcile what they would like to do, as described by their tastes or preferences, and what the market will allow them to do, as described by their incomes and the prices of different goods. The model allows us to predict how consumers will respond to changes in market conditions. It helps to make sense of the price and income elasticities examined in Chapter 5.

6-1 The theory of consumer choice

The model's four elements describe both the consumer and the market environment:

1 The consumer's income
2 The prices at which goods can be bought
3 The consumer's tastes, which rank different bundles of goods by the satisfaction they yield
4 The behavioural assumption that consumers do the best they can for themselves. Of the affordable consumption bundles, the consumer picks the bundle that maximizes her own satisfaction.

Each element in the model requires detailed discussion.

The budget constraint

Together, elements (1) and (2) define the consumer's budget constraint.

The **budget constraint** describes the different bundles that the consumer can afford.

Table 6-1	Affordable consumption baskets		
Quantity of meals (Q_M)	Spending on meals ($£5 \times Q_M$)	Quantity of films (Q_F)	Spending on films ($£10 \times Q_F$)
0	0	5	50
2	10	4	40
4	20	3	30
6	30	2	20
8	40	1	10
10	50	0	0

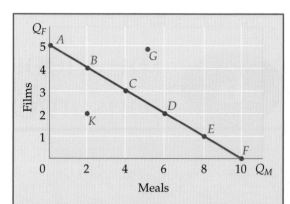

The budget line shows the maximum combinations of goods that the consumer can afford, given income and the prevailing prices. Points on the budget line use up the entire consumer budget. Points above the budget line are unaffordable. Points inside the budget line would allow additional spending.

Figure 6-1 The budget line

Which bundles are feasible, or can be afforded, depends on two factors: the consumer's income and the prices of different goods.

Consider a student with a weekly budget (income, allowance, or grant) of £50 which can be spent on meals or films.[1] Each meal costs £5 and each film £10. What combination of meals and films can she afford? Completely going without films, she can spend £50 on 10 meals at £5 each. Completely going without meals, she can buy 5 cinema tickets at £10 each. Between these two extremes lies a range of combinations of meals and films that together cost exactly £50. These combinations are called the budget constraint.

The budget constraint shows the *maximum* affordable quantity of one good given the quantity of the other good being purchased.[2] Table 6-1 shows the budget constraint for the student. Each row shows an affordable consumption bundle. Row 4 shows that 6 meals (costing £30) and 2 films (costing £20) use up all available income. Other rows are calculated in the same way.

Table 6-1 shows the *trade-off* between meals and films. Higher quantities of meals require lower quantities of films. For a given income, the budget constraint shows how much of one good must be sacrificed to obtain larger quantities of the other good. It is because there is a trade-off that she must *choose between* meals and films.

The budget line

It is useful to depict the budget constraint of Table 6-1 as a *budget line*. Plotting the data of Table 6-1, the budget line in Figure 6-1 shows the maximum combinations of meals and films that the student can purchase out of available income.

The position of the budget line is determined by its end-points *A* and *F*, which have a simple economic

[1] When there are more than two goods, we can think of 'films' as standing for 'all goods other than meals'.
[2] We assume that all income is spent on goods. There is no saving. We defer analysis of the important choice between spending and saving until later.

interpretation. Point *A* shows the maximum quantity of films (5) that the budget will purchase if the student does without meals: £50 buys at most 5 tickets at £10 each. Point *F* shows that £50 buys at most 10 meals at £5 each if she goes without films. The budget line joins up points *A* and *F*. Intermediate points such as *B* and *C* show more balanced purchases of meals and films.

The slope of the budget line indicates how many meals must be sacrificed to get another film. Moving from point *F* to point *E* reduces the quantity of meals from 10 to 8 but increases the quantity of films from 0 to 1. This trade-off between meals and films is constant along the budget line. Giving up two meals always provides the extra £10 to buy an additional cinema ticket.

We now see the crucial role of prices. It is because film tickets cost twice as much as meals that two meals must be sacrificed to purchase another film ticket. *The slope of the budget line depends only on the ratio of the prices of the two goods.* The slope of a line is the change in the vertical distance divided by the corresponding change in the horizontal distance. In Figure 6-1 the slope of the budget line is $-\frac{1}{2}$. A positive change of 1 film must be divided by the corresponding negative change of -2 meals.

This example illustrates the general rule

$$\text{Slope of the budget line} = -P_H/P_V$$

where P_H is the price of the good on the horizontal axis and P_V is the price of the good on the vertical axis. In our example, the price of meals P_H is £5 and the price of films P_V is £10. Formula (1) confirms that the slope of the budget line is $-\frac{1}{2}$ and the minus sign reminds us that there is a trade-off. We have to *give up* one good to get more of the other good.

Thus, the two end-points of the budget line (here, A and F) show how much of each good the budget will buy if the other good is not purchased at all. The slope of the budget line joining these end-points, depends only on the relative prices of the two goods.

Any point above the budget line (such as G in Figure 6-1) is unaffordable. The budget line shows the maximum quantity of one good that can be afforded, given the quantity purchased of the other good and given the budget available for spending. Given an income of £50, the point G is out of reach since it requires £25 to buy 5 meals and £50 to buy 5 cinema tickets. Points such as K, which lie inside the budget line, leave some income unspent. Only on the budget line is there a trade-off where the student must choose *between* films and meals.

Tastes[3]

The budget line summarizes the market environment (income and prices) of the consumer. We now consider the consumer's *tastes*. We make three assumptions that seem rather plausible. First, the consumer can rank alternative bundles of goods according to the satisfaction or *utility* they provide. It is unnecessary to quantify this utility, for example to decide that one bundle yields twice as much utility as another bundle. We only require that the consumer can decide that one bundle is better than, worse than, or exactly as good as another. We assume that this ranking of possible bundles is internally consistent: if bundle A is preferred to bundle B and bundle B is preferred to bundle C, then bundle A had better be preferred to bundle C.

Second, we assume that the *consumer prefers more to less*. If bundle B offers more films but the same number of meals as bundle K we assume that bundle B is preferred. How do we handle things like pollution, which are not goods but 'bads'? Consumers do not prefer more pollution to less. We get round this problem by redefining commodities so that the assumption will be satisfied. We analyse clean water rather than polluted water. More clean water is better, other things equal.

Figure 6-2 examines the implications of these assumptions about tastes. Each point shows a particular consumption bundle of meals and films. We begin at bundle a. Since more is preferred to less, any point such as c to the

---

[3] The Appendix to this chapter presents an alternative approach to tastes based on measurable utility. It is less satisfactory, but you may find it easier.

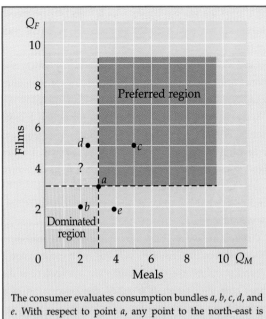

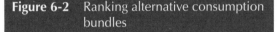

The consumer evaluates consumption bundles a, b, c, d, and e. With respect to point a, any point to the north-east is preferred and any point to the south-west is dominated by a. Points such as d or e in the other two regions may or may not be preferred to a, depending on the consumer's tastes.

Figure 6-2   Ranking alternative consumption bundles

north-east of a is preferred to a. Point c offers more of *both* goods than a. Conversely, points to the south-west of a offer less of both goods than a. Point a is preferred to points such as b.

Without knowing the consumer's exact tastes we cannot be sure how points in the other two regions (north-west and south-east) will compare with a. At points such as d or e the consumer has more of one good but less of the other good than at a. Someone who really likes food might prefer e to a, but an avid film buff would prefer d to a. Others might be indifferent between d, a, and e.

We now introduce the concept of the marginal rate of substitution of meals for films.

The **marginal rate of substitution** of meals for films is the quantity of films the consumer must sacrifice to increase the quantity of meals by one unit *without changing total utility*.

Since consumers prefer more to less, an additional meal tends to increase utility. To hold utility constant, when one meal is added the consumer must simultaneously sacrifice some quantity of the other good (films). The marginal rate of substitution tells us how many films the consumer could exchange for an additional meal without changing total utility.

Suppose the student begins with 5 films and no meals. Having already seen 4 films that week, she probably does not enjoy the fifth film very much. With no meals, she is *very* hungry. The utility of this bundle is low: being so hungry, she cannot really enjoy the films anyway. For the same amount of utility she could give up a lot of films for a little food.

Suppose instead that the student is consuming a large number of meals but seeing few films. She will be reluctant to sacrifice much cinema attendance to gain yet another meal. It makes sense to sacrifice abundant films for scarce meals. Conversely, when the ratio of films to meals is already low, it does not make sense to sacrifice scarce films for yet more meals.

Economists believe that this common-sense reasoning about tastes or preferences is very robust. It can become a general principle, the third assumption we need to make about consumer tastes. It is called the assumption of a diminishing marginal rate of substitution.

Consumer tastes exhibit a **diminishing marginal rate of substitution** when, to hold utility constant, diminishing quantities of one good must be sacrificed to obtain successive equal increases in the quantity of the other good.

Our student might be equally happy with bundle $X =$ (6 films, 0 meals), bundle $Y =$ (3 films, 1 meal), and bundle $Z =$ (2 films, 2 meals). Beginning from bundle X, a move to Y sacrifices 3 films for 1 meal, but a further move from Y to Z sacrifices only 1 film for 1 extra meal. Such tastes satisfy the assumption of a diminishing marginal rate of substitution.

These three assumptions – that consumers prefer more to less, can rank alternative bundles according to the utility provided, and have tastes satisfying a diminishing marginal rate of substitution – are all we shall require. It is now convenient to show how tastes can be represented as *indifference curves*.

Representing tastes as indifference curves

If we join up all the many points the student likes equally, we obtain an indifference curve.

An **indifference curve** shows all the consumption bundles which yield the same utility.

Figure 6-3 shows three indifference curves labelled U_1U_1, U_2U_2, and U_3U_3.

Every point on U_2U_2 yields the same utility. Point C offers a lot of meals and few films, and point A offers many films but few meals. Because the consumer prefers more to less, *indifference curves must slope downwards*. Since more meals

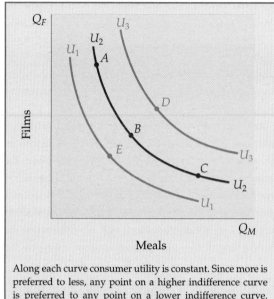

Along each curve consumer utility is constant. Since more is preferred to less, any point on a higher indifference curve is preferred to any point on a lower indifference curve. Indifference curves slope downwards. Otherwise the consumer would have more of both goods and be better off. Diminishing marginal rates of substitution imply that each curve becomes flatter as we move along it to the right.

Figure 6-3 Representing consumer tastes by indifference curves

tend to increase utility, some films must simultaneously be sacrificed to hold utility constant.

The slope of each indifference curves gets steadily flatter as we move to the right. This follows immediately from the assumption of a diminishing marginal rate of substitution. At point A, where films are relatively abundant compared with meals, the consumer will sacrifice a lot of films to gain a little more food. At the point B, where films are less abundant relative to meals, she will sacrifice a smaller quantity of films to gain the same additional quantity of meals. And at the point C she now has so many meals that hardly any films will be sacrificed for additional meals. In fact, we now recognize that the marginal rate of substitution of meals for films is simply the slope of the indifference curve at the point from which we begin. These two properties of a single indifference curve – its downward slope and its steady flattening as we move to the right – follow directly from the assumptions that consumers prefer more to less and that their tastes satisfy the assumption of diminishing marginal rates of substitution.

Now consider the point D on indifference curve U_3U_3. D offers more of both goods than B. Since consumers prefer more to less, utility at D must be higher than utility at B. By definition, all points on U_3U_3 yield the same utility. Every point on U_3U_3 yields more utility than every point on U_2U_2. Conversely, E must yield less utility than B since it offers less of both goods. Every point on U_1U_1 yields less utility than every point on U_2U_2.

Although Figure 6-3 shows only three indifference curves, we can draw in other indifference curves as well. Higher

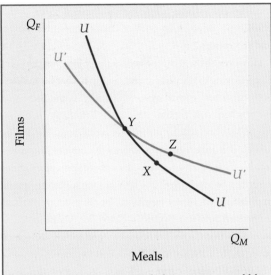

If indifference curves intersected, the consumer would be indifferent between X and Y on the indifference curve UU, and between Y and Z on $U'U'$, and hence indifferent between X and Z. Since Z offers more of both goods than X, this violates the assumption that consumers prefer more to less. Indifference curves cannot intersect.

Figure 6-4   Indifference curves cannot intersect

indifference curves are better because the consumer prefers more to less.

Is it a coincidence that we have not drawn any indifference curves that cross each other? It is not: indifference curves cannot cross. Figure 6-4 shows why. Suppose the indifference curves UU and $U'U'$ were to intersect. Since X and Y lie on the same indifference curve UU, the consumer is indifferent between these points. But Y and Z both lie on the indifference curve $U'U'$. Hence the consumer is indifferent between Y and Z. Together these imply that the consumer is indifferent between X and Z. But this is impossible, since the consumer gets more of both goods at Z than at X. Hence intersecting indifference curves would violate our assumption that consumers prefer more to less. Our assumptions about consumer tastes rule out intersecting indifference curves.

We can represent the tastes of any consumer by drawing the complete *map* of indifferent curves. Figure 6-5 shows two consumers with different tastes. In each case, moves to a higher indifference curve imply an increase in utility. In Figure 6-5(a) we show the indifference map for a glutton prepared to give up a lot of films to gain a little extra food. Figure 6-5(b) shows the indifference map for a weight-watching film buff, who will give up large quantities of food to increase the quantity of films by even a small amount. Both indifference maps are valid: they satisfy our three basic assumptions about consumer tastes. Our theory can cope with extreme kinds of preferences as well as with more typical preferences which lie in between.

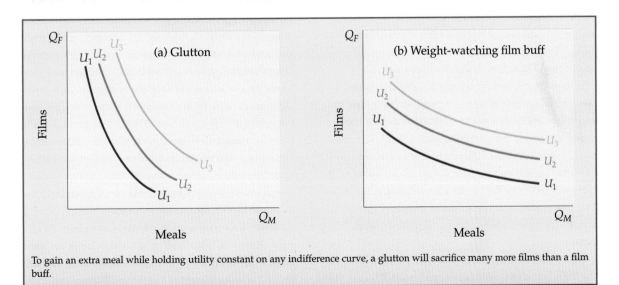

To gain an extra meal while holding utility constant on any indifference curve, a glutton will sacrifice many more films than a film buff.

Figure 6-5   Different tastes

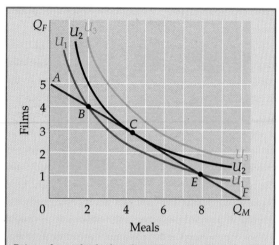

Points above the budget line *AF* are unaffordable. The consumer cannot reach the indifference curve U_3U_3. Points such as *B* and *E* are affordable but only allow the consumer to reach the indifference curve U_1U_1. The consumer will choose the point *C* to reach the highest possible indifference curve U_2U_2. At the chosen point *C*, the indifference curve and the budget line just touch and their slopes are equal.

Figure 6-6   Consumer choice in action

Utility maximization and choice

The budget line shows affordable bundles given the consumer's market environment (the budget for spending and the price of different goods). The indifference map shows the tastes of the consumer. To complete the model, we assume that *the consumer chooses the affordable bundle that maximizes her utility*.

The consumer cannot afford points that lie above the budget line, and will never choose points that lie below the budget line where it is possible to purchase more of one good without sacrificing any of the other good.

Thus we know the consumer will select a point on the budget line. To determine which point on the budget line maximizes utility we need to think about the consumer's tastes. We expect our glutton to pick a point with more meals and less films than the point our film buff will select. We begin by showing in general how to use indifference curves to determine the bundle the consumer will choose. Then we confirm that our model of consumer choice can capture the different behaviour of the glutton and the film buff.

Figure 6-6 shows the budget line *AF* for the student who has £50 to spend on films (£10 each) and meals (£5 each). The indifference curves U_1U_1, U_2U_2, and U_3U_3 are part of the indifference map describing her tastes.

Since U_3U_3 lies everywhere above the budget line *AF*, all points on U_3U_3 are unattainable, however much the student would like to obtain this amount of utility. Suppose she considers the attainable point *B* on the indifference curve U_1U_1. This will certainly be preferred to the point *A*, which must lie on a lower indifference curve (since indifferent curves cannot intersect, the indifference curve through *A* must lie everywhere below the indifference curve U_1U_1). Similarly, *F* must lie on a lower indifference curve than *E* and she prefers *E* to *F*.

However, she will choose neither the point *B* nor the point *E*. By moving to the point *C* she can reach a higher indifference curve and obtain more utility, so *C* is the point that the student will choose. Any other affordable point on the budget line will be on a lower indifference curve. The assumption that consumers choose the bundle that maximizes their utility given the affordable possibilities described by the budget line thus has the following simple implication: *the chosen bundle will be the point at which an indifference curve just touches the budget line*. Mathematicians would say that the budget line is a *tangent* to the indifference curve U_2U_2 at the point *C*. The budget line never crosses a higher indifference curve, such as U_3U_3, and crosses twice every lower indifference curve, such as U_1U_1. Point *C* is the point of maximum utility given the budget constraint.

It is helpful to reach the same conclusion by a slightly different chain of reasoning. Consider again point *B* in Figure 6-6. The slope of the budget line indicates the trade-off between affordable quantities of films and meals that the market environment will allow. When films cost £10 and meals £5, two meals can be traded for one film. The slope of the indifference curve at *B* (the marginal rate of substitution of meals for films) shows how the consumer would trade meals for films to preserve a constant level of utility. At the point *B* the budget line is flatter than the indifference curve. Moves to the left would take the student on to a lower indifference curve because the market trade-off is less than the required utility trade-off. Similarly, beginning at the point *E* it cannot make sense to move to the right along the budget line. The market trade-off of meals for films is less than the utility trade-off required to hold utility constant. Moves from *E* to the right must reduce utility and take the consumer on to a lower indifference curve.

However, it makes sense to consider a move from *B* to the right. The market trade-off of affordable meals for films exceeds the utility trade-off required to maintain constant utility. The student reaches a higher indifference curve and increases her utility. Similarly, it makes sense to consider a move from *E* to the left. Again the market trade-off, this time

---

| BOX 6-1 | The one that I want |

Comedienne Ruby Wax earns a fortune from her commercials for the Vauxhall Corsa. If Kate Moss is seen in a particular outfit, sales take off. Every newcomer who wins a major sporting event knows the prize money will be dwarfed by subsequent advertising and marketing fees. Why do the manufacturers pay supersalaries to superstars to promote their wares? They are trying to change your tastes. There are lots of small cars, but only one with the big personality. It's the one to have. No other will do.

You could of course buy a car magazine and find out how fast the Corsa goes in comparison with its rivals, whether it really is bigger inside, and how much that sporty sunroof costs. But that's not the point. Much of this advertising is about *style*. Not what you think is nice, but what *other people* think is nice. Ruby is assuring you that other people, stylish people like herself, think it's cool to drive a Corsa. Do so and you can be cool too. This *interdependence* of tastes is what opens the door for so much advertising and PR.

---

increasing the quantity of affordable films in exchange for less meals, more than compensates for the utility trade-off, the slope of the indifference curve, required to maintain utility at a constant level. Moves from *E* leftwards along the budget line increase utility and allow her to reach a higher indifference curve.

In fact, we can make a general principle out of these examples. Wherever the budget line crosses an indifference curve, a move along the budget line in one direction will increase utility since the market trade-off is better than the utility trade-off required to maintain constant utility.

Viewed in these terms, *the point C, which maximizes utility, is the point at which the slope of the budget line and the slope of the indifference curve coincide.* At all other points on the budget line the slope of the indifference curve through such points differs from the slope of the budget line: a move in one or other direction will increase utility. Only at point *C* are there no feasible or affordable moves along the budget line that increase utility. The student will choose point *C* since it maximizes utility.

To check that our model of consumer choice makes sense, we consider what it implies for the observable behaviour of our glutton and film buff whose tastes between meals and films differ. In Figure 6-5 we represented the indifference curves of the glutton as steep and those of the film buff as flat. To maintain a constant level of utility along a particular indifference curve, the glutton will always sacrifice a lot of films for more food but the film buff will hardly sacrifice any films for a lot more food.

In Figure 6-7 we give these two students the same budget line. They have the same income and face the same prices for food and films. Only their tastes differ. Figure 6-7(a)

shows that the chosen point *C* for the glutton occurs at a combination of a lot of meals but few films. Figure 6-7(b) confirms that the film buff will choose a point *C* with many more films but much less food. The theory of consumer choice based on individual utility maximization successfully translates differences in tastes into differences in revealed or observable demands for the two goods.

Each student will choose a point *C* at which their marginal rate of substitution equals the slope of the budget line, which depends only on the relative price of films and meals. Because the glutton has a strong preference for food (steep indifference curves), the chosen point must lie far to the right to give the indifference curve a long time to flatten out. Because the film buff has flat indifference curves, the chosen point must lie well to the left before indifference curves can become flatter than the budget line.

6-2 Adjustment to income changes

In the previous chapter we introduced the concept of the income elasticity of demand to describe, other things equal, the response of quantity demanded to changes in consumer incomes. Now we can use our model of consumer choice to analyse this response in greater detail.

For given tastes and prices, Figure 6-8 shows the adjustment to a change in income. The student has an income of £50, faces the budget line *AF*, and chooses the point *C* at which utility is maximized. Now suppose her income rises from £50 to £80. Prices of meals and films remain unchanged at £5 and £10 respectively. With higher income, she can afford more of one or both of the goods. The budget line shifts outwards from *AF* to *A'F'*. To find the exact position

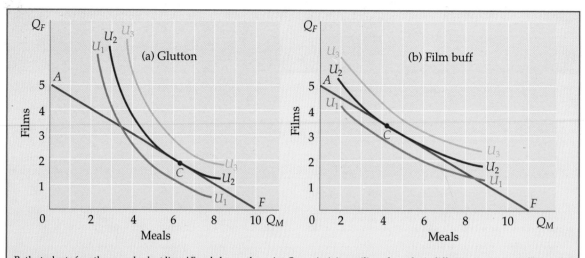

Both students face the same budget line AF and choose the point C, maximizing utility where the indifference curve is tangent to the budget line. The glutton has steep indifference curves and must consume a lot of meals before the diminishing marginal rate of substitution flattens the indifference curve sufficiently. The film buff has flat indifference curves and the point of tangency occurs much further to the left. The glutton chooses more meals but fewer films than the film buff.

Figure 6-7   The effect of tastes on consumer choice

of this new line we have to calculate the purchasing power of the new income in terms of the two goods. Again we calculate the end points at which all income is spent on a single good. The point A' shows that at most £80 buys 8 films at £10 each. The point F' shows that £80 buys at most 16 meals at £5 each. Joining these points yields the new budget line $A'F'$. Since the slope of a budget line depends only on the relative prices of the two goods, which remain unchanged, the new budget line $A'F'$ is parallel to the old budget line AF.

Which point on $A'F'$ will the student choose? She will choose the point C' at which the new budget line is tangent to the highest attainable indifference curve. However, the position of C' depends on the map of indifference curves that describe her tastes.

For most consumers food is a normal good but a necessity whereas entertainment is a luxury good. Figure 6-8 shows the case in which the student's tastes have these properties. A rise in income from £50 to £80 moves her from the point C (2 films, 6 meals) to the point C' (4 films, 8 meals). Thus, a 60 per cent rise in income induces a 100 per cent increase in the quantity of films demanded, confirming that films are a luxury good with income elasticity in excess of unity. Similarly, the 60 per cent rise in income induces a 33 per cent increase in the quantity of meals demanded. Thus, the income elasticity of demand for food is $(0.33/0.6) = 0.55$, confirming that food is a normal good (income elasticity

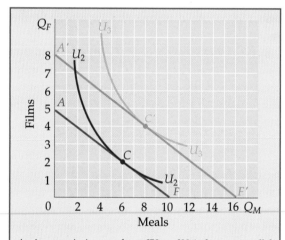

An increase in income from £50 to £80 induces a parallel shift in the budget line from AF to $A'F'$. The new end points A' and F' reflect the increase in purchasing power if only one good is purchased. The slope remains unaltered since prices have not changed. At the higher income the consumer chooses C'. Since both goods are normal, higher income raises the quantity of each good demanded but the percentage increase in film quantity is larger since its income elasticity is higher.

Figure 6-8   An increase in consumer income

greater than zero) but a necessity (income elasticity less than unity).

In contrast, Figure 6-9 illustrates the case in which the student's tastes make food an inferior good, for which quantity demanded declines as income rises. At the point C'

on the budget line $A'F'$ fewer meals are demanded than at the point C on the budget line AF, corresponding to the lower income.

The effects of a fall in income are, of course, exactly the opposite. The budget line shifts inwards but remains parallel to the original budget line. When both goods are normal, lower consumer income reduces the quantity demanded for both goods. If one good is inferior, the quantity demanded will actually rise as income falls. Notice both goods cannot be inferior: when income falls but prices remain unchanged it cannot be feasible for the consumer to consume more of both goods.

Income expansion paths

Thus far we have considered the response of demand to a particular change in income, other things equal. We might wish to know the response of demand to income over all possible variations in income. To study this we can trace out the *income expansion path*. The income expansion path shows how the chosen bundle of goods varies with consumer income levels.

Look again at Figure 6-8. The budget lines AF and $A'F'$ correspond to incomes of £50 and £80 respectively. With yet higher incomes we could draw more budget lines, parallel to AF and $A'F'$ but higher up. We could then find the points on these new budget lines which the consumer would choose at these higher income levels. Joining up the chosen points (C and C' in Figure 6-8) and these new points (say C'' and C'''), we obtain the income expansion path. Try drawing it for yourself.

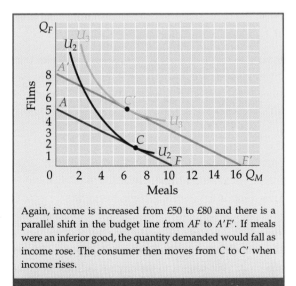

Again, income is increased from £50 to £80 and there is a parallel shift in the budget line from AF to $A'F'$. If meals were an inferior good, the quantity demanded would fall as income rose. The consumer then moves from C to C' when income rises.

Figure 6-9 An increase in income reduces demand for the inferior good

6-3 Adjustment to price changes

Having studied the effects of changing tastes and changing income on quantity demanded, we now isolate the effect of a price change. Relying on common sense, in Chapter 5 we argued that an increase in the price of a good will reduce the quantity demanded, other things equal. The own price elasticity of demand measures this response, and will be larger the easier it is to substitute towards goods whose prices have not risen.

We also introduced the cross price elasticity of demand to measure the response of the quantity demanded of one good to a change in the price of another good. An increase in the price of good j tends to increase the quantity demanded of good i when the two goods are substitutes but tends to reduce the quantity demanded of good i when the two are complements. The empirical evidence was presented in Tables 5-3 and 5-7.

Are those propositions invariably true, or did the evidence we examined just happen to confirm our commonsense reasoning? To answer this question we now offer a more formal analysis based on the model of consumer choice we have now developed.

Price changes and the budget line

In Figure 6-10 we draw the budget line AF for a consumer with an income of £50 facing prices of £10 and £5 for films and meals respectively. Now suppose that meal prices

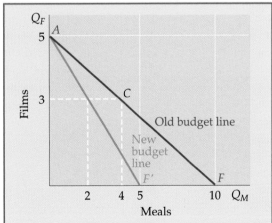

The consumer begins at the point C on the budget line AF. Doubling meal prices halves the amount that can be spent on meals when no films are bought. The point F shifts to F'. The budget line rotates around the point A at which no meals are bought. Along the new budget line the consumer can no longer afford the original consumption bundle C. Consumption of one or both commodities must be reduced.

Figure 6-10 An increase in meal prices

BOX 6-2   Internet music sales

Digital distribution via the Internet is forecast to reach 8 per cent of worldwide recorded music sales by 2004 and 20 per cent by 2010. Countries with high incomes and large populations provide most of the likely consumers. On-line discounting is likely to eat into the existing high profit margins of the CD industry.

Internet sales (£ m)	1997	2004
USA	24	1420
Japan	–	250
UK	1	135
Germany	1	130

Source: *Financial Times*, 26 May 1999.

increase to £10. Since the price of films remains unaltered, £50 still buys 10 films when all income is spent on films. The point A must lie on the new budget line as well as the old budget line. But when all income is spent on meals, £50 buys only 5 meals at £10 each instead of the 10 meals it used to buy at £5 each. Thus the other extreme point on the budget line shifts from F to F' when meal prices double. As usual, we join up these end-points to obtain the new budget line AF'. Thus the effect of an increase in meal prices is to *rotate* the budget line inwards around the point A, at which no meals are bought and meal prices are irrelevant.

Except at the point A itself, at the higher meal prices the consumer can now afford fewer meals for any given number of films purchased, or fewer films for any given number of meals. The new budget line AF' lies inside the old budget line AF. The consumption bundles lying between AF' and AF are no longer affordable at the higher price of meals. In particular, the chosen point on the old budget line is no longer affordable unless it happened to be the extreme point A. This analysis shows how a price increase makes the consumer worse off by reducing consumption opportunities out of a fixed money income. The consumer's standard of living will fall.

To check that you understand, try drawing diagrams to illustrate the effect on the budget line of: (1) a reduction in the price of meals (*hint*: Figure 6-10 can be used. How?); (2) an increase in the price of films (*hint*: around which point does the budget line rotate?).

Substitution and income effects

Our model of consumer choice is based on the interaction of affordable opportunities represented by the budget line, and tastes represented by indifference curves. To analyse the effect of price changes on the actual quantity of goods demanded, we must now study how rotations of the budget line affect the highest indifference curve that the consumer can reach.

An increase in the price of meals has two distinct effects on the budget line in Figure 6-10. First, the budget line becomes steeper, reflecting the increase in the relative price of meals. To obtain an additional meal a larger quantity of films must now be sacrificed. Second, in general the budget line AF' lies inside the original budget line AF. The purchasing power of a given money income has been reduced by the price increase. Economists therefore break up the effect of a price increase into these two distinct effects: the change in the relative prices of the two goods, and the reduction in the purchasing power of the given money income.

The **substitution effect** of a price change is the adjustment of demand to the relative price change alone. The **income effect** of a price change is the adjustment of demand to the change in real income alone.

Figure 6-11 shows the response of demand quantities to an increase in the price of meals. At the original prices the consumer faces the budget line AF and chooses C to reach the highest possible indifference curve U_2U_2. At the higher meal price the budget line rotates to AF' and the consumer chooses E to reach U_1U_1, the highest indifference curve now possible. In this example, the doubling of meal prices reduces the quantity of meals demanded and the quantity of films demanded.

The substitution effect To isolate the effect of relative prices alone, imagine drawing the *hypothetical* budget line HH, parallel to AF' but tangent to the original indifference curve U_2U_2. Because HH is a parallel to the new budget line AF' its slope reflects the new relative prices of films and meals after the price of meals has risen. Because HH is tangent to the old

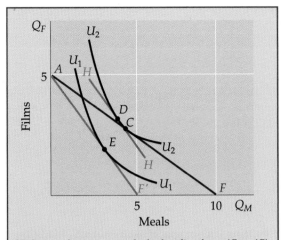

Higher meal prices rotate the budget line from *AF* to *AF'*. The consumer moves from *C* to *E*. This can be decomposed into a pure substitution effect, from *C* to *D*, the response to relative price changes at the old standard of living, plus a pure income effect, from *D* to *E*, the response to a fall in real income at constant relative prices. The substitution effect reduces the quantity of meals demanded. The income effect also reduces the quantity of meals demanded if meals are a normal good. Under these circumstances, price increases reduce the quantity demanded and demand curves slope downwards.

Figure 6-11   Income and substitution effects

indifference curve U_2U_2, it allows the consumer to attain the original level of utility and standard of living that, by definition, is constant along U_2U_2.

If confronted with the hypothetical budget line *HH* the consumer would choose *D*. The move from *C* to *D* is the pure substitution effect, the adjustment of demand to relative prices when income is adjusted to maintain the old standard of living in the face of the new higher prices. *The substitution effect of an increase in the price of meals unambiguously reduces the quantity of meals demanded.* This result is perfectly general.[4] As meals become relatively more expensive, the consumer has an incentive to switch towards films, which have become relatively cheaper.

The income effect   To isolate the effect of the reduction in real income, holding relative prices constant, consider now the parallel shift in the budget line from the hypothetical position *HH* to the actual new position *AF'*. The consumer moves from the point *D* to the point *E*. When both goods are

---

[4] With only two goods, substitution away from meals must imply substitution towards films However, when there are more than two goods, we cannot be sure that the substitution effects will tend to increase the quantity demanded for all other goods. We discuss this shortly under the heading 'Complements and substitutes'.

normal goods, a reduction in real income will reduce the quantity demanded of both goods. Thus in Figure 6-11 we show the point *E* lying to the south-west of the point *D*.

The net effect of a price increase on the quantity demanded The consumer moves directly from the original point *C* to the new point *E*. We can interpret this as a pure substitution effect from *C* to the hypothetical point *D* plus a pure income effect from *D* to *E*. Provided the good whose price has risen is a normal good, demand curves slope downwards as we asserted in Chapter 5.

The substitution effect from *C* to *D* must reduce the quantity of meals demanded. When the price of meals rises, the budget line becomes steeper and we must move along U_2U_2 to the left to find the point at which it is tangent to *HH*. Similarly, the income effect must further reduce the quantity of meals demanded if meals are a normal good. *E* must lie to the left of *D*.

Inferior goods   Although the substitution effect is guaranteed to reduce the quantity of meals demanded when the price of meals increases, the income effect will go in the opposite direction when we examine a good that is inferior. Then reductions in real income increase the quantity demanded. We can even imagine a perverse case in which this effect is so strong that price rises actually increase the quantity of that good demanded. Demand curves then slope *upwards*! This possibility is illustrated in Figure 6-12. An increase in the price of the inferior good rotates the budget line from *AF* to *AF'*. The substitution effect, from *C* to *D*, tends to reduce the quantity of the inferior good demanded, but is outweighed by the income effect, from *D* to *E*. Since *E* lies to the right of *C*, the net effect of the increase in price of the inferior good has been to increase the quantity demanded. Economists refer to such goods as 'Giffen goods', after a nineteenth century economist who claimed that increases in the price of bread increased the quantity of bread demanded by the poor.

Even though a good is an inferior good it need not be a Giffen good. It requires a very strong income effect – here an increase in demand in response to real income reductions – to offset the substitution effect, which must be negative. When goods are inferior, theoretical reasoning alone cannot establish which affect will dominate. We have to look at the empirical evidence. After many decades of empirical research, economists are convinced that the possibility of Giffen goods is largely a theoretical *curiosum*. In practice, goods are rarely sufficiently inferior that the income effect can reverse the substitution effect.

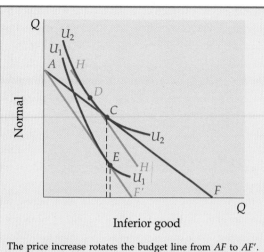

Inferior good

The price increase rotates the budget line from AF to AF'. The substitution effect, from C to D, reduces the quantity of the inferior good demanded. Since the good is inferior, the income effect, from D to E, increases the quantity of the inferior good demanded. For a Giffen good, the income effect dominates and E lies to the right of C. In practice, the income effect for inferior goods is less strong and the point E, although to the right of D, usually lies to the left of C so that the quantity demanded falls as the price of the inferior good rises.

Figure 6-12   A price increase increases the quantity of a Giffen good demanded

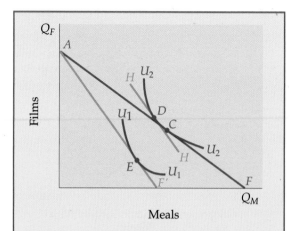

Meals

An increase in the price of meals rotates the budget line from AF to AF'. The substitution effect from C to D is small. Indifference curves have large curvature since the two goods are poor substitutes in utility terms. The income effect from D to E implies a large reduction in films for two reasons. First, the reduction in real income is larger the further to the right the initial point C. Second, films are a luxury good whose quantity demanded is sensitive to changes in real income. Thus the income effect outweighs the substitution effect. E lies below C.

Figure 6-13   A negative cross price elasticity of demand

Thus, as an empirical judgement, economists have concluded that for inferior goods, the substitution effect outweighs the income effect and demand curves will slope downwards as price is increased. For the much more common case in which goods are normal, having a positive income elasticity of demand, the income and substitution effects both act to reduce the quantity demanded, as in Figure 6-11. The proposition that demand curves slope downwards can then be established by theoretical reasoning alone.

Cross price elasticities of demand

We now investigate the effect of an increase in the price of one good on the quantity of another good demanded. In Chapter 5 we suggested that cross price elasticities might be negative or positive, and we now illustrate these two possibilities, highlighting the different roles played by substitution and income effects.

Figure 6-13 illustrates the case where the cross price elasticity is negative. A rise in the price of meals leads to a reduction in the quantity of films demanded. Figure 6-13 has three properties. First, the two goods are poor substi-

tutes. Indifference curves are very curved. Moving away from balanced combinations of the two goods requires very large additional quantities of one good to compensate for small losses of the other good if a constant level of utility is to be preserved. When the price of meals is increased, the substitution effect towards films is very small. Moving leftwards along U_2U_2, we quickly attain the slope required to match the new relative prices of the two goods. The substitution effect from C to D adds little to the quantity of films demanded.

Second, films have a high income elasticity of demand. They are a luxury good. Hence the income effect, the move from D to E in response to the parallel downward shift in the budget line from HH to AF', leads to a large reduction in the quantity of films demanded.

Finally, the point C lies well to the right on the original budget line AF. Meal expenditure takes up a large part of consumer budgets. Hence changes in meal prices lead to large changes in the purchasing power of consumer income. Not only is the quantity of films demanded very responsive to given changes in consumer real income, but in addition a given increase in meal prices has a large effect on consumer real income because meals are a large part of consumer budgets.

These last two effects lead to a large income effect, which reduces the quantity of films demanded. Because the substitution effect in favour of films is small, the net effect is a reduction in the quantity of films demanded. An increase in meal prices reduces the quantity of films demanded. The cross price elasticity of demand is negative.

Figure 6-14 illustrates the opposite case, in which the cross price elasticity is positive. We now suppose the consumer is choosing between bread and other food and examine the effect of an increase in the price of bread. First, there are quite good substitutes for bread, for example potatoes. To preserve a given level of utility consumers do not require large additional amounts of one good to depart from balanced combinations of the two goods. Indifference curves have much less curvature than in Figure 6-13.

Second, other food has a relatively low income elasticity of demand. To the extent that higher bread prices reduce real consumer income, this has a relatively small income effect acting to reduce the quantity of other food demanded. Third, since bread forms a relatively small share in consumer budgets, the increase in bread prices has a relatively small effect in reducing consumer purchasing power. Comparing Figures 6-13 and 6-14, the parallel shift from HH to AF' is much smaller in the latter.

These last two effects mean that there is only a small income effect acting to reduce the quantity of other food demanded. In contrast, the substitution effect in favour of other food is large. Hence a rise in bread prices increases the quantity of other food demanded. The cross price elasticity is positive. This positive effect would be even stronger if 'other food' were an inferior good. The income effect would then act to increase the quantity of other food demanded, thereby reinforcing the substitution effects in this direction.

Table 6-2 summarizes the implications of our model of consumer choice for the demand response to a price change.

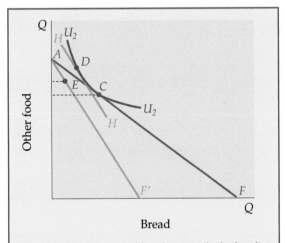

An increase in the price of bread rotates the budget line from AF to AF'. The substitution effect from C to D is large. Indifference curves have little curvature since the two goods are good substitutes in utility terms. The income effect from D to E is relatively small because the income elasticity of demand for other food is low and because the reduction in real income is small since bread forms a small share of the consumer budget. The substitution effect outweighs the income effect. E lies above C.

Figure 6-14   A positive cross price elasticity of demand

6-4 The market demand curve

We have now established the foundations for the proposition that individual demand curves slope downwards. For the rest of this book we assume that this proposition is correct. We consider now what this implies for the market demand curve.

The **market demand curve** is the sum of the demand curves of all individuals in that market.

It is obtained by asking, at each price, how much each person demands. By adding the quantities demanded by all consumers at that price we obtain the total quantity demanded at each price, the market demand curve. Since, as price is reduced, each person increases the quantity demanded, the total quantity demanded must also increase

Good	Type	Substitution effect	Income effect	Total effect
I	Normal	Negative	Negative	Negative
	Inferior	Negative	Positive	Ambiguous (usually negative)
J	Normal	Positive	Negative	Ambiguous
	Inferior	Positive	Positive	Positive

Table 6-2   The effect of an increase in the price of good I on the quantity demanded of goods I and J

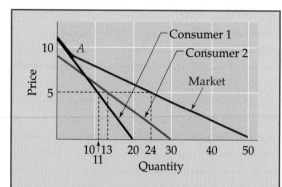

The market demand curve is the horizontal sum of individual demand curves. For example, if the price is £5, the quantity demanded by consumer 1 is 11 units, and the quantity demanded by consumer 2 is 13 units. The total quantity demanded in the market at £5 is thus 24 units, as shown in the market demand curve. The market demand curve is kinked at point A, the price at which consumer 2 first comes into the market.

Figure 6-15   Individual demand curves and the market demand curve

as price falls. The market demand curve also slopes downwards.

We sometimes say that the market demand curve is the *horizontal addition of individual demand curves*. With prices on the vertical axis, we must add together individual quantities demanded at the same price. Figure 6-15 illustrates this idea for two consumers.

6-5 Complements and substitutes

We have now given many illustrations of how income and substitution effects may be used to understand the consequences of a price change. Whatever the direction of the income effect, when there are only two goods the substitution effect is always unambiguous. The pure relative price effect leads the consumer to substitute away from the good whose relative price has risen towards the good whose relative price has fallen. In this sense, abstracting from income effects, goods are necessarily substitutes for one another in a two-good world.

When there are more than two goods we must recognize the possibility that some goods are consumed jointly – pipes and pipe tobacco, bread and cheese, electric cookers and electricity. We therefore have to recognize the possibility of *complementarity*.

When there are many goods it is still possible to prove that there will be a substitution effect *away* from the goods whose relative price has risen. However, it is not necessarily

true that there is a substitution *towards* all other goods. Consumers will tend to substitute *away* from goods consumed jointly with the good whose price has risen.

Suppose the price of pipes rises. What will happen to the demand for pipe tobacco? (We ignore the income effect since expenditure on pipes is a tiny fraction of household budgets, so real incomes are only slightly reduced. Since pipes and pipe tobacco are used jointly, we expect the demand for pipe tobacco will fall along with the quantity of pipes demanded. The demand curve for pipe tobacco shifts to the left in response to the increase in pipe prices.

Whenever goods are complements, an increase in the price of one good will reduce the demand for the complement both through the substitution effect (substituting away from the higher priced activity) and of course through the income effect (provided goods are normal).

6-6 Transfers in kind

A transfer is a payment, usually by the government, for which no corresponding service is provided by the recipient. Social security payments are an example. Wages are not: the recipient is providing labour services in exchange for wages.

A **transfer in kind** is the gift of a good or service.

For example, the poor may be given food stamps entitling them to buy food, but only food. The stamps cannot be spent on films or petrol. In this section we use the model of consumer choice to ask whether an in-kind transfer payment is preferred by the consumer to a cash transfer payment of equivalent monetary value.

The consumer has £100 to spend on food or films, each costing £10 per unit. Figure 6-16 shows the budget line AF. Now suppose the government issues the consumer with food stamps worth four food units. For any point on the old budget line AF the consumer can now have an additional four units of food by using the food stamps. Moving horizontally to the right a distance of four food units we obtain the new budget line BF'. To remind ourselves that food stamps cannot buy films, we can think of the new budget line as ABF'. The consumer can still consume at most 10 films.

Suppose the consumer had originally chosen point e on the old budget line AF. Since both goods are normal, the parallel shift in the budget line to ABF' – effectively, an increase in real income – will lead the consumer to choose a point to the north-east of e. This is precisely the point the consumer would have chosen had the transfer been in cash.

BOX 6-3

Substitution: even rats do it

The diagram shows the substitution effect in action. A consumer was offered a choice between a Tom Collins cocktail and root beer. Facing the budget line *AF* with equal prices for the two drinks, the consumer chose the point *e*. Then the relative price of Tom Collins was increased fourfold but the consumer's income was adjusted, so that the new budget line *A'F'* went through the point *e* originally chosen. Although still possible to consume *e*, the consumer chose *e'*, substituting root beer for Tom Collins in response to the lower relative price of root beer.

The consumer who illustrated the substitution effect so well was a white male albino rat. The budget line was the number of times it had to push on levers to get the two kinds of drink. The quantity per push changed with the price of the drink. The experiment is reported in a paper by Professor John Kagel and others, 'Experimental Studies of Consumer Demand Behaviour Using Laboratory Animals' (*Economic Inquiry*, March 1975).

The authors report one other fascinating finding. When large changes were made in relative prices, there were 'severe disruptions' in the rat's consumer choice behaviour. Many humans feel the same way.

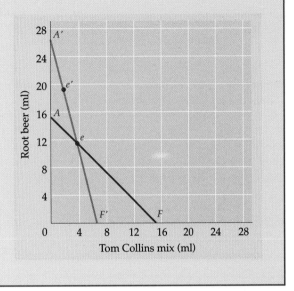

A food transfer in kind may leave consumers less satisfied than a cash transfer of the same value. A consumer at *e'* might wish to spend less than the full allowance on food moving to *c*. The budget line is *A'BF'* under a cash transfer. The in-kind transfer restricts the budget line to *ABF'*, ruling out points *A'B'*.

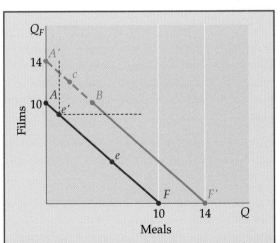

Figure 6-16 Transfers in cash and in kind

When food costs £10 per unit, the cash equivalent of four food units is £40, shifting the budget line to *A'F'*. Thus, if the consumer begins at *e* it makes no difference whether the transfer is in cash or in kind.

Suppose, however, that the consumer had begun at point *e'*. With a cash payment, the consumer might have wished to move to point *c* on the budget line *A'F'*. The transfer in kind, by restricting the consumer to the budget line *ABF'*, prevents the consumer reaching the preferred point *c*. Perhaps instead the consumer moves to the point *B*, which can be reached. The point *B* must yield the consumer less utility than point *c*: when the consumer was given a cash payment and could choose either, *c* was preferred to *B*.

Cash transfers allow consumers to spend the extra income in any way that they desire. Transfers in kind may limit the consumer's option. Where they do, the increase in consumer utility will be less than under a cash transfer of the same monetary value.

Yet transfers in kind are politically popular. The electorate wants to know that money raised in taxation is being wisely spent. Some who favour transfers in kind will argue that the poor really do not know how to spend their money wisely and may spend cash transfers on 'undesirable' goods such as alcohol or entertainment rather than on 'desirable' goods such as food or housing.

One view says that people can best choose for themselves, whereas the other says that people may not act in their own best interests. This issue is not merely one of economics but also of philosophy, involving wider questions such as liberty and paternalism. In so far as people are capable of judging their own self-interest, economic analysis is clear: people will be better off, or at least no worse off, if they are given transfers in cash rather than in kind.

SUMMARY

● The theory of demand is based on the assumption that the consumer, given the budget constraint, seeks to reach the maximum possible level of utility.

● The budget line shows the maximum affordable quantity of one good for each given quantity of the other good. The position of the budget line is determined by income and prices alone. Its slope reflects only relative prices.

● Because the consumer prefers more to less, he or she will always select a point on the budget line. The consumer has a problem of choice. Along the budget line, more of one good can be obtained only by sacrificing some of the other good.

● Consumer tastes can be represented by a map of non-intersecting indifference curves. Along each indifference curve, utility is constant. Higher indifference curves are preferred to lower indifference curves. Since the consumer prefers more to less, indifference curves must slope downwards. To preserve a given level of utility, increases in the quantity of one good must be offset by reductions in the quantity of the other good.

● Indifference curves reflect the principle of a diminishing marginal rate of substitution. Their slope becomes flatter as we move along them to the right. To preserve utility, consumers will sacrifice ever smaller amounts of one good to obtain successive unit increases in the amount of the other good.

● Utility-maximizing consumers choose the consumption bundle at which the highest reachable indifference curve is just tangent to the budget line. At this point the market trade-off between goods, the slope of the budget line, just matches the utility trade-off between goods, the slope of the indifference curve.

● At constant prices, an increase in income leads to a parallel outward shift in the budget line. If goods are normal, the quantity demanded will increase.

● A change in the price of one good rotates the budget line around the point at which none of that good is purchased. Such a price change has an income effect and a substitution effect. The income effect of a price increase is to reduce the quantity demanded for all normal goods. The substitution effect, induced by relative price movements alone, leads consumers to substitute away from the good whose relative price has increased.

● In a two-good world, the goods are necessarily substitutes. The substitution effect is unambiguous. With many goods, the pure substitution effect of a price increase will also reduce the demand for goods that are complementary to the good whose price has risen.

● A rise in the price of a normal good must lower its quantity demanded. For inferior goods, the income effect operates in the opposite direction but rarely seems to dominate the substitution. Demand curves slope downwards.

● The market demand curve is the horizontal sum of individual demand curves, at each price adding together the individual quantities demanded.

● Consumers prefer to receive transfers in cash rather than in kind, if the two transfers have the same monetary value. A transfer in kind may restrict the choices a consumer can make.

REVIEW QUESTIONS

1 A consumer's income is £50. Food costs £5 per unit and films cost £2 per unit. (a) Draw the budget line. Choose a point e for the optimal initial consumption bundle. (b) Suppose now the price of food falls to £2.50. Draw the new budget line. What can be said about the new consumption point if both goods are normal? Label the new consumption point e'. (c) Suppose the price of films also falls to £1. Draw the new budget line and indicate where the consumer now chooses. Label this point e". (d) How does e" differ from e? Explain your answer.

2 The own price elasticity of demand for food is negative. The demand for food is inelastic. An increase in food prices raises spending on food. Hence higher food prices imply that less is spent on all other goods and that the quantity demanded of each of these other goods must fall. Discuss carefully these statements and identify any that you think might be wrong.

3 Suppose films are normal but transport is inferior. Draw the income expansion path for films and transport as incomes rise.

4 'If an increase in the price of drinks raises the demand for chocolate, an increase in the price of chocolate must increase the demand for drinks.' Is this true?

5 Suppose Londoners have a given income. They consume a large variety of goods, including petrol and weekend trips to the countryside (a three-hour drive). Now let the price of petrol double. (a) What is the effect on the demand for weekend trips to the countryside? Discuss both the income and substitution effects. (b) Use a demand and supply diagram to show what happens to the price of hotel rooms in the countryside at weekends. (c) Suppose there is a holiday place closer to London. What happens to the demand for hotel rooms there?

6 *Common fallacies* Show why the following statements are incorrect: (a) The average consumer has never heard of an indifference curve or a budget line. Consumers don't choose the point on the budget line which is tangent to the highest possible indifference curve. (b) If inflation leads to a doubling of all incomes and prices, the budget line will shift and consumers will reduce quantities of each good demanded. (c) If in (b) consumers demand the same quantities as before, this proves that income effects can be neglected.

Appendix: Consumer choice with measurable utility

We developed the theory of consumer choice under the very general assumption that consumers could rank or order different bundles according to the utility or satisfaction they gave. Saying bundle A gave higher utility than bundle B just meant that the consumer preferred A to B. Nothing we said required the consumer to decide *by how much* A was preferred to B. Higher indifference curves were better, but we did not need to know how much better.

In the nineteenth century, some economists believed that utility levels could actually be measured. It was as if each consumer had a *utility meter* measuring his happiness. The further to the right the needle on his utility meter, the happier he was. The units on this meter were traditionally marked off in *utils*. Nowadays this seems a bit strange: are you 2.9 times as happy if you get an extra week's holiday?

Nevertheless, analysing consumer choice when utility *is* measurable in this way is quite interesting, even though we have been able to derive all the main propositions in the text without this additional assumption. The (rather robot-like) individual whose utility can be exactly calibrated in utils we shall call Fred.

Fred goes to rock concerts and eats hamburgers. His utility depends on the bundle of hamburgers and concerts he consumes. For a given consumption of one of these goods, he prefers more of the other to less. His utility goes up; he gets more utils.

The **marginal utility** of a good is the increase in total utility obtained by consuming one more unit of that good, for given consumption of other goods.

Thus, if Fred gets 67 utils of utility from consuming 10 hamburgers and 1 rock concert, and 70 utils of utility from 11 hamburgers but still 1 rock concert, his marginal utility of the eleventh hamburger is $(70 - 67 = 3)$ utils.

Fred was hardly going hungry. He had 10 hamburgers at his only concert. He cannot have got much from an extra one; indeed, he got only an extra 3 utils. In contrast, if Fred had only 2 hamburgers at one concert (say, giving him 20 utils), he might rather have enjoyed one more hamburger (say, taking his utils to 27). The marginal utility of that extra hamburger is $(27 - 20 = 7)$ utils. Fred's tastes obey the law of diminishing marginal utility.

A consumer has **diminishing marginal utility** from a good if each extra unit consumed adds successively less to total utility.

Figure 6-A1 plots Fred's marginal utility of hamburgers. He gets fewer *extra* utils from extra consumption of hamburgers, the more he is already consuming; we show this as the downward-sloping schedule *MU*.

Fred has a given income to spend. Once we know the prices of rock concerts and hamburgers, we can work out his budget line. How does Fred choose the affordable point on this line at which to consume? He maximizes his utility.

Suppose the price of hamburgers in pounds is P_H and the price of concerts is P_C. Thus, if MU_H is the marginal utility Fred gets from another hamburger, he gets an extra number of utils equal to MU_H/P_H for each extra pound spent on hamburgers. And he gets an extra MU_C/P_C for each extra pound spent on concerts.

Suppose MU_H/P_H is bigger than MU_C/P_C. An extra pound spent on hamburgers increases Fred's utility more than an

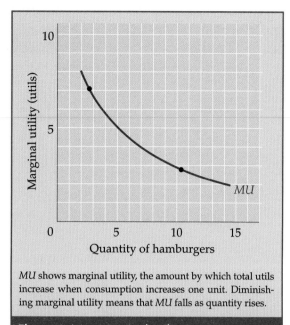

MU shows marginal utility, the amount by which total utils increase when consumption increases one unit. Diminishing marginal utility means that *MU* falls as quantity rises.

Figure 6-A1 Marginal utility

extra pound spent on concerts. More importantly, if Fred spends one extra pound on hamburgers and one less pound on concerts his total utils will rise: he gains more from hamburgers than he loses from concerts. He can increase utility *without spending more*. He will always want to transfer spending towards the good that yields more marginal utility per pound spent. It is easy to see how Fred maximizes his utility. He spends all his income (he is on rather than inside his budget line), and he adjusts his spending between hamburgers and concerts until

$$MU_H/P_H = MU_C/P_C \qquad (A1)$$

Only when this condition holds can Fred not rearrange the division of his total spending to increase his utility.[5]

The consumer maximizes utility by choosing the consumption bundle which satisfies the budget constraint and for which the ratio of marginal utility to price is the same for every good.

---

[5] Equation (A1) implies $MU_H/MU_C = P_H/P_C$. Multiplying both sides by (-1), the right-hand side is simply the slope of the budget line, which we know depends only on relative prices. The left-hand side is simply the marginal rate of substitution: if the marginal utility of one hamburger is 2 and of one concert is 4, then $-MU_H/MU_C = -\frac{1}{2}$. Equivalently, we can exchange 1 hamburger for ½ a concert without altering total utility, which is precisely what the marginal rate of substitution measures. Hence equation (A1) is equivalent to saying that the slope of the indifference curve, measured by the marginal rate of substitution, must equal the slope of the budget line. This is precisely the tangency condition we derived in the text without the use of measurable utility!

BOX 6-4

Marginal utility and the water diamond paradox

Nineteenth-century economists were puzzled as to why the price of water, essential for survival, was so much lower than that for decorative diamonds. One answer is that diamonds are scarcer than water. Yet consumers clearly get more total utility from water (without it they die) than from diamonds. The concept of marginal utility solves the problem.

Equation (A1) tells us that consumers keep buying a good until the ratio of its *marginal* utility to price equals that for other goods. *At the margin*, the last litre of water

we drink or use in the shower gives very little extra utility. At the margin, the last diamond still makes a big difference. People are willing to pay more for extra diamonds than for extra water.

In terms of a figure like Figure 6-A1, the marginal utility schedule *MU* is *very* high for the first few drops of water. Not dying is worth lots of utils. But most of us are a long way down this schedule, using lots of water to the point where its marginal value to us has become quite low.

Given Fred's *utility function* (the meter from which we read off utils depending on the quantities of hamburgers and concerts Fred consumes), the prices P_H and P_C for hamburgers and concerts, and his income, we can now derive Fred's demand curves for hamburgers and concerts.

Deriving demand curves

Suppose the price of hamburgers falls. For given hamburger consumption, MU_H/P_H has risen because hamburger prices have fallen. MU_H/P_H now exceeds MU_C/P_C for concerts. This violates equation (A1). To maximize utility, Fred will have to change the quantities he demands.

If Fred buys *more* hamburgers when the price *falls*, the law of diminishing marginal utility implies that MU_H will fall as Fred increases the quantity of hamburgers demanded in response to their cheaper price. MU_H/P_H moves towards MU_C/P_C, as required by equation (A1). We call this the *substitution effect* of the relative change in the price of hamburgers and concerts. On its own, the substitution effect suggests that *demand curves slope down*: when the price of hamburgers falls, the quantity demanded increases.

However, we must be careful; a second effect is at work. Cheaper hamburger prices increase the purchasing power of Fred's given money income. We need to think about the effect of this on Fred's marginal utility. Suppose first that hamburgers are a normal good; Fred wants more when the purchasing power of his income rises. We can think of higher income as shifting Fred's marginal utility schedule upwards in Figure 6-A2.

This *income effect* means that Fred finds that MU_H/P_H rises not only because P_H falls but also because, with a higher marginal utility schedule for hamburgers, MU_H rises at any

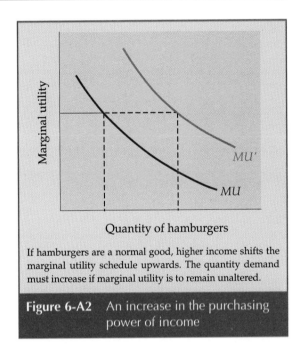

If hamburgers are a normal good, higher income shifts the marginal utility schedule upwards. The quantity demanded must increase if marginal utility is to remain unaltered.

Figure 6-A2   An increase in the purchasing power of income

particular level of hamburger consumption. Fred will have to increase his hamburger demand yet further to slide down the higher schedule (diminishing marginal utility) to restore MU_H/P_H to equality with MU_C/P_C. Thus, for normal goods the income effect reinforces the substitution effect. Demand curves must slope down.

Suppose however that hamburgers are an inferior good. In Figure 6-A2 we could show this as a downward shift in the marginal utility schedule when the purchasing power of Fred's income increases. At his original consumption bundle, it is now possible that MU_H has fallen a lot; specifically, it could have fallen more than P_H the price of hamburgers. If so, Fred will have to *reduce* his hamburger consumption in order to increase its marginal utility and restore MU_H/P_H to equality with MU_C/P_C as utility maximization requires.

Thus, for inferior goods the income effect goes in the opposite direction to the substitution effect. If the income effect is powerful enough, it could win out. Lower hamburger prices would then reduce the quantity of hamburgers demanded. Demand curves would slope upwards! As we discuss in the text, we call such goods Giffen goods. In practice they are rarely if ever found. It is safe to assume that demand curves slope down in practice.

Modern economists are pretty sniffy about measurable utility, preferring the more general indifference curve analysis we used in the text. But indifference curves seem a bit tricky the first time you meet them, and you need to practice using them before you get comfortable with them. In contrast, measurable utility and the simple idea of diminishing marginal utility allows an easier introduction to the basic properties of demand curves and consumer choice we have developed in this chapter.

7 Business organization and behaviour

LEARNING OUTCOMES

When you have finished this chapter, you should be able to:

- Explain the different legal forms in which a business can be owned and run
- Define revenue, cost, profit, and cash flow
- Construct balance sheets, both for flows within a year and for net wealth at a point in time
- Distinguish economic and accounting definitions of cost
- Discuss the assumption that a firm's output level is chosen to maximize profits
- Relate this output choice to marginal cost and marginal revenue

Having analysed demand, we turn now to supply. How do firms decide how much to produce and offer for sale? Can a single theory of supply describe the behaviour of a wide range of different producers, from giant companies such as Shell to the self-employed ice cream vendor with a van?

For each possible output level a firm needs to answer two questions: how much will it *cost* to produce this output and how much *revenue* will be earned by selling it. For each output level, production costs depend on technology that determines how many inputs are needed to produce this output, and on input prices that the firm has to pay for these inputs. The revenue obtained from selling output depends on the demand curve faced by the firm. The demand curve determines the price for which any given output quantity can be sold and hence the revenue that the firm will earn. Figure 7-1 emphasizes the interaction of costs and revenues that determines how much output firms wish to supply.

Profits are the excess of revenues over costs. The key to the theory of supply is the assumption that all firms have the same objective: to make as much profit as possible. By examining how revenues and costs change with the level of

output produced and sold, the firm can select the output level which maximizes its profits. To understand how firms make output decisions we must therefore analyse the determination of revenues and costs.

We introduce two essential concepts in the theory of supply, *marginal cost* and *marginal revenue*. Finally, because the assumption of profit maximization forms the cornerstone of this approach, we discuss the plausibility of this assumption and examine alternative views of what firms' aims might be.

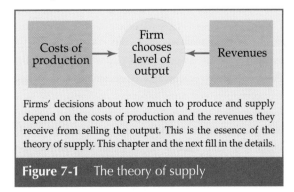

Firms' decisions about how much to produce and supply depend on the costs of production and the revenues they receive from selling the output. This is the essence of the theory of supply. This chapter and the next fill in the details.

Figure 7-1 The theory of supply

7-1 Business organization

Businesses are self-employed sole traders, partnerships, or companies. Sole traders are by far the commonest type of business organization, though each sole trader operates on a relatively small scale. Partnerships operate on a larger scale and companies are larger still. The largest companies have sales measured in billions of pounds.

A **sole trader** is a business owned by a single individual.

A sole trader is entitled to the income or revenue of the business and responsible for any losses the business suffers. You might open a health food shop, renting the premises and paying someone to stand at the till. Although you can keep the profits, if the business makes losses that you cannot meet you will have to declare bankruptcy. Your remaining assets, including personal assets such as your house, will then be sold and the money shared out between your creditors.

However, your health food shop may prosper. You need money to expand, to buy bigger stocks, a delivery van, and office furniture. To raise all this money, you may decide to go into partnership with other people.

A **partnership** is a business jointly owned by two or more people, sharing the profits and jointly responsible for any losses.

Not all the partners need be active. Some may put up some money for a share of the profits but take no active part in running the business. Some large partnerships, such as famous law and accounting firms, have hundreds of partners, all taking an active interest in the business.

Partnerships have *unlimited liability*. In the last resort, the owners' personal assets must be sold to cover losses that cannot otherwise be met. This is one reason why firms where trust is involved – for example, solicitors or accountants – are partnerships. It is a signal to the customers that the people running the business are willing to put their own wealth behind the firm's obligations.

Any business needs some financial capital, money to start the business and finance its growth, paying for stocks, machinery, or advertising before any revenue is earned. Firms of lawyers, accountants, or doctors, businesses that rely primarily on human expertise, need relatively little money for such purposes. The necessary funds can be raised from the partners and, possibly, by a loan from the bank. Businesses that require large initial expenditure on machinery, or are growing very rapidly, may need much larger amounts of initial funds. Because of legal compli-cations, it may not make sense to take on an enormous number of partners. Instead, it makes sense to form a company.

A **company** is an organization legally allowed to produce and trade.

Unlike a partnership, it has a legal existence distinct from that of its owners. Ownership is divided among share-holders. The original shareholders are the people who started the business, but now they have sold shares of the profits to outsiders. By selling these entitlements to share in the profits, the business has been able to raise new funds.

For *public companies* these shares can be resold on the *stock exchange*. Trading on the stock exchange, reported in most daily newspapers, is primarily the sale and resale of existing shares in public companies. However, even the largest company occasionally needs to issue additional new shares to raise money for especially large projects.

To buy into a company, a shareholder must purchase shares on the stock exchange at the equilibrium share price, which just balances buyers and sellers of the company's shares on that particular day. Shareholders earn a return in two ways. First, the company makes regular *dividend* payments, paying out to shareholders that part of the profits that the firm does not wish to re-invest in the business. Second, the shareholders may make *capital gains* (or losses). If you buy ICI shares for £700 each and then everyone decides ICI profits and dividends will be unexpectedly high, you may be able to resell the shares for £750, making a capital gain of £50 per share on the transactions.

The shareholders of a company have **limited liability**. The most they can lose is the money they originally spent buying shares.

Unlike sole traders and partners, shareholders cannot be forced to sell their personal possessions when the business cannot pay. At worst, the shares merely become worthless.

Companies are run by boards of directors who decide how the firm is run but must submit an annual report to the shareholders. At the annual meeting the shareholders can vote to sack the directors, each shareholder having as many votes as the number of shares owned. Companies are the main form of organization of big businesses.

7-2 Revenues, costs, and profits

A firm's **revenue** is the amount it earns by selling goods or services in a given period such as a year. The firm's **costs**

Revenue	£1 000 000
(100 000 hours, £10/hour)	
Deduct expenses (costs)	
Wages	£700 000
Advertising	50 000
Office rent	50 000
Other expenses	100 000
	£900 000
Profits before tax	£100 000
Taxes paid	£25 000
Profits after tax	£75 000

Figure 7-2   Rent-a-Person income statement year ending 31 December 2000

are the expenses incurred in producing goods or services during the period. **Profits** are the excess of revenues over costs.

Although these ideas are simple, in practice the calculation of revenues, costs, and profits for a large business is complicated. Otherwise we would not need so many accountants. We begin with a simple example.

Rent-a-Person is a firm that hires people whom it then rents out to other firms that need temporary workers. Rent-a-Person charges £10 per hour per worker but pays its workers only £7 per hour. During 2000 it rented 100 000 hours of labour. Business expenses, including leasing an office, buying advertising space, and paying telephone bills, came to £200 000. Figure 7-2 shows the *income statement* or *profit-and-loss account* for 2000. Profits or net income before taxes were £100 000. Taxes came to £25 000. Rent-a-Person's after-tax profits were £75 000. Now we discuss some of the complications in calculating profits.

Outstanding bills

People do not always pay their bills on time. At the end of 2000, Rent-a-Person has not been paid for all its workers hired out during the year. On the other hand, it has not paid its telephone bill for December. From an economic viewpoint, the right definition of revenues and costs relates to the activities during the year whether or not payments have yet been made.

This distinction between economic revenues and costs and actual receipts and payments raises the important concept of cash flow.

A firm's **cash flow** is the net amount of money actually received during the period.

Profitable firms may still have a poor cash flow, for example when customers are slow to pay.

Capital and depreciation

Physical capital is the machinery, equipment, and buildings used in production.

Rent-a-Person owns little physical capital. Instead, it rents office space, typewriters, and desks. In practice, businesses frequently buy physical capital. Economists use 'capital' to denote goods not entirely used up in the production process during the period. Buildings and lorries are capital because they can be used again in the next year. Electricity is not a capital good because purchases during 2000 do not survive into 2001. Economists also use the terms 'durable goods' or 'physical assets' to describe capital goods.

How should the cost of a capital good be treated in calculating profits and costs? It is the cost of using rather than buying capital equipment that is part of the firm's costs within the year. If Rent-a-Person leases all its capital equipment, its costs include merely the rentals paid in leasing capital goods.

Suppose Rent-a-Person buys eight computers at the beginning of the year for £1000 each. It should not count £8000 as the cost of computers in calculating costs and profits for that year. Rather, the cost is the reduction in the value of the computers over the year. Suppose the wear-and-tear on the computers over the year has reduced their value from £1000 to £700 each. The economic cost of the use of eight computers over the year is £2400 (8 × £300). This depreciation is the cost during the year.[1]

Depreciation is the loss in value resulting from the use of machinery during the period.

The cost *during the period* of using a capital good is the depreciation or loss of value of that good, not its purchase price.

Depreciation leads to a difference between economic profits and cash flow. When a capital good is first purchased there is a large cash outflow, much larger than the depreciation cost of using the good during the first year. Profits may be high but cash flow low. However, in subsequent years the firm makes no further cash outlay, having already paid for the capital goods, but must still calculate depreciation as an economic cost since the resale value of goods is reduced still further. Cash flow is now higher than economic profit.

Treating depreciation rather than purchase price as the true economic cost spreads the initial cost over the life of the

---

[1] There is a *second* economic cost – the interest payments on the money used to buy the computers – which we discuss shortly.

BOX 7-1

What a good name is worth

The consultancy Interbrand tries to calculate how much of a company's revenue is due simply to the marketing value of its brand image as distinct from other inputs such as capital and labour employed. US giants such as Coca-Cola top the worldwide list, but Microsoft, Nokia, and Yahoo! are well up there already. So are Nike and Adidas. Interestingly, the big banks fare poorly in this ranking.

Rank	Company	Industry	Brand value (£ bn)
1	Coca-Cola (www.coca-cola.com)	Drinks	50
2	Microsoft (www.microsoft.com)	Software	35
3	IBM (www.ibm.com)	Computers	25
5	Ford (www.ford.com)	Cars	20
6	Disney (www.disney.com)	Entertainment	19
11	Nokia (www.nokia.com)	Mobile phones	12
18	Sony (www.sony.com)	Electronics	8
25	Citibank (www.citibank.com)	Banking	6
28	Nike (www.nike.com)	Sports goods	5
45	BP (www.bpamoco.com)	Oil	2
52	Heineken (www. heineken.com)	Beer	1

Source: Financial Times, 22 June 1999.

capital goods; but that is not the reason for undertaking the calculation in this way. Rent-a-Person could have sold its computers for £5600 after one year, restricting its costs to £2400. Since it chose to keep them for re-use in the next year, the latter strategy is even more profitable. Hence the true economic cost of using the computers in the first year can be at most £2400.

Inventories

Inventories are goods held in stock by the firm for future sales.

If production were instantaneous, firms could produce to meet orders as they arose. In fact, production takes time. Firms hold inventories to meet future demand.

Suppose at the beginning of 2000 Rover has a stock of 100 000 cars completed and available for sale. During the year it produces 1 million new cars and sells 950 000. By the end of the year its inventories of finished cars have risen to 150 000. How does this complicate the profit calculation? Revenues accrue from the sale of 950 000 cars. Should costs be based on sales of 950 000 cars or the 1 million actually made?

The answer is that costs should relate to the 950 000 cars actually sold. The 50 000 cars added to stocks are like capital the firm made for itself, available for sale in the following period. There was a cash outflow to pay for the manufacture of 1 million cars but part of this cash outflow was for the purchase of inventories which will provide cash revenue the following year without requiring any cash outlay on production.

Borrowing

Firms usually borrow to finance their set-up and expansion costs, buying capital goods, solicitors' fees for the paperwork in registering the company, and so on. There is interest to be paid on the money borrowed. This interest is part of the cost of doing business and should be counted as part of the costs.

The balance sheet

The income statement or profit-and-loss account of Figure 7-2 tells us about the flow of money during a given year. We also paint a picture of the position the firm has reached as a result of all its past trading operations. The *balance sheet* lists

ASSETS		LIABILITIES	
Cash	£40 000	Accounts payable	£90 000
Accounts receivable	70 000	Salaries payable	50 000
Inventories	100 000	Mortgage	150 000
Factory building (original value £250000)	200 000	Bank loan	60 000
Other equipment (original value £300000)	180 000		
			350 000
		Net worth	240 000
	590 000		590 000

Figure 7-3　Snark International balance sheet 31 December 2000

the assets the firm owns and the liabilities for which it is responsible at a point in time.

Figure 7-3 is a balance sheet for Snark International on 31 December 2000.

Assets are what the firm owns.

Assets are shown on the left. Snark has some cash in the bank, is owed money by customers which is entered as 'accounts receivable', and has large inventories in its warehouses. It owns a factory which originally cost £250 000 but is now worth only £200 000 because of depreciation. Its other equipment has also depreciated and is now worth £180 000. The total value of Snark assets is £590 000.

Liabilities are what the firm owes.

Liabilities, shown on the right, include unpaid bills and salaries, the mortgage on the factory, and a bank loan for short-term cash needs. The total value of debts is £350 000. The *net worth* of Snark International is £240 000, its assets minus its liabilities.

We show net worth on the liabilities side. Because the firm is owned by the shareholders, the net worth is really a liability of the firm to the shareholders.

You make a takeover bid for Snark International. Should you offer £240 000, the net worth of the company? Probably not. Snark International is a live company with good prospects for future growth and a proven record. You are bidding not merely for its physical and financial assets minus liabilities but also for the firm as a going concern. You will also get its reputation, customer loyalty and a host of intangibles which economists call *goodwill*. If Snark is a sound company, bid more than £240 000.

Alternatively, you may feel that Snark's accountants have undervalued the resale value of its assets. If you can buy the company for close to £240 000 you might make a profit

selling off the separate pieces of equipment and buildings, a practice known as 'asset-stripping'.

Earnings

Finally, we must consider what the firm does with its profits after taxes. It can pay them out to shareholders as dividends, or keep them in the firm as retained earnings.

Retained earnings are the part of after-tax profits that is ploughed back into the business rather than paid out to shareholders as dividends.

Retained earnings affect the balance sheet. If they are kept as cash or used to purchase new equipment, they increase the asset side of the balance sheet. Alternatively, they may be used to reduce the firm's liabilities, for example by repaying the bank loan. Either way, the firm's net worth is increased.

Opportunity cost and accounting costs

The income statement and the balance sheet of a company provide a useful guide to how that company is doing. Economists and accountants do not always take the same view of costs and profits. Whereas the accountant is interested in describing the actual receipts and payments of a company, the economist is interested in the role of costs and profits as determinants of the firm's supply decision, the allocation of resources to particular activities. Accounting methods can mislead in two ways.

Economists identify the cost of using a resource not as the payment actually made but as its opportunity cost.

Opportunity cost is the amount lost by not using the resource (labour or capital) in its best alternative use.

To show that this is the right measure of costs, given the questions economists wish to study, we give two examples.

BOX 7-2

Corporate finance and corporate control

Corporate finance refers to the ways companies raise money by ploughing back profits, issuing new shares, or borrowing. Borrowing can be from banks or by selling pieces of paper (corporate debt) whereby the firm promises to pay interest for a specified period and then to pay off the debt. Different countries have very different systems of corporate finance.

The United States and the UK have market-based or *outsider* systems, relying on active stock markets trading existing shares and debt, and available for launching new shares and debt. Japan and much of continental Europe, most notably Germany, have an *insider* system, in which financial markets play only a small role. German companies get long-term loans from banks, who then sit on company boards with access to inside information about how the firm is doing.

DISTINGUISHING FINANCE AND CONTROL

Large firms finance most of their new investment from their own retained profits. Professor Colin Mayer of Oxford University has calculated that over 91 per cent of UK corporate investment is financed in this way; less then 7 per cent comes from sales of new shares on the stock market. The key difference in the two systems of corporate finance lies not in the ease with which they provide firms with finance, but in the way they award *control rights* to those providing that finance.

Under the bank-based insider system, representatives of the bank sit on the firm's board, and can use this inside position to press for changes in company policy or top management when mistakes are made. The market-based system entails a much smaller role for banks, and a more significant role for stock markets and debt markets. Failure to meet interest payments on debt usually gives debtholders the right to force the company into bankruptcy, a radical transfer of corporate control in which the existing management rarely survives. Similarly, the existence of publicly quoted shares raises the possibility of a stock market takeover in which a new management team effectively buys control on the open market. Outsider market-based systems of corporate finance thus become markets for corporate control itself.

HOSTILE TAKEOVERS: GOOD OR BAD?

In Germany, hostile takeovers have been rare. In contrast, a large fraction of UK takeover activity reflects hostile bids uninvited by existing managers. Some economists see hostile bids as a vital force for efficiency. The separation of ownership and control of public companies leads to a *principal–agent problem*. The agents (here, the managers) are tempted to act in their own interests rather than those of their principals (the shareholders). The threat of hostile takeovers may deter managers from departing too much from the profit-maximizing policies desired by shareholders.

However, hostile takeovers also undermine the existing managers. Suppose you want workforce co-operation in moving to new production methods. You promise to reward employees handsomely in the future once all the changes have been made and productivity has risen. The workers know you always keep your word. Even so, they may feel unable to trust you. While the changes are being made, profits will temporarily fall and you may become the victim of a takeover raid. The new owner may start firing workers to save money. So the workers reject your plan to bring changes to the company.

Hostile takeovers, by undermining the ability of managers to make commitments to their workers, may thus inhibit investment and encourage *short-termism*. It is Germany and Japan, with bank-based systems of corporate finance, and not the UK and the United States, with market-based systems, that are noted for strategic planning and the ability to think long-term.

Interlocking share ownership, where firm A owns part of firm B but B also owns part of A, can be an effective defence against outside takeover raiders. Similarly, US shareholders sometimes volunteer a 'supermajority clause', which states that a raider needs to buy, say, 75 per cent of the shares before it can displace the existing managers. Why do shareholders offer managers protection from the discipline of the market-place? The shareholders must think that the gains to profits from allowing managers to take a longer-term view outweigh the danger that they may use greater security to opt for the easy life.

Any persons working in their own businesses should take into account the cost of their own labour time spent in the business. A self-employed sole trader might draw up an income statement such as Figure 7-2, find that profits were £20 000 per annum, and conclude that this business was a good thing. But this conclusion neglects the opportunity cost of the individual's labour, the money that could have been earned by working elsewhere. If that individual could have earned a salary of £25 000 working for someone else, being self-employed is actually losing the person £5000 per annum even though the business is making an accounting profit of £20 000. To understand the incentives that the market provides to guide people towards particular occupations, we must use the economic concept of opportunity cost, not the accounting concept of actual payments.

The second place where opportunity cost must be counted is with respect to capital. Somebody has put up the money to start the business. In calculating accounting profits, no cost is attached to the use of owned (as opposed to borrowed) financial capital. This financial capital could have been used elsewhere, in an interest-bearing bank account or perhaps to buy shares in a different company. The opportunity cost of that financial capital is included in the *economic* costs of the business but not its accounting costs. If the owners could have earned 10 per cent elsewhere, the opportunity cost of their funds is 10 per cent times the money they put up. If, after deducting this cost, the business still makes a profit, economists call this 'supernormal profit'.

Supernormal profit is the profit over and above the return which the owners could have earned by lending their money elsewhere at the market rate of interest.

Supernormal profits are the true indicator of how well the owners are doing by tying up their funds in the business. Supernormal profits, not accounting profits, are the incentive to shift resources into or out of a business.

These are the two most important adjustments between accounting and economic notions of costs and profits. In other cases there may be minor differences – for example, since it is hard to calculate the resale value of a second-hand factory, economic and accounting approaches to depreciation may vary slightly. In many cases the two approaches are the same – for example, the wages paid by farmers to students for help in picking crops are not only an accounting cost but an economic cost. Without making these payments, farmers would not have been able to attract temporary student labour resources to the activity of crop picking.

Figure 7-4 summarizes the key adjustments to accounting

ACCOUNTING COSTS: INCOME STATEMENT		
Revenues		£80 000
Costs		50 000
Accounting profit		£30 000

OPPORTUNITY COSTS: INCOME STATEMENT		
Revenues		£80 000
Costs:		
Accounting costs	£50 000	
Cost of owner's time	25 000	
Opportunity cost of		
financial capital (£30 000)		
used in firm, at 10%	3 000	78 000
Economic (supernormal) profit)		£2 000

Economic costs are the opportunity costs of resources used in production. Accounting costs are likely to omit costs of the owner's time and the opportunity cost of financial capital used in the firm. Economic (supernormal) profit deducts the right measure of economic costs from revenues.

Figure 7-4 Accounting and opportunity costs: two important adjustments

costs and profits to get economic measures of costs and profits.

7-3 Firms and profit maximization

Firms are in business to make money. Economists assume that firms make supply and output decisions so as to *maximize profits*.

Some economists and business executives question the assumption that firms have the sole aim of maximizing profits. The last section described a self-employed individual making £20 000 per annum who could have made £25 000 per annum in a different job. Individuals who like to be their own boss may happily exchange the extra £5000 for the additional independence. Such a business is maximizing not the net income but the total satisfaction of its owner.

Ownership and control

A more significant reason to question the assumption of profit maximization is that large firms are not run by their owners. A large company is run by a salaried board of directors and by the managers this board appoints. Although at the annual meeting the shareholders may dismiss the board, in practice this happens rarely. The directors are the experts with the information; it is hard for the shareholders, even in bad times, to be sure that different directors would raise the profitability of the company.

Economists call this a separation of ownership and

control. Although shareholders want the maximum possible profit, the directors who actually make the decisions can pursue different objectives. Do the managers and directors have an incentive to act other than in the interests of the shareholders?

Managers' salaries are usually higher the larger is the firm. This may lead managers to aim for size and growth rather than the maximum possible profit. Managers may spend large sums on advertising even though this achieves only a small addition to sales.

Nevertheless, there are two reasons why the assumption of profit maximization is a good place from which to begin. Even if the shareholders cannot recognize that profits are lower than they might be, other firms with experience in the industry may catch on faster. If profits are low, share prices will be low. By mounting a takeover, another company can buy the shares cheaply, sack the existing managers, restore profit-maximizing policies, and make a handsome capital gain as the share prices rise once the stock market sees the improvement in profits.

Alternatively, being aware of the opportunity for managerial discretion, shareholders may try to ensure that the interests of the managers and the shareholders coincide. By giving senior managers a quantity of shares that is small relative to the total number of shares but large relative to managerial salaries, shareholders can try to ensure that senior managers care about profits as much as other shareholders do.

For these reasons, the assumption that firms try to maximize profits is more robust than might first be imagined. We now use this assumption to develop the theory of supply.

7-4 The firm's production decisions: an overview

We first focus on how much output should be produced. Many details are left for later chapters, but we introduce the key ideas of marginal cost and marginal revenue.

Imagine a firm that makes snarks. Of the many ways to make snarks, some use a lot of labour and few machines, others a lot of machines but little labour. Not only does the firm know the different techniques for making snarks, it also knows the wage rate for a skilled snark lathe operator and the rental on a snark lathe. The firm also knows its demand curve – how much it would earn by selling different quantities of snarks at each possible price.

The objective is to maximize profits by choosing the best level of output. Changing the output level affects both the costs of production and the revenues from sales. Production costs and demand conditions interact to determine the output chosen by a profit-maximizing firm.

Cost minimization

Any firm maximizing profits certainly wants to produce its chosen output level at the minimum possible cost. Otherwise, by producing the same output at lower cost it could increase profits. Thus a profit-maximizing firm must produce its output at minimum cost.

The total cost curve

Knowing the available production methods and the costs of hiring labour and machinery, the firm's managers can calculate the least cost at which each level of output can be produced. To make a few snarks per annum it is probably cheapest to use some workers but hardly any machinery. To make more snarks, it probably makes sense to use more machinery per worker.

Table 7-1 shows the minimum costs at which each output level can be produced. The firm incurs a cost of £10 even when no output is produced. This cost is the expenses of being in business at all – running an office, renting a telephone, and so on. Thereafter, costs rise with output. Costs in the table include the opportunity costs of all resources used in production. Total costs are higher the more is produced. At levels of output, such as 4 or 5 units per week, costs rise quite slowly as output rises. At high levels of output, such as 9 units per week, costs rise sharply as output increases. At high output the firm has to pay the workers extra money to work at weekends.

Total revenue

Information on costs is not sufficient to assess profits. The firm must also think about its revenue, which depends on demand. Table 7-2 shows the demand curve facing the firm.

Table 7-1 Total costs of production

Output (goods produced/week)	Total costs (£/week)
0	10
1	25
2	36
3	44
4	51
5	59
6	69
7	81
9	95
9	111
10	129

BOX 7-3   **Shares in the business**

The *Financial Times* [27 April 1998 (www.ft.com)] surveyed the finance directors of the UK's top 100 companies to ask what they really thought of their institutional shareholders, the pension funds and insurance companies which own most of their assets. Somewhat surprisingly, 98 per cent replied that their institutional investors did take a long-term view and were not a force for short-termism. Yet only 69 per cent thought these investors understood their business 'well' or 'very well'; 91 per cent thought investor comments about the business were hardly ever useful.

Table 7-2   Revenues, costs, and profits

(1) Output (goods/week)	(2) Price per unit (£)	(3) Total revenue (price × output) (£/week)	(4) Total costs (from Table 7-1) (£/week)	(5) Profits (total revenue minus total costs)
0	–	0	10	−10
1	21	21	25	−4
2	20	40	36	4
3	19	57	44	13
4	18	72	51	21
5	17	85	59	26
6	16	96	69	27
7	15	105	81	24
8	14	112	95	17
9	13	117	111	6
10	12	120	129	−9

At a price of £21 it can sell only one snark. The lower the price, the more snarks it can sell: its demand curve slopes down. Table 7-2 shows the firm's total revenue from selling different quantities of snarks. Total revenue is price times quantity, shown in the third column.

The fourth column shows the total cost of producing each output level. The last column shows profits, the difference between revenues and costs. At low output, profits are negative. At the highest output, 10 units per week, profits are again negative. At intermediate levels of output, the firm is making profits.

The highest level of profits is £27 per week and the corresponding output is 6 snarks per week. To maximize profits the firm produces 6 snarks per week. At £16 each, this brings in £96 in total revenue. Costs of production, properly calculated to include the opportunity cost of all resources used, are £69 per week, leaving a profit of £27 per week. The level of output and profits chosen by the firm are shown in row 6 in Table 7-2.

Maximizing profit is not the same as maximizing revenue. By selling 10 snarks a week the firm could earn £120, but its costs would be £129. Making the last few snarks is very expensive and brings in little extra revenue. It is more profitable to make a few less.

To sum up, the firm calculates the level of profit associated with each possible output level. To do this, it must know both the revenue received at each output and the cost of producing each output. From revenues and costs it calculates profit, and selects the output that maximizes total economic profit.

7-5 Marginal cost and marginal revenue

It is helpful to view the same problem from a different angle. At each output level we now ask whether the firm should increase output still further. Suppose the firm produces 3 snarks and considers moving to 4 snarks. From Table 7-2, we reproduce the relevant cost and revenue data in Table 7-3. Increasing output from 3 to 4 snarks will raise total cost from £44 to £51, a £7 increase in total cost. Revenue will increase from £57 to £72, an increase of £15 in total revenue. Increasing output from 3 to 4 snarks adds more to revenue than costs. Profit will rise by £8 (£15 of extra revenue less

Table 7-3 Effects of output changes on costs and revenues

Output (snarks/week)	Total cost (£/week)	Cost increase (£/week)	Total revenue (£/week)	Revenue increase (£/week)
3	44		57	
4	51	7	72	15

£7 of extra costs). Having decided that it is profitable to increase production from 3 to 4 snarks, we can repeat the exercise, asking whether it is profitable to move from 4 to 5, and so on.

This approach – examining how the production of 1 more unit of output will affect profits – focuses on the marginal cost and marginal revenue of producing one more unit.

Marginal cost is the increase in total cost when output is increased by 1 unit. **Marginal revenue** is the increase in total revenue when output is increased by 1 unit.

So long as marginal revenue exceeds marginal costs, the firm should increase its output. Producing and selling 1 more unit adds more to total revenue than to total cost, thereby increasing total profit.

Conversely, if marginal cost exceeds marginal revenue, the extra unit of output reduces total profit. Thus we can use marginal cost and marginal revenue to calculate the output level that maximizes profit. So long as marginal revenue exceeds marginal cost, keep increasing output. As soon as marginal revenue falls short of marginal cost, stop increasing output. To clarify this argument, we look more closely at marginal revenue and marginal cost.

Marginal cost

Table 7-4 uses Table 7-1 to calculate the marginal cost of producing each extra unit of output. Increasing output from 0 to 1 increases total costs from £10 to £25. The marginal cost of the first unit is £15. In Table 7-4 we show the marginal cost on a line between 0 and 1 snark to make clear that it is the cost of increasing output from 0 to 1 snark. All other marginal costs in the table are calculated in the same way.

The marginal cost of increasing output by 1 unit at each output level is shown in Figure 7-5(b), taken from Table 7-4. But it can also be calculated from Figure 7-5(a) taken from Table 7-2. In Figure 7-5(a) we show the total cost of producing each output level. Marginal cost is the amount total cost rises when output is increased 1 unit. For example, going from 0 to 1 unit, total costs rise by £15, shown by the shaded area *ABCD*, the marginal cost of producing 1 more unit. Figure 7-5(b) could be taken from Figure 7-5(a) as well as Table 7-2.

Table 7-4 Total and marginal costs of production

Output (snarks/week)	Total cost (£/week)	Marginal cost (£/week)
0	10	
1	25	15
2	36	11
3	44	8
4	51	7
5	59	8
6	69	10
7	81	12
8	95	14
9	111	16
10	129	18

Either way, marginal cost is high when output is low but also when output is high. Marginal cost is lowest for the production of the fourth unit, which adds only £7 to total costs.

Why do marginal costs start high, then fall, then rise again? The answer depends mainly on the different production techniques for making snarks. At low output, the firm is using simple techniques. As output rises more sophisticated machines can be used, which make extra units of output quite cheaply. Automated production lines make additional units cheaply but are prohibitively expensive at small output levels. As output rises still further, the difficulties of managing a large firm begin to emerge. Increased output is now expensive and marginal costs rise.

The relation of marginal costs to output vary from firm to firm. In a coal mine that is nearly worked out, marginal costs rise steeply with additional output. In mass production industries, marginal costs may have the pattern of Figure 7-6, starting out high but declining to a constant level.

Marginal revenue

Table 7-5 shows marginal revenue, the increase in total revenue when an additional unit of output is sold. Increasing output from 0 to 1 unit increases revenue from 0 to £21. Thus £21 is the marginal revenue of the first unit. Increasing output from 7 to 8 units increases revenue from £105 to £112 so marginal revenue is £7. Total and marginal

BOX 7-4   So what is a firm anyway?

It sounds like a simple enough question, but it has intrigued economists for decades. Why are some activities conducted by trading in markets while other activities are organized by hierarchical command within a firm before trade ever takes place. When the boss wants a photocopy of a document, she doesn't hold an auction; she simply tells her secretary to make a copy.

One view of firms is that they capture 'static synergies', benefits from undertaking closely related activities and from doing them repeatedly. Just as it makes little sense to have separate markets for left and right shoes – people usually want a pair – so it may make sense to bundle together related production activities before selling the package. Chapter 8 discusses such economies of scale and of scope in more detail.

A second view of firms, often associated with Professor Oliver Williamson, is that they involve relationships, like trust or teamwork, that are intrinsically long-run relationships. When all workers are easily replaceable, one might have a daily auction for unskilled workers, as used to take place in docks and coal mining. However, if jobs require that workers develop specific skills, in relation to the firm and to each other, yesterday's team is not easily replaced today. Firms then become devices to cement together the long-run relationships that efficiency requires.

The third and most recent view of firms, associated with Professor Oliver Hart, is that they reflect incomplete contracts. Where people can foresee what may happen, they could, in principle, engage in a market transaction, signing a contract specifying what happens in each possible situation. But some future situations cannot even be contemplated today: no contract can take them into account. Authority – the hierarchy of decision-making within the firm – is an arrangement that specifies today who will adjudicate if some strange future contingency arises. This idea that markets are necessarily incomplete is one to which we will return in later chapters.

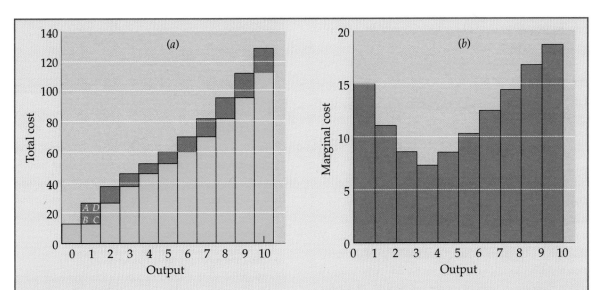

Part (a) shows total costs of production for each level of output. The shaded parts show the amount by which total costs go up when the level of output increases by 1 unit. Thus, total costs rise from 10 to 25 when output increases from 0 to 1 unit. This increase in total costs, at each level of output, is the marginal cost of increasing output by 1 unit. The marginal costs are shown in part (b), which uses a larger vertical scale.

Figure 7-5   Total and marginal costs of production

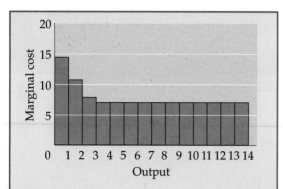

In Figure 7-5, marginal costs decline output increases, but then increase. A different possibility is that marginal costs at first decline, then become constant: any further increases in output can be produced at the same addition to cost per unit. Which pattern applies in practice depends on the techniques of production available to the firm. The pattern of marginal costs varies from firm to firm and industry to industry.

Figure 7-6   Marginal costs: a different pattern

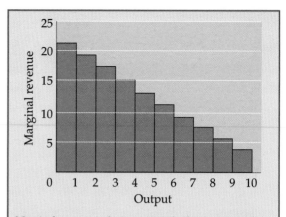

Marginal revenue is the increase in the firm's revenue from an increase in sales by one unit. If the firm can sell more output only by reducing its price, marginal revenue declines as output rises.

Figure 7-7   Marginal revenue

Table 7-5   Price, total revenue and marginal revenue

Output (snarks/week)	Price received (£/snark)	Total revenue (£/week)	Marginal revenue (£/week)
0	–	0	
1	21	21	21
2	20	40	19
3	19	57	17
4	18	72	15
5	17	85	13
6	16	96	11
7	15	105	9
8	14	112	7
9	13	117	5
10	12	120	3

revenue depend on the demand curve for the firm's product.

Marginal revenue is also shown in Figure 7-7 and is falling throughout. It can even become negative at high output levels. Suppose that 11 snarks per week can be sold only at a price of £10 each. Total revenue would then be £110 per week. Table 7-5 implies that the marginal revenue from moving from 10 to 11 snarks per week would be −£10 per week.

To understand how marginal revenue changes with output, we keep track of two separate effects

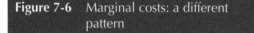

Marginal revenue = change in total revenue from selling 1 more unit of output
(additional revenue earned on last unit alone)
= − (revenue lost by selling existing output at a lower price)   (1)

Demand curves slope down. To sell more output, the price must be cut. Selling an additional unit of output at this lower price is the first component of marginal revenue in equation (1). However, we must also take account of the fact that, in selling additional output, we bid down the price for which *all* previous units of output can be sold. This effect acts to reduce the additional revenue obtained from selling an extra unit of output.

In Table 7-5 the firm can sell 5 snarks at £17 each or 6 snarks at £16 each. Increasing output from 5 to 6, the firm earns £16 from selling the extra snark at £16, but it also loses

£5 by cutting the price £1 on the 5 snarks it was already selling. Marginal revenue is thus £11.

Marginal revenue falls steadily for two reasons. First, because demand curves slope down, the extra unit must be sold at a lower price. Second, successive price reductions reduce the revenue earned from *existing* units of output. When the firm's demand curve slopes down, we have thus established two propositions.

(i)   Marginal revenue falls as output rises.
(ii) Marginal revenue must be less than the price for which the last unit is sold. From this we must subtract the effect of lower prices on revenue earned from previous units of output.

The shape of the marginal revenue curve depends only on the shape of the firm's demand curve. A small firm in a huge

Table 7-6   Using marginal revenue and marginal cost to determine output

Output (units/wk)	Marginal revenue (£/wk)	Marginal cost (£/wk)	Marginal revenue minus marginal cost (£/wk)	Output decision
0				
1	21	15	6	Increase
2	19	11	8	Increase
3	17	8	9	Increase
4	15	7	8	Increase
5	13	8	5	Increase
6	11	10	1	Increase
7	9	12	−3	Decrease
8	7	14	−7	Decrease
9	5	16	−11	Decrease
10	3	18	−15	Decrease

market may be able to sell as much output as it wishes without affecting the existing market price. A single wheat farmer's output may be insignificant relative to the total supply of wheat. Although the market demand curve for wheat slopes down, the individual farmer can sell wheat without bidding down the price. For the individual farmer, the demand curve is horizontal at the equilibrium price of wheat. Each extra unit of output by the individual farmer earns the same marginal revenue, the wheat price itself. In terms of equation (1), the first term is constant and the second term, 'revenue lost on existing units', is zero.

Using marginal revenue and marginal cost to determine the level of output

Combining marginal cost and marginal revenue, Table 7-6 examines the output that maximizes the firm's profits. If marginal revenue exceeds marginal cost, a 1-unit increase in output will increase profits. The last column shows that this reasoning will lead the firm to produce at least 6 units of output.

Suppose the firm now considers increasing output from 6 to 7 units. Marginal revenue is £9 and marginal cost £12, so profits would fall by £3. Output should *not* be expanded to 7 units. Similar reasoning rules out expansion to any output level above 6 units. If marginal cost exceeds marginal revenue the firm will save money by reducing output. The firm should expand up to 6 units of output but no further. This is the output that maximizes profits, as we know already from Table 7-2.

Total cost and revenue versus marginal cost and revenue

Table 7-2, based on total cost and total revenue, and Table 7-6, based on marginal cost and revenue, are different ways of examining the same problem. Economists use marginal analysis more frequently because it suggests a useful way of thinking about the decision problem faced by firms or consumers. Is there a small change that could make the firm (or the consumer) better off? If so, the current position cannot be the best possible one and changes should be made.

Marginal analysis should be subjected to one very important check. It may miss an all-or-nothing choice. For example, suppose that marginal revenue exceeds marginal cost up to an output level of 6 units but thereafter marginal revenue is less than marginal cost. This suggests that 6 units should be produced. Producing 6 units is certainly better than producing any other output level. However, if the firm incurs large costs whether or not it produces (for example a vastly overpaid managing director), the profit earned from producing 6 units may not cover these fixed costs. Conditional on paying these fixed costs, an output level of 6 units is then the loss-minimizing output level. However, the firm might do better to shut down altogether. We examine this issue in greater detail in the next chapter.

In summary, a profit-maximizing firm should expand output so long as marginal revenue exceeds marginal cost but should stop expansion as soon as marginal cost exceeds marginal revenue. This rule guides the firm to the best positive level of output. If the firm is not making profits even in this position, it might do better to close down altogether.

7-6 Marginal cost and marginal revenue curves: $MC = MR$

Thus far we have assumed that the firm can produce only an integer number of goods, such as 0, 1 or 7, rather than a

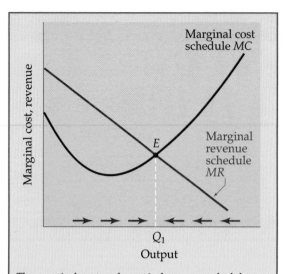

The marginal cost and marginal revenue schedules are shown changing smoothly. The firm's optimal output is Q_1, at which marginal revenue is equal to marginal cost. Anywhere to the left of Q_1, marginal revenue is larger than marginal cost and the firm should increase output, as shown by the arrows. Where output is greater than Q_1, marginal revenue is less than marginal cost and profits are increased by reducing output. If the firm is losing money at Q_1 it has to check whether it might be better not to produce at all than to produce Q_1.

Figure 7-8   Marginal cost and marginal revenue determine the firm's output

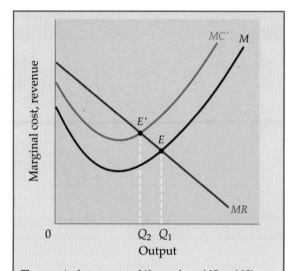

The marginal cost curve shifts up from MC to MC' as a result of an increase in the costs of using a factory of production: for instance, the wage may have risen. This upward shift moves the intersection of MC and MR curves from E to E'. Output falls from Q_1 to Q_2. Thus, when the firm's costs rise, it decides to produce less.

Figure 7-9   An increase in marginal cost reduces output

quantity such as 1.5 or 6.7. In most cases output is not confined to integer levels, for two reasons. First, for goods such as wheat or milk, there is no reason to think that only 1 kilogram or 1 litre units can be sold. The firm can sell in odd amounts. Second, even for goods such as cars, which are necessarily sold in whole units, the firm may be selling 75 cars every four weeks, or 18.75 cars per week. Thus it is convenient to imagine that firms can vary production levels and sales almost continuously.

If so, we can draw smooth marginal cost (MC) and marginal revenue (MR) schedules as in Figure 7-8. Profits are maximized where the schedules cross, at the point E. The output Q_1 maximizes profits (or minimizes losses). At smaller outputs, MR exceeds MC and expansion increases profits (or reduces losses).

To the right of Q_1, MC exceeds MR. Expansion adds more to costs than revenue and contraction saves more in costs than it loses in revenue. The profit incentive to increase output to the left of Q_1 and to reduce output to the right of Q_1 is shown by the arrows in Figure 7-8. This incentive guides the firm to choose the output level Q_1, provided the

firm should be in business at all. At Q_1 marginal revenue is exactly equal to marginal cost.

Table 7-7 summarizes the conditions for determining the output that maximizes profits.

The effect of changing cost on output

Suppose the firm faces a price increase for a raw material. At each output level, marginal costs will rise. Figure 7-9 illustrates this change by an upward shift from MC to MC'. Choosing output to set $MC = MR$, the firm now produces at E'. Higher marginal costs reduce profit-maximizing output from Q_1 to Q_2.

The effect of a shift in the demand curve on output

Suppose that the firm's demand curve and marginal revenue curve shift upwards. At each output level, price and marginal revenue are higher than before. In Figure 7-10 the MR curve shifts out to MR', inducing the firm to move from E to E''. Higher demand has led the firm to expand output from Q_1 to Q_3.

Table 7-7 Determining the firm's output level		
Marginal condition	Decision	Check
$MR > MC$	Increase output	
$MR < MC$	Cut output	
$MR = MC$	Optimal output	If positive profits, produce this output level. If not, consider closing down for a while or going out of business altogether

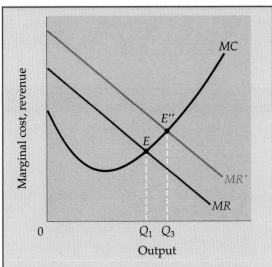

When the MR curve shifts upward from MR to MR', the intersection point between MR and MC curves shifts from E to E''. The firm's optimal level of output increases from Q_1 to Q_3. The upward shift in the marginal revenue curve could result, for instance, from an increase in the number of customers in the firm's market.

Figure 7-10 An upward shift in marginal revenue increases output

Do firms know their marginal cost and revenue curves?

By now you may be wondering if firms in the real world know their marginal cost and marginal revenue curves, let alone go through some sophisticated calculations to make sure output is chosen to equate the two.

Such thought experiments by firms are not necessary for the relevance of our model of supply. If, by luck, hunch, or judgement, a manager succeeds in maximizing the firm's profits, marginal cost and marginal revenue will *necessarily* be equal. What we have been doing is to develop a formal analysis by which to track the hunches of smart managers who get things right on average and survive in a tough business world.

In this chapter we gave an overview of cost and revenue conditions. Although later chapters will fill in the picture, we already have the basis for a theory of how much output firms choose to supply. Firms choose the output that will maximize profits, the output level at which marginal cost equals marginal revenue.

SUMMARY

● The theory of supply is the theory of how much output firms choose to produce.

● There are three types of firm: self-employed 'sole traders', partnerships, and companies. Sole traders are the most numerous but are often very small. The large firms are companies.

● A company is an organization set up to conduct business. Companies are owned by their shareholders but run by managers responsible to the board of directors.

● Shareholders have limited liability. Partners and sole traders have unlimited liability.

● Revenue is what the firm earns from sales. Costs are the expenses incurred in producing and selling. Profits are the excess of revenue over costs.

● Costs should include opportunity costs of all resources used in production. Opportunity cost is the amount an input could obtain in its next highest paying use. In particular, economic costs include the cost of the owner's time and effort in running a business. Economic costs also include the opportunity cost of financial capital used in the firm. Supernormal profit is the pure profit accruing to the owners after allowing for all these costs.

● Firms are assumed to aim to maximize profits. Even though the firm is run by its managers, not its owners, profit maximization is a useful assumption in under-standing the firm's behaviour. Firms that make losses cannot continue in business indefinitely.

● In aiming to maximize profits, firms necessarily produce each output level as cheaply as possible. Profit maximization implies minimization of costs for each output level.

● Firms choose the optimal output level to maximize total economic profits. This decision can be described equivalently by examining marginal cost and marginal revenue. Marginal cost is the increase in total cost when one more unit is produced. Marginal revenue is the corresponding change in total revenue and depends on the demand curve for the firm's product. Profits are maximized at the output at which marginal cost equals marginal revenue. If profits are negative at this output, the firm should close down if this reduces losses.

● An upward shift in the marginal cost curve reduces output. An upward shift in the marginal revenue curve increases output.

● It is unnecessary for firms to calculate their marginal cost and marginal revenue curves. Setting MC equal to MR is merely a device that economists use to mimic the hunches of smart firms who correctly judge, by whatever means, the profit-maximizing level of output.

KEY TERMS

◆ Sole trader 92

◆ Partnership 92

◆ Company 92

◆ Limited liability 92

◆ Revenue 92

◆ Costs 92

◆ Profits 93

◆ Cash flow 93

◆ Physical capital 93

◆ Depreciation 93

◆ Inventories 94

◆ Assets and liabilities 95

◆ Retained earnings 95

◆ Opportunity cost 95

◆ Supernormal profits 97

◆ Marginal cost 100

◆ Marginal revenue 100

REVIEW QUESTIONS

1 (a) What are the main advantages of a company over a large partnership as a way of doing business? (b) List five companies whose products you buy. (c) Do you buy goods or services from any partnerships or sole traders? Say which goods and firms.

2 How would each of the following affect the income statement for Rent-a-Person presented in Figure 7-2? (a) Rent-a-Person still owes £70 000 to the people it rented out during the year. (b) Instead of renting an office, the company owns its office. (c) During the year Rent-a-Person was paid by one of the people who owed it money at the end of 2000.

3 (a) Suppose Rent-a-Person is run by an owner, who could be paid £40 000 per year to manage another firm. Suppose also that she has invested £200 000 of her own in the company, on which she could earn 12 per cent elsewhere. What are the economic profits earned by Rent-a-Person? (Use Figure 7-2.) (b) What is the general principle underlying the adjustments made to accounting costs?

4 (a) Suppose that Snark International borrows another £50 000 from the bank and increases its inventories. How is its balance sheet affected? (Refer back to Figure 7-3.) (b) Explain how the interest paid on the loan would appear in the income statement of Snark International.

5 (a) Do firms aim to maximize profits? Explain. (b) Do you think firms *should* aim to maximize profits, or should they do things like support charities, the arts, and political campaigns? Explain.

6 In Table 7-2, assume that total costs of producing each level of output are higher by £40 than the costs shown in the fourth column of the table. What level of output should the firm produce? Explain. (You can work out the answer using the table – no need to draw graphs.)

7 Suppose that a firm that has the same costs as those shown in Table 7-4 can sell as much output as it wants at a price of £13. (a) Draw *MR* and *MC* curves. (b) Show the level of output that the firm will produce.

8 *Common fallacies* Show why the following statements are incorrect: (a) Firms which show an accounting profit must be thriving. (b) Firms do not know their marginal costs. It is unreasonable to base the theory of supply on the assumption that firms set marginal revenue equal to marginal cost. (c) The way to make the most profit is to sell as much output as possible.

8 Developing the theory of supply: costs and production

LEARNING OUTCOMES

When you have finished this chapter, you should be able to:

● Explain the production function and its relation to the avoidance of waste
● Define technology and a technique of production
● Show how a firm's choice of production technique is affected by prices of the inputs that it purchases
● Distinguish total, average and marginal cost, both in the long run and in the short run
● Consider different returns to scale and their relation to the shape of average cost curves
● Distinguish fixed and variable factors in the short run, and explain the law of diminishing returns
● Derive a firm's chosen output level, in the short run and in the long run, including temporary shutdown and permanent exit

Firms don't always close down when they start losing money. Sometimes they expect demand to increase, or they may think that, given time, they can reduce their production costs enough to get back into profit. This chapter takes a closer look at costs and their influence on the output that firms wish to produce.

In Chapter 7 we introduced the theory of supply. Firms choose the output at which marginal cost equals marginal revenue. This maximizes profits (or minimizes losses). If profits are positive, the firm produces this output level. If profits are negative, it checks whether losses could be reduced by not producing at all.

In this chapter we distinguish between the *short-run* and the *long-run* output decisions of firms. No firm will stay in business if it expects to make losses for ever. We show how and why cost curves differ in the short run, when the firm

cannot fully react to changes in conditions, and the long run in which the firm can fully adjust to changes in demand or cost conditions. In fact, we have to consider the short-run and long-run versions of three different cost curves: total cost; marginal cost; and average cost.

Figure 8-1 summarizes the material of this chapter. The new material is all on the cost side. Because there are so many different cost curves, you may find all this confusing at first. It will be useful to check back to Figure 8-1. We start at the left of Figure 8-1 by introducing the *production function*, which describes the firm's technology.

8-1 Inputs and output

An **input** (or **factor of production**) is any good or service used to produce output.

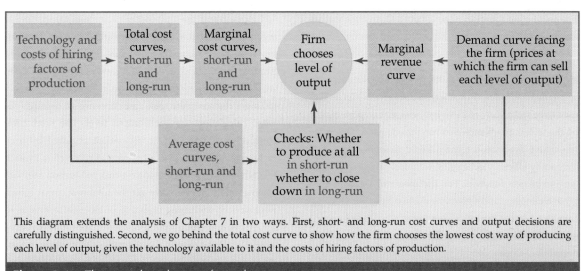

This diagram extends the analysis of Chapter 7 in two ways. First, short- and long-run cost curves and output decisions are carefully distinguished. Second, we go behind the total cost curve to show how the firm chooses the lowest cost way of producing each level of output, given the technology available to it and the costs of hiring factors of production.

Figure 8-1   The complete theory of supply

Inputs include labour, machinery, buildings, raw materials, and energy. The term 'input' covers everything from senior management to bandages in the first-aid room.

Suppose our firm uses inputs to make snarks. This is an engineering and management problem. The recipe for making snarks is largely outside the field of economics and is a matter of technology and on-the-job experience. The economist takes the recipe as given, subject to one important qualification: *no waste*. We explain this qualification in discussing the *production function*.

The **production function** specifies the maximum output that can be produced from any given amount of inputs.

The production function summarizes the *technically efficient* ways of combining inputs to produce output. A production method is technically *inefficient* if, to produce a given output, it uses more of some inputs and no less of other inputs than some other method that makes the same output. Since profit-maximizing firms will not be interested in wasteful production methods, we restrict our attention to those that are technically efficient.

For example, method A produces 1 snark from 2 hours of labour and 1 hour of machine time. Method B produces 1 snark from 2 hours of labour and 2 hours of machine time. Method B is less efficient than method A since it uses more machine time but the same amount of labour to produce the same output as method A. Method B is not one of the production methods summarized in the production function.

Table 8-1 summarizes the technically efficient techniques listed by the production function. The first two rows of the

Table 8-1   The production function gives the output levels produced by different quantities of inputs

Output level (snarks/wk)	Capital input (no. of machines*)	Labour input (no. of workers*)
100	4	4
100	2	6
106	2	7
200	4	12

*Machines and labour are each used 40 hours per week.

table show two different ways to produce 100 snarks: 4 machines and 4 workers, or 2 machines and 6 workers. Beginning from the latter, the third row shows the effect of adding an extra worker. Output rises 6 snarks per week. The last row shows that doubling both the inputs in the second row also doubles the output, though this need not be so. For example, overcrowding a small factory can slow people down.

Table 8-1 could be enlarged to include other combinations of labour and capital that are also technically efficient. How does the firm discover its production function, the complete set of technically efficient production techniques? In part, it will ask its engineers, designers, and time-and-motion experts. In part, it may experiment with different techniques and observe the results.

Before turning to a detailed analysis of this choice of technique, we summarize the terms we have used so far.

A **technique** is a particular method of combining inputs to make output. **Technology** is the list of all known techniques.

The **production function** is the list of all techniques that are technically efficient.

By *technical progress* economists mean an invention or improvement in organization that allows a given output to be produced with fewer inputs than before. A technique that used to be technically efficient has been rendered inefficient by the technical advance that has introduced a new, more productive production technique. By changing the set of technically efficient techniques, technical progress changes the production function. For the moment, we assume a given technology and a given production function. Once we have filled in the theory of supply for a given technology, we can consider how technical progress affects the output decisions of firms.

8-2 Costs and the choice of production technique

In Chapter 7 we showed how the firm's output level is determined by marginal cost and marginal revenue curves. We now wish to get behind the marginal cost curve and the total cost curve from which it is derived.

Minimizing costs: the choice of technique

The production function relates volumes of inputs to volume of output. However, costs are values. To go from the production function to a cost curve, we need to know the price that the firm pays for inputs.

Consider the lowest-cost way to produce 100 snarks per week. We assume that there are only two technically efficient techniques, the first two rows of Table 8-1, reproduced in the first two columns of Table 8-2 and labelled techniques A and B. Either technique makes 100 snarks per week. The firm knows the cost of renting a machine (£320 per week) and of hiring labour (£300 per week). From the production function the firm knows the quantities of labour and capital required to make 100 snarks per week using each technique. Table 8-2 shows that the total cost of this output is £2480 per week using technique A and £2440 per week using technique B. The firm will choose

technique B and the total cost of producing 100 snarks per week will be £2440. We now have one point on the total cost curve for snarks: to produce 100 units the total cost is £2440. This is the *economically efficient* (lowest-cost) production method at the rental and wage rates in Table 8-2.

To get the complete total cost curve we go through the same calculations for each output level. The production function gives the input combinations required by each technique. We then work out the cost of production by each technique and choose the lowest-cost production method. Joining up these points we get the total cost curve, which may embody switching from one production technique to another at different output levels. From the total cost curve we calculate the marginal cost curve – the increase in total costs at each output level as output is increased by one more unit.

Factor intensity

A technique using a lot of capital and little labour is 'capital-intensive'. Conversely, a technique using a lot of labour but relatively little capital is 'labour-intensive'. In Table 8-2, technique A is more capital-intensive and less labour-intensive than technique B. The ratio of the units of capital input to labour input is 1 (= 4/4) in technique A but only 1/3 (= 2/6) in technique B.

Factor prices and the choice of technique

At the factor prices (costs per input unit) in Table 8-2, the more labour-intensive technique is cheaper. Suppose the wage rises from £300 to £340 per week: labour has become more expensive but the rental on capital is unchanged. The *relative price* of labour has risen.

We ask two questions. First, what happens to the total cost of producing 100 snarks per week? Second, is there any change in the preferred production technique? Table 8-3 recalculates the costs of production at the new factor prices. Because both techniques use some labour, the total cost of producing 100 snarks by each technique has risen. Repeating this argument for all other output levels, this implies that the total cost curve for snark production shifts

Table 8-2   Choosing the lowest-cost production technique

	Capital input	Labour input	Rental rate per machine (£/wk)	Wage rate (£/wk)	Capital cost (£/wk)	Labour cost (£/wk)	Total cost (£/wk)
Technique A	4	4	320	300	1280	1200	2480
Technique B	2	6	320	300	640	1800	2440

Table 8-3 The effect of an increase in the wage rate

	Capital input	Labour input	Rental rate (£/wk)	Wage rate (£/wk)	Capital cost (£/wk)	Labour cost (£/wk)	Total cost (£/wk)
Technique A	4	4	320	340	1280	1360	2640
Technique B	2	6	320	340	640	2040	2680

upwards at each output level when the wage rate (or the price of any other input) rises.

In this example, the rise in the relative price of labour leads the firm to switch techniques: it switches to the more capital-intensive technique A.

8-3 Long-run total, marginal, and average costs

Faced with an upward shift in its demand and marginal revenue curves, a firm will want to expand production, as we explained in the previous chapter. However, adjustment takes time. In the first few months, the firm can get its existing workforce to do overtime. Over a longer period it may be cheaper to build a new factory and increase capacity.

The **long run** is the period long enough for the firm to adjust all its inputs to a change in conditions.

In the long run the firm can vary its factory size, switch techniques of production, hire new workers and negotiate new contracts with suppliers of raw materials.

The **short run** is the period in which the firm can make only *partial* adjustment of its inputs to a change in conditions.

The firm may have the flexibility to vary the shift length almost immediately. Hiring or firing workers takes longer, and it might be several years before a new factory is designed, built, and fully operational.

In this section we deal with long-run cost curves, when the firm is able to make all the adjustments it desires.

The **long-run total cost curve** describes the minimum cost of producing each output level when the firm can adjust all inputs.

Total and marginal costs in the long run

Table 8-4 shows long-run total costs (*LTC*) and long-run marginal costs (*LMC*) of producing each output level. *LTC* reflects the lowest-cost method of producing each output level and is shown in the second column of the table. Since

Table 8-4 Long-run costs

(1) Output (goods/wk)	(2) Total cost (£/wk)	(3) Marginal cost (£/wk)	(4) Average cost (£/wk)
0	0		–
1	30	30	30
2	54	24	27
3	74	20	24.67
4	91	17	22.75
5	107	16	21.40
6	126	19	21.00
7	149	23	21.29
8	176	27	22.00
9	207	31	23.00
10	243	36	24.30

there is always an option to close down entirely, the *LTC* of producing zero output is zero. *LTC* describes the eventual costs after all adjustments have been made.

Table 8-4 also shows the *LMC* of production.

Long-run marginal cost is the increase in long-run total cost if output is permanently increased by one unit.

LTC must rise with output. It must cost more to produce more output than less. How fast do total costs increase with output? Can large firms produce goods at a lower unit cost than small firms? Might it be a disadvantage to be large?

Long-run average costs

To answer these questions it is convenient to examine the cost per unit of output or the average cost of production.

The **long-run average cost of production** is the total cost divided by the level of output.

The last column of Table 8-4 shows long-run average cost (*LAC*). *LAC* is *LTC* divided by output.

The *LAC* data of Table 8-4 are plotted in Figure 8-2. Average cost starts out high, then falls, then rises again. This common pattern of average costs is called the U-shaped average cost curve. To see why the U-shaped average cost curve is common in practice we examine 'returns to scale'.

8-4 Economies and diseconomies of scale

There are **economies of scale** (or **increasing returns to scale**) when long-run average costs decrease as output rises. There are **constant returns to scale** when long-run average costs are constant as output rises. There are **diseconomies of**

scale (or **decreasing returns to scale**) when long-run average costs increase as output rises.

In these definitions scale refers to the size of the firm as measured by its output. The three cases are illustrated in Figure 8-3.

In Figure 8-2 the U-shaped average cost curve has increasing returns to scale up to the point A, where average cost is lowest. At higher output levels there are decreasing returns to scale. Why should there be economies of scale at low output levels but diseconomies of scale at high output levels?

We draw a cost curve for given input prices. Hence changes in average costs as we move along the LAC curve cannot be explained by changes in factor prices. (Changes in factor prices *shift* cost curves.) The relationship between average costs and output as we move along the LAC curve must be explained by the relation between physical quantities of inputs and output summarized in the production function. At given factor prices, does the firm use more or fewer inputs per unit of output as output rises? This is a technological question about the most efficient production techniques.

Economies of scale

There are three reasons for economies of scale. The first is *indivisibilities* in the production process, some minimum quantity of inputs required by the firm to be in business at all whether or not output is produced. These are sometimes

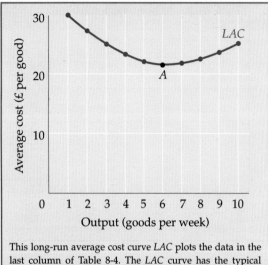
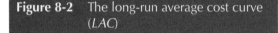

This long-run average cost curve LAC plots the data in the last column of Table 8-4. The LAC curve has the typical U-shape. The minimum average cost of production is at point A, with output level of 6 and average cost of £21.

Figure 8-2   The long-run average cost curve (LAC)

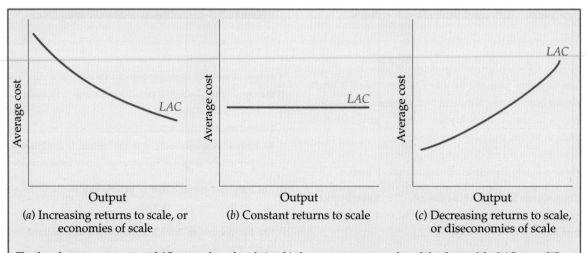

(a) Increasing returns to scale, or economies of scale

(b) Constant returns to scale

(c) Decreasing returns to scale, or diseconomies of scale

The three long-run average cost LAC curves show the relationship between returns to scale and the shape of the LAC curve. When LAC is declining, average costs of production fall as output increases and there are economies of scale. When LAC is increasing, average costs of production increase with higher output, and there are decreasing returns to scale. The intermediate case, where average costs are constant, has constant returns to scale.

Figure 8-3   Returns to scale and long-run average cost curve

called *fixed costs*, because they do not vary with the output level. To be in business a firm requires a manager, a telephone, an accountant, a market research survey. The firm cannot have half a manager and half a telephone merely because it wishes to operate at low output levels. Beginning from small output levels, these costs do not initially increase with output. The manager can organize three workers as easily as two. As yet there is no need for a second telephone. There are economies of scale because these fixed costs can be spread over more units of output as output is increased, reducing average cost per unit of output. However, as the firm expands further, it has to hire more managers and telephones and these economies of scale die away. The average cost curve stops falling.

The second reason for economies of scale is *specialization*. A sole trader must undertake all the different tasks of the business. As the firm expands and takes on more workers, each worker can concentrate on a single task and handle it more efficiently. Adam Smith, the father of economics, emphasized the gains from specialization in *The Wealth of Nations* (1776). His example (he calls it a 'very trifling manufacture') is the pin industry:

A workman not educated to this business . . . could scarce . . . make one pin a day, and certainly could not make twenty. But in the way in which this business is now carried on, . . . it is divided into a number of branches. . . . One man draws out the wire, another straightens it, a third cuts, a fourth points it. . . .

There were 18 stages in making a pin, and Smith estimated average output per worker at 4800 pins per day. These economies of scale from specialization are impressive. Similar benefits from specialization occur in assembly line work, for example in the car industry.

The third reason for economies of scale is closely related. Large scale is often needed to take advantage of better machinery. Engineers have a rule of two-thirds that applies to many factories and machines: the cost of building a factory or a machine rises only by two-thirds as much as the output of the factory or machine. Sometimes this rule has a physical basis. Oil tankers are essentially cylinders: as volume rises the surface area rises only by around two-thirds. Tankers and storage containers require proportionately less steel the larger their volume.

Sophisticated but expensive machinery also has an element of indivisibility. No matter how productive a robot assembly line is, it is pointless to install one to make five cars a week. Average costs would be enormous. However, at high output levels the machinery cost can be spread over a large number of units of output and this production technique may produce so many cars that average costs are low.

Diseconomies of scale

With such powerful reasons for economies of scale, why does the U-shaped average cost curve turn upward again as diseconomies of scale set in? Notice first that the second and third reasons for economies of scale are much more prevalent in manufacturing than in service industries such as restaurants and laundries.

The main reason for diseconomies of scale is that management becomes more difficult as the firm becomes larger: there are *managerial diseconomies of scale*. Large companies need many layers of management, which themselves have to be managed. The company becomes bureaucratic, co-ordination problems arise, and average costs may begin to rise.

Geography may also explain diseconomies of scale. If the first factory is located in the best site, to minimize the cost of transporting goods to the market, the site of a second factory must be less advantageous. To take a different example, in extracting coal from a mine, a firm will extract the easiest coal first. To increase output, deeper coal seams have to be worked and these will be more expensive.

The shape of the average cost curve thus depends on two things: how long the economies of scale persist, and how quickly the diseconomies of scale occur as output is increased. The balance of these two forces is an empirical question. It will vary from industry to industry and firm to firm.

Returns to scale in practice

To gather evidence on the shape of long-run average cost curves we can talk to design engineers to get an idea of the direct production cost of producing different output levels in different kinds of factory. It is much harder to quantify the managerial diseconomies that set in with the cost of operating a large and unwieldy firm. Almost all the empirical research focuses only on the direct production cost of different output levels. Because it ignores managerial diseconomies of scale it overestimates the falling range of average cost curves.

Figure 8-4 shows data on average costs for firms in the cement industry in the United States and in the brewing industry in the UK. Average costs fall steadily as output increases. Even at large output levels, the forces inducing economies of scale dominate the forces inducing diseconomies of scale. Many studies of manufacturing

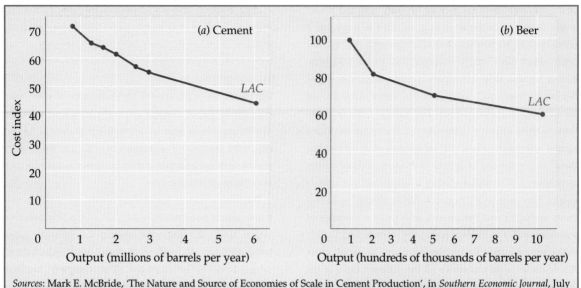

Sources: Mark E. McBride, 'The Nature and Source of Economies of Scale in Cement Production', in *Southern Economic Journal*, July 1981, pp. 105–115. C. F. Pratten, *Economies of Scale in Manufacturing Industry*, Cambridge University Press, 1971, p. 75.

Figure 8-4   Average cost curves in the long run

industry confirm this pattern of falling average costs as output rises.[1]

For such firms the typical pattern of the *LAC* curve is that of Figure 8-3(a). At low output levels, average costs fall rapidly. As output rises, average costs fall but more slowly. Economists have tried to measure the output level at which further economies of scale become unimportant for the individual firm, the point at which the average cost curve first becomes horizontal. This output level is called the *minimum efficient scale* (*MES*).

Table 8-5 contains some estimates of the MES for firms operating in different industries in the UK and the United States. The first column gives an idea of how steeply average costs fall before minimum efficient scale is reached. It shows how much higher average costs are when output is one-third of the output at minimum efficient scale. The second and third columns show the *MES* output level relative to the output of the industry as a whole. This provides a benchmark of the importance of economies of scale to firms in each industry. Since firms in the UK and the United States essentially have access to the same technical know-how, differences between the second and third columns primarily reflect differences in the size of the industry in the two countries rather than differences in the *MES* output level for an individual firm.

Table 8-5   Minimum efficient scale for selected industries in the UK and the USA

Industry	% increase in average costs at ⅓ MES	MES as % of market in	
		UK	USA
Cement	26.0	6.1	1.7
Steel	11.0	15.4	2.6
Glass bottles	11.0	9.0	1.5
Bearings	8.0	4.4	1.4
Fabrics	7.6	1.8	0.2
Refrigerators	6.5	83.3	14.1
Petroleum refining	4.8	11.6	1.9
Paints	4.4	10.2	1.4
Cigarettes	2.2	30.3	6.5
Shoes	1.5	0.6	0.2

Source: F. M. Scherer *et al.*, *The Economics of Multiplant Operation*, Harvard University Press, Tables 3.11 and 3.15.

These figures suggest that in heavy manufacturing industries economies of scale are substantial. At low outputs, average costs are much higher than at minimum efficient scale. We would expect similar effects in aircraft and motor car manufacture, which have very large fixed costs for research and development of new models and which can take advantage of highly automated assembly lines if output is sufficiently high. Yet in a large country such as the United States, minimum efficient scale for an individual firm occurs at an output that is small relative to the industry as a whole. Most firms will be producing on a

---

[1] See F. M. Scherer and D. Ross, *Industrial Market Structure and Economic Performance* (3rd edn.), Houghton Mifflin, 1990.

BOX 8-1   Scale economies and the internet

The information revolution is so important that we devote the whole of Chapter 11 to it. Here is a sneak preview. Producing information products like films, music, and news programmes has a high fixed cost, but distributing these products digitally has almost a zero marginal cost and no capacity constraint. Scale economies are therefore very large. Moreover, if marginal cost is close to zero, smart suppliers will price their products so that marginal revenue is also tiny. In Chapter 11 we describe how the introduction of Microsoft's encyclopaedia software *Encarta* forced *Encyclopaedia Britannica* into a 95 per cent price cut.

---

relatively flat part of their averge cost curve with few economies of scale still to be exploited.

In smaller countries such as the UK, the point of minimum efficient scale may be large relative to the industry as a whole. Table 8-5 implies that if there is more than one refrigerator manufacturer in the UK it is impossible for every firm in the refrigerator industry to be producing at minimum efficient scale.

However, Table 8-5 suggests that there are many industries, even in the manufacturing sector, where minimum efficient scale for a firm is small relative to the market as a whole and average costs are only a little higher if output is below minimum efficient scale. These firms will be producing in an output range where the *LAC* curve is almost horizontal.

Finally, there are a large number of firms, especially those outside the manufacturing sector, whose cost conditions are well represented by a U-shaped average cost curve. With only limited opportunities for economies of scale, these firms run into rising average costs even at quite moderate levels of output.

We begin by discussing the output decision of a firm with a U-shaped average cost curve. Then we show how this analysis must be amended when firms face significant economies of scale. In later chapters which discuss the structure of different types of industry it will be important to remember which shape of average cost curve we think of relevance for the industry we are studying.

8-5 Average cost and marginal cost

In Table 8-4 we showed long-run marginal costs (*LMC*) and long-run average costs (*LAC*). We now want to connect these two cost measures whose behaviour is closely related.

The last two columns of Table 8-4 are plotted in Figure 8-5. At each output *LAC* is simply total cost divided by that

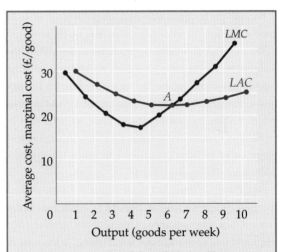

These cost data are plotted from Table 8-4. There are two special features of the relationship between the marginal cost curve (*LMC*) and the average cost curve (*LAC*). First, *LAC* is declining whenever *LMC* is below *LAC*, and rising whenever *LMC* is above *LAC*. Second, the *LMC* curve cuts the *LAC* curve at the minimum point of the *LAC* curve – in other words, at the point where output is produced at lowest unit cost.

Figure 8-5   Average and marginal cost curves

output level. However, marginal costs are incurred by moving from one output level to another so we plot *LMC* at points halfway between the corresponding output levels. For example the *LMC* of £30 for the first output unit is plotted at the output level half way between 0 and 1.

Two facts stand out from the table and diagram.

1 *LAC* is falling when *LMC* is less than *LAC*, and rising when *LMC* is greater than *LAC*.
2 *LAC* is at a minimum at the output level at which *LAC* and *LMC* cross.

Neither of these facts is an accident. The relation between average and marginal is a matter of arithmetic, as relevant

Table 8-6	Marginal and average cost		
	MC < AC	MC = AC	MC > AC
AC is:	falling	minimum	rising

for football as for production costs. A footballer with 3 goals in 3 games is averaging 1 goal per game. Two goals in the next game, implying 5 goals from 4 games, would raise the average to 1.25 goals per game. In the fourth game the marginal score is 2 goals, the increase in total goals from 3 to 5. Because the marginal score exceeds the average score in previous games, the extra game must drag up the average.

The same relation holds for production costs. When the marginal cost of the next unit exceeds the average cost of the existing units, making the next unit must drag up average cost. Conversely, when the marginal cost of the next unit lies below the average cost of existing units, an extra unit of production drags down average costs. When marginal and average cost are equal, adding a unit leaves average cost unchanged. This explains fact 1.

Fact 2 follows from fact 1. In Figure 8-5 average and marginal cost curves cross at the point A, which must be the point of minimum average cost. Why? To the left of A, LMC lies below LAC so average cost is still falling. To the right of A, LMC lies above LAC so average cost is rising. A must be the output level at which average costs are at a minimum.

As in the football example, this relation rests purely on arithmetic. Although Figure 8-5 refers to long-run average and marginal cost, the same reasoning will hold when we discuss short-run average and marginal cost in section 8-7. With a U-shaped average cost curve, the marginal cost curve lies below the average cost curve to the left of minimum average costs but above the average cost curve to the right of minimum average cost. The marginal cost curve crosses the average cost curve from below at the point of minimum average cost.

Table 8-6 summarizes this important relationship. It is true both for the relationship between LMC and LAC and for the relationship between short-run average cost (SAC) and short-run marginal cost (SMC).

8-6 The firm's long-run output decision

We can now analyse the firm's long-run output decision. Figure 8-6 shows smooth LAC and LMC curves for a firm not restricted to produce integer units of output. It also shows the marginal revenue (MR) curve. From Chapter 7 we

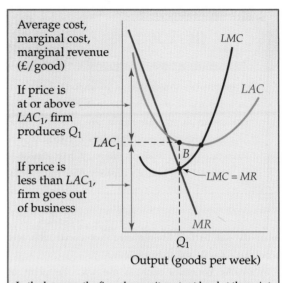

In the long run the firm chooses its output level at the point B where MR is equal to LMC. It has then to check whether it is making losses at that output level Q_1. If price is equal to or more than LAC_1, the long-run average cost corresponding to output Q_1, the firm is not making losses and stays in business. If the price is less than LAC_1, the firm's long-run output decision should be zero – it closes down permanently.

Figure 8-6　The firm's long-run output decision

already know that the output level of maximum profit or minimum loss occurs at B, the output at which marginal revenue equals marginal cost. The firm then has to check whether it makes profits or losses at this output. It should not stay in business if it makes losses for ever.

Total profits are average profits per unit of output multiplied by the number of units of output. Hence total profits are positive only if average profits per unit of output exceed zero. Average profits are average revenue per unit minus average cost per unit. But average revenue per unit is simply the price for which each output unit is sold. Hence *if long-run average costs at B exceed the price for which the output Q_1 can be sold, the firm is making losses even in the long run* and should close down. If, at this output, price equals LAC, the firm just covers its costs and breaks even. And if price exceeds LAC at this output, the firm is making long-run profits and should happily remain in business.

Notice that this is a two-stage argument. First we use the *marginal condition* ($LMC = MR$) to find the profit maximizing or loss minimizing output provided the firm stays in business, *then* we use the *average condition* (the comparison of LAC at this output with the price or average revenue received) to determine whether the profit maximizing or loss minimizing output in fact yields profits and hence allows the firm to stay in business in the long run. If even the best output from the firm's viewpoint yields losses, then the firm should close down.

8-7 Short-run cost curves and diminishing marginal returns

The short run is the period in which the firm cannot fully adjust to a change in conditions. In the short run the firm has some fixed factors of production.

A **fixed factor of production** is a factor whose input level cannot be varied. A **variable factor** can be adjusted, even in the short run.

How long this short run lasts depends on the industry. It might take ten years to build a new power station but only a few months to open new restaurant premises if an existing building can be bought, converted, and decorated.

The existence of fixed factors in the short run has two implications. First, in the short run the firm has some fixed costs.

Fixed costs are costs that do not vary with output levels.

These fixed costs must be borne even if output is zero. If the firm cannot quickly add to or dispose of its existing factory, it must still pay depreciation on the building and meet the interest cost of the money it originally borrowed to buy the factory.

Second, because in the short run the firm cannot make all the adjustments it would like, its short-run costs of production must be different from its long-run production costs, and must be higher. When adjustment eventually becomes possible, the firm has an incentive to make this adjustment only if it can get on to a lower cost curve by doing so. We now study these short-run costs in more detail.

Short-run fixed and variable costs of production

Table 8-7 presents data on short-run costs. The second column shows the fixed costs, which are independent of the output level. The third column shows the variable costs.

Variable costs are costs that change as output changes.

Variable costs are the costs of hiring variable (non-fixed) factors of production, typically labour and raw materials. Although firms may have long-term contracts with workers

and material suppliers, which tend to reduce the speed at which adjustment of these factors can be accomplished, in practice most firms retain important elements of flexibility through overtime and short time, hiring or non-hiring of casual and part-time workers, and raw material purchases in the open market to supplement contracted supplies.

The fourth column of Table 8-7 shows short-run total costs

$$\begin{array}{ccc} \text{Short-run} & \text{short-run} & \text{short-run} \\ \text{total cost} = \text{fixed cost} + \text{variable cost} & \quad (1) \\ \text{(STC)} & \text{(SFC)} & \text{(SVC)} \end{array}$$

The final column shows short-run marginal costs (*SMC*). Since fixed costs do not increase with output, *SMC* is the increase both in short-run total costs and in short-run variable costs as output is increased by 1 unit.

Whatever the output level, fixed costs are £30 per week. Because marginal costs are always positive, short-run total costs rise steadily as output rises. Extra output adds to total cost, and adds more the higher is the marginal cost. In the last column of Table 8-7, as output increases, marginal costs first fall then rise again. The short-run marginal cost curve has the same general shape as the long-run marginal cost curve shown in Figure 8-7, but for a very different reason.

In the long run the firm can vary all factors freely. As output expands, it may become cost-minimizing to install a sophisticated assembly line which then allows extra output to be produced quite cheaply. Then diseconomies of scale set in and marginal costs of further output increases start to rise again.

The short-run marginal cost curve assumes that there is at least one fixed factor, probably capital. Suppose there are only two inputs in the short run, fixed capital and variable labour. To change output as we move along the short-run marginal cost curve, the firm must be adding

Table 8-7 Short-run costs of production

(1)	(2) (SFC) short-run fixed cost	(3) (SVC) short-run variable cost	(4) (STC) short-run total cost	(5) (SMC) short-run marginal cost
Output				
0	30	0	30	
1	30	22	52	22
2	30	38	68	16
3	30	48	78	10
4	30	61	91	13
5	30	79	109	18
6	30	102	132	23
7	30	131	161	29
8	30	166	196	35
9	30	207	237	41
10	30	255	285	48

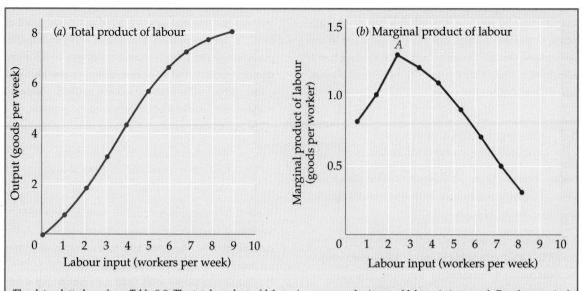

The data plotted are from Table 8-8. The total product of labour increases as the input of labour is increased. But the marginal product of labour first increases and then decreases. Beyond point *A* in part (b) the marginal product of labour is decreasing, as more and more workers work with the same stock of machines.

Figure 8-7   The productivity of labour and diminishing marginal returns

ever-increasing amounts of labour to a given amount of plant and machinery. It is here we must seek the explanation for the shape of the short-run marginal curve.

The marginal product of labour and diminishing marginal productivity

Table 8-8 shows how output increases as variable labour input is added to the fixed quantity of capital. With no workers, the firm produces no output. The first unit of labour increases output by 0.8 units.

The **marginal product** of a variable factor (in this example, labour) is the increase in output obtained by adding 1 unit of the variable factor, holding constant the input of all other factors (in this example the fixed factor, capital).

The first unit of labour has a marginal product of 0.8 units. The third unit of labour has a marginal product of 1.3 units since output increases from 1.8 units with 2 labour units to 3.1 with 3 labour units.

At low levels of output and labour input, the first worker has a whole factory to work with and has to do too many jobs to produce very much. A second worker helps, and a third helps even more. Suppose the factory has three machines and the three workers are each specializing in fully running one of the factory's machines. The marginal product of the fourth worker is lower. With only three machines, the fourth worker gets to use one only when

Table 8-8   Total and marginal products of labour

Labour input (workers/wk)	Output (goods/wk)	Marginal product of labour (goods/wk)
0	0	
1	0.8	0.8
2	1.8	1.0
3	3.1	1.3
4	4.3	1.2
5	5.4	1.1
6	6.3	0.9
7	6.3	0.7
8	7.5	0.5
9	7.8	0.3

another worker is having a rest. There is even less useful machine work for the fifth worker to do. In fact, beyond a labour input of 3, the marginal product of each additional worker decreases steadily as the number of workers is increased. We say that there are diminishing returns to labour.

Holding all factors constant except one, **the law of diminishing returns** says that, beyond some level of the variable input, further increases in the variable input lead to a steadily decreasing marginal product of that input.

This is a law about technology. Adding ever-increasing numbers of workers to a fixed quantity of machinery gets less and less useful. The ninth worker's main role in production is to get coffee for the others operating the machines. This contributes to output but not a great deal. Figure 8-7 summarizes our discussion of marginal productivity. If capital happened to be the variable factor and labour the fixed factor, a similar argument would obtain. Adding more and more machines to a given labour force might initially lead to large increases in output but would quickly encounter diminishing returns as machines became under-utilized. Thus the schedule in Figure 8-7 showing the marginal product of labour when labour is the variable factor could equally well describe the behaviour of the marginal product of capital when capital is the variable factor.[2]

Before we show the relevance of marginal products for short-run marginal cost, notice that this concept is *not* the everyday meaning of 'productivity' which refers to the *average* product. For example, the average product of labour, what is most commonly meant by 'productivity', is output divided by total labour input. The same old arithmetic holds good. If the marginal product of labour lies above the average product, adding another worker will raise the average product and 'productivity'. When diminishing returns set in, the marginal product will quickly fall below the average product and the latter will fall if further workers are added. If you do not see why this must be true, try calculating output per unit of labour input as an extra column in Table 8-8.

Finally, as usual, we must distinguish between movements along a curve and shifts in a curve. The marginal product curve is drawn for given levels of the other factors. For a higher given level of the fixed factors, the marginal product curve would be higher. With more machinery to work with, an extra worker will generally be able to produce more extra output than previously. The numbers in Table 8-8 and the height of the marginal product curve in Figure 8-7 depend on the amount of fixed factors with which the firm began.

Short-run marginal costs

Table 8-7 shows that, as output is increased, short-run marginal costs first fall then rise. Every worker costs the

firm the same wage. While the marginal product of labour is increasing, each worker adds more to output than previous workers. Hence the extra cost of making extra output is falling. *SMC* is falling so long as the marginal product of labour is rising.

Short-run marginal cost is the extra cost of making one extra unit of output in the short-run while some inputs remain fixed.

Once diminishing returns to labour set in, the marginal product of labour falls and *SMC* starts to rise again. It takes successively more workers to make each extra unit of output.

Thus the shape of the short-run marginal cost curve and hence the short-run total cost curve is determined by the shape of the marginal product curve in Figure 8-7, which in turn depends on the technology facing the firm.

Short-run average costs

Table 8-9 shows short-run *average* cost data corresponding to Table 8-7.

Short-run average fixed cost (*SAFC*) equals short-run fixed cost (*SFC*) divided by output. **Short-run average variable cost** (*SAVC*) equals *SVC* divided by output and **short-run average total cost** (*SATC*) equals *STC* divided by output.

Each number in Table 8-9 is obtained by dividing the corresponding number in Table 8-7 by the output level. (The first row is omitted: dividing by zero output does not make sense.) The table also shows short-run marginal costs, taken from Table 8-7.

Table 8-9　Short-run average costs of production

Output	(SAFC) short-run average fixed cost	(SAVC) short-run average variable cost	(SATC) short-run average total cost	(SMC) short-run marginal cost
0	–	–	–	
				22
1	30.00	22.00	52.00	
				16
2	15.00	19.00	34.00	
				10
3	10.00	16.00	26.00	
				13
4	7.50	15.25	22.75	
				18
5	6.00	15.80	21.80	
				23
6	5.00	17.00	22.00	
				29
7	4.29	18.71	23.00	
				35
8	3.75	20.75	24.50	
				41
9	3.33	23.00	26.33	
				48
10	3.00	25.50	28.50	

---

[2] Notice that economists use *diminishing* returns to describe the addition of one variable factor to other fixed factors in the short run, but *decreasing* returns to describe diseconomies of scale when *all* factors are freely varied in the long run.

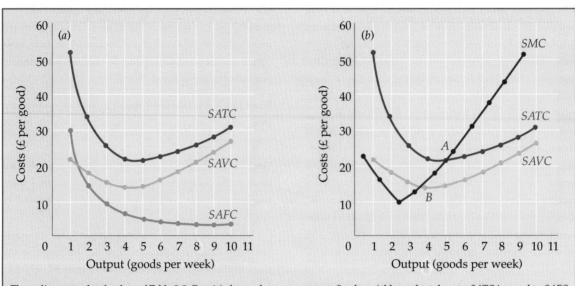

These diagrams plot the data of Table 8-9. Part (a) shows short-run average fixed, variable, and total costs. SATC is equal to SAFC plus SAVC. The shape of the SATC curve is a result of the shapes of its two components. When both SAVC and SAFC are declining, so is SATC. When SAVC starts rising, the shape of SATC depends on whether SAVC is rising more rapidly than SAFC is falling. In part (b) the relationship between marginal and average cost curves established for the long-run applies also to the short-run curves. The SMC curve goes through the minimum points of both the SAVC curve, at B, and the SATC curve, at A.

Figure 8-8   Short-run average cost and marginal cost curves

Figure 8-8 plots the three short-run average cost measures from Table 8-9.

$$\begin{array}{ccc} \text{Short-run} & \text{short-run} & \text{short-run} \\ \text{average} = \text{average} + \text{average} & & (2) \\ \text{total cost} & \text{fixed cost} & \text{variable cost} \\ (SATC) & (SAFC) & (SAVC) \end{array}$$

This follows from dividing each term in equation (1) by the output level.

Look first at Figure 8-8(b). We already understand the shape of the SMC curve that follows from the behaviour of marginal labour productivity. The usual arithmetical relation between marginal and average explains why SMC passes through the lowest point A on the short-run average total cost curve. To the left of this point, SMC lies below SATC and is dragging it down as output expands. To the right of A the converse holds. That explains the shape of the SATC curve in Figure 8-8.

Variable costs are the difference between total costs and fixed costs. Since fixed costs do not change with output, marginal costs also show how much total *variable* costs are changing. The same arithmetic relation between marginal costs and average *variable* costs must hold and the usual reasoning implies that SMC goes through the lowest point B on SAVC. To the left of B, SMC lies below SAVC and SAVC

must be falling. To the right of B, SAVC must be rising. Finally, since average total costs exceed average variable costs by average fixed costs, SAVC must lie below SATC. Hence point B must lie to the left of point A. That explains the shape of SAVC and its relation to SATC in Figure 8-8(b).

In Figure 8-8(a), SAFC falls steadily because the same total fixed cost (what firms call 'overheads') is being spread over ever larger output levels, thereby reducing average fixed costs. The reasoning of Figure 8-8(b) is easily confirmed in Figure 8-8(a). Carrying over from Figure 8-8(b) the SATC and SAVC curves we can check that, at each output level, SATC = SAVC + SAFC as in equation (2).

By now any reasonable person is asking two questions: how can anyone remember all these curves, and what use are they? To answer the 'how' question, go back to Figure 8-1, which shows the three basic costs: total, marginal, and average. We must distinguish between the short and long run, and between fixed and variable costs. With these distinctions we generate all the cost curves we have examined.

The second question is more important. We make these distinctions not to exercise the mind but because they are necessary to understand the firm's output decision. We have already used long-run cost curves to analyse the firm's long-

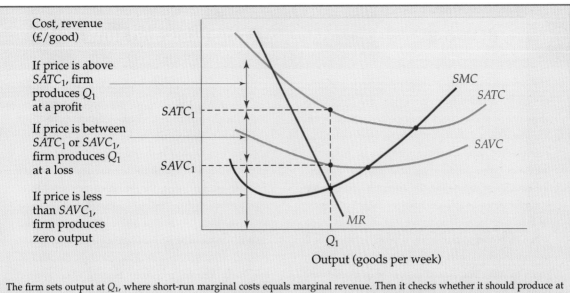

The firm sets output at Q_1, where short-run marginal costs equals marginal revenue. Then it checks whether it should produce at all. If price is above $SATC_1$, the level of short-run average total cost at output Q_1, the firm is making a profit and should certainly produce Q_1. If price is between $SATC_1$ and $SAVC_1$, the firm partly covers its fixed costs, even though it is losing money. It should still produce output Q_1. Only if the price is below $SAVC_1$ should the firm produce zero. At those prices, the firm is not even covering its variable costs.

Figure 8-9   The firm's short-run output decision

run output decision. Now we use short-run cost curves to analyse the firm's output decision in the short run.

8-8 The firm's output decision in the short run

Figure 8-9 illustrates the firm's choice of output in the short run. Since fixed factors cannot be varied in the short run, it is short-run marginal cost that must be set equal to marginal revenue to determine the output level Q_1 which maximizes profits or minimizes losses.

Next, the firm decides whether or not to stay in business in the short run. Again, profits are positive at the output Q_1 if the price p at which this output can be sold covers average total costs. It is the short-run measure $SATC_1$ at this output that is relevant. If p exceeds $SATC_1$, the firm is making profits in the short run and should certainly produce Q_1.

Suppose p is less than $SATC_1$. The firm is losing money because p does not cover costs. In the long run the firm closes down if it keeps losing money, but there the difference between the long run and the short run appears. Even at zero output the firm must pay the fixed costs in the short run. The firm needs to know whether losses are bigger if it produces at Q_1 or produces zero.

If revenue exceeds variable cost the firm is earning

Table 8-10   The firm's output decisions

	Marginal condition	Check whether to produce
Short-run decision	Choose the output level at which $MR = SMC$	Produce this output unless price lower than $SAVC$. If it is, produce zero.
Long-run decision	Choose the output level at which $MR = LMC$	Produce this output unless price is lower than LAC. If it is, produce zero.

something towards paying its overheads. Thus the firm will produce Q_1 provided revenues exceed variable costs even though Q_1 may involve losses. The firm produces Q_1 if p exceeds $SAVC_1$. If not, it produces zero.

The firm's **short-run output decision** is to produce Q_1, the output at which $MR = SMC$, provided the price at least equals the short-run average variable cost ($SAVC_1$) at that output level. If the price is less than $SAVC_1$ the firm produces zero.

Table 8-10 summarizes the short-run and long-run output decisions of a firm. The Economics in Action that follows draws attention to two principles that are central to making good decisions.

BOX 8-2   Marginal conditions and sunk costs

The analysis of supply illustrates two principles of good decision-making which are frequently encountered in economics and in other aspects of life. The first is the *marginal principle*. If the best position has been reached, there cannot be even a small change that improves things. In deciding how much to produce, the firm keeps examining the effect on profits when output is increased or decreased by 1 unit. If profits can be increased by such a change, the change is made. When no further improvement is possible, the point of maximum profits has been found. To decide how many hours to study, you should assess the extra costs and benefits of studying another hour. If the benefits outweigh the costs, consider studying yet another hour. When you reach the point at which the two are equal, you have found the best position.

Of course it is also necessary to examine the big picture. Not only does the firm have to set marginal cost equal to marginal revenue; it must check that it is not better to close down completely. Similarly, the marginal principle will guide you to the best number of hours for which to study economics, but you must look at the big picture to assess whether you should be studying economics in the first place.

The second general principle is that *sunk costs are sunk*. If certain costs have already been incurred and cannot be affected by your decision, ignore them. They should not influence your future decisions. In deciding how much to produce in the short run, the firm ignores its fixed costs which must be incurred anyway. It finds the best output using the marginal principle, then examines whether the price at which this output can be sold will cover its variable costs in the short run, the costs that still can be affected by the decision the firm is making now. You have read nearly eight chapters of this book: should you keep reading? The answer depends entirely on the costs and benefits you will get from the rest of the book, not on the time you have already spent.

The *sunk cost fallacy* is the view that sunk costs matter. It may seem a pity to abandon a project on which a lot of money has already been invested. Poker players call this throwing good money after bad. If you do not think it will be worth reading the next ten chapters in their own right, you should not do it merely because you have put a lot of effort into the first eight chapters. Bygones should be bygones.

8-9 Short-run and long-run costs

Even if it is making losses in the short run, a firm will stay in business if it is covering its variable costs. Yet in the long run it must cover all its costs to remain in business. In this section we discuss how a firm may reduce its costs in the long run, converting a short-run loss into a long-term profit.

Figure 8-10 shows a U-shaped *LAC* curve. At each point on the curve the firm is producing a given output at minimum cost. The *LAC* curve describes a time scale sufficiently long that the firm can vary *all* factors of production, even those that are fixed in the short run.

Suppose, for convenience, that 'plant' is the fixed factor in the short run. Each point on the *LAC* curve involves a particular quantity of plant. Holding constant this quantity, of plant, we can draw the short-run average total cost curve for this plant size. Thus, the $SATC_1$ curve corresponds to the plant size at point *A* on the *LAC* curve and the $SATC_2$ and

$SATC_3$ curves correspond to the plant size at points *B* and *C* on the *LAC* curve. In fact, we could draw an *SATC* curve corresponding to the plant size at each point on the *LAC* curve.

By definition, the *LAC* curve describes the minimum-cost way to produce each output when all factors can be freely varied. Thus, point *B* describes the minimum average cost way to produce an output Q_2. Hence it *must* be more costly to produce Q_2 using the wrong quantity of plant, the quantity corresponding to point *E*. For the plant size at *A*, $SATC_1$ shows the cost of producing each output including Q_2. Hence $SATC_1$ must lie above *LAC* at every point except *A*, the output level for which this plant size happens to be best.

This argument can be repeated for any other plant size. Hence $SATC_3$ and $SATC_4$ corresponding respectively to the fixed plant size at *C* and at *D*, must lie above *LAC* except at points *C* and *D* themselves. In the long run the firm can

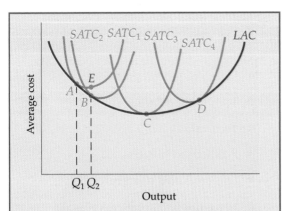

Suppose the plant size is fixed in the short run. For each plant size we obtain a particular *SATC* curve. But in the long run even plant size is variable. To construct the *LAC* curve we select at each output the plant size which gives the lowest *SATC* at this output. Thus points such as *A, B, C,* and *D* lie on the *LAC* curve. Notice the *LAC* curve does not pass through the lowest point on each *SATC* curve. Thus the *LAC* curve shows the minimum average cost way to produce a given output when all factors can be varied not the minimum average cost at which a given plant can produce.

Figure 8-10   The long-run average cost curve *LAC*

vary all its factors and will generally be able to produce a particular output more cheaply than in the short run, when it is stuck with the quantities of fixed factors it was using previously. A firm currently suffering losses because demand has fallen can look forward to future profits after it has had time to build a plant more suitable to its new output.

⊕ SUMMARY

● This chapter develops the distinction between short-run and long-run cost curves and output decisions. The long-run is a period over which the firm can fully adjust all its inputs to a change in conditions. The short run is a period in which the firm cannot fully adjust all its inputs to changed conditions. The length of calendar time corresponding to the long run varies from industry to industry.

● The production function specifies the maximum amount of output that can be produced using any given quantities of inputs. The inputs are machines, raw materials, labour, and any other factors of production. The production function summarizes the technical possibilities open to the firm.

● The total cost curve is derived from the production function, for given wages and rental rates of factors of production. The long-run total cost curve is obtained by finding, for each level of output, the method of production that minimizes costs when all inputs are fully flexible. When the relative price of using a factor of production rises, the firm substitutes away from that factor in its choice of production techniques. If the wage rate rises, the firm tends to use more machines and less labour.

● Average cost is total cost divided by output. The long-run average cost curve is derived from the long-run total cost curve, allowing full flexibility of all inputs.

● The long-run average cost curve (*LAC*) is typically drawn as U-shaped. The falling part of the U is the result of indivisibilities in production, the benefit of specialization, and some engineering advantages of large scale. There are increasing returns to scale on the falling part of the U. The rising part of the U is a result of managerial diseconomies of scale.

● Data from manufacturing typically show that the *LAC* decreases with high levels of output, or that there are economies of scale. For some industries the economies of scale become small at levels of output that are only a small percentage of total industry output.

● When marginal cost is below average cost, average cost is falling. When marginal cost is above average cost, average cost is rising. Average and marginal cost are equal only at the lowest point on the average cost curve.

● In the long run the firm produces at the point where long-run marginal cost (*LMC*) equals *MR* provided price is not less than the level of long-run average cost at that level of output. If price is less than long-run average cost, the firm goes out of business.

● In the short run the firm cannot adjust some of its inputs. But it still has to pay for them. It has short-run fixed costs (*SFC*) of production. The cost of using the variable factors is short-run variable cost (*SVC*). Short-run total costs (*STC*) are equal to *SFC* plus *SVC*.

● The short-run marginal cost curve (*SMC*) reflects the marginal product of the variable factor holding other factors fixed. Usually we think of labour as variable, but capital as fixed in the short run. When very little labour is used, the plant is too big for labour to produce much. Increasing labour input leads to large rises in output and *SMC* falls. Once machinery is fully manned, extra workers add progressively less to output. *SMC* begins to rise.

● Short-run average total costs (*SATC*) are equal to short-run total costs (*STC*) divided by output. *SATC* is equal to short-run average fixed costs (*SAFC*) plus short-run average variable costs (*SAVC*). The *SATC* curve is U-shaped. The falling part of the U results both from declining *SAFC* as the fixed costs are spread over more units of output and from declining *SAVC* at low levels of output. The *SATC* continues to fall after *SAVC* begins to increase, but eventually increasing *SAVC* outweighs declining *SAFC* and the *SATC* curve slopes up.

● The *SMC* curve cuts both the *SATC* and *SAVC* curves at their minimum points.

● The firm sets output in the short run at the level at which *SMC* is equal to *MR*, provided price is not less than short-run average variable cost. In the short run the firm is willing to produce at a loss provided it is recovering at least part of its fixed costs.

● The *LAC* curve is always below the *SATC* curve, except at the point where the two coincide. This implies that a firm is certain to have higher profits in the long run than in the short run if it is currently producing with a plant size that is not best from the viewpoint of the long run.

KEY TERMS

REVIEW QUESTIONS

1 (a) What information does the production function provide? (b) Explain why the production function does not provide enough information for anyone actually to run a firm.

2 (a) What are economies of scale and why might they exist? (b) The following table shows how output changes as inputs change. Assume the wage rate is £5 and the rental rate of capital is £2. Calculate the lowest-cost method of producing, 4, 8, and 12 units of output. (c) Do you have increasing, constant, or decreasing returns to scale between those output levels? Which applies where?

Capital input	Labour input	Output
4	5	4
2	6	4
7	10	8
4	12	8
11	15	12
8	16	12

3 (a) For each output in the above table, say which technique is more capital intensive. (b) Does the firm switch towards or away from more capital-intensive techniques as output rises?

4 Suppose the rental rate of capital in question 2 rose to £3. (a) Would the firm change its method of production for any levels of output? Say which, if any. (b) How do the firm's total and average costs change when the rental rate of capital rises?

5 (a) Calculate the marginal and average costs for each level of output from the following total cost data. (b) Show how marginal and average costs are related. (c) Are these short-run or long-run cost curves? Explain how you can tell.

Output	0	1	2	3	4	5	6	7	8	9
Total cost (£)	12	27	40	51	60	70	80	91	104	120

6 (a) Why does a firm have fixed costs of production in the short run? (b) Explain the typical shape of *SAFC*, *SAVC*, and *SATC* curves. (c) Why does the law of diminishing marginal productivity have anything to do with short-run cost curves?

7 (a) Explain why it might make sense for a firm to produce goods that it can only sell at a loss. (b) Can it keep on doing this for ever? Explain.

8 *Common fallacies* Show why the following statements are incorrect: (a) Firms which make losses are lame ducks who should be closed down at once. (b) The long-run average cost curve passes through the lowest point on each short-run average cost curve. (c) Larger firms can always produce more cheaply than smaller firms.

9 Perfect competition and pure monopoly: the limiting cases of market structure

LEARNING OUTCOMES

When you have finished this chapter, you should be able to:

- Understand the concepts of perfect competition and pure monopoly
- Show why a perfectly competitive firm chooses the output at which price equals marginal cost
- Relate entry and exit to the level of profits of existing firms
- Derive industry supply curves from the marginal cost curves of perfectly competitive firms
- Master comparative static analysis of shifts in demand or supply
- Analyse a market in which international trade takes place
- Explain why a monopolist chooses output to equate marginal cost and marginal revenue
- Compare a monopolist's output with that of a perfectly competitive industry
- Show how the ability to price discriminate affects a monopolist's output and profits

An industry is the set of all firms making the same product. The output of an industry is the sum of the outputs of its firms. Yet different industries have very different numbers of firms. Letters in the UK are delivered by the Post Office, which we call a nationalized industry because it is owned and run by the state. However, some sole suppliers are private firms. Eurostar is the only supplier of train journeys from London to Paris. In contrast, the UK has 200 000 farms and 30 000 grocers.

We now derive the industry supply curve and examine its interaction with the market demand curve to determine price and output for the industry as a whole.

What about the size and number of firms in an industry?

Why indeed do some industries have many firms but others only one? These are questions about market structure.

The **market structure** is a description of the behaviour of buyers and sellers in that market.

In the next chapter we develop a general theory of market structure, showing how demand and cost conditions together determine the number of firms and their behaviour. First it is useful to establish two benchmark cases, the opposite extremes between which all other types of market structure must lie. These limiting cases are *perfect competition* on the one hand and *monopoly* or *monopsony* on the other hand.

A **perfectly competitive** market is one in which both buyers and sellers believe that their own buying or selling decisions have no effect on the market price. A *monopolist* is the only seller or potential seller of the good in that industry. A *monopsonist* is the only buyer or potential buyer of the good in that industry.

In this and the following chapter we are interested primarily in the relationship between the number of sellers and the behaviour of sellers. We assume that there are many buyers whose individual downward-sloping demand curves can be aggregated to yield the market demand curve. At present we assume that the demand side of the market is competitive, and we contrast the limiting cases on the supply side.

The economist's definition of perfect competition is different from the meaning of competition in everyday usage. The economist means that each individual, recognizing that his own quantities supplied or demanded are trivial relative to the market as a whole, acts on the assumption that his actions will have no effect on the market price. This assumption is built into our model of consumer choice in Chapter 6. Each consumer constructs a budget line on the assumption that market prices are given and unaffected by the quantities he chooses. Changes in *market* conditions, applying to all firms and consumers, change the equilibrium price and hence individual quantities demanded, but each individual neglects any feedback from his own actions to market price.

This concept of competition, which we now extend to firms, differs from everyday usage. Ford and Renault are fighting each other vigorously for the European car market, but an economist would not call them perfectly competitive. Each commands such a large share of the total market that changes in their quantities supplied affect the market price. Each must take account of this in deciding how much to supply. They cannot regard themselves as *pricetakers*. Only under perfect competition can individuals make decisions that treat the price as independent of their own actions.

9-1 Perfect competition

In a **perfectly competitive industry** nobody believes that their own actions affect the market price.

Such an industry must have many buyers and many sellers. In London the New Covent Garden fruit market confronts many buyers with many sellers. Neither buyers nor sellers believe their own actions affect the market price.

Firms in a perfectly competitive industry face a horizontal demand curve as in Figure 9-1. However much the firm sells, it gets exactly the market price. If it tries to charge a price in excess of P_0 it will not sell any output: buyers will go to one of the other firms whose product is just as good. Since the firm can sell as much as it wants at P_0, there is no point charging less than P_0. The individual firm's demand curve is *DD*.

This horizontal demand curve is the crucial feature of a perfectly competitive firm. For this to be a plausible description of the demand curve facing the firm, we really need to have in mind an industry with four characteristics. First, there must be a large number of firms in the industry so that each is trivial relative to the industry as a whole. Second, the firms must be making a reasonably standard product, such as wheat or potatoes. Even if the car industry had a large number of firms it would not be sensible to view it as a competitive industry. A Ford Mondeo is not a perfect substitute for a Vauxhall Vectra. The more imperfect they are as substitutes, the more it will make sense to view Ford as the sole supplier of Mondeos and Vauxhall as the sole supplier of Vectras. Each producer will cease to be trivial relative to the relevant market and will no longer be able to act as a price-taker.

This example alerts us to the problem of which goods can be grouped together within the same market or industry. We return to this issue in the next chapter. For the moment we can evade this issue. In a perfectly competitive industry all

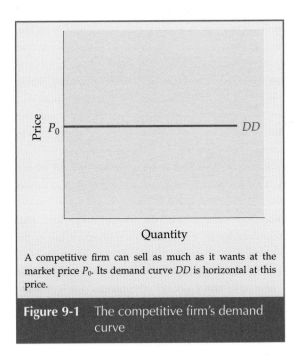

A competitive firm can sell as much as it wants at the market price P_0. Its demand curve *DD* is horizontal at this price.

Figure 9-1   The competitive firm's demand curve

firms must be making essentially the same product, *for which they all charge the same price.*

Even if all firms in an industry made *homogeneous* or identical goods each firm might have some discretion over the price it charged if buyers have imperfect information about the quality or characteristics of products. If you don't know much about cars you may *think* that a 1990 Ford Sierra being sold for £1000 must be in a *better* condition than a 1990 Ford Sierra being sold for £500. Hence, if no firm in a competitive industry can affect the price for which it sells its output, we must assume that buyers have almost perfect information about the products being sold. They know the products of different firms in a competitive industry really are identical.

Why don't all the firms in the industry do what OPEC did in 1973–74, collectively restricting supply, to increase the price of their output by moving the industry up its market demand curve?

One answer is that, with so many firms in the industry, the costs of organizing themselves into a cohesive group might be prohibitive. Managers might spend more time negotiating with other firms than organizing production. Nevertheless, if the market demand curve is very inelastic, the potential increase in revenue from such co-operation could be enormous, as OPEC discovered. We need a more profound answer to rule out co-operation.

Thus the fourth crucial characteristic of a perfectly competitive industry is *free entry and exit.* Even if existing firms could organize themselves to restrict total supply and drive up the market price, the consequent increase in revenues and profits would simply attract new firms into the industry, thereby increasing total supply again and driving the price back down. Conversely, as we shall shortly see, when firms in a competitive industry are losing money, some firms will close down and, by reducing the number of firms remaining in the industry, reduce the total supply and drive the price up, thereby allowing the remaining firms to survive.

To sum up, each firm in a competitive industry faces a horizontal demand curve for its product at the going market price. To be a reasonable description of the demand conditions facing a firm, the industry must have four characteristics: (1) many firms, each trivial relative to the industry as a whole; (2) a standardized or homogeneous product, so that it is legitimate to examine the industry as a whole rather than a series of subindustries each with many fewer firms; (3) perfect customer information about product quality so that buyers recognize that the identical products of different firms really are the same; and (4) free entry

and exit so there is no incentive for existing firms to collude.[1]

9-2 The firm's supply decision under perfect competition

In Chapter 8 we developed a general theory of the supply decision of the individual firm. First, the firm uses the marginal condition ($MC = MR$) to find the best positive level of output; then it uses the average condition to check whether the price for which this output is sold covers average cost.

This general theory must hold for the special case of perfectly competitive firms. *The special feature of perfect competition is the relationship between marginal revenue and price.* The competitive firm faces a horizontal demand curve as in Figure 9-1. Unlike the more general case, in which the firm faces a downward-sloping demand curve, the competitive firm does *not* bid down the price as it sells more units of output. Since there is no effect on the revenue from existing output, the marginal revenue from an additional unit of output is simply the price received.

This special feature of a perfectly competitive firm has far-reaching consequences. It is so important we show this feature as equation (1):

$$\text{(Marginal revenue)} \ MR = P \ \text{(price)} \qquad (1)$$

The firm's short-run supply curve

Figure 9-2 shows again the short-run cost curves – marginal cost SMC, average total cost $SATC$, and average variable cost $SAVC$ – from Chapter 8. From equation (1) the marginal condition for the best level of positive output now implies

$$SMC = MR = P \qquad (2)$$

Suppose the firm faces a horizontal demand curve at the price P_4 in Figure 9-2. Equation (2) implies that the firm chooses the output level Q_4 to reach the point D, at which price equals marginal cost.

Next, the firm checks whether it would rather shut down in the short run. It will shut down only if the price P_4 at which output can be sold fails to cover short-run variable costs of producing this output. In Figure 9-2 P_4 exceeds

---

[1] Many factors may inhibit entry and exit. Until 1980 de Beers controlled virtually all diamond mines in the non-communist world, preventing new firms entering the diamond industry. In many countries doctors and lawyers, acting through their professional bodies, have restricted entry to the medical and legal professions. Governments may also urge firms *not* to exit from an industry in which they provide a lot of jobs.

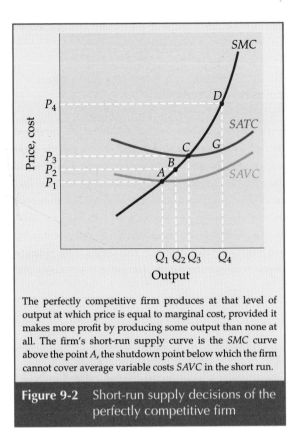

The perfectly competitive firm produces at that level of output at which price is equal to marginal cost, provided it makes more profit by producing some output than none at all. The firm's short-run supply curve is the *SMC* curve above the point *A*, the shutdown point below which the firm cannot cover average variable costs *SAVC* in the short run.

Figure 9-2 Short-run supply decisions of the perfectly competitive firm

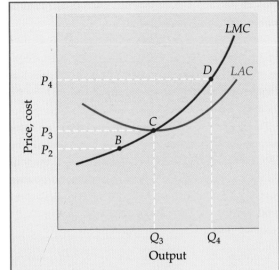

The perfectly competitive firm produces at that level of output at which *P* is equal to marginal cost, provided it makes more profit by producing some output than none at all. It therefore chooses points on the *LMC* curve. At any price above P_3 the firm makes profits because price is above long-run average cost (*LAC*). At any price below P_3, such as P_2, the firm makes losses because price is below long-run average cost. It therefore will not produce any output at prices below P_3. The long-run supply curve is the *LMC* curve above point *C*.

Figure 9-3 Long-run supply decisions of the perfectly competitive firm

SAVC at the output level Q_4. Not only does the firm wish to produce this output, it also makes profits in the short run. The point *D* lies above the point *G*, the short-run average total cost (including overheads) of producing Q_4.

Suppose the firm had faced a different price. In the short run the firm should produce positive output for any price above P_1. Any price below P_1 lies below the minimum point on the *SAVC* curve and the firm cannot find an output at which price covers *SAVC*. Given any price such as P_2, above P_1, the firm produces Q_2, the output at which price equals marginal cost.

The curve showing the quantity the firm wants to produce at each price is the firm's **supply curve**.

The short-run supply curve is thus the *SMC* curve above point A, the point at which the *SMC* curve crosses the lowest point on the *SAVC* curve.

Between points *A* and *C* the firm will be making short-run losses, since price is less than average total cost. But it will be recouping some of its overheads. At any price above P_3, the point at which the *SMC* curve crosses the lowest point on the *SATC* curve, the firm is making short-run profits. For example, at the price P_4 the profit per unit of output is the

distance *DG*, the difference between price and average total cost per unit of output. Remember that these are economic or supernormal profits after allowing for the economic costs, including the opportunity costs of the owners' financial capital and work effort, summarized in the *SAVC* and *SATC* curves.

The price P_1 is called the **shutdown price**, the price below which the firm reduces its losses by choosing not to produce at all.

The firm's long-run supply curve

The same principles apply in deriving the long-run supply curve of the perfectly competitive firm. Figure 9-3 shows the firm's average and marginal costs in the long run. Remember that the long-run marginal cost curve *LMC* will be flatter than the *SMC* curve since the firm can freely adjust all factors of production only in the long run.

Facing a price P_4, the marginal condition leads the firm to choose the long-run output level Q_4 at the point *D*. Again we must check whether it is better to shut down than to produce this output. In the long run, shutting down means leaving the industry altogether.

The firm exits from the industry only if price fails to cover long-run average cost *LAC* at the best positive output level. At the price P_2 the marginal condition leads to the point *B* in Figure 9-3, but the firm is losing money and should leave the industry in the long run.

Thus the firm's *long-run supply curve*, the schedule relating output supplied to price in the long run, is the portion of the *LMC* curve to the right of point *C* corresponding to the price P_3. At any price below P_3 the firm can find no positive output at which price covers *LAC*. At the price P_3 the firm produces Q_3 and just breaks even after paying all its economic costs. It makes only normal profits.[2]

When economic profits are zero we say the firm is making **normal profits**. Its accounting profits just pay the opportunity cost of the owner's money and time.

Entry and exit

The price P_3 corresponding to the minimum point on the *LAC* curve is called the *entry or exit price*. Firms are making only normal profits. There is no incentive to enter or leave the industry. The resources tied up in the firm are earning just as much as their opportunity costs, what they could earn elsewhere.

Entry is when new firms join an industry. **Exit** is when existing firms leave.

Any price less than P_3 will induce the firm to exit from the industry in the long run. At any price above P_3 the firm can find a long-run output level, such as Q_4, that yields supernormal profits. P_3 is the minimum price required to keep the firm in the industry.

However, we can also interpret Figure 9-3 as the decision facing a potential entrant to the industry. The cost curves now describe the post-entry costs. P_3, the price that just covers the lowest average cost at which the entrant could produce, is the critical point at which entry becomes attractive. Any price above P_3 yields supernormal profits

and means that the return on the owners' time and money will be higher than their opportunity costs.

The long-run and short-run supply decisions of the competitive firm

Figure 9-4 summarizes the preceding discussion. For each level of fixed factors there exists a different *SMC* curve and short-run supply curve (*SRSS*). The long-run supply curve (*LRSS*) is flatter than *SRSS* because extra factor flexibility in the long run makes the *LMC* curve flatter than the *SMC* curve. The *SRSS* curve starts from a lower shutdown price because in the short run the firm will produce if it can cover average variable costs. In the long run all costs are variable and must be covered if the firm is to remain in the industry. In either case, the competitive firm's supply curve is the part

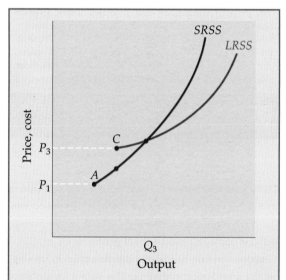

Taken from the two previous figures, the short-run supply curve is the firm's *SMC* curve above *A* and the long-run supply curve *LRSS* is the firm's *LMC* curve above *C*. P_1 is the shutdown price in the short run and P_3 the entry and exit price in the long run. If the firm happens to begin with the stock of fixed factors it would choose at the lowest point on its *LAC* curve, then *C* will actually lie on the *SRSS* curve.

Figure 9-4 Short- and long-run supply curves of the competitive firm

[2] The firm's behaviour in the short run and in the long run is rather like the behaviour of a good poker player. In the short run the poker player is dealt a particular hand and plays the hand if it is likely to be profitable. If not, the player temporarily shuts down by throwing in the hand. Over time the player gets new hands just as a firm can gradually rearrange its factors of production. When the poker player realizes that, whatever the cards, the long-run outlook is bad because other players are better, the player should leave the game altogether. Similarly, if a firm realizes that, however it adjusts its factors of production, it is going to make losses in the long run, it should leave the industry.

Table 9-1 The supply decision of the perfectly competitive firm

Marginal condition	Average condition	
	Short-run	Long-run
Produce output where $P = MC$	If $P < SAV$ shut down temporarily	If $P < LAC$ leave industry

of the marginal cost curve above the point at which it is better to produce no output at all. Table 9-1 sets out this principle.

9-3 Industry supply curves

A competitive industry comprises many firms. In the short run two things are fixed: the quantity of fixed factors employed by each firm, and the number of firms in the industry. In the long run, each firm can vary all its factors of production, but the number of firms can also change through entry and exit from the industry.

The short-run industry supply curve

Just as we can add individual demand curves by buyers to obtain the market demand curve, we can add the individual supply curves of firms to obtain the industry supply curve. Figure 9-5 shows how. At each price we add together the quantities supplied by each firm to obtain the total quantity supplied at that price.

In the short run the number of firms in the industry is given. Suppose there are two firms, A and B. Each firm's short-run supply curve is the part of its SMC curve above its shutdown price. Figure 9-5 assumes that firm A has a lower shutdown price than firm B. Firm A has a lower $SAVC$ curve, perhaps because of a more favourable geographical location

or superior technical know-how. Each firm's supply curve is horizontal at the shutdown price. At a lower price, no output is supplied.

At each price, the industry supply Q is the sum of Q^A, the supply of firm A, and Q^B, the supply of firm B. Thus at the price P_3, $Q_3 = Q^A_3 = Q^B_3$. The industry supply curve is the horizontal sum of the separate supply curves. The industry supply curve is discontinuous at the price P_2. Between P_1 and P_2 only the lower-cost firm A is producing. At P_2 firm B starts to produce as well.

When there are many firms, each with a different shutdown price, there are a large number of very small discontinuities as we move up the industry supply curve. In fact, since each firm in a competitive industry is trivial relative to the total, the industry supply curve is effectively smooth.

Comparing short- and long-run industry supply curves

Figure 9-5 may also be used to derive the long-run industry supply curve. For each firm the individual supply curve is the portion of the LMC curve above the firm's entry and exit price. However, unlike the short run, the number of firms in the industry is no longer fixed. Not only can existing firms leave the industry, but also new firms can enter. Instead of horizontally aggregating at each price the quantities

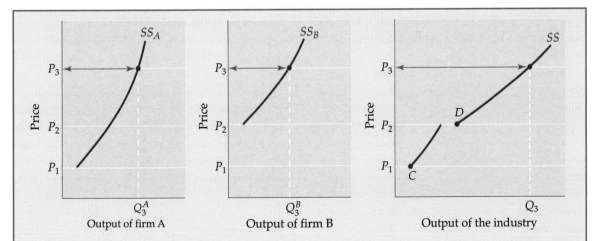

The industry supply curve SS shows the total quantity supplied at each price by all the firms in the industry. It is obtained by adding at each price the quantity supplied by each firm in the industry. With only two firms A and B the figure shows how at a price such as P_3 we add Q^A_3 and Q^B_3 to obtain the output Q_3 on the industry supply curve. Since firms can have different shutdown prices or entry and exit prices, the industry supply curve can have step jumps at points such as C and D where an extra firm starts production. However, with many firms in the industry, each trivial relative to the industry as a whole, the step jumps in the industry supply curve when another starts production are so small that we can effectively think of the upward sloping industry supply curve as smooth.

Figure 9-5   Deriving the industry supply curve

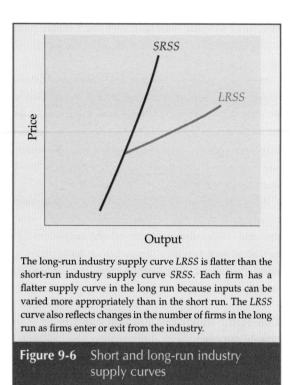

The long-run industry supply curve *LRSS* is flatter than the short-run industry supply curve *SRSS*. Each firm has a flatter supply curve in the long run because inputs can be varied more appropriately than in the short run. The *LRSS* curve also reflects changes in the number of firms in the long run as firms enter or exit from the industry.

Figure 9-6   Short and long-run industry supply curves

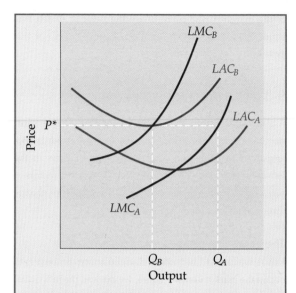

Suppose firms have different cost curves. Firm A, the lowest-cost firm in the industry, has long-run average costs LAC_A and marginal costs LMC_A. Firm B faces much higher costs LAC_B and LMC_B. Other firms have intermediate costs. At the price P^* firm A produces Q_A and makes profits. Firm B produces Q_B and just breaks even. Firm B is the marginal firm, the highest-cost producer that can remain in the industry in the long run.

Figure 9-7   The marginal firm in the industry

supplied by the existing firms in the industry, we must horizontally aggregate the quantities supplied by existing firms *and firms that might potentially enter the industry.*

At a price below P_2 in Figure 9-5 firm B will not be in the industry in the long run. As we contemplate prices above P_2 we must recognize that firm B *will* wish to enter the industry in the long run. As the market price rises, the total industry supply rises in the long run for two distinct reasons: each existing firm will move up its long-run supply curve, and new firms will find it profitable to enter the industry.

Conversely, at lower prices, higher-cost firms lose money and leave the industry. Entry and exit in the long run play a role analogous to shutdown in the short run. In the long run, entry and exit affect the number of producing firms whose output must be horizontally aggregated to obtain the industry supply. In the short run, although the number of firms in the industry is given, the fraction that is producing rather than being temporarily shut down is not. Again, the industry supply curve is the horizontal sum of the outputs of those actually producing at the given market price.

Figure 9-6 illustrates what these arguments imply about the relation between short- and long-run industry supply curves. The long-run supply curve is flatter for two reasons: each firm can vary its factors more appropriately in the long run and has a flatter supply curve (Figure 9-4); and higher

prices attract additional firms into the industry, causing industry output to rise by more than the additional output supplied by the firms previously in the industry.

Conversely, when the price falls firms initially move down their (relatively steep) short-run supply curves. If short-run average variable costs are covered firms will continue to produce and may not reduce output very much. In the long run each firm will reduce output further since all factors of production can now be varied. In addition some firms will leave the industry since they are no longer covering long-run average costs. Thus, a price reduction reduces industry output by more in the long run than in the short run.

The marginal firm   Suppose there are many firms, each making the same product for sale at the same price but having slightly different cost curves. Figure 9-7 shows the cost curves for two firms, a low-cost firm A and a high-cost firm B. Some firms have costs lying between those of A and B, others have even higher costs than B.

The long run is the period in which all adjustment – both in factors and in number of firms – has been completed. There is no further entry and exit. Suppose the long-run price is P^* in Figure 9-7. The low-cost firm A is producing Q_A and making healthy profits, since P^* exceeds LAC at the output Q_A. Slightly higher-cost firms are making slightly less profit. Firm B is the last firm that can survive in the industry.

The **marginal firm** in an industry is just breaking even.

All firms with higher costs than firm B cannot compete in the industry if the long-run price is P^*. Suppose one potential entrant has an LAC curve whose lowest point is only slightly above P^*. It is the marginal firm waiting to enter the industry. If anything causes P^* to rise a little, this marginal firm can enter.

The horizontal long-run industry supply curve

Each firm has a rising LMC curve and hence a rising long-run supply curve. The industry supply curve is somewhat flatter. Higher prices not merely induce existing firms to produce more; they also induce new firms to enter the industry. In the extreme case the industry long-run supply curve is horizontal. This case occurs when all existing firms and potential entrants have *identical cost* curves. This is illustrated in Figure 9-8. Below P^* no firm will wish to supply. Although it takes a price above P^* to persuade each

individual firm to produce Q_1, no higher price than P^* is required to expand industry output.

Consider any price such as P_2 above P^*. Each firm produces Q_2 and makes supernormal profits since point D lies above point E. Since potential entrants face the same cost curves, there would be a flood of new firms entering the industry.

Hence the industry supply curve is horizontal in the long run at the price P^*. It is not necessary to offer a higher price to bribe existing firms to move up their individual supply curves. Industry output can be expanded by the entry of new firms alone. In Figure 9-8 we show the long-run industry supply curve $LRSS$ as a horizontal line at the price P^*.

There are two reasons why the general case of a rising long-run industry supply curve is much more likely than the special case of a horizontal long-run supply curve for a competitive industry. First, it is unlikely that every firm and potential firm in the industry has identical cost curves.

Second, even if all firms face the same cost curves, we draw a cost curve for given technology *and* given input prices. Although each small firm can affect neither output prices nor input prices, the collective expansion of output by all firms may bid up input prices. If so, it requires a higher output price to allow an increase in industry output that will bid up input prices and shift the cost curves for each individual firm upwards. Thus in general we expect the long-run supply curve of the industry to be rising. It requires a higher price to call forth a higher total output.

9-4 Comparative statics for a competitive industry

Having discussed the industry supply curve, we can now examine how supply and demand interact to determine equilibrium price in the short run and the long run.

In **short-run equilibrium** the market price equates the quantity demanded to the total quantity supplied by the given number of firms in the industry when each firm produces on its short-run supply curve.

In **long-run equilibrium** the market price equates the quantity demanded to the total quantity supplied by the number of firms in the industry when each firm produces on its long-run supply curve. Since firms can freely enter or exit from the industry, the marginal firm must make only normal profits so that there is no further incentive for entry or exit.

We now examine equilibrium in a competitive industry and apply the method of comparative static analysis introduced in Chapter 3.

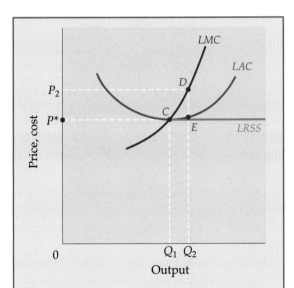

When all existing firms and potential entrants have identical costs, industry output can be expanded without offering a price higher than P^*. The long-industry supply curve is the horizontal line $LRSS$ at P^*. Industry output can be indefinitely expanded at this price by increasing the number of firms that each produce Q_1.

Figure 9-8　The horizontal long-run industry supply curve

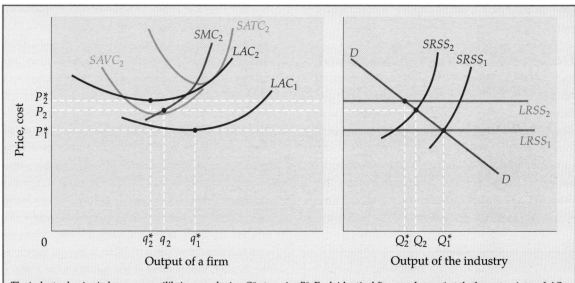

The industry begins in long-run equilibrium producing Q_1^* at a price P_1^*. Each identical firm produces q_1^* at the lowest point on LAC_1. The long-run supply curve $LRSS_1$ is horizontal at P_1^*. When costs increase, firms have fixed factors and the number of firms is given in the short run. Each firm produces q_2 where the short-run equilibrium price P_2 equals SMC_2. Together these firms produce Q_2. Since firms are losing money, in the long run some firms leave the industry. The new long-run supply curve $LRSS_2$ for the industry is horizontal at P_2^*, the minimum point on each firm's new long-run average cost curve LAC_2. Each firm produces q_2^*. Industry output is Q_2^*.

Figure 9-9   The effect of a cost increase on a competitive industry

Comparative statics examines how equilibrium changes when there is a change, for example, in demand or cost conditions.

The effect of an increase in costs

First we discuss the effect of an increase in costs that hits all firms: an increase in the price of a raw material, or in the wage rate which must be paid in the industry. For simplicity, we discuss the case in which all firms face the same costs and the long-run supply curve of the industry is horizontal.

Figure 9-9 summarizes the implications of our analysis of a competitive industry. The industry faces the downward-sloping demand curve DD. Initially, the long-run supply curve is $LRSS_1$ and the market clears at the price P_1^* and the total output Q_1^*. The short-run industry supply curve is $SRSS_1$. The market is in both short-run and long-run equilibrium.

The left-hand figure shows that each firm is producing q_1^* at the lowest point on its average cost curve LAC_1. This must also be the lowest point on its $SATC$ curve and hence also lies on its SMC curve, though the initial position of these two curves is not shown in Figure 9-9. If there are N_1 firms in the industry, total output Q_1^* is N_1 times the individual firm's output q_1^*.

Now suppose an increase in input prices raises costs for all firms. LAC_2 is the new long-run average cost curve for a firm. In the short run the firm has some fixed factors. $SATC_2$

and $SAVC_2$ depict average total and average variable costs at this level of fixed factors. Short-run marginal costs SMC_2 pass through the lowest point of both these curves. The part of SMC_2 above $SAVC_2$ is the firm's short-run supply curve. In the short run the number of firms remains fixed.

Horizontally adding these short-run supply curves for the given number of firms, we obtain the new industry short-run supply curve $SRSS_2$. The new short-run equilibrium occurs at P_2, where $SRSS_2$ crosses the demand curve. Each firm sets P_2 equal to SMC_2 and produces an output q_2. Together the N_1 firms produce Q_2. Firms now cover variable costs but not fixed costs at the price P_2. They are losing money.

As time elapses two things happen: fixed factors are varied, and firms leave the industry. Long-run equilibrium occurs at the price P_2^* since the new long-run industry supply curve $LRSS_2$ is horizontal at P_2^*, which just covers minimum long-run average costs. Each firm produces q_2^*. The number of firms N_2 is such that Q_2^* equals q_2^* times N_2.

Figure 9-9 makes two points about the change in the long-run equilibrium. First, the rise in average costs is eventually passed on to the consumer in higher prices. In long-run equilibrium the marginal firm (here, all firms, since they are identical) must make only normal profits to prevent an incentive for further entry or exit. To allow normal profits, prices rise to cover the increase in minimum average costs.

Second, since higher prices reduce the total quantity demanded, industry output must fall.

A shift in the market demand curve: an example from the coal industry

Figure 9-10 illustrates the effect of a shift up in the market demand curve from DD to $D'D'$. We show the effects at the industry level. Try to draw your own diagram showing what is happening for the individual firm, as we did in Figure 9-9.

The industry begins in long-run equilibrium at the point A. Overnight, each firm has fixed factors and the number of firms is fixed. Horizontally adding their short-run supply curves, we obtain the industry supply curve $SRSS$. The new short-run equilibrium occurs at the point A'. When demand first increases it requires a large price rise to persuade individual firms to move up their steep short-run supply curves with given fixed factors.

In the long run, firms can adjust all factors and move on to their flatter long-run supply curves. In addition, super-normal profits attract extra firms into the industry. Figure 9-10 assumes that the long-run industry supply curve is rising. Either it takes higher prices to attract higher-cost

firms into the industry, or the collective expansion bids up some input prices, or both. The new long-run equilibrium occurs at A''. Relative to short-run equilibrium at A' there is a further expansion of total output but a more appropriate choice of factors of production and the entry of new firms combine to increase supply and reduce the market-clearing price.

The most spectacular example of a demand curve shift is probably provided by the oil price shock in 1973–74 when oil prices tripled. Since oil and coal are substitutes as energy sources, we should expect a large outward shift in the demand for coal. In many European countries the coal industry was regulated by the government. The best example of a competitive coal industry was the case of the United States.

How did higher oil prices affect the US coal industry? Table 9-2 presents some statistics for the 1970s which confirm the prediction of Figure 9-10. In 1974–77, immediately following the oil price shock, there was a 52 per cent rise in the real price of coal but only a modest 12 per cent rise in production of coal. This matches the move from A to A' in Figure 9-10.

For the period 1978–80 output rises a lot but the real price falls back, as the move from A' to A'' predicts. Table 9-2 confirms that firms were being attracted into the industry as

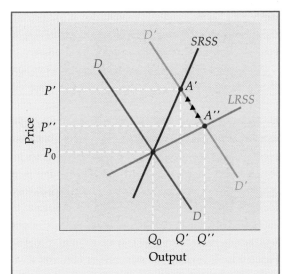

The industry begins in long-run equilibrium at A. When the demand curve shifts from DD to $D'D'$ the new short-run equilibrium occurs at A'. As fixed factors are gradually adjusted and new firms enter the industry, equilibrium gradually moves from A' towards A'', the new long-run equilibrium.

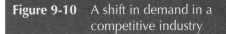

Figure 9-10 A shift in demand in a competitive industry

Table 9-2	The coal industry in the United States		
Years	Real price*	Output	
1970–73	100	100	
1974–77	152	112	
1978–80	145	129	
Year	Real price	Number of Firms	Workers
1972	102	3365	155 000
1977	147	5275	242 000

*Index for 1970–73 = 100.
Sources: *Survey of Current Business* (various issues), and *Statistical Abstract of the United States*, 1981.

the theory implies. These additional firms provide a substantial amount of the increase in total output. Many of these new coal mines were quite small relative to the large mines previously in operation. We see from Table 9-2 that the addition of these new smaller mines actually reduced average output per mine. Only at the higher prices could these small, higher-cost mines survive in the coal industry.

Thus the messages of Figure 9-10 are confirmed. When demand increases there must be a rise in the price. This has three effects which act to restore long-run equilibrium. First, by moving consumers up the demand curve, the price rise partly mitigates the increase in quantity demanded. Second, the price rise induces existing firms to produce more output. Finally, the price rise entices new firms into the industry.

In the short run the price *overshoots* its long-run position. In Figure 9-10 the point A' lies above the point A''. Consumers may well complain about the large price increase in the short run, especially since firms in the industry are temporarily making large profits. But these profits fulfil an important role in the adjustment process, for they act as the signal to potential entrants that this is an industry that can profitably be entered. Entry helps increase long-run supply and mitigate the initial price increase. As entry takes place and existing firms adjust their previously fixed factors, the industry gradually moves from A' to A'' in Figure 9-10. Eventually, the extra output competes away the supernormal profits by bidding the price down. The industry reaches A'', its new long-run equilibrium position.

9-5 Competition in world markets

Changes in conditions in domestic markets are often the result of events in other countries. Fish prices in Western Europe fell in the 1990s after suppliers from the ex-USSR

joined the world economy. Wool prices in the European Union rise when there is a drought in Australia, one of the world's largest wool suppliers. We now discuss how competitive markets in different countries are linked together and show why shifts in foreign conditions affect domestic markets.

When a commodity is internationally traded, its price in one country cannot be independent of its price in another country. In the extreme case, the 'Law of One Price' will hold.

If there were no obstacles to trade and no transport costs, the **Law of One Price** implies that the price of a given commodity will be the same all over the world.

Without trade barriers and transport costs, suppliers sell in the market with the highest price but consumers purchase in the market with the lowest price. The commodity can simultaneously be traded in two different countries only if its price is the same in both markets.

In practice, transport costs and trade restrictions such as tariffs (taxes levied on imports) allow international differences in the price of a commodity. Nevertheless, unless these costs and restrictions are prohibitive, international competition will ensure that prices of the same good in different countries generally move together.

We now show how international trade affects competitive markets. To highlight this issue, we assume transport costs and trade restrictions are negligible. Producers and consumers throughout the world are essentially part of a unified world market for the commodity.

Equilibrium in the domestic market

Figure 9-11 shows the domestic supply curve SS and the domestic demand curve DD for such a commodity. Suppose first that there is no international trade, perhaps because the domestic country has enormous tariffs on imports. The domestic market will be in equilibrium at the point A, at which price is P^* and quantity is Q^*.

Now suppose tariffs are abolished. There is a world supply curve, which horizontally aggregates the supply curve of each country, and a world demand curve, which horizontally aggregates the demand curve of each country. Together these determine a world price for the commodity. Suppose the domestic country is small relative to the world and must take the world price as given.

One of three things can happen, and Figure 9-11 illustrates each of these cases. Suppose, first, that the world equilibrium price is P^*, exactly the price that would have cleared the domestic market in isolation. Point A continues to describe equilibrium in the domestic market. The Law of One Price is satisfied. Consumers cannot buy the good more cheaply abroad and producers cannot sell the good at a higher foreign price. Domestic supply exactly caters for domestic demand and the domestic country neither imports nor exports the good.

Now suppose the given world price is P_1^*. If domestic suppliers attempt to charge a higher price domestic consumers will simply import the good and pay P_1^*. But domestic suppliers will produce at Q_1 since they can always export the good if domestic consumers will not buy it. Hence the domestic market is in equilibrium at the price P_1^*, at which producers supply Q_1, consumers demand Q'_1, and the quantity $(Q'_1 - Q_1)$, corresponding to the horizontal distance between C and C', is imported from abroad. Conversely, if the given world price is P_2^*, domestic consumers will demand the quantity Q_2 but domestic producers will supply Q'_1. The quantity $(Q'_1 - Q_1)$ corresponding to the horizontal distance between B and B' will now be exported to consumers abroad.

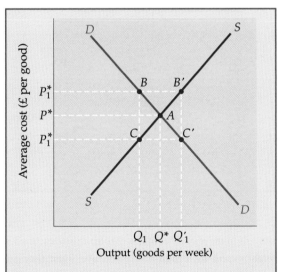

DD and SS show the domestic supply and demand curves for a commodity competitively traded in world markets. In the absence of trade, domestic equilibrium occurs at A. When trade is possible at the world price P^*, equilibrium occurs at A. When trade is possible at the given world price P_1^*, domestic producers supply Q_1 and domestic consumers demand Q'_1. The excess demand (the horizontal distance between C and C') is met from imports. Conversely, when world prices are P_2^*, domestic producers supply Q_1, domestic consumers demand Q_1, and the excess supply (the horizontal distance between B and B') is exported.

Figure 9-11   Domestic equilibrium and world prices

The effect of changes in world conditions on the domestic market

When our industries compete in world markets, a change in the world price, reflecting a shift in world supply or world demand, will affect the domestic market. Figure 9-11 may be used to show why.

Suppose a drought in Australia reduces the world supply of wool. The world price of wool rises. Suppose originally the world price was P_1^* in Figure 9-11. British farmers were producing Q_1 but clothing manufacturers in Britain were additionally importing $(Q'_1 - Q_1)$ since their total quantity demanded was Q'_1. The Australian drought raises the world price above P_1^* and this has two effects. First, it reduces the quantity of wool demanded by British clothing manufacturers. Second, it allows British farmers to charge higher prices and move up their supply curve, expanding output and attracting new resources into the farming industry.

Since the domestic quantity demanded has declined but the domestic quantity supplied has increased, the higher world price of wool has led to a fall in imports. Indeed, if the world price rises sufficiently, Figure 9-11 implies that the UK would become a net exporter of wool.

This first look at international trade also reminds us that the relevant definition of the market or the industry may be a good deal wider than that of the domestic economy. When transport costs are low and trade restrictions unimportant, it is in the world market that we must seek the forces that determine the equilibrium price of a good.

9-6 Pure monopoly: the opposite limiting case

The perfectly competitive firm is too small to worry about the effect of its own output decision on industry supply. It can sell as much as it wants at the market price. Before setting out a general theory of market structure, we discuss the opposite limiting case on the supply side, the case of pure monopoly.

A **monopolist** is the sole supplier and potential supplier of the industry's product.

The firm and the industry coincide. The sole national supplier need not be a monopolist if the good or service is internationally traded. The Post Office is the sole supplier of UK stamps and is a monopolist. British Steel, although effectively the sole UK steel supplier, is not a monopolist since it must compete with imports. Some monopolists are nationalized industries. The state makes price and output

BOX 9-2

The elasticity of supply

The elasticity of supply measures the responsiveness of the quantity supplied to a change in the price of that commodity.

$$\text{Supply elasticity} = \frac{(\% \text{ change in quantity supplied})}{(\% \text{ change in price})}$$

Because supply curves slope upwards, the elasticity of supply is *positive*. As we move along a supply curve, positive price changes are associated with positive output changes. The more elastic is supply the larger the percentage increase in quantity supplied in response to a given percentage change in price. Thus, elastic supply curves are relatively flat and inelastic supply curves relatively steep.

The diagram shows a typical supply curve SS with a positive supply elasticity and also shows the two limiting cases. The vertical supply curve $S'S'$ has a zero supply elasticity. A given percentage change in price is associated with a zero percentage change in quantity supplied. The horizontal supply curve $S''S''$ has an infinite supply elasticity. Any price increase above the price P^* would lead to an infinite increase in quantity supplied.

The elasticity of supply tells us how the equilibrium price and quantity will change when there is a shift in demand. The diagram shows that a demand shift from DD to $D'D'$ leads to higher price rises and lower quantity rises the more inelastic is supply.

Supply elasticities Along the supply curve SS the supply elasticity is positive. Higher price is associated with higher output. The vertical supply curve $S'S'$ has a zero supply elasticity. The supply curve $S''S''$ has an infinite supply elasticity. Beginning from equilibrium A, a demand shift from DD to $D'D'$ leads to a new equilibrium at B', B, or B'' depending on the elasticity of supply. The more inelastic is supply the more the demand increase leads to higher prices rather than higher quantities. In the extreme cases, the move from A to B' reflects only a price increase and the move from A to B'' reflects only a quantity increase.

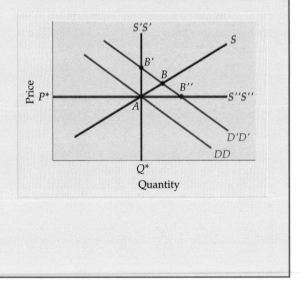

decisions and may not aim primarily to maximize profits. The behaviour of nationalized industries will be discussed in Chapter 18.

Here we are concerned with the decisions of a private profit-maximizing monopolist. Bricks are so heavy that huge transport costs effectively insulate national markets from one another. Since 1968 the London Brick Company has been the sole UK supplier of fletton bricks. Based on a particular clay, these bricks enjoy a substantial cost advantage over all other bricks because their higher carbon content greatly reduces the cost of firing the clay. Other examples of *private* monopolists can be given, but the analysis of this section has a wider significance. Many countries aim to 'privatize' state-run monopolies. The

analysis in the remainder of this chapter illustrates how we might expect such industries to behave when they are restored to private ownership.

9-7 Profit-maximizing output for a monopolist

To maximize profits a firm chooses the output at which marginal revenue MR equals marginal cost MC (SMC in the short run and LMC in the long run). The firm then checks that it is covering average costs ($SAVC$ in the short run and LAC in the long run).

The special feature of a competitive firm is that MR equals price. Selling an extra unit of output does not bid down the price and reduce the revenue earned on previous units. The price at which the extra unit is sold is the change in total revenue.

In contrast, the monopolist's demand curve is the industry demand curve, which slopes down. This implies *MR* is less than the price at which the extra unit of output is sold. The monopolist recognizes that extra output reduces revenue from *previous* units because price falls as we move down the demand curve.

Figure 9-12 reminds you of our previous discussion of the relationship between price, marginal revenue, and total revenue when the demand curve slopes down. The more inelastic the demand curve, the more an extra unit of output will bid down the price and reduce revenue from existing units. At any output, *MR* lies further below the demand curve the more inelastic is demand. Also, the larger the existing output, the larger the revenue loss from existing units when the price is reduced to sell another unit. For a given demand curve, *MR* falls increasingly below price the higher the output level from which we begin.

Beyond a certain output (4 units in Figure 9-12), the revenue loss on existing output exceeds the revenue gain from the extra unit itself. Marginal revenue becomes negative. Further expansion reduces total revenue.

On the cost side, there is only one producer, and the discussion of the cost curves for a single firm in Chapter 8 carries over directly. The monopolist has the usual cost curves, average and marginal, short-run and long-run. For simplicity we discuss only the long-run curves.

There is one other crucial aspect of our definition of monopoly. Not only is a monopoly the sole existing supplier, it need take no account of new entrants to the industry. When existing suppliers take account of the threat of new firms entering the industry they are *not* monopolists.

Profit-maximizing output

In Chapter 7 we showed why setting *MR* equal to *MC* would lead to the profit-maximizing level of positive output. When *MR* exceeds *MC*, an additional unit of output will add more to revenue than to costs and will increase profits. When *MC* exceeds *MR*, the last unit has added more to costs than to revenue. Profits would be increased by cutting back output. When *MR* equals *MC* output is at the profit-maximizing or loss-minimizing level, given that the firm produces anything at all.

Then the monopolist must check whether at this output the price (or average revenue) covers average variable costs in the short run and average total costs in the long run. If not, the monopolist should shut down in the short run and

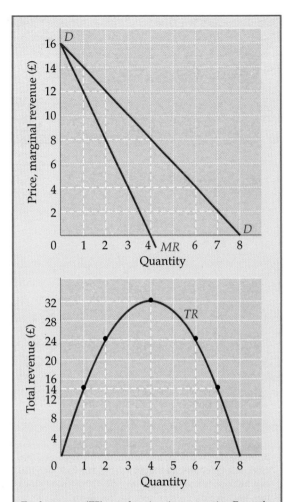

Total revenue (*TR*) equals price times quantity. From the demand curve *DD* we can plot the *TR* curve at each quantity. Maximum *TR* occurs at £32, when 4 units are sold for £8 each. Marginal revenue (*MR*) shows how *TR* changes when quantity is increased a small amount. *MR* lies below the demand curve *DD*. From the price of the extra unit we must subtract the loss in revenue from existing units as the price is bid down. This effect is larger the higher is existing output and the more inelastic is the demand curve. The *MR* curve lies further below *DD* the larger is output and the more inelastic the demand curve. Beyond an output of 4 units, *MR* is negative and further expansion reduces total revenue.

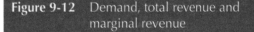

Figure 9-12   Demand, total revenue and marginal revenue

leave the industry in the long run. Table 9-3 summarizes the criteria by which a monopolist decides how much to produce.

Figure 9-13 shows the average cost curve *AC* with its usual U-shape. The marginal cost curve *MC* passes through the lowest point on the *AC* curve. Marginal revenue *MR*

Table 9-3 Monopolists' criteria for maximizing profits

	Marginal condition			Average condition			
				Short-run		Long-run	
	$MR > MC$	$MR = MC$	$MR < MC$	$P \geq SAVC$	$P < SAVC$	$P \geq LAC$	$P < LAC$
Output decision	Raise	Optimal	Lower	Produce	Shut down	Stay	Exit

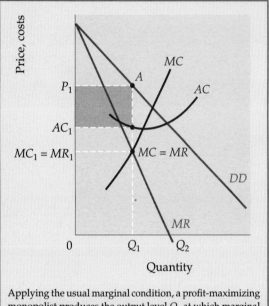

Applying the usual marginal condition, a profit-maximizing monopolist produces the output level Q_1 at which marginal cost MC equals marginal revenue MR. Then it must check that price covers average cost. In this figure, Q_1 can be sold at a price P_1 in excess of average costs AC_1. Monopoly profits are the shaded areas $(P_1 - AC_1) \times Q_1$.

Figure 9-13 The monopoly equilibrium: $MC = MR$

lies below the down-sloping demand curve DD. Setting $MR = MC$, the monopolist chooses the output level Q_1. However, to find the price for which Q_1 units can be sold we must look at the demand curve DD. The monopolist sells Q_1 units of output at a price P_1 per unit. Profit per unit is given by $P_1 - AC_1$, price minus average cost when Q_1 is produced. Total profits are the shaded area $(P_1 - AC_1) \times Q_1$.

Even though we are studying the long run, the monopolist continues to make these *supernormal* profits. They are sometimes called *monopoly* profits.

Supernormal profits are pure profit after making all cost deductions for the opportunity cost of the owner's time and money.

Unlike the competitive industry, supernormal profits of a monopolist are not eliminated in the long run. An industry is a monopoly only if the sole existing supplier need take no account of the possibility of entry. By ruling out the possibility of entry, we remove the mechanism by which supernormal profits tend to disappear in the long run. In Figure 9-13 the monopolist is on to a good thing for ever.

Price-setting Whereas the competitive firm is a *price-taker*, taking as given the equilibrium price determined by the interaction of market supply and market demand, the monopolist actually sets prices and is a price-setter. Having decided to produce Q_1 in Figure 9-13, what the monopolist actually does is to quote a price P_1 knowing that customers will then demand exactly Q_1 units of output.

Elasticity and marginal revenue In Chapter 5 we saw that when the (own-price) elasticity of demand lies between 0 and -1 demand is inelastic and an increase in output will reduce total revenue. Marginal revenue is negative. In percentage terms, the fall in price exceeds the rise in quantity. All outputs to the right of Q_2 in Figure 9-13 have negative MR. The demand curve is inelastic at quantities above Q_2. At quantities below Q_2 the demand curve is elastic. Higher output leads to higher revenue.

The monopolist sets MC equal to MR. Since MC must be positive, so must MR. The chosen output must lie to the left of Q_2. Hence, we say that *a monopolist will never produce on the inelastic part of the demand curve*.

Price, marginal cost, and monopoly power At any output, price exceeds the monopolist's marginal revenue since the demand curve slopes down. Hence, in setting MR equal to MC the monopolist sets a price that exceeds marginal cost. In contrast, a competitive firm always equates price and marginal cost, since its price is also its marginal revenue.

The excess of price over marginal cost is a measure of **monopoly power**.

The competitive firm cannot raise price above marginal cost and has no monopoly power.

Comparative statics for a monopolist

Figure 9-13 may also be used to analyse the effect of changes in costs or demand. Suppose there is a change in costs, for example an increase in input prices, which shifts the MC and AC curves upwards. The higher MC curve must cross the MR curve at a lower level of output. Provided the monopolist can sell this output at a price that covers average costs, the effect of the cost increase must be to reduce output. Since the demand curve slopes down, this reduction in output will be accompanied by an increase in the equilibrium price.

Now suppose for the original cost curves shown in Figure 9-13 that there is an outward shift in demand and marginal revenue curves. MR must now cross MC at a higher level of output. Thus an increase in demand leads the monopolist to increase output.

9-8 Output and price under monopoly and competition

We now compare a perfectly competitive industry with a monopoly. For this comparison to be of interest the two industries must face the same demand and cost conditions. We are interested in how the *same* industry would behave if it were organized first as a competitive industry then as a monopoly.

Clearly this is a tricky comparison. In the next chapter we develop a theory of market structure that aims to explain why some industries are competitive but others are monopolies. If this theory has any content, can it be legitimate to assume that the same industry could be competitive or monopolized? The answer turns out to be yes in some circumstances but no in other circumstances. We now distinguish these two cases.

Comparing a competitive industry and a multi-plant monopolist

Consider a competitive industry in which all firms and potential entrants have the same cost curves. From our earlier discussion of the horizontal $LRSS$ curve for a competitive industry we know this case can be analysed using Figure 9-14.

Facing the demand curve DD, the industry is in long-run equilibrium at A where the price is P_1 and total output is Q_1. The industry $LRSS$ curve is horizontal at P_1, the lowest point on the LAC curve of each firm. Any other price would eventually lead to infinite entry or exit from the industry. $LRSS$ is the industry's long-run marginal cost curve LMC_1 of expanding output by enticing new firms into the industry.

Each firm is producing at the lowest point on its LAC curve and breaking even. Since marginal cost curves pass through the point of minimum average costs, each firm is also on its SMC and LMC curves. Horizontally adding the SMC curves of each firm, we obtain $SRSS$, the short-run industry supply curve. We can regard this as the industry's short-run marginal cost curve SMC_1 of expanding output from existing firms with temporarily fixed factors. Since $SRSS$ crosses the demand curve at P_1, the industry is both in short-run and long-run equilibrium.

Beginning from this position, suppose the competitive industry became a monopoly. The monopolist takes over each plant (firm) but makes centralizing pricing and output decisions.

Overnight the monopolist still has the same number of factories (ex-firms) as in the competitive industry. Since the firm and the industry now coincide, SMC_1 remains the short-run marginal cost curve for the monopolist taking all plants together.[3] However, the monopolist makes centralized decisions which recognize that higher output reduces the revenue earned from previous units.

In the short run the monopolist equates SMC_1 and MR, reaching equilibrium at B. Q_2 units are produced at a price P_2. Relative to competitive equilibrium at A, *the monopolist raises price and reduces quantity*.

In the long run the monopolist can enter or set up new factories and can exit or close down existing factories. Even though the monopolist may be making short-run profits at B (we need to draw in the $SATC$ curve to confirm this) nevertheless, in complete contrast to a competitive industry, the monopolist will decide to exit or retire some factories from the industry in the long run.

The monopolist wants to cut back output to force up the price. Yet in the long run it makes sense to operate each factory at the lowest point on its LAC curve. To reduce total output some factories must be retired. In the long run the monopolist sets LMC_1 equal to MR and reaches the equilibrium position C. *Price has risen yet further to P_3 and output has fallen to Q_3*. Long-run supernormal profits are

---

[3] In a competitive industry each firm equates the given price to its own marginal cost. Hence firms produce at the same marginal cost. Thus we horizontally add individual SMC curves (i.e. at the same price) to get the industry SMC curve. A multi-plant monopolist need not equate MC across all plants but will always find it profitable to do so. Why? If marginal costs in two plants differed, the monopolist could always produce the same total output more cheaply by producing an extra unit in the low MC plant and one less unit in the high MC plant. Thus SMC for the monopolist across all plants remains the horizontal sum of the SMC curves for individual plants, as in a competitive industry.

Before 1997 many countries' domestic markets for telecommunications were heavily regulated. Previous editions of our book often used the national phone company as a good example of a monopoly. Some countries, such as Britain and the United States, had been deregulating telecoms for some time, but the 1997 deal, embracing 68 countries, went much further. For example, the entire European Union (www.eu.int) committed itself to complete liberaliz-ation of basic telecoms, including satellite networks and mobile phones, by 2003. The World Trade Organ-ization (www.wto.org) estimated that the additional trade generated across national borders could be worth 4 per cent of the world's output in the following decade.

The table below shows how much national mon-opolies have been eroded by international competition. It shows how the cost of an off-peak 3-minute long-

distance call came tumbling down during 1995–99 (cost in pence).

This example reminds us of two things. First, many monopolies are the result of government policy to license only one supplier; such policies can change. Second, firm size must always be considered in relation to the relevant market. When technical breakthroughs in telecom technology made the relevant market much larger – satellites are no respecters of national boundaries – the national phone company was suddenly playing in a much larger game. Sooner or later policy-makers have to recognize such realities.

	France	Germany	Italy	Portugal	Spain	UK
1995	25	35	48	56	48	14
1999	18	11	24	25	38	12

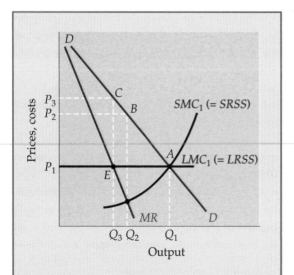

Long-run equilibrium in a competitive industry occurs at A. Total output is Q_1 and the price P_1. A monopolist sets MR equal to SMC_1, restricting output to Q_2 and increasing price to P_2. In the long run the monopolist sets MR equal to LMC_1, reducing output to Q_3 and increasing the price again to P_3. There are no entrants to compete away supernormal profits P_3CEP_1 by increasing the industry output.

Figure 9-14 A monopolist produces a lower output at a higher price

given by the area P_3CEP_1 since P_1 remains the long-run average cost when all plants are at the lowest point on their LAC curve.

Although it is the recognition that MR is less than price that provides the incentive for a monopolist to produce less than a competitive industry and charge a higher price, in this example it is the legal prohibition on entry by competitors that allows the monopolist to succeed in the long run. In a competitive industry supernormal profits are competed away by the new entrants that they attract to the industry. That is why we have insisted that the absence of entry is intrinsic to the model of monopoly we have developed.

The social cost of monopoly Should society mind that a monopolist restricts output and drives price above marginal cost? This is not an issue in positive economics, the description of actual behaviour, but rather an issue in normative economics, which deals in recommendations and policy prescriptions. We deal with such questions at length in Part 3.

At this point we merely sketch how that argument might go. The marginal cost measures the resources used to make the last unit of the good. Since consumers voluntarily buy the good, the price of the good must measure the marginal benefit to consumers of buying the last unit of the good. If the marginal benefit were higher than the price, consumers would buy even more at that price. If the marginal benefit were less than the price, consumers would not demand that last unit at that price.

Society should want to equate the marginal cost of the good and its marginal benefit. If marginal cost is less than marginal benefit, society will be better off with more of the good. Whereas a competitive industry automatically sets marginal cost equal to price (equal to presumed marginal consumer benefit) monopoly does not. It sets marginal cost less than price and, by implication, produces less of the good than society might wish.

Comparing a single-plant monopolist with a competitive industry

In the previous example we examined a multi-plant monopolist who took over a large number of previously competitive firms. Now we examine a monopolist meeting the entire industry demand from a single plant. This is most plausible when there are large economies of scale. There are huge costs in setting up a national telephone network. Yet the cost of connecting a marginal subscriber is low once the network has been set up.

Monopolies enjoying huge economies of scale – falling *LAC* curves over the entire range of output – are called *natural monopolies*. As we shall see in the next chapter, large scale-economies may explain why there is a sole supplier who need not worry about entry. Smaller new entrants would be at a prohibitive cost disadvantage.

Figure 9-15 illustrates the long-run equilibrium for a natural monopoly. In the long run the natural monopoly faces average and marginal cost curves *LAC* and *LMC*. Given the position of the demand curve, *LAC* is declining over the entire range of outputs that might be sold. The monopoly produces at *LMC* equal to *MR*, selling output Q_1 for a price P_1. At this output, price exceeds *LAC*. The monopoly makes supernormal profits and is happy to remain in business.

It does not make sense to compare this equilibrium with how the industry would behave if it were competitive. With such economies of scale, there should be only one firm in the industry. *LAC* is the cost curve for each possible firm. If there were only one firm, it would be crazy not to recognize that its output decisions affected price. If it were stupid enough to try to set price equal to *LMC* it would reach the point *B*, conclude that it was not covering average costs, and leave the industry.[4] If a lot of small firms produced a small

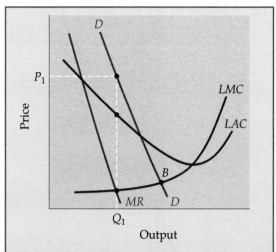

The *LAC* curve is falling throughout the relevant range of output levels. Economies of scale are large relative to the market size. The monopoly produces Q_1 at a price P_1 and makes profits. If it tried to behave like a price-taking competitive firm it would produce at *B* where price equals *LMC* and make losses. By recognizing the effect of output on price the single firm monopoly can do much better. This industry cannot support a lot of small firms. Each would have very high average costs at low output. This cannot be a competitive industry.

Figure 9-15   A natural monopoly with economies of scale

fraction each of total demand, their average costs would be enormous. A single large firm could undercut them and wipe them out. This industry must have a sole supplier, and that natural monopoly will maximize profits only by recognizing that its marginal revenue is not its price.

It is this insight that we develop in the next chapter to provide a general theory of market structure. Turning to the normative issue, society may still be interested in forcing the monopolist to produce at a price closer to marginal cost. In the extreme case, society might order the monopoly to price at marginal cost, produce at the point *B*, make losses, and receive a government subsidy. We return to this issue in Part 3.

9-9 The absence of a supply curve under monopoly

A competitive firm sets price equal to marginal cost if it supplies at all. If we know its marginal cost curve we know

---

[4] From Chapter 8 we know that marginal cost lies below average cost at all points left of the point of minimum average cost. Since the *LAC* curve is still falling in Figure 9-15 it must lie above *LMC*. Pricing at marginal cost *must* yield losses at point *B*.

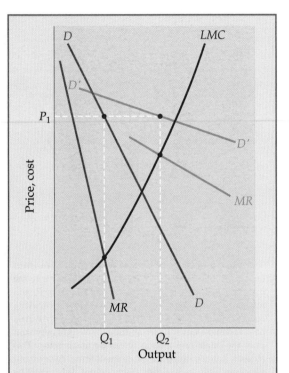

Given the demand curve *DD* and the corresponding marginal revenue curve *MR*, the monopolist produces Q_1 at a price P_1. However, facing $D'D'$ and MR', the monopolist produces Q_2 at a price P_1. Knowing the price, we cannot uniquely infer the quantity supplied unless we also know demand and marginal revenue. Because the monopolist knows that output affects both marginal cost and marginal revenue, the two must be considered simultaneously.

Figure 9-16   Absence of a supply curve under monopoly

how much it supplies at each price. Aggregating across firms, we also know how much the industry supplies at each price. We can draw the supply curve without knowing anything about the market demand curve. We then analyse how supply and demand interact to determine equilibrium price and quantity.

The monopolist recognizes that output affects marginal cost and marginal revenue simultaneously. Figure 9-16 shows a given *LMC* curve. How much will the monopolist produce at the price P_1? It all depends on demand and marginal revenue. When demand is *DD* and the corresponding marginal revenue *MR*, the monopolist produces Q_1 and charges a price P_1. However, when demand is $D'D'$ and marginal revenue MR', the monopolist produces Q_2 but still charges P_1.

The monopolist does not have a supply curve independent of demand conditions. What we can say is that the

monopolist simultaneously examines demand (hence marginal revenue) and cost (hence marginal cost) when deciding how much to produce and what to charge.

Discriminating monopoly

Thus far we have assumed that all consumers must be charged the same price, although this price will depend on the level of output and the position of the demand curve. Unlike a competitive industry, where competition prevents any individual firm charging more than its competitors, a monopolist may be able to charge different prices to different customers.

A **discriminating monopoly** can charge different prices to different people.

This is attractive when it can identify different types of customer whose demand curves are quite distinct.

Consider an airline monopolizing flights between London and Rome. It has business customers whose demand curve is very inelastic. They have to fly. Their demand and marginal revenue curves are very steep. The airline also carries tourists whose demand curve is much more elastic. If flights to Rome get too expensive tourists can holiday in Athens instead. Tourists have much flatter demand and marginal revenue curves.

Recall why the marginal revenue curve lies below the demand curve. Adding an extra unit of output and sales bids down the price for which existing output can be sold. The more inelastic is the demand curve the more the marginal revenue curve must lie below the demand curve because the higher will be the reduction in revenue from existing output units.

Suppose the airline charges tourists and business travellers the same price. From the separate demand curves we can read off at each price the number of each type of traveller and add these to obtain the total number of travellers at each price. However since the demand curve of business travellers is less elastic, the marginal revenue obtained from the last business traveller must be lower than the marginal revenue obtained from the last tourist.

Whatever the total number of passengers (and hence total cost of carrying them), the airline is carrying the wrong *mix* between tourists and business travellers. Since the marginal revenue from the last tourist exceeds the marginal revenue from the last business traveller the airline would gain revenue without adding to cost by carrying the same number of passengers but carrying more of the group with the higher marginal revenue and less of the group with the lower marginal revenue. And it will pay to keep changing

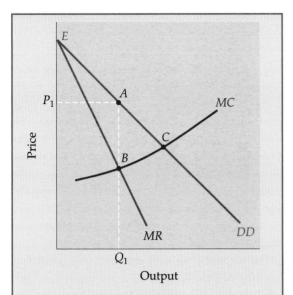

Charging all customers the same price the monopolist will produce at B where MC = MR. If each output unit can be sold for a different price, the revenue from existing units is not reduced by cutting the price to sell another unit. The demand curve DD is the marginal revenue curve and the perfectly discriminating monopolist will produce at C. Output is higher and profits are higher. By price discrimination the monopolist gains an extra revenue EP_1A from selling Q_1 but also increases output beyond this level making a marginal profit of ABC in expanding from A to C.

Figure 9-17   Perfect price discrimination

between London and Brussels, almost exclusively an expense account business trip, are among the highest in Europe, but package holidays are much cheaper. Rail companies charge rush-hour commuters a higher fare than midday shoppers whose demand for trips to the city is much more elastic.

Many of the best examples of price discrimination refer to services which must be consumed on the spot rather than to goods which can be resold. Price discrimination in a standardized commodity is unlikely to work. The group buying at the lower price have an incentive to resell to the group paying the higher price thus undercutting the attempt to charge some customers a higher price. Effective price discrimination is feasible only when the submarkets can be isolated from one another to prevent resale.

What does price discrimination have to do with the absence of a supply curve under monopoly? Figure 9-17 illustrates this most clearly for the case of *perfect price discrimination* where we assume that it is actually possible to charge each and every customer a different price for the same good.

Suppose first that the monopolist charges every customer the same price. The profit-maximizing output is Q_1 where MR equals MC and the corresponding price is P_1.

Now suppose the monopolist can perfectly price discriminate, charging a different price for each unit of output sold. The very first can be sold for a price E. Having sold this output to the highest bidder, the customer most desperate for the good, the next unit can be sold to the next highest bidder and so on. As we move down the demand curve DD we can read off the price for which each extra unit can be sold. However, in reducing the price to sell that extra unit, the monopolist no longer reduces revenue from previously sold units. *Hence the demand curve is the marginal revenue curve under perfect price discrimination*. The marginal revenue of the last unit is simply the price for which it can be sold.

Treating DD as the marginal revenue curve we conclude that a perfectly price discriminating monopolist will produce at point C where marginal revenue and marginal cost are equal. Two points follow immediately. First, if price discrimination is possible it is profitable to employ it. In moving from the uniform pricing point A to the price discriminating point C the monopolist adds the area ABC to profits. This represents the excess of additional revenue over additional cost when output is increased. But the monopolist makes a second gain from price discrimination. Even the output Q_1 now brings in more revenue than under uniform pricing. The monopolist also gains the area EP_1A by

the mix until the marginal revenue of the two groups is equated.

To do this, the airline must charge the two groups *different* prices. Since tourist demand is elastic the airline wants to charge tourists a low fare to increase tourist revenue. Since business demand is inelastic the airline wants to charge business travellers a high fare to increase business revenue.

Profit-maximizing output will satisfy two separate conditions. First, business travellers with inelastic demand will pay a fare sufficiently higher than tourists with elastic demand that the marginal revenue from the two separate groups is equated. Then there is no incentive to rearrange the mix by altering the price differential between the two groups. Second, the general level of prices and the total number of passengers will be determined to equate marginal cost to both these marginal revenues. This ensures that the airline operates on the most profitable scale as well as with the most profitable mix.

When a producer charges different customers different prices we say that the producer *price discriminates*. There are many examples of this in the real world. Air fares per mile

being able to charge different prices on the first Q_1 units of output rather than the single price P_1. In practice, when firms call in economic consultants one of the main ways these consultants manage to increase the profits of the firm is by devising new ways in which the firm can price discriminate.

Second, whether or not the firm is able to price discriminate affects the output it will choose to produce even if demand and cost conditions remain unaltered. Earlier in this section we said there was no unique supply curve relating output to price for a monopolist. We also had to know the elasticity of the demand curve and hence how far marginal revenue would lie below the price. Figure 9-17 shows it is not even sufficient to know the total demand curve facing a firm. In addition we need to know whether the market can be segmented enough to allow price discrimination. Uniform and discriminatory pricing will lead to very different outputs because they affect the marginal revenue obtained from any given total demand curve facing a monopolist.

9-10 Monopoly and technical change

In Section 9-8 we compared a monopoly and a perfectly competitive industry. When such a comparison was meaningful we discovered two things: (1) a monopoly will restrict output and drive up prices; and (2) in consequence a monopoly will make economic profits in the short run, and need not fear the erosion of these profits by entrants in the long run.

Joseph Schumpeter (1883–1950) argued that this comparison ignores the possibility of technical advances, which reduce costs and may allow price reductions and output expansion. A large monopolist with steady profits may find it much easier to fund the research and development (R&D) necessary to make cost-saving breakthroughs. Second, and completely distinct, a monopolist may have a greater *incentive* to undertake R&D.

In a competitive industry a firm with a technical advantage has only a temporary opportunity to earn high profits to recoup its research expenses. Imitation by existing firms and new entrants gradually compete away any supernormal profits. In contrast, by shifting down all its cost curves, a monopoly may be able to enjoy higher supernormal profits for ever. Schumpeter argued that these two forces – greater resources available for R&D and a higher potential return on any successful venture – tend to make monopolies more innovative than competitive industries. Taking a dynamic long-run view, rather than a snapshot static picture, monopolists tend to enjoy lower cost curves which lead them to charge lower prices thereby increasing the quantity demanded.

This argument has some substance. Very small firms typically do little R&D. Many of the largest firms have excellent research departments. Many small firms complain about the problem of trying to raise bank loans for risky research projects. Nevertheless, the Schumpeter argument may overstate the case.

Most Western economies operate a *patent* system. Inventors of new processes acquire a temporary legal monopoly for a fixed period. By temporarily excluding entry and imitation the patent laws increase the incentive to conduct R&D without establishing a monopoly in the long run. Over the patent life the inventor can charge a higher price and make handsome profits. Eventually the patent expires and competition from other firms leads to higher output and lower prices. The real price of copiers and microcomputers fell significantly when the original patents of Xerox and IBM expired.

The patent laws can provide an R&D incentive even in industries that are not permanent monopolies. Nor does the empirical evidence show unusually high R&D expenditure in industries that are monopolies. What the evidence does show is that small firms do little research. But above a certain size of firm there is no further correlation between the size of the firm and its research expenditure.

SUMMARY

● In a competitive industry each buyer and seller acts as a price-taker, believing that individual actions have no effect on the market price. Competitive supply is most plausible when a large number of firms make a standard product under conditions of free entry and exit from the industry, and customers can easily verify that the products of different firms really are the same.

● For a competitive firm, marginal revenue and price coincide. Output is chosen to equate price to marginal cost. The firm's supply curve is its *SMC* curve above *SAVC*. At any lower price the firm temporarily shuts down. In the long run, the firm's supply curve is its *LMC* curve above its *LAC* curve. At any lower price the firm eventually leaves the industry.

● Adding at each price the quantities supplied by each firm, we obtain the industry supply curve. It is flatter in the long run both because each firm can fully adjust all factors and because the number of firms in the industry can vary. In the extreme case where all potential and existing firms have identical costs, the long-run industry supply curve is horizontal at the price corresponding to the lowest point on each firm's *LAC* curve.

● An increase in demand leads to a large price increase but only a small increase in quantity. The existing firms move up their steep *SMC* curves. Price exceeds average costs and the ensuing profits attract new entrants. In the long run output increases still further but the price falls back. In the long-run equilibrium the marginal firm makes only normal profits and there is no further change in the number of firms in the industry.

● An increase in costs for all firms reduces the industry's output and increases the price. In the long run the marginal firm must break even. A higher price is required to match the increase in its average costs.

● Markets for the same good in different countries will be closely linked if transport costs are small and there are no trade restrictions. In a competitive world market each country takes the world price of the commodity as given. Discrepancies between domestic supply and domestic demand are met through imports or exports. Foreign trade transmits foreign shocks to the domestic economy but acts as a shock absorber for domestic shocks.

● A pure monopoly is the only seller or potential seller of a good and need not worry about entry even in the long run. Though rare in practice, this case offers an important benchmark against which to compare less extreme forms of monopoly power.

● A profit-maximizing monopolist has a supply rule: choose output to set *MC* equal to *MR*, but not a supply curve uniquely relating price and output. The relation of price and *MR* depends on the demand curve.

● Where a monopoly and a competitive industry can meaningfully be compared, the monopolist produces a smaller output at a higher price. However, natural monopolies with large economies of scale could not exist as competitive industries.

● A discriminating monopolist charges different prices to different customers. To equate the marginal revenue from different groups, groups with an inelastic demand must pay a higher price. Successful price discrimination requires that customers cannot trade the product among themselves.

● Monopolies may have more internal resources available for research and may have a higher incentive for cost-saving research because the profits from technical advances will not be eroded by entry. Although small firms do not undertake much expensive research, it appears that the patent laws provide adequate incentives for medium- and larger-sized firms. There is no evidence that an industry has to be a monopoly to undertake cost-saving research.

REVIEW QUESTIONS

1 Draw a diagram such as Figure 9-9 showing the position of a competitive firm and the industry in long-run equilibrium. Suppose this is the wool industry. The development of artificial fibres reduces the demand for wool by the clothing industry. Show what happens in the short run and the long run if all sheep farmers have identical costs. What happens if there are high-cost and low-cost sheep farmers?

2 Suppose the wheat crop is hit by a drought. Explain the adjustment in the price of wheat in the short run and the long run. How is the price of bread affected in the short run and the long run?

3 A country can trade at given world prices. Draw the domestic supply and demand curves. Show a price that would make the country an importer of the good. The government now taxes imports adding to their price in the domestic market. Show what happens to the quantities demanded and supplied in the domestic market. What happens to the quantity of imports?

4 The table shows the demand curve facing a monopolist who produces at a constant marginal cost of £5.

Price (£)	9	8	7	6	5	4	3	2	1	0
Quantity	0	1	2	3	4	5	6	7	8	9

Calculate the monopolist's marginal revenue curve. What is the equilibrium output? What is the equilibrium price? What would be the equilibrium price and output for a competitive industry? Explain in words why the monopolist produces a lower output and charges a higher price.

5 Now suppose that, in addition to the constant marginal cost of £5, the monopolist has a fixed cost of £2. What difference does this make to the monopolist's output, price, and profits? Why do we get this answer?

6 The Royal Economic Society in the UK has different membership rates for students, university lecturers, and professional economists working outside universities. Why do you think the RES pursues this policy?

7 *Common fallacies* Show why the following statements are incorrect: (a) Since competitive firms break even in the long run there can be no incentive to be a competitive firm. (b) Monopolists always make profits. (c) By introducing a law to break up every monopoly into smaller companies society could always obtain more output at a lower price. (d) Perfect competition is possible only if all firms face the same cost curves.

10 Market structure and imperfect competition

When you have finished this chapter, you should be able to:

● Define imperfect competition, oligopoly, and monopolistic competition
● Show how differences in cost and demand lead to different market structures
● Analyse the tangency equilibrium in monopolistic competition
● Consider the tension between collusion and competition within a cartel
● Analyse games, and define the concepts of commitment and credibility
● Explain why there is little market power in a contestable market
● Define innocent entry barriers and analyse how strategic entry barriers can be created

Perfect competition and pure monopoly are useful benchmarks of extreme kinds of market structure. Most markets lie somewhere between these two extremes. In nearly half the 800 major product categories in UK manufacturing 70 per cent of the market is shared by the five largest firms in the industry.

What determines the structure of a particular market? Why are there 10 000 florists but only a handful of chemical producers? How does the structure of an industry affect the behaviour of its constituent firms?

A perfectly competitive firm faces a horizontal demand curve at the going market price. It is a price-taker. Any other type of firm faces a downward sloping demand curve for its product and is called an *imperfectly competitive* firm.

An **imperfectly competitive firm** cannot sell as much as it wants at the going price. It must recognize that its demand curve slopes down and that its output price will depend on the quantity of goods produced and sold.

For a pure monopoly the demand curve for the firm is the industry demand curve itself. We now distinguish two intermediate cases of an imperfectly competitive market structure, an *oligopoly* and a *monopolistically competitive* industry.

An **oligopoly** is an industry with only a few producers, each recognizing that its own price depends not merely on its own output but also on the actions of its important competitors in the industry. An industry with **monopolistic competition** has many sellers producing products that are close substitutes for one another. Each firm has only a limited ability to affect its output price.

In most countries the car industry is a good example of an oligopoly. The price Rover can charge for its cars depends not only on its own production levels and sales, but also on the decisions taken by major competitors such as Ford and Toyota. The corner grocer's shop is a good example of a monopolistic competitor. Its output is a subtle package of physical goods such as jars of coffee, personal service and extra convenience for those customers who live nearby.

Table 10-1	Market structure			
	Number of firms	Ability to affect price	Entry barriers	Example
Perfect companies	Many	Nil	None	Fruit stall
Imperfect competition:				
Monopolistic competition	Many	Small	None	Corner shop
Oligopoly	Few	Medium	Some	Cars
Monopoly	One	Large	Huge	Post Office

It can charge a few pence more for a jar of coffee than the supermarket in the main shopping area some distance away. But, if prices are higher by more than a few pence, even shoppers who live nearby will make the trip to the supermarket.

As with most definitions, the lines between these types of market structure are a little blurred. A major reason is the ambiguity about the relevant definition of the market. Is British Gas a monopoly in gas or an oligopolist in energy? Similarly, when a country trades in a competitive world market, even the sole domestic producer may have little influence on market price. We can never fully remove these ambiguities, but Table 10-1 shows some things to bear in mind as we proceed through this chapter. Notice that the table includes the ease with which new firms can enter the industry. This has a crucial bearing on the ability of existing firms to maintain high prices and supernormal profits in the long run.

10-1 Why market structures differ

We have already drawn attention to the influence of government legislation on market structure. Some industries are legal monopolies, the sole licensed producers. Patent laws may confer temporary monopoly on producers of a new process. Ownership of a raw material may confer monopoly status on a single firm. We now develop a general theory of how the economic factors of demand and cost interact to determine the likely structure of each industry.

The car industry is not an oligopoly one day but perfectly competitive the next. It is long-run influences that induce different market structures. Similarly, although a particular firm may have a temporary advantage in technical know-how or workforce skill, in the long run one firm can hire another's workers and learn its technical secrets. In the long run all firms or potential entrants to an industry essentially have access to the same cost curves.

Figure 10-1 shows the demand curve DD for the output of an industry. Suppose first that in the long run all firms and potential entrants face the average cost curve LAC_1. At the price P_1, free entry and exit ensures that each firm produces q_1. Given the demand curve DD, the industry output is Q_1 and the industry can support N_1 firms where $N_1 = Q_1/q_1$. If q_1, the minimum average cost output on LAC_1, lies sufficiently far to the left relative to DD, then N_1 will be a very large number of firms. Each firm will have a trivial effect on industry supply and market price. We have discovered a perfectly competitive industry.

Now suppose that each firm has the cost curve LAC_3. Economies of scale are very large relative to the market size. The lowest point on LAC_3 occurs at an output large relative to the demand curve DD. Suppose initially there are two producers each producing q_2. Market output Q_2 is twice as large. The market clears at P_2 and both firms break even. However, if one firm expands a little its average costs will fall. It will also bid the price down. With lower average costs, that firm will survive and the other firm will lose money. The firm that expands will gobble up the whole market, undercut its competitor, and eventually drive the other firm out of business.

Such an industry is a natural monopoly. Suppose that Q_3 is the output at which its marginal cost and marginal revenue coincide. The price is P_3 and the natural monopoly makes supernormal profits. Yet there is no room in the industry for other firms with access to the same LAC_3 curve. A new entrant needs a large output to get average costs down. Extra output on this scale would so depress the price that both firms would make losses. The potential entrant is powerless to break in.

A **natural monopoly** enjoys such scale economies that there is no fear of entry by others.

Finally, we show the LAC_2 curve with more economies of scale than a competitive industry but fewer than a natural monopoly. This industry will support at least two firms enjoying economies of scale near the lowest point of their LAC_2 curves. It will be an oligopoly. Attempts to expand either firm's output beyond q_4 quickly encounter decreasing

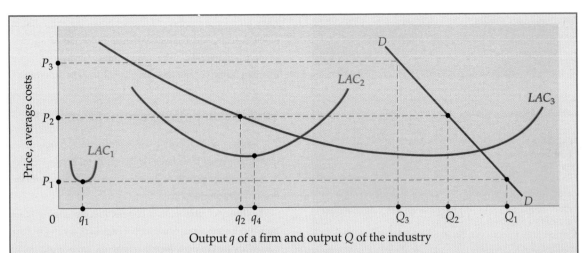

DD is the industry demand curve. In a competitive industry, minimum efficient scale occurs at an output level q_1 when firms have average cost curves LAC_1. The industry can support a very large number of firms whose total output is Q_1 at the price P_1. When LAC_3 describes average costs, the industry will be a natural monopoly. When a single firm produces the entire industry output, no other firm can break into the market and make a profit. For intermediate positions such as LAC_2 the industry can support a few firms in the long run, and no single firm can profitably meet the entire demand. The industry will be an oligopoly.

Figure 10-1   Demand, costs, and market structure

Table 10-2   Demand, costs, and market structure

Minimum efficient scale relative to market size		
Tiny	Intermediate	Large
Perfect competition	Oligopoly	Natural monopoly

returns to scale and prevent it from expanding to drive its competitor out of business.

The **minimum efficient scale** is the output at which a firm's long-run average cost curve stops falling.

The crucial determinant of market structure is the output at minimum efficient scale relative to the size of the total market as represented by the demand curve. Table 10-2 summarizes our discussion. It is the interaction of market size and the output at minimum efficient scale that matters. When the demand curve shifts to the left, an industry previously supporting many firms may have room for only a few. Similarly, an increase in fixed costs which increases the output at minimum efficient scale will reduce the number of producers. In the 1950s there were a large number of European aircraft manufacturers. Today, the research and development costs of a major commercial airliner are enormous. Apart from the co-operative European venture Airbus Industrie, subsidized by European governments, only the American giant Boeing-McDonnell-Douglas survives.

Monopolistic competition lies midway between oligopoly and perfect competition. But it is the fact that monopolistic competitors all supply slightly different products, such as the location in which you shop, that makes them special.

Evidence on market structure

The larger the minimum efficient scale relative to the market size, the fewer will be the number of plants – and probably the number of firms – in the industry. What is the number of plants (NP) operating at minimum efficient scale that the current market size could allow? In Chapter 8 we discussed how economists have tried to estimate the minimum efficient scale for plants in different industries. By looking at the total quantity of consumption of a product we can estimate the market size. Hence we can construct estimates of NP for each industry.

How do we measure how many firms there are in an industry? Even industries that essentially have only a few very large firms may have some small firms on the fringe. The number of firms in the industry tells us nothing about their size or importance. It might be a misleading indicator of the essential structure of the industry. For this reason, economists use the N-firm concentration ratio to measure the number of important firms in the industry.

Table 10-3	Concentration and scale economies in three European countries					
	UK		France		Germany	
Industry	CR	NP	CR	NP	CR	NP
Refrigerators	65	1	100	2	72	3
Cigarettes	94	3	100	2	94	3
Petroleum refining	79	8	60	7	47	9
Brewing	47	11	63	5	17	16
Fabrics	28	57	23	57	16	52
Shoes	17	165	13	128	20	197

CR = % market share of 3 largest firms; NP = markets size divided by output of minimum efficient scale.
Sources: F. M. Scherer et al., *The Economics of Multiplant Operation*, Harvard University Press, 1975, and F. M. Scherer, *Industrial Market Structure and Economic Performance*, Rand McNally, 1980.

The **N-firm concentration ratio** is the market share of the largest N firms in the industry.

Thus the 3-firm concentration ratio tells us the percentage of the total market supplied by the largest three firms in the industry. If there are basically only three firms that matter, they will supply almost the whole market for the product. If the industry is perfectly competitive, the largest three firms will still account for only a tiny share of the total market for the product.

Table 10-3 looks at the evidence for the UK, France, and Germany. CR is the 3-firm concentration ratio, the market share of the top three firms. NP is the number of plants at minimum efficient scale which the market size would allow. Nothing guarantees that all plants are being operated at minimum efficient scale. Nevertheless, if our theory of market structure is correct, industries with large economies of scale relative to the market size – a very low value of NP – should exhibit a large CR. Such industries should have only a few important firms. Conversely, where NP is very high, economies of scale are relatively unimportant and the largest three firms should control a much smaller market share. CR should be much lower.

Table 10-3 confirms that our theory of market structure is compatible with the facts. In industries such as refrigerator and cigarette manufacture there is room for only very few plants operating at minimum efficient scale, and these industries exhibit high degrees of concentration. The largest three firms control almost the whole market. Economies of scale are still substantial in industries such as brewing and petroleum refining and the top three firms control around half the market. Industries such as shoe manufacture quickly encounter rising average cost curves; they have room for a large number of factories operating at minimum efficient scale, and consequently are much closer to competitive industries. The top three firms in shoe manufacturing control less than one-fifth of the market.

10-2 Monopolistic competition

The essence of oligopoly is interdependence. Large firms must guess what their large rivals are up to. Before turning to this exciting branch of economic analysis, however, we begin with a simpler case.

The theory of monopolistic competition envisages a large number of quite small firms so that each firm can neglect the possibility that its own decisions provoke any adjustment in other firms' behaviour. We also assume free entry and exit from the industry in the long run. In these respects the framework resembles our earlier discussion of *perfect* competition. What distinguishes monopolistic competition is that each firm faces a *downward*-sloping demand curve.

Monopolistic competition describes an industry in which each firm can influence its market share to some extent by changing its price relative to its competitors. Its demand curve is not horizontal because different firms' products are only limited substitutes. We have given one example, the location of corner grocers. A lower price attracts some customers from another shop, but each shop will always have some local customers for whom the convenience of a nearby shop is more important than a few pence on the price of a jar of coffee.

Monopolistically competitive industries exhibit *product differentiation*. For corner grocers this differentiation is based on location, but in other cases it is based on brand loyalty. The special features of a particular restaurant or hairdresser may allow that firm to charge a slightly different price from other producers in the industry without losing all its customers.

Although brand loyalty and product differentiation may also be important in many other industries these need not be monopolistically competitive. Brand loyalty limits the substitution between Ford and Rover in the car industry but, with so few producers, the key feature of the industry remains the oligopolistic interdependence of the decisions of different firms. Monopolistic competition requires not merely product differentiation, but also limited opportunities for economies of scale so that there are a great many producers who can largely neglect their interdependence with any particular rival. Many examples of monopolistic competition are service industries where economies of scale are small.

BOX 10-1 — Packaging holidays

In the UK the market for package summer holidays is now worth £7bn a year as people jet off in search of sand and sun. Whereas in 1986 the top 5 chains of travel agents had a combined market share of 25%, by 1998 this had soared to 87%. Evidence of huge economies of scale? Not necessarily.

The industry has been integrating vertically, as travel agents (retail outlets) combine with tour operators (producers of airline and hotel services). Vertical integration can cut costs by allowing better coordination between different stages of the production chain, but it can also enhance market power. The two largest tour operators (Thomson (www.thomson-holidays.com) and Airtours (www.airtours.com)) now own the two largest travel agents (Lunn Poly and Going Places). These two firms have a market share of 49%.

The market leaders have been accused of unfair practices. In 1996 Lunn Poly refused to display brochures of First Choice for four months until a new agreement on commissions for travel agents was reached. Small operators claimed to have to pay up to 19% commission to Lunn Poly, while Thomson paid only 10%. Thomson and Airtours argued that their size allowed them to keep prices lower, and that smaller competitors couldn't compete.

UK package tours (% market share 1998)	
Thomson (www.thomson-holidays.com)	28
Airtours (www.airtours.com)	21
Thomas Cook (www.thomascook.com)	19
First Choice (www.firstchoice.co.uk)	17
Other	15

Sources: *Financial Times*, 8 November 1996; *Observer*, 19 September 1999.

The industry demand curve shows the total industry output which would be demanded at each price if every firm in the industry charged that price. The market share of each firm depends on the number of firms in the industry and on the price it charges. For a given number of firms, a shift in the industry demand curve will shift the demand curve for the output of each individual firm. For a given industry demand curve, an increase (decrease) in the number of firms in the industry will shift the demand curve of each firm to the left (right) as its market share falls (rises). But each firm faces a downward-sloping demand curve. For a given industry demand curve, number of firms, and price charged by all other firms, a particular firm can increase its market share to some extent by charging a lower price.

Figure 10-2 shows the supply decision of a firm. Given its own demand curve DD and marginal revenue curve MR the firm produces Q_0 at a price P_0 making short-run profits equal to $Q_0 \times (P_0 - AC_0)$. In the long run these profits attract new entrants, who dilute the market share of each firm in the industry, shifting their demand curves to the left. Entry stops when each firm's demand curve has shifted so far to the left that price equals average cost and firms are just breaking even. In Figure 10-2 this occurs when demand has

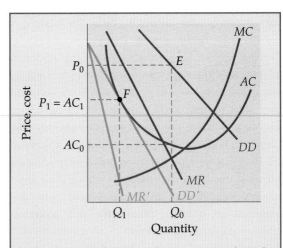

In the short run the monopolistic competitor faces the demand curve DD and sets MC equal to MR to produce Q_0 at a price P_0. Profits are $Q_0 \times (P_0 - AC_0)$. Profits attract new entrants and shift each firm's demand curve to the left. When the demand curve reaches DD' we reach the long-run tangency equilibrium at F. The firm sets MC equal to MR' to produce Q_1 at which P_1 equals AC_1. Firms are breaking even and there is no further entry.

Figure 10-2 Equilibrium for a monopolistic competitor

shifted to DD' and the firm produces Q_1 at a price P_1 to reach the tangency equilibrium at F.

In monopolistic competition the long-run **tangency equilibrium** occurs where each firm's demand curve is tangent to (just touches) its AC curve at the output level at which MC equals MR. Each firm is maximizing profits but just breaking even. There is no further entry or exit.

Notice two things about the firm's long-run equilibrium at F. First, the firm is *not* producing at minimum average cost. It has excess capacity. It could reduce average costs by further expansion. However, its marginal revenue would be so low this would not be profitable. Second, the firm retains some monopoly power because of the special feature of its particular brand or location. Price exceeds marginal cost.

This helps explain why firms are usually eager for new customers prepared to buy additional output at the *existing* price. It explains why we are a race of eager sellers and coy buyers. It is purchasing agents who get Christmas presents from sales reps, not the other way round. Remarkably enough, under perfect competition the firm does not care if another buyer shows up at the existing price. With price equal to marginal cost, the firm is already selling as much as it wants.

The theory of monopolistic competition yields interesting insights when there are many goods each of which is a close but not perfect substitute for the other. For example, it explains why Britain exports Jaguars and Rovers to Germany and Sweden but simultaneously imports Volvos and Mercedes. There are large economies of scale in making cars. In the absence of trade the domestic car market would have room for only a few varieties. Producing a large number of brands at low output would enormously raise average costs. International trade allows each country to specialize in a few types of car and produce a much larger output of that brand than the home market alone could support. By swapping these cars between countries, consumers get a wider choice while each individual producer enjoys economies of scale, holding prices down.

10-3 Oligopoly and interdependence

Under perfect competition or monopolistic competition, there are so many firms in the industry that no single firm need worry about the effect of its own actions on rival firms. However, the essence of an oligopolistic industry is the need for each firm to consider how its own actions affect the decisions of its relatively few competitors.

Although in the last chapter we used a hypothetical example of a *monopoly* airline, in practice of course airlines are oligopolists. Even on the popular transatlantic routes, British Airways, Air France, and Virgin have significant market shares, and the position of each of their demand curves depends crucially on how their rivals behave and can be induced to behave. In contemplating a cut-price deal, each airline needs to consider whether or not other airlines will follow suit. When new airlines try to break into the market by offering cheap fares – Laker in the 1970s and People's Express in the 1980s – these entrants' prospects depend on how existing airlines respond. Laker, for example, miscalculated how other airlines would react, failing to foresee the extent to which they would cut prices to drive it out of business.

What makes oligopoly so fascinating is that the supply decision of each firm depends on its guess about how its rivals will react. Exciting recent developments in economics shed important insight into what constitutes a smart guess. First, however, we introduce the basic tension between competition and collusion in all oligopolistic situations.

Collusion is an explicit or implicit agreement between existing firms to avoid competition with one another.

Initially, for simplicity, we neglect the possibility of entry and focus only on the behaviour of existing firms.

The profits from collusion

The existing firms will maximize their *joint* profits if they behave as if they were a multi-plant monopolist. A monopolist or sole decision-maker would organize the output from the industry to maximize total profits. Hence, if the few producers in an industry collude to behave as if they were a monopolist, their *total* profit will be maximized.

Figure 10-3 shows an industry where each firm, and the entire industry, has constant average and marginal costs at the level P_c. In the last chapter we saw that a competitive industry would produce Q_c at a price P_c but a multi-plant monopolist would maximize profits by producing Q_m at a price P_m. If the oligopolists collude jointly to produce Q_m we say they are acting as a *collusive monopolist*. Having thus decided industry output, there will then be some negotiation backstage to divide up output and profits between individual firms.

However, it is hard to stop individual firms cheating on the collective agreement. In Figure 10-3 joint profit is maximized when aggregate output is restricted to Q_m and the price forced up to P_m. Yet each firm can expand at marginal cost P_c. If one firm expands production by under-cutting the agreed price P_m, its profits will rise since its

marginal revenue will exceed its marginal cost. But this firm's gain is at the expense of its collusive partners. Industry output is higher than Q_m, total profits are lower, and other firms suffer.

Hence oligopolists are torn between the desire to collude, thus maximizing joint profits, and the desire to compete, in the hope of increasing market share and profits at the expense of rivals. Yet if all firms compete, joint profits will be low and no firm is likely to do very well. Therein lies the dilemma.

Cartels

Collusion or co-operation between firms is easiest when formal agreements are legally permitted. Such arrange- ments are called *cartels*. In the late nineteenth century cartels were common, and they agreed market shares and prices in many industries. Such practices are now outlawed in Europe, the United States, and many other countries. Although there are usually large penalties for being caught, informal agreements and secret deals in smoke-filled rooms are not unknown even today.

The most famous cartel is OPEC, the Organization of Petroleum Exporting Countries. Active since 1973, its members meet regularly to set price and output levels. Initially, OPEC was very successful in organizing quantity reductions to force up the price of oil. Real OPEC revenues rose 500 per cent between 1973 and 1980. Yet almost from

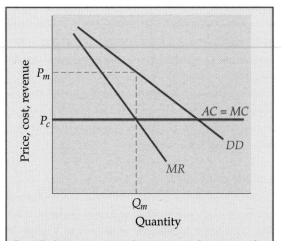

By colluding to restrict industry output Q_m, joint profits are maximized and equal to those which a multi-plant monopolist would obtain. But each firm, with a marginal cost of P_c, has an incentive to cheat on the collusive agree- ment and expand its output.

Figure 10-3 Collusion versus competition

the start, many economists predicted that OPEC, like most cartels, would quickly collapse. Usually, the incentive to cheat is too strong to resist, and once somebody breaks ranks others tend to follow.

In practice, one reason OPEC was successful for so long was the willingness of Saudi Arabia, the largest oil producer, to restrict its output further when smaller members insisted on expansion. By 1986 Saudi Arabia was no longer prepared to play by these rules, and refused to prop up the price any longer. The oil price collapsed from just under $30 to $9 a barrel. Since then, apart from a brief period during the Gulf War, oil prices have fluctuated between $10 and $20 a barrel. OPEC has never recovered the cohesion it had during 1973–85.

The oligopoly kinked demand curve

Collusion is much harder if there are many firms in the industry, if the product is not standardized, and if demand and cost conditions are changing rapidly. In the absence of collusion, each firm's demand curve depends on how competitors react. Firms must guess how their rivals will behave. Before undertaking a serious analysis of how firms might make intelligent guesses, we introduce a simple model which highlights the key feature of this inter- dependence.

Suppose that each firm believes that its own price cut will be matched by all other firms in the industry but that an increase in its own price will induce no price response from competitors. Figure 10-4 shows the demand curve DD that each firm would then face. The current price is P_0 and the firm is producing Q_0. Since competitors do not follow suit, a price increase will lead to a large loss of market share to other firms. The firm's demand curve is elastic above A at prices above the current price P_0. Conversely, a price cut is matched by other firms and market shares are unchanged. Sales increase only because the industry as a whole moves down the market demand curve as prices fall. The demand curve DD is much less elastic for price reductions from the initial price P_0.

The key feature of Figure 10-4 is that the marginal revenue curve MR is discontinuous at the output Q_0. Below Q_0 the elastic part of the demand curve is relevant, but at the output Q_0 the firm hits the inelastic portion of its kinked demand curve and marginal revenue suddenly falls. Q_0 is the profit-maximizing output for the firm, given its belief about how competitors will respond.

The model has one important implication. Suppose the MC curve of a single firm shifts up or down by a small amount. Since the MR curve has a discontinuous vertical

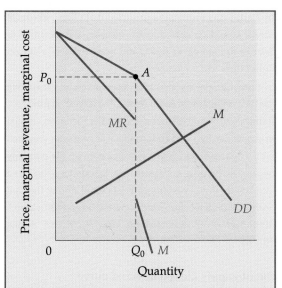

An oligopolist believes rivals will match price cuts but not price rises. The oligopolist's demand curve is kinked at A. Price rises lead to a large loss of market share, but price cuts increase quantity only by increasing industry sales. Marginal revenue is discontinuous at Q_0. The oligopolist produces Q_0, the output at which MC crosses the MR schedule.

Figure 10-4   The kinked demand curve

10-4 Game theory and interdependent decisions

A good poker player sometimes bluffs. Sometimes you can clean up with a bad hand, provided your opponents misread it for a good hand. Similarly, by having bluffed in the past and been caught, you may persuade them to keep betting even when you have a terrific hand.

Like poker players, oligopolists have to try to second-guess their rivals' moves to determine their own best action. To study how such interdependent decisions are made, we use *game theory*.

A **game** is a situation in which intelligent decisions are necessarily interdependent.

The *players* in the game try to maximize their own *payoffs*. In an oligopoly, the firms are the players and their payoffs are their profits in the long run. Each player must choose a strategy.

A **strategy** is a game plan describing how the player will act or move in every conceivable situation.

Being a pickpocket is a strategy. Lifting a particular wallet is a move.

As usual, we are interested in equilibrium. In most games, each player's best strategy depends on the strategies chosen by other players. It is silly to be a pickpocket in an area where the police have TV cameras. Equilibrium occurs when each player chooses the best strategy, *given* the strategies being followed by other players. This description of equilibrium, invented by John Nash, is called Nash equilibrium. Nobody wants to change their strategy, since other people's strategies have already been figured into the calculation of each player's best strategy.

Sometimes, but not usually, a player's best strategy is independent of those chosen by others. If so, it is called a *dominant strategy*. We begin with an example in which each player has a dominant strategy.

Collude or cheat?

Figure 10-5 shows a game[1] which we can imagine is between the only two members of a cartel like OPEC. Each firm can select a high-output or low-output strategy. In each box of Figure 10-5 the coloured number shows firm A's

segment at the output Q_0, it will remain optimal to produce Q_0 and charge the price P_0. In contrast, a monopolist facing a continuously downward-sloping MR curve would adjust quantity and price when the MR curve shifted. The kinked demand curve model may explain the empirical finding that firms do not always adjust prices when costs change.

It does not explain what determines the initial price P_0. One interpretation is that it is the collusive monopoly price. Each firm believes that an attempt to undercut its rivals will provoke them to co-operate among themselves and retaliate in full. However, its rivals will be happy for it to charge a higher price and see it lose market share.

One advantage of interpreting P_0 as the collusive monopoly price is that it contrasts the effect of a cost change for a single firm and a cost change for all firms. The latter will shift the marginal cost curve up for the industry as a whole and increase the collusive monopoly price. Each firm's kinked demand curve will shift upwards since the monopoly price P_0 has increased. Thus we can reconcile the stickiness of a single firm's prices with respect to changes in its own costs alone, and the speed with which the entire industry marks up prices when all firms' costs are increased by higher taxes (as in the cigarette industry) or inflationary wage settlements in the whole industry.

---

[1] The game is usually called the Prisoners' Dilemma, because it was first used to analyse the choices facing two people arrested and in different cells, each of whom could plead guilty or not guilty to the only crime that had been committed. Each prisoner would plead innocent if only he or she knew the other would plead guilty.

profits and the black number, firm B's profits for that output combination.

When both have high output, industry output is high, the price is low, and each firm makes a small profit of 1. When each has low output, the outcome is more like the collusive monopoly of Figure 10-3. Prices are high and each firm does better, making a profit of 2. Each firm does best (a profit of 3) when it alone has high output; for then, the other firm's low output helps hold down industry output and keep up the price. In this situation we assume the low-output firm makes a profit of 0.

Now we can see how the game will unfold. Consider firm A's decision. If firm B has a high-output strategy, firm A does better also to have high output. In the two left-hand boxes of Figure 10-5, firm A gets a profit of 1 by choosing high but a profit of 0 by choosing low. Now suppose firm B chooses a low-output strategy. From the two right-hand boxes. Firm A still does better by choosing high, since this yields it a profit of 3 whereas low yields it a profit of only 2. Hence firm A has a dominant strategy. Whichever strategy B adopts, A does better to choose a high-output strategy.

Firm B also has a dominant strategy to choose high output. Use Figure 10-5 to check for yourself that B does better to go high whichever strategy A selects. Since both firms choose high, the equilibrium is the top left-hand box. Each firm gets a profit of 1.

Yet both firms would do better, getting a profit of 2, if they colluded to form a cartel and both produced low – the bottom right-hand box. But neither can afford to take the risk of going low. Suppose firm A goes low. Firm B, comparing the two boxes in the bottom row, will then go high, preferring a profit of 3 to a profit of 2. And firm A will

get screwed, earning a profit of 0 in that event. Firm A can figure all this out in advance, which is why its dominant strategy is to go high.

This is a particularly clear illustration of the tension between collusion and competition. In this example, it appears that the output-restricting cartel will never get formed, since each player can already foresee the overwhelming incentive for the other to cheat on such an arrangement. How then can cartels ever be sustained? One possibility is that there exist binding pre-commitments.

A **pre-commitment** is an arrangement, entered into voluntarily, which restricts one's future options.

If both players in Figure 10-5 could simultaneously sign an enforceable contract to produce low output they could achieve the co-operative outcome in the bottom right-hand box, each earning profits of 2. Clearly, they then do better than in the top left-hand box, which describes the non-co-operative equilibrium of the game. Without any pre-commitment, neither player can go low because then the other player will go high. Binding pre-commitments, by removing this temptation, enable both players to go low, and both players gain.

This idea of pre-commitment is important, and we shall encounter it many times. Just think of all the human activities that are the subject of legal contracts, a simple kind of pre-commitment simultaneously undertaken by two parties or players.

Although this insight is powerful, its application to oligopoly requires some care. Cartels within a country are usually illegal, and we don't seriously believe that OPEC is held together by a signed agreement which could be upheld in international law! Is there some less formal way in which oligopolists can pre-commit themselves not to cheat on the collusive low-output solution to the game?

If the game is played only once, this may be difficult. In the real world, the game is repeated many times: firms choose output levels day after day. Suppose two players try to collude on low output. Furthermore, each announces a *punishment strategy*. Should firm A ever cheat on the low-output agreement, firm B promises that it will subsequently react by raising its output. Firm A makes a similar promise.

Suppose the agreement has been in force for some time and both firms have stuck to their low-output deal. Firm A assumes that firm B will go low as usual. Figure 10-5 shows that firm A will make a *temporary* gain today if it cheats and goes high. Instead of staying in the bottom right-hand box with a profit of 2, it can move to the top right-hand box and make 3. However, from tomorrow onwards, firm B will also

		Firm B output			
		High		Low	
Firm A output	High	1	1	3	0
	Low	0	3	2	2

The coloured and black numbers in each box indicate profits to firms A and B, respectively. Whether B pursues high or low output, A makes more profit going high; so does B, whichever A adopts. In equilibrium both go high. Yet both would make greater profits if both went low!

Figure 10-5 The Prisoners' Dilemma Game

BOX 10-2   Rubber cartel collapses

In February 1999 Thailand, the world's largest rubber producer, decided to pull out of the International Natural Rubber Organization, claiming that INRO had failed to prop up rubber prices adequately. Thailand complained that large members of INRO had borne too much of the burden of trying to hold down production to boost prices.

---

go high, and firm A can then do no better than continue to go high too, making a profit of 1 for evermore. But if A refuses to cheat today it can continue to stay in the bottom right-hand box and make 2 forever. In cheating, A is swapping a temporary gain for a permanent reduction in profits, and it may well conclude that this is a poor deal. Thus, punishment strategies can sustain an explicit cartel or implicit collusion even when no formal mechanism of pre-commitment exists.

It is all very well to say that you will adopt a punishment strategy in the event that the other player cheats. But you can expect this to have an effect on the other player's behaviour only if your threat is not an empty one.

A **credible threat** is one which, after the fact, you would then find it optimal to carry out.

In the preceding example, once firm A has cheated and gone high, it is then in firm B's interest to go high anyway. Hence a threat to go high if A ever cheats is a credible threat.

Let us see if we can use these insights to interpret the actual behaviour of OPEC in 1986, when Saudi Arabia dramatically raised its output leading to a collapse of oil prices. During the 1980s, other members of OPEC had gradually cheated on the low-output agreement, trusting that Saudi Arabia would continue to produce low, and perhaps even cut its output, to sustain a high price and the cartel's prestige. They hoped Saudi threats to adopt a punishment strategy were empty threats. And they were wrong. Figure 10-5 shows that, once the others go high, Saudi Arabia may as well go high too. Moreover, since the top left-hand box is clearly less desirable than the bottom right-hand box, the Saudi action may then have persuaded other players to return to the co-operative low-output solution. If so, the temporary period of high output and low prices was a good investment for the Saudis, and was a good reason why its punishment strategy should have been viewed as a credible threat. Although OPEC never regained its position of the 1970s, the Saudi's action did at least ensure that the cartel continued to survive.

10-5 Entry and potential competition

So far in this chapter we have discussed imperfect competition between existing firms. To complete our understanding of such markets, we must also think about the effect of potential competition from new entrants to the industry on the behaviour of existing or incumbent firms. Three cases must be distinguished: where entry is trivially easy, where it is difficult by accident, and where it is difficult by design.

Contestable markets

In the previous chapter we saw that free entry to, and exit from, the industry was a key feature of perfect competition, a market structure in which each firm is tiny relative to the industry. Suppose, however, that we observe an industry with few incumbent firms. Before assuming that our previous analysis of oligopoly will be required, we must think hard about entry and exit. It is possible that this industry is a contestable market.

A **contestable market** is characterized by free entry and free exit.

By free entry, we mean that all firms, including both incumbents and potential entrants, have access to the same technology and hence have the same cost curves. By free exit, we mean that there are no *sunk* or irrecoverable costs; on leaving the industry, a firm can fully recoup its previous investment expenditure, including money spent on building up knowledge and goodwill.

A contestable market allows *hit-and-run* entry. If the incumbent firms, however few, are not behaving as if they were a perfectly competitive industry at long-run equilibrium ($p = MC = $ minimum AC), an entrant can step in, undercut them, and make a temporary profit before quitting again.

The theory of contestable markets is controversial. There are many industries in which sunk costs are hard to recover or where the initial expertise may take an entrant some time

BOX 10-3

Freezing out new entrants?

Unilever (www.unilever.com) is a major player in many consumer products from toothpaste to soap powder. One of its big winners is Wall's ice cream, which has two thirds of the UK market and generates profits of £100 mn/year; retailers' markups can also be as high as 55%. In addition to established rivals such as Nestlé (www.nestle.com) and Haagen Dazs (www.haagen.dazs.com), Unilever has faced new challenges from frozen chocolate bars. Mars has 18% of the market.

A critical aspect of these 'bar wars' is the freezer cabinets in which small shops store ice cream. As the leading incumbent, Unilever, 'loans' these cabinets free of charge to small retailers. Unilever has contended that its high market share reflects its marketing expertise (just one Cornetto); Mars has argued that Unilever erected strategic barriers to entry, particularly effective in small shops that have space for only one freezer cabinet, by requiring that only Unilever products were stocked in the cabinet they loaned to retailers.

In January 2000 the UK government finally ordered Unilever to stop freezing out competitors.

Source: *Economist*, 13 January 1996.

to acquire, placing it at a temporary disadvantage against incumbent firms. Nor, as we shall shortly see, is it safe to assume that incumbents will not change their behaviour when threatened by entry. But the theory does vividly illustrate that market structure and incumbent behaviour cannot be deduced simply by counting the number of firms in the industry.

In the previous chapter, we were careful to stress that a monopolist is a sole producer *who can completely discount fear of entry*. We now refine the classification of Table 10-1 by discussing entry in more detail.

Innocent entry barriers

Our discussion of entry barriers distinguishes those that occur anyway and those that are deliberately erected by incumbent firms.

An **innocent entry barrier** is one not deliberately erected by incumbent firms.

In his pioneering study in 1956, the American economist Joe Bain highlighted three types of entry barrier: product differentiation, absolute cost advantages, and scale economies. The first of these is not an innocent barrier, as we shall shortly explain. Absolute cost advantages, where incumbent firms have lower cost curves than those that entrants will face, may be innocent. If it takes time to learn the business, incumbents will face lower costs, at least in the short run; if they are smart, they may already have located in the most advantageous site. In contrast, if incumbents have undertaken investment or R&D specifically with a

view to deterring entrants, this is not an innocent barrier. We take up this issue shortly.

Figure 10-1 showed the role of scale economies as an innocent entry barrier. If minimum efficient scale is large relative to the industry demand curve, an entrant cannot get into the industry without considerably depressing the market price, and it may prove simply impossible to break in at a profit.

The greater are such innocent entry barriers, the more appropriate it will be to neglect potential competition from entrants. The oligopoly game then reduces to competition between incumbent firms along the lines we discussed in the previous section. Where innocent entry barriers are low, one of two things may happen. Either incumbent firms accept this situation, in which case competition from potential entrants will prevent incumbent firms from exercising much market power – the outcome will be closer to that of perfect competition – or else incumbent firms will try to design some entry barrier of their own.

10-6 Strategic entry deterrence

We defined a strategy as a game plan when decision-making is interdependent. The word 'strategic' is used in everyday language, but it has a precise meaning in economics.

A **strategic move** is one that influences the other person's choice, in a manner favourable to one's self, by affecting the other person's expectations of how one's self will behave.

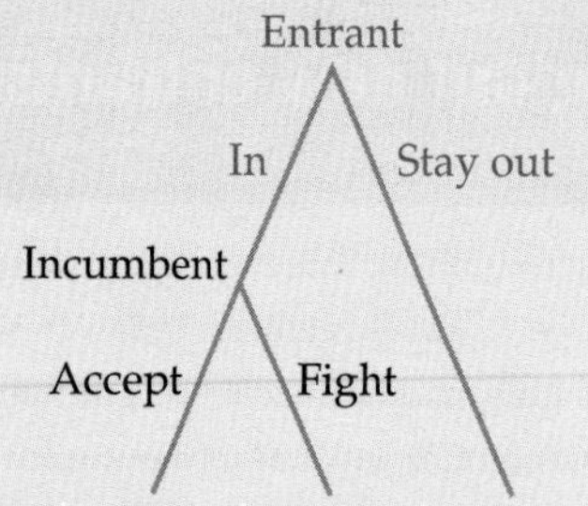

In the absence of deterrence, if the entrant enters, the incumbent does better to accept entry than to fight. The entrant knows this and enters. Equilibrium is the top left-hand box, and both firms make a profit of 1. But if the incumbent pre-commits an expenditure of 3 which is recouped *only* if there is a fight, the incumbent resists entry, the entrant stays out, and equilibrium is the bottom right-hand box. The incumbent does better, making a profit of 2.

Figure 10-6 Strategic entry deterrence

We have already introduced pre-commitment as a strategy move, and we now extend that idea to entry deterrence.

To do so we use Figure 10-6. For simplicity, there is only one incumbent firm and the game is against a potential entrant. The entrant can choose to come in or stay out. If the entrant comes in, the incumbent can either opt for the easy life, accept the new rival, and agree to share the market – or it can fight. If the entrant is large, the easy life may actually involve an output reduction by the incumbent, so that the two firms' joint output will not depress the price too much. Fighting entry means producing at least as much as before, and perhaps considerably more than before, so that the industry price collapses. In this *price war*, sometimes called *predatory pricing* by the incumbent, both firms do badly and make losses. The top row of boxes in Figure 10-6 show the profits to the incumbent (in black) and the entrant (in colour) in each of the three possible outcomes.

If the incumbent is unchallenged it does very well, making profits of 5. The entrant of course makes nothing. If they share the market, both make small profits of 1. In a price war, both make losses. How should the game go?

Suppose the entrant comes in. Comparing the left two boxes of the top row, the incumbent does better to cave in than to fight. The entrant can figure this out. Any threat by the incumbent to resist entry is not a credible threat – when it comes to the crunch, it will be better to cave in. Much as

the incumbent would like the entrant to stay out, in which case the incumbent would make profits of 5, the equilibrium of the game is that the entrant will come in and the incumbent will not resist. Both make profits of 1, the top left-hand box.

The incumbent, however, may have got its act together before the potential entrant appears on the scene. It may be able to invent a binding pre-commitment which forces itself to resist entry and thereby scares off any future challenge. The incumbent would be ecstatic if a Martian appeared and guaranteed to shoot the incumbent's directors if they ever allowed an entry to be unchallenged. The entrants would expect a fight, would anticipate a loss of 1, and would stay out, leaving the incumbent with a permanent profit of 5.

In the absence of Martians, the incumbent may be able to achieve the same effect by economic means. For example, suppose the incumbent invests in spare capacity. This capacity is expensive, and is unused at low output. The incumbent has low output in the absence of entry or if an entrant is accommodated without a fight. Suppose in these situations the incumbent loses 3 by carrying this excess capacity. The second row of boxes in Figure 10-6 reduces the incumbent's profits by 3 in these two outcomes. In a price war, however, the incumbent's output is high and the spare capacity is no longer wasted; hence we do not need to reduce the incumbent's profit in the middle column of boxes in Figure 10-6. Now consider the game again.

If the entrant comes in, the incumbent loses 2 by caving in but only 1 by fighting. Hence entry is resisted. Foreseeing this, the entrant does not enter, since the entrant loses money in a price war. Hence the equilibrium of the game is the bottom right-hand box and no entry takes place. Strategic entry deterrence has been successful. It has also been profitable. Even allowing for the cost of 3 of carrying the spare capacity, the incumbent still makes a profit of 2, which is better than the profit of 1 in the top left-hand box when no deterrence was attempted and the entrant came in.

Strategic entry deterrence is behaviour by incumbent firms to make entry less likely.

Does deterrence always work? No. Suppose in Figure 10-6 we change the right-hand column. In the top row the incumbent gets a profit of 3 if no entry occurs. Without the pre-commitment, the equilibrium is the top left-hand box as before. But if the incumbent has to spend 3 on a spare capacity pre-commitment, it now makes a profit of 0 in the bottom right-hand box when entry is deterred. The entrant is still deterred, but the incumbent would have done better not to invest in spare capacity but to let the entrant in.

BOX 10-4 Why advertise so much?

Advertising is not always intended to erect entry barriers to potential new producers. Sometimes it really does aim to influence consumers, not so much by trying to influence their tastes as by acting as a channel for revealing the inside information that producers have about the quality of their own goods.

When consumers can tell at a glance the quality of the product, even before they buy it, there is not much to be gained by advertising. Rotten bananas go black and it is futile to advertise them as fresh. Information is freely available, and any attempt to deceive consumers is instantly detected. However, for most goods consumers cannot detect quality before they buy, but find this out only after using the good for a while.

Now the firm has inside information over first-time buyers. A conspicuous (expensive) advertising campaign *signals* to potential consumers that the firm believes in its product and expects to make repeat sales for a long time to recoup the fixed cost of initial advertising. Firms that know that customers will soon discover they have been misled about quality do not invest much in advertising. It does not take consumers long to decide if they are satisfied with a particular brand of biscuit.

Some goods have to be used for a very long time before consumers can establish their true quality. Even if Magicbrand toothpaste really does give you stronger teeth, you can hardly confirm this in a few weeks. Consumers now have a lot to gain from truthful advertising, but lying advertisers could get away with

it for quite a while. The solution for producers who know they have good products is to raise the stakes and commit a lot of money to advertising. This can make sense only if they expect the product to be successful for a very long time, long enough for consumers to discover the truth. It rules out hit-and-run advertising, whereby lying advertisers expect to quit before consumers discover the truth.

Finally, what about goods like refrigerators, which are essentially a once-off purchase, usually not replaced for a decade or more? Consumers would really love truthful advertising, which would have a big benefit for them, but producers of high-quality goods have no incentive to advertise. In such a situation it would pay lying advertisers to advertise too (since it will be a long time till they are found out), so a willingness to advertise no longer signals that a product must be high-quality. But that was the reason for advertising in the first place. So little advertising occurs.

Much of modern economics emphasizes the costs of acquiring information. Signalling is often employed by those who want to convey their own above-average quality. We shall meet this idea again in Chapter 13 when discussing the incentive to go to university. First, we confirm that the theory helps us understand advertising. The table below shows advertising spending as a fraction of sales revenue for the four types of good identified above. The theory fits the facts rather well.

Advertising spending as a percentage of sales revenue for four types of good			
Quality detected	Time until purchase again	Examples	Advertising as % of sales revenue for these goods
Before purchase	Irrelevant	Bananas, posters	0.4
Soon after purchase	Soon	Biscuits, stationery	3.6
Long after purchase	Irrelevant	Fridge, CD player	1.8

Source: E. Davis, J. Kay, and J. Star, 'Is Advertising Rational?', *Business Strategy Review*, Autumn 1991, Oxford University Press.

We can extend this analysis in two ways. First, the above model suggests that price wars should never happen. If the incumbent is really going to fight, then the entrant should not have entered. This of course requires that the entrant knows accurately the profits of the incumbent in the different boxes and therefore can correctly predict its behaviour. In the real world, entrants sometimes get it wrong. Moreover, if the entrant has much better financial backing than the incumbent, a price war may be a good investment for the entrant. The incumbent will exit first, and thereafter the entrant will be able to cash up and get its losses back with interest.

Second, is spare capacity the only kind of pre-commitment available to incumbents? Pre-commitments must be irreversible, otherwise they are an empty threat; and they must increase the chances that the incumbent will fight. Generally, anything with the character of fixed and sunk costs will be of interest: fixed costs artificially increase scale economies and make the incumbent more keen on high output, and sunk costs cannot be reversed. Advertising to invest in goodwill and brand loyalty is a good example. So is product proliferation. If the incumbent has only one brand, an entrant may hope to break in with a different brand. But if the incumbent has a complete range of brands or models, an incumbent will have to compete across the whole product range.

10-7 Summing up

Few industries in the real world closely resemble the textbook extremes of perfect competition and pure monopoly. Most are imperfectly competitive. In this chapter, we have introduced you to some developments in how to think about imperfect competition. Game theory in general, and notions such as pre-commitment, credibility, and deterrence in particular, have allowed economists to analyse many of the practical concerns of big business.

What have we learned? First, market structure and the behaviour of incumbent firms are determined *simultaneously*. Economists used to start with a market structure, determined by the extent of scale economies relative to the industry demand curve, then deduce how the incumbent firms would behave (monopoly, oligopoly, perfect competition), then check out these predictions against performance indicators, such as the extent to which prices exceeded marginal cost. Now we realize that strategic behaviour by incumbent firms can affect entry, and hence market structure, except where entry is almost trivially easy.

Second, and related, we have learned the importance of *potential* competition, which may come from domestic firms considering entry, or from imports from abroad. The number of firms observed in the industry today conveys little information about the extent of the market power they truly exercise. If entry is very easy, even a single incumbent or apparent monopolist may find it unprofitable to depart significantly from perfectly competitive behaviour.

Finally, we have seen how many business practices of the real world – price wars, advertising, brand proliferation, excess capacity or excessive research and development – can be understood as strategic competition in which, to be effective, threats must be made credible by precommitments.

SUMMARY

● Imperfect competition exists when individual firms believe they face downward-sloping demand curves. The most important forms are monopolistic competition, oligopoly, and pure monopoly.

● Pure monopoly status can be conferred by legislation, as when an industry is nationalized or a temporary patent is awarded. When minimum efficient scale is very large relative to the industry demand curve, this innocent entry barrier may be sufficiently high to produce a natural monopoly in which all threat of entry can be ignored.

● At the opposite extreme, entry and exit may be costless. The market is contestable, and incumbent firms must mimic perfectly competitive behaviour, otherwise they would be undercut by a flood of entrants. With intermediate degrees of innocent entry barrier, the industry is likely to be an oligopoly.

● Monopolistic competitors face free entry and exit to the industry, but are individually small and make similar though not identical products. Each has limited monopoly power in its special brand. In long-run equilibrium, price equals average cost but exceeds marginal revenue and marginal cost at the tangency equilibrium.

● Oligopolists face a tension between collusion to maximize joint profits and competition for a larger share of smaller joint profits. Collusion may be formal, as in a cartel, or informal. Without credible threats of punishment by other collusive partners, each firm faces a temptation to cheat.

● Game theory describes interdependent decision-making in which each player chooses a strategy. In the Prisoners' Dilemma game, each firm has a dominant strategy but the outcome is disadvantageous to both players. With binding pre-commitments, both could be better off by guaranteeing not to cheat on the collusive solution.

● Innocent entry barriers are made in heaven, and arise from scale economies or absolute cost advantages of incumbent firms. Strategic entry barriers are made in boardrooms and arise from credible pre-commitments to resist entry if challenged. Only in certain circumstances is strategic entry deterrence profitable for incumbents.

KEY TERMS

◆ Imperfect competition   149

◆ Oligopoly   149

◆ Monopolistic competition   149

◆ Natural monopoly   150

◆ Minimum efficient scale   151

◆ N-firm concentration ratio   152

◆ Tangency equilibrium   154

◆ Collusion   154

◆ Game   156

◆ Strategy   156

◆ Pre-commitment   157

◆ Credible threat   158

◆ Contestable market   158

◆ Innocent entry barrier   159

◆ Strategic move   159

◆ Strategic entry deterrence   160

REVIEW QUESTIONS

1 An industry faces the demand curve:

Price	1	2	3	4	5	6	7	8	9	10
Quantity	10	9	8	7	6	5	4	3	2	1

(a) Suppose it is a monopolist whose constant MC equals 3: what price and output are chosen? (b) Now suppose there are two firms, each with $MC = AC = 3$: what price and output will maximize joint profits if they collude? (c) Why do the two firms have to agree on the output each will produce? (d) Why might each firm be tempted to cheat if it can avoid retaliation by the other?

2 Suppose in the above problem the two firms, call them A and Z, begin with half the market each when charging the monopoly price. Z decides to cheat and believes A will stick to its old output level. (a) Show the demand curve Z believes it faces. (b) What price and output would Z then choose? (c) How is A likely to respond if Z does cheat in this way?

3 Go back to problem 1 with a sole supplier producing at $MC = AC = 3$. Suppose there are potential entrants who can produce at $MC = AC = 5$. (a) What price will the sole supplier charge? (b) If entry became prohibited, what would the sole supplier do?

4 Vehicle repairers have sometimes suggested that mechanics should be licensed so that repairs are done only by qualified people. Some economists argue that customers can always ask whether a mechanic was trained at a reputable institution without needing to see any licence. (a) Evaluate the arguments for and against licensing car mechanics. (b) Are the arguments the same for licensing doctors?

5 Think of five adverts on television. Do you think their function is primarily informative, or the erection of entry barriers to the industry?

6 A good-natured parent knows that children sometimes need to be punished, but also knows that, when it comes to the crunch, the child will be let off with a warning. Can the parent undertake any pre-commitment to make the threat of punishment credible?

7 *Common fallacies* Show why the following statements are incorrect: (a) Competitive firms should get together to restrict output and drive up the price. If they don't do this they cannot be maximizing profits. (b) Firms wouldn't advertise unless they expected it to increase sales. (c) Monopoly power is measured by the extent to which firms can raise price above marginal costs. Average costs don't come into it. Hence market structure has nothing to do with economies of scale.

11 The information economy

The computer you use is probably driven by a chip made by Intel (www.intel.com). The boss of Intel is fond of saying: 'There is no such thing as an internet company. All companies will be internet companies'. Electronic commerce is booming. Revenues from e-commerce are forecast to rise during 1999–2002 from £70 billion to £550 billion in the United States, and from £13 billion to £150 billion in Western Europe. Just as the service economy displaced the industrial economy in the 20th century, the information economy will dominate the 21st century.

A century ago, fortunes were made in railways, mining, and the oil business. Then people like Richard Branson became rich in the service sector. But the richest person on the planet is currently Bill Gates of Microsoft (www.microsoft.com). When he is overtaken, it is likely to be by someone in the e-business. The information revolution is

here. It is big business, and changing people's lives in remarkable ways. Yet the laws of economics continue to provide a reliable framework in which to understand what is going on. This chapter is about microeconomics in action.

First, we discuss the key attributes of information products. Then we examine how consumers and producers of these products behave, and hence how the market will develop. How does competition occur? What forms of pricing and other strategic behaviour emerge?

11-1 E-products

Table 11-1 documents the rise of the internet. Table 11-2 illustrates the dramatic cost reductions that e-commerce can achieve in distributing business products. Figure 11-1 compares the stock market value of four companies: the US

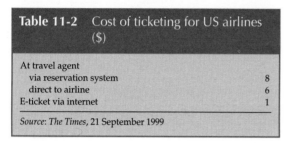

Table 11-1	Business use of the internet			
	1997	1999	2001	2003
Business to business (£bn)	<5	40	320	1130
Business to consumer (£bn)	<5	10	60	150
Millions of devices	100	210	400	720
Milliions of users	100	190	320	490

Source: Financial Times, 24 March 1999.

Table 11-2	Cost of ticketing for US airlines ($)
At travel agent	
via reservation system	8
direct to airline	6
E-ticket via internet	1

Source: The Times, 21 September 1999

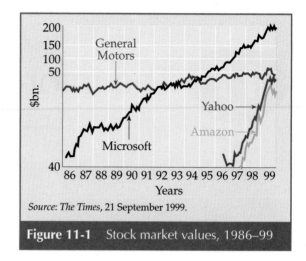

Source: The Times, 21 September 1999.

Figure 11-1   Stock market values, 1986–99

industrial giant, General Motors (www.generalmotors.com), Microsoft, the internet search engine Yahoo! (www.yahoo.co.uk), and the internet book distributor Amazon (www.amazon.com). General Motors has already been overtaken by Microsoft. In a handful of years, Yahoo! and Amazon have almost caught up. Electronic information products are booming.

An **e-product** can be digitally encoded then transmitted rapidly, accurately and cheaply.

Examples include music, films, magazines, news, books, and sport. Information is expensive to assemble and produce but very cheap to distribute. The fixed cost of creating a usable product is large, the marginal cost of distributing it is tiny. This cost structure implies vast scale economies in production. We discuss the implications for market structure and competition in Section 11-3. Before that, we examine the key attributes of information products as viewed by users. Table 11-1 shows that these users or consumers of information are not merely households but businesses themselves.

11-2 Consuming information

From the viewpoint of users, e-products have four key features: experience, overload, switching costs, and network externalities.

Experience
We first encountered experience in Box 10-4 on page 161, where we discussed its role in explaining advertising expenditure. Information is an experience product.

An **experience good or service** is one that must be sampled before the user knows its value.

The first time we try something we find out how useful it is to us. Most goods and services that we buy are repeat purchases. We no longer buy them just to find out what they are like. What is different about information is that it is nearly always new. If we already had the information, we would not need to buy it! We say 'nearly always' because we all have a favourite film or sporting contest that we like to watch more than once. People buy videos of Manchester United's Cup triumph to watch over and over again, but rent videos or suspense thrillers from Blockbuster (www.blockbuster.co.uk), from whom a new thrill is rentable the next night.

The importance of experience in assessing the demand for information products gives rise to many familiar tactics of suppliers, who look for ways to whet your appetite without revealing so much of their information that there is then no need for you to buy it. Free samples, previews, headlines, opportunities to browse are marketing tactics for experience goods and services. Suppose you supply such a product. If you don't give any free samples, people may never discover how great your product really is. But how do you decide how many free samples to give away?

To keep things simple, suppose the marginal cost of reproducing the information product is zero, so your only aim is to maximize revenue. Giving away more samples reduces sales you might have made today but, by raising awareness of the quality of your product, enhances the demand for your product in the future. You give away free copies up to the point at which the marginal loss of sales revenue today equals the (present value of) the marginal revenue you obtain from induced extra sales in the future.

BOX 11-1 — Been here, got the e-shirt

The production and distribution of information dates back to the first conversation between our most primitive ancestors. Distribution costs have been falling ever since. The printing press slashed costs – think of those monks previously transcribing by hand – and so did the postal service and the telephone. Mail order catalogues are a century old. Browsing did not begin on the internet, it has merely been taken to another dimension. The information economy is different not merely because the distribution costs are dramatically lower but because the distribution of information is now interactive. Customers can manipulate the information they receive and follow-up questions can be processed instantly and cheaply.

A second way in which suppliers of experience products increase the demand for their output, and make a market in information itself, is through branding and reputation. Think first of a one-off deal. Do you want to buy a particular piece of information that costs £100? Without seeing the information, you do not know what it is worth; but, having seen it, you no longer need to buy it! If every deal were a one-off, sellers would face big temptations to rip off customers and customers would be so wary that few trades would ever take place. Firms invest in reputation (by previous good behaviour) in order to earn trust that yields returns in the present and the future. The demand curve for their products is higher the higher the reputation they have previously established.

Information overload

Families that get two Sunday newspapers rarely read the six sections in each paper. On the internet, the problem is compounded many times. There is so much information available, it is hard to know where to start. Box 1-4 on page 10 highlighted information overload as one of the fault lines running through central planning in the Soviet bloc. Search is much easier when someone else has narrowed down the options for you. Rich people looking for a house don't spend weeks driving round Knightsbridge and Belgravia. They hire an agent to narrow things down, and look only at the agent's shortlist. Similarly, when a firm is seeking to fill a top management post, it often employs a specialist 'headhunter' to produce a shortlist of suitable candidates.

Just as the agent can charge a fee for the screening service, so suppliers of internet screening have a valuable product that they can sell. Search engines such as Yahoo! are among the most visited websites on the internet, and hence offer valuable opportunities to advertisers. Similarly, the data-

base of users is a scarce commodity that other firms may be willing to purchase.

Information overload arises when the volume of available information is large but the cost of processing it is high. Screening devices are then very valuable.

Pre-screening explains why makers of yachts advertise in yachting magazines not football club fanzines. In effect, the internet allows the yacht producer to target customers even more accurately. One reason why internet firms may supply services without charge is that their register of customers, with customers' permission, can be retailed not just to advertisers but to others doing internet business. Similarly, the next time you buy a TV and complete your personal details on the 'free' guarantee form, just remember that the guarantor is really 'purchasing' information about TV customers – where they live, and what they spend. This information helps other businesses target their sales more accurately. It is a valuable commodity.

Switching costs

Whereas compilation of a customer database may provide a permanent reason to subsidize an information product, a second motive is strictly temporary. Suppliers may provide free services during some initial period in order to lock users into a particular supplier. Such users face switching costs.

Switching costs arise when existing costs are sunk. Changing supplier then incurs additional costs.

If Britain had to start from scratch, it might decide to drive not on the left but on the right. British cars would no longer be different from those in continental Europe. Manufacturers would find it much harder to charge British people premium prices for cars if similar cars could be easily and cheaply imported across the channel. However, the UK has made many investments in driving on the left. Any switch would entail changing street signs and motorway slip roads, scrapping most of the existing stock of left-hand-drive cars, and teaching drivers to do things the other way round. During the transition there would be accidents as well as expense. Even though Britons would benefit from cheaper right-hand-drive cars, switching costs may be so high that it is better to leave things unaltered.

Similarly, the costs of switching out of nicotine dependence are large. Someone who has never smoked and someone smoking 20 cigarettes a day will make different decisions. The past matters. So does the future. Switching costs should force users and suppliers to take a long-run view in the first place. Don't start smoking on the assumption it is easy to quit. You get locked in.

In Chapter 10 we distinguished innocent and strategic entry barriers, one made by nature the other planned in boardrooms. Switching costs also have both aspects. Smart suppliers devise many strategies for locking in users. Air miles and reward points are obvious examples made possible by the information economy. Previously, it was simply too expensive to keep separate track of individual retail customers.

A modern computer changes all that. Once individuals can be distinguished, they can be 'incentivized'. Reward points offer customers a small reward for volunteering to be

locked in to a particular supplier. The customer may care little whether she flies BA or Virgin, or shops at Tesco or Sainsbury, but to the airline or supermarket it makes a huge difference. Yahoo! and Freeserve may be free today, but once you are familiar with their systems they may be able to charge you for the *same* services in the future.

The information economy did not invent these practices but is pushing to the limit things done more crudely for years. For decades, high street banks have known that today's students are tomorrow's profitable customers. Banks compete for space on campus and offer students subsidized banking, relying on the later cost of switching banks to lock in the customer and offer subsequent opportunity to get back their original investment with interest. Banks could always tell the difference between students and non-students. The information economy takes this principle to the limit, distinguishing individual customers and working out when early subsidies earn later returns.

Network externalities

From the user viewpoint, the final attribute of information products is that they have network externalities.

A **network externality** arises when an additional network member conveys benefits to those already on the network.

There is no point having a phone if nobody else has one, nor any reason to master Esperanto if this new language fails to catch on with other people. The fax technology was invented in 1843 and the first e-mail was sent in 1969, yet it was not until other people adopted the technologies that they became popular.[1]

Figure 11-2 shows how usage affects demand for a product exhibiting network externalities. It parallels our discussion of costs in Chapter 8. There, we saw that firms have different cost curves in the short run and long run. Even when short-run cost curves are U-shaped, long-run average costs may fall for a long time, exhibiting scale economies in production. Producing more can lower average costs.

Network externalities give rise to a similar phenomenon on the demand side: cutting prices can boost demand a lot, especially in the long run. Figure 11-2 shows the initial short-run demand curve D_1D_1, the demand for the product for a *given* number of users already on the network. Suppose

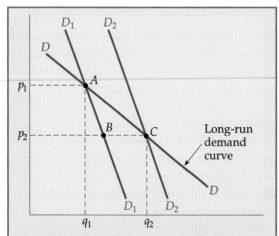

Each short-run demand curve reflects the number of people already using the network. Reducing the price from p_1 to p_2 not only causes a move from A to B it also induces a shift in demand curve since the network is more valuable. The long-run demand curve, joining points such as A and C, is more elastic.

Figure 11-2   A demand curve with network externalities

---

[1] These, and many other, fascinating examples are quoted in Carl Shapiro and Hal Varian, *Information Rules*, Harvard University Press, 1999.

BOX 11-2	Britannica shelved

Serious parents used to purchase their children a bookshelf filled with *Encyclopaedia Britannica* (www.britannica.co.uk). This prestige reference work was the market leader for two centuries after its launch in 1768, despite commanding a premium price, which peaked at £1000. Annual sales reached £450 million in 1990. Since 1990 sales revenue has collapsed by over 80 per cent. The CD-ROM destroyed the printed encyclopaedia. The marginal cost of making a CD-ROM is about £1. The marginal cost of *Encyclopaedia Britannica* had been about £150 for the books, plus several hundred pounds in commission for the door-step salesforce.

The main challenge came when Microsoft decided to produce software for an encyclopaedia, called *Encarta*, at a thirtieth of the price of *Britannica*. *Encarta* was not only cheaper but also easier to carry around. Being shorter, it fitted on a single CD-ROM. *Britannica* was not brought down by a new entrant to the 24-volume book business but by a new technology that changed the nature of the niche.

During the 1990s, *Britannica* gradually figured out how best to respond to *Encarta*'s entry. It produced its own CD-ROM. The door-to-door salesforce got fired. Those using computers pay more attention to website advertising than doorstep sales patter. *Britannica* has tried to emphasize that, now with similar technology to *Encarta*, it remains longer and therefore more informative. *Encarta* is trying to get bigger to undermine the new niche that *Britannica* is hoping to create.

Sources: P. Evans and T. Wurster, *Blown to Bits*, Harvard Business School Press, 1999; R. Melcher, 'Dusting off the Britannica', *Business Week*, 20 October 1997.

A is the point at which the number of people using the network is the same as in the previous period. There is no reason for the demand curve to shift.

Now, however, suppose the supplier cut the price and induced extra customers today, moving down the demand curve D_1D_1 from *A* to *B*. With more people on the network, the product is now more valuable to everyone and the demand curve shifts up next period to D_2D_2. At the price p_2 the quantity demanded then rises to q_2. Further reductions in the price will shift the short-run demand curve even further to the right. The long-run demand curve *DD*, formed by joining up points such as *A* and *C*, is more elastic than the short-run demand curve.

Even without switching costs, network externalities may justify the subsidization of price – even free provision – early in the life of a product. The supplier is investing in enhancing the network. Once customers build up and demand strengthens, the price can then be raised. Network externalities explain why users herd together, being slow to take up the new product then crossing over all at once. Even if you know e-mail is wonderful, it is little use until all your friends (and customers) are connected. When everyone thinks everyone else is ready, people all switch within a very short time.

These four characteristics – experience, overload, switching costs, and network externalities – are key features of information products from the users' viewpoint. We turn now to the special features of costs, production, and competition between suppliers.

11-3 Distributors of information

The key characteristics of information from the suppliers' viewpoint is that it is expensive to create but very cheap to distribute: for an information product, fixed costs are large but marginal costs tiny. Hence there are large-scale economies. While expansion of output by industrial monopolists is eventually limited by their existing capacity, the reproduction of information products faces no such capacity constraint. The industrial economy was made up largely of oligopolists – Ford, Vauxhall, Fiat, etc. – but we should expect the information economy to be made up largely of monopolies. Moreover, as demonstrated by the birth and precocious childhood of companies like Amazon, Yahoo!, and Freeserve, even existing monopolists are always under threat from unexpected newcomers.

From our discussion in Chapters 9 and 10, you would expect – correctly – that these monopolies would take one of two forms. The first is a dominant firm with a fringe of smaller competitors. Microsoft, inventor of DOS and then Windows, fits the bill well. Microsoft's income stream is now so large that, like Boeing in the airliner business, it can devote vast sums to R&D. Both take advantage of huge scale economies to become the lowest-cost producer of the industry's standard product.

Other forms of monopoly have to operate in smaller, niche markets, carefully targeted on particular groups of consumers whose diversity of preferences allows these niches to co-exist. Internet firms distribute many products, from airline tickets to dealings in stocks and shares. Monopolistic competition describes these market structures well. However, since the incumbent's advantage is dependent on the segmentation of the market into small niches, its temporary monopoly is vulnerable to competitors who manage to jump across niches. For example, Amazon has recently realized that there is no reason it should confine its activities to taking internet orders for books alone.

Pricing information products

Armed only with the preceding chapters, you set up as a consultant (on the internet, of course) to advise firms on how to price information products. Since marginal cost is very low, you expect to drive marginal revenue down almost to zero. But you also want to make profits. Like the phone company, perhaps you should use a two-part tariff.

A **two-part tariff** levies an annual charge to cover fixed costs, and a small price per unit related to marginal costs.

Does anyone implement this on the internet? The two most visited UK websites, AOL and CompuServe (early entrants, both American companies, available to subscribers only) charge an annual membership fee and then provide free services. It will be interesting to see whether competition from newer entrants such as Freeserve (www.freeserve.net) leads AOL and CompuServe to abolish annual charges or whether new entrants are simply offering loss leaders to try to overcome switching costs. Economic theory suggests that in the long run some form of annual fee may be part of the solution. Internet suppliers need to earn revenue just like every other business. Unless they can make this revenue from advertising or from selling customer information to other suppliers, membership fees may become part of how pricing develops.

Another lesson you will remember from Chapter 9 is that a monopolist earns more by price discriminating than by charging a uniform price. In revenue terms, the latter allows it to earn the best available rectangle price (price × quantity) under the demand curve, whereas perfect price discrimination – a different price for each customer – would allow the monopolist the entire (much larger) area under the demand curve.

Where suppliers simply quote a price without knowing the characteristics of the buyer that will show up, it is very difficult to price discriminate. Sometimes, differences in buyers are very obvious, as with package holidaymakers and business travellers. We return to the airline example shortly. However, in many instances, suppliers of goods and services have simply not been able to engage in much price discrimination.

The information revolution has changed all that, since suppliers will frequently have very detailed data on individual purchasers. This allows them to price discriminate, quoting different prices to different customers based on the actual or likely characteristics of the customer. It is precisely because this yields so much more revenue that suppliers are willing to buy lists of customer information from other suppliers. So far, Chapters 9 and 10 are standing you in pretty good stead. Let's look at price discrimination in more detail.

What we have described to date is customer-specific price discrimination. Nice work if you can get it. However, distributors of information products have two other tricks even when they cannot buy or establish information about particular customers.

Versioning

Why do publishers supply both hardback and paperback versions of a book, and at very different prices? It is a form of price discrimination that increases total sales revenue. Note that the 'benefit' of the hardback, that justifies the higher price, is not simply its superior physical quality. It is also the fact that it comes out several months earlier. In the information business, old news is no news.

Versioning is the deliberate creation of different qualities in order to facilitate price discrimination.

We'll take a bet that you are reading a paperback version of this textbook. It is a pretty safe bet, since there is no hardback version! Delaying publication makes little sense when a student's course starts at a particular time; nor do students need the book to last for 20 years (even though the principles will continue to be relevant!). So little *additional* benefit can be created for a hardback version; given the additional production costs it is not worth doing it.

On the internet, the cost calculation is a little different. Once the product exists, packaging it in various forms incurs little extra cost. Marginal cost of all versions is close to zero. Even small revenue gains from differentiating the product to achieve price discrimination are worthwhile.

Sometimes this involves making one version of the

BOX 11-3 — EMI quit making CDs

In response to internet-induced changes to the music industry, in November 1999, EMI (www.emigroup.com), the world's third largest music company, announced its intention to stop making and distributing compact discs. Having decided CDs had been made obsolete by the ability to download tracks direct from the internet, EMI decided to concentrate on developing and producing music, rather than the business of distributing it. The table below shows how the economics of music distribution are expected to change, with the artist and record label grabbing revenue formerly going to distributors.

Costs and profits on a $15 CD

$ spent on	Traditional retail CD	Internet CD
Promotion	2.50	2.50
Manufacturing	1.00	1.00
Web promotion		1.00
Shipping		1.00
Distribution	3.50	
Retail store	2.00	
Royalty and label profit	6.00	9.50

Source: Financial Times, 3 March 1999.

---

product deliberately worse than it could be in order to enhance the value of the premium version. Think again about airlines, who on scheduled flights have economy class and business class. Do businessmen really need a continuous diet of smoked salmon? Is it really optimal to squeeze economy passengers in quite so tight?

Even within Europe, business fares can cost double an economy fare; on transatlantic flights the difference can be between £3000 for a business fare and £500 for standard economy fare. Anything that makes people choose business class rather than economy is very profitable. It may actually be revenue enhancing to deliberately make economy worse than it need have been.[2] Once again, suppliers of information products who have made a fine art out of versioning are merely taking previous ideas to their logical conclusion.

Bundling

Versioning creates different qualities of the same product in order to allow price discrimination. It occurs when suppliers do not know the characteristics of any individual, but can make guesses about differences across groups of potential purchaser. A different tactic of suppliers is bundling.

---

[2] This trick is over 100 years old. Dupuit, the famous 19th-century French economist who was an early advocate of marginal cost pricing in state-run activities, noted that railway companies deliberately provided no roof for third-class carriages in order to boost the demand for second class, where much more revenue could be earned (quoted in Hal Varian, 'Versioning Information Goods', mimeo, University of California at Berkeley, 1997).

Table 11-3   Bundling TV channels (user value in £000s)

	News	Sports
Edward	6	10
Camilla	10	6

Bundling is the joint supply of more than one product in order to reduce the need for price discrimination.

Price discrimination is only necessary when different customers behave differently. Suppose one really wants a news channel and another really wants a sports channel. Table 11-3 shows the valuations Edward and Camilla put on each channel. Their tastes for a particular channel differ a lot. Perhaps their tastes for a bundle of channels are more similar.

If Sky TV (www.sky.co.uk) knows the exact characteristics of each viewer, it gets £32 000 in revenue by perfect price discrimination. How? By charging Edward £6000 to receive the news channel, and £10 000 for the sports channel; and by charging Camilla £10 000 for the news channel and £6000 for the sports channel. If the prices were any higher, Edward and Camilla would simply refuse to sign up to take the channel.

Now assume Sky executives don't have enough detailed information about users to charge different prices to different people. They have to set a single price per channel. For the news channel, if they charge £10 000 only Camilla

BOX 11-4	The hub with the hubbub

Gatwick Airport's (www.gatwickairport.co.uk) proud boast is 'the hub without the hubbub'. Like airline traffic, internet traffiic needs high-quality infrastructure to convey business across the Atlantic and distribute it within Europe. Gatwick's advantage as a European airline hub is based partly on location. UK hopes of becoming Europe's internet hub are based on the UK's lead in telecommunications. Other indicators (in 1998) of the UK's lead in telecoms within Europe – a legacy of early liberalization of the telecoms industry in the UK – are shown below.

	UK	Sweden	Netherlands	France	Germany
Transatlantic 'backbone' capacity (megabits/second)	1514	776	600	245	205

Source: *Financial Times*, 23 June 1999

	US	Japan	UK	France	Germany
% of firms using e-mail	65	72	63	41	48
% of firms with Web site	41	45	37	14	30
% of population on-line	21	6	10	1	5

Source: http://www.dti.gov.uk/cii

will sign up. If they charge £6000 they can get both to sign up. Sky does best by charging £6000 for each channel, making £24 000 total revenue (2 × 2 × £6000). But this is a lot worse than the £32 000 that price discrimination would yield. The problem is that to sell a channel to the second subscriber, Sky has to cut the price a lot for the person who would have happily paid more.

Bundling reduces this diversity of people's tastes. Suppose Sky now offers only the two channels as a package. Edward would pay up to £16 000 to get both, so would Camilla. Sky gets £32 000. Bundling is just as good as perfect price discrimination in this example because Edward and Camilla place the same total value on the total package. By bundling news, sports, and movie channels, Sky TV can get more revenue than by selling channels separately at a uniform price to each user.

Although bundling beats uniform pricing across users, it is usually less effective than perfect price discrimination. Suppose in Table 11-3 that the sports channel is worth £4000 rather than £6000 to Camilla. The most she will pay for a total package is £14 000. Selling a package for £14 000 to each of Edward and Camilla earns Sky £28 000. Note that since Edward still values the total at £16 000, price discrimination across users would earn Sky (£16 000 + £14 000), an extra £2000 in revenue for Sky.

However, Sky's informational requirement about indi-vidual customers would then be huge. Bundling is therefore often the best suppliers can do in the circumstances. You get bundled all the time. That's why the Sunday papers have all these sections, and why tour operators offer holidays with a week in Florence plus a week on an Adriatic beach. Perhaps Camilla likes frescoes more than Edward, whose own preference tends more towards swimming.

Competition versus collaboration

Bundling suggests that most products have more than one attribute or component. From this it is only a short step to the idea that these different components may be produced by *different* firms. More generally, the production and sales of products that are complements rather than substitutes is becoming increasingly prevalent.

Software and hardware is an obvious example. Most Microsoft products are operated in computers driven by Intel chips. Nowadays, Apple (www.apple.com) is unusual in producing both hardware and software. Apple's early success was gradually overhauled by the strategic alliance of Microsoft and Intel.

A **strategic alliance** is a blend of co-operation and competition in which a group of suppliers provide a range of products that partly complement one another.

Strategic alliances are occurring in other industries, such

as airlines, where BA (www.british-airways.com) is currently in the One World partnership with Canadian Airlines (www.cdnair.com), Quantas (www.quantas.com), Finnair (www.finnair.com), Iberia (www.iberia.com), and American Airlines (www.AA.com). These alliances allow the different partners to specialize in segments that largely complement one another – travel within the Americas, travel across the Atlantic and within Europe, and travel within Asia and Australasia.

Alliances seek many of the benefits that occur when vertical integration of different production stages occurs within any firm – cost reduction from closer co-ordination and greater specialization. However, an alliance is not a complete merger. It preserves a degree of competition, even between the partners. This may keep all partners on their toes and help assure customers that future profit margins will not become excessive. Whenever switching costs plays a prominent role, current users will pay considerable attention to such signals about possible future behaviour of suppliers.

11-4 Setting standards

One process in which strategic alliances may be especially useful is in the competition to set standards, norms around which economic behaviour is organized.

A **standard** is the technical specification that is common throughout a particular network.

The UK decision to drive on the left is one such standard, the width of railway tracks another, the type of electric plug socket a third. Each is a very strong example of a network externality. There is little point having an AC power supply if the rest of the country has DC power supply.

But how are standards originally determined? Usually, as the outcome of competition, which may be economic, political, or both. Strategic alliances help tip the balance in favour of the standard those partners want by demonstrating that a major number of key players are already on this particular network. Underpopulated networks are not worth joining, and sometimes differences in standards are the easiest way to distinguish one network from another.

Typically, as a result of this initial competition to set the standard, one standard is increasingly adopted by everyone. For some of the early networks, this is a valuable triumph as their own standard becomes adopted more widely. Other networks wither as theirs is rejected. Sony (www.sony.com) ploughed a lot of R&D into the Betamax technology for video cassette recorders, but the world adopted its rival, the VHS system that you now have at home.

Alliances, explicit or implicit, help resolve the standards war in favour of the well organized. Why did UK mobile phone company Vodafone (www.vodafone.com) launch a takeover bid for its US counterpart Air Touch, rather than the other way round? The answer lies in standard setting. Early in the 1990s the Europeans managed to resolve the standard that would apply to mobile telephony, creating sufficient of a single market to allow European firms to grow rapidly and enjoy scale economies. American firms were not late into the game. Rather they had three competing standards and never managed to agree which to adopt. While US firms competed with one another inside fragmented regional markets, the Europeans forged ahead to such an extent that their standard was quickly adopted in other continents.

Once standards have been set, competition switches from rivalry over standards to rivalry within the standard. As we explained earlier, this often leads either to a dominant firm (e.g. Microsoft, Intel) using its scale to achieve cost advantages over rivals in current production and greater R&D to sustain this position in the future; or else to a series of temporary monopolies in niche markets, well described by the monopolistic competition model in Chapter 10.

11-5 Understanding the e-economy

In this chapter, we have described what is special about the information economy, and how these characteristics affect the behaviour of both users of information and providers of information. Two lessons stand out.

First, while the information revolution is truly changing our lives, few of its activities or market tactics are unprecedented. The cost of distributing information has been falling since the printing press was invented. The history of industries such as newspapers, book publishing, and telephones already contains examples of most of the phenomena we described in the chapter. Standards, bundling, versioning, alliances, price discrimination, selling customer lists, switching costs – we've seen them all before. What is new about the information economy is the extent to which they are now routinely practised. And, because marketing is part of every business, these practices are now widespread in every industry.

Second, the revolution in technology has not required any corresponding revolution in economic theory. The existing laws of economics work just fine. Indeed, they are much the best way to make sense of what is happening.

SUMMARY

● Information is expensive to produce but very cheap to copy and distribute.

● From the users' viewpoint, e-products have four key attributes: experience, overload, switching costs, and network externalities. Buyers' need to experience explains why sellers allow sampling and browsing. Sellers also invest in a good reputation to reduce the need for buyers to sample. Potential information overload explains why specialist agents develop to pre-screen material.

● Switching costs make future opportunities depend on current choices. Users should therefore take a long-run view from the outset. It is optimal for sellers to subsidize initial use, and to manufacture artificial switching costs using reward schemes for loyalty.

● Network externalities arise when the value of a network depends on how densely it is populated. Producers will respond by subsidizing early entry to the network.

● Information products, with high fixed costs but low marginal cost, are potential monopolies. R&D, learning by doing, switching costs, and network externalities may lead to natural monopolies. Where niche markets are smaller, monopolistic competition may prevail. Many existing markets are contestable by new entrants, so many monopolies are temporary.

● Monopolists want to price discriminate when users differ. Information technology may allow personalized pricing. Otherwise, sellers produce different versions of the product, to make discrimination easier, or bundle different products to reduce the need for discrimination.

● Standards are a key feature of a network. Initially, there is competition between networks to set the standard. Once one standard is dominant, there is competition within the network to supply according to that standard.

KEY TERMS

◆ E-product   166

◆ Experience good or service   166

◆ Information overload   167

◆ Switching cost   167

◆ Network externality   168

◆ Two-part tariff   170

◆ Versioning   170

◆ Bundling   171

◆ Strategic alliance   172

◆ Standard   173

REVIEW QUESTIONS

1 You get invited to a free day 'trial membership' of a David Lloyd Sports Club. Is this because the product (a) has aspects of an experience good (b) has network externalities, or (c) to combat switching costs?

2 Why do most undergraduate courses require students to take particular courses in their first year but give them a wide range of options in their final year? Of which supplier tactic in the chapter is this an example?

3 Give three of your own examples of versioning.

4 'If price discrimination is good for producers, it must be bad for consumers.' Do you agree? Does it matter which consumer you are?

5 What is the difference between a strategic alliance and a cartel?

6 You are Chief Justice of the newly appointed Global Supreme Court, and you have just argued in favour of allowing Microsoft's dominant position to continue. What arguments did you use?

7 *Common fallacies* Show why the following statements are incorrect: (a) The internet is free, so fortunately it has little to do with economics. (b) Price discrimination requires monopoly and must therefore be bad. (c) Firms currently losing money cannot justify high share prices. (d) Because sales by internet are small relative to those in the high street, high street shops are as yet unaffected.

12 The analysis of factor markets: labour

LEARNING OUTCOMES

When you have finished this chapter, you should be able to:

- Analyse the firm's demand for factors in the long run and in the short run
- Define marginal value product, marginal revenue product, and marginal cost of a factor, and relate these to the structure of input and output markets
- Derive the industry demand for labour from that of individual firms in the industry
- Discuss labour supply decisions, both for labour force participation and for hours of work
- Distinguish transfer earnings and economic rent
- Analyse labour market equilibrium and discuss processes that prevent labour markets clearing continuously
- Explain how minimum wages affect employment
- Define isoquants and examine their role in the choice of production technique

In winning a golf tournament, a top professional earns more in a weekend than a professor earns in a year. Students studying economics can expect higher career earnings than those of equally smart students studying philosophy. An unskilled worker in the EU earns more than an unskilled worker in India. Few market economies manage to provide jobs for all their citizens wanting to work. How can we explain these aspects of the real world?

In each case the answer depends on the supply and demand for that particular type of labour. In this chapter and the next we discuss the supply and demand for labour. We begin our analysis of the markets for the factors of production – labour, capital and land. We discuss what determines the equilibrium prices and quantities of factors of production in different industries and in the economy as a whole. Although we begin with the factor called 'labour', we shall see in Chapter 14 that many of the same principles apply in analysing the markets for other factors of production.

We have already studied the market for goods. There is nothing intrinsically different about our approach to factor markets. You should be able to guess the structure of this chapter: demand, supply, equilibrium, problems of disequilibrium and adjustment.

Table 12-1 gives data on UK earnings (for full-time males) in 1998 and compares these with inflation-adjusted data for 1986. By 1998 workers in financial services earned over £200 a week more than the national average, and nearly £350 a week more than workers in the textile industry. Real earnings of textile workers stagnated during 1986–98.

Table 12-1	Weekly real earnings in the UK (full-time males, £ 1998)	
	1986	1998
Whole economy	340	437
Financial services	496	656
Textiles	279	323
Energy and water	368	496

Source: ONS, Labour Market Trends.

Another question considered in this chapter is why different methods of production are used in different countries. A snack bar in a poor country has several waiters; in a rich country it has vending machines. The relative cost of using capital and labour in rich and poor countries affects the way in which goods and services (here, fast food) are produced. How does this work?

The economics of factor markets differ from the economics of output markets not because we depart from the usual reliance on supply and demand, but because there is something special about demand in factor markets. It is not a direct or final demand, but a derived demand. It is only because firms want to produce output that they demand factors of production.

The demand for factors of production is a **derived demand** because it is derived from the demand for the output that the factors are used to produce.

Each firm simultaneously decides how much output to supply and how many factors to demand. The two are inextricably interlinked. But it is the demand for the firm's output that drives the whole process.

On the supply side we distinguish between the supply of factors to the whole economy and to an individual firm or industry. It takes a long time to train helicopter pilots. Thus the supply of helicopter pilots is almost fixed in the short run. But this total supply of pilots can choose in which industry to work. They will tend to work in the industry offering the highest wages.

Must all industries pay the same wage rate for pilots if they wish to stop pilots moving to higher paying industries? Not quite. Different jobs have different non-monetary characteristics. Helicopter flights to offshore oil rigs are dangerous because of bad weather, and may involve working irregular shifts that make it hard to plan leisure activities during time off. To attract pilots to this industry, it is necessary to pay a higher than average wage rate to offset these disadvantages of the job.

An **equalizing wage differential** is the monetary compensation for differential non-monetary characteristics of the same job in different industries so that workers have no incentive to move between industries.

Thus, unpleasant or dangerous jobs pay more than the national average for that skill and pleasant jobs pay less than the national average. The total returns, monetary and non-monetary, are equated in different industries and workers with that skill have no incentive to move.

In the short run, with an almost fixed supply of pilots to the economy as a whole, any increase in the total demand for pilots (e.g. the discovery of North Sea oil) raises the equilibrium wage of pilots in all industries. To retain some of their pilots, other industries have to match the total rewards (lucrative wages adjusted for non-monetary drawbacks) offered by the North Sea oil industry. But in the longer run the supply of pilots is not fixed. High wages act as a signal for young workers to abandon plans to train as fixed-wing pilots or engine drivers and move instead into the lucrative helicopter business. Another theme of our analysis of factor markets will be the need to distinguish between supply possibilities in the short run and in the longer run.

Putting demand and supply together we can determine equilibrium prices and quantities in different factor markets. But are these markets always in equilibrium? When examining goods markets we showed how excess supply or excess demand would lead to changes in price that tend to restore equilibrium. In the labour market the wage rate is the price of labour. Are wages sufficiently flexible to restore labour market equilibrium, or might wage responses be sluggish and the labour market out of equilibrium for some time? How does this relate to unemployment? These are questions we examine in more detail towards the end of the chapter.

12-1 The firm's demand for factors in the long run

We begin by discussing the long run in which all factors of production can be fully adjusted. In Chapter 8 we discussed the firm's long-run average cost curve and long-run marginal cost curve. In Chapters 9 and 10 we considered various descriptions of the demand curve facing the firm and showed how the firm would choose output supplied to maximize profits.

Although it is all part of the same decision, we now switch our attention from the firm's behaviour in the output market to its behaviour in the corresponding input markets. Recall that a firm's cost curves show the minimum cost way to produce each possible output level. The minimum cost method for producing any output level depends on two things: the production function, summarizing the alternative production techniques available, and the prices at which different factors of production can be employed.

Table 12-2 shows data for two possible ways to make 100 snarks. Technique A is more capital intensive than technique B. In technique A the ratio of capital to labour input quantities is 1 to 1. In technique B the ratio is 1 to 3. Technique A uses relatively more capital and relatively less labour to make 100 snarks.

To construct the total cost curve the firm chooses the minimum cost technique at each possible output level. Table 12-2 is relevant to the particular output level of 100 snarks. When each unit of capital input costs £320 per week and each unit of labour input £300 per week, the cheapest way to produce 100 snarks is to use technique B. The total cost is then £2440.

The second two rows show what happens when each unit of labour now costs £340 per week. Technique A is now the cheapest way to produce 100 snarks per week. But the total cost of producing 100 snarks has risen to £2640 per week.

This simple example illustrates a general principle. In producing a *given* output by the cheapest available technique, a rise in the price of a unit of labour relative to the price of a unit of capital will lead the firm to switch to a more capital-intensive technique. Conversely, if capital becomes relatively more expensive, the cost-minimizing technique to produce a given output will now be a more labour-intensive technique. The firm substitutes away from the factor of production that has become relatively more expensive.

This principle helps explain differences across countries in the capital–labour ratios in the same industry. In the European Union, farmers face high wages relative to the cost of renting a combine harvester. Mechanized farming economizes on expensive workers. In contrast, India has cheap and abundant labour, but capital is relatively scarce and expensive. Indian farmers use much more labour-intensive techniques. Workers with scythes and shovels perform tasks undertaken by combine harvesters and bulldozers in the EU.

Table 12-2 shows that when output is 100 snarks per week the firm will demand 4 units of labour and 4 units of capital when a unit of capital costs £320 per week and a unit of labour £340 per week. When output is 100 snarks per week, but the cost of labour is only £300 per week, the firm will demand 6 units of labour and 2 units of capital. This

Table 12-2 Factor prices and the choice of technique

Technique	Input Capital	Labour	Rental rate (£)	Wage rate (£)	Total cost (£)
A	4	4	320	300	2480
B	2	6	320	300	2440
A	4	4	320	340	2640
B	2	6	320	340	2680

suggests that the demand for factors of production depends on the level of output and the relative price of the factors themselves.

However, this is not a helpful way to think about the demand curve for factors of production. Although Table 12-2 tells us how the firm selects the minimum cost technique to produce a given output, it does not tell us which output the firm will choose. To determine profit-maximizing output, and the corresponding quantities of factors demanded, we have to repeat the calculations of Table 12-2 for each and every output, calculate the entire total cost curve for all output levels, and then choose profit-maximizing output by equating marginal cost and marginal revenue.

An increase in the wage rate will cause the firm to substitute away from labour and towards capital in producing a given output level. But it will also raise the total cost of producing each and every output level. Even with more capital-intensive techniques firms will still use some labour for which they have now to pay more. With higher marginal costs, but unchanged demand and marginal revenue curves, firms will produce less output.

Although it is tempting to say that a decrease in output, an increase in wage rate, or a fall in the price of capital, will decrease the quantity of labour demanded, we can now see the problem. A change in the price of one factor not merely changes factor intensity at a given output, but changes marginal output costs and hence the profit-maximizing level of output itself.

When we studied consumer decisions in Chapter 6 we saw that a change in the price of a good has both a substitution effect and an income effect. The substitution effect reflects the change in relative prices of different goods and the income effect reflects changes in real income as a result of the price change. We have now established that the demand for factors works exactly the same way.

Table 12-2 illustrates the pure substitution effect at a given level of output. A higher relative price of labour leads firms

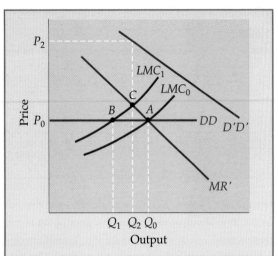

A wage increase will have a substitution effect leading firms to substitute relatively more capital-intensive techniques. Nevertheless, total costs and marginal costs of producing output will be greater than before. Facing the horizontal demand curve DD, a shift from LMC_0 to LMC_1 will lead the firm to move from A to B and output will fall from Q_0 to Q_1. This tends to reduce the demand for all factors of production. Facing the demand curve $D'D'$ and corresponding marginal revenue curve MR', the upward shift from LMC_0 to LMC_1 leads the firm to move from A to C at which marginal cost and marginal revenue are again equal. The output effect reduces output only from Q_0 to Q_1.

Figure 12-1   The output effect of a wage increase

to substitute towards the factor that has become relatively cheaper. But there is also an income or output effect. By shifting the marginal cost of producing output, a change in a factor price leads to a different profit-maximizing output.

In the long run an increase in the wage rate will reduce the quantity of labour demanded. The substitution effect leads to more capital-intensive techniques at each output level and the higher marginal cost of output will reduce the amount of output it is most profitable to supply. Similarly, an increase in the price of capital will reduce the quantity of capital demanded. The substitution effect and the output effect go in the same direction.

What about the effect of a higher wage rate on the quantity of capital demanded? There is a substitution effect towards more capital-intensive techniques, but an output effect tending to reduce output and the quantity of all factors demanded. The easier it is to substitute capital for labour the more likely is the substitution effect to dominate. Firms will substitute a lot of capital for labour. With much less labour than before, marginal output costs will rise only

a little and the profit-maximizing output is likely to fall only a little. The quantity of capital demanded is likely to rise.

We began the chapter by pointing out that the demand for factors of production is a derived demand. It depends on demand for the firm's output. The output demand curve plays a large part in determining the output effect of a change in the price of a factor.

Figure 12-1 shows the shift upwards in the long-run marginal cost curve LMC when there is an increase in the wage rate. At the old wage rate the marginal output cost curve is LMC_0 but at the higher wage rate the marginal cost curve is LMC_1. The original profit-maximizing point is A. If the firm faces a horizontal demand curve DD, the upward shift in marginal costs leads to a new profit-maximizing output at B. Output falls from Q_0 to Q_1. With the much less elastic demand curve $D'D'$, the firm is still initially at A where LMC_0 equals MR' the marginal revenue curve corresponding to $D'D'$. Now the shift to LMC_1 leads to a much smaller reduction in profit-maximizing output. The new output is Q_2 and the firm is at C.

Hence, the more elastic is the demand curve for the firm's output, the more a given increase in the price of a factor of production, and a given shift in the long-run marginal cost curve for output, will lead to a large reduction in the quantity of output produced. And the larger the output effect, the greater will be the reduction in the quantity of all factors demanded.

Box 12-1 that follows summarizes our analysis of the influences determining the firm's long-run demand for factors and the associated choice of technique.

Since we have emphasized the substitution and output effects of a change in the price of a factor of production, you may be wondering if we can analyse factor demands using analytical techniques resembling the indifference curve–budget line techniques we used to study household demands for goods in Chapter 6. The answer is 'yes' and the Appendix to this chapter shows how to do this.

12-2 The firm's demand for labour in the short run

In the long run the firm can vary its factor intensity by switching from one production technique to another. But in the short run the firm has some fixed factors of production. We now consider the firm's short-run demand for labour when the quantity of capital it employs, and thus the cost of that capital, are fixed.

Table 12-3 extends the ideas we introduced in Chapter 8 in looking at the firm's short-run output decision with a fixed

BOX 12-1   The firm's long-run factor demands and the choice of technique

In the long run all factors can be varied. The firm's long-run total cost curve, and the average and marginal cost curves derived from it, embody the minimum cost production technique at each output level. At each output level the minimum cost technique reflects both the technical possibilities summarized in the production function and the prices of the factors employed. For a given long-run cost curve, the firm supplies the output at which long-run marginal cost is equal to marginal revenue. Knowing this output, we can determine the technique chosen and the quantity of each factor employed.

An increase in the price of one factor will have both a substitution effect and an output effect. The substitution effect leads the firm to produce a given output using a technique which economizes on the factor that has become relatively more expensive. A rise in the wage rate leads to a substitution effect towards more capital-intensive production methods at each output.

But an increase in the price of a factor will also increase both total costs and marginal costs. Since the marginal revenue curve is unaltered the profit-maximizing output must fall. This is the pure output effect. It tends to reduce the quantity demanded for all factors. The output effect is larger the more elastic is the demand for the firm's output.

For a given output demand curve, an increase in the price of one factor will reduce the quantity of that factor demanded. The substitution effect and output effect operate in the same direction. But the effect on the quantity of the other factor demanded is ambiguous. A rise in the wage rate leads to substitution towards more capital-intensive techniques but also leads to lower total output.

Table 12-3   Output and employment in the short run

(1) Labour input (workers)	(2) Output (goods)	(3) Marginal product of labour (MPL) (goods/extra worker)	(4) Marginal value product ($MPL \times £500$)	(5) Wage rate (£)	(6) Extra profits (£)
0	0				
1	0.8	0.8	400	300	100
2	1.8	1.0	500	300	200
3	3.1	1.3	650	300	350
4	4.3	1.2	600	300	300
5	5.4	1.1	550	300	250
6	6.3	0.9	450	300	150
7	7.0	0.7	350	300	50
8	7.5	0.5	250	300	−50

capital stock. Now we focus on the implications for labour demand. From columns (1) and (2) we calculate the marginal product of labour, how much each extra worker adds to total output. The marginal product increases as the first workers are added because it is hard for the first and second worker to handle all the machinery. Once the third worker is added, the *diminishing marginal productivity* of labour has set in. With existing machines fully utilized, there is less and less for each new worker to do.

As in our discussion of output, we concentrate on the *marginal principle*. Does the cost of a new worker exceed the benefit from having an extra worker? Table 12-3 assumes we

are discussing a competitive firm which can hire as many workers as it wishes at the wage rate of £300 and can sell as much output as it wishes at a price of £500. Column (4) shows the extra revenue from taking on another worker.

The **marginal value product of labour** is the extra revenue obtained by selling the output an extra worker produces.

Since the firm is perfectly competitive, the marginal value product of another worker is simply the marginal product in physical goods multiplied by the price for which these extra goods can be sold. From this extra revenue from an additional worker, the firm must subtract the extra wage

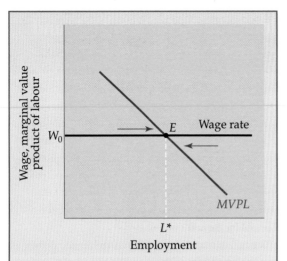

The firm sells output for a given price and hires labour at the given wage W_0. Diminishing marginal productivity makes the MVPL schedule slope down. Below L^* extra employment adds more to revenue than labour costs. Above L^* extra employment adds more to costs than revenue. L^* is the profit maximizing employment level where the wages equals the MVPL.

Figure 12-2   The firm's choice of employment

cost. The final column of Table 12-3 shows the increase in profits when an extra worker is taken on.

The firm keeps expanding employment so long as the marginal value product of another worker exceeds the wage cost. After the third worker, diminishing returns set in. Further employment expansion starts to reduce the marginal product of labour in physical goods and hence its marginal value product. It is profitable to expand as far as 7 workers. The seventh worker has a marginal value product of £350, which just covers the wage of £300 for this extra worker. But the eighth worker's marginal value product is only £250. The optimal level of employment is 7 workers.

Note that the firm is simultaneously choosing the employment level and the output level: 7 workers make 7 units of output. In moving from 6 workers and 6.3 units of output to 7 workers and 7 units of output, the firm's marginal revenue is £350 (= 0.7 × £500). Labour is the only variable factor and the marginal cost of the extra 0.7 output unit is just the wage rate £300 of the extra worker. Seven units of output is the level to which the profit-maximizing firm would be led by thinking about marginal cost and marginal revenue. The marginal revenue of moving from 7 to 7.5 output units would not cover the marginal labour cost. It is just another way of looking at the same thing.

The firm's employment rule is thus: expand (contract) employment if the marginal value product of labour is greater than (less than) the wage of a extra worker. When labour can be smoothly adjusted, as for example when the correct measure of labour input is workers times hours worked, the firm's demand for labour must satisfy the condition:

$$\text{wage} = \text{marginal value product of labour} \qquad (1)$$

Figure 12-2 illustrates this principle when we can assume that there is diminishing marginal productivity at all employment levels. The marginal value product of labour (MVPL) slopes down. A competitive firm can hire labour at the constant wage rate W_0 since it is a price-taker in the labour market. Below L^* profits can be increased by expanding employment, since MVPL exceeds the wage rate or marginal cost of taking on extra labour. Above L^* it is profitable to contract employment, since the wage exceeds the MVPL. L^* is the profit-maximizing level of employment.

Monopoly and monopsony power

This theory is easily amended when the firm has *monopoly power* in its output market (a downward-sloping demand curve for its product) or *monopsony power* in its input markets (an upward-sloping supply curve for its inputs so that the firm must offer a higher factor price the more of a factor it wishes to employ).

A firm with **monopsony power** is not a price-taker in its input markets. It faces an upward-sloping factor supply curve, and must offer a higher factor price to attract more factors. Hence the **marginal cost of an additional unit of the factor** *exceeds* the factor price. In expanding its factor use, the firm bids up the price paid to all units of the factor already employed.

For a perfectly competitive firm, the MVPL schedule depicts its marginal revenue from taking on an extra worker. We usually reserve the term *marginal value product of labour* (MVPL) for competitive firms who are price-takers in their output markets. MVPL is simply the marginal product of labour in physical goods MPL multiplied by the output price. We reserve the term *marginal revenue product of labour* (MRPL) for firms facing a downward-sloping demand curve for their output.

To calculate the **marginal revenue product of labour** we first find the marginal physical product of labour MPL and then calculate the change in the firm's total revenue when it sells these extra goods.

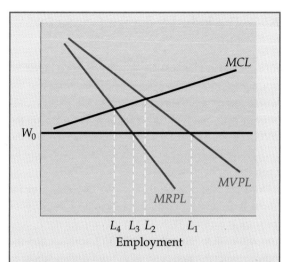

A perfectly competitive firm sets MVPL equal to W_0 and employs L_1 workers. Facing a downward-sloping demand curve in its output market, an imperfectly competitive firm recognizes that its marginal revenue from extra output will be less than MVPL. It sets MRPL equal to W_0 and employs L_3 workers. A monopsonist recognizes that additional employment bids up wages for existing workers so that MCL depicts the marginal cost of an extra worker. Facing a given goods price, the monopsonist sets MCL equal to MVPL to employ L_2 workers, but facing a downward-sloping demand curve in the output market, the monopsonist would set MCL equal to MRPL to employ L_4 workers. Thus, monopoly and monopsony power tend to reduce the firm's demand for labour.

Figure 12-3   Monopoly and monopsony power

Figure 12-3 shows the MVPL and MRPL schedules for two firms with the same technology. Both schedules slope down because of diminishing marginal productivity – a technical property of production – but the MRPL schedules slopes down more steeply because the firm faces a downward-sloping demand curve for its output and recognizes that additional output reduces the price and hence the revenue earned on previous units of output.

Similarly, although W_0 is the marginal cost of a unit of labour for a competitive firm that is a price-taker in its input market, a monopsonist must recognize that an expansion of employment will bid up the wage rate. Since all workers must be paid the same wage, the marginal cost of an extra worker is not merely the wage paid to that worker but the increase in the wage bill for previously employed workers. The monopsonist's marginal cost of labour exceeds the wage rate and increases with the level of employment. It is shown in Figure 12-3 as the MCL schedule.

Any firm will maximize profits when the marginal

revenue from an extra worker equals its marginal cost. Otherwise, the firm has the wrong employment level. Thus, a firm that is a price-taker in both its output and input markets will set W_0 equal to MVPL to employ L_1 workers in Figure 12-3. A firm that is a price-taker in the labour market but not in the output market will set MRPL equal to W_0 and use L_3 workers. A firm that is a price-taker in its output market but not in the labour market will set MVPL equal to MCL to employ L_2 workers. And a firm that is both a monopolist and a monopsonist will set MCL equal to MRPL to employ L_4 workers.

Thus the general principle is straightforward: choose employment such that the marginal cost of the last unit of labour equals the marginal revenue earned from that last unit of labour. Formally, we can say the firm should set

$$MCL = MRPL \qquad (2)$$

When the firm is a price-taker in the labour market, MCL is just the wage rate itself. When the firm is a price-taker in the output market, MRPL is simply the marginal value product of labour MVPL. For a perfectly competitive firm, equation (2) thus reduces to equation (1). For the rest of this chapter we assume that both output and labour markets are competitive. The analysis is easily amended when it is known that the firm has monopoly power in its output market or monopsony power in the labour market.

Changes in the firm's demand for labour

Consider the effect of a rise in the wage W_0 faced by a competitive firm. Using Figure 12-2 or 12-3, the firm now employs fewer workers than before. The marginal cost of labour has risen, but diminishing labour productivity makes the MVPL schedule slope down. Hence it requires a reduction in employment to raise the marginal value product of labour in line with its higher marginal cost. The marginal revenue earned from the last workers in the original position no longer covers their marginal cost.

Next, suppose that the competitive firm faces a higher output price. Although the MPL remains unaltered in physical goods, this output brings in more money. The MVPL schedule shifts up at each level of employment. Hence in Figure 12-2 or 12-3 the horizontal line through the wage W_0 crosses the new MVPL schedule at a higher employment level. With the marginal cost of labour unaltered and the marginal revenue from labour increased, output and employment expand until diminishing marginal productivity drives MVPL back down to the wage W_0.

Finally, suppose the firm had begun with a higher capital stock. Each worker has more machinery with which to work and will be able to make more output. Although wages and prices remain unchanged, there is an increase in MPL in physical goods at each employment level. Hence the MVPL schedule shifts upwards, since MVPL equals MPL times output price. As in the case of an increase in output price, this upward shift in the MVPL schedule leads the firm to expand employment and output.[1]

For a competitive firm there is a neat way to combine our first two results. Noting that MVPL equals the output price P times MPL, the extra physical product of another worker, we can write the firm's profit-maximizing condition as wage $W = P \times MPL$. Dividing both sides of this equation by P, we obtain

$$W/P = MPL \qquad (3)$$

Equation (3) says that a profit-maximizing competitive firm will demand labour up to the point at which the marginal physical product of labour equals its *real* wage, its nominal or money wage divided by the firm's output price.

The position of the MPL schedule depends on technology and the existing capital stock. Since these are fixed in the short run we can alter MPL only by moving along the schedule. Diminishing returns imply that, with more workers, the marginal physical product of the last worker is lower. From the particular level of the marginal physical product of labour we can deduce how many workers are being employed. Equation (3) tells us that if nominal wages and output prices both double, real wages and employment will both be unaffected. But changes in either the nominal wage or the output price, if not matched by a corresponding change in the other, will alter employment by affecting the real wage. Lower real wages move the firm down its MPL schedule, taking on more workers until the marginal physical product of labour equals the real wage.

Having studied the firm's demand for labour in the short run, we now turn to the demand by the industry as a whole. Although each competitive firm regards itself as a price-taker in both its output and input markets, an expansion by the whole industry is likely to change output prices and wage rates. In moving from the firm's demand curve to the industry demand curve for labour, we need to take account of these effects.

12-3 The industry demand curve for labour

For a given price P_0 and wage W_0 each firm in a competitive industry chooses employment to equate the wage and the MVPL. In Figure 12-4 we horizontally add the marginal value product of labour curves for each firm to obtain the $MVPL_0$ schedule for the industry. At the wage W_0 and the price P_0, the industry will choose the point E_0. This must be a point on the industry demand curve for labour.

However, $MVPL_0$ is *not* the industry demand curve for labour. It is drawn for a particular output price, P_0. Suppose the wage is cut from W_0 to W_1. At the output price P_0 each firm will wish to move down its MVPL schedule and the industry will wish to expand output and employ labour to the point E_1 in Figure 12-4. In terms of the supply and demand for output, the cut in wages has shifted the industry supply curve to the right.

At the price P_0 there will now be an excess supply of goods. The increase in supply must bid down the equilibrium price for the industry's product to some lower

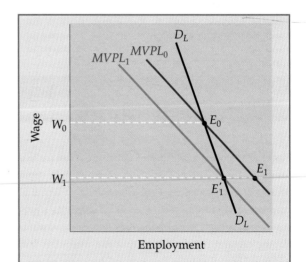

MVPL$_0$ is the horizontal sum of each firm's MVPL schedule at the price P_0. Each firm and the industry as a whole sets MVPL equal to W_0. Hence E_0 is a point on the industry demand curve for labour. A lower wage W_1 leads each firm and the industry as a whole to move down their MVPL schedules to a point E_1. Extra employment and output by the whole industry (a shift to the right in the industry supply curve of goods) leads to excess goods supply at the original price P_0. To clear the output market the price must fall, and this shifts to the left each firm's MVPL schedule. The new industry schedule is $MVPL_1$ and the chosen point is E'_1. Joining all the points such as E_0 and E'_1, we obtain the industry demand curve $D_L D_L$.

Figure 12-4   The industry demand for labour

---

[1] These three employment predictions carry over to firms with monopoly and monopsony power. An upward shift in the output demand curve or a larger capital stock will shift the MRPL curve upwards, increasing the labour demanded by a firm with monopoly power. An upward shift in the MCL schedule reduces the labour demanded by a monopsonist.

Help wanted? or just Help!

The world does not stand still. Technical progress, changing culture and tastes, and easier transport and communications are contributing to the rise and fall of particular industries and skills. The following figure shows forecasts by the US Bureau of Labor Statistics about likely employment trends in the USA.

Source: *Economist*, 28 September 1996.

---

price P_1. The lower price shifts each firm's *MVPL* schedule to the left. $MVPL_1$ is thus the new *MVPL* schedule for the industry at the new price P_1. Hence the industry chooses the point E'_1 at the new wage W_1.

By connecting points such as E_0 and E'_1, we obtain the *industry demand for labour schedule* $D_L D_L$ in Figure 12-4. Although each firm constructs its *MVPL* schedule as if it were a price-taker, the industry demand curve has a steeper slope, since a lower wage will shift the industry output supply curve to the right and reduce the equilibrium price.

Production technology determines how steep the *MVPL* schedules are. The faster the *MPL* diminishes as labour is increased, the steeper will be the *MVPL* schedule of the firm and of the industry. But the slope of the industry demand curve for labour depends on a second influence, the elasticity of the market demand curve for the industry's product. The more inelastic is market demand, the more a wage cut – through increasing the supply of output – will reduce market price and shift *MVPL* schedules to the left; and the steeper will be the industry demand curve $D_L D_L$ for labour.

This last observation takes us back to where we began the chapter. The demand for factors of production is a *derived* demand. Firms want factors only because they perceive a demand for their output that it is profitable to supply. It is unsurprising that the elasticity of demand for labour in a particular industry should reflect the elasticity of demand for the product the industry supplies.

12-4 The supply of labour

In this section we discuss the supply of labour, beginning with the decision of an individual and ending with the supply of labour to an industry and to the economy as a whole. It will then be possible to put together the labour demand curve and the labour supply curve to determine the equilibrium level of wages and employment.

The individual's labour supply decision: hours of work

The effective labour input to the production process is the number of workers multiplied by the number of hours they work. We approach the analysis of labour supply in two stages: how many hours people wish to work given that they are in the labour force, and whether or not people wish to be in the labour force at all.

The **labour force** is all individuals in work or seeking employment.

Suppose the individual is in the labour force: how many hours will she wish to work?

Note first that this will depend on the *real* wage, W/P, the nominal wage divided by the price of goods. If both W and P double, the individual will be able to buy exactly as many goods as before. It is the real wage that measures the amount of goods that can be bought, so it is the real wage that should influence labour supply decisions.

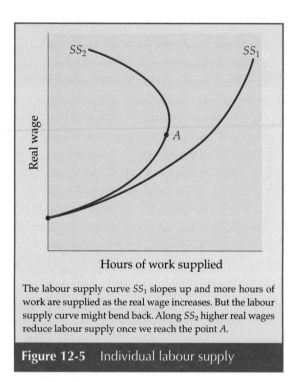

The labour supply curve SS_1 slopes up and more hours of work are supplied as the real wage increases. But the labour supply curve might bend back. Along SS_2 higher real wages reduce labour supply once we reach the point A.

Figure 12-5   Individual labour supply

Figure 12-5 shows two possible labour supply curves relating hours of work supplied to the real wage. The curve SS_1 slopes upwards. Higher real wages make people want to work more. But the labour supply curve SS_2 is *backward-bending*. Beyond A, further real wage increases make people want to work fewer hours.

Do labour supply curves usually correspond to SS_1, where higher real wages always increase hours of work supplied? The alternative to working another hour is staying at home and having fun. Each of us has only 24 hours a day and we have to decide how to divide these hours between work and leisure. More leisure is nice but by working longer we can get more real income with which to buy consumer goods. How should an individual trade off leisure against consumer goods in deciding how much to work?

This is a straightforward application of the model of consumer choice developed in Chapter 6. The choice is no longer between one good and another good, but between goods as a whole and leisure. An individual will want to work until the marginal utility derived from the goods an extra hour of work will provide is just equal to the marginal utility from the last hour of leisure.

A higher real wage increases the quantity of goods an extra hour of work will purchase. This makes working more attractive than before and tends to increase the supply of hours worked. But there is a second effect. Suppose you

work to get a target real income or a target bundle of goods. You work to get enough to be able to eat, pay the rent, run a car, and have a holiday. With a higher real wage you can have your cake and eat it too. You can work less hours to earn the same target real income and have more time off for fun.

These two effects are precisely the *substitution and income effects* we introduced in the consumer choice model of Chapter 6. An increase in the real wage increases the relative return on working. It leads to a substitution effect or pure relative price effect that makes people want to work more. But a higher real wage also tends to raise people's real income. This has a pure income effect. Since leisure is probably a luxury good, the quantity of leisure demanded increases sharply when real incomes increase. This income effect tends to make people work less. The overall effect of a real wage increase, and the shape of the supply curve for hours worked, depends on which of these effects is larger.

To decide whether or not the substitution effect will dominate the income effect, we must look at actual data on what people do. Economists have tried three techniques in an attempt to discover how people actually behave. Interview studies simply ask people how they behave. Econometric studies of the kind discussed in Chapter 2 try to disentangle the separate effects from data on actual behaviour. And experiments have been conducted by giving different people different amounts of take-home pay and recording their behaviour.

The empirical evidence for the UK, the United States, and most other Western economies is as follows. For adult men, the substitution effect and the income effect almost exactly cancel out. A change in the real wage has almost no effect on the quantity of hours supplied. The supply curve of hours worked is almost vertical. In terms of Figure 12-5, adult men are on the part of the supply curve to the point A where changes in the real wage have almost no effect on hours supplied.[2]

For women, the substitution effect just about dominates the income effect. The supply curve for hours slopes upward. Higher real wages make women work longer hours.

Workers care about take-home pay after deductions of income tax. A reduction in income tax rates thus serves to raise after-tax real wages. For the moment we merely note

---

[2] This conclusion applies to relatively small changes in real wage rates. In most Western countries, the large rise in real wages over the last 100 years has been matched by reductions of ten hours or more in the working week.

Table 12-4	UK participation rates (%)		
	1971	1985	1996
Men	92	89	84
Unmarried women	72	74	67
Married women	50	62	72

Source: General Household Survey.

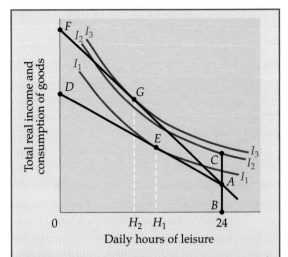

With a non-labour income *BC* the individual can do no work and consume at *C* on the indifference curve I_2I_2. Any work incurs the fixed cost *AC*. At a low hourly wage rate the total budget line is *CAD* and the best point attainable by working is *E*. Thus this lies on the indifference curve I_1I_1 and the individual is better off at *C* where no work is done. At a higher hourly wage rate the new budget line is *CAF*. By working $(24 - H_2)$ hours the individual can reach *G* on the indifference curve I_3I_3 which is better than being at *C*. The higher the real hourly wage rate the more likely is the individual to participate in the labour force.

Figure 12-6   Labour force participation

that the empirical evidence on labour supply implies that lower income tax rates should not be expected to lead to a dramatic increase in the supply of hours worked. In fact, for adult men, changes in income tax rates should have almost no effect on hours of work supplied.

Individual labour supply: participation rates

If the effect of real wages on the supply of hours is smaller than is often supposed, the more important effect of real wages on labour supply may be the effect on the incentive to enter or participate in the labour force.

The **participation rate** is the percentage of a given group of the population of working age who decide to enter the labour force.

Table 12-4 presents UK data on participation rates for different groups of the population of working age. Most men are in employment or are seeking employment. A smaller but still quite stable percentage of unmarried women are in the labour force. Table 12-4 shows that there has been a substantial increase in the number of married women in the labour force, a trend continuing steadily since 1951 when only 25 per cent of married women were in the UK labour force. Similar patterns are observed in other Western countries. Can our model of consumer choice explain these trends?

We now develop a model of consumer choice with the following properties: individuals are more likely to participate in the labour force (*a*) the more they like the benefits of working (ability to buy goods or job status) relative to the benefits of leisure, (*b*) the lower their income from non-work sources, (*c*) the lower the fixed costs of working, and (*d*) the higher the real wage rate.

In Figure 12-6 we plot leisure on the horizontal axis. The maximum possible leisure per day is 24 hours. On the vertical axis we plot total real income from work and other sources. This shows the ability to buy consumer goods and services. We begin with budget constraint. Suppose the individual has a non-labour income represented by the vertical distance *BC*. This may be income earned by a

spouse, income from rent or dividends, or welfare payments received from the government.

Thus an individual who is not working at all can have 24 hours of leisure a day plus a daily income *BC*. The individual can consume at the point *C*. Now suppose the individual works. There may be fixed costs in working. Unemployment benefit from the government may be lost immediately, the right clothes or uniform must be purchased, and travel expenses must be incurred to get to the place of work. These costs are independent of the number of hours worked provided any work is done. They are a fixed cost of working.

Figure 12-6 shows these costs as the vertical distance *AC*. Instead of being able to consume at *C*, the net non-labour income *BC* is reduced to *BA* after these fixed costs of working are incurred. Having decided to work, the individual can then move along the budget line *AD* sacrificing hours of leisure to gain wage income. The higher the real wage the steeper will be the budget line *AD*. Giving up a given number of leisure hours earns a higher real income when the real wage is higher.

Because of the fixed costs of working, the individual faces the kinked budget line *CAD*. Thus working a small number of hours can actually reduce total real income. The small wage income is insufficient to cover the fixed costs of working. The lower the real wage rate, the flatter will be the line AD, and the more hours an individual will have to work merely to recoup the fixed costs. This phenomenon is sometimes called the *poverty trap*. Unskilled workers may be offered such a low wage rate that they actually lose out by working.

To complete the model of consumer choice we must superimpose an indifference map on the kinked budget line CAD. Individuals like both leisure and the goods that real income can buy. Each indifference curve has the usual slope and curvature discussed in Chapter 6, and a higher indifference curve means that the individual is better off. We can now give a general analysis of the participation decision and establish the four effects we cited above.

The indifference curve I_2I_2 shows how well off the individual will be by refusing to participate and consuming at the point C. Given the budget line CAD, the best the individual can do by working is to work $(24 - H_1)$ hours, consume H_1 hours of leisure, and choose the point E to reach the highest possible indifference curve I_1I_1 given that some work is done. But the individual can reach a higher indifference curve I_2I_2 by refusing to participate. This individual will choose not to work.

Now suppose the real wage rate rises. Each hour of leisure now earns a higher real wage income. The budget line AD rotates to AF and the complete budget line is now CAF. Figure 12-6 shows that by choosing the point G the individual can now reach the indifference curve I_1I_3 and be better off than at C. Hence higher real wages tend to increase the number of people wishing to participate in the labour force. As the real hourly wage rises, the fixed costs of working become less important.

A reduction in AC, the fixed cost of working, also tends to increase participation. The point C remains fixed but the point A shifts up. Hence there is a parallel upward shift in the sloping part of the budget line such as AD or AF. It is more likely that the highest indifference curve attainable by working will lie above the indifference curve I_2I_2 through the point C at which no work is done.

Although we do not show it in Figure 12-6, a decrease in non-labour income BC will also lead to an increase in labour force participation. Changes in non-labour income have no effect on the relative return of an hour's work and an hour's leisure. There is no substitution effect, but there is an income effect. Lower non-labour income tends to reduce the quantity demanded of all normal goods including leisure. People are more likely to work.

Finally, consider the effect of a change in tastes. Suppose people decide leisure is less important and work more important. Each indifference curve in Figure 12-6 is flatter. To preserve a given level of utility along an indifference curve, people are prepared to sacrifice more leisure in exchange for the direct and indirect benefits of extra work. Consider again the budget line CAD. The flatter are all indifference curves the more likely it is that the indifference curve through C will cross the portion of the budget line AD on which work is done. But if it crosses AD there must be another point on AD yielding even higher utility. Figure 12-6 shows the indifference curve I_2I_2 crossing the budget line AF and shows that it is possible to attain a higher indifference curve by choosing the point G on AF. Exactly the same argument applies if the flatter indifference curve through C crosses the line AD.

Thus labour force participation is increased by (a) an increase in the real hourly wage rate, (b) a reduction in the fixed costs of working, (c) lower income from non-labour sources, and (d) changes in tastes in favour of more work and less leisure. Can we use these propositions to explain the steady increase of participation by married women?

First, there has been an important change in social attitudes to work, especially to work by married women. Their indifference curves have become flatter. Second, the pressure for equal opportunities for women has tended to increase women's real wages towards the higher levels earned by men. It is as if the budget line for women working has rotated from AD to AF in Figure 12-6. Finally, the fixed costs of working may have been reduced for married women. Automatic ovens, labour-saving devices for housework, a second family car, and many other changes, not least in the attitude of husbands, may have made it possible for married women to contemplate working. It is as if the fixed cost of working had been substantially reduced.

Hence we are thinking about labour supply in the right way. For the remainder of the chapter the most important conclusion of our analysis of labour supply is that a higher real wage rate will increase total labour supply. And the most important effect of higher real wages on the total supply of people times hours is the participation effect on the supply of people rather than the effect on the supply of hours by those already in the labour force.

It is best to think of this analysis as relating to the supply of unskilled workers. Acquiring skills takes time. We examine decisions about whether or not to acquire training and skills in the next chapter.

BOX 12-3

Boosting UK labour supply

New Labour's labour market policies fall under two main headings, *Welfare to Work* and *Making Work Pay*. Both are based on the belief that work allows people to acquire skills and new opportunities: work is a ladder allowing people gradually to climb out of poverty. If this strategy succeeds, the policies will boost UK labour supply. Is this likely?

Welfare to Work has two elements, more help in finding a job and possible loss of benefits for those making little effort to find work. The budget line changes from *CAD* to *FGH*. The fall from *C* to *F* reflects lower benefits for those out of work, and the rise from *A* to *G* the lower fixed cost of working once the

government helps. In diagram (*a*) we show the choice of someone drawn into the labour force by the change in policy.

Making Work Pay deals with the part of the budget line once some work is being done. The Working Families Tax Credit gives money to *workers* with children, provided the parent is working a minimum number of hours a week. Diagram (*b*) shows the discontinuity *JK* when the benefit kicks in. The indifference map shows a person who would not work facing *CAD* but for whom *K* is better than *F* once the budget line becomes *FGJKM*. Or so the government hopes! (see www.newdeal.gov.uk)

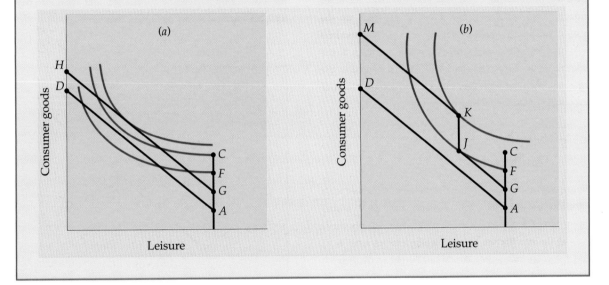

The supply of labour to an industry

So far we have discussed the economy as a whole. Now we discuss the supply of labour to an individual industry. Suppose that the industry is very small relative to the economy as a whole and that it wishes to employ workers with very common skills.

Essentially there are economy-wide markets for welders, drivers, and other types of worker. The small individual industry will have to pay the going rate. Jobs in different industries have different non-monetary characteristics, such as risk, comfort, or anti-social hours like night shifts. The idea of the going wage rate must be adjusted industry by industry to allow for the *equilibrium wage differential* which

offsets these non-monetary characteristics and makes workers indifferent about the industry in which they work.

Given this adjustment, a small industry will be able to hire as many workers as it wants from the economy-wide labour pool. At this wage rate the industry faces a horizontal labour supply curve.

In practice, few industries are this small relative to all the skills they wish to employ. The steel industry is a significant user of welders and the freight industry a significant user of lorry drivers. When an industry is a significant user of a particular skill, an expansion of employment in the industry will tend to bid up the wages of that particular skill whose short-run supply is relatively fixed to the economy as a whole. In the short run it will generally be correct to assume that expansion of the industry will bid up the wages of at least some of the workers it employs. The industry's labour supply curve slopes upwards.

In the long run the industry's labour supply curve may be a little flatter. When short-run expansion bids up the wages of computer programmers, more school-leavers will start to train in this skill. In the long run the economy-wide supply will increase and the wages that these workers can earn will fall back again. The individual industry will not have to offer such a high wage in the long run to increase the supply of that type of labour to the industry.

To sum up, real wages determine total labour supply to the economy. In the short run the supply of a given skill may be relatively fixed. To obtain a larger share of the total pool an individual industry will typically have to offer higher relative wages than other industries to bid workers into that industry. In depleting the labour pool available for other industries, expansion by one industry also bids up the wages that other industries will have to pay for workers who have become more scarce in the whole economy. To the extent that the supply of scarce skills is augmented in the long run, each industry may face a flatter long-run labour supply curve than in the short run.

12-5 Industry labour market equilibrium

Figure 12-7 shows equilibrium in the labour market for a particular industry. Its labour demand curve D_LD_L slopes down and crosses the upward-sloping labour supply curve S_LS_L at the equilibrium point E where employment is L_0 and the wage rate is W_0. We do not bother to distinguish long-run and short-run supply curves though this is easily done.

Suppose wages and prices are fixed in all other industries. We can think of W as the nominal wage the industry must pay to attract workers away from other industries. Since other wages and prices are fixed, a higher nominal wage W also implies a higher real wage. We now use this model of industry equilibrium in the labour market to investigate demand and supply shocks to the industry.

We draw the industry labour demand curve D_LD_L for a given output demand curve. Suppose there is a recession in the building industry which shifts the demand curve for cement to the left. The equilibrium price of cement falls. This shifts to the left the marginal value product of labour curve $MVPL$ for each cement manufacturer. Hence D_LD_L shifts to $D'_LD'_L$ for the cement industry. At the new equilibrium E_1 in

the labour market for the cement industry, wages and employment are reduced in the industry.

Conversely, suppose there is a spurt of investment in new machinery in every industry except cement. With more capital to work with, labour becomes more productive in all other industries. Setting wages equal to the $MVPL$, these industries now pay a higher wage rate. This shifts the supply curve of labour to the cement industry to the left to $S'_LS'_L$. For each wage rate in the cement industry, the industry now attracts fewer workers from the general pool than before.

The new equilibrium for cement workers occurs at E_2. Employment has contracted from L_0 to L_2. Since the remaining workers have more capital to work with they have a higher marginal product. In addition, the contraction in cement output shifts the output supply curve to the left and bids up the cement price. Together these effects move the industry up its demand curve D_LD_L and allow it to pay a higher wage rate to its remaining workers.

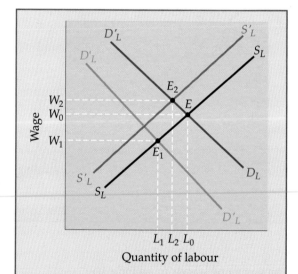

The industry labour market supply curve S_LS_L slopes up. Higher wages are needed to attract workers into the industry. For a given output demand curve, the industry's labour demand curve D_LD_L slopes down because of diminishing marginal labour productivity and because higher industry output bids down its output price. A leftward shift in the output demand curve thus shifts the derived demand for labour from D_LD_L to $D'_LD'_L$ and moves labour market equilibrium from E to E_1. An increase in wages elsewhere in the economy shifts the industry's labour supply curve from S_LS_L to $S'_LS'_L$ and shifts equilibrium from E to E_2.

Figure 12-7 Equilibrium in an industry labour market

Thus wage increases in one industry spill over into other industries. The crucial link between industries is the assumption of labour mobility. It is because cement workers are lured away from the industry by wage rises elsewhere that the cement industry's labour supply curve shifts to the left in Figure 12-7. The degree of labour mobility between industries affects not only how much an industry's labour supply curve will shift when conditions change elsewhere, it also affects the slope of the industry's labour supply curve. This can be understood most easily by considering the two extreme cases.

Suppose first that workers can move effortlessly between similar jobs in different industries. If each industry is small relative to the economy, it will face a completely elastic (horizontal) labour supply curve at the going wage rate (adjusted for non-monetary advantages). When all other industries pay higher wages, the horizontal supply curve of labour to the cement industry shifts up by the full amount of the wage increase elsewhere. Unless the cement industry matches the going rate, it loses all its workers.

At the opposite extreme, consider the market for concert pianists. Suppose there is no other job they are capable of doing. They have to work in the music industry. The industry faces a vertical supply curve of concert pianists at the given number of pianists currently in existence. Even if all other industries pay higher wages this will have no effect on the equilibrium in the market for concert pianists. In the short run there is no question of anyone entering or leaving the occupation of concert pianists.

The general case depicted in Figure 12-7 lies between these extremes. With limited mobility between industries, the cement industry can attract more workers if it offers higher wages. But, because it is not insulated from other industries, its labour supply curve will shift to the left when wages rise in other industries.

12-6 Transfer earnings and economic rents

Top pianists and top footballers are doubtless delighted with the high salaries they can earn, but they would almost certainly choose the same career even if the pay was less good. Why then do they get paid so much? We need to distinguish between transfer earnings and economic rent.

The **transfer earnings** of a factor of production in a particular use are the minimum payments required to induce that factor to work in that job. **Economic rent** (not to be confused with income from renting out property) is the

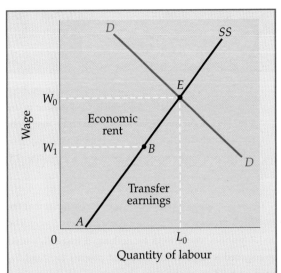

DD is the industry demand curve for labour. A quantity A of labour would work in the industry even at a zero wage. Higher wages attract additional workers to the industry. SS is the industry labour supply curve. If each worker were paid only the transfer earnings requires to attract them to the industry (to keep them on their supply curve), the industry need only pay AEL_0 in wages. If all workers must be paid the highest wage rate necessary to attract the last worker to the industry, equilibrium at E implies workers as a whole derive economic rent $OAEW_0$. For workers who would work for a zero wage rate, W_0 is economic rent, a pure bonus.

Figure 12-8   Transfer earnings and economic rent

extra payment a factor receives over and above the transfer earnings required to induce the factor to supply its services in that use.

Figure 12-8 helps make sense of these concepts. DD is the labour demand curve for concert pianists and SS the supply of pianists to the music industry. Even at a zero wage some dedicated musicians would be concert pianists. Higher wages attract into the industry concert pianists who could have done other things. The supply curve slopes upwards.

Because all workers must be paid the same wage rate, equilibrium occurs at E where the wage is W_0 and the number of pianists is L_0. In the market for concert pianists or footballers W_0 may be a very large wage. Each firm in the music industry is happy to pay W_0 because their workers are very talented. They have a high marginal product. In the output market (concerts) firms can earn a large revenue. The derived demand curve DD for concert pianists is very high.

BOX 12-4 — Premiership wages

The wage bill in UK Premier League football rose from £50 million in the 1992–93 season to £190 million in the 1988–98 season, while income of the clubs rose from £464 million to £569 million. Spiralling club incomes reflect not only increasing demand as satellite TV retails football to ever wider (and more profitable) audiences, but also greater proficiency in marketing ancillary products like replica shirts. Competition for top talent has seen players get their hands on all of the club's additional revenue.

The supply curve SS shows the transfer earnings that the industry may pay to attract pianists into the industry. The first A pianists would work for nothing. A wage W_1 would be required to expand the supply of pianists to B and W_0 must be paid to increase supply to L_0. If the industry as a whole could make separate wage bargains with each individual pianist, paying each the minimum required to attract them into the industry, the triangle AL_0E is the total transfer earnings the industry would need to pay to attract L_0 pianists.

At the equilibrium position E the last pianist enticed into the industry has transfer earnings W_0 since E lies on the supply curve SS. And it is just worth employing this last pianist, since his or her marginal value product is also W_0. E lies on the demand curve DD. However, because the industry typically has to pay all workers the same wage, all previous workers must also be paid W_0 even though the labour supply curve SS implies these workers would have worked for less than W_0. These workers whose transfer earnings are less than W_0 are earning *economic rent*, a pure surplus arising because W_0 is needed to attract the last pianist. Rent reflects differences in pianists' *supply* decisions not their *productivity* as musicians.

Thus in Figure 12-8 the industry as a whole makes total wage payments equal to the rectangle OW_0EL_0. It pays L_0 workers W_0 each. But these payments can be divided into the total transfer earnings AL_0E and the economic rent $OAEW_0$.

Economic rent arises whenever the supply curve of a factor is not horizontal. Try drawing a horizontal supply curve SS in Figure 12-8. No worker earns more than the going rate required to keep pianists in the industry. All earnings are transfer earnings. When the factor supply curve to the industry slopes up, any further expansion of supply can be achieved only by higher payments to entice additional factor supply into the industry. This is a pure bonus or economic rent for those already happily working in the industry.

Notice the distinction between the firm and the industry. Economic rent is an unnecessary payment as far as the industry is concerned. By colluding to wage-discriminate, paying each worker his or her transfer earnings alone, the industry could retain all its workers without paying them economic rent. But the entire wage W_0 is a transfer earning as far as a single competitive firm is concerned. If the firm does not match the going rate for the industry, its workers will go to another firm who will employ them, since their marginal value product covers the wage at the equilibrium position E.

In the UK football industry[3] and the US baseball industry, it is currently being asserted that high player salaries are bankrupting the industry. What light does our analysis shed on this issue? First, wages are high because the derived demand is high – crowds at the ground and television rights make it profitable to supply this output – and because the supply of talented players is scarce. The supply curve of good players is steep: even by offering very high wages the industry cannot increase the number of good players by much. Thus there is no simple link between high salaries and the ruin of the game. If supplying the output were not profitable, the derived demand for players would be lower and their wages would be correspondingly reduced.

12-7 Do labour markets clear?

Thus far we have assumed that wage flexibility ensures that labour markets for each industry and for the economy as a whole are in equilibrium. Each market clears at the equilibrium wage and employment level that equates supply and demand. In Part 4 we shall see that many questions in macroeconomics turn on whether or not it

___
[3] Football clubs pay transfer fees to another club from whom they wish to take over a player. This idea of transfer fees between clubs should not be confused with the economist's concept of transfer earnings of players, the amount necessary to keep them in the industry.

is correct to assume that wage flexibility is sufficient to maintain labour markets close to their equilibrium positions. We now examine why it may not be possible to take labour market equilibrium for granted.

Minimum wage agreements

The UK minimum wage is £3.60 an hour. Figure 12-9 shows the demand curve $D_L D_L$ and the supply curve $S_L S_L$ for a particular labour skill in a particular industry. Free market equilibrium is at E. For skilled workers the equilibrium wage W_0 is likely to exceed a minimum wage agreement at the level W_1 so the agreement is irrelevant. At W_1 there would be excess labour demand $L_2 - L_1$, which would bid wages back to their equilibrium level W_0. Putting the argument differently, at the minimum wage W_1 the labour supply L_1 would have a marginal value product equal to W_2, the height of the industry labour demand curve at L_1. Firms have an incentive to pay higher wages to attract additional workers until the differential between the wage and the $MVPL$ is eroded.

For low-skill labour the situation may be very different. Assume that the minimum wage W_2 exceeds the free market equilibrium wage W_0. At W_2 there is an excess labour supply $L_2 - L_1$. Since firms cannot be forced to employ workers they do not want, employment will be L_1 and the quantity of workers $L_2 - L_1$ will be involuntarily unemployed.

Workers are **involuntarily unemployed** if they are prepared to work at the going wage rate but cannot find jobs.

Thus, for low-skill occupations a minimum wage in excess of the free market equilibrium wage will raise the wage for those lucky enough to find jobs but will reduce the total amount of employment relative to the free market equilibrium level of employment. Minimum wage agreements may explain involuntary unemployment among low-skilled workers.

Trade unions

A strong trade union may act in a similar way. Figure 12-9 implies that, if unions in an industry are successful in forcing employers to pay a wage W_2 which is higher than the wage W_0 that would have prevailed under free competition, the consequence will be a lower level of employment in the industry. By forcing the wage up from W_0 to W_2, the union must accept a loss of employment from L_0 to L_1. How unions trade off higher wages for lower employment is a question we consider in the next chapter. However, the consequence of such behaviour is already

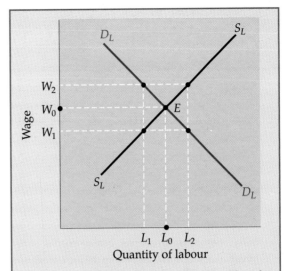

Free market equilibrium occurs at the wage W_0 and a quantity of employment L_0. A minimum wage W_1 below W_0 is irrelevant. However, a minimum wage W_2 above W_0 will restrict the actual quantity of employment to L_1, leaving a quantity $L_2 - L_1$ of workers involuntarily unemployed. They would like to work at this wage rate but cannot find jobs.

Figure 12-9 A minimum wage

clear. If the union chooses a wage W_2, the resulting unemployment is collectively voluntary for the union – it chose this action – but may be involuntary for some of the unlucky union members who lose their jobs. To say more, we need to develop models of how decisions are made within unions.

Scale economies

Involuntary unemployment may arise from the interaction of scale economies and imperfect competition, which we discussed in Chapter 10. We saw how these would create entry barriers and prevent new firms from joining an industry. These entry barriers may prevent the unemployed from starting new firms even if these unemployed workers were prepared to work for a wage below that earned by workers in existing firms.

Insider–outsider distinctions

Whereas the previous explanation emphasizes entry barriers in the formation of new firms, the insider–outsider theories emphasize barriers to entering employment in existing firms.

Insiders have jobs and are represented in wage bargaining. **Outsiders** do not have jobs and are unrepresented in wage bargaining.

BOX 12-5 — Minimum wages hurt jobs, don't they?

A minimum wage prices some workers out of a job: by raising wages it slides employment up the demand curve. It must reduce jobs. One of the few certainties in economics. Even politicians understand. Right?

Not so fast. The 'proof' relies on a diagram of a perfectly competitive labour market. People's intuition about economics is often based on perfect competition. But there are other kinds of market structure. What happens when there is a monopsonist, a sole employer in the relevant labour market. A monopsonist recognizes that additional hiring bids up the price of existing workers making the marginal cost of labour exceed the wage. The diagram shows $MRPL$ the marginal revenue product of labour, LS the labour supply curve facing the firm, and MCL the marginal cost of labour to the monopsonist. Equilibrium is where $MRPL$ equals MCL. Employment is N_1 and a wage W_1 is necessary to attract this labour. Crucially, this combination is not on the monopsonist's $MRPL$ curve. The vertical gap between LS and $MRPL$ shows workers are being paid less than their marginal product. Sometimes this is called *exploitation*.

Now suppose the government imposes a minimum wage at W_2. Effectively, the monopsonist will face a *horizontal* labour supply at this wage, at least until N_2 people are hired. Since W_2 is now the relevant marginal cost of labour, the firm will indeed hire N_2 workers to equate the marginal cost and marginal benefit of hiring. The minimum wage has increased employment, from N_1 to N_2! In effect it has countered the exploitation.

Notice that, beginning at free market equilibrium at a wage W_1, steadily increasing the minimum wage will *increase* employment (sliding the market along the labour supply curve LS) until the minimum wage

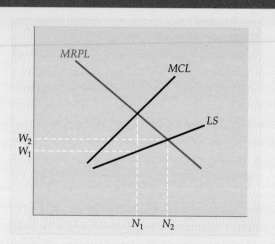

reaches W_2 at which point employment is maximized. Further increases in the minimum wage now slide the market up the demand curve, steadily *reducing* employment thereafter. Thus, when employers have some monopsony power, a minimum wage slightly above the free market equilibrium is good for employment – it offsets the distortion caused by the market power of firms in this situation – but a minimum wage substantially above the free market equilibrium is likely to reduce employment. The employment effect of a minimum wage is therefore an *empirical* question. A study of four EU countries found that there is no evidence minimum wages have reduced adult employment but some evidence they have reduced youth employment, presumably because the productivity of the young and unskilled is lower so minimum wages, even lower rates for youths, are often above the intersection of LS and $MRPL$.

Source: Dolado *et al.*, 'The Economic Impact of Wages in Europe', *Economic Policy, 1996*.

Entry barriers may take several forms: the cost of advertising for workers, interviewing them, and evaluating what sort of job they should be offered; costs of training new workers in activities specific to the firm; and the time taken to build up teamwork and for new employees to master their new jobs. In the terminology of Chapter 10, these are innocent entry barriers.

But existing workers (insiders) may also succeed in erecting strategic barriers to entry by outsiders, even with-

out the presence of formal trade unions at plant level. For example, they may threaten various forms of industrial disruption if too many outsiders are admitted too quickly, and in many circumstances they would find it easy to obtain mass insider support for such threats if there were any proposal to admit outsiders at a lower wage than that currently being paid to insiders.

When such entry barriers confront outsiders, the insiders will be able to raise their own wage above that for which outsiders would be prepared to work *without* inducing a spate of hiring of outsiders. The outsiders might like to work at the wage currently enjoyed by insiders, but outsiders do not find it attractive to work for the very much lower wage that would be necessary to induce firms to hire them when the economic cost of these various entry barriers is large. Just as in the discussion of new entry by firms in Chapter 10, the market power of the incumbents or insiders will depend on the size of the entry barriers.

Efficiency wage explanations

Thus far, we have assumed that information is trivially easy (i.e. cheap) to come by. In the real world, employers face two kinds of problem: they find it hard to tell whether an applicant for a job will be a productive or unproductive worker (a matter of innate ability); and they find it hard to monitor whether workers are trying or shirking even once they are employed.[4]

Given the costs of evaluating or screening new workers, and the subsequent costs of monitoring their performance on the job, what is the best policy for a firm? The efficiency wage theory argues that it will be profitable for firms to respond by paying existing workers a wage which on average exceeds the wage for which workers as a whole are prepared to work.

Efficiency wages are high wages which increase productivity through their incentive effect.

First, to the extent workers may quit their job if they find a more attractive offer elsewhere, if firms pay a wage that is the average of that required by productive and unproductive workers, it is the productive workers who are more likely to find better offers elsewhere and quit. Eventually, the firm will be left only with the low-quality workers. Paying a wage premium is a device to help retain high-quality workers, even in a world where the firm has some trouble distinguishing between high- and low-quality workers.

Second, when workers shirk on the job there is a small chance they will get caught. Suppose they get sacked if caught: how big is the penalty for being caught? It is the difference between what the worker currently earns and what the worker will get in unemployment benefit or in some subsequent job. The higher the wage paid by the existing employer, the larger the penalty of being caught shirking. Hence the efficiency wage theory concludes that,

to increase the penalty and reduce the incentive to shirk, firms will pay existing workers a higher wage than on average would be necessary to get them to supply their labour. Again, the implication is that some workers may be involuntarily unemployed, in the sense that they might be happy to work for wages at or below those paid to existing workers, but have little practical chance of actually securing a job at such wages.

Minimum wage agreements, trade union power, scale economies, insider–outsider distinctions, and efficiency wages are all *possible* explanations for insufficient wage flexibility in the short run to maintain the labour market in continuous equilibrium. Whether the labour market is always in equilibrium, and the length of time for which any disequilibrium might persist, are questions to which we return repeatedly in Part 4.

12-8 UK wages and employment

We began the chapter by looking at real earnings in energy, financial services, and textiles. We end the chapter by re-examining earnings in these industries. It allows us to draw together some of the themes of the chapter.

Table 12-5 shows changes in real earnings and employment during 1986–98. Throughout the economy, real earnings rose 26 per cent. Technical advances, better machinery, and an improvement in workforce skills and practices tended to increase labour's marginal value product and shift the derived demand curve for labour to the right. But this process was very different in different industries.

Facing severe international competition, especially from the Far East, the textile industry's output demand curve shifted to the left. This shifted its derived demand curve for labour to the left and reduced the equilibrium real wage in the textile industry relative to the economy as a whole. Textile wages rose less than wages elsewhere. In consequence, the supply of workers to the textile industry fell

---

[4] Economists refer to these problems as adverse selection and moral hazard. We discuss them in detail in Chapter 15 when we turn to the interesting issues that arise in the economics of information.

Table 12-5 UK jobs and real earnings (% growth during 1986–98)

	Real earnings	Jobs
Whole economy	+26	+9
Financial services	+32	+16
Textiles	+16	−32
Energy and water	+34	−54

Source: ONS, *Labour Market Trends.*

and textile employment became a smaller fraction of employment in the whole economy.

Financial services (such as banking and insurance) boomed. The demand for these products increased sharply as the industry was deregulated and as it took advantage of its stronger position in world markets. There were large increases in both employment and real earnings per person. Technical progress and continuing physical investment helped boost productivity in energy and water, but privatization and greater international competition led to rapid job losses, especially in the coal industry.

SUMMARY

● In the long run, the firm chooses the technique of production to minimize the cost of producing a particular output. From the total cost curve showing the cheapest way to produce each output level the firm then calculates long-run marginal cost and equates this to marginal revenue to determine the profit-maximizing output. An increase in the relative price of one factor of production will tend to reduce the intensity with which that factor is used. Thus a rise in the wage rate relative to the rental cost of capital will tend to lead firms to choose more capital-intensive techniques in the long run. The capital–labour ratio will rise.

● In the long run, a rise in the price of labour (capital) will have both a substitution effect and an output effect. The substitution effect reduces the quantity of labour (capital) demanded as the capital–labour ratio rises (falls) at each output. But total costs and marginal costs of output increase. The more elastic is the firm's demand curve and marginal revenue curve, the more this upward shift in the marginal cost curve will reduce output, and this will tend to reduce the demand for both factors. For an increase in the own price of a factor the substitution and output effects work in the same direction to reduce the quantity of that factor demanded in the long run.

● In the short run, the firm has fixed factors and probably has a fixed production technique. The firm can vary short-run output by varying its variable input, labour. But labour is subject to diminishing returns when other factors are fixed. The marginal physical product of labour falls as more labour is employed.

● A profit-maximizing firm produces the output at which marginal output cost equals marginal output revenue. Equivalently, it hires labour up to the point where the marginal cost of labour equals its marginal revenue product. One implies the other. If the firm is a price-taker in its output market, the marginal revenue product of labour is its marginal value product, the output price times its marginal physical product. If the firm is a price-taker in the labour market, the marginal cost of labour is the wage rate. A perfectly competitive firm equates the real wage to the marginal physical product of labour.

● Thus the downward-sloping marginal physical product of labour schedule is the short-run demand curve for labour (in terms of the real wage) for a competitive firm. Equivalently, the marginal value product of labour schedule is the demand curve in terms of the nominal wage. The $MVPL$ schedule for a firm shifts up if the output price increases, the capital stock increases, or if technical progress makes labour more productive.

● The industry's labour demand curve is not merely the horizontal sum of firms' $MVPL$ curves. Higher industry output in response to a wage reduction will also reduce the output price in equilibrium. The industry labour demand curve is steeper (less elastic) than that of each firm and is more inelastic the more inelastic is the demand curve for the industry's output.

● Thus labour demand curves are derived demands. A shift in the output demand curve for the industry will shift the derived factor demand curve in the same direction.

● For an individual already in the labour force, an increase in the hourly real wage has a substitution effect tending to increase the supply of hours worked, but an income effect tending to reduce the supply of hours worked. For men, the two effects cancel out almost exactly in practice, but the empirical evidence suggests that the substitution effect dominates for women. Thus women have a rising supply curve for hours but the supply curve for men is almost vertical.

● Individuals with non-labour income may prefer not to work. In theory, four factors increase the participation rate in the labour force: higher real wage rates, lower fixed costs of working, lower non-labour income, and changes in tastes in favour of working rather than staying at home. These forces help explain the steady trend for increasing labour force participation by married women over the last few decades.

● For a particular industry the supply curve of labour depends on the wage paid relative to wages in other industries using similar skills. Equilibrium wage differentials are the monetary compensation for differences in non-monetary characteristics of jobs in different industries undertaken by workers with the same skill. Taking monetary and non-monetary considerations together, there is then no incentive to move between industries.

● When the labour supply curve to an industry is less than perfectly elastic, the industry must pay higher wages to expand employment. For the marginal worker, the wage is a pure transfer earning required to induce that worker into the industry. For workers prepared to work in the industry at a lower wage, there is an element of economic rent. Economic rent is the difference between income received and transfer earnings for that individual. Economic rent is highest when the supply curve is steep and when the derived demand curve for labour is high. Economic rent explains the extremely high salaries in sports, entertainment, and related industries.

● In free market equilibrium, some workers will choose not to work at the equilibrium wage rate. They are voluntarily unemployed. Involuntary unemployment is the difference between desired supply and desired demand at a disequilibrium wage rate. Workers would like to work but cannot find a job.

● There is considerable disagreement about how quickly labour markets can get back to equilibrium if they are initially thrown out of equilibrium. Possible causes of involuntary unemployment are minimum wage agreements, trade unions, scale economies, insider–outsider distinctions, and efficiency wages.

KEY TERMS

◆ Derived demand   176

◆ Equalizing wage differentials   176

◆ Marginal value product of labour   179

◆ Monopsony power   180

◆ Marginal revenue product of labour   180

◆ Marginal cost of labour   180

◆ Labour force   183

◆ Participation rate   185

◆ Transfer earnings   189

◆ Economic rent   189

◆ Involuntary unemployment   191

◆ Insiders and outsiders   191

◆ Efficiency wages   193

◆ Isoquant   196

REVIEW QUESTIONS

1 In what sense is it true that a firm's decision on how much output to produce is the same thing as its decision on how much labour to demand?

2 (a) Suppose in Table 12-2 that there is a third way of making 100 snarks per week. The third technique uses 4 units of capital and 5 units of labour. Would this technique ever be used? Explain. (b) Suppose that there is another technique using 1 unit of capital and 8 units of labour. Are there any levels of the wage rate at which this technique would be used assuming that the rental rate for capital stays at £320 per week?

3 (a) Explain why the marginal product of labour eventually declines. (b) Show in a diagram the effect of an increase in the firm's capital stock on its demand curve for labour.

4 Over the last 100 years the real wage has risen but the length of the working week has fallen. (a) Explain this result using income and substitution effects. (b) Explain how an increase in the real wage could cause everyone in

employment to work fewer hours but still increase the total amount of work done in the economy.

5 Why should the labour supply curve to an industry slope upwards even if the aggregate labour supply to the economy is fixed?

6 A film producer says that the industry is doomed because film stars are paid an outrageous amount of money. Evaluate the argument being sure to discuss economic rent.

7 Answer the questions with which we began the

chapter: (a) Why can a top golfer earn more in a weekend than a university professor earns in a year? (b) Why can students studying economics expect to earn more than equally smart students studying philosophy?

8 *Common fallacies* Show why the following statements are incorrect: (a) There is no economic reason why a sketch that took Picasso one minute to draw should fetch a price of £100 000. (b) Higher wage rates must increase incentives to work. (c) Unemployment can result only from greedy and unrealistic wage claims by workers.

Appendix: isoquants and the choice of production technique

In the text we used Table 12-2 to describe how a firm chooses the production technique. We now show that this problem of producer choice can be examined using techniques similar to the indifference curve–budget line approach we used to study consumer choice in Chapter 6.

Figure 12-A1 plots input quantities of capital K and labour L. Points A, B, C, and D show the *minimum* input quantities required to produce 1 unit of output using each of four different techniques of production. Technique A is the most labour-intensive, requiring L_A units of labour and K_A units of capital to produce 1 unit of output. Technique D is the most capital intensive. Connecting A, B, C, and D yields a schedule called an *isoquant* ('iso' meaning 'the same' and 'quant' meaning 'quantity').

An **isoquant** shows the different minimum combinations of inputs to produce a given level of output. Different points on an isoquant reflect different production techniques for making the same output level.

Although Figure 12-A1 shows only four production techniques we can imagine that there are many more available techniques. Figure 12-A2 shows smooth isoquants. Isoquant I corresponds to a particular output level. Each point on isoquant I corresponds to a different production technique, ranging from the very capital intensive to the very labour intensive. The higher isoquant I' shows the different input combinations needed to produce a higher output level. Higher isoquants reflect higher output levels since more inputs are required. Each isoquant shows different input combinations to produce a given output level.

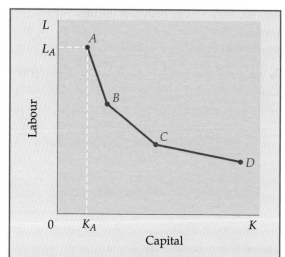

Points A, B, C, and D show different input combinations required to produce 1 unit of output. By connecting them we obtain an isoquant that shows the different input combinations which can produce a particular level of output.

Figure 12-A1   An isoquant

The successive isoquants constitute an isoquant map. Three properties of isoquants are important. First, they cannot cross. Each isoquant refers to a different output level. Second, each isoquant slopes down. To make a given output, a firm will consider a technique using more capital only if it uses less labour, and vice versa. Hence isoquants must slope down.

Third, Figure 12-A2 shows each isoquant getting flatter as we move along it to the right. Moving down a given isoquant, it takes more and more extra capital input to make equal successive reductions in the labour input required to produce a given output.

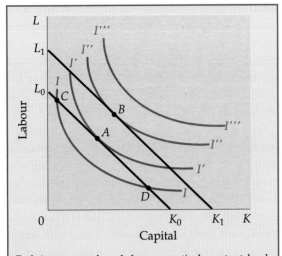

Each isoquant such as I shows a particular output level. Higher isoquants such as I'' show higher output levels. Straight lines such as L_0K_0 are isocost lines showing different input combinations having the same total cost. The slope of an isocost line depends only on relative factor prices. A higher isocost line such as L_1K_1 implies a larger total cost. To produce a given output, such as that corresponding to the isoquant I', the firm chooses the point of tangency of that isoquant to the lowest possible isocost line. Thus point A is the cost minimizing way to produce the output level on I' and point B the cost minimizing way to produce the output level on I''.

Figure 12-A2   Cost minimization

In Figure 12-A2 the line L_0K_0 is called an *isocost* line. It shows different input combinations with the *same* total cost. With a given amount of money to spend, the firm can use more units of capital only if it uses less units of labour. Facing given prices at which different inputs may be hired, we can say two things about isocost lines. First, the slope of the isocost line reflects the relative price of the two factors of production. Beginning at K_0, where all the firm's money is spent on capital the firm can trade off 1 unit of capital for more units of labour the cheaper is the wage rate relative to the rental cost of capital. Second, facing given factor prices, if the firm spends more on inputs it can have larger quantities of both labour and capital. An isocost line parallel to but above L_0K_0 thus represents a larger expenditure on hiring inputs. Thus along the isocost line L_1K_1 the firm is spending a larger amount on inputs than along the isocost line L_0K_0.

We now can examine the firm's decision problem.

To minimize the cost of producing a given output level, the firm chooses the point of tangency of that isoquant to the lowest possible isocost line.

At the cost-minimizing point the (negative) slope of the isocost line is exactly equal to the (negative) slope of the isoquant.

If w is the wage rate and r the rental cost of a unit of capital, the slope of the isocost line is $-r/w$. What about the slope of the isoquant?

By using an extra unit of capital (a change of $+1$) the firm gains MPK units of output, where MPK is the marginal physical product of capital. But along an isoquant output is constant. By shedding a unit of labour the firm gives up MPL units of output. Hence a negative change in labour input equal to $-MPK/MPL$ will maintain output constant when capital input is increased by 1 unit. Thus the slope of an isoquant is given by $-MPK/MPL$ since it tells us by how much labour must be changed to preserve a constant output level when capital is increased by 1 unit. Hence the tangency condition in Figure 12-A2 implies:

$$\text{Slope of isocost line} = -r/w = -MPK/MPL$$
$$= \text{slope of isoquant} \qquad (A1)$$

The point A in Figure 12-A2 tells us the cost-minimizing way to produce the output level corresponding to the isoquant I'. We can repeat this analysis for every other isoquant corresponding to every other output level. That is how we build up the total cost curve which we discussed in the text. How does the firm find the profit-maximizing output?

Suppose at point A, the marginal product of labour exceeds the wage rate w. Equation (A1) tells us that in the long run the marginal product of capital must also exceed the rental rate r. Only then can the factor price ratio r/w equal the ratio of the marginal products MPK/MPL. But if the marginal product of each factor exceeds the price at which the firm can hire that factor, it will clearly be profitable to expand output. In the long run, the firm will expand output and factor use until the marginal product of each factor equals the price for which that factor can be hired. Thus, in Figure 12-A2, long-run profit-maximizing output will occur at a point such as B at which

$$MPL = w \text{ and } MPK = r \qquad (A2)$$

If equation (A2) holds, equation (A1) must necessarily be satisfied. Profits can be maximized only if the chosen output is produced in the cost-minimizing way.

Finally we show the effect of an increase in the price of one factor. Figure 12-A3 shows the initial position at B where the isocost line L_1K_1 is tangent to the isoquant I''. Now suppose the wage rate rises. Each isocost line then becomes less steep. Sacrificing a unit of capital will allow less

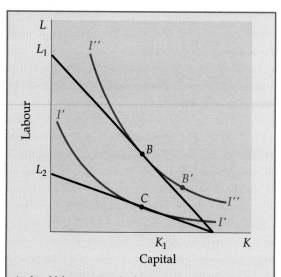

At the old factor prices the firm's output level corresponds to the isoquant I''. All isocost lines have the same slope as L_1K_1 and the firm produces its given output most cheaply by choosing the point B where the isoquant is tangent to the lowest possible isocost line L_1K_1. A wage increase makes all isocost lines flatter, parallel to L_2K_1. Each unit of capital sacrificed now allows the purchase of less additional labour. The wage increase has a pure substitution effect from B to B' where the original isoquant I'' has the same slope as the new isocost lines. Firms substitute capital for labour. But with higher marginal costs at each output level, the firm's profit-maximizing output is reduced, say to the level corresponding to the isoquant I'. On this isoquant, costs are minimized by producing at C to reach the lowest possible isocost line L_2K_1 at the new factor prices. The move from B' to C is the pure output effect induced by the shift in the firm's marginal cost curve for its output.

Figure 12-A3   The effect of a wage increase

additional labour while preserving total cost. At the original output level on isoquant I'' this leads to a pure substitution effect from B to B' the point on the old isoquant tangent to an isocost line with the new flatter slope. But a higher wage rate also shifts up the total cost curve and the marginal cost curve for output and leads to a reduction in the output which maximizes profits.

The lower isoquant I' shows the new profit-maximizing output at this lower level. L_2K_1 is the lowest attainable isocost line embodying the flatter slope corresponding to the new relative input prices. The firm will thus choose the point C. The move from B' to C is the pure output effect of a higher wage-rate. The actual move from B to C can thus be decomposed into a substitution effect from B to B' and an output effect from B' to C. Both effects tend to reduce the quantity of labour demanded.

13 Human capital, discrimination, and trade unions

LEARNING OUTCOMES

When you have finished this chapter, you should be able to:

- Show how workers differ, and explore consequences of these differences
- Analyse how investment in human capital allows workers to be more productive and earn more
- Explain how signalling may identify differences in workers, allowing the more skilled to be allocated to more demanding and more valuable jobs
- Study different forms of direct and indirect discrimination, both in the labour market and before people become workers
- Examine the role of trade unions, both in restricting labour supply to force up the wage and in co-ordinating helpful changes that enhance productivity and the value of workers

In most European countries men earn more than women and whites earn more than non-whites. Do these stark facts reflect discrimination in the labour market, or simply differences in the productivity of different workers?[1]

The theme of this chapter is that labour is heterogeneous. Workers differ not merely in sex and race but in age, experience, education, training, innate ability, and in whether or not they belong to a trade union. How do these differences affect pay? Table 13-1 emphasizes the difference between men and women. Women earn only two-thirds as much per hour as men. These differences partly reflect continuity of employment. Single women do considerably

better than married or divorced women and earn almost 90 per cent as much per hour as men. Whether we regard this as discrimination against women who take time off to raise a family is an issue that goes to the heart of our view about how society should be organized.

Table 13-2 considers some of the factors that influence pay differentials for men, the group on which most data are available. It shows separate estimates for workers in trade unions and not in unions. The effect of unions themselves is considered later in the chapter.

---

[1] By 'discrimination' we mean failure to pay the going rate for the job and skill characteristics merely because a worker is female or black. However, other kinds of discrimination may also exist. Discrimination in education might imply that blacks are less qualified than whites. Discrimination in education would reduce the earnings of blacks.

Table 13-1 Hourly earnings in the UK, 1998

	Men	Women
Manual	£7.1	£5.2
Non-manual	£12.9	£8.9

Source: Department of Employment, *New Earnings Survey*.

Table 13-2   Pay differentials for UK men

% extra pay for	Union	Non-union
Education and training		
GCSE	+5	+13
A-levels	+16	+21
University degree	+32	+47
Postgraduate degree	+50	+50
Other higher education	+18	+21
Apprenticeship	+11	+9
Personal		
Ethnic minority	−1	−5
Profit share	+2	+11
Years experience		
5	+13	+10
10	+23	+20
15	+30	+28
30	+35	+32
Job character		
South East	+15	+16
London	+23	+15
Manual	−17	−21
Shift work	+12	+8
% overtime	+52	+47

Source: A. Booth, 'Seniority, Earnings and Unions', *Economica*, 1996.

Table 13-2 highlights four sources of pay differentials. People with more education and training earn more money, and these returns to education do not depend much on whether the worker is in a union or not. Notice that it is not just vocational degrees, such as engineering, that enhance earning power. All graduates, including, for example, history and philosophy graduates, seem to earn more than their less educated counterparts.

Personal characteristics also matter. Table 13-2 shows that ethnic minorities earn lower pay even *after allowing for differences in education and work experience*. This is *prima facie* evidence of discrimination. And it may understate the true disadvantage of such minorities if they also enjoy lower educational achievement and work experience because of discrimination elsewhere, for example, in schools.

Work experience generally adds to earnings, though at a diminishing rate, especially in manual work, where older workers may not be able to perform all the tasks of which their strong, young colleagues are capable. But experience still matters, even in manual work. Table 13-2 shows that job characteristics also have important effects on pay. Shift work and overtime typically involve additional payments (equalizing wage differentials). Manual workers, perhaps with fewer skills, earn less than non-manuals. And firms in the busy (and expensive) South East region, including London, also have to pay workers more.

Section 13-1 examines how education, experience and skill contribute to earning by increasing workers' *human capital* – the stock of relevant expertise they have accumulated. We then examine the role of education as a filter that screens out the high-ability workers with high career potential. History degrees may *signal* general intelligence, even though they provide little training of direct relevance for many jobs.

Section 13-2 examines in more detail discrimination and equality of opportunity in the labour market. The final section studies the role of trade unions in the labour market.

13-1 Human capital

Human capital is the stock of expertise accumulated by a worker. It is valued for its income-earning potential in the future.

As with physical capital, human capital is the result of past investment and its purpose is to generate future incomes. To invest in another year of school education or a further qualification people may have to make a direct payment, as with fees for private schools, but they also forgo the opportunity to earn immediate income by working. The anticipated benefit of this initial expenditure is either a higher future monetary income or a future job yielding greater job satisfaction.

The human capital approach assumes that wage differentials reflect differences in the productivity of different workers. Skilled workers have a higher marginal value product and earn more. The problem for workers is to decide how much to invest in improving their own productivity.

Age–earnings profiles and education

Table 13-2 shows that education and work experience contribute to higher earnings. Figure 13-1 shows how earnings change with age for workers with three different levels of educational qualification: university or other higher degrees, A-levels or other qualifications equivalent to the best school-leavers, and those without any formal qualifications at all.

The figure makes two points. People with more educational qualifications typically earn more, but the disparity grows steadily with age and experience. Healthy young people without qualifications can work hard and make quite good money. But they cannot look forward to steadily rising real wages. Indeed, by the age of 30 their earnings have already peaked. In contrast, the most highly educated start at wage rates only a little above those of the unqualified

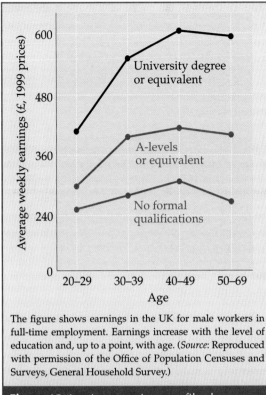

The figure shows earnings in the UK for male workers in full-time employment. Earnings increase with the level of education and, up to a point, with age. (*Source*: Reproduced with permission of the Office of Population Censuses and Surveys, General Household Survey.)

Figure 13-1   Age–earnings profiles by highest educational attainment

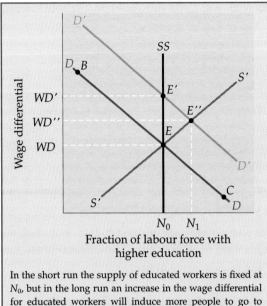

In the short run the supply of educated workers is fixed at N_0, but in the long run an increase in the wage differential for educated workers will induce more people to go to university. The long-run supply curve is $S'S'$. DD is the downward-sloping demand curve for educated workers. From the initial equilibrium at E, with a wage differential WD, an upward shift in the demand for educated workers leads initially to a sharp increase in the differential to WD'. Gradually more people get higher education, and the new long-run equilibrium is at E''.

Figure 13-2   The market for highly educated workers

but they then face steadily rising incomes over most of their working lifetime. Figure 13-1 suggests that the most highly educated go into the most difficult jobs which take a long time to master. With increasing experience, productivity and salaries rise steadily.

There are two completely different interpretations of why the most educated get the highest earnings. One is that education directly increases workers' productivity and allows them to command higher earnings sooner or later. The other is that education does *not* contribute the expertise that increases worker productivity. Rather, people have different innate abilities. High-ability people have high productivity because they can learn difficult jobs. Also, they like studying and are good at it. They happen to amass a lot of educational qualifications, but they earn good money because of the skills they were born with. We return to this view later in the section.

The market for educated workers

Suppose higher education contributes to productivity. Figure 13-2 shows the market for workers with higher education. The vertical axis plots the difference between

wages for workers with higher education and for workers without higher education. It is the *wage premium* for higher education. The horizontal axis shows the fraction of the workforce with higher education.

DD is the demand curve for workers with higher education. At point B the wage differential is high and firms want only a small proportion of their workers to have this extra education. At the lower differential at point C the demand for educated workers is much higher. The demand curve DD thus assumes that workers with higher education are more productive but that firms face diminishing returns in employing educated workers. At any instant, the supply of such workers is fixed by past education decisions. The short-run supply curve SS is vertical.

In the long run, the supply curve $S'S'$ of workers with higher education slopes upwards. The greater the payoff to higher education, as measured by the wage differential, the more school leavers will delay working and acquire more education. The long-run supply curve of educated workers slopes up.

Suppose the market begins in short-run and long-run

equilibrium at *E*. The wage differential *WD* just compensates workers for the cost of acquiring further qualifications and for the wages they forgo while they are being educated.

Now suppose the demand curve for educated workers shifts up to *D'D'*. For example, there may be an expansion of high-technology firms which use educated workers intensively. In the short run, with a fixed supply *SS* of such workers, the differential rises to *WD'*. In competing for scarce educated workers firms bid up their wages. The economy is at *E'*.

The premium on higher education is now so high that more people decide to acquire education. Over the long run the supply of educated workers increases. As this happens the premium on scarce workers falls back. In the long run equilibrium occurs at *E"* with a higher number of educated workers and a wage differential *WD"*.

Investing in human capital: cost–benefit analysis

Consider the decision of a school-leaver whether to continue in education or take a job immediately. Does investment in further education make sense? There are two costs and two benefits. The immediate costs are for books and fees to continue in education, and the income that could have been earned (the opportunity cost) by taking a job immediately rather than remaining unpaid while in further education, *minus* any income received from the government as an educational grant.

The first benefit occurs in the future and is the stream of *extra* wages that workers with higher education can earn. The second occurs immediately but in a non-monetary form. It is the fun or consumption value of going to college or university. Most students have a good time. They meet new people, try new sports, discover new rock bands, and do whatever students do.

Like any investment decision, the decision whether or not to continue in higher education rests on comparing current costs and benefits (usually a net cost) with the stream of future costs and benefits (usually a stream of net benefits). Figure 13-3 compares the income profile of a school-leaver entering the labour force at 18 with the income profile of a university graduate entering the labour force at 21. The cost of higher education, the grey area, is the income forgone by not being in the labour force between 18 and 21, *plus* the direct cost of fees and books, *minus* the sum of money that the school-leavers would have paid to enjoy the pleasures of being a student. The benefit, the coloured area, is the stream of extra income earned after the age of 21.

It makes sense to go on to further education if the benefits

outweigh the costs. But the benefits accrue in the future. Most people would prefer £100 today than a promise of £100 in five years' time. To compare like with like, it is necessary to *discount* or reduce the value of future benefits (or future costs) to place them on a par with benefits or costs incurred today. In the next chapter we discuss in detail how this should be done.

For the moment we can skip the technical details. The general idea will suffice. If the present value, however calculated, of the benefits outweighs the present value of the costs incurred, the educational investment in improving human capital by further education makes sense. If the present value of the benefits is less than the present value of the costs, higher education is a bad investment. It is better to start work immediately.

Cost–benefit analysis computes the stream of costs and benefits of an action.

It is a procedure for making long-run decisions such as whether to build a factory or go to university. In either case, present actions have implications far into the future. The correct way to make a decision is to compare the present

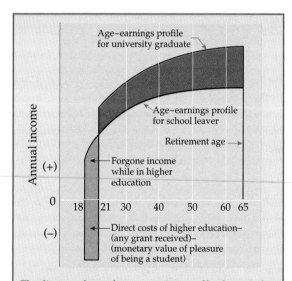

The diagram shows the age–earnings profiles for a worker leaving school at 18 to enter the labour force and for a student who delays working until 21. The coloured area shows how much extra the student will eventually earn. The grey area above 0 shows the income forgone while at university. The grey area below 0 shows the money value of the other costs and benefits of being at university: the diagram assumes that these costs outweigh the benefits. The decision whether or not to go to university depends on comparing the coloured area with the total grey area.

Figure 13-3   Investment in higher education

BOX 13-1   Good economists in short supply

In June 1999 the Bank of England warned that it was having difficulty recruiting staff with good post-graduate degrees in economics. British students account for only 10 per cent of PhD students in economics in leading UK universities. Why so low? Partly because a good undergraduate economics degree is now worth so much in the City. Professor

Andrew Oswald of Warwick University has estimated that economics undergraduates earn about £35 000 a year in their mid-twenties, rising to over £100 000 a year by retirement. The Bank of England can't match these salaries. Nor incidentally can universities. Some of us have to write textbooks to make a decent living!

value of the costs with the present value of the benefits. The action should be undertaken only if the present value of the benefits exceeds the present value of the costs.

The demand for higher education

The analysis behind Figure 13-3 can explain real-world data. We need to add one complication: the minimum age for leaving school is below 18. In countries like Britain it is 16. So 16-year-olds must decide to leave school at 16 to seek a job; to continue at school to 18, sit A-level exams, but then seek a job; or to sit A-levels and try for university.

The fraction of 16-year-olds staying on at school at 16 is well explained by three things: (1) a measure of expected future income in general, (2) the level of unemployment, and (3) as viewed from 16, the present value of the *extra* income enjoyed by university graduates minus the income lost between 16 and 21 by not taking a job at 16. Factor (3) is exactly the effect examined in Figure 13-3.

Higher unemployment makes more people stay on at school. High youth unemployment reduces the chances of finding a job at 16. It reduces the opportunity cost of invest-ing in education. How do we explain point (1)? Education is not just an investment in human capital to increase future income; it also has consumption value. Students usually have fun. Moreover, going to university may broaden the mind, enabling people to get more out of life. If this is a normal good, demand for it rises with income, as (1) suggests.

Table 13-3 shows some estimates of the annual rate of return, spread over one's future lifetime, on two decisions: staying at school from 16 to 18 to sit A-level exams, and going to university at 18. Education beyond 16 yields more than sufficient benefits to pay for the costs: the return is generally positive. Two features deserve further comment.

First, the socio-economic background of the family matters a lot. Children whose fathers work in unskilled or

Table 13-3 Expected return on education (% per annum over rest of life)

	Father's occupation	
	Professional or manager	Manual or unskilled
Men		
A-level only	6	−1
University	7	25
Women		
A-level only	10	13
University	6	8

Source: R. Bennett, H. Glennerster, and D. Nevison, 'Investing in Skill: To Stay On or Not to Stay On', *Oxford Review of Economic Policy*, 1992.

manual get nothing out of A-levels if they then go out to work at 18. Presumably, many of them end up in similar jobs to their fathers. Children from more privileged backgrounds leaving school at 18 get better jobs provided they acquire A-level qualifications.

This is compatible with the second feature of Table 13-3, the huge payoff enjoyed from university by children of unskilled or manual fathers. For such children, university is the stepping stone to much better career prospects.

On-the-job training and age–earnings profiles

Figure 13-1 shows that education increases future earning power. But earnings also rise with experience on the job, especially in the difficult jobs usually done by workers of higher ability and education. Learning on the job is central to the age–earnings profiles of the better educated but much less important for the unqualified who frequently do relatively routine jobs which can be mastered quickly.

If on-the-job training increases worker productivity, why don't workers pay firms for the valuable learning oppor-tunities that firms provide? In part they do. To understand how and why we must distinguish between two kinds of skills.

Firm-specific skills help increase a worker's productivity only if he or she works for that particular firm.

Firm-specific human capital could be something as simple as knowing how the filing system works or something as complicated as mastering the most efficient way to combine the various production processes of a particular factory. In either case, the skill is virtually worthless to any other firm.

General skills are those that can be transferred to work for another firm.

Examples are learning how to be a welder or understanding how the stock market works.

The firm can afford to pay for on-the-job training in firm-specific skills. Workers' productivity will be much higher with that firm than with any other firm. The firm is unlikely to lose the worker. The more general or transferable the skill, the more the firm will want the worker to pay the cost of training. No firm will want to invest heavily in training its workers only to see them move to other firms.

Thus, firms offering general or transferable training try to make the workers pay for this. How? By offering an age–earnings profile that starts off lower than the worker's marginal product, but is guaranteed to rise steeply over time. Examples are apprentice schemes, both in industry and in professional jobs such as accountancy. The worker is paying for training by working for less than his immediate marginal product. Workers are prepared to pay this cost of investing in human capital because the firm is committed to an age–earnings profile that will allow the worker to recoup the initial investment with interest at a later date. Hence in Figure 13-1 age–earnings profiles rise much more steeply for people with more education, likely to be doing jobs that involve more training, than they do for unqualified workers whose training is likely to be limited.

Signalling

Why can a history graduate go on to earn big money in banking? The theory we have just developed says that education and training on the job raise worker productivity. But there is an alternative theory of investment in education, the theory of *signalling*. This theory says that it could be rational to invest in costly education *even if education adds nothing directly to a worker's marginal product*. This theory may be more helpful in explaining why history graduates go on to earn big money in banking.

The theory assumes that people are born with different innate ability. Some people are good at most things, other people are less smart and on average less productive. But smart people do not all have blue eyes and less smart people brown eyes. The problem for firms is to tell which applicants will turn out to be the smart ones with high productivity. Looking at their eyes is not enough.

For the sake of the argument, suppose higher education contributes nothing to productivity. Before making this costly investment in human capital, how can school-leavers be assured that they will earn wages in future to offset the initial cost?

Signalling is the decision to undertake an action in order to reveal inside information.

Signalling theory says that, in going on in education, the smart people are sending a signal to employers that they are the high-productivity workers of the future. Higher education is *screening out* the smart high-productivity workers. Firms can pay university graduates more because they can be assured that they are the high-ability workers.

Screening is the process of learning inside information by observing differences in behaviour.

To be effective, the screening process must separate the high-ability workers from the others. Why don't lower-ability workers go to university and fool firms into offering them high wages? Lower-ability workers could not be confident of passing. Here we have an interesting comparison between the two theories of investment in education. If it is studying that adds to productivity, firms should offer higher wages to people who have *attended* university, whether or not they pass the final exam. But if university works by screening out the good people, firms should be interested not in attendance but in *passing*.

Some firms hire university students before they sit their final exams. Is this evidence against the signalling theory? Not necessarily, for screening works in a second way. The lower-ability people may decide not to go to university: they may not expect to pass, or may feel that to scrape through they will have to work enormously hard. Since most people know their own ability, firms may take it on trust that people who have stuck it out till their final year at university believe themselves to be at the higher end of the ability range.

It seems quite probable that education (even at the highest levels) contributes something to productivity. But there may also be an element of screening in all except purely vocational courses. Engineering, law, and business degrees presumably contribute more to productivity than philosophy, history, or politics.

There is one final issue to consider before we leave investment in education. It concerns the distinction between what is good for the individual and what is good for society as a whole. If education raises productivity directly, it is good for society. It raises the amount of output that the labour force can eventually produce.

Suppose the only function of higher education was to signal which were the higher-ability workers. It still makes sense for individuals to go to university, but does it make sense for society as a whole? There is a social gain to learning which are the smart workers. By matching smart workers to difficult jobs, society will achieve a higher output. It will not give lower-ability people jobs they are unable to do. Nor will it lead higher-ability workers to become bored in jobs that are too easy for them. But if the only function of higher education is to screen out the high-ability workers, there may be a cheaper way for society to achieve the same result. A national IQ test, with results adjusted for disadvantages of background and previous opportunity to learn, might screen as well (possibly even better!) at much less cost to society as a whole.

13-2 Discrimination

Table 13-1 showed that women's hourly earnings in the UK are only two-thirds those of men. Table 13-2 showed that ethnic minorities earn less than whites. Do these numbers provide evidence of sex and race discrimination in the UK labour market?

For all the reasons we analysed in the last chapter, some jobs pay more than others. Differences in average earnings of different sexes or races can thus arise for two distinct reasons. The first reason is that different groups may get different shares of the high-paying jobs. They have different employment patterns. The second reason is that different groups may get paid different amounts for doing each kind of job. We begin by examining the difference between men and women of adult age in full-time employment.

Differences between men and women

Table 13-4 shows the weekly earnings in 1998 in different occupations and the pattern of male and female employment. Part-time working is excluded. The table shows that the patterns of male and female employment do differ. Most men are industrial manual workers or belong to the professional and managerial occupations. Many women do secretarial or selling jobs. Yet the pattern of employment is not the major cause of the fact that women as a whole earn £7500 a year less than men. If women had the employment pattern shown for men in Table 13-4 but were paid the rates shown for women the overall earnings of women would hardly change. In contrast, if women maintained their employment pattern but earned the pay rates shown for men, women as a whole would earn more than men. Does this evidence indicate pure discrimination against women, i.e. a failure to pay them the same rate as men for doing the same job?

Table 13-4 certainly suggests this at first sight. However, we should need a more detailed analysis to confirm this impression. There is a big difference between a skilled manual worker and an unskilled one, or between a top manager in charge of a major company and a junior supervisor. What we can conclude from Table 13-4 is that either women get paid less than men for the identical job, however narrowly that job is defined, or else men get promoted and trained faster within these broad occupational classifications. For example, the percentage of women in full-time employment in the professional or managerial occupations is comparable with that for men; but the proportion of women on the boards of major companies is much smaller than the proportion of men.

Why should companies promote or train women more slowly? Is this overt discrimination, subtle discrimination or neither? Does our analysis of human capital and signalling in the previous section help us to make sense of this?

Suppose firms bear some of the cost of training. The firm makes a hard-nosed investment decision. Assuming that men and women are of inherently equal ability and educational attainment, it costs the firm the same to train either sex. Suppose that on average firms believe that women are more likely than men to interrupt or even end their careers at a young age. As a matter of biology, it is women who have babies. Firms may conclude that the present value of the extra productivity benefits in the future is lower for women than men simply because they are likely to work fewer years in the future. It is more profitable to train and promote men purely as a financial calculation.

Table 13-4	UK annual pay and employment in 1998 (full-time adult workers)			
Occupation	Male pay (£)	% of male employment	Female pay (£)	% of female employment
Non-manual	26 580	71	16 580	90
Manual	16 390	29	10 320	10

Source: Department of Employment, *New Earnings Survey*.

Some women plan to have a full-time career, either remaining childless or returning to work almost immediately after any children are born. It would make sense for firms to invest in such people but there is a huge problem: how is a firm to tell which young women are planning to stay and which are planning to work only a few years and then have a family? Asking is no good because there is an incentive for young women not to tell the truth.[2]

Can firms and workers co-operate to devise a screening procedure that will persuade young women to reveal their true career plans? Suppose firms offer young workers the choice between a relatively flat age–earnings profile and a much steeper profile that begins at a lower wage but pays a higher wage later in a worker's career. By making the wages in later years sufficiently high, firms could ensure that the two profiles were equally valued by someone planning a lifetime career. The early sacrifice of lower wages would be recouped with interest later. But someone planning to quit the labour force, say at the age of 30, would never opt for the steeper profile: she wouldn't expect to work long enough at the higher wage to recoup the early sacrifice.

By observing whether new recruits accept the steeper age–earnings profile, it might be possible for firms to persuade recruits to reveal their career plans. If women, or any other group with a high risk of quitting at a young age, accept the steeper profile, the firm can embark on training with some confidence that its investment would not be wasted.

There is, of course, an issue of credibility. Young workers would need to be assured that they really were exchanging low wages in the early years for suitably higher wages later in their career. And, initially, even career women might be reluctant to accept the steeper profile until they could see a generation of women who, having accepted such a profile and induced the firm to place its training bets, had succeeded in being promoted through the company to earn the suitably higher earnings in the later years of their career.

We suspect that there are still a few firms who try to pay female workers less than male workers who are identical in every respect, including the risk of quitting. We might call this overt discrimination.

Discrimination is the different treatment of people whose relevant characteristics are identical.

[2] This is a version of the problem of *moral hazard* that we discuss in detail in Chapter 15. However, single women are less likely to interrupt their career than married women. Since firms can discover a woman's marital status, single women on average earn much more than married women. Firms are more likely to invest in training for single women.

In other cases, traditional age–earnings profiles may give firms a purely economic reason to be cautious about investment in the education and training of women. We have indicated how this more subtle form of discrimination might be changed. But society may discriminate against women in even more subtle ways.

For example, our analysis suggests that paternity leave for fathers, the provision of crèches for working parents, or a greater acceptance of part-time working by both sexes, would reduce the incentive for hard-nosed firms to conclude that it is more profitable to train and promote men than women. Whether or not society wishes to organize its work and home life along such principles remains a controversial issue. Pay differentials between men and women depend on much wider factors than the labour market in isolation.

Access to education

Thus far we have discussed sex discrimination by firms assuming that they receive male and female applicants of equal calibre. However, it may be that firms treat workers of equal calibre equally but pay men more on average because male workers have more educational qualifications than female workers. If so we must seek the root cause of pay differences by sex not in the labour market, but in education itself.

Table 13-5 shows full-time and part-time UK students in three types of education: FE colleges, university undergraduates, and postgraduates. In 1971 male students greatly outnumbered female students in all forms of further and higher education. By 1998 the gender gap had closed significantly. Women had overtaken men in FE colleges, but still lagged behind in universities: despite catching up quickly, they were coming from a low baseline in the past.

Table 13-5	UK students 1971–98 (thousands)			
	Male		Female	
	71	98	71	98
Further education				
Full time	116	414	95	445
Part time	891	638	630	938
Undergraduate				
Full time	241	491	173	528
Part time	127	168	19	224
Postgraduate				
Full time	33	75	10	63
Part time	15	112	3	102

Source: ONS, *Social Trends*.

Why do fewer women continue in higher education? There are three possible explanations. First, there may be genuine discrimination in education. In schools teaching boys and girls, teachers may try harder with boys or encourage more of them to think about further education.

Second, women may have different tastes. The old stereotype of school, marriage, motherhood, and domesticity may still survive in some cases, but this is hard to square with the large number of female students in FE colleges.

Finally, we can think about the return to this initial investment in higher education. Equal opportunity legislation and social pressure have increased wages for women, both by reducing sex discrimination for a given job and by increasing the chances of female promotion. Women may now feel that there has been an increase in the future benefits through higher salary opportunities. If so, we should expect more and more women to decide to invest in education. Note, however, the crucial role of expectations or perceptions. Until it becomes evident that women really are being promoted and enjoying the benefits of higher education, the perceived return on higher education may continue to be lower for women than for men, and fewer women than men will invest in further education.

Racial discrimination

Exactly the same general principles may be used to analyse racial discrimination and differences in the earnings of whites and non-whites. West Indians, Indians and Pakistanis are the most important racial minority groups in the UK. Many studies have confirmed the suggestion in Table 13-2 that on average non-whites earn less than whites.

The age–earnings profiles for non-white males are much flatter than the corresponding profiles for white males. White men are much more likely to achieve steady promotion and rising earnings. From our discussion of age–earnings profiles in the previous section, this is likely to imply that whites do more difficult jobs where training and experience are important.

Part of the problem for non-white men is not so much the amount of education but the type of education they receive. The payoff to education is very low for non-whites who attend a typical state-run inner-city school.

Two interpretations are possible. Either the quality of education in inner-city schools with predominantly non-white children is poor, or attendance at such schools tends to act as a signal to firms that these children are likely to come from disadvantaged backgrounds. Firms may believe that these potential workers will have lower productivity and be more expensive to train.

Table 13-6	Ethnic groups, UK, 1995			
	Participation rate (%)		Unemployment rate (%)	
	Men	Women	Men	Women
Whites	86	72	9	7
Blacks	79	65	24	22
Indian	82	63	14	11
Pakistani/Bangladeshi	68	23	29	29

Source: ONS, *Labour Market Trends*.

Both interpretations imply that firms will be less inclined to employ such workers in jobs that are difficult and require extensive on-the-job training. White workers or non-whites from other educational backgrounds are much more likely to be given the skilled and demanding jobs with which the steeply rising age–earnings profiles are associated. A higher proportion of non-whites will be restricted to unskilled and low-paying jobs.

Table 13-6 completes our examination of racial discrimination. It shows involuntary inactivity rates across ethnic groups. Muslim women from Pakistan and Bangladesh have much lower rates of labour force participation. However, this seems to reflect a different attitude to the willingness to supply labour as much as any evidence of discrimination in the demand for their labour. Most minority groups also have unemployment rates well above those for white men or women.

As in our discussion of sex discrimination, it is hard to draw a line between discrimination in the labour market and elsewhere in society. The responsibility of managers is to maximize profits for their shareholders. So long as managers perceive that different groups of workers have already acquired different characteristics, or will tend to behave differently during their working lifetimes, managers will wish to treat different groups differently. Unless society as a whole removes the differences in characteristics, opportunities and behaviour of different groups of workers, the eradication of blatant racism or sexism will go only part of the way to eliminating pay differentials between groups of workers.

13-3 Trade unions

Trade unions are worker organizations designed to affect pay and working conditions. Do unions protect workers from exploitation by powerful employers or do they use their power to secure unjustified pay increases and oppose

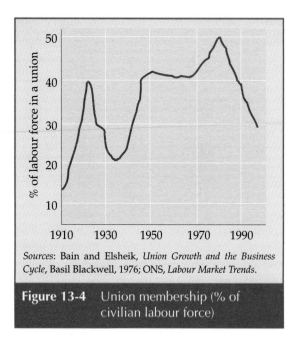

Sources: Bain and Elsheik, *Union Growth and the Business Cycle*, Basil Blackwell, 1976; ONS, *Labour Market Trends*.

Figure 13-4 Union membership (% of civilian labour force)

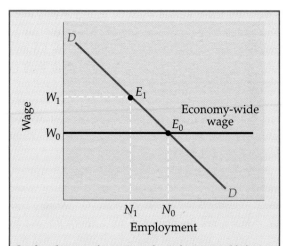

In the absence of a union, the industry would face a horizontal labour supply curve at the wage W_0. Given the industry demand curve *DD* for labour, equilibrium would occur at E_0. By restricting the industry labour supply to N_1, the union can increase the wage to W_1. It can trade off lower employment in the industry for higher wages.

Figure 13-5 Unions in the labour market

technical changes and productivity improvements which might threaten the employment of their members? Before examining these questions we give a brief outline of the importance of unions in the British economy.

By 1980 just over half the civilian labour force in the UK belonged to a trade union. Figure 13-4 shows changes since 1910. After the steady increase in union membership until 1920 there was a massive decline and then recovery in the degree of unionization of the labour force during the inter-war years. Thereafter, there was a long period during which unionization was fairly constant until the late 1960s. The 1970s saw a sharp rise in union membership, which peaked in 1979, since when it has been falling sharply.

With rising female participation in the labour force, there was a much faster growth of union membership by women than men. The pattern of industrial growth may also be important. The period saw an expansion of industries, for example those in the public sector, in which unions are traditionally well organized and the degree of unionization is high. Privatization and cuts in the size of the public sector tend to reduce the degree of unionization in the economy as a whole.

What unions do

The traditional view of unions is that they offset the power that a firm enjoys in negotiating wages and working conditions. A single firm has many workers. If each worker must make a separate deal with the firm, the firm can make a take-it-or-leave-it offer. A worker with firm-specific

human capital, which will be pretty useless in any other firm, may face a large drop in productivity and wages if she rejects the firm's offer. The firm is in a strong bargaining position if it can make separate agreements with each of its workers. In contrast, by presenting a united front, the workers may be able to impose large costs on the firm if they *all* quit. The firm can replace one worker but not its whole labour force. The existence of unions evens up the bargaining process.

Once a union is established, it aims not merely to protect its members but to improve their pay and conditions. To be successful the union must be able to restrict the firm's labour supply. If the firm can hire non-union labour, unions will find it hard to maintain the wage above the level at which the firm can hire non-union workers. This is one reason why unions are keen on closed-shop agreements with individual firms.[3]

A **closed shop** is an agreement that all a firm's workers will be members of a trade union.

We now analyse how unions raise wages by restricting supply. Figure 13-5 shows an industry's downward-sloping

---

[3] Unions frequently argue that, in the absence of a closed shop, non-union workers will benefit from improvements in pay and conditions achieved through the efforts of the union. Non-union members are getting a 'free ride' without paying their union subscriptions.

labour demand curve DD. The wage in the rest of the economy is W_0, and we assume that the industry faces a perfectly elastic labour supply curve at this wage rate. The labour supply curve to the industry is the horizontal line through W_0. In the absence of unions, equilibrium would occur at E_0 with employment N_0.

Now suppose everyone in the industry must belong to a trade union and that the union restricts labour in this industry to N_1. The industry faces a vertical labour supply curve at N_1. Equilibrium occurs at E_1. By sacrificing employment in the industry the union has raised the wage for each employed member from W_0 to W_1. At a higher wage and marginal cost of production, each firm will be forced to raise its price. The full effect of the trade union is not merely to raise wages and lower employment in the industry but also to raise the output price and lower equilibrium output of the industry.

This analysis raises two questions. What determines how far the union will trade off lower employment for higher wages in the industry? And what determines how much power unions have to control the supply of labour to particular industries?

Assume that the union has full control over the supply of labour to a firm or an industry. It can trade off employment for wage rises. How far it will go depends on the preferences or tastes of the union and its members. It might try to maximize total income (wage times employment) of its members, or it might try to maximize per capita income (wages) of those in employment. A lot depends on the power and decision structure within the union.

The more the union cares about its senior members, the more it is likely to maximize the wage independently of what happens to employment. Senior workers have the most firm-specific human capital and are the least likely to be sacked if total employment in the industry must fall. Conversely, the more the union is democratic and the more it cares about its potential members as well as those actually in employment, the less likely it is to restrict employment to ensure higher wages for those who remain employed in the industry.

When does restricting labour supply by a given amount lead to the largest rise in wages? When the demand for labour is most inelastic. For example, in the last 20 years workers in the electricity supply industry have secured large wage increases. Power stations are very capital-intensive, so the wage bill is a relatively small component of total costs in the industry. Moreover, the consumer demand for electricity is relatively price-inelastic in the short run. For both these reasons, the industry was prepared to meet high

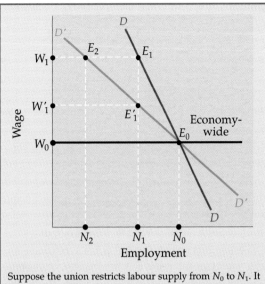

Suppose the union restricts labour supply from N_0 to N_1. It drives up wages in the industry and its members enjoy a wage differential compared with non-union workers elsewhere in the economy. The differential is larger, for any given reduction in industry employment, the more inelastic is the industry demand curve for labour.

Figure 13-6 Wage differentials and the demand for labour

wage claims which did not add much to total costs and could in any case be passed on to the consumer.

Figure 13-6 illustrates this general point. In the absence of unions industry equilibrium occurs at E_0, where the horizontal labour supply curve intersects the labour demand curve. DD shows an inelastic labour demand curve and $D'D'$ a more elastic labour demand curve. The more inelastic is labour demand, the larger the wage increase a union will secure by restricting labour supply from N_0 to N_1.

Suppose the car industry is unionized. Initially the derived demand curve for car workers is quite inelastic, and by restricting employment to N_1 the unions are able to increase car workers' wages from W_0 to W_1. Then Japanese car producers start vigorously competing in the domestic market. Each firm's output demand curve becomes more price-elastic since domestic models must compete with imports. Hence, for the reasons set out in the previous chapter, the derived demand curve for labour by domestic car manufacturers becomes more elastic. It rotates from DD to $D'D'$ in Figure 13-6. At the wage rate W_1 domestic producers lose market share and union employment falls from the level N_1 to the level N_2. Eventually, if the unions wish to maintain employment in the car industry at N_1 they will have to accept a wage cut to W'_1 on the new demand curve for labour $D'D'$.

Unionization and wage differentials

Table 13-7 shows estimates of the union–non-union wage differential. It shows how much more an individual union member typically earns than a non-union worker. Union members earn 7.5 per cent more than people not belonging to a union in unskilled jobs, but only 1.5 per cent extra in skilled jobs. Union power has been falling over time. So has the union wage differential.

Trade union power also varies across industries. Figure 13-6 identified the slope of the labour demand curve as the key determinant of trade union power to raise wages without too great a loss of employment. In the previous chapter we stressed that the demand for labour is a derived demand which depends on the demand for a firm's output.

Consider first an industry that is not very competitive, with few domestic firms and little foreign competition. Firms in this industry are making substantial supernormal profits. We would expect unions to get their hands on some of these through higher wages which eat into healthy profit margins.

At the other extreme, in a perfectly competitive industry, if a union in a single firm raises wages it will simply drive that firm out of business. Only if the union can organize across *the whole industry*, which can then pass these increases on in part to consumers, does the union stand a chance of raising wages.

Studying a large number of industries, Mark Stewart of Warwick University has shown that this is exactly what happens in practice![4] In competitive industries facing significant foreign competition, unions get no wage differential at all. In industries sheltered from foreign competition but with a large number of domestic firms, union differentials exist only when the whole industry is unionized. But unions get substantial markups in industries with few domestic firms and little foreign competition.

Union wages as compensating differentials

Union wage differentials arise not only from the successful restriction of labour supply. Union work has certain characteristics – a structured work setting, inflexibility of hours, employer-set overtime, and a faster work pace – a whole set of conditions that might be regarded as unpleasant. Perhaps higher wages in such industries are merely *compensating wage differentials* for these non-monetary aspects of the job?

There are two competing views. The first is that, after unions take over and raise wages, firms respond by taking

Table 13-7 Union wage differentials		
% extra for union in	1984	1990
Unskilled	10.5	7.5
Semi skilled	10.5	6.5
Skilled	3.5	1.5

Source: M. Stewart, 'Union wage differentials in an era of declining unionisation', *Oxford Bulletin of Economics and Statistics*, 1995.

advantage of unions to raise productivity. Work patterns are standardized and the union assists in implementing these new practices. Firms finance higher wages by making workers operate in less pleasant but more productive ways.

The alternative view is that the change in work practices is not an employer *response* to a successful union restriction of labour supply to raise wages, but rather the rationale for the union's existence. Unions emerge in industries where large productivity gains would result from the introduction of unpleasant working conditions. The union exists not to restrict labour supply in total, but to negotiate productivity gains, ensuring that workers receive proper compensating differentials for the unpopular changes in working practices that employers find it profitable to introduce. On this view, the unions do not make separate deals for pay and working conditions; rather, their role is to secure pay increases for changes in working conditions.

To sum up, unions secure higher wages for their members for two distinct reasons. First, they restrict labour supply, trading off lower employment in the industry for higher wages. But they also play an important role in negotiating changes in working practices, securing higher productivity and appropriate part of this gain for the workforce.

Bargaining and strikes

How serious are strikes? Table 13-8 shows the days of work lost per employee because of industrial disputes. Notice that in most countries strikes cost the whole economy less than one workday per employee per year. Even this is probably an overestimate, since employees sometimes work extra overtime after a strike to make up some of the lost production. Days lost through industrial disputes have been falling since the 1970s.

Why do strikes occur? Although employers and workers are fighting for a share of the firm's total revenue, they have a common interest too. If the firm does better, there may be more for employers and workers. Typically the bargaining process between a firm and a union is completed without a strike. If strikes can be avoided, there is potentially

---

[4] See M. Stewart, 'Union Wage Differentials, Product Market Influences and the Division of Rents', *Economic Journal*, 1990.

	1975–79	1985–89	1990–94	1995–97
Table 13-8 Industrial disputes: workdays lost per year per 1000 employees				
Italy	1510	300	240	94
Canada	940	424	231	230
UK	510	180	37	29
USA	260	86	43	43
France	210	57	30	172

Source: As in Table 13-6.

more money to divide between the shareholders and the workers.

Given this common interest, why do strikes occur at all? If both parties knew the settlement that would be reached after a strike it would be better to settle immediately on the same share out and avoid the loss of output and revenue that the strike induces. One reason for strikes is that one party misjudges the other's position. As the strike proceeds each party becomes aware of the requirements of the other party.

But not all strikes are mistakes that could have been avoided with better initial perceptions of the other side's requirements. Strikes may also occur because of issues of long-term credibility. If a firm believes that the workers will strike unless they get a fair deal, the firm may offer a fair deal immediately. After a few years of co-operation the firm begins to feel that the union is a pushover. The union may then strike not merely because of the current dispute, but to remind the firm that it will strike unless the firm is fair. Thus, one strike might earn the union a fair deal for many years to come because the firm believes that the union will strike unless the firm is fair.

SUMMARY

● Different workers get different pay. This reflects personal characteristics such as education, job experience, sex, race, and union status.

● Skills or human capital are the most important source of wage differentials. Human capital formation includes both formal schooling and on-the-job training. Earnings profiles confirm that workers with more education and training earn higher lifetime incomes.

● How much more employers pay for skilled workers depends on the production technology. The demand for skilled workers depends on the extent to which skilled and unskilled workers can be substituted and on the output demand for industries that use skilled workers relatively intensively.

● Skilled labour is relatively scarce because it is costly to acquire human capital. Education beyond minimum age has not only direct costs but the opportunity cost of earnings forgone by not working immediately. The investment decision for human capital involves comparing the present costs with the present value of extra income or other benefits in the future.

● These considerations are reinforced by the role of education as a screening or signalling device, which indicates to employers the workers of innate ability. Thus education has a return to high-ability workers even if it does not directly increase their productivity.

● Women and non-whites on average receive lower incomes than white men. Women and non-whites are concentrated in relatively unskilled jobs with fewer opportunities for promotion. This need not reflect blatant sexism or racism by employers. It may reflect educational or other disadvantages before young workers reach the labour market. It may also reflect a low perceived rate of return by firms on the money spent in training such workers or by such workers on the time spent in education and skill acquisition.

● Under a third of the UK labour force now belongs to a trade union. Unions restrict the labour supply to firms or industries, thereby raising wages but lowering employment. Unions move firms up their demand curve for labour.

● Unions achieve a higher wage differential for their members the more inelastic the demand for labour and the more they are willing or able to restrict the supply of labour. However, some union wage differentials should be viewed as compensating wage differentials, which unions have secured in return for changes in work practices that raise productivity but reduce the pleasantness of the job.

KEY TERMS

REVIEW QUESTIONS

1 University-educated workers now earn a larger wage differential than in the 1960s. (a) What effect would this have on the incentive to go to university? Why? (b) Suppose it was shown that going to university added nothing to life-time income potential. Would anyone still go to university? Why?

2 A worker can earn £20 000 a year for the next 40 years. Alternatively, the worker can take three years off to go on a training course whose fees are £7000 per year. If the government provides an interest-free loan for this training, what future income differential per year would make this a profitable investment in human capital?

3 Suppose economists form a union and establish a certificate that is essential for practising economics. How would this help to raise the relative wage of economists? How would the union restrict entry to the economics profession?

4 Apprentices are typically paid low wages. Using the concept of human capital, explain this observation.

5 Who benefits if there is economic discrimination against women? Why?

6 Show in a diagram of the labour market how a policy of restricting flight time for pilots to a specified monthly maximum number of hours affects the wage differential of unionized pilots. Why is a restriction on the number of working hours an important part of the union's attempt to raise wage differentials for pilots?

7 *Common fallacies* Show why the following statements are incorrect: (a) Women earn less than men. Employers must be sexists. (b) People who study ancient history at university learn nothing about running a business. They would earn higher salaries if they joined companies at the age of eighteen. (c) Free schooling between sixteen and eighteen means that children from poor families can stay on in education as easily as children from wealthy families. (d) Since many low-paid workers belong to a trade union, this proves that unions have little effect on improving pay and conditions for their members.

14 Capital and land: completing the analysis of factor markets

LEARNING OUTCOMES

When you have finished this chapter, you should be able to:

- Study the markets for inputs of capital and land, and to analyse how incomes of factors are therefore determined
- Define and study the functional and personal distributions of income
- Distinguish flows over time and stocks measured at a point in time
- Conduct simultaneous analysis of the market for renting capital services and the market for buying new capital assets
- Explain the concept of present values, which collapse future flows into their equivalent stock value today
- Consider the difference between nominal and real interest rates
- Analyse how saving and investment, or thrift and productivity of new capital formation, determine the equilibrium real interest rate
- Show how land is allocated between competing uses

Industry needs to increase its capital stock – its machinery, equipment, factory and office buildings. The car industry has to invest to compete with heavily mechanized foreign producers, the steel industry has to modernize its capital equipment, and the new growth industries such as information technology need to invest for future production. Investment adds to the stock of capital in the economy.

In the last two chapters our analysis of factor markets has focused on labour. In this chapter we turn our attention to the other factors of production with which labour must co-operate in the productive process. Some issues can be dealt with rather briefly. We have already studied how a firm chooses its production technique in the long run, when all factors can be freely varied, and we are already familiar with the concept of a factor's marginal product. These ideas carry over from the analysis of labour markets to the examination of markets for other factors of production.

Apart from the irreversible decision to acquire education and skills, many aspects of labour market behaviour can be conveniently analysed within a relatively short-run time horizon. This simplification does not distort the picture too much since labour is the most variable factor of production in the short run. Since it takes much longer to adjust other factor inputs, decisions about their use must necessarily take a longer view. One theme of this chapter will be the role of time and the future in economic behaviour.

In developing this analysis, we confront explicitly the question of how decision makers today should value future benefits and costs, and we show how to discount future payments or receipts to calculate their *present value*.

Our interest in the markets for capital and land goes beyond a curiosity about the equilibrium quantity of capital or the equilibrium price of land. There are two reasons to be interested in how the complete set of factor markets work as a whole. First, firms rarely use a single factor of production in isolation. Decisions about inputs of capital and land affect the demand curve for labour and the equilibrium wage rate, just as decisions about labour inputs will feed back upon the demand for other factors of production.

Second, having completed our analysis of factor markets, we shall be able to discuss what determines the *income distribution* in an economy. The price of a factor multiplied by the total quantity of the factor employed gives us the earnings or income of that factor. We need to know the prices and quantities of all productive factors if we are to understand how the economy's total income is distributed.

We conclude this chapter by pulling together our analysis in Chapters 12–14 to examine the income distribution in the UK. We shall distinguish two measures of income distribution, *functional* and *personal*.

The **functional income distribution** tells us how an economy's total income is divided between the different factors of production. For example it tells us the share going to labour through wages and salaries and the share going to landowners through property rents.

Understanding the functional income distribution might allow us to determine whether trade unions have secured a larger share of the national cake at the expense of profits or rents earned by landowners. But an individual may supply the services of several different factors of production. Individuals may supply labour services through work, capital services by renting out machinery which they own, and the services of land by renting out property.

The **personal income distribution** tells us how national income is divided between different individuals, regardless of the factor services from which they earn their income.

The personal income distribution tells us whether some people are better off than others.

Having indicated the topics we shall cover in this chapter, we begin by defining our terms. We concentrate on the factors of production that economists call capital and land.

Physical capital is the stock of produced goods that contribute to the production of other goods and services.

The stock of physical capital includes the assembly line machinery used to make cars, railway lines that produce transport services, school buildings that produce education

services, dwellings that produce housing services, and consumer durables such as televisions that produce entertainment services.

Physical capital is distinguished from land by the fact that the former is produced.

Land is the factor of production that nature supplies.

Clearly, this distinction between land and capital can become blurred. By applying labour to extract weeds or fertilizer to improve the soil balance, farmers can 'produce' better land. Because land and capital are sometimes hard to disentangle we discuss these two factors of production in the same chapter. Nevertheless, the distinction is often useful, as we shall see.

In Chapter 7 we introduced the idea of *depreciation*, the extent to which an asset or durable good is used up within the time period over which we study and measure the production of goods and services. Capital and land are both assets. They do not completely depreciate during the time period during which we examine production decisions by firms.

Together, capital and land make up the **tangible wealth** of the economy.

They are wealth or assets because they are durable. They are tangible because they are physical goods which we could literally touch. Financial wealth, such as a sum of money in the bank, is not tangible wealth. It cannot directly produce goods and services though it can be used to purchase factors of production which can produce goods and services. Similarly, we must distinguish between *physical* capital – plant, machinery, and buildings, which henceforth we refer to simply as 'capital' – and *financial* capital, or money and paper assets.

14-1 Physical capital

Table 14-1 shows the level and composition of physical capital in the UK in 1996. (Data on capital take a long time to collect!) 'Dwellings' are primarily owned by private individuals, but some is state owned. Productive fixed capital is plant, machinery and buildings. Inventories are stocks of manufactured goods awaiting sale, partially finished goods (work in progress), and raw materials held for future production. Inventories are capital because they are produced goods which contribute to future production.

To assess how physical capital is combined with labour in the production process, Table 14-2 examines physical capital after subtracting dwellings. The first row shows physical capital used in production (CP) in the UK in 1981 and 1996. The second row shows the ratio of CP to real national output. The capital input to the production process is about three times the value of annual national output. The final row shows that (at 1996 prices) the quantity of capital available per employed worker rose from £70 000 to £88 000 between 1981 and 1996.

Table 14-2 confirms that investment in physical capital is increasing the capital input to the UK's national production, not only in absolute terms but also relative to the number of workers employed. Even over a period as short as a decade, there has been a significant change in production techniques. The economy is becoming more *capital-intensive*. Each worker has more capital with which to work.

In practice, it is difficult to measure the stock of capital exactly. Capital depreciates over time, becoming less productive and less valuable. The official statistics estimate as best they can the rate at which depreciation occurs. Because capital depreciates, it takes some investment in new capital goods merely to stand still.

Gross investment is the production of new capital goods and the improvement of existing capital goods. **Net invest-**

ment is gross investment minus the depreciation of the existing capital stock.

If net investment is positive, gross investment more than compensates for depreciation and the effective capital stock is increasing. However, very small levels of gross investment may fail to keep pace with depreciation and the capital stock will then be falling over time. In the next few sections we concentrate on capital, the produced goods that are inputs to subsequent production. Later in the chapter we discuss the special features of the input that economists call 'land'.

14-2 Rentals, interest rates, and asset prices

To clarify our discussion of capital we use Table 14-3 to emphasize two crucial distinctions: between *stocks* and *flows*, and between *rental payments* and *asset prices*. We begin with the example of labour input.

The labour market trades a commodity called 'hours of labour services'. The corresponding price is the hourly wage rate. Rather loosely, we sometimes call this the 'price of labour'. Strictly speaking, the hourly wage is the *rental payment* that firms pay to hire an hour of labour. There is no asset price for the durable physical asset called a 'worker' because modern societies do not allow slavery, the institution by which firms actually own workers.

Since capital can be bought and sold – there are markets for new and used vehicles and buildings – we shall have to be more careful.

A **stock** is the quantity of an asset at point in time, such as 100 machines on 1 January 2000. A **flow** is the stream of services that an asset provides during a given interval, such as 40 labour hours per week per person.

The distinction between rental payments and asset prices follows immediately from this distinction between stocks and flows.

The cost of using capital services is the **rental rate** for capital.

Table 14-1	UK capital stock, 1996	
	£bn	%
Dwellings	1192	34.0
Productive fixed capital	2144	61.2
Inventories	168	4.8
Total capital stock	3504	100.0

Source: ONS, *UK National Accounts 1998*.

Table 14-2	Capital input to UK production	
	1981	1996
Capital input to production (CP)*	1518	2312
CP/national output	3	3
CP per employed worker*	70	88

*CP and national output in £ billion. CP per employed worker in £ thousand. All in 1996 prices.
Source: ONS, *UK National Accounts*.

Table 14-3	Stock and flow concepts		Capital	Labour
Flow input to hourly production			Capital services	Labour services
Payment for flow			Rental rate (£/machine hour)	Wage rate (£/labour hour)
Asset price			£/machine	£/slave, if purchase allowed

For example, travellers pay a rental rate to hire a car for the weekend. Building contractors pay a rental rate to lease earth-moving equipment. Sometimes there is no rental or leasing market for a type of capital good. It is impossible to rent a power station. When firms make a once-and-for-all purchase of a capital asset or stock they must calculate how much it is implicitly costing them day by day to use their capital. We return to this question in Section 14-4.

Unlike labour, capital goods can be purchased and have an asset price.

The **price of an asset** is the sum for which the stock can be purchased outright. By owning a capital asset the purchaser acquires title to the future stream of capital services that the stock will provide.

Buying a car for £9000 entitles a household to a stream of future transport services. Buying a factory for £100 000 entitles the owner to a stream of future rental payments on the capital services that the factory provides.

What will a purchaser be prepared to pay for a capital asset? The answer depends on the value of the rental payments that will be paid in the future for the capital services that the asset stock provides. Can we simply add together the future rental payments over the life of the capital asset to calculate its current asset price or value? Not quite. We have to pay attention to the role of *time* and *interest payments*.

Interest and present values

Suppose a lender makes a loan to a borrower. At the outset the borrower agrees to pay the initial sum (the principal) *with interest* at some future date. If the loan is £100 for one year at 10 per cent interest per annum, the borrower must repay £110 at the end of the year. The extra £10 (10 per cent of £100) is the interest cost of borrowing £100 for a year. *Interest rates* are usually quoted as a percentage per annum. Thus, an interest rate of 20 per cent means that the borrower must pay an additional annual payment of 20 per cent of the principal at the end of the loan contract.

Suppose we lent £1 and re-lent the interest as it accrued. The first row of Table 14-4 shows what would happen if the interest rate were 10 per cent per annum. After one year we should have £1 plus an interest payment of £0.10. Re-lending the whole £1.10, we should have £1.21 by the end of the second year. The concept of *compound interest* reminds us that the absolute amount by which our money grows increases every year. The first year we increase our money by £0.10, which is 10 per cent of £1. Since we re-lend the interest, our money grows by £0.11 in the next year since

Table 14-4 Interest and present value (PV)

	Year		
	0	1	2
At 10% interest rate:			
value of £1 lent today in:	£1	£1.10	£1.21
PV of £1 earned in:	£1	£0.91	£0.83
At 5% interest rate:			
value of £1 lent today in:	£1	£1.05	£1.10
PV of £ earned in:	£1	£0.95	£0.91

we earn 10 per cent on £0.10. If we lend for yet another year, our money will grow by £0.121 to £1.331 at the end of the third year.

At 10 per cent interest per annum, £1 on year 0 is worth £1.10 in year 1 and £1.21 in year 2. Now let us ask the question the other way round. If we offered you £1.21 in two years' time, what sum today would be just as valuable? The answer is £1. If you had £1 today you could always lend it out to get exactly £1.21 in two years' time. The second row of Table 14-4 extends this general idea. If £1.21 in year 2 is worth £1 today, then £1 in year 2 must be worth £1/1.21 =£0.83 today. £0.83 today could be lent out at 10 per cent interest to accumulate to £1 in year 2. Similarly, £1 in year 1 is worth only £1/1.10 = £0.91 today.

The **present value** of £1 at some future date is the sum that, if lent out today, would accumulate to £1 by that future date.

The law of compound interest implies that lending £1 today accumulates to ever larger sums the further into the future we maintain the loan and re-lend the interest. Conversely, the present value of £1 earned at some future date becomes smaller the further into the future the date at which the £1 is earned.

The present value of a future payment also depends on the interest rate. The third row of Table 14-4 shows that a loan of £1 will accumulate less rapidly over time if the interest rate is lower. At 5 per cent interest a loan of £1 cumulates to only £1.10 after two years, compared with £1.21 after two years when the interest rate was 10 per cent in row 1. Hence the fourth row of Table 14-4 shows that the present value of £1 in year 1 or year 2 is larger when the interest rate is only 5 per cent than in the corresponding entry in row 2 where the interest rate is 10 per cent.

Figure 14-1 makes the same points in a diagram. It shows how lending £1 today would accumulate at compound interest rates of 5 and 10 per cent. After 10 years the loan fund is worth £2.59 at 10 per cent interest but only £1.62 at 5 per cent interest. Higher interest rates imply more rapid

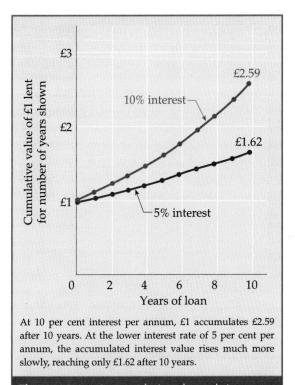

At 10 per cent interest per annum, £1 accumulates £2.59 after 10 years. At the lower interest rate of 5 per cent per annum, the accumulated interest value rises much more slowly, reaching only £1.62 after 10 years.

Figure 14-1   Accumulation through interest

Table 14-5	Present values and asset prices (at annual interest rate of 10%)		
Year	Rental (£)	Scrap value (£)	Present value (£)
1	4000		3 640
2	4000	+ 10 000	11 620
Asset price			15 260

Note: From Table 14-4, the present value of each £1 in year 1 is £0.91 and in year 2 is £0.83.

Valuing an asset: an example

How much would you bid for a machine that earns £4000 in rental for two years and can then be sold for scrap for £10 000? If you bid anything before asking what the interest rate is you have not understood the previous section! Suppose the interest rate is 10 per cent per annum. The first two rows of Table 14-5 show the money received in each year. The final column shows the present value of receipts from years 1 and 2. From Table 14-4 we know that each £1 next year is worth only £0.91 today, and £1 in year 2 only £0.83 today. The present value of £4000 in year 1 is £3640 (£4000 × 0.91), and the present value of the £14 000 received from rental earnings and sale for scrap in year 2 is £11 620 (£14 000 × 0.83). Adding together these present values for years 1 and 2, the asset price should be £15 260.

Why do we get £15 260, a much smaller figure than the £18 000 actually earned from two years of rental income and the resale value from scrap? Again, because at any positive interest rate £1 tomorrow is worth less than £1 today. £1 today would accumulate to more than £1 tomorrow. We convert future payments to current values by *discounting* the future.

A useful way to understand the role of interest rates in present-value calculations is to realize that the interest rate represents the *opportunity cost* of the money used to buy the asset. The same money could have been lent to a bank or a building society to earn interest. At an interest rate of 10 per cent per annum a payment next year of £110 has a present value of £100 today. We would not bid more than £100 today for the entitlement of £110 next year: we can get at least £110 next year by lending £100 to a bank today.

The principles we have outlined can be used to calculate the present value of any future income stream once the interest rate is known. We go into more detail in the appendix to this chapter. The calculation is particularly simple in one special case, when the asset lasts for ever and the income stream per time period is constant. For example, governments sometimes borrow by selling a *perpetuity*, a

accumulation through lending. The same diagram can be used for present values. A payment of £2.59 in 10 years' time has a present value of £1 if the interest rate is 10 per cent. Thus the present value of £1 in 10 years' time is £1/2.59 = £0.386. If interest rates are only 5 per cent the value of £1 in 10 years' time is £1/1.62 = £0.617.

Using interest rate to calculate present values of future payments tells us the right way to add together payments at different points in time. For each payment at each date we calculate its present value. Then we add together the present values of the different payments.

Now we see how the price of a capital asset should be related to the stream of future payments that will be earned from the capital services it provides. We calculate the present value of the rental payment earned by the asset in each year of its working life and add these present values together. This tells us what the asset is worth today. In equilibrium it should be the asset price. If you can buy an asset for a lower price than the present value of its future stream of rental earnings, you have got a good deal. Unfortunately, others are likely to reach the same conclusion. If you all try to buy the asset you will bid up its price. Where does the process end? When the asset price equals the present value of the stream of future rental earnings and the equilibrium price is reached.

BOX 14-1   The future's orange, but the present was in the red

How would you like to start a company, make a loss of £229 million pounds in your first year of trading, and watch your share price rise on the stock market? Not a bad beginning.

The Financial Times (12 February 1997) reported that Orange, the mobile phone operator launched in the mid 1990s, 'claimed to have overtaken Vodaphone, the industry leader, in terms of quality, revenues per subscriber and customer churn' (the rate at which existing customers leave the network for bad debt or fraud). Because, like biotechnology, telecommunications seems to many a growth area, stock market analysts often forecast profits in the future even when a young company is making massive losses in its early years. 'Analysts forecast a pre-tax loss of about

£150 million for 1997 and a small profit in the following year' the Financial Times reported. Orange's share value is simply the present value of the stream of future profits that shareholders expect to receive. The share price is the present value divided by the total number of shares. Orange's shares rose 5 pence to £2.19 following the 1997 announcement of the £229 million loss, which was lower than the loss shareholders had been expecting! Since Orange's total share value was then £2.6 billion shareholders were obviously doing the present value calculations using expectations of some pretty big profits in the not too distant future.

Nor were they disappointed. By October 1999 Orange was worth £20 million after a takeover by German competitor Mannesmann.

bond (simply a piece of paper) promising to pay the owner a constant interest payment (called the 'coupon') for ever. In the UK these are called 'consols' (after a famous bond issue called Consolidated Stock). The present value of a consol, the price the stock market will offer for this piece of paper, obeys the formula

$$\text{Present value of a perpetuity} = \frac{\text{constant coupon payment per annum}}{\text{interest rate per annum}} \quad (1)$$

If you look in the financial pages of a newspaper you will find 2½ per cent consols. This perpetuity promises to pay £2.50 per annum for ever. (£2.50 was 2½ per cent of the price the government happened to sell the bonds for many years ago.) Suppose the current rate of interest is 10 per cent. You should find that 2½ per cent consols are worth around £25 (£2.5, the annual coupon, divided by 0.1, the annual interest rate expressed as a decimal fraction).

If interest rates fall to 5 per cent per annum the 2½ per cent consols will be worth £50 (= £2.5 divided by 0.05). Although government bonds are pieces of financial paper and not physical capital, exactly the same principles of present values apply. Calculating present values and asset prices of real capital goods is more difficult than for government bonds. Whereas the latter have a known future coupon or rental payment, the rental rates on physical capital in the future will depend on the state of the economy, the level of production, and so on. Nevertheless, the formula given in

equation (1) is useful in calculating the asset price of some long-lived physical asset such as land if the annual rental is expected to remain roughly constant over time.

Real and nominal interest rates: inflation and present values

Thus far we have discussed future payments valued in nominal terms. The first column of Table 14-5 shows rental receipts in actual pounds without any adjustment for inflation between years. Similarly, the interest rate of 10 per cent tells us how many actual pounds we will earn by lending £1 for a year.

The **nominal interest rate** tells us how many actual pounds will be earned in interest by lending £1 for one year.

At a nominal interest rate of 10 per cent, £100 lent today will accumulate to £110 by next year. But we may well be interested in how many goods that £110 will then buy.

The **real interest rate** measures the return on a loan as the increase in goods that can be purchased rather than as the increase in the nominal or the money value of the loan fund.

The distinction between nominal and real interest rates is very important. Suppose the nominal interest rate is 10 per cent and inflation is 6 per cent, so that goods prices rise by 6 per cent each year. Lending £1 for a year gives us £1.10, but after a year it also costs us £1.06 to buy the goods we could have bought for £1 today. With £1.10 to spend next year, we can increase the number of goods we can purchase by only 4 per cent. We say that the real interest rate is 4 per cent because that is the number of extra goods we can buy next year as a result of lending our money for a year. Thus we can use the general formula

$$
\begin{aligned}
\text{Real interest rate} &= \text{inflation adjusted} \\
&\quad \text{interest rate} \\
&= \text{nominal interest rate} \\
&\quad - \text{inflation rate} \qquad (2)
\end{aligned}
$$

To confirm this formula, let us try a second example. Nominal interest rates are 17 per cent and the inflation rate is 20 per cent. Lending £100 for a year, you can have £117. But it will cost you £120 to buy the goods you could have bought this year for £100. You are actually worse off by delaying purchases for a year and lending out your money at the apparently high rate of 17 per cent. In fact, real interest rates are *negative*. Equation (2) says that the real interest rate is (17–20) per cent = −3 per cent. In real terms it is *costing* you to be a lender. The nominal interest you receive will not compensate for rises in the prices of goods you ultimately wish to purchase.

What determines the real interest rate?

Most lenders and borrowers are capable of working out the real interest rate involved in a loan agreement. Do we expect real interest rates to be positive or negative? There are two forces that tend to lead to positive real interest rates.

First, people are impatient by nature. Given the choice of an equal number of goods tomorrow or today, they would rather have them today. To delay spending on goods and services, lenders usually have to be bribed with a positive real interest rate which allows them to consume *more* goods in the future if they postpone consumption and lend today. But wanting a positive real interest rate is not enough; there also has to be a way of earning positive real returns, or borrowers would never wish to borrow. Investing in physical capital is a way of making a real return even after paying back interest. Thus borrowers are willing to pay positive real interest rates because they can find investment

opportunities in physical capital goods that provide a stream of returns more than sufficient to meet the interest cost.

Impatience to consume and the productivity of physical capital are thus the two forces that lead us to expect a positive real interest rate. Table 14-6 shows data on nominal interest rates, inflation, and real interest rates over three decades. The table confirms the pattern found in many countries in many decades. Real interest rates are usually small and positive though they can occasionally be negative. Since real interest rates change only a little, large changes in nominal interest rates occur specifically to offset large changes in inflation rates, preserving real interest rates in their normal range as determined by the forces of impatience and capital productivity. The proposition that a 1 per cent increase in inflation will be matched by a 1 per cent increase in nominal interest rates to leave real interest rates unchanged is a useful rule of thumb.

What is the implication of this distinction between nominal and real interest rates for the calculation of present values? It is necessary only to be consistent. If we wish to calculate the present value of a future payment expressed in nominal terms, we should use the discount factor based on the current nominal interest rate. However, if the future payment is expressed in real terms, we should use a discount factor based on the real interest rate.

What we must not do is confuse the two. The following is quite a common mistake. You want to buy a farm whose rental this year is £10 000. Today's interest rate is 20 per cent. You reckon that the farm's output should not change much over time. Hence you apply the formula of equation (1) for a perpetuity, divide £10 000 by 0.2, and get £50 000. The farmer wants £100 000 for the farm so you decide not to buy. The present value of the rental stream is only £50 000.

You have just missed a financial killing. Current interest rates are 20 per cent only because the market believes that inflation on average will be something like 17 per cent, leaving a real interest rate of 3 per cent. Doing the calculation in real terms at constant prices, we should divide £10 000 for ever by 0.03 to obtain £333 000 as the correct price

Table 14-6	Nominal and real interest rates and inflation in the UK, 1966–99 (% per annum)							
	66	71	76	81	85	91	95	99
Nominal interest rate	6.9	8.9	14.4	13.8	10.6	10.8	6.4	6.0
Inflation rate	3.9	9.4	16.5	11.9	6.1	5.9	2.7	2.2
Real interest rate	3.0	−0.5	−2.1	1.9	4.5	4.9	3.7	3.8

Source: IMF, *International Financial Statistics*.

for the farm. Equivalently, if we wish to calculate in nominal terms, we can use discount factors based on the 20 per cent nominal interest rate, but we must remember that the likely inflation rate of around 17 per cent will steadily increase the nominal farm rental over time. If we do this calculation, we shall again conclude that at £100 000 asking price the farm is a real bargain. Would you have got the right answer?

14-3 Saving, investment, and the real interest rate

Figure 14-2 shows the production possibility frontier AA', feasible combinations of current and future consumption goods that the economy can produce. At A the economy only produces for current consumption, at A' only for future consumption.

The frontier AA' shows the consequences of devoting different amounts of current resources to *investment* in the capital stock. At A not only is no investment being undertaken, the existing capital is also being sold off (perhaps to foreigners) to finance imports for immediate consumption.

At A' all current resources are going to investment to increase the capacity to produce consumption goods in the future. But people are starving today. Moving down AA', more and more resources are being transferred from future to current consumption. As usual, the curvature of the production possibility frontier reflects diminishing returns in this tradeoff.

The slope of the frontier shows the additional future consumption obtained by sacrificing one unit of current consumption. The slope has magnitude $-(1 + i)$ where i is the rate of return on investment. The minus sign reminds us that we have to sacrifice current consumption to add to future consumption.

If the real return on investment is zero, we can exchange £1 of current consumption for £1 of future consumption. Positive rates of return allow us to get additional future consumption by sacrificing £1 of current consumption.

What about consumer tastes? Both current and future consumption are desirable, so we can superimpose on Figure 14-2 a standard indifference map. The more impatient are consumers for current consumption, the steeper will be their indifference curves. Impatient people will give up lots of future consumption to get a bit more today. Thrifty people have flatter indifference curves.

In Figure 14-3 UU is the highest indifference that can be reached and E is the point of maximum welfare, the allocation of current resources between consumption and investment that delivers the best combination of consumer goods now and in the future. E is the point a benevolent central planner would choose.

In a market economy, the real interest rate may adjust to accomplish precisely the same outcome, even though

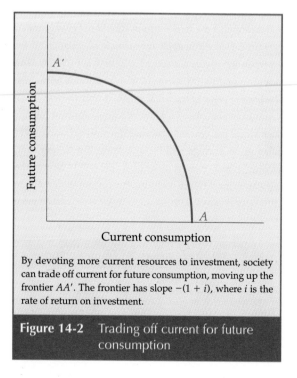

By devoting more current resources to investment, society can trade off current for future consumption, moving up the frontier AA'. The frontier has slope $-(1 + i)$, where i is the rate of return on investment.

Figure 14-2   Trading off current for future consumption

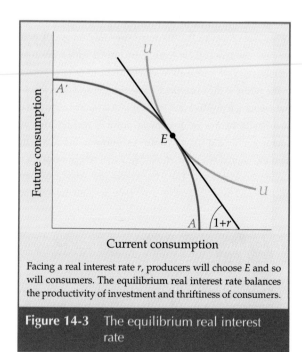

Facing a real interest rate r, producers will choose E and so will consumers. The equilibrium real interest rate balances the productivity of investment and thriftiness of consumers.

Figure 14-3   The equilibrium real interest rate

decisions to add to the capital stock are taken by firms and decisions about saving are taken by households.

Saving is the difference between current income and current consumption.

Firms will invest up to the point at which the real rate of return i equals the real interest rate r at which they can borrow money. When households save, they exchange £1 of consumption today for £$(1 + r)$ of consumption in the future. They will choose to save up to the point at which these market terms of exchange just equal the relative utility valuation on current and future consumption, which is precisely what the slope of the indifference curve tells us. Households save up to the point their indifference curve is tangent to their 'budget line' with slope $-(1 + r)$. Production determines the level of national output to which this line is tangent.

Equilibrium occurs where saving equals investment and both households and firms are happy with the same transfer of resources from the present to the future. Thus, Figure 14-3 shows the equilibrium real interest rate r. Firms wish to be at E where the rate of return i equals the cost of borrowing r [the slope of the frontier $-(1 + i)$ is tangent to the line $-(1 + r)$]. Households want to be at the *same* point E, where their indifference curve UU is tangent to the line $-(1 + r)$.

14-4 The demand for capital services

The analysis of the demand for capital services by an industry closely parallels the analysis of labour demand in Chapter 12. The rental rate for capital takes the place of the hourly wage rate. Each represents the cost of employing or using factor services. We emphasize the *use* of *services* of capital. The example to bear in mind is a firm renting a vehicle or leasing office space.

We begin the demand for capital services by a firm. As with labour, the firm considers how much one more hour of capital services will add to the value of the firm's output.

The **marginal value product of capital** is the increase in the value of the firm's output when one more unit of capital services is employed.

As in our discussion of labour in Chapter 12, we can generalize our analysis to the case where the firm has monopoly power in its output market or monopsony power in its input markets. Having discussed that extension in Chapter 12, we confine our discussion of capital services to the simpler case in which the firm is competitive.

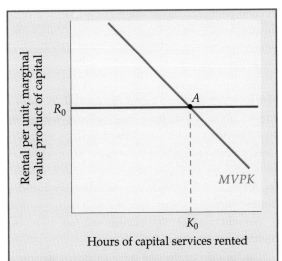

Diminishing marginal productivity implies a falling *MVPK* schedule as capital input is increased holding constant the quantity of other inputs. At any given rental, the firm hires capital services up to the point at which the rental per unit equals the *MVPK*. Thus the *MVPK* curve is also the firm's demand curve for capital services. For example, at a rental rate R_0 the firm will hire K_0 capital services.

Figure 14-4   The demand for capital services

Given the amounts of labour (and any other factor, such as land) that the firm employs, the marginal value product of capital *MVPK* declines as the amount of capital per worker increases. Although the firm's output price is fixed since it is competitive, the marginal physical product of capital is subject to diminishing returns. Figure 14-4 shows a downward-sloping *MVPK* curve just like the *MVPL* curve in Chapter 12.

Suppose the firm can rent units of capital at the rental rate R_0. We can think of this as the monthly payment for leasing an office. The firm will rent capital up to the point at which its marginal cost – the rental rate – equals its marginal value product. It will demand K_0 units of capital services at the rental rate R_0.

For a given price and quantity of other factors of production, *MVPK* is the firm's demand curve for capital services. For any rental rate we can read off the profit-maximizing level of capital services from the *MVPK* curve. As with the firm's *MVPL* curve, showing its labour demand, the firm's *MVPK* curve showing its capital demand curve can be shifted outwards by one of three things: (1) an increase in its output price, which makes the marginal *physical* product of capital more valuable, (2) an increase in the level of other factors (chiefly labour) with which capital works to produce output, thus increasing the marginal physical product of capital and hence its marginal value product, and (3) a technical advance, which increases the physical productivity of capital for any given quantity of other factor inputs.

The industry demand curve for capital services

As with labour, we can move from the firm's demand for capital services to the industry demand curve for capital services by horizontally adding the marginal value product of each firm. As in Figure 12-4, which added together the $MVPL$ curves of each firm to obtain the industry demand curve for labour, again we must recognize that, in expanding output, the industry will bid down the equilibrium price of its output.

Thus the industry demand curve for capital services is steeper than the horizontal sum of each firm's $MVPK$ curves. The industry demand curve recognizes that output prices will change when industry output is changed. The more inelastic is the demand curve for the industry's output the more inelastic will be the industry's derived demand curve for capital services.

14-5 The supply of capital services

Capital services are produced by capital assets. Owning or renting a machine allows a firm to use the input machine-hours. The economist's approach to capital is first to analyse the market for capital services used in production, then to consider what this implies for the market for machines themselves. In so doing, we usually assume that the flow of capital services is directly determined by the stock of capital assets such as machines.

It should be remembered that this is only a first approximation. By working overtime shifts, a firm can alter the effective flow of machine services it gets from a given machine bolted to the factory floor. Even if firms cannot quickly change the stock of machines, it may thus be possible to vary, at least in part, the flow of capital services derived from these assets, even in the short run.

Nevertheless, in normal times firms have only a limited ability to vary the flow of capital services that can be extracted from a given capital stock. We shall understand the most important features of the market for capital if we assume that the flow of capital services is essentially determined by the stock of capital available. We must now distinguish between the long run and the short run, and between the supply of capital services to the whole economy and to a particular industry.

The short-run supply of capital services

In the short run the total supply of capital assets (machines, buildings, and vehicles), and thus the services they provide, is fixed to the economy as a whole. It takes time to change the capital stock. New factories cannot be built overnight. For the whole economy, it makes sense to think of the supply of capital services as fixed in the short run. The supply curve is vertical at a quantity determined by the existing stock of capital assets.

Some types of capital are fixed even for the individual industry. The steel industry cannot change overnight its number of blast furnaces. However, some industries may be able to increase their supply of some types of capital, even in the short run. By offering a higher rental rate for delivery vans, the supermarket industry can attract a larger share of the total quantity of delivery vans that the economy currently possesses. For such types of capital services the industry faces an upward-sloping supply curve. By offering a higher rental rate the industry can increase the supply of delivery van services to that industry.

The supply of capital services in the long run

In the long run the total quantity of capital in the economy can be varied. New machines and factories can be built. Conversely, with no new investment in capital goods the existing capital stock will depreciate and be effectively reduced. Similarly, individual industries can adjust their stocks of capital.

The required rental on capital   To discuss the supply side of the market for capital, we consider the rental rates at which owners or potential owners of capital would be willing to buy or build.

The **required rental on capital** is the rental rate that just covers the opportunity cost of owning the capital.

Suppose you buy a machine to rent out as a business. The machine costs £10 000, which you have to borrow. How much must the machine earn if you are to break even as a machine services supplier? First you have to cover the interest cost. Suppose the *real*, or inflation-adjusted, interest rate is 5 per cent. You have to pay the bank £500 (£10 000 × 0.05) a year in real terms.

Then you have expenditure on maintenance. You must also recognize that the resale value of the machine is depreciating each year. Suppose that in real terms maintenance and depreciation cost you £1000 per annum. This is 10 per cent of the purchase price, and we say the depreciation rate is 10 per cent per annum. Thus your annual cost of renting out a machine in working order is

$$\frac{\text{Annual}}{\text{cost}} = \frac{\text{interest} + \text{maintenance and}}{\text{cost} \quad \text{depreciation}}$$

$$= \frac{\text{asset}}{\text{price}} \times \left\{ \frac{\text{interest}}{\text{rate}} + \frac{\text{depreciation}}{\text{rate}} \right\}$$

$$= £10\,000 \times (0.05 + 0.1)$$

$$= £1500 \tag{3}$$

The required rental if you are to break even must therefore be £1500 at constant prices. Frequently we show the required rental as a percentage of the purchase price of the capital good. In this example the required *real rate of return* is 15 per cent per annum.[1] It is worth borrowing from a bank to buy a machine if, after allowing for inflation, its rental is at least £1500 per annum. You will at least cover the costs, including interest and depreciation, of being in the business of renting out machines.[2]

What determines the required rental? Equation (3) shows that the required rental rate or cost of capital depends on three things: the price of the capital good, the real interest rate, and the depreciation rate. Depreciation depends largely on technology; on how fast the machine wears out with use and age. The real interest rate is determined by economy-wide forces. Table 14-6 shows that it changes only slowly. Treating the depreciation rate and the real interest rate as given, we examine how the purchase price of capital goods affects the required rental on capital.

The long-run supply curve for the economy In the long run, a given quantity of capital services is supplied to the economy only if it earns the required rental. If it earns more, people will build new capital goods. If it earns less, owners of capital will allow their goods to depreciate without building new ones.

Figure 14-5 shows the long-run supply curve of capital services to the economy. Imagine that these are industries

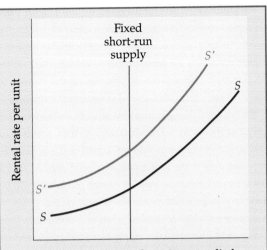

In the short run, the stock of capital goods, and the services they supply, is fixed by past investment decisions. New capital goods cannot be produced overnight. In the long run, a higher rental rate is required to call forth a higher supply of capital services and a permanently higher capital stock. The higher rental rate just offsets the higher price for capital goods required to induce higher output of new capital goods to match the higher total depreciation of a larger capital stock. Thus the required rate of return is met at all points on *SS*. If real interest rates increase, the required rate of return will also increase to match the opportunity cost of funds tied up in capital goods. Hence the long-run supply curve of capital services shifts up to *S'S'* providing a higher rental level at each level of the capital stock and its corresponding purchase price. Each point on *S'S'* matches the new required rate of return.

Figure 14-5 The supply of capital services to the economy

that produce capital goods. For example, the construction industry produces buildings and the motor industry produces container lorries. Each industry has an upward-sloping supply curve. The higher the price of the capital good, the more the capital goods producing industry will choose to supply.

In the long run there can be a larger flow of capital services only if there is a permanently higher capital stock. But capital depreciates. The higher the capital stock the larger will be the total amount of depreciation. With a 10 per cent depreciation rate, the depreciation per annum on a stock of £200 million is £20 million or twice the depreciation of £10 million per annum on a capital stock of only £100 million. Thus, a higher long-run flow of capital services requires a permanently higher capital stock, which in turn requires a higher flow of new capital goods to offset depreciation and maintain the capital stock intact.

---

[1] To simplify the calculation, we assumed that both the machine and the bank loan last for ever. You may be wondering if equation (3) has any connection with our earlier discussion of the present value of a perpetuity. Equation (1) said that the price p of a perpetuity should equal the annual payment c divided by the required rate of return r that lenders could get by lending to a bank. If $p = c/r$, then $r = c/p$. Equation (3) says that when c is the annual cost and p is the initial price of a machine, you need a rate of return $r = c/p$ to decide to go into the business of renting out machines.

[2] If the firm using the capital services also owns the capital good, the required rental is the cost the firm should charge itself for using the capital when calculating economic costs. You might like to refer back to our discussion of accounting costs and economic costs in Chapter 7.

But producers of new capital goods require a higher price for capital goods to produce a larger quantity of new capital goods. To maintain the required rate of return we require a higher rental rate for capital services. A higher rental rate divided by a higher purchase price for capital goods will leave the rate of return unaltered as equation (3) implies.

Because, in the long run, capital services will be supplied only if capital earns the required rate of return, we now see that a higher long-run flow of capital services will be supplied only if the rental rate on capital rises to match the increased purchase price of capital goods that will be necessary to persuade producers of new capital goods to keep pace with higher absolute levels of depreciation. Thus in Figure 14-5 we show the supply curve for capital services sloping upwards in the long run when plotted against the rental rate on capital.

We draw the upward-sloping supply curve for capital services SS for a given real interest rate. What happens if the real interest rate increases? Equation (3) says that, for a given purchase price of capital goods, the required rental must increase. Suppliers of capital services need a higher return to offset the higher opportunity cost of the money they tie up in purchasing capital goods. Unless the rental rate rises the required rate of return cannot rise to match the increase in the opportunity cost of funds, namely the real interest rate.

Hence, in Figure 14-5 we show an increase in real interest rates as shifting upwards the long-run supply curve for capital services, from SS to S'S'. At each level of capital services, and corresponding price of capital goods necessary to persuade producers of new capital goods to produce just enough to maintain the corresponding capital stock intact in spite of depreciation, the rental rate on capital services, and hence the rate of return, is now higher.

The long-run supply curve for the industry Again, our discussion parallels the discussion of labour supply in Chapter 12. The preceding analysis determines the supply of capital services to the whole economy. In the long run a very tiny industry can obtain as much of this capital as it wishes, provided it pays the going rental rate. A larger industry may have to pay an increasing rental rate per unit of capital services the larger the fraction of the economy-wide supply it wishes to attract. Thus an industry whose use of capital is significant relative to the whole economy will face an upward-sloping supply curve for capital services.

We now analyse the case of a small industry facing a horizontal long-run supply curve for capital services at the going rental per unit. The analysis is easily extended to an industry facing an upward-sloping long-run supply curve for capital services.

14-6 Equilibrium and adjustment in the market for capital services

Figure 14-6 shows the market for capital services for an industry. Long-run equilibrium occurs at E, where the horizontal supply curve SS crosses the industry demand curve DD derived from firms' MVPK curves. The industry employs K_0 capital services and pays the going rental per unit R_0.

Adjustments in the market for capital services

Suppose workers in this industry now secure a wage increase. If you mastered Chapter 12 you should already be able to analyse the long-run effect on the quantity of capital services demanded by the industry.

In the long run all factors of production can be freely varied. A higher wage rate has a *substitution effect* and an *output effect*. A higher wage rate increases the cost of labour services relative to capital services. The substitution effect leads firms to switch to more capital-intensive techniques to economize on labour that is now more expensive, thus increasing the quantity of capital services demanded at any rental rate.

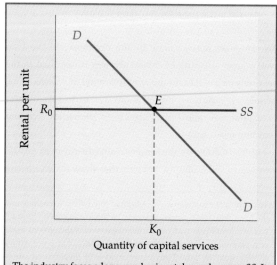

The industry faces a long-run horizontal supply curve SS. It must pay the going rental for capital services. DD is the industry demand curve derived from individual firms' MVPK curves. Equilibrium for the industry occurs at E with a quantity K_0 of capital services.

Figure 14-6 Equilibrium in the market for capital services

But there is also an output effect. By raising costs, a wage increase causes an upward shift in the industry supply curve for output and reduces the quantity of output supplied. This tends to reduce the quantity of all factors demanded by the industry. The more elastic is the demand curve for the industry's output, the more a given upward shift in its supply curve will reduce the equilibrium quantity of output and the larger will be the output effect on the quantity of capital demanded.

This analysis is based on our discussion of the choice of technique in Chapter 12. It concludes that a wage increase is more likely to reduce the demand for capital services the more elastic is the industry's output demand curve. We can reach the same conclusion by arguing directly from marginal product schedules.

We draw the marginal product of capital schedule for a given quantity of other factors including labour. A rise in the wage rate will reduce the quantity of labour demanded. This effect tends to cause a leftward shift in the marginal value product of capital by reducing the marginal physical product of capital, which now has less labour with which to work. However, a wage increase also shifts the industry supply curve upwards and raises the equilibrium price for the industry's output. This tends to increase the marginal value product of capital and shift the schedule to the right. This effect will be smaller the more elastic is the demand curve for the industry's output. Again, we reach the conclusion that the demand for capital services is more likely to shift to the left the more elastic is the demand for the industry's output.

Short-run and long-run adjustment

The above analysis applied only in the long run when the industry can completely adjust to the wage increase. Figure 14-7 examines short-run and long-run adjustment to a wage increase for the case in which the long-run effect is to shift the demand curve for capital services inwards from DD to $D'D'$.

Originally the industry was in equilibrium at E. Overnight, capital is a fixed factor and the industry supply of capital services is vertical at the initial quantity K_0. Thus, when the demand curve first shifts from DD to $D'D'$, the firm cannot immediately respond by cutting its input of capital services. With a vertical short-run supply curve, the new short-run equilibrium occurs at E'. The rental on capital falls from R_0 to R_1.

However, this small industry faces a long-run supply curve $S'S'$ for capital services. Eventually it must pay the going rate. At E' owners of capital are not receiving the

required rental for the capital services they supply. They allow their existing capital stock to depreciate without taking steps to maintain it, let alone replace it. Over time, the industry's capital stock and supply of capital services fall until equilibrium is reached at E''. The capital services used by the industry have fallen to K_1. For a given quantity of labour, lower capital means a higher marginal product of capital. In the long-run equilibrium at E'', users of capital are once more prepared to pay the required rental R_0.

The arrows in Figure 14-7 show the dynamic path that the industry will follow. When demand for capital is first reduced there is a sharp fall in the rental on capital, but owners of the fixed factor can't adjust the quantity of capital services they supply. As time elapses it is possible to adjust the quantity, in this instance by allowing capital goods to depreciate, and the rental gradually recovers.

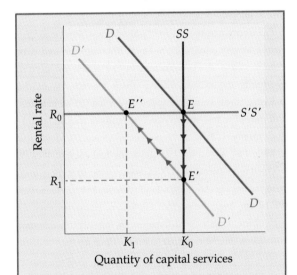

The industry begins in equilibrium at E. Overnight its short-run supply of capital is fixed at K_0, but in the long run it faces the horizontal supply curve $S'S'$ at the going rental R_0. Suppose a wage increase shifts the demand curve for capital from DD to $D'D'$. The new short-run equilibrium is at E'. Since the rental R_1 fails to provide the required rate of return, owners of capital goods allow these goods slowly to depreciate without buying any new capital goods. The industry's capital stock and the services it provides gradually fall back. Eventually the industry reaches long-run equilibrium at E''. Since capital is again earning the required rate of return, owners of capital goods now replace goods as they depreciate.

Figure 14-7   Short- and long-run adjustment of capital to a wage rise

Table 14-7	UK real capital, 1985–96	
	85	96
Whole economy	1563	2144
Financial services	145	266
Agriculture, forest, fish	46	46

Note: 1996 £ bn, excluding inventories and dwellings.
Source: ONS, UK National Accounts.

More examples of adjustment

Suppose competition from imports reduces the demand for domestically produced textiles. A lower output price shifts the derived demand curve for capital services to the left. Figure 14-7 again describes the short-run and long-run response we should expect. In the short run capital is mostly fixed and the rental is demand-determined. The rental is high only if the derived demand for capital is high. Over the long run the stock of capital can be adjusted, and the supply of capital services changed, to restore the required return on capital goods.

The German textile industry provides a striking example. Facing severe competition from imports, the industry experienced a sharp reduction in the rental on capital. Gradually the existing capital stock moved out of the industry. It was literally stripped down, loaded on to trains, and moved to low-wage Greece to produce textiles for sale in Germany.

Table 14-7 shows the change in the real capital stock of selected industries in the UK in recent years. To some extent, rising real wages have led all industries to substitute capital for labour over the period. However, industries such as agriculture, forestry, and fisheries, facing difficult demand conditions in their output market, have increased their capital stock, despite the national trend. In contrast, industries such as financial services, experienced rapid increases in their capital stock, as the analysis of derived demand in this chapter would lead us to expect.

14-7 The price of capital assets

Having studied the market for capital services, we now ask: what is going on in the market for capital goods themselves? Capital goods are the output of the capital goods producing industries, which have the usual upward-sloping output supply curve. They supply more capital goods if the price is higher.

Capital goods are demanded by firms who wish to supply capital services. Think of Hertz renting out cars, or property companies renting out office space. Anticipating a stream of rentals, the suppliers of capital services work out the present value of this stream of rentals at the going interest rate. This tells us how much they should be prepared to pay to obtain a capital good today. Each potential supplier of capital services will be prepared to pay a higher purchase price for a capital asset the higher the anticipated rental stream or the lower the interest rate. Both tend to increase the present value of the future rental stream.

People anticipating a higher stream of rental earnings will be prepared to pay a high purchase price for capital assets. At a lower price, people with slightly lower anticipated streams will now find it profitable to demand capital goods. Hence we have the downward-sloping demand curve for capital goods. The lower the price, the higher the quantity demanded, since more potential suppliers of capital services are able to cover the purchase price by the present value of the rental earnings that the capital good will provide. The upward-sloping supply curve and downward-sloping demand curve together determine the equilibrium price and quantity of capital goods for the economy. The quantity determines the flow supply of capital services that this stock will provide.

What happens when an individual industry faces a leftward shift in its derived demand for capital services, as in Figure 14-7? In the short run the rental per unit of capital services falls to R_1. Moreover, everyone can work out that it will take some time before the rental rate climbs back to R_0. At the going interest rate the present value of rental earnings on new capital goods in this industry falls.

But the industry is small relative to the economy. To buy capital goods it has to pay the going price. Since the price this industry is prepared to pay has fallen below the going price, the industry buys no new capital goods. Nor does it replace existing goods that depreciate. The capital stock falls until the rental rate has climbed back to the rate prevailing throughout the economy. The present value of anticipated future rentals once more matches the price of capital goods in the whole economy. The industry now buys capital goods to replace goods as they depreciate. The capital stock is maintained, and we have reached the new long-run equilibrium for the industry.

Thus, for the industry and the economy, the long-run equilibrium price of a capital asset is both the price of inducing the capital-producing industries to supply capital goods and the price that buyers of capital goods are prepared to pay, namely the present value of the anticipated rental stream for capital services discounted at the going rate of interest.

14-8 Land and rents

The distinguishing feature of land is that it is essentially in fixed supply to the whole economy even in the long run. This is not literally true. For example, the Dutch have been able to reclaim from the sea some areas of low-lying land. Similarly, fertilizers may enhance the effective input of land for farming. Nevertheless, it makes sense to think about a factor whose total long-run supply is fixed as a guide to the most important single feature on the market for land.

Figure 14-8 shows the derived demand curve for land DD exactly analogous to the derived demand for capital services. With a fixed supply the equilibrium rental per acre is R_0. An increase in the derived demand, for example because wheat prices has risen, leads only to an increase in the rental to R_1. The quantity of land services is fixed by assumption.

Consider a tenant farmer who rents land. Wheat prices have risen but so have rents. Not only may the farmer be no better off, but the connection between the two rises may not even be recognized. The farmer may complain that high rents are making it hard to earn a decent living. As in our discussion of footballers' wages in Chapter 12, it is the high

derived demand combined with the inelastic factor supply that cause the high payments for factor services.

Because land is traditionally viewed as *the* asset in fixed supply, economists have taken over the word 'rent', the payment for land services, to the concept of *economic rent*, the excess of actual payments over transfer earnings, which we introduced in Chapter 12.

14-9 Allocating a fixed land supply between competing uses

Land can be used for crops, for grazing, for housing or offices, and even for building roads. How do land prices and land rentals guide the allocation of the fixed total supply between the different possible uses?

Suppose there are two industries, housing and farming. Given each industry's output demand curve, we can derive its demand curve for land. Figure 14-9 shows $D_H D_H$ the demand curve for housing land and $D_F D_F$ the demand curve for farming land. SS shows the fixed total supply of land to be allocated between the two industries.

Although in the long run the supply in total is fixed, its allocation between the two industries is not. If rentals are different in the two industries, owners of land will transfer their supplies of land services from the low-rental to the high-rental industry. Hence, rentals must be equal in the two industries in the long run. Moreover, the rental must equate the fixed supply of land with the total quantity demanded. Hence equilibrium occurs at the rental R_0 at which the quantity of land L_H demanded by the housing industry plus the quantity L_F demanded in farming together equal the fixed total supply L.

Now suppose the government subsidizes housing. The demand for housing land shifts up from $D_H D_H$ to $D'_H D'_H$. The vertical shift is the amount of the subsidy. At the quantity L_H households are paying R_0 per unit as before but the government is contributing $R_1 - R_0$ to owners of land, who receive R_1 in total.

At the original allocation of L_H and L_F landowners have an incentive to transfer land services from farming to housing, from which they now receive a higher rental. The new equilibrium occurs at R_2, which again equalizes rentals earned in the two sectors while ensuring that the total quantity demanded equals the total quantity supplied. The housing subsidy increases general land rentals and leads farmers to economize on land until its marginal value product once more equals the rental per unit of land services.

What about land prices? When rentals were R_0 the land

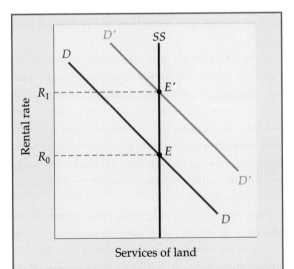

The total supply of land is fixed to the economy. The supply curve is vertical. The derived demand curve for land services reflects the marginal value product of land. Its derivation is exactly the same as the demand curves for labour and capital from the *MVPL* and *MVPK* schedules. The demand curve DD for land services determines the equilibrium land rental rate R_0. If the derived demand curve for land services shifts up to $D'D'$, the equilibrium land rental will increase to R_1.

Figure 14-8   The market for land services

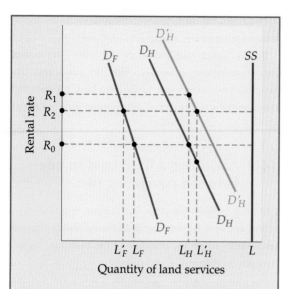

The vertical supply curve SS shows that the total supply of land is fixed. $D_F D_F$ is the demand curve for farming land and $D_H D_H$ the demand curve for housing land. In the long run, landowners will transfer land services between industries unless the rental in the two industries is the same. The equilibrium rental R_0 ensures that the total quantity of land services demanded $L_F + L_H$ just equals the total supply. With a government housing subsidy, $D_H D_H$ still shows the demand curve for housing land net of the subsidy and $D'_H D'_H$ shows the rental the housing landowners will receive inclusive of the subsidy. Overnight, the supply of land to the two industries is fixed (at L_F and L_H) and the subsidy merely raises the rental received by owners of housing land to R_1. It is they not households who benefit. Since the rental for farmland remains R_0 in the short run there is an incentive to transfer land from farming to housing. The new long-run equilibrium occurs at rental R_2 though households pay less than this because the government subsidizes housing land. The total demand $L'_F + L'_F$ again just equals the total supply of land.

Figure 14-9   Allocating land between competing uses

Table 14-8   Real fixed capital per worker, 1996 (£000 per worker, 1996 prices)

Energy and water	873
Agriculture, forestry, fishing	84
Manufacturing	107
Distribution, hotels, catering	39
Construction	14

Source: ONS, *UK National Accounts*.

14-10 The facts again

The economy is becoming more capital-intensive in its production techniques, a general phenomenon in industrial economies. How does the analysis of this chapter help us make sense of the facts?

Table 14-8 shows UK data on capital intensity in different sectors in 1996. It shows the amount of fixed capital (productive capital minus inventories) available per production worker in each sector.

Let us assume that all industries are in long-run equilibrium so we can neglect any short-run adjustment problems. For the questions we are now asking, this seems a reasonable simplification. The ranking of industries by capital intensity in 1996 is very similar to the position 10 years earlier.

In the long run we expect the rental on capital to be equalized in different sectors. Otherwise capital would move between sectors in search of a higher return. Similarly, long-run wage differentials should primarily reflect non-monetary job characteristics, so there is no incentive for labour to move between sectors. We should not be surprised that miners earn more than farm labourers; other things being equal, people would rather work in the fields than in a dangerous mine shaft.

These offsetting wage differentials apart, different sectors face the same relative factor rentals in the long run. Our model of the choice of technique predicts that the main determinant of different capital–labour ratios across sectors will be differences in technology. It all depends on the technical ease with which labour can be substituted for capital.

Table 14-8 confirms this prediction. A modern power station or sewage plant can be run by a few technical supervisors who keep an eye on the computer screens. Although a large capital-intensive plant is expensive, it can produce a large output at low average cost. It would be much more expensive to produce the same output in a labour-intensive

price was the present value of this rental stream at the going interest rate. When rentals rise to R_2 the present value of the stream increases and prices rise correspondingly.

Again, we should distinguish between short- and long-run adjustment. Overnight the land supplied to each industry is fixed. When housing is first subsidized landowners can immediately charge at rental R_1 to the housing industry at the original quantity L_H. This high rental provides the incentive for landowners to transfer land from farming to housing, bidding up farm rentals but bidding down housing rentals. In the short run housing rentals received by landowners actually overshoot the increase required in the long run.

way. Thus it makes sense to choose very capital-intensive production techniques in the gas, electricity, and water industries.

Conversely, construction is very labour-intensive and capital per employee very low. Building a factory involves a number of different tasks that are not easily automated. Service industries such as restaurants, theatres, and hairdressing are also labour-intensive. Human contact and personal services cannot be reproduced by machines.

Why does capital intensity increase in every decade? Two separate reasons can be given. First, the wage–rental ratio increased, leading industries to substitute capital for labour. In the long run the supply of labour is less elastic than the supply of capital, so real wages rise more than the real rental on capital. This change in relative factor rentals causes further substitution towards capital-intensive techniques.

Second, the steady stream of new inventions led to technical advances in production methods. To take advantage of these improvements, firms have to install new capital that *embodies* the latest techniques. There is no point knowing that a breakthrough has been made in robot assembly-line technology unless the robot assembly is actually installed. Labour-saving inventions thus provide an incentive to introduce more capital-intensive methods.

14-11 Income distribution in the UK

The income of a factor is simply its rental rate multiplied by the quantity of the factor that is employed. In this final section we pull together our discussion of factor markets to examine the distribution of income in the UK.

The functional distribution of income

The *functional income distribution* shows the division of national income between the different factors of production. Table 14-9 shows the total earnings of the different factors of production in the UK in 1996 and compares their shares of national income with the shares they received during 1981–89.

Table 14-9	UK functional income distribution, 1981–98 (% of national income)	
Source (factor of production)	1981–89 average	1998
Employment	64.3	63.4
Self-employment	6.4	5.9
Profits and property rents	29.3	30.7
Source: ONS, *UK National Accounts*.		

The most interesting feature of Table 14-9 is that there has been relatively little change in the shares of the different factors of production over the last two decades. As the real incomes increased, the real incomes of the different factors of production broadly kept pace.

In Chapter 12 we saw that the aggregate labour supply curve to the economy is relatively inelastic. With an almost vertical labour supply curve, the total number of employed workers was little higher in 1998 than in 1981. Table 14-2 shows that the UK capital stock grew considerably faster than the UK labour force. With more capital to work with, labour's marginal product schedule shifted outwards and upwards. When confronted with an almost vertical labour supply curve, the consequence of this steady increase in the demand for labour was to increase the equilibrium real wage. And the combination of real wage growth and a slight increase in the labour force has increased real income from employment since 1981, though the share of income from employment in national income fell over this period.

Table 14-9 shows that the share of income from profits and rents grew slightly during 1981–98. From Table 14-2, we know that the quantity of capital employed has been steadily rising, but at roughly the same rate as national output. Since the ratio of capital to output has been fairly constant, a relatively constant share of profits in national income suggests that the rate of return on capital has also been fairly constant over a long period.

If the quantity of capital has increased without a permanent fall in its rate of return, the economy cannot simply have moved down a given marginal product of capital schedule; otherwise, the rental on capital and its rate of return would have been reduced. Rather, the marginal product schedule must have shifted outwards.

This outward shift in the marginal product of capital schedule was chiefly caused not by an increase in the quantity of labour employed, which scarcely changed, but by technical progress. Technical progress both directly increased the productivity of capital for a given effective quantity of labour input, and increased the quantity of labour effectively employed by raising its productivity.

We know that the supply of land is very inelastic and that the demand for land is a derived demand. As national income increases the derived demand curve for land will shift upwards. Thus it is not surprising that property rents have risen at least in line with national income.

The personal income distribution

The *personal income distribution* shows how national income is divided between different individuals, regardless of the

---

BOX 14-2   Factor markets: a summary

In the last three chapters we have studied the markets for the factors of production – labour, capital, and land. In the long run when all inputs can be freely varied, the firm's choice of technique at each output level will be determined by relative factor prices or rentals. At a given output level, an increase in the relative price of one factor will lead the firm to substitute towards techniques that use that factor less intensively. The long-run total cost curve shows the cheapest way to produce each output level when the production technique is optimally chosen. From long-run total cost we can then determine long-run marginal cost and hence the profit-maximizing output at which marginal cost and marginal revenue are equal.

For each factor, the firm's demand curve is a derived demand that depends on the factor's marginal physical product in making extra output and on the marginal revenue that the firm obtains by selling that extra output. For a competitive firm, the demand curve for a factor is precisely its marginal value product schedule. We construct a marginal value product schedule for a given output price, given quantities of all other factors of production, and a given technology. Changes in any of these three things will shift the marginal value product schedule. In the short run, a competitive firm will demand that quantity of its variable factor that equates the factor's marginal value product and its factor price or rental. But in the long run, every factor can be freely varied. Each factor will be demanded up

to the point at which its factor rental equals its marginal value product *given that the quantity of all other factors has already been optimally adjusted to the same criterion.*

What then distinguishes the three factors of production we call labour, capital, and land? Primarily the speed with which the supply of that factor can adjust. At one extreme we have casual labour employed on a day-to-day basis on construction sites or on farms during the crop picking season. The supply of this factor to the firm, the industry, and possibly even to the economy as a whole, is quite free to vary even in the short run. The supply of highly skilled workers with extensive training can be changed less quickly and the supply of many capital goods, such as factories and power stations, takes even longer to adjust. And land is the factor the supply of which to the whole economy is essentially fixed, even in the long run. The slower is the speed of adjustment, and the more irreversible the process, the more current decisions must be based on future as well as present conditions. Beliefs about future conditions, and estimates of the rate of return over a long future period, could be neglected in our discussion of unskilled labour in Chapter 12, but were intrinsic to our discussion of investment in human capital in Chapter 13 and in physical capital in the present chapter.

These general principles form the basic toolkit for thinking about factor markets.

---

factor services from which these individuals earn their income. The personal income distribution is relevant to issues such as equality and poverty.

Table 14-10 does not show people whose income is so low that the Inland Revenue do not need to record what their income actually is. Even confining our attention to people with sufficiently high pre-tax incomes that they may be liable for income tax, we can see that pre-tax income is quite unequally distributed in the UK. Looking at the bottom of Table 14-10, 9 per cent of all taxpayers earn 29 per cent of national income. Why should some people earn so much while others earn so little?

Table 14-10   UK personal income distribution, 1998

Income range (£000)	Percentage of	
	Taxpayers	National income
Under 8	24.6	8.6
8–12	23.0	13.7
12–15	13.6	10.9
15–20	15.6	16.2
20–30	14.6	21.3
30+	8.6	29.3

Based on 25 million taxpayers.
Source: ONS, *Social Trends*.

Table 14-11 UK wealth distribution	
% of population	% of total wealth
Richest 1%	19
5%	38
10%	51
25%	73
50%	93

Source: ONS, Social Trends, 1998.

Chapters 12 and 13 discussed some of the reasons why people earn different wages and salaries. Unskilled workers have little training and low productivity. Workers with high levels of training and education earn much more. Some jobs, such as coal mining, pay high compensating differentials to offset unpleasant working conditions. Very pleasant, but unskilled, jobs pay much less since many people are prepared to do them. Talented superstars in scarce supply but strong demand may earn very high economic rents.

However, Table 14-10 refers not just to income from the supply of labour services. A major reason why the distribution of personal income is so unequal is that the ownership of wealth, which provides income from profits and rents, is even more unequal. Table 14-11 shows details for the UK for 1994.

Table 14-11 shows that the most wealthy 1 per cent of the population owns 19 per cent of the nation's marketable wealth and the most wealthy 25 per cent of the population own 73 per cent of the nation's marketable wealth. The stream of profit and rent income to which such wealth gives rise lays a large part in determining the personal distribution of pre-tax *income*.

SUMMARY

● Physical (as opposed to financial) capital comprises real assets yielding useful services to producing firms or consuming households. The main categories of physical capital are plant and machinery, residential structures, other buildings, consumer durables, and inventories. Tangible wealth is physical capital plus land.

● Present value calculations convert future receipts or payments into current values. Because lenders can earn – and borrowers must pay – interest over time, a pound tomorrow is worth less than a pound today. How much less depends on the interest rate. The higher the interest rate, the lower the present value of any future payment.

● Since lending or borrowing cumulates at compound interest, for any given annual interest rate the present value of a given sum is smaller the further into the future that sum is earned or paid.

● The present value of a perpetuity is the constant annual payment divided by the rate of interest. At a 10 per cent interest rate per annum a payment of £100 per annum for ever is worth £1000 today.

● Nominal interest rates measure the monetary interest payments on a loan. The real, or inflation-adjusted, interest rate measures the extra goods a lender can buy by lending for a year and delaying purchases of goods. The real rate of interest is the nominal interest rate minus the inflation rate over the same period.

● In the long run, the real interest adjusts to make investment equal to saving, and, hence, is determined by the return on firms' investment and the degree of impatience of households.

● The demand for capital services is a derived demand. The firm's demand curve for capital services is its marginal value product of capital curve. Higher levels of the other factors of production and higher output prices shift the derived demand curve up. The industry demand curve is less elastic than the horizontal sum of each firm's curve because it also allows for the effect of an industry expansion in bidding down the output price.

● In the short run the supply of capital services is fixed. In the long run it can be adjusted by producing new capital goods or allowing the existing capital stock to depreciate.

● The required rental is the rental that allows a supplier of capital services to break even on the decision to purchase the capital asset. The required rental is higher the higher is the interest rate, the depreciation rate, or the purchase price of the capital good.

● A rise in the industry wage has two effects on the derived demand curve for capital services. By reducing labour input it reduces the marginal physical product of capital. By reducing the industry output it increases the output price. When output demand is very inelastic the latter effect will dominate. The derived demand curve for capital services shifts up. Essentially the industry substitutes capital for labour to produce almost the same output. When output demand is very elastic the former effect dominates. The demand curve for capital services shifts down. The industry contracts its use of labour and capital and produces a much lower output.

● The asset price is the price at which a capital good is bought and sold outright rather than rented. In long-run equilibrium it is both the price at which suppliers of capital goods are willing to produce and the price at which buyers are willing to purchase. The latter is merely the present value of anticipated future rentals earned from the capital services that the good provides in the future.

● Land is the special capital good whose supply is fixed even in the long run. However, land and capital can move between industries in the long run until rentals on land or on capital are equalized in different industries.

● Technology and the ease of factor substitution dictate the very different capital intensity of different industries in the long run. Although most industries are becoming more capital-intensive over time, the rate of change is different in different industries. In part this reflects the ease with which industries can substitute capital for labour as wage rates rise relative to capital rentals. In part it is a reflection of the discovery and implementation of technical advances in different industries.

● The functional distribution of income shows how national income is divided between the factors of production. The share of each factor has remained fairly constant over time. This conceals a rise in the quantity of capital relative to labour and a corresponding fall in the ratio of capital rentals to labour wages.

● The personal distribution of income shows how national income is divided between different individuals regardless of the factor services from which income is earned. A major cause of income inequality in the UK is a very unequal distribution of income-earning wealth.

KEY TERMS

◆ Functional income distribution 214
◆ Personal income distribution 214
◆ Physical and financial capital 214
◆ Land 214
◆ Tangible wealth 214
◆ Gross and net investment 215
◆ Asset stocks and service flows 215
◆ Asset prices and rental rate 214–215
◆ Present value 215
◆ Nominal and real interest rates 218
◆ Saving 220
◆ Marginal value product of capital 221
◆ Required rental 222

REVIEW QUESTIONS

1 Rich countries tend to have a relatively large share of the capital stock in the form of consumer capital. Why do you think this is?

2 (a) Consumer durables – washing machines, televisions, etc. – are part of the capital stock but do not generate any financial income for their owners. Why do we include consumer durables in the capital stock? (b) To wash your clothes you can take them to a laundromat and spend £2 per week indefinitely or buy a washing machine for £400. It costs £1 per week (including depreciation) to run a washing machine, and the interest rate is 10 per cent per annum. Does it make sense to buy the washing machine? Does this help you answer part (a).

3 A bank offers you £1.10 next year for every £0.90 you give it today. What is the implicit interest rate?

4 A firm buys a machine for £10 000, earns rentals of £3600 for each of the next two years, and then sells it for scrap for £9000. Use the data of Table 14-4 to determine if the machine is worth buying when the interest rate is 10 per cent per annum.

5 Discuss the main determinants of the firm's demand curve and the industry's demand curve for capital services. How do these determinants affect the way a tax on the industry's output will shift the industry demand for capital services?

6 The interest rate falls from 10 to 5 per cent. Discuss in detail how this affects the rental on capital services and the level of the capital stock in an industry in the short and long run.

7 Suppose a plot of land is suitable only for agriculture. Can it be true that the farming industry will experience financial distress if there is an increase in the price of land? How would your answer be affected if the land could also be used for housing?

8 *Common fallacies* Show why the following statements are incorrect: (a) Inflation makes nominal interest rates go up. This must reduce the present value of future income. (b) If the economy continues to become more capital-intensive, eventually there will be no jobs left for workers to do. (*Hint*: what happens to labour productivity, wage income, and consumer demand?) (c) Since the economy's supply of land is fixed, it would be supplied even at a zero rental. Land rents should therefore be zero in long-run equilibrium. (*Hint*: is land supply fixed to each firm in the long run?)

Appendix: The simple algebra of present values and discounting

Suppose we lend £K today at an annual interest rate i. For example, K might be 100 and i might be 0.1, an annual interest rate 10 per cent. After one year our money has grown to £$K(1 + i)$. With $K = 100$ and $i = 0.1$, we get £110 back after a year. Suppose we re-lend the money for another year at the same interest rate. By the same principle we get back £$\{K(1 + i)\}(1 + i)$ at the end of the second year. For example, our £100 has grown to £121 after two years. If we lend this sum for yet another year we get back £$K(1 + i)^3$ at the end of the third year.

The law of compound interest makes this into a general principle. Lending an initial sum £K (the *principal*) for a period of N years at an annual interest rate of i, we get back £$K(1 + i)^N$ after N years.

Let us call £X the amount we get after N years. The law of compound interest promises us that

$$£X = £K(1 + i)^N \qquad \text{(A1)}$$

Beginning with £K we can get exactly £X after N years. Since one can be converted into the other, they are worth the same amount. If we divide through (A1) by $(1 + i)^N$ get

$$£X \left\{ \frac{1}{(1 + i)^N} \right\} = £K \qquad \text{(A2)}$$

£K is the present value of a payment £X in N years' time if the interest rate is i. We call $1/\{(1 + i)^N\}$ the discount factor. Since i is a positive number, the discount factor must be a positive fraction. For example, with $i = 1$ (an interest rate of 100 per cent per annum) and $N = 3$, the discount factor is $(\frac{1}{2})^3 = \frac{1}{8}$. It discounts or reduces the value of £X in three years' time to give a present value only one-eighth as large.

Equation (A2) is the general formula to calculate the present value of a payment received in N periods' time. The table shows the present value of £1 N years from now using this formula when the interest rate is 10 per cent per annum and $i = 0.1$.

Present value (*PV*) of £1 *N* years from now when annual interest rate is 10 per cent						
	$N = 1$	$N = 5$	$N = 10$	$N = 20$	$N = 30$	$N = 40$
PV	£0.91	£0.62	£0.39	£0.15	£0.06	£0.02

To calculate the present value of a whole stream of future payments, we simply multiply the face value of each payment by the relevant discount factor. Thus the present value of £100 after 10 years and £200 after 40 years is (£100 × 0.39 + (£200 × 0.02) = £43. Notice that payments will not be received or made for many years have a very small present value.

Finally, we can relate our general formula to the formula we gave in equation (1) of the text for the value of a perpetuity. Suppose an asset earns £K per annum for ever. Letting PV_N be the present value of £1 received after N years the present value of the constant stream £K per annum is $K(PV_0 + PV_1 + PV_2 + PV_3 + PV_4 + \ldots)$. Fortunately we do not have to add up every term in this series. The algebra of geometric series promises us that the answer to this infinite sum is given by $£K(1 + i)/i$. If each payment is made more frequently than once a year, we must use the interest rate i (expressed as a decimal) over this shorter period. Thus, the more frequent the payments, the lower the interest rate. When the money is paid almost continuously, i will be very small per period and $(1 + i)$ is very close to 1. We then obtain the formula for the present value of a perpetuity paying $£K$ per period:

$$\text{Present value of } £K \text{ per period for ever} = £K/i \qquad \text{(A3)}$$

15 Coping with risk in economic life

LEARNING OUTCOMES

When you have finished this chapter, you should be able to:

- **Distinguish risk aversion, risk neutrality, and risk loving**
- **Show why diminishing marginal utility leads to risk aversion**
- **Explain how insurance reduces risk through risk pooling, and reduces the cost of bearing risk through risk spreading**
- **Analyse how inside information about one's own opportunities or characteristics gives rise to moral hazard and adverse selection**
- **Show that the return on an asset is not just the cash flow in dividends or interest but also capital gains (losses) while the asset is held**
- **Consider how positive, zero, or negative correlation of asset returns affects the possibility of risk pooling through diversification**
- **Discuss an efficient asset market**
- **Define spot and forward markets, and explain how hedging can shift the burden of risk on to someone prepared to bear it at a smaller price**

The only certainties are death and taxes. Nevertheless, you do not know when you are going to die or the extent of the taxes you will pay. *Every* action we take today has a future outcome that is less than perfectly certain. It is risky. When we add to our bank account we do not know how much the money will buy when we want to use it because we are not certain how much the prices of goods will rise in the meantime. When we start a job we do not know how fast we will be promoted. When we start studying economics we have only a rough idea what is involved and even less idea about the purpose to which we shall put this skill once we have acquired it.

In this chapter we ask two questions: How does the presence of risk affect our actions? And how have economic institutions evolved to help us deal with the risky environment in which we are forced to live?

Although there is a degree of risk in everything we do, some activities increase the risk we face while other activities reduce it. UK citizens spend billions of pounds on insurance, which reduces the net risks they face, but they also spend billions on legal forms of betting and gambling, such as horse racing and the lottery, activities that artificially increase the risks people face. Can we deduce anything about people's general attitude to risk by examining their revealed behaviour in gambling and insurance activities?

We shall argue that people generally dislike risk and are therefore prepared to pay to have their risks reduced. We shall see that this idea allows us to explain the existence of many economic institutions that, at a price, allow those people who dislike risk most to pass on their risks to others who are more willing or more able to bear these risks. Before the end of the chapter, we will have to explain why the lottery is so popular!

15-1 Individual attitudes to risk

A risky activity has two characteristics: the likely outcome and the degree of variation in all the possible outcomes. Suppose we are offered a 50 per cent chance of making £100 and a 50 per cent chance of losing £100. On average you will make no money by taking such gambles. We call them fair gambles.

A **fair gamble** is one which on average will make exactly zero monetary profit.

In contrast, a 30 per cent chance of making £100 and a 70 per cent chance of losing £100 is an unfair gamble. On average you will lose money. With the probabilities of winning and losing reversed, the gamble would on average be profitable. The odds on this gamble are *favourable*. Now compare a gamble offering a 50 per cent chance of making or losing £100 with a gamble with the same chances of winning or losing £200. Both are fair gambles, but we say the second is *riskier*. Depending on the outcome you will either do better or do worse, but the range of possible outcomes is greater.

Having discussed the type of gambles the market may offer, we turn now to individual tastes. Economists classify individuals as risk-averse, risk-neutral, or risk-loving. The crucial question is whether or not the individual would accept a fair gamble. A *risk-neutral* person pays no attention to the degree of dispersion of possible outcomes, betting if and only if the odds on a monetary profit are favourable. Although any individual bet may turn out to be a loser, and there may even be quite a long string of unlucky losing bets.

A **risk-neutral** person is interested only in whether the odds will yield a profit *on average*. A **risk-averse** person will refuse a fair gamble.

This does not mean he or she will never bet. If the odds are sufficiently favourable the probable monetary profit will overcome the inherent dislike of risk. But the more risk-averse the individual, the more favourable must the odds be before that individual will take the bet.

A **risk-lover** will bet even when a strict mathematical calculation reveals that the odds are unfavourable.

The more risk-loving the individual, the more unfavourable must the odds be before the individual will not bet.

Some people play poker for high stakes because they know that by superior card play and psychology they can turn the odds in their favour. People with perfect memories have the odds very slightly in their favour when they play blackjack in a casino. Perhaps such gamblers are risk-lovers, or perhaps they merely reckon that the odds are sufficiently favourable to offset their relatively low degree of risk-aversion. But we all know the inveterate gambler who will bet on almost anything, even when the odds are clearly unfavourable. Such people are definitely risk-lovers.

Insurance is the opposite of gambling. Suppose you own a £50 000 house and there is a 10 per cent chance it will burn down by accident. Thus you have a 90 per cent chance of continuing to have £50 000 but a 10 per cent chance of having nothing. Our risky world is forcing you to take this bet. On average, you will end up with £45 000 which is 90 per cent of £50 000 plus 10 per cent of nothing.

An insurance company offers to insure the full value of your house for a premium of £10 000. Whether or not your house burns down, you pay the insurance company the £10 000 premium, but they pay you £50 000 if it does burn down. Whether or not your house burns down, you will end up with £40 000.

Would you insure? The insurance company is offering you unfavourable odds, which of course is how they make their money. If you do nothing the average outcome is £45 000 but the actual outcome could be £50 000 or zero. Insuring guarantees you £40 000 either way. A risk-neutral person would decline the insurance company's offer. The straight mathematical calculation in monetary terms says it is on average better to stand the risk of a fire. The risk-lover will also decline. Not only is the insurance company offering bad odds, there is also the added enjoyment of standing the risk. But a person who is sufficiently risk-averse will accept the offer, happy to give up £5000 on average to avoid the possibility of catastrophe. Table 15-1 summarizes this discussion of attitudes to risk.

Table 15-1	Behaviour towards risk	
Type of person	Betting	Insurance at unfair premium
Risk-averse	Needs favourable odds	May buy
Risk-neutral	Except at unfavourable odds	Will not buy
Risk-lover	Even if odds against	Will not buy

BOX 15-1   What a lottery

The UK's National Lottery, played twice weekly since February 1997, is based on drawing 6 balls without replacement from a stock of 49 balls. The odds on matching all 6 balls are about 1 in 14 million. In addition to the jackpot, there are also smaller consolation prizes for matching 3 or more balls. Only 45 per cent of all sales revenue is returned as prizes, much worse odds than would be received by a blind punter at a horse race. You get better odds still in a casino playing roulette: even with a 0 and a 00 on a roulette wheel with 36 other numbers, the casino only systematically makes money on 2 of the 38 possible outcomes. So why are lotteries so popular?

One possibility is that people like the idea of giving to good causes. Since a fraction of lottery profits go to charitable works, people buy lottery tickets instead of giving to OXFAM or Comic Relief. This is a testable hypothesis. And the evidence is that charities' other sources of revenue did fall when the lottery was introduced. So did the revenue of betting shops such as Ladbrokes. The thrill of the lottery draw acted as a substitute for the thrill of the 3.30 at Newmarket.

But this is not the whole story. Purchasers of lottery tickets are not a random sample of the population. They tend to be disproportionately concentrated among the poor. The poorest 20 per cent of the population account for over ⅓ of all spending on the UK National Lottery. Lotteries are an inferior good. This raises a big issue for government policy. If we really think that almost everyone has diminishing marginal utility, extensive gambling (even at fair odds) should be a bad investment for poor people as well as rich people. One concern is that those with less access to education may simply be less able to calculate the true chances of winning. Another possibility is that the poor may have less to lose: those who fall below some minimum level of income, at whatever level society decides to draw the line, may then be entitled to welfare support from the state. For people just above the welfare minimum, the state is then effectively insuring their losses from gambling. But those *already* receiving welfare support get no additional payments from the state if their gambles do not succeed. Their behaviour can be reconciled with diminishing marginal utility only if we regard them as 'paying' for leisure thrills..

Risk aversion and diminishing marginal utility

Decisions about gambling or insurance depend on two distinct considerations. First, there is the pleasure or pain from the risk itself. The thrill of the occasional flutter on the Grand National resembles the pleasure of seeing a good film. Having a lottery ticket increases the fun of watching the draw of the winning numbers. It has a component of pure entertainment. For other people the stress in not knowing the outcome is painful. Occasional gambling for the sheer fun of it is a legitimate form of consumption for people who enjoy it, and the standard model of consumer choice suggests that people will be prepared to pay for this modest form of entertainment. A roulette wheel does not quite offer fair odds. Yet many of us would play roulette on our birthday and regard the slightly unfavourable odds as the implicit price of our fun.

Such leisure activities form only a trivial part of the risk that we face in our everyday lives. This approach is not helpful in thinking about the risk of our house burning down or the risk a firm takes in deciding whether or not to build a new factory. It is not the spectacle that counts but the fact that different outcomes will have different implications for the financial well-being of the household or the firm.

At given prices, you calculate how much utility or happiness £1000 would yield through the goods it would let you buy. Now calculate your utility if you had £2000 to spend. Since you have more goods, we can assume your utility has gone up. How much it goes up is the marginal utility of the extra £1000 which increased your wealth from £1000 to £2000.

Now you get another £1000. You have more goods and your utility rises still further. What about the marginal utility of this extra £1000? When you had only £1000 you could only just afford the essential of life. Another £1000 allowed you to buy some things you really needed but could not previously afford. Yet another £1000 allows you to buy some nice things, but they are really luxuries that you could have done without. As we gave you more and more money in blocks of £1000 a time, you find fewer and fewer things to spend it on.

Thus the marginal utility of the first £1000 is very high. You really needed it. The marginal utility of the next £1000 is not quite so high. As you get more, the marginal utility of the extra money tends to diminish.

Economists assume that individual tastes satisfy the principle of **diminishing marginal utility of wealth**. Successive increases of equal monetary value add less and less to total utility.

Of course, we can all think of exceptions to this general rule. Some people *really* want a yacht, and their utility takes a huge jump when they are finally rich enough to afford one. But most of us first spend our money on the things we most need and get less and less extra satisfaction out of successive equal increases in our spending power.

Suppose you own £15 000 and you are then offered an equal chance of winning or losing £10 000. This is a fair bet in money terms since the average profit is £0. But it is not a fair bet in utility terms. Diminishing marginal utility implies that the extra utility you enjoy if the bet wins, taking your total wealth from £15 000 to £25 000, is much smaller than the utility you sacrifice if the bet loses, taking your wealth from £15 000 to £5000. You get a few extra luxuries with the £10 000 you might win, but you have to give up a lot of essential goods if you lose and have to cut back to only £5000.

We said a person is risk-averse if he or she declines a fair bet in money terms. We can now see that the hypothesis of diminishing marginal utility implies that, except for the occasional small gamble for pure entertainment, people should generally be risk-averse. They should refuse fair money gambles because they are not fair utility gambles. As we shall see, this story seems to fit many of the facts.

Two implications of this analysis recur throughout the chapter. First, *risk-averse individuals will devote resources to finding ways to reduce risk*. As the booming insurance industry confirms, people will be prepared to pay to get out of some of the risks that our environment would otherwise force them to bear. Second, *individuals who take over or bear the risk will have to be rewarded for doing so*. Many economic activities consist of the more risk-averse bribing the less risk-averse to take over the risk.

15-2 Insurance and risk

We begin with a simple example of home-made insurance. A farmer and an actress have risky incomes which fluctuate from month to month. But these risks are *independent*. Whether or not the farmer has a good month is completely

Table 15-2   Risk-pooling

	Farmer	
	Good month	Bad month
Actress		
good month	I	II
bad month	III	IV

unconnected with whether or not the actress has a good month. Table 15-2 shows what happens if the two get together to *pool* their incomes and their risks. Suppose they share out their total incomes in proportion to their average earnings over the past few years. If they have a good month (case I) or both have a bad month (case IV), the pooling arrangement makes no difference. They each get what they would have got on their own. But in cases II and III the success of one partner offsets the failure of the other. Together they have a more *stable* income than they would have as individuals. If the farmer and the actress are risk-averse, they can gain by pooling their risky incomes. If it were not so hard to set up such deals (lawyers' fees, the problem of cheating, tax problems) we would see a lot more of them.

Pooling of independent risks is the key to the insurance business. Suppose we look up the mortality tables and see that on average 1 per cent of people aged 55 will die during the next year. Deaths result from heart disease, cancer, road accidents, and other causes but in fairly predictable proportions.

Now let us randomly choose any 100 people aged 55 knowing nothing about their health. Throughout the nation 1 per cent of such people will die in the next year. But in our sample of 100 people it could be 0, 1, 2, or even more. The larger we make our sample of 55-year-olds, the more likely it is that around 1 per cent will die in the next year. With 1 million 55-year-olds we could be pretty confident that around 10 000 would die, though we could not of course say which ones. By putting together more and more people we reduce the risk or dispersion of the aggregate outcome.[1]

Suppose these 100 people would like to leave their family some money in the event that they die in the next year. Each person puts up £100 to give a total of £10 000 to be shared out among the families of those who die in the next year. If this small sample of 100 55-year-olds behaves like the

---

[1] This proposition is called the 'Law of Large Numbers'. A proof can be found in most statistics textbooks.

national average, one person will die and that family will get £10 000. But four people might die and their families would get only £2500 each. The payment to the family of someone dying in the next year is risky. It cannot be forecast for sure. But if 1 million people enter the scheme, almost exactly 10 000 will die and their families will get almost exactly £10 000 each. The risk has been slashed.

Life assurance companies take in premium payments in exchange for a promise to pay a much larger amount to the family if the insured person dies. The company can make this promise with a high degree of certainty because it pools its risks over a huge number of clients. Since the company cannot guarantee that precisely 1 per cent of its large number of 55-year-olds will die in any one year, there is a small element of residual risk for the company to bear and it will make a small charge for this in calculating its premiums. However, the company's ability to pool the risk means that it will make only a *small* charge. If life assurance companies try to charge more, new entrants will join the industry knowing that the profits more than compensate for the small residual risk to be borne.

Risk-pooling works only when the risk can be spread over a large number of individuals, each of whose risks are essentially independent of the risks faced by all other individuals. It works in our example because the risk that one person is run over by a bus makes no difference to another person's risk of getting cancer or being run over by a bus. Risk-pooling will not work when all individuals face the *same* risk.

Suppose there is a 10 per cent risk of a nuclear war in Europe alone during the next 10 years. If it happens everyone in Europe will die. In that event they would like to leave some money to their nearest surviving relative in the rest of the world. Ten million people in Western Europe offer to pay £100 each to an American insurance company. Since 10 million is a large number, they expect the insurance premium to be small. Surely the residual risk for the insurance company is very small if it can spread the risk over this many people?

Not so. Since *everybody* in Europe dies if *anybody* dies, the insurance company either pays out to everybody's relatives or it pays nothing. In the aggregate there is exactly a 10 per cent chance of having to pay out, just as the individual faced a 10 per cent chance of disaster. When the same thing happens to everybody if it happens at all, the aggregate behaves like the individual. There is no risk reduction from pooling.

This explains why many insurance companies will not provide insurance against what they call 'acts of god' –

floods, earthquakes, epidemics. Such disasters are no more natural or unnatural than a heart attack. But they affect large numbers of the insurance company's clients if they happen at all. Their risk cannot be reduced by pooling. Companies cannot quote the low premium rates that apply for heart attacks, where one person's outcome has no implication for the outcome of others and the aggregate outcome is relatively certain.

Risk-pooling works by aggregating independent risks to make the aggregate more certain.

But there is another way to reduce the cost of risk-bearing. This is known as *risk-sharing*, and the most famous example is the Lloyd's (www.lloyds.com) insurance market in London. Risk-sharing is necessary when it has proved impossible to reduce the risk by pooling. Lloyd's offer insurance on earthquakes in California, and one-off deals such as insurance of a film star's legs.

To understand risk-sharing we must return to diminishing marginal utility. We argued that the utility from an extra £10 000 was less than the utility sacrificed when £10 000 must be given up. However, this difference in marginal utility for equivalent financial gains and losses is smaller, the smaller the gain and loss. The marginal utility from an extra £1 is only fractionally less than the utility lost by sacrificing £1. When the stakes are very small people are close to being risk-neutral. You would probably toss a coin with us to win or lose £0.10, but not to win or lose £10 000. The larger the stake, the more diminishing marginal utility bites.

Risk-sharing works by reducing the stake.

You go to Lloyd's to insure the US space shuttle launch for £20 billion. That is a big risk. Only part of this risk can be pooled as part of a larger portfolio of risks. It is too big for anyone to take on at a reasonable premium.

The Lloyd's market in London is a big room with hundreds of 'syndicates', each a group of 20 or so individuals who have each put up £100 000. Each syndicate will take perhaps 1 per cent of the £20 billion deal and then resell some of the risk to yet other people in the insurance industry. By the time the deal has been subdivided and subdivided again, each syndicate or insurance company is holding only a tiny share of the total. And each syndicate risk is further subdivided among its 20 members. The risk has been shared out until each individual's stake has been so reduced that there is only a small difference between the marginal utility in the event of a gain and the marginal loss of utility in the event of a disaster. It now requires only a small premium to cover this risk, and the whole package can be sold to the client at a premium that is low enough to attract the business.

By pooling and sharing risks, insurance allows individuals to deal with many risks at affordable premiums. But there are two interesting and complicating factors which further inhibit the operation of insurance markets, tending to reduce the extent to which individuals can use insurance to buy their way out of risky situations.

Moral hazard

Insurance companies employ actuaries to calculate the average or statistical chances for aggregate behaviour. They work out how many houses per million will have a fire next year. Since fires in different houses are independent risks, we expect insurance firms to be able to pool the risk over a large number of clients and charge low premiums for fire insurance.

You are sitting in a restaurant and remember you left your car unlocked. Do you abandon your nice meal and rush outside to lock it? You are less likely to if you know the car is fully insured against theft. With full health insurance you are less likely to bother about precautionary check-ups. If the act of insuring increases the likelihood of the occurrence of the thing you wish to insure against, we call this the problem of *moral hazard*.[2]

Moral hazard is the exploiting of inside information to take advantage of the other party to the contract.

Actuarial calculations for the whole population, many of whom are uninsured and will take greater care, are no longer a reliable guide to the risks the insurance company faces and the premiums it should charge. Moral hazard makes it harder to get insurance and more expensive when you do get it.

Frequently insurance companies will insure your property only up to a certain percentage of its replacement cost. They will take a large part of the risk, but you will still be worse off if the nasty thing happens. The company is providing you with an incentive to take care and hold down the chances of the nasty thing happening. On average, they pay out less frequently and can charge you lower premia.

Adverse selection

Suppose some people smoke cigarettes but others do not. People who smoke are more likely to die young. Individuals know whether they themselves smoke, but suppose the insurance company cannot tell the difference and must charge all clients the same premium rate for life assurance.

Suppose the premium is based on mortality rates for the nation as a whole. People who do not smoke know they have an above-average life expectancy and will find the premium too expensive. Smokers know their life expectancy is lower than the national average and realize that the premium is a bargain. Even though the insurance company cannot tell the difference between the two groups, it can work out that if it charges the premium based on the national average it will attract only smokers and will pay out more than it expected.

Adverse selection occurs when individuals use their inside information to accept or reject a contract, so that those who accept are not an average sample of the population.

One solution is to assume that all clients are smokers and charge the correspondingly high premium to all clients. Non-smokers find it impossible to get insurance at what they believe is a reasonable price. They might be able to volunteer a medical examination in an attempt to prove they are low-risk clients who should be charged a lower price. Medical examinations are in fact compulsory for many insurance contracts now.

To check that you understand the difference between moral hazard and adverse selection, say which is which in the following examples. (1) A person with a fatal disease signs up for life insurance. (2) Reassured by the fact that he took out life assurance to protect his dependants, a person who has unexpectedly become depressed decides to commit suicide. (The first was adverse selection, the second moral hazard.)

Discrimination or sound insurance?

Risk-pooling and risk-sharing allow companies to offer cheap insurance against some important risks. But when all clients must be charged the same premium rate for apparently similar risks, moral hazard and adverse selection make things much harder for the insurance companies. They may refuse to insure at all, or may charge such high premiums that even risk-averse clients find there is little gain in taking out an insurance policy.

In the previous section we argued that the solution might lie in *price discrimination*. If insurance companies can distinguish between low-risk non-smokers and high-risk

---

[2] Similarly for safety regulations. It has been argued by Professor Sam Peltzman that the introduction of safety belts resulted in more accidents since drivers thought they could safely go faster. See 'The Effects of Automobile Safety Regulations', *Journal of Political Economy*, 1975.

smokers they can quote them different premium rates. High-risk clients will pay a higher premium which properly reflects their greater risk. But price discrimination raises issues of fairness.

Women live longer than men. In 1999 the life expectancy at birth was about 70 years for a male child in many Western countries including the UK, but the life expectancy of a female child was six or seven years longer. Since insurance companies can easily tell the difference between men and women, life insurance premiums should be lower for women than for men. Nor does this seem particularly unfair.

But now consider retirement pensions, typically paid for as long as the person lives after retiring from a job. Suppose a man and a woman have been earning the same amount each year in a job and have paid the same amount towards a pension. If they retire at the same age, on average the woman will live longer. If they receive the same annual pension, on average the woman will receive more pension income over the rest of her life than the man although they made the same contributions to the pension plan while in employment. Is that fair? There is no easy answer.

This example reminds us that pricing policies are not always exclusively determined by the market forces of supply and demand. Social considerations such as fairness sometimes have to be taken into account. This forms an important theme in welfare economics, which we begin to study in the next chapter.

15-3 Uncertainty and asset returns

There are many ways of carrying wealth from the present to the future. People can hold money, government bills or bonds, company shares, housing, gold, and so on. We now compare the rates of return on shares and Treasury bills, two particular ways in which wealth might be held. In the next section we discuss the general problem faced by a wealth-holder trying to decide how to choose the composition of that wealth portfolio.

Treasury bills are issued by the government usually for a period of three months. The government sells a bill for say £97 and simultaneously promises to buy back the bill for £100 in three months' time. People who buy the bill and sell it back to the government earn just over 3 per cent on their money in three months. By re-investing the proceeds to buy three more bills in the course of the year, they will earn something over 12 per cent during the year. Each time an individual buys a bill, the implicit nominal interest rate over the three-month period is known for certain since the

government has guaranteed the price at which the bill will be re-purchased.

The real return on Treasury bills is a little less certain. The *real return* is the nominal return minus the inflation rate over the period the bill is held. People do not know what the inflation rate will be over each three-month period during which the bill is held. On the other hand, they have a pretty good idea about what inflation is *likely* to do over the next three months. Hence even the real return on Treasury bills is not very risky.

Company shares pay out a return in two different ways. First, shareholders are entitled to dividend payments. *Dividends* are the regular payments that the firm makes out of profits after deciding how much to keep back to finance future spending on plant and machinery. Second, shareholders may make *capital gains* or suffer *capital losses*.

The **capital gain** is the increase in the share price during the period in which the share is held.

If a share can be bought at a low price and subsequently sold at a higher price, this contributes to the return earned while holding the share.

We express the rate of return as a percentage of the money initially laid out. Again we are interested in the real wage of return after allowing for inflation. Thus the general formula for the real rate of return during a given period is

$$\frac{\text{Real rate}}{\text{of return}} = \frac{\text{nominal rate}}{\text{of return}} - \frac{\text{inflation rate}}{\text{over period}}$$

$$= \frac{\text{dividend} + \text{capital gain}}{\text{purchase price}} - \frac{\text{inflation}}{\text{rate}} \quad (1)$$

Figure 15-1 shows the annual real rate of return on Treasury bills and on company shares in the UK during 1960–98. There are two important points to note about the figure. First, the rate of return on company shares has been enormously more variable than that on Treasury bills. In fact, as we argued in the previous chapter, the real rate of return on Treasury bills is relatively constant over time. The real rate of return on shares was as high as 130 per cent during 1975 and as low as −70 per cent in 1974. Even excluding these two years, there are several years when the real return on shares exceeded 20 per cent and some years in which it was worse than −10 per cent. Shares are much riskier than Treasury bills.[3]

---

[3] There are strong grounds for believing the large positive or negative returns on shares were unanticipated by the market. Why? Because if the market had foreseen a return to say 30 per cent in real terms it would surely have seen people trying to buy these

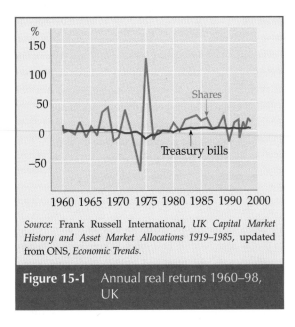

Source: Frank Russell International, *UK Capital Market History and Asset Market Allocations 1919–1985*, updated from ONS, *Economic Trends*.

Figure 15-1   Annual real returns 1960–98, UK

The second thing to note about Figure 15-1 is the average real rate of return on the two assets over the whole period. The real rate of return on Treasury bills is very close to zero on average. In contrast, shares on average yield around 10 per cent per annum in real terms. Why such a discrepancy?

Figure 15-1 shows that shares were very much riskier than Treasury bills. The person who buys shares has to take a much bigger risk but is compensated *on average* by a higher return. Since the risk is quite a big one – many people lost huge sums of money in 1974 – it requires the carrot of a large real return on average to induce people to take this risk.

Shares are riskier for two reasons. First, nobody is quite sure what dividend the firm will announce during the year. It all depends how much profit it makes and how confident it is about the future. The more they anticipate bad times in the future, the more inclined firms may be to pay a low dividend in order to keep a contingency reserve within the firm.

Second, views about the likely capital gains may change quite radically. If people thought firms were doing well they will have anticipated rising share prices. They expect to make capital gains. Equation (1) shows that these add to the return people expect to make in shares. If the shares are offering a higher expected return, people will want to buy

them and the current share prices will be bid up. Thus one reason why share prices may be high is because people have bought the shares in anticipation of capital gains.

If it suddenly becomes apparent that the company's prospects are less good, the happy scenario of steadily rising share prices can quickly vanish. Share prices may collapse. We discuss this phenomenon in more detail in Section 15-5 under the heading of 'speculative bubbles'. For the moment we merely note that current share prices and current returns are crucially dependent on current expectations of future share prices and hence capital gains. In speculative markets there can be little certainty that current views about future share prices will persist without revision. It is revisions in beliefs about likely capital gains which lead to volatile share prices and share returns.

15-4 Portfolio selection

The *portfolio* of a financial investor is the collection of financial and real assets – bank deposits, Treasury bills, government bonds, ordinary shares of industrial companies, gold, works of art – in which the financial investor's wealth is held. How does a risk-averse investor select her portfolio or wealth composition?

In Chapter 6 we set out the basic model of consumer choice among goods. The budget line summarized the market opportunities, the goods that a given income would buy. Indifference curves represented individual tastes, and the consumer chose the bundle that was on the highest possible indifference curve given the budget constraint describing which bundles were affordable. We use the same basic approach to the choice of a portfolio.

Instead of the choice between two different goods, we now focus on the choice between the average or expected return on the portfolio and risk that the portfolio embodies.

The risk–return choice

Tastes The risk-averse consumer (or financial investor) prefers a higher average return on the portfolio but dislikes higher risk. To take more risk he needs to think they will receive a higher average return. By 'risk' we mean the variability of returns on the whole portfolio. From the previous section, we know that a portfolio composed exclusively of industrial shares would be much riskier than a portfolio composed exclusively of Treasury bills.

Opportunities To highlight the problem of portfolio selection we assume there are only two possible assets in which to invest. Bank deposits are a relatively safe asset. The

bargain stocks. Their prices would have been bid up, and equation (1) tells us that this increase in the purchase price would have reduced the real return to a more typical level. Similarly, if large capital losses have been foreseen, share prices would already have been lower, and the return higher, as people tried to dump these shares.

investor has a relatively good idea of the rate of return on bank deposits. The other asset is company shares, which are much riskier since their return is more variable.

The investor has a given wealth to invest. If all wealth is put into bank deposits the whole portfolio will earn the return on bank deposit and this will be relatively riskless. The higher the fraction of the portfolio held in industrial shares, the more closely the return on the whole portfolio resembles the return on shares and the riskier it becomes.

Portfolio choice   Suppose the average return on the risky asset (shares) is lower than the average return on the safe asset (bank deposits). Putting more of the portfolio into bank deposits both increases the portfolio return *and* reduces the risk of variability of the return on the whole portfolio. The risk-averse investor will put the whole portfolio into the safe asset.

To consider buying the risky asset, the investor must believe the average return on the risky asset exceeds the average return on the safe asset. Suppose this is the case. How much of the portfolio will be put into the risky asset? It all depends how risky the risky asset is and how big the differential is between the average return on the two assets. Generally, however, the fraction of the portfolio held in the risky asset will be higher (1) the higher the average return on the risky asset compared with the safe asset, (2) the less risky is the risky asset, and (3) the less risk-averse is the investor.

Diversification

When there are several risky assets the investor may be able to reduce the risk on the whole portfolio *without* having to accept a lower average return on the portfolio. We illustrate this possibility using Table 15-3 whose structure resembles the problem of the actress and the farmer we studied in Table 15-2. There are two risky assets, say, oil shares and banking shares. Each has two possible returns: £4 if things go well and £2 if things go badly. Each industry has a 50 per cent chance of good times and a 50 per cent chance of bad times. Finally, we assume that the returns in the two

industries are independent. Good times in the oil industry tell us nothing about whether the banking industry is having good or bad times.

You have £2 to invest, and oil and bank shares each cost £1. Which portfolio gives the best risk–return combination? First note that both shares have the same payoff characteristics – the same returns and the same chances. You should be indifferent between buying only oil shares and only bank shares. But a superior strategy is to buy one of each and *diversify* the portfolio.

Diversification is the strategy of reducing risk by risk-pooling across several assets whose individual returns behave differently from one another.

Diversification means not putting all your eggs into one basket. Suppose you buy only one kind of share. Buying two shares for your £2, you have a 50 per cent chance of earning £8 and a 50 per cent chance of earning £4. It all depends whether the industry in which you invest has good or bad times. The average return is £6, but the actual return will either be £4 or £8.

Table 15-3 shows the payoffs from the diversified portfolio with one of each share. If both industries do well you will make £8, but this is only a 25 per cent chance. There is a 50 per cent chance of oil doing well but, since returns in the two industries are independent, on only half of those occasions will banking also be having good times. Similarly, there is a 25 per cent chance of both industries doing badly at the same time. There is also a 25 per cent chance that one industry does well while the other one does badly. Each of the four portfolio returns shown in Table 15-3 is a 25 per cent chance.

The average return on the portfolio is still £6, just as when you put all your £2 into one kind of share, but the variability of portfolio returns has been reduced. Instead of a 50/50 chance of £4 or £8, you now have only a 25 per cent chance of each of the extreme outcomes and a 50 per cent chance of earning the average return of £6.

Diversification reduces the risk by pooling it without altering the average rate of return. It offers you a better deal. As in our earlier discussion of risk-pooling by insurance companies, the greater the number of risky assets with independent returns across which the portfolio pools the risk, the lower will be the total risk of the portfolio.

Figure 15-2 shows the typical relationship between the total portfolio risk and the number of independent assets in the portfolio. The figure not only shows that portfolio risk declines as the number of independent risky assets is increased; it also shows that most of the gains of risk

Table 15-3	A diversified portfolio		
		Banking	
		Good	Bad
Oil	good	£8	£6
	bad	£6	£4

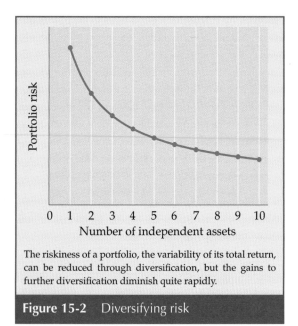

The riskiness of a portfolio, the variability of its total return, can be reduced through diversification, but the gains to further diversification diminish quite rapidly.

Figure 15-2   Diversifying risk

Table 15-4	Share returns and beta		
	Returns (%)		
Asset	Boom	Normal	Slump
Stock market	14	6	−2
High beta	20	10	−8
Beta = 1	14	6	−2
Low beta	5	4	3
Negative beta	2	3	5

reduction through diversification come very quickly. Even a few assets cut the total risk a lot. (This explains why people carry one spare tyre in their cars rather than five.)

Because it is more expensive to buy in quantities of under 100 shares, small investors typically hold a dozen different shares rather than a hundred. They get many of the benefits of diversifying without having to buy too few shares at a time. People who are even more risk-averse and really want to hold a large number of shares are better advised to buy shares in a mutual fund or unit trust, a professionally run fund that buys large quantities of many different shares and then retails small shares in the total fund to small investors.

Diversification when asset returns are correlated

Risk-pooling works because asset returns are independent of each other. When asset returns move together, we say that they are *correlated*. When returns on two assets tend to move in the same direction we say they are *positively correlated*. For example, a general expansion of the whole economy will tend to be good for bank shares and shares of motor car manufacturers. If returns tend to move in opposite directions, we say they are *negatively correlated*. For example, if people buy gold shares during financial crises, gold shares will tend to rise when other shares are falling and vice versa.

Positive and negative correlations have different implications for the effect of diversification in reducing risk. Suppose bank shares have good times only when oil shares have good times and vice versa. Buying one of each is

just like putting all your money in one kind of share. Diversification achieves nothing. When returns are perfectly positively correlated risk-pooling does not work, just as it did not work in the 'acts of God' example we discussed for the insurance industry.

Conversely, diversification is a spectacular success when returns are negatively correlated. Suppose bank shares do well only when oil shares are doing badly and vice versa. Buying one of each, you earn either £4 from oil and £2 from banking or £2 from oil and £4 from banking. On the diversified portfolio you earn £6 for certain. You have diversified away all the risk, even though each of the individual shares is quite risky.

In practice, returns on different shares are never perfectly correlated. Some *tend* to vary together and some *tend* to vary in opposite directions, but over any particular period actual returns on two shares may not exhibit their usual correlation. Thus it is impossible to completely diversify away all portfolio risk. But smart fund managers are always on the lookout for an asset that tends to have a negative correlation with the assets in the existing portfolio. On average, extending the portfolio to include this asset will improve the risk–return characteristics of the portfolio.

Beta

Beta is a measurement of the extent to which a particular share's return moves with the return on the whole stock market.

Table 15-4 gives some examples. The first row shows returns on the market as a whole in booms, normal times, and slumps. A share with beta = 1 moves exactly the same way as the whole market. A high beta share does even better when the market is up but even worse when the market is down. A low beta share moves in the same general direction as the market but more sluggishly than the market. Negative beta shares move against the market.

Most shares move pretty much with the market and have a beta close to one. There are not too many negative beta

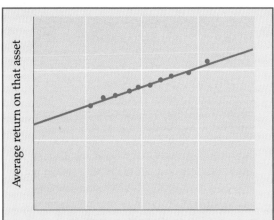

Riskiness of each asset (beta)

Each share's risk is measured by its beta, which shows how that share's returns move with returns in the market as a whole. The higher the beta, the more the inclusion of the share in a portfolio will increase the total portfolio risk. The data show that riskier shares with higher betas must offer a higher return on average to compensate for this disadvantage.

Figure 15-3   Risk–return relationship for company shares

shares, but some gold shares have betas that are close to zero. This suggests that most people should have some gold shares in their portfolios.

Bankers and stockbrokers calculate betas from the past behaviour of individual shares and the whole stock market. Ideally, they are looking for negative beta shares which will greatly reduce the risk of a portfolio whose other components vary with the market as a whole. Even low beta shares are partly independent of the rest of the market and allow some risk to be pooled. High beta shares are doubly undesirable. Not only are their own returns highly variable but, because they vary in the same direction as the whole market, they cannot be used to pool risk.

A share with a low (or even negative) beta will be in high demand. Risk-averse purchasers are anxious to buy low beta shares whose inclusion in their portfolios will reduce the total portfolio risk. High demand will bid up the share price and reduce the average return, but investors are happy to trade off a lower return for the success of low beta shares in reducing the total risk of their portfolios.

Hence in stock market equilibrium low beta shares should have high prices and low rates of return on average. High beta shares add to investors' portfolio risk and will be purchased only because they have low prices and high rates of return on average which compensate for their

undesirable risk characteristics. Figure 15-3 shows the results of a pioneering study by Professors Black, Jensen, and Scholes using stock market data from 1931 to 1965. Average returns on individual shares rise steadily with the shares' beta as the theory predicts.

To sum up, in stock market equilibrium individual share prices depend both on expected or average returns and on risk characteristics. The risk characteristics of the firm's shares determine the expected return the share must offer if it is to compete with other shares. For a given required return, equation (1) implies that higher anticipated dividends or capital gains will mean a higher current share price. Unless shares with anticipated high dividends or capital gains have high share prices, they will have above-average expected rates of return for their risk characteristics. They will be a bargain and people will buy them, bidding up the share price until it reaches its equilibrium level.

In considering the risk characteristics of the firm's shares the crucial point is that we are not concerned with the variability of the share's return in isolation from the rest of the market. This is why beta matters. Adding a risky asset to the portfolio will reduce the risk of the portfolio provided the share's beta is less than 1. Low beta shares can be individually risky; nevertheless, taken with other shares they reduce portfolio risk and are therefore desirable since people are risk-averse. In equilibrium, low beta shares will have an above-average price and a below-average rate of return to offset this advantage.

Diversification in other situations

Diversification is an important facet of behaviour by risk-averse people in many other situations. Countries diversify their sources of supply of raw materials. No country likes buying all its oil, copper, or titanium from a single producer. If anything disrupts that producer's ability or willingness to sell, the country may face a disaster. Similarly, an individual farmer will be reluctant to rely on a single crop.

It may be much better for a navy to have two small aircraft carriers than one large one. If the only aircraft carrier is sunk the navy will be completely without air cover.

15-5 Efficient asset markets

There are two basic images of the stock market. One is that of a casino, where there is no rational basis for speculation; it is all a matter of luck. The other view – the theory of *efficient markets* – is that the stock market is a sensitive processor of information, quickly responding to new information to adjust share prices correctly.

BOX 15-2

The crash of '98

A financial asset is actually a bundle of different characteristics, which people gradually realized they could unbundle and trade separately. Derivative markets boomed for financial products such as options (the right to buy or sell in the future at a particular price) and swaps (decoupling ownership of an asset from ownership of the income stream it generates). Like a giant game of fantasy football, participants bought and sold hypothetical teams of players and made side bets whose outcome depended on what happened in the real match.

When the price of the same characteristic differed in different markets, you could arbitrage, buying in one market and selling in others to make sure profits. These trades exploited market inefficiencies. Traders boasted that, in making fortunes, they helped make financial markets more efficient.

Long-Term Capital Management (LTCM) was a dream team of Wall Street bond dealers and hot-shot academics (in 1997 Bob Merton and Myron Scholes won the Nobel Prize in economics). Using fancy mathematics and huge computers, they exploited small arbitrage opportunities other people missed. Betting billions at a time, they turned small profit margins into

huge earnings. Between February 1994 and April 1998, LTCM made a profit of $95 million a *month*!

In August 1998 LTCM had huge quantities of Russian bonds and complicated offsetting contracts to insure against changes in the rouble exchange rate and other risks. It looked safe to LTCM. They had not reckoned on a Russian default. LTCM lost $1.8 billion in August 1998.

Markets began to panic. Who had lent to LTCM? Who else had lost money in Russia? Asset prices collapsed and people became reluctant to trade. LTCM was unable to trade in sufficient volume to insure some of its other supposedly riskless bets. By late September LTCM had lost $4.6 billion and was out of business.

How was confidence restored? The Fed (the US equivalent of the Bank of England) 'persuaded' leading private banks to stump up for LTCM losses, and Fed Chairman Alan Greenspan said he would cut interest rates as much as needed to restore market confidence. The Fed cut interest rates by 0.25 per cent on 29 September, 14 October, and 17 November. Markets got the message and the general crisis subsided.

An **efficient asset market** already incorporates existing information properly in asset prices.

The second view recognizes that share prices fluctuate a lot but argues that these fluctuations are the appropriate response to new information as it becomes available.

Shares are claims on future dividends of companies. Individuals, and society, should value a company more highly (1) the higher the profits the company earns and hence the dividends it can pay its shareholders, and (2) the lower its beta. Companies that do well when everyone else is in a slump not merely reduce the risk of portfolios that include their shares; they also help to stabilize the economy. They are providing high output, employment, and profits when other firms are doing badly.

If companies with high average returns and low betas have high share prices, it is easier for these companies to

expand by issuing new shares. The higher the share price, the more money the company will raise by floating a new share issue and the more likely the company is to invest in plant and machinery financed by a new share issue. Share prices are guiding the right firms to invest. Companies with low average returns and high betas are valued neither by financial investors nor by society at large. Low share prices make it hard for them to raise money to finance new plant and equipment, and they will tend to contract.

Hence it matters which of the two views of the stock market is correct. If share prices correctly reflect prospective dividends and risk characteristics – the efficient market view – a free market in industrial shares is essentially guiding society's scarce resources towards the right firms. But if share prices are purely pot luck, as in a casino, the wrong firms may expand just because their share prices are high.

Testing for efficiency

Suppose everybody has all the information available today about the likely risks and returns on different shares. Equilibrium share prices should equate the likely return on all shares with the same risk characteristics. Otherwise there would be an obvious opportunity to switch from the low return shares to higher return shares with equivalent risk characteristics. If the market has got it right, it does not matter which share you buy in any risk class. They are all expected to yield the same return. The efficient market view says there is no way of beating the market to earn an above-average return on a share of a given risk class.

If the market neglects some available information you could use this information to beat the market. For example, if the market failed to spot that hot weather increases ice cream sales it would never mark up share prices in ice cream companies when good weather occurred. By buying ice cream shares when the sun shone you would make money and beat the market. The market would be surprised by high dividends from ice cream companies and realize too late that it would have been a bargain to have bought ice cream shares for the price being quoted. But you bought them, having figured all this out by using extra information. You knew ice cream shares would pay a higher rate of return than the market thought. You spotted an inefficiency in the market.

In contrast, the efficient market view says that all the relevant available information is immediately incorporated in the share price. Given the long-range weather forecast, the market makes the best guess about profits and dividends in the ice cream industry and sets the current price to give the required rate of return for shares with the same risk characteristics as ice cream shares. If the weather forecast is correct, the return will be as predicted. If unexpectedly there is a hot spell, the market will immediately mark up ice cream shares to reflect the new information that ice cream profits will be higher than previously expected. How high are ice cream shares marked up? To the price that reduces the expected rate of return back to the average for that risk class.

Thus the crucial implication of the efficient market theory is that asset prices correctly reflect all existing information. It is unforeseen new information that changes share prices as the market quickly incorporates this unanticipated development to restore expected returns to the required level. Existing information cannot systematically be used to get above-average returns for that risk class of asset.

The theory of efficient markets has been tested extensively to see whether there is any *currently available* information

that would allow an investor systematically to earn an above-average return for that risk class. The vast majority of all empirical studies conclude that there is no readily available information that the market neglects. In particular, rules of the form 'buy shares when the price has risen two days in a row' do not work. Nor do rules that use existing information about how the economy or the industry is doing. Smart investors have taken this information on board as it became available. It is already in the price.

The empirical literature usually concludes you may as well stick a pin in the financial pages of a newspaper as employ an expensive financial adviser. Paradoxically, it is because the market has *already* used all the relevant economic information correctly that there are no bargains around. The theory of efficient markets does not say share prices and returns are unaffected by economics; it says that, because the economics has been correctly used to set the price, there are no easy pickings.

Financial newspapers and stock market institutions run competitions for the investor of the year. If the theory of efficient markets is right, why do some portfolios do better than others? Why, indeed, are financial portfolio advisers in business at all? The world is uncertain, and there will always be new surprises that could not have been previously forecast. As this new information is incorporated in share prices some lucky investors will find they happen to have already invested in shares whose price has unexpectedly risen. Others are unlucky, holding shares whose price unexpectedly falls.

Thus one interpretation of why some investors do better than others is pure chance. This story could even explain why some investors have above-average returns for several years in a row. Even with a fair coin there is roughly one chance in a thousand of tossing ten consecutive heads. Even if there is no systematic way to beat the market, there are thousands of investors, and someone is going to have a lucky streak for ten years.

But there is also a more subtle interpretation. When a piece of new information first becomes available someone has to decide *how* share prices should be adjusted. The price does not change by magic. And there is an incentive to be quick off the mark. The first person to get the information, or correctly to calculate where the market will soon be setting the price, may be able to buy a share just before everyone else catches on and the share's price rises. The empirical evidence is compatible with the view that the non-specialist investor cannot use *past* information to make above-average profits. But it is also compatible with the view that the specialist investors, by reacting very quickly, can make capital gains or avoid capital losses within the first few hours of new information becoming available. It is their actions that help to change the price, and the small profits that they make from fast dealing are what pay the portfolio industry's salaries. It is the economic return to their time and effort in gathering and processing information.

Speculative bubbles

Consider the market for gold. Unlike shares or bonds, gold pays no dividend or interest payment. Its return accrues entirely through the capital gain element in equation (1). Today's prices depend on the anticipated capital gain, which in turn depends on expectations of tomorrow's price. But tomorrow's price will depend on the capital gain then expected, which will depend on expectations of the price the day after; and so on.

In such markets there is no way for the *fundamentals*, the economic calculations about future dividends or interest payments, to influence the price. It all depends on what people today think people tomorrow will expect people the next day to expect. Such a market is vulnerable to *speculative bubbles*. If everyone believes the price will rise tomorrow, it makes sense to purchase the asset today. So long as people expect the price to keep rising, it makes sense to keep buying even though the price may already have risen a lot.

A famous example of a speculative bubble is the South Sea Bubble of 1720. A company was set up to sell British goods to people in the South Seas and to bring home the wonderful and exotic goods produced there. The shares were issued long before any attempt was made actually to trade these goods. It sounded a great idea and people bought the shares. The price rose quickly, and soon people were buying not in anticipation of eventual dividends but purely to resell the shares at a profit once the price had gone even higher. The price rose even faster, till one day it became apparent that the company's proposal was a fiasco with no chance of success and the bubble burst. Sir Isaac Newton lost £2000 (over half a million pounds at today's prices).

More recently the great English economist John Maynard Keynes has argued that the stock market is like a casino because it is dominated by short-term speculators who buy not in anticipation of future dividends but purely to resell at a quick profit. In terms of equation (1) again, it is capital gains not dividends that matter. Since next period's share price depends on what people then think the following period's share price will be, Keynes likened the stock market to a beauty competition in a newspaper, where the winner is the reader who guesses the beauty who will receive most votes from all readers. Thus, Keynes argued, share prices will reflect what average opinion expects average opinion to be.

Keynes made a lot of money on the stock market, so his views deserve some attention. Nor does the empirical evidence on the 'efficient market' theory necessarily reject the 'casino' theory. If share prices are set by beliefs or whims about what other investors will think, share prices will move quite randomly and empirical investigators will conclude that no available information can be used to systematically beat the market.

Undoubtedly, financial markets do sometimes exhibit temporary bubbles. Nevertheless, they *are* usually temporary. Eventually it becomes obvious that the share price has moved away from the price that could be justified by fundamentals. Bubbles are less likely the larger the share of the total return that comes in the form of dividends rather than capital gains. And we do have some evidence that, although there are no systematic opportunities to beat the market, market prices themselves are more compatible with the efficient market theory than the pure casino theory. For example, the relation between share prices and betas shown in Figure 15-3 is evidence in favour of efficient markets and against the pure 'casino' theory.

15-6 More on risk

Risk is a central characteristic of economic life. Every topic in this book could be extended to include uncertainty. Although individual applications differ, two features recur: individuals try to find arrangements to reduce risk, and those who take over the risk-bearing have to be compensated for so doing. In this section we develop these themes.

Hedging and forward markets

A **spot market** deals in contracts for immediate delivery and payment. A **forward market** deals in contracts made today for delivery of goods at a specified future date at a price agreed to day.

There are forward markets for many commodities and assets including corn, coffee, sugar, copper, gold, and foreign currencies.

Suppose the current price of copper is £800 a ton and people expect the price to rise to £880 a ton after 12 months. Some people will hold copper in their portfolios. The expected capital gain is 10 per cent of the purchase price, and it may be interesting to diversify a portfolio by including copper. However, that is not our concern at present.

BOX 15-3   Spot markets and forward markets

At first most people find it hard to keep track of all the different terms – spot price, future spot price, expected future spot price, and forward price. Here is a chance to see if you have got them straight. Suppose there is a spot market for copper and a forward market for copper. For simplicity, suppose the only type of forward contract that exists is for delivery of copper one year after the deal is struck but at a price agreed immediately. However, the money only changes hands when the copper is delivered in one year's time. Suppose today is 1 June 2001.

Term	Definition	Example
Today's spot price	Price of copper on 1/6/01 for delivery and payment on 1/6/01.	£800/ton
Future spot price	Price of copper in the spot market in the future, say 1/6/02.	Whatever it then is, say £900/ton
Expected future	The best guess today (1/6/01) about the spot price at 1/6/02.	£880/ton
Forward price	Price in forward market on 1/6/02 at which copper is being traded for delivery and payment on 1/6/02.	£860/ton
Risk premium	Difference between expected future spot price and the current forward price. The amount of money a hedger expects on average to lose by making a forward contract on 1 June 2001 to sell copper which is delivered on 1 June 2002 rather than by taking a chance on the spot price that will be prevailing on 1 June 2002 when the copper is actually available for delivery and sale. The amount the hedger is prepared to pay to get out of the risk. Also, the amount the speculator expects to make by offering the forward contract and then reselling the copper in the spot market on 1 June 2002.	£880 − £860 = £20/ton

Suppose you own a copper mine and know you will have 1 ton of copper to sell in 12 months' time. The *spot* price of copper is the price for immediate delivery. Today's spot price is £800 and people expect the spot price to be £880 at this time next year. One option is for you simply to sell your copper at the spot price at this time next year. You expect that to be £880 but you cannot be sure today what the price next year will actually be. It is risky.

Alternatively, you can *hedge* against this risk in the forward market for copper.

Hedging is the use of forward markets to shift risk on to somebody else.

Suppose today you can sell 1 ton of copper for delivery in 12 months' time at a price of £860 agreed today. You have hedged against the risky future spot price. You know for certain what you will receive when your copper is available for delivery. But you have sold your copper for only £860, even though you expect copper then to sell for £880 on the spot market. You regard this as an insurance premium to get out of the risk associated with the future spot price.

To whom do you sell your copper in the forward market? You sell it to a trader whom we can call a *speculator*.

A **speculator** temporarily holds an asset in the hope of making a capital gain.

The speculator has no interest in 1 ton of copper *per se*. But the speculator, having promised you £860 for copper to be delivered in one year's time, currently expects to resell that copper immediately it is delivered. The speculator expects to get £880 for that copper in the spot market next year. He or she expects to make £20 as compensation for bearing your risk. If spot copper prices turn out to be less than £860 next year the speculator will lose money. £20 is the risk premium necessary to attract enough speculators into the forward market to take up the risky positions that hedgers wish to avoid.

Whereas someone buying spot copper today at £800 for possible resale next year at £880 must compare the expected capital gain of 10 per cent with returns and interest rates on offer in other assets – copper must cover the opportunity cost of the returns that could have been earned by using this money elsewhere – the speculator in the forward market need not make this comparison. No money is currently tied up in the forward contract. Although the price has been agreed today at £860, the money is handed over only next year when the copper is delivered. Provided the speculator then resells in next year's spot market, no money is actually tied up. All the speculator has to think about is the likely spot price in 12 months' time and how much it could vary either side of this estimate. The riskier the future spot price, the larger premium the speculator will need and the more the current forward price will lie below the expected future spot price.

In the previous example, the speculator had an open position. The speculator had taken forward delivery of copper only in order to resell it at a likely profit. Suppose you use copper as an input to a production process. You may wish to *buy* copper for delivery in 12 months' time at a price agreed today. Again, you wish to hedge against the risky future spot price. A speculator who can make two forward contracts, one to take delivery of copper from the copper miner, the other to sell copper to a copper user, does not have an open position. The speculator's book is balanced and there is no residual risk. The risky future spot price is irrelevant, since the speculator need neither buy in the future spot market (to find copper for people the speculator has contracted to deliver to in 12 months' time) nor sell in the future spot market (to offload copper which the speculator has promised to accept in 12 months' time).

In forward markets with roughly equal numbers of people wishing to hedge by buying and hedge by selling, speculators' books will roughly balance and the residual risk is small. Hence the speculators need only a little compensation to cover this residual risk and the administration costs. The current price of forward copper should be close to the expected future spot price. This seems to fit the facts. There is little systematic discrepancy between today's forward price and the spot price that subsequently transpires. Among other things, this suggests that speculators on average guess future spot prices correctly. However, it is a risky business if buyers and sellers cannot be matched up in the forward market. In practice, the spot prices that subsequently transpire can vary by a large amount on either side of the estimate implicitly contained in the current forward price.

Why are there forward markets for copper and silver but not for cars and washing machines? Again, we return to the questions of moral hazard and adverse selection which we said could inhibit the development of insurance markets. Suppose today you make a contract for delivery of a new car model in 12 months' time. Suppose the motor car manufacturer has sold 5 million of its new model in today's forward market. At £10 000 each, the company has a guaranteed revenue of £50 billion next year whatever kind of car it develops. You thought you were buying a de luxe family saloon, but the company brings out a low-quality car and says 'this is our new model'. Either you pay up or there is an expensive court wrangle. By making all these forward contracts the motor car manufacturer has affected its own quality incentives.

Forward markets do not exist for the vast majority of goods because it is impossible to write legally binding and cheaply enforceable contracts that specify the characteristics of the commodity being traded. Where forward markets do exist they are for very standardized commodities – 18-carat gold, copper of a certain grade, Japanese yen – which are easily defined. Thus, although forward markets are an important mechanism by which individuals can reduce the risks they face, there are only a limited number of risks that can be hedged in this way.

Compensating differentials in the return to labour

Since people are risk-averse, we expect people with risky jobs to earn more on average than people whose jobs are safe. Broadly speaking this seems confirmed by the facts. Divers who inspect North Sea oil pipelines earn high hourly rates because the death rate in this activity is high in comparison with other jobs of equivalent skill and unpleasantness. University academics earn relatively low wages in the UK because many of them have secure jobs, unlike industrial managers who face the sack if their company has a bad spell.

At a broad level, profits are often seen as a reward given to entrepreneurs, individuals who set up and run firms, for taking big risks. The average person who starts a business works long hours for small rewards initially. In the early stages there is the continual threat of failure, and many small firms never get off the ground. The possibility of becoming a millionaire, like Richard Branson of Virgin or Bill Gates of Microsoft, is the carrot that is required to persuade people to embark on this risky activity.

SUMMARY

● Uncertainty pervades economic life. Although some people gamble occasionally for fun and some addicts gamble in spite of themselves, most people seem to be risk-averse. They volunteer to take risks only if they are offered favourable odds which on average will yield a profit. Conversely, most people insure at less than fair odds in order to reduce some of the risks they would otherwise face.

● Risk-aversion may be explained by diminishing marginal utility of wealth. A fair gamble in monetary terms yields less extra utility when it succeeds than it sacrifices when it fails. Hence people usually refuse fair gambles except for very small stakes. The prevalence of risk aversion implies that individuals look for ways to reduce risk and must compensate people who take over their risk-bearing.

● Insurance schemes work by pooling risks that are substantially independent to reduce the aggregate risk, and by spreading any residual risk across a large number of people so that each insurer has a very small stake in the risk that cannot be pooled away.

● Insurance markets are inhibited by adverse selection and moral hazard. The former means that high-risk clients are more likely to take out insurance; the latter means that the act of insuring may increase the likelihood that the undesired outcome will in fact occur.

● Company shares have a higher average return but a much more variable return than that on Treasury bills or bank deposits.

● Portfolio choices depend on the investor's tastes – the trade offs between risk and average return that yield equal utility – and on the opportunities that the market provides – the risk and return combinations on existing assets.

● When risks on different asset returns are independent, the risk of the whole portfolio can be reduced by diversification across assets.

● The risk that an asset contributes to a portfolio is not measured by the variability of that asset's own return. Much more important is the correlation of its return with the return of other available assets. An asset that is negatively correlated with other assets will actually reduce the risk on the whole portfolio even though its own return is risky. Conversely, assets with a strong positive correlation with the rest of the portfolio will increase the overall risk. The value of beta for an asset measures its correlation with other assets.

● In equilibrium risky assets can earn higher rates of return on average to compensate portfolio holders for bearing this extra risk. High beta assets have high returns. If an asset is offering too high an expected return for its risk class, people will buy the asset, bidding up its price until the expected return is forced back to its equilibrium level.

● In an efficient market assets are priced to reflect the latest available information about their risk and return. There are no easy systematic investment opportunities to beat the market unless you systematically get or use new information faster than other people. Evidence from share prices is compatible with stock market efficiency, but speculative bubbles sometimes occur.

● Forward markets set a price today for future delivery of and payment for goods. They allow people to hedge against risky spot prices in the future by making a contract today. Speculators take over the hedgers' risk and will require a premium unless they can match buyers and sellers. In practice, matching is quite close and forward prices agreed today on average are close to today's expectation of the spot price in the future. But over the life of the forward contract there will usually be a lot of new information which leads the spot price to deviate from the level previously expected.

KEY TERMS

REVIEW QUESTIONS

1 A fair coin is to be tossed. If it comes down heads the player wins £1. If it comes down tails the player loses £1. Person A doesn't mind whether or not she takes the bet. Person B will pay £0.02 to play the game. Person C demands £0.05 before being willing to play. Characterize the three people's attitude to risk. Which would be most likely to take out insurance for car theft?

2 It is sometimes said that the family is one of the main forms of insurance. Can you give several reasons why people might think this?

3 You hear a radio commercial for life insurance for anyone over 45 years old. No medical examination is required. Do you expect the premium rates to be high, low, or average? Why?

4 In which of the following are the risks being pooled: (a) life insurance?; (b) insurance against the Thames flooding?; (c) insurance for a pop star's voice?

5 You set up a firm to advise the unemployed on the best way to use their time to earn money. Your firm issues shares on the stock market. In equilibrium, will your shares be expected to earn a higher or lower return than the stock market average? Why?

6 Why did the US stock market fall when it was announced that President Kennedy had been shot?

7 Someone gives you a tip that a firm has invented a fine new product. (a) Assuming that you are an active investor, what do you do about it? (b) Why are stock markets regulated to prevent 'inside trading' where a firm's managers use inside information about the firm to buy and sell its shares?

8 *Common fallacies* Show why the following statements are incorrect: (a) Economists cannot predict changes in the stock market. This proves that economics is useless in thinking about share prices. (b) It is silly to take out insurance. If the insurance company is making a profit on average its clients must be losing money. (c) Prudent investors should not buy shares whose returns are more volatile than those of the 'blue chip' companies such as GEC and ICI. (d) You make money by buying at the bottom and selling at the top. Hence you should buy shares whose price has fallen a lot and sell shares whose price has risen a lot.

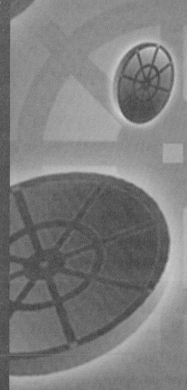

part 3

Welfare Economics

Normative or welfare economics is concerned with making value judgements and using these to recommend what policies are desirable. Much of economics is about reconciling the goals of efficiency and equity (fairness). Part 3 discusses reasons for market failures that give rise to inefficiencies, then investigates how government might intervene to improve the market. Government intervention may itself be subject to failures; well-meaning intervention can sometimes make things worse. Globalization is also undermining the economic sovereignty of nation states, sometimes making cross-border co-operation desirable.

Chapter 16 introduces welfare economics, defines efficiency and equity, and examines reasons for market failure. Chapter 17 focuses on direct government intervention through taxes and public spending. Chapter 18 deals with government attempts to influence the market through industrial policy and competition policy. Chapter 19 discusses whether natural monopolies should be taken over by the state or regulated in the private sector.

16 Introduction to welfare economics

In Chapter 1 we pointed out that markets are not the only way society can resolve what, how, and for whom to produce. Communist economies, for example, rely much more heavily on central direction or command. Are markets a good way to allocate scarce resources? What does 'good' mean? Is it fair that some people earn much more than others in a market economy? These are not positive issues about how the economy works but normative issues about how well it works. They are normative because the assessment will depend on the value judgements adopted by the assessor.

Welfare economics is the branch of economics dealing with normative issues. Its purpose is not to describe how the economy works but to assess how well it works.

Left and right wing parties fundamentally disagree about how well a market economy works. The right believes the market fosters choice, incentives and efficiency. The left stress the market's failings and the need to supplement it with regulations to protect people from its consequences. How do we cut through the political rhetoric to see what lies behind the disagreement? Two themes recur throughout our discussion of welfare economics in Part 3. The first is *allocative efficiency*. Is the economy getting the most out of its scarce resources or are they being squandered? The second is *equity*. How fair is the *distribution* of goods and services between different members of society?

16-1 Equity and efficiency

We begin by defining these terms.

Equity

Economists use two different concepts of equity or fairness.

Horizontal equity is the identical treatment of identical people. **Vertical equity** is the different treatment of different people in order to reduce the consequences of these innate differences.

Whether or not either concept of equity is desirable is a pure value judgement. Horizontal equity would rule out racial or sexual discrimination between people whose economic characteristics and performance were literally identical. Vertical equity is the Robin Hood principle of taking from the rich to give to the poor.

Many people would agree that horizontal equity is a good thing. In contrast, although few people believe that the poor should starve, the extent to which resources should be redistributed from the 'haves' to the 'have-nots' to increase vertical equity is an issue on which different people take very different positions.

Efficient resource allocation

By a *resource allocation* for an economy we mean a list or complete description of who does what and who gets what. To emphasize that markets are not the only possible allocation devices, we begin by assuming that allocations are chosen by a central dictator. Feasible or producible allocations depend on the technology and resources available to the economy. The ultimate worth of any allocation depends on consumer tastes, which determine how people value what they are given.

Figure 16-1 shows an economy with only two people, David and Susie. The initial allocation at point A gives David a quantity of goods Q_D and Susie a quantity of goods Q_S. Are society's resources being wasted? Suppose by reorganizing production it was possible to produce at point B to the north-east of A. If David and Susie assess their own utility by the quantity of goods they themselves receive, and if they would each rather have more goods than less, B is a better allocation than A since both David and Susie get more. It is inefficient to produce at A if production at B is possible. Similarly, a move from A to C makes both David and Susie worse off. If it is possible to be at A, it is definitely inefficient to be at C.

But what about a move from A to E or F? One person gains but the other person loses. Whether we judge such a change desirable depends on how we value David's utility relative to Susie's. If we think David's utility is terribly important we might consider a move from A to F a good thing, even though Susie's utility will be severely reduced.

Value judgements about equity, the fairness of the distribution of goods between people, have got mixed up with our attempt to make statements about waste or inefficiency. Since different people will make different value judgements, there can be no unambiguous answer to the question of whether a move from A to D, E, or F is desirable. It all depends who is making the assessment.

In an effort to separate as far as possible the discussion of equity from the discussion of efficiency, modern welfare economics uses the idea of *Pareto-efficiency* named after the economist Vilfredo Pareto whose *Manuel D'Economie Politique* was published in 1909.

An allocation is **Pareto-efficient** for a given set of consumer tastes, resources, and technology, if it is impossible to move to another allocation which would make some people better off and nobody worse off.

In terms of Figure 16-1 a move from A to B or A to G is a *Pareto gain*. In either case Susie is better off and David no worse off. If B or G is a feasible allocation which could be produced then point A is *Pareto-inefficient*.

How about a move from A to D? David is better off but Susie is worse off. The Pareto criterion has nothing to say about such a change. Without bringing in an explicit value judgement about the relative importance of David's and

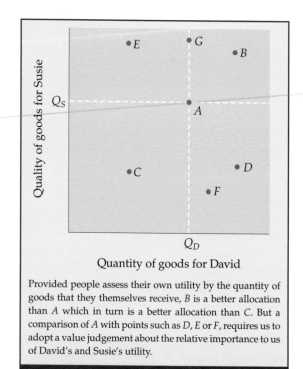

Provided people assess their own utility by the quantity of goods that they themselves receive, B is a better allocation than A which in turn is a better allocation than C. But a comparison of A with points such as D, E or F, requires us to adopt a value judgement about the relative importance to us of David's and Susie's utility.

Figure 16-1   Allocating goods to two people

Susie's utility we cannot evaluate this change. Thus the Pareto principle is of only limited use in comparing allocations on efficiency grounds. It only allows us to evaluate moves to the north-east or the south-west in Figure 16-1, but it is the most we can say about efficiency without becoming entangled in value judgements about equity.

Figure 16-2 takes the argument one stage further. Suppose by all possible reorganizations of production, the dictator decides that the economy can produce anywhere inside or on the frontier *AB*. From any allocation inside the frontier it is always possible to achieve a Pareto gain by moving to the north-east on to the frontier. Hence any point inside the frontier must be Pareto-inefficient. It is possible to make one person better off without making the other person worse off. But *all* points on the frontier are Pareto-efficient. Beginning at a point such as *C*, it is possible to give one person more only by giving the other person less. Since no Pareto gain is possible, every point such as *C* lying on the frontier must be Pareto-efficient.

Thus the dictator should never choose an inefficient allocation inside the frontier. Which of the Pareto-efficient points on the frontier is most desirable will depend on the dictator's value judgement about the relative importance of David's and Susie's utility. It is purely a judgement about equity.

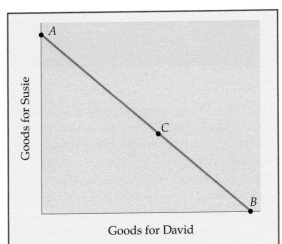

The frontier *AB* shows the maximum quantity of goods which the economy can produce for one person given the quantity of goods being produced for the other person. All points on the frontier are Pareto-efficient. David can only be made better off by making Susie worse off, and vice versa. The distribution of goods between David and Susie is much more equal at point *C* than at points *A* or *B*.

Figure 16-2   The efficient frontier

16-2 Perfect competition and Pareto-efficiency

Will a free market economy find a Pareto-efficient allocation on its own, or must it be guided there by government intervention? An answer to this question will shed light on the different claims made in the Conservative and Labour manifestos. Under certain conditions, soon to be elaborated, we can prove the following result: *If every market in the economy is a perfectly competitive free market, the resulting equilibrium throughout the economy will be Pareto-efficient.* Formalizing Adam Smith's remarkable insight of the Invisible Hand, this result is the foundation of modern welfare economics.

Competitive equilibrium in free markets

Suppose there are many producers, many consumers, but only two goods, meals and films. Each market is a free, unregulated market and is perfectly competitive. Suppose in equilibrium the price of meals is £5 and the price of films is £10. Finally, assume that labour is the variable factor of production and that workers like equally the non-monetary aspects of jobs in the film and meal industries.[1] We now argue through seven stages:

1   The last film produced yields consumers £10 worth of extra utility. If it yielded less (more) extra utility than its £10 purchase price, the last consumer would buy less (more) films. Similarly, the last meal purchased must yield consumers £5 worth of extra utility. Hence consumers could swap 2 meals (£10 worth of utility) for 1 film (£10 worth of utility) without changing their utility.

2   Since each firm sets price equal to marginal cost, the marginal cost of the last meal must be £5 and the marginal cost of the last film must be £10.

3   The variable factor (labour) must earn the same wage rate in both industries in competitive equilibrium. Otherwise there would be an incentive for workers to transfer their labour to the industry offering higher wages.

4   The marginal cost of output in either industry is the wage divided by the marginal physical product of labour. Higher wages increase marginal cost, but a higher marginal physical product of labour means that less extra workers are needed to make an additional unit of output, thus reducing marginal cost.

---

[1] Otherwise the analysis is more complicated because we need to keep track of changes in job satisfaction when workers transfer between industries.

5 Since wages are equal in the two industries and the marginal cost of meals (£5) is half the marginal cost of films (£10), the marginal physical product of labour must be twice as high in the meal as in the film industry.

6 Hence reducing film output by 1 unit and transferring the labour thus freed to the meals industry would increase the output of meals by 2 units. The marginal physical product of labour is twice as high in meals as in films. Feasible resource allocation between the two industries thus allows society to exchange 2 meals for 1 film.

7 Stage (1) says that consumers can swap 2 meals for 1 film without changing their utility. Stage (6) says that, by reallocating resources, producers swap an output of 2 meals for 1 film. Hence there is no feasible reallocation of resources that can make society better off. Since no Pareto gain is possible, the initial position – competitive equilibrium in both markets – is Pareto-efficient.

Notice the crucial role that prices play in this remarkable result. Prices do two things. First, they ensure that the initial position of competitive equilibrium is indeed an *equilibrium*. By balancing the quantities supplied and demanded, prices ensure that the final quantity of goods being consumed can be produced. They ensure that it is a feasible allocation.

But in *competitive* equilibrium prices are performing a second role. Each consumer and each producer is a price-taker and each knows that they cannot affect market prices. In our example, each consumer knows that the equilibrium price of meals is £5 and the equilibrium price of films is £10. Knowing nothing about the actions of other consumers and producers, each consumer automatically ensures that the last film purchased yields twice as much utility as the last meal purchased. Otherwise that consumer could rearrange purchases out of a given income to make himself or herself better off.[2]

Thus by their individual actions facing given prices, every consumer automatically arranges that 1 film could be swapped for 2 meals with no change in utility. Similarly, every producer, merely by setting their own marginal cost equal to the price of their output, ensures that the marginal cost of films is twice the marginal cost of meals. Thus it takes society twice as many resources to make an extra film rather

---

[2] A formal proof was given in Chapter 6 where we showed each consumer would maximize her own utility by choosing the point on the budget line tangent to the highest possible indifference curve. The slope of the indifference curve – the utility trade off between films and meals – must equal the relative price of films and meals.

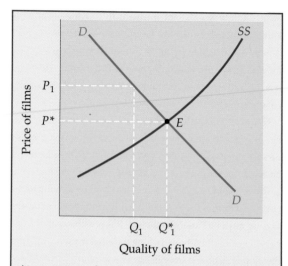

At any output such as Q_1 the last film must yield consumers P_1 pounds worth of extra utility; otherwise they would not demand Q_1. The supply curve SS for the competitive film industry is also the marginal cost of films. If the meals industry is in competitive equilibrium, the price of a meal is also the value of its marginal utility to consumers. Thus the marginal cost of a film is not only its opportunity cost in meals but is also the value of the marginal utility consumers would have derived from those meals. Hence at any film output below Q^* the marginal utility of films exceeds the marginal utility of meals sacrificed to produce an extra film. Above Q^* the marginal utility of films is less than the marginal utility of meals sacrificed. The equilibrium point E for films and the corresponding equilibrium point in the market for meals thus ensure that resources are efficiently allocated between the two industries. No reallocation could make all consumers better off.

Figure 16-3   Competitive equilibrium and Pareto-efficiency

than an extra meal. By rearranging production, transferring labour between industries, society can swap 2 meals for 1 film, exactly the trade off that would leave consumer utility unaffected.

Thus, as if by an Invisible Hand, prices are guiding individual consumers and producers, each acting only in their own self-interest, to an allocation of the economy's resources that is Pareto-efficient. Nobody can be made better off without someone else worse off.

Figure 16-3 makes the same point. *DD* is the market demand curve for one of the goods, say films. At a price P_1 a quantity of films Q_1 is demanded. But the last film demanded must yield consumers exactly P_1 pounds worth of utility; otherwise they would buy more films or less films than the quantity Q_1. Hence *DD* shows also the marginal utility of the last unit of films which consumers purchase.

When a total quantity of Q_1 films is purchased the last film yields exactly P_1 pounds worth of extra utility to consumers.

In a competitive industry, the supply curve for films SS is also the marginal cost of films. Variable factors (labour in our example) are paid not only their marginal value product in the film industry, but also their marginal value product in the meals industry: labour mobility ensures that wage rates are equated in the two industries. Hence the marginal cost of producing the last film must be the value of the meals sacrificed by using the last units of labour to make films rather than meals.

Prices ensure that both industries are in equilibrium. Figure 16-3 shows that at the equilibrium point E the marginal utility of the last film equals its marginal cost. But the marginal cost of the last film equals the value of meals sacrificed, the price of meals multiplied by the quantity of meals forgone by using labour to make that last film. However, the meals industry is also in equilibrium. An equivalent diagram for the meals industry shows that the equilibrium price of meals is also the marginal utility of the last meal purchased. Hence the value of meals sacrificed to make the last film is also the marginal utility of the last meal times the number of meals sacrificed.

Thus, provided the *meals* industry is in competitive equilibrium, the marginal cost curve for the *film* industry is simply the extra pounds worth of utility sacrificed by using scarce resources to make another film instead of extra meals. It is the opportunity cost in utility terms of the resources being used in the film industry. And equilibrium in the film industry, by equating the marginal utility of films to the marginal utility of the meals sacrificed to make the last film, guarantees that society's resources are allocated efficiently.

At any output of films below the equilibrium quantity Q^*, the marginal consumer benefit of another film would exceed the marginal consumer valuation of the meals that would have to be sacrificed to produce that extra film. At any output of films in excess of Q^*, society would be devoting too many resources to the film industry. The marginal value of the last film would be less than the marginal value of the meals that could have been produced by transferring resources to the meals industry. Competitive equilibrium ensures that there is no resource transfer between industries that would make all consumers better off.

Equity and efficiency

In the previous section, we saw that there is an infinity of Pareto-efficient allocations, each with a different distribution of utility between different members of society. We have now discovered that a competitive equilibrium in all markets generates one particular Pareto-efficient allocation. What determines which Pareto-efficient allocations it picks out?

People have different innate abilities. At any instant, people also have different amounts of human capital and financial wealth. These differences allow people to earn very different income levels in a market economy. They also affect the pattern of consumer demand.

Brazil, with a very unequal distribution of income and wealth, has a high demand for luxuries such as servants. In Sweden, with a much more equal distribution of income and wealth, almost nobody can afford servants. Thus, the initial distribution of abilities, human capital and wealth, by affecting income-earning potential, determines the pattern of consumer demand in the economy. Different patterns imply different demand curves for individual goods and services and determine different equilibrium prices and quantities. In principle, by varying the distribution of initial income-earning potential, we could induce the economy to pick out each of the possible Pareto-efficient allocations at its competitive equilibrium.

Now we come to a very attractive idea. The government is elected to express the value judgements of the majority. Ideally, we should like the government to ensure that the economy is on the Pareto-efficient frontier, shown in Figure 16-2, but take responsibility for making the value judgement about which point on this frontier the economy should attain. Since every competitive equilibrium is Pareto-efficient, and since different Pareto-efficient allocations correspond to different initial distributions of income-earning potential in a competitive economy, it seems that the government can confine itself to redistributing income and wealth through income and inheritance taxes or welfare benefits *without having to worry about interventions to ensure that resources are allocated efficiently*. Free competitive markets take care of allocative efficiency.

This seems like a pretty powerful case for the free enterprise ideal espoused by the right. The government should let markets get on with the the job of allocating resources efficiently. It should not interfere by introducing regulations, investigatory bodies, or state-run enterprises. Nor need the free enterprise ideal be uncompassionate. The government can make its value judgements about distribution or equality and can pursue its views about the desirable degree of vertical equity without impairing the efficient functioning of a free market economy. The right-wing case is more than a political ideal: it can be backed up by rigorous economic arguments.

But surely the left must be aware of these arguments?

Before you conclude that the case of free markets has been convincingly made you should remember to read the fine print. We began this section by stating that *under certain conditions* we could show that free markets led to a Pareto-efficient allocation. It is time to study these conditions in more detail. In so doing, we shall begin to understand the difference between the two views of how a market economy works. One believes that these are *minor* qualifications that do not seriously challenge the case for a free market economy. The other believes that these qualifications are so serious that they remove any presumption that the government can rely on a free market economy. Accordingly, it considers that a considerable amount of government intervention is necessary to *improve* the way the economy works.

16-3 Distortions and the second best

Competitive equilibrium is Pareto-efficient because the independent actions of producers setting marginal cost equal to price, and consumers setting marginal benefits equal to price, ensure that the marginal cost of producing a good just equals its marginal benefit to consumers.

A **distortion** exists whenever society's marginal cost of producing a good does not equal society's marginal benefit from consuming that good.

In the previous section we suggested that a government could use taxes and welfare benefits to redistribute income-earning potential and thereby enforce its value judgements about equity while leaving the market economy to take care of allocative efficiency. This neat solution may not in fact be possible.

Taxation as a distortion
Suppose the government wishes to subsidize the poor. To pay for these subsidies the government must tax the rich by taxing the incomes of rich people or the goods that rich people buy. As in the previous section, suppose there are only two goods, films and meals. Suppose everyone buys meals, but only the rich can afford to go to the cinema. If the government wishes to raise tax revenue in order to subsidize the poor, it should levy a tax on films.

Figure 16-4 shows a tax on films makes the gross-of-tax price of films to consumers exceed the net-of-tax price received by producers of films. The difference between the two prices is exactly the amount of the tax on each unit of films sold. Consumers equate the gross price to the value of the marginal benefit they receive from the last film, but

producers equate the marginal cost of films to the lower net-of-tax price of films.

Hence in competitive equilibrium the price system no longer equates the social marginal cost of producing films with the social marginal benefit of consuming films. In this example, the marginal benefit of another film exceeds the marginal cost of producing another film. The tax on films is causing too few films to be produced. Producing another film would add more to social benefit than to social cost.

When the other industry (meals) is untaxed and in competitive equilibrium, we showed in the last section that the marginal cost of producing films is exactly the value of the marginal utility sacrificed by not using the same resources to produce more meals. But when films are taxed the marginal social benefit of another film exceeds its marginal cost. Hence the marginal value to consumers of another film exceeds the marginal value of the last meal currently being produced by the resources that would be

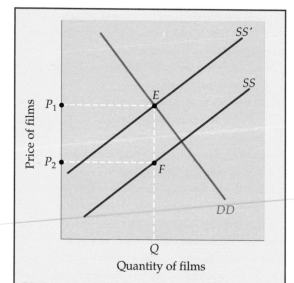

DD shows the demand for films and the marginal benefit of the last film to consumers. *SS* shows the quantity of films supplied at each price received by producers and is also the marginal social cost of producing films. Suppose each unit of films bears a tax equal to the vertical distance *EF*. To show the tax-inclusive price required to induce producers to produce each output, we must draw the new supply curve *SS'* that is a constant vertical distance *EF* above *SS*. The equilibrium quantity of films is Q. Consumers pay a price P_1, producers receive a price P_2, and the tax per film is the distance *EF*. At the equilibrium quantity Q the marginal consumer benefit is P_1 but the marginal social cost is P_2. Society would make a net gain by producing more films. Hence the equilibrium quantity Q is socially inefficient.

Figure 16-4   A tax on films

necessary to make another film. By transferring resources from meals into films, consumers of extra films could compensate meals consumers for the meals sacrificed *and still have some extra utility left over*. It would be possible to make a Pareto gain, making some people better off without making anyone else worse off.

A similar argument holds for any other commodity we tax. A tax causes a discrepancy between the price the purchaser pays and the price the seller receives. Suppose there is an income tax. Firms equate the marginal value of labour to the gross wage rate, but suppliers of labour equate the after-tax wage rate to the marginal value of the leisure that they sacrifice to work another hour. The income tax ensures that the marginal value product of labour, society's benefit from another hour of work, now exceeds the marginal value of the leisure being sacrificed in order to work. Again this is inefficient. With another hour of work, society would gain more than sufficient to compensate workers fully for the value of the extra leisure forgone.

We can now pose the choice between efficiency and equity in a stark form. If the economy is perfectly competitive, and if the government is happy with the distribution of income-earning potential that currently exists, the government need raise no taxes. Perfectly competitive free market equilibrium then allocates resources efficiently. It is impossible to reallocate resources to make some people better off without making others worse off. The economy is not wasting resources.

However, if as a pure value judgement the government considers that this distribution of income-earning potential is inequitable, the government will need to raise taxes from some people in order to provide subsidies for others. Yet the very act of raising taxes introduces a *distortion*. The price system, operating through competitive free markets, no longer equates the marginal benefits of taxed commodities with their marginal cost. The resulting equilibrium in the economy is allocatively inefficient. Society will be wasting resources by producing the wrong output levels of different goods.

What should the government do? The answer depends a good deal on the value judgements of the government in power. The more it dislikes the income distribution thrown up by the free market, a distribution reflecting differences in innate ability, human capital, and financial wealth, the more the government is likely to judge that the inefficiency costs of distortionary taxes are a price worth paying to secure a more equitable distribution of income and utility. Conversely, the more the government feels able to tolerate the income distribution thrown up in a free market

economy, the more it can resist distortionary taxation and allow competitive free markets to allocate resources as efficiently as possible.

Thus one explanation for the differing attitudes to the market economy expressed in the election manifestos at the start of the chapter is a difference in value judgements about equity. Caricaturing the argument so far, the right supports a free enterprise economy because it considers the most important objective is to maximize the size of the national cake by allocating resources as efficiently as possible. The left supports considerable state intervention because it considers that it is more important to divide the cake more fairly, even if this means having more allocative inefficiency and a smaller cake to share out.

But this is only part of the disagreement. The pursuit of equity through redistribution taxation is not the only distortion that can lead to allocative inefficiency. We consider distortions in the next section. Before leaving our tax example, there is one final point to make.

The second best

Thus far we have shown that when there is no distortion in the market for *meals*, a tax on *films* will lead to an inefficient allocation. Because the market for meals is in competitive equilibrium we saw that the marginal cost curve for films also told us the marginal value of the meals being sacrificed to make the last film. Hence, any tax on films, by driving a wedge between the marginal value of films and the marginal cost of films, drives a wedge between the marginal benefit of employing scarce resources in the film industry and employing these same resources in the meals industry.

Suppose, however, that there is a tax on *meals*. What should we do in the film industry? If we could abolish the tax on meals, then we could get back to free competitive equilibrium in both industries which we know is Pareto-efficient. We call this the *first-best* allocation to remind ourselves that it is fully efficient.

Suppose, however, that we cannot get rid of the tax on meals. The government needs some tax revenue to pay for national defence or its budget contribution to the European Union. Given that there is an unavoidable tax on meals, do we allocate resources more efficiently by ensuring that at least there are no distortions in the film industry?

In a seminal article Professors Richard Lipsey and Kelvin Lancaster showed that the answer is 'No!'[3] Suppose both industries are in equilibrium but there is a tax on meals. The

[3] R. G. Lipsey and K. Lancaster, 'On the General Theory of the Second Best', *Review of Economic Studies*, 1956–57.

marginal cost curve for films shows the opportunity cost to private producers of the resources they employ to make films rather than meals. But this is no longer society's opportunity cost of these resources in the film industry. Why not? Because producers are valuing the resources in terms of the price *producers* could get by transferring them to the meals industry. But the price of meals to consumers is higher than the price of meals received by producers. To check you understand this, try drawing a diagram like Figure 16-4 for the meals industry.

Since consumers of meals equate the value of the marginal utility of the last meal to the tax-inclusive price that must be paid, society's valuation of the last meal exceeds the net-of-tax price to which producers of meals equate marginal cost. Hence the private producers' marginal cost curve for films reflects the market value to producers of using these resources to make meals instead, but no longer reflects the opportunity cost or utility valuation of forgone meals to society. It understates the social value of meals forgone. Figure 16-5 shows what happens in the market for films when there is a tax-induced distortion in the market for meals. *DD* is the demand curve for films and reflects the marginal valuation of the last film by consumers of films. *MPC* is the marginal private costs to film producers of using resources to make films. It shows what the resources could have earned in producing meals on which meal producers would receive the net-of-tax price. *MSC* is the marginal *social* cost of using these resources to make films rather than meals. It exceeds the marginal private cost to producers because the consumer benefits of extra meals exceed the value of extra meals to producers.

With no tax on films, competitive equilibrium in the film industry occurs at E' where the demand curve crosses the private marginal cost curve which is also the competitive supply curve of the film industry. At this output Q' the marginal social cost exceeds the marginal social benefit as given by the height of the demand curve *DD*. To equate the marginal social cost of films and their marginal social benefit it is necessary to levy a tax FE^* on films. Competitive film producers then produce Q^*, receiving a net-of-tax price P_1^* equal to their marginal private cost at this output. Consumers would pay the tax-inclusive price P_2^*. Marginal social cost and marginal social benefit are equated at the point E^*.

In contrast to the *first-best* allocation, when we achieve full efficiency by removing all distortions, we have now developed the principle of the *second best*. The principle of the second best says the following. Suppose we are interested only in allocative efficiency. However, there is an

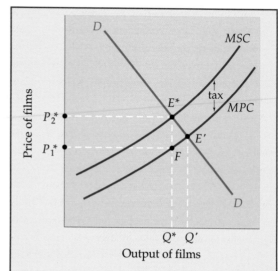

DD shows the demand curve and marginal consumer benefit of films. *MPC* is the marginal private cost of films and reflects what the resources could earn for producers if they were employed in the meals industry. With a tax on meals, the consumer price and marginal consumer benefit of meals will exceed the net-of-tax price received by producers of meals. Hence the social opportunity cost of using resources in films, the value of the marginal consumption benefits of meals forgone, exceeds the private producers' opportunity cost of using these resources in films. *MSC* shows the marginal social cost of the forgone utility by using resources in films rather than meals. With no film tax, competitive equilibrium is at E'. At the output Q' the marginal social benefit of films is less than the marginal social cost of films. Q^* is the efficient output of films at which marginal social cost and marginal social benefit of films are equal. A tax on films equal to the distance E^*F would induce a competitive film industry to produce Q^*. Consumers would pay P_2^* and producers would receive P_1^*.

Figure 16-5   The second best

inevitable distortion somewhere else in the economy that we are unable to remove. It is inefficient to treat other markets as if that distortion did not exist. Thus in the film industry it is inefficient to aim to equate private marginal cost and private marginal benefit, the efficient outcome in the absence of a meals tax. Rather, it is efficient to deliberately introduce a new distortion to the film industry to help counterbalance the inevitable distortion in the meals industry.

The **first-best** removes all distortions. The **second-best** is the most efficient outcome that can be achieved conditional on being unable to remove some distortions.

In effect, the theory of the second best says that if there must be a distortion, for example if the government has to raise some taxes, it is a mistake to concentrate the distortion in one market. It is more efficient to spread its effect more thinly over a wide range of markets. In the example of Figure 16-5 a tax on meals leads to too few meals being produced. The only place the resources can go is the film industry, so too many films are being produced. A tax on films helps redress the balance.

Several applications of this general principle will be found in the ensuing chapters. The real world in which we live unfortunately provides us with several inevitable distortions. Given their existence, the argument of this section implies that the government may *increase* the overall efficiency of the whole economy by introducing *new* distortions to offset distortions that already exist. By now you will rightly be wanting to know the source of these inevitable distortions that the government should take action to offset.

16-4 Market failure

We began by showing that in the absence of any distortions a freely competitive equilibrium would ensure allocative efficiency. We use the term *market failure* to cover all the circumstances in which equilibrium in free unregulated markets (i.e. markets not subject to direct price or quantity regulation by the government) will fail to achieve an efficient allocation. Market failure describes the circumstances in which distortions prevent the Invisible Hand from allocating resources efficiently.

We now list the possible sources of distortions that lead to market failure.

1 *Imperfect competition*   It is perfect competition that leads firms to set marginal cost equal to price and thus to marginal consumer benefit. Under imperfect competition, producers set marginal cost equal to marginal revenue, which is less than the price at which the last unit is sold. Since consumers equate price to marginal benefits derived from the last unit, in general marginal benefit will exceed marginal cost in imperfectly competitive industries. Such industries will tend to produce too little. Expanding output would add more to consumer benefit than it would to production costs or the opportunity cost of the resources used. This idea forms the theme of Chapter 18.

2 *Social priorities such as equity*   Redistributive taxation in the pursuit of equity induces allocative distortions by driving a wedge between the price the consumer pays and the price the producer receives. We study the principles of taxation more fully in Chapter 17.

3 *Externalities*   Externalities are things like pollution, noise, and congestion. What they have in common is that one person's actions have direct costs or benefits for other people which that individual does not take into account. Much of the remainder of this chapter is devoted to analysing this distortion. The problem arises because there is neither a market nor a market price for things like noise. Hence we cannot expect markets and prices to ensure that the marginal benefits of making a noise are equated to the marginal cost of that noise to other people.

4 *Other missing markets: future goods, risk, and information*   These are further examples of commodities for which markets are absent or limited. In Chapter 14 we saw how moral hazard and adverse selection inhibit the setting up of insurance markets to deal with risk. As with externalities, we cannot expect markets to allocate resources efficiently if the markets do not exist. We pursue this theme at the end of this chapter. First, we look more closely at the problem of externalities.

16-5 Externalities

An **externality** arises whenever an individual's production or consumption decision directly affects the production or consumption of others **other than through market prices**.

Suppose a chemical firm discharges waste into a lake, polluting the water and directly imposing an additional production cost on anglers (fewer and smaller fish, which are harder to catch) or a consumption cost on swimmers (less pleasant swimming and a dirty beach). If there is no 'market' for pollution, the firm can pollute the lake without cost. Its self-interest will lead it to pollute until the marginal benefit of polluting (a cheaper production process for chemicals) equals its own marginal cost of polluting, which is zero. It takes no account of the marginal cost its pollution imposes on anglers and swimmers.

Conversely, by painting your house you make the whole street look nicer and give consumption benefits to your neighbours. But you paint only up to the point on which your own marginal benefit equals the marginal cost of the paint you buy and the time you spend. Your marginal costs are also society's marginal costs, but society's marginal benefits exceed your own: there is too little house-painting.

In both cases there is a divergence between the individual's comparison of marginal costs and benefits and society's comparison of marginal costs and benefits. Free markets cannot induce people to take account of these

BOX 16-1   Rent-seeking

In America, lobbyists catch the early morning plane to Washington DC. In Europe, they find their way to Brussels. Over expense-account lunches, the business of persuasion is conducted. What does all this have to do with the efficiency of the economy?

Where the process is largely one of providing information to policy makers, it is possible that, like informative advertising, it increases the efficiency of decision making. But of course it goes way beyond this. Suppose a lecturer walks into a class and deposits on the table an open suitcase in which you can all see £10 000 in used banknotes. She gives a brilliant class for an hour, but nobody is listening. All the students are working out if there is any way they can make off with the loot. Nor are they likely to be co-operating. Ian Ironfists is chiefly worried about how to stop his main rival Sam Slugger. Indeed, Ironfists and Slugger can be observed in the lecture parting with their own hard-earned cash to assemble rival teams of students to fight the inevitable lunchtime battle for the suitcase. Micro-economic theory absorbed during the hour's lecture? Zero.

Sources of inefficiency? First, the lecturer's time was *wasted*. Second, at the beginning of the class, society has one suitcase with £10 000, plus the loose change in people's pockets that became used to pay for lunchtime mercenaries. At the end of the lunchtime fight, society will still have one suitcase, £10 000, and some loose change. Total increase in goods and services as a result of the morning's effort? Nothing. It was a zero-sum game that had no net value added for society. The prospect of *economic rent* or pure surplus – a suitcase worth £10 000 – has led the students to spend their valuable resources (cash in their pocket, time that could have been spent learning more economics) trying to compete for and capture the jackpot.

While government intervention in the economy to offset market failures can, in principle, improve efficiency, intervention can also create opportunities for rent-seeking. Suppose the government regulates the award of franchises to operate railway lines or TV stations. Rival bidders may use up huge amounts of real resources trying to outdo one another. Privately, being in the winning team is so important that it is worth spending a lot to increase your team's chances of winning. But socially it may be close to a zero-sum game. One supplier of railway services or TV programming may be scarcely any better than the other; and encouraging competition between prospective suppliers is good only so long as the improvements society thereby receives outweigh the social value of the resources the two sides use up their trench warfare while fighting one another to a standstill. Where society decides that some form of intervention is necessary to combat market failure, it should still give considerable thought to how to design intervention to minimize government failure. Substantial rent-seeking is one channel through which such government failure may occur.

---

indirect effects on other people if there is no market in these indirect effects.

Divergences between private and social costs and benefits

Suppose a chemical firm discharges a pollutant into a river, the quantity of pollutant discharged being in proportion to the level of chemical production. Further down the river there are food-processing companies using river water as an input in making sauce for baked beans. There are also farmers with agricultural land.

At small levels of chemical output, pollution is negligible.

The river can dilute the small amounts of pollutant discharged by the chemical producer. But as the discharge rises the costs of pollution rise sharply. Food processors must worry about the purity of their water intake and build expensive purification plants. Still higher levels of pollution start to corrode pipes and contaminate agricultural land.

Figure 16-6 shows the marginal private cost MPC of producing chemicals. For simplicity, we assume that MPC is constant. It also shows the marginal *social cost MSC* of chemical production. The divergence between marginal private cost and marginal social cost reflects the marginal cost imposed on other producers by an extra unit of the

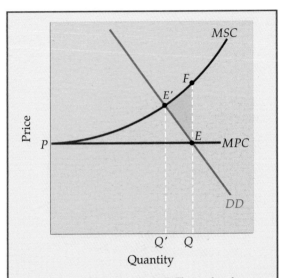

Competitive equilibrium occurs at E. The market clears at a price *P* which producers equate to marginal private cost *MPC*. But pollution causes a production externality which makes the marginal social cost *MSC* exceed the marginal private cost. The socially efficient output is at *E'* where marginal social cost and marginal social benefit are equal. The demand curve *DD* measures the marginal social benefit because consumers equate the value of the marginal utility of the last unit to the price. By inducing an output *Q* in excess of the efficient output *Q'*, free market equilibrium leads to a social cost equal to the area of the triangle *E'FE*. This shows the excess of social cost over social benefit in moving from *Q'* to *Q*.

Figure 16-6   The social cost of a production externality

production externality of pollution that the chemical producer disregards. The demand curve *DD* shows how much consumers are willing to pay for the output of the chemical producer. If that producer acts as a price-taker, equilibrium is at *E* and the chemical producer's output is *Q* at which the marginal private cost equals the price received by the firm for its output.

However, at this output *Q* the marginal social cost *MSC* exceeds the marginal social benefit of chemicals as given by the corresponding point on the demand curve *DD*. The market for chemicals takes no account of the production externality inflicted on other firms. Since at the output *Q* the marginal social benefit of the last output unit is less than the marginal social cost inclusive of the production externality, the output *Q* is not socially efficient. By reducing the output of chemicals society would save more in social cost than it would lose in social benefit. It would allow society to make some people better off without making anyone worse off.

In fact the socially efficient output is *Q'*, at which the marginal social benefit of the last output unit equals is marginal social cost. *E'* is the efficient point. How much does society lose by producing at the free market equilibrium *E* rather than at the socially efficient point *E'*? The vertical distance between the marginal social cost *MSC* and the marginal social benefit as given by *DD* shows the marginal social loss of producing the last output unit. Hence, by expanding from *Q'* to *Q*, society loses a total amount equal to the triangle *E'EF* in Figure 16-6. This measures the social cost of the market failure caused by the production externality of pollution.[4]

Production externalities lead to a divergence between marginal private production costs and marginal social production costs. Similarly, a consumption externality leads to a divergence between marginal private benefits and marginal social benefits. Figure 16-7 illustrates a beneficial consumption externality as when painting your house or planting roses in your front garden gives pleasure also to your neighbours.

Since there are no production externalities *MPC* is both the marginal private cost and the marginal social cost of making your house and garden look nicer. It is the cost of the paint and plants plus the opportunity cost of your time. *DD* is the marginal private benefit of house improvements and, comparing your own costs and benefits, you will undertake a quantity *Q* of improvements.

But you do not take account of the consumption value these improvements have for your neighbours. Since these are benefits too, the marginal social benefit *MSB* is greater than your marginal private benefit. In comparison with the free market equilibrium at *E*, the socially efficient quantity of improvements is *Q'*. At *E'* the marginal social benefit and marginal social cost are equated.

Free market equilibrium leads to too few improvements. Society could gain the triangle *EFE'*, measuring the excess of social benefits over social costs, by increasing the quantity of improvements from *Q* to *Q'*. Alternatively, this same triangle measures the social cost of the market failure that leads free market equilibrium to a social inefficient allocation.

---

[4] Conversely, some production externalities have beneficial effects on other producers. A farmer who spends money on pest control on his or her property may reduce the cost of pest control on neighbouring farms. When production externalities are beneficial the marginal social cost will lie *below* the marginal private cost. Suppose we re-label the *MSC* curve as *MPC* in Figure 16-6 and re-label the *MPC* curve as *MSC*. Free market equilibrium will then occur at *E'* but *E* will now be the socially efficient allocation.

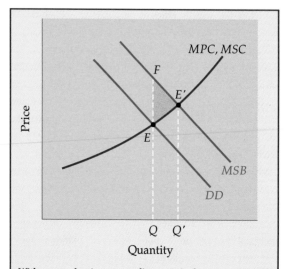

With no production externality, marginal private cost and marginal social cost coincide. *DD* measures the marginal private benefit and free market equilibrium occurs at *E*. The beneficial consumption externality makes marginal social benefit *MSB* exceed marginal private benefit. *E'* is the socially efficient point. By producing *Q* instead of the efficient output *Q'*, free market equilibrium wastes the triangle *EFE'*.

Figure 16-7   A beneficial consumption externality

Property rights and externalities

Suppose your neighbour's tree grows into your garden, obscuring your light and giving you a harmful consumption externality. If the law says that you must be compensated for any damage suffered, your neighbour will either have to pay up or cut back the tree. What is the smart thing for your neighbour to do, and how much compensation will you get?

Your neighbour really likes the tree and wants to know how much it would take to compensate you to leave the tree at its current size. Figure 16-8 shows the marginal benefit *MB* that your neighbour gets from the last inch of tree size and the marginal cost *MC* to you of that last inch of tree size. At the tree's current size S_1 the total cost to you is the area $OABS_1$. You simply take the marginal cost *OA* of the first inch, then add the marginal cost of the second inch, and so on till you get to the existing size S_1. The area $OABS_1$ is what you require in compensation if the tree size is S_1.

Your neighbour is about to pay up this amount. But he has a daughter studying economics. She points out that at the size S_1 the marginal benefit of the last inch is less than the marginal cost to you, which is also the amount you must be compensated for that last inch on the tree. It is not worth your neighbour having a tree this big. Nor, she points out, is

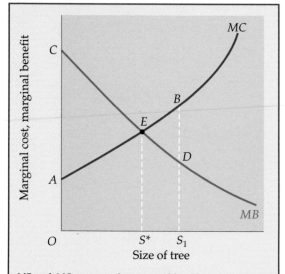

MB and *MC* measure the marginal benefit to your neighbour and marginal cost to you of a tree of size *S*. The efficient size is *S** where the marginal cost and benefit are equal. Beginning from a size S_1 you might bribe your neighbour the value S^*EDS_1 to cut back to *S**. Below *S** you would have to pay more than it is worth to you to have the tree cut back further. Alternatively, your neighbour might pay you the value $OAES^*$ to have a tree of size *S**. Property rights, in this case whether you are legally entitled to compensation for loss of light to your garden, determine who compensates whom but not the outcome *S** of the bargain.

Figure 16-8   The efficient quantity of an externality

it worth cutting the tree down altogether. The first inch yields a higher marginal benefit to your neighbour than the amount that you require in compensation to offset the marginal cost to you of that first inch. A tiny tree has little effect on your light and makes the garden next door look nicer.

At the efficient allocation or tree size *S** the marginal benefit to your neighbour equals the marginal cost to you. Above *S** the neighbour cuts back the tree since the marginal cost (and compensation) exceeds the marginal benefit. Below *S** he or she increases the tree size and pays the marginal compensation that is less than the marginal benefit. At the efficient size *S** your total cost is the area $OAES^*$ and this is the compensation you will be paid.

Notice that since a larger tree benefits one party but hurts the other party, *the efficient tree size and efficient quantity of the externality will not be zero*. Rather, it occurs where the marginal benefits equals the marginal cost.

Property rights are the power of residual control of an asset, including the right to be compensated for externalities.

First, they affect who compensates whom. They have a distributional implication. Suppose there was no law requiring compensation. Would you just sit there and allow your neighbour's tree to grow to a size S_1 that inflicts a huge cost on you? Of course not. You would bribe your neighbour to cut it back. You would compensate your neighbour for the loss of his marginal benefit. It would be worth you paying to have the tree cut back as far as S^* but no further. Beyond that size, you pay more in compensation for the loss of marginal benefit than you save yourself in reduced cost of the externality. So you would pay your neighbour a *total* of EDS_1S^* to compensate for the loss of benefit in cutting the tree back from S_1 to S^*. Who has the property rights determines who must compensate whom, but it does not affect the quantity that the bargain will determine. It must pay to reach the point at which the marginal benefit to one of you equals the marginal cost to the other.

Property rights thus have a distributional implication – who compensates whom – but also act to achieve the socially efficient allocation. They implicitly set up the 'missing market' for the externality. The market ensures that the price equals the marginal benefit and the marginal cost, and hence equates the two.

Sometimes economists say that property rights are a way to 'internalize' the externality. If people must pay for it they will take its effects into account in making private decisions and there will no longer be market failure. Why then do externalities like congestion and pollution remain a problem? Why don't private individuals establish the missing market through a system of bribes or compensation?

There are two obvious reasons why it may be hard to set up this market. The first is the cost of organizing the market. If a factory chimney dumps smoke on a thousand gardens nearby it may be very expensive to collect £1 from each household to bribe the factory to cut back to the socially efficient amount.

Second, there is the *free-rider* problem.

A **free-rider**, recognizing that he cannot be excluded from consuming a good, has no incentive to offer to purchase it.

Suppose someone knocks on your door and says: 'I am collecting bribes from people who mind the factory smoke falling on their gardens. The money I collect will be paid to bribe the factory to cut back. Do you wish to contribute? I am going round 5000 houses in the neighbourhood.' Whether you mind or not, you say: 'I don't mind and won't contribute.' Provided everybody else pays, the factory will cut back and you cannot be prevented from getting the benefits. The smoke will not fall exclusively on your garden

merely because you alone did not pay up. Regardless of what other people contribute, there is no incentive for you to contribute: you are a *free-rider*. But everyone else will reason similarly; hence no one will pay, even though you would all have been better off paying and getting the smoke cut back.

16-6 Environmental issues

When, for either reason, there is no implicit market for pollutants, there will be overproduction of pollutants. Because private producers fail to take account of the costs they impose on others, in equilibrium social marginal cost will exceed social marginal benefit.

If the private sector cannot organize charges for the marginal externalities pollution creates, perhaps the government can? By charging (through taxes) for the divergence between marginal private and social cost, the government could then induce private producers to take account of the costs inflicted on others. This argument for government intervention through taxes is examined in the next chapter.

Pollution taxes, especially for water pollution, have been used in France, Italy, Germany, and the Netherlands. But most policy takes a different approach, the imposition of pollution standards that regulate the maximum amount of allowed pollution.

Air pollution

Since the Clean Air Act of 1956, UK governments have designated clean air zones in which certain types of pollution, notably the smoke caused by burning coal, are illegal. The number of designated clean air zones has increased steadily, and Table 16-1 shows the dramatic reduction in smoke pollution in the UK.

Adding lead to petrol improves the fuel economy of cars. However, lead emissions from car exhausts are an atmospheric pollutant harmful to people's health. Since 1972 the UK government has steadily reduced the quantity of lead permitted in petrol. Table 16-2 shows that lead emission

Table 16-1	Smoke emission in the UK (million tonnes per annum)		
1958	1974	1995
2.0	0.8	0.4

Sources: Digest of Environmental Protection and Water Statistics; ONS, *Social Trends.*

Table 16-2	Lead emissions
	Thousand tonnes
1975	8.3
1980	6.7
1986	2.8
1996	1.2

Source: ONS, *Social Trends*.

from vehicles fell dramatically, even though consumption of petrol has risen dramatically.

Water pollution

Since 1951 governments in the UK have imposed increasingly stringent controls on discharges into inland waters. Although we tend to think of *industrial* effluent, sewage is a more important source of pollution. Since 1970 regional water authorities in England and Wales spent (at 1997 prices) an annual average of £3 billion on water purification and sewage treatment. This expenditure was only moderately successful in reducing water pollution. By the late 1980s an even more important problem had been recognized: water pollution from nitrates used as fertilizers on agricultural land. The European Union has laid down tough standards for water purity which will take many years to achieve.

Evaluating pollution policy in the UK

Direct regulation of pollution has met with mixed success over the last 30 years. In some cases, for example, the smoke pollution which used to be acute in winter when smoke and fog mixed to produce dense 'smog', tougher standards have led to dramatic improvements in environmental quality. Many rivers are also cleaner, and fish have reappeared.

In other cases, governments have tried to regulate but often been ineffective; it is hard to enforce regulations such as those that prevent ships discharging oil at sea. In yet other cases there has been little attempt to intervene. For example, coal-fired power stations continue to emit large quantities of sulphur dioxide, which the high chimneys are only partially successful in dispersing. And ecologists continue to oppose government policies that allow new coal mines in previously green countryside, or permit the disposal of nuclear waste at sea.

Has the government been tough enough on polluters? Recall from Figures 16-6 and 16-8 that the efficient quantity of pollution is not zero. The fact that pollution still exists is not sufficient to establish that policy has not been tough enough.

Where pollution control has been attempted it has usually been crude and simple. Calculations of the social marginal costs and benefits of cutting back pollution tend to be conspicuous by their absence. In part this reflects the difficulty in measuring costs and benefits. For example, in considering how much to reduce lead emissions from cars it is not impossible to calculate the marginal social cost of producing cars with anti-pollution exhaust systems and the marginal social cost of cars that use more fuel per mile. But even if doctors were unanimous about the effects of lead emission on health, how should society value a marginal increase in the health of current and future generations?

This is not merely a question of efficiency, which we might answer by considering the resources tied up in looking after the sick or the extra output that healthier workers could produce. It is also a question of equity, both within the current generation – poor inner-city children may be most vulnerable to arrested development caused by inhaling lead-polluted air – and across generations. Devoting more resources to reducing lead pollution today reduces the resources producing consumer goods for today's consumers, but improves the quality of life for tomorrow's consumers.

Prices versus quantities

Although it is hard to judge whether there is enough pollution control, we can discuss whether the current mechanism of pollution control is sensible. If free markets tend to overpollute, society can reduce pollution either by regulating the quantity of pollution (as it does) or by using the price system to discourage such activities by taxing them. Would it be more sensible to intervene through the tax system than to regulate quantities directly?

Many economists believe the answer to this question is yes. One reason is that, if each firm were charged the same price or tax for a marginal unit of pollution, then every firm equate the marginal cost of reducing pollution to the price of pollution. Any allocation in which different firms have different marginal costs of reducing pollution is socially inefficient. By having the firms with low marginal reduction costs contract further and firms with high marginal reduction costs contract less, the same total reduction in pollution could be achieved at less cost.

However, there are two important qualifications to this argument. First, it would be necessary to monitor the quantity of pollution of each firm in order to assess its tax liability. Second, in order to assess the tax rate or charge for pollution it would still be necessary to calculate the overall costs and benefits of marginal changes in the amount of

BOX 16-2   Acid rain: a bitter controversy

Gases such as sulphur dioxide and oxides of nitrogen are discharged into the atmosphere, dissolved in water vapour, and fall as acid rain. Acid rain poisons fish, destroys forests, and corrodes buildings. The following table shows data for European emissions of sulphur.

It reveals the appalling pollution in Eastern Europe and the ex-USSR, mainly from power stations fuelled by low-grade coal. In Western Europe, the UK is a big exporter of acid rain: prevailing winds blow it east, and Scandinavia is a big loser.

Installing and operating enough flue gas desulphurization plants to cut UK power station emissions of sulphur dioxide by 50 per cent would add 6 per cent to UK electricity prices. Since much of the damage occurs in Swedish lakes and German forests, UK voters are unwilling to pay the extra cost. It needs a concerted European policy, perhaps even with transfer payments between governments, to deal with externalities across national borders.

Europe is trying to agree a 20 per cent cut in sulphur dioxide emissions and a freeze on emissions of oxides of nitrogen (mainly from car exhausts). But when different countries face a different marginal cost of pollution abatement, and inflict different amounts of marginal damage (polluting unpopulated areas is less costly than polluting densely populated areas), equal cutbacks for all is not the efficient solution. For a given overall reduction, the efficient solution equates the marginal net benefit (damage reduction minus abatement cost) across different polluters. The following table shows estimates by Professor David Newbery of Cambridge University of the efficient way to achieve a 30 per cent reduction in sulphur dioxide emissions in Europe.

Sulphur emissions	Million tonnes a year	
	Produced	Received
E. Europe	6.6	3.7
UK	1.3	0.7
France, Italy, W. Germany	2.3	2.1
Ex-USSR in Europe	2.6	3.5
Scandinavia	0.1	0.5
Other Europe	2.6	3.1

Note: 2 million tonnes received cannot be traced to any particular emitting country.

Efficient cuts in sulphur dioxide emissions (%) (selected countries)

Belgium	69	Austria	16
Holland	65	Spain	10
France	40	Hungary	8
UK	31	Poland	3
Italy	27	Norway	3
Denmark	18	Ex-USSR	3

Data from D. Newbery, 'Acid Rain', *Economic Policy*, October 1990.

pollution. If the government has to make a decision on the socially efficient level of pollution anyway, it may be simpler to regulate the quantity directly.

Finally, there is the issue of the uncertainty of the effect of the legislation. Suppose pollution beyond a certain critical level has disastrous consequences, for example irreversibly damaging the ozone layer. By regulating the quantity directly it is at least possible to ensure that the disaster is avoided. Indirect control through taxes or charges runs the risk that the government might do its sums wrong and set the tax too low. Pollution will then be higher than intended, and possibly disastrous.

Thus, regulating the total quantity of pollution and conducting a series of spot checks on individual producers to see that they are not violating agreed standards is a relatively simple policy which may avoid the worst outcomes. However, by ignoring differences in the marginal cost of reducing pollution across different polluters, it does not reduce pollution in the manner that is cost-minimizing to society. There is no simple answer in an uncertain world where monitoring and enforcement also use up society's scarce resources.

Lessons from the United States

The United States has gone furthest in trying to use property rights and the price mechanism to cut back pollution in a manner that is economically efficient. The US Clean Air Acts (1955, 1970, 1977) have established an environmental policy that includes an *emissions trading programme* and *bubble policy*.

BOX 16-3

A lot of hot air?

Chlorofluorocarbons (CFCs) are gases used in things like aerosols. There is increasing evidence that they may destroy the ozone layer that protects the earth from the sun's rays. Without this sunscreen, more people will get skin cancer. But organizing international cutbacks in atmospheric pollution is difficult: each country is tempted to act as a free-rider, enjoying the benefits of other countries' reductions but making no contribution of its own. The Montreal Protocol on Substances that deplete the Ozone Layer was concluded in 1987 with nearly 50 countries signing. Before the Protocol, projected ozone depletion was 5 per cent by the year 2025 and 50 per cent by the year 2075. In the Protocol, countries agreed to take steps to reduce ozone depletion to 2 per cent by 2025 with no further deterioration thereafter. Such optimistic aims will be hard to achieve.

A second type of atmospheric pollution is potentially more important, though it remains the subject of scientific controversy. The greenhouse effect arises from emissions of CFCs, methane, nitrous oxide and, especially, carbon dioxide. Greenhouse gases are the direct result of pollution and the indirect result of a reduction in the atmosphere's ability to absorb them. Plants convert carbon dioxide into oxygen. Chopping down forests to clear land for cattle, as the world demand for hamburgers increases, may be good business in the short run, but has a significant effect on the long-run cumulation of greenhouses gases.

The consequence is global warming. People in London and Stockholm get better suntans; people in Africa face drought and famine; and, as icecaps melt, the sea-level rises, flooding low-lying areas. In 1990 the Intergovernmental Panel on Climate Change forecast that by 2070 the temperature would have risen by 3.5°C, and the sea by 45 centimetres. As with acid rain and CFCs, organizing collective international cutbacks has proved difficult because of the free-rider problem.

In 1997 the Kyoto Protocol finally agreed national targets for lower emissions of greenhouse gases. Becoming binding in 2008–12, the agreement will cut emissions by 5 per cent relative to the 1990 level, but by much more relative to the growth that a do-nothing policy would have allowed. The table below shows 1990 levels, actual behaviour in the 1990s, and the target for 2012. The targets shown in the table are partly the outcome of political compromise. However, in practice different countries face different marginal costs of abatement (cutbacks). It would therefore be more efficient to issue pollution licences and allow these to be traded. Producers facing large marginal costs of cutbacks could buy licences from producers quite happy to do an above-average share of abatement because they face low marginal costs of abatement. By choosing the number of licences, the overall target can be met. By allowing trading in licences, the cutbacks can be allocated to those who can bear them most cheaply.

'Economists back call for new carbon taxes' reported the *Financial Times* (14 February 1997), citing a statement signed by 2000 economists including 6 Nobel Prize winners. The proposal called for an international auction of emission permits, and argued that the economic cost of doing nothing about global warming outweighed the cost of taking action.

	1990 emissions (million tonnes)	Change 1990–95 (%)	2012 target (relative to 1990) (%)
Japan	1190	+8	−6
USA	5713	+5	−7
Germany	1204	−12	−21
UK	715	−9	−12
Italy	532	+2	−6
France	498	0	0
Spain	301	+2	+15

The Acts lay down a minimum standard for air quality, and impose pollution emission controls to particular polluters. Any polluter emitting less than their specified amount obtains an *emission reduction credit* (ERC), which can be sold to another polluter which wants to go over its allocated pollution limit. Thus, the total quantity of pollution is regulated, but firms that can cheaply reduce pollution have an incentive to do so, and sell off the *ERC* to firms for which pollution reduction is more expensive. In this way we get closer to the efficient solution in which the marginal cost of pollution reduction is equalized across firms.

When a firm has many factories, the bubble policy applies pollution controls to the firm as a whole rather than individual factories. The firm can cut back most in the plants in which pollution reduction is cheapest.

Thus, the US policy manages to combine 'control over quantities' for aggregate pollution, where the risks and uncertainties are greatest, with 'control through the price system' for allocating efficiently the way these overall targets are achieved.

16-7　Other missing markets: time and risk

The previous two sections have been devoted to a single idea. When externalities exist, free market equilibrium is inefficient because the externality itself does not have a market or a price. People take no account of the costs and benefits their actions inflict on others. Without a market for externalities the price system cannot bring marginal costs and marginal benefits of these externalities into line. In this section we discuss two other types of 'missing market', those associated with time and with risk.

The present and the future are linked. People save, or refrain from consumption, today in order to consume more tomorrow. Firms reduce current output by devoting resources to training or building in order to produce more tomorrow. How should society make plans today for the quantities of goods to be produced and consumed in the future? Ideally we should like to organize everyone's plans today so that the social marginal cost of goods in the future just equals the social marginal benefit.

In Chapter 15 we introduced the concept of a *forward market*, in which buyers and sellers make contracts today for goods to be delivered in the future at a price agreed today. Suppose there was a forward market for delivery of copper in 2004. Consumers would equate the marginal benefit of copper in 2004 to the forward price, which producers would equate to the marginal cost of producing copper for 2004. A complete set of forward markets for all commodities for all future dates would lead producers and consumers today to make consistent plans for future production and consumption of all goods, and the social marginal benefit of every future good would equal its social marginal cost.

In Chapter 15 we explained why only a very limited set of future markets actually exists. You can trade gold one year forward but not cars or washing machines. Since nobody knows the characteristics of next year's model of a car or a

washing machine, it is impossible to write legally binding contracts which could be enforced when the goods are delivered. Without these forward markets the price system cannot equate the marginal cost and marginal benefits of planned future goods.

There is also a limited set of *contingent* or insurance markets for dealing with risk. In Chapter 15 we argued that people typically dislike risk. Risk is costly to individuals because it reduces their utility. But does society undertake the efficient amount of risky activities?

A complete set of insurance markets allows risk to be transferred from those who dislike risk to those who will bear risk at a price. The equilibrium price or insurance premium would equate the marginal cost and marginal benefit of risk-bearing. The price system would equate social marginal costs and benefits of risky activities.

However, problems of adverse selection and moral hazard inhibit the organization of private insurance markets. If some risky activities are uninsurable at any price, the price system cannot guide society to equate social marginal costs and benefits.

Future goods and risky goods are examples of commodities with missing markets. Like externalities, they induce market failure. Free market equilibrium will not generally be efficient. One problem which inhibits the development of forward and contingent markets is *information*. For example, it is the problem of acquiring the relevant information about purchasers of insurance policies that leads insurance companies to face problems of moral hazard and adverse selection. We now study some practical examples of how informational problems affect the way in which markets work.

16-8　Quality, health, and safety

Information is incomplete because gathering information is costly. This may lead to inefficient allocations. A worker unaware that exposure to benzene might cause cancer will be willing to work for a lower wage than if this information were widely available. The firm's production cost will understate the true social cost and the good will be over-produced.

In most countries, governments have accepted an increasing role in regulating health, safety, and quality standards because they have recognized the danger of market failure.

Examples of government regulation in the UK are the Health and Safety at Work Acts, legislation controlling food and drugs production, the Fair Trading Act which governs consumer protection, and the various traffic and motoring regulations. The purpose of such legislation is twofold: to encourage the provision of information that will allow individuals more accurately to judge costs and benefits, and to set and enforce standards designed to reduce the risks of injury or death.

Providing information

Figure 16-9 shows the supply curve *SS* for a drug that is potentially harmful. *DD* is the demand curve when consumers are unaware of the danger. In equilibrium at *E* the quantity *Q* is produced and consumed. With full information about the dangers, people would buy less of the drug. The demand curve *DD'* shows the marginal consumer benefit with full information. The new equilibrium at *E'* avoids the deadweight burden *EE'F* from overproduction of the drug.

If information were free to collect, everyone would already know the true risks. From the social gain *EE'F* we should subtract the resources that society expends in discovering this information. In saying free market equilibrium would be at *E*, we are really saying that it would not be worth while for each individual to check up privately on

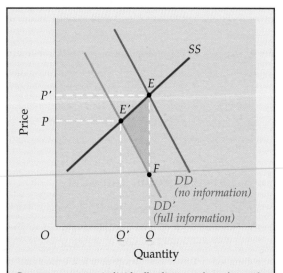

Consumers cannot individually discover the safety risks associated with a particular good. Free market equilibrium occurs at *E*. A government agency now provides information about the product. As a result, the demand curve shifts down and the new equilibrium is at *E'* where the *true* or full information value of an extra unit of the good equals its marginal social cost. Providing information prevents a welfare cost *E'EF* that arises when uninformed consumers use the wrong marginal valuation of the benefits of the good.

Figure 16-9　Information and unsafe goods

each and every drug on the market. But it makes sense for society to have a single regulatory body that does the checking and a law whose enforcement entitles individuals to assume that drugs being sold have been checked out as safe.

Certification of safety or quality need not be carried out by the government. Sotheby's certify the quality of Rembrandts, and the private University College at Buckingham certifies educational attainments of its students. People arrested on suspicion of drunk driving in the UK are allowed to send half their blood sample to a private certification agency to corroborate the results of the police analysis.

Nevertheless, two factors tend to inhibit the use of private certification in many areas of health and safety. The first concerns the incentive to tell the truth. If private certification firms are in business to earn profits, which they do by charging firms for a certificate attesting the quality or safety of a product, which then allows firms to sell more of the product at any given price, will not firms have an incentive to bribe the certifier to obtain the certificate? And even if they do not, will people believe that they have not? Firms issuing false certificates might be sued, but that is expensive. Private individuals might be too poor to sue, and society might not wish to devote lots of resources to court cases.

Second, a private certification agency would have to decide on standards. What margin of error should be built into safety regulations? How safe must a drug be before it receives a certificate? These are questions on which society has views. They involve externalities and have important distributional implications. Even where society relies on private agencies to *monitor* regulations, it will probably want to set the standards itself.

Imposing standards

The public interest may be especially important when little is known about a product and where the consequences for society of any error may be catastrophic. Few believe that safety standards for nuclear power stations can be adequately determined within the private sector.

In imposing standards, governments increase the private cost of production by preventing firms from adopting the cost-minimizing techniques they would otherwise have employed. Sometimes the justification is that the government has access to better information than the private sector and judges the true social cost to be in excess of the private cost.

Frequently, however, the imposition of standards reflects

a pure value judgement based on distributional consider-ations. One particularly contentious area is the valuation of human life itself.

Politicians often claim that human life is beyond economic calculation and must be given absolute priority at any cost. For example, the UK government repeated this assurance after the Paddington rail disaster in October 1999. An economist will raise two points in reply. First, it is quite impossible to implement such an objective. It is simply too expensive in resources to attempt to eliminate *all* risks of premature death, and in fact we do not do so. Second, in making occupational and recreational choices, for example being a racing driver or going climbing, people do take risks. Society must ask how much more risk-averse it should be than the people it is trying to protect.

Thus, beyond a certain point the marginal social cost of further risk reduction will exceed the marginal social benefit. It will take an enormous effort to make the world just a little safer, and the resources might have been used elsewhere to greater effect. Zero risk does not make economic sense. Economists have long been calling for safety regulations to be subject to cost–benefit analysis. We need to know the costs of making the world a little safer, and we need to encourage society to decide how much it values the benefits.

However, society decides to value the benefit of saving human life, an efficient allocation would adopt health and safety regulations up to the point at which the marginal social cost of saving life by each and every means was equal to the marginal social benefit of saving life. By shying away from the 'unpleasant' task of spelling out the costs and benefits, society is likely to produce a very inefficient allocation in which the marginal costs and marginal benefits are very different in different activities.

Suppose we assume that each regulation is enforced up to the point at which the marginal cost and marginal benefit of saving life are equal *for that activity*. If we can measure the marginal cost directly, we can infer the implicit marginal benefit from saving life through that activity. Economists frequently complain that such calculations reveal very different implicit marginal benefits across activities, which is unsurprising when those responsible for safety standards in building, motoring, medicine, and other areas make no attempt to reach a common view of the marginal social benefit from saving life. For example, estimates for the implicit marginal social benefit from saving life in the UK range from £20 million in the case of building regulations introduced after the Ronan Point disaster to £50 for a rarely used test in pregnant women that might prevent some still-births.[5] Such wide disparities in the social marginal cost of life-saving suggest that society might make big efficiency gains by adopting an integrated approach to cost–benefit analysis of health and safety regulations.

---

[5] See C. Mooney, 'Human Life and Suffering', in D. W. Pearce (ed.), *The Valuation of Social Cost*, George Allen and Unwin.

SUMMARY

● Welfare economics deals with normative issues or value judgements. Its purpose is not to describe *how* the economy works but to assess *how well* it works.

● Horizontal equity is the equal treatment of equals, and vertical equity the unequal treatment of unequals. Equity is concerned with the distribution of welfare across people. The desirable degree of equity is a pure value judgement.

● A resource allocation is a complete description of what, how, and for whom goods are produced. To separate as far as possible the concepts of equity and efficiency, economists use Pareto efficiency. An allocation is Pareto-efficient if no reallocation of resources would make some people better off without making some people worse off.

If an allocation is inefficient it is possible to achieve a Pareto gain, making some people better off and none worse off. Many reallocations make some people better off and others worse off. We cannot say whether such changes are good or bad without making value judge-ments about the comparison of different people's welfare.

● For a given level of resources and a given technology, the economy has an infinite number of Pareto-efficient allocations which differ in the distribution of welfare across people. For example, every allocation that gives all output to one individual is Pareto-efficient. But there are many more allocations that are inefficient.

● Under strict conditions, competitive equilibrium is Pareto-efficient. Different initial distributions of human and physical capital across people generate different competitive equilibria corresponding to each possible Pareto-efficient allocation. When price-taking producers and consumers face the same prices, marginal costs and marginal benefits are equated to prices (by the individual actions of producers and consumers) and hence to each other.

● In practice, governments face a conflict between equity and efficiency. Redistributive taxation drives a wedge between prices paid by consumers (to which marginal benefits are equated) and prices received by producers (to which marginal costs are equated). Free market equilibrium will not equate marginal cost and marginal benefit and there will be inefficiency.

● Distortions occur whenever free market equilibrium does not equate marginal social cost and marginal social benefit. Distortions lead to inefficiency or market failure. Apart from taxes, there are three other important sources of distortions: imperfect competition (failure to set price equal to marginal cost), externalities (divergence between private and social costs or benefits), and other missing markets in connection with future goods, risky goods, or other informational problems.

● When only one market is distorted the first-best solution is to remove the distortion, thus achieving full efficiency. The first-best criterion relates only to allocative efficiency. Governments caring sufficiently about redistribution might still prefer inefficient allocations with greater vertical equity. However, when a distortion cannot be removed from one market it is not generally efficient to ensure that all other markets are distortion-free. The theory of the second best says that it is more efficient to spread inevitable distortions thinly over many markets than to concentrate their effects in a few markets.

● Production externalities occur when decisions by one producer affect the production costs of another producer directly, as when one firm pollutes another's water supply. Consumption externalities imply that one person's decisions affect another consumer's utility directly, as when my garden gives pleasure to the neighbours. Externalities shift indifference curves or production functions.

● Externalities lead to divergence between private and social costs or benefits because there is no implicit market

for the externality itself. When only a few people are involved, a system of property rights may establish the missing market. The direction of compensation will depend on who has the property rights. Either way, it achieves the efficient quantity of the externality at which marginal cost and marginal benefit are equated. The efficient solution is rarely a zero quantity of the externality. Transactions costs and the free-rider problem may prevent implicit markets being established. Equilibrium will then be inefficient.

● When externalities lead to market failure the government could set up the missing market by pricing the externality through taxes or subsidies. If it was straightforward to assess the efficient quantity of the externality and hence the correct tax or subsidy, and straightforward to monitor the quantities produced and consumed, such taxes or subsidies would allow the market to achieve an efficient resource allocation.

● In practice, governments often regulate externalities such as pollution or congestion by imposing standards that affect quantities directly rather than by using the tax system to affect production and consumption indirectly. Overall quantity standards may fail to equate the marginal cost of pollution reduction across different polluters, in which case the allocation will not be efficient. However, simple standards may use up less resources in monitoring and enforcement and may prevent disastrous outcomes when there is uncertainty.

● Moral hazard, adverse selection, and other informational problems prevent the development of a complete set of forward and contingent markets. Without these markets the price system cannot equate social marginal cost and benefit for future goods or risky activities.

● Incomplete information may lead to private choices which do not represent the best interests of individuals or society as a whole. Health, quality, and safety regulations are designed both to provide information and to express society's value judgements about intangibles such as life itself. By avoiding explicit consideration of social costs and benefits, government policy may be inconsistent in its implicit valuation of health or safety in different activities under regulation.

KEY TERMS

◆ Welfare economics 257

◆ Horizontal and vertical equity 258

◆ Pareto-efficiency 258

◆ Distortions 262

◆ First-best and second-best efficiency 264

◆ Externality 265

◆ Property rights 268

◆ Free-rider 269

REVIEW QUESTIONS

1 An economy has 10 units of goods to share out between two people. (x, y) denotes that the first person gets a quantity x and the second person a quantity y. For each of the following allocations say whether they are (i) efficient and (ii) equitable: (a) (10,0) (b) (7,2) (c) (5,5) (d) (3,6) (e) (0,10). What does 'equitable' mean? If you were making the choice, would you prefer allocation (d) to allocation (e)?

2 Suppose the equilibrium price of meals is £1 and of films £5. There is perfect competition and no externality. What can we say about (a) the relative benefit to consumers of a marginal film and a marginal meal?; (b) the relative marginal production cost of films and meals?; (c) the relative marginal product of variable factors in the film and meal industries? Hence explain why competitive equilibrium is Pareto efficient.

3 In deciding whether or not to drive your car during the rush hour, you think about the cost of petrol and the time of the journey. Do you slow other people down by driving in the rush hour? Is this an externality? Does this mean that too many or too few people drive cars in the rush hour? Would it make sense for city authorities to restrict commuter parking in cities during the day?

4 Explain how an economist might defend laws making it compulsory to wear seat belts in cars.

5 In 1885, 200 people died when the steam boiler exploded on a Mississippi river boat. This prompted Jeremiah Allen and three friends to form a private company offering to insure any boiler that they had inspected for safety. The idea of boiler inspections caught on and boiler explosion rates plummeted. (a) Would Jeremiah Allen's company have been so successful if it had certified boilers but not insured them as well? Explain. (b) Could this idea be carried over from boiler inspections to drug inspections? If not, why not?

6 (a) Why might society wish to ban drugs that neither help nor harm the diseases they are claimed to cure? (b) It is sometimes argued that regulatory bodies will be blamed for bad things that happen in spite of the regulations (e.g. a plane crash) but not blamed so much for good things that are prevented (e.g. the quick availability of a safe and useful drug) by stringent tests and regulations. Does this mean that regulatory bodies will tend to over-regulate the activities under their scrutiny?

7 Why is it inefficient for different government departments to have different rules of thumb about the marginal value of human life?

8 *Common fallacies* Show why the following statements are incorrect. (a) Irresponsible firms discharge toxic waste with no thought for the damage inflicted on others. Society should ban all such discharges. It would be much better off without them. (b) Anything governments can do the market can do better. (c) Anything the market can do the government can do better.

17 Taxes and government spending

LEARNING OUTCOMES

When you have finished this chapter, you should be able to:

- ● **Discuss types of government spending and the different motives for them**
- ● **Show why pure public goods cannot be provided by a market**
- ● **Distinguish average and marginal tax rates; and direct and indirect taxes**
- ● **Analyse tax incidence, and relate the size of a tax distortion to the elasticities of supply and demand of the commodity being taxed**
- ● **Show how taxes can compensate for externalities**
- ● **Explain what is meant by supply-side economics**
- ● **Develop the Laffer curve, and analyse why there is a limit to the maximum revenue that can be raised by any tax**
- ● **Discuss how mobility of people, capital, and products across political jurisdictions may limit economic sovereignty**

By the 1980s many people felt that the government had become too big. High government spending was pre-empting resources that could be used more productively in the private sector, high taxes were stifling private enterprise. Curtailing the complex system of government regulations, interventions, and subsidies would unleash private initiative and energy. These were not quack ideas that never made it in practice. Electorates in many countries turned to the political leaders who promised to implement these new policies. New Labour continues this approach in the UK.

This chapter is about government involvement in the economy. How much should the government raise in taxation? Are there good taxes and bad taxes? If taxes are needed to pay for government spending, why do we need government spending in the first place?

We begin with three tables that provide some historical perspective. Table 17-1 shows the scale of government spending over four decades. It is important to distinguish government spending on goods and services – schools, defence, the police, and so on – from government spending on *transfer payments*, such as social security, state pensions, and debt interest. Whereas spending on goods and services directly uses up factors of production that could otherwise be employed in the private sector, transfer payments do not directly pre-empt society's scarce resources. Rather, they

Table 17-1	UK government spending (% of GDP)		
Spending on	1956	1976	1999
Goods and services	20.7	25.9	20.8
Transfer payments	13.2	21.0	17.9
Total spending	33.9	46.9	38.7

Sources: ONS, *UK National Accounts*; HM Treasury, *Budget 1999*.

Table 17-2	UK income tax rates, 1978–2000		
Taxable income (000s of 1999 £)	Marginal tax rate (%) 78–79	86–87	99–00
1 500	34	29	10
5 000	34	29	20
10 000	34	29	20
20 000	45	29	20
30 000	50	40	40
40 000	70	50	40
70 000	83	60	40

Sources: HMSO, *Financial Statement & Budget Report*; ONS, *Budget 1999*.
Note: Taxable income after deducting allowances. In 1999–2000 a single person's allowance was £4335.

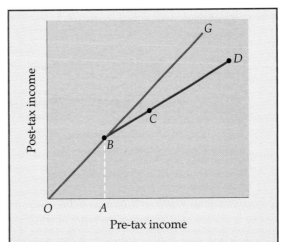

The 45 per cent line *OG* shows zero taxes or transfers so that pre-tax and post-tax income coincide. With an allowance *OA* then a constant marginal tax rate *t*, the post-tax income schedule is *OBCD*. The slope depends only on the marginal tax rate [on *BCD* it is $(1 − t)$]. The average tax rate at any point *D* is the slope of *OD*. A tax is progressive if the average tax rate rises with pre-tax income.

Figure 17-1   A progressive income tax

transfer purchasing power from consumers paying taxes to consumers in receipt of transfer payments or subsidies.

Table 17-1 shows that between 1956 and 1976 there was an increase in the share of national resources directly pre-empted by the government through spending on goods and services. Successive governments have reversed this trend. The second row of Table 17-1 shows government spending on transfer payments. The last row shows the turnaround in total spending since 1976.

One reason for trying to reduce government spending is to make room for tax cuts. Table 17-2 picks out the most controversial aspect of the tax system, the *marginal rate of income tax*.

The **marginal rate of income tax** is the percentage taken by the government of the last pound that an individual earns. In contrast, the **average** tax rate is the percentage of total income that the government takes in income tax.

A *progressive* tax structure is one in which the average tax rate rises with an individual's income level. The government takes proportionately more from the rich than from the poor. A *regressive* tax structure is one in which the average tax rate falls as income level rises, taking proportionately less from the rich.

Table 17-2 shows that, as in most countries, the UK has a progressive income tax structure. Figure 17-1 explains why. We plot pre-tax income on the horizontal axis and post-tax income on the vertical axis. The line *OG* with a slope of 45 degrees would correspond to no taxes. A pre-tax income *OA* on the horizontal axis corresponds to the same post-tax income *OA* on the vertical axis. Now suppose there is an income tax with a tax allowance *OA*. The first *OA* pounds of income are untaxed. If the marginal tax rate on taxable income is constant, individuals face a schedule such a

OBCD. The individual gets to keep only a constant fraction of each pound of pre-tax income above *OA*. The higher the marginal tax rate the flatter the portion *BC* of the schedule.

How do we calculate the average tax rate at a point such as *D*? We join up *OD*. The flatter the slope of this line the higher the average tax rate. Hence, even with a constant marginal tax rate and a constant slope of the portion *BC* of the tax schedule, the presence of an initial tax allowance makes the tax structure progressive. The higher an individual's gross income, the smaller is the tax allowance as a percentage of this gross income so the larger is the percentage of total income on which the individual is paying tax.

But Table 17-2 shows that *marginal* tax rates may also rise with income. As individuals move into higher tax bands they may pay higher marginal tax rates and move on to even flatter portions of the tax schedule. The average tax rate now rises sharply with income.

Table 17-2 shows that UK marginal tax rates fell substantially, especially for the very rich. A millionaire paying an 83 per cent tax rate on all taxable income except the first £70 000 in 1978 was paying only 40 per cent in 1999.

Table 17-3 shows a worldwide move to cut tax rates, especially for the very rich. Were the tax cuts designed to make the rich richer? Or was their purpose to revive hard work and enterprise? If so, will they work? These questions go to the heart of the current debate and form the background to much of the discussion of this chapter.

17-1 Taxation and government spending

Table 17-1 shows that government spending, and the taxation that finances it, are now 39 per cent of national output. Table 17-4 shows the composition of government spending and revenue in 1998.

£161 billion, almost half of total government spending, went on transfer payments such as unemployment benefit and debt interest. Of the remaining £167.9 billion spent directly on goods and services, the most important spending categories were health, defence, and education.

Why is the government directly involved in providing defence, schools, and health services? How much of each should be provided? Would it make sense for these activities to be provided by the private sector in the same way as haircuts and cars? If refuse collection can be 'privatized', why not defence?

Table 17-4 shows that most government spending is financed through taxation. The most important taxes are income tax and expenditure taxes such as value added tax (VAT). Since state provision of retirement pensions is included on the expenditure side under transfer payments, the pension contributions under the National Insurance Scheme must be included on the revenue side.

Against this background, we begin by discussing the reasons for government spending. Then we ask how spending should be financed. Are there good and bad taxes? The answer depends on the criteria of efficiency and equity that we developed in the last chapter.

17-2 The government in the market economy

How do we justify government spending in a market economy? We begin with public goods.

Public goods

A **private good**, if consumed by one person, cannot be consumed by another person.

Ice cream is a private good. If you eat an ice cream it prevents anyone else from eating the same ice cream. For any given supply of ice cream, your consumption reduces the quantity available for others to consume. Most goods are private goods.

A **public good**, even if consumed by one person, can still be consumed by other people.

Clean air and defence are examples of public goods. If the air is pollution-free, your consumption of it does not interfere with our consumption of it. If the Navy is patrolling coastal waters, your consumption of national defence does not affect our quantity of national defence. In fact, for a *pure public good* we must all necessarily consume

Table 17-3	Income tax reform 1975–90 (marginal tax rates, %)			
	Initial rate		Top rate	
	1975	1990	1975	1990
Holland	27	35	71	60
France	5	5	60	57
Germany	22	19	56	53
Italy	10	10	72	50
Japan	10	10	75	50
Australia	20	24	65	49
Sweden	35	25	56	42
UK	35	25	83	40
USA	14	15	70	33
New Zealand	19	24	56	33

Source: J. Kay, 'Tax Policy: A Survey', *Economic Journal*, 1990.

Table 17-4 Expenditure and revenue of UK central and local government 1998			
Expenditure	£ billion	Revenue	£ billion
Health	46.3	Income tax	86.5
Education	38.1	Corporation tax	30.8
Defence	24.2	Expenditure taxes	103.6
Other current spending	45.0	Social security contributions	54.1
Capital investment	14.3	Taxes on capital	2.0
All goods and services	167.9	Council tax, rates, fees	27.9
Social security	106.1	Other revenue	26.9
Debt interest	30.0	TOTAL REVENUE	331.8
Other transfer payments	25.6	NET SURPLUS	2.2
All transfer payments	161.7		
TOTAL EXPENDITURE	329.6		

Source: ONS, *UK National Accounts*.

the same quantity, namely, whatever quantity is supplied in the aggregate. We may of course get different amounts of utility if our tastes differ, but we all consume the same quantity.

The key aspects of public goods are (1) that it is technically possible for one person to consume without reducing the amount available for someone else, and (2) the impossibility of excluding anyone from consumption except at a prohibitive cost. A football match could be watched by a lot of people, especially if it is televised, without reducing the quantity consumed by any individual; but *exclusion* is possible – the ground holds only so many, and the club can refuse to allow the game to be televised. The interesting issues arise when, as with national defence, exclusion of certain individuals from consumption is impossible.

Free-riders   In the last chapter we introduced the *free-rider problem* when discussing why bribes and compensation for externalities might not occur. Public goods are especially vulnerable to the free-rider problem if they are supplied by

the private sector. Since you get the same quantity of national defence as everyone else, *whether or not you pay for it*, you never purchase national defence in a private market. Everybody else would adopt similar reasoning, and no defence would be demanded even if we all wanted defence.

Public goods are like a strong externality. If you buy defence everyone else gets the benefits. Since marginal private and social benefits diverge, private markets will not produce the socially efficient quantity. There is a case for government intervention to equate marginal social cost and marginal social benefit.

The marginal social benefit   Suppose the public good is the purity of the public water supply. The more infected the water, the more likely that everyone will be hit by an epidemic of cholera or some other disease. Figure 17-2 supposes there are two people. The first person's demand curve for water purity is D_1D_1. Each point on the demand curve shows what the individual would pay for the last unit of purer water. It shows the marginal benefit to the individual. D_2D_2 shows the marginal benefit of purer water to the second individual.

Curve DD gives the marginal social benefit of purer water. At each output level for the public good, we *vertically* sum the marginal benefit of each individual to get the social marginal benefit. Thus at the output Q the social marginal benefit is $P = P_1 + P_2$. We sum vertically at *a given quantity* because everyone consumes the same quantity of a public good.

Figure 17-2 also shows the marginal cost of producing the public good. If there are no production externalities the marginal private cost and marginal social cost of production coincide. The socially efficient output of the public good is at Q^*, where the marginal social benefit equals the marginal social cost.

What would happen if the good were privately produced and marketed? Person 1 might pay P_1 to have a quantity Q produced by a competitive supplier pricing at marginal cost. At the output Q the price P_1 just equals the marginal private benefit which person 1 derives from the last unit of the public good. Would person 2 pay to have the output of the public good increased beyond Q? No. Because it is a public good, person 2 cannot be excluded from consuming the output Q which person 1 has commissioned. But, at the output Q, person 2's marginal private benefit is only P_2, which is less than the current price P_1. Person 2 would not pay the higher price necessary to induce a competitive supplier to expand production beyond Q. Person 2 is a free-

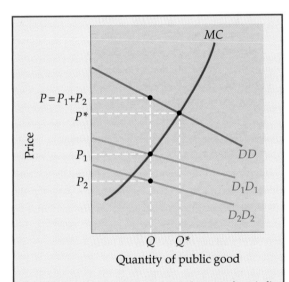

D_1D_1 and D_2D_2 are the separate demand curves of two individuals and show the marginal private benefit of the last unit of the public good to each individual. What is the social marginal benefit of the last unit to the group as a whole? Since both individuals consume whatever quantity of the good is produced, we must add up *vertically* the price each is prepared to pay for the last unit. At the output Q the marginal social benefit is thus $P_1 + P_2$. The curve DD showed the marginal social benefit and is obtained by vertically adding the demand curves of the two individuals. If MC is the private and social marginal cost of producing the public good the socially efficient output is Q^* at which social marginal cost and social marginal benefit are equal.

Figure 17-2   A pure public good

rider enjoying person 1's purchase Q. And the total quantity privately produced and consumed in a competitive market lies below the socially efficient quantity Q*.

Revelation of preferences By constructing the marginal social benefit curve DD, the government can decide how much of the public good it is socially efficient to produce. But how does the government find out the individual demand curves that must be vertically added to get DD? If people's payments for the good are related to their individual demand curves everyone has an incentive to lie because of the free-rider problem. People will understate how much they value the good in order to reduce their own payments, just as in a private market.

Conversely, if payments are divorced from the question of how much people would like, people will overstate their private valuations. We are all for safer streets if we do not have to contribute to the cost. In practice, democracies try to resolve this problem through elections of governments. Different parties offer different quantities of public goods together with a statement of how the money will be raised through the tax system. By asking the question, 'How much would you like, given that everyone will be charged for the cost of providing public goods?' society can come closer to providing the efficient quantities of public goods. However, since there are only a few parties competing in the election and many different aspects of government on which they offer a position, this is a crude way to elicit people's view of how much of any particular public good should be provided.

Government production The economist's definition of public goods relies solely on the fact that everyone consumes the same quantity. The free-rider problem implies that private markets will not produce the socially efficient level. There is a case for government intervention on efficiency grounds. This merely says that the government must determine how much is produced. It does not imply that the government must produce the goods itself. Public goods are not necessarily produced by the government.

National defence is a public good and is also produced largely within the public or government sector. We have few private armies. On the other hand, street-sweeping, though a public good, can be subcontracted to private producers, even if local government determines its quantity and pays for it out of local tax revenue. Conversely, state hospitals involve public sector production of private goods. One person's hip replacement operation certainly prevents the busy surgeon from doing something else at the same time.

In the next chapter we examine why the public sector may wish to produce private goods. Whether public goods need be produced by the public sector depends not on their consumption characteristics, on which our definition of public good relies, but on their production characteristics. There is nothing special about street sweeping, and it can as easily be produced by the public or the private sector. In contrast, armies and navies rely on discipline and secrecy. Generals and admirals may believe, and society may agree, that offences against these regulations should receive unusual penalties which would not be generally sanctioned in private firms. Few people believe that insubordination is an important offence for street sweepers. Hence it may make more sense for soldiers to be in the public sector than street sweepers.

Transfer payments and income redistribution

The government spends money on public goods because there is a market failure when public goods are left to private markets. Thus the motivation for this intervention is social efficiency. In contrast, government spending on transfer payments is primarily concerned with *equity* and *income redistribution*. By spending money on the unemployed, the old, and the poor, the government seeks to ensure that the distribution of income and welfare that a totally free market economy would otherwise have produced is at least truncated: there is a minimum standard of living below which no citizen should fall. The specification of this standard is a pure value judgement.

Where does the money come from to pay the poor and the disadvantaged? Primarily from those who can most afford to pay. Table 17-2 shows that the income tax system in the UK is *progressive*. Increasing marginal tax rates on income ensure that each individual's average tax rate, the proportion of total income paid in taxes, increases with income. Taken as a whole, the tax and transfer system takes money from the rich and gives to the poor. The poor receive not merely the direct financial transfer in the form of transfer payments such as supplementary benefit, but also the consumption of public goods that have been paid for by income taxes raised from the rich.

Not only is the amount of redistribution to be undertaken a pure value judgement on which different individuals and different political parties will disagree, but there is an inevitable trade-off between the competing objectives of efficiency and equity. To undertake more redistribution the government will have to increase tax rates, thereby driving a larger wedge between the price paid by the purchaser and the price received by the seller of the good or service. Since the price system achieves Pareto efficiency by inducing each individual to equate marginal cost or marginal benefit to the price received or paid, and hence to one another, taxes are generally distortionary and tend to reduce efficiency.

In Table 17-3 we saw that governments succeeded in reducing marginal tax rates, especially for the very rich. Opponents argued that the objective as well as the consequence of the legislation was to increase the after-tax incomes of the rich at the expense of the poor. Government argued that reducing distortions in the labour market by cutting income tax would lead to efficiency gains that would far outweigh the valuation that society should put on a more equal income distribution. If society's resources could be used to make more output, even the poor might be better off in the long run.

Merit goods and bads

Merit goods (bads) are goods that society thinks everyone ought to have (ought not to have) regardless of whether they are wanted by each individual.

Examples of merit goods are education and health. Merit bads are products such as cigarettes. Since society places a different value on these goods from the value placed on them by the individual, individual choice within a free market leads to a different allocation from the one that society wishes to see.

There are two distinct reasons for merit goods. The first is a version of the externality argument examined in the previous chapter. If more education raises the productivity not merely of an individual worker but of all other workers with whom this worker co-operates, there is a production externality that the individual does not take into account in choosing how much education to purchase. If individuals demand too little education, society should encourage the provision of education. Free schooling to ensure a minimum level of education, communication, and social interaction might be one way to achieve this.

Conversely, if people take account of the costs to them-

selves but not the burden on state hospitals in deciding whether or not to smoke and damage their health, society may regard smoking as a merit bad to be discouraged. We shall shortly see how the tax system, in this case a tax on cigarettes, may offset externalities that individuals fail to take into account.

The second aspect of merit goods is where society believes that individuals no longer act in their own best interests. Addiction to drugs, tobacco, or gambling are examples. Economists rarely subscribe to the value judgement of paternalism. The function of government intervention is less to tell people what they ought to like than to allow them better to achieve what they already like. However, the government will sometimes have more information or be in a better position to take a decision. Much as some people hate going to school, they will frequently be glad afterwards that they were made to do so.

Thus the government may spend money on compulsory education or compulsory vaccination because it recognizes that otherwise individuals act in a way they will subsequently regret.

17-3 The principles of taxation

This section is in three parts. First we consider different taxes through which the government can raise revenue. Then we consider again the equity implications of taxation. Finally, we examine the efficiency implications of taxation.

Variety of taxes

Governments can raise tax revenue only if they can identify the activities on which the tax rates apply. Before sophisticated records of income or sales were ever kept, governments raised most of their revenue through customs duties and road tolls, the two places where transactions could be easily monitored. Income tax in peacetime was not introduced in the UK until the 1840s, and VAT not until the 1970s. We briefly outline the main taxes shown in Table 17-5, grouped under three headings.

Table 17-5 Sources of tax revenue (% of total taxes)

Taxes	USA	UK	Germany	France	Sweden	Japan
Direct	45	38	30	22	42	34
Indirect	29	43	30	34	32	28
Social security contributions	25	18	40	43	26	36
Capital	1	1	0	1	0	2

Source: ONS, *Economic Trends*, March 1999.

Direct taxes are taxes on income, **indirect taxes** are taxes on spending, and **wealth taxes** are taxes on the value of assets.

Direct taxes Individuals pay income tax on earnings from labour, rents, dividends, and interest. In Chapter 15 we saw that the return on an asset is not just the dividend or interest payment but also the capital gain. Although many economists would argue that capital gains are as much income as the dividend component of the return on an asset, in practice the Inland Revenue assesses and taxes capital gains separately. National insurance contributions by individuals are also a form of direct personal taxation.

Companies pay corporation tax calculated on their taxable profits after allowance for interest payments and depreciation. They also make a national insurance contribution on behalf of their employees.

Indirect taxes Indirect taxes are taxes levied on expenditure on goods and services. The most important tax is value added tax (VAT), which is effectively a retail sales tax. Whereas a sales tax is collected only at the point of final sale to the consumer, VAT is collected at different stages of the production process.

Suppose a firm mines iron ore and converts it into £200 worth of high-grade steel, which is then sold to a car producer. The car producer converts the steel into a car costing £3200. A simple sales tax levied at 15 per cent would raise the cost to the consumer to £3200 + £480 (15 per cent of £3200) or £3680. In contrast, VAT works as follows. The steel firm has a value added or net output of £200 on which it pays 15 per cent or £30 in tax. Passing the tax on to the car producer, the steel is sold for £230. The car producer has a value added or net output of £3000 and pays 15 per cent or £450 in tax. Since the car firm paid £230 for the steel, the final price to the consumer is £230 + £3000 + £450 = £3680. As far as the consumer is concerned this is just the same as a 15 per cent sales tax.

This example makes it seem that the consumer price is raised by the full amount of the tax. But a higher consumer price will reduce the quantity demanded. In turn this will move producers back down their marginal cost curves and alter the net-of-tax price producers require. Later in this section we show how to analyse these induced effects to determine how the burden of the tax is ultimately divided between producers and consumers.

Revenue from VAT is supplemented by other indirect taxes including special duties on tobacco and alcohol,

licence fees for motor cars and televisions, and customs duties on imports.

Wealth taxes In the UK there are two taxes on wealth *per se* rather than on the income derived from wealth. The first is the tax on property values, the main source of revenue for local government. The second is capital transfer tax, which applies to transfers of wealth between individuals, whether as gifts during life or as inheritances after death.

How does the UK tax structure compare with that in other countries? Table 17-5 shows data for several advanced countries. The most notable feature of the UK tax system appears to be its low reliance on social security contributions. Table 17-5 also suggests that the UK relies quite heavily on indirect taxes on spending.

Tax revenue is necessary to pay for government expenditure. We now assess the UK tax system against our two welfare criteria, equity and efficiency.

How to tax fairly

The last chapter gave two notions of equity: *horizontal equity*, or the equal treatment of equals, and *vertical equity*, the redistribution from the 'haves' to the 'have-nots'.

In Table 17-2 we showed that income tax is progressive.

In taking proportionately more from the rich than from the less well off, income tax reflects the principle of **ability to pay**.

The principle of ability to pay thus reflects a concern about vertical equity.

A second principle is sometimes applied in discussing the extent to which unequal people should be treated unequally.

The **benefits principle** argues that people who receive more than their share of public spending should pay more than their share of tax revenues.

Car users should pay more towards public roads than people without a car should pay.

However, the benefits principle often conflicts directly with the principle of ability to pay. If people who are most vulnerable to unemployment must pay the highest contributions to the government unemployment insurance scheme, it is difficult to redistribute income, wealth, or welfare. If the main objective is vertical equity, the ability to pay principle must usually take precedence.

Although UK income tax is progressive, it is the entire structure of taxes, transfers, and public spending that we must examine before we can judge how much the government is effectively redistributing from the rich to the poor.

Two factors make the entire structure more progressive than an examination of income tax alone would suggest. First, transfer payments actually give money to the poor. The old get pensions, the unemployed get unemployment benefit, and, as a final safety net, anyone whose income falls below a certain minimum is entitled to supplementary benefit. Second, the state provides public goods that can be consumed by the poor, even if they have not paid any taxes to finance these goods. In addition to pure public goods, such as defence, the state also makes free provision of certain goods, such as parks and swimming pools, which have part of the characteristics of a pure public good. Although the whole population cannot squeeze into a park, quite a few people can enjoy its amenities without spoiling the enjoyment of others. Since the rich tend to sit in their own gardens, public parks help redistribute enjoyment to the poor.

As against these progressive elements of the tax, transfer, and spending structure, there are some *regressive* elements that take proportionately more from the poor. Beer and tobacco taxes are huge earners for the government. Yet the poor spend a much higher proportion of their income on these goods than do the rich. Such taxes reduce the effectiveness of the tax, transfer and spending structure in redistributing from the rich to the poor.

Tax incidence

The **incidence** of a tax measures the final tax burden on different people once we allow for all effects of the tax.

The ultimate effect of a tax can be very different from its apparent effect. Thus to see how taxes (or subsidies) alter people's spending power and welfare, we need to examine tax incidence in more detail.

Figure 17-3 shows the market for labour. *DD* is the demand curve and *SS* the supply curve. In the absence of an income tax (a tax on wages), the labour market will be in equilibrium at *E*.

Now suppose the government imposes an income tax. If we measure the gross wage on the vertical axis, the demand curve *DD* is unaltered since it is the comparison of the gross wage with the marginal value product of labour that determines the quantity of labour demanded by firms. Workers' preferences or attitudes are also unchanged, but it is the wage net of tax that workers compare with the marginal value of their leisure in deciding how much labour to supply. Thus, although *SS* continues to show the labour supply curve in terms of the after-tax wage, we must draw in the higher schedule *SS'* to show the supply of labour in

terms of the gross or pre-tax wage. The vertical distance between *SS'* and *SS* measures the amount of tax being paid on earnings from the last hour's work.

DD and *SS'* show the behaviour of firms and workers at any gross wage. The new equilibrium is at *E'*. The gross wage is W' at which firms demand *L'*. The vertical distance between *A'* and *E'* measures the tax being paid on earnings from the last hour of work. Thus the after-tax wage is W" at which workers are happy to supply a quantity of hours *L'*.

Relative to the original equilibrium, the tax on wages has raised the pre-tax wage to W', but lowered the after-tax wage to W". It has raised the wage that firms pay but lowered the take-home wage for workers.

The **tax wedge** is the gap between the price paid by the buyer and the price received by the seller.

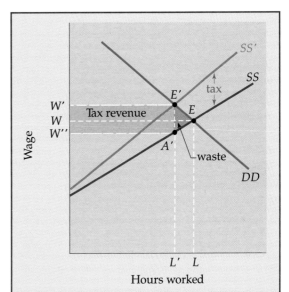

With no tax, equilibrium is at *E* and the wage is W. A wage tax raises the gross wage paid by firms above the net wage received by workers. Measuring gross wages on the vertical axis, the demand curve *DD* is unaltered by the imposition of the tax. Firms demand labour to equate the gross wage to the marginal value product of labour. SS continues to show labour supply, but as a function of the *net* wage. To get labour supply in terms of the gross wage we draw the new supply curve *SS'*. *SS'* lies vertically above SS by a distance reflecting the tax on the last hour worked. The new equilibrium is at *E'*. The hourly wage paid by firms is W' but the net wage received by workers is W". The vertical distance *A'E'* shows the tax rate. Whether the government *collects* the tax from firms or from workers, the *incidence* of the tax is the same. It falls partly on firms, who pay a higher gross wage W', and partly on workers, who receive the lower net wage W". The area of pure waste *A'E'E* is discussed in the text.

Figure 17-3 A tax on wages

The incidence of the tax has fallen on *both* firms and workers even though, for administrative convenience, the tax may be collected directly from workers.

The lesson from Figure 17-3 is an important one: the incidence or burden of a tax cannot be established by looking at who actually hands over the money to the government. Taxes usually alter equilibrium prices and quantities and these induced effects must also be taken into account. However, we can draw one very general conclusion. The more inelastic the supply curve and the more elastic the demand curve, the more the final incidence will fall on the seller rather than the purchaser.

Figure 17-4 depicts the extreme case in which the supply curve is completely inelastic. In the absence of a tax, equilibrium is at E and the wage is W. Since the vertical supply curve SS implies that a fixed quantity of hours L will be supplied whatever the after-tax wage, the imposition of a tax on wages leads to a new equilibrium at A'. Only if the pre-tax wage is unchanged will firms demand the quantity L that is supplied. Hence the entire incidence falls on the workers.

To check you have grasped the idea of incidence, draw for yourself a market with an elastic supply curve and an inelastic demand curve. Show that the incidence of a tax will now fall mainly on the purchaser.[1]

Taxation, efficiency, and waste

We have been considering the equity implications of a tax. But we must also think about the efficiency implications of a tax. We can use Figure 17-3 again.

Before the tax is imposed, labour market equilibrium is at E. The wage W measures both the marginal social benefit of the last hour of work and its marginal social cost. The demand curve DD tells us the marginal value product of labour, the extra benefit society could have from extra goods produced. The supply curve SS tells us the marginal value of the leisure being sacrificed in order to work another hour, the marginal social cost of extra work. At E marginal social cost and benefit are equal, which is socially efficient.

---

[1] By now you may be wondering whether we always show the effect of a tax as a shift in the supply curve. We do, provided we wish to measure the pre-tax price of the good or service on the vertical axis. If we want to measure the after-tax price on the vertical axis, the effect of the tax will be to shift not the supply curve but the demand curve. In Figures 17-3 and 17-4, you can see that in terms of the after-tax wage, the demand curve must shift down until it passes through the point A'. The distance between A' and E still measures the tax and we get exactly the same conclusions as before.

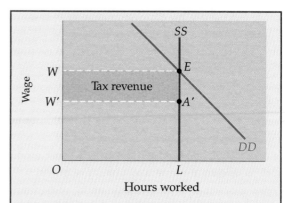

If the supply curve SS is vertical, a tax $A'E$ per unit leaves the quantity L unaffected. Since the demand curve DD is unaltered, the tax has no effect on the pre-tax wage rate. The full incidence of the tax falls on workers whose after-tax wage is reduced by the full amount of the tax.

Figure 17-4   Taxing a factor in inelastic supply

When the tax is imposed, the new equilibrium is at E'. The tax $A'E'$ increases the wage to firms to W' but reduces the after-tax wage for workers to W''. But there is an additional tax burden or deadweight loss that is pure waste. It is the triangle $A'E'E''$. By reducing the quantity of hours from L to L', the tax causes society to stop using hours on which the marginal social benefit, the height of the demand curve DD, exceeds the marginal social cost, the height of the supply curve SS. By driving a wedge between the wage firms pay and the wage workers receive, the tax induces a distortion destroying the efficiency of free market equilibrium.

Must taxes be distortionary?

Government needs tax revenue to pay for public goods and to make transfer payments. Must taxes create distortions and lead to inefficiency in Figure 17-3?

Figure 17-4 shows what happens when a tax is levied but the supply is completely inelastic. There is no change in the equilibrium quantity. Since the quantity is unchanged, there is no distortionary triangle or deadweight burden. The equilibrium quantity remains the socially efficient quantity.

We can make this into a general principle. When either the supply or the demand curve for a good or service is very inelastic, the imposition of a tax will lead only to a small change in quantity. Hence the deadweight burden triangle must be small. Given that the government must raise some tax revenue, the smallest amount of total waste will be achieved when the goods that are most inelastic in supply or demand are taxed most heavily.

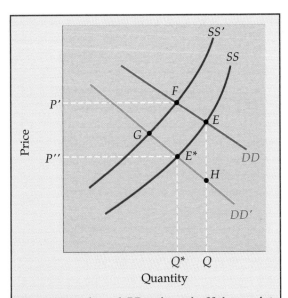

Given private demand *DD* and supply *SS* free market equilibrium is at *E* with a quantity *Q*. With a negative consumption externality, the social marginal benefit is *DD'* lying below *DD*. *E** is the socially efficient point at which output is *Q**. At this output the marginal externality is *E*F*. By levying a tax of exactly *E*F* per unit, the government can shift the private supply curve from *SS* to *SS'* leading to a new equilibrium at *F* at which the socially efficient quantity *Q** is produced and the deadweight burden of the externality *E*HE* is eliminated.

Figure 17-5   Taxes to offset externalities

This principle finds practical expression in the UK tax system. The most heavily taxed commodities are alcohol and tobacco. Alcohol and tobacco have an inelastic demand.

So far, we have discussed the taxes that would do least harm to the allocative efficiency of the economy. Sometimes the government can levy taxes which actually improve efficiency and reduce waste. The most important example is when externalities exist.

Cigarette smokers pollute the air for other people but take no account of this in deciding how much to smoke. They give rise to a harmful consumption externality. Figure 17-5 shows the supply curve *SS* of cigarette producers. Since there are no production externalities, *SS* is also the marginal social cost curve. *DD* is the private demand curve showing the marginal benefit of cigarettes to smokers. Because there is a harmful consumption externality, the marginal social benefit *DD'* of cigarette consumption is lower than *DD*.

In the absence of a tax, free market equilibrium is at *E*, but there is over-consumption of cigarettes. The socially efficient quantity is *Q** since marginal social cost and marginal social benefit are equated at *E**. Suppose the

government levies a tax, equal to the vertical distance *E*F*, on each packet of cigarettes. With the tax-inclusive price on the vertical axis, the demand curve *DD* is unaffected, but the supply curve shifts up to *SS'*. Each point on *SS'* then allows producers to receive the corresponding net-of-tax price on *SS*.

After the tax is introduced, equilibrium is at the point *F*. The socially efficient quantity *Q** is produced and consumed. Consumers pay the price *P'* and producers receive the price *P"* after tax has been paid at the rate *E*F* per unit.

Only the tax rate *E*F* per unit guides the free market to the efficient allocation. A lower tax rate (including zero) leads to too much consumption and production of cigarettes. A higher tax rate than *E*F* will move consumers further up their demand curve and lead to under-consumption and under-production.

Why must the tax rate be exactly *E*F* if the efficient quantity is to be achieved? Because this is exactly the amount of the externality on the last unit when the efficient quantity *Q** is produced. By levying a tax at precisely this rate, consumers are induced to behave as if they took account of the externality, though in fact they take account only of the tax-inclusive price.

Whenever externalities induce distortions, the government can improve efficiency by levying taxes. The fact that alcohol and tobacco have harmful externalities provides a reason for taxing them heavily.

17-4 Taxation and supply-side economics

Many Western countries became disenchanted with the extent of government involvement in the economy. In part, it was felt that governments were spending too much. Resources used to produce goods and services for the government cannot be used to make goods in the private sector. We have more to say about this in the next chapter. However, the major objection to high government expenditure seems to have been the need for correspondingly high levels of revenue collection. Table 17-3 reminds us that some government expenditure is financed by borrowing. In Part 4 we examine the argument that high borrowing leads to high inflation, high interest rates, or both. For the moment we ignore government borrowing and consider the argument that high taxation to pay for high spending necessarily strangles the economy.

Suppose the government adopts a less ambitious spending programme and is therefore able to reduce income tax rates. What will be the consequences?

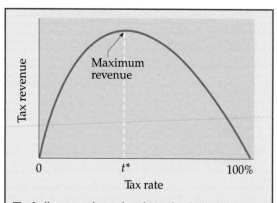

The Laffer curve shows the relationship between tax rates and tax revenue. Moderate tax rates raise some revenue. Beyond t^*, higher tax rates reduce revenue because disincentive effects greatly reduce the supply of the quantity being taxed. At 100 per cent tax rate, supply and revenue will be zero again.

Figure 17-6 The Laffer curve

First, by spending less on goods and services, the government will free some resources for use by the private sector. If it were true that the private sector uses resources more productively than the public sector, the transfer of resources might directly produce more output. The total supply of goods and services would rise. Whether or not the private sector does use resources more productively than the government remains a contentious issue.

What about the effects of lower tax rates? Figure 17-3 suggests that income taxes introduce a distortion that leads to a level of work that is socially inefficient. With lower taxes and a smaller distortion there would be a lower deadweight burden. Since the distortion leads to a level of work that is lower than the socially efficient amount, cutting income taxes would also increase the amount of work done in the economy.

How large could this effect be? It all depends on the elasticity of labour supply. The more inelastic the labour supply, the lower is the distortion introduced by any particular income tax rate. When labour supply is completely inelastic as in Figure 17-4, income tax does not induce any distortion at all and there will be no allocative gain in reducing income tax rates.

In Chapter 12 we showed that an increase in the after-tax wage (as for example when income tax rates are cut) will have a substitution effect, tending to make people work longer hours, but an income effect, tending to make them work fewer hours. With higher after-tax wages it takes fewer hours to earn any given target income. Hence we argued that, for people already in work, changes in after-tax wages have only a small effect on hours of work supplied. Then we showed that increasing the after-tax wage *would* encourage labour force participation by those not currently in the labour force. Hence, taking hours and participation together, the supply curve of labour input (hours times people) will not be completely vertical. Cutting income tax *will* increase the supply of labour input, chiefly by attracting new workers into the labour force. But the total effect on labour supply might not be as large as some proponents of tax cuts believe.

In contrast, the tax cut enthusiasts believe that income tax is a major distortion and labour supply is very elastic. The socially efficient quantity of labour input would then be much larger than the equilibrium level under current tax rates. One illustration of this view is the famous Laffer curve, named after one of President Reagan's most influential advisers.

The **Laffer curve** shows how much tax revenue is raised at each possible tax rate.

Suppose that all government tax revenue was raised through income tax. Figure 17-6 shows that with a zero tax rate the government would raise zero revenue. At the opposite extreme, with a 100 per cent income tax rate, there would be no point working and again tax revenue would be zero. Beginning from a zero rate, a small increase in the tax rate will yield some tax revenue. Initially revenue rises with the tax rate, but beyond the tax rate t^* higher taxes have major disincentive effects on work effort and revenue falls.

Professor Laffer's idea was that many 'big government–big tax' countries are now at tax rates above t^*. If so, tax cuts would be the miracle cure. The government would actually raise *more* revenue by cutting taxes. By reducing the tax distortion and increasing the amount of work *a lot*, lower taxes would be more than compensated by the extra work and incomes to which the tax rates were applied.

It is not the shape of the Laffer curve that is in dispute. Rather, what many professional economists have disputed is that these economies do *in fact* have tax rates above t^*. Most economists' reading of the empirical evidence is that our economies lie to the left of t^*. Cutting income tax rates may eliminate some of the deadweight burden of distortionary taxation, but governments should probably expect their tax revenue to decline if such policies are put into effect. Hence, if governments do wish to reduce tax rates without adding to government borrowing it is essential that they reduce their spending.

17-5 Local government

Thus far we have been chiefly interested in the principles of central government. In this section we examine the economics of local government. Local government expenditure may cover a variety of things, from sweeping the streets to providing local schooling. In turn this must be financed through taxes. Some of these taxes will be local, but some will come from central government revenue raised through the national tax system. Finally, local government is responsible for some types of regulation, for example land use or *zoning* laws.

Economic principles

Why don't we make central government responsible for everything? First, diversity matters. People are different and don't want to be treated the same. Civic pride is necessarily local. Second, people feel that central government is remote from their particular needs. Even if central government paid attention to local considerations, it would find it hard to do so efficiently.

We turn now to two important models of local government. The first is the Tiebout model.[2] This model emphasizes diversity. Some people want a lot of local expenditure on public services and are prepared to pay high local taxes; others want to pay lower local taxes even though this means lower public services. If all local governments are the same, everyone is unhappy with the compromise. The Tiebout model is sometimes called the *invisible foot*: people will cluster in the area providing the package of spending and taxes they want. The invisible foot brings about an efficient allocation of resources through competition between local governments.

In practice, the invisible foot is sometimes a very imperfect incentive structure. First, it may be hard to move between local authorities. For example, being born in a neighbourhood may entitle you to a higher place in the queue for housing provided by that local authority. Second, if much of local authority revenue comes from central government, the levels of spending and taxes may be insensitive to the wishes of local residents.

Earlier in the chapter, we stressed the distinction between efficiency and equity. Even if the invisible foot led to efficiency, it might also lead to inequity. The rich are likely to cluster together in suburbs. Then they pass zoning laws specifying a minimum size for a house and its garden. This makes it impossible for the poor to move to that neighbourhood. By forming an exclusive club, the rich ensure that their taxes do not go to supporting the poor. And the poor get stuck with one another in inner-city areas whose governments face the biggest social needs but the smallest local tax base.

The Tiebout model assumes that residents mainly consume the public services provided by their own local authority. But when each unit of local government is responsible for a small geographical area, this may be a bad assumption. If an inner-city supplies free art galleries, financed out of taxes on inner-city inhabitants, the rich still come in from the suburbs to make use of these facilities. Conversely, inner-city inhabitants spend their Sundays enjoying countryside facilities supported by taxes raised out of town. In these cases, provision of public services in one area confers a beneficial externality on neighbouring areas.

Economic theory suggests the right answer to this problem. Unless the externality can be priced (charging suburban users but not city dwellers for entry to subsidized galleries and opera houses), the most efficient solution is to widen the geographical area of each local government until it includes most of the people who will use the public services it provides. Thus, for example, it may make sense to have an integrated commuter rail service and inner-city subway, and to subsidize it to prevent people driving through congested streets; but only a local government embracing both the suburbs and the inner city is likely to get close to the efficient policy.

These two theories of local government pull in opposite directions, and the right answer lies somewhere in between. The assumptions of the Tiebout model favour a lot of small local government jurisdictions to maximize choice and competition between areas. The model emphasizing externalities across areas suggests larger jurisdictions to 'internalize' externalities than would otherwise occur.

17-6 Economic sovereignty

Thus far, we have discussed a single country in isolation. Although we examine the relationship between different countries in Part 5, some issues are best discussed immediately. In a democratic country insulated from the rest of the world, the government is sovereign: while it retains democratic support and observes existing laws, it has the final say in policy design. Where it dislikes existing laws it may also be able to initiate legislation to amend previous laws. Sometimes central government chooses to delegate powers to local government. Section 17-5 discussed when it

---

[2] Charles Tiebout, 'A Pure Theory of Local Expenditures', *Journal of Political Economy*, 1956.

would be efficient to do so. What this account ignores is the existence of other countries. We now ask how interactions with the rest of the world affect the sovereignty of national governments.

Economic sovereignty is the power of national governments to make decisions independently of those made by other governments.

Even in an economy closed to the outside world, governments cannot do anything they like. Within market economies they have to work within the forces of supply and demand. For example, in Section 17-3 we argued that it would generally be more efficient to have high tax rates on things for which the demand or supply was inelastic: high tax rates on things with elastic supply and demand induces large distortions since equilibrium quantity is very sensitive to the price. We now apply this insight to economies open to interactions with the rest of the world.

International capital is now highly mobile across countries. Suppose the UK government tries to levy a large tax on capital in Britain. Lots of capital will quickly move elsewhere to escape the high taxes. The *tax base*, in this example the quantity of capital available for taxing in Britain, quickly shrinks. So the high tax *rates* may raise little tax *revenue*. In contrast, since people are much less mobile than capital across national boundaries, the tax base for taxation of workers' incomes in Britain is much less sensitive to tax rates than the tax base for capital taxes.

Even people are more mobile across national boundaries than they were a few decades ago. Communication is easier, transport costs are lower, satellites pay no attention to national frontiers on a map. Migration affects not just taxation but government spending. Suppose a country wishes to implement a generous welfare state. As a closed economy, all it has to worry about is how much of its tax base disappears from work into leisure. If welfare is too generous, people may not work enough. As an open economy, it also has to worry whether more generous welfare provision will lead to more migration into the country as foreigners take advantage, legally or illegally, of the generous welfare provision.

Thus closer economic integration with other countries – through trade in goods and movement of factors of production – effectively undermines the sovereignty of nation states. If the rate of income tax was 80 per cent in Liverpool but 20 per cent in Manchester, one would expect some pretty dramatic movement of capital and of people from Liverpool to Manchester. The tax base in Liverpool

would evaporate (even die-hard Everton supporters could commute from Manchester for Everton's home games). The local government of Liverpool has limited local sovereignty because it is effectively in competition with Manchester.

As modern technology undermines even barriers between countries, the same process is at work. The economic sovereignty of nation states, their freedom to do what they want, is steadily being constrained by the pressure of competition from foreign countries. More than one in ten beer cans now sold in England was bought by British households in France, hopping across the English Channel to take advantage of lower rates of alcohol taxation in France. UK Chancellors, caught between the pressure to raise revenue to close the budget deficit and the need to reduce alcohol taxes to prevent the UK booze business being undercut, have recently opted for a compromise and made little changes to alcohol taxes. They have already lost the sovereignty to set tax rates at the high levels that they would have liked.

National sovereignty is undermined not merely by competition between countries for tax bases but by two other considerations. The first is other sorts of cross-country spillovers such as acid rain, greenhouse gases, or the threat of pollution from a nuclear accident. Banning nuclear power generation in southern England may have limited value if northern France is studded with nuclear power stations.

The second is the scope for redistribution. Economics is about equity as well as efficiency. In an important sense, the right jurisdiction for government is the area within which citizens feel sufficient identity with one another that the rich are prepared to pay for the poor, and the fortunate are prepared to assist the unlucky, without resentment becoming entrenched. Many of the nation states of Europe have long histories and retain strong national identities. But these are not always set in stone. The Irish question has troubled Britain for centuries. More recently, countries such as Belgium and Italy have faced strong internal pressures for division. In the opposite direction, some Europeans now feel as much a citizen of Europe as of their own particular nation state.

It is clearly not the case that nation states are obsolete. But they are beginning to come under pressure. And further developments in technology are likely to increase the transnational scope both of economic interactions and of cultural identity. The proliferation of e-commerce and the use of the internet for entertainment will only accelerate this process.

SUMMARY

● In industrialized economies, government revenues come mainly from direct taxes on personal incomes and company profits, indirect taxes on purchases of goods and services, and contributions to state-run social security schemes. Government spending comprises spending on goods and services and transfer payments.

● Government intervention in a market economy should be assessed against the criteria of distributional equity and allocative efficiency. A progressive tax and transfer system takes most from the rich and give most to the poor. The UK tax and transfer system is mildly progressive. The less well off do receive transfer payments and the rich face the highest rates of income tax. Although some necessities, notably food, are exempt from VAT, other goods intensively consumed by the poor, notably cigarettes and alcohol, are heavily taxed.

● Externalities are cases of market failure where intervention may improve efficiency. By taxing or subsidizing goods that involve externalities, the government can induce the private sector to behave as if it takes account of the externality, eliminating the deadweight burden arising from the misallocation induced by the externality distortion.

● A pure public good is a good for which one person's consumption does not reduce the quantity available for consumption by others. Together with the impossibility of effectively excluding people from consuming it, this implies that all individuals consume the same quantity, although they may attach different utility to this consumption if their tastes differ.

● A free market will undersupply a public good because of the free-rider problem. Individuals need not offer to pay for a good that they can consume if others pay for it. The socially efficient quantity of a public good equates the marginal social cost of production to the *sum* of the marginal private benefits over all people at this output level. Diagrammatically, this implies that individual demand curves are vertically added to get the social demand or marginal benefit curve.

● Except for taxes designed to offset externalities, taxes are generally distortionary. By driving a wedge between the selling price and the purchase price, they prevent the price system achieving the equality of marginal costs and marginal benefits. The amount of the deadweight burden is higher the higher is the marginal tax rate and the size of the wedge, but it also depends on supply and demand elasticities for the taxed commodity or activity. The more inelastic are supply and demand, the less the tax will change equilibrium quantity and the smaller will be the deadweight burden.

● The incidence of tax describes who ultimately pays the tax. The more inelastic is demand relative to supply, the more a tax will fall on purchasers as opposed to sellers.

● Rising tax rates initially increase tax revenue but eventually lead to such large falls in the equilibrium quantity of the taxed commodity or activity that revenue starts to fall again. Cutting tax rates will usually reduce the deadweight tax burden but might increase revenue if taxes had initially been sufficiently high. Most Western economies do not appear to have reached this position. If governments wish to reduce the deadweight tax burden and balance spending and revenue, they must cut government spending in order to cut taxes.

● The economic sovereignty of nation states is being affected by increasing integration of countries within the world economy. As national tax bases become more mobile they become more elastic and harder to tax by a single country. Pollution spillovers also inflict transnational externalities. In both cases, co-operation between countries is needed for a more efficient solution. However, national policies also reflect national identities. A tension exists between the appropriate jurisdiction for efficiency and the appropriate jurisdiction to support legitimacy and willingness to redistribute.

KEY TERMS

◆ Marginal and average tax rate   279

◆ Private and public goods   280

◆ Merit goods   283

◆ Direct, indirect and wealth taxes   284

◆ Ability to pay   284

◆ Benefits principle   284

◆ Tax incidence   285

◆ Tax wedge   285

◆ Laffer curve   288

◆ Economic sovereignty   290

REVIEW QUESTIONS

1 Which of the following are public goods? (a) the fire brigade; (b) clean streets; (c) refuse collection; (d) cable television; (e) social toleration; (f) the postal service. Explain and discuss alternative ways of providing these goods or services.

2 Why does society try to ensure that every child receives an education? Discuss the different ways this could be done and give reasons for preferring one method of providing such an education.

3 How would you apply the principles of horizontal and vertical equity in deciding how much to tax two people, each capable of doing the same work, but one of whom chooses to devote more time to sun-bathing and therefore has a lower income?

4 Whereas a progressive tax takes proportionately more of a rich person's income, a regressive tax takes proportionately more of a poor person's income. Classify the following taxes as progressive or regressive. (a) 10 per cent tax on all luxury goods; (b) taxes in proportion to the value of owner-occupied houses; (c) taxes on beer; (d) taxes on champagne.

5 There is a flat-rate 30 per cent income tax on all income over £2000. Calculate the average tax rate (tax paid divided by income) at income levels of £5000, £10 000, and £50 000. Is the tax progressive? Is it more or less progressive if the exemption is raised from £2000 to £5000?

6 (a) Suppose labour supply is completely inelastic. Show why there is no deadweight burden if wages are taxed. Who bears the incidence of the tax? (b) Now suppose labour supply is quite elastic. Show the area that is the deadweight burden of the tax. How much of the tax is ultimately borne by firms and how much by workers? (c) For any given supply elasticity show that firms bear more of the tax the more inelastic is the demand for labour.

7 *Common fallacies* Show why the following statements are incorrect: (a) The only reason for taxation is to provide for shirkers by penalizing people who do an honest day's work. (b) It is obvious that the government is supplying too many goods and services. In a free enterprise economy it would be profitable only to supply a fraction of the amount to which the government is currently committed. (c) The government spends all its revenue. Taxes cannot be a burden on society as a whole.

18 Industrial policy and competition policy

LEARNING OUTCOMES

When you have finished this chapter, you should be able to:

● Explain and contrast the ways in which competition policy and industrial policy seek to offset market failures and improve efficiency
● Discuss the role of patents in stimulating investment in R&D
● Examine why sunrise and sunset industries are vulnerable to market failures
● Consider why a firm's costs might depend on its location and identify reasons for locational externalities
● Define consumer surplus and producer surplus, and use them to analyse the social cost of monopoly power
● Examine the principles behind UK competition policy and evaluate its success in practice
● Distinguish different types of merger and explain why merger booms have occurred
● Examine the regulation of potential mergers, both in theory and in practice

What do Durex, Valium, and Cornflakes have in common with household gas supplies and mobile phones? The answer is that the London Rubber Company, Hoffman LaRoche, Kelloggs, British Gas, Cellnet and Vodafone have all been the subject of investigations by the Competition Commission, which exists to monitor the behaviour of large firms and check the possible abuse of monopoly power.[1] In this and the following chapter we examine government intervention to enhance market efficiency.

Competition policy aims to enhance economic efficiency by promoting or safeguarding competition between firms.

---

[1] Prior to 1999, the Competition Commission was known as the Monopolies and Mergers Commission.

The instruments of competition policy include rules about conduct of firms and rules about the structure of industries. The former aims to prevent abuse of a monopoly position. The latter seeks to prevent monopolies arising, for example by breaking up existing monopolies or by stopping mergers that create new monopolies.

Some industries were traditionally viewed as natural monopolies: scale economies were so large that breaking them up made no sense and competition from other firms provided no competitive discipline. In many countries, especially in Europe, these had become nationalized industries, run by the state to provide continuous supervision in the social interest. Since 1980 the UK has pioneered the privatization of many of the state-owned firms, and other countries have followed. Since scale economies do not vanish with privatization, continuing regulation has been necessary in many instances. We describe this regulatory revolution in the next chapter. First, we deal with cases in which scale economies are less acute and competition policy therefore offers a more promising avenue for intervention.

Before so doing, we discuss other motives for intervention to increase the efficiency of industrial production. Broadly speaking, if this is not motivated by scale economies and market power, nor by environmental externalities of the type discussed in Chapter 16, what other market failures do we have in mind? Essentially all the other externalities associated with production.

Industrial policy aims to offset externalities that affect production decisions by firms.

We discuss four such channels for market failure: invention and knowledge creation, in which it is difficult to prevent hard-earned progress being pirated by others; spillovers into other countries, which provide opportunities for policy competition between governments; capital market failures, which explain why new businesses are so hard to start; and locational externalities that explain why car stylists cluster in Turin and why Chinese restaurants cluster in London's Soho district.

18-1 Industrial policy

Inventions and the patent system

In Chapter 15 we saw that information is a very special economic commodity which frequently causes indigestion in freely competitive markets. It is hard to trade information: the buyer needs to see it, and having seen the information then has no incentive to pay for it!

Inventions – the discovery of new information about production – are a particular example of this general theme. Suppose a company develops a product in secret, and then markets it. If other firms quickly imitate the new invention, competition will rapidly compete away the profits on this new product. Since everyone can foresee that this will occur, few resources will be devoted to searching for inventions, even though they are socially valuable.

Inventions are an example of a public good, which we discussed in Chapter 17. The problem arises because the inventor cannot privately appropriate the benefits since imitators cannot be excluded. The solution to this market failure is a patent system.

A **patent** is a temporary legal monopoly awarded to an inventor who registers the invention.

The temporary monopoly provides, before the fact, the assurance that if the search for a new discovery is successful the inventor will be able to cash up after the fact. In the language of Chapter 10, it is a credible pre-commitment.

Why is the legal monopoly only temporary? Otherwise, successful inventors would have an entrenched entry barrier which would prevent competition for all time. The trick in designing a successful patent system is to provide a big enough incentive for invention, but not such a large and long-lived cushion that the benefits of competition are suppressed for ever.

This is not a trivial problem, especially when considerations of strategic competition are introduced. For example, there are documented cases of pre-emptive patenting by incumbent firms. The incumbent may discover a new process or product, patent it, but *not* actually introduce it. Potential entrants are aware that any attempt at entry will be met with the launch of this new product, which will place the entrant at a disadvantage. Thus, pre-emptive patenting can be a highly effective strategic entry barrier. This example shows that intelligent industrial policy and competition policy must work hand in hand. Evidence of pre-emptive patenting is the type of information the Competition Commission seeks in evaluating whether incumbents are abusing their market power.

Research and development (R&D)

Research is the process of invention. **Development** makes research commercially viable.

In many countries, including the UK, one aim of industrial policy is to promote R&D. In Western Europe, the United States, and Japan, R&D accounts for between 2 and 3 per cent of national output. Why should governments, even those committed to allowing market forces to work, spend several billion pounds of taxpayers' money promoting R&D?

This seems to indicate widespread agreement that there are market failures in R&D which the patent system alone is insufficient to offset. Economics provides several insights into what may go wrong with market forces in R&D.

First, large projects can be very risky for an individual company, nowhere more so than in the development of a major new commercial airliner. The chief executive of Boeing, the largest plane manufacturer in the world, has described each new project as 'betting the company': failure on one new project could threaten the very existence of the company. In Chapter 15 we described why private individuals may be risk-averse, and this applies even to

---

BOX 18-1   Turning research into business success

Harvard Business School guru Professor Michael Porter is famous for his work on what gives countries a competitive edge. He gives the UK pretty low marks, calculating that it is only the thirteenth most effective of the industrial nations at deriving commercial benefit from science and technology.

He recommends slashing barriers to risk taking. 'In the UK, people say we want more entrepreneurs but we don't want them to become rich.' Porter advocates a reduction in capital gains tax faced by successful entrepreneurs, and better tax breaks for research and development expenditure. The table below shows the ratio of patents (a measure of commercial application of ideas) to citations (the number of academic references to scientists' work, an indicator of scientific research output). The UK scores only 87 patents per 100 citations, compared with over 250 in Japan, Germany, or Switzerland.

International patents per 1000 scholarly citations, 1975–95			
Japan	267	Italy	108
Germany	266	Canada	97
Switzerland	266	Finland	89
Austria	150	UK	87
France	135	Denmark	57
Sweden	130	Australia	46
Netherlands	120	Spain	25

Source: *Financial Times*, 11 December 1998.

---

executives of large corporations. Consequently, private firms may undertake less R&D than is socially desirable.

This implies that the social return on such projects exceeds the private return to those making the decisions. If the private decision-makers require a large risk premium, or on average a high expected return, before being willing to assume such risks, why should society demand any less? Essentially for two reasons. First, the government can *pool* the risks across a large number of projects in its portfolio. Second, even if projects go wrong, the government can spread the burden very thinly across the population: 1 per cent on everybody's income tax rate for a year should cover even the biggest disaster. Thus, the population as a whole should require only a small risk premium, much smaller than that required by executives in an individual company who may face personal disaster if the project turns sour. And these arguments have generally been found persuasive by governments. Hence their provision of public subsidies for R&D.

It should also be noted that no patent system can be watertight. Indeed, as we remarked above, to make it so would effectively be to suppress all future competition indefinitely. In these circumstances, a further argument for public support of R&D may be because private firms realize they will not be able to appropriate for themselves all the benefits of their efforts. Some imitation will occur, but it will be insufficiently clear-cut to guarantee that a law suit will not be protracted and expensive. Moreover, other inventors may be stimulated by what they see to make a breakthrough

in an entirely different area. New breakthroughs build on past discoveries. These provide additional motives for R&D support as part of an effective industrial policy.

Strategic international competition

In Chapter 10 we discussed how individual firms might try to erect strategic entry barriers to preserve and enhance their market power. Such considerations also apply in international competition between large firms.

For a concrete example, consider again the commercial airliner industry. Effectively, there are two large firms left in the world market. Boeing (www.boeing.com) is much the largest and has an entire product range, from the relatively small twin-engined 737 to the 747, the Jumbo. Another American firm, McDonnell-Douglas (www.boeing.com), had a smaller product range, and in 1996 decided to merge with Boeing. The other major player is the European consortium Airbus Industrie (www.airbus.com), in which British Aerospace (BAe) (www.bae.co.uk) has a stake.

Airbus Industrie asked the governments of its member producers (Germany, France, the UK, and Spain) for *launch aid*, a grant or loan on favourable terms to help with R&D on new aircraft. In addition to the standard arguments for R&D support, what extra issues does international competition raise? What must the UK government consider in deciding whether to put in taxpayers' money?

First, will Airbus succeed even without government support? If the answer is yes, public subsidies are simply a

BOX 18-2   State Aids in the EU

Every time an EU government gives yet another 'final subsidy' to its ailing national airline, there is a howl of protest from other airlines trying to compete. The European Union has been trying, with modest success, to crack down on the practice of State Aids. These arise when the government of a member state gives preferential treatment to one or more firms in such a way as to distort competition and trade within the EU. Examples include outright subsidies to ailing firms, but also other forms of discriminatory treatment such as special tax breaks. Not all forms of government support qualify as State Aids. If support is non-discriminatory, it does not qualify. Thus, disaster relief after flooding, or provision of roads freely open to everyone, would not count. Politicians, of course, face intense lobbying on particular issues. Getting rid of State Aids is not easy. But they have been falling slowly, and have gone in the UK.

EU competition policy, by viewing transfers to individual firms as distortions, clearly takes the view that State Aids are bad for efficiency within the Single Market. This has been the traditional view of economists. However, economics is like a sausage machine: you get out what you put in. Within models with few market failures, State Aids add an unnecessary market failure and diminish efficiency.

However, within the last decade, two new areas of economic analysis have shown how a useful role for State Aids might exist. The first is the new industrial economics, for example strategic international competition between firms, as between Boeing and Airbus, where knowledge that Airbus has State Aids may affect the behaviour of Boeing in ways favourable to Europe. The second is the new economic geography, where locational externalities may provide incentives for governments to bid for inward investment (e.g. of Japanese car producers) which then augments the industrial base of its host nation. From the viewpoint of the EU as a whole, it is desirable that such inflows go to the place where their contribution will be largest. An implicit auction, in which member states each bid to attract investment (by offering tax advantages, investment grants, etc.) may then be quite an efficient mechanism for revealing where the locational externalities are greatest.

State aid to manufacturing, 1994–96 (% of net output)	
6	Greece, Italy
4	Germany
3	Belgium, Denmark, Spain
2	Luxembourg, Portugal, France, Ireland, Finland
0	UK

transfer payment to Airbus shareholders, for which there is no strong rationale. Second, will other European governments support Airbus even if the UK does not? If so, the UK government may be able to act as a free-rider. However, governments that systematically try to do this will eventually get a bad reputation.

Suppose the UK government has decided that it cannot free-ride on other governments: either it pays its share of launch aid or the whole project collapses. What are the benefits of providing launch aid?

If Airbus pulls out, Boeing-McDonnell-Douglas will be the sole producer without fear of competition. In that event, Boeing will surely cash up, raising the price of aircraft. British airlines and ultimately British consumers will pay high prices, and Boeing can earn monopoly profits. It may well be worth preventing this.

If the UK could have been sure that McDonnell-Douglas would have stayed independent, and provided effective competition to Boeing, it *might* have been worth allowing Airbus to fold: European consumers would still have got the benefit of cheaper planes. But this strategy would have been risky.

Launch aid may be seen as a pre-commitment by European governments not to allow Airbus to be bullied out of the industry. Boeing may conclude that there is no point attempting a price war to try to force Airbus out. If European governments can display the credible threat to back Airbus if necessary, Boeing shareholders are only going to lose by an unsuccessful price war. Hence, the pre-commitment may *prevent* a price war which might otherwise occur.

This example draws on the ideas of Chapter 10 to show how strategic international competition can provide a rationale for strategic industrial policy. Just as industrial policy is related to competition policy, so it is closely related to international trade policy, an issue to which we return in Chapter 33.

Sunrise and sunset industries

The next aspect of industrial policy which we examine concerns dynamic change, the rise and fall of industries and the firms within them.

Sunrise industries are the emerging new industries of the future. **Sunset** industries are those in long-term decline.

Currently, sunrise industries include information technology and genetics. Sunset industries in Western economies include the old heavy industries such as steel and shipbuilding which are now suffering from massive excess capacity as these industries have been undercut by more efficient producers in the Pacific basin.

Why not leave such changes to market forces? What are the market failures that might justify government intervention through industrial policy? We begin with the sunrise industries.

Two types of market failure have sometimes been put forward to justify the case for intervention, though it should be stressed that those who believe in the efficiency of market forces would argue that it is easy to exaggerate the importance of these factors. First, there may be imperfections in the market for lending to new companies and new industries. Banks and other lenders may be too risk-averse, or too unfamiliar with the new business, to lend the money needed through the early loss-making years. Second, the market may be slow to provide the relevant training and skills: Catch 22 (until the industry exists, people won't perceive the need for developing such skills; but without the skills, the industry cannot exist).

These arguments suggest that it may be possible to provide a rationale for an industrial policy to subsidize sunrise industries. But certain questions must be answered satisfactorily. First, why are markets so short-sighted and uninformed? If existing lenders or trainers get it wrong, why don't new firms come in and do a better job? If the answer is entry barriers, this confirms the close relation between industrial policy and competition policy.

Second, even if markets get it wrong, can the government do better? The strategy of trying to outguess the market by 'picking winners' is now highly discredited. It seems implausible that civil servants or politicians can do better than trained analysts in industry and finance. Rather, if such industrial policy is to be attempted, it seems preferable to diagnose the cause of the market failure and provide a generalized incentive which market decision-makers then take into account when undertaking their professional analysis.

Sunset industries present different problems. For example, the government may or may not attach importance to local unemployment when industries with a heavy geographical concentration are allowed to go under all at once. It *may* be desirable to spend what could otherwise be dole money on temporarily subsidizing lame ducks to ease the transition. Sometimes, however, a sharp shock is required to signal the extent of the adjustment eventually required and the government's commitment to seeing that adjustment is actually made.

Strategic considerations may be important here too. Suppose for example there are two remaining producers in an industry which has now contracted to the point when it can profitably support only one firm. Each firm would like to be the one to survive. They are playing an exit game of chicken. One of two things may happen, neither of which is socially desirable. First, the industry survives with two firms for much longer than is socially efficient. Second, the firm with the smaller financial backing will be the first to crack, even though it may be able to produce at slightly lower cost than its richer rival. In such circumstances, an industrial policy that seeks faster and more efficient rationalization of the sunset industry may be advantageous.

Strategic international considerations may also apply. The European steel industry has an enormous over-capacity, partly because it has been undercut by Korean, Japanese, and now Czech producers, partly because of a wave of added Italian steel capacity in the 1970s. Clearly, the European governments are engaged in a game to see who will close capacity to leave a profitable market share for the survivors. In such circumstances, each country's steel industry needs effective government representation, and *laissez-faire* industrial policy may be a poor policy. In fact, since 1980 British Steel (www.corusgroup.com) achieved a larger reduction in its capacity than the steel industry in any other major EC country. Far from being a free-rider, British Steel actually eased the adjustment problem for other European steel producers.

18-2 Economic geography

Consumer electronics – TVs, sound systems, home computers – can be found in many ring-road superstores, but people from all over south-east England may still go to Tottenham Court Road, London, for cheap deals, just as in the 1960s their parents bought flower-power clothes in

Carnaby Street. Ferrari apart, most Formula 1 racing teams have their production headquarters in the Thames Valley.

The term 'economic geography', to capture the idea that locational externalities are significant and require special analysis, was coined by Professor Paul Krugman in the early 1990s, but the idea dates back at least to Alfred Marshall, Cambridge Professor and teacher of Keynes, who was one of the fathers of twentieth century economics.

Economic geography means that a firm's location affects its production costs. A beneficial **locational externality** occurs when a firm's production costs are reduced by locating near similar firms.

Why might a firm's costs of production depend on its geographical proximity to other firms? Explanations fall under three headings: the interaction of scale economies and risk, transport and transactions costs, and technological spillovers.

Suppose a worker invests in very specific skills, such as designing racing cars or explaining to customers why flower shirts are essential (!), and there is only one employer in the local labour market. The worker is very dependent on the particular employer: having skills this specific is risky. With a cluster of similar employers, risks of workers fall. They no longer require such a large 'risk premium' or 'compensating differential' in their wage. Labour is therefore cheaper for firms. Where did scale economies come into the argument? Without them, each locality could have a tiny smattering of every firm. It is the presence of (some) scale economies that forces firms into all or nothing choices between different locations.

A second reason for clustering of producers is transport costs. Shops may cluster because of transport costs for consumers – one trip gets you to a street with lots of shops stocking what you want – but larger producers cluster because of features of production. Closeness to raw materials is an obvious example. Discovering a coal seam or iron ore leads to a profusion of heavy industrial businesses in the locality.

Most significant of all is probably the spillover in technology itself. In addition to Formula 1 car producers, famous examples include Silicon Valley in California and Route 128 around Boston, clusters of computer-based producers who find it advantageous to be in proximity. Although they are in competition with one another, they also feed off each other's ideas just as the most competitive of university professors still attend each other's seminars. Although articles get published two years later in journals, at which point ideas become accessible worldwide,

discussions with the professor next door about some state of the art idea may yield a huge competitive edge over professors (research producers) elsewhere. The same holds good in businesses from software design to satellite technology.

What these examples have in common is that one firm's cost curve depends on how many other similar firms are nearby. This concept of a locational externality allows us to make clearer a concept that politicians have discussed for years but which previously economists have had considerable trouble providing with a coherent interpretation.

The **industrial base** of a country or region is a measure of the stock of existing producers available to provide such locational externalities.

The emphasis on 'industrial' carries the presumption that the externalities are more significant for producers than for consumers, because of the specificity of investments required and minimum size that scale economies impose. Although ring-road superstores cluster together to offer adjacent carpet stores, DIY shops, and garden centres, competition between *different* local clusters is intense. The degree of market failure is small.

In contrast, where the minimum efficient scale of specific investments is large, countries or regions may find there are two equilibria – one in which nobody enters and one in which many firms enter, each enjoying benefits from the presence of the other. Yet achieving the second outcome efficiently requires co-ordination of the entry decision of different producers to internalize the externality facing each firm: it neglects the benefits that its own entry creates for other firms.

Before this is taken as a blank cheque to pursue industrial subsidies, it should be recalled that in the 1970s and 1980s industrial policy had some spectacular failures in many countries. Any time a large private firm experienced difficulties, this was prima facie evidence that intervention was required to 'preserve skills', 'maintain an international presence' in the industry, or 'take account of the needs of suppliers'. The new economic geography is not an alibi for backing losers or for freezing the industrial structure in a changing world.

18-3 The social cost of monopoly power

Chapter 16 showed that, in the absence of market failure, competitive equilibrium would be Pareto-efficient. Competitive equilibrium would ensure that each industry expanded its output up to the point at which price equals marginal cost and therefore social marginal benefit equals social marginal cost. No resource reallocation would make consumers as a whole better off.

When an industry is imperfectly competitive each firm in the industry enjoys a degree of *monopoly power*. Equating marginal cost and marginal revenue, each firm will produce an output at which price exceeds marginal cost. This excess of price over both marginal revenue and marginal cost is a measure of the firm's monopoly power.

When firms have monopoly power, price and social marginal benefit of the last output unit exceed the private and social marginal cost of producing that last output unit. From society's viewpoint the industry is producing too little. Expanding output would add more to social benefit than to social cost. How should we measure the social cost of monopoly power and inefficient resource allocation?

In Chapter 19 we take up the case of natural or pure monopoly. We begin with a more general discussion of all forms of imperfect competition and monopoly power. Intermediate forms of imperfect competition require some economies of scale to limit the number of firms an industry can support. Nevertheless, to introduce the idea of the social cost of monopoly power it is convenient to ignore economies of scale altogether. We thus ask the following question: what would happen if a competitive industry were taken over by a single firm which then operated as a multi-plant monopolist? Figure 18-1 shows how this question may be answered. Under perfect competition *LMC* is both the industry's long-run marginal cost curve and its supply curve. With constant returns to scale, *LMC* is also the long-run average cost curve of the industry. Given the demand curve *DD*, competitive equilibrium is at *B*. The competitive industry produces an output Q_C at a price P_C.

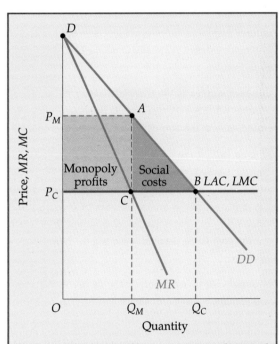

The industry has horizontal long-run average and marginal costs. A perfectly competitive industry produces at *B*, but a monopolist sets *MR* = *MC* to produce only Q_M at a price P_M. The monopolist earns excess profits $P_M P_C CA$, but there is a social cost or deadweight burden equal to the triangle *ACB*. Between Q_M and Q_C social marginal benefit exceeds social marginal cost and society would gain by expanding output by Q_C. The triangle *ACB* shows how much society would gain by this expansion.

Figure 18-1   The social cost of monopoly

Now the industry is taken over by a monopolist, who produces an output Q_M at a price P_M thus equating marginal cost and marginal revenue. The area $P_M P_C AC$ shows the monopolist's profits from selling Q_M at a price in excess of marginal and average cost. The triangle *ACB* shows the deadweight burden or social cost of monopoly power. Why? Because at Q_M the social marginal benefit of another unit of output is P_M but the social marginal cost is only P_C. Society would like to expand output up to the competitive point B at which social marginal benefit and social marginal cost are equal. The triangle ACB measures the social profit or excess of benefits over costs from such an output expansion. Conversely, by reducing output to Q_M the monopolist imposes a social cost equal to the area ACB.

Since the demand curve measures the marginal benefit to consumers of each unit of output and the marginal cost curve measures the extra resources used to make each unit of output, the area between DD and LMC up to that output always measures the total surplus to be divided between producers and consumers.

Producer surplus is the excess of revenue over total costs. Total costs are shown by the area under the LMC curve up to this output.

Consumer surplus is the triangle showing the excess of consumer benefits over spending. It is the area under the demand curve at this output minus the spending rectangle.

In Figure 18-1, at the output Q_M producer surplus is the rectangle labelled profits and consumer surplus is the triangle DAP_M above this. But this output is inefficient because it does not maximize the sum of consumer and producer surplus. That is maximized at output Q_C at which the area between the demand curve and the LMC curve is maximized.

The **social cost of monopoly** is the failure to maximize social surplus.

For the whole economy the social cost of monopoly power is obtained by adding together the deadweight burden triangles such as ACB for all industries in which marginal cost and marginal revenue are less than price and social marginal benefit.

When output is below the socially efficient level, the **deadweight burden** triangle shows the social surplus that has been sacrificed.

An early study by Professor Arnold Harberger suggested that the social cost of monopoly power, as measured by these deadweight burden triangles, was considerably less than 1 per cent of national income.[2] If social costs are really

this small, perhaps there are more important things for the government to worry about in designing economic policy. Professor George Stigler, a Nobel Prize winner, has argued that 'Economists might serve a more useful purpose if they fought fires or termites instead of monopoly.'[3]

However, other economists believe that the social costs of monopoly cannot be ignored. Professor F. M. Scherer of Yale, whose work on industrial structure we cited in Chapters 8–10, has argued that in the United States the social cost of monopoly is large enough 'to treat every family in the land to a steak dinner at a good restaurant'.[4] Professors Keith Cowling and Dennis Mueller have argued that the social cost of monopoly could be as high as 7 per cent of national income.[5]

Why is there such disagreement about the cost of monopoly? First, the area of the deadweight burden triangle in Figure 18-1 depends on the elasticity of the demand curve. In calculating the size of deadweight burden triangles under monopoly, different economists have used different estimates of the elasticity of demand.

Second, the welfare cost of monopoly is greater than the deadweight burden triangle itself. Since monopoly may yield high profits to the firm, firms will expend large quantities of resources in trying to acquire and secure monopoly positions. In Chapter 10 we saw that existing oligopolists would have an incentive to advertise too much, not to provide information about the product, but to raise the fixed cost of being in the industry, thereby making it harder for new firms to enter.

Similarly, firms may devote large quantities of resources trying to influence the government in order to obtain favourable judgements which enhance or preserve their monopoly power. They may also deliberately maintain extra production capacity so that potential entrants can see that any attempt at entry will be matched by a sharp increase in production by existing firms, forcing price reductions which in the short run will be unprofitable for all but which may bankrupt the entrant first. From the economy's viewpoint, resources devoted to lobbying the government or maintaining over-capacity may also be largely wasted.

Modern economic analysis emphasizes yet another consideration, the role of information. Those running a

---

[2] Arnold Harberger, 'Monopoly and Resource Allocation', *American Economic Review*, 1954.

[3] The quotation comes from J. Siegfried and T. Tiemann, 'The Welfare Cost of Monopoly: An Interindustry Analysis', *Economic Inquiry*, Journal of the Western Economic Association, 1974.

[4] As footnote 3.

[5] Keith Cowling and Dennis Mueller, 'The Social Costs of Monopoly Power', *Economic Journal*, 1978.

monopoly are likely to have inside information about the firm's true cost opportunities. They know more than either the shareholders or any potential regulator. Perhaps the monopolist could really have lower costs than it has, but the managers can't be bothered putting in the effort. Economists sometimes call this 'managerial slack' or 'X-inefficiency'. The failure of competition effectively gives the firm an 'information monopoly' on its own cost possibilities. Outsiders can't find out.

When a competitive firm gets lazy it loses market share and may even go out of business. When a monopoly gets lazy it simply makes a little less profit than it might. From the social viewpoint, its cost curves are unnecessarily high. Society is spending more resources on producing this output than would be the case if the X-inefficiency could be eliminated.

In Figure 18-2 LMC is the marginal cost of a firm striving for cost efficiency. The monopolist takes advantage of its information monopoly to enjoy an easy life and has higher costs LMC'. Suppose the monopolist could be broken up into identical firms (in the example there are constant returns to scale). Competition between firms would not merely make each set price equal to marginal cost, it would reveal managerial slack and force firms to attain the lower cost curve LMC. The monopolist would produce output Q_M at a price P_M. The competitive industry produces Q_C at a price P_C. Thus the economy moves from E' to E. Notice that the social gain is hugely larger than the triangle $E'FG$.

At the monopoly output Q_M, consumer surplus, the excess of their benefits over what they paid, was $P_M JE'$. $HFE P_M$ was the declared profit of the monopolist, $KFHP_C$ the hidden profit that the monopolist took as the easy life, and OQ_MKP_C the costs that even an efficient firm would have had to incur. In contrast, when equilibrium moves from E' to E, the *additional* social profits are the whole triangle $E'KE$. With the industry now competitive, and the cost curve LMC, total consumer surplus is JEP_C, since this is the gap between the demand curve and the rectangle OQ_CEP_C that consumers actually pay. Notice that the rectangle $HFKP_C$ has effectively been redistributed from the slack monopolist to consumers once society finds out that true costs are LMC and prices accordingly.

So far we have assumed monopolists are lazy 'fat cats'. If it takes resources (effort, investment, etc.) to lower costs, the gain from abolishing monopoly will be smaller than in Figure 18-2 but still larger than the triangle $E'FG$.

For these reasons, the precise extent of the social cost of monopoly remains a subject of continuing controversy. Nevertheless, few governments believe that the social cost of monopoly is sufficiently small that it can safely be ignored. We shortly examine the policies which have been adopted to restrict the degree of monopoly power exercised by large firms.

Our discussion relates only to the efficiency losses arising from imperfect competition. Society might also have views on two other aspects on monopoly performance: the amount of *political* power that large companies are in a position to exert, and the *distributional* issue of fairness in relation to the large supernormal profits that a monopolist can earn.

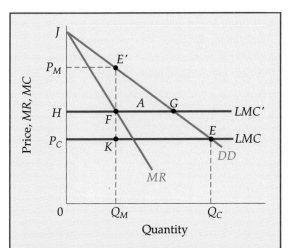

A monopolist with inside information about costs may allow LMC to rise to LMC', and produce at E'. A competitive industry would produce at E and reveal that true costs were LMC.

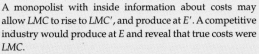

Figure 18-2   An information monopoly

The distribution of monopoly profits

In Figure 18-1 the area $P_M P_C CA$ showed pure monopoly profits after all economic costs. Should society tolerate such privately collected taxes? Whether the high price P_M charged by a monopolist is a rip-off or the just reflection of what consumers are prepared to pay is a value judgement about equity. It is worth remarking that the ultimate recipients of monopoly profits are the monopolist's shareholders. Since a large fraction of the stock market is held by pension funds and insurance companies which will eventually make payments to workers, monopoly profits may indirectly pay income to some relatively poor people.

Nevertheless, society may decide that it dislikes monopoly profits purely on the grounds of equity. Suppose the government imposes a profits tax: what effect would this have on the monopolist's output decision?

The simple answer is that it would have no effect! Whatever the tax rate (assuming it is less than 100 per cent), the way to maximize after-tax profits is to maximize pre-tax profits. Provided the government does not take all the extra pre-tax profit in taxes, increasing pre-tax profits must always increase post-tax profits. Hence the monopolist will produce exactly the same output as in the absence of a profits tax and, facing the same demand curve, will charge the same price as before.

One last issue. A monopolist may have sunk costs in the past, for example in R&D or in building factory capacity. Viewed from today, these have already been incurred and the position of today's cost curve is independent of whether or not the government taxes monopoly profits. However, had the firm known that profits would be subject to a windfall tax, perhaps the monopolist would never have incurred large R&D costs in the first place.

Thus, an occasional surprise windfall tax may be able to remove monopoly profits without any adverse incentive effects on efficiency.[6] However, the expectation that there would be regular resort to such a device would undermine incentives to invest. Costs would become higher than they need have been.

Must liberalization help?

By now you may be assuming that more competition is always better. But in Chapter 16 we introduced the theory of the second best. Beginning from a distorted position, elimination of all market failures would always increase efficiency. But partial elimination or reduction can occasionally make things worse: sometimes two distortions somewhat offset each other. Removing just one makes the other one worse.

Here is the first example. Unlike Figures 18-1 and 18-2 suppose there are large economies of scale and a falling average cost curve. A monopolist is bad for the reasons outlined already, but it does at least produce on a large scale and allow society to benefit from scale economies. Suppose the government insists on more competition, say entry of a second producer. Dividing the market, both firms fail to reap many scale economies. More competition may reduce profit margins and drive price closer to marginal cost; it may also reduce information monopolies (we can see what the

other firm is charging), forcing more expenditure on cost reduction to shift cost curves down. But if scale economies are big enough, both producers will still have larger costs than the original monopolist. Society may be worse off because it has to spend more resources on production.

The second example is called cream skimming

Cream skimming is entry only in the profitable parts of the business, thereby undermining scale economies elsewhere.

Suppose a postal monopoly is required to have a uniform service provision: it has to deliver throughout the UK at a uniform price. A private entrant would want to take on profitable parcel delivery in cities but not unprofitable parcel delivery to remote rural areas. If it is allowed to cream skim the profitable bits alone, it reduces the scale economies of the large producer in other areas and might even jeopardize the entire operation.

With this brief discussion of market power, we can now understand more clearly the role of competition policy.

18-4 Competition policy

Figure 18-3 provides a convenient guide to the remainder of this chapter and the chapter that follows. It divides possible outcomes into four regions. In the top left box, competition is possible and desirable, what we might call the normal case. In the top right box, some kind of competition would be possible but it is not desirable. In this box, scale economies are important and entry by other firms would lead to cream skimming or to small-scale high-cost activities by all firms. In the bottom right, the situation is one of natural monopoly. Huge scale economies preclude any possiblility of open competition. In the bottom left box, the incumbent has sufficient power to deter entry if things are

---

[6] For example, in 1997 the incoming Labour government levied a once-off tax on the profits of the privatized utilities, arguing that they had made more profits than anyone had anticipated at the time of their privatization.

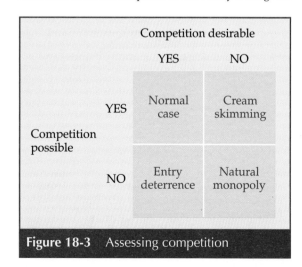

		Competition desirable	
		YES	NO
Competition possible	YES	Normal case	Cream skimming
	NO	Entry deterrence	Natural monopoly

Figure 18-3   Assessing competition

left to the market. But scale economies are not that significant. Society would gain more from greater competition, if only it could be secured, than it would lose from giving up economies of large scale by allowing entry.

Figure 18-3 divides up our analysis into competition policy, the topic in the remainder of this chapter, and regulation, the topic of the next chapter. Competition policy is about the two boxes in the left-hand column. It concerns situations in which promotion of competition is likely to be beneficial. This can be achieved by setting rules for conduct or by taking steps to ensure a market structure in which competition can then take place.

In the United States, much of competition policy has been based on achieving a structure favourable to competition. UK competition policy has been more pragmatic, assessed on a case by case basis, without any prior presumption that the existence of monopoly power is against the public interest.

Competition law in the UK

Legislation has been steadily extended since the Monopoly and Restrictive Practices Act of 1946. Restrictive practices have been separately examined since the establishment of the Restrictive Practices Court in 1956. Monopoly policy was comprehensively reassessed in the 1973 Fair Trading Act and amended in the Competition Acts of 1980 and 1998.

The 1973 Act introduced a Director-General of Fair Trading to supervise many aspects of competition and consumer law including the regulation of quality and standards discussed in Chapter 16. The Director-General is responsible for monitoring company behaviour and, subject to a ministerial veto, can refer individual cases to the Competition Commission for a thorough investigation.

A company can be referred if it supplies more than 25 per cent of the total market. The Commission can also be given cases where two or more distinct firms by implicit collusion operate to restrict competition.

The **Competition Commission** is charged to investigate whether or not a monopoly, or potential monopoly, acts against the public interest.

There is no presumption that monopoly is necessarily bad, and the Commission is charged to investigate whether or not the monopoly acts against the public interest, a brief that may be widely interpreted though in recent years there has been increasing emphasis on the 'maintenance and promotion of effective competition'.

The Restrictive Practices Court examines agreements between firms supplying goods and services in the UK, for example agreements on collusive pricing behaviour. All agreements must be notified to the Director-General of Fair Trading, who will refer them to the Court unless they are voluntarily abandoned or judged of trivial significance. The Court will find against these agreements unless they satisfy one of eight 'gateways' or justifications, for example that their removal would cause serious and persistent unemployment in the area. Thus for restrictive practices the burden of proof lies on the companies to show that they are acting in the public interest: in contrast, the legislation on monopolies is more open-minded, requiring the Commission to make the case that companies are acting against the public interest.

The UK is subject to the monopoly legislation of the European Union as well. Article 85 of the Treaty of Rome is rather similar to the UK legislation on restrictive practices. Agreements have to be notified and they are likely to be outlawed. Article 86 bans the abuse of a 'dominant position' as a monopolist.

The 1998 Competition Act sought to bring UK policy more in line with European Law. In particular, the previous terms of reference of the Competition Commission were supplemented by two new Prohibitions. Essentially, there is a ban on agreements that prevent, restrict, or distort competition in the UK (though exemptions can still be granted if this is judged in the public interest), and a ban on conduct that amounts to abuse of a dominant position within the UK.

UK competition policy in practice

The Competition Commission (www.competition-commission.gov.uk) has wide powers to make recommendations, and the Secretary of State to act on these recommendations, yet only a few companies have been penalized as a result of investigations. More frequently, the Commission has relied on informal assurances that criticized behaviour will be discontinued.

The Commission has investigated a wide range of cases, from beer to breakfast cereals and from contraceptives to cross-Channel ferries. Because the Commission is charged to investigate each case with an open mind, its judgements have tended to stress different aspects of behaviour in different cases. Certainly a high market share has not been sufficient to attract an unfavourable judgement.

On the other hand, cost reduction has not been sufficient to avoid censure by the Commission. Hoffman LaRoche was praised as 'a highly competent organization with a product range of high quality', but its enormous profits, sometimes as high as 60 or 70 per cent on capital employed, were held to be unjustified and the Commission recommended that the price of both Librium and Valium be halved.

Box 10-3 on page 160 described the ice cream wars in which Unilever subsidiary Birds Eye Wall's (BEW) was accused of freezing out the competition by distributing wrapped ice cream primarily through dedicated distribution outlets on terms that did not allow these outlets to handle products that competed with BEW. The case was eventually referred to the Competition Commission.

In 1998 the Commission ruled that there was no evidence that BEW had refused to supply other wholesalers, but that BEW had supplied some regional wholesalers on less favourable terms than those granted to its own distributors. The Commission concluded that BEW had restricted and distorted competition, found no offsetting benefits to the public interest, and recommended that BEW be required to supply wholesalers on the same terms as its dedicated distributors.

The Commission also has the power to investigate regulated industries such as utilities that we discuss more fully in Chapter 19. In 1999 it reported on claims that charges by Cellnet, Vodafone, and BT for calls from fixed phones to mobile phones were too high. It concluded that emerging competition in telecommunications was not yet sufficient to discipline these powerful suppliers, and that at the end of 1998 charges made by Vodafone and Cellnet were 22 per cent above the public interest benchmark – calculated for a hypothetical supplier, with the scale economies corresponding to a 25 per cent market share, and a 16.5 per cent return on capital – and that BT charges for calling into a mobile phone were 50 per cent above a public interest benchmark. The Commission recommended that the licences of Cellnet, Vodafone, and BT be modified to impose price ceilings on these particular charges.

Restrictive practices

Since restrictive practices legislation was first introduced, over 5000 agreements have been registered, the vast majority of which were abandoned even before they were taken to the Court. Most explicit price-fixing has gone. These facts look impressive but overstate the success of policy against restrictive practices.

First, they may simply have forced collusive agreements underground. Where oligopolistic market structures remain it seems likely that some firms will resort to informal agreements and the other collusive devices examined in Chapter 10. An important aspect of recent legislation and policy has been to tighten up on 'information agreements', which could form the basis of secret collusion.

Second, the various 'gateways' have permitted some agreements to be ratified, and the wisdom of some of these ratifications has been challenged. Finally, it is possible that tighter control of restrictive practices agreements between firms is one of the factors that provide an incentive for mergers, a subject we take up in the next section. By formally merging, companies could continue their old practices within the merged company and take their chance if they got investigated by the Commission.

Assessing UK competition policy

To assess competition policy we need to compare the evolution of the economy under the policy with the evolution that would have occurred under some different policy, for example a policy of *laissez-faire* or complete non-intervention. That would be a major undertaking.

At a more modest level, we can say that legislation on restrictive practices has eliminated many cases of blatant anti-competitive behaviour and that the Director-General of Fair Trading now has powers to promote the provision of better consumer information (e.g. the Trade Descriptions Act) and to monitor general company behaviour. And the Competition Commission has identified some practices that many regard as undesirable.

If these seem modest benefits, would a more radical and comprehensive anti-monopoly policy have been better for society?

Large scale may be necessary to achieve minimum efficient plant size, and the cost of breaking up large companies may be considerable. Large scale may also promote better management, co-ordination, and research. Co-ordination via cartels or single ownership may facilitate better planning when products are close complements in production.

As we stressed in Chapter 9, Rover may produce a large share of the cars made in the UK but this need not mean it has significant market power. When tariffs on imports are low and transport costs are moderate, domestic producers may face severe international competition. Without knowing the size of the relevant market in which firms are competing, large size cannot immediately be equated with uncompetitive behaviour.[7]

Nor is it obvious that the government should always oppose large profits. Profits are the carrot that encourages firms to take risks in a market economy. Many firms take

---

[7] More generally, in Chapter 10 we argued that *potential* competition (from new firms as well as imports) is important.

risks that do not come off. But if potential risk-takers are assured that success will immediately invite investigation by the Competition Commission and an order to cut prices and eliminate excess profits, there will be less risk-taking in the economy. Society has to decide how much risk-taking it wishes to encourage and to allow a proper return to risk-taking as an economic cost against accounting profits.

These doubts about the merit of a blind pursuit of perfect competition lie behind the UK policy and the judgements of the Competition Commission. Thus policy has considered each case on its merits. Notice, finally, that this approach suggests that monopoly policy should not be independent of other aspects of government policy. Large firms make more sense when the UK is competing within a large European market. We might wish to be tougher on large firms if the government is pursuing a policy of protection with high import tariffs.

18-5 Mergers

Two existing firms can join together in two different ways.

One firm may make a **takeover bid** for the other by offering to buy out the shareholders of the second firm.

Managers of the 'victim' firm will usually resist since they are likely to lose their jobs, but the shareholders will accept if the offer is sufficiently attractive.

A **merger** is the voluntary union of two companies where they think they will do better by amalgamating.

We must ask whether mergers are in the public interest, since mergers help to create monopoly power.

It is important to distinguish three types of merger. The production process typically has several stages. For example, the first stage might be iron ore extraction, the second stage steel manufacture from iron ore, and the third stage production of cars from steel.

By a **horizontal merger** we mean the union of two firms at the same production stage in the same industry. By a **vertical merger** we mean the union of two firms at different production stages in the same industry. In **conglomerate mergers**, the production activities of the two firms are essentially unrelated.

What do firms think they stand to gain by merging? A horizontal merger may allow exploitation of economies of scale. One large car factory may be better than two small ones. (Notice that this requires that each of the original companies were producing below minimum efficient scale.)

In vertical mergers it is often claimed that there are important gains to co-ordination and planning. It may be easier to make long-term decisions about the best size and type of steel mill if a simultaneous decision is taken on the level of car production to which steel output forms an important input. Since conglomerate mergers involve companies with completely independent products, these mergers have only small opportunities for a direct reduction in production costs.

Two other factors are frequently mentioned as potential benefits of mergers. First, if one company has an inspired management team it may be more productive to allow this team to run both businesses. Managers of course are very fond of this explanation for mergers. Economists have tended to be more sceptical. Second, by pooling their financial resources, the merging companies may enjoy better credit-worthiness and access to cheaper borrowing, enabling them to take more risks and finance larger research projects. There may also be some economies of scale in marketing effort. Managerial and financial gains could explain why mergers make sense even for firms producing completely distinct products.

If companies achieve any of these benefits, they will increase productivity and lower the cost of making any specified output level. These private gains are also social gains, since society can use less resources to achieve the same output. If these were the only considerations, social and private calculations would coincide.

However, there are two reasons for private and social assessments to diverge. First, the merger of two large firms will give them the monopoly power that derives from a large market share. The merged company is likely to restrict output and increase prices, a deadweight burden for society as a whole.

Second, the merged company may be able to use its *financial* power as distinct from its power derived from current market share. This danger is especially apparent in conglomerate mergers. A car producer and a food manufacturer cannot merge to gain economies of scale in production or any direct reduction in costs; but they can use their joint financial resources to start a price war in one of these industries. Because they have extra financial resources they will not be the first company to go bust. By forcing out some existing competitors, or merely holding this increased threat over potential entrants, they may be able to increase their market share in the long run, deter entry, and charge high prices for evermore.

In framing merger policy, the government must therefore decide whether the potential social gains from reduced costs

Table 18-1   UK takeovers and mergers 1972–98 (annual averages)

	Number	Value (1998 £bn)
1972–78	640	1.4
1979–85	490	4.2
1986–89	1300	43.1
1990–94	590	9.5
1995–98	580	31.2

Sources: *British Business 1989; Business Trends 1997;* ONS, *First Release 1999.*

Table 18-2   UK takeovers and mergers 1997–99 (domestic and cross-border, £bn)

Nationality of firms (acquired by acquirer)	97	98	99 (to Sept only)
UK by UK	26.5	29.5	23.0
Overseas by UK	19.2	54.3	88.1
UK by overseas	15.7	32.0	25.2

Source: ONS, *First Release.*

and more efficient production are outweighed by the social costs of monopoly power that might arise.

Mergers in practice

Table 18-1 shows annual averages of takeovers and mergers involving only UK firms. It shows dramatic merger booms in the late 1980s and again after 1995. What was going on?

First, the two merger booms coincided with high values of the stock market, when the cost of financing mergers was low. Since one way in which a firm finances a takeover is by giving some of its shares to shareholders in the other company, a booming stock market raises both the bidding power of takeover raiders and the value of the companies for which they are bidding.

Table 18-1 shows it was the value of the mergers, even more than the number of them, which was the key aspect of the merger booms. Conversely, 1990–94 was a period of recession, high real interest rates and expensive borrowing. The benefit of mergers was reduced and the cost increased.

Second, mergers are often associated with opportunities to rationalize industrial structure. Two major developments in European markets have been the run up to the creation of the Single European Market in 1992, and the corresponding reorganization that took place before the euro was launched in 1999. A larger market increases opportunities for scale economies (a greater private incentive to create large firms) and enhances competition (reducing the need for society to worry about mergers creating monopoly power).

Third, the combination of new technology and deregulation has been changing market structure both in the UK and in its main trading partners. Segmentation of national markets has been breaking down in telecoms, financial services, and many other industries. Cross-border mergers have allowed leading players to respond to larger markets. Table 18-2 confirms that cross-border activity has been substantial, including the spectacular acquisition of US

mobile phone company AirTouch by Vodafone (www.vodafone.com) for £39 billion.

The increase in effective market size in the last 15 years has also influenced the type of mergers taking place. Conglomerate mergers had grown steadily in the 1960s and 1970s, becoming a third of all mergers by the early 1980s. However, financial deregulation has made it easier to raise finance and reduced the importance of the financial muscle that provided one of the motives for conglomerate mergers. Disappointing performance of these hybrid companies has increasingly led to demerger and a renewed focus on the original core business. In contrast, the erosion of segmented national markets has led to a boom in horizontal mergers.

Merger policy

The proliferation of large companies through merger would not have been possible had the government been operating a tough anti-merger policy. Individual cases have been scrutinized to see if they were against the public interest.

Indeed, it is only since 1965 that mergers have been subject to public scrutiny at all. There are now two grounds for referring a prospective merger to an investigation by the Competition Commission: (1) that the merger will promote a new monopoly as defined by the 25 per cent market share used in deciding references for existing monopoly positions, or (2) that the merger involves the transfer of at least £70 million worth of company assets.[8]

Since the legislation was introduced in 1965, only about 4 per cent of all merger proposals have been referred to the Competition Commission. Thus for much of the period government policy has been to consent to, or actively encourage, mergers.

In believing that the benefits would outweigh the costs,

---

[8] The asset valuation was £5 million during 1965–80, £15 million during 1980–84, and £30 million during 1984–94.

| BOX 18-4 | Sky's the limit for Man United |

In late 1998, British Sky Broadcasting launched a huge bid to take over UK football giants Manchester United. The bid was referred to the Competition Commission, which turned it down. The Commission emphasized Premier League matches. TV rights, for the whole Premier League, are sold collectively by the Premier League to various TV companies. Much the largest fees are paid by BSkyB (www.sky.co.uk). Its very high market share of premium football viewing gives it market power.

The Commission argued that if collective selling of Premier League rights continued, BSkyB would gain an unfair advantage over other TV bidders through the influence and information it would acquire as a result of merger with Man United. Aware of this, potential bidders would be reluctant to bid, further enhancing BSkyB's dominant position. If, instead, the collective sale of Premier League rights was replaced by deals between individual clubs and broadcasters, merger of the top club and top broadcaster would again have adverse effects on competition.

The Commission also considered that the merger would have adverse effects on football itself. It would reinforce the existing gap between rich and poor clubs, even within the Premier League. And it would give BSkyB too much influence over regulation of football by the Premier League. Moreover, if the merger then provoked a small number of other clubs and broadcasters into similar mergers, the rich–poor gap would widen still further.

The Commission's judgement was based on its assertion that 'the relevant football market in which Manchester United operates is no wider than the matches of Premier League clubs' (http://www.mmc.gov.uk/bskyb.htm). But was this correct? In 1999 Man United were European champions and won the world cup championship in Tokyo, but they did it on the cheap, partly because so many of their young stars had grown up in the Man United youth programme. BSkyB's money would have allowed Man United to match salaries in Series A in Italy. The Premier League has never been able to (afford to) attract the top Brazilian stars.

Whereas European club teams simultaneously compete in national and European competitions, most American sports are hermetically sealed. World Series baseball is strictly a US affair. The same goes for basketball or American football. This makes it easier to have salary caps and other rules for redistributing between clubs to prevent wide gaps persisting (the worst teams one year get the pick of the newcomers the next year). Within Europe, penalizing the top team within a country may be good for the country's club competition, but it threatens to deprive their country's clubs of honours on the European stage.

This example shows again the difficulty in defining the relevant market in which to assess competition policy. Should it be the UK, Europe, or the global market? Once it extends beyond a single country, which competition authority should have jurisdiction? Easy questions with difficult answers.

British merger policy reflected two underlying assumptions. The first was that the cost savings from economies of scale and more intensive use of scarce management talent could be quite large. The second was that the UK was effectively part of an increasingly competitive world market so that the monopoly power of the merged firms, and the corresponding social cost of the deadweight burden, would be small. Large as they were, the merged firms would still be small in relation to European or world markets, and would face relatively elastic demand curves which gave little scope for raising price above marginal cost.

Nevertheless, it would be wrong to suppose that all mergers were approved. Nearly half of the mergers actually referred to the Competition Commission were found to be against the public interest, and the effects of the legislation went beyond the cases actually referred. Investigation was a lengthy process taking many months, a delay during which company share prices could move considerably and upset the original negotiations about the terms on which the relative shares of the companies should be valued. In practice, even the threat that a merger might be referred was often sufficient to induce the companies to abandon the merger.

BOX 18-5   A single European merger policy

In 1990 the first step was taken towards a European merger policy implemented through the European Commission. The idea was not to supplant national regulation of mergers, but to examine mergers whose significance extended beyond national boundaries. Mergers are examined if worldwide turnover of the merged firms would exceed 5 billion Euros (about £3 billion); if their EU turnover exceeds 250 billion Euros; and if at least one partner does not have two-thirds of its turnover in a single EU country. The EU Commission should block mergers 'creating or strengthening a dominant position'.

Of the first 140 mergers examined, only one was stopped: the proposed merger of De Havilland and Aerospatiale/Alenia, which together would have dominated production of 60-seater short-haul passenger aircraft. Yet, as the accompanying table shows, other mergers, achieving a huge market share, have been approved. Can such decisions be justified?

The Commission has not been unduly worried about a large market share provided either that vigorous actual competition already exists (as in the decision that a merger of Renault and Volvo truck businesses would face stiff competition from Mercedes despite its 18 per cent market share); or that prospects for potential competition (new entry) look good. Even where both of these factors were absent, some mergers

went ahead subject to conditions or 'remedies', typically a requirement that part of the business be hived off to provide additional competition.

In watching future merger regulation unfold, it is useful to keep in mind three themes of our previous analysis. First, how do we define the market, and hence market share? How much competition is likely from other countries, from other products, and from new producers? Second, we should expect firms to behave strategically. If domestic German control of mergers is tougher than that of the EU Commission, we should expect German firms to adopt tactics (i.e. where to sell output, which firms to pursue for merger talks) which ensure that they are investigated by the EU and not domestic German regulators. Third, there may well be a regulatory game between EU countries. Those with more lax merger controls may give their national firms a strategic advantage as EU superfirms are created by marriage. Under-regulating imposes a harmful externality on other EU countries. That is quite a powerful argument for a centralized European merger policy to internalize this externality.

Material in this box from: D. Neven, R. Nuttall and P. Seabright, *Merger in Daylight*, Centre for Economic Policy Research.

Merger	Product	Market share	EU decisions
Air France/Sabena	Brussels–Lyon flights	100%	Yes, subject to remedy
TetraPak/Alfa Laval	Food packaging	90%	Yes: no change in market share (Alfa Laval began with 0%)
Alcatel/Telettra	Microwaves	83%	Yes: potential competition OK
Courtaulds/SHIA	Manmade fibres	65%	Yes: strong actual and potential competition
Aerospatiale/Alenia/De Havilland	60 seat aircraft	64%	No: weak competition
Renault/Volvo	Trucks	54%	Yes: strong actual competition

SUMMARY

● The social cost or deadweight burden of monopoly power arises because marginal cost is set equal to marginal revenue, which is less than price and marginal consumer benefit. The social cost is the cumulative difference between the value that consumers place on the lost output and its marginal production cost. The social cost is higher still if oligopolists waste society's resources lobbying for monopoly power or incurring unnecessary expenditure to deter entrants, both of which shift cost curves upwards.

● Monopolists usually have inside information about their true costs, which neither shareholders nor regulators can easily discover. The easy life may lead monopolists to make inadequate efforts to reduce costs, adding to the social cost of monopoly.

● Industrial policy seeks to offset market failures in production which do not arise from scale economies in the domestic market and the imperfect competition to which these give rise; offsetting the latter is the object of competition policy. The two are frequently related.

● Patents provide a temporary legal monopoly for successful inventors, and hence an incentive to look for inventions. Otherwise the incentive for inventors would be low since they could foresee that profits on successful inventions would quickly be competed away by imitators.

● Many governments believe that the social return on R&D exceeds its private return. Some benefits of R&D spill over to other firms, creating an externality.

● When international competition is strategic between superfirms, the industrial policies of national governments towards their own 'national champions' may be an important pre-commitment which affects the bargaining power of their firms in the international market.

● Sunrise and sunset industries may involve other market failures. Before taking this as a general licence for an active industrial policy to manage change, governments must ask why the market is not doing a better job, and whether intervention can itself improve on the existing situation. Generally, picking winners has not been a success, but decentralized incentives may be effective if their rationale has been clearly identified.

● Economic geography is based on locational externalities arising in training, transport, and knowledge creation. The industrial base is the existing locational stock available. Such externalities may justify intervention to offset these market failures; they are not an excuse for blanket industrial subsidies.

● In the UK any firm with more than 25 per cent of the market can be referred to the Competition Commission, which must then consider whether or not the monopoly is against the public interest. The Commission takes account of a wide range of factors in making a judgement.

● Anti-competition agreements between firms, such as collusive price-fixing, must be notified and are generally outlawed. The Restrictive Practices Court does recognize certain gateways through which such agreements may be ratified as being in the public interest.

● Mergers may be horizontal, vertical, or conglomerate. Conglomerate mergers have the smallest scope for economies of scale. The recent merger boom has largely been in horizontal mergers to take advantage of larger markets caused by globalization, European integration, and deregulation.

● In principle, mergers can be referred to the Competition Commission if they will create a firm with a 25 per cent market share or if they involve assets of over £70 million. In practice, few mergers satisfying these criteria are actually referred. In part this may be justified because the UK competes in large world markets where the firms will have little monopoly power.

KEY TERMS

♦ Competition policy 293

♦ Industrial policy 294

♦ Patents 294

♦ Research and development (R&D) 294

♦ Sunrise and sunset industries 297

♦ Economic geography 298

♦ Locational externality 298

♦ Industrial base 298

♦ Producer surplus 300

♦ Consumer surplus 300

♦ Social cost of monopoly 300

♦ Deadweight burden 300

♦ Cream skimming 302

♦ Competition Commission 303

♦ Takeovers and mergers 305

♦ Horizontal, vertical and conglomerate mergers 305

REVIEW QUESTIONS

1 With constant AC and MC equal to £5, a competitive industry produces 1 million output units. Taken over by a monopolist, output falls to 800 000 units and the price rises to £8. AC and MC are unchanged. How would you calculate the social cost of monopoly? What is it?

2 Now suppose, when the monopolist takes over, AC and MC increase to £6 and ouput falls to 600 000 units at a price of £11. What is the social cost of monopoly now?

3 Explain the difference between UK and US policy towards monopolies and mergers.

4 Compared with other countries, a relatively large fraction of UK R&D expenditure by the government is devoted to defence projects. Is this necessarily economically undesirable?

5 Quite apart from aid to sunrise industries, UK policy provides substantial tax breaks for those investing in small firms. Do you think the issues discussed in this chapter can be used to justify such a policy?

6 Most footballs in the world are made in a small village in Pakistan. Why do football producers cluster together? Why not in Switzerland?

7 *Common fallacies* Show why the following statements are fallacious. (a) Monopolies make profits and must therefore be well-run companies. (b) Monopolies create social waste. Society should prohibit any firm from having more than 20 per cent of the domestic market. (c) It does not matter what other governments do; ours should not get involved in industrial policy. (d) Mergers are obviously beneficial; otherwise companies would not bother merging.

19 Privatization and regulation

LEARNING OUTCOMES

When you have finished this chapter, you should be able to:

- Study the problem of natural monopoly and interpret nationalization, regulation, and market enlargement as possible solutions
- Discuss the ideal of social marginal cost pricing, combined with social cost–benefit analysis of investment decisions
- Examine how two-part tariffs and peak-load pricing add to social efficiency (and to private profits if the company remains in the private sector)
- Explore how problems of nationalized industry performance gave rise to pressures for the alternative strategy of privatization and regulation
- Consider arguments for and against privatization, and relate these to the Private Finance Initiative
- Study issues arising in regulation of privatized natural monopolies
- Discuss whether globalization or European integration can solve the problem of natural monopoly by enlarging the market adequately

'In every great monarchy in Europe the sale of the Crown lands would deliver a much greater revenue than any which these lands ever afforded to the Crown. When the Crown lands had become private property, they would, in the course of a few years, become well improved and well cultivated.'

Adam Smith, *The Wealth of Nations* (1776)

This chapter deals with the boundary between the public sector and the private sector. As suggested by Adam Smith, the controversy is over 200 years old.

Chapter 18 discussed the role of policy in cases where promoting competition was feasible and likely to enhance efficiency. Now, we discuss industries in which scale economies are considerable. Competition may not be feasible or may require sacrificing scale economies to an extent that makes competition undesirable. Before 1980 such industries were thought to require so much regulation that they might as well be state owned.

Nationalization is the acquisition of private companies by the public sector.

Since 1980 the UK has pioneered a programme of privatization that has now been emulated in countries as diverse as France, Japan, Mexico and Hungary. Some countries, like the Czech Republic which began the 1990s with 97 per cent of its economy in state hands, were so keen to privatize quickly that they gave away state enterprises to private shareholders for only a nominal price!

Privatization is the return of state enterprises to private ownership and control.

It was the intention in the UK that subsequent regulation of privatized companies would be as light and unintrusive as possible. For this reason, the changes were sometimes called deregulation. In industries without big scale economies this was indeed possible. In the industries on which we mainly focus in this chapter – utilities such as electricity, gas, water, telecommunications – more extensive regulation, with regard to structure not just conduct, is required whenever international competition is not vigorous.

19-1 Natural monopoly

Figure 19-1 shows an industry with steadily decreasing long-run average costs reflecting the technological advantages of producing a very large output. Only one private firm could survive in such an industry. With many firms, the firm that expands output will always be able to reduce costs and undercut its rivals. Facing a demand curve DD and marginal revenue curve MR, the resulting monopolist will produce Q_M and earn profits P_MCBE.

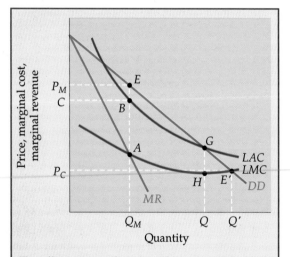

The efficient point E' equates long-run marginal cost LMC and marginal benefit DD. A private monopolist sets $MR = MC$, produces Q_M and earns profits P_MCBE. The deadweight loss under private monopoly is AEE'. If by law the monopolist was forced to charge a fixed price P_C, the monopolist would face a horizontal demand curve P_CE' up to the output Q'. Since P_C would then also be marginal revenue, the monopolist would produce at E where the marginal revenue and marginal cost coincide. Although efficient, society cannot force the monopolist to produce here in the long run. Since E' lies below LAC the monopolist is making losses and would rather go out of business.

Figure 19-1   Natural monopoly

A **natural monopoly**'s average costs keep falling as its output rises. It can undercut all smaller competitors. Since LMC lies below LAC while LAC is falling, a natural monopoly makes losses if forced to adopt uniform pricing at marginal cost.

At this output the social marginal benefit P_M exceeds the social marginal cost at A. The monopolist produces too little. Social marginal cost and marginal benefit are equal at the output Q' and the efficient point for society is E'. The private monopoly creates a deadweight burden AEE'.

Suppose you sat on the Competition Commission investigating this monopolist. What are your options? If you split the firm up you will have a lot of small firms each producing at higher average cost, a waste of society's resources. You could order the firm to produce at the socially efficient point E'. Then you will get the desired output Q'. However, the price P_C will be less than the firm's average costs at Q' so it will be making losses. You cannot force private firms to make losses. They will shut down instead.

Few countries allow unregulated natural monopolies to produce at E and impose the full deadweight burden AEE' on society. The first solution is a regulatory body such as OFTEL, which regulates British Telecom. The aim is to get as close as possible to the socially efficient allocation E' while allowing the monopolist to break even after allowing a proper deduction for all economic costs. For example, by ensuring that the monopolist produces Q at the price corresponding to average cost at this output, the social cost of the deadweight burden can be reduced from AEE' to GHE'.

An even better solution is to allow the monopolist to charge a two-part tariff.

A **two-part tariff** is a price system where users pay a fixed sum for access to the service and then pay a price per unit which reflects the marginal cost of production.

Thus the aim of a two-part tariff is to use fixed charges to pay for fixed costs and then to levy marginal charges to cover marginal costs. It acts as a lump-sum tax on users of the system.

Hence in Figure 19-1 the monopolist can be instructed to charge P_C for each unit of the good. Consumers will demand the socially efficient quantity Q'. Since the monopolist is now a price-taker at the controlled price P_C, it will be loss-minimizing for the monopolist to produce Q', at which both price and marginal revenue equal marginal cost. If the regulatory body does its sums correctly, it will then allow the monopolist to levy the minimum fixed charge necessary

BOX 19-1

Airline deregulation

Lessons from the United States   Internal US flights were deregulated in 1978. Entry barriers were removed, and by 1984 the number of airlines had risen from 36 to 120, fares were down 30 per cent, and passenger use was up 50 per cent. Fuller planes meant lower costs. More frequent service meant greater passenger convenience. Free marketeers rejoiced as their predictions came true.

The story changed after 1984. Cutthroat competition led to bankruptcies and mergers. By 1989 only 27 airlines survived. The top 12 controlled 97 per cent of the market. Fares rose. By 1997 airline profits reached $5 bn. Powerful incumbent airlines erected strategic entry barriers to consolidate their market share. They moved to a single airport (the hub) out of which long-haul flights operated. A system of feeder services (the spokes) first flew passengers to the hub. The hub-and-spoke system made it hard for small airlines to challenge the major airlines. Second, the majors also owned the reservation system used by travel agents to locate empty seats. By programming the computer to show their own flights first, they put new entrants at a disadvantage. Finally, they offered air miles that could be cashed in only with the same airline.

Regulation in Europe   European scheduled air travel was extensively regulated until 1997. Flights between European capitals were often restricted to one airline from each of the two countries, such as Iberia and Alitalia on the Madrid–Rome route. Competition was sometimes nominal; the two airlines divided their joint revenue equally. Fares were strictly controlled. Scheduled air travel was specifically exempt from EC Competition Law.

The consequence? High fares. Moreover, in Chapter 13 we argued that, when firms have extensive product

market power, trade unions will grab a big slice of these excess profits: lack of competition will show up as much in inflated costs as in high profits. The table shows how beautifully this theory fits the facts. Apart from the UK, where domestic deregulation had begun in the 1980s, all continental airlines paid much more than their US counterparts, despite average living standards being much higher in the USA than in, say, Spain or Portugal.

In the 1990s, European airlines were increasingly subject to normal competition law. 'EU completes air travel deregulation programme' reported *The Times* (2 April 1997) but then pointed out that, because of congestion at major airports, new entrants would have to operate out of secondary airports. While incumbents retain access to prime 'landing and takeoff slots' at favoured airports, life will remain difficult for new entrants. In March 1999, the High Court in London ruled that slots at Heathrow could be traded freely for cash. The European Commission thinks small airlines will be unable to afford to buy these slots.

Labour costs per worker, 1987 (USA = 100)		
	Cockpit staff	Cabin crew
8 US airlines	100	100
British Airways	120	68
Sabena (Belgian)	307	139
UTA (French)	298	161
Lufthansa (German)	325	143
Alitalia (Italian)	232	211
TAO (Portuguese)	167	93
SAS (Scandinavian)	258	146
Iberia (Spanish)	200	132

Sources: F. McGowan and P. Seabright, 'Deregulating European Airlines', *Economic Policy*, 1990; *The Times*, 2 April 1997; *Financial Times*, 10 February 1998.

to ensure that the monopolist breaks even after allowing for all relevant economic costs.

The two-part tariff is not always a feasible solution. If the fixed charge has to be *very* high it may induce people to abandon consumption of the commodity altogether. Moreover, whereas it may be easy to collect fixed charges from consumers with telephone or gas installations, it is harder to

enforce a fixed charge for the right to travel by rail and a fare per journey reflecting marginal cost. The costs of enforcing such a system might be enormous.

The third solution to the natural monopoly problem is to order the monopolist to produce at the socially efficient point E' and the corresponding price P_C but to provide a government subsidy to cover the losses that this will inevitably imply. However, the government will wish to be closely concerned with the operation of the company to ensure that this does not provide a blanket guarantee to underwrite whatever losses the company makes through its own stupidity or inefficiency. It is still socially desirable to produce the efficient output Q' in the cost-minimizing way. Thus, where the subsidy solution is adopted there is a pressure for the government to become involved in the entire running of the industry so that all operations can be carefully monitored.

We have just demonstrated that natural monopolies cannot both survive as profit-making industries and produce the socially efficient output by pricing at marginal cost unless they have very favourable opportunities for levying two-part tariffs. If such industries are nationalized so they can produce closer to the socially efficient output, it is inevitable that they will make losses and require a subsidy.

The fact that nationalized industries make losses is *not* sufficient to prove that they are not minimizing costs or producing the wrong output from society's viewpoint.

Three problems recur in attempts to adopt any of the above solutions to the problem of natural monopoly. First, once information is costly for monitors to acquire it is hard to ensure that the industry does minimize costs. Unnecessarily high costs can be passed on under average cost pricing (solution 1), can result in a higher fixed charge to ensure break-even under a two-part tariff (solution 2), or can require a larger subsidy (solution 3). In each case the regulatory body has the difficult task of trying to ensure that the management of the natural monopoly is as efficient as possible.

The second problem is regulatory capture.

Regulatory capture implies that the regulator gradually comes to identify with the interests of the firm it regulates, eventually becoming its champion, not its watchdog.

Clearly, the regulated devote considerable time, effort, and money to lobbying and otherwise trying to influence the regulator. A sense of public duty is the only reason for the regulator to resist. It can become an unequal contest.

More subtly, the regulated firm has all the inside information about its own activities, information which it is the whole purpose of the regulatory to try to acquire. Of necessity, regulators build up contacts with the regulated. At the end of long conversations, the regulator can feel quite sympathetic to the problems as perceived by the regulated.

Third, regulators may have difficulty making credible commitments about their future behaviour. For example, the regulator may seek to encourage the monopolist to invest by promising 'light' regulation in the future. But once the investment is made and a cost sunk, the regulator then faces temptations to change the ground rules, toughening requirements. Foreseeing all this, the monopolist never invests in the first place. The equilibrium is one of underinvestment because the regulator faces commitment problems.

During 1945–80, many European governments concluded that the least bad solution to these three problems was nationalization.

19-2 Nationalized industries

By nationalized industries we mean not the state provision of public goods, such as defence, nor of goods services supplied without charge, such as state education, but of private goods for sale in the market-place. Even by 2000 some UK firms remained under state control (e.g. the Post Office and Nuclear Electric).

Although natural monopoly was the commonest reason for nationalization, three other motives sometimes played a role. The first was externalities. One reason the London Underground has yet to be privatized is that the failure of politicians to price roads properly allows huge pollution and congestion externalities to go unchecked. Subsidizing public transport may then be the second-best policy. A second reason was value judgements about equity or fairness. A private profit-maximizing railway would close many rural lines. Society may think this would severely reduce the welfare of citizens in remote areas and undermine national unity. If so, its choices are to legislate that private suppliers must subsidize rural railways if they wish to be in the train business, or to nationalize the whole thing.

Third, it may be important to co-ordinate different parts of a network. As a nationalized industry, British Rail could think about the entire system. The fragmentation of the industry after privatization has led to externalities. For example, when Railtrack (www.railtrack.co.uk) invests in better infrastructure, the main gain may accrue to train operators not Railtrack itself.

We now discuss in more detail how society might wish investment and pricing decisions to be made within the public sector.

Investment decisions

Chapter 14 discussed the demand for capital and investment decisions by private firms. An investment project is profitable if the present value of the stream of future operating profits exceeds the initial cost of the new capital. Since firms do the most profitable projects first, investment proceeds until the marginal project is reached. At this point the present value of future profits just equals the cost of the capital. The same statement can be made using flows instead of stocks. Investment proceeds as long as the rate of return exceeds the interest rate that represents the opportunity cost of the funds tied up.

The same principles carry over into social investment decisions provided we use social not private measures of costs, benefits and the discount rate.

The initial cost of capital good　In the absence of other distortions, this is simply the private cost of the capital project. However, if externalities exist they should be taken into account. Local unemployment might reduce the social opportunity cost of construction workers below the market wage. Without the project the people would have made nothing else. Even the Treasury understands that where projects reduce unemployment they also reduce payments for unemployment benefit. A second possible externality arises from economic geography. Where *building* capital goods fosters production externalities (e.g. skill development), the right place to take this into account is in adjusting the 'social price' of the capital good.

Valuing the stream of future costs and benefits　Society will wish to use social not private values of costs and benefits. Externalities are one source of divergence between private and social. Consumer surplus is another. A private firm thinks the annual benefit is the steam of profits. For society the benefit is the entire area under the demand curve up to this ouput. Social profit coincides with monopoly profits only when the monopolist can price discriminate. With uniform pricing, the profit rectangle ($OP \times OQ$) is always smaller than the total consumer benefit. Notice, for later, that even when we measure *total* social benefit by the area under the demand curve, the *marginal benefit* is still given by the height of the demand curve at the output actually produced.

Choosing the discount rate　If public sector projects use a different discount rate from private sector projects, this will lead to a distortion between public and private investment.

The **discount rate** is the interest rate used in calculating present values of future streams of benefits or costs.

However, there are two reasons why the (second-best) compromise still involves public-sector discount rates below private ones. First, the public sector handles risk better. Even a huge loss on a major project would imply only a tiny change in income tax rates. The risk is spread more thinly: the public sector has more 'shareholders'.

Second, public investment displaces not just private investment but private consumption. Governments finance public-sector investment out of taxation that reduces take-home pay and high-street spending. Households can shift resources between current and future consumption by saving today to accumulate wealth for tomorrow. The after-tax interest rate shows the terms on which one can be swapped for the other. For efficiency, public sector investment should offer the same rate of return.

First best would thus be the same return on public investment, private investment and private saving. Distortions from tax rates and differences in ability to handle risk make this unattainable. The most efficient compromise (the second best) involves a public sector discount rate below the private rate but above the post-tax interest rate.

Pricing decisions

But for distortions elsewhere in the economy, nationalized industries should set prices at marginal cost. Private marginal cost should be adjusted for any production or consumption externalities that arise, thus ensuring that society equally values the marginal cost and marginal benefit from the last unit of output. Social marginal cost also takes account of any distributional value judgements the government wishes to impose.

We now consider some special aspects of nationalized industry pricing.

Short-run or long-run marginal cost pricing?　The once-and-for-all cost of building a plant is a *stock* concept. The cost is incurred at the point in time when the plant is built. But *LMC* is a *flow* concept, relating to the cost *per period* of producing output. In Chapter 14 we explained how stocks and flows are related. At the discount rate r the present value PV (a stock concept) of a permanent flow of c_k per period is given by the perpetuity formula $PV = c_k/r$. Conversely, the per period cost c_k of an initial outlay PV can be expressed as $c_k = r \times PV$. The flow cost is the opportunity cost of the money or social resources tied up in the plant and is measured by the initial capital cost multiplied by the discount rate r.

Figure 19-2 shows the short-run marginal cost SMC_0 of producing output. For simplicity, we assume that existing plant has a maximum capacity of Q_0 and the SMC_0 is

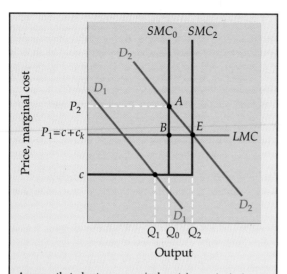

Assume that short-run marginal cost is constant at c up to full capacity and then vertical. SMC_0 corresponds to capacity Q_0 and SMC_2 to capacity Q_2. Suppose SMC_0 is relevant and demand is D_1D_1. In the short run the efficient output is Q_1 and price should be set at c. If demand is D_2D_2, pricing at short-run marginal cost leads to a price P_2 on the vertical part of SMC_0. LMC also includes the capital charge c_k. Beginning from the plant size Q_0, in the long run society can gain the triangle ABE by expanding capacity until LMC equals social marginal benefit at E. At plant size Q_2 the price P_1 still lies on the short-run marginal cost curve which is now SMC_2. Short-run marginal cost pricing equates immediate marginal costs and marginal benefits. In the long run it is by efficient investment decisions that capacity is adjusted to ensure that this price also reflects long-run marginal cost.

Figure 19-2   Marginal cost pricing

constant at the level c up to full capacity and then becomes vertical. No matter how much is spent, output cannot be increased beyond Q_0 given the existing level of plant capacity.

Since SMC_0 measures the marginal social opportunity cost in the short run of the resources used to produce this good, price should be set at SMC_0 to equate marginal social cost and marginal social benefit. Thus if demand is low the industry should produce Q_1 and will operate at less than full capacity. Given the higher demand curve D_2D_2, short-run marginal cost pricing will lead to a price P_2 and the industry will produce at full capacity. Since output cannot be increased above Q_0, a price P_2 higher than c is required to keep the quantity demanded equal to the maximum quantity that can be supplied.

Suppose in the long run the industry can build more identical factories. For example, with a slightly higher capital stock the industry will then face the short-run

marginal cost curve SMC_2 with constant marginal cost c up to the new level of full capacity Q_2, after which marginal costs become vertical.

But LMC also includes the per-period opportunity cost of the resources tied up in the capital stock, what we might call the capital charge c_k, whose calculation we described above. Figure 19-2 assumes that this capital charge c_k is given by the vertical distance $P_1 - c$. Thus we draw the LMC curve as a horizontal line at the height $P_1 = c + c_k$. The long-run marginal cost of another output unit is both the marginal operating cost and the capital charge c_k per unit of output.

Suppose the demand curve, reflecting social marginal benefit, is given by D_2D_2 and that the industry begins with the capital stock for which Q_0 is the maximum output and SMC_0 the short-run marginal cost curve. Pricing at short-run marginal cost, the industry charges a price P_2. Although this is the socially efficient output in the short run it is not efficient in the long run. Once capacity can be varied society will wish to produce at E, where marginal social benefit equals long-run social marginal cost LMC. By increasing the capital stock until its maximum output is Q_2 society can gain the area of the triangle ABE, the excess of marginal benefit over marginal cost when output is increased from Q_0 to Q_2.

Pricing and investment decisions are interconnected. In the short run output should be priced at SMC, the social opportunity cost of the resources employed. However, in the long run society should invest if the present value of future benefits exceeds the cost of adding to the capital stock. Instead of this stock evaluation of investment decisions we can use the equivalent flow evaluation. The capital stock should be increased if the marginal social benefit exceeds the long-run marginal cost inclusive of the capital charge. Thus, although prices are set according to SMC, in the long run investment will change capacity and shift the SMC curve.

Hence, although prices are set according to SMC, in the long run investment will adjust the capital stock and full capacity output until price also equals LMC. In the long run the efficient allocation is at point E in Figure 19-2, where marginal benefit, SMC, and LMC coincide.

Peak load pricing   In Chapter 9 we argued that a private monopolist would make higher profits if it were possible to price-discriminate, charging different prices to customers whose demand curves were effectively distinct. The problem with price discrimination in *goods* is that low-price customers resell to higher-price customers, thus tending to equalize the prices customers actually pay. Resale is not a problem when the commodity is a service (train journeys, electricity supply), which must be consumed as it is purchased.

A producer of electricity faces a high demand for electricity at breakfast time and dinner time, moderate demand throughout the rest of the day, and very little demand at night. To cater for demand at peak times it has to build extra power stations, which are idle when demand is lower. Thus in the long run, taking account of the capacity cost of building the extra power stations, the marginal cost of supplying peak users is very high.

Users at different times impose very different marginal costs on society. It makes sense to charge peak users higher prices to reflect the higher marginal costs they impose.

Peak load pricing is a system of price discrimination whereby peak time users pay higher prices to reflect the higher marginal cost of supplying them.

Peak load pricing has two attractive consequences. Not only are peak users paying for the high marginal costs they impose, but also those users who would not mind consuming at a different time (e.g. households with night storage heaters, who can use electricity at a time when marginal costs are low) are induced by cheaper prices to switch to consuming at off-peak times. By spreading total daily consumption more evenly, society reduces peak demand and has to devote less resources to building power stations whose number is determined by peak usage.

In Figure 19-2, the efficient pricing policy makes prices vary with short-run marginal cost. Off-peak users, with the demand curve D_1D_1, do not exhaust full capacity and pay the marginal operating cost c exclusive of capacity charges for the marginal plant. Peak users with the demand curve D_2D_2, pay a higher price P_2 on the vertical part of the SMC curve through which their demand curve passes.

Given this efficient pricing structure, what is the efficient quantity of investment? Investment should increase capacity up to the point at which the once-and-for-all cost of a new plant equals the present value of operating profits when the efficient pricing structure is in operation. Equivalently, on a flow basis, the average daily price (in Figure 19-2, the average of the prices P_2 and c, weighted by the fraction of the day for which the demand curves D_1D_1 and D_2D_2 are relevant) should cover long-run marginal cost inclusive of capacity costs. Thus in Figure 19-2 the efficient level of capacity might be Q_0 if the weighted average of P_2 and c is equal to $P_1 = c + c_k$.

To sum up, prices should be set at short-run marginal cost, the actual opportunity cost of the resources to society. When there is a daily or seasonal pattern in demand, peak load pricing reflects the different short-run marginal costs of supplying different customers at different times of day or times of year. The amount of total demand met on the vertical part of short-run marginal cost curves will then depend on the level of total capacity. At low capacity, prices will frequently be high since they are set on the vertical part of the short-run marginal cost curves. In the long run, investment and the efficient level of capacity should be determined to ensure that, when pricing at short-run marginal cost, average daily or yearly prices equal long-run marginal cost.

Telephone pricing in the UK   Peak load pricing and two-part tariffs try to get the relevant price as close to marginal cost as possible. In discussing nationalized industries, or natural monopolies that have been privatized and are regulated by government agencies, the objective of this price discrimination is to minimize social inefficiency. However, in Chapter 9 we showed that price discrimination, if it is possible, will also add to the profits of a private unregulated monopolist. We should not expect privatization to make much difference to the general structure of prices of natural monopolies such as electricity, gas, and telecommunications.

Next time you or your family get the quarterly telephone bill, take a look at it in closer detail. You will find you have been charged a quarterly rental independent of the number of calls made, and then in addition a charge per minute that you make a call: a two-part tariff. Since the telephone regulator OFTEL cares about efficiency, the rental should roughly cover the capacity charge in Figure 19-2, while the price per unit should cover short-run marginal cost SMC. This in turn should follow the principle of peak load pricing.

Households and businesses wake up in the morning and want to get started on a new day's communication by phone. By evening, there are fewer people left to call, and by the middle of the night most of us are asleep. Figure 19-2 implies that those who wish to make daytime calls should pay the high price required to choke off demand at full capacity. Conversely, when the weekend network is deserted because business is asleep, SMC and price should be much lower. Table 19-1 shows that actual prices of British

Table 19-1 BT price of a local call, 2000			
	Day	Evening	Weekend
Pence/minute	4	1	1

Note: Quarterly fixed rental £23.63.
Source: British Telecommunications.

Telecom closely follow both principles: two-part tariff and peak-load pricing.

Nationalized industries' performance

By 1967 the large UK public sector was being run according to sophisticated principles of pricing and investment as set out above. Civil servants who helped run these industries were masters of the intricacies of the social discount rate, peak-load pricing, two-part tariffs and consumer surplus. So what went wrong?

Three things. First, the analysis assumed perfect (i.e. costless) information. In practice, firms always had inside information and the government became worried that there were insufficient ways of preventing unnecessary cost escalation. Cost curves were thought to be higher than they should be.

Second, there were several types of commitment problem. The government found it difficult to pre-commit to resist pressure for wage increases in the public sector. Managers of nationalized industries couldn't argue that the 'shareholders' couldn't afford it. The shareholder was the Treasury and it could always find more money. Hence managers in nationalized industries found it hard to resist wage claims. They also found it hard to fire people. Strikes against dismissals made politicians nervous. Sometimes the minister would pick up the phone and find a way to do a deal.

Commitment problems also applied to investment. Investment by the nationalized industries is part of government spending and contributes to the budget deficit. Of course it also contributes to future government earnings but politicians under short-term pressure had a habit of cancelling long-term investment plans by nationalized industries. So nationalized industries had inefficient levels of investment. However much the privatized utilities are now blamed for poor infrastructure in railway signalling or water supply, half a century of under-investment while they had been nationalized obviously contributed to the problem.

There were other types of 'government failure'. Politicians wanted plants located in their constituencies, wanted wage freezes during periods of overheating, wanted additional spending during recessions, all of which distorted decision making within nationalized industries. They had been nationalized to solve a market failure: now they were at least as vulnerable to government failure.

Third, people began to realize that a goldfish might look big in a small jar but small in a large lake. Increasing integration of different national economies began to introduce competition through imports or entry by foreign companies. As the size of the relevant market increased, the potential market power of firms of a given size diminished. Industries previously viewed as natural monopolies might be subject to more competition in the future, reducing the case for state control.

19-3 Public versus private

Efficiency does not fall like rain from the sky. It needs sustained effort and leadership by management. How do incentives differ in the public and private sectors?

Incentives for private managers

In theory, private managers' performance is monitored by actual and potential shareholders. If managers do badly, the company's directors may be voted out of office at the annual general meeting of shareholders. Moreover, if bad management is perceived by the stock market, share prices will be lower than they might have been and a takeover raider may see an opportunity to buy up the company, install a better management, improve profits, and hence make capital gains when share prices subsequently rise. Together, these threats are supposed to discipline managers and keep them on their toes.

In practice, these threats are weak and not very credible. In the first place, individual shareholders face a free-rider problem: provided other shareholders monitor the management, everything will be fine. So everyone tends not to bother. Second, takeover raids typically bid up the share price significantly; the incumbent management has considerable leeway before it is likely to get into trouble and be out of a job. Finally, incumbent managers have a lot of insider information about the true state of the firm, information not available to existing shareholders or potential raiders.

Because shareholders know all this, they try to give managers a direct incentive to care about profits and cost reduction. Senior executives get large profit-related bonuses. These are a carrot, for those who like carrots; but shareholders have no accompanying stick, which effective two-handed discipline would require.

In these circumstances, we cannot guarantee that private management will be efficient unless it is subject to effective competition and challenge, either from other competitors in the market-place or from a tough and watchful regulatory body. When the private firm is very large, and therefore subject to little domestic competition, and also produces in a sector sheltered from imports and foreign competition, it is quite likely to be a relatively sleepy monopolist unless it has regulators to whom it must account. And these regulators must be capable of resisting the regulatory capture we discussed in Chapter 18.

Incentives for public managers

If private managers sometimes face a weak market mechanism for discipline and control, public sector managers face no market mechanism at all. Everything depends on the effectiveness of the government as a watchdog.

In principle, the government might do this at least as effectively as private markets. It too can offer performance-related bonuses, and it does not face the free-rider problem which confronts individual shareholders. On the other hand, its civil servants probably have less training in business evaluation than do private sector analysts, and, of greatest importance, there is the overwhelming political temptation for the government to hijack the nationalized industries and make them an instrument of whatever is the pressing problem of the day.

The importance of ownership

It follows from the arguments above that the transfer of *ownership* from public to private sector may not in itself be the most important issue. Neither public nor private owners are good at monitoring managements. If ownership transfer to the private sector has any direct benefit, it is the one we cited above: it makes it less easy for governments to use industries to meet the requirements of other political dictates.

On the other hand, it should not be imagined that private industries are immune from such considerations. If you doubt this, talk to any private oil company involved in the North Sea. Such companies have at times faced a petroleum revenue tax rate of over 90 per cent, way above anything they were led to expect when they first went into the North Sea.

Thus, most economists agree that the key issue is not ownership itself but rather the severity of the market competition, or its substitute regulatory policy, which the industry faces. Sheltered monopolies will be sleepy and slack no matter who owns them. Conversely, the major benefits of privatization are likely to stem not from literally returning ownership to the private sector, but rather from associated measures which make it clear to managers that they are expected to compete effectively and efficiently. The litmus test of this assertion is the fact that so many UK nationalized industries managed to improve their performance in the run-up to privatization, *while they were still in*

public ownership. However, over the longer run, privatization may represent a useful commitment by government not to interfere too closely in the day-to-day running of the industry.

Selling the family silver?

Some people worry that selling off state assets mortgages the country's future. Others think privatization makes the state better off. Is there any simple way through the confusion in the public debate?

You already know enough to work out the answer for yourself. The market price of an asset is simply the present value of the income stream to which it entitles the owner. Suppose a fair price is £100. If we sell you the asset, we get £100 in cash but you get an asset worth £100. Neither of us is better or worse off than before. Of course, if we underprice the asset we are selling, perhaps because we want large queues of buyers so we can claim how popular it is, we make a loss on the sale and you make a profit. That is one way the government could be worse off by privatization.[1]

How could the government be better off by privatization? Essentially for the reason first advanced by Adam Smith in the quotation at the start of this chapter. If nationalized industries previously had bad performances, they would have been worth little had they been sold at that stage. If management policy is changed *prior* to privatization, the present value of future profits rises at this point, and it is this that is the source of improvement to the public finances, not the subsequent change of ownership.

Finally, notice that the question of mortgaging the future hinges crucially on what is done with the privatization revenue. If it is invested in physical capital for the public sector or used to retire outstanding government debt, it is not at all imprudent. Only if it is 'blown', for example on a tax-cut-financed consumer boom, can the government be said to be piling up financial trouble for future governments.

19-4 Privatization in practice

Table 19-2 shows average annual real revenues from privatization under the Conservative Government during 1980–97 from sales of nationalized industries such as British Telecom, British Gas, British Airways, British Steel, the

---

[1] Most UK privatizations do seem to have been underpriced. The government believed there was an externality in encouraging wider share ownership, and was prepared to subsidize this activity.

BOX 19-2   The private finance initiative

In 1992, when two years of UK recession had undermined tax revenue and caused government borrowing to mushroom, the government introduced the Private Finance Initiative (PFI). The government claimed it was an innovative way of drawing on private-sector expertise to finance and manage public projects. Critics claimed it was largely a scam for lowering the apparent size of the budget deficit. The argument has been raging ever since.

The PFI transforms government departments and agencies from owners and operators of assets to ongoing purchasers of services from the private sector. Private firms become long-term service providers not just upfront asset builders. Rather than paying for the capital cost of road building, the government becomes a continuing purchaser of miles of maintained highway.

During 1992–98 £11 billion such deals were signed, of which 27 per cent was accounted for by the Channel Tunnel Rail Link alone; another 33 per cent by other transport schemes such as roads, bridges, and rail and tram developments; and 12 per cent by hospitals and other health-sector projects. The remainder went on IT, defence, education, and prison and other accommodation. In 1996 the scheme was extended to local authorities under the name Public Private Partnership Programme. The table below shows projections for 1998–99 to 2001–02.

The Treasury insists the principal aim is to draw on private-sector management expertise and risk control. The government was fed up with cost overruns on public projects. Under the PFI, the private sector is responsible for risks within its control. The government is only responsible for overruns arising from wider risks outside the contractors' control. Of course, the dividing line is ambiguous. London and Continental Railway, responsible for the largest PFI project, the Channel Tunnel Rail Link, has kept asking for more money than the level specified in its original bid.

What about the budgetary implications? First, any benefit of private-sector efficiency has to be set against the fact that the government can borrow more cheaply than the private sector. The private sector bears the initial construction costs, which it finances by borrowing. Yet the lower credit rating of privately financed projects (compared with a government rating of AAA, Greenwich Hospital's bonds are rated BBB, and Docklands Light Railway bonds rated A), can mean anything up to an extra one percentage point on the interest rate that must be paid. When average interest rates are only 6 or 7 per cent, this can add quite a lot to the cost of a project. Private-sector efficiency has to offset more than this if the government is to benefit by the arrangement.

Second, the PFI allows the government to escape the initial capital cost of building a road or a prison in exchange for incurring two future costs: the ongoing cost of 'renting' the road or prison service from the asset provider, and the possible liability for cost increases outside the control of the private supplier. Making proper allowance for the latter in today's budget estimates is no easy matter.

What about exchanging the capital cost for a future liability to rent the service instead? Suppose a road costs £100 million to build, and interest rates are 10 per cent. The private provider will have to charge £10 million a year just to cover the opportunity cost of the money tied up in the project. In the early years, the government has its road and is spending a lot less than the £100 million it would have to spend to build the road. Initially, it needs less tax revenue. It is like hidden borrowing. The present value of the future road rental charges it will have to pay does not show up in government debt.

Many future flows are not properly accounted for in the government accounts. When the UK first discovered North Sea Oil, the present value of all the future tax levied on oil extraction was not immediately included as a government asset. This is not how the stock market behaves. Think of all these internet companies currently valued at billions of pounds merely because they will earn revenues at some future date.

Conversely, many governments already know that they face huge future pension obligations, because of ageing populations and generous state pensions (not

Planned PFI private sector capital investment (£m), 1998/99 to 2001/02				
Department	98/99	99/00	00/01	01/02
Environment, Transport, Regions	470	1050	940	1160
Health	310	610	740	690
Local authorities	300	600	600	600
Defence	340	300	220	220
Scotland	310	520	320	60
Wales	110	150	120	70
Home Office	70	270	280	190
Other	290	500	360	100
Total	2200	4020	3580	3090

Sources: *Financial Times*, 11 December 1998
http://www.treasury-projects-taskforce.gov.uk

a feature of the UK!), yet this liability does not show up anywhere in their accounts today. It should be recorded not in the flow account of current income and spending, but ideally in the current assessment of assets and liabilities. Since it is not, as PFI projects gradually build up the flow of fees to be paid to private-service providers of what were previously public projects, this will automatically tend to raise the flow of government spending in the future.

water companies and most of electric power. At 1997 prices, almost £67 billion in revenue was raised during 1980–97.

People quickly figured out that buying shares at the offer price was a good deal; hence the queues of eager buyers featured on the TV news. However, the attempt to encourage wider share ownership was substantially frustrated. Having made their capital gains, individuals soon sold their shares to the big pension funds and insurance companies that were eager to have a portfolio close to the market average.

Earlier, we stressed the importance of the extent of competition that the newly privatized companies would face. We distinguish two cases.

Enough competition, little market failure

Examples in this group include Jaguar, Cable & Wireless, British Aerospace, and British Airways. Some firms were not that large, but many were huge. We place them in this group because they were subject to acute international competition. In general, firms in this group have been quite successful after privatization.

Market power and regulation

Having privatized most of the smaller companies first, by 1984 the government turned to sales of the giant corporations that were close to natural monopolies. Whereas water and electricity were broken up into different private companies between which there might be a degree of competition, British Telecom (BT) and British Gas were privatized intact. The privatizing of giant firms not subject to severe international competition is unlikely to be attractive unless accompanied by regulation.

Table 19-2 UK privatization revenues 1980–97 (annual averages, 1997 £bn)				
80–83	84–86	87–90	91–93	94–97
0.2	1.5	4.5	7.8	5.0

Source: HM Treasury.

Will national markets survive?

We argued that regulation of private companies as large as British Steel was not necessary on natural monopoly grounds: they play not in an insulated national market but in a global market in which there is cutthroat competition. However, other markets, such as gas and water, seem to remain nationally insulated from one another.

When natural monopoly exists, allowing private firms to exploit market power is inefficient. Yet an underlying theme of the last two chapters is that the policy response of nationalization was not an unmitigated success, and we are gradually learning in Europe that the alternative policy response – leave natural monopolists in the private sector but regulate their activities – is also full of difficulties. In the United States, where regulation was always preferred to public ownership, the same conclusion was reached long ago: regulatory capture and informational problems create serious difficulties for public policy.

Perhaps a bit of lateral thinking is needed. Instead of imperfectly intervening to control a monopolist within a small market, why not try to expand the market? A large market may support competition between many firms

---

BOX 19-3	The biggest privatizer of all?

Table 19-2 showed how the UK pioneered privatization under Margaret Thatcher and John Major. By 1997 the UK did not have that much left to sell. Continental Europe has been catching up fast, and countries such as Italy and France may eventually raise even more from privatization than the UK did. So far, the UK has resisted privatizing the Post Office, but the Dutch post office has already been sold, and Germany's giant `Bundespost, Europe's biggest letter carrier, is scheduled for sale in 2000.

Source: *Observer*, 7 March 1999.

Privatization receipts 1993–98 (£bn)

Italy	56	UK	22
France	36	Sweden	12
Spain	28	Holland	11
Germany	23	Portugal	10

Top 10 sales of 1999 (£bn)

Deutsche Telekom	German telecoms	4.4
ENI	Italian oil & gas	3.8
Credit Lyonnais	French bank	2.5
Iberia	Spanish airline	1.3
Autostade	Italian motorways	1.3
Portugal Telecom	Portuguese telecoms	1.3
Monte dei Paschi	Italian bank	1.2
Alitalia	Italian airline	1.1
Aerospatiale	French defence	0.9
Telecom Eireann	Irish telecoms	0.9

where each of them has to be large to take advantage of economies of scale. This is a key aspect of the programme to 'complete the internal market' within Europe, discussed in Chapter 35.

How easily the market can be widened affects the regulatory strategy that should be adopted for a particular industry. For example, gas and telecommunications should not be treated similarly, as our previous discussion suggests. For some time to come, British Gas (www.britishgas.co.uk) will inevitably have a powerful market position within the UK, although it will of course face competition from other energy sources. In contrast, exciting changes are taking place in telecommunications, which are likely to promote much greater competition.

Within the UK, Mercury succeeded in securing 10 per cent of the market (Mercury is now part of Cable & Wireless, see www.cwcom.co.uk). More significantly, mobile phones and data services through cable TV have become big business and present a challenge even to BT (www.bt.co.uk). Data transmission is a rapidly growing market, and satellites are no respecters of national boundaries. Driven by the new technological opportunities, the European Commission is now discussing how to dismantle many of the national regulations of telecommunications. If this occurs, the significance of national markets will be substantially reduced.

19-5 Regulatory reform

What lessons should have been learned from the experience of nationalizing natural monopolies? First, regulators need to be independent of government to make credible the promise not to interfere all the time. This has been accomplished by establishing the independent regulators whose acronyms punctuate the financial media: OFTEL, OFWAT, OFGEM, and so on. Each regulatory agency has objectives clearly laid down by Parliament but is responsible for their implementation through regulatory policy.

Second, attention must be paid to information asymmetries and possible cost escalation by natural monopolists. In essence, two systems of regulation of *conduct* are possible: a price ceiling or a ceiling on the rate of return (sometimes called 'cost-plus'). Regulatory design faces a tradeoff when the firm has an information monopoly on its true costs. A price ceiling gives the monopolist all the benefit of cost reduction that is unobservable by the regulator; a cap on the rate of return would force prices down with costs.

If that was the only problem, a price cap offers much better incentives. But if the monopolist faces other risks, rate of return regulation enables unforeseen developments to be passed on to consumers, whereas a price cap makes the monopolist bear all of the risk. Efficient risk-sharing might employ at least some elements of rate-of-return regulation.

Despite the case for some compromise between these two methods, UK regulation has plumped entirely for the price-cap method, putting the full force of regulation behind the pressure for cost reduction. This was pioneered with the privatization of BT in 1984 which has been subject to an '$RPI - X$' price ceiling. What this means is that its *nominal* prices can rise by the same percentage as the retail price index, minus X per cent. X is therefore the annual rate of reduction in *real* prices. Since the telecommunication industry is enjoying rapid technical progress, it should be able to reduce costs year after year. The regulator sets X. During 1984–89, X was 3 per cent. It was then raised to 4.5 per cent and then 6.25 per cent. During its first ten years as a private company, BT was supposed to reduce its real prices by a cumulative 45 per cent. In fact they fell by 43 per cent.

Subsequent regulators have used a similar approach. For example, in regulating the water companies, OFWAT (www.open.gov.uk/ofwat) adopted '$RPI + K$' to reflect the fact that the real price of water needs to increase if water companies are to improve quality (and indeed quantity!) by undertaking the substantial investment that was for so long neglected when water was a nationalized industry. The level of K averaged around 5.5 per cent during 1990–95 although it varied slightly across the different regional water companies according to OFWAT's assessment of the need for investment.

In 1999, after an investigation by the Competition Commission was critical of charges for mobile phones, Vodafone and Cellnet were set a price ceiling of RPI − 9 during each of 1999 and 2000.

Regulating conduct is not the only option available to regulators. It would also be possible to think about breaking up the company to change the structure of the industry. In the 1980s, the US phone company AT&T (www.att.com) was broken up into 'baby Bells', each serving a region of the US but sharing the same network for interregional calls.

The problems of regulating giant companies has led regulators to think harder and harder about whether some parts of the business could survive competition. When BT was privatized in 1984, Mercury was licensed as a smaller competitor. BT had to provide Mercury with access to its network at reasonable prices.

Many industries are vertically integrated, combining an upstream facility, the basic transmission network, with downstream activities such as local distribution. The basic network is a natural monopoly – we only want one national grid for electricity – but downstream activities may offer more opportunities for competition. Obviously, access to the network has to be available at reasonable prices, and the regulator needs to monitor this. A key issue is whether the firm that runs the network should also be allowed to compete with other downstream distributors. The answer depends on whether either vertical externalities or opportunities for strategic behaviours give the network monopolist undue power in the downstream market.

In privatizing BT, the government decided to allow BT to compete in downstream activities. Subsequent experience has shown that Mercury offered only limited competition; BT may now be facing tougher competition from cable TV companies that are now allowed simultaneously to offer phone calls down the same cable. Indeed, after more than a decade of regulatory experience, UK practice has moved steadily towards greater regulation of structure, which began with the electricity privatization in which the grid and the distribution companies were kept clearly distinct.

Similarly, the privatization of British Rail led to the creation of Railtrack to supply the infrastructure network, and the award of regional operating franchises to companies such as Virgin Trains and Connex.

SUMMARY

● Nationalization is the acquisition of private companies by the public sector. Privatization is the sale of public-sector firms to the private sector.

● A natural monopoly faces a falling average cost curve. Marginal cost lies below average cost. Pricing at marginal cost implies losses.

● A two-part tariff allows the monopolist to set the appropriate marginal charge and recover losses via the fixed charge. With an information monopoly, however, the firm could be inefficient and seek to recover unnecessary losses via this fixed charge.

● Ideally, state-run firms should price at marginal social cost and invest until price just covers long-run marginal social cost, including the annual interest cost of the initial capital expenditure.

● Regulatory capture occurs when the regulator becomes the champion of the industry that it is supposed to regulate.

● Privatization was a response to the view that some state companies were not natural monopolies, and that even natural monopolies were better handled by arms' length regulation that committed the government not to intervene perpetually.

● Transfer of ownership makes credible the fact that the firm does not have limitless government backing (though governments do bail out even private companies from time to time!).

● Selling assets at a fair price leaves government wealth unaltered. If prospects of tougher treatment in the future lead to productivity improvements in state firms, the government becomes better off when the productivity improves not when (or if) the firm is sold.

● Many privatized firms now face intense competition, often from abroad. However, natural monopolies have required a new framework of regulation. This has favoured price-capping, administered by independent regulatory agencies and subject to periodic review.

● Increasingly, the UK has been driven to regulate not merely conduct but structure. This presupposes that some parts of a natural monopoly can be hived off and become suitable for competition. In practice, this has usually been downstream activities in a vertically-related industry.

● The Private Finance Initiative uses private finance to build projects and private management to run them. The government then pays a service charge to use the asset.

KEY TERMS

◆ Nationalization   311

◆ Privatization   312

◆ Natural monopoly   312

◆ Two-part tariff   312

◆ Regulatory capture   314

◆ Discount rate   315

◆ Peak-load pricing   317

REVIEW QUESTIONS

1 Why do sports clubs have both an initial membership fee and an annual subscription for people who are already members?

2 An MP has suggested that since British Telecom is regulated by OFTEL it would make sense to establish OFAIR to regulate British Airways. Would it?

3 'Cheap season tickets keep commuters off congested rush-hour roads.' 'Commuters should pay extra since most trains lie idle the rest of the day.' Adjudicate between these views. Does the answer depend on how cars and parking are being priced?

4 'The Channel Tunnel, built with private money, was then unable to keep up the interest payments on its debts. It should never have been built.' Discuss.

5 Did you remember the distinction between private and social valuation of costs and benefits in answering question 4? Identify five sources of difference between private and social?

6 Suppose competition from the tunnel also bid down prices on cross-channel ferries. Is this socially desirable or not? How does it affect questions 4 and 5?

7 When the Ministry of Defence orders the design and manufacture of a new fighter aircraft, it could issue a fixed-price contract or a cost-plus contract. Explain how incentives differ in the two contracts. When would cost-plus be socially desirable?

8 Why is the Private Finance Initiative a compromise between fixed-price and cost-plus contracts?

9 *Common fallacies* Show why the following statements are fallacious. (a) Nationalized industries that lose money must be inefficient and should be privatized. (b) A private monopoly is always inferior to a public monopoly. (c) Since conduct can always be regulated, there is no need ever to break up monopolies.

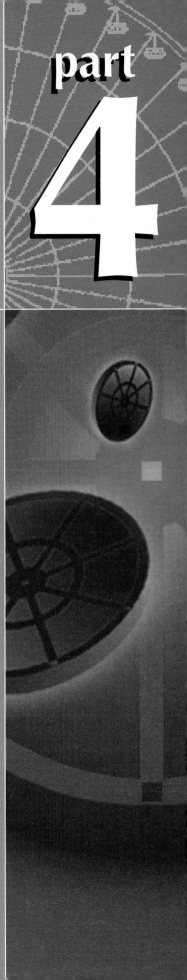

part 4

Macroeconomics

Part 4 builds a picture of the national economy as a system in which feedbacks occur. Sluggish adjustment of wages and prices allows output to deviate from full capacity. We analyse why booms and slumps occur. Demand for national output depends on private demand, government demand, and from foreigners. Since interest rates affect demand, the financial sector interacts with the real economy. Price and wage adjustment allows eventual convergence of output on full capacity.

Economic growth changes this capacity over time. Business cycles refer to shorter-term movements of output around its long-run trend.

Chapter 20 introduces macroeconomic accounting. Chapters 21–22 develop the basic model of output determination in the short run. Chapters 23–25 introduce the financial sector, and show how interest rates balance the supply and demand for money, and examine how output and interest rates are determined together. Chapter 26 analyses how wage and price adjustment bring output to its full-capacity level. Chapters 27–28 discuss implications for unemployment and inflation. Chapter 29 explores the role of the exchange. Chapters 30–31 examine long-run growth cycles, and Chapter 32 takes stock of positive macroeconomics.

20 Introduction to macroeconomics and national income accounting

LEARNING OUTCOMES

When you have finished this chapter, you should be able to:

● **Recall that macroeconomics simplifies the components of the economy to study interaction and feedback within the whole system**
● **Construct an internally consistent set of national accounts**
● **Explain how the circular flow between households and firms keeps track of real resource flows and the corresponding financial payments**
● **Bring in the government and the foreign sector, and show the equality of leakages from, and injections to, the circular flow**
● **Recognise that national income and output are poorly measured, and discuss what more comprehensive measures might be included**

Macroeconomics is the study of the economy as a whole.

Macroeconomics is concerned not with the details of individual products or industries but with the economy as a whole. We now turn to the big issues such as unemployment, inflation, and economic growth.

The distinction between microeconomics and macroeconomics is more than the difference between economics in the small and economics in the large, which the Greek prefixes *micro* and *macro* suggest. The purpose of the analysis is also different.

A model is a deliberate simplification to enable us to pick out the key elements of a problem and think about them clearly. Although we could study the whole economy by piecing together our microeconomic analysis of each and every market, the resulting model would be so cumbersome that it would be hard to keep track of all the economic forces at work.

Microeconomics and macroeconomics take different approaches to keep the analysis manageable. Microeconomics places the emphasis on a detailed understanding of particular markets. To achieve this amount of detail or magnification, many of the interactions with other markets are suppressed. In saying that a tax on cars reduces the equilibrium quantity of cars, we ignore the question of what the government does with the tax revenue. If the government has to borrow less money, interest rates and the exchange rate may fall, boosting competitiveness and car output.

Microeconomics is a bit like looking at a horse race through a pair of binoculars. It is great for details, but sometimes we get a clearer picture of the whole race by using the naked eye. Because macroeconomics is concerned with the interaction of different parts of the economy, it relies on a different simplification to keep the analysis manageable. Macroeconomics simplifies the building blocks in order to focus on how they fit together and influence one another.

Macroeconomics is concerned with broad aggregates

such as the total demand for goods by households or the total spending on machinery and building by firms. As in watching the horse race through the naked eye, our notion of the individual details is more blurred but we can give our full attention to the whole picture. We are more likely to notice the horse sneaking up on the rails.

20-1 The issues

We now introduce some of the main issues in macroeconomics. We pose a series of questions which form the theme on the analysis in Part 4.

The annual **inflation rate** is the percentage increase per annum in the average price of goods and services.

In Chapter 2 we introduced the retail price index (RPI), a weighted average of the prices households pay for goods and services. The percentage annual growth in the RPI is the most commonly used measure of inflation in the UK.

What causes inflation? The money supply? Trade Unions? Why do people mind so much about inflation? Does inflation cause unemployment? These are among the questions we shall seek to answer.

Unemployment is a measure of the number of people registered as looking for work but without a job.

The *unemployment rate* is the percentage of the labour force that is unemployed. The *labour force* is the number of people working or looking for work. It excludes all those, from rich landowners to heroin addicts, who are neither working nor looking for work.

Unemployment is still high. Why has it increased so much since the late 1970s? Are workers pricing themselves out of jobs by greedy wage claims? Is high unemployment necessary to keep inflation under control, or could the government create more jobs?

Real gross national product (real GNP) measures the total income of the economy. It tells us the quantity of goods and services the economy as a whole can afford to purchase. It is closely related to the total output of the economy.

Increases in real GNP are called **economic growth**.

What determines real GNP? Does unemployment mean that real GNP is lower than it might be? Why do some countries grow faster than others?

Macroeconomic policy Almost every day the newspapers and television refer to the problems of inflation, unemployment, and slow growth. These issues are widely discussed;

they help determine the outcome of elections, and make some people interested in learning more about macroeconomics.

The government has a variety of policy measures through which it can try to affect the performance of the economy as a whole. It levies taxes, commissions spending, and influences the money supply, interest rates, and the exchange rate.

What the government can and should do is the subject of lively debate both within economics and in the country at large. It is important to distinguish between positive issues relating to how the economy works and normative issues relating to priorities or value judgements. In the ensuing chapters we try to make clear which aspects of the policy debate reflect differing beliefs about how the economy works and which reflect differences in value judgements.

20-2 The facts

We begin with some key facts on recent inflation, economic growth, and unemployment.

Prices and inflation

Table 20-1 shows recent inflation rates in several countries. It gives a fair picture of what has been happening in prices in general. How did this inflation compare with other countries and other decades? The first column of Table 20-2 shows that the average annual inflation rate has varied greatly from country to country. Although the UK has experienced higher inflation than Switzerland, Japan, or the United States, its inflation rate has still been much lower than that of many other countries. Figure 20-1 shows the annual inflation rate in the UK over a much longer period.

Economic growth

Table 20-2 also shows the average annual rate of growth of real output in selected countries. Again, the performance of different countries has varied greatly. Korea and Israel have

Table 20-1	Inflation rates (%)	
	1990	1998
USA	4.3	1.6
Japan	2.3	0.6
Germany	3.2	0.9
France	3.1	0.8
Italy	7.6	1.7
UK	6.4	3.4
Netherlands	2.3	2.0

Source: OECD, *Economic Outlook*.

Table 20-2	Inflation and real output growth, 1980–97 (% per annum)	
Country	Inflation	Growth
Argentina	234	0.9
Brazil	362	2.9
Israel	65	4.7
Korea	6	8.5
Italy	8	1.9
UK	5	2.6
Sweden	5	1.7
France	4	1.5
USA	3	2.8
Japan	1	2.9
Switzerland	3	0.8

Source: World Bank, *World Development Report*.

Table 20-3	Unemployment (% of labour force)		
	1980	1989	1998
USA	7.2	5.3	4.5
Japan	2.0	2.2	4.1
France	5.8	9.3	11.7
Italy	5.6	10.0	11.9
UK	6.2	7.3	6.3
Belgium	9.3	7.5	9.5
Holland	6.0	6.9	4.0
Sweden	2.0	1.5	8.3

Source: OECD, *Economic Outlook*.

Table 20-4	Inflation, unemployment, and real GNP growth 1960–98 (% per annum)		
	UK	USA	Germany
Inflation			
1960–73	5	3	3
1973–81	15	9	5
1981–90	6	5	3
1990–98	4	3	3
Unemployment			
1960–73	3	5	1
1973–81	6	7	3
1981–90	10	7	7
1990–98	9	6	7
Real growth			
1960–73	3	4	5
1973–81	1	2	2
1981–90	3	3	2
1990–98	2	3	3

Sources: *Economic Report of the President of the United States*; OECD, *Economic Outlook*.

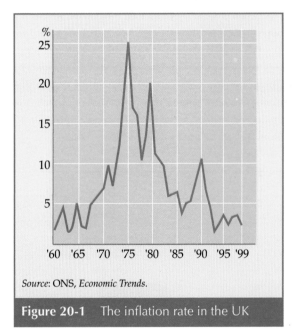

Source: ONS, *Economic Trends*.

Figure 20-1   The inflation rate in the UK

grown significantly faster than the European countries such as the UK, Switzerland and France.

The table gives strong evidence against the popular myth that countries with high inflation rates always grow slowly. Switzerland, with the lowest inflation rate, has almost the *lowest* growth rate of real output. Brazil, with an inflation rate 100 times as large, grew three times as quickly.

Unemployment

Since 1980 Europe has faced high unemployment. Table 20-3 shows that unemployment rates increased much more in Europe than in Japan or the United States.

Recent years in perspective

The 1970s was a period of poor macroeconomic performance throughout the world. In almost every country there was a decline in the growth of both real GNP and real GNP per person, a rise in unemployment rates, and an increase in inflation. Table 20-4 contrasts the good years 1960–73 with the difficult years 1973–81.

In the 1980s and 1990s many people became disenchanted

with the old economic policies. Chapter 17 described moves away from government intervention in the economy, moves to cut taxes and public spending and 'get the government off the backs of the people'. Table 20-4 helps provide the background to this wave of popular feeling. As Western economies started to slow down and both inflation and unemployment rose, people began to feel that the old policies were no longer working.

Table 20-4 shows that since 1981 government have

steadily brought inflation under control. However, unemployment has remained stubbornly high and growth has not recovered to the pace seen before 1973.

20-3 An overview

The complete economy comprises many millions of individual economic units: households, firms, and the departments of central and local government. Together, their individual decisions determine the economy's total spending, its total income, and its total level of production of goods and services.

The circular flow

We begin by ignoring the government sector and the possibility of making transactions with foreigners in other countries. Table 20-5 presents a simple classification of the different transactions between households and firms within an isolated economy which also has no government. Households own the factors of production or inputs to the production process. They own their own labour, which they can rent out to firms in exchange for wages. In Chapter 7 we saw that households are also the ultimate owners of firms. It is households who put up the money as sole-traders, partners, or shareholders in exchange for the final entitlement to the firms' profits. Hence, although other factors of production such as capital and land appear to be held by firms, they are ultimately owned by households.

The first row of Table 20-5 shows that households supply factor services to firms which use these factors to produce goods and services. The second row shows the corresponding payments. Households earn factor incomes (wages, rents, profits), payments by firms for these factor services. The third row shows that households use their incomes to buy goods and services from firms, thereby giving firms the money to pay for the factor services used in production.

Figure 20-2 shows this *circular flow* between households and firms.

The **circular flow** shows how real resources and financial payments are exchanged between firms and households.

The inner loop shows the transfers of real resources between

Table 20-5	Transactions by households and firms
Households	**Firms**
Own factors of production which they supply to firms	Use factors of production supplied by households to produce goods and services
Receive incomes from firms in exchange for supplying factors of production	Pay households for use of factors of production
Spend on goods and services produced by firms	Sell goods and services to households

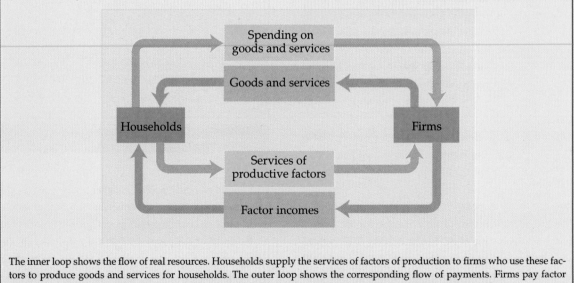

The inner loop shows the flow of real resources. Households supply the services of factors of production to firms who use these factors to produce goods and services for households. The outer loop shows the corresponding flow of payments. Firms pay factor incomes to households but receive revenue from households' spending on goods and services that the firms produce.

Figure 20-2 The circular flow between firms and households

BOX 20-1 — Macroeconomics without binoculars

Macroeconomics is about the economy as a system. It is helpful to glance ahead at the chapters in Part 4:

20	defining and measuring macro variables;
21–22	determining national output in the short run;
23–24	financial markets, interest rates and monetary policy . . . ;
25	and how they affect output and employment
26	wage and price adjustments, consequences for ouput; the limiting case of instant flexibility;
27	what all this means for unemployment . . . ;
28	and inflation . . . ;
29	but the story is incomplete without exchange rates and the external dimension;
30	what determines long-run growth . . . ;
31	and why we get short-run cycles;
32	summing it all up.

the two sectors and the outer loop shows the corresponding flows of money. These monetary payments are only one of many ways in which an economy could allocate inputs and outputs. A centrally planned economy could arrange for the resource transfers on the inner loop without the use of markets, prices, or payments.

Figure 20-2 suggests that there are three ways of measuring the amount of economic activity in an economy: (*a*) the value of goods and services produced, (*b*) the level of factor earnings, which represent the value of factor services supplied, or (*c*) the value of spending on goods and services. Since all payments are the counterparts of real resources, and since for the moment we assume that all payments must be spent on purchasing real resources, we must get the same estimate of total economic activity whether we measure the value of production, the level of factor incomes, or spending on goods and services.

It is worth restating this important point. Factor incomes must equal household spending since we assume that all income is spent. The value of production or output must equal total spending on goods and services since we assume that all goods are sold. The value of output must equal the value of household incomes: since profits are residually defined as the value of output sales minus the direct payments to hire land, labour, and capital, and since these profits ultimately accrue to the households which own the business, it follows that household incomes – derived either from supplying land, labour, and capital or from entitlements to the firms' profits – must exactly equal the value of production.

Our model is still very simple. What happens if firms do not sell all their output? What happens if firms sell output not to households but to other firms? What happens if

households do not spend all their incomes? In the next section we take account of all these possibilities. Having done so, our conclusion will be unchanged: the level of economic activity can be measured by valuing total spending, total output, or total earnings. All three methods give the same answer.

Once we have learned to measure the level of economic activity through this system of *national income accounting*, we can begin the analysis of the basic macroeconomic issues such as inflation, unemployment, and economic growth. We will have a coherent framework in which to relate the flows of payments to the flows of factor inputs and outputs of goods and services.

The circular flow diagram in Figure 20-2 allows us to keep track of the interactions that are so important in studying the economy as a whole. But the diagram is too simple. It leaves out too many of the important features of the real world: saving and investment, government spending and taxes, transactions between firms and with the rest of the world. Our first priority must be a comprehensive system of national accounting which addresses all these complications.

20-4 National income accounting

Measuring GDP

Gross domestic product (GDP) measures the output produced by factors of production located in the domestic economy regardless of who owns these factors.

GDP measures the value of output produced within the economy. Most of this output will be produced by domestic factors of production but there are exceptions. Suppose

(1)	(2)	(3)	(4) Transaction value	(5) Value added	(6) Expenditure on final goods	(7) Factor earnings
Table 20-6 Calculating GDP						
Good	Seller	Buyer				
Steel	Steel producer	Machine producer	£1 000	£1 000	–	£1 000
Steel	Steel producer	Car producer	£3 000	£3 000	–	£3 000
Machine	Machine producer	Car producer	£2 000	£1 000	£2 000	£1 000
Tyres	Tyre producer	Car producer	£500	£500	–	£500
Cars	car producer	Consumers	£5 000	£1 500	£5 000	£1 500
Total value of transactions			£11 500			
Gross domestic product (GDP				£7 000	£7 000	£7 000

Nissan or Peugeot builds a car factory in the UK. They employ UK workers and use machines made in the UK. Their output is part of GDP for the UK. However, the company's profits are owned by shareholders in Japan or France. Hence the value of the factory's output cannot be the same as the value of incomes earned by UK households. Initially we discuss a country with no links with the rest of the world. Then we introduce the rest of the world, show how to treat payment of profits and other income to foreigners, and explain why we have to distinguish GDP from GNP. When an economy has no transactions with the rest of the world we say that it is a *closed economy*.

First, we extend our simple circular flow diagram to recognize that transactions do not take place exclusively between a single firm and a single household. Firms hire labour services from households but buy raw materials and machinery from other firms.

To avoid double counting, we use the concept of value added.

Value added is the increase in the value of goods as a result of the production process.

Value added is calculated by deducting from the value of the firm's output the cost of the input goods used up in producing that output. Closely related is the distinction between final goods and intermediate goods.

Final goods are goods purchased by the ultimate user, either consumer goods purchased by households or capital goods such as machinery purchased by firms. **Intermediate goods** are partly finished goods which form inputs to another firm's production process and are used up in that process.

Thus, ice cream is a final good but steel is an intermediate good which some other firm uses as an input to its pro-

duction process. In classifying capital goods as final goods we suppose they are not used up in subsequent production. In the language of Chapter 7, we suppose that they do not depreciate or wear out. Shortly, we shall see how depreciation may be handled within this framework.

The following example should help you sort out these concepts and it is important that you study it until you have mastered these ideas. We assume that there are four firms in the economy: a steel producer, a producer of capital goods (machines) used in the car industry, a tyre producer, and a car producer who sells cars to the final consumers, the households. Table 20-6 shows how we may calculate GDP for this simple economy.

The steel producer makes £4000 worth of steel, one-quarter of which is sold to the firm that makes machines and three-quarters of which is sold to the car producer to make cars. If the steel producer also mines the iron ore from which the steel is produced, then the entire £4000 is value added or net output by the steel firm. This revenue is directly paid out in wages and rents or is residual profits which also accrue to households as income. Hence the first two rows of the last column also add up to £4000. Although firms have spent £4000 buying this steel output, this does not show up as expenditure on final goods since steel is entirely an inter-mediate good, to be used up in later stages of the production process.

The machine manufacturer spends £1000 buying steel input which is then converted into a machine to be sold to the car producer for £2000. The value added by the machine manufacturer is £2000 less the £1000 spent on steel inputs. And this net revenue of £1000 accrues directly or indirectly to households as income or profit. Since the car firm intends to keep the machine, its full value of £2000 is shown under 'Final expenditure'.

Like the steel producer, the tyre manufacturer produces

an intermediate output which does not show up under final expenditure. If the tyre manufacturer also owns the rubber trees from which the tyres were made, the entire output of £500 is value added and will contribute directly or indirectly to household incomes. If the tyre company bought rubber from a domestic rubber producer, we subtract the input value of rubber from the tyre manufacturer's output to obtain value added or net output, but we add another row showing the value added of the company producing the rubber for sale to the tyre company.

The car producer spends £3000 on steel and £500 on tyres. Since both are used up during the period in which cars are made, we subtract £3500 from the car output of £5000 to obtain the value added of the car producer. This net revenue pays households for factor services supplied, or is paid to them as profits.

Finally, the car producer sells the car for £5000 to the final consumer-households. Only now does the car become a final good and its full price of £5000 is entered as final expenditure.

Table 20-6 shows that the gross value of all the transactions is £11 500, but this overstates the value of the goods the economy has actually produced. For example, the £3000 that the steel producer earned by selling steel to the car producer is already included in the final value of car output. It is double-counting to count this £3000 twice.

Column (5) shows the value added at each stage in the production process. £7000 is the correct measure of the net output of the economy. Since each producer pays the corresponding net revenue to households either as direct factor payments or indirectly as profits, household earnings also equal £7000 in the last column of the table. If we simply counted up the payments made to households as income and profits we would get the same measure of GDP.

Table 20-6 confirms that we also get the same answer if we measure spending on *final* goods and services. In this case the final users are the households buying cars and the car producer buying the (everlasting) machinery used to make cars.

Investment and saving

This example not only allows us to explain value added and the distinction between intermediate and final goods, but also allows us to deal with a second complication. Total output and household incomes are each equal to £7000, but households spend only £5000 on cars. What are they doing with the rest of their incomes? And who is doing the rest of the spending? To resolve these issues we need to introduce investment and saving.

Investment is the purchase of new capital goods by firms. **Saving** is that part of income which is not spent buying goods and services.

Households are consuming £5000, the value of their expenditure on consumer goods (cars). Since their income is £7000 they are saving £2000. The car manufacturer is spending £2000 on investment (the purchase of new machinery). Figure 20-3 shows how we must amend the circular flow diagram of Figure 20-2. The bottom half of the figure shows that incomes and the value of factor services are each £7000. But £2000 leaks out from the circular flow when households save. Only £5000 finds its way back to firms as households spending on consumer goods (cars).

The top half of the figure shows that £5000 is the value of output of consumer goods and of household spending on these goods. Since GDP is £7000, where does the other £2000 come from? If not from household spending, it must come from spending by firms themselves. It is the £2000 of investment expenditure made by the car producer in purchasing machinery for use in car manufacturing.

The numbers in Table 20-6 relate to flows of output, expenditure, and income in a particular time period such as a year. During the same time the economy goes once round the inner and outer loops of Figure 20-3. On the inner loop firms produce an output of £5000 for consumption by households and an output of £2000 of capital goods for investment by firms. On the outer loop, which relates to money payments, saving is a *leakage* of £2000 from the circular flow and investment spending by firms on new machinery is an *injection* of £2000 to the circular flow.

A **leakage** from the circular flow is money no longer recycled from households to firms. An **injection** is money that flows to firms without being cycled through households.

Two questions immediately arise. First, is it coincidental that household savings of £2000 exactly equal investment expenditure of £2000 by firms? Second, if not, how is the money saved by households transferred to firms to allow them to pay for investment spending?

Suppose we use Y to denote GDP which is also the value of household incomes. If C denotes household spending on consumption and S denotes saving, then by definition savings are the part of income not spent,

$$S \equiv Y - C \text{ and } Y \equiv C + S \qquad (1)$$

The symbol $\equiv$ means 'is identically equal to, as a matter of definition'. Since GDP Y can be measured as the sum of final expenditure

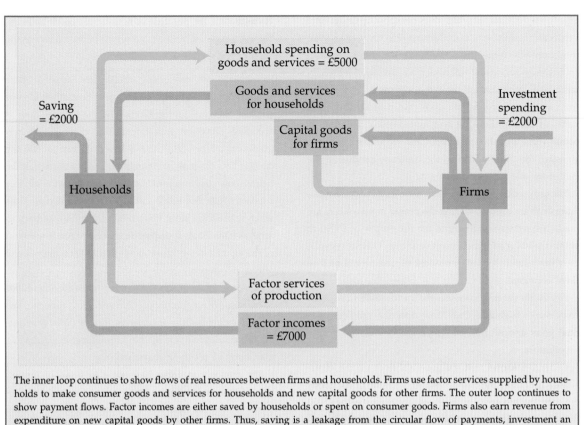

The inner loop continues to show flows of real resources between firms and households. Firms use factor services supplied by households to make consumer goods and services for households and new capital goods for other firms. The outer loop continues to show payment flows. Factor incomes are either saved by households or spent on consumer goods. Firms also earn revenue from expenditure on new capital goods by other firms. Thus, saving is a leakage from the circular flow of payments, investment an injection into the circular flow.

Figure 20-3 Investment, saving, and the circular flow

$$Y \equiv C + I \qquad (2)$$

it follows purely from the national accounting definitions we have adopted that

$$Y \equiv C + S \equiv C - I$$

Hence

$$S \equiv I \qquad (3)$$

It is no accident that saving and investment are each £2000 in our example. Equation (3) tells us that saving will equal investment in any example we construct. Look again at the outer loop of Figure 20-3. All consumption expenditure in the top half of the figure finds its way back to households as income in the bottom half of the figure. Investment spending by firms is matched by an income flow to households in excess of their consumption expenditure. Since saving is defined as the excess of income over consumption, investment and savings must always be equal.

These are purely accounting identities which follow from our definitions of investment, savings, and income. We have shown that *actual* saving must equal *actual* investment. As

yet we have said nothing about *desired* savings or *desired* investment; nor have we claimed that there will always be an equilibrium between the two. To investigate these issues we need to develop models or theories of desired savings and investment, a task we begin in the next chapter.[1]

Injections are payments to firms not originating from households. **Leakages** are uses of income that do not return as revenue to domestic firms.

What connects the leakage of saving and the injection of investment? Since firms are making income payments to households of £7000 but receiving only £5000 from households through spending on consumption, they must be

---

[1] It helps to think of analogous concepts in microeconomics. The demand curve shows desired purchases at any price and the supply curve shows desired sales at any price. Equilibrium occurs at the price at which desired purchases equal desired sales. When the price is too high there is excess supply and some desired sales will be frustrated. But since there is a buyer and a seller in every transaction that takes place, actual purchases equal actual sales whether or not the market is in equilibrium.

borrowing £2000 to pay for the new capital goods they are purchasing. Since households are saving £2000, they must be lending it to firms for investment.

In a market economy, financial institutions and financial markets – the banks that take household savings as deposits and grant overdraft facilities to firms, and the stock market on which firms raise money by selling new shares to households – play a key role in channelling household saving to the firms that wish to borrow to invest in new capital goods.

Investment allows us to deal with another problem glossed over in our simpler circular flow diagram. What happens if firms cannot sell all the output that they produce? Surely this leads to a difference between the output and expenditure measures of GDP?

Final goods are goods not used up in the production process during the period. In Table 20-6 steel was an intermediate good used up in making cars and machines, but machines were a final good because the car producer could use them again in the next period.[2] Suppose that the car producer's sales were not £5000 but only £4000. The producer is left with £1000 worth of cars which must be stockpiled.

Inventories or **stocks** are goods currently held by a firm for future production or sale.

Thus the car producer may hold stocks of steel, which will form an input to production of cars in the next period, or stocks of finished cars awaiting sale to consumers in the next period.

In Chapter 7 we described stocks as *working capital*. Because they have not been used up in production and sale during the current period, stocks are classified as capital goods. Adding to stocks is investment in working capital. When stocks are run down, we treat this as negative investment or disinvestment.

Now we can keep the national accounts straight. When the car producer sells only £4000 of the £5000 worth of cars produced in the period, we treat the inventory investment of £1000 by the car producer as final expenditure. As in Table 20-6, the output and expenditure measures of GDP are each £7000 including the output and expenditure on the machinery for making cars. But spending on final goods now comprises: car producer (£2000 on machines, £1000 on stocks), household-consumer (£4000 on cars).

Many people find this confusing. The trick is to distinguish between classification by commodity and

classification by economic use. Steel is clearly an intermediate commodity but that is not important. When a steel producer makes *and sells* steel we show this as production of an intermediate good. Since it has been passed on to someone else, our expenditure measure will pick it up further up the chain of production and sales. But when a firm adds to its stocks we must count that as final expenditure because it will not show up anywhere else in the national accounts. The firm is temporarily adding to its capital, and when it subsequently uses up these stocks we treat this as negative investment to keep the record straight.

We now introduce the government sector.

The government

Governments raise revenue both through direct taxes T_d levied on incomes (wages, rents, interest, and profits) and through indirect taxes or expenditures taxes T_e (VAT, petrol duties, cigarette taxes). Taxes are raised to meet two kinds of expenditure. Government spending on goods and services G comprises purchases by the government of physical goods and services. It includes spending on the wages of civil servants and soldiers, the purchase of typewriters, tanks, and military aircraft, and investment in roads and hospitals.

But governments also spend money financing *transfer payments* or benefits, B. These include pensions, unemployment benefit, and subsidies to private firms (investment grants) and to state-owned firms (covering losses). Transfer payments are payments that do not require the provision of any goods or services in return.

Transfer payments add to neither national income nor national output. They are not included in GDP. There is no corresponding value added or net output produced. Taxes and transfer payments merely redistribute existing income and spending power away from people being taxed and towards people being subsidized. In contrast, spending G on goods and services produces net output, gives rise to factor earnings in the firms supplying this output, and hence to additional spending power of the households receiving this income. Hence government spending G on goods and services should be included in GDP.

The purpose of national income accounting is to provide a logically coherent set of definitions and measures of national output. However, taxes drive a wedge between the price the purchaser pays and the price the seller receives. Thus we can choose to value national output either at market prices inclusive of indirect taxes on goods and services, or at the prices received by producers after indirect taxes have been paid.

---

[2] Of course, the machine gradually wears out with use. We deal with depreciation shortly.

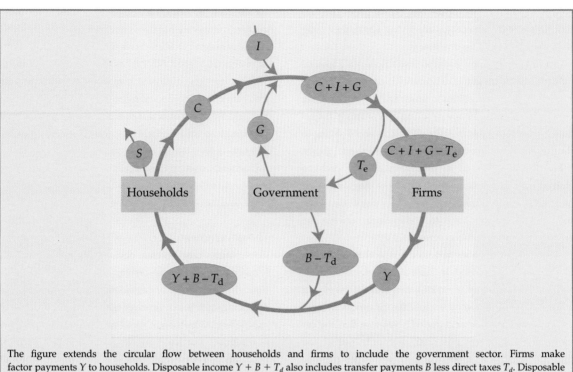

The figure extends the circular flow between households and firms to include the government sector. Firms make factor payments Y to households. Disposable income $Y + B + T_d$ also includes transfer payments B less direct taxes T_d. Disposable income goes on savings S or consumption C. This spending is augmented by injections of government spending G on goods and services and by investment spending I. From $C + I + G$ or GDP at market prices, we must subtract the leakage of indirect taxes T_e to get GDP at basic prices Y which firms pay out to households.

Figure 20-4   The government and the circular flow

GDP at market prices measures domestic output inclusive of indirect taxes on goods and services. **GDP at basic prices** measures domestic output exclusive of indirect taxes on goods and services. Thus GDP at market prices exceeds GDP at basic prices by the amount of revenue raised in indirect taxes (net of any subsidies on goods and services).

Our national accounts may now be constructed as follows. Measuring consumption C, investment I, and government spending G on goods and services, at market prices inclusive of indirect taxes, the value added or net output of the economy is given by $(C + I + G)$. Hence

$$\text{GDP at market prices} \equiv C + I + G \qquad (4)$$

Higher indirect taxes increase the price of goods and services. Although the value of output increases at market prices, the physical quantity of output is unchanged. Hence it makes more sense to measure GDP at basic prices Thus, subtracting indirect taxes (net of subsidies) T_e,

$$Y \equiv \text{GDP at basic prices} \equiv C + I + G - T_e \qquad (5)$$

This measure is independent of indirect taxes. Higher tax rates increase the value of $(C + I + G)$ but leads to an equivalent rise in T_e, leaving GDP at basic prices unchanged.

We now use Y to denote GDP at basic prices. The right-hand side of equation (5) is the final expenditure measure of GDP and the net output measure of GDP, each at basic prices. The left-hand side is the income measure of GDP at basic prices. Through factor payments and profits, firms pay households the exact value of net output measured at the prices, net of indirect taxes, that firms actually receive. The output, expenditure, and income measures of GDP at basic prices are all equal.

Figure 20-4 shows that direct taxes and transfer benefits do affect the circular flow of payments, which we now extend to take account of the government sector. Household incomes at basic prices Y are supplemented by benefits B less direct taxes T_d. This gives us personal disposable income.

Personal disposable income is household income after direct taxes and transfer payments. It shows how much households have available for spending and saving.

Personal disposable income equals $(Y + B - T_d)$.

We must now amend our definition of savings S when there is a government sector. Saving is the amount of disposable income that is not spent on consumption.

$$S \equiv (Y + B - T_d) - C \qquad (6)$$

Proceeding round the top loop of Figure 20-4, consumption C at market prices is now supplemented by injections of investment spending I and government spending G. From $(C + I + G)$ or GDP at market prices, we subtract indirect taxes T_e to get back to Y or GDP at basic prices.

Equation (6) implies that Y is given by

$$Y \equiv C + S - B + T_d$$

Comparing this with our definition of Y in equation (5),

$$C + S - B + T_d \equiv Y \equiv C + I + G - T_e$$

Since these expressions are identically equal,

$$S + T_d + T_e \equiv I + G + B \qquad (7a)$$

and

$$S - I \equiv G + B - T_d - T_e \qquad (7b)$$

Equations (7a) and (7b) confirm that our national income accounts make sense. The left-hand side of (7a) tells us the total leakages or withdrawals from the circular flow of payments. Money leaks out through household savings and taxes to the government. The right-hand side of (7a) tells us the injections to the circular flow. Investment spending by firms and government spending on goods and services and on transfer benefits put money back into the system. Total leakages must equal total injections; otherwise we would have made a bookkeeping error and the sums would not add up.[3]

Equation (7b) makes a similar point. Taking firms and households together, net withdrawals from the circular flow $S - I$ (the financial surplus of the private sector) must be exactly offset by net injections $G + B - T_d - T_e$ from the government sector (the financial deficit of the government). The private sector can run a surplus only if the government runs a deficit, and vice versa.

The foreign sector

Thus far we have considered a closed economy, which does not transact with the rest of the world. We now consider

an *open economy*, which does have dealings with other countries.

Exports (X) are goods that are domestically produced but sold abroad. **Imports (Z)** are goods that are produced abroad but purchased for use in the domestic economy.

Households, firms, and the government may purchase imports Z that are not part of domestic output and do not give rise to domestic factor incomes. These goods will not show up in the output measure of GDP, which relates only to the *value added* by domestic producers. However, imports do show up in final expenditure. There are two solutions to this problem. We could subtract the import component separately from C, I, G, and X and measure only final expenditure on the domestically produced component of consumption, investment, government spending, and exports. But it is much easier to continue to measure total final expenditure on C, I, G, and X and then subtract total expenditure on imports from $(C + I + G + X)$. It comes to exactly the same thing. It is also the same as adding net exports NX to $C + I + G$.

Hence in an open economy we recognize foreign trade by redefining GDP at factor cost as

$$Y \equiv C + I + G + X - Z - T_e$$
$$\equiv C + I + G + NX - T_e \qquad (8)$$

which directly extends to equation (5).

What about leakages from and injections to the circular flow? Imports represent a leakage, but exports are an injection. Combining equation (8) with equation (6), which remains unchanged, we now get

$$S + (T_d + T_e - B) + Z \equiv I + G + X \qquad (9a)$$

and

$$S - I \equiv (G + B - T_e - T_d) + NX \qquad (9b)$$

Equation (9a) makes the usual point that total leakages must equal total injections. Imports are an extra source of leakages and exports an extra source of injections of money to the circular flow.

Equation (9b) extends (7b) to an open economy. A private sector surplus $S - I$ is a leakage from the circular flow. It must be matched by an injection of the same amount. This injection can come either from a government deficit $(G + B - T_e - T_d)$ or from net exports NX, the excess of export earnings over import spending. Since our trade surplus is foreigners' trade deficit, we can summarize (9b) by saying that the surplus of the private sector must be matched by the budget deficit of the government plus the trade deficit of foreigners.

---

[3] Notice that when $T_d = T_e = G = B = 0$ there is no government sector and equation (7a) implies $S = I$, as in equation (3).

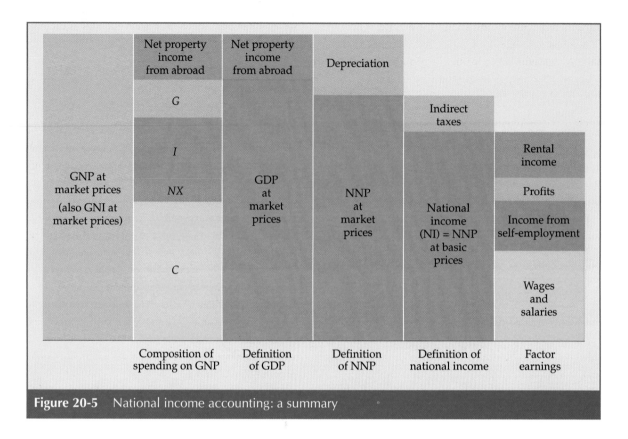

Figure 20-5   National income accounting: a summary

From GDP to GNP or GNI

To complete the national accounts we must deal with two final problems. Thus far we have assumed that all factors of production are domestically owned: all net domestic output accrues to domestic households as factor incomes. But this need not be the case. When Nissan or Peugeot owns a car factory in the UK, some of the profits will be sent back to Japan or France to be spent or saved by Japanese or French households. Similarly, when immigrant workers send some of their wages back home to support relatives, or foreign owners of UK property or shares in UK companies send home some of their income from property rents or company dividends, there is a discrepancy between the factor incomes earned in the UK and the factor incomes accruing to UK households.

Conversely, UK households earn income from factor services that they supply in foreign countries. Since most income flows between countries are not labour income but income from interest, dividends, profits, and rents, they are shown in the national accounts as the flow of *property income* between countries. The net flow of property income into the UK is the excess of inflows of property income from factor services supplied abroad over the outflows of property income from factor services by foreigners in the UK.

When there is a net flow of property income between the UK and the rest of the world, the output and expenditure measure of GDP will no longer equal the total factor incomes earned by UK citizens. We use the terms *gross national product* (GNP) or *gross national income* (GNI) to measure GDP adjusted for net property income from abroad.

GNP (or GNI) measures total income earned by domestic citizens regardless of the country in which their factor services were supplied. GNP (or GNI) equals GDP plus net property income from abroad.

Thus, if the UK has an inflow of £2 billion of property income from abroad but an outflow of £1 billion of property income accruing to foreigners, UK GNP, measuring income earned by UK citizens, will exceed UK GDP, measuring the value of goods produced in the UK, by £1 billion.

From GNP to national income

The final complication is depreciation.

Depreciation or capital consumption measures the rate at which the value of the existing capital stock declines per period as a result of wear and tear or of obsolescence.

Table 20-7   UK national accounts (£ billion, current prices)

Expenditure measure		Income measure	
At market prices		Income source	
C	545	Employment	463
I	151	Mixed (self-employment)	43
G	153	Profits and rent	223
NX	−8		
Statistical discrepancy	2	GDP at basic prices	729
		Indirect taxes	114
GDP at market prices	843		843
Net property income from abroad	12		
GNP (GNI) at market prices	855		
less depreciation	−89		
NNP at market prices	766		
less indirect taxes	−114		
National income at basic prices	652		

Source: ONS, *UK National Accounts*.

Depreciation is a flow concept telling us how much our effective capital stock is being used up in each time period. Depreciation is an economic cost because it measures resources being used up in the production process.

In our simple example of Table 20-6 we ignored depreciation completely. We assumed that the machine purchased by the car producer would last for ever. We now recognize that machinery wears out. In consequence, the *net* output of the economy is reduced. Some of the economy's gross output has to be used merely to replace existing capital, and this part of gross output is not available for consumption, investment in net additions to the capital stock, government spending, or exports. Similarly, we need to reduce our measure of the incomes available for spending on these goods.

Accordingly, we subtract depreciation from GNP to arrive at net national product (NNP) or national income.

National income is the economy's net national product. It is calculated by subtracting depreciation from GNP at basic prices.

National income measures the amount of money the economy has available for spending on goods and services after setting aside enough money to maintain its capital stock intact by offsetting depreciation.

Summary

We have now developed a complete set of national accounts. You are probably wondering how you are going to

remember all these new concepts. Figure 20-5 may help to keep you straight. Table 20-7 fills in the actual numbers for the UK in 1998.

20-5 What GNP measures

A company's accounts provide a picture of how the company is doing. Our system of national income accounting allows us to assess the performance of the economy as a whole. But, just as a company's accounts may conceal as much as they reveal, we must interpret the national income accounts with some care.

We concentrate on GNP as a measure of national economic performance. National income, or net national product at basic prices, differs from GNP at basic prices only because the former subtracts an estimate of the economic depreciation of the capital stock. Since depreciation is rather difficult to measure, and consequently may be treated differently in different countries or during different time periods, in practice most economists make comparisons using GNP, which avoids the need to argue about depreciation.

In this section we make three points. First, we recall the distinction between nominal and real variables. Second, we show how per capita GNP can take account of population growth and provide a more accurate picture of the standard of living of a representative person in the economy. Finally, we discuss the incompleteness of GNP as a measure of the activities that provide economic welfare or satisfaction to members of society.

BOX 20-2 — GNP is underestimated, but don't tell the government!

The famous gangster Al Capone was never charged with murder or gun running, but he was eventually convicted of income tax evasion. Taxes are evaded not only by smugglers and drug dealers but also by gardeners, plumbers, street vendors, and many others offering goods and services 'for cash'. Since government estimates of GNP are derived from tax statistics, the 'hidden' or 'underground' economy is not reported in GNP.

Economists have devised various ways to come up with some rough estimates of the size of the hidden economy. One way is to keep track of the circulation of large-denomination banknotes. People with fistfuls of £50 notes are often engaged in tax evasion. Another possibility is to guess people's income by keeping track of what they spend. A study by Maria Lacko uses the stable relationship between household consumption of electricity and its two main determinants – income

and weather temperature – to estimate incomes by studying available data on electricity consumption and temperature. She confirms two popularly held views. The hidden economy is large both in the former communist economies, where the new private sector is not yet part of official statistics, and in several Mediterranean countries that have a long history of having trouble getting their citizens to pay their taxes.

Estimated size of the hidden economy (% of GNP)

Poland	34	Denmark	16	Netherlands	8
Hungary	31	Finland	11	Australia	7
Spain	21	Germany	11	France	6
Greece	20	USA	10	Japan	3
Italy	16	UK	10		

Source: M. Lacko, *Hungarian Hidden Economy in International Comparisons*, Institute of Economics, Budapest, 1996.

Nominal and real GNP

Nominal GNP measures GNP at the prices prevailing when income was earned.

Since it is physical quantities of output that yield people utility or happiness, it can be very misleading to judge the economy's performance by looking at nominal GNP.

Real GNP, or GNP at constant prices, adjusts for inflation by measuring GNP in different years at the prices prevailing at some particular calendar date known as the *base year*.

Table 20-8 presents a simple hypothetical example of a whole economy. Nominal GNP increases from £600 to £1440 between 1980 and 2000. If we take 1980 as the base year we can measure real GNP in 2000 by valuing output quantities in that year at 1980 prices. Thus, real GNP increases only from £600 to £860. This increase of 43 per cent in real GNP provides a much more accurate picture of the change in the total quantity of goods produced by the economy as a whole.

The GNP deflator   In Chapter 2 we introduced the retail price index (RPI), an index of the average price of goods purchased by consumers. The most common measure of the

Table 20-8   Nominal and real GNP

		1980	2000
Quantity:	apples	100	150
	chickens	100	140
Price (£):	apples	2	4
	chickens	4	6
Value (current £):	apples	200	600
	chickens	400	840
	Nominal GNP	600	1440
Value (1980 £):	apples	200	300
	chickens	400	560
	Real GNP	600	860

inflation rate in the UK is the percentage increase in the RPI over its corresponding value in the same month one year earlier.

However, consumption expenditure is only one component of GNP. GNP also includes investment, government spending, and net exports. To convert nominal GNP to real GNP we need to use an index that reflects what is happening to the price of all goods. This index is called the GNP deflator.

Table 20-9   Nominal and real GNP, UK, 1960–98 (at market prices)

	1960	1970	1980	1990	1998
Nominal GNP (current £bn)	25.6	51.7	227.9	548.8	855.4
GNP deflator (1995 = 100)	8.1	12.3	45.5	84.2	106.8
Real GNP (£bn, 1995 prices)	316.0	420.0	500.9	653.3	800.7

Source: ONS, *Economic Trends*.

Table 20-10   Growth rates, 1980–96 (% per year)

	Real GNP	Per capita real GNP
Denmark	2.4	2.3
UK	2.7	2.5
Jordan	4.3	0.2

Source: World Bank, *World Development Report*.

The **GNP deflator** is the ratio of nominal GNP to real GNP expressed as an index.

Expressing the deflator as an index means that the ratio of nominal to real GNP is multiplied by 100. In Table 20-8, nominal and real GNP coincide in the base year 1980. Their ratio is 1 and the index is 100. For 2000 the ratio of nominal to real GNP is 1.674 (= 1440/860) and the value of the index is 167.4. According to the GNP deflator, prices for the economy as a whole increased from 100 to 167.4, a 67.4 per cent increase from 1980 to 2000.

Table 20-9 presents actual numbers for the UK over four decades. Nominal GNP in the UK rose from £25 billion in 1960 to over £855 billion in 1998. Yet without knowing what happened to the price of goods in general it is impossible to judge what happened to the quantity of output over this period. The second row of Table 20-9 answers this question. On average, prices in 1998 were 13 times those in 1960. In consequence, the change in real GNP was much less dramatic than the change in nominal GNP over the same period. Hence we see the vital importance of distinguishing between nominal and real GNP.[4]

Per capita real GNP

Real GNP gives us a simple measure of the real income of an economy, and the annual percentage increase in real GNP

gives us an idea of how fast an economy is growing. Table 20-10 shows the average annual growth rate of real GNP in three countries. The first column shows that the annual growth rate of real GNP during 1980–96 was highest in Jordan and lowest in Denmark. Although this tells us about the growth of the whole economy, we may be interested in a different question: what was happening to the standard of living of a representative person in each of these countries? To answer this question we need to examine per capita real GNP.

Per capita real GNP is real GNP divided by the total population. It is real GNP per head.

For a given level of real GNP, the larger the population, the smaller will be the quantity of goods and services available for each individual. Table 20-10 shows what was happening to per capita real GNP. Notice that the ranking is largely reversed: GNP per person hardly growing in Jordan. Thus, if we wish to get a simple measure of the standard of living enjoyed by a person in a particular country, it is better to look at per capita real GNP, which adjusts for population growth, than to look at total real GNP.

Even per capita real GNP is only a crude indicator. Table 20-10 does *not* say that every person in Denmark obtained 2.3 per cent more goods and services each year. It only indicates what was happening on average. Some people's real incomes increased by a lot more than 2.3 per cent per annum and some people became absolutely poorer. The more the income distribution is changing over time, the less reliable is the change in per capita real GNP as an indicator of what is happening to any particular person.

A comprehensive measure of GNP

Because we use GNP to measure the production of goods and services in the economy, it is desirable that the coverage of the GNP accounts should be as comprehensive as possible. In practice, we encounter two problems in including all production in GNP. First, some outputs, such as noise, pollution, and congestion, are nuisances. We should make an adjustment for these 'bads' by subtracting from the traditional GNP measure an allowance for all the

---

[4] Even after many years of inflation this point is not universally understood. How many times have you heard statements such as 'Today the stock market hit an all-time high'? Frequently such statements refer to the *nominal* value of a variable. For many purposes it is *real* values that are of interest in assessing economic performance.

BOX 20-3   The quality of life

Since data collection is itself expensive, national statistics are often the by-product of other activities such as tax collection. Unmarketed activities are often unrecorded. Familiar statistical measures, such as GDP, omit many of the things we really care about. However, governments could decide to spend more money collecting statistics. In 1998, UK Deputy Prime Minister John Prescott announced plans to produce a 'happiness index' measuring the quality of life. The index includes 13 'headline indicators': economic growth, social investment, health, education and training, employment, housing quality, climate change, air pollution, transport, water quality, land use, waste disposal, and wildlife. Many of these indicate aspects of 'environmental capital'. Keeping track of depreciation of, and investment in, environmental capital may be one way to promote sensible use of natural resources.

nuisance goods created during the production process. This is a perfectly sensible suggestion but it is almost impossible to implement. These nuisance goods are not traded through markets, so it is hard to quantify the level of their output or the costs they impose on society.

Many valuable goods and services are excluded from GNP because they are not marketed and therefore hard to measure accurately. These activities include household chores, do-it-yourself activities, and unreported jobs.

Deducting the value of nuisance outputs and adding the value of unreported and non-marketed incomes would make GNP a more accurate measure of economy's production of goods and services. But there is another important adjustment that must be made if we are to use GNP as the basis for calculations of national economic welfare. People get enjoyment not merely from goods and services, but also from leisure time.

Suppose people in Leisuria value leisure more highly than people in Industria. Other things equal, people in Industria will work more hours and produce more goods and services. Industria will have a higher measured GNP. It would be silly to say this proves that people in Leisuria have a lower level of enjoyment. By choosing to work less hard they are revealing that the extra leisure is worth at least as much as the extra goods that could have been produced by working longer hours.

Because it is difficult and expensive to collect regular measurements on non-marketed and unreported goods and bads and to make regular assessments of the implicit value of leisure, real GNP inevitably remains the most commonly used measure of economic activity. Although far from ideal, it is the best measure we have that is available on a regular basis.

SUMMARY

● Macroeconomics is the study of the working of the economy as a whole. Inflation, unemployment, and growth are three key macroeconomic issues.

● Macroeconomics sacrifices aspects of individual detail to concentrate on the interaction of broad sectors of the economy. Households supply the services of factors of production to firms that use them to produce goods and services. Firms pay factor incomes to households, who in turn use this money to purchase the goods and services produced by firms. This process is called the circular flow of payments.

● Gross domestic product (GDP) is the value of output of the factors of production located in the domestic economy. It can be measured in three equivalent ways: value added in production, factor incomes including profits accruing to entrepreneurs, or final expenditure.

● Leakages from the circular flow are those parts of payment by firms to households that do not automatically return to firms as spending by households on the output of firms. Savings and taxes net of subsidies are leakages. Injections are sources of revenue to firms that do not arise from household spending. Investment expenditure by firms, spending on goods and services by the government, and net exports are all injections. As a matter of definition or national income accounting, total leakages must equal total injections.

● GDP at market prices values domestic output at prices inclusive of indirect taxes. GDP at basic prices measures domestic output at prices exclusive of indirect taxes. Gross national product (GNP), also called gross national income (GNI), adjusts GDP for net property income from abroad.

● National income is net national product (NNP) at basic prices. NNP is GNP minus the depreciation of the capital stock during the period. In practice, many assessments of economic performance are based on GNP since it is not always easy to measure depreciation accurately and the treatment of this item varies across time periods and across countries.

● Nominal GNP measures income at current prices. Real GNP measures income at constant prices. It adjusts nominal GNP for changes in the general price level as a result of inflation. The index of prices used to make this adjustment is called the GNP deflator.

● Per capita real GNP divides real GNP by the population. It is a more reliable indicator of the goods and services available per person in an economy, but only an average measure of what people get. The goods and services available to particular individuals also depends on the income distribution.

● Real GNP and per capita real GNP are still very crude measures of national and individual welfare. GNP takes no account of non-market activities, bads such as pollution, valuable activities such as work in the home, and production unreported by tax evaders. Nor does GNP measure the value of leisure.

● Because it is expensive, and sometimes impossible, to make regular and accurate measurements of all these activities, in practice GNP is the most widely used measure of national performance.

KEY TERMS

REVIEW QUESTIONS

1 Explain what is meant by each of the terms 'inflation', 'unemployment', and 'economic growth'. Table 20-4 shows that many countries have had higher inflation, higher unemployment, and lower growth since 1973. Why might economic performance have deteriorated since 1973?

	Final sales	Intermediate goods purchases
Car producer	1000	270
Windscreen producer	199	12
Tyre producer	83	30
Car radio producer	30	5
Steel producer	47	0

2 This question deals with the value added accounting. The table shows final sales and purchases of intermediate goods by firms connected with car production:
What is the contribution of the car industry to GNP?

3 GNP at market prices is £300 billion. Depreciation is £30 billion and indirect taxes are £20 billion. There are no subsidies. (a) What is the value of national income? (b) Explain why and how depreciation leads to a discrepancy between GNP and national income. (c) Explain why indirect taxes enter the calculation.

4 (a) Suppose the crime rate falls and the police force can be halved. Former police officers get jobs in private industry at the same wage as police officers. Explain why there is no change in GNP. (b) Is society better or worse off? (c) What does this suggest about including police expenditure as part of GNP?

5 Suppose GNP = 2000, C = 1700, G = 50, and NX = 40. (a) What is investment I? (b) Suppose exports are 350. What are imports? (c) Suppose depreciation is 130. What is national income? (d) In this example net exports are positive. Could they be negative?

6 Consider an economy with the following data:

	Nominal GDP	GNP Deflator
1999	2000	100
2000	2400	113

(a) What is 2000 GNP in constant (1999) prices? (b) What is the growth rate of real GNP from 1999 to 2000? (c) What is the inflation rate? (d) Suppose 2000 nominal GNP was 2240 with all other data above unchanged. What would 2000 real GNP be? What would the growth rate of real GNP be?

7 Explain whether the following activities should appear in a comprehensive measure of GNP: (a) time spent by students in lectures; (b) the income of muggers; (c) the time spent by boxing match spectators; (d) the wage paid to traffic wardens who issue parking tickets; (e) dropping litter.

8 *Common fallacies* Explain why the following statements are incorrect: (a) If a country concentrates its production on goods with a high selling price, it will automatically increase its national income. (b) Unemployment benefit helps prop up national income in years when employment is low. (c) A higher level of per capita real GNP is always a good thing. (d) In 2000 *Crummy Movie* earned £1 million more at the box office than *Gone With The Wind* has earned over the last 50 years. *Crummy Movie* is already a bigger box office success.

21 The determination of national income

LEARNING OUTCOMES

When you have finished this chapter, you should be able to:

● Distinguish actual output and potential output
● Develop the concept that output is demand determined in the short run, and define short-run equilibrium output
● Explain the determinants of desired consumption and desired investment
● Derive the level of short-run equilibrium output and show how it changes when there is a shift in aggregate demand
● Define the multiplier, and relate its size to the slope of the consumption function
● Discuss the paradox of thrift

Since 1960 real GNP in the UK has grown on average at 2.3 per cent per annum. But there have been marked cycles around this rising trend in real GNP. Real GNP actually fell during 1973–75, 1979–81, and 1989–92. In between, it grew 10 per cent during 1975–79, 26 per cent during 1981–89, and 24 per cent during 1992–98.

Technical words used by economists to describe the fluctuations – 'recession' and 'recovery', 'boom' and 'slump' – have passed into everyday language. One aim of macroeconomics is to explain why real GNP fluctuates as it does. In this chapter we analyse the forces determining real GNP.

To construct a simple model, we ignore the discrepancies between national income, real GNP, and real GDP. Henceforth, we use national income, total output, and GNP interchangeably. We begin by distinguishing *actual* output from *potential* output.

Potential output is the output the economy would produce if all factors of production were fully employed.

Potential output tends to grow smoothly over time as the economy's stock of factors of production increases. Population growth adds to the labour force. Investment in education, training, and new machinery gradually increases the stock of human and physical capital. Technical advances allow any given stock of factors to produce more output. Together, these explain why the UK has grown on average at 2.3 per cent per annum since 1960.

We examine the theory of long-run economic growth in potential output in Chapter 30. For the moment we are more interested in why the economy's actual output can deviate from potential output in the short run.[1] Since potential output changes only slowly, we begin with a short-run analysis of an economy with a given level of potential output.

Potential output is not the maximum output the economy could conceivably produce – if compelled to work 18 hours

---

[1] In Chapter 31 we also consider the idea that short-run output fluctuations might be caused by *fluctuations* in potential output.

a day, doubtless we could all produce more. Rather, it is the output that could be sustained if every market in the economy were in long-run equilibrium. Every worker who wanted to work at the equilibrium wage rate could find a job, and every machine that could profitably be employed at the equilibrium rental for machinery was indeed being used. Thus, potential output includes an allowance for 'normal unemployment'. Some people don't want to work at the equilibrium wage rate, and, in a constantly changing economy, others are temporarily in between jobs. Potential output in the UK, and in many other countries of Western Europe, probably corresponds to an unemployment rate of between 5 and 10 per cent.

Suppose actual output falls below potential output. Workers become unemployed and firms have idle machines or spare capacity. A key issue in macroeconomics is how quickly market forces will return output to its potential or full employment level. In microeconomics, when we studied a single market in isolation we assumed that excess supply would quickly put downward pressure on the price of that product, eliminating excess supply and restoring equilibrium. In macroeconomics, this argument cannot be taken for granted. Macroeconomics emphasizes how disturbances in one part of the economy induce changes in other parts of the economy which may feed back on the first part, exacerbating the original disturbance.

We cannot examine this important issue by *assuming* that the economy is always at its full employment potential output, for that would be to assume that the problem could never arise. Instead, we must construct a model in which departures from potential output are a logical possibility, examine the market forces that would then be set in motion, and form a judgement about the success or otherwise of market forces in restoring output to its full employment potential.

Thus we begin by studying a model with two crucial properties. First, all prices and wages are fixed at a given level. Second, at these prices and wage levels, there are workers without a job who would like to work and firms with spare capacity they would find profitable to use. Thus the economy has spare resources. Under these circumstances, we do not need to analyse the supply side of the economy in detail. Any increase in output and employment will happily be supplied by firms and workers until full employment is reached.

Since, below potential output, firms happily supply as much output as is demanded, the actual quantity of total output is *demand-determined*. It depends only on the level of *aggregate demand*, the total amount that people want to

spend on goods and services in the economy as a whole. This is the essence of the model of income and output determination in the next few chapters.

Of course, we shall want to relax the assumption that prices and wages are fixed. Not only do we want to study the important problem of inflation, but we also want to examine how quickly market forces, acting through changes in prices and wages, can eliminate the problems of unemployment and spare capacity. But first we must learn to walk. We postpone the analysis of price and wage adjustment until Chapter 26.

Until then, we focus on the demand-determined model of output and employment first developed by John Maynard Keynes in *The General Theory of Employment, Interest, and Money*, published in 1936. Keynes used the model to explain the high levels of unemployment and low levels of output that persisted in most industrial countries throughout the 1930s in the Great Depression. The unemployment rate was persistently above 10 per cent. In the UK and the United States it reached over 20 per cent in the early 1930s.

After the publication of the *General Theory* in 1936, most young economists became Keynesians, advocating government intervention to keep output close to potential. In the 1950s and 1960s, this approach was challenged by *monetarists*, whose intellectual leader was Milton Friedman. They argued, correctly, that even if Keynesian analysis helped us think about depressions it was a poor tool for understanding inflation, which monetarists attribute to a growth in the money in circulation. We develop an approach that builds on the best insights of both Keynesians and monetarists.

In the 1970s unemployment also started to rise. Some economists, concluding that Keynesian economics must be fundamentally flawed, returned to the pre-Keynesian classical model, to which they added some important modern insights. These *new classical* and *real business cycle* approaches deny the effectiveness of many simple types of government intervention aiming to stabilize national output. Indeed, they conclude stablizing output may not even be desirable.

The increasing popularity of these recent approaches has now prompted a fightback by *new Keynesians*, who believe that the central messages of Keynes were right all along and can be understood better by drawing on modern microeconomics to explain the market failures that ultimately justify Keynesian intervention.

By the end of Part 4 you will be able to understand these frontiers of research in economics. First, you must learn to walk. For the next few chapters we develop a simple but useful approach that builds on the key ideas of both Keynesians and monetarists.

21-1 The circular flow

Chapter 20 introduced the circular flow of income and payments between households and firms. Households spend money purchasing the output of firms. Firms pay factor incomes to households. In this chapter we build a simplified model of the interaction of households and firms. In the next chapter we introduce the government and the foreign sector.

Since we assume output is demand-determined, the aggregate demand or spending plans of households and firms determine the output produced, which in turn generates the income from which households spend. Suppose households decide to save more of their income and spend less. Firms can now sell fewer goods and cut back on output and employment. But this reduces household incomes, so households further reduce their spending. Output and employment fall yet again.

The Great Depression is evidence that the economy can spiral down far below its potential output. Fortunately, we can show that the spiral cannot go on for ever. We now explain why.

21-2 Components of aggregate demand or planned spending

In the absence of the government and the foreign sector, there are two sources of demand for goods: consumption demand by households, and investment demand for new machines and buildings by firms. Using AD to denote aggregate demand, C to denote consumption demand, and I to denote investment demand,

$$AD = C + I \qquad (1)$$

Consumption demand and investment demand are determined by different economic groups and depend on different things.

Consumption demand

Households buy goods and services ranging from cars and food to cricket bats, theatre performances, and electricity. In practice, these consumption purchases account for about 90 per cent of personal disposable income.

Personal disposable income is the income households receive from firms, plus transfer payments received from

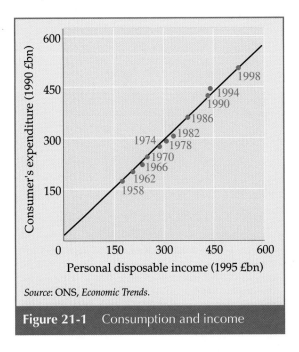

Source: ONS, *Economic Trends*.

Figure 21-1   Consumption and income

the government, minus direct taxes paid to the government. It is the income that households have available for spending or saving.

Given its disposable income, each household must decide how to divide this income between spending and saving. A decision about one is necessarily a decision about the other. One family may be saving to buy a bigger house; another may be spending more than its income, or 'dissaving', by taking the round-the-world trip it has always wanted.

Many factors affect the consumption and savings decisions of each household and thus the aggregate level of planned consumption and planned savings. We examine these in detail in Chapter 25. But to get started, a single simplification will take us a long way. We assume that, in the aggregate, households' consumption demand is larger the larger is aggregate personal disposable income.

Figure 21-1 shows the relationship between real consumption and real personal disposable income in the UK. Because the scatter of points lies close to the line summarizing this relationship, our simplification is helpful. Nevertheless, the points do not lie *exactly* along the line. Our simplification is missing some of the other influences on consumption demand which we take up in Chapter 25.

The consumption function   Figure 21-2 shows a hypothetical example of the relationship between desired aggregate consumption and total income that we assume in the rest of this chapter. It resembles the line actual data in Figure 21-1 and is called the *consumption function*.

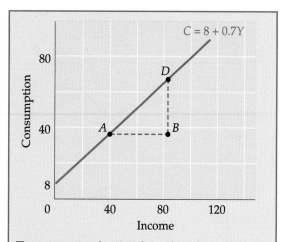

The consumption function shows desired aggregate consumption at each level of aggregate income. With zero income, desired consumption is 8. This is autonomous consumption unrelated to the level of income. The marginal propensity to consume is 0.7. Of each extra pound of income, 70 pence is consumed and the other 30 pence saved. When income rises by 40 (from *A* to *B*) consumption rises by $0.7 \times 40 = 28$ (from *B* to *D*).

Figure 21-2   The consumption function

The **consumption function** shows the level of aggregate consumption desired at each level of personal disposable income.

Recall from Chapter 2 that a function is a rule for going from a value of one variable to the corresponding value of another. The consumption function tells us how to go from personal disposable income to desired consumption.

Our simplified model has no government, no transfer payments, and no taxes. Hence personal disposable income equals national income. Figure 21-2 shows desired consumption at each level of *national* income. The consumption function is a straight line, and any straight line is completely described by its intercept – the height at which it crosses the vertical axis – and its slope – the amount it rises for each unit we move horizontally to the right. In Figure 21-2 the intercept is 8. We call this *autonomous* consumption demand. By autonomous we mean unrelated to the level of income. Households wish to consume 8 even when income is zero.[2] The slope of the consumption function is the marginal propensity to consume.

---

[2] This minimum consumption is needed for survival. How do households finance this spending when their incomes are zero? In the short run they dissave and run down their existing assets. But they cannot do so for ever. The consumption function may be different in the short run from in the long run, an idea we discuss in Chapter 25.

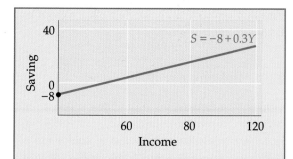

The saving function shows desired saving at each income level. Since all income is saved or spent on consumption, the saving function can be derived from the consumption function or vice versa.

Figure 21-3   The saving function

The **marginal propensity to consume** is the fraction of each extra pound of disposable income that households wish to consume.

In Figure 21-2 the marginal propensity to consume (*MPC*) is 0.7. If income rises by £1, desired consumption rises by 70p.

Saving is income that is not consumed. Figure 21-2 implies what when income is zero, saving is −8. Households are dissaving, or running down their assets.

Moreover, since 70p of every pound of extra income is consumed, 30p of every extra pound of income must be saved. The *marginal property to save* (*MPS*) is 0.3. Since every extra pound of income leads either to extra desired consumption or to extra desired saving, *MPC* = *MPS* must always equal unity. Figure 21-3 shows the *saving function* corresponding to the consumption function in Figure 21-2.

Investment spending

Income is the key determinant of household consumption or spending plans as described by the consumption function. What about the factors determining the investment decision by firms?

Investment demand consists of firms' desired or planned additions to physical capital (factories and machines) and to their inventories.

Inventories are goods held for future production or sale.

Firms' demand for investment depends chiefly on firms' current guesses about how fast the demand for their output will increase. There is no close connection between the current *level* of output and current guesses about how demand and output will *change*. Sometimes output is high and rising, sometimes it is high and falling. Since there is no

| BOX 21-1 | Movements along the aggregate demand schedule and shifts in the schedule |

The aggregate demand schedule is a straight line whose position depends on its intercept and its slope. The intercept is the total amount of autonomous spending: autonomous consumption demand plus investment demand. The slope is the *MPC*. For a given level of autonomous demand, changes in income lead to *movements along* a given *AD* schedule.

The level of autonomous demand is influenced by many things which we examine in Chapter 25. It is not fixed for all time. But it *is* independent of income. The purpose of the *AD* schedule is to separate out the change in demand directly induced by changes in income. All other sources of changes in aggregate demand must be shown as *shifts* in the *AD* schedule. For example, if firms get more optimistic about future demand and decided to invest more, autonomous demand increases and the new *AD* schedule is parallel to, but higher than, the old *AD* schedule. It crosses the vertical axis at a higher point, reflecting the increase in autonomous demand.

close connection between the current level of income and firms' guesses about how the demand for their output is going to change, we begin our analysis of aggregate demand by making the simple assumption that investment demand is autonomous. We assume that desired investment *I* is constant, independent of current output and income. In Chapter 25 we discuss investment demand in more detail.

21-3 Aggregate demand

Aggregate demand is the amount that firms and households plan to spend on goods and services at each level of income.

In our simplified model, aggregate demand is simply households' consumption demand *C* plus firms' investment demand *I*.

The aggregate demand schedule

Figure 21-4 shows the *aggregate demand schedule*. In this example, the given amount *I* that firms wish to spend on investment is 22. Given the consumption function $C = 8 + 0.7Y$, the aggregate demand schedule *AD* is a vertical distance 22 higher than the consumption function at each income level. Since each extra unit of income adds 0.7 to consumption demand and nothing to investment demand, aggregate demand increases by 0.7. The *AD* schedule is parallel to the consumption function and the slope of both is given by the marginal propensity to consume.

We now show how aggregate demand determines the level of output and income.

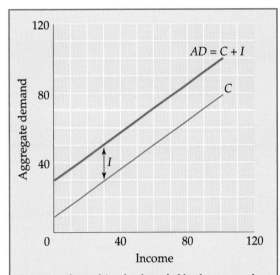

Aggregate demand is what households plan to spend on consumption and firms plan to spend on investment. Since we assume investment demand is constant, consumption is the only part of aggregate demand that increases with income. Vertically adding the constant investment demand to the consumption function *C* gives the aggregate demand schedule *AD*.

Figure 21-4   Aggregate demand

21-4 Equilibrium output

In our simplified model there is no government, no foreign sector, and no depreciation. National income, GNP, GDP, and personal disposable income are all equal. Firms produce output and pay the proceeds to households as factor incomes.

Wages and prices are *fixed* and output is demand-determined. Whenever aggregate demand falls below its full employment level, firms can't sell as much as they would like. We say there is *involuntary* excess capacity. Workers can't work as much as they would like. There is *involuntary* unemployment.

We now require a definition of short-run equilibrium. We cannot use the definition that we used in microeconomics, namely the output at which both suppliers and demanders were happy with the quantity being purchased and sold. We now wish to contemplate a situation in which firms and workers would be delighted to produce more goods and supply more labour. Suppliers are frustrated. But we can at least require that demanders are happy.

When prices and wages are fixed, the output market is in **short-run equilibrium** when aggregate demand or planned aggregate spending just equals the output that is actually produced.

Thus, spending plans are not being frustrated by a shortage of goods. Nor are firms producing more output than they can sell. In short-run equilibrium the output produced exactly equals the output demanded by households as consumption and by firms as investment.

Figure 21-5 shows income on the horizontal axis and planned spending on the vertical axis. It also includes the 45° line, which reflects any point on the horizontal axis on to the same point on the vertical axis. Beginning, for example, at an income of 40 on the horizontal axis, we go vertically up to B on the 45° line, then horizontally along to the same value of 40 on the spending axis.

We draw in the AD schedule from Figure 21-4. This crosses the 45° line at E. Since E in on the 45° line, the value of income on the horizontal axis equals the value of spending on the vertical axis. Since E is the *only* point on the AD schedule that is also on the 45° line, it is the only point at which income and desired spending are equal.

Hence Figure 21-5 shows that equilibrium output at E. Firms are producing 100. That output is equal to income. At an income of 100 we can read from the AD schedule that the demand for goods is 100. At E the planned spending on goods or the demand for goods is exactly equal to the quantity produced.

At any other output, output is not equal to aggregate demand. Suppose output and income are only 40. Since the consumption function is $C = 8 + 0.7Y$, consumption demand is $8 + (0.7 \times 40) = 8 + 28 = 36$. But investment demand is always 22; aggregate demand is 58; but output is only 40. There is excess demand, and spending plans cannot be realized at this output level.

Indeed, Figure 21-5 shows that, for all output levels below the equilibrium level of 100, aggregate demand will exceed income and output. The AD schedule lies *above* the 45° line along which spending and output would be equal. Conversely, at all outputs above the equilibrium level of 100, aggregate demand will be less than income and output.

Adjustment towards equilibrium

Suppose the economy begins with an output of 30, below the equilibrium output. Table 21-1 shows that aggregate demand is 51. Aggregate demand exceeds production. If firms have inventories they can sell more than they have produced by running down stocks for a while. Note that this destocking is *unplanned*; planned changes of stocks are already included in the total investment demand I.

If firms cannot meet aggregate demand by unplanned destocking, they have to turn away customers. Either response – unplanned destocking or turning away customers – is a signal to firms that they should increase their output levels. Thus the first row of Table 21-1 shows how firms react when output is 30 but aggregate demand is 51.

Any *any* output level below 100, aggregate demand exceeds output firms get signals to start raising their output.

The fourth row of Table 21-1 illustrates what happens when output is initially above its equilibrium level. Output

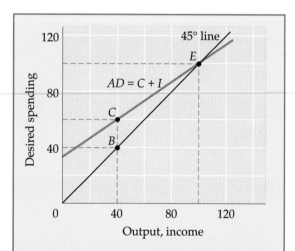

The 45° line reflects any value on the horizontal axis on to the same value on the vertical axis. The point E, at which the AD schedule crosses the 45° line, is the only point at which aggregate demand AD is equal to income. Hence E is the equilibrium point at which planned spending equals actual output and actual income.

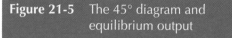

Figure 21-5   The 45° diagram and equilibrium output

BOX 21-2   Spending like there's no tomorrow

Nowadays Nigel Lawson advertises diets. He used to be Chancellor of the Exchequer. At the height of the Lawson boom in the late 1980s, heady optimism and easy access to credit made UK consumers spend a lot. Personal saving collapsed as people bought champagne, sports cars, and houses. The boom years didn't last long. As inflation got out of control, the government had to take action to slow the economy down. House prices fell. People found their mortgages were larger than the value of their houses. To pay off this 'negative equity', householders had to raise saving sharply in the early 1990s. By 1999 personal saving was collapsing again. . . .

Although in this chapter we assume a constant marginal propensity to save, Chapter 25 discusses more sophisticated theories of consumption and saving.

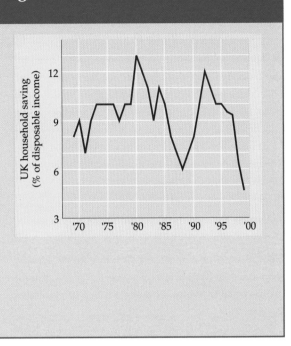

Table 21-1   Aggregate demand and output adjustment

Y	I	C = 8 + 0.7Y	AD = C + I	Y − AD	Unplanned stocks	Output
30	22	29	51	−21	Falling	Rising
80	22	64	86	−6	Falling	Rising
100	22	78	100	0	Zero	Constant
120	22	92	114	+6	Rising	Falling

exceeds aggregate demand. Firms cannot sell all they have produced, make *unplanned* additions to inventories, and respond by making plans to cut output.

Hence, when output is below its equilibrium level, firms have an incentive to start raising output. When output is above its equilibrium level, firms have an incentive to start reducing output. As the third row of Table 21-1 shows, when output is at its equilibrium level of 100, firms are selling all their output and making no unplanned changes to their stocks. There is no incentive to change output levels.

Equilibrium output and employment

In this example the equilibrium level of income and output is 100. Firms sell all the goods they produce and households and firms buy all the goods they want. But there is nothing that guarantees that 100 is the level of full employment or potential output.

The whole point of our analysis is that the economy can end up with an output level below potential without any forces being present to move output towards the potential level. Firms have no incentive to hire unemployed workers since there is no prospect of increasing the level of output beyond its existing level of 100. At the given level of prices and wages, the lack of aggregate demand blocks an expansion of output to the full-employment level.

21-5 Another approach: planned saving equals planned investment

Equilibrium income equals planned investment plus planned consumption. Equivalently, planned investment equals equilibrium income minus planned consumption.

$$I = Y - C \qquad (2)$$

However, planned saving S is the part of income Y not devoted to planned consumption C. Thus $S = Y - C$. Using equation (2), we see that equilibrium occurs where planned investment equals planned savings:

$$I = S \qquad (3)$$

In modern economies, firms make investment decisions, and the managers of these firms are not the same decision-units as the households making savings and consumption plans. But household plans depend on the level of income. Equation (3) says that equilibrium income makes households plan to save as much as firms are planning to invest.

Figure 21-6 shows how this works out. Using the data in Figure 21-5, since the consumption function is $C = 8 + 0.7Y$, the saving function must be $S = -8 + 0.3Y$.

The **saving function** shows desired saving at each income level.

Since planned investment I is 22 whatever the level of income, the equilibrium level of income that makes planned savings equal to planned investment is $Y = 100$, exactly as in Figure 21-5.

If income exceeds its equilibrium level of 100, households want to save more than firms want to invest. But savings is the part of income not consumed. Thus, households are not planning enough consumption, together with firms' investment plans, to purchase the total amount of output being produced. Unplanned inventories pile up and firms reduce output. Conversely, when output is below its equilibrium level, planned investment exceeds planned saving. Together, planned consumption and planned investment exceed actual output. Firms make unplanned inventory reductions and increase output. Either way, output tends to adjust towards its equilibrium level of 100.

A pitfall: remembering the distinction between planned and actual

We have shown that the equilibrium level of output and income will satisfy one of two equivalent conditions. Aggregate demand must equal income and output. In other words, planned consumption plus planned investment must equal actual income, output, and spending. Equivalently, planned investment must equal planned saving.

In the last chapter we showed that *actual* investment is *always* equal to *actual* saving, purely as a consequence of our national income accounting definitions. When the economy is not in equilibrium, unplanned investment or disinvestment in stocks or unplanned saving (frustrated consumers) always ensures that actual investment, planned plus unplanned, equals actual saving, planned plus unplanned.

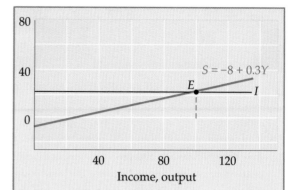

Equilibrium output is 100, at which planned investment equals planned saving. Planned investment is 22, as in Figure 21-5. The saving function $S = -8 + 0.3Y$ is implied by the consumption function in that figure. To the right of E, households plan to save more than firms plan to invest. Deficient consumption demand causes unplanned stock-building, and firms cut production. To the left of E, households save less than firms want to invest. Stocks are run down and firms increase output.

Figure 21-6 At equilibrium output planned investment equals planned saving

21-6 A fall in aggregate demand

Figure 21-5 shows equilibrium output for a particular aggregate demand schedule AD. What might lead to a shift in the AD schedule, and what would happen to equilibrium output?

The slope of the AD schedule depends only on the marginal propensity to consume (MPC). For a given MPC it is the level of *autonomous* spending that determines the position of the AD schedule. Autonomous spending is spending unrelated to income. In Figure 21-5 there are two items of autonomous spending, the autonomous consumption spending of 8 and the autonomous investment spending of 22.

Changes in autonomous spending lead to parallel shifts in the AD schedule. We have argued that investment demand depends chiefly on current guesses by firms about the future demand for their output. Since there is no way of knowing for sure what future demand will be, Keynes argued that investment demand was likely to fluctuate significantly, being strongly influenced by current pessimism or optimism about the future – what he called the *animal spirits* of investors.[3]

---

[3] Similarly, a collapse of consumer confidence, and hence a fall in autonomous consumption demand, was widely blamed for the recession in the early 1990s.

Suppose firms became pessimistic about the future demand for their output. In consequence they reduce their current investment demand. Specifically, suppose planned investment falls from 22 to 13. Since autonomous consumption remains 8, the aggregate demand schedule is now 13 rather than 22 above the consumption function at each income level. Figure 21-7 shows this shift in the aggregate demand schedule from *AD* to *AD'*.

Before we go into the details, think about what is likely to happen to output. It will certainly fall, but how much? When investment demand falls by 9, firms cut back production. Households have lower incomes and cut back their consumption demand. Firms cut back production again. Thus output will probably fall by more than 9. But how far will it fall, and what brings the process of falling output and income to an end?

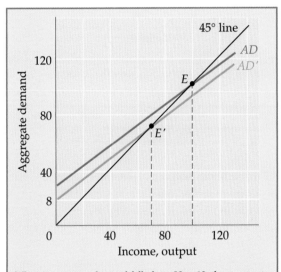

When investment demand falls from 22 to 13, the aggregate demand schedule shifts down from *AD* to *AD'* and is 9 lower at each output level. The equilibrium point moves from *E* to *E'*. Equilibrium output falls from 100 to 70. The fall of 9 in investment demand is multiplied into a fall of 30 in equilibrium output.

Figure 21-7   A fall in investment demand

Figure 21-7 shows that a downward shift of the aggregate demand schedule by 9 reduces equilibrium output from 100 to 70. Equilibrium moves from *E* to *E'*. Although equilibrium output falls by considerably more than the reduction of 9 in investment, it does not fall all the way to zero. The new equilibrium level of output is 70.

Table 21-2 explains. Step 1 shows the original equilibrium from Table 21-1 with investment demand still at 22 and output at the equilibrium level of 100. In step 2 investment demand falls to 13. We assume that firms did not expect demand to change and therefore still produce 100. Output exceeds aggregate demand by 9. Firms add these goods to their inventories and then cut back production.

Step 3 shows firms producing 91, the level that would just have met demand in step 2. But when firms reduce output, income falls. Step 3 shows consumption demand reduced to 71.7. This fall is caused entirely by firms cutting back output by 9. Since the *MPC* is 0.7, a cut in income by 9 causes a fall in consumption demand by 6.3, from 78 to 71.7. But this induced fall in consumption demand means that output at 91 still exceeds aggregate demand, which is now 84.7. Again inventories pile up, and again firms respond by cutting output.

At step 4 firms are producing enough to meet demand at step 3. Output is 84.7, but again this leads to a further reduction in consumption demand so output still exceeds aggregate demand. However, comparing steps 2, 3, and 4, we can see that the excess of output over aggregate demand is gradually getting smaller. The process will keep going until it reaches the new equilibrium, an output level of 70. Only at that level does aggregate demand equal output. There is no unplanned stockbuilding and output is constant.

How long it takes for the economy to reach the new equilibrium depends on how well firms figure out what is going on. If they mechanically produce during each period to meet the level of demand in the previous period, it can take a long time to adjust. But smart firms will recognize that, period after period, they are producing too much and adding to unwanted inventories. They start to anticipate

Table 21-2   Adjustment to a shift in investment demand

	Y	I	C = 8 + 0.7Y	AD = C + I	Y − AD	Unplanned stocks	Output
Step 1	100	22	78	100	0	Zero	Constant
Step 2	100	13	78	91	9	Rising	Falling
Step 3	91	13	71.7	84.7	6.3	Rising	Falling
Step 4	84.7	13	67.3	80.3	4.4	Rising	Falling
New equilibrium	70	13	57	70	0	Zero	Constant

that demand is still falling and cut back output more quickly than Table 21-2 suggests.

Why does equilibrium output fall by a larger amount than 9, the reduction in investment demand? Because this fall in investment demand induces a reduction in income which then induces an additional reduction in consumption demand. Total demand falls by more than the original fall in investment demand.

The reduction in equilibrium output is exactly 30. Output does not fall for ever.

The **multiplier** is the ratio of the change in equilibrium output to the change in autonomous spending that causes the change in output.

In our example, the initial change in autonomous investment demand is 9 and the final change in equilibrium output is 30. The multiplier is thus $(30/9) = 3.33$.

21-7 The multiplier

The multiplier tells us how much output changes when there is a shift in aggregate demand. The multiplier is larger than 1 because any given change in autonomous demand sets off further changes in consumption demand. This gives us a clue about the size of the multiplier. It must depend on the marginal propensity to consume. The initial effect of a 1-unit increase in investment demand is to increase output and income by 1 unit. If the *MPC* is large, this increase in income will lead to a large increase in consumption and the multiplier will be large. If the *MPC* is small, a given change in investment demand and output will induce only small changes in consumption demand and the multiplier will be small.

To obtain the exact formula for the multiplier, we go through a series of steps like those in Table 21-3, which begins with a 1-unit *increase* in investment demand. In step 2, firms react by increasing output by 1 unit. Consumption rises by 0.7, the marginal propensity to consume times the 1-unit change in income and output. At step 3, firms increase output by 0.7 to meet the increased consumption

demand in step 2. In turn, consumption demand is increased by 0.49 (the *MPC* 0.7 times the 0.7 increase in income) leading to step 4 to an increase in output of $(0.7)^2$ or 0.49. Consumption increases again and the process continues.

To find the value of the multiplier, we add together all the increases in output from each step in the table and then we keep going:

$$\text{Multiplier} = 1 + 0.7 + (0.7)^2 + (0.7)^3$$
$$+ (0.7)^4 + (0.7)^5 + \dots \qquad (4)$$

The dots at the end mean that we keep adding terms such as $(0.7)^6$ and so on. The right-hand side of equation (4) is called a geometric series. Each term is (0.7) times the previous term. Fortunately, we do not have to keep adding these up indefinitely. Mathematicians have shown that there is a general formula for the sum of all the terms in such a series. It is given by

$$\text{Multiplier} = \frac{1}{1 - 0.7} \qquad (5)$$

Since the formula applies whatever the (constant) value of *MPC*, it is useful to remember that the multiplier will always be given by

$$\text{Multiplier} = \frac{1}{1 - MPC} \qquad (6)$$

For the particular value of 0.7 for the *MPC*, equation (5) tells us that the multiplier equals $1/(0.3) = 3.33$. Hence an initial reduction in investment demand by 9 will lead to a final reduction in equilibrium output by $(9 \times 3.33) = 30$, as Figure 21-7 confirms.

The marginal propensity to consume tells how much of each additional unit of income is spent on consumption. Thus the marginal propensity to consume will usually be a number between zero and unity. The higher the *MPC*, the lower will be $(1 - MPC)$. Dividing 1 by a smaller number leads to a larger answer; dividing 1 by 0.3 yields 3.33, whereas dividing 1 by 0.5 yields only 2. Hence the general formula for the multiplier shown in equation (6) confirms

Table 21-3	Calculating the multiplier							
Change in	Step 1	Step 2	Step 3	Step 4	Step 5	*	*	*
I	1	0	0	0	0	*	*	*
Y	0	1	0.7	$(0.7)^2$	$(0.7)^3$	*	*	*
C	0	0.7	$(0.7)^2$	$(0.7)^3$	$(0.7)^4$	*	*	*

that the larger the *MPC*, the larger will be the value of the multiplier.

The multiplier and the MPS   Any part of an extra unit of income not spent on extra consumption must be saved. Hence $(1 - MPC)$ equals *MPS*, the marginal propensity to save.

The **marginal propensity to save** is the fraction of each extra unit of income that households wish to save.

Equation (6) says that we can think of the multiplier as $1/MPS$. The higher the marginal propensity to save, the more of each extra unit of income leaks out of the circular flow into savings and the less goes back round the circular flow to generate further increases in aggregate demand, output, and income.

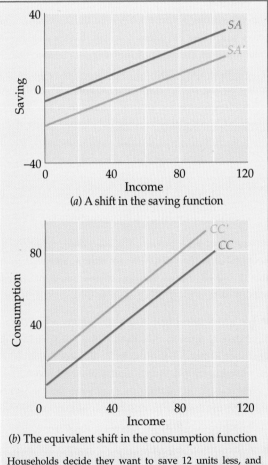

(a) A shift in the saving function

(b) The equivalent shift in the consumption function

Households decide they want to save 12 units less, and consume 12 units more, at each income level. The saving function shifts down by 12 from *SA* to *SA'* and the consumption function shifts up by 12 from *CC* to *CC'*.

Figure 21-8   A shift in the consumption and the saving functions

21-8 The paradox of thrift

In the previous section we analysed a parallel shift in the aggregate demand schedule caused by a change in autonomous investment demand. We now investigate a parallel shift in the aggregate demand schedule caused by a change in the autonomous component of planned consumption and savings.

Previously, we assumed that at zero income households plan to consume 8, which they finance by a corresponding dissaving of 8. Suppose households decide they now wish to save 12 *less* at each level of income. Equivalently, they wish to consume 12 more at each income level. Figure 21-8 shows the saving function shifting down from *SA* to *SA'* and the consumption function shifting from *CC* to *CC'*.

What happens to *actual* saving when households want to save less? Figure 21-9 shows that the aggregate demand schedule shifts up by 12 from *AD* to *AD'* because of the upward shift in the consumption function. The equilibrium shifts from *E* to *E'*. Equilibrium income and output increase from 100 to 140. The increase in autonomous consumption acts like an increase in autonomous investment. Since the marginal propensity to consume remains 0.7 we can use our previous analysis of the multiplier to say immediately that the change in equilibrium output will be 40, the change in autonomous consumption, times $1/(1 - 0.7)$ or 3.33, the

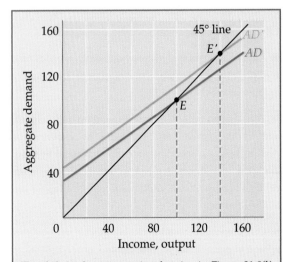

The shift in the consumption function in Figure 21-8(*b*) shifts the aggregate demand schedule from *AD* to *AD'*. Equilibrium output rises from 100 to 140. Although households want to save less at each income level, equilibrium saving is 22 at both *E* and *E'*. Income rises to maintain the equality of desired savings and desired investment.

Figure 21-9   The paradox of thrift

multiplier. Thus equilibrium income and output increase by $12 \times 3.33 = 40$.

Since the new consumption function is $C = 20 + 0.7Y$, at the equilibrium income of 140 consumption demand is 118. Hence saving is $140 - 118 = 22$. This should come as no surprise. We already know that in equilibrium planned investment equals planned saving. Since investment demand remains at 22, equilibrium planned saving must also remain at 22.

A change in the amount households wish to save at each income leads to a change in equilibrium income. There is no change in equilibrium saving, which must still equal planned investment. This is the **paradox of thrift**.

The paradox of thrift helps us to understand an old debate about the virtues of saving and spending. Does society benefit from thriftiness and a high level of desired saving at each income level? The answer depends on whether or not the economy is at full employment.

When aggregate demand is low and the economy has spare resources, the paradox of thrift shows that a *reduction* in the desire to save will increase spending and increase the equilibrium income level. Society will benefit from higher output and employment. And since investment demand is autonomous, a change in the desire to save has no effect on the desired level of investment.

Suppose, however, that the economy is at full employment. In Chapter 26 we discuss how this might come about in the longer run once prices and wages have time to adjust. If the economy is in long-run equilibrium at full employment, an *increase* in the desire to save at each income level must lead to an increase in the level of savings at full-employment income. Consumption demand must fall but investment demand may increase to restore aggregate demand to its full-employment level. In the next few chapters we discuss the forces that could induce this change in autonomous investment demand in the long run. Hence, in the long run society may benefit from an *increase* in the desire to save. Investment will increase and the economy's capital stock and full-employment output level may grow more quickly.

In this chapter we have focused on the short run before prices and wages have time to adjust. Saving and investment decisions are made by different people, and there is no automatic mechanism to translate higher saving into a corresponding rise in investment demand. Since planned saving depends on the level of income, it is income that adjusts to equate planned saving and planned investment.

⊕ SUMMARY

● Aggregate demand is planned spending on goods (and services). The *AD* schedule shows aggregate demand at each income level.

● This chapter neglects planned spending by foreigners and by the government. We focus on consumption demand by households and investment demand by firms. We treat investment demand as constant. Investment demand is firms' *desired* additions to physical capital and to inventories.

● Consumption demand is closely though not perfectly related to personal disposable income. In the absence of taxes and transfers, personal disposable income and total income coincide.

● Autonomous consumption is desired consumption at zero income. The marginal propensity to consume (MPC) is the fraction by which consumption rises when income rises by a pound. The marginal propensity to save (MPS) is the fraction of an extra pound of income that is saved. Since income is consumed or saved, MPC + MPS = 1.

● For given prices and wages, the goods market is in equilibrium when output equals planned spending or aggregate demand. Equivalently, at the equilibrium level of income, planned saving equals planned investment. Goods market equilibrium does not mean that income is at its full-employment level. Rather, it means that planned spending is equal to actual spending and actual output.

● The equilibrium level of output is demand-determined because we assume that prices and wages are fixed at a level that implies an excess supply of goods and labour. Firms and workers are happy to supply whatever output and employment is demanded.

● When aggregate demand exceeds actual output there is either unplanned disinvestment (inventory reductions) or unplanned saving (frustrated customers). Actual investment always equals actual savings as a matter of national income accounting. Unplanned inventory reductions or frustrated customers act as a signal to firms to increase output when aggregate demand exceeds actual output. Similarly, unplanned additions to stocks occur when aggregate demand is less than actual output.

● A rise in planned investment increases equilibrium output by a larger amount. The initial increase in income to meet investment demand leads to further increases in consumption demand.

● The multiplier is the ratio of the change in output to the change in autonomous demand which caused output to change. In the simple model of this chapter, the multiplier is 1/(1 − MPC) or 1/MPS. The multiplier exceeds 1 because MPC and MPS are positive fractions.

● The paradox of thrift shows that a reduced desire to save leads to an increase in output but no change in the equilibrium level of planned savings, which must still equal planned investment. Higher output is needed to offset the reduced desire to save at each output level.

KEY TERMS

◆ Potential output   347

◆ Personal disposable income   349

◆ Consumption function   350

◆ Marginal propensity to consume (MPC)   350

◆ Investment demand   350

◆ Aggregate demand   351

◆ Short-run equilibrium output   352

◆ Saving function   354

◆ Multiplier   356

◆ Marginal propensity to save (MPS)   357

◆ Paradox of thrift   358

REVIEW QUESTIONS

1 Suppose the consumption function is C = 0.7Y and planned investment is 45. (a) Draw a diagram showing the aggregate demand schedule. (b) If actual output is 100, what unplanned actions will occur? (c) What is equilibrium output?

2 Suppose the MPC is 0.6. Beginning from equilibrium, investment demand then rises by 30. (a) How much does equilibrium output increase? (b) How much of that increase is extra consumption demand? (c) Construct a table like Table 21-2 to show how adjustments take place over time.

3 Planned investment is 150. People decide to save a higher proportion of their income: the consumption function changes from C = 0.7Y to C = 0.5Y. (a) What happens to equilibrium income? (b) What happens to the equilibrium proportion of income saved? Explain. (c) Using a saving-investment diagram, show the change in equilibrium output.

4 Which part of actual investment is not included in aggregate demand? Why not?

5 (a) Find equilibrium income when investment demand is 400 and the consumption function is C = 0.8Y. (b) Would output be higher or lower if the consumption function were C = 100 + 0.7Y?

6 This question looks ahead to the next chapter. Suppose equilibrium output is below the full-employment level. The government is a potential source of demand for goods. Can the government increase the equilibrium level of output?

7 *Common fallacies* Show why the following statements are incorrect: (a) If only people were prepared to save more, investment would increase and we could get the economy moving again. (b) Lower output leads to lower spending and yet lower output. The economy could spiral downwards for ever. (c) A market economy cannot guarantee that saving and investment are equal. That is why we need central planning.

22 Aggregate demand, fiscal policy, and foreign trade

LEARNING OUTCOMES

When you have finished this chapter, you should be able to:

● Examine how government spending and taxes affect aggregate demand
● Derive short-run equilibrium output when the model is extended to include the government
● Explain the balanced budget multiplier
● Discuss automatic stabilisers and how the government budget is affected by output fluctuations
● Construct the structural budget and the inflation-adjusted budget
● Consider the link between budget deficits and the build up of the national debt
● Explain the limits to active fiscal policy
● Extend the model of output determination to include the foreign sector

In most European countries, governments directly purchase about one-fifth of national output. They spend about the same on transfer payments, and raise taxes to pay for both types of spending. What is the macroeconomic impact of government fiscal policy?

Fiscal policy is the government's decisions about spending and taxes.

We extend our model of income determination to include the effects of fiscal policy, then take up three issues in fiscal policy.

Stabilization policy consists of government actions to try to keep output close to potential output.

We analyse both the possibilities and the difficulties of using fiscal policy for stabilization.

The second issue is the significance of the government's budget deficit.

The **budget deficit** is the excess of government outlays over government receipts.

When the government is running a deficit, it is spending more than it is taking in. In the last forty years, 1969–70, 1988–90, and 1999 are the only periods when the UK government has *not* been in deficit. Deficits worry people. They wonder how the government can keep spending more than it receives year after year without something terrible happening. We examine the size of the deficit and ask how much we should worry about it.

The government finances its deficit mainly by borrowing from the public through selling bonds, which are promises to pay specified amounts of interest payments at future

Table 22-1   UK public finances 1999/2000

Revenue	£bn	Expenditure	£bn
Direct taxes		Goods and services	
Income tax	88	Health	61
Corporation tax	30	Education	41
Social security contributions	56	Defence	26
		Law and order	19
Indirect taxes		Housing and environment	13
VAT	54		
Excise duties	36	Transfer payments	
Property taxes	29	Social security	102
		Debt interest	26
Other taxes and receipts	56		
		Other spending	61
Total revenue	349	Total spending	349
		Deficit	0
		Net borrowing	0

Source: HM Treasury, *Budget 99*.

dates. As a result of this borrowing, the government builds up its debts to the public.[1]

The **national debt** is the stock of outstanding government debt.

As deficits have continued, the national debt has risen to apparently astronomical levels. By 1999 the UK national debt was £350 billion, or about £5900 per person. The third fiscal policy issue we examine is the effects of the national debt.

Most of this chapter is about the government and aggregate demand. We know from Chapter 20 that GDP is not equal to $C + I + G$ but rather to $C + I + G + X - Z$. To complete our model of income determination we must add not merely the government but also the effect of foreign trade. Exports X and imports Z are each nearly 30 per cent of UK GDP. The UK is a very open economy, and the effects of foreign trade are too important to be ignored even in a simple model.[2] We conclude this chapter by discussing income determination when foreign trade is included.

22-1 The government in the circular flow

Figure 20-4 showed how the government gets into the circular flow of payments. Government spending G on

goods and services contributes directly to aggregate demand. The government also withdraws money from the circular flow through indirect taxes T_e on expenditure and through direct taxes T_d on factor incomes (less transfer benefits B that augment factor incomes).

Table 22-1 provides a useful summary of UK government activity in 1999/2000. The major components of direct spending on goods and services are health, education and defence. Social security payments – state pensions, unemployment benefit, and child support – and interest payments on government debt are the major components of transfer payments.

The main sources of direct tax are income tax, corporation tax, and national insurance contributions to state schemes for pensions and unemployment benefit. Indirect taxes include value added tax (VAT), specific duties on tobacco, alcohol, and fuel, and the property taxes levied by local government.

22-2 The government and aggregate demand

We now extend our model of income determination to include the government sector. Since it is cumbersome to keep distinguishing between GDP at market prices and GDP at basic prices, we assume all taxes are direct taxes. In the absence of indirect taxes, measurements at market prices and at basic prices coincide. Until the final section of this chapter, we continue to ignore foreign trade.

In this simplified model, aggregate demand AD equals

---

[1] Government is responsible not merely for its own deficits but also for losses made by nationalized industries. The public sector net cash requirement (PSNCR) is the government deficit plus net losses of nationalized industries.

[2] In contrast, net property income is 1 per cent of GNP. We continue to treat GNP and GDP as equivalent.

consumption demand C, plus investment demand I plus government demand G for goods and services.[3]

$$AD = C + I + G \qquad (1)$$

In the short run government spending G need not vary with the level of output and income. We assume G is fixed by the government. This level reflects how many hospitals the government wishes to build, how large it wants defence spending to be, and so on. Thus we now have three autonomous components of aggregate demand which do not directly vary with current income and output: the autonomous component of consumption demand, investment demand I, and government demand G.

The government also levies taxes and pays out transfer benefits. *Net taxes* are taxes minus transfers. Since we are assuming that there are no indirect taxes, net taxes NT are simply direct taxes T_d minus transfer benefits B. Net taxes reduce personal disposable income – the amount available for spending or savings by households – relative to national income and output. Letting YD denote disposable income, Y denote national income and output, and NT denote net taxes,

$$YD = Y - NT \qquad (2)$$

For simplicity, we assume that net taxes are proportional to national income. If t is the *net tax rate*, the total revenue from net taxes is

$$NT = tY \qquad (3)$$

For the UK, taxes net of transfer benefits come to about 20 per cent of national income. Thus we can think of the (net) tax rate t as 0.2. For this tax rate, equation (3) says that if national income Y rises by £1, net tax revenue will rise by 20p. The government's revenue from direct taxes rises and the government pays out less in unemployment benefit since fewer people are unemployed.

Disposable income YD is national income Y minus net taxes NT. Hence when the net tax rate is t, disposable income is related to national income by the formula

$$YD = Y - NT = Y - tY = Y(1 - t) \qquad (4)$$

Households are allowed to keep only the fraction $(1 - t)$ of each pound of pre-tax income. When the net tax rate t is 0.2, or 20 per cent, households' after-tax or disposable income is only 80 per cent of their pre-tax income Y. The other 20 per cent goes to the government.

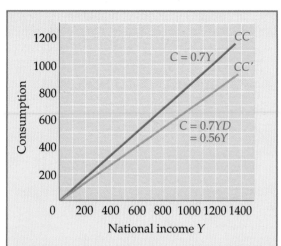

In the absence of taxation, national income Y and disposable income YD are the same. The consumption function CC shows how much households wish to consume at each level of national income. With a proportional net tax rate of 0.2, households still consume 70p of each extra pound of disposable income. Since YD is now only $0.8Y$, households consume only $0.7 \times 0.8 = 0.56$ of each extra unit of national income. Relating consumption to national income, the effect of net taxes is to rotate the consumption function downwards from CC to CC'.

Figure 22-1   Net taxes and consumption

We continue to assume that households' desired consumption is proportional to their personal disposable income. For simplicity, suppose that autonomous consumption is zero but that, as in the previous chapter, the marginal propensity to consume out of disposable income is 0.7. Households wish to consume 70p of each extra pound of disposable income. Thus the consumption function is now $C = 0.7YD$.

Figure 22-1 shows the consumption function CC when net taxes are zero. Disposable income and national income coincide. Each extra pound of national income raises consumption demand by 70p. With a net tax rate t, equation (4) says that disposable income YD is only $(1 - t)$ times national income Y. To relate consumption demand to *national* income, we write

$$C = 0.7YD = 0.7(1 - t)Y \qquad (5)$$

If national income rises by £1, consumption demand rises by only 0.7 times $(1 - t)$ of a pound. If the net tax rate t is 0.2, consumption demand rises by only $0.7 \times 0.8 = 0.56$ pounds. Each extra pound of national income increases disposable income by only 80p, out of which households wish to consume only an additional 56p. Figure 22-1 shows this consumption function CC' relating consumption demand to national income.

In general, let MPC be the marginal propensity to consume out of disposable income and MPC' the marginal propensity to consume out of national income. With a proportional net tax rate t, disposable income will always be (1 − t) times national income and MPC' will always be related to MPC by the formula

$$MPC' = MPC \times (1 - t) \qquad (6)$$

We now show how the government affects equilibrium national income and output. We start with an example in which autonomous investment demand $I = 300$ and the consumption function in terms of disposable income is $C = 0.7YD$.

The effect of government spending on output

Suppose government spending G on goods and services is 200 but there are no taxes. National income and disposable income coincide. Figure 22-2 shows that an increase in government spending from zero to 200 has precisely the same effects as an increase in investment spending from 300 to 500. With the multiplier equal to $1/(1 − MPC) = 3.33$, an increase in government spending G from zero to 200 increases income and output by 666, from 1000 to 1666. In Figure 22-2 equilibrium moves from E to E' when the aggregate demand schedule shifts from AD to AD'.

Thus, an increase in G leads to an increase in equilibrium

output equal to the multiplier times the increase in G. In a recession, when output is low, increased government spending on goods and services will increase aggregate demand and equilibrium output.

The effect of net taxes on output

Now we ignore government spending and focus on net taxes. The *net* tax rate t is increased when the government raises tax rates or reduces the rate of subsidies. Either way, net tax revenue increases at each level of national income.

Figure 22-1 shows that an increase in the net tax rate from zero to 0.2 causes the consumption function to pivot downward from CC to CC'. Its slope, the marginal propensity to consume out of national income, falls from MPC to MPC'. To draw the aggregate demand schedule we add the constant investment demand to consumption demand at each income level. Hence Figure 22-3 shows that the rise in the net tax rate rotates the aggregate demand schedule from AD to AD'. The point at which it crosses the 45° line – where planned spending equals actual output – moves from E to E'. Equilibrium income and output fall from 1000 to 682.

Raising the net tax rate reduces equilibrium output. When aggregate demand and equilibrium output are below the full-employment level, lower tax rates or higher transfer

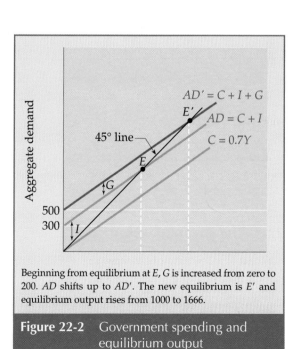

Beginning from equilibrium at E, G is increased from zero to 200. AD shifts up to AD'. The new equilibrium is E' and equilibrium output rises from 1000 to 1666.

Figure 22-2   Government spending and equilibrium output

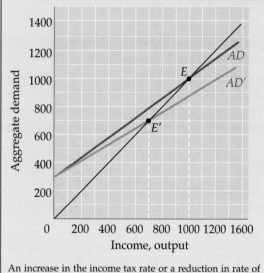

An increase in the income tax rate or a reduction in rate of unemployment benefit will increase the net tax rate t. The consumption function rotates from CC to CC' in Figure 22-1. With constant investment demand, the aggregate demand schedule rotates from AD to AD' in Figure 22-3. The equilibrium level of output falls from 1000 to 682 and the equilibrium point moves from E to E'.

Figure 22-3   Increasing the net tax rate

benefits will increase aggregate demand and equilibrium output.

The combined effects of government spending and taxation

Now put the two changes together. Government spending increases from zero to 200 and the tax rate increases from zero to 0.2. Investment remains at 300 and the *MPC* out of disposable income is still 0.7. Taxation makes the marginal propensity to consume out of national income drop to 0.56.

Figure 22-4 shows that the tax and spending package increases equilibrium output from 1000 to 1136.

The balanced budget multiplier

The economy began at an equilibrium output of 1000. With a proportional tax rate of 20 per cent, revenue was 200, precisely the amount of government spending.

You may think an equivalent increase in government spending and taxes would leave aggregate demand and equilibrium output unchanged. But Figure 22-4 shows that equilibrium output increases. The increase of 200 in government spending raises aggregate demand by 200. The tax increase reduces disposable income by 200. But since the *MPC* out of disposable income is only 0.7, this reduction in disposable income reduces consumption demand by only 140 (0.7 × 200).

Thus the initial effect of the tax and spending package is to increase aggregate demand by 200 because of government spending but to reduce aggregate demand by only 140 because higher taxes reduce consumption demand. On balance, aggregate demand is increased by 60. Output increases, and this induces further increases in consumption demand. When the new equilibrium is reached, output has risen a total of 136. This example illustrates the famous balanced budget multiplier.

The **balanced budget multiplier** states that an increase in government spending plus an equal increase in taxes leads to higher output.

The multiplier with proportional taxes

The multiplier relates changes in autonomous demand to changes in equilibrium *national* income and output. The formula in Chapter 20 still applies, except we must now use *MPC'*, the marginal propensity to consume out of national rather than disposable income.

$$\text{Multiplier} = \frac{1}{1 - MPC'} \qquad (7)$$

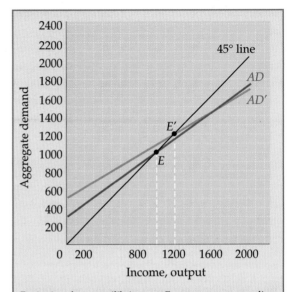

Beginning from equilibrium at *E*, government spending rises from zero to 200, shifting the *AD* schedule upwards, and the tax rises from zero to 0.2, making the new schedule *AD'* flatter. Equilibrium moves from *E* to *E'* where *AD'* intersects the 45° line. Equilibrium output increases from 1000 to 1136.

Figure 22-4   The combined effects of higher spending and taxes

Table 22-2   Values of the multiplier

MPC	t	MPC'	Multiplier
0.9	0	0.90	10.00
0.9	0.2	0.72	3.57
0.7	0	0.70	3.33
0.7	0.2	0.56	2.27
0.7	0.4	0.42	1.72

With proportional taxes, we know that *MPC'* equals *MPC* × (1 − *t*). For a given marginal propensity to consume out of disposable income, a higher tax rate *t* reduces *MPC'*, increases (1 − *MPC'*), and thus reduces the multiplier. Table 22-2 illustrates this.

22-3 The government budget

A **budget** is a description of the spending and financing plans of an individual, a company, or a government.

The government budget describes what goods and services the government will buy during the coming year, what transfer payments it will make, and how it will pay for them. Usually the government plans to pay for most of its

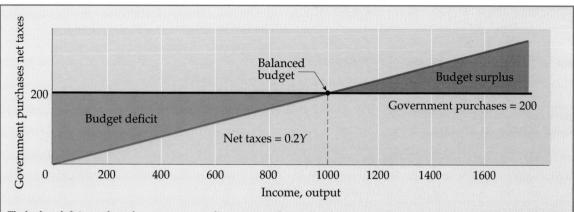

The budget deficit equals total government spending minus total tax revenue, or government purchases of goods and services minus net taxes. Government purchases are shown as constant, independent of income, while net taxes are proportionate to income. Thus at low levels of income the budget is in deficit; at high income levels, the budget is in surplus.

Figure 22-5   The government budget

spending by making people pay taxes. When spending exceeds taxes, there is a budget deficit. When taxes exceed spending there is a budget surplus. Continuing to use G to denote government spending on goods and services, and NT to denote net taxes or taxes minus transfer payments,

$$\text{Government budget deficit} = G - NT \qquad (8)$$

Figure 22-5 shows government purchases G and net taxes tY in relation to national income. We assume G is fixed at 200. With a proportional net tax rate of 0.2, net taxes are $0.2Y$. Taxes are zero when income is zero, 100 when income is 500, and 200 when income is 1000. At income levels below 1000, the government budget is in deficit. At an income of 1000 the budget is balanced, and at higher incomes the budget is in surplus. Given G and t, the budget deficit or surplus depends on the level of income. The higher the income level, the smaller the deficit or the larger the surplus.

The budget surplus or deficit is thus determined by three things: the tax rate t, the level of government spending G, and the level of income. With a given tax rate, an increase in G will increase equilibrium income tax revenue. Could the budget deficit be *reduced* by higher spending? We now show that this is not possible.

Investment, savings, and the budget

Chapter 20 showed that, by definition, actual leakages from the circular flow must always equal actual injections to the circular flow. Payments cannot vanish into thin air. Our model now has two leakages – saving by households and net taxes paid to the government – and two corresponding injections – investment spending by firms and government

spending on goods and services. Thus *actual* savings plus *actual* net taxes must always equal *actual* government spending plus *actual* investment spending.

In the last chapter we saw that, when the economy is not at equilibrium income, actual saving and investment will differ from *desired* or *planned* saving and investment. Firms make unplanned changes in inventories, and households may be forced to make unplanned savings if demand exceeds the output actually available.

We defined the economy as being in equilibrium when all quantities demanded or *desired* are equal to *actual* quantities. Hence we can now say that, in equilibrium, planned saving S plus planned net taxes NT must equal planned government purchases G plus planned investment I. Planned leakages equal planned injections.

$$S + NT = G + I \qquad (9)$$

In the absence of the government, this reduces to the equilibrium condition, planned saving equals planned investment, used in the last chapter. Equation (9) implies that in equilibrium desired saving minus desired investment equals the government's desired budget deficit.

$$S - I = G - NT \qquad (10)$$

Equation (10) tells us immediately that an increase in planned government spending G must *increase* the budget deficit. Why? For a given tax rate, an increase in G leads to a parallel upward shift in the aggregate demand schedule. This raises equilibrium income. Provided the tax rate is less than 100 per cent, disposable income must rise. Since households increase both desired consumption and desired saving when disposable income rises, some of this extra disposable income will go on extra desired saving.

Since desired investment I is independent of income, this increase in desired saving must increase the left-hand side of equation (10). Hence on the right-hand side of equation (10), net taxes NT cannot have increased by as much as the original increase in G. Equation (10) promises us that the equilibrium budget deficit rises.

An **increase in government spending on goods and services** increases equilibrium output. With a given tax rate, tax revenue rises. But the budget deficit increases (or the budget surplus falls).

We can analyse the effect of an increase in the tax rate in a similar way. We know from Figure 22-3 that a rise in the tax rate will cause the aggregate demand schedule to pivot downwards. Equilibrium income must fall. Disposable income falls both because equilibrium national income has fallen and because the tax rate is higher. With lower equilibrium disposable income, desired saving must fall. Hence the left-hand side of equation (10) must fall.

For a given level of government spending G, an **increase in the tax rate** reduces both equilibrium output and the budget deficit.

22-4 Deficits and the fiscal stance

Is the size of the budget deficit a good measure of the government's *fiscal stance*? Can we tell from the size of the deficit whether fiscal policy is *expansionary* and aiming to increase national income, or *contractionary* and trying to reduce national income?

In itself, the deficit is *not* a good measure of the government's fiscal stance. The deficit can change for reasons that have nothing to do with fiscal policy. Even though government spending and tax rates remain unaltered, if investment demand drops income will fall. In turn this will reduce the government's net tax revenue and increase the budget deficit. The government will take in less revenue from taxes and have to pay out more transfer payments such as unemployment benefit.

In particular, for given levels of government spending and tax rates, we expect the budget to show larger deficits in recessions, when income is low, than in booms, when income is high. Suppose aggregate demand suddenly falls. The budget will go into deficit. Someone looking at the deficit might conclude that fiscal policy was expansionary and that there was no case for further tax cuts or further

increases in government spending on goods and services. But that might be wrong. The deficit may exist because of the recession.

The structural budget

We can use the budget deficit as an indicator of the fiscal stance by calculating the *structural* or *cyclically-adjusted budget*.

The **structural budget** shows what the budget would have been if output had been at full-employment output.

Suppose government spending is 200 and the tax rate is 0.2. As in Figure 22-5, the budget will be in deficit at any income level below 1000 and in surplus at any income level above 1000. If, given the other components of aggregate demand, the equilibrium level of income is 800, the actual budget will be in deficit. Net tax revenue will be 0.2 × 800 or 160. With government spending at 200, there is a budget deficit of 40.

However, equilibrium output is the level at which desired spending equals actual income and spending. Suppose the equilibrium output of 800 lies well below the full-employment output of the economy, say 1200. Would the government still be running a deficit if the other components of aggregate demand were higher and the economy was at full-employment output?

With output and income at 1200 and a tax rate of 0.2, net tax revenue would be 240. There would be a budget *surplus* at full-employment output. Looking at the deficit of 40 when the actual income level is 800, we might be tempted to conclude that fiscal policy is too expansionary and that the government should be raising taxes or cutting its spending levels. Once we realize that the main cause of the deficit is the low level of income, we are less likely to reach this conclusion. We might even argue that taxes should be reduced or spending increased despite the deficit in the actual budget, believing that when the economy returns to full employment, the deficit will disappear.[4]

Inflation-adjusted deficits

A second reason why the actual government deficit may be a poor measure of fiscal stance concerns the distinction between real and nominal interest rates. Official measures of the deficit treat the whole of the nominal interest paid by the government on the national debt as an item of government

---

[4] We should emphasize that in this chapter we are concerned only with the impact of fiscal policy on aggregate demand. There may be other reasons to worry about the consequences of a deficit. We examine these in more detail in Chapter 28.

BOX 22-1 — Better measures of fiscal stance

During the mid 1970s, Britain's Labour government had budget deficits of around 5.5 per cent of GDP. But the oil price shocks and trade union power in wage bargaining combined to give the UK double-digit inflation during this period. Although nominal interest rates were 15 per cent during 1975–77, annual inflation averaged 16 per cent during the same period: real interest rates were negative. Begg (1987) shows that the inflation correction alone – counting real not nominal interest in the budget deficit – reduced it from 5.5 per cent to only 1 per cent during 1975–77. Quite a difference!

Now inflation is much better under control, so the inflation correction is much less important.

Even so, one should still remember the other correction – for the effect of the business cycle on tax

revenues. Remember that the UK experienced the Lawson boom in the late 1980s, then the Major slump in the early 1990s, before enjoying steady growth after 1993. Thus the structural budget deficit should be larger than the actual deficit in the late 1980s (when boom conditions temporarily boosted government revenues), smaller than the actual deficit in the early 1990s (the recession cut tax revenue and boosted unemployment benefit). After several years of steady recovery, the discrepancy between the two should have been much smaller by the late 1990s. The table below confirms these predictions.

Recent estimates by the UK Treasury suggest that, after two years, a 1 per cent increase in output (relative to potential output) leads to an improvement in the budget deficit or surplus by 0.75 per cent of GDP.

Average annual deficit (central and local government)	1988–90	1991–94	1995–97	1998–2000
Actual deficit (% of GDP)	0.2	5.8	4.6	−0.1
Structural deficit (% of GDP)	2.5	4.6	3.8	−0.3

Sources: OECD, *Economic Outlook*; D. Begg, 'UK Fiscal Policy since 1970', in R. Dornbusch and R. Layard (eds.), *The Performance of the UK Economy*, Oxford University Press, 1987; HM Treasury, *Budget 99*.

expenditure. It would make more sense to count only the *real* interest rate times the outstanding government debt as an item of expenditure which contributes to the deficit.

The **inflation-adjusted budget** uses real not nominal interest rates to calculate government spending on debt interest.

Suppose inflation is 10 per cent, nominal interest rates are 12 per cent, and real interest rates are 2 per cent. From the government's viewpoint, the interest burden is only really 2 per cent on each £1 of debt outstanding. Putting the matter differently, although nominal interest rates are 12 per cent, even at constant tax rates inflation will inflate future nominal tax revenue at 10 per cent a year, providing most of the revenue required to meet the high nominal interest rates. Similarly, from the private sector's viewpoint, although bondholders are getting a nominal income of 12 per cent from the government, this represents a real return of only 2 per cent, and it is the latter that will determine the real value of the fiscal stimulus the government is providing via

transfer payments in the form of debt interest to the private sector.

22-5 Automatic stabilizers and active fiscal policy

In Table 22-2 we showed that a higher net tax rate t reduces the multiplier. For example, when MPC is 0.7, the multiplier is 3.33 when the tax rate is zero but is only 2.27 when the tax rate is 0.2.

Suppose the economy is hit by a fall of 100 in investment demand. With a zero tax rate, equilibrium output falls by 333. However, with a tax rate of 0.2, equilibrium output falls by only 227. Similarly, if investment increases, the higher the tax rate the more damped is the multiplier effect on equilibrium output. The proportional tax rate is an automatic stabilizer.

Automatic stabilizers are mechanisms in the economy that reduce the response of GNP to shocks.

BOX 22-2 — The limits on active fiscal policy

WHY CAN'T SHOCKS TO AGGREGATE DEMAND IMMEDIATELY BE OFFSET BY FISCAL POLICY?

1 Time lags It takes time to recognize that aggregate demand has changed. It may take six months to collect reliable statistics on national output. Even then, it takes time to change fiscal policy. Long-term spending plans on hospital construction or on defence cannot be changed overnight. And once the policy change has been implemented it takes time to work through all the steps of the multiplier process shown in Table 21-2 before the full effect of the new fiscal policy is felt.

2 Uncertainty The government faces two major sources of uncertainty in deciding how much fiscal policy should be changed. First, it does not know for certain the values of key magnitudes such as the multiplier. It only has estimates obtained from past data. Mistakes in estimating the multiplier induce incorrect decisions about the extent of the fiscal change required to change equilibrium output by a given amount. Second, since fiscal policy takes time to work, the government has to forecast the level that aggregate demand will have reached by the time fiscal policy has had its full effects. If investment is currently low but about to increase dramatically, it may be unnecessary to begin fiscal expansion today. Mistakes in forecasting non-government sources of autonomous demand, such as investment, may lead to incorrect decisions about the fiscal changes currently required.

3 Induced effects on autonomous demand Our simple model treats investment demand and the autonomous component of consumption demand as given. But this is only a simplification. Changes in fiscal policy may lead to offsetting changes in other components of autonomous demand. If the government estimated these induced effects incorrectly, fiscal changes will not have the expected effects. To discuss this important issue, we extend our model of aggregate demand in Chapter 25.

WHY DOESN'T THE GOVERNMENT EXPAND FISCAL POLICY WHEN UNEMPLOYMENT IS PERSISTENTLY HIGH?

1 The budget deficit When output is low and unemployment is high, the budget deficit is likely to be large. Fiscal expansion will make the deficit even larger. The government may refuse to undertake a fiscal expansion either because of worries about the size of the deficit itself, an issue we discuss in Section 22-6, or because of worries that a large deficit will lead to inflation, an issue we explore in Chapter 28.

2 Maybe we're at full employment! Our simple model assumes that there are resources involuntarily unemployed that would like to work. Output is demand-determined. Fiscal expansion raises demand and output. Suppose however that we are in full long-run equilibrium at potential output. People are unemployed, and machines idle, only because they do not wish to supply their factor services at the going wages or rentals. Now there are no spare resources to be mopped up by expansion of aggregate demand. If the government believes that high unemployment and low output are not the result of a fall in aggregate demand, but rather the result of a decline in the willingness to work or to supply output, it may conclude that fiscal expansion is pointless. Chapters 26, 27, and 31 discuss the supply side of the economy and explore this argument in greater detail.

By 'shocks' we mean events such as an oil price increase or a war. Shocks change the autonomous components of aggregate demand and shift the aggregate demand schedule.

Income tax, VAT, and unemployment benefit are important automatic stabilizers. Whenever income and output fall, government payments of unemployment benefits rise and government receipts of income tax and VAT fall. These factors help to ensure that the net tax rate is sufficiently high to reduce the size of the multiplier by a considerable amount. And this means that a given shift of the aggregate demand schedule will have a smaller effect on the equilibrium level of income and output.

Automatic stabilizers have one great advantage. They

work automatically. Nobody has to decide whether there has been a shock to which the government should now respond. By reducing the responsiveness of the economy to shocks, automatic stabilizers help ensure that output does not fall to catastrophic levels. In an open economy, imports are another automatic stabilizer.

Active or discretionary fiscal policy

Although automatic stabilizers are always at work, governments also use *active* or *discretionary* fiscal policies which alter spending levels or tax rates in order to stabilize the level of aggregate demand close to full-employment output. When other components of aggregate demand are abnormally low, the government stimulates demand by cutting taxes, increasing spending, or both. Conversely, when other components of aggregate demand are abnormally high, the government raises taxes or reduces spending.

By now you ought to be – and probably are – asking yourself two questions. First, why can't fiscal policy be used to stabilize aggregate demand completely? Surely, by maintaining aggregate demand at its full-employment level, the government could eliminate booms and slumps altogether? Second, why have governments become reluctant to adopt an expansionary fiscal policy which might have offset the reductions in other sources of aggregate demand and prevented the rise in unemployment? Box 22-2 provides some of the answers to these two questions about fiscal policy.

22-6 The national debt and the deficit

The government's total outstanding debts are called the *national debt*.

The UK government ran large actual deficits in the 1970s. Hence the nominal value of its debt increased sharply during the 1970s, from £33 billion in 1971 to £113 billion in 1981.

Yet in many of these years the nominal deficit was actually a real surplus once the appropriate inflation-accounting is employed. This suggests that the *real* debt must have been falling, not rising. And this in fact is the case. Even if it were not, we should remember that, when the economy is growing in *real* terms, real tax revenue will be rising, and the public sector can service a growing real debt without having to increase *tax rates*.

These two arguments – inflation adjustment of the deficit and the growth of real incomes and the real tax revenue from given tax rates – suggest that in many countries debt may not be out of control. Although nominal deficits have

Table 22-3	UK national debt, 1969–97 (net public sector debt as % of GDP)			
1973	1979	1985	1991	1999
60	48	46	28	41

Source: OECD, *Economic Outlook*; HM Treasury, *Budget 99*.

dramatically raised the nominal debt, the ratio of nominal debt to nominal GDP may well have *fallen*. Table 22-3 confirms that this reasoning is correct. In fact, the debt/GDP ratio in 1999 was two-thirds of its level 30 years earlier. Public fears of a UK debt explosion were misplaced.

There are two theoretical reasons why concerns about the national debt may be overstated. First, the vast majority of UK debt is owed to UK citizens who hold government bonds. It is a debt we owe ourselves as a nation. Second, some of the money which the public sector has borrowed in the past has been used to finance physical investment or investment in human capital, which will raise *future* tax revenue and help pay off the debt. Prudent businesses sometimes borrow to finance profitable investment, and there is no reason why a prudent public sector should not do likewise.

Why, then, should a sensible economist worry about the scale of the public debt at all? Two reasons. First, *if* the debt becomes large relative to GNP, high tax rates may be required to meet the debt interest burden. High tax rates may have disincentive or distortionary effects.

Second, if the government is unwilling to raise tax rates beyond a certain point (perhaps because of the adverse effects mentioned above) or is unable to raise tax rates beyond a certain point (perhaps because businesses and rich individuals would then emigrate), a sufficiently large debt may lead to large deficits which the government can finance only by borrowing or printing money. Since borrowing merely compounds the problem, eventually the temptation to print money on a massive scale may become irresistible. That is how hyperinflations start. We discuss hyper-inflations in Chapter 28.

By the late 1990s, UK government debt, as a percentage of GDP, was lower than in 1970. In many European countries, it has risen steadily for two decades. Table 22-4 shows that the debt has now reached massive proportions in countries like Belgium and Italy. Such high debt levels are especially worrying when real interest rates are high.

This completes our introduction to fiscal policy, aggregate demand, and the economy. We conclude the chapter by

BOX 22-3   'You've never had it so prudent'

This is what Prime Minister Tony Blair told the Labour Party Conference in 1999. His Chancellor, Gordon Brown, not only gave the Bank of England independent control of interest rates (to stop politicians being tempted to boost the economy too much), but also introduced a Code for Fiscal Stability (for the same reason).

The **Code for Fiscal Stability** commits the government to a medium-run objective of financing all current government spending out of current revenues.

Borrowing-financed deficits are allowed only to finance public-sector investment (which should eventually pay for itself by raising future output and hence future tax revenues). A medium-run perspective is needed because the actual deficit fluctuates over the business cycle even if tax rates remain constant. Chancellor Brown's 'golden rule' means that government debt accumulation in the long run (because of borrowing to finance investment) should be accompanied by higher output and tax revenue without requiring any change in tax rates.

Table 22-4	Government net debt (% of GDP)	
	1981	2000
Belgium	84	107
Italy	53	104
Netherlands	25	52
USA	22	36
UK	38	40
France	0	46
Germany	12	49
Japan	19	48
Sweden	−6	5

Source: OECD, *Economic Outlook*.

Table 22-5	UK foreign trade, 1950–98 (percentage of GDP)		
	Exports	Imports	Net exports
1950	23	23	0
1960	20	21	−1
1970	22	21	1
1980	27	25	2
1998	26	27	−1

Source: ONS, *Economic Trends*.

extending our model of aggregate demand and income determination to include the one sector we have so far neglected – foreign trade with the rest of the world.

22-7 Foreign trade and income determination

In this section we take account of the economy's exports X, goods domestically produced to be sold to the rest of the world, and its imports Z, goods produced by the rest of the world but purchased by domestic residents. Table 22-5 shows UK exports, imports, and net exports $X - Z$. Two points should be noted.

Net exports are very small relative to GDP. Roughly speaking, exports and imports are equal in magnitude. The UK has tended to have a roughly balanced trade with the rest of the world.

The **trade balance** is the value of net exports. When exports exceed imports the economy has a **trade surplus**. When imports exceed exports, the economy has a **trade deficit**.

When a household spends more than its income, it dissaves, or is in deficit, and must run down its assets (in bank accounts or holdings of industrial shares) to meet this deficit. Similarly, when a country runs a trade deficit with the rest of the world, the country as a whole must sell off some assets to foreigners to pay for this deficit. In Chapter 29 we explain how this occurs.

Second, Table 22-5 shows that the UK is a very open economy. Exports and imports are each over a quarter of GDP. In the United States, exports and imports are about 12 per cent of GDP. Foreign trade is much more important for most European countries than for a very large country like the United States.

Chapter 20 explained that net exports $X - Z$ add to our income and expenditure measures of GDP. Hence, the

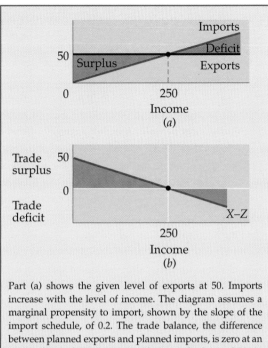

Part (a) shows the given level of exports at 50. Imports increase with the level of income. The diagram assumes a marginal propensity to import, shown by the slope of the import schedule, of 0.2. The trade balance, the difference between planned exports and planned imports, is zero at an income level of 250. Imports and exports both equal 50. At higher levels of income, imports exceed 50 and there is a trade deficit. The net export schedule $X - Z$ in part (b) shows the difference between export and import demand.

Figure 22-6   Exports, imports, and the trade balance

equilibrium condition for the goods market must now be expanded to[5]

$$Y = C + I + G + X - Z \qquad (11)$$

What determines the desired levels of exports and imports? The demand for our exports depends chiefly on what is happening in foreign economies. For a small country like the UK, the level of foreign income and foreign demand for our exports is largely unrelated to the level of income in our domestic economy. Hence we treat the demand for our exports as autonomous. At any particular instant it is at a given level but this level will change when demand conditions alter in the rest of the world.

Imports from the rest of the world may be raw materials for domestic production or items consumed directly by households, such as a Japanese television or a bottle of French wine. Demand for imports is likely to rise when domestic income and output rise. Figure 22-6 shows the

---

[5] This condition also implies $Y + Z = C + I + G + X$. Domestic output Y plus output Z from abroad equals final demand or final expenditure $C + I + G + X$.

behaviour of export, import, and net export demand as domestic income changes.

The export demand schedule is horizontal since export demand is independent of domestic income. The level of desired imports is zero when income is zero but rises steadily as incomes rises. The slope of the import demand schedule is the marginal propensity to import.

The **marginal propensity to import (MPZ)** is the fraction of each additional pound of national income that domestic residents wish to spend on extra imports.

The import demand schedule in Figure 22-6 assumes a value of 0.2 for the marginal propensity to import. Each additional pound of national income adds 20p to desired imports. One of the problems facing the UK is that the marginal propensity to import MPZ is higher than 0.2, so that any increase in national income leads to a large increase in the demand for imports.

At each income level, the difference between export demand and import demand is the demand for net exports. At low levels of income, net exports will be positive. There will be a trade *surplus* with the rest of the world. At high levels of income, there will be a trade *deficit* and net exports will be negative. By raising import demand while leaving export demand unchanged, an increase in income will reduce the trade surplus or increase the trade deficit.

Net exports and equilibrium income

Figure 22-7 shows how equilibrium income is determined when foreign trade is included in the model. We start from the schedule $C + I + G$, described earlier in the chapter. At low income levels, net export demand is positive. Aggregate demand $C + I + G + X - Z$ will then exceed $C + I + G$. As income rises, import demand rises and the desired level of *net* exports falls. At the income of 250, Figure 22-6 tells us that net export demand is zero. Figure 22-7 shows the new aggregate demand schedule AD crossing $C + I + G$ at an income of 250. Beyond this income, net export demand is negative and the aggregate demand schedule is below $C + I + G$.

At a zero income, Figure 22-7 shows autonomous demand equal to 150, made up of $I + G = 100$ and 50 of export demand. We assume that the marginal propensity to consume out of national income MPC' is 0.7. The $C + I + G$ schedule has a slope of 0.7, but the aggregate demand schedule AD a slope of only 0.5. Although each extra pound of national income adds 70p to desired consumption, it also adds 20p to desired imports, since $MPZ = 0.2$. Each extra pound of national income adds only 50p to aggregate

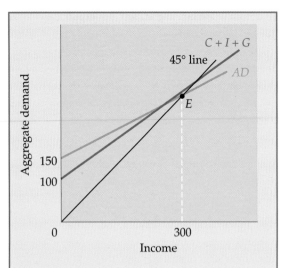

Net exports $(X - Z)$ must be added to $C + I + G$ to obtain aggregate demand AD. When export demand is 50 and the marginal propensity to import 0.2, the gap between the $C + I + G$ schedule and the AD schedule is precisely the net export schedule in Figure 22-6. The $C + I + G$ schedule crosses the AD schedule at an income of 250 where net exports equal zero. Equilibrium occurs at the income 300 and point E, where the AD schedule crosses the 45° line.

Figure 22-7   Equilibrium income in an open economy

demand for domestic output. The AD schedule has a slope of 0.5.

In Figure 22-7 equilibrium occurs at E, where aggregate demand equals domestic income and output. Only at that point do planned spending and actual incomes and output coincide. The equilibrium level of domestic income is 300. Investment and government spending account for 100, exports are 50. Consumption is 210 (0.7 × 300), of which 150 is spent purchasing domestically produced goods. The remaining 60 (0.2 × 300) is import spending, which exceeds exports of 50. At the equilibrum output, there is a trade deficit of 10.

The multiplier in an open economy

Each additional pound of national income raises consumption demand *for domestically produced goods* not by MPC', the marginal propensity to consume goods from whatever source, but only by $(MPC' - MPZ)$. Hence in an open economy, the formula for the multiplier must be amended to

$$\text{Multiplier} = \frac{1}{1 - (MPC' - MPZ)} \qquad (12)$$

With a value of 0.7 for MPC', the value of the multiplier in the absence of foreign trade would be 3.33. When the value

of the marginal propensity to import is 0.2, the multiplier is reduced to $1/0.51 = 2$. Higher values of the MPZ reduce the multiplier still further.

An increase in exports

An increase in export demand leads to a parallel upward shift in the aggregate demand schedule AD. Hence equilibrium income must increase. A higher aggregate demand schedule must cross the 45° line at a higher level of income. With a higher income, desired imports rise. The analysis of what happens to net exports is very similar to our analysis of the effect of an increase in government spending on the budget deficit.

As a matter of national income accounting, total leakages from the circular flow must always equal total injections to the circular flow. And in equilibrium desired spending must coincide with actual income and spending on domestic goods. Hence the amended equilibrium condition for an open economy is

$$S + NT + Z = I + G + X \qquad (13)$$

Desired savings plus net taxes plus desired imports equal desired investment plus desired government spending plus desired exports. An increase in export demand X increases equilibrium domestic income and output. In turn, this raises desired savings, and net tax revenue at constant tax rates, and desired imports.[6] Since S, NT, and Z all increase, the increase in desired imports must be smaller than the increase in desired exports X. Hence an increase in export demand raises the equilibrium level of desired imports but still increases the desired level of net exports. The domestic country's trade balance with the rest of the world improves.

Import spending and employment

A common view is that imports steal jobs from the domestic economy. Final expenditure demand $C + I + G + X$ is met partly through goods produced abroad rather than through goods produced at home. Thus, by reducing imports, we can create extra output and employment at home. This view is correct, but also dangerous. It is correct because higher consumer spending on domestic rather than foreign goods *will* increase aggregate demand for domestic goods and therefore increase domestic output and employment. In Figure 22-7, a reduction in the marginal propensity to import makes the AD schedule steeper and raises equilibrium income and output.

---

[6] Since tax rates remain constant, higher domestic income raises disposable income, desired consumption, and savings.

There are many different ways to restrict import spending at each level of output. In Chapter 29 we begin the analysis of how the exchange rate affects the demand for imports (and exports). However, imports can also be restricted directly. For example, the United States has *import quotas*, or maximum quantities, on steel imports from European or Japanese producers.

The view that import restrictions are always good for domestic output and employment is dangerous because it ignores the possibility of retaliation by other countries. By reducing our imports, we cut the exports of others. If they retaliate by doing the same thing, the demand for our exports will fall. In the end, nobody gains employment but world trade disappears. When the whole world is in a recession, what is needed is a worldwide expansion of fiscal policies, not a collective, and ultimately futile, attempt to steal employment from other countries.

SUMMARY

● The government enters the circular flow by purchasing goods and services, and by levying taxes (net of transfer benefits) which reduce disposable income below national income and output.

● Proportional taxes lower the marginal propensity to consume out of national income. Households get only a fraction of each extra pound of national income to use as a disposable income.

● An increase in government purchases of goods and services increases aggregate demand and equilibrium output. An increase in the tax rate reduces aggregate demand and equilibrium output.

● An equal initial increase in government spending and taxes raises aggregate demand and output. This is the balanced multiplier.

● The government budget is in deficit (surplus) when spending is larger (smaller) than tax revenue. Higher government spending increases the budget deficit. An increase in the tax rate reduces the budget deficit.

● In equilibrium in a closed economy, desired savings and taxes equal desired investment and government spending. Any excess of desired savings over desired investment must be offset by an excess of government spending on goods and services over net tax revenue.

● The budget deficit is not a good indicator of the fiscal stance. Recessions make the budget go into deficit. The structural budget calculates whether the budget would be in surplus or deficit if income were at its full-employment level. It is a better measure of the fiscal stance than the actual surplus or deficit. It is also important to inflation-adjust the deficit.

● Automatic stabilizers reduce fluctuations in GNP by reducing the multiplier. Leakages act as automatic stabilizers.

● In addition, the government may also use active or discretionary fiscal policy to try to stabilize output. In practice, we should not expect active fiscal policy to be capable of perfect stabilization of output.

● The national debt grows as a result of budget deficits. Since the debt is mainly owed to the citizens of the country, it may pose fewer problems for the economy than is often supposed. However, the national debt may be a burden if the government is unable or unwilling to raise taxes to meet high interest payments on a large national debt.

● Deficits are not necessarily bad. Particularly in a recession, any move to reduce the deficit might lead the economy further away from its full-employment output. But extremely large deficits create the possibility of a vicious circle of extra borrowing, extra interest payments, and yet more borrowing.

● In an open economy, exports are a source of demand for domestic goods but imports are a leakage from the circular flow since they represent a demand for goods produced abroad.

● Exports are determined mainly by conditions abroad and can be treated as autonomous spending unrelated to domestic income. Imports are assumed to increase in line with domestic income. The marginal propensity to import *MPZ* tells us how much of each extra pound of national income goes on additional demand for imports.

● The marginal propensity to import reduces the value of the multiplier from $1/(1 - MPC')$ to $1/(1 - MPC' + MPZ)$.

● An increase in exports increases domestic output and income. An increase in the marginal propensity to import reduces domestic output and income.

● The trade surplus is the excess of exports over imports. The trade surplus is larger the smaller is the level of income. An increase in exports increases the trade surplus, and an increase in the marginal propensity to import reduces it.

● In equilibrium, desired leakages $S + NT + Z$ must equal desired injections $G + I + X$. This means that any surplus $S - I$ desired by the private sector must be offset by the sum of the government deficit $G - NT$ and the desired trade surplus $(X - Z)$.

KEY TERMS

REVIEW QUESTIONS

1 Suppose equilibrium output in a closed economy is 1000, consumption is 800 and investment is 80. (a) What is the level of government spending on goods and services? (b) Suppose investment rises by 50 and the marginal propensity to consume out of national income is 0.8. What is the new equilibrium level of C, I, G, and Y? (c) Suppose instead that G had risen by 50. What would be the new equilibrium of C, I, G, and Y? (d) Suppose full-employment output is 1200. By how much would G now have to be raised to get the economy to full-employment output?

2 (a) Explain why the multiplier is lower when there is a proportional tax rate. (b) Relate your answer to automatic stabilizers.

3 The government makes a transfer payment of £5 billion to the elderly. The income tax rate is 0.2 and the MPC is 0.8. (a) What is the effect of the transfer payment on equilibrium income and output? (b) Does the budget deficit rise or fall as a result of the transfer? Explain.

4 In equilibrium, desired savings equal desired investment. True or false? Explain.

5 Why does the government bother to raise taxes when it could borrow to cover its spending?

6 The MPC' is 0.8. MPZ, the marginal propensity to spend on imports, is 0.4. Suppose investment demand rises by 100. (a) What happens to the equilibrium level of income and the equilibrium level of net exports? (b) Suppose exports, rather than investment, increase by 100. How does the trade balance change?

7 The EU's trade partners have a recession. (a) What happens to the EU's trade balance? (b) What happens to the equilibrium level of EU income? Explain.

8 *Common fallacies* Show why the following statements are incorrect: (a) The Chancellor raised taxes and spending by equal amounts. It will be a neutral budget for employment and output. (b) Government policy should aim to balance exports and imports but ensure that the government follows the prudent example of the private sector in spending less than it earns. (c) To reduce the budget deficit by £1 billion it is necessary to cut government spending by £1 billion.

23 Money and modern banking

LEARNING OUTCOMES

When you have finished this chapter, you should be able to:

- Define the medium of exchange, the key attribute of money
- Consider other functions of money
- Analyse how banks create money by holding fewer reserves than they create deposits
- Relate the monetary base to the money supply via the money multiplier
- Explain different measures of money in the UK and discuss why different measures have been emphasized as the financial sector has changed
- Analyse how modern banks compete for deposits and loans by choosing the interest rates they pay depositors and charge lenders

In songs and popular language, 'money' stands for many things. It is a symbol of success, it is a source of crime, and it makes the world go around.

Money is any generally accepted means of payment for delivery of goods or settlement of debt. It is the **medium of exchange**.

Dog's teeth in the Admiralty Islands, sea shells in parts of Africa, gold during the nineteenth century: all are examples of money. What matters is not the physical commodity used but the social convention that it will be accepted without question as a means of payment.

We now begin our study of the role of money in the economy. We explain why society uses money and how money helps us to economize on scarce resources used in the transacting process. By the end of Chapter 24 we will understand how modern banks play a key role in determining the total quantity of money and how the government, operating through profit incentives or direct controls on the banking system, seeks to control the quantity of money in the economy.

As macroeconomists, we are interested in how the financial markets interact with the 'real economy', the markets for output of goods and inputs of factors such as labour. We begin by showing the relation between money and interest rates. Then in Chapter 25 we show how interest rates can affect aggregate demand and hence output and employment. In Chapters 26–28 we examine the relation between money, prices, and output. By then we shall be in a position to discuss the major issues of unemployment and inflation. And in Chapter 29 we discuss the relation between money, interest rates, prices, and the exchange rate, showing how international competitiveness can affect the demand for exports and imports, and hence aggregate demand.

We study the financial markets in some detail. We begin by asking why society uses money at all.

23-1 Money and its functions

Although the crucial feature of money is its acceptance as the means of payment or medium of exchange, money has three other functions. It serves as a unit of account, as a store of value, and as a standard of deferred payment.

The medium of exchange

Money, the medium of exchange, is used in one-half of almost all exchange. Workers exchange labour services for money. People buy or sell goods in exchange for money. We accept money not to consume it directly but because it can subsequently be used to buy things we do wish to consume. Money is the medium through which people exchange goods and services.[1]

To see that society benefits from a medium of exchange, imagine a barter economy.

A **barter economy** has no medium of exchange. Goods are simply swapped for other goods.

In a barter economy, the seller and the buyer *each* must want something the other has to offer. Each person is simultaneously a seller and a buyer. To see a film, you must hand over in exchange a good or service that the cinema manager wants. There has to be a *double coincidence of wants*.

Trading is very expensive in a barter economy. People spend a lot of time and effort finding others with whom they can make mutually satisfactory swaps. Since time and effort are scarce resources, a barter economy is wasteful. The use of money – any commodity *generally* accepted in payment for goods, services, and debts – makes trading simpler and more efficient. By economizing on time and effort spent in trading, society can use these resources to produce extra goods or leisure, making everyone better off.

Other functions of money

The **unit of account** is the unit in which prices are quoted and accounts are kept.

In Britain prices are quoted in pounds sterling; in the United States in dollars. It is usually convenient to use the units in which the medium of exchange is measured as the unit of account as well. However, there are exceptions. During the rapid German inflation of 1922–23 when prices in marks were changing very quickly, German shopkeepers found it more convenient to use dollars as the unit of account. Prices were quoted in dollars but payment was made in marks, the German medium of exchange.

Money is a **store of value** because it can be used to make purchases in the future.

To be accepted in exchange, money *has* to be a store of value. Nobody would accept money as payment for goods supplied today if the money was going to be worthless when they tried to buy goods with it tomorrow. But money is neither the only nor necessarily the best store of value. Houses, stamp collections, and interest-bearing bank accounts all serve as stores of value. Since money pays no interest and its real purchasing power is eroded by inflation, there are almost certainly better ways to store value.

Finally, money serves as a *standard of deferred payment* or a unit of account over time. When you borrow, the amount to be repaid next year is measured in pounds sterling. Although convenient, this is not an essential function of money. UK citizens can get bank loans specifying in dollars the amount that must be repaid next year. Thus the key feature of money is its use as a medium of exchange. For this, it must act as a store of value as well. And it is usually, though not invariably, convenient to make money the unit of account and standard of deferred payment as well.

Different kinds of money

In prisoner-of-war camps, cigarettes served as money. In the nineteenth century money was mainly gold and silver coins. These are examples of *commodity money*, ordinary goods with industrial uses (gold) and consumption uses (cigarettes) which also serve as a medium of exchange. To use a commodity money, society must either cut back on other uses of that commodity or devote scarce resources to additional production of the commodity. But there are less expensive ways for society to produce money.

A **token money** is a means of payment whose value or purchasing power as money greatly exceeds its cost of production or value in uses other than as money.

A £10 note is worth far more as money than as a 7.5 × 14 cm piece of high-quality paper. Similarly, the monetary value of most coins exceeds the amount you would get by melting them down and selling off the metals they contain. By collectively agreeing to use token money, society economizes on the scarce resources required to produce money as a medium of exchange. Since the manufacturing cost is tiny, why doesn't everyone make £10 notes? The essential

---

[1] For an interesting account of how cigarettes became used as money in prisoner-of-war camps, see R. A. Radford, 'The Economic Organisation of a POW Camp', *Economica*, 1945.

The following contrast between a monetary and barter economy is reproduced from the World Bank, *World Development Report*, 1989.

LIFE WITHOUT MONEY
'Some years since, Mademoiselle Zelie, a singer, gave a concert in the Society Islands in exchange for a third part of the receipts. When counted, her share was found to consist of 3 pigs, 23 turkeys, 44 chickens, 5000 cocoa nuts, besides considerable quantities of bananas, lemons and oranges . . . as Mademoiselle could not consume any considerable portion of the receipts herself it became necessary in the meantime to feed the pigs and poultry with the fruit.' W. S. Jevons (1898)

MARCO POLO DISCOVERS PAPER MONEY
'In this city of Kanbula [Beijing] is the mint of the Great Khan, who may truly be said to possess the secret of the alchemists, as he has the art of producing money . . . He causes the bark to be stripped from mulberry trees . . . made into paper . . . cut into pieces of money of different sizes. The act of counterfeiting is punished as a capital offence. This paper currency is circulated in every part of the Great Khan's domain. All his subjects receive it without hesitation because, wherever their business may call them, they can dispose of it again in the purchase of merchandise they may require.' *The Travels of Marco Polo*, Book II

condition for the survival of token money is restriction of the right to supply it. Private production is illegal.[2]

Society enforces the use of token money by making it *legal tender*. The law says it must be accepted as a means of payment. However, laws cannot always be enforced. When prices are rising very quickly, domestic token money is a poor store of value and people are reluctant to accept it as a medium of exchange. Shops and firms give discounts to people paying in gold or in foreign currency, as in the later stages of the great German inflation in 1923.

In modern economies, token money is supplemented by IOU money.

An **IOU money** is a medium of exchange based on the debt of a private firm or individual.

A bank deposit is IOU money because it is a debt of the bank. When you have a bank deposit the bank owes you money. You can write a cheque and the bank is obliged to pay whenever the cheque is presented. Bank deposits are a medium of exchange because they are generally accepted as payment. To examine how IOUs of private firms came to serve as money, we now turn to the development of the banking system.

23-2 Goldsmiths and early banking

Once upon a time people used gold bullion as money. Wanting a safe place to store this bullion, people deposited it with goldsmiths – people who worked with gold and had vaults for storing it safely – and picked it up when needing to make payments.

Banking

Two developments turned goldsmiths from safekeepers into bankers. First, people found that, instead of physically handing over gold as a means of payment, they could give the seller of goods a letter transferring the ownership of the gold held by the goldsmith. This letter was what today we would call a cheque.

Once cheques became acceptable in payment of purchases, people felt that the gold at the goldsmith's was as good as gold in their pocket. To figure out how much money they had, people would count both gold in their pockets and gold held by the goldsmith.

The amount at the goldsmith's for safekeeping was called a **deposit**.

People's money holdings were gold in their pockets plus their deposits. Since letters of gold ownership were more convenient to carry around than heavy gold, the invention of deposits made the payments system more efficient.

Second, and of greater significance, the goldsmiths had a

[2] The existence of forgers shows that society is economizing on scarce resources by producing money whose value as a medium of exchange exceeds its direct production cost.

lot of gold lying idle in their vaults. People swapped titles of ownership much more frequently than they came to withdraw gold from the vaults.

The first bank loan

Suppose a firm asks a goldsmith for a loan. The goldsmith realizes some of the gold in the vault can be lent to the firm, which will eventually repay it with interest. Although the goldsmith is temporarily short of gold, it is unlikely that all depositors of gold will suddenly ask for it back at the same time.

Table 23-1 shows what happens. Originally, the goldsmith had assets of £100 of gold in the vault and a corresponding liability of £100 owed to people who had deposited gold. Then the goldsmith lends £10 in gold to a firm. The goldsmith's assets are still £100 but only £90 of this is now gold in the vault, while the other £10 is the value of the outstanding loan. Deposits still equal £100. The goldsmith expects to get the gold loan back with interest and is happy about the deal.

Lending a bank deposit Since gold is difficult to carry around, the firm might be happier if, instead of borrowing physical gold, it can borrow from the goldsmith by being given a deposit. Today we call this an overdraft. The third row shows what happens when the goldsmith keeps all the gold but grants the firm a deposit of £10 and simultaneously records this loan as an asset of the goldsmith

The borrower wants the loan to buy a carriage. The new deposit of £10 is used to pay for the carriage by writing a cheque. The last row of the table shows the goldsmith's balance sheet when the seller of the carriage brings in the cheque and asks for £10 in gold. Assets fall £10 as the gold is paid out, but liabilities fall £10 because the borrower has used up the deposit. Notice that rows (2) and (4) of the table are identical. It makes no difference to the goldsmith whether the loan is initially in gold or in the form of a deposit or overdraft.

Reserves

People originally deposited £100 of gold, but, having made the loan, the goldsmith has only £90 of gold in the vault. If all depositors were suddenly to want their gold again, the goldsmith is unlikely to be able to get back at short notice the missing £10 of gold that has been lent out. As a banker, the goldsmith is relying on the fact that depositors will not all reclaim their gold simultaneously.

The **reserves** are the gold immediately available to meet depositors' demands. The **reserve ratio** is the ratio of reserves to deposits.

The old-fashioned goldsmith in Table 23-1 has a 100 per cent reserve ratio. Depositors could be paid in full but, making no loans, the goldsmith is making no profits from the lending business. The goldsmith-banker in row (2) has a reserve ratio of 90 per cent. There is a small profit from lending out gold but only a small risk of being unable to pay depositors if some of them want their gold back. The lower the reserve ratio, the more the goldsmith is lending. Interest payments will be higher but, with less gold in the vaults, there will be a greater risk of being unable to meet depositors' claims for their gold back.

How much of the gold dare the goldsmith lend out? The more unpredictable the withdrawals by depositors, and the less able are borrowers to repay loans at short notice, the more cautious must the goldsmith be and the higher must be the reserve ratio. Conversely, the larger the interest rate, the more likely the goldsmith is to take a chance and the lower will be the desired reserve ratio.

Financial panics

Everybody knows what the goldsmith-banker is up to. Most of the time people don't mind. Cheques are easier to use as a medium of exchange than gold. But if people believe that the goldsmith has lent too much, and will be unable to meet depositors' claims, there will be a *run* on the bank. If the goldsmith is not going to be able to repay all depositors, it

Table 23-1	Goldsmiths as bankers		
		Assets	Liabilities
(1) Old-fashioned goldsmith		Gold £100	Deposits £100
(2) Gold lender		Gold £90 + loan £10	Deposits £100
(3) Deposit lender: Step 1		Gold £100 + loan £10	Deposits £110
(4)	Step 2	Gold £90 + loan £10	Deposits £100

makes sense to get your gold out first while the goldsmith can still pay. Since everyone is doing the same thing, they ensure that the goldsmith will be unable to pay. Whenever the goldsmith has lent at all, and the reserve ratio is less than 100 per cent, it is impossible to meet the claims of all depositors at once.

A **financial panic** is a self-fulfilling prophecy. People believe that the bank will be unable to pay. In the stampede to get their money out, they ensure that the bank cannot pay. It will go bankrupt.

Today, financial panics are rare.[3] One important reason for this, which we discuss in the next chapter, is that the Bank of England stands ready to lend to banks who get into temporary difficulties. And the mere knowledge that this is the case helps prevent the self-fulfilling stampede to withdraw deposits before bankruptcy is declared.

Goldsmith banking and the money supply

The **money supply** is the value of the total stock of money, the medium of exchange, in circulation.

In our simple example, the money supply is gold coins in people's pockets plus the amount of deposits at the goldsmiths. Deposits are money because cheques against these deposits are accepted as a means of payment. Thus

$$\text{Money supply} = \text{gold in circulation} + \text{deposits at goldsmith} \quad (1)$$

Table 23-1 shows that goldsmiths' liabilities are always equal to their assets. Deposits are liabilities. Assets are gold in the vaults plus the value of loans. Thus,

$$\text{Money supply} = \text{gold in circulation} + \text{gold at goldsmiths} + \text{goldsmiths' loans} \quad (2)$$

The total gold stock is gold in circulation plus gold in goldsmiths' vaults. Thus

$$\text{Money supply} = \text{gold stock} + \text{goldsmiths' loans} \quad (3)$$

The importance of this result cannot be overstated. *Loans by goldsmith-bankers increase the stock of money in the economy.* Go back to Table 23-1. When the goldsmith first lends £10, the borrower received extra money. But nobody else had

any less money than before. Existing depositors could still write cheques against the gold originally deposited. The goldsmith took £10 out of the vaults and put it back into circulation. By making loans and putting gold back into circulation, the goldsmith increased the money supply.

Before leaving this example, we note two things. First, the money supply is larger than the gold stock. Second, the money supply is larger the more goldsmiths lend. The lower their reserve ratio, the higher the money stock.

23-3 Modern banking

The goldsmith-bankers were an early example of a financial intermediary.

A **financial intermediary** is an institution that specializes in bringing lenders and borrowers together.

A *commercial bank* borrows money from the public, crediting them with a deposit. The deposit is a liability of the bank. It is money owed to depositors. In turn the bank lends money to firms, households, or governments wishing to borrow.

Banks are not the only financial intermediaries. Insurance companies, pension funds, and building societies also take in money in order to relend it. The crucial feature of banks is that some of their liabilities are used as a means of payment, and are therefore part of the money stock.[4]

Commercial banks are financial intermediaries with a government licence to make loans and issue deposits, including deposits against which cheques can be written.

We begin by looking at the present-day UK banking system. Although the details vary from country to country, the general principle is much the same everywhere. It is basically the principle discovered by the goldsmith-bankers example of the previous section.

In the UK, the commercial banking system comprises several hundred registered banks, the National Girobank operating through post offices, and about a dozen trustee savings banks. Much the most important single group is the clearing banks. The clearing banks are so named because they have a central clearing house for handling payments by cheque.

---

[3] For a highly readable account of the more spectacular panics, see Charles Kindleberger, *Manias, Panics, and Crashes*, Basic Books, 1979.

[4] In fact, building societies now issue cheque books to their depositors. Although official UK statistics do not classify building societies as banks, this example illustrates the practical difficulty in deciding which intermediaries are banks and which of their deposits in practice are accepted as a medium of exchange. Many building societies are now changing their legal status to that of banks.

BOX 23-2　　　　Sainsbury's ready at the cheque outs

When is a bank not a bank? Building societies have for years been giving depositors chequebooks and access to 'hole-in-the-wall' cash dispensers. In 1997, a wave of building societies, including the very biggest such as the Halifax, followed Abbey National's earlier example and formally converted to the legal status of banks. And it is not just building societies that have been entering the banking industry, as the following piece makes clear:

'Sainsbury's Bank, the joint venture set up by the J Sainsbury supermarket group and Bank of Scotland has won its banking licence. . . . Tesco's Clubcard Plus account, managed by National Westminster Bank, is already running, . . . and has already attracted a large deposit base. . . . Safeway and Abbey National meanwhile yesterday announced details of the ABC Bonus Account . . . Some bankers worry, however, that, by helping supermarkets to break into their core business, they may have allowed a cuckoo into their nest. Barclays and Lloyds TSB have, so far at least, stayed aloof from the market.'

Source: *Financial Times*, 11 February 1997.

Table 23-2　Balance sheet of UK commercial banks, March 1999

Assets	£bn	Liabilities	£bn
In foreign currency		In foreign currency	
Securities	242	Deposits and money market instruments	1050
Loans	883	Other liabilities	93
Other assets	24		
In sterling		In sterling	
Securities	71	Deposits and money market instruments	832
Loans	861	Other liabilities	146
Other assets	40		
	2121		2121

A **clearing system** is a set of arrangements in which debts between banks are settled by adding up all the transactions in a given period and paying only the net amounts needed to balance inter-bank accounts.

Suppose you bank with Barclays but visit a supermarket that banks with Lloyds. To pay for your shopping you write a cheque against your deposit at Barclays. The supermarket pays this cheque into its accounts at Lloyds. Lloyds presents the cheque to Barclays which will credit Lloyds' account at Barclays and debit your account at Barclays by an equivalent amount. A transfer of funds between the two banks is required. Crediting or debiting one bank's account at another bank is the simplest way to achieve this.

However, on the same day someone else is probably writing a cheque on a Lloyd's deposit account to pay for her stereo equipment from a shop banking with Barclays. The stereo shop pays the cheque into its Barclays' account, increasing its deposit. Barclays then pays the cheque into

its account at Lloyds where her account is simultaneously debited. Now the transfer flows from Lloyds to Barclays.

Although in both cases the cheque writer's account is debited and the cheque recipient's account is credited, it does not make sense for the two banks to make two separate inter-bank transactions between themselves. The clearing system calculates the *net* flows between the member clearing banks and these are the settlements that they make between themselves. Thus the system of clearing cheques represents another way society reduces the costs of making transactions.[5]

---

[5] Society continues to find new ways to save scarce resources in producing and using a medium of exchange. Already many people use credit cards. Some supermarket tills directly debit customers' bank accounts. And shopping by TV and telephone and the internet is growing rapidly.

Balance sheet of the UK banks

Table 23-2 shows the balance sheet of the UK banks. Although more complex, it is not fundamentally different from the balance sheet of the goldsmith-banker shown in Table 23-1. We begin by discussing the asset side of the balance sheet.

Commercial banks hold some cash reserves in their vaults, just as the goldsmiths held gold in their vaults. However, modern banks' reserves also include money deposited with the Bank of England (usually known as the Bank), the *central bank* that acts as banker to the other banks and is responsible for monetary policy. We discuss the role of the central bank in the next chapter. Note that modern banks get by with very few reserves. In Table 23-2 they are so small that they are put into the 'other sterling assets' of the commercial banks.

Their balance sheet shows separately assets and liabilities in sterling and in foreign currency. Banks normally reduce their exposure to exchange rate changes by keeping assets and liabilities in foreign currency roughly in balance.

Whether in sterling or in foreign currency, loans are the principal asset of banks and the tough part of their business, because they are frequently not very liquid.

Liquidity refers to the speed and certainty with which an asset can be converted back into money. Money is the most liquid asset of all.

A bank that lends to a business may have little prospect of getting its money out until the project has been completed, and may lose everything if the business goes bankrupt.

The other main asset of banks is securities, various kinds of loans for which a second-hand market exists and in which trade is carried out all the time. Box 23-3 offers an introduction to these bills and bonds. Because a well-developed market exists, they are much more liquid than the loans recorded separately on the balance sheet.

Liabilities of commercial banks include sight and time deposits. Sight deposits mean the depositor can withdraw money 'on sight' without any notice; chequing accounts are sight deposits. Time deposits, which pay higher interest rates, require the depositor to give a period of notice before withdrawing money. Banks then have more time to organize the sale of some of their high-interest assets in order to have the cash available to meet these withdrawals. Certificates of deposit (CDs) are large 'wholesale' time deposits, a one-off deal with a particular client for a specified period, usually paying quite generous interest rates. The other liabilities of banks are various 'money

market instruments', short-term and highly liquid borrowing banks.

Banks as financial intermediaries

In what sense are banks financial intermediaries standing between lenders and borrowers? A bank is a business and its owners or managers aim to maximize profits. A bank makes profits by lending and borrowing. To get money in, the bank offers favourable terms to potential depositors. British banks increasingly offer interest on sight deposits and usually offer free chequing facilities to people whose sight deposits or current accounts do not fall below a certain level. They do not charge directly for the expenses of clearing and processing cheques. And they offer better interest rates on time deposits.

Next, the banks have to find profitable ways to lend what has been borrowed. Table 23-2 shows how the banks lend out their money. In sterling, most is lent as advances of overdrafts to households and firms, usually at interest rates well in excess of the rate simultaneously being paid to the bank customers with time deposits. Some is used to buy securities such as long-term government bonds. Some is more prudently invested in liquid assets. Although these do not pay such a high rate of interest, the bank can get its money back quickly if people start withdrawing a lot of money from their sight deposits. And some money is held as cash, the most liquid asset of all.

What economic services does the bank provide? It is transforming household loans to the bank into bank loans to a wide range of people – governments wishing to finance a budget deficit, firms borrowing to build a new factory, and individuals borrowing to start a new business or buy a new home. The bank is using its specialist expertise to acquire a diversified portfolio of investments though depositors merely observe that they get an interest rate on their time deposits or free chequing facilities. Without the existence of the intermediary, depositors would have neither the time nor the expertise to decide which of these loans or investments to make. That is the economic service that the bank as an intermediary provides.

Fractional reserve banking

Later in the chapter we show that UK banks hold reserves that are only 2 per cent of the sight deposits that could be withdrawn at any time. If only 2 per cent of people holding sight deposits denominated in pounds withdrew their money, banks would not have enough cash to meet these withdrawals.

This shows the importance of the other liquid assets in

BOX 23-3

A beginner's guide to the financial markets

Financial asset A piece of paper entitling the owner to a specified stream of interest payments for a specified period. Firms and governments raise money by selling financial assets. Buyers work out how much to bid for these assets by calculating the present value of the promised stream of payments. Assets are frequently retraded between individuals before the date at which the original issuer is committed to repurchase the piece of paper for a specified price.

Cash Notes and coin, paying zero interest. The most liquid asset.

Bills Financial assets with less than one year until the known date at which they will be repurchased by the original borrower. Suppose the government sells three-month Treasury bills. In April the government sells a piece of paper simultaneously promising to repurchase it for £100 in July. Bills do not pay interest, but if people bid £97 in April they will effectively make 3 per cent by holding the bill till July, quite a decent annual return. As July gets nearer the price at which the bill is retraded will climb towards £100. Buying it from some-one else in June for £99 and reselling to the government in July for £100 still yields 1 per cent in a month, or over 12 per cent a year at compound interest. Because Treasury bills can easily be bought and sold, and because their price can only fluctuate over a small range (say, between £97.5 and £98 in May when they expire in July), they are highly liquid. People can get their money back quickly and have a good idea how much they would get if they had to sell.

Bonds Longer-term financial assets. If you look under government bonds in the *Financial Times* you will find a bond listed as Treasury 5% 2004. In the year 2004 the government guarantees to repurchase this bond for £100 (the usual repurchase price). Until then the person owning the paper will get interest payments of £5 a year. Bonds are less liquid than bills, not because they are hard to sell, but because the price for which they could be sold, and the amount of cash this would

generate, is more uncertain. We now explain why by looking at the most extreme kind of bond.

Perpetuities Bonds that are never repurchased by the original issuer, who pays interest for ever. Usually called Consols (consolidated stock) in the UK. Consols 2.5% pay £2.5 a year for ever. Most consols were issued when interest rates were very low. People originally would have bid around £100 for this consol. Suppose interest rates on other assets rise to, say, 10 per cent. Consols are traded between people at around £25 each so that new purchasers of these old bonds get about 10 per cent on their financial investment. Notice two things. The person *holding* a bond makes a capital loss when other interest rates rise and the price of the bonds falls. Second, since the price of Consols was once £100 and is now only £25, there is much more volatility in Consol prices than in the price of Treasury bills. In fact, the longer the period until the original issuer is committed to buying the bond back for £100, the more its current price can move around as existing bond-holders attempt to sell out to new buyers and offer them a rate of return in line with other assets today. Hence although bonds can easily be bought and sold, they are not very liquid. If you buy one today, you do not have a very good idea exactly how much you would get if you had to sell out in six months' time.

Gilt-edged securities Government bonds in the UK. Gilt-edged because there is no danger of the govern-ment going bust and refusing to meet the interest payments.

Industrial shares (equities) Entitlements to receive corporate dividends, the part of firms' profits paid out to shareholders rather than retained to finance new investment in machinery and buildings. In good years, dividends will be high, but in bad years dividends may be zero. Hence a risky asset which is not very liquid. Firms could even go bust, making the shares completely worthless.

which banks have invested. At very short notice, they could cash in much of the money shown under 'Banks and market loans'. That is precisely why banks hold some of their money in liquid assets when they could get a higher interest rate by making less liquid advances to firms and households or by purchasing less liquid securities. The skill in running a bank entails being able to judge how much must be held in liquid assets including cash, and how much can be lent out in less liquid forms that earn higher interest rates.

23-4 Commercial banks and the money supply

Today, we define money as those generally accepted means of payments that are usable for *unrestricted* payments. We can use them at any time to pay any amount to anyone. They are measured as notes and coin in circulation with the general public plus deposits with the banking system. Exactly how we measure these deposits is discussed shortly.

Banks as creators of money

Like goldsmiths, modern banks create money by granting overdraft facilities, issuing sight deposits in excess of the cash reserves in the bank vaults. Without depositing any cash, some people are told they now have money in their bank accounts. These bank accounts are money because people can write cheques against them and use them as a means of payment.

Modern fractional reserve banking is an intrinsic part of the process of money creation. Assume that there are ten banks, each prepared to expand lending up to the point at which cash reserves in the vaults or with the central bank equal 10 per cent of all deposits.[6] Suppose one of the ten banks now has a client who pays an additional £100 in cash into her chequing account. That bank's cash assets and its deposit liabilities each rise by £100.

Is this an equilibrium position for a profit-maximizing bank? No. The bank will want to increase the lending on which it earns interest. In assuming a cash reserve ratio of 10 per cent, we assume that the bank's initial reaction is to increase lending by £90 or 90 per cent of the extra cash reserves it has just received.

To show how the banks interact, suppose first that only *one* bank increases its lending. Table 23-3 shows Bank A took in £100 in cash in exchange for a deposit of £100. In step 1, the bank lends out £90 or 90 per cent of its extra cash

Table 23-3	Direct expansion by a single bank	
Step	Assets	Liabilities
1	Cash £100, loans £90	Deposits £190
2	Cash £10, loans £90	Deposits £100
3	Cash £19, loans £90	Deposits £109
4	Cash £19, loans £98.10	Deposits £117.10

reserves. Suppose it gives you a deposit overdraft of £90 against which you can write cheques. Assets are £100 in cash plus the loan for £90. Deposits are also £190, comprising the £100 of the original cash depositor plus the additional £90 deposit you have been allowed to write cheques on.

In step 2 you blow your loan of £90, running down your deposit account to zero. The shops to which you wrote the cheques have collected their £90 in cash from your bank. Although the bank has reached its desired position of holding cash equal to 10 per cent of its total deposits, that is not the end of the story. The shops now have an extra £90 in cash. If in total they use the ten banks equally, your bank will get a new deposit of £9 in cash as shopkeepers put their money in their bank accounts. This is shown in step 3.

Step 4 shows that your bank will now lend out 90 per cent of this new deposit of £9. Its cash reserves are now £19 and its loans £98.10, the original loan to you of £90 plus a new loan of £8.10, or 90 per cent of the new cash deposit of £9. Since you have completely used up your deposit overdraft, total deposits of £117.10 are made up of the £100 deposits of the original cash deposit, £9 of new deposits when the shops paid in £9 in cash, and the new overdraft deposit of £8.10.

When this overdraft is spent, the bank will lose £8.10 in cash as people present their cheques for payment. However, it can hope to get back 10 per cent of this as a new cash deposit if it gets its share of new cash deposits across the whole banking system. And against this new cash of £0.81 it can lend a little more. You can fill in the next few steps in the table yourself.

Table 23-3 shows that even a single bank can create money. A single client began the process by depositing £100 in cash. By step 4 there is £81 of this cash outside the bank and there are deposits of £117.10. The money supply has increased from £100 to £198.10.[7] It may seem as if a single

---

[6] We use 10 per cent to keep the arithmetic simple.

[7] Even if the outstanding cash of £81 has been deposited in other banks, there will be corresponding deposit accounts. Either way we add this £81 to £117.10 to obtain £198.10.

Table 23-4	Deposit expansion by the banking system as a whole	
Step	Assets	Liabilities
1	Cash £100, loans £90	Deposits £190
2	Cash £100, loans £180	Deposits £280
3	Cash £100, loans £900	Deposits £1000

bank, acting in isolation, has created a lot of money. However, this is nothing compared with the money that the banking system can create when all banks act together.

When a single bank expands deposits, it loses most of its cash as people write cheques against their new deposits. Although this cash will be redeposited with the banking system as a whole, a single bank will get only a small share of this redepositing. Suppose, however, that all the other banks also increase deposits and lending when they get additional cash.

What happens to the £81 withdrawn from our bank in step 2 and not redeposited in step 3? It gets deposited in other banks, which then increase their lending. As people cash in cheques written against these deposits, our bank will get its share of the redeposits of this cash. Provided all withdrawn cash is redeposited in banks, *the banking system as a whole does not lose cash as it expands deposits*. Table 23-4 shows how the banking system expands deposits when it receives £100 of extra cash.

Suppose initially that each bank lends out 90 per cent of the value of its new cash. Step 1 shows that the banking system lends out £90 and creates £90 of new deposits when it begins with £100 in cash and equivalent deposits.

However, the system as a whole does not lose cash. In step 2, banks find that their cash assets are undiminished. They try lending out some more and creating even more deposits. Still they will find their cash reserve undiminished. They will try lending even more. In fact, lending will expand until £900 has been lent out and total deposits are the £900 corresponding to these loans plus the original £100 of deposits corresponding to the initial cash of £100 paid in. By the last row of Table 23-4 each bank, and the banking system as a whole, has succeeded in attaining its desired 10 per cent ratio of cash reserves to total deposits.

Originally, the money supply was the £100 of cash in people's pockets. This money is no longer in circulation. But bank deposits are now £1000, and this is the value of the money supply. The banking system has converted £100 of cash in circulation into £1000 of bank deposits against which

people can write cheques as a means of payment. Thus banks play a crucial role in determining the level of the money supply.

23-5 The monetary base and the money multiplier

Because the cash reserves of commercial banks are only a small fraction of total bank deposits, bank-created deposit money forms by far the most important component of the money supply in modern economies. Although we have now mastered the basics, it is important to tie up the loose ends, which we do in this section. Banks' deposits depend on the cash reserves in the banking system. To complete our analysis of how the money supply is determined we need to examine what determines the amount of cash that will be deposited with the banking system.

Through the *central bank*, the Bank of England in the UK, the government controls the issue of token money in a modern economy. We have already seen that private creation of token money must be outlawed when its value as a medium of exchange exceeds the direct cost of its production.

The **monetary base** or stock of **high-powered money** is the quantity of notes and coin in private circulation plus the quantity held by the banking system.

How much of the monetary base will be held by commercial banks as cash reserves? In the simplified example of the previous section, we assumed that the general public deposited all its cash with the banks. But this is only a simplification. Even people with deposit accounts and cheque-books carry some money around in their pockets. We do not write out a cheque for a bus fare. And how many times have you stood behind someone writing a cheque for a rail ticket and wished that they had been paying in cash, which can be dealt with more quickly?

But there are other reasons why people hold cash. Many people do not trust banks. They keep their savings under the bed. Remarkably enough, only three-quarters of British households have chequing accounts. Other people hold cash because they wish to make illegal or unreported transactions in the 'black economy'.

How is the money supply related to the monetary base, the amount of notes and coin issued by the central bank? The answer to this question is the money multiplier.

The **money multiplier** gives the change in the money stock for a £1 change in the quantity of the monetary base.

Thus we can write

$$\text{Money stock} = \text{money multiplier} \times \text{monetary base} \quad (4)$$

The value of the money multiplier depends on two key ratios, the banks' desired ratio of cash reserves to total deposits, and the private sector's desired ratio of cash in circulation to total bank deposits.

Banks' desired ratio of cash reserves to total deposits determines how much they will multiply up any given cash reserves into deposit money. The *lower* the desired cash reserves ratio, the larger the quantity of deposits the banks will create against given cash reserves and the *larger* will be the money supply.

Similarly, the *lower* the private sector's desired ratio of cash in circulation to private sector bank accounts, the *larger* will be the money supply for any given quantity of high-powered money issued by the central bank. Since a higher fraction of the monetary base is deposited in the banking system, the banks are able to create more bank deposits.

We give an exact formula for the money multiplier in Box 23-4 on page 387. To give an idea of its possible magnitude, suppose that banks wish to hold cash reserves equal to 1 per cent of their total deposits and that the private sector wishes to hold cash in circulation equal to 3 per cent of the value of private sector sight deposits. The formula given implies that the money multiplier would be 27. Each £100 increase in the monetary base leads to a rise of £2700 in the money supply.

At present, it is more important to remember that an increase in either the banks' desired cash reserves ratio or the private sector's desired ratio of cash to chequing account balances will reduce the value of the money multiplier. For a given monetary base, the money supply will fall.

We have seen what determines the cash reserves ratio desired by banks. The higher the interest rate banks can earn by lending relative to the interest rate (if any) that banks must pay depositors, the more banks will wish to lend and the more they will take chances with a low ratio of cash reserves to outstanding sight deposits. Conversely, the more unpredictable are withdrawals from sight deposits and the fewer lending opportunities the banks have in very liquid loans, the higher cash reserves they will have to maintain for any level of deposit lending.

What about the public's desired ratio of cash in circulation to deposits? In part this depends on institutional factors, for example whether firms pay wages by cheque or cash. In part it depends on tax rates and the incentive to hold cash to

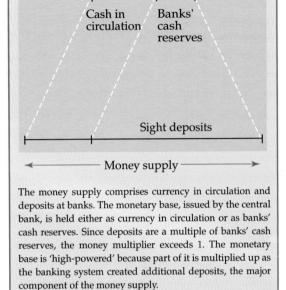

The money supply comprises currency in circulation and deposits at banks. The monetary base, issued by the central bank, is held either as currency in circulation or as banks' cash reserves. Since deposits are a multiple of banks' cash reserves, the money multiplier exceeds 1. The monetary base is 'high-powered' because part of it is multiplied up as the banking system created additional deposits, the major component of the money supply.

Figure 23-1   Money supply determination

make untraceable payments in the process of tax evasion. Credit cards reduce the amount of cash used. Credit cards are a temporary means of payment, a *money-substitute* rather than money itself. When you sign a credit card slip, the slip itself cannot be used to make further purchases. Within a short period you have to settle your account by using cash or a cheque, the ultimate means of payment. Nevertheless, since credit cards allow people with chequing accounts to carry less cash in their pocket, their increasing use will probably reduce the desired ratio of cash to sight deposits with banks.

Figure 23-1 summarizes our discussion of the relation between the monetary base and the level of the money supply. The monetary base or stock of high-powered money is held either as cash reserves by the banks or as money in circulation. Since bank deposits are a multiple of banks' cash reserves, the money multiplier exceeds unity. The money multiplier will be larger (*a*) the lower the private sector's desired ratio of cash to bank deposits, thus giving the banks more cash with which to create a multiplied deposit expansion, and (*b*) the lower is the banks' desired ratio of cash to deposits, thus leading them to create more deposits for any given cash reserves.

23-6 Measures of money

Money is the medium of exchange, and the money supply is cash in circulation (outside banks) plus bank deposits. It sounds simple, but it isn't. Two issues arise: which bank deposits, and why only bank deposits?

We can think of a spectrum of liquidity. Cash, by definition, is completely liquid. Sight deposits (chequing accounts) are almost as liquid, though all of us can remember a situation in which we met problems trying to pay by cheque. Time deposits (savings accounts) used to be much less liquid, but nowadays many people have provisions for automatic transfer between savings and chequing accounts when the latter runs low. Savings deposits are almost as good as chequing accounts.

UK statistics now also distinguish between *retail* and *wholesale* deposits. Retail deposits are those made in high street branches at the advertised rate of interest. Wholesale deposits are big one-off deals where the (corporate) depositor negotiates an interest rate with the bank. But these too can be quite liquid.

Until the 1980s, everyone was pretty clear what a bank was, and hence whose deposits counted towards the money supply. Financial deregulation has blurred this distinction, both in the UK and the USA, and is starting to do so in continental Europe. Until about 1980, UK banks did not lend for house purchase and cheques on building society deposits could not be used at the supermarket checkout. Now 'banks' compete vigorously for house mortgages, and building society cheques are widely accepted as a means of payment. The case for excluding building society deposits from measures of the money supply has gradually collapsed.

Figure 23-2 shows different monetary aggregates and their relation to one another. M0 is the wide monetary base: cash in circulation outside the banks, cash inside banks, and the banks' own accounts with the Bank of England. M0 is the narrowest measure of money. Wider measures begin from cash in circulation. Adding all sight deposits, we get the M1 measure, which used to be considered a good measure of narrow money. Augmenting that by UK private sector time deposits and CDs gives M3 which used to be called sterling M3. That used to be considered the best definition of broad money.

Since there is a spectrum of liquidity, there may be no good place to draw a line and say that everything narrower than this is money, everything wider than this is not. We used to keep track of M0, M1, and M3. All of these measures ignore balances in foreign currency and refer purely to cash and deposits in sterling.

This approach has been made obsolete by the increasing use of building society deposits as means of payment, and by the conversion of many building societies to commercial banks.

To reflect the new reality, monetary statistics now combine banks and building societies, as shown in Figure 23-2. M2 is cash in circulation plus retail sight deposits at banks and retail deposits and shares in building societies. M4 is the old M3 plus UK private sector deposits and shares in building societies, minus building society holds of cash bank deposits and bank CDs.

Now the government routinely publishes statistics only on M0 and M4. Advances in technology, and financial deregulation (which led to greater competition and many more financial products on offer), have made it increasingly easy for customers to substitute between 'broad' and 'narrow' money. Once we leave the monetary base, the first sensible place to stop is M4. Table 23-5 gives actual data for 1999.

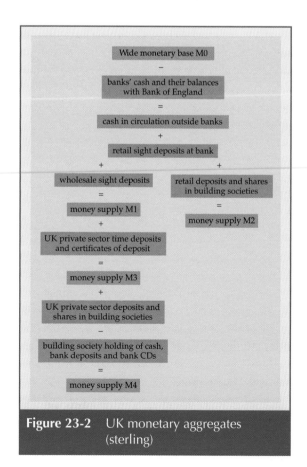

Figure 23-2   UK monetary aggregates (sterling)

BOX 23-4 — The money multiplier

Suppose banks wish to hold cash reserves R equal to some fraction c_b of deposits D, and that the private sector holds cash in circulation C equal to a fraction c_p of deposits D. Thus

$$R = c_b D \quad \text{and} \quad C = c_p D$$

The monetary base, or stock of high-powered money, H, is either in circulation or in bank vaults. Hence

$$H = C + R = (c_p + c_b)D$$

Finally, the money supply is circulating currency C plus deposits D. Hence

$$M = C + D = (c_p + 1)D$$

These last two equations give us the money multiplier, the ratio of M to H

$$M/H = (c_p + 1)/(c_p + c_b) > 1$$

Using the data of Table 23-5,

$$c_p = 22.8/750.5 = 0.03 \qquad c_b = 6/750.5 = 0.008$$

and the money multiplier is

$$M/H = (1.03)/(0.038) = 27$$

which of course is simply $(783.3)/(28.8)$, the ratio of $M4$ to $M0$.

Table 23-5 Narrow and broad money in the UK, June 1999, sterling (£ billion)

	wide monetary base M0	28.8
−	banks' cash and balance at bank	−6.0
=	cash in circulation	22.8
+	banks' retail deposits	404.5
+	building society's deposits and shares	104.7
+	wholesale deposits	266.3
	money supply M4	798.3

Source: ONS, *Financial Statistics*.

23-7 Competition between banks

Financial deregulation, allowing the new entry of more and more banks, has made modern banking a very competitive business. Banks compete with one another both in the interest rates they offer to attract deposits and in the interest rates they charge borrowers for loans.

The **interest rate spread** is the gap between the interest rate a bank pays on deposits and the higher rate it charges for loans.

The spread covers the cost of providing banking services. When spreads exceed this amount, they generate profits for banks. Profits act as a signal for new banks to enter, which tends to compete away spreads. With more banks, interest rates on bank loans fall. Increased competition for deposits also raises interest rates paid to depositors. Both effects reduce the spread.

Equilibrium in the banking industry occurs at the point at which it is not worth attracting any more deposits in order to make more loans. The marginal cost of funds, the deposit interest rate, plus the marginal cost of doing banking business, plus any equilibrium profit margin, just equals the marginal revenue that can be earned on making new bank loans (inclusive of any appropriate allowance for possible default). In a perfectly competitive industry, any super-normal profits are competed away eventually by free entry.

Although regulated less than before, banking regulation has not completely disappeared. Moreover, there are substantial scale economies in banking, and competition is therefore imperfect. For both reasons, equilibrium profit margins in banking are usually positive. Nevertheless, once we know the exact market structure, we have a good idea of how interest rates on deposits and loans are likely to be related. And, other things equal, further deregulation of banks is likely to reduce interest rate spreads further.

Competition between banks and the influence of regulation therefore affect how much cash it is *optimal* for profit-maximizing banks to suck into the banking system. These two forces also affect the size of cash reserves it is optimal for banks to hold. The key ratios c_p and c_b that determine the size of the money multiplier in Box 23-4 are not fixed constants but the outcome of the competitive behaviour of banks themselves.

SUMMARY

● Money has four functions: a medium of exchange or means of payment, a store of value, a unit of account, and a standard of deferred payment. It is its use as a medium of exchange that distinguishes money from other assets.

● In a barter economy, trading is costly because there must be a double coincidence of wants. Using a medium of exchange reduces the costs of matching buyers and sellers and allows society to devote scarce resources to other things. A token money has a higher value as a medium of exchange than in any other use. Because its value greatly exceeds its production cost, token money economizes still further on the resources required to facilitate trading.

● Token money is accepted either because people believe it can subsequently be used to make payments or because the government declares it legal tender. The government controls the supply of token money.

● The story of the goldsmith-banker illustrates the role of modern banks. Goldsmiths create money by making loans, either by releasing into circulation gold previously held in vaults or by increasing the value of deposits. The choice of how much reserves to hold involves a trade-off between interest earnings and the danger of insolvency.

● Modern banks attract deposits by acting as financial intermediaries. A national system of clearing cheques, a convenient form of payment, attracts funds into sight deposits. Interest-bearing time deposits attract further funds. In turn, banks lend out money as short-term liquid loans, as longer-term less liquid advances, or by purchasing securities.

● Sophisticated financial markets for short-term liquid lending allow modern banks to operate with very low cash reserves relative to deposits. The money supply is currency in circulation plus deposits.

● The monetary base M0 is currency in circulation plus banks' cash reserves. The money multiplier is the ratio of the money supply to the monetary base, and exceeds unity. The money multiplier is larger (a) the smaller is the desired cash ratio of the banks and (b) the smaller is the private sector's desired ratio of cash in circulation to deposits.

● Financial deregulation has allowed building societies into the banking business. M4 is a broad measure of money and includes deposits at both banks and building societies.

KEY TERMS

◆ Money   375

◆ Medium of exchange   375

◆ Barter economy   376

◆ Unit of account   376

◆ Store of value   376

◆ Token money   376

◆ IOU money   377

◆ Deposit   377

◆ Reserves   378

◆ Financial panic   379

◆ Money supply   379

◆ Financial intermediary   379

◆ Commercial bank   379

◆ Clearing system   380

◆ Liquidity   382

◆ Monetary base or high-powered money   384

◆ Money multiplier   384

◆ Interest rate spreads   387

REVIEW QUESTIONS

1 (a) A person trades in a car when buying another. Is the used car a medium of exchange? Is this a barter transaction? (b) Could you tell by watching someone buying mints (white discs) with coins (silver discs) which one is money?

2 A goldsmith holds 100 per cent reserves against deposits. What happens to the money supply when a customer withdraws gold from the vault?

3 Initially gold coins were used as money but people could melt them down and use the gold for industrial purposes. (a) What must have been the relative value of gold in these two uses? (b) Explain the circumstances in which gold could (i) become a token money, and (ii) disappear from monetary circulation completely.

4 In what sense do commercial banks create money? (a) Use a balance sheet to show how cheque clearance works. (b) What difference does this make to the resources that society uses in trading?

5 (a) Would it make sense to include travellers' cheques in measures of the money supply? (b) season tickets for the train? (c) credit cards?

6 Sight deposits = 30, time deposits = 60, banks' cash reserves = 2, currency in circulaton = 12, building society deposits = 20. Calculate M0 and M4.

7 *Common fallacies* Show why the following statements are incorrect: (a) Since their liabilities equal their assets, banks cannot create anything. (b) The money supply has gone up because of the expansion of the black economy. Since cash transactions are untraceable, people are putting less in the banks. (c) Since the government is responsible for printing money, it always knows the exact quantity of the money supply in the UK.

24 Central banking and the monetary system

LEARNING OUTCOMES

When you have finished this chapter, you should be able to:

- Explain the key roles of the central bank as banker to the commercial banks and setter of monetary policy
- Examine the channels through which the central bank can affect the money supply
- Explore the role of the central bank as lender of last resort
- Discuss motives for holding money and their relation to the determinants of money demand
- Note that people care about the size of real money balances not nominal balances
- Analyse how money market equilibrium is achieved and recognize that this implies equilibrium in other financial markets as well
- Analyse comparative static experiments that alter money market equilibrium
- Consider why a nominal anchor is needed to tie down the price level, and examine how the central bank uses the interest rate instrument to pursue intermediate targets

Today every country of any size has a central bank.

A **central bank** acts as banker to the commercial banks and is responsible for setting interest rates.

Originally private institutions in business for profit, central banks came under public control as their activities as bankers to their respective governments grew, and as governments have placed increasing emphasis on manipulating interest rates. Founded in 1694, the Bank of England (www.bankofengland.co.uk) was not nationalized until 1947. The Federal Reserve System (www.federal reserve.gov), the central bank in the United States, was not set up until 1913.

In this chapter we look in detail at the role of the central bank, and show how it influences equilibrium in the markets for financial assets in general and money in particular. Since the central bank influences the supply of money, it is necessary to consider what determines the demand for money before analysis of monetary equilibrium can be undertaken.

We conclude the chapter by discussing the techniques of monetary control available to the central bank and showing the problems that arise in practice when it attempts to implement monetary policy. This chapter discusses the central bank in relation to financial markets. Later chapters discuss how monetary policy affects the real economy. By

Chapter 28 we will be able to examine the role of the Bank in inflation control.

24-1 The Bank of England

The Bank of England, usually known simply as the Bank, is the central bank of the UK. For historical reasons, it is divided into Issue and Banking Departments, each with separate balance sheets shown in Table 24-1.

The Issue Department is responsible for issuing banknotes, shown as liabilities in Table 24-1. To introduce notes into circulation, the Issue Department purchases financial securities: bills and bonds issued by the government, commercial firms, or local authorities. These are shown as assets of the Issue Department in Table 24-1. The exchange of high-powered money for financial securities is called an *open market operation*.

The Banking Department acts as banker to the commercial banks and to the government. Public deposits and bankers' deposits are deposits by the government and the commercial banking system. Reserves and other accounts are deposits by central banks of other countries, by domestic local authorities, and by nationalized industries.

Assets are government securities (loans to the government) and advances. Advances are loans to the banks. Other assets include physical capital, buildings and equipment, and securities issued by private firms or local authorities.

In practice, the activities of the Issue Department and the Banking Department are carefully co-ordinated. Although much of Table 24-1 resembles the balance sheet of a commercial bank, there is one crucial difference. *There is no possibility that the Bank can go bankrupt.* A £50 note is a liability of the Issue Department. Suppose you take it along to the Bank and say you want to cash it in for £50. At best, the Bank would simply give you 50 new £1 coins. The central bank's liabilities can be created in unlimited quantities without fear of bankruptcy.

24-2 The Bank and the money supply

In this section we study the ways in which a central bank can affect the supply of money in the economy. The money supply is currency in circulation outside the banking system plus the deposits of commercial banks and building societies. (Henceforth we talk only of 'banks'.) Thus the money supply is partly a liability of the Bank (currency in private circulation) and partly a liability of banks (bank deposits).

In the last chapter we introduced the *monetary base*, the currency supplied by the Bank both to the commercial banks and to private circulation, and the *money multiplier*, the extent to which the money supply is a multiple of the monetary base. We saw that the money multiplier was larger the smaller the cash reserve ratio of the commercial banks and the smaller the private sector's desired ratio of cash to bank deposits.

We now describe the ways in which the Bank *might* seek to affect the money supply: reserve requirements, the discount rate, and open market operations.

Reserve requirements

A **required reserve ratio** is a minimum ratio of cash reserves to deposits that the central bank requires commercial banks to hold.

If a reserve requirement is in force, banks can hold more than the required cash reserves but they cannot hold less. If their cash falls below the required amount, they must immediately borrow cash, usually from the central bank, to restore their required reserve ratio.

Suppose the banking system has £1 million in cash and for strictly commercial purposes would normally maintain cash reserves equal to 5 per cent of deposits. Since deposits will be 20 times cash reserves, the banking system will create £20 million of deposits against its £1 million cash reserves.

Table 24-1 Balance sheet of the Bank of England, June 1999

Department	Assets	£b	Liabilities	£b
Issue	Government securities	19.5	Notes in circulation	24.0
	Other securities	4.5		
Banking	Government securities	1.2	Public deposits	0.2
	Advances	46.2	Bankers' deposits	1.7
	Other assets	2.6	Reserves and other accounts	48.1

Source: ONS, *Financial Statistics*.

Suppose the Bank now imposes a reserve requirement that banks must hold cash reserves of at least 10 per cent of deposits. Now banks can create only £10 million deposits against their cash reserves of £1 million.

Thus, when the central bank imposes a reserve requirement in excess of the reserve ratio that prudent banks would anyway have maintained, the effect is to reduce the creation of bank deposits, reduce the value of the money multiplier, and reduce the money supply for any given monetary base. Similarly, when a particular reserve requirement is already in force, any increase in the reserve requirement will reduce the money supply.

When the central bank imposes a reserve requirement in excess of the reserves that banks would otherwise have wished to hold, the banks are creating fewer deposits and undertaking less lending than they would really like. Thus a reserve requirement acts like a tax on banks by forcing them to hold a higher fraction of their total assets as bank reserves and a lower fraction as loans earning high interest rates. Can the banks do anything about it?

Although there are profitable lending opportunities, the banks can take advantage of them only if they can increase their cash reserves. In principle, they could try to borrow cash from the central bank. If the point of a reserve requirement is to reduce the money supply, the central bank will be reluctant to lend banks the cash they want to make additional loans, increase deposits, and expand the money supply. With lucrative lending opportunities around, the banks may be able to induce the private sector to exchange cash in circulation for bank deposits. Banks can offer more generous interest rates on time deposits or stay open later to encourage people to make greater use of chequing facilities. By attracting more cash from the general public, banks may then be able to restore former levels of deposit lending, though there is then the danger that the central bank will raise the reserve requirement still higher.

One form of reserve requirement that used to be popular in the UK was the use of *special deposits*. Commercial banks were required to deposit some of their cash reserves in a special deposit at the Bank, and this money could *not* be counted as part of the banks' cash reserves in meeting their reserve requirements. Varying the amount required as special deposits gave the Bank another lever for controlling deposit creation by the banking system and the size of the money multiplier.

The discount rate

The second instrument of monetary control available to the central bank is the discount rate.

The **discount rate** is the interest rate that the Bank charges when the commercial banks want to borrow money.

When the discount rate was an important part of monetary control in the UK it used to be known as the Bank Rate, or Minimum Lending Rate (MLR).

Suppose banks think the *minimum* safe ratio of cash to deposits is 10 per cent. It does not matter whether this figure is a commercial judgement or a required ratio imposed by the Bank. On any particular day, banks are likely to have a bit of cash in hand. Say their cash reserves are 12 per cent of deposits. How far dare they let their cash reserves fall towards the minimum level of 10 per cent?

Banks have to balance the interest rate they will get on extra lending with the dangers and costs involved if there is a sudden flood of withdrawals which push their cash reserves below the critical 10 per cent figure. This is where the discount rate comes in. Suppose market interest rates are 8 per cent and the central bank makes it known it is prepared to lend to commercial banks at 8 per cent. Commercial banks can lend up to the hilt and drive their cash reserves down to the minimum 10 per cent of deposits. The banks are lending at 8 per cent and, if the worst comes to the worst and they are short of cash, they can borrow from the Bank at 8 per cent. Banks cannot lose by lending as much as possible.

Suppose, however, that the Bank announces that, although market interest rates are 8 per cent, it will lend to commercial banks only at the penalty rate of 10 per cent. Now a bank with cash reserves of 12 per cent may conclude that it is not worth making the extra loans at 8 per cent interest that would drive its cash reserves down to the minimum of 10 per cent of deposits. There is too high a risk that sudden withdrawals will force it to borrow from the Bank at 10 per cent. It will have lost money by making these extra loans. It makes more sense to hold some excess cash reserves against the possibility of a sudden withdrawal.

Thus, by setting the discount rate at a penalty level in excess of the general level of interest rates, the Bank can induce commercial banks voluntarily to hold additional cash reserves. Since bank deposits now become a lower multiple of banks' cash reserves, the money multiplier is reduced and the money supply is lower for any given level of the monetary base.

Open market operations

An **open market operation** occurs when the central bank alters the monetary base by buying or selling financial securities in the open market.

BOX 24-1 — The repo market

In American movies, people falling into arrears on their loans have their cars repossessed by the repo man. In the mid 1990s, London finally established a repo market. Other European financial centres, such as Frankfurt and Milan, had operated repo markets for years. Surely the ultracautious Bundesbank was not a major player in dubious car loans?

A gilt repo is a *sale and repurchase agreement*. For example, a bank sells you a gilt with a simultaneous agreement to buy back the gilt at a specified price on a particular future date. You pay cash to the bank today and get a predictable amount of cash (plus interest) back at a known future date. You have effectively made a deposit in the bank and your short-term loan is secured or 'backed' by the gilt which is temporarily registered in your ownership. Thus repos use the outstanding stock of *long-term* assets (here gilts) as backing for a new set of secured *short-term* loans.

Reverse repos are the other way round. Now you get a short-term loan from the bank by initially selling gilts to the bank, accompanied by an agreement for you to repurchase the gilts at a specified date in the near future at a price agreed now. Just as repos are secured temporary fixed-term deposits, reverse repos are

effectively secured temporary fixed term loans by the bank.

Repos and reverse repos are clearly very like other short-term loan lending and borrowing. They can even be used as the basis for open market operations by the central bank. In the UK, the Bank of England used to conduct open market operations by buying and selling Treasury Bills; the Bundesbank and Banca d'Italia made much more extensive use of repo and reverse repo transactions. But they achieved much the same purpose. Now the Bank of England also uses the repo market for open market operations designed to alter the monetary base.

The repo market allowed gilts to be used as collateral for more liquid short-term lending and borrowing. It increased the extent of financial intermediation. As the cost of lending and borrowing fell, more people made deposits to banks and borrowed from banks. The Bank of England estimated that this increased the money supply M4 by as much as £6 billion at the start of 1996 when the gilt repo market began in the UK.

(Bank of England, *Inflation Report*, May 1996.)

Whereas the previous two methods of monetary control operate by altering the value of the money multiplier, open market operations alter the monetary base. Since the money supply is the monetary base multiplied by the money multiplier, they alter the money supply.

Suppose the Issue Department of the Bank prints £1 million of new banknotes and uses them to purchase government securities on the open market. There are now £1 million fewer securities in the hands of the banks or the private sector, but the monetary base has increased by £1 million. There has been an injection of £1 million of cash into the economy. Some will be held in private circulation but most of it will be deposited with the banking system, which can now expand deposit lending against its higher cash reserves. Conversely, if the Issue Department of the Bank sells £1 million of government securities from its existing stock, exactly £1 million of cash must be withdrawn from private circulation or the banks' cash reserves. The

monetary base falls by £1 million. Since banks lose cash reserves, they have to reduce deposit lending and the money supply falls.

Notice that it makes little difference whether the Bank transacts with banks directly or with members of the non-bank public. If the Bank sells securities directly to the banking system, banks' cash reserves are immediately reduced. If the Bank sells securities to the general public, individuals will write cheques on their bank accounts and banks' cash reserves are again reduced. Either way, by open market operations in financial securities, the Bank alters the monetary base, banks' cash reserves, deposit lending, and the money supply.

24-3 Lender of last resort

Modern fractional reserve banking allows society to produce the medium of exchange with relatively small

BOX 24-2

Financial regulation or lifeboat operations?

Systemic risk provides a powerful rationale for government intervention in financial markets: externalities matter. Allowing one institution to go under may bring down many others, either because they themselves have deposited money or because their potential customers have done so. While a similar argument applies in many industries (e.g. networks of engineering suppliers), it is plausible that externalities are especially large when the payments mechanism itself is at stake.

Any intervention carries its own risk, often one of moral hazard. Standing ready to intervene may itself encourage inadequate prudence by financial institutions. Automatic federal deposit insurance was a key element in the collapse of savings and loan associations (building societies) in the United States in the late 1980s. Insuring depositors against loss removes their incentive to monitor the institutions' management, and gives managers perverse incentives to go for broke. They cash up if things go well, but the government pays if things go badly.

One solution is *capital adequacy* requirements. In the UK, regulation of banks is now the responsibility of the Financial Services Agency. Capital adequacy requirement ensure that shareholder capital has to be sufficient to stand a pretty large loss, thereby reducing the chance of bankruptcy and a financial panic. If shareholders stand to lose from bad managerial decisions, they are more likely to provide the right incentives for managers.

Even so, there may still be a case to supplement this with last-resort lending by the central bank. In the UK, with its seafaring tradition, this is called a 'lifeboat operation'. The Bank either lends directly to the troubled institution or simply floods the market with money which, as we shall shortly see, causes a reduction in interest rates. The reduction may increase both asset prices and business confidence to an extent sufficient to remove the source of the crisis. When the panic dies down, the Bank will typically undo this temporary injection of liquidity so there are no long-run effects on the money supply.

---

inputs of scarce resources: land, labour, and capital. However, there is a price to be paid for this efficient production of the medium of exchange. In the last chapter we saw that any system of fractional reserve banking will be vulnerable to financial panics. Since banks have insufficient reserves to meet a simultaneous withdrawal of all their deposits, any hint of large withdrawals is likely to become a self-fulfilling prophecy as people scramble to get their money out before the banks go bust.

To avoid financial panics, it is necessary to ensure that people believe that banks can never get into trouble in the first place. There must be a guarantee that banks can get cash if they really need it. And there is only one institution that can manufacture cash in indefinite quantities: the central bank. The threat of financial panics can be avoided, or at least greatly diminished, if it is known that the Bank of England stands ready to act as a lender of last resort.

The **lender of last resort** stands ready to lend to banks and other financial institutions when financial panic threatens the financial system.

The Bank's role as lender of last resort does not merely preserve a sophisticated and interconnected system of modern finance in which the failure of one bank would bring many others crashing down. It also reduces one major uncertainty in the day-to-day process of monetary control. If depositors were subject to fluctuating moods of optimism and pessimism about the solvency of banks, there would be wild swings in the private sector's desired ratio of cash in circulation to bank deposits and corresponding fluctuations in the value of the money multiplier. For a given monetary base, the fraction being held as banks' cash reserves would constantly be varying, and it would be difficult for the Bank to predict the money supply with any accuracy. By acting as a lender of last resort, the Bank can maintain confidence in the banking system and relatively stable values of the private sector's desired ratio of cash to deposits and hence of the money multiplier.

Although the mere knowledge that the Bank stands ready to act as a lender of last resort prevents most panics from arising, occasionally the Bank is required to act (see Box 24-2).

24-4 The demand for money

In 1965 the amount of money (M4) in the UK was £17 billion. By 1999 it was £783 billion. Why were UK residents prepared to hold 46 times as much money in 1999 as in 1965? We single out three variables that determine money demand: interest rates, the average price of goods and services, and real income. Before examining whether movements in these variables can explain the increase in money holdings since 1965, we reconsider why people hold money at all.

The motives for holding money

Money is a stock. It is the quantity of circulating currency and deposits *held* at any given time. Holding money is not the same as *spending* money when we go to the cinema. We hold money now to spend it later.

Money is the medium of exchange, for which it must also serve as a store of value. In these two functions of money we must seek the reasons why people wish to hold it. People can hold their wealth in various forms – money, bills, bonds, equities, and property. For simplicity we assume that there are only two assets: money, the medium of exchange that pays no interest, and bonds, which we use to stand for all other interest-bearing assets that are not directly a means of payment. As people earn income, they add to their wealth. As they spend, they deplete their wealth. How should people divide their wealth at any instant between money and bonds?

There is an obvious cost in holding money.

The **opportunity cost of holding money** is the interest given up by holding money rather than bonds.

People will hold money only if there is a benefit to offset this cost. We now consider what that benefit might be.

The transactions motive Without money, making transactions by direct barter would be costly in time and effort. Holding money economizes on the time and effort involved in undertaking transactions.

If all transactions were perfectly synchronized, we would earn revenue from sales of goods and factor services at the same instant we made purchases of the goods and services we wish to consume. Except at that instant, we need hold no money at all.

The **transactions motive** for holding money reflects the fact that payments and receipts are not perfectly synchronized.

We need to hold money between receiving payments and making subsequent purchases. Or do we?

We could use all receipts immediately to purchase interest-earnings assets to be resold only at the instant we need money to make expenditures. Corporate treasurers of large companies try to implement this policy, but for most of us it does not make sense. Every time we buy and sell assets there are brokerage and banking charges, which tend to be proportionally larger the smaller the transaction. And it takes an eagle eye to keep track of incomings and outgoings to judge the precise moment at which money is needed and assets must be sold. When small sums are involved, the extra interest does not compensate for the brokerage charges and the extra time and effort required to implement such a policy. It is simpler and cheaper to hold at least some money.

How much money we need to hold depends on the value of the transactions we wish to make and the degree of synchronization of our payments and receipts. Money is a nominal variable not a real variable. We do not know how much £100 will buy until we know the price of goods. If all prices double, both our receipts and our payments will double in nominal terms. To make the same transactions as before we will need to hold twice as much money.

The **demand for money** is a demand for *real* money balances.

We need a given amount of real money, nominal money deflated by the price level, to undertake a given quantity of total transactions. Hence when the price level doubles, other things equal we expect the demand for nominal money balances to double, leaving the demand for real money balances unaltered. People want money because of its purchasing power in terms of the goods it will buy.

People hold real money balances because they want to make transactions. Real national income is a good proxy for the total real value of the transactions people undertake. Thus we assume that the transactions motive for holding real money balances will increase when real national income increases.

The second factor affecting the transactions motive for holding money is the synchronization of payments and receipts. Suppose that, instead of shopping throughout the week, households do all their shopping on the day they get a salary cheque from their employers. Over the week, national income and total transactions are unaltered, but people now *hold* less money over the week.[1]

A nation's habits for making payments change only

---

[1] By allowing us to pay all at once when the statement arrives monthly, credit cards have this effect.

slowly. In our simplified model we assume that the degree of synchronization remains constant over time. Thus we focus on real national income as *the* measure of the transactions motive for holding *real* money balances.

The precautionary motive   Thus far we have assumed that people know exactly when they will obtain receipts and make payments. But, of course, we live in an uncertain world. This uncertainty about the precise timing of receipts and payments gives rise to a precautionary motive for holding money.

Suppose you buy a lot of interest-earning bonds and try to get by with only a small amount of money. You are walking down the street and spot a great bargain in a shop window. But you do not have enough money to take advantage immediately of this opportunity. By the time you arrange to cash in some bonds, the sale may be over. Someone else may have snapped up the video recorder on sale at half price. This is the precautionary motive for holding money.

In an uncertain world, there is a **precautionary motive** to hold money. In advance, we decide to hold money to meet contingencies the exact nature of which we cannot yet foresee.

If we did not have to take advantage of the transactions opportunity immediately, it would not matter that it was unforeseen: we could still cash in our bonds at our leisure and buy the half-price video recorder. We forgo interest and carry money for precautionary reasons, because having ready money allows us to snap up unforeseen bargains, or stave off unforeseen crises by making immediate payments.

How can we measure the benefits from holding money for precautionary reasons? The payoff to having ready money available is likely to be larger the larger the volume of transactions we undertake and the greater the degree of uncertainty. If the degree of uncertainty remains roughly constant over time, it is the volume of transactions that will determine the benefits from holding real money balances for precautionary reasons. As with the transactions motive, we use the level of real national income to measure the volume of transactions. Thus, other things equal, the higher is real national income the stronger will be the precautionary motive for holding money.

Together, the transactions and precautionary motives provide the main reasons for holding the medium of exchange. They are the motives most relevant to the benefits from holding a narrow measure of money. The wider measure, M4, includes interest-earning deposits. The wider the definition of money, the less important will be the trans-

actions and precautionary motives that relate to money as a medium of exchange, and the more we must take account of money as a store of value in its own right.

The asset motive   Suppose we forget all about the need to transact. We think of a wealthy individual or a firm deciding in which assets to hold wealth. At some distant date there may be a prospect of finally spending some of that wealth, but in the short run the objective is to earn a good rate of return.

Some assets, such as industrial shares, on average pay a high rate of return but are also quite risky. Some years their return is *very* high but in other years it is negative. When share prices fall, shareholders can make a capital loss which swamps any dividend payment to which they are entitled. Other assets are much less risky, but their rate of return tends to be much lower than the average return on risky assets.

How should people divide their portfolios of financial investments between safe and risky assets? You might like to reread Chapter 15. We concluded that, since people dislike risk, they will not put all their eggs in one basket. As well as holding some risky assets, they will keep some of their wealth in safe assets.

The **asset motive** for holding money arises because people dislike risk. People are prepared to sacrifice a high average rate of return to obtain a portfolio with a lower but more predictable rate of return.

The asset motive for holding money is important when we consider why people hold broad measures of money such as M4.

The demand for money: prices, real income, and interest rates

The transactions, precautionary, and asset motives suggest that there are benefits to holding money. But there is also a cost, the interest forgone by not holding interest-earning assets instead. People hold money up to the point at which the marginal benefit of holding another pound just equals its marginal cost. Figure 24-1 illustrates how much money people will choose to hold.

People want money only because of its purchasing power over goods. Hence, on the horizontal axis we plot quantities of real money balances, nominal money in current pounds divided by the average price level of goods and services. The horizontal line *MC* shows the marginal cost of holding money, the interest forgone by not holding bonds. The height of *MC* depends on the level of interest rates.

The *MB* schedule shows the marginal benefit of holding money. We draw the *MB* schedule for a given level of real national income measuring the level of transactions undertaken. For this given level of transactions, it is possible to get by with a low level of real money holdings, but we have to work hard. We have to keep watching our purchases and receipts, being quick to invest money as it comes in and being ever ready to sell off bonds just before we make a purchase. And we do not have much money holdings for precautionary purposes. We may be frustrated or inconvenienced if, unexpectedly, we wish to or need to make a purchase or settle a debt.

With a low level of real money holdings, the marginal benefit of another pound is high. We don't need to put so much effort into timing our transfers between money and bonds and we have larger precautionary balances to deal with unforeseen contingencies. For a given level of real income and real value of transactions, the marginal benefit of the last pound of money holdings declines as we hold more real money. With very high real money balances, we have plenty of money both for precautionary purposes and

for transactions purposes to meet our planned purchases. We have given up leaping in and out of bonds, and life is much easier. The marginal benefit of yet more money holdings is very low.

Given the level of our real income and transactions, desired money holdings occur at point *E*. For any level of real money below the level *L*, the marginal benefit of another pound exceeds its marginal cost in interest forgone. We should hold more money. Above *L*, the marginal cost exceeds the marginal benefit and it is not worth holding as much money as this. The optimal level of money holding is *L*.

To emphasize the effect of prices, real income, and interest rates on the quantity of money demanded, we now consider changing each of these variables in turn. If all prices of goods and services double but interest rates and real income remain unaltered, neither the *MC* schedule nor the *MB* schedule shift. The desired point remains *E* and the desired level of *real* money remains *L*. Since prices have doubled, individuals will hold twice as much nominal money to preserve the level of their real money balances at *L*.

If interest rates on bonds increase, the opportunity cost of holding money rises. Figure 24-1 shows this as an upward shift from *MC* to *MC'*. The desired point is now *E'* and the desired quantity of real money holdings has fallen from *L* to *L'*. Higher interest rates reduce the quantity of real money balances demanded.[2]

Finally, we consider the effect of an increase in real income. At each level of real money holdings, the marginal benefit of the last pound is higher than before. With more transactions to undertake and a greater need for precautionary balances, a given quantity of real money does not make life as easy as it did when transactions and real income were lower. The benefit of a bit more money is now greater. Hence we show the *MB* schedule shifting up to *MB'* when real income increases.

At the original interest rate and *MC* schedule, the desired

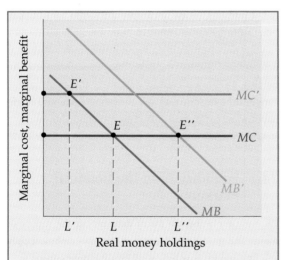

The horizontal axis shows the purchasing power of money in terms of goods. The *MC* schedule shows the interest sacrificed by putting the last pound into money rather than bonds. The *MB* schedule is drawn for a given real income and shows the marginal benefits of the last pound of money. The marginal benefit falls as money holdings increase. The desired point is *E*, at which marginal cost and marginal benefit are equal. An increase in interest rates, a rise in the opportunity cost schedule from *MC* to *MC'*, reduces desired money holdings from *L* to *L'*. An increase in real income increases the marginal benefit of adding to real balances. The MB schedule shifts up to *MB'*. Facing the schedule *MC*, a shift from *MB* to *MB'* increases real money holdings to *L''*.

Figure 24-1   Desired money holdings

---

[2] Chapter 14 distinguished nominal interest rates and real interest rates which subtract the inflation rate from the nominal interest rate over the same period. It is nominal interest rates that affect the demand for money. Why? Because the opportunity cost of holding money is the extra return between bonds and money. If π is the inflation rate and r the nominal interest rate on bonds, the real return on bonds is $r - \pi$. But in purely financial terms the real return on money is $-\pi$. That is the rate at which the purchasing power of money is being eroded by inflation. Hence the differential real return between bonds and money is $(r - \pi) - (-\pi) = r$. The nominal interest rate is the opportunity cost with which the transactions and precautionary benefits of money must be compared.

Table 24-2	The demand for money		
	Effect of increase in		
	Price level	Real income	Interest rates
Quantity of nominal money demanded	Increases proportionately	Increases	Falls
Quantity of real money demanded	Unaffected	Increases	Falls

level of money balances is L''. Thus an increase in real income increases the quantity of real money balances demanded. Table 24-2 summarizes our discussion of the demand for money as a medium of exchange.

Thus far we have focused on the demand for M0, the narrowest measure of money as a medium of exchange. Wider definitions of money must also recognize the asset motive for holding money. To explain the demand for M4 we interpret MC as the *extra* return that could be obtained on average by putting the last pound into risky assets rather than time deposits, which are safe but yield a lower return. For a given wealth, MB shows the marginal benefit of time deposits in reducing the riskiness of the portfolio. When no wealth is invested in time deposits the portfolio is very risky. A bad year could be a real disaster. There is a high benefit in taking out insurance by having at least some time deposits. As the quantity of time deposits increases, the danger of a disaster recedes and the marginal benefit of more time deposits falls.

An increase in the average *interest differential* between risky assets and time deposits shifts the opportunity cost schedule from MC to MC' and reduces the quantity of time deposits demanded. An increase in wealth shifts the marginal benefits schedule from MB to MB' and increases the quantity of time deposits demanded.

Explaining the rise in money holdings from 1965 to 1999

We now return to the question with which we began this section. Why did nominal money holdings increase from £17 billion in 1965 to £873 billion in 1999? Our discussion has identified three factors: prices, real income, and nominal interest rates. Table 24-3 shows how these variables changed over the period.

Although nominal money holdings grew 46-fold, the average price level also grew between 1965 and 1999. Once we divide nominal money by the price index to obtain real money, Table 24-3 shows that real money balances quadrupled over the period. Yet real GDP more than doubled. Higher real income and real output increase the quantity of

Table 24-3	Holdings of M4, 1965–99	
	1965	1999
Index of:		
Nominal M4	100	4605
Real M4	100	413
Real GDP	100	235
Interest rate (%)*	6	5

*Interest rate on Treasury bills.
Source: ONS, *Economic Trends*.

real money demanded. Nominal interest rates hardly changed. Why then has real money demand increased much more than real GDP?

The intense increase in competition forced banks to pay ever more generous interest rates on *deposits*, thereby *reducing* the cost of holding broad money, most of which is now interest-bearing deposits. The opportunity cost of holding an interest-bearing deposit is the small spread between the deposit rate and the interest rate you might have earned on Treasury bills. This cost of holding money is now much smaller than the 5 per cent shown in Table 24-3.

24-5 Equilibrium in the financial markets

We have explained the forces determining the supply of money and the demand for money. We now combine supply and demand to show how equilibrium is determined.

The monetary base is the outstanding stock of currency plus commercial banks' deposits at the Bank. Through open market operations the central bank can determine the level of the monetary base. The money supply, currency in private circulation plus private sector sight deposits with the banking system, equals the monetary base multiplier by the money multiplier. The size of the money multiplier depends on the cash reserves ratio of the banks and the cash–deposits ratio of the private sector.

The central bank can affect the banks' cash reserves ratio, and hence the money multiplier, in two ways: by imposing required reserves ratios on the banking system, or by setting the discount rate – the interest rate at which the central bank will lend to commercial banks – at a penalty level which induces banks to play safe and hold extra cash reserves to minimize the risk of having to borrow from the central bank. Apart from small fluctuations in the cash–deposits ratio desired by the private sector, the central bank can in principle control the level of the money supply.

The real money supply L is the nominal money supply M divided by the price level P. We now issue a warning that should never be forgotten.

The central bank controls the *nominal* money supply. When we simplify by assuming that the price of goods is fixed, the central bank also controls the *real* money supply. But in later chapters, when we allow the price level to change, changes in nominal money will tend to lead to changes in the price level. It is then much harder for the central bank to control the real money supply.

For the moment we ignore this difficulty. With given prices, the central bank can determine both the nominal and the real money supply.

In the last section we emphasized that the demand for money is a demand for real money balances. The quantity of real money demanded increases with the level of real income but decreases with the level of nominal interest rates. For the moment, we focus exclusively on the financial markets for money and bonds. We examine market equilibrium for a *given* level of real income and real output of goods and services. Having mastered this analysis, in the next chapter we can study how the financial markets interact with the markets for goods and labour to determine the equilibrium level of real income itself.

Money market equilibrium

The **money market** is in **equilibrium** when the quantity of real balances demanded equals the quantity supplied.

Figure 24-2 shows the demand curve LL for real money balances for a given level of real income. The higher the interest rate and the opportunity cost of holding money, the lower the quantity of real money balances demanded. With a given price level, the central bank controls the quantity of nominal money and real money. The supply curve is vertical at this quantity of real money L_0. Equilibrium is at the point E. At the interest rate r_0 the quantity of real money that people wish to hold just equals the outstanding stock L_0.

Suppose the interest rate is r_1, lower than the equilibrium level r_0. There is an excess demand for money given by the

distance AB in Figure 24-2. How does this excess demand for money bid the interest rate up from r_1 to r_0 to restore equilibrium? The answer is rather subtle.

Strictly speaking, there is no such thing as a market for money. Money is the medium of exchange. It is what we use for payments or receipts when making transactions in *other* markets. A market for money would involve buying and selling pounds with other pounds.

The other market of relevance to Figure 24-2 is the market for bonds. In saying that the interest rate is the opportunity cost of holding money, we are saying that people who don't hold money will hold bonds instead. What is happening explicitly in the market for bonds determines what is happening in the implicit market for money shown in Figure 24-2.

The stock of real wealth W is equal to the total outstanding stock or supply of real money L_0 and real bonds B_0. People decide how they wish to divide up their total wealth W between desired real bond holdings B^D and desired real money holdings L^D. *Whatever determines this division, it must be true that*

$$L_0 + B_0 = W = L^D + B^D \tag{1}$$

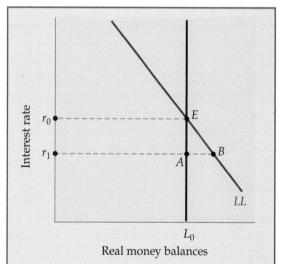

The demand schedule LL is drawn for a given level of real income. The higher the opportunity cost of holding money, the lower the real balances demanded. The real money supply schedule is vertical at L_0. The equilibrium point is E and the equilibrium interest rate, r_0. At a lower interest rate r_1 there is excess demand for money AB. There must be a corresponding excess supply of bonds. This reduces bond prices and increases the return on bonds, driving the interest rate up to its equilibrium level at which both markets clear.

Figure 24-2　Money market equilibrium

The total supply of real assets determines the wealth to be divided between real money and real bonds. And people cannot plan to divide up wealth they do not have. Since the left-hand side of equation (1) must equal the right-hand side, it follows that

$$B_0 - B^D = L^D - L_0 \qquad (2)$$

An excess demand for money must be exactly matched by an excess supply of bonds. Otherwise people would be planning to hold more wealth than they actually possess.

This insight allows us to explain how an excess demand for money at the interest rate r_1 in Figure 24-2 sets in motion forces that will bid up the interest rate to its equilibrium level r_0. With excess demand for money, there is an excess supply of bonds. To induce people to hold more bonds, suppliers of bonds must offer a higher interest rate.[3] As the interest rate rises, people switch out of money and into bonds. The higher interest rate reduces both the excess supply of bonds and the excess demand for money. At the interest rate r_0 the supply and demand for money are equal. Since the excess demand for money is zero, the excess supply of bonds is also zero. The money market is in equilibrium only when the bond market is also in equilibrium. People wish to divide their wealth in precisely the ratio of the relative supplies of money and bonds.

For the rest of this chapter, we focus on the implicit market for money. However, equations (1) and (2) imply that, once we know total wealth, any statement about what is happening in the money market is simultaneously a statement about what is happening in the bond market. That is why we called this section 'Equilibrium in the financial markets' rather than simply 'Money market equilibrium'.

Changes in equilibrium

A shift in either the supply curve or the demand curve for money will alter the equilibrium in the money market (and the bond market). These shifts are examined in Figure 24-3.

[3] A bond is a commitment by the issuer to pay a given stream of interest payments over a given time period. Chapter 14 explained that the price of a bond should be the present value of this stream of payments. The higher the interest rate at which this stream is being discounted, the lower the price of a bond. Equivalently, the lower the price of a bond, the higher the rate of return that the promised stream of payments will yield. With excess supply in the bond market, bond prices fall and the interest rate or rate of return on bonds rises.

A fall in the money supply Suppose the central bank reduces the money supply, either by undertaking an open market sale of securities to reduce the monetary base or by taking steps to make banks increase their cash reserve ratios and reduce the value of the money multiplier. Given our assumption that the price level is given, this contraction in nominal money will also reduce the real money supply. Figure 24-3 shows this as a leftward shift in the supply curve. The real money stock falls from L_0 to L'. The equilibrium interest rate rises from r_0 to r'. It takes a higher interest rate to reduce the demand for real balances in line with the lower quantity supplied. Hence a reduction in the real money supply leads to an increase in the equilibrium interest rate. Conversely, an increase in the real money supply reduces the equilibrium interest rate.

An increase in real income In Figure 24-3 we draw the demand curve for real balances LL for a given real income. An increase in real income increases the marginal benefit of holding money at each interest rate, and increases the quantity of real balances demanded. Hence in Figure 24-3

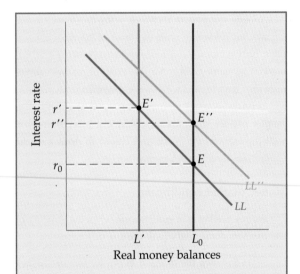

With a given real income, LL is the demand schedule for real money balances. A reduction in the real money supply from L_0 to L' moves the equilibrium interest rates from r_0 to r' to reduce the quantity of money demanded in line with the fall in the quantity supplied. With a given supply of real money L_0, an increase in real income shifts the demand schedule from LL to LL''. The equilibrium interest rates must increase from r_0 to r''. Higher real income tends to increase the quantity of real money demanded and higher interest rates are required to offset this, maintaining the quantity of real money demanded in line with the unchanged real supply.

Figure 24-3 Equilibrium interest rates

BOX 24-3 — The big issue

Like the UK, Japan had a huge property price boom in the late 1980s and then an even more severe collapse in the early 1990s. Japanese banks took a big hit as the value of their loans and other assets fell drastically. Fears about the health of the banking system then led to a loss of consumer confidence and a collapse of private spending.

The Bank of Japan (www.boj.or.jp/en) eased monetary policy to try to help banks and get people spending again. Interest rates fell steadily as the Bank printed money. On 3 March 1999 it issued 1800 billion yen (about £9 billion), driving short-term interest rates to 0.02 per cent!

With interest rates down to zero, further open-market operations between money and short-term securities were pretty pointless. The Bank of Japan then started discussing whether it should buy government bonds as a device for pumping yet more money into the economy.

---

we show the money demand schedule LL shifting to LL'', when real income increases. Since people wish to hold more real balances at each interest rate, the equilibrium interest rate must rise from r_0 to r'' to keep the quantity of real balances demanded equal to the unchanged real supply L_0. Conversely, a reduction in real income will shift the LL schedule to the left and reduce the equilibrium interest rate.

An increase in banking competition   In Figure 24-3 we also draw the demand curve LL for a given interest rate paid on bank deposits. Holding this rate constant, an increase in market interest rates r reduces the quantity of money demanded. A once-and-for-all increase in banking competition, reflected by a permanent increase in interest rates paid on bank deposits, will increase the demand for bank deposits at any level of market interest rates r. Again, the demand curve shifts from LL to LL''. For a given money supply, this bids up equilibrium market interest rates.

To sum up, an increase in the real money supply reduces the equilibrium interest rate. A lower interest rate reduces the attractiveness of bonds and induces people to switch from bonds to money. It is necessary to induce people to hold the higher real money stock. An increase in real income increases the equilibrium interest rate. A higher interest rate offsets the tendency of higher real income to increase the quantity of real money balances demanded, and thus maintains the demand for real balances in line with the unchanged supply. An increase in banking competition has similar effects.

24-6 Monetary control

We begin by examining the practical problems entailed when the Bank tries to implement the textbook theory of monetary control, namely the use of open market operations to determine the monetary base and the use of reserve requirements and the discount rate to influence the size of the money multiplier.

Monetary base control

Suppose first that the Bank imposes a cash reserve requirement on the banks. This acts as a tax on banks, preventing them from undertaking business that they would otherwise have found profitable. Modern banks, with access to sophisticated telecommunications, will try to find ways round these controls. They may well conduct lending business with domestic firms through markets in Frankfurt or New York.

To avoid this problem, the Bank can dispense with a *required* cash ratio and rely on open market operations and changes in the monetary base to work through a money multiplier whose size is determined by the cash ratio that banks wish to hold for purely commercial purposes. This is one reason why UK formal reserve requirements were scrapped in the early 1980s.

Nevertheless, the Bank argues that there is one key problem in trying to work through the monetary base: the Bank's role as lender of last resort. When the banks wish to increase lending and deposits they can *always* get extra cash from the Bank. That was why, until the 1980s, the Bank imposed *liquid assets* ratio requirements. The idea was that

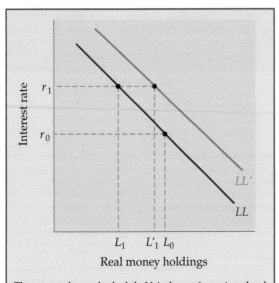

The money demand schedule LL is drawn for a given level of real income. If the Bank can fix the real money supply at L_0 the equilibrium interest rate will be r_0. Alternatively, if the Bank sets the interest rate r_0 and provides whatever money is demanded, the money supply will again be L_0. To control the money supply by using interest rates, the Bank must know the position of the demand schedule. Fixing an interest rate r_1, the resulting money supply will be L_1 if the demand schedule is LL but will be L'_1 if the demand schedule is LL'.

Figure 24-4   Interest rates and monetary control

the Bank would control the total supply of liquid assets, basically cash plus short-term government bills, and the banks could always sell bills to the Bank when they were short of cash. Since the exchange of cash for bills would not alter the outstanding stock of liquid assets, the Bank could control the money supply through a liquid assets multiplier instead of a money multiplier.

In such a system, we can think of the money supply as the liquid assets multiplier multiplied by the liquid assets base or stock of liquid assets outstanding. The liquid assets multiplier is larger (a) the lower the banks' ratio of liquid assets to deposits and (b) the lower the fraction of outstanding liquid assets held by the non-bank public and the higher the fraction held by the banks. How would the Bank control the liquid assets base? Not by buying and selling bills, which simply exchanges one liquid asset for another, but by buying and selling long-term bonds, which are not liquid assets. Sales of long-term bonds take cash out of the system and reduce the liquid assets base.

But this system also has difficulties. Although the non-bank private sector holds cash in a very stable ratio to

deposits, its demand for other liquid assets is sensitive to interest rates. By offering generous interest rates, banks can acquire liquid assets from the private sector and give them time deposits instead. By getting a larger share of the outstanding liquid assets, banks increase the size of the liquid assets multiplier.

How can banks afford to pay such generous rates on time deposits? Because the demand for bank loans is not very sensitive to interest rates. If a company is in trouble it will be happy to borrow at almost any interest rate the banks charge. When the demand for loans is strong, banks increase their overdraft charges. With correspondingly high rates on time deposits, banks can induce the private sector to swap holdings of liquid assets for holdings of time deposits without any cash drain on the banking system. Thus banks acquire the extra liquid assets they need to expand lending and create new overdraft sight deposits.

Can't the central bank do anything to prevent banks expanding lending and deposits whenever they wish? One possibility is a more vigorous use of the discount rate for last-resort loans.

Nevertheless, there are tricky problems in trying to implement the textbook account of monetary control in the real world. In practice, the Bank has judged these difficulties to be quite important and has leant towards an alternative method of monetary control.

Control through interest rates

Figure 24-4 shows again the market for money. We draw the money demand schedule LL for a given level of real income. If the central bank were able to control the money supply, then, for a given level of goods prices, it could fix the real money supply, say at L_0. The equilibrium interest rate would be r_0.

Alternatively, the central bank can fix the interest rate at r_0 and provide whatever money is required to clear the market at this interest rate. The central bank announces that it is ready to deal in interest-bearing assets in unlimited quantities at r_0. In equilibrium, the central bank will end up supplying exactly the quantity of money demanded at the interest rate r_0. The money supply will be L_0.

The central bank can fix the money supply and accept the equilibrium interest rate implied by the money demand equation, or it can fix the interest rate and accept the equilibrium money supply implied by the money demand equation.

Faced with all the problems in trying to control the money supply directly, the Bank has preferred to set interest rates and then provide the money the market demanded. This is one reason why, in practice, the Bank has frequently been prepared to act as lender of last resort without charging a penalty rate.

24-7 Targets and instruments of monetary policy

When the position of the money demand schedule is uncertain, fixing the money supply makes the interest rate uncertain, whereas fixing the interest rate makes the money supply uncertain. If the *effects* of monetary policy on the rest of the economy operate primarily through the interest rate, this is an important reason to view monetary policy as the choice of interest rates rather than the choice of money directly. In any case, the latter is almost impossible. Table 23-5 showed that 97 per cent of M4 is bank deposits, and only 3 per cent is cash directly issued by the central bank. In practice, therefore the central bank always conducts monetary policy by choosing interest rates. Interest rates are the instrument of monetary policy.

The **monetary instrument** is the variable over which the central bank exercises day to day control.

Two other concepts lie behind our discussion of monetary policy in later chapters. One is the *ultimate objective* of monetary policy in macroeconomics. Objectives could include price stability, output stabilization, manipulation of the exchange rate, and reducing swings in house prices. We return to objectives in Chapter 28.

In pursuing its ultimate objective, what information does a central bank use at its frequent meetings to decide about interest rates? It probably tries to get up-to-date forecasts of as many variables as possible. Sometimes, however, it concentrates on one or two key indicators, such as the recent behaviour of prices, the exchange rate, or the money supply.

An **intermediate target** is the key indicator used as an input to frequent decisions about where to set interest rates.

Although every central banker knows that interest rates are the instrument about which policy decisions are made, interest rates may be chosen to try to keep the intermediate target on track. New data on the money supply (largely bank deposits) comes out faster than new data on the price level. In the heyday of monetarism, central banks responded to new information by changing interest rates to try to meet medium-run targets for money growth. In terms of Figure 24-4 it was as if they were fixing the money supply not interest rates.

Throughout the world, over the last decade there have been two key changes in the design of monetary policy. First, central banks have been told that their ultimate objectives should concentrate more on inflation control and less on other things. Second, money has become less important as an intermediate target. The financial revolution has reduced its reliability as a leading indicator of what is happening to inflation. Increasingly, central banks are using *inflation forecasts* as the intermediate target to which interest rate policy responds. The next four chapters help explain why these changes took place.

SUMMARY

● The Bank of England is the UK central bank acting as banker to the banks and to the government. Because it can print money it can never go bust. It acts as lender of last resort to the banks.

● The Bank is responsible for implementing the government's monetary policy. It controls the monetary base through open market operations, purchases and sales of government securities. In addition, the Bank can affect the size of the money multiplier by imposing reserve requirements on the banks, or setting the discount rate for last resort loans at a penalty level which encourages banks to hold excess reserves.

● The demand for money is a demand for real balances. Money is valued for its subsequent purchasing power over goods. The demand for the medium of exchange depends on comparing the transactions and precautionary benefits of holding another pound with the interest sacrificed by not holding interest-bearing assets instead. The quantity of real balances demanded falls as the interest rate rises. Increases in real income increase the quantity of real balances demanded at each interest rate.

● For wider definitions of money such as M4, the asset motive for holding money is also relevant. When other interest-bearing assets are risky, people diversify their portfolios by holding some of the safe asset, money. When there is no immediate need to make transactions, this leads to a demand for holding interest-bearing deposits. This demand is larger the larger the total wealth to be invested and the lower the interest differential between deposits and risky assets.

● There is no explicit market in money. Because people can only plan to hold the total supply of assets that they own, any excess supply of bonds must be exactly matched by an excess demand for money. Interest rates adjust to clear the market for bonds. In so doing, they ensure that the money market is in equilibrium.

● An increase in the real money supply reduces the equilibrium interest rate. An increase in real income increases the equilibrium interest rate.

● In practice, the Bank finds it difficult to control the money supply exactly. Imposing artificial regulations drives banking business into unregulated channels. Monetary base control is difficult since the Bank is committed to act as a lender of last resort and supply cash when needed.

● In practice, the Bank has preferred to control the money supply by operating directly on interest rates and allowing the demand for money to determine the quantity of money that must then be supplied. Interest rates are the instrument of monetary policy.

● Because interest rates take time to affect the economy, intermediate targets are used as leading indicators relevant to the interest rate decision.

KEY TERMS

◆ Central bank   390

◆ Required reserve ratio   391

◆ Discount rate   392

◆ Open market operation   392

◆ Lender of last resort   394

◆ Opportunity cost of holding money   395

◆ Transactions motive   395

◆ Demand for money   395

◆ Precautionary motive   396

◆ Asset motive   396

◆ Money market equilibrium   399

◆ Monetary instrument   403

◆ Intermediate target   403

REVIEW QUESTIONS

1 Suppose the Bank conducts a £1 million open market sale of securities to Mr Jones who banks with Barclays. (a) If Mr Jones pays by cheque, show the effect of the deal on the balance sheets of the Bank of England and Barclays Bank. (b) What happens to the money supply? (c) Would the answer be the same if Mr Jones had paid in cash?

2 Suppose the Bank required commercial banks to hold 100 per cent cash reserves against deposits. Repeat your answers to question 1. What is the value of the money multiplier?

3 What effect do you expect the widespread adoption of credit cards to have on the precautionary demand for money by households? Explain. Be sure to take account of the demand for sight deposits as well as the demand for cash.

4 Suppose banks raise interest rates on time deposits whenever interest rates on bank loans and other assets rise. (a) Will a rise in the general level of interest rates have a large or a small effect on the demand for time deposits? (b) If the government is worried about the effect of high interest rates on electors who have large loans to finance house purchases, does this imply that it will be easy or difficult for the government to reduce M4 by a large amount?

5 How does a repo differ from an unsecured deposit?

6 What are the desirable properties of a good leading indicator?

7 *Common fallacies* Explain why the following statements are incorrect: (a) The abolition of reserve requirements implied that the Bank had given up any attempt to control the money supply. (b) When inflation exceeds nominal interest rates, real interest rates are negative. People are actually being paid to hold money. (c) Interest rates are high. This proves that the money supply has been tightly controlled.

25 Monetary and fiscal policy in a closed economy

LEARNING OUTCOMES

When you have finished this chapter, you should be able to:

- Develop theories of consumption that allow household borrowing against future incomes, and explore motives to smooth out fluctuations in consumption
- Study how interest rates and expected future profits affect investment demand by firms
- Analyse simultaneously the markets for output and money, realizing output affects money demand and interest rates affect goods demand
- Derive *IS* and *LM* curves, combinations of output and interest rates that lead to goods market and money market equilibrium
- Manipulate the *IS–LM* model to show how output and interest rates react to shocks in either the goods market or the money market
- Recognize that different mixes of monetary and fiscal policy can achieve the same output but at different interest rates

In this chapter we extend the simple model of income determination developed in Chapters 20 and 21. For the moment we assume a closed economy. Exports, imports, and the foreign sector will be reintroduced in Chapter 29 once we have mastered the analysis of a closed economy. First, we relax the simple assumptions with which we began our study of aggregate demand and income determination. We give a more complete account of the determinants of consumption and investment demand and explain why lower interest rates boost aggregate demand and national income.

Then we start to use the analysis of money and interest rates developed in the last two chapters. We now discuss a model in which the level of income affects interest rates but the level of interest rates also affects aggregate demand and

equilibrium income. We explain how the money market and the output market interact to determine simultaneously the equilibrium level of income *and* interest rates.

We then examine how the government can affect equilibrium income by altering interest rates and aggregate demand. We also reassess the role of fiscal policy in this extended model. Finally, we discuss how the government can use a mix of monetary and fiscal policy to manage or control the level and composition of aggregate demand.

In this chapter, we persist with the assumption that prices remain fixed. The interest rate is the key variable connecting the markets for money and output. In the following chapter, we allow prices to change and show that the price level is a second variable relating the markets for money and output. Chapter 29 shows that, in an open economy such as the UK, the foreign sector provides a third linkage between the financial markets and the 'real economy' in which output and employment are determined.

25-1 The consumption function again

We begin our re-examination of aggregate demand by looking again at the consumption function. In Chapter 21 we used a very simple consumption function: an upward-sloping straight line relating aggregate consumption to the disposable income of households. The slope of this line, the marginal propensity to consume, showed the fraction of each extra pound of disposable income that households would spend rather than save. The height of the consumption function depended on autonomous consumption demand. It captured all determinants of consumption spending except personal disposable income. Changes in disposable income moved households along the consumption function. Changes in autonomous demand shifted the consumption function. What factors shift the consumption function?

Determinants of autonomous consumption

Household wealth Suppose there is an increase in the real value of household wealth, for example a boom on the stock market which increases the value of company shares held by households. If households never spend this extra wealth, they will have to leave it all to their children. In practice, households are likely to use some of their extra wealth to pay for a new car or an extra holiday. For a given level of disposable income, consumption spending will increase. Since this happens whatever the level of disposable income, the entire consumption function shifts up when household wealth increases.

The **wealth effect** is the upward (downward) shift in the consumption function when household wealth increases (decreases) and people spend more (less) at each level of personal disposable income.

Can money and interest rates affect household wealth and hence consumption and aggregate demand? Yes, in two different ways. First, since money is one of the assets in which households hold their wealth, an increase in the real money supply adds directly to household wealth. Second, interest rates affect household wealth indirectly. Using the concept of present values explained in Chapter 14, the market price of corporate shares and long-term government bonds is the present value of the expected stream of divided earnings or promised coupon payments. When interest

rates fall, future earnings must now be discounted at a lower interest rate and are worth more today. Thus, reductions in interest rates make the price of bonds and corporate shares rise and make households wealthier.[1]

Durables and consumer credit When rich people spend more than their current disposable income they run down their wealth, selling off some company shares or using up money in their bank account. Poorer people don't have spare assets to finance an excess of spending over disposable income. They have to borrow.

Although some people borrow money to spend on things like holidays, most consumer borrowing finances purchases of *consumer durables*, household capital goods such as televisions, furniture, and cars. Splashing out on a new car can cost a whole year's income.

Two aspects of consumer credit or borrowing possibilities affect consumption spending. First, there is the quantity of credit on offer. If banks decide to give more generous overdrafts or retailers extend more generous loans to customers, more people are likely to overspend their current disposable income and buy the car, stereo, or dream kitchen they have always wanted. An increase in the supply of consumer credit shifts the consumption function upwards. People spend more at any level of disposable income. Second, the cost of consumer credit matters. The higher the interest rate, the lower the quantity that households can borrow while still being able to make repayments out of their future disposable incomes.

Money and interest rates thus affect consumer spending by affecting both the quantity of consumer credit and the interest rates charged on it. An increase in the monetary base increases the cash reserves of the banking system and allows it to extend more consumer credit in the form of overdrafts. And by reducing the cost of consumer credit, lower interest rates allow households to take out bigger loans while still being able to meet the interest and repayments.

Those two forces – wealth effects and changes in consumer credit – account for most of the shifts in the consumption function. They are part of the *transmission mechanism* through which changes in the financial sector affect output and employment in the real economy. Operating through wealth effects or the supply and cost

---

[1] When interest rates are 10 per cent, a bond promising to pay £2.50 for ever will trade today for about £25 so that new buyers get about 10 per cent a year on their investment. If interest rates fall to 5 per cent, bond prices must rise to £50 if new buyers are to get an annual return in line with interest rates on other assets. A similar argument applies to company shares, even though share prices are based upon guesses about future dividend payments.

BOX 25-1   Do tax cuts work?

Present consumption demand depends partly on expectations about future income. Two hundred years ago, the English economist David Ricardo noticed that this has a striking implication. Suppose the path of government spending on goods and services through time is fixed. Today, the government cuts taxes and sells extra bonds to cover the deficit thus induced. The tax cut is a fiscal expansion and boosts aggregate demand. Doesn't it?

Ricardo spotted that the answer is less obvious than it looks. Suppose a tax cut is £1 billion. Thus, £1 billion of bonds is issued. But the market value of a bond is simply the present value of future interest payments to bondholders. Since, by assumption, the path of government spending is fixed, it will take higher future taxes to pay the future interest on these new bonds. Hence £1 billion is the value of the tax cut, the value of the bond issue, *and* the value of the extra future taxes thus incurred. The private sector gets a handout today (the tax cut) matched by a future penalty (higher taxes) of identical present value. Since the private sector is neither richer nor poorer as a result, it should not change its desired spending. There is *no* effect on aggregate demand.

Looking at the same thing from another angle, the fall in government saving (larger deficit today) is exactly offset by a rise in private saving: private spending is unaltered, and larger disposable incomes (because of the tax cut) go entirely in extra saving (anticipating the future taxes).

In modern macroeconomics, this *Ricardian equivalence* has been advocated by Professor Robert Barro of Harvard. Ricardo himself thought it would not hold in the real world. Since his time, economists have been pondering how much Ricardian equivalence should hold.

INCORRECT OBJECTIONS TO RICARDIAN EQUIVALENCE

It says government spending on roads has no effect, which is obviously wrong! Not true. It acknowledges that real government spending has real effects. Rather, it asserts that, for a given programme of real government spending over time, it doesn't matter when people pay for it, provided we recognize that the interest rate is the price for converting today into tomorrow. People can pay less today (lower taxes) provided they pay equivalently more (the taxes saved plus interest) tomorrow. The government is retiming when it collects the money. Since the rest of us can also lend and borrow, we simply use the financial markets to have the money available when the government wants it.

Some of us will be dead before these future taxes are levied. Tax cuts today make us better off! Not necessarily. Barro proved that all that is necessary is that people have children and care about them. Suppose you know you will die next year, but that future tax increases will occur only after 40 years. Do you spend more after a tax cut today? Barro noted that the taxes will fall on your grandchildren, who are cared about by their parents, your children. Your kids save extra to let their kids afford the taxes; you save extra to allow your kids to do this. Your extra disposable income goes entirely in saving to raise the bequest for your children.

VALID OBJECTIONS TO RICARDIAN EQUIVALENCE

Breakdowns in intergenerational transfers Some people are not planning to have children. Some people have had a family fight, hate their kids, and aim to spend all their money before they die. Breakdowns in Barro's chain of intergenerational bequests cause a breakdown in Ricardian equivalence. The practical issue is whether this is rare or commonplace.

Distortions of taxation As we explained in Part 3, most taxes have to be marginal taxes, and marginal taxes drive distortionary wedges between the price paid and the price received. In aggregate, these have supply-side effects on the level of potential output.

Capital market imperfections Most of the time the government can borrow as much as it wants provided it pays the market interest rate. Because governments can raise taxes and print money, there is usually little danger of default on the loan. Ricardian equivalence requires that private citizens be able to borrow as easily as the government. If only this were true!

Lenders usually consider households and firms more risky than the government, for two reasons. First, there is more information about the financial position of the government than about a private citizen or company. Second, private people have no residual power to tax or print money when things go wrong. Hence, lenders charge private borrowers a higher rate of interest than the government, and sometimes they refuse to lend at all to private borrowers. Since borrowers are no longer price-takers in the borrowing or capital market, we say the capital market is imperfect.

Now let's do the sums again. £1 billion is simultaneously the value of the tax cut, the extra government bonds, and the present value of extra tax payments *discounted at the interest rate faced by the government*. But the rest of us face a higher interest rate when we try to borrow. *As viewed by us, the present value of our extra future taxes is less than £1 billion.*

Thus, the tax cut *is* a fiscal expansion because in effect the government is acting as a financial intermediary. It borrows on the good terms it enjoys and then lends to us at better terms than the capital market. It gives us a loan, tax cuts today, which we repay later in higher taxes. But we are charged only the government's lower interest rate for our loan. We are better off and raise our desired spending. Aggregate demand increases.

EVIDENCE ON RICARDIAN EQUIVALENCE
UK evidence over the last 40 years shows that private saving (firms + households) is not closely connected with government saving, though there is evidence of some weaker relationship – for example the high government saving in the late 1980s coincides with a dip in private saving.

SUMMING UP
Theory and evidence suggest that complete Ricardian equivalence is much too extreme to describe the real world. So tax cuts *do* boost aggregate demand today (though the higher future taxes will reduce demand at some future date). But, if Ricardian equivalence is not completely right, it is certainly not completely wrong either. It reminds us that expectations of future conditions affect current behaviour. Private saving rises a bit when public saving falls. The private sector can and does substitute between present and future, despite all the obstacles to doing this easily. And it is these obstacles that make consumption demand much more sensitive to *current* disposable income than it would be in the world of Friedman and Barro, where only permanent income matters.

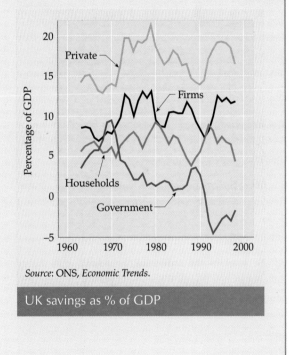

Source: ONS, *Economic Trends*.

UK savings as % of GDP

---

of consumer credit, changes in the money supply and in interest rates can shift the consumption function and the aggregate demand schedule, thus affecting the equilibrium level of income and output.

Modern theories of consumption demand
Two closely related theories of the consumption function re-interpret these phenomena and make some of their subtleties more explicit.

The permanent income hypothesis Developed by Professor Milton Friedman, this hypothesis starts from two propositions: first, people's incomes fluctuate; second, people dislike fluctuating consumption. A few extra bottles of champagne in the good years is little compensation for going hungry in the bad years. Rather than allowing fluctuations in income to be reflected in fluctuations in consumption, people have an incentive to even out fluctuations in consumption.

People will go without champagne to avoid ever being hungry.

What determines the consumption that people can afford on average? Friedman coined the term *permanent income* to describe people's average income in the long run. And he argued that consumption depends not on current disposable income but on permanent income.

The **permanent income hypothesis** says that consumption is based on long-run or permanent income.

When people believe that current income is unusually high they will recognize that this temporarily high income makes little difference to their permanent income or the amount of consumption they can afford in the long run. Since their permanent income has hardly risen, they will hardly increase their current consumption. Rather, they will save most of their temporary extra income and put money aside to see them through the years when income is unusually low. Only if people believe that a rise in today's income is likely to be sustained as higher future incomes will they believe that their permanent income has significantly increased. And only then will a large rise in current income be matched by a large rise in current consumption.

The life-cycle hypothesis   Developed by Professors Franco Modigliani and Albert Ando, this theory is very similar to the permanent income hypothesis.

The **life-cycle hypothesis** argues that people form a lifetime consumption plan (including any bequests to their children) which can just be financed out of lifetime income (plus any initial wealth or inheritances).

At the level of the individual household, this theory does not require that each household plans a constant consumption level over its lifetime. There may be years of heavy expenditure (splashing out on a round-the-world cruise or sending the kids to private school) and other years when spending is a bit less. However, such individual discrepancies tend to cancel out in the aggregate. As with the permanent income hypothesis, the life-cycle hypothesis suggests that it is average long-run income that is likely to determine the total demand for consumer spending.

Figure 25-1 shows a household's actual income over its lifetime. Income rises with career seniority until retirement, then drops to the lower level provided by a pension. The household's permanent income is *OD*. Technically, this is the constant annual income with the same present value as the present value of the actual stream of income. If the household consumed exactly its permanent income, it

would consume *OD* each year and die penniless. The two shaded areas labelled *A* show when the household would be spending more than its current income and the area *B* shows when the household would be saving.

Although the household spends its income over its lifetime, the area *B* is not the sum of the two areas *A*. We must also take account of interest. In the early years of low income, the household borrows. The area *B* shows how much the household has to save to pay back the initial borrowing *with interest* and accumulate sufficient wealth to see it through the final years when it is again dissaving.

Now let's think about wealth effects and consumer credit again. With more initial wealth, a household can spend more in every year of its lifetime without ever going broke. We can shift the permanent income line in Figure 25-1 upwards and consumption will rise. Although the area *B* is now smaller and the areas *A* are now larger, the household can use its extra wealth to meet this shortfall between the years of saving (the area *B*) and the years of dissaving (the two areas *A*).

Although we again conclude that higher wealth leads to more consumption at any level of current disposable income, we pick up something we missed earlier. If house-

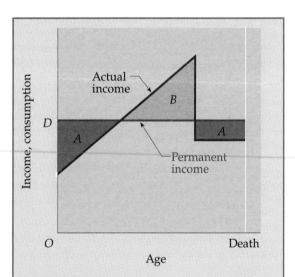

Actual disposable income rises over a household's lifetime until retirement, then falls to the pension level. Permanent income is the constant income level *OD* with the same present value as actual income. Suppose consumption equals permanent income. The areas *A* show total dissaving and the area *B*, total saving. In the absence of inherited wealth and bequests, *B* must be large enough to repay borrowing with interest and also build up enough wealth to supplement actual income during retirement.

Figure 25-1   Consumption and the life-cycle

holds believe their *future* income will be higher than they had previously imagined, this also raises their permanent income. Households can spend more in every year and still expect to balance their lifetime budget. And they will increase *current* consumption as soon as they upgrade their estimates of their future incomes. We now see that the present value of future income plays a role very similar to wealth. It is money to be shared out in consumption over the lifetime. Friedman called it 'human wealth', to distinguish it from financial and physical assets. But the important point is that increases in expected future incomes will have wealth effects; they will shift up the simple consumption function relating *current* consumption to *current* disposable income.

How about consumer credit? An increase in interest rates reduces the present value of future incomes and makes households worse off today. In terms of Figure 25-1, households must enlarge area *B* to meet the extra interest costs of paying back money borrowed in area *A* during the early years of the lifetime. We must shift the permanent income line downwards. Thus, an increase in interest rates reduces current consumption not merely by reducing the market value of financial assets such as company shares, but also by reducing the present value of future labour income. By reducing human wealth, it shifts the simple consumption function downwards.

Finally, how about an increase in the quantity of consumer credit on offer? Figure 25-1 assumes that people can spend more than their incomes in the early years of their lifetime. Students run up overdrafts knowing that, as rich economists, they can pay them back later. But what if nobody will lend? Then people without wealth are restricted by their actual incomes, although people with wealth can lend to themselves by running down their wealth. Hence an increase in the availability of consumer credit allows people who would like to dissave in the early years to do so without being forced to keep consumption in line with their low current incomes. Total consumption will rise. More students will run up overdrafts and buy cars.

What about fiscal policy? A tax cut that is expected to be permanent will increase people's current and future disposable incomes. Hence it will shift their average or permanent income by quite a lot. However, a tax cut that is known to be temporary will affect only current disposable income. Since it has no effect on expected future disposable incomes, it will have little effect on permanent income. Hence *temporary* tax cuts will have little effect on current consumption; permanent tax cuts will have a much larger effect. And it is whether or not people *believe* that the tax cut is permanent that counts.

25-2 Investment demand

In earlier chapters we treated investment demand as autonomous, or independent of the current level of income and output. In this section we begin to analyse the forces that determine the level of investment demand. Here we focus on the role of interest rates. Other determinants of investment demand are considered in greater detail in Chapter 30.

Total investment spending comprises investment in fixed capital and investment in working capital. Fixed capital includes factories, houses, plant, and machinery. Working capital consists of stocks or inventories. Figure 25-2 shows recent UK data measured in billions of pounds at 1995 prices.

Total investment has fluctuated between £69 billion and £132 billion. These numbers imply that the share of investment in GDP fluctuates between 10 and 20 per cent.[2] Although the total volume of stockbuilding or destocking is quite small, this component of total investment is volatile

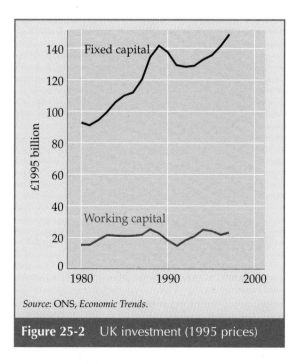

Source: ONS, *Economic Trends.*

Figure 25-2   UK investment (1995 prices)

---

[2] These numbers refer to *gross* investment or the production of *new* capital goods. Since the capital stock is depreciating, or wearing out, it now takes something like £70 billion of gross investment per annum merely to maintain the existing capital stock intact.

and contributes significantly to changes in the total level of investment.

How are we to organize our thoughts about investment? Our model of aggregate demand in a closed economy distinguishes consumption C, investment I, and government spending G on goods and services. Public investment is part of G, and we continue to treat government demand as part of the government's general fiscal policy. Thus we assume that G is fixed at a level determined by the government. In this section it is the determination of private investment demand I on which we focus.

Investment in fixed capital

Firms add to their plant and equipment because they foresee profitable opportunities to expand their output, or because they can reduce costs by moving to more capital-intensive production methods. British Telecom needs new equipment because it is developing new products for data transmission. Rover needs new assembly lines because it is substituting robots for workers in car production.

In each case, the firm has to weigh the benefits from new plant or equipment – the increase in profits – against the cost of investment. But the benefit occurs only in the future, whereas the costs are incurred immediately as the plant is built or the machine purchased. The firm must compare the value of extra future profits with the current cost of the investment.

The firm has to ask whether the investment will return enough extra profits to pay back *with interest* the loan used to finance the original investment. Equivalently, if the project is funded out of existing profits, the firm has to ask whether the new investment will yield a return at least as great as the return that could otherwise have been earned by lending the money out at interest. The higher the interest rate, the larger must be the return on a new investment before it will match the opportunity cost of the funds tied up in it.

At any instant there is a host of investment projects that the firm *could* undertake. Suppose the firm ranks these projects, from the most profitable to the least profitable. At a high interest rate, only a few projects will earn enough to cover the opportunity cost of the funds employed. As the interest rate falls, more and more projects earn a return at least as great as the opportunity cost of the funds used to undertake the investment. Hence the firm will undertake more investment.

Figure 25-3 plots the investment demand schedule *II* describing this relationship between interest rates and investment demand.

The **investment demand schedule** shows how much investment firms wish to make at each interest rate.

If the interest rate rises from r_0 to r_1, fewer investment projects will cover the opportunity cost of the funds tied up, and desired investment will fall from I_0 to I_1.

What determines the height of the schedule *II*? Two things: the cost of the new machines, and the stream of profits to which new machines give rise. For a given stream of expected future profits, an increase in the purchase price of new capital goods will reduce the rate of return earned on the money tied up in investment. Hence fewer projects will match the opportunity cost of any particular interest rate. Since the level of desired investment will be lower at each interest rate, an increase in the cost of new capital goods will shift the investment demand schedule *II* downwards.

Similarly, if the firm becomes less optimistic about future demand for its output, it will reduce its estimates of the stream of profits that will be earned on each of the possible investment projects. For a given cost of new capital goods, the return on each project will fall. At each interest rate there will now be fewer projects matching the opportunity cost of the funds. Since desired investment will fall at each interest rate, a lower level of expected future demand

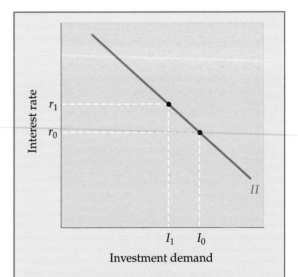

For a given price of capital goods and given expectations about the profit stream to which new investments give rise, a higher interest rate reduces the number of projects that can provide a return matching the opportunity cost of the funds used. As interest rates rise from r_0 to r_1, desired investment falls from I_0 to I_1.

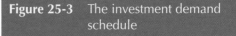

Figure 25-3   The investment demand schedule

and profits will shift the investment demand schedule downwards.[3]

The investment demand schedule II can be used to analyse both business investment in plant and machinery and residential investment in housing. Can we say anything about the slope of the schedule? There is an important difference between a machine that wears out in three years and a house or a factory lasting, say, 50 years. The longer the economic life of the capital good, the larger the fraction of its total returns that will be earned in the relatively distant future and the more the original cost of the goods will have accumulated at compound interest before the money can be repaid. Hence a small change in interest rates has a more important effect, the longer the economic life of the capital good. The investment demand schedule will be flatter for long-lived houses and factories than for very short-term machinery.[4] A rise in interest rates is more likely to choke off long-term than short-term projects.

Inventory investment

There are two reasons why firms plan to hold inventories or stocks of raw materials, partly finished goods, and finished goods awaiting sale. First, the firm may be speculating, or betting on price increases. When oil prices were rising sharply, many firms bought large stocks of oil, believing it would be cheaper to buy it now rather than later. Similarly, firms may hold finished goods off the market hoping to get a better price for them in the near future.

Second, firms may plan to hold stocks for the same reasons households plan to hold money. Corresponding to the transactions motive for holding money is the fact that

many production processes take time. A ship cannot be built in a month, or even a year in many cases. Some stocks are simply the throughput of inputs on their way to becoming outputs. But there is also a motive corresponding to the precautionary motive for holding money. Suppose demand for the firm's output suddenly increases. Since plant capacity cannot be changed overnight, the firm may have to pay large overtime payments if it is to meet the upsurge in its order book; so it may be cheaper to carry some stocks in reserve with which to meet any sudden upswing in demand. Similarly, in a temporary downturn, it may be cheaper to continue production and pile up stocks of unsold goods than to incur expensive redundancy payments in order to reduce the workforce and cut back production.

These are the benefits of holding inventories. What about the costs? By holding on to goods that could have been sold, or purchasing goods whose purchase could have been delayed, the firm is tying up money that could have been used elsewhere to earn interest. Hence the cost of holding inventories is the interest paid on the money that could have been earned by selling them or that was laid out to purchase them.

Thus we can also regard the investment demand schedule II in Figure 25-3 as being relevant to investment in increasing inventories. For any given assessment of the speculative profits to be earned from holding inventories, or of the cost savings and additional profits accruing from using inventories to smooth out production when demand is varying, an increase in the interest rate increases the marginal cost of holding inventories relative to this given marginal benefit. Hence an increase in interest rates makes firms reduce desired investment in inventories and move up the investment demand schedule. But a rise in potential speculative profits or cost reductions shifts the schedule upwards and increases inventory investment at each interest rate.

We conclude by noting two special features of inventory investment. First, unlike other components of investment, inventory investments can be negative. Firms can reduce stocks, as Figure 25-2 makes clear. Second, we must remember that the investment demand schedule shows desired or planned investment, a component of aggregate demand. For investment in fixed capital, there is probably little difference between desired investment and actual investment. Firms rarely build factories they do not want at the time.

However, firms do get forced into unplanned inventory changes. In Chapter 21 we saw that, when aggregate demand is not equal to actual output, unplanned inventory

---

[3] If you have mastered Chapter 14, you may have realized that we can make the same points a different way. Knowing the stream of future profits and the interest rate, the firm can calculate the present value of the extra profits on a project. It will undertake all the projects for which the present value exceeds the initial price of the capital goods required. A higher interest rate reduces the present value of the profits, and some projects no longer cover the purchase price of the capital goods. Hence, higher interest rates reduce desired investment. Similarly, downgrading the stream of expected future profits, or increasing the purchase price of capital goods, reduces the present value of the extra profits relative to the purchase price, and some projects are not profitable enough to undertake.

[4] Equivalently, using present values, a 1 per cent rise in the interest rate has only a small effect on the present value of earnings over a three-year period but a much larger effect on the present value of earnings over the next 50 years. Note that this is exactly the same argument as we used in Chapter 23, in saying that a change in interest rates would have little effect on the price (the present value of promised payments) of a short-term bond but a much larger effect on the price of a long-term bond.

BOX 25-2

Investment, the stock market, and interest rates

Firms will invest in projects whose rate of return exceeds the opportunity cost of the funds used. But which is the correct interest rate for firms to use in calculating this cost? In the UK, some investment is financed by bank borrowing through overdrafts. Since firms deduct interest payments from profits before paying corporation tax, a tax on profits at the rate t (currently about 0.3), the opportunity cost of each pound is £$(1 - t)r$ where r is the interest rate charged by the bank.

What if the firm has no profits on which to offset the interest? Then it does a deal with a bank. The bank buys the capital good and leases it to the firm. The bank gets the tax break instead of the firm (and banks are careful always to make profits!). Since competition between the banks for leasing business ensures that they have to pass on most of the tax break to the firms, effectively the opportunity cost to the firm remains close to £$(1 - t)r$.

Some really large projects are financed not by normal borrowing or leasing, but by selling new company shares on the stock market. If Shell wants a lot more investment money it will sell new shares. The higher the Shell share price, the more money it can raise from a new share issue. But the share price is the present value of expected Shell dividends discounted at the interest rate. Hence an increase in interest rates reduces share prices and reduces the amount of investment Shell will wish to undertake. Thus, even when investment is financed through the stock market, our investment demand schedule in Figure 25-3 remains relevant. Higher interest rates reduce desired investment. And higher expected future profits and dividends, by raising share prices, lead to more investment at any interest rate and shift up schedule II just as when the investment is financed by bank borrowing. Neither leasing nor the use of the stock market alters the usefulness of the investment demand schedule in analysing investment decisions.

changes take much of the strain until output and aggregate demand are brought into equilibrium. It is partly these unanticipated developments that lead to the volatility of actual inventory investment, brought out so clearly in Figure 25-2. Although it would be wrong to infer that fluctuations in interest rates lead to fluctuations in inventory investment demand of the order shown in Figure 25-2, inventory *plans* do respond to the opportunity cost of the funds tied up.

In this section we have established two points. First, an increase in interest rates will affect all types of investment decisions. From now on we suppose there is an aggregate investment demand schedule relating planned investment to the level of the interest rate. Precisely which interest rate is a question we discuss in Box 25-2. Second, an increase in the cost of capital goods or a reduction in expected future profit opportunities will lead to a downward shift in the investment demand schedule. A decrease in the cost of capital goods or greater optimism about future profits will shift the schedule upwards. Since ideas about future profits can sometimes be revised quite drastically, it is possible that the investment demand schedule could shift around quite a lot.

25-3 Money, interest rates, and aggregate demand

A fall in interest rates increases the level of investment demand by moving firms down their investment demand schedule. And from Section 25-1 we know that a fall in interest rates will also increase consumption demand by increasing household wealth and shifting the consumption function upwards.

How will monetary policy set interest rates? Treating interest rates as exogenous ignores the fact that monetary policy reacts to changes in economic conditions. The central bank pursues an intermediate target. Until Chapter 26 we treat the price level as fixed. It does not yet make sense to assume the Bank has an inflation target. For the moment, we assume the intermediate target is a fixed path for the money supply.

The implication is shown in Figure 25-4. For simplicity we assume that government spending G is zero. Initially, the consumption function is CC_0, investment demand is I_0 and the aggregate demand schedule AD_0. The equilibrium point is E_0 where the AD_0 schedule crosses the 45° line. Aggregate demand or planned spending equals actual income and output. What is the effect of a higher money supply target? A lower interest rate is needed to increase money demand in line with the higher money supply. Lower interest rates increase investment demand to I_1 and shift the consumption function from CC_0 to CC_1. The aggregate demand schedule shifts from AD_0 to AD_1.

You may be thinking that the new equilibrium point is E_1. However, this is not quite right. *Before* reading further, see if you can work out for yourself why not.

Damping effects   In the last chapter we pointed out that the quantity of money demanded depends both on interest rates and on the level of income. The immediate effect of an increase in the money supply target is to reduce interest rates to maintain equilibrium in the money market. Figure 25-4 shows that the consequence of lower interest rates is to shift aggregate demand upwards. As firms gradually revise their investment plans upwards and households decide to consume more, income increases. But as income increases, so does the demand for money.

There is now excess demand for money, and interest rates have to rise a bit to choke this off and maintain money market equilibrium. And since interest rates have risen a bit,

the aggregate demand schedule must fall back a bit. Hence the final position of the aggregate demand schedule is higher than its original position AD_0 but lower than AD_1, in Figure 25-4. Thus the new equilibrium will be between E_0 and E_1. We discuss these damping effects more fully in Section 25-5.

25-4 Fiscal policy and crowding out

In Chapter 22 we showed that an expansionary fiscal policy, through tax cuts or additional government spending, leads to higher aggregate demand and an increase in equilibrium income and output. We must now modify our analysis. An increase in government spending will shift the aggregate demand schedule upwards and will tend to increase income and output. But with an unchanged real money supply, higher income will increase the demand for money and raise interest rates. This reduces investment demand and shifts the consumption function downwards. These effects tend to offset the original upward shift in aggregate demand caused by the increase in government spending, though they cannot offset it completely.[5] Figure 25-5 illustrates this.

Beginning from the aggregate demand schedule AD, the immediate effect of higher government spending is to shift aggregate demand to AD', as in Chapter 22. In that chapter we said that the equilibrium point moved from E to E' and that equilibrium income increased from Y to Y'. Now we must recognize that higher income will increase the demand for money. To meet the monetary target, the Bank must raise interest rates, thus shifting the aggregate demand schedule down, say to AD''. The final equilibrium point will be E'' and equilibrium income will increase only from Y to Y''.

In Chapter 21 we introduced the concept of the output multiplier, and in Chapter 22 we calculated the multiplier for government spending as the ratio of the increase in equilibrium income to the increase in government spending that caused it. Figure 25-5 tells us that, once we include the money market and the effect of interest rates on aggregate demand, the multiplier on government spending will be *lower* than our earlier discussion suggests. Government spending crowds out private expenditure.

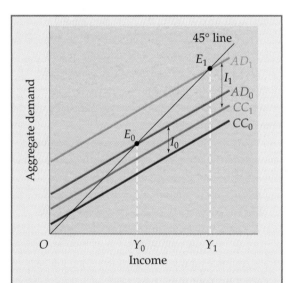

Initially the consumption function is CC_0, investment demand is I_0, and equilibrium is at E_0, where aggregate demand AD_0 crosses the 45° line. A fall in interest rates shifts the consumption function to CC_1 and increases investment demand to I_1, shifting aggregate demand up from AD_0 to AD_1. Hence an increase in the money supply target lowers interest rates, shifts aggregate demand upwards, and increases income and output.

Figure 25-4   Interest rates and aggregate demand

[5] If falls in consumption and investment demand completely offset higher government demand, aggregate demand would then be unchanged. With unchanged income, there would be no upward pressure on the demand for money and interest rates. Without higher interest rates, investment and consumption demand would not have been reduced. Hence, increased government spending must lead to some upward shift in the aggregate demand schedule, some increase in interest rates, and to only partially offsetting falls in consumption and investment demand.

Table 25-1 Government spending and crowding out			
(1)	(2)	(3)	(4)
Higher government spending raises output and income.	Higher income raises desired real money balances.	Higher real money demand and unchanged supply bid up interest rates.	Higher interest rates crowd out consumption and investment, damping the expansion.

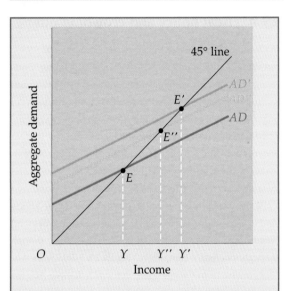

Increased government spending initially shifts the aggregate demand schedule from AD to AD'. But higher income raises money demand and interest rates rise, thus reducing investment demand and shifting the consumption function downwards. The final aggregate demand schedule is thus AD" and the new equilibrium point is E". Fiscal policy with a constant money supply target is less expansionary than it would be if the money supply were increased to keep interest rates constant as income expanded.

Figure 25-5   Crowding out

Crowding out is the reduction in private demand for consumption and investment caused by an increase in government spending, which increases aggregate demand and hence interest rates.

In the model of this chapter, government spending does not completely crowd out private consumption and investment spending. On balance, the aggregate demand schedule still shifts upwards. But, by increasing interest rates, reducing investment demand, and shifting the consumption function downwards, the expansionary effect of higher government spending is partially damped. Similarly, although a tax cut initially causes an upward rotation of the consumption function plotted against national income, the induced rise in income bids up interest rates, again damping the final effect of the fiscal stimulus.

Table 25-1 summarizes the steps in the crowding-out argument for the case of higher government spending. Try constructing your own table for the case of an income tax cut.

Finally, to check you have fully understood, how much crowding out is caused by higher government spending in the case in which the central bank abandons its money supply target and simply fixes interest rates exogenously? (*Answer given as Review question 8 at the end of the chapter.*)

25-5 The *IS–LM* model

In the previous two sections we have analysed the interaction of income and interest rates using the familiar aggregate demand schedule and the 45° line. Equilibrium income is the level at which the aggregate demand schedule crosses the 45° line. Although it is possible to use this framework to analyse the effects of the government's fiscal and monetary policy, the framework is a bit cumbersome. Any initial shift in the aggregate demand schedule induces interest rate changes and hence further shifts in the aggregate demand schedule.

In this section we introduce a different way to study the same issues. The advantage of this method is that we can see immediately how the equilibrium levels of income and interest rates are simultaneously determined. The trick is to consider the *combinations* of income and interest rates that would lead to equilibrium in each of the two markets, goods and money, and thus determine the unique combination of income and interest rates that leads to equilibrium in both markets at the same time.

The *IS* schedule

The goods market is in equilibrium when the aggregate demand and actual income are equal. In Chapter 21 we saw that this would occur at the point at which planned investment *I* equals planned savings *S*. For this reason, the set of different combinations of interest rates and income compatible with equilibrium in the goods market is called the *IS* schedule.

The **IS schedule** shows the different combinations of income and interest rates at which the goods market is in equilibrium.

Figure 25-6 constructs the *IS* schedule. We begin with a particular interest rate, call it r_0. For this interest rate, we know the level of investment demand and autonomous consumption demand. Thus we know the height of the aggregate demand schedule, which we plot as AD_0 in the top diagram. The equilibrium output in the top diagram is Y_0. Hence in the bottom diagram we plot the corresponding point E_0. The goods market is in equilibrium if the interest rate is r_0 and income is Y_0.

Now imagine a lower interest rate r_1. Since investment demand will now be higher and the consumption function will have shifted upwards, we plot the higher aggregate demand schedule AD_1. AD_1 is higher than AD_0 only because of the effect of lower interest rates. The new equilibrium point is E_1 and the bottom diagram shows that the combination of r_1 and Y_1 would also lead to equilibrium in the goods market. By repeating this exercise for all possible interest rates, we can trace out a whole series of combinations of interest rates and income levels compatible with goods market equilibrium. Joining up all these points in the bottom half of the diagram we obtain the *IS* schedule.

The slope of the IS *schedule*   The *IS* schedule slopes downwards. For goods market equilibrium, a higher interest rate must be accompanied by a lower income level since the aggregate demand schedule must be lower. How steep will the *IS* schedule be? This depends on the sensitivity of aggregate demand to interest rates. The more investment demand and autonomous consumption demand are reduced by a given increase in interest rates, the more a rise in interest rates will reduce the equilibrium level of income and the flatter will be the slope of the *IS* schedule. Conversely, if changes in interest rates lead to only small shifts in the aggregate demand schedule, the equilibrium level of income will hardly be affected and the *IS* schedule will be very steep.

Shifts in the IS *schedule*   The purpose of the *IS* schedule is to illustrate the effect of interest rates *alone* in shifting the aggregate demand schedule and changing the equilibrium level of income. Anything else that would have shifted the aggregate demand schedule will also shift the *IS* schedule. For a *given* level of interest rates, an increase in firms' optimism about future profits will shift the investment demand schedule upwards, increasing autonomous

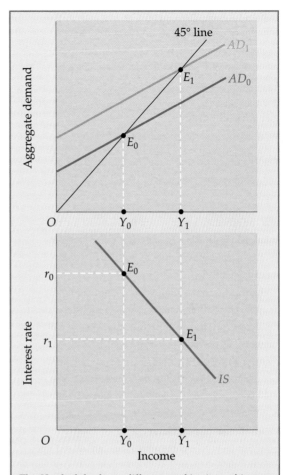

The *IS* schedule shows different combinations of income and interest rates at which the goods market is in equilibrium. At the interest rate r_0 aggregate demand is AD_0. The top figure tells us that equilibrium income is then Y_0. This combination is shown as E_0 in the bottom figure. At the lower interest rate r_1, the aggregate demand schedule is higher, say AD_1. Equilibrium income is now Y_1 and the point E_1 plots this combination in the bottom figure. Repeating this exercise for all possible interest rates, we can join up all the points such as E_0 and E_1 in the bottom figure to obtain the *IS* schedule.

Figure 25-6   The *IS* schedule

investment demand; an increase in households' estimate of future incomes will shift the consumption function upwards, increasing autonomous consumption demand; or an increase in government spending could increase the government component of autonomous demand directly. Any of these would shift the aggregate demand schedule upwards at a given interest rate. Hence equilibrium income would increase at any interest rate. We would show this as an *upward shift in* the *IS* schedule, telling us that equilibrium income is now higher at any particular interest rate.

To sum up, movements along the *IS* schedule tell us about shifts in equilibrium income caused by shifts in aggregate demand as a result only of changes in interest rates. Any other cause of a shift in the aggregate demand schedule must be represented as a shift in the *IS* schedule.

The *LM* schedule

We now consider money market equilibrium.

The ***LM* schedule** shows the combinations of interest rates and income compatible with equilibrium in the money market.

It is the schedule along which the demand for real money balances, which Keynes originally called liquidity prefer-ence, is equal to the supply of real money balances, which we can denote by *L*.

Figure 25-7 shows how we construct the *LM* schedule. Suppose the central bank has a given monetary target. In Figure 25-7(a) we show a fixed supply of real money balances L_0. For a given income level Y_0, we plot the money demand schedule LL_0. Higher interest rates reduce the quantity of real money balances demanded. The equilib-rium point is E_0 and the equilibrium interest rate, r_0. Hence in Figure 25-7(b) we show the corresponding point E_0 at which the money market is in equilibrium with the combination of an income level Y_0 and an interest rate r_0.

At the higher income level Y_1, the demand for money will be greater at each interest rate. Plotting the new money demand schedule LL_1, we see that the equilibrium interest rate is now r_1 and we plot the point E_1 in Figure 25-7(b), showing that the combination r_1 and Y_1 also leads to money market equilibrium. With a higher income, tending to increase the quantity of money demanded, and a higher interest rate, tending to reduce the quantity of money demanded, the quantity of money demanded remains in line with the unchanged quantity supplied. Considering each income level in turn, plotting the corresponding money demand schedule in Figure 25-7(a), and plotting the corresponding equilibrium points in Figure 25-7(b), we can trace out the entire *LM* schedule.

The slope of the* LM *schedule The *LM* schedule slopes upwards. With a higher income level it requires a higher interest rate to choke off money demand and maintain money market equilibrium with an unchanged money supply. The more a given increase in income tends to increase the quantity of money demanded, the larger will be the increase in the interest rate required to maintain money market equilibrium and the steeper will be the *LM* schedule. Similarly, the less responsive the quantity of money demanded to a given rise in interest rates, the larger will be the increase in interest rates required to choke off money demand for a given increase in income, and the steeper will be the *LM* schedule. Conversely, the more the quantity of money demanded responds to interest rates and the less it responds to income, the flatter will be the *LM* schedule.

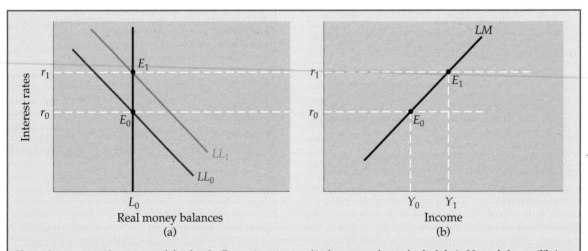

The real money supply is assumed fixed at L_0. For a given income Y_0 the money demand schedule is LL_0 and the equilibrium interest rate r_0. Point E_0 in figure (b) shows that r_0 and Y_0 lead to money market equilibrium. If income is Y_1, the money demand schedule in (a) shifts up to LL_1 and the equilibrium interest rate is r_1. This combination of income and interest rates is shown as point E_1 in (b). Repeating the analysis for all income levels and joining up the points such as E_0 and E_1 in (b), we get the *LM* schedule showing the different combinations of interest rates and income compatible with money market equilibrium.

Figure 25-7   The *LM* schedule

Shifts in the LM schedule We construct a given *LM* schedule for a given supply of *real* money balances. Suppose we now increase the target money supply. Real money balances therefore increase. For a given income level and a given height of the money demand schedule in Figure 25-7(a), the equilibrium interest rate will now be lower since the vertical supply curve has shifted to the right. At each income level, a lower interest rate is required to induce people to hold the additional supply of real balances. Hence in Figure 25-7(b) we must represent an increase in the supply of real money balances as a shift to the right in the *LM* schedule, showing that the equilibrium interest rate is lower at each income level, or, equivalently, that at each interest rate it requires a higher income level to induce people to hold the additional supply of real balances. Conversely, a reduction in the real money supply shifts the *LM* schedule to the left. To reduce the quantity of real balances demanded and maintain money market equilibrium with a lower real money supply, it now takes a higher interest rate at each income level.

To sum up, we draw an *LM* schedule for a given real money supply. Moving along the schedule, higher interest rates must be accompanied by higher income to maintain the quantity of real balances demanded in line with the fixed supply. Increases in the real money supply shift the *LM* schedule to the right. Although the real money supply can be increased either by an increase in the nominal money supply at constant goods prices or by a fall in goods prices with a given nominal money supply, we consider only the former mechanism in this chapter since we are still assuming that goods prices are fixed. The role of changing goods prices is examined in the next chapter.

Equilibrium in the goods and money markets

Instead of having two separate but interrelated diagrams to illustrate the markets for goods and money, the *IS–LM* model allows us to think about both markets in the same diagram. Figure 25-8 plots both the *IS* schedule, showing goods market equilibrium, and the *LM* schedule, showing money market equilibrium. Only at *E* are both markets in equilibrium. Goods and money markets interact to determine the level of equilibrium interest rate r^* and the equilibrium income Y^*.

Suppose the interest rate is r_1. At the income Y_1 we would be at the point *A* on the *IS* schedule. The combination r_1 and Y_1 lead to goods market equilibrium. But at the interest rate r_1 it would require an income Y_2 for money market equilibrium, at *B* on the *LM* schedule. Given the interest rate r_1, the income level Y_1 is too low for money market equilibrium.

With too low an income level, there is not enough money demand to match the given quantity of money supply. With excess supply of money, interest rates will have to be cut to achieve the money supply target. We can repeat this argument until interest rates fall to r^*. At that level, aggregate demand and income have risen sufficiently to increase money demand enough to lead to equilibrium in the money market as well as the goods market.

Conversely, with an interest rate r_2, the income Y_2 required for goods market equilibrium at *C* is greater than the income Y_1 required for equilibrium in the money market at *D*. With income too high for money market equilibrium, there is excess demand for money, bidding up interest rates. Again, the process continues until interest rates are r^*, income is Y^*, and both markets are in equilibrium.

Now we rework the analysis of monetary and fiscal policy that we undertook earlier in the chapter using the more cumbersome framework of the aggregate demand schedule and the 45° line. Previously we had to concentrate on the goods market in our diagram, but, by keeping the money market at the back of our minds, we had to remember that changes in income would alter equilibrium interest rates and induce further shifts in the aggregate demand schedule. The *IS* schedule now captures interest-rate-induced shifts in the aggregate demand schedule; and, by plotting the *LM* schedule on the same diagram, we can now explicitly keep track of both markets at once.

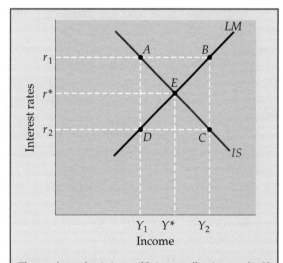

The goods market is in equilibrium at all points on the *IS* schedule. The money market is in equilibrium at all points on the *LM* schedule. Hence only at point *E* are both markets in equilibrium.

Figure 25-8 Equilibrium in the goods and money markets

Fiscal policy: shifting the *IS* schedule

Any change, other than a fall in interest rates, that shifts the aggregate demand schedule upwards will also shift the *IS* schedule upwards. Figure 25-9 analyses the consequences of an increase in government spending, though the same diagram can be used also to discuss the effect of an increase in firms' optimism about future profits or an increase in households' estimates of their future disposable incomes.

The economy begins with the *IS* schedule IS_0 and the *LM* schedule LM_0. Initial equilibrium is at *E*. Suppose first that the government increases government spending *G* and finances the extra government deficit by selling bonds. Thus the money supply target remains unchanged and *LM* schedule remains LM_0. However, the additional government spending shifts the *IS* schedule upwards, say from IS_0 to IS_1. At each interest rate the equilibrium level of income is increased, since higher government spending tends to shift the aggregate demand schedule upwards.

Given the schedules IS_1, and LM_0 the new equilibrium point is E_1. Thus the effect of bond-financed government spending increases is to increase the equilibrium level of income from Y_0 to Y_1. With a fixed supply of real money balances, interest rates must rise from r_0 to r_1 to prevent the higher income level from increasing the quantity of real balances demanded. Although higher interest rates crowd out consumption and investment spending, higher government spending is not completely offset by crowding out and equilibrium income increases.

Figure 25-9 allows us to make two interesting points. First, crowding out would be complete only if the *LM* schedule were vertical. Then, an upward shift in the *IS* schedule would lead to higher interest rates but not to higher income. A vertical *LM* curve implies that interest rates have *no effect* on the quantity of money demanded. Under this extreme assumption, any increase in income would lead to excess demand in the money market that could no longer be eliminated by higher interest rates. Hence, no increase in equilibrium income would be possible. Interest rates would simply increase until private consumption and investment had fallen by the amount of the original increase in government spending. Crowding out would be complete.

In practice, this is most unlikely. The demand for money is not completely insensitive to interest rates, and the *LM* schedule is not completely vertical. However, the less sensitive is money demand to interest rates, the steeper will be the *LM* schedule, and the more a bond-financed increase in government spending will lead to higher interest rates rather than higher income.

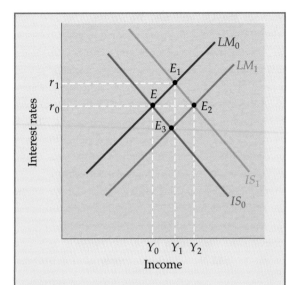

A bond-financed increase in government spending shifts the *IS* curve from IS_0 to IS_1 but leaves the money supply target unaltered. Hence the *LM* schedule remains LM_0. Thus, fiscal expansion moves the equilibrium from *E* to E_1. Income increases to Y_1 even though the increase in interest rates partly crowds out private investment and autonomous consumption demand. However, by simultaneously increasing the money supply target, the government could shift the *LM* curve from LM_0 to LM_1, thus preventing a rise in interest rates. The equilibrium income level would then increase to Y_2, since private investment and consumption would no longer be crowded out.

Figure 25-9   Fiscal expansion shifts the
                          IS schedule

Second, in Figure 25-9 we show what would happen if the increase in government spending were accompanied by an increase in the money supply target. Suppose, in addition to raising spending and shifting the *IS* schedule upwards, the money supply rises just enough to keep interest rates at their original level while income expanded. By providing enough extra money to shift the *LM* schedule as far as LM_1, the fiscal expansion induces a new equilibrium at E_2, with interest rates unchanged at r_0.

By increasing the money supply target in line with the income-induced increase in money demand, the Bank prevents interest rates from rising and crowding out private investment and consumption. In fact, the ratio of the increase in income from Y_0 to Y_2 to the increase in government spending that had shifted the *IS* curve would then be exactly the value of the multiplier calculated in Chapter 22 for an increase in government spending. There, we *ignored* the possibility that interest rates could affect aggregate demand. Here, we consider the change in the money supply target that would *prevent* interest rates from affecting aggregate demand.

Thus we conclude that an increase in government spending increases the equilibrium level of income even when we take account of the money market and the effect of interest rates on aggregate demand. However, the exact value of the government spending multiplier depends on the monetary policy in force when the fiscal expansion is undertaken. If the money supply is held constant, interest rates will rise, crowd out private expenditure, and partially offset the fiscal stimulus. If the money supply is increased to hold interest rates constant as output increases, the multiplier will be larger. Thus government spending financed by printing money tends to be more expansionary than government spending financed by issuing bonds.

Monetary policy: shifting the *LM* schedule

Figure 25-9 can also be used to discuss monetary policy. Suppose fiscal policy is held constant and the *IS* schedule is fixed at IS_0. Given the initial level of the real money supply target, the *LM* schedule is LM_0 and equilibrium occurs at *E*. An increase in the money supply target, with given goods prices, will shift the *LM* schedule to the right, say to LM_1. Figure 25-9 shows that the new equilibrium occurs at E_3.

The increase in the real money supply requires a reduction in interest rates to induce people to hold the extra real money balances. Overnight, before income has time to change, there will be a large drop in interest rates. If the money market is continuously in equilibrium, in Figure 25-9 the economy will move from point *E* to the point on the new schedule LM_1 vertically below *E*. But this point is not on the fixed schedule IS_0. Lower interest rates will increase consumption and investment spending, increase income, and hence increase the demand for money. At the new equilibrium in both markets, the economy will be at E_3 with the corresponding income and interest rates.

Thus, Figure 25-9 summarizes our discussion of the transmission mechanism through which an increase in the money supply target reduces interest rates, increases consumption and investment demand, and hence increases the equilibrium level of income. Although the final effect of an increase in the real money supply is to increase income, interest rates must nevertheless be lower in the new equilibrium than in the original one. Without a reduction in the equilibrium interest rate, there would be nothing to make aggregate demand and equilibrium income increase. With neither lower interest rates nor higher income, the demand for money would not have increased in line with the increase in its supply. Figure 25-9 summarizes this argument

by noting that the new equilibrium point E_3 lies to the southeast of the original equilibrium at *E*. It promises us that an increase in the real money supply increases the equilibrium level of income and reduces the equilibrium interest rate.

25-6 Demand management and the policy mix

Fiscal policy is the set of decisions the government makes about taxation and spending. Through such decisions, the government can shift the *IS* schedule. Monetary policy is the corresponding set of decisions about the money supply target and interest rates. Monetary policy can shift the *LM* curve. Although fiscal decisions will determine the government's budget deficit, it is not essential to finance the deficit by printing money. The government can also sell bonds and borrow from the private sector. Hence, if it chooses, the government can pursue independent monetary and fiscal policies.

Demand management is the use of monetary and fiscal policy to stabilize the level of income around a high average level.

Thus, if pessimism about the future leads the private sector (firms and households) to spend less, the government can use an expansionary fiscal policy to shift the *IS* schedule upwards, an expansionary monetary policy to shift the *LM* curve to the right, or some combination of these two policies. Nevertheless, monetary and fiscal policy are not interchangeable. They affect aggregate demand through different routes and have different implications for the *composition* of aggregate demand.

Figure 25-10 can be used to analyse the mix of monetary and fiscal policy. Suppose the government aims to stabilize income at the level Y^*. The figure shows two different ways in which this can be done. One option is to have an expansionary or *easy* fiscal policy with high government spending, low tax rates, or both. This leads to a high *IS* schedule, which we show as IS_1. To keep income in check with such an expansionary fiscal policy, it is necessary to have a *tight* monetary policy. With a low money supply the *LM* schedule lies far to the left, which we show as LM_1.

Equilibrium at E_1 meets the objective of attaining an income level Y^*. Since government spending is a large component of aggregate demand, it requires a high equilibrium interest rate to keep investment and consumption demand in check so that total income is no larger than Y^*. Thus the mix of easy fiscal policy and tight monetary policy means that government spending *G* will be a relatively large

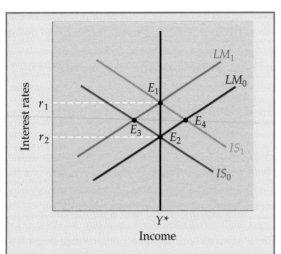

The target income Y^* can be attained by easy fiscal policy and tight monetary policy. Equilibrium at E_1, the intersection of LM_1 and IS_1, implies high interest rates r_1 and a low share of private sector investment and consumption in GNP. Alternatively, with easy monetary policy and tight fiscal policy, equilibrium at E_2, the intersection of LM_0 and IS_0, still attains the target income but at lower interest rates r_2. The share of private sector investment and consumption in GNP will be higher than at E_1.

Figure 25-10   The policy mix and the composition of aggregate demand

share of national income Y^* and private spending $(C + I)$ a relatively small share.

Alternatively, the government can adopt a tight fiscal policy (a lower IS schedule, IS_0) and an easy monetary policy (a schedule LM_0, further to the right). The target income Y^* is still attained but at the lower interest rate r_2 corresponding to the new equilibrium E_2. With easy monetary policy and tight fiscal policy, the share of private expenditure $(C + I)$ will be higher and the share of government expenditure lower than at E_1. With lower interest rates, there is less crowding out of private expenditure.

Of course, easy monetary policy and easy fiscal policy together are highly expansionary. With the schedules IS_1 and LM_0 the equilibrium point in Figure 25-9 is E_4, where income is much higher than Y^*. Conversely, with tight monetary policy and tight fiscal policy, the schedules LM_1 and IS_0, the equilibrium point is E_3, where income lies well below Y^*.

In the UK the Heath government in the early 1970s adopted a mix of easy monetary policy and easy fiscal policy in a famous attempt at 'a dash for growth'. Real national income rose by over 8 per cent in 1972. And easy fiscal and monetary policy during the Lawson boom of

1987–88 achieved real growth rates of over 6 per cent a year. Conversely, both fiscal and monetary policy were tight during the early 1980s and the early 1990s. In both cases, real national income fell. The subsequent periods of output growth were achieved against a background of gradual easing of both fiscal and monetary policy.

When aggregate demand is too low, easy monetary and fiscal policies can help to raise it. When aggregate demand is too high, tight monetary and fiscal policies can help reduce it. But when aggregate demand is about right, what should determine the mix of fiscal and monetary policy?

In the short run, the government may care about the total level of aggregate demand, income, and employment, but in the longer run it may also care about economic growth. High levels of investment are good for growth because they increase the capital stock more quickly, giving workers more equipment with which to work and raising their productivity. Figure 25-10 suggests that it is better to choose a tight fiscal policy and an easy monetary policy than the other way round. With lower interest rates, firms will invest more, and in the long run the economy's productive potential will grow more quickly.

However, this argument is less clear-cut than it first appears. Government spending G includes not only wages of civil servants but capital investment in roads, hospitals, and many other things, such as spending on education. Thus, tight fiscal policy typically involves cutting back on such spending, and this must be set against any benefits from higher private investment that a correspondingly easier monetary policy and lower interest rate allows.

Three other issues play a large role in the practical judgements of governments about the desirable mix of fiscal and monetary policies. First, there is the question of predictability. In practice, neither monetary nor fiscal policy ever has exactly the effects the government anticipated. Our model is only a simplification of the complex world in which we live. Fiscal actions such as higher government expenditure do have one major advantage over monetary actions. Higher government spending adds directly to aggregate demand. In contrast, monetary policy must work indirectly through the transmission mechanism set out in this chapter.

The other two issues take us beyond the scope of our simple model. First, there may be a reluctance to embark on an easy monetary policy because it is feared that an increase in the money supply target will lead to inflation. Moreover, if it does, the induced rise in prices may offset the initial increase in the nominal money supply, leaving the real money supply unaltered. If so, the LM schedule reverts to its original position. Easy monetary policy has brought on inflation but no stimulus to aggregate demand, income, and employment. To examine this important issue, we begin in the next chapter the analysis of how the price level is determined.

Second, in deciding the appropriate fiscal policy, the government may be concerned not merely with the effects of spending and taxes on aggregate demand but also with the *microeconomic* effects of fiscal policy. For example, it is commonly held that high tax rates discourage the incentive to work and reduce the economy's productive potential. Supply-side economics argues that the effects of fiscal policy on aggregate supply may be as important as its effects on aggregate demand.

These two issues introduce us to the material we shall be studying in the next few chapters. We now take stock of what we have learned so far in macroeconomics and indicate the ground we have still to cover.

25-7 Keynesian economics and activism

In the last five chapters we have developed the Keynesian theme that aggregate demand determines output and employment. We have seen how the government can use fiscal and monetary policy to manipulate or manage aggregate demand and can aim to stabilize the economy close to its full-employment level. During periods of recession, when aggregate demand is insufficient, monetary and fiscal expansion can boost demand, output, and employment.

Britain was partly pulled out of the slump of the 1930s by the inadvertently Keynesian policy of heavy government spending on rearmament as the threat of war loomed. However, in the three decades after 1945 governments of both political parties in Britain (and other countries) attempted to implement the Keynesian policy prescription and to manage the level of aggregate demand. The government accepted responsibility for preserving a high and stable level of demand and employment, intervening actively to offset shocks to private demand.

But the policy did not work perfectly. In the decade after 1965, both inflation and unemployment grew fairly steadily. That build-up of inflation proved to be a costly after-effect of Keynesian policies. Today we are more doubtful about the success of the activist period of the 1950s and 1960s.

We have already mentioned the two main worries that have developed about the pursuit of Keynesian activism. First, simple Keynesian economics proceeds on the assumption that the price level is given. But what happens when the price level can change, for example when the economy is near full employment and there is no longer spare capacity to make firms think twice about raising prices or paying higher wages? Then a monetary expansion may lead not to higher employment but only to higher prices, leaving the real money supply unaltered. The analysis of prices and inflation is central to a fuller understanding of macroeconomics. We begin this task in the next chapter.

Second, Keynesian economics discusses an economy with spare capacity and workers who would like to work but cannot find a job. But it says little about what determines full-employment output or the economy's productive potential. On the one hand, the high tax rates that accompany a government sector of ever-increasing size may provide a disincentive to work. On the other hand, the very promise of a Keynesian government to take care of the unemployment problem through demand management may make people slack and complacent. Both these effects *could* so reduce the level of productive potential that it is no longer legitimate to look at low actual output levels and conclude that we must be way below full-employment output. And if we are really close to full-employment output, we had better start to pay attention to the supply bottlenecks that can make productive potential so low, rather than focusing exclusively on aggregate demand on the happy assumption that the economy has plenty of scarce resources which can easily be put to work if only demand is increased.

Although these are important topics yet to be covered, by now we have completed the first major stage of macroeconomics. We have learned how to analyse the demand side of the economy. Even when we have mastered the analysis of supply, adjustment, and price behaviour, we shall see that the demand analysis we have mastered plays an important part in the story, especially in the short run.

✳ SUMMARY

● An increase in interest rates reduces household wealth and also makes borrowing more expensive. Together, these effects reduce autonomous consumption demand and shift the consumption function downwards.

● Modern theories of the consumption function emphasize long-run disposable income and the incentive to smooth out short-run fluctuations in consumption. They suggest that higher interest rates also reduce consumption demand by reducing the present value of expected future labour income. They also suggest that temporary tax changes are likely to have less effect on consumption demand than tax changes that are expected to be permanent.

● For a given cost of new capital goods and expected stream of future profits, an increase in interest rates reduces the number of investment projects that earn a rate of return at least as great as the opportunity cost of the funds employed. The investment demand schedule shows this negative relationship between the interest rate and the demand for investment. Higher expected future profits or a lower cost of new capital goods will shift the investment demand schedule upwards.

● Together, these effects of interest rates on consumption and investment spending show the transmission mechanism through which an increase in the money supply and a reduction in interest rates affect aggregate demand.

● With a given real money supply, a fiscal expansion increases output, money demand, and interest rates, thus crowding out or partially displacing private consumption and investment demand. Thus the government spending multiplier is smaller than its value in the case where the money supply is simultaneously increased to prevent interest rates from rising as output increases.

● The *IS* schedule shows the combinations of interest rates and income compatible with goods market equilibrium. As interest rates increase, equilibrium income falls. At given interest rates, an increase in expected future consumer incomes, higher expected profits on investment, or higher government spending would shift the aggregate demand schedule upwards. Hence they shift the *IS* schedule upwards showing higher equilibrium income at each interest rate.

● The *LM* schedule shows combinations of interest rates and income compatible with money market equilibrium. With a given money supply target, higher income must be accompanied by higher interest rates to keep money demand unchanged. An increase in the supply of real money shifts the *LM* schedule to the right. Equilibrium in both markets occurs at the point at which the *IS* and *LM* schedules intersect.

● A given income level can be attained by easy monetary policy and tight fiscal policy or by the converse. In the latter case the equilibrium interest rate is higher and private spending will be a lower share of the given level of income and spending.

REVIEW QUESTIONS

1 Before the 1976 election in the United States President Ford tried to get unemployment down by giving everyone a once-off tax rebate. Most people saved their government rebate and spending hardly increased. Can modern theories of the consumption function explain why?

2 Suppose people not previously allowed bank overdrafts get credit cards on which they can borrow up to £500 each. What happens to the consumption function? Why?

3 Why do higher interest rates reduce investment demand? Be sure to discuss all the different ways in which firms might finance their investment projects.

4 'Higher money supply increases consumption and investment, and hence income. Higher income increases interest rates. Hence higher money supply increases interest rates.' Evaluate this proposition using diagrams to check your answer.

5 Fiscal policy takes the form of government subsidies to firms undertaking investment. Monetary policy involves an open market sale of government bonds. Explain what this policy mix does to the level of GNP and to its composition as between consumption, investment, and government expenditure on goods and services.

6 Suppose firms expect a huge boom in a couple of years. What happens today to investment, income, and interest rates?

7 What is active Keynesian demand management? Give two reasons why some people believe it might not always work.

8 Answer to text question in Section 25-4: no crowding out since interest rates don't change!

9 *Common fallacies* Show why the following statements are incorrect: (a) Consumers must have gone crazy. Their take-home pay is down yet their spending is up. (b) Interest rates affect investment only if firms have to borrow. In practice, many firms finance investment out of existing profits. Hence we should not expect interest rates to have much effect on investment. (c) Keynesians believe only in fiscal policy. They ignore monetary policy.

26 Aggregate supply, the price level, and the speed of adjustment

When you have finished this chapter, you should be able to:

- Derive the macroeconomic demand schedule, explaining the roles of the real balance effect and the credit channel
- Examine how labour supply and labour demand lead to labour market equilibrium
- Analyse determinants of the equilibrium or natural rate of unemployment
- Show how the equilibrium price level is determined in the classical model
- Explain why price adjustment, and especially wage adjustment, may not be rapid
- Use short-run and long-run aggregate supply to trace out the adjustment process
- Explore the effect of a supply shock, both in the short run and the long run

By assuming that prices are fixed and that the economy has spare resources, Keynesian models suggest that boosting aggregate demand will always lead to higher output. But prices are not fixed for ever. Inflation is one of the key macroeconomic issues. And, with only finite resources, the economy cannot expand output indefinitely. By introducing aggregate supply, or firms' willingness and ability to produce, we now show how demand and supply determine both the price level and the level of output.

We shall see that steadily increasing the money supply must eventually create inflation since output and employment cannot expand for ever. Similarly, fiscal expansion must eventually increase prices and interest rates rather than continue to increase output. To introduce these ideas we move from the Keynesian extreme, in which wages and prices are fixed, to the opposite extreme, in which wages and prices are fully flexible.

The **classical model** of macroeconomics analyses the economy when wages and prices are fully flexible.

In the classical model, the economy is *always* at its full-employment output. Monetary and fiscal policy then affects prices but not output and employment.

In the very short run, before prices and wages have time to adjust fully to the pressures of demand and supply, the Keynesian model remains relevant. In the long run, after all prices and wages have adjusted, the classical model is relevant. A key issue in the modern macroeconomic debate is how quickly prices and wages *actually* adjust in the real world. Taken by themselves, neither the Keynesian nor the classical model is a complete description of how the economy works.

In seeking to understand macroeconomics, the challenge is to master the analysis of how the economy makes the transition from the Keynesian short run to the classical long run. Many of the policy issues most keenly debated today turn on differing assessments of how quickly the economy makes this transition. Hence in the second part of the chapter we examine in detail the process through which the economy responds to shocks to aggregate demand or aggregate supply.[1]

In this chapter we shall study the interaction of three markets: the markets for goods, money, and labour. This sounds more complicated than it is. The analysis breaks down into two parts. Aggregate demand depends on the interaction of the markets for goods and money. That is the part we have already learned. The new element is the introduction of aggregate supply, which involves the interaction of the markets for goods and labour.

26-1 The price level and aggregate demand

In this section we show that the real money supply is the key variable linking the aggregate demand for goods and the price level.

The **price level** is the average price of all the goods produced in the economy.

The real money supply is the nominal money supply divided by the price level. It shows the quantity of goods that nominal money will purchase. When the price level is fixed, the real money supply increases (decreases) only if the nominal money supply increases (decreases). But when the price level can change, the real money supply will rise (fall) if the price level falls (rises) while the nominal money supply remains unchanged.

In Figure 26-1(a) we plot real income against interest rates, and in Figure 26-1(b) we plot the price level against real income. Since we wish to isolate the effect of prices alone on aggregate demand, we hold constant all other determinants of aggregate demand such as the nominal money supply target, government spending, tax rates, and private sector expectations of future profits and future incomes.

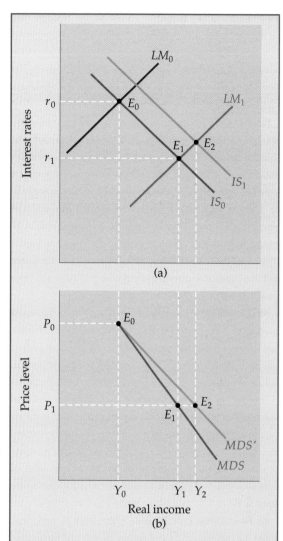

(a)

(b)

For a given nominal money supply, a lower price level increases the real money supply, shifts the LM schedule to the right, and increases equilibrium income. Given the IS schedule IS_0, a fall from P_0 to P_1 induces the shift from LM_0 to LM_1 and an increase from Y_0 to Y_1. The macroeconomic demand schedule MDS shows combinations of prices and income at which the money market is in equilibrium and actual output satisfies the aggregate demand for goods.

Figure 26-1   The macroeconomic demand schedule

Suppose the economy begins with a price level P_0. Given the fixed nominal money supply, P_0 determines the real money supply and hence the position of the LM schedule, say LM_0. Given the level of government spending and all other variables relevant to aggregate demand, we can draw the IS schedule, say IS_0, showing the different combinations of interest rates and income at which planned spending on goods equals actual output of goods. Notice crucially that for the moment we continue to assume that output is demand-determined and that firms will happily produce whatever output is demanded. Exploring whether this is true is precisely where we are going to use the aggregate supply schedule later in the chapter.

Planned spending on goods equals actual output of goods at all points on the IS schedule. And the money market is in equilibrium at all points on the LM schedule. Hence only at the intersection of the IS schedule (assumed for the moment to be IS_0) and the LM schedule (assumed for the moment to be LM_0) is the money market in equilibrium and the planned spending on goods equal to the actual output of goods. In Figure 26-1(a) this point is E_0. Hence in Figure 26-1(b) we draw E_0 showing that the money market clears and that planned and actual output are equal when the price level is P_0 and aggregate demand is Y_0.

Now consider a lower price level P_1. Given the fixed nominal money supply, the lower price level means a higher real money supply and shifts the LM schedule from LM_0 to LM_1. At each interest rate it takes a higher income level to induce people to hold the larger real money stock. Since the IS schedule remains IS_0, the point E_1 in Figure 26-1(a) now shows the combination of interest rates and income at which the money market is in equilibrium, and planned spending equals actual income *and* output. In Figure 26-1(b) we draw E_1 showing that, when the price level is P_1, the level of income at which planned spending and actual spending are equal is Y_1.

By considering each possible price level in turn, and hence the corresponding real money supply and position of the LM schedule, we trace out a set of points such as E_0 and E_1 in Figure 26-1(b). Joining these up, we obtain the macroeconomic demand schedule.

The **macroeconomic demand schedule MDS** shows the different combinations of the price level and real income at which planned spending equals actual output once interest rates are set at the level required to keep the money market in equilibrium.

The macroeconomic demand schedule slopes downwards because a lower price level increases the real money supply, reduces equilibrium interest rates, and increases aggregate demand. It is drawn for a given level of the nominal money supply target, government spending, and all other variables relevant to the level of aggregate demand. Real changes, such as an increase in government spending, which would shift the IS schedule upwards also shift upwards the MDS. At each price level – and hence each level of the real money

supply and position of the LM schedule – higher government spending will increase aggregate demand and income in the short run. Hence the macroeconomic demand schedule must shift upwards, showing a higher income at each price level. Similarly, for each price level, a higher nominal money supply target will imply an LM schedule further to the right and higher aggregate demand and actual income. Again, the macroeconomic demand schedule will shift upwards.

The macroeconomic demand schedule shows how lower prices increase aggregate demand by increasing the real money supply and reducing the equilibrium interest rate.

In Figure 26-1 the macroeconomic demand schedule MDS slopes down because a lower price level shifts the LM schedule as a higher real money supply reduces interest rates. This moves us down a given IS schedule.

The real balance effect

The IS schedule isolates the effect of interest rates on aggregate demand. Lower interest rates increase aggregate demand both by increasing investment demand and by shifting the consumption function upwards, through increasing the value of household wealth and also by making consumer borrowing cheaper. However, consumer wealth may increase for a reason not directly connected with the fall in interest rates. This extra wealth effect is the real value of that part of household wealth held in money. A lower price level increases the value of households' real money balances, adding directly to their wealth.

The **real balance effect** is the increase in consumption demand when the value of consumers' real money balances increases.

Because the IS schedule isolates the increase in aggregate demand due to interest rates *alone*, we must show the real balance effect as an upward shift in the IS schedule. At each interest rate, aggregate demand and output increase when real balances are higher. Figure 26-1 shows the consequence of including the real balance effect. If we begin with the price level P_0 and the schedules LM_0 and IS_0. E_0 remains the equilibrium in the goods and money markets. However, at the lower price level P_1, not only does the real money supply increase and the LM schedule shift from LM_0 to LM_1, but the real balance effects shifts the IS schedule from IS_0 to IS_1. Hence the new equilibrium is E_2, which we also plot in Figure 26-1(b).

Repeating the analysis for all price levels, we now get the macroeconomic demand schedule MDS'. It is flatter than MDS because a fall in prices increases aggregate demand not only through lower interest rates, but also through the real balance effect.

The credit channel

Recent research has emphasised another channel through which monetary policy can affect aggregate demand. It is called the credit channel of monetary policy. It acts to supplement the real balance effect.

The **credit channel** emphasises the effect of monetary policy on the value of collateral for loans, and hence on the supply of credit.

When you try to borrow money, the first thing the lender usually asks for is collateral – assets that can be taken for sale if you fail to repay the loan. Collateral is how lenders try to cope with the moral hazard and adverse selection arising from inside information. You know more about your ability and willingness to repay than they do.

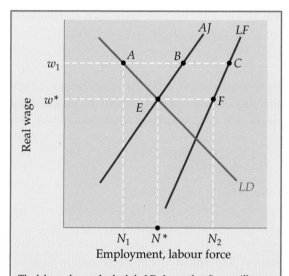

The labour demand schedule *LD* shows that firms will want more workers the lower is the real wage. The schedule *LF* shows that more people wish to be in the labour force the higher is the real wage. The schedule *AJ* shows how many workers have actually chosen to accept a job at each real wage. Labour market equilibrium occurs at *E*, where the employment demanded by firms equals the number of jobs that people wish to accept. The horizontal distance between the *AJ* and *LF* schedules shows voluntary unemployment at each wage rate. At the equilibrium wage rate the level of voluntary unemployment *EF* as a percentage of the labour force N_2 is called the natural rate of unemployment. When the real wage exceeds w^*, some people are involuntarily unemployed. They would like to take a job but can't find one. At the real wage w_1, involuntary unemployment is *AB* and voluntary unemployment is *BC*.

Figure 26-2   The labour market

Suppose the price of goods falls, increasing the real value of nominal assets. People now have more collateral they can offer banks and other lenders, who are therefore prepared to lend more than before at any particular interest rate. The supply of credit shifts and aggregate demand for goods increases.

There are really two types of credit channel, since there are two sources of changes in the value of collateral. First, as above, changes in goods prices can change the real value of nominal assets. Second, and quite distinct, changes in interest rates may affect the present value of future income from assets and hence the market value of assets themselves.

Both effects make the macroeconomic demand schedule have a flatter slope. As prices fall, they boost collateral directly. In addition, a higher real money stock requires a lower interest rate to achieve a corresponding increase in real money demand. The lower interest rates further boost the value of some collateral and encourage additional lending and spending.

Even after recognising both the real balance effect and the credit channel, the main conclusion of this section is unaffected. The macroeconomic demand schedule – the set of points at which the money market clears *and* planned spending on goods equals actual income and output – is a downward-sloping schedule relating the price level and the level of real income.

To determine which combination of prices and real income is relevant, we now turn to the link between the goods and labour market, summarized in the aggregate supply schedule.

26-2 The labour market and aggregate supply

The **aggregate supply schedule** shows the output that firms wish to supply at each price level.

Since output will depend on the inputs employed, we begin our analysis of aggregate supply by examining the labour market.

Labour demand

Firms have a given amount of machines, buildings, and land – we shall call these resources capital – which can be combined with labour to produce output for sale in the goods market. Figure 26-2 plots the labour demand schedule *LD* showing how much labour firms demand at each real wage.

The **real wage** is the nominal wage divided by the price level. It shows the quantity of goods that the nominal wage will buy.

We briefly review the analysis of Chapter 12 explaining why a fall in the real wage increases the quantity of labour demanded.

The **marginal product of labour** is the increase in output produced from a given capital stock when an additional worker is employed.

If the marginal product of labour exceeds the real wage, firms will increase profits by expanding employment, since the marginal benefit of another worker (the extra output) exceeds the marginal cost (the real wage). If the marginal product of labour is less than the real wage, firms will reduce employment, thereby avoiding the losses made by hiring the last worker whose marginal cost exceeded the marginal benefit. Hence firms maximize profits by increasing employment up to the point at which the marginal product of labour just equals the real wage.

With a fixed capital stock, the marginal product of labour falls as extra workers are hired. More and more workers have to share the same capital, and an extra worker can add less and less to total output. Hence firms demand a higher quantity of labour only if the real wage falls to compensate for the reduction in the marginal product of the last worker when more workers were employed. Figure 26-2 shows a down-sloping LD schedule for a given capital stock. An increase in the capital stock would shift the LD schedule upwards. Hence firms would demand more labour at each real wage.

Labour supply

We must distinguish between the people wishing to register as being in the labour force and the people who actually accept a job.

The **registered labour force** is the number of people registered as wishing to work. It is the number of people in employment *plus* the *registered unemployed*, those without a job who are registered as seeking a job.

In Figure 26-2 the schedule LF shows that more people join the labour force as the real wage increases. Being in the labour force has certain costs. People have to commute to work or spend time job hunting. They must give up leisure, and possibly hire babysitters or buy special clothing. As the real wage rises, more people find it worthwhile to enter the labour force in search of a job. We discussed the decision to join the labour force in Chapter 12.

The schedule AJ shows that as the real wage rises more people will accept jobs. Note that the AJ schedule is getting closer to the LF schedule as the real wage increases. For a given level of unemployment benefit, a higher percentage of the labour force are likely to accept jobs the higher is the real wage relative to the level of unemployment benefit.

The horizontal distance between the job acceptances schedule AJ and the labour force schedule LF shows how many people are unemployed because they refuse jobs at that real wage even though they are in the labour force and registered as seeking employment. Some people will inevitably be in between jobs. They will be temporarily unemployed in a world where the pattern of employment is continually changing. Others may have been tempted into the labour force at a particular wage rate in the hope of finding an unusually good offer, above the average wage. They are still searching for better offers.

An increase in the population of working age shifts both the LF and the AJ schedules to the right. More people enter the labour force and more will accept jobs. An increase in the real level of unemployment benefit will shift the AJ schedule to the left since people in the labour force can be more choosy about which job offer to accept. In the UK, people whose income from whatever source falls below a national minimum are entitled to income support. An increase in this benefit shifts the LF and AJ schedules to the left. Working is less attractive relative to not working, and fewer people will join the labour force or accept job offers.

Labour market equilibrium

In Figure 26-2 labour market equilibrium occurs at the real wage w^*. The quantity of employment N^* that firms demand equals the number of people wishing to take jobs at the real wage w^*. Everyone who wants a job at this real wage has found a job. Although we call this position the *full-employment equilibrium*, registered unemployment is not zero. Figure 26-2 shows that EF people are registered as unemployed. They want to be in the labour force but do not want a job at this real wage.

The **natural rate of unemployment** is the percentage of the labour force that is unemployed when the labour market is in equilibrium. They are **voluntarily unemployed** because they choose not to work at that wage rate.

At any real wage above w^* some people are *involuntarily unemployed*.

People are **involuntarily unemployed** when they would like to work at the going real wage but cannot find a job.

At the real wage w_1 there are thus two kinds of unemployment. A number of workers AB are involuntarily unemployed. They would like to accept jobs but firms are only offering N_1 jobs at this real wage. In addition a number of workers BC are voluntarily unemployed. The real wage $w1$ has tempted them into the labour force, perhaps in the hope of securing an unusually good offer in excess of w_1, but they are not actually prepared to take a job at the wage rate w_1.

When the labour market clears at the real wage w^*, employment can be increased only if firms are prepared to take on more workers at each wage rate (a rightward shift in the labour demand schedule) or if workers are prepared to work for lower wages (a rightward shift in the job acceptance schedule). Moreover, since the AJ schedule is probably quite steep in practice, the main consequence of a rightward shift in labour demand will probably be to bid up the equilibrium real wage rather than to increase equilibrium employment by very much. In contrast, when the real wage exceeds w^* and there are involuntarily unemployed workers, an increase in labour demand will lead to an increase in employment without increasing the real wage. In Figure 26-2 the number of workers AB would be happy to work at the real wage w if only firms offered more jobs.

Money wages, prices, and real wages   Figure 26-2 says that it is *real* and not *nominal* wages that matter in the labour market. Real wages tell firms the cost of a worker relative to the extra output that he or she can produce, and real wages tell households how many goods they can buy if they supply their labour. If all prices and all money wages double, nothing real changes. Workers can still buy as many goods with their wage income and firms' money wage costs have risen exactly in line with their output prices. Firms and workers who recognize that it is real wages that matter are said not to suffer from money illusion.

Money illusion exists when people confuse nominal and real variables.

Suppose all wages and prices double. If firms reduce employment because *money wages* have risen, they are suffering from money illusion. In fact, real wages are no higher than before.

If prices and money wages are fully flexible, real wages are also fully flexible. In the classical model this means that the labour market is *always* in equilibrium. Any excess supply of labour or demand for labour will (instantaneously) bid real wages back to their equilibrium level. Combining the assumption of full flexibility with the assumption of an absence of money illusion has two strong

implications. First, only real changes (a higher capital stock, higher population, etc.) shift labour demand and supply schedules and alter the equilibrium real wage. Hence any price increase *not* caused by a shift in these schedules must be matched by an equivalent change in money wages to leave real wages at their unchanged equilibrium level. Second, because real wages are unchanged, equilibrium employment must also be unchanged. We now develop these two points which are central to the classical model of output determination.

Suppose that output prices double but neither the labour supply nor labour demand schedules shift. At the original money wages the real wage has been halved. Hence there is excess demand for labour which bids up the money wage as firms compete for scarce workers. Only when the money wage doubles will real wages be restored to the equilibrium level and excess labour demand be eliminated. Employment will have returned to its equilibrium level. Thus, if neither the labour supply nor the labour demand schedules shift, and if wages are instantly and fully flexible, a change in prices will be instantly matched by a change in money wages precisely because both firms and workers care about real wages rather than money wages. And prices will have no effect on either the real wage or the level of employment. This is the strong result obtained in the classical model.

Employment, output, and prices

The last step on the supply side is to link employment, output, and prices. In the classical model, where both prices and money wages are flexible, real wages adjust to keep the labour market in equilibrium continuously. Employment is always at its full-employment level, where nobody is involuntarily unemployed. And this employment level is unaffected by changes in prices in the absence of any real shocks to the labour market.

Together with the existing capital stock, this full-employment level determines the quantity of output firms are willing and able to produce. *Potential output* is the output produced when labour is fully employed. Since the level of full employment is unaffected by changes in prices alone, we conclude that the level of output supplied by firms must also be independent of prices alone. Firms always supply full employment output or potential output in the classical model. In Figure 26-3 we show this result as a vertical aggregate supply schedule at the level of potential output Y_p.

The **aggregate supply schedule AS** shows the quantity of output firms wish to supply at each price. In the classical model there is no money illusion and money wages are flexible. The quantity of output supplied is then independent of prices, and the aggregate supply schedule is vertical at the level of potential output.

Before reading the next sentence, explain to yourself why in the classical model a fall in prices does *not* result in a reduction in the output that firms wish to supply. The answer? Beginning from labour market equilibrium, a fall in prices with a given money wage would increase the real wage, causing excess labour supply. Flexible money wages are immediately bid down until the real wage is restored to its equilibrium level and the excess supply is eliminated. Thus employment remains at its full-employment level and output at the potential output level.

Full wage flexibility is the critical assumption. Later in the chapter we examine how realistic an assumption it is.

26-3 The equilibrium price level

We have developed the macroeconomic demand schedule *MDS* and, for the classical model, the vertical aggregate supply schedule *AS*. Figure 26-3 shows that these two schedules intersect at *E*: output is at its potential level and the equilibrium price level is *P*.

The *equilibrium price level P* does a lot of work. It clears the markets for goods, labour, and money. The labour market is in equilibrium anywhere on the classical aggregate supply schedule. But at *E* we are also on the macroeconomic demand schedule along which the money market clears and aggregate demand for goods equals the actual output of goods.

Suppose prices were higher than *P*. The real money stock would be lower and interest rates higher. Hence aggregate demand would be lower. At any price above *P*, firms could not sell the output Y_p they wish to produce. In the classical model, firms immediately cut prices to eliminate excess demand. In so doing, they increase the real money supply, lower interest rates, and boost aggregate demand until they get back to equilibrium at *E* again. Conversely, if prices were below *P*, real money supply would be higher, interest rates lower, and aggregate demand would exceed potential output. Excess demand would bid up prices and return the economy to equilibrium at the point *E*, at the equilibrium price level *P*. Given this price level, we can calculate the money wage level that secures the real wage required for equilibrium in the labour market.

What determines prices?

The equilibrium price level *P* depends on a number of factors reflected in the positions of the macroeconomic demand schedule and the aggregate supply schedule. On the supply side, the level of potential output Y_p depends

chiefly on the labour supply and demand schedules that determine the equilibrium level of employment. If more workers want to work at each real wage, the labour supply schedule shifts to the right and the equilibrium level of full employment and potential output increases. Similarly, if firms have a larger capital stock, the marginal product of labour will rise at each level of employment, shifting the labour demand schedule to the right and increasing the level of equilibrium employment and potential output. Thus an increase in the willingness to work, or an increase in the stock of capital available, will increase potential output, shift the aggregate supply schedule to the right in Figure 26-3, and reduce the equilibrium price level. Lower prices boost aggregate demand in line with the increase in the potential output that firms wish to supply.

Although many factors can affect the macroeconomic demand schedule, we concentrate on those under government control. Other changes may be analysed in a similar manner. Under Keynesian assumptions, with prices given

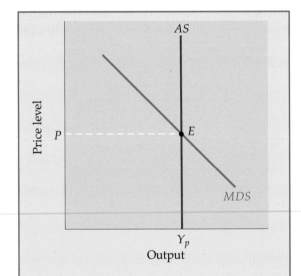

With flexible wages and prices, the real wage always adjusts to maintain full employment in the labour market. Given this labour input, firms produce potential output Y_p. The classical aggregate supply schedule *AS* is vertical at Y_p. Any change in prices is immediately reflected in a change in wages to maintain equilibrium real wages, full employment, and potential output. The macroeconomic demand schedule *MDS* shows points at which money demand equals money supply and planned spending on goods equals actual output. Hence, at *E* the markets for labour, goods, and money are all in equilibrium. The equilibrium price level is *P*, determined jointly by aggregate supply and macroeconomic demand.

Figure 26-3   Full equilibrium in the classical model

and output determined *only* by demand, we showed in the previous chapter that an increase in the nominal money supply, or in government spending, boosts aggregate demand and increases output. The situation is very different under the assumptions of the classical model.

26-4 Monetary and fiscal policy

Movements along the macroeconomic demand schedule show how changes in prices alter the real money supply, thus changing aggregate demand both by altering the interest rate and through the real balance effect on consumption demand. But changes in the nominal money supply target, or in fiscal policy, *shift* the macroeconomic demand schedule by altering the level of aggregate demand at each price level.

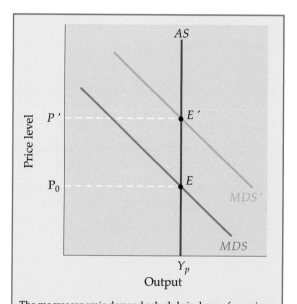

The macroeconomic demand schedule is drawn for a given nominal money supply target and a given fiscal policy. A doubling of the nominal money supply target increases aggregate demand at each price level, shifting MDS to MDS'. Since the equilibrium moved from E to E', in the classical model an increase in the money supply leads to higher prices but not higher output, which remains Y_p. In fact, if nominal money doubles, equilibrium prices must also double. Only then is the real money supply unaltered. Since interest rates are unaltered, aggregate demand will remain exactly Y_p as required. Fiscal expansion also shifts the macroeconomic demand schedule upwards. Since output supply remains Y_p, in the classical model prices must rise just enough to reduce the real money supply and increase interest rates enough to completely crowd out private expenditure, leaving aggregate demand unaltered at Y_p.

Figure 26-4 Monetary and fiscal expansion

Monetary policy

Suppose the economy begins in equilibrium at E in Figure 26-4 and that the nominal money supply target is doubled. Interest rates are cut to increase money demand. At each price level, the real money stock is now higher than before and the macroeconomic demand schedule shifts upwards from MDS to MDS'. At each price level, interest rates are lower and there is also a real balance effect on consumption.

The new equilibrium is E'. When all wages and prices have adjusted, the only effect of an increase in the nominal money supply is to increase the price level. There is no effect on output, which remains Y_p since the classical aggregate supply schedule is vertical. We can be even more specific. When the nominal money supply doubles, the macroeconomic demand schedule in Figure 26-4 must shift up from MDS to a position MDS' such that the equilibrium price level exactly doubles in moving from P_0 to P'. Why?

With a vertical supply schedule, real aggregate demand must remain unchanged at Y_p in the new equilibrium. This can happen only if the *real* money supply also remains unchanged. Otherwise interest rates would change, thus affecting aggregate demand. There would also be a real balance effect on consumption if the real money balances of households changed.

In the classical model, a change in the nominal money supply leads to an equivalent percentage change in nominal wages and the price level. The real money supply, interest rates, output, employment, and real wages are unaffected.

This proposition, that changes in the nominal money supply lead to changes in prices and wages, rather than to changes in output and employment, is one of the central tenets of the *monetarists*. Figure 26-4 shows that the proposition is correct in the classical model in which there is full wage and price flexibility and an absence of money illusion.

It is helpful to spell out the process through which the economy adjusts (instantaneously in the classical model) from E to E' when the nominal money supply is increased. Beginning from E, where the price level is P_0, an increase in nominal money increases the real money supply, lowers interest rates, and increases aggregate demand. Aggregate demand exceeds potential output but firms wish to supply Y_p whatever the price level. Excess demand for goods instantaneously bids up the price level until equilibrium is restored. Higher prices have offset the initial increase in the nominal money supply. The real money supply and interest rates have returned to their original level. And in the labour market, higher money wages have matched the increase in the price level, maintaining real wages at their original level.

BOX 26-1

Anchors away!

Now that we allowed the price level to be determined by market forces, we can finally explain why the economy needs a *nominal anchor*.

A **nominal anchor** eventually determines the level of other nominal variables. Market forces determine real variables.

Some real variables are the ratio of two nominal variables. If one nominal variable is fixed, this determines what level other nominal variables have to reach in order to achieve the correct real value in equilibrium. In this chapter the money supply target fulfils this role.

Imagine the Bank had no intermediate target. It simply set interest rates exogenously. In the classical model, money market equilibrium occurs when the real money supply M/P equals real mney demand, which depends on real output (fixed at Y_p) and interest rates (chosen exogenously).

The Bank passively supplies nominal money to achieve money market equilibrium but what is the equilibrium price level? If the market decides to make this larger, the Bank simply supplies more nominal money to maintain the correct real money stock. *Any* price level can be the equilibrium price level. There are an infinite number of possible equilibria! The economy has no nominal anchor.

An intermediate target of nominal money is one possible nominal anchor. Later chapters discuss other possibilities, notably a target for the price level or for the nominal exchange rate.

The economy has returned to full employment and potential output. In the classical model all these adjustments happen instantaneously.

Fiscal policy

Figure 26-4 may also be used to examine a fiscal expansion. At each price level, and corresponding value of the real money supply, an increase in government spending (or a cut in taxes) will increase aggregate demand, shifting MDS to MDS'. Again, since the classical aggregate supply schedule is vertical, the consequence of fiscal expansion must be a rise in prices from P_0 to P' but not an increase in output, which remains at its full-employment level Y_p.

The impact of the fiscal expansion is to increase aggregate demand if prices remain unchanged. But since firms wish to supply potential output, there is excess demand. Prices are bid up (instantaneously) until excess demand for goods is eliminated. Since firms wish to supply Y_p whatever the price level, higher prices must eliminate excess demand entirely by reducing the demand for goods. With a given nominal money supply, higher prices reduce the real money supply, drive up interest rates, and reduce private expenditure on consumption and investment. When aggregate demand has fallen to its full-employment level again, full equilibrium is restored. The economy has higher prices and nominal wages, a lower real money stock, and higher interest rates. Government spending is higher but private consumption and investment are sufficiently lower that aggregate demand remains at its full-employment level. The increase in government spending is exactly offset by a reduction in private expenditure on consumption and investment.

An increase in government spending **crowds out** an equal amount of private expenditure in the classical model, leaving aggregate demand unaltered at potential output.

There is a subtle difference between partial crowding out in the Keynesian model and this complete crowding out in the classical model. In the Keynesian model discussed in the previous chapter, prices and wages were fixed and output was demand-determined in the short run. Although the nominal and real money supplies were both fixed, an increase in government expenditure bid up equilibrium interest rates through its effect on aggregate demand and actual output. Higher output increased the demand for money and required a higher interest rate to maintain money market equilibrium. In turn, the higher interest rate reduced consumption and investment demand and partly offset the expansionary effect of higher government spending on aggregate demand and output.

In the classical model the mechanism is quite different. Now full-employment aggregate supply is the binding constraint. Whenever aggregate demand does not equal the potential output that firms wish to produce, excess supply or demand for goods will alter the price level and the real money supply until aggregate demand is restored to its full-employment level. Hence an increase in government expenditure (in real terms) must reduce consumption and investment together by exactly the same amount (in real terms). Only then can aggregate demand $C + I + G$ remain equal to the constant aggregate supply Y_p.

A moment for perspective

Before proceeding, it is worth stopping for a moment to take stock. Figure 26-5 is useful. Suppose the economy begins with the macroeconomic demand schedule *MDS* and is in full equilibrium at *E*. Then aggregate demand falls, say because firms get pessimistic about future profits and reduce investment demand. So the macroeconomic demand schedule shifts down from *MDS* to *MDS'*.

In the classical model, prices fall from *P* to *P'*. There is a corresponding fall in money wages to maintain real wages at the full-employment level. Lower prices increase the real money supply. The real balance effect on consumption, together with the lower interest rates required to induce people to hold the larger real money supply, increase aggregate demand again. They completely offset the initial downward shock to aggregate demand, restoring it to Y_p. The new equilibrium is at *E'*.

In contrast, the Keynesian model assumes that wages and prices are fixed. Beginning from equilibrium at *E*, the downward shift in *MDS* leads to a new equilibrium at *A*, with the price level still at *P*. This is an equilibrium in the sense that the money market clears and that planned spending on goods equals actual output of goods. But it is not a *full* equilibrium. Suppliers would really like to be producing Y_p but are only producing *Y*. Output is demand-determined.

What happens next in this story? One of two things. First, a Keynesian government may adopt an expansionary fiscal or monetary policy to shift the macroeconomic demand schedule up from *MDS'* to *MDS*, in which case suppliers will happily produce the extra output, taking them back on to their desired supply curve. Income will increase from *Y* to Y_p. Fiscal or monetary policy will be capable of increasing output precisely because the economy had spare resources at *A*. Suppliers were producing less than they wished. In consequence, they were demanding less labour than households wished to supply. At *A* there was involuntary unemployment in the labour market, since the quantity of employment had been reduced but the real wage was unchanged.

Alternatively, in the absence of a government boost to aggregate demand, it is possible that firms will begin to cut prices to try to raise output towards the level they would like to produce, and that workers will accept nominal wage

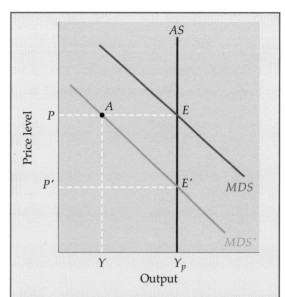

The economy begins in equilibrium at *E*. A downward shock shifts *MDS* to *MDS'*. In the classical model prices fall from *P* to *P'* to keep aggregate demand equal to potential output. Money wages fall to maintain equilibrium real wages in the labour market. In the Keynesian model, the failure of prices and wages to adjust leads to equilibrium at *A*. The money market clears and planned spending on goods equals actual output. But this is less than the output that firms wish to supply. With lower output and employment, but unchanged real wages, there is involuntary unemployment. Output and employment are demand-determined. Fiscal and monetary policy can shift *MDS'* to *MDS*. In the classical model this leads only to higher prices and higher money wages, a move from *E'* to *E*. In the Keynesian model it leads to an expansion of output and employment, a move from *A* to *E*.

Figure 26-5 Keynesian and classical models compared

cuts as involuntary unemployment puts downward pressure on wage rates. Thus it is possible that the economy will gradually drag its way down the schedule *MDS'* from *A* to *E'*, where full employment and equilibrium in all markets are restored.

Thus, on the one hand the classical model asserts that these price and wage adjustments happen immediately, or at least sufficiently quickly that, for the purpose of practical analysis, we can ignore the short time interval during which adjustment occurs. On the other hand, the extreme Keynesian model assumes that, in spite of the fact that at point *A* firms are not selling as much output as they wish and workers are not finding as many jobs as they wish, there is nevertheless no downward movement of prices and wages.

Viewed in this way, we can regard the Keynesian story as

BOX 26-2 — OECD estimates of output gaps 1980–2000

The output gap is the percentage deviation of actual output Y from potential output Y_P. Actual output is (relatively) easily measured. Potential output is not actually observed, but it is possible to make an educated guess about its level. Each year the Paris-based Organization for Economic Cooperation and Development (OECD) makes such estimates for all its member countries. The charts below show estimates for the UK, Germany and Finland.

The figure shows the UK slump of the early 1980s, as the Thatcher government fought to conquer inflation caused by previously high demand plus the second oil shock to the supply side; the boom of the mid 1980s; which in turn prompted another recession as government tightened policy to control inflation; and the steady recovery since 1993.

Germany also experienced a recession in the early 1980s as the Bundesbank raised interest rates to fight inflation from the second oil shock. At the end of the 1980s, German Unification led to a massive boost to demand as the government ran a large budget deficit in

order to finance restructuring in East Germany. Again, the Bundesbank responded to overheating by raising interest rates, causing a subsequent contraction of demand. We also show data for Finland, which initially benefited from an opening of trade to the east, but then suffered a dramatic collapse in its export markets in the early 1990s as the former Soviet Union imploded.

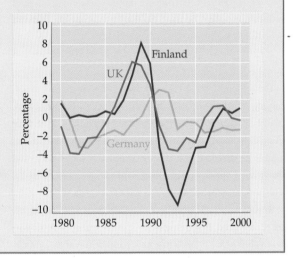

describing the behaviour of the economy in the short run, before prices and wages have time fully to adjust, and the classical story as describing the behaviour in the long run, after all wages and prices have had time to adjust. The crucial issue is how quickly this adjustment takes place in practice. The analysis of this issue is the focus of the rest of the chapter. How quickly does the classical long run become relevant?

Before leaving Figure 26-5 we should note two final points. First, there is no disagreement between the Keynesian model and the classical model about the fact that monetary and fiscal policy can shift the macroeconomic demand schedule. Expansionary policies shift the schedule upwards. In the Keynesian model the economy has spare resources which the expansion can mop up; below full employment, output is demand-determined. In contrast, in the classical model we are always at full employment; the aggregate supply schedule is vertical at this output, and the only consequence of expansionary policy is to bid up prices to knock out the effect of the expansion on aggregate demand and maintain demand at potential output Y_P.

Finally, in the classical model in which output is always Y_P, the way for the government to increase output and employment is not to adopt demand management policies to boost demand, but to adopt supply-side policies to boost full-employment output.

Supply-side economics is the pursuit of policies aimed not at increasing aggregate demand but at increasing aggregate supply.

Supply-side policies include measures such as tax cuts (designed to increase households' willingness to work), increasing equilibrium employment in the labour market, and shifting the aggregate supply curve for goods to the right. We discuss such policies in the next chapter, when we examine employment and unemployment in greater detail.

The rest of this chapter focuses on the adjustment process by which the economy responds to an initial shock. How does the economy make the transition from the Keynesian short run, before prices and wages have time to adjust, to the classical long run, in which all prices and wages have fully adjusted and full equilibrium in all markets has been restored?

26-5 The labour market and wage behaviour

In modern economies such as Western Europe and the United States, downward shocks to aggregate demand are followed by periods of unemployment that can be severe and persistent. Recessions are measured in years rather than weeks or months. Although the classical model is a useful guide to the long-run equilibrium to which the economy is adjusting, that adjustment can be slow and painful.

Adjustment is not immediate because prices and wages do not leap immediately to their new long-run equilibrium positions as the extreme classical model suggests. But why don't they? We must now come to grips with how wages and prices are actually set in the short run. Since firms must cover their costs of production, and since wages are usually the most important component in these costs, it is sluggish wage adjustment that is the most likely cause of a slow adjustment of prices to changes in aggregate demand. Thus we begin by examining how wages are actually set in the labour market.

To examine wage-setting behaviour we must think about the general relationship between firms and their work-forces.

Long-term job commitments

From the viewpoint of both firms and workers, a job is typically a long-term commitment. For the firm, it is expensive to hire and fire workers. Firing an existing worker usually means a severance or redundancy payment. It also means the loss to the firm of whatever special expertise the worker has built up on the job. Hiring a worker means advertising, interviewing, and training the new worker in the special features of work within that firm. Thus, firms are reluctant to hire and fire workers merely because of short-term fluctuations in demand and output.

From the worker's viewpoint, looking for new jobs is costly in time and effort. It can also mean beginning from scratch, throwing away experience, seniority, and perhaps the high wages that go with the high productivity that comes from having mastered a particular job in a particular firm. Like firms, workers are concerned with long-term arrangements. Since both firms and workers view job arrangements as long term, both want to reach some explicit or implicit understanding about the terms of work. This includes agreements about wages and how to handle fluctuations in the output produced by the firm.

Adjustments in labour input

A firm and its workers have *explicit* or *implicit labour contracts* specifying working conditions. These include normal hours, overtime requirements, regular wages, and pay schedules for overtime work. It is then up to the firm to set the number of hours, within the limits of these conditions, depending on how much output it wishes to produce in that week.

The firm's **labour input** is the total number of labour hours it employs in a given period.

Labour input may be changed by changing the number of hours worked by a given number of people, by changing the number of workers employed to work a given number of hours, or by some combination of the two. When the firm wishes to change its output, and hence its labour input, how does it choose whether to change the hours worked or the number of workers it employs?

Suppose the demand for a firm's output falls. Given the costs of hiring and firing labour, in the short run the firm's first reaction will be to abolish overtime and try to get by with the same labour force but a shorter working week. Factories may even close before the end of a normal working day. If demand does not recover, or declines still more, firms may then lay off some of their workers.

A **lay-off** is a temporary separation of workers from the firm.

Workers are made unemployed but they are not fired. Given their skills are specialized to that firm, there is a mutual understanding that the workers will be rehired when demand improves. The lay-off makes sense for the firm, which does not lose its skilled workers for ever, and makes sense for the workers, who need not look for jobs in which they will have to start learning skills from scratch. But when the firm finally concludes that demand prospects are poor, it may make workers redundant, or fire them permanently.

Conversely, during a boom a firm's reaction will be to get its existing workforce to work overtime. Then it may seek temporary workers to supplement the existing labour force. Only when the firm is confident that higher sales can be sustained is it likely to embark on a major recruiting programme. We now discuss the implications of this pattern of hours and employment adjustment for wage settlements.

Wage adjustment

In modern industrial economies, wages are not set in a daily auction in which the equilibrium wage clears the market for labour. We have explained that firms and workers both stand to gain by reaching long-term understandings. To some extent this mutual commitment insulates a firm and its workforce from conditions in the labour market as a whole.

Nor can a firm and its workforce spend every day haggling about terms and conditions of employment. Bargaining is a costly process, using up valuable time which workers and managers could have been using to produce and sell output. Although there may be regular meetings to deal with minor grievances, in practice the costs of bargaining about the firm's general wage structure mean that such negotiations can be undertaken only infrequently. In the UK this usually means once a year. In the United States many bargains are for a three-year period.

The existence of bargaining costs (which may include the use of strikes initiated by the workforce or lock-outs initiated by the managers) provides a microeconomic rationale for wage changes only at discrete intervals. The macroeconomic consequence is that immediate wage adjustment to demand shocks is ruled out. At best, many firms will have to wait until the next scheduled date for a revision in the wage structure. In practice, complete wage adjustment is unlikely to take place even then. Why is adjustment even more sluggish?

Suppose there is a fall in aggregate demand and some firms have made workers unemployed. Other firms may still be doing all right. Merely because there is a pool of involuntarily unemployed workers prepared to work at, or even below, the going wage it does not mean that all firms will use this excuse to reduce wages. First, a new worker is a poor substitute for an existing worker familiar with the job and the firm. Second, long-term co-operation between a firm and its workforce is more important than short-term gains from forcing wages down a little. The reputation of a firm as an employer is an important determinant of the firm's ability to attract and retain its skilled workers in the long run.

If its existing labour force dislikes fluctuations in the wage rate, the firm may smooth out wages in the long run to keep its labour force happy. The firm will lose out in the times when it would like to be cutting wages, but it will gain in the

times when demand is high and labour market pressures are tending to raise wages. Thus, firms and workers may reach an implicit understanding that wages will neither be drastically cut during slumps nor drastically raised during booms.

In Section 12-7 we discussed other reasons why involuntary unemployment might not be immediately eliminated by instantaneous wage adjustment. We grouped these arguments under the headings of trade union effects, the effect of scale economies, insider–outsider effects, and arguments based on efficiency wages when information on worker quality and effort is expensive for the firm to collect. If you do not recall these arguments in detail, we strongly suggest that you go back to Section 12-7 before continuing with this chapter.

Recap

Table 26-1 summarizes our discussion and provides a road map for the rest of the chapter. The table lays out the labour market adjustment in the short run, the medium run, and the long run. Based on our reading of the empirical evidence, we also indicate how long each of these 'runs' might be. We suggest three months for the short run, one year for the medium run, and four to six years for the long run. We should emphasize that it is precisely on this assessment that many macroeconomists disagree. Many monetarists think that adjustment will be faster than we have suggested and some Keynesians think it will be considerably slower than we have suggested. But the assessment of Table 26-1 corresponds to the view of many mainstream economists.

In the short run, variations in labour input largely take the form of changes in hours, perhaps supplemented by lay-offs or recalls from lay-offs. In the medium run, as changes in labour demand persist, the firm begins to alter its permanent workforce. The alternative, continuing to run a factory with large overtime or short-time working, is simply too expensive. In the long run adjustment becomes complete. By then, firms have adjusted to the new long-run equilibrium and the classical model becomes relevant.

In the short run the wage structure within a firm is largely

Table 26-1	Adjustment in the labour market		
	Short-run (3 months)	Medium-run (1 year)	Long-run (4–6 years)
Wages	Largely given	Beginning to adjust	Clearing the labour market
Hours	Demand-determined	Hours/employment	Normal work week
Employment	Largely given	mix adjusting	Full employment

given. The firm has a bit of flexibility over earnings as distinct from negotiated wage rates, because fluctuations in overtime and short time affect average hourly earnings. But this flexibility is limited. In the medium run the firm begins the process of adjusting the wage structure, and in the long run this process has been completed and the economy as a whole is back on the vertical classical aggregate supply schedule at full-employment output.

Although the table suggests that firms will be slow to fire workers, the fact that firms make long-run decisions means that they will also be slow to take on new workers when demand picks up or wages are reduced. While this means that involuntary or Keynesian unemployment may be slow to build up, it also means that it is not quickly eliminated once it has built up.

Having examined behaviour in the labour market, we turn now to the link between the labour market and the goods market.

26-6 Wages, prices, and aggregate supply

Figure 26-6 shows the implications of our discussion of short-term wage adjustment. Suppose the economy begins at full employment at A. In the short run there is a very flat wage schedule WW. If firms wish to produce more output, their first reaction will be to use overtime payments to get more labour input out of their existing labour force, producing at a point such as C. Conversely, if demand for their output falls, firms will initially meet this reduction in demand and output by reducing the working week, ending overtime, and slightly reducing hourly earnings in consequence. Faced with this reduction in demand, the short-term response will be to produce at a point such as B.

If demand does not pick up, in the medium run firms will begin making workers unemployed and cutting wages. However, wage rates are unlikely to be reduced all the way to W_2, the level we assume would restore full employment in the classical long run. Rather, in the medium run there will be partial adjustment, say to the wage schedule WW_1. As we shall shortly explain, lower wages will allow lower prices, and this will partly restore the level of aggregate demand by increasing the real money supply and reducing interest rates. But sluggish wage adjustment implies that this adjustment will not be accomplished fully in the medium run. Hence firms will still be producing an output below potential output Y_p.

Only in the long run is the wage schedule finally reduced to WW_2. Now, wages and prices have fallen sufficiently to

increase the real money supply and lower interest rates to the extent required to restore aggregate demand to its full-employment level. In the absence of any further shock to aggregate demand, firms will now be at the new long-run equilibrium A_2 at the wage rate W_2. Any temporary fluctuations in demand around this new full-employment position will be met by temporary movements along the new wage schedule WW_2.

Now we make explicit the link between wages in the labour market and prices in the goods market.

The short-run aggregate supply schedule

Only in some markets, notably agricultural markets such as wheat and soya beans, where there is a standardized product, are prices set in a competitive auction. In most cases prices are set by sellers. Ford sets the price of its cars and Sony the price of its televisions. How are prices set in practice?

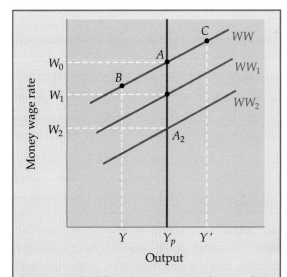

Beginning at the full employment point A, there is a short-run money wage schedule WW along which output changes are met primarily by changing hours of work and overtime bonuses. A permanent fall in aggregate demand initially will be met by a move from A to B. Output is cut and short-time working introduced. As time elapses, workers are fired and wage adjustment begins. The new wage schedule is WW_1. Since wages have not fallen enough to restore full employment, the economy is at a point on WW_1 to the left of Y_p. Only in the long run do money wages and prices fall enough to restore aggregate demand and attain full employment and potential output, at the point A_2. Temporary fluctuations in demand around full employment will then be met by movements along WW_2 and will be reflected chiefly in temporary fluctuations in hours worked.

Figure 26-6   Wage adjustment

In Part 2 we examined a number of microeconomic theories of pricing and saw that market structure would play an important role. In some market structures, such as perfect competition or pure monopoly, prices were related to the marginal cost of producing the last unit of output, with the mark-up of price over marginal cost being determined by the extent of the firm's monopoly power, if any. In other theories, such as the limit pricing model of competition between a few firms in an industry, prices were set as a mark-up on average costs, with the size of the mark-up depending on the threat of entry of new firms to the industry if profits became too large.

Whether we base our analysis of pricing on rigorous microeconomic analysis or on the view of pragmatic managers that prices should cover costs and overheads and leave a reasonable profit margin, we reach the same conclusion: when firms' costs rise, they have to raise prices.

In modern economies, labour costs are the major part of the costs of production. Of course raw materials, land, and capital are also important. But for the moment we concentrate on wages as the chief determinant of costs.

With this simplification we can move directly from a wage schedule WW in Figure 26-6 to an equivalent short-run aggregate supply schedule SAS in Figure 26-7. All we do is change the vertical axis from 'wages' to 'prices'.

The **short-run aggregate supply schedule** shows the prices charged by firms at each output level, given the wages they pay.

Figure 26-7 shows the short-run aggregate supply schedule SAS corresponding to the wage schedule WW. Suppose we begin at A in both diagrams. The economy is at full employment and all markets clear. Prices are P_0 in Figure 26-7 because negotiated money wages are W_0 in Figure 26-6. Beginning from this inherited level of money wage settlements, firms will move along the supply schedule SAS in the short run. Firms can supply a lot of extra output in the short run at only a slightly higher price. A slightly higher price allows firms to cover the overtime payments needed to produce extra output. But, facing a lower price, firms will want to cut back output a lot. At the inherited wage rates, firms have only limited scope for cutting costs, and will have to reduce output a lot if prices fall. In the medium run, however, negotiated wage rates gradually adjust. If demand and output remain low, wage rates will gradually fall, allowing firms to move on to a lower wage schedule in Figure 26-6 and a lower short-run aggregate supply schedule such as SAS_1 in Figure 26-7. And if full employment and potential output are still not restored, in the longer

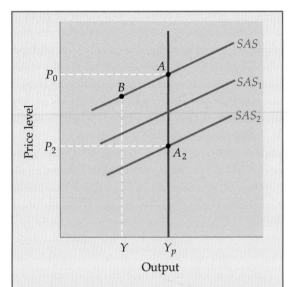

Firms base prices on wage costs. The short-run aggregate supply schedules correspond to the wage schedules in Figure 26-6. For a given negotiated money wage rate and height of the wage schedule, firms can vary labour costs only by affecting overtime payments and other bonuses. Hence, in the short run they require only a small increase in price to produce more output but can afford to charge only a slightly lower price when producing less output. In the longer term, as firms negotiate lower wages and move on to lower wage schedules, they can also cut their prices. The short-run supply schedule shifts down. At A_2 prices have fallen enough to restore the full-employment level of aggregate demand, and full equilibrium is restored.

Figure 26-7   Short-run aggregate supply

run negotiated wage rates will fall yet again, leading to a short-run aggregate supply schedule such as SAS_2.

Thus, if demand falls, firms cannot cut their prices much in the short run. They can only move back along the relatively flat short-run supply schedule SAS. In the medium run, firms will be able to negotiate lower wage settlements if demand remains low and they have to start sacking workers. When the wage schedule shifts down to WW_1 in Figure 26-6, firms can cut prices much more. Corresponding to this wage schedule, the short-run aggregate supply schedule in Figure 26-7 will now be SAS_1. And in the long run, with the wage schedule down to WW_2, the short-run aggregate supply schedule will be SAS_2. Firms have reached A_2, at which they are back on their vertical long-run aggregate supply schedule. There is full employment, and firms are producing potential output. Prices have fallen to increase the real money supply and reduce interest rates to the extent required to restore aggregate demand to its full-employment level.

We now use the short-run aggregate supply schedule to develop a realistic picture of the adjustment of the economy to disturbances. Anticipating our main results, we shall show the following. Because the short-run aggregate supply schedule is very flat, a shift in aggregate demand will lead mainly to changes in output rather than changes in prices in the short run. This is the Keynesian feature. But because deviations from full employment gradually change wages and prices over time, the economy gradually works its way back to full employment. That is the classical feature.

26-7 The adjustment process

We now combine the macroeconomic demand schedule with the short-run aggregate supply schedule to show how demand or supply disturbances work themselves out in the adjustment process. In combining the macroeconomic demand schedule and the short-run aggregate supply schedule, we are assuming that even in the short run the goods market clears. Demand for goods and supply of goods are equal. But short-run aggregate supply gradually changes over time as firms are able to secure wage adjustment towards the level of wages that will restore full employment and potential output, placing firms eventually on their long-run aggregate supply schedule.

In this more sophisticated analysis, we have finally abandoned the simplifying assumption that output is demand-determined when aggregate demand lies below the level of potential output. In the short run, firms are also on their short-run supply schedules producing as much as they wish, *given the inherited level of money wage bargains*.

Which market is not clearing in the short run? The labour market. Sluggish wage adjustment is preventing immediate adjustment back to full-employment equilibrium. As we shall see, when aggregate demand for goods is reduced, firms cut back on the output they wish to produce and the jobs they wish to offer. Since wages do not fall immediately, there is involuntary unemployment. Until wages fall in the long run to restore full employment, there will be more people wishing to take a job than there are jobs on offer. Some people will want to take a job at the going wage but be unable to find a job. Since there is excess supply of labour at the wage rate ruling in the short run, *employment* is demand-determined in the short run. Only when wages have eventually fallen to eliminate involuntary unemployment will full employment be restored.

We can use Figure 26-8 to analyse a shift in the macroeconomic demand schedule. To be specific, suppose there is a once-and-for-all reduction in the nominal money supply

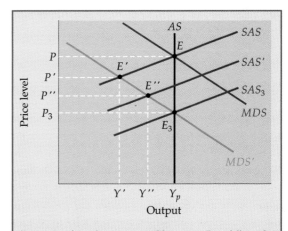

Beginning from long-run equilibrium at E, a fall in the nominal money supply shifts MDS to MDS'. Given the inherited money wage level, and the short-run supply schedule SAS, the goods market clears at E'. There is a large output fall, from Y_p to Y'. Since prices fall from P to P' but money wages are unaltered, real wages rise. There is involuntary unemployment in the labour market. Gradually this leads to reductions in money wages. Hence the short-run supply schedule for goods shifts from SAS to SAS' and the goods market now clears at P''. As money wages keep falling, the short-run aggregate supply schedule shifts down until it reaches SAS_3. Money wages and prices have now fallen in the same proportion as the original reduction of the nominal money supply. Full equilibrium is re-established at E_3.

Figure 26-8   A fall in the nominal money supply

target. Initially the economy is at E in full equilibrium, producing potential output Y_p at an equilibrium price level P. Money wages W clear the labour market at the equilibrium real wage $w = W/P$. The point E lies on the macroeconomic demand schedule MDS along which the money market clears and actual output equals planned spending. It also lies on the long-run aggregate supply schedule which is vertical at potential output Y_p.

When the nominal money supply is reduced, aggregate demand falls and the macroeconomic demand schedule shifts down from MDS to MDS'. In the classical model there is immediate price and wage adjustment to maintain the economy at full employment and potential output. The equilibrium price level falls immediately to P_3 and the level of money wages falls to W_3 such that the real wage W_3/P_3 remains at its unchanged full-employment level. The new equilibrium point is E_3.

The reduction in the price level from P to P_3 has just matched the reduction in the nominal money supply. The real money supply is unaltered. Interest rates are unaltered.

Aggregate demand is unaltered. No real variables have changed. That is why the economy is able to remain at its full-employment position.

Now we recognize that the classical results will be valid only in the long run. Eventually the economy will move from E to E_3 in Figure 26-8, but we wish to study the adjustment process while wages, and hence prices, are slow to adjust. When the money supply is first reduced, the economy faces the short-run aggregate supply schedule SAS, reflecting the money wage settlements already in force.

In the short run, the downward shift in MDS is met by a move from E to E'. Since firms have few opportunities for reducing costs per unit output, they will want to cut back output a lot. At E' the goods market is clearing. We are on both the demand schedule MDS' and the supply schedule SAS but prices have not fallen much. Output has fallen a lot. Since money wages have not yet adjusted, *real* wages have actually risen. The money wage is unaltered and the price level is lower. Once firms start adjusting employment, they will be offering fewer jobs but more workers will want to take a job. There will be involuntary unemployment.

In the medium run this starts to bid down money wages. With a lower wage settlement, firms move on to a lower short-run aggregate supply schedule, say SAS'. The goods market now clears at E''. Lower goods prices mean that the original money wage cut turns out not to have reduced real wages so much. Some involuntary unemployment persists. But since prices are lower at E'' than E', aggregate demand for goods has increased. The real money supply has begun to increase, interest rates have fallen, and the economy has moved down the demand schedule MDS', showing that output has begun to move back towards its full-employment level.

Only in the long run is full adjustment completed. Money wages have fallen in proportion to the original reduction in the nominal money supply. And so have prices. The short-run aggregate supply schedule has shifted down to SAS_3 in Figure 26-8 and the economy is in full equilibrium at the point E_3, lying both on the short-run and the long-run aggregate supply schedules. Prices have fallen sufficiently to restore the real money supply, interest rates and aggregate demand to their original full-employment position. And in the labour market, the real wage has returned to its full-employment level. Involuntary unemployment has been eliminated.

Figure 26-9 shows how the decrease in the nominal money supply has affected output and prices. At time t_0 there was a once-and-for-all reduction in the nominal money supply. Initially output fell sharply to Y' but then it

began to move back towards its full-employment level as wage and price reductions increased the real money supply, reduced interest rates and boosted aggregate demand. Once wages and prices had fallen in proportion to the original fall in the nominal money supply, all real variables were back to their original position and full equilibrium had been restored.

Figure 26-9 shows how the real world lies between the extreme simplifications adopted by the simple Keynesian model and the simple classical model. In practice, prices and wages are neither fully flexible nor fully fixed. A monetary contraction has real effects in the short run since output and employment are reduced. But after wages and prices have fully adjusted, the only consequence of a monetary

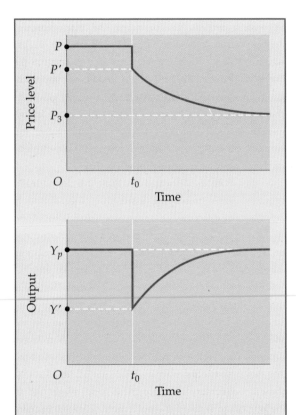

The economy begins at potential output Y_p with an equilibrium price level P. At time t_0 there is a once-and-for-all reduction in the nominal money supply. In Figure 26-8 the economy moves from E to E'. Here this is shown as falls in the price level to P' and in output to Y'. Thereafter, as wages slowly fall, the price level gradually falls to its new long-run equilibrium level P_3. As the real money supply gradually increases again, output rises slowly back to Y_p. Employment follows a path similar to that shown for output.

Figure 26-9   Adjustment paths for prices and output

contraction is a reduction in nominal wages and prices. No real variables have changed, and the economy has returned to full employment and potential output.

Similar conclusions apply in other contexts. We strongly suggest that you use a figure like Figure 26-8 to analyse for yourself the short-run and long-run effects of a change in fiscal policy.

This analysis also demonstrates the possibility of a *business cycle*. An initial expansion (a boom) or an initial contraction (a slump) will set in motion forces that gradually reverse the initial movement and bring the economy back to full employment and potential output. But it takes time. We examine business cycles in detail in Chapter 30.

26-8 A shift in aggregate supply

When aggregate demand increases and the *MDS* schedule shifts upwards, output and employment temporarily increase until a temporary period of inflation has reduced the real money supply sufficiently to restore aggregate demand to the level of potential output. The effect of a shift in aggregate supply is very different. Suppose a change in social attitudes towards women working leads to more people wishing to work at each real wage rate. The labour supply schedule shifts to the right, increasing the level of equilibrium employment in the long run. Figure 26-10 shows this as an increase in potential output from Y_p to Y'_p.

Until this pool of extra labour starts to reduce wage settlements, there will be no effect on the short-run aggregate supply schedule. Beginning from the point *E*, the schedule remains *SAS* in the short run. Prices, output, and employment are unaffected. Since more people wish to work, recorded unemployment will rise.

Over time, this bids down wages, and the short-run aggregate supply schedule will shift from *SAS* to *SAS'*. With lower wages and prices, the real money supply and aggregate demand increase and the new equilibrium will be *E'*. Unemployment has been reduced but not eliminated. Only in the long run do wages and prices fall sufficiently to

establish equilibrium at *E**. Output and employment are permanently lower than at the original equilibrium *E*. Table 26-2 summarizes the important differences in the way the economy reacts to a supply shift and a demand shift.

An adverse supply shock

So far, wages have been the only determinant of costs, prices, and the aggregate supply schedule. We now recognize other cost items. Suppose the price of oil increases. In Figure 26-11 we begin from long-run equilibrium at *E*. Even with given wage rates, the schedule *SAS* no longer allows firms to cover costs when oil prices increase. At any output level firms have to charge a higher price, thus passing on the increase in the price of oil inputs.

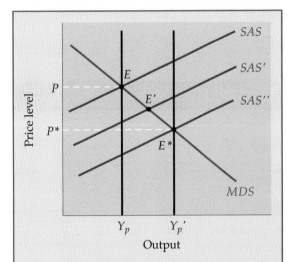

An increase in the willingness to work increases the level of full employment and increases potential output from Y_p to Y'_p. Beginning from *E*, initially there is no effect on output or prices, so unemployment increases. Gradually this leads to lower wages. The short-run aggregate supply schedule shifts from *SAS* to *SAS'* and the new equilibrium is *E'*. Eventually wages fall sufficiently to shift *SAS'* to *SAS''*, and full employment is attained at *E**. Prices are permanently lower and output permanently higher in the long run.

Figure 26-10   An increase in potential output

Table 26-2   Reactions of the economy to shifts in demand and supply

	Effect on output		Effect on price level	
Rightward shift of:	Short run	Long run	Short run	Long run
Aggregate demand	Rise	Zero	Rise	Higher
Aggregate supply	Zero	Higher	Zero	Lower

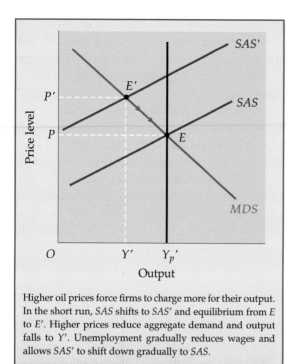

Higher oil prices force firms to charge more for their output. In the short run, *SAS* shifts to *SAS'* and equilibrium from *E* to *E'*. Higher prices reduce aggregate demand and output falls to *Y'*. Unemployment gradually reduces wages and allows *SAS'* to shift down gradually to *SAS*.

Figure 26-11   An adverse supply shock

This shifts *SAS* up to *SAS'*. The new short-run equilibrium is at *E'*. Prices rise but output and employment fall. Higher prices reduce the real money supply and aggregate demand.

An **adverse supply shock** increases prices and reduces output in the short run.

In the long run, one of two things may happen. Figure 26-11 illustrates the case in which unemployment gradually bids down wages, *SAS'* gradually shifts downwards, and the economy gradually moves down the *MDS* schedule back to the original equilibrium at *E*.

Although oil prices are permanently higher, wages and other prices have fallen sufficiently that the aggregate price level has returned to *P*, thus restoring aggregate demand to the level of potential output Y_p.

In practice, a second outcome is more probable. Since the price of oil has risen relative to other commodities, firms will try to get by with less oil. Since oil is one of the inputs with which labour works to produce output, labour will now have fewer materials with which to work in producing output. Thus, at each employment level the marginal product of labour is likely to be reduced. The labour demand schedule will shift downwards. Because it will now cross the labour supply schedule at a lower level of employ-

ment, full employment and potential output will be reduced. Hence a more complete analysis of an oil shock would take account not merely of the short-term effect of higher prices in reducing aggregate demand, as shown in Figure 26-11, but also of the possibility that potential output Y_p may be permanently reduced. If so, the new long-run equilibrium will occur at a point higher up the *MDS* schedule than *E* in Figure 26-10. Output will be lower and the price level higher in the long run.

A wage increase   Figure 26-11 can also be used to show the effect of an increase in trade union power. Beginning from *E*, an 'unjustified' wage increase will force firms to raise prices and will move *SAS* to *SAS'*. Output will fall and unemployment increase. Gradually, this is likely to put downward pressure on wages and to allow the supply schedule to shift back to *SAS* again. Workers who keep their jobs during the transitional period will temporarily have higher real wages, but other workers will be temporarily priced out of a job while aggregate demand is reduced by higher prices and a lower real money supply. Nevertheless, those who expected (correctly or mistakenly) to keep their jobs during the transitional period may succeed in outvoting the other workers and forcing the union to press for the wage increase.

26-9 The business cycle

Shifts in aggregate supply and demand generate changes in the level of output and prices during transitional periods of adjustment. Shifts in aggregate supply and demand are thus the underlying source of the business cycle.

The **business cycle** is the tendency for output and employment to fluctuate around their long-term trends.

Although the economy is continuously buffeted by small shocks, major shocks are infrequent. However, in both 1973 and 1979 there were major supply-side shocks in the form of the oil price increases. In the UK the latter was exacerbated by an increase in VAT from 8 to 15 per cent, which dramatically increased the prices that suppliers had to charge their customers.

Figure 26-12 shows that these two supply-side shocks, displayed as temporary increases in the annual inflation rate, were quickly followed by sharp rises in unemployment, as Figure 26-11 predicts. But we can also identify periods in which demand-side shocks were occurring.

Figure 26-12 shows clearly the Heath boom of 1972–73 and the Lawson boom of 1986–88, two periods when

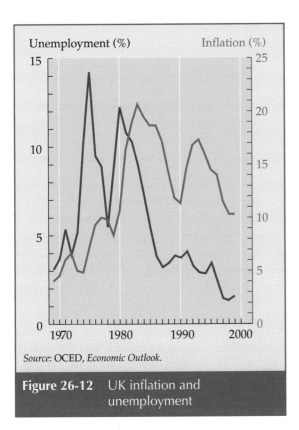

Source: OCED, *Economic Outlook.*

Figure 26-12 UK inflation and unemployment

better understanding of the exact timing of the adjustment responses. But the big picture comes through clearly. The rate of inflation and the level of output are being moved around by shifts in aggregate supply and aggregate demand to which the economy responds only sluggishly.

Persistent inflation A close look at Figure 26-12 leaves us with one remaining puzzle. Although swings in unemployment reflect shifts in aggregate supply or demand, there is *always* inflation. Inflation slows down when unemployment is high but prices never actually fall. Since prices rise essentially because wages rise, this means that money wages are rising even when unemployment is 10 per cent of the labour force. Why aren't workers taking wage cuts?

The answer in part is that they are. It is real wages that firms and workers care about. Suppose inflation is 10 per cent. Workers need a 10 per cent rise in money wages just to maintain real living standards. If workers settle for 7 per cent, they are taking a 3 per cent cut in real wages. But to expect workers actually to cut *money* wages by, say, 5 per cent when prices are rising at 10 per cent would be to suppose that workers would accept a 15 per cent reduction in real wages in the course of a single year. In practice, the labour market rarely adjusts this quickly.

Hence, money wages continue to increase, even during a slump, because prices have been rising and are expected to continue to rise. And in seeking money wage increases that, at least in part, allow them to protect their living standards, workers reach deals with firms that ensure that wage costs will keep rising and that prices will have to be raised again. We examine the interaction of rising wages and rising prices at length in Chapter 28, where we deal explicitly with the question of inflation.

expansionary policy led to sharp falls in unemployment which then increased the inflation rate. Equally, we can see that deliberately tight policy in 1980–82 and 1990–92 did succeed in getting inflation down, but only at the cost of a temporary increase in unemployment.

Thus recent economic history illustrates the usefulness of the supply and demand apparatus we have developed in this chapter to analyse short-run adjustment. We could have made the theory more sophisticated, allowing for example a

SUMMARY

● The classical model of macroeconomics assumes full flexibility of wages and prices, and the absence of money illusion.

● The macroeconomic demand schedule shows at each price level the income at which planned spending on goods equals actual output when the money market is also in equilibrium. The schedule slopes downward. Lower prices increase the real money supply, increasing aggregate demand both through lower interest rates and through the real balance and credit channel effects.

● An increase in the real wage increases the quantity of labour supplied but reduces the quantity of labour demanded. Since the marginal product of labour declines as employment increases, firms need a lower real wage to match the declining marginal product of labour when more workers are employed.

● In the classical model, there is always full employment and the aggregate supply schedule is vertical at the corresponding level of potential output. The equilibrium price level is determined by the intersection of the aggregate supply schedule and the macroeconomic demand schedule. The markets for goods, money, and labour are all in equilibrium.

● In this model, fiscal or monetary expansion cannot increase output. Rather, they increase prices until the real money supply has fallen to restore aggregate demand to the level of potential output that firms wish to supply.

● Supply-side economics considers how to increase potential output by providing incentives to increase the supplies of factor inputs.

● In practice, wages change only slowly in response to shocks since job arrangements are long term. Firms incur costs in hiring and firing, and workers lose seniority when they switch jobs and have to learn particular skills afresh. Firms and workers reach implicit understandings about terms and conditions of work.

● In the short run, variations in labour input are met chiefly by changing hours. Only in the longer run is the quantity of workers adjusted.

● Wage adjustment is sluggish not merely because wage bargaining is infrequent, but because workers prefer their long-term employers to smooth wages. Trade unions, scale economies, insider–outsider distinctions, and efficiency wages may all act to reduce short-run wage flexibility.

● Prices are based chiefly on labour costs. The short-run aggregate supply schedule shows how much firms wish to produce given the wage settlement in force. Output is responsive to small price changes since small variations in overtime and other bonuses allow firms to produce the extra output at only slightly different labour costs. As wage adjustment takes place, the short-run supply schedule shifts and prices change much more.

● Thus, in the short run prices and wages are capable only of small changes. In the long run, a period of several years, they are fully flexible. Hence the Keynesian model is a good guide to short-term behaviour but the classical model describes behaviour in the long run.

● A shift in the macroeconomic demand schedule, whether caused by changes in private expenditure or by changes in fiscal and monetary policy, will thus affect output more than prices in the short run. But in the long run the economy returns to potential output as induced prices changes alter the real money supply and the level of aggregate demand.

● A shift to the right in the aggregate supply schedule may have little short-run effect, but in the long run output is permanently higher at the new level of potential output and prices are permanently lower, thus ensuring a corresponding increase in aggregate demand.

● Sluggish adjustment implies that shocks to aggregate demand or aggregate supply set off a business cycle. Because shocks are irregular, the business cycle is also irregular.

KEY TERMS

- Classical model 426
- Price level 427
- Macroeconomic demand schedule 428
- Credit channel 429
- Real balance effect 429
- Aggregate supply schedule 429
- Real wage 429
- Marginal product of labour 430
- Registered labour force 430
- Natural rate of unemployment 430
- Voluntary and involuntary unemployment 430–431
- Money illusion 431
- Nominal anchor 434
- Crowding out 434
- Supply-side economics 436
- Labour input 437
- Lay-off 437
- Short-run aggregate supply schedule 440
- Adverse supply shock 444
- Business cycle 444

REVIEW QUESTIONS

1 (a) Define the macroeconomic demand schedule. (b) What happens to the schedule if (i) consumers' propensity to save increases? (ii) prices fall? (iii) investment demand increases?

2 Explain how and whether an increase in the money supply affects prices and output in the classical model.

3 How does a larger capital stock affect the long-run aggregate supply schedule?

4 How do the following affect the short-run supply schedule and hence output and prices in the short run: (a) a higher income tax rate? (b) an increase in labour productivity? (c) an increase in the money supply?

5 'Higher unemployment means lower inflation.' Is this true for (a) a supply schedule shift? (b) a demand schedule shift?

6 Using aggregate supply and demand schedules, explain why a cut in the money supply aimed at reducing the price level could be costly to society in the short run.

7 Draw a diagram showing how you expect the economy to react to a big increase in the VAT rate.

8 *Common fallacies* Show why the following statements are incorrect: (a) The money supply affects only the price level. (b) Fiscal expansion would increase output for ever. (c) The government can do nothing about the level of unemployment. (d) Higher unemployment always means lower inflation.

27 Unemployment

LEARNING OUTCOMES

When you have finished this chapter, you should be able to:

- Distinguish classical, frictional and structural unemployment
- Define voluntary and involuntary unemployment
- Explore determinants to the changing UK unemployment rate
- Assess the success of tax cuts and other supply-side policies in reducing the natural rate of unemployment
- Discuss the private and social costs of unemployment, and relate them to the source of unemployment
- Discuss the concept of hysteresis and outline channels through which a temporary recession could permanently reduce aggregate supply

In the early 1930s, more than one-quarter of the UK labour force was unemployed. In particular regions and occupations the unemployment rate was very much higher. High unemployment means that the economy is throwing away output by failing to put its people to work. It also means misery, social unrest, and hopelessness for the unemployed. Over the following 40 years, macroeconomic policy was geared to avoiding a rerun of the 1930s. Figure 27-1 shows that it succeeded.

In the 1970s views about unemployment began to change. People began to reject the Keynesian pessimism about the ability of the economy to respond to shocks by quickly restoring full employment. The classical model began to be more widely accepted as a description of the way the economy works even in the fairly short run.

By the 1970s governments in many countries began to perceive an even greater danger to economic and social stability, the danger of high and rising inflation. Thus by the 1980s many governments had embarked on tight monetary

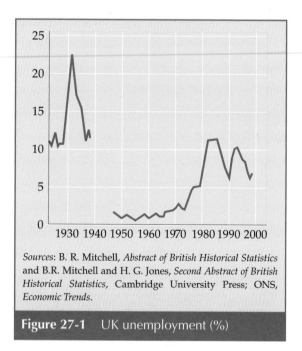

Sources: B. R. Mitchell, *Abstract of British Historical Statistics* and B.R. Mitchell and H. G. Jones, *Second Abstract of British Historical Statistics*, Cambridge University Press; ONS, *Economic Trends*.

Figure 27-1 UK unemployment (%)

Table 27-1	Unemployment (%)		
	1972	1982	1999
UK	4.0	11.3	6.7
Ireland	8.0	13.5	6.4
Italy	6.3	8.4	12.3
Sweden	2.7	3.2	5.6
France	2.8	8.1	12.4
EU	3.2	9.4	11.2
USA	5.5	9.5	4.2

Source: OECD, *Economic Outlook*.

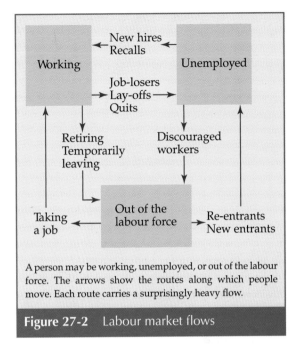

A person may be working, unemployed, or out of the labour force. The arrows show the routes along which people move. Each route carries a surprisingly heavy flow.

Figure 27-2 Labour market flows

and fiscal policies to try to keep inflation under control. The combination of restrictive demand policies and adverse supply shocks led to a dramatic increase in unemployment in most of the industrial countries in the 1980s. Figure 27-1 shows data for the UK. Data for other countries are shown in Table 27-1.

In the 1990s, high unemployment has receded a bit in the UK and the United States but in Continental Europe remains a major problem. Will high unemployment continue? Is it a drain on society or a signal that at last people are getting out of dead-end jobs into something better? What can and should the government be doing? These are the questions we set out to answer in this chapter.

27-1 The facts

Not everyone wants a job. Those people who do are called the labour force.

The **labour force** comprises all those people holding a job or registered as being willing and available for work.

The *participation rate* is the percentage of the population of working age who declare themselves to be in the labour force. Chapter 12 pointed out that the postwar growth of the labour force has been caused less by an increase in the population of working age than by an increase in participation rates by married women.

The **unemployment rate** is the percentage of the labour force without a job but registered as being willing and available for work.

Of course, some people without a job are really looking for work but have not bothered to register as unemployed. These people will not be included in the official statistics for the registered labour force, nor will they appear as registered unemployed. Yet from an economic viewpoint, such people *are* in the labour force and *are* unemployed. This

is an important phenomenon to which we return shortly. For the moment, when we present evidence on the size of the labour force or the number of people unemployed, it should be understood that data refer to the registered labour force and the registered unemployed.

Figure 27-1 makes several main points about the unemployment rate in the UK. Unemployment was high during the interwar years, especially during the Great Depression of the 1930s. It was the persistence of high unemployment that led Keynes to develop his *General Theory*. By comparison, the postwar unemployment rate was tiny until the late 1970s. By the early 1980s it was starting to get back to prewar levels, and it has fallen further in the 1990s. This pattern in other industrial countries is shown in Table 27-1.

Stocks and flows

Unemployment is a stock concept measured at a point in time. Like a pool of water, its level rises when inflows (the newly unemployed) exceed outflows (people getting new jobs or quitting the labour force altogether). Figure 27-2 illustrates this important idea.

Beginning with people working, there are three ways to become unemployed. Some people are sacked or made redundant (job-losers); some are temporarily laid off but expect eventually to be rehired by the same company; and some people voluntarily quit their existing jobs. But the inflow to unemployment can also come from people not

Table 27-2	Flows into and out of unemployment (millions of people)
	1998
Inflow to unemployment	3.2
Outflow from unemployment	3.3
Stock of unemployed	1.8

Source: ONS, *Labour Market Trends*.

Table 27-3	Long-term unemployed (over 1 year as % of all unemployed)	
	1980	1998
Italy	51	66
UK	29	33
France	32	44
Netherlands	35	48
Norway	3	9
Sweden	5	33

Source: OECD, *Employment Outlook*.

Table 27-4	Unemployment rates (percentage of relevant group)			
	Men		Women	
Age	1985	1998	1985	1998
Under 25	24	13	18	10
25–59	16	6	9	4

Source: ONS, *Labour Market Trends*.

previously in the labour force: school-leavers (new entrants), and people who once had a job, then ceased even to register as unemployed, and are now coming back into the labour force in search of a job (re-entrants).

People leave the unemployment pool in the opposite directions. Some get jobs. Others give up looking for jobs and leave the labour force completely. Although some of this latter group may simply have reached the retirement age at which they can draw a pension, many of them are discouraged workers.

Discouraged workers are pessimistic about finding a job and leave the labour force.

Table 27-2 shows that the pool of unemployment is not stagnant. Even with 1.8 million unemployed, this number is less than the number of people entering and leaving the pool *every* year.

The duration of unemployment When unemployment is high, people have to spend longer in the pool before they find a way out. Table 27-3 gives data on the duration of unemployment. Unemployment is no longer a temporary stopover on the way to better things.

The composition of unemployment

Table 27-4 gives a recent breakdown of unemployment by sex and by age. A recession hits young workers badly. Unlike established workers with accumulated skills and job experience, young workers have to be trained from scratch, and firms frequently cut back on training when times are tough. Table 27-4 shows that youth unemployment exceeds the national average.

Table 27-4 also shows that the unemployment rate is lower for women than for men. In part this may reflect the fact that employment in the declining heavy engineering industries had traditionally been predominantly male, so men are worst hit by redundancies in steelworks and shipyards.

Labour economists believe that the discrepancy between male and female workers is smaller than the table suggests, because unemployed women are less likely than unemployed men to register as unemployed. Hence the true unemployment rates for women are probably higher than the table suggests.

27-2 The framework

We now develop a theoretical framework in which to discuss the subject. We begin with the old-style classification of types of unemployment, which emphasizes the source of the problem. Then we discuss the modern approach to unemployment which emphasizes the way people in the labour market are behaving.

Types of unemployment

Economists used to classify unemployment as frictional, structural, demand-deficient, or classical.

Frictional unemployment is the irreducible minimum level of unemployment in a dynamic society.

It includes people whose physical or mental handicaps make them almost unemployable, but it also includes the people spending short spells in unemployment as they hop between jobs in an economy where both the labour force and the jobs on offer are continually changing.

In the longer run, the pattern of demand and production is always changing. In recent decades industries such as textiles and heavy engineering have been declining in the UK.

Structural unemployment refers to unemployment arising because there is a mismatch of skills and job opportunities when the pattern of demand and production changes.

For example, a skilled welder may have worked for 25 years in shipbuilding but is made redundant at 50 when the industry contracts in the face of foreign competition. That worker may have to retrain in a new skill which is more in demand in today's economy. But firms may be reluctant to take on and train older workers. Such workers become the victims of structural unemployment.

Demand-deficient unemployment occurs when output is below full capacity.

In Chapter 26 we saw that, until wages and prices have adjusted to their new long-run equilibrium level, a fall in aggregate demand will lead to lower output and employment. Some workers will want to work at the going real wage rate but will be unable to find jobs. Only in the longer run will wages and prices fall enough to boost the real money supply and lower interest rates to the extent required to restore aggregate demand to its full-employment level, and only then will demand-deficient unemployment be eliminated.

Since the classical model assumes that flexible wages and prices maintain the economy at full employment, classical economists had some difficulty explaining the high unemployment levels of the 1930s. Their diagnosis of the problem was partly that union power was maintaining the wage rate above its equilibrium level and preventing the required adjustment from occurring.

Classical unemployment describes the unemployment created when the wage is deliberately maintained above the level at which the labour supply and labour demand schedules intersect.

It can be caused either by the exercise of trade union power or by minimum wage legislation which enforces a wage in excess of the equilibrium wage rate.

The modern analysis of unemployment takes the same types of unemployment but classifies them rather differently in order to highlight their behavioural implications and consequences for government policy. Modern analysis stresses the difference between *voluntary* and *involuntary* unemployment.

The natural rate of unemployment

Figure 27-3 shows the market for labour. The labour demand schedule LD slopes downwards, showing that firms will take on more workers at a lower real wage. The schedule LF shows how many people want to be in the labour force at each real wage. We assume that an increase in the real wage increases the number of people wishing to work. The schedule AJ shows how many people accept job offers at each real wage. The schedule lies to the left of the LF schedule, both because some people are inevitably between jobs at any instant, and because a particular real wage may tempt some people into the labour force even though they will accept a job offer only if they find an offer with a rather higher real wage than average. Labour market equilibrium occurs at the point E. The employment level N* is the equilibrium or full-employment level. The distance EF is called the natural rate of unemployment.

The **natural rate of unemployment** is the rate of unemployment when the labour market is in equilibrium.

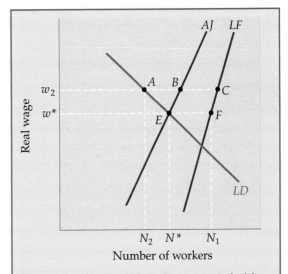

The schedules LD, LF, and AJ show, respectively, labour demand, the size of the labour force, and the number of workers willing to accept job offers at any real wage. AJ lies to the left of LF both because some labour force members are between jobs and because optimists are hanging on for an even better job offer. When the labour market clears at E, EF is the natural rate of unemployment, the people in the labour force not prepared to take job offers at the equilibrium wage w*. If union power succeeds in maintaining the wage w_2 in the long run, the labour market will be at A, and the natural rate of unemployment AC now shows the amount of unemployment chosen by the labour force collectively by enforcing the wage w_2.

Figure 27-3 The natural rate of unemployment

BOX 27-1

The lump-of-labour fallacy

Those without an economics training often think there is one really simple solution for reducing unemployment. Shorten the working week, so that the same amount of total work is shared between more workers, leaving fewer people unemployed. What's wrong with this argument?

It presumes the demand for labour (hours × people) is fixed, independent of either the cost of hiring workers or their benefit in goods produced and revenue earned. In practice, both would be affected by the proposal.

You go to work for say 7 hours, but probably have an hour of dead time (coffee breaks, tidying up at the end

of the day, being nice to colleagues, talking about sport, sneaking out to the shops). In effect this is a fixed cost. There are probably economies of scale to shift length. Shortening the shift length adds to the cost of labour, making firms less competitive, and hence reducing their demand for labour. Moreover, if you only work 20 hours a week instead of 37, you have less money to spend. If everyone in the economy spends less, then firms sell less and need fewer not more workers.

Few economists think compulsory reductions in the length of the work week is a promising solution to the problem of high unemployment.

This unemployment is entirely *voluntary*. At the equilibrium real wage w^*, N_1 people want to be in the labour force but only N^* want to accept job offers; the remainder don't want to work at the equilibrium real wage.

Which of our earlier types of unemployment must we include in the natural rate of unemployment? Certainly all frictional unemployment. But we should also include structural unemployment. Suppose a skilled welder earned £150 a week before being made redundant. The issue is not why the worker became redundant (the decline of the steel industry), but why the worker refuses to take a lower wage as a dishwasher in order to get a job, or why steelworkers as a whole did not take a sufficient wage cut to allow the steel industry to remain profitable and competitive at its former levels of output and employment. If the answer is that steelworkers refuse to accept that the equilibrium wage for their skill has fallen, and refuse to work at wages lower than those to which they have been accustomed, then we must count this unemployment as voluntary and include it in the natural rate. They are not prepared to work at the going wage rate but still want to be considered part of the labour force.

What about classical unemployment, for example where unions maintain wages above their equilibrium level? This is shown in Figure 27-3 as a wage rate w_2 above w^*. Total unemployment is now given by the distance AC. As individuals, a number of workers AB would like to take jobs at the wage rate w_2 but will be unable to find them since firms will wish to be at the point A. As individuals, these workers are involuntarily unemployed.

A worker is **involuntarily unemployed** if he or she would accept a job offer at the going wage rate.

However, through their unions, workers collectively decide to opt for the wage rate w_2 in excess of the equilibrium wage, thereby reducing the level of employment. Hence for workers as a whole we must regard the extra unemployment as voluntary. Thus we also include classical unemployment in the natural rate of unemployment. If in the long run unions maintain the wage w_2, the economy will remain at A and AC is the natural rate of unemployment.

This leaves only Keynesian or demand-deficient unemployment. Such unemployment is involuntary, being caused by sluggish labour market adjustment beyond the control of individual workers or unions. Thus we can divide total unemployment into the equilibrium or natural rate – the equilibrium level determined by normal labour market turnover, structural mismatch, union power, and incentives in the labour market – and Keynesian unemployment, sometimes called demand-deficient or cyclical unemployment – the disequilibrium level of involuntary unemployment caused by the combination of low aggregate demand and sluggish wage adjustment.

This division helps us think clearly about the government policies required to tackle the unemployment problem. Since we have argued that in the long run the economy will gradually manage to get back to full employment through a slow process of wage and price adjustment, Keynesian unemployment will eventually get rid of itself. But in the short run, Keynesian unemployment is the part of total unemployment that the government could help mop up by using fiscal and monetary policy to boost aggregate *demand*, rather than waiting for wage and price reductions to increase the real money supply and lower interest rates.

In contrast, the natural rate of unemployment tells us the part of unemployment that will not be eliminated merely by restoring aggregate demand to its full-employment level. The natural rate is the 'full-employment' level of unemployment. To reduce the natural rate, *supply-side* policies operating on labour market incentives will be needed.

This is the framework we employ for the rest of the chapter. We begin by investigating the high unemployment over the last decade, in order to understand its causes more fully. Then we discuss the prospects for unemployment during the 1990s and the policy options open to the government.

27-3 Why is unemployment so high?

The task for empirical economists is to try to say how much of high unemployment was caused by an increase in the natural rate of unemployment and how much was caused by deficient demand and sluggish wage adjustment. In Table 27-5 we give some estimates by Stephen Nickell, Richard Layard and Richard Jackman of the London School of Economics.

Table 27-5 shows the average unemployment rate during seven periods, from 1956–59 through to 1991–95. The top row shows the steady rise in the average unemployment rate in successive periods. Figure 27-1 implies further fluctuations within each period, which we ignore here.

The second row shows that there has been a steady rise in the natural or equilibrium rate of unemployment, which quadrupled between the 1950s and the 1980s. Indeed, until the start of the 1980s, almost *all* the increase in unemployment reflected a deterioration of supply-side factors and the consequent rise in the natural rate of unemployment. Since the early 1980s, the natural rate of unemployment has remained obstinately high.

Increasing skill mismatch has contributed to a higher natural rate of unemployment. Recent research emphasizes that the labour market is not very good at processing workers as they step out of one job and hope to step into another. The larger is mismatch, the harder the task we are asking the market to perform, and the more likely it is that people will get stuck in unemployment.

More generous unemployment benefit may entice more people into the labour force, shifting *LF* to the right in Figure 27-3. More significantly, it shifts *AJ* to the left. People spend longer in unemployment searching for the right job. For both reasons, equilibrium unemployment increases. Higher benefits caused some of the increase in equilibrium unemployment, though less than is sometimes supposed.

Rises in trade union power, especially in the 1970s, had a marked effect on equilibrium unemployment, as did the tax wedge between the cost of labour to the firm and the take-home pay of the worker.

Table 27-5 shows that up to 1980 actual unemployment was very close to its equilibrium rate – hardly surprising, since this was the objective of the demand management policies in force. However, while the rise in unemployment up to 1980 was due to supply-side factors, since 1980 the story is rather different. The determined attempt of governments to improve the supply side did halt the decline, which may have been quite an achievement.

Table 27-5 also shows that, when actual unemployment rose to 10 per cent and above, much of the unemployment was Keynesian, or due to deficient demand. For example, during 1981–87, of the actual unemployment rate of 11.1 per cent, only 8.7 per cent was equilibrium unemployment: the rest was due to insufficient demand. Given the depth of the recession during 1990–92, when unemployment rates again reached double digits, the UK again experienced significant Keynesian unemployment.

27-4 Supply-side economics

Keynesians believe that the economy can deviate from full employment for quite a long time, certainly for a period of

Table 27-5   UK unemployment 1956–95

Unemployment rate (%)	56–59	60–68	69–73	74–80	81–87	88–90	91–95
Actual rate	2.2	2.6	3.4	5.2	11.1	7.3	9.3
Estimated natural rate	2.2	2.5	3.6	7.3	8.7	8.7	8.9

Sources: R. Layard, S. Nickell, and R. Jackman, *Unemployment*, Oxford University Press, 1991; S. Nickell, 'Inflation and the UK Labour Market' in T. Jenkinson, *Readings in Macroeconomics*, Oxford University Press, 1996.

BOX 27-2

Did the tax carrot work?

The evidence from the past

A lower *marginal* tax rate makes people *substitute* work for leisure. But tax cuts also make workers better off. This *income effect* makes them want to consume more leisure, and hence work less. The combined effect on hours of work is small for those already in work. Of more importance is the decision about whether to work at all. In Chapter 12 we showed that higher take-home pay, for example because of tax cuts, *will* encourage more people to join the labour force by reducing the significance of the fixed costs of working (commuting, babysitters, giving up social security).

The UK evidence shows that tax cuts have a negligible effect on the labour supply decision of men and single women. But for married women, higher take-home pay does encourage labour force participation, if only a little.

The Thatcher programme

During the 1980s the Thatcher government embarked on a major programme of tax cuts and tax reforms. The real value of personal allowances – how much you can earn before paying income tax – rose by 25 per cent. The basic rate of income tax fell from 33 to 25 per cent and for top income-earners from 83 to 40 per cent. Many politicians anticipated a considerable increase in the labour supply, yet most economists were pessimistic because of the evidence from the past.

The effect of the Thatcher programme is assessed by C. V. Brown, 'The 1988 Tax Cuts, Work Incentives and Revenue', *Fiscal Studies*, 1988. Brown finds that the substantial increase in tax allowances led to less than 0.5 per cent extra hours of labour supply. The cut in the basic rate of income tax had no detectable effect at all. The massive cut in the marginal tax rate of top earners had a small effect in stimulating extra hours of work by the rich. The evidence from the past stood up well to this major change of tax policy.

several years. Monetarists believe that the classical full-employment model is relevant much more quickly. But everyone agrees that in the long run the performance of the economy can be changed only by affecting the level of full employment and the corresponding level of potential output.

Supply-side economics is the use of microeconomic incentives to alter the level of full employment, the level of potential output, and the natural rate of unemployment.

Although in this section we are interested chiefly in how to change the natural rate of unemployment, it is convenient to discuss some of the wider implications of supply-side economics at the same time. We return to the determination of potential output in Chapter 31.

Income tax cuts

One of the key themes of supply-side economists is the benefits that stem from reducing the marginal rate of income tax.

The **marginal rate of income tax** is the fraction of each extra pound of income that the government takes in income tax.

We discussed tax rates and work incentives in detail in Chapter 12. We pointed out that a cut in marginal tax rates, and a consequent increase in the take-home pay derived from the last hour's work, tend to make people substitute work for leisure. But against this *substitution effect* must be set an *income effect*. To the extent that people now pay less in taxes, they will have to do less work to obtain any given target living standard. Thus, theoretical economics cannot prove that income tax cuts increase the desired labour supply, and in fact most empirical studies confirm that, at best, tax cuts lead to only a small increase in the supply of labour. We gave some details in Chapter 12 and more in the Economics in Action that follows.

Figure 27-4 may be used to analyse the effect of a cut in marginal tax rates. The labour demand schedule *LD* shows that firms demand more workers at a lower real wage. We draw a steep schedule *LF* showing that higher after-tax real wage rates, at best, lead to only a small increase in the number of people wishing to be in the labour force. The schedule *AJ* shows how many people wish to accept job offers at each real wage. It is drawn for a given (real) level of unemployment benefit. Hence the horizontal distance between the *AJ* and *LF* schedules – the number of people in the workforce refusing to work at each real wage, or the amount of voluntary unemployment – decreases as the real wage rises relative to the given level of unemployment benefit. The figure assumes that a lower replacement ratio, the ratio of unemployment benefit to wage rates, reduces voluntary unemployment.

Suppose there is a marginal income tax rate equal to the vertical distance *AB*. Equilibrium employment will then be N_1. Why? Because income tax drives a wedge between the gross-of-tax wages paid by firms and the net-of-tax wages received by workers. At the employment level N_1 firms are happy to hire this quantity of labour at the gross wage w_1. Subtracting the income tax rate *AB*, N_1 workers want to take job offers at the after-tax wage w_3. Thus N_1 is the equilibrium level of employment. The horizontal distance *BC* shows the natural rate of unemployment, the number of workers in the labour force not wishing to work at the going rate of take-home pay.

To show the effect of a cut in marginal tax rates, suppose

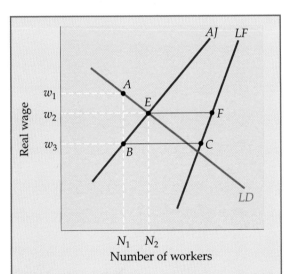

An income tax makes the net-of-tax wage received by households lower than the gross wage paid by firms. *AB* measures the amount each worker pays in income tax, and equilibrium employment is N_1, the quantity that households wish to supply at the after-tax wage w_3 and that firms demand at the gross wage w_1. At the after-tax wage w_3 the natural rate of unemployment is *BC*. If income tax were abolished, equilibrium would be at *E*. Employment would rise from N_1 to N_2 and the natural rate of unemployment would fall from *BC* to *EF*. Relative to the fixed level of unemployment benefit, the rise in take-home pay from w_3 to w_2 reduces voluntary unemployment.

Figure 27-4   A cut in marginal income tax rates

income taxes were abolished. The gross wage and the take-home pay now coincide, and the new labour market equilibrium is at *E*. Note that two things have happened. First, equilibrium employment has risen. Second, although more people wish to be in the labour force because take-home pay has increased from w_3 to w_2, the natural rate of unemployment has fallen from the distance *BC* to the smaller distance *EF*. A rise in take-home pay relative to unemployment benefit reduces voluntary unemployment.

Similar effects would be obtained if, instead of cutting income tax, the level of unemployment benefit were cut. For a given labour force schedule *LF*, fewer people would now wish to be unemployed at any real wage. Hence the schedule *AJ*, showing acceptances of job offers, would shift to the right. Again, the effect would be both to increase the equilibrium level of employment (and hence of potential output) and to reduce the natural rate of unemployment by reducing the replacement ratio.

What about the effect of changes in the national insurance contributions paid both by firms and by workers? These are mandatory contributions to state schemes which provide unemployment and health insurance. They act like an income tax in driving a wedge *AB* between the total cost to a firm of hiring another worker and the net take-home pay of a worker. Figure 27-4 shows that a reduction in these contributions will increase the equilibrium level of employment, increase the equilibrium level of take-home pay, reduce the replacement ratio, and reduce the natural rate of unemployment.

Other policies aimed at labour supply

Figure 27-3 showed that, by restricting labour supply, unions force firms up the labour demand schedule. The equilibrium real wage is higher but equilibrium employment lower. Since a higher real wage reduces employment but (slightly) increases the number of people wishing to be in the labour force, in raising real wages unions increase the natural rate of unemployment. Collectively, labour opts for higher wages and more unemployment.

Conversely, the natural rate of unemployment will be reduced if the power of organized labour is weakened. Unions will be less successful in restricting labour supply and forcing up wages. Government intervention in the labour market to weaken the monopoly power of trade unions should be classified as a supply-side policy aimed at reducing the natural rate of unemployment and increasing equilibrium employment and potential output.

Earlier, we pointed out that frictional and structural unemployment are important components of the natural

BOX 27-3   'The graphs the EU Commission dare not publish'

'Brussels riven by job market row – A controversial report linking unemployment to rigidities in the labour market has split the Commission' reported the *Financial Times*, giving details of a row between those believing less regulation of the labour market would reduce European unemployment (and therefore wanting the two figures shown below to be published by the Commission) and those believing there is no simple link between labour market regulation and equilibrium unemployment (and therefore wanting these figures suppressed since they were 'misleading'). The first graph shows, for 14 EU members, the correlation between the degree of labour market regulation and the percentage of the labour force with jobs. The second graph shows, for some OECD countries, the correlation between the employment rate and the cost of firing a worker. The figures show a high degree of regulation and high costs of dismissal are each associated with a lower employment rate. If correlation proved causality, this would clinch the case for deregulation.

Suppose you had to make the case for continuing labour market regulation. Where would you begin? You'd acknowledge that if the labour market worked perfectly there would be no need for intervention, and that regulations might be designed to *offset* existing market failures thereby enhancing efficiency. The countries with the largest market failures might thus have the largest distortions and lowest employment rates, but also the largest degree of regulation as governments intervened to ameliorate the worst consequences of these distortions. Of course, to be persuasive, you'd have to identify exactly what these distortions were (market power of large employers, externalities in training, etc.) and explain why the particular forms of regulation made things better not worse. You might or might not be able to show this. The debate about labour market regulation continues in Europe . . .

Source: *Financial Times*, 8 November 1996.

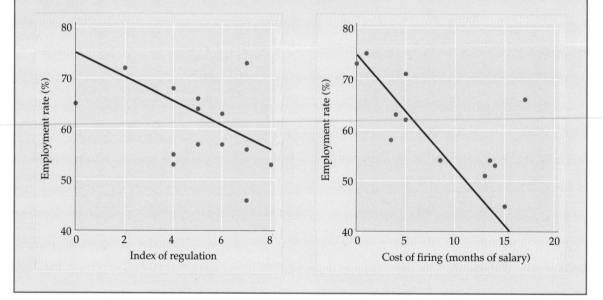

rate of unemployment. Policies aimed at reducing frictional and structural unemployment should also be included in supply-side economics. Their objective is to shift the *AJ* schedule to the right relative to the labour force schedule *LF*.

Among such policies we include grants that allow

redundant workers to retrain in relevant skills, various government measures introduced to help school-leavers develop skills and job experience for the first time, and special measures to encourage the long-term unemployed back into the labour force. By making the labour force more suited to employers' needs, such policies aim to allow firms to make wage offers that unemployed workers will find acceptable. Hence such measures reduce voluntary unemployment. Chapter 12 contains more details of recent policies to boost labour supply. To refresh your memory, reread the Box 12-3 on page 187.

Policies aimed at the demand for labour

Thus far, we have emphasized policies aimed at the supply of workers for employment. We now turn to the demand for workers by firms. In the previous chapter we saw that an adverse supply shock could reduce the derived demand for labour, shifting the LD schedule downwards. This can be represented in Figure 27-4 by a downward shift in the labour demand schedule LD.

Try constructing your own diagram to show the effect of this. (Forget about income taxes and start from the point E in Figure 27-4.) If you draw the diagram correctly you will discover two things. First, the downward shift in the LD schedule reduces equilibrium employment. Second, because equilibrium real wages fall, the replacement ratio must rise and the natural rate of unemployment must increase. Some redundant workers decide to go on the dole rather than work for lower wages.

Supply-side economics aims to reverse this effect. If firms can be encouraged to install modern capital equipment, the labour demand schedule will shift upwards. Hence the equilibrium wage rate will rise and the natural rate of unemployment will fall. What kind of policies could induce this favourable outcome?

We saw that firms' investment demand depends on three things: future output and profit prospects, the cost of new capital goods, and the rate of interest. The government can affect the price of new capital goods by grants (investment subsidies) or tax breaks. For example, firms can be allowed to set the cost of buying new capital goods against their pre-tax profits, thus reducing their liability to corporation tax on profits.

Second, the government can try to get interest rates down.

Surely interest rates come under the heading of demand management rather than supply-side policies?

Not in the long run. If the economy is at full employment, the purpose of lower interest rates is not to increase aggregate demand. Rather, it is to alter the *composition* of full-employment aggregate demand, allowing the share of investment to increase. Of course this means that some other components of aggregate demand must fall; otherwise excess demand for goods will simply bid up prices, reduce the real money supply, and bid up interest rates again.

In this section we have discussed how supply-side policies could be used to reduce the natural rate of unemployment. Supply-side policies may offer some hope in the long run, but many of them, for example measures to increase the capital stock, cannot be expected to have a dramatic effect in the short run. Slashing the level of unemployment benefit is one supply-side policy that would have an immediate effect. However, it would make life pretty miserable for those who still could not find a job.

27-5 Eliminating Keynesian unemployment

Suppose the government boosts aggregate demand: what effect will this have on employment and unemployment if the economy begins with spare capacity and Keynesian unemployment? The answer depends in part on which components of aggregate demand are increased.

Government expenditure on extra police officers will add more to employment than an equivalent increase in spending on nuclear electricity, whose production is very capital-intensive.

It is also extremely important to understand the cyclical relationship between demand and output, employment, and unemployment. On average, boosting aggregate demand by 1 per cent will not increase employment by 1 per cent or reduce unemployment by 1 percentage point. Table 27-6 shows two periods of demand growth and two periods of rapid demand decline. In practice, booms lead initially to

Table 27-6 Output, employment, and unemployment				
Cumulative change in	79ii–81ii	86ii–88ii	90ii–91ii	92iv–98ii
Real GDP (%)	−7.8	+9.1	−3.4	+16.8
Employment (%)	−6.3	+2.5	−2.9	+6.8
Employed (million)	−1.7	+0.5	−0.7	+1.5
Unemployed (million)	+1.4	−0.9	+0.6	−1.2
Source: ONS, *Economic Trends*.				

BOX 27-4   Hysteresis and high unemployment in Europe

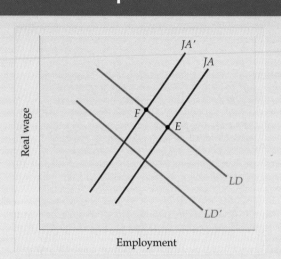

Supply and demand curves are supposed to be independent of one another. The labour supply curve or job acceptances schedule *JA* shows the number of people willing to work at each real wage whatever the position of the labour demand curve *LD*, and vice versa. But this assumption may be wrong.

In the diagram, the initial equilibrium is at *E*. Something then makes the labour demand curve shift left to *LD'*. Suppose this in turn *causes* a permanent reduction in labour supply: *JA* shifts to *JA'*. When labour demand reverts to its original level *LD*, the new equilibrium is at *F*, not *E*. The short-run history of the economy has affected its long-run equilibrium.

An economy experiences **hysteresis** when its long-run equilibrium depends on the path it has followed in the short run.

Hysteresis is a possible explanation of high and persistent unemployment in Europe. We now examine some channels through which it might work.

The insider–outsider distinction   Outsiders are the unemployed without jobs. Only insiders with jobs participate in wage bargaining. At the original equilibrium *E*, there are lots of insiders in work and they ensure that real wages are low enough to preserve their own jobs. When a recession occurs, *LD* shifts to *LD'*. Some insiders get fired and become outsiders. Eventually, as we explained in Chapter 26, market forces will restore labour demand to *LD* again. But now there are fewer insiders than originally. They exploit their scarcity by pressing for higher wages for themselves, rather than encouraging their firms to rehire. The economy gets trapped in the high-wage, low-employment equilibrium at *F* instead of the low-wage, high-employment equilibrium at *E*. Thereafter, only long-run supply-side measures aimed at breaking down insider power (e.g. less job protection) can gradually break the economy out of this low-employment equilibrium.

Discouraged workers   Again, the economy begins at *E*. It has a skilled and energetic labour force. A temporary recession leads to unemployment. If the recession is protracted, we see the emergence of the long-term unemployed and a culture in which people stop looking for jobs. Again, when demand picks up, labour supply has been permanently reduced and equilibrium reverts to *F*, not *E*. Only long-term supply-side measures to restore the work culture will succeed.

Search and mismatch   When unemployment is low at *E*, firms are busily trying to find scarce workers and potential workers are searching hard for a good job. A recession makes firms advertise fewer vacancies, and workers realize it is a waste of time searching for jobs. When demand picks up again, both firms and workers have become accustomed to low levels of search; so new jobs don't get created.

The capital stock   At *E* the economy has a lot of capital, so labour productivity is high and firms want lots of workers. During a temporary recession, firms save money by abandoning investment. When the demand for goods picks up again, firms have permanently lower capital. Hence the demand for labour, which depends on the marginal product of labour, never rises to its original level. Again, the economy returns to an equilibrium with lower employment than at *E*.

Policy implications of hysteresis   All these explanations imply that a temporary fall in demand leads to a permanently lower level of employment and output, and a rise in the natural rate of unemployment. There are two policy implications. First, once the problem has emerged, it is dangerous to try to break out of it simply by expanding aggregate demand. Before long-run supply can respond, you get a major bout of inflation. Supply-side policies, needed to restore aggregate supply, take a long time to work.

Second, precisely because the problem is so hard to cure once it occurs, it is even more important not to let demand fall in the first place. The payoff to demand management is higher than in an economy with a *unique* long-run equilibrium, where all that is at stake is how quickly the economy gets back to its original point.

a sharp increase in shift lengths and hours worked; slumps lead to the abolition of overtime, the introduction of short time, and a marked decline in hours worked.

Hence the table confirms that changes in demand and output lead to smaller changes in the level of employment. For example, when output grew 17 per cent between the second quarter of 1992 and the second quarter of 1998 employment increased by only 7 per cent. Moreover, changes in employment do not lead to corresponding changes in unemployment. The last two rows of the table show that rapid expansion or contraction of employment leads to significantly smaller changes in unemployment.

One reason for this result is the 'discouraged worker effect'. When unemployment is high and rising, some people who would really like to work get so pessimistic that they give up looking for a job. Since they are no longer registered as looking for work, they are not recorded in the labour force or considered to be among the unemployed. Conversely, in a boom many people who had previously given up looking for work come back into the labour force since there is now a good chance of finding a suitable job. Hence in booms and slumps recorded employment data change by more than recorded unemployment data.

27-6 The private and social cost of unemployment

In this section we discuss the private and social cost of unemployment. We begin with the private cost.

The private cost of unemployment

It is important to distinguish between voluntary and involuntary unemployment. When individuals are voluntarily unemployed, they reveal that they do better by being unemployed than by accepting the job offers that they face at the going wage rate. Under these circumstances the private cost of unemployment (the wage forgone by not working) is less than the private benefits for being unemployed. What are these benefits?

First, the individual is entitled to transfer payments from the government. These are of two kinds. Workers who have previously contributed to the national insurance scheme are entitled to unemployment benefit for the first 12 months after they become unemployed. Thereafter they become entitled to supplementary benefit, the ultimate backstop in the British welfare state.

Are there any other benefits to be had from being unemployed? First, there is the value of leisure. By refusing a job, some people are revealing that the extra leisure is worth more to them than the extra disposable income if they took a job. Second, some people expect to get a better job after a temporary spell of unemployment. These future benefits must be set against the current cost of lower disposable income.

When people are involuntarily unemployed, the picture changes. Involuntary unemployment means that people would like to work at the going wage but cannot find a job because there is excess labour supply at the existing wage rate. These people are worse off as a result of being unemployed.

The distinction between voluntary and involuntary unemployment is important because it may affect our value judgement about how much attention should be paid to the unemployment problem. When unemployment is involuntary, people are suffering more and the case for helping them is stronger.

The social cost of unemployment

Again we distinguish between voluntary and involuntary unemployment. When unemployment is voluntary, individuals prefer to be unemployed. Does this mean that unemployment is also good for society as a whole?

There is one obvious discrepancy between individual benefit and social benefit. For an individual, unemployment and supplementary benefit are part of the benefits of being unemployed. But these transfer payments give no corresponding benefit to society as a whole. They may ease the collective conscience about poverty and income inequality, but they are not payments for the supply of any goods or services that other members of society may consume. To this extent, the value judgement that we ought to support the unemployed inevitably entails a cost in allocative inefficiency. It encourages too many people to be voluntarily unemployed.

However, this does not mean that society should go to the opposite extreme and try to eliminate voluntary unemployment completely. First, society is perfectly entitled to adopt the value judgement that it will maintain a reasonable living standard for the unemployed, whatever the cost in resource misallocation. Second, even in terms of allocative efficiency, the efficient level of voluntary unemployment is certainly above zero.

In a changing economy, it is important to match up the right people to the right jobs. Getting this match right allows society as a whole to produce more output. Freezing the existing pattern of employment in a changing economy will eventually lead to a mismatch of people and jobs. The flow through the pool of unemployment is one of the mechanisms through which society reallocates people to more suitable jobs and increases total output in the long run. If unemployment benefits make this transition smoother, society may gain.

Two points from our earlier discussion are also relevant here. First, even when unemployment is high, flows both in and out of the pool are large relative to the pool itself. Second, people who do not get out of the pool quickly are in danger of stagnating when unemployment is high: the fraction of the unemployed who have been unemployed for over a year is higher in the 1990s than it was at the end of the 1970s when unemployment was much lower.

Involuntary or Keynesian unemployment has an even higher social cost. Since the economy is producing below capacity, it is literally throwing away output that could have been made by putting these people to work. Moreover, since Keynesian unemployment is involuntary, it may entail more human and psychological suffering than voluntary unemployment. Although this is hard to quantify, it is also part of the social cost of unemployment.

SUMMARY

● People are either employed, unemployed, or out of the labour force. The level of unemployment rises when inflows to the pool of the unemployed exceed outflows. Inflows and outflows are large relative to the level of unemployment.

● As unemployment has risen, the average duration of unemployment has increased.

● Women face lower unemployment rates than men. The unemployment rates for old workers, and especially for young workers, are well above the national average.

● Unemployment can be classified as frictional, structural, classical, and demand-deficient. In modern terminology, the first three types are voluntary unemployment and the last is involuntary, or Keynesian, unemployment. The natural rate of unemployment is the equilibrium level of voluntary unemployment.

● In the long run, sustained rises in unemployment must reflect increases in the natural rate of unemployment. During temporary recessions, Keynesian unemployment is also important.

● Supply-side economics aims to increase equilibrium employment and potential output, and to reduce the natural rate of unemployment, by operating on incentives at a microeconomic level. Supply-side policies include income tax cuts, reductions in unemployment benefit, retraining and relocation grants, investment subsidies, and policies such as lower interest rates coupled with lower government spending, aimed at 'crowding in' investment's share of full-employment aggregate demand.

● A 1 per cent increase in output is likely to lead to a much smaller reduction in Keynesian unemployment. Some of the extra output will be met by longer hours. And as unemployment falls some people, effectively in the labour force but not registered, look for work again.

● Hysteresis means that short-run changes can move the economy to a different long-run equilibrium. It may explain why European recessions have raised the natural rate of unemployment substantially.

● Although people who are voluntarily unemployed reveal that the private benefits from unemployment exceed the private cost in wages forgone, society derives no direct return from the payment of unemployment benefit which individuals regard as a private benefit from being unemployed. Nevertheless, society would not benefit by driving the natural rate of unemployment to zero. Some social gains in higher productivity are derived from the improved matching of people and jobs that temporary spells of unemployment allow.

● Keynesian unemployment is involuntary and therefore a disadvantage to private individuals who would prefer to be employed. Socially it represents wasted output. Society may also care about the human misery inflicted by involuntary unemployment.

● In most European countries unemployment has been high for some time.

KEY TERMS

◆ Labour force   449

◆ Unemployment rate   449

◆ Discouraged workers   450

◆ Frictional and structural
   unemployment   450–451

◆ Demand-deficient unemployment
   451

◆ Classical unemployment   451

◆ Natural rate of unemployment   451

◆ Involuntary unemployment   452

◆ Supply-side economics   454

◆ Marginal rate of income tax   454

◆ Hysteresis   458

 REVIEW QUESTIONS

1 What is the discouraged-worker effect? Suggest two reasons why it occurs.

2 'The average duration of an individual's unemployment rises in a slump. This suggests that the problem is a lower outflow from the pool of unemployment, not a higher inflow.' Do you agree?

3 Why is teenage unemployment so high?

4 'The microchip has caused a permanent increase in the level of unemployment.' Carefully examine this assertion.

5 How would high unemployment be explained by (a) a Keynesian, (b) a classical economist?

6 Shouldn't we pay the unemployed an amount equal to the after-tax wage they earned in their last job, thereby eliminating the disadvantage they suffer on becoming unemployed?

7 *Common fallacies* Show why each of the following statements is incorrect. (a) Unemployment is always a bad thing. (b) So long as there is unemployment, there should be pressure on wages to fall. (c) Unemployment arises only because greedy workers are pricing themselves out of a job.

28 Inflation

LEARNING OUTCOMES

When you have finished this chapter, you should be able to:

- Analyse the quantity theory of money and discuss when it implies that a higher money supply will simply cause higher prices
- Consider the relation between inflation and nominal interest rates
- Analyse seigniorage, the inflation tax, and why hyperinflations occur
- Examine whether budget deficits lead to increases in the nominal money supply
- Use long-run and short-run Phillips curves to examine the relation between inflation and unemployment
- Explain how the costs of inflation depend on whether or not it was anticipated
- Discuss how central banks' independence may remove political temptations to inflate, allowing the private sector to reduce inflation expectations
- Study the Monetary Policy Committee of the Bank of England

One of the first acts of the Labour government in 1997 was to make the Bank of England independent, with a mandate to achieve low inflation.

Inflation is a rise in the average price of goods over time. **Pure inflation** is the special case in which all prices of goods and factors of production are rising at the same rate.

Persistent inflation over many years is in fact quite a recent phenomenon. Before 1950, prices tended to rise in some years but fall in other years. In the UK the *price level* – the average price of goods as a whole – was no higher in 1950 than it had been in 1920. Figure 28-1 shows that the UK price level fell quite sharply during some of the interwar years when inflation was negative. Yet after 1945 there was not a single year in which the price level fell. Since 1950 the price level has increased by a factor of 20, more than its increase over the previous three centuries. This broad picture applies in most of the advanced economies.

Inflation does have bad effects, but some of the popular criticisms of inflation are based on spurious reasoning. It requires care to distinguish between the good and bad arguments about why inflation is costly for the economy as a whole.

To understand the costs of inflation we need to understand its effects. But these effects may depend on what is causing the inflation in the first place. First we examine the causes of inflation.

We then turn to the consequences of inflation. How does it affect the markets for goods and labour? Is high inflation bad for output and employment? And does it matter whether the inflation was previously expected or whether it takes people by surprise?

To what extent is inflation a bad thing? We distinguish the costs that inflation might impose on individuals and the costs it might impose on society as a whole. We conclude by considering what the government can do about inflation.

28-1 Money and inflation

In this section we develop the basic link between the nominal money supply and the price level. In turn, this provides a link between the rate of growth of nominal money and inflation.

The analysis focuses on the market for money which we discussed in Chapters 24 and 25.

The **real money supply** M/P is the nominal money supply M divided by the price level P.

People demand money because of its purchasing power in terms of goods. In Chapter 24 we explained that the demand for money will be a demand for *real* money balances. Because Keynes used the term *liquidity preference* to mean the demand for money, economists often use the symbol L to denote the demand for real money balances. We use the symbol $L(Y, r)$ to denote the quantity of real balances demanded when real income is Y and the interest rate is r.

An increase in real income increases the quantity of real balances demanded since people are undertaking more transactions. By increasing the opportunity cost of holding money rather than interest-bearing assets, an increase in the interest rate r will reduce the quantity of real balances demanded.

If the money market is in equilibrium, the supply of real balances M/P must equal the quantity of real balances demanded.

$$M/P = L(Y, r) \qquad (1)$$

Throughout this chapter we assume that flexible interest rates keep the money market continuously in equilibrium. Equation (1) holds at all points in time.

Suppose that nominal wages and prices are slow to adjust in the short run. An increase in the nominal money supply M leads initially to an increase in the real money supply M/P since prices P have not yet had time to adjust fully. The excess supply of real money balances bids interest rates down. Lower interest rates boost aggregate demand for goods. Gradually this excess demand for goods bids up goods prices, and in the labour market the increased demand for employment starts to bid up money wages. In Chapter 26 we saw that, when wages and prices have fully adjusted, a once-and-for-all increase in the nominal money supply leads to an equivalent once-and-for-all increase in wages and prices. Output, employment, interest rates, and real money are restored to their original levels.

Equation (1) allows us to state this argument succinctly. When adjustment is complete the demand for real balances is unchanged. Hence the price level must have changed in proportion to the original increase in the nominal money supply. This is the quantity theory of money.

The **quantity theory of money** says that changes in the nominal money supply lead to equivalent changes in the price level (and money wages) but do not have effects on output and employment.

The theory is at least 500 years old and may date from Confucius. Today the quantity theory is defended by monetarists, who argue that *most* changes in prices are due to changes in the nominal money supply.

However, the theory must be interpreted with care. Effectively, the quantity theory says that, since the demand for real balances must always be constant, the supply of real balances must also be constant. Hence changes in nominal money must be matched by equivalent changes in prices. There are two issues we must now investigate. First, even if the demand for real balances does remain constant, is it

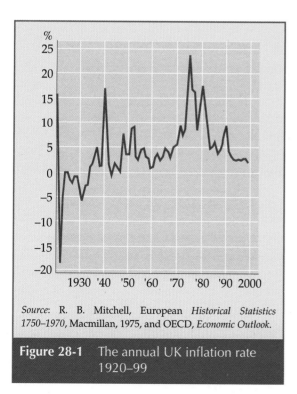

%
25
20
15
10
5
0
−5
−10
−15
−20
        1930 '40   '50   '60   '70   '80   '90 2000

Source: R. B. Mitchell, European *Historical Statistics 1750–1970*, Macmillan, 1975, and OECD, *Economic Outlook*.

Figure 28-1   The annual UK inflation rate 1920–99

changes in nominal money that cause changes in prices, or changes in prices that cause changes in nominal money? Second, is the demand for real money balances remains constant?

Money, prices, and causation

Suppose the demand for real balances is constant over time. We can say that a change in the money supply causes a change in prices. Now ask the question the other way round. Suppose workers secure higher money wages from firms. In consequence, firms put their prices up to cover their costs. What happens next?

Equation (1) says that one of two things can happen. If the nominal money supply does not increase, the real money supply will be reduced. Interest rates will increase to maintain money market equilibrium. But higher interest rates reduce aggregate demand for goods and create excess goods supply, putting downward pressure on goods prices and the quantity of employment demanded. Eventually, prices and wages will fall back to their original level. Full-employment equilibrium is then restored. Prices, wages, the real money supply, and interest rates are back to their original level. The attempt to raise wages and prices will be defeated once full adjustment has taken place.

Alternatively, the government may react to the initial rise in wages and prices by *accommodating* this shock.

Monetary policy **accommodates** a shock when a change in prices induces the government to provide a matching change in the nominal money supply to avoid any change in the real money supply or interest rates in the short run.

When a rise in prices is accommodated by an increase in the money supply, the real money stock remains constant. There is no change in equilibrium interest rates. The economy remains at full employment but with a higher level of nominal money, prices and nominal wages.

We can now understand Milton Friedman's claim that inflation is a monetary phenomenon. Once wages and prices have had time to adjust, the economy will always be at full-employment output. If the demand for real balances is always the same at full employment, any increase in prices must have been accompanied by an increase in nominal money.

The demand for real money balances

Table 28-1 shows the behaviour of nominal money, prices, real money, and real income over a 38-year period. The simple quantity theory is not a good approximation to reality. Nominal money rose six times as much as prices in

Japan but only twice as much in France. Changes in real income were very different in the three countries. Real income growth increases real money demand and requires a matching increase in the real money supply. Nominal money must grow more quickly than prices.

Two other forces help to explain the data of Table 28-1. First, although real income grew slowly in the UK, financial deregulation and competition between banks offered depositors attractive interest rates on bank deposits. This helps explain why real money demand increased so much in the UK. Second, we must take account of other effects of interest rates on real money demand. We investigate the role of interest rates in the next section.

Already, we can reach one conclusion: even in the long run, changes in real income and interest rates significantly alter real money demand. However, one cannot dispute the theoretical proposition that, *if* real income and interest rates were unaltered, changes in nominal money would eventually lead to equivalent change in money wages and prices.

Inflation

So far we have talked about levels. Now we talk about rates of change. Equation (1) implies that the growth in real money demand must equal the growth in the real money supply, namely the excess of nominal money growth over the growth in prices. But inflation is the growth in prices. Thus,

$$
\begin{matrix} \text{Inflation} \\ \text{rate} \end{matrix} = \begin{bmatrix} \text{nominal} \\ \text{money} \\ \text{growth} \end{bmatrix} - \begin{bmatrix} \text{real money} \\ \text{demand} \\ \text{growth} \end{bmatrix} \qquad (2)
$$

When the growth of real money demand is zero, the inflation rate equals the rate of nominal money growth. Table 28-1 showed how this prediction gets screwed up by the fact that real money demand does change. Could changes in real money demand be small relative to changes in nominal money and prices? Yes. Since real income and interest rates *usually* change only a few percentage points a

Table 28-1	Nominal money and prices, 1999 (1962 = 100)		
	Japan	France	UK
Nominal money	3021	1477	5039
Prices	474	730	1198
Real money	637	202	421
Real income	1290	290	235

Source: IMF, *International Financial Statistics*.

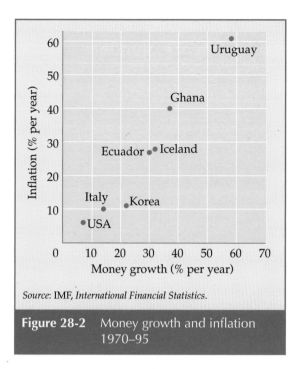

Source: IMF, *International Financial Statistics.*

Figure 28-2   Money growth and inflation 1970–95

Table 28-2	Inflation and interest rates 1998 (% per annum)	
	Inflation	Interest rate
Turkey	85	75
Ecuador	36	50
Jamaica	14	25
Nigeria	10	14
South Africa	7	17
Switzerland	0	1

Source: IMF, *International Financial Statistics.*

year, real money demand usually changes only slowly.[1] When nominal money is growing rapidly it will essentially have to be matched by rapidly growing prices to make sure that the real money supply changes only slowly in line with real money demand.

Figure 28-2 shows some countries with high inflation and high nominal money growth. Inflation and money growth are very similar, as equation (2) predicts. The points in Figure 28-2 lie close to the line along which inflation and nominal money growth are equal.

The essential insight of the quantity theory of money is that real variables usually change slowly. Hence very large changes in one nominal variable (nominal money supply) must be accompanied by very large changes in other nominal variables (prices and money wages) in order to maintain real money supply (and real wages) at their equilibrium values. This is a useful first look at inflation, but we have simplified too much. We now put this right.

28-2 Inflation and interest rates

Table 28-2 shows interest and inflation rates for selected countries for 1998. Countries with high inflation have high interest rates. In fact, the data suggest that a 1 per cent higher inflation rate is pretty much accompanied by a 1 per cent higher interest rate, a proposition first suggested by Professor Irving Fisher.

The **Fisher hypothesis** says that a 1 per cent increase in inflation will be accompanied by a 1 per cent increase in interest rates.

$$\begin{matrix} \text{Real} & & \text{nominal} & & \\ \text{interest} & = & \text{interest} & - & \text{inflation rate} & \quad (3) \\ \text{rate} & & \text{rate} & & \end{matrix}$$

The Fisher hypothesis says that *real* interest rates do not change much. Otherwise there would be large excess supply or demand for loans. Higher inflation must largely be offset by higher nominal interest rates to maintain the equilibrium real interest rate. Table 28-2 shows that the hypothesis is not a bad approximation.

Hence an increase in the rate of money growth will lead to an increase not merely in inflation but also in nominal interest rates. This will alter the demand for real money balances and hence will require money and prices to grow at *different* rates until the real money supply has adjusted to the change in real money demand. To show how this works, we consider a spectacular example, the German hyperinflation.

Hyperinflation

Hyperinflations are periods when inflation rates are very large.

Bolivian inflation reached 11 000 per cent in 1985, and Ukraine's inflation topped 10 000 per cent in 1993. The most famous example is Germany in 1922–23.

Germany lost the First World War. The German government had a big deficit, which it financed largely by printing money. Table 28-3 shows what happened. The sixteenfold increase in the nominal money supply in 1922 was tiny compared with the increase in 1923. The government had to buy faster printing presses. In the later stages of the hyperinflation they took in old notes, stamped on some more zeros, and reissued them as larger-denomination notes in the morning.

---
[1] An exception is the hyperinflation example of the next section.

BOX 28-1 — The quantity theory of money

The quantity theory of money says:

$$MV = PY$$

The velocity of circulation V is the ratio of nominal income PY (prices P times real income Y) to nominal money M. When prices adjust to maintain real income at its full employment level, assumed constant, a change in M leads to an equivalent change in P, *provided velocity V stays constant*. What is velocity? It is the speed at which the stock of money is passed round the economy as people transact. If everyone holds money for a shorter period and passes it on more quickly, the economy can get by with a lower money stock relative to nominal income. But how do we assess whether velocity is likely to remain constant, as the simple quantity theory requires?

The quantity theory equation can be rearranged as

$$M/P = Y/V$$

The left-hand side is the real money supply. We can think of the right-hand side as real money demand. It rises if real income rises and falls if velocity rises. But we have argued that real money demand is determined by real income and nominal interest rates, which measure the opportunity cost of holding money. Hence velocity just measures the effect of interest rates on the demand for real money balances. Higher nominal interest rates reduce real money demand. People *hold* less money relative to income. Velocity rises. Hence, while inflation and nominal interest rates are increasing, velocity is rising. But if inflation and nominal interest rates settle down at some particular level, velocity will become constant. For a given income level, changes in money will then be accompanied by equivalent changes in prices and the simple quantity theory once more applies.

This assumes that prices (and wages) are fully flexible. In the short run, if prices are sluggish, changes in nominal money must change the real money supply. Changes in interest rates or real income will be required to change the quantity of real balances demanded and maintain money market equilibrium. Changes in nominal money will not be immediately matched by changes in prices. The quantity theory of money will not hold in the short run.

Table 28-3 The German hyperinflation, 1922–23 (January 1922 = 1)

	Currency	Prices	Real money	Inflation (% per month)
January 1922	1	1	1.00	5
January 1923	16	75	0.21	189
July 1923	354	2 021	0.18	386
September 1923	227 777	645 946	0.35	2 532
October 1923	20 201 256	191 891 890	0.11	29 720

Source: Data adapted from C.L. Holtfrerich, *Die Deutsche Inflation 1914–23*, Walter de Gruyter, 1980.

Prices increased by a factor of 75 in 1922 but by considerably more in 1923. By October 1923 it took 192 million reichmarks to buy a drink that had cost 1 reichmark in January 1922. People carried money around in wheelbarrows when they went shopping. According to the old joke, thieves used to steal the barrows but leave the almost worthless money behind.

The flight from money When the inflation rate is π and the nominal interest rate r, the real interest rate is $(r - \pi)$ but the real return on non-interest-bearing money is simply $-\pi$, which shows how quickly the real value of money is being eroded by inflation. The extra real return on holding interest-bearing assets rather than money is $(r - \pi) - (-\pi) = r$. Even though people care about real rates of return, the *nominal* interest rate measures the cost of holding money.

Nominal interest rates rise with inflation. During the German hyperinflation the cost of holding money became enormous.

The **flight from money** is the dramatic reduction in the demand for real money when high inflation and high nominal interest rates make it very expensive to hold money.

The third column of Table 28-3 shows that by October 1923 real money holdings were only 11 per cent of their level in January 1922. How did people get by with such small holdings of real money?

People were paid twice a day so they could shop in their lunch hour before the real value of their cash depreciated too much. Any money not immediately spent was quickly deposited in a bank where it could earn interest. People spent a lot of time at the bank.

What lessons can we draw? First, *rising* inflation and *rising* interest rates can significantly reduce the demand for *real* money balances. Hyperinflations are a rare example in which a real quantity (real money balances) can change quickly and by a large magnitude.[2] Second, and as a direct result, money and prices can get quite out of line when inflation and nominal interest rates are rising. Table 28-3 shows that prices rose by six times as much as nominal money between January 1922 and July 1923, thus reducing the real money supply by 82 per cent, in line with the fall in real money demand.

Box 28-1 covering the quantity theory of money summarizes our discussion to date.

28-3 Inflation, money, and deficits

Persistent inflation must be accompanied by continuing money growth. Printing money to finance a large deficit may be the source of inflation. Do large budget deficits necessarily lead to inflation by forcing the government to print large quantities of extra money to finance these deficits? If so, tight *fiscal* policy will be required to fight inflation by keeping the deficit small and the rate of money growth low.

Figure 28-3 shows that there is no obvious link between the size of the budget deficit and the inflation rate. If we are to establish a relation between the deficit and inflation, we shall have to analyse the linkage or transmission mechanism more carefully.

Deficits and money growth

A deficit by the government or the public sector can be financed in two ways. First, the government can borrow from the private sector by selling bonds. The money received can then be used to meet the excess of expenditure over revenue. Second, the government can print money and spend it directly.

In a hyperinflation it is quite clear what is happening: deficits are being financed by printing large quantities of money. But this need not be the case. It is logically possible for the government to finance a deficit entirely by selling bonds. Although the government *might* decide to finance a constant fraction of its deficit by printing money, it need not do so. Figure 28-4 shows data for the UK. It shows the deficit as a percentage of GDP, and the corresponding annual rates of growth in nominal money, measured both by the narrow M0 and the broad M4 definitions. Particularly on the wider definitions, there seems little short-run relation between money and the deficit even when we average annual data over four-year periods.

In the longer run, the relationship between the size of the public sector deficit and the growth of the money supply is more likely to be significant. Suppose the government tries to run a persistently high deficit and finance it by bond issues alone. As the stock of bonds increases, interest payments on existing government debts rise. This tends to

---

[2] Even if nominal interest rates keep up with inflation and the real interest rate on bonds remains unchanged, the real return on cash is the negative of the inflation rate. Because changes in inflation affect this *real* return, large changes in inflation lead to large changes in *real* money demand.

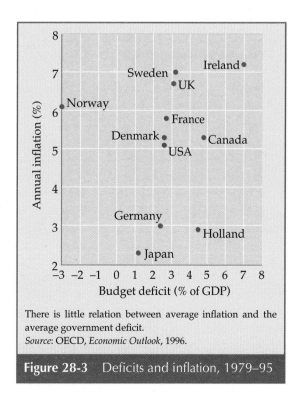

There is little relation between average inflation and the average government deficit.
Source: OECD, *Economic Outlook*, 1996.

Figure 28-3 Deficits and inflation, 1979–95

BOX 28-2 — Seigniorage, the inflation tax, and hyperinflation

The government has a monopoly on the creation of notes and coin. As an efficient token money, its production cost is tiny relative to its value as money. *Seigniorage* is value of real resources acquired by the government through its ability to print money. Real money demand M/P rises with real income. Thus, long-run economic growth provides the government with an opportunity to increase M without adding to P. A second potential source of seigniorage is the *inflation tax*.

Suppose real income and output are constant but that the government is politically weak and unable to raise sufficient taxes to cover all its spending commitments. It has little credibility and nobody will allow it to borrow. So it prints money to cover the budget deficit. If ΔM is the amount of high-powered money created (to pay for a nominal deficit of the same size), the real seigniorage is thus $(\Delta M)/P$, which is the same as $\Delta M/M \times (M/P)$, the growth rate of cash times the real demand for cash. Since real income is constant, the increase in nominal money must feed into prices sooner or later. Hence

$$\frac{\text{real revenue from}}{\text{inflation tax}} = \frac{\text{inflation}}{\text{rate}} \times \frac{\text{real cash}}{\text{demanded}}$$

This confirms that inflation helps the government by reducing the real value of the non-interest-bearing part of the government debt, namely cash. We can think of inflation as the tax rate and real cash as the tax base for the tax.

Now for the part you may not have thought of before. If money growth and inflation rise, does the government get more *real* revenue from the inflation tax? Remember that higher inflation will raise nominal interest rates and hence reduce the real demand for

cash. The figure shows the answer. At low inflation, real cash demand is high, but the multiple of the two is small. Similarly, at high inflation, although inflation tax rate is high the tax base – real cash demand – is now very low because nominal interest rates are so high. So the real revenue raised through the inflation tax cannot be increased indefinitely. After a certain point, faster money growth and higher inflation shrink the tax base more than they raise the tax rate.

The figure has two implications. First, if the government needs to cover a particular *real* deficit d by printing money, there may be two rates of money growth and inflation rate that will do the job. Either is a long-run equilibrium in which inflation will be constant. Second, if for political reasons the government has a real deficit as large as D, printing money cannot do the job. The economy explodes into hyperinflation. At high inflation, real cash demand is already low. Raising inflation further causes such a large percentage fall in the tiny demand for real cash that inflation tax revenue falls, the government prints even more cash, and the problem gets even worse.

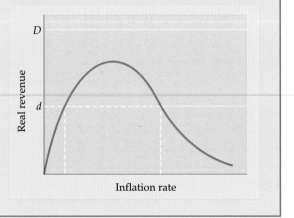

increase the government deficit, requiring yet more bond issues. And the government may have to offer higher interest rates to induce people to hold ever larger stocks of government debt. Thus it is possible that interest payments on existing debt, and hence the size of the public sector deficit, become so large that they cannot be met by new bond issues alone. If so, then unless the government takes

fiscal action to reduce the deficit, it will have no option but to resort to financing the deficit by printing money. That is how hyperinflation starts.

Money growth and inflation in the UK

We conclude this section by looking at the short-run relationship between money growth and inflation, each

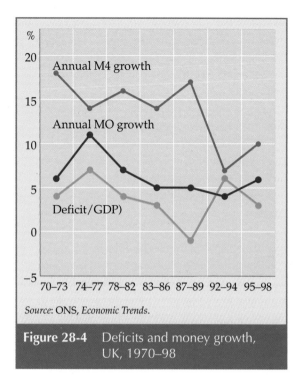

Source: ONS, *Economic Trends*.

Figure 28-4 Deficits and money growth, UK, 1970–98

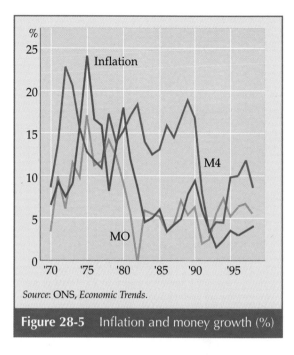

Source: ONS, *Economic Trends*.

Figure 28-5 Inflation and money growth (%)

expressed in percentage per annum, between 1970 and 1998. Figure 28-5 shows data comparing inflation in the UK with the annual growth rate of M0 and M4.

UK inflation peaked at 24 per cent in 1975. Figure 28-5 shows why in the late 1970s many people believed that UK inflation was determined by the rate of growth of broad money two years earlier. This view depended heavily on the behaviour of M4 and inflation in the mid-1970s. The relationship has been much less close since then.

Looking at the whole period shown in Figure 28-5, we can draw two conclusions. First, there is no simple relation between nominal money growth and inflation: changes in interest rates and in real income lead to changes in real money demand that destroy any simple relationship in the short run.

Second, since changes in nominal money are not immediately reflected in changes in prices, the evidence of Figure 28-5 is compatible with the account of sluggish adjustment we developed in Chapter 26. In the short run, changes in nominal money lead to changes in the real money supply, inducing changes in interest rates and income. Only in the longer run is there a tendency for prices and wages to adjust fully to restore full employment and potential output.

Recap

The demand for real money balances changes with changes in real income and in interest rates. In the long run, changes

in real money demand are usually quite small. Hence the equilibrium real money supply usually changes slowly. Thus persistent inflation is possible only if the government is printing money. High budget deficits may increase the temptation to print money in the long run, but there need not be a close short-run relation between the budget deficit and money growth.

Having examined the causes of inflation, we now turn our attention to its consequences. We have already seen the effect of inflation on nominal interest rates. When inflation is high, nominal interest rates must increase to protect the real rate of return earned by lenders. Otherwise there won't be many people in the lending business. In the next section we look at the effect of inflation on output and employment.

28-4 Inflation, unemployment, and output

We begin by discussing one of the most famous and infamous relationships in postwar macroeconomics. It is known as the Phillips curve.

The Phillips curve

In 1958 Professor A. W. Phillips of the London School of Economics demonstrated a strong statistical relationship between annual inflation and annual unemployment in the UK. Similar relationships were found to hold in other

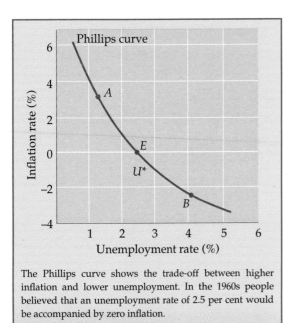

The Phillips curve shows the trade-off between higher inflation and lower unemployment. In the 1960s people believed that an unemployment rate of 2.5 per cent would be accompanied by zero inflation.

Figure 28-6 The Phillips curve

countries and this relationship quickly became known as the Phillips curve. It is shown in Figure 28-6.

The **Phillips curve** shows that a higher inflation rate is accompanied by a lower unemployment rate. It suggests we can *trade off* more inflation for less unemployment, or vice versa.

The Phillips curve seemed the answer to the problem of choosing macroeconomic policy in the 1960s, when Keynesian economics was at its most fashionable and economists were pessimistic about the speed with which the economy was capable of returning to full employment automatically through wage and price adjustments.

Keynesian governments saw the policy choice as follows. By selecting fiscal and monetary policy, the government could determine the level of aggregate demand and the extent of involuntary unemployment. The Phillips curve showed the level of inflation that would then ensue: higher aggregate demand put upward pressure on wages and prices and led to higher inflation but lower unemployment. It showed the menu of choices available. Governments simply had to decide how much extra inflation to tolerate in exchange for lower unemployment. They picked a point on the Phillips curve and set fiscal and monetary policies to achieve the corresponding level of aggregate demand and hence unemployment.

The Phillips curve in Figure 28-6 shows the trade-off that people believed they faced in the 1960s. In those days UK

unemployment was scarcely ever over 2 per cent of the labour force. But people sincerely believed that if they did the unthinkable, and cut back aggregate demand until unemployment rose to 2.5 per cent, the inflation rate would fall to zero.

Today, of course, we know that there have been years since 1970 when *both* inflation and unemployment were over 10 per cent. Something happened to the Phillips curve. The rest of this section explains why the simple Phillips curve of Figure 28-6 ceased to fit the facts.

Many of the important clues were discovered by Milton Friedman. However, let's try to work it out for ourselves using the analysis of aggregate demand and aggregate supply developed in Chapter 26. Suppose the level of full employment and potential output are fixed in the long run, but there is sluggish wage and price adjustment. In response to an initial shock, wages and prices change only slowly and the economy gradually works its way back to full employment as changes in prices alter the real money supply.

We begin by assuming that *in the long run* the nominal money supply is fixed. When the economy gets back to full employment, inflation will eventually be zero, maintaining the real money supply in line with the quantity of real money demanded when income equals potential output and nominal interest rates are at their long-run equilibrium level.

From an initial position of equilibrium in all markets, suppose there is a once-and-for-all increase in the nominal money supply. Since prices and wages do not immediately increase much, the real money supply increases and it takes lower interest rates to induce people to hold a larger quantity of real money. In the short run, higher aggregate demand for goods leads to higher output. Unemployment falls.

In Figure 28-6, we begin in equilibrium at E with zero inflation and unemployment equal to its natural rate U^*. The immediate effect of the increase in aggregate demand is to move the economy to a point such as A on the Phillips curve. Since prices have risen a bit, inflation is greater than zero, but higher aggregate demand has reduced unemployment below the natural rate U^*.

However, this is only the first step. The economy does not stay at A for ever. Gradually wages rise in response to higher demand for workers, and prices rise as firms pass on these wage increases. In Chapter 26 we described this response as a slow shift upwards in the short-run aggregate supply schedule. What happens as this process continues? First, higher prices reduce real money supply and push up interest rates to choke off the demand for real money.

Aggregate demand starts to fall and unemployment starts to rise again. Second, although wages and prices are still rising, they are rising at an ever slower rate. Since a higher price *level* is reducing the real money supply and aggregate demand relative to the level of potential output that firms wish to supply in the long run, there is less and less additional upward pressure on money wages and prices the longer adjustment continues.

In Figure 28-6 the economy is moving down the Phillips curve from *A* back to long-run equilibrium at *E*. When prices and money wages rise sufficiently to reduce the real money supply and raise interest rates to the levels that equate aggregate demand and potential output, the economy is back to long-run equilibrium. Since the nominal money supply is constant thereafter, inflation is then zero. There is no further pressure for wages or prices to change.

The same story may be told in reverse. If the initial shock is a downwards shift in aggregate demand, two things will happen in the short run. A partial fall in wages and prices will make inflation negative in the short run. But because wage and price adjustment is only partial, lower aggregate demand will increase unemployment. The economy will move to a point such as *B* on the Phillips curve in Figure 28-6. Thereafter, involuntary unemployment will gradually bid down wages and prices, thereby increasing the real money supply, lowering interest rates, and increasing aggregate demand. The economy will gradually move back up the Phillips curve from *B* to *E*, where full employment is restored and inflation is zero again.

We draw two conclusions. First, it was wrong to interpret the Phillips curve as a *permanent* trade-off between inflation and unemployment. Rather, it shows the temporary trade-off while the economy is adjusting to a shock to *aggregate demand*. An increase in aggregate demand requires a *temporary* period of inflation to reduce real money balances and get aggregate demand back to its full-employment level.

Second, the speed with which the economy moves back along the Phillips curve depends on the degree of flexibility of money wages, and hence of prices. Extreme monetarists believe that this flexibility is almost instantaneous. In this extreme version, it is only the fact that workers make annual wage settlements that prevents the economy from being continuously at its long-run equilibrium position. Changes in aggregate demand that were not foreseen when money wages were set mean that money wages and prices are temporarily at the wrong level to secure the real money supply which will equate aggregate demand and potential output. But such mistakes are rectified as soon as wages are

renegotiated. In contrast, the model of more sluggish wage adjustment that we developed in Chapter 26 means that the economy takes much longer to adjust fully to any shock to aggregate demand. Movements along the Phillips curve back to long-run equilibrium take much longer.

This examination of short-run adjustment is a useful beginning to our analysis. But it is only a beginning. First, we have assumed that the long-run equilibrium involves a constant nominal money supply and zero inflation. Second, we have assumed that all shocks are to aggregate demand rather than to aggregate supply. And, finally, we have assumed that the natural rate of unemployment remains constant over time. Once we recognize these three complications we shall be able to understand the complete picture.

The vertical long-run Phillips curve

The nominal money supply need not be constant in the long run. Suppose in long-run equilibrium the nominal money supply is growing at 20 per cent per annum. Inflation is 20 per cent per annum and nominal interest rates are, say, 22 per cent, so that the real interest rate is 2 per cent. Money wages are also growing at 20 per cent every year, so that real wages remain constant at their full-employment level. The real money supply is constant, since prices and nominal money are growing at the same rate, and equals the level of real balances demanded given the nominal interest rate of 22 per cent and the real income corresponding to full-employment output.

Is there any reason why output, employment, and unemployment in this long-run equilibrium should differ from the levels that these variables would attain if there were no inflation? In the absence of money illusion, people care about real variables not nominal variables. In long-run equilibrium, nominal money and money wages are growing at the *same* rate as prices. Neither the real money supply nor real wages are being eroded by inflation. And if nominal interest rates rise in line with inflation to maintain the real interest rate, neither lenders nor borrowers are doing better or worse as a result of inflation.

In thinking about the Phillips curve, Milton Friedman suggested that we recognize that the long-run equilibrium values of full employment, potential output, real wages, and unemployment will be unaffected by the inflation rate. Since all nominal variables can keep up with inflation and maintain the values of the corresponding real variables, and since people care only about real variables, the equilibrium values of these real variables will be unaffected by inflation in the long run when everyone has had the chance to adjust fully to the equilibrium inflation rate.

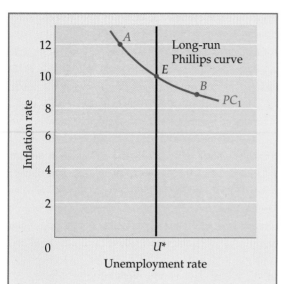

Since people care about real variables not nominal variables, when full adjustment has been completed people will arrange for all nominal variables to keep up with inflation. The vertical long-run Phillips curve shows that eventually the economy gets back to the natural rate of unemployment U^*, whatever the long-run inflation rate. There is no long-run trade-off between inflation and unemployment. The short-run Phillips curve PC_1 shows short-run adjustment as before. The height of the short-run Phillips curve depends on the rate of inflation and nominal money growth in long-run equilibrium, as shown by the position of the point E on the long-run Phillips curve.

Figure 28-7   The long-run Phillips curve

In Figure 28-7 we show this as a vertical long-run Phillips curve. Whatever the long-run rate of money growth and inflation, eventually everyone can adjust to it and the economy will get back to the natural rate of unemployment U^*. Thus, if the money supply grows at 10 per cent a year for ever, eventually the economy will reach long-run equilibrium at E. Inflation will be 10 per cent, money wages will grow at 10 per cent, and unemployment will be U^*.

Suppose we begin from long-run equilibrium at E. We can repeat the analysis of short-run adjustment we discussed using Figure 28-6. Any stimulus to aggregate demand will temporarily reduce unemployment, and will put upward pressure on wages and prices until a temporary period of extra inflation, during which prices grow faster than nominal money, reduces the real money supply and restores aggregate demand to its full-employment level.

Hence we draw the short-run Phillips curve, PC_1. The long-run equilibrium point E is a point on this Phillips curve. But in the short run, a boost to aggregate demand will take the economy to A. Thereafter, pressure on wages and

prices will reduce the real money supply and aggregate demand and take the economy back along PC_1 to E again. Conversely, any drop in aggregate demand will initially take the economy to B. Higher unemployment will then moderate the rate of growth of money wages and prices, boost the real money supply and aggregate demand, and move the economy along PC_1 back to E.

As in Figure 28-6, the short-run Phillips curve describes the temporary trade-off between inflation and unemployment *while the economy is adjusting to a change in aggregate demand*. But the height of the short-run Phillips curve is determined by the height of the point at which it crosses the vertical long-run Phillips curve, namely the rate of money growth and inflation in long-run equilibrium.

Friedman's insight explains why most economies had higher inflation at each unemployment rate in the 1970s and 1980s: the short-run Phillips curve had shifted upwards. Why? Because governments were printing money at a faster rate than before. Hence the long-run equilibrium inflation rate had risen. The point E lay further up the long-run Phillips curve in Figure 28-7. The short-run Phillips curve passing through this point had shifted upwards.

Expectations and credibility

Figure 28-8 allows us to put this apparatus to work to discuss what happens when a new government is elected with a commitment to get inflation down.

Suppose the economy begins in long-run equilibrium at E facing the short-run Phillips curve PC_1. Nominal money, prices, and money wages are all rising at the rate π_1. The government believes that inflation is unacceptably high and in the long run wants to get inflation down to the lower rate π_2. It wants to get to position F. The day the government is elected it announces that money growth is to be permanently reduced from π_1 to π_2.

In the short run, firms are locked into their previous agreements to increase money wages at the old inflation rate π_1. They have little scope for reducing the rate at which prices are rising in the short run. Hence a reduction in nominal money growth leads to a reduction in the real money supply. Prices are rising faster than nominal money. Aggregate demand falls and there is involuntary unemployment. The economy moves along the short-run Phillips curve PC_1 to A. Unemployment is higher and inflation is only slighly reduced. The key question is, what happens next?

On the optimistic scenario, workers believe that the government will stick to its tighter monetary policy and inflation will quickly fall. In the next round of wage

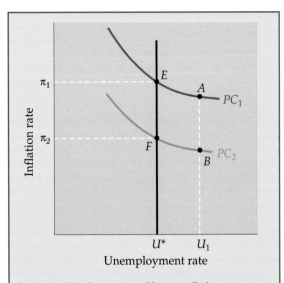

Beginning from long-run equilibrium at E, the government cuts the rate of money growth from π_1 to π_2. Initially this reduces the real money supply and moves the economy from E to A. Unemployment increases to U_1. If people believe that money growth will remain π_2, they realize that the new long-run equilibrium will be at F. The short-run Phillips curve shifts from PC_1 to PC_2 and the economy moves from A to B. There is a sharp fall in money wage growth because people realize that inflation will be lower and cost of living wage claims can be moderated. Thereafter the economy moves up PC_2 from B to F. However, if people believe that the rate of money growth will soon return to its original level π_1, they cannot moderate wage increases in anticipation of falling inflation. The short-run curve remains PC_1. In the short run, nominal money is growing at π_2, but inflation is higher. Hence the Keynesian slump intensifies since the real money supply is still being reduced.

Figure 28-8   Expectations and credibility

bargaining, they can afford to ask for a much lower rate of increase in money wages without expecting any reduction in real wages, since they expected inflation to fall quickly. Because unemployment has now reached U_1, in excess of the equilibrium rate U^*, there will be *additional* downward pressure on wages. Hence the economy moves from A to B on the new short-run Phillips curve PC_2 corresponding to the new long-run inflation rate π_2. Inflation has indeed fallen quickly. The economy then moves from B to F. While inflation is less than the rate of money growth π_2, the real money supply is expanding to boost aggregate demand and restore unemployment to the natural rate U^*.

Now for the pessimistic scenario. Suppose that, when the economy first reaches A, workers do not believe that the government will persevere with its new tough monetary policy. They think π_1 will remain the equilibrium inflation

rate in the long run. Since they think inflation will remain high, workers cannot afford to take nominal wage cuts in anticipation of lower inflation. They believe that it is the short-run Phillips curve PC_1 not PC_2 that is relevant. But if the economy stays at A while the government in fact is only increasing the money supply at the lower rate π_2, in the short run prices are rising more quickly than nominal money. The real money supply is falling yet again, aggregate demand is further reduced, and unemployment increases as the economy moves further down PC_1. Moreover, the worse this slump becomes, the more likely it is that the government's nerve will crack and it will conclude that unemployment has reached such unacceptable proportions that the money supply must be increased to boost aggregate demand again. A belief that the government's nerve will crack can become a self-fulfilling prophecy. The economy will stay on PC_1, and the attempt to reduce inflation substantially will have failed. Gradually the economy will move back along PC_1 to equilibrium at E.

This insight explains why governments go to such lengths to proclaim that there will be no U-turn from the tight monetary policy. The sooner people accept that the long-run inflation rate really will be lower, the sooner wage claims will moderate. To help convince people that the government will stick to its tight monetary targets, governments often announce a commitment to low money growth targets for several years into the future.

Changes in the natural rate of unemployment

In the long-run, the Phillips curve is vertical at the natural rate of unemployment U^*, the level of voluntary unemployment when the labour market is in equilibrium. In the previous chapter we discussed the forces that could change the natural rate of unemployment. We also argued that the natural rate had steadily increased since the mid-1960s. Structural unemployment had increased, and organized workers had secured real wage increases in excess of their productivity increases.

In terms of Figure 28-8, an increase in the natural rate of unemployment shifts the vertical long-run Phillips curve to the right. It continues to pass through the natural rate of unemployment, which has increased.

Inflation and unemployment since 1960

The original Phillips curve seemed to offer a permanent trade-off between inflation and unemployment. Moreover, it suggested that both inflation *and* unemployment could be extraordinarily low.

In the 1960s and the early 1970s, many governments were committed to maintaining full employment even in the short run. Any shock that tended to increase inflation – whether a wage claim by a trade union or a rise in the cost of a raw material – was accommodated by an increase in the money supply to prevent a reduction of the real money supply in the short run. Since governments were often raising the rate of money growth but rarely reducing it, money growth and inflation gradually increased. That explains why inflation rose above its level of the 1960s. Since the mid-1970s, government policy has changed in many countries. The emphasis is now on keeping inflation down. That is why inflation has fallen since the early 1980s.

What about unemployment? We now understand that the Phillips curve is vertical in the long run at the natural rate of unemployment. An increase in the natural rate of unemployment in many countries is an important component of the rise in actual unemployment in those countries. But it is not the whole story. We understand now that the short-run Phillips curve shows the *temporary* trade-off between inflation and unemployment while the economy is adjusting to an aggregate demand shock and gradually working its way back to potential output and the natural rate of unemployment. The height of the short-run Phillips curve depends on current expectations about future inflation and money growth.

At the beginning of the 1980s, inflation was high because it had been high in the past. Anti-inflation policies were only just beginning to bite. When tight money was first introduced, the real money supply was cut since inflation did not fall immediately. Aggregate demand fell and the economy moved to the right along the short-run Phillips curve. In addition to a high natural rate of unemployment, many countries were experiencing a short-run Keynesian slump. Involuntary unemployment was also high.

In the 1990s, many European economies were trying to reduce inflation to very low levels to show they were fit candidates for monetary union. Even countries such as the UK that were undecided about whether to join still pressed ahead with tight policies to get inflation down. These policies helped keep European unemployment at high levels. But once inflation had been defeated, continuing tight policies was unnecessary. British unemployment has fallen a lot since 1993.

An aggregate supply shock

What is the effect of an aggregate supply shock such as the doubling of oil prices? Overnight, inflation increases as firms pass on increased costs in higher prices. Suppose

there has not yet been time for employment to change. What happens next depends on what the government does, and on what people expect the government to do.

Suppose the government does *not* accommodate the shock. Money growth remains unchanged. With higher inflation, the real money supply is reduced, interest rates rise, and aggregate demand falls. There is a Keynesian slump and stagflation.

Stagflation is a period of both high inflation and high unemployment. It is often caused by an adverse supply shock.

Gradually, involuntary unemployment bids down wages or moderates wage increases. The inflation rate falls below the fixed rate of money growth, and the real money supply starts to expand again. Eventually the economy gets back to the natural rate of unemployment. Since money growth has remained unchanged, in the long run the inflation rate has not been altered by the adverse supply shock.

Suppose instead that the government *had* accommodated the aggregate supply shock. When inflation first increased, the government simply raised permanently the rate of money growth to match this higher inflation rate. There would be no reduction in the real money supply, even in the short run. Aggregate demand would not be reduced in the short run and there would be no increase in unemployment. But the economy would be left with permanently higher rates of money growth and inflation.

This example highlights the policy dilemma. If the government refuses to accommodate the shock, it will take a painful period of unemployment before wage and price adjustment restores the economy to its original equilibrium position in the long run. But long-run inflation will not have increased. However, by accommodating the original supply shock to prices, the government can avoid the Keynesian slump by maintaining aggregate demand; but only at the price of permanently higher inflation.

Again, the credibility of policy is crucial. Before the Thatcher government took office in the UK, workers recognized that governments were so frightened of high unemployment that they would accommodate almost any shock. Extravagant wage claims would buy temporarily higher real wages until prices adjusted fully. And in the long run the government would increase the money supply to maintain aggregate demand at full employment, so there was little danger of additional Keynesian unemployment. By refusing to accommodate high money wage claims, the Thatcher government gradually convinced workers that such claims reduce the real money supply, reduce aggregate demand, and push up unemployment. Since 1980 many union leaders have found little support from their members when they proposed large wage increases.

Once the Thatcher government had established the credibility of its determination to fight inflation, it was then able to relax policy a bit in the mid-1980s and achieve a sustained boom. For five or six years inflation remained low. Wage-setters believed that, in spite of a monetary and fiscal expansion, any outbreak of inflation would quickly be met by a return to restrictive policies. But the longer policy remained looser, the more wage-setters began to wonder whether the government really would tighten policy if required. When inflation began to climb again in 1989, the government was forced to raise interest rates substantially to try to restore its credibility.

It was against this background that the UK decided to join the Exchange Rate Mechanism (ERM) of the European Monetary System (EMS) in 1990. At the time, it seemed likely to enhance the credibility of monetary policy by tying UK interest rates to those of EMS partners, notably Germany. In practice, for reasons we explain in later chapters, the high interest rates that the German economy required at this time proved unacceptably tough medicine for many EMS countries.

A speculative run forced sterling out of the EMS in September 1992. Since by then the UK was in a deep recession, an immediate outbreak of inflationary expectations was not likely against a background of high and rising unemployment. But to keep inflation expectations in check in the longer run, the UK had to move towards greater independence for the Bank of England. We discuss central bank independence in Sections 28-6 and 28-7.

Recap of the relation between inflation and unemployment

We have reached the following conclusions. There is essentially *no* long-run trade-off between inflation and unemployment. The long-run Phillips curve is vertical at the natural rate of unemployment. The short-run Phillips curve is a temporary trade-off between inflation and unemployment when the economy is adjusting to shocks to aggregate demand. The height of this short-run trade-off depends on beliefs about money growth and inflation in the long run. But there is no trade-off *between* inflation and unemployment in the short run when shocks come from the supply side. Initially, higher inflation is likely to be accompanied by higher unemployment. What happens next depends crucially on the extent to which the government accommodates the supply-side shock.

28-5 The costs of inflation

People dislike inflation. And governments think it worth while to adopt tight fiscal and monetary policies aimed at reducing inflation, even though in the short run these policies may mean higher unemployment and lower output. Why exactly is inflation such a bad thing? Now that we understand what causes inflation and what some of its effects are, we are in a much better position to answer this question.

Inflation illusion?

Some of the arguments most commonly used to show why inflation is a bad thing are in fact quite spurious, and suggest that people may suffer from inflation illusion.

People have **inflation illusion** when they confuse nominal and real changes. People's welfare depends on real variables, not nominal variables.

It is incorrect to say that inflation is bad because it makes goods more expensive. If *all* nominal variables are increasing at the same rate, people have larger nominal incomes and can buy the same physical quantity of goods as before. If people think about their nominal expenditure without recognizing that their nominal incomes are also increasing, they have inflation illusion. It is real incomes that tell us how many goods people can afford to buy.

A second kind of illusion is more subtle. Suppose there is a sharp increase in the real or relative price of oil. In countries that import large quantities of oil, people will now be worse off. The country as a whole has to divert goods from domestic consumption to exports in order to earn the extra foreign currency with which to purchase the more expensive oil imports. Hence domestic consumption per person has to fall. However, it can fall in one of two ways.

The first way is if workers do not ask for 'cost-of-living' wage increases to cover the higher cost of oil-related products. Real wages fall since the old level of money wages now buys fewer goods. Suppose also that domestic firms absorb the increase in their oil-related fuel costs and do not pass on these costs in higher prices. There is no increase in either domestic prices or domestic money wages. The domestic economy has adjusted to the adverse supply shock without inflation. And people are inevitably worse off.

Suppose instead that people try to maintain their old standard of living. Workers put in for cost-of-living increases to restore their real wages, and firms protect their profit margins by increasing prices in line with higher wage and fuel costs. There is a lot of domestic inflation, which the government accommodates by printing extra money. Eventually the economy settles down in its new long-run equilibrium position, but what does this new equilibrium look like?

People must still be worse off. The rise in the real oil price has not disappeared by magic. It still takes more domestic exports, made possible by lower domestic consumption, to pay for the more expensive oil imports. Hence in the new long-run equilibrium workers will find that their real wages have been reduced and firms may find that their profit margins have been squeezed. This is the market mechanism that brings about the required fall in domestic expenditure and allows resources to be transferred to the export industries.

What people notice is that there has been a period of rising wages and rising prices, but that somehow wages did not manage to keep up with price rises. Real wages fell. But people draw the wrong conclusion. It was not the inflation that made them worse off, but the rise in oil prices. Real wages would have fallen whether or not there had been a domestic inflation. When inflation is caused by an adverse supply shock, and is allowed to persist because the government adopts an accommodating monetary expansion, it is neither the inflation nor the monetary expansion that makes people worse off: it is the adverse supply shock. The inflation is merely a symptom of the initial refusal to accept the new reality.

So far, we have examined some spurious arguments about why inflation is a bad thing. We now turn to more serious arguments. The subsequent discussion has two central themes. First, was the inflation fully expected in advance? Or are people still adjusting to inflation which took them by surprise? Second, do our institutions, including government regulations and the tax system, enable people to adjust fully to inflation once they have come to expect it? The costs of inflation depend on the answer to these two questions.

Complete adaptation and full anticipation

Imagine an economy in which inflation is 10 per cent a year for ever. Everybody knows it, anticipates its continuation, and can take it into account when making wage bargains or lending money. All prices, money wages, and the nominal money supply grow at 10 per cent a year. Inflation is eroding neither real incomes nor the real money supply. The economy is at full employment. Government policy is also fully adjusted. Nominal taxes are being changed every year to keep real tax revenue constant. Nominal government spending is increasing at 10 per cent a year so that real government spending is constant.[3]

Nominal interest rates have risen to the constant level necessary to maintain the equilibrium real interest rate when inflation is 10 per cent a year. Share prices are rising with inflation to maintain the real value of company shares on the stock exchange. The tax treatment of interest earnings and capital gains has been adjusted to take account of inflation. In real terms, taxation of interest earnings and capital gains remains unaffected by inflation.[4] Pensions and other transfer payments are being raised every year, in line with expected inflation.

This economy does not suffer from inflation illusion. Individuals and the government fully expect a 10 per cent inflation and have adjusted as fully as they can to minimize its effect on real variables. This was the insight that lay behind the long-run vertical Phillips curve in the previous section. But even in this ideal world, is complete adjustment possible?

Shoe-leather costs   Earlier in this chapter, we explained that nominal interest rates usually rise with inflation to preserve the real rate of interest. But the nominal interest rate is the opportunity cost of holding money. Hence when inflation is higher, people hold less money balances. Section 28-2 examined the flight from money during hyperinflation as an extreme example of this relation between inflation and the demand for real balances.

We began our study of money in Chapter 23 by showing that society uses money to economize on the time and effort involved in undertaking transactions. When high nominal interest rates induce people to economize on holding real money balances, society must use a greater quantity of resources in undertaking transactions and therefore has less resources available for production and consumption of goods and services. We call this the *shoe-leather cost* of higher inflation.

Shoe-leather costs stand for all the extra time and effort people put into transacting when they try to get by with lower real balances.

---

[3] For simplicity we assume there is no productivity growth, no changes in supply or demand conditions, and hence a given level of full employment and potential output. Pure inflation could also happen, of course, in an economy with underlying real growth of output and employment.

[4] During times of inflation, amy people worry about a country's international competitiveness. We discuss this in the next chapter. We shall see that it is also possible to adjust the exchange rate over time so that a country's real competitiveness remains unaffected by inflation.

Menu costs   When prices are rising, price labels have to be changed. For example, menus have to be reprinted to show the higher price of meals.

The **menu costs** of inflation refer to the physical resources required to reprint price tags when prices are rising (or falling).

The faster the rate of price change, the more frequently menus have to be reprinted if real prices are to remain constant.

Among the menu costs of inflation we should probably include the effort of doing mental arithmetic. When the inflation rate is zero it is easy to walk into a shop and see that a pound of steak costs the same as it did three months ago. But when inflation is 25 per cent a year, it takes a bit more effort to compare the price of steak today with that of three months ago so as to see what has happened to the real or relative price of steak. Although people without inflation illusion try to think in real terms, the mental arithmetic required involves real time and effort.

How significant are menu costs? In supermarkets it may be relatively easy to change price tags. But the cost of changing parking meters, pay telephones, and slot machines are more substantial. In fact, in countries where inflation rates are high, pay telephones usually take tokens whose price can be easily changed without having to physically alter the machines.

Even when inflation is perfectly anticipated and the economy has fully adjusted to inflation, it is impossible to avoid shoe-leather costs and menu costs. Although these costs become very significant when the inflation rate reaches hyperinflation levels, they suggest that the social cost of living with 20 per cent inflation for ever might not be too large. However, this applies to the case in which society is best able to adjust to inflation. As we now see, the costs of inflation will be larger in other situations.

Fully anticipated inflation when institutions fail to adapt fully

In this section we assume that the inflation is fully anticipated but that institutional factors prevent people from implementing some of the changes that would be required if nominal variables are to adjust in line with expected inflation. Because nominal variables are prevented from fully adjusting, inflation then affects more real variables than the shoe-leather and menu effects identified above.

Interest rate controls   To preserve real interest rates, nominal interest rates must be allowed to rise in line with

inflation. If chequing accounts paid interest, shoe-leather costs would apply only to cash itself since, as yet, we have found no way to pay interest on cash.

In many countries chequing accounts either pay no interest or pay a small interest rate which typically does not rise with inflation.

Whether these are permanent costs of inflation remains to be seen. One effect of persistently high inflation is that people start pressing for institutional changes to allow nominal variables to keep up with inflation. The longer high inflation continues, the more likely it is that banks and other institutions will be forced to pay competitive nominal interest rates on various kinds of bank deposits. But since institutional change is usually quite slow, in the short run the effect of a move from low inflation to high inflation may be to reduce real interest rates on many kinds of borrowing and lending, thereby benefiting borrowers and penalizing lenders.

Taxes   The second major effect of fully anticipated inflation when institutional adjustment is incomplete is that tax rates may not be fully inflation-adjusted. The first problem is fiscal drag.

Fiscal drag is the increase in real tax revenue when inflation raises nominal incomes and pushes people into higher tax brackets in a progressive income tax system.

Here is a simple example. Suppose income below £2000 is untaxed but people pay income tax at 30 pence in the pound on all income over £2000. Initially, a person with an income of £3000 pays tax at 30 per cent on the income over £2000. Thus income tax paid is £300. Suppose that after ten years of inflation all wages and prices have doubled but the tax brackets and tax rates remain as before. The person's income is now £6000. Nominal tax paid is 30 per cent on the £4000 by which nominal income exceeds £2000. Hence nominal tax paid is £1200. Thus, although wages and prices have only doubled, nominal taxes paid have increased fourfold. Fiscal drag has increased the real tax burden. The government is benefiting from the inflation at the expense of private individuals.

To make the tax system inflation-neutral, nominal tax brackets must be increased in line with inflation. In the above example, if the real tax exemption limit had been preserved by raising the nominal limit from £2000 to £4000 when other nominal variables doubled, everything would be inflation-adjusted.

When governments adjusted the nominal tax bands upwards to offset inflation this used to be portrayed as a cut in income tax or increased government generosity. This is pure inflation illusion. The adjustments are required merely to maintain the real burden of income tax unchanged. In countries such as the UK and the United States, this logic has now been accepted. Tax bands are now automatically increased in line with inflation unless a deliberate government policy to the contrary is adopted.[5]

Taxing capital   Income tax levied on interest income is also affected by inflation. Suppose there is no inflation and the nominal and real interest rates are both 4 per cent. With a 30 per cent tax rate, the after-tax real return on lending is 2.8 per cent a year. Now suppose inflation is 10 per cent a year and nominal interest rates rise to 14 per cent to maintain the pre-tax real interest rate of 4 per cent. But in the current tax system in most countries, lenders must pay income tax at 30 per cent on nominal income. Hence the after-tax nominal interest rate is 9.8 per cent (0.7×14). Subtracting the 10 per cent inflation rate, the after-tax *real* interest rate is actually *negative*. This compares with the 2.8 per cent after-tax real interest rate when inflation was zero.

What goes wrong? When inflation is 10 per cent, nominal interest rates are 14 per cent. But 10 per cent of this is not real income, merely a payment for keeping up with inflation. Only 4 per cent is the real interest rate providing real income. But income tax applies to the whole 14 per cent. Hence higher inflation reduces the real return on lending because the tax system is not properly inflation-adjusted.

Higher inflation rates must have real effects in such a system. If, as we have assumed, the pre-tax nominal interest rate rises fully in line with inflation to preserve the pre-tax interest rate to borrowers, then higher inflation makes lenders lose out. Conversely, higher inflation *could* lead to even higher nominal interest rates to preserve the real after-tax interest rate to lenders. But then the real pre-tax interest rate to borrowers would rise with inflation. Either way, the government is benefiting by higher real tax revenue. Individual borrowers or lenders are losing out.

Capital gains taxation provides another example. Suppose people have to pay the government 30 per cent of any capital gains they make when buying and selling

shares. When inflation is zero only real gains are taxed. But when inflation is 10 per cent, nominal share prices must rise merely to preserve their real value. People have to pay capital gains tax even though they are not making real capital gains.

Taxing profits   Inflation may also increase the real burden of taxation on company profits. Here is a simple example. Suppose a company holds some stocks of finished goods awaiting sale. In an inflationary world, the nominal value of these stocks will increase over time. If these capital gains are treated as taxable company profits, firms will have to pay more taxes even though the real value of their stocks remains unchanged. Such inconsistencies in the tax system would disappear if firms and the government moved over to inflation accounting.

Inflation accounting is the adoption of definitions of costs, revenue, profit and loss that are fully inflation-adjusted.

Thus institutional imperfections help explain why inflation can have real effects even when individuals have fully anticipated that inflation. Until institutions are fully adjusted to inflation, these effects can be significant. In many instances it is the government that stands to gain most by inflation.

Earlier in the chapter we argued that a period of high unemployment and lower output may be required if inflation is to be reduced. Before assuming that the economy should pay this price for reducing the costs of inflation, it is important to ask whether it might not be cheaper to adjust the institutions so that inflation no longer imposed these costs. We discuss 'living with inflation' later in the chapter. For the moment we merely note that institutional adjustment would imply both the once-and-for-all cost of thinking how to design inflation-adjusted institutional rules, and the menu costs of calculating and implementing adjustments as they were required to offset steadily rising prices.

Unexpected inflation

Previously, we assumed that inflation was fully anticipated. Now we discuss problems that arise when inflation takes people by surprise.

Redistribution   When prices rise unexpectedly, the losers are people who own nominal assets and the gainers are people with nominal liabilities. The terms of the original nominal contract to buy or sell, lend or borrow, may have been written to take full account of expected inflation, but

---

5 How about indirect taxes? Percentage taxes on value, such as VAT, automatically increase nominal tax revenue in proportion to inflationary rises in the price level. However, *specific* duties, such as £5 a bottle on whisky, need to be raised as the price level rises. In the UK there is no *automatic* formula for raising such duties. Each year the government makes a decision about how much to raise them.

they cannot have incorporated inflation that subsequently takes people by surprise.

Suppose you expect inflation to be 10 per cent and agree to lend £100 for a year at 12 per cent, expecting a real interest rate of 2 per cent. Unexpectedly, inflation jumps to 20 per cent. You thought you would have £112 next year with which to buy goods whose price had risen from £100 to £110. In fact, goods cost £120 next year and you have lost out by lending. The real interest rate is −8 per cent. Conversely, the borrower has gained. Having borrowed £100 today and promised to repay £112 next year, the borrower suddenly finds that all nominal variables, including the borrower's nominal income, have risen by 20 per cent. The real interest rate of −8 per cent tells us that, if the borrower had put the £100 into durable goods today, these could be sold for £120 the next year, allowing the borrower to repay £112 as promised, leaving a profit of £8.

In one sense, since to every borrower there corresponds a lender, one person's gain is another person's loss. In the aggregate the two cancel out. But unexpected inflation results in a redistribution of income and wealth, in this case from lenders to borrowers. This has two consequences. First, it may lead to economic dislocation. For example, some people may have to declare bankruptcy, which in turn may affect other people. Second, we have to adopt a value judgement about whether we like the redistribution that is taking place. For example, if rich lenders are losing out to poor borrowers, political parties that believe in a more equal income distribution may not mind this effect, whereas political parties supported by the rich may think this a very bad thing.

One of the most important redistributions is between the government and the private sector. Unexpected inflation reduces the real value of all outstanding nominal government debt. Not only is the real money supply reduced, but the real price at which the government has to buy back its bonds is reduced. Equivalently, the government has a higher nominal tax revenue with which to buy back bonds at the already agreed nominal price.[6]

Does this redistribution matter? This is a tricky question. If the government is better off it may be able to cut taxes and undo the effect of such a redistribution. But typically, the people who lent to the government and lost out through unexpected inflation tend not to be the same people who will benefit from any tax cuts the government then can offer.

The old and the young   In practice, many of the people who lend by buying nominal assets are the old. Having paid off their mortgages and built up savings during their working life, they may well have put their wealth into nominal bonds to provide income during retirement. These people lose out when there is unexpected inflation and the real value of the bonds falls. They also lose out if they keep their wealth in non-interest-bearing money, either in a current account or under the bed.

The nominal debtors are the young, and especially those just entering middle age, who have a large mortgage to move into a large house to see them through the process of bringing up a family. Having borrowed a fixed sum to buy a house, they gain when unexpected inflation increases house prices and nominal incomes without any matching increase in the nominal sum they owe the bank or building society.

Unexpected inflation redistributes from the old to the young. If we believe in equality, this redistribution is undesirable. With technical progress and productivity increases, each generation is already likely to have a higher lifetime standard of living than its predecessor. Further redistribution from the old to the young accentuates inequality between generations.

Uncertainty about inflation

Uncertainty about future inflation rates imposes two kinds of costs. First, it increases the complexity of making long-term plans since a much wider range of possible (nominal) outcomes must be investigated. As with shoe-leather costs, this increases the real resources that society must expend in making plans, undertaking transactions, and doing business. Second, people dislike risk. Chapter 15 explained why. Briefly, the extra benefits of the champagne years are poor compensation for the years of starvation. People would rather average out these extremes and live comfortably all the time. The psychic costs of worrying about how to cope with the bad years may also be important.

When people must enter into nominal contracts, an increase in uncertainty about the inflation rate increases the uncertainty about the eventual real value of the nominal bargains that people are currently making. This is a genuine cost of inflation. However, the next stage in the argument is more tricky. It is frequently argued that reducing the average level of inflation also reduces the uncertainty about inflation. In fact, it is hard to show in any theoretical model

---

[6] Why do we emphasize unexpected inflation? Because expected inflation was already built into the terms on which bonds were originally issued. Since expected inflation is incorporated into nominal interest rates, either the government had to offer a high nominal payment per annum or it had to issue the bonds at a lower price than it promised to repurchase them at, so that people could make capital gains to offset expected inflation.

why, if people expect 2 per cent inflation but think it could be as high as 4 per cent or as low as zero, then when people expect 20 per cent inflation the same range of outcomes (namely as high as 22 per cent or as low as 18 per cent) should not apply. Nevertheless, there is some empirical evidence that inflation rates change by more when inflation is already high. Hence higher average inflation rates may be accompanied by more uncertainty about inflation. If so, this imposes a real cost. It may be a very important cost.

28-6 Defeating inflation

In the long run the inflation rate will be low if the rate of money growth is low. For this it may be necessary to keep fiscal policy fairly tight so that deficits are also low. However, to get to this position from an initial position of high inflation, it may be necessary to get through an intermediate period of high unemployment. Until prices and wages adjust to the new tight monetary and fiscal policies, real aggregate demand will fall. We have argued that this recession could last for a period of years rather than months. To incur the permanent benefits of lower inflation, the economy must first undergo a period of low output and employment.

Could this transition be made more quickly and less painfully? We have already explained that, the more credible the new policy, the faster is likely to be the speed of adjustment of wages and prices. We now examine other policies designed to speed up the process.

Incomes policies

Incomes policy is the attempt to influence wages and other incomes directly.

Suppose the government wishes to get inflation down from 10 per cent to 2 per cent. If, by explicit legislation or implicit pressure, it can persuade everyone to seek wage increases of only 2 per cent, price inflation will quickly fall to 2 per cent. If this transition happens quickly enough, *real* wages need not suffer.

It is commonly said, and essentially correct, that all previous attempts at incomes policy have been a failure, at best lasting for a short time before a new explosion of wages and prices took place. However, this need not be inevitable. We discuss several reasons why past incomes policies have been unsuccessful.

First, when governments have been in the business of direct intervention in the labour market, they have often been unable to resist pursuing other aims at the same time.

For example, in the UK in the 1970s the Labour government tried to reduce the differential between high-wage jobs and low-wage jobs by adopting an incomes policy that allowed an absolute rather than a percentage increase: £6 a week means much more to a worker getting £40 a week than to a worker getting £100 a week. By changing relative wages, such policies alter real wages from their equilibrium levels, lead to excess supply in some skills and excess demand in others, and set up pressures to circumvent or break the policy. But it is possible to introduce incomes policies to reduce nominal wage increases and inflation *without* attempting to tinker with real wages.

Second, one might suggest incomes policy as a temporary adjustment device. In the long run, slow nominal money growth is essential if low inflation is to be maintained. Some incomes policies have failed because governments hoped that long-term incomes policy could hold down money wages and prices even though nominal money was still growing at a rapid rate. Since real aggregate demand then quickly expands, wages and prices have to rise to reduce aggregate demand to its full employment level again.

Similarly, long-term incomes policies are hard to administer when equilibrium real wages for particular skills are changing over time. Freezing the existing wage structure by awarding everyone an equal cost-of-living wage increase will gradually set up powerful market forces of excess supply and excess demand.

These three important sources of past breakdowns in incomes policy might not apply if the policy were known to be a temporary device to speed up the adjustment of wages to an underlying change in nominal money growth that was widely believed to be permanent.

Institutional reform

This approach takes a long run view. It is concerned not with the temporary costs of first getting inflation down, but with how to *keep* inflation down. Box 28-3 provides evidence that central bank independence is a useful pre-commitment to tight monetary policy and low inflation.

Indeed, institutional pre-commitment was a favourite theme of the 1990s as the following examples show.

The Maastricht Treaty Signed in 1991, the treaty set out conditions both for entering EMU and after admission to EMU. The first requirement was to avoid loose fiscal policy: a ceiling of 3 per cent on budget deficits relative to GDP (though this may yet be interpreted in relation to the structural budget to allow some modest and temporary overshoot during recessions). High-debt countries were also

BOX 28-3   Central bank independence

Central bankers are cautious people unlikely to favour rapid money growth and inflation. So why do these occur? Either because the government cares so much about unemployment that it never tackles inflation, or because it is politically weak and ends up with a budget deficit which it finances, at least to some extent, by printing money. Essentially, inflation arises when governments overrule cautious bankers. Proposals for central bank independence mean *independence from the government*.

Suppose this could be achieved, and monetary policy on average was tighter. In the short run this might cause a recession, but in the long run prices and wages adjust and the economy returns to full employment. Hence, in the long run, where it is the level of full capacity output that counts, independent central banks should lead to lower inflation without any reduction in real output. That, after all, is what the vertical long-run Phillips curve is all about. Central bank independence is a pre-commitment by government to keep money tight and inflation low.

The two figures below, taken from an article by Harvard's Professors Alberto Alesina and Larry Summers (Summers is now US Secretary for the Treasury, shows that both predictions of the theory work out in practice – countries with more independent central banks have lower average inflation, yet there is no evidence that real output growth is lower in the long run.

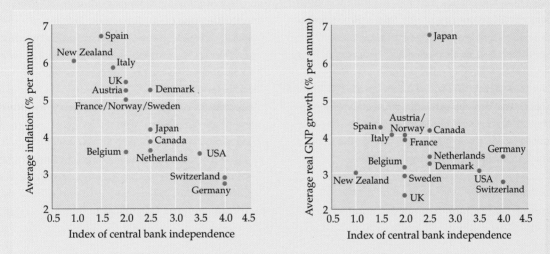

Source: A. Alesina and L. Summers, 'Central bank independence and macroeconomic performance: some comparative evidence', *Journal of Money, Credit, and Banking*, May 1993.

supposed to initiate actions to bring their debt/GDP levels below 60 per cent. Moreover, EMU entrants first had to succeed in disinflating to low levels, measured both directly by changes in price indexes and indirectly by nominal interest rates (the Fisher effect again!).

Not only did EU governments have to sign up for tight policy in the 1990s and beyond, EMU hopefuls had to undertake institutional reform, making their national central banks formally independent. And the Maastricht Treaty confirmed that the new European Central Bank will be constitutionally independent and mandated to pursue price stability.

Outside Europe   The US central bank – the Federal Reserve – is already pretty independent, and many other central banks, from Canada to New Zealand have also seen their independence enhanced. Within the United States, a succession of Congressional resolutions have also forced the

United States to end large budget deficits and move much closer to budget balance.

UK policy 1992–97   Despite losing the peg to the Deutsch-mark, since 1992 UK inflation has been remarkably low. UK monetary policy worked as follows. First, the Chancellor announced his inflation target for the coming years. Second, each month Treasury and Bank officials tried to agree on a recommendation about the stance of monetary policy that would achieve this medium-run objective while looking after the short-term needs of the real economy. At the monthly meeting of Chancellor and Governor (the Ken & Eddie show) the arguments would be considered *then the Chancellor alone would decide.*

Since previous Chancellors always 'took the Bank's views into account', what was new about this procedure? Two things. First, since the minutes of the Governor–Chancellor meeting were published a few weeks later, any objections by the Bank were highly publicized. Second, and formally separate from the monthly meetings, the Bank was given responsibility to produce a quarterly *Inflation Report*, openly published and *completely free from any Treasury control.* The Report quickly became very influential, because of its clear analysis, and the envy of other central banks. Despite the UK's success in maintaining low inflation since 1992, there were some who thought high European unemployment, an absence of adverse supply shocks, and the need to keep open the possibility of joining EMU had made this a period in which high inflation was in any case unlikely.

UK policy since 1997   On taking office in May 1997, the new Chancellor, Gordon Brown, quickly announced that the Bank of England would acquire 'operational independence' in deciding the level at which interest rates should be set. The Bank would endeavour to achieve an inflation target laid down by the Chancellor. Thus, the Bank would not itself choose this target. For example, in an emergency (e.g. a doubling of oil prices) the government could announce a temporarily higher target rather than force the Bank to initiate a drastic recession simply to bid prices down again very quickly. Nevertheless, any such change in the target would be politically difficult except in truly exceptional circumstances. Operational independence would thus act as a pre-commitment to policies favouring low inflation.

28-7 The Monetary Policy Committee

Since 1997 UK monetary policy has been set by the Bank of England's Monetary Policy Committee [MPC (www.

bankofengland.co.uk)], which meets monthly to set interest rates to try to hit the inflation target laid down by the Chancellor. Currently the target is 2.5 per cent annual inflation, plus or minus 1 per cent. If the MPC misses its target range, the Governor is obliged to write to the Chancellor explaining why.

An **inflation target** is an intermediate target for setting interest rates. It serves as a nominal anchor.

In this section, we discuss three questions. Why was the MPC given an inflation target rather than a target for the path of nominal money. How does it work? And how easy has it been for the MPC to decide where to set interest rates?

Inflation targets

Chapter 24 explained that, without a nominal anchor, there is nothing to die down the price level or any other nominal variable. Market forces determine real variables such as money M divided by prices P. Setting interest rates can influence M/P but not separately determine M and P. An intermediate target – an announced path for one of the nominal variables – is also required. For example, for a given path for M, once we know interest rates and output we know money demand M/P and can therefore work out the price level P.

Chapters 25 and 26 discussed what happens when the intermediate target is a path for nominal money. An inflation target is instead a path for prices themselves. It is an alternative to a nominal money target. Two reasons have made inflation targets increasingly popular. First, since we care about inflation, it seems natural to target inflation itself. Second, changes in banking behaviour caused by changes in competition and regulation have led to quite large and unpredictable changes in the demand for money. When banks offer better interest rates on deposits, they cut the cost of holding money. If the central bank has difficulty forecasting the demand for real money balances, it may be unsure what target for nominal money growth will achieve the path of inflation rate it really desires.

Because this seems obvious, why were money growth targets ever popular? Partly because data on money supply comes out much faster than data on the price level. However, given the headache of trying to forecast money demand, central banks would rather predict what the price level data is going to be.

Back to the future

Not only do lags in data mean that the MPC has to forecast where the economy is today, it also has to recognize that

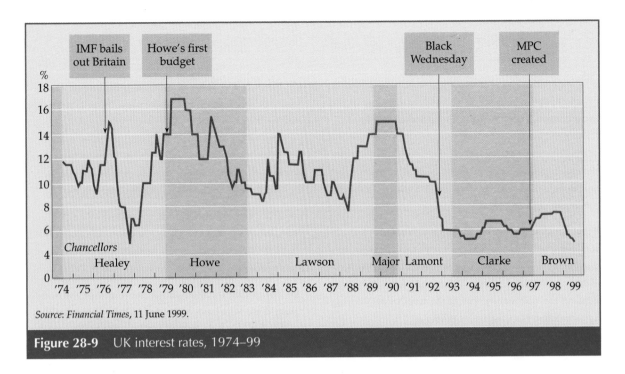

Figure 28-9   UK interest rates, 1974–99

interest rate medicine does not work immediately. In fact, it can take up to two years for a change in interest rates to have its full effect on private behaviour. Hence the MPC has to *forecast* the path of prices at least two years into the future merely to know where to set interest rates *today*!

On occasion, the MPC may raise interest rates even though current inflation is under control. This means that, in the absence of any change in interest rates, the MPC is forecasting that inflation will be too high. It then has to act quickly to keep inflation on track.

So far so good
Most people give the MPC high marks for their performance so far. It was prepared to change interest rates even when this was unpopular, and inflation remained close to 2.5 per cent as a result. Since inflation expectations were therefore low, nominal interest rates were low relative to the bad old days when inflation was high.

Figure 28-9 shows the history of UK interest rates since 1974. Although the Bank's operational independence in setting interest rates was granted in 1997, Figure 28-9 shows that the decisive break actually occurred in 1992 when sterling left the Exchange Rate Mechanism and changed nominal anchors from a pegged exchange rate to an inflation target. The MPC has been building on the earlier success during 1992–97.

SUMMARY

● The quantity theory of money asserts that changes in prices are caused chiefly by equivalent changes in the nominal money supply. In practice, prices cannot immediately adjust to changes in nominal money, so interest rates or income alter to change money demand. In the long run, changes in real income and interest rates can change real money demand and break any simple relation between nominal money and prices.

● A 1 per cent increase in inflation leads roughly to a 1 per cent increase in nominal interest rates so real interest rates are roughly unchanged. Since the nominal interest rate is the cost of holding money, higher inflation reduces the demand for real money. The flight from money during hyperinflation is a spectacular example.

● In the short run, there need be no close relation between the size of the budget deficit and the growth of the nominal money supply. In the long run, persistent use of bond finance to meet large deficits may so increase the government's interest payments that the government must resort to printing money if fiscal action is not taken to cut the deficit.

● The original Phillips curve showed a trade-off between inflation and unemployment. We now recognize that the short-run Phillips curve is a temporary trade-off showing how unemployment and inflation adjust to shocks to aggregate demand. Adverse supply shocks lead to higher inflation and higher unemployment when wage and price adjustment is sluggish.

● In the long run the Phillips curve is vertical. If people can completely adjust to inflation, it has no real effects. The economy returns to a natural rate of unemployment whatever the inflation rate.

● The height of the short-run Phillips curve depends on underlying money growth and expected inflation. To shift the Phillips curve downwards people must believe inflation will be lower in the future.

● Some of the claimed costs of inflation are illusory. Some people forget that their nominal incomes are rising; others fail to see that inflation may be the consequence of a shock that would have reduced real incomes in any case. The true costs of inflation depend on whether it was anticipated and on the extent to which the economy's institutions allow complete inflation-adjustment.

● Shoe-leather costs and menu costs are unavoidable costs of inflation and are larger the larger the inflation rate. Failure fully to inflation-adjust the tax system may also impose costs, even if inflation is anticipated.

● Unexpected inflation redistributes income and wealth from those who have contracted to receive nominal payments (lenders and workers) to those who have contracted to pay them (firms and borrowers).

● Uncertainty about future inflation rates imposes costs on people who dislike risk. Uncertainty may be greater when inflation is already high.

● Incomes policies might temporarily speed the transition to a lower inflation rate and reduce the extent of the Keynesian recession required. But they are unlikely to succeed in the long run. Low money growth is necessary for low inflation in the long run.

● Operational independence of central banks is designed to remove the temptation faced by politicians to boost the economy too much.

● Inflation targets are an alternative nominal anchor to targets for nominal money.

KEY TERms

REVIEW QUESTIONS

1 Suppose your real income is constant. This year you earn £10 000 and want to borrow £20 000 for ten years to buy a house, paying all the money back at the end. Make a list of your annual incomings and outgoings for each of these years if inflation is zero and the nominal interest rate is 2 per cent a year. Repeat the exercise when inflation is 10 per cent a year and the nominal interest rate is 12 per cent a year. Are the two situations the same?

2 Does your answer to question 1 explain why voters mind about high inflation even when nominal interest rates rise in line with inflation?

3 (a) How do you explain the following data? (b) Is inflation always a monetary phenomenon?

1996	Money growth	Inflation
	%	%
France	4	2
Japan	11	1
Germany	10	1
Holland	13	2
USA	−5	3
Italy	4	3

Source: The Economist.

4 Looking at data on inflation and unemployment over ten years, could you tell the difference between supply shocks and demand shocks?

5 Name five groups which lose out during inflation. Does it matter whether this inflation was anticipated?

6 How much of the popular dislike of inflation do you think is due to illusion?

7 Common fallacies Show why the following statements are incorrect. (a) Getting inflation down is the only way to cure high unemployment. (b) Inflation stops people saving. (c) Inflation stops people investing. (d) Without a budget deficit, there could be no inflation.

29 Open economy macroeconomics

LEARNING OUTCOMES

When you have finished this chapter, you should be able to:

- Describe the forex market and discuss how exchange rate regimes differ
- Develop balance of payments accounting, and explain key determinants of current account flows
- Analyse how perfect capital mobility leads speculators to equate expected returns on assets in different currencies
- Define the concepts of internal and external balance
- Analyse the effects of monetary and fiscal policy under fixed exchange rates
- Explore the effects of devaluation in the short run, medium run, and long run
- Analyse what determines floating exchange rates
- Explain how floating rates are affected by changes in monetary policy, fiscal policy, and resource discoveries

Exports and imports are each about 10 per cent of the size of GNP in the United States, 20 per cent in Japan, and 30 per cent in the UK, France, and Germany. Even in the United States, the exchange rate, international competitiveness, and the trade deficit are major issues. International considerations will be even more important in more open economies such as the UK, Germany, and Holland.

Open economy macroeconomics is the study of economies in which international transactions play a significant role.

In the early 1980s, President Mitterrand was elected in France on a socialist programme of fiscal expansion to reduce high unemployment. The value of the French franc quickly fell on the foreign exchange market and the French government was forced to abandon its election promises.

The UK recession of the early 1990s was exacerbated by high interest rates while the government (vainly) tried to defend the pound within the exchange rate mechanism of the EMS. International considerations have a major role in the formulation of domestic macroeconomic policy in open economies.

In this chapter we show how international transactions affect the domestic economy. The effects of monetary and fiscal policy are very different in an open economy from the effects we discussed in a closed economy. The international environment is not merely an afterthought which can be discussed separately from macroeconomics: in open economies it is intrinsic to the way these economies work. That is why we discuss these issues in Part 4. Wider issues of how the world economy behaves as a system are examined in Part 5.

29-1 The foreign exchange market

Different countries use different national currencies. In the UK, goods, services, and assets are bought and sold for pounds sterling; in the United States they are bought and sold for dollars.

The **foreign exchange (forex) market** is the international market in which one national currency can be exchanged for another. The price at which the two currencies exchange is the **exchange rate**.

For UK residents, an exchange rate of $1.6/£ measures the international value of sterling; the number of units of foreign currency (dollars) that exchange for one unit of the domestic currency (pounds).[1]

As in any market, the equilibrium price depends on supply and demand. If there are only two countries, the UK and the United States, who is bringing a supply of dollars to the forex market wishing to exchange them into pounds? This demand for pounds comes from two sources. First, American consumers pay in dollars but British exporters want to be paid in pounds. Second, American residents wishing to buy British assets (shares in ICI or UK Treasury bills) must convert their dollars into pounds before these assets can be purchased. Conversely, a supply of pounds arises from UK imports of goods produced in the United States, and from UK residents wishing to purchase assets in the United States.

Figure 29-1 shows the supply and demand for pounds in the forex market. We begin with the demand. Suppose the UK produces whisky at £8 a bottle. At $2/£, a bottle of whisky costs $16, but at $1.50/£ it costs only $12. Hence at a lower exchange rate, and a lower dollar price of whisky and other UK goods, the UK will export a larger quantity of goods to the United States. American consumers will buy more at a lower dollar price.

If the price in pounds of British goods is constant, UK export revenue in pounds must increase as the exchange rate falls. Since the export revenue is initially earned in dollars which must subsequently be converted into pounds, Figure 29-1 shows that the demand schedule for pounds, *DD*, slopes downwards. A larger quantity of pounds is demanded at a lower dollar–sterling exchange rate.

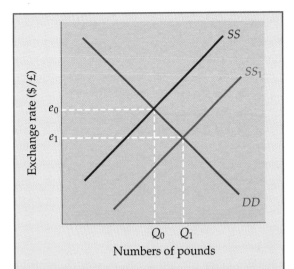

DD shows the demand for pounds by Americans wanting to buy British goods or assets. SS shows the supply of pounds by British residents wishing to buy American goods or assets. The equilibrium exchange rate is e_0. If British residents want more dollars at each exchange rate, the supply of pounds will shift from SS to SS_1 and the equilibrium international value of the pound will fall.

Figure 29-1   The forex market

The supply schedule for pounds, *SS*, depends on the quantity of dollars UK residents require to pay for UK imports or purchases of dollar assets. Suppose a holiday in Florida costs $600: at $2/£ it costs £300, but at $1.50/£ it costs £400. A lower $/£ exchange rate increases the price in pounds, and reduces the quantity of Florida holidays demanded by UK residents. Whether it reduces the number of pounds spent depends on the elasticity of demand.

Figure 29-1 assumes that the demand for Florida holidays and other British imports is price-elastic. A rise in the sterling price reduces both the quantity demanded and the total spending in pounds on such goods and services. A lower exchange rate reduces the quantity of pounds supplied to the forex market. The supply schedule *SS* slopes upward. However, if the British demand for American goods, services, and assets were price-inelastic, a lower exchange rate and higher sterling price would actually increase sterling spending on these things, and the supply schedule of pounds to the forex market would slope downwards.[2]

---

[1] With many foreign currencies – US dollars ($), German Deutschmarks (DM), French francs (FF), and Japanese yen (¥) – sterling's effective exchange rate is an index of its international value, an average of the $/£, DM/£, FF/£, and ¥/£ exchange rates, weighted by the relative importance of each country in Britain's international trading transactions.

[2] The supply and demand for cars refers to physical quantities supplied or demanded at each price. However, the supply and demand schedules for pounds sterling refer to values of pounds supplied and demanded at each exchange rate. That is why the analysis is a bit more tricky than the analysis of the supply and demand for physical goods such as cars.

At the equilibrium exchange rate of e_0 the quantity of pounds supplied and demanded is equal. What would change this equilibrium rate? If, at each sterling price, the demand by Americans for British goods or assets increases, the demand schedule for pounds, DD, will shift to the right, increasing the equilibrium dollar–sterling exchange rate. Similarly, if the British demand for goods and assets denominated in dollars is reduced at each sterling price, the supply schedule for pounds, SS, will shift to the left, and the equilibrium dollar-sterling exchange rate will again increase.

When the dollar–sterling exchange rate increases we say the pound has *appreciated*, because the international value of sterling has risen. Conversely, when the dollar–pound exchange rate falls we say that the pound has *depreciated*. Its international value is lower.

Alternative exchange rate regimes

An **exchange rate regime** is a description of the conditions under which national governments allow exchange rates to be determined.

In Chapter 34 we discuss the different exchange rate regimes that have been adopted to handle international transactions in the world economy. Here we concentrate on the two extreme cases. These cases allow us to grasp the basics of how the macroeconomics of an open economy differs from the macroeconomics of a closed economy.

In a **fixed exchange rate** regime, national governments agree to maintain the convertibility of their currency at a fixed exchange rate.

A currency is **convertible** if the government acting through the central bank, agrees to buy or sell as much of the currency as people wish to trade at the fixed exchange rate.

Suppose the exchange rate is fixed at e_0. For example, between 1949 and 1967 the dollar–pound exchange rate was fixed at \$2.80/£. In Figure 29-2 the fixed exchange rate e_1 would be the free market equilibrium rate if the supply schedule were SS and the demand schedule DD. With neither an excess supply of pounds nor an excess demand, nobody would be wanting to buy or sell pounds to the central bank. The market would clear on its own.

Suppose now that the demand for pounds shifts from DD to DD_1. Americans get hooked on whisky and need more pounds to pay for extra imports of UK whisky. In a free market, the equilibrium point would now be B and the pound would appreciate against the dollar. At the fixed

exchange rate e_1 there is an excess demand for pounds equal to AC. Since the currency is convertible, this excess demand is satisfied by people asking the Bank of England for AC pounds which the Bank is committed to supply on demand.

The Bank prints AC additional pounds and sells them in exchange for ($e_1 \times AC$) dollars, which are added to the UK foreign exchange reserves.

The **foreign exchange** reserves are the stock of foreign currency held by the domestic central bank.

Now suppose the demand schedule for pounds shifts to the left to DD_2. Few foreigners want British goods or assets, and the demand for pounds is correspondingly low. The free market equilibrium exchange rate would lie below e_1 in the absence of any intervention by the central bank. However, the central bank is committed to defending the fixed exchange rate e_1. At this rate, there is an excess supply of pounds EA. Because the currency is convertible, the central bank must demand EA pounds, which it pays for by selling ($EA \times e_1$) dollars from the foreign exchange reserves. When the central bank is forced to buy or sell pounds to support

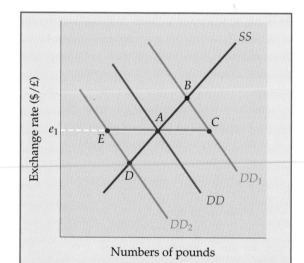

Suppose the exchange rate is fixed at e_1. When demand for pounds is DD_1, there is an excess demand AC. The Bank of England intervenes by supplying AC pounds in exchange for dollars, which are added to the UK foreign exchange reserves. When demand is DD_1, the Bank sells foreign exchange reserves in exchange for pounds. It demands EA pounds to offset the excess supply EA. When demand is DD, the market clears at the exchange rate e_1 and no intervention by the Bank is required.

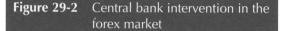

Figure 29-2   Central bank intervention in the forex market

the fixed exchange rate, we say that the central bank *intervenes* in the forex market.

If the demand for pounds fluctuates between DD_1 and DD_2, the Bank of England can sustain the exchange rate e_1 in the long run. When the demand schedule is DD_1 the UK will be adding to its foreign exchange reserves, but when the schedule is DD_2 it will be running down its reserves. In the long run, the UK will neither run out of foreign exchange reserves nor accumulate reserves indefinitely.

However, if the demand for pounds on average is DD_2, the Bank will be running down the UK foreign exchange reserves to support the pound at e_1. Under these circumstances, we say that the pound is overvalued, or at a higher international value than is warranted by its long-run equilibrium position. As reserves start to run out, the government may try to borrow foreign exchange reserves from the International Monetary Fund [IMF (www.imf.org)], an international body which exists primarily to lend to countries in short-term difficulties. But at best this is only a temporary solution. Unless the demand for pounds increases in the long run, it will be necessary to *devalue* the pound.

In a fixed exchange rate regime, a **devaluation (revaluation)** is a reduction (increase) in the exchange rate that governments commit themselves to maintain.

Thus, in November 1967 the UK government, after consultations with other governments, devalued the pound from \$2.80/£ to \$2.40/£.

In a **floating exchange rate regime**, the exchange rate is allowed to attain its free market equilibrium level *without* any government invervention using the foreign exchange reserves.

Thus, in Figure 29-2 the demand schedule shifts from DD_2 to DD to DD_1 would be allowed to move the equilibrium point from D to A to B.

Of course, it is not necessary to adopt the extreme regimes of pure or clean floating on the one hand and perfectly fixed exchange rates on the other hand. *Dirty floating* describes a regime in which intervention is used to offset large and rapid shifts in supply or demand schedules in the short run, but where the exchange rate is gradually allowed to find its equilibrium level in the longer run.

There are many kinds of exchange rate regime. If we understand the two polar cases – fixed exchange rates and freely floating exchange rates – we can see how the intermediate cases would work. Before studying macro-economics under each of these regimes, we explain balance of payments accounting.

29-2 The balance of payments

The **balance of payments** is a systematic record of all transactions between residents of one country and the rest of the world.

Taking the UK as the domestic country and the United States as the 'rest of the world', all international transactions that give rise to an inflow of pounds to the UK are entered as credits in the UK balance of payments accounts. Outflows of pounds are shown as debits, and are entered with a minus sign. Similarly, inflows of dollars to the United States are credits in the US balance of payments accounts but outflows are debits. Table 29-1 shows the actual UK balance of payments accounts in 1998.

We begin with the current account.

The **current account** of the balance of payments records international flows of goods, services, and transfer payments.

Visible trade refers to exports and imports of goods (cars, food, steel). *Invisible trade* refers to exports and imports of services (banking, shipping, tourism). Together, these make up the trade balance or net exports of goods and services. In Chapter 20 we discussed net exports and the definition of GDP in an open economy, and in Chapter 22 we began the analysis of how net exports affect aggregate demand.

However, the trade balance is not identical to the current account on the balance of payments. We must also take account of transfer payments between countries (foreign aid, budget contribution to the EU) and of the net flow of property income (interest, profits, dividends) which arises

Table 29-1	UK balance of payments, 1998 (£bn)
Visible exports	169
Visible imports	−190
Invisibles: credits	182
Invisibles: debits	−160
(1) CURRENT ACCOUNT	1
(2) CAPITAL ACCOUNT	−9
(3) Balancing item	8
(4) UK BALANCE OF PAYMENTS (1 + 2 + 3)	0
(5) Official financing	0

Source: IMF, *International Financial Statistics*.

when residents of one country own income-earning assets in another country. In Chapter 20 we showed that the flow of net property income leads to a discrepancy between GDP and GNP.

Table 29-1 combines exports of services with transfer payments and property income received from abroad to give total credits from invisibles as £182 billion. We combine imports of services with transfer payments and property income paid to foreigners to obtain total debits on invisibles of – £160 billion. Combining visibles and invisibles, the current account on the balance of payments was £1 billion in surplus in 1998, measuring net exports of goods and services, plus net transfers and property income from abroad.

Now we turn to transactions on the capital account of the balance of payments.

The **capital account** of the balance of payments records international transactions in financial assets.

Table 29-1 shows a net outflow of £9 billion in 1988. The outflow of money from the UK to buy physical and financial assets abroad exceeded the inflow of money to the UK as foreigners bought assets in the UK.

The balancing item is a statistical adjustment, which would be zero if all previous items had been correctly measured. It reflects a failure to record all transactions in the official statistics. Estimating implicit changes in the value of foreign investments, which the statistics treat as money reinvested abroad, is particularly tricky. Adding together the current account (1), the capital account (2), and the adjustment (3) we obtain the UK *balance of payments* in 1998. It so happens it just balanced in 1998.

The balance of payments shows the net inflow of money to the country when individuals, firms, and the government make the transactions they wish to undertake under existing market conditions. It is in surplus (deficit) when there is a net inflow of money (outflow of money). It takes account of the transactions that individuals wish to make in importing and exporting and in buying and selling foreign assets, and the amount of transactions that governments wish to make in the form of foreign aid (transfer payments to foreigners), military spending (maintaining military bases abroad), and so on.

The final entry in Table 29-1 is *official financing*. This is always of equal magnitude and opposite sign to the balance of payments in the line above, so that the sum of all the entries in Table 29-1 is *always* zero. Official financing measures the international transactions that the government must take to *accommodate* all the other transactions shown in the balance of payments accounts. What is this official financing?

Floating exchange rates

Suppose first that the exchange rate is freely floating and there is no government intervention in the forex market. The government neither adds to nor runs down the foreign exchange reserves. The exchange rate adjusts to equate the supply of pounds and the demand for pounds in the forex market.

The supply of pounds arises from imports to the UK or purchases of foreign assets by UK residents. It measures the outflows from the UK, the negative items on the balance of payments accounts of the UK. Conversely, the demand for pounds arises from UK exports and purchases of UK assets by foreigners, and measures the inflows to the UK, the positive items on the UK balance of payments accounts. With a freely floating exchange rate, the quantities of pounds supplied and demanded are equal. Hence inflows equal outflows and the balance of payments is exactly zero. There is no government intervention in the forex market and no official financing.

Since the balance of payments is the sum of the current account and the capital account, under floating exchange rates a current account surplus must be exactly matched by a capital account deficit, or vice versa. What is true for the country as a whole is also true for an individual. Think of your own balance of payments account with all other individuals. If your income exceeds your spending, you run a current account surplus in your transactions with other people. This surplus adds to your assets. You add to your cash balances or your bank account, or buy shares or property. The increase in your asset holdings matches the excess of your income over your spending.

Similarly, for the country as a whole a current account surplus, or net inflow from abroad, must be matched by an increase in the country's holding of foreign assets. Since the government is not adding to the foreign exchange reserves, this must show up in the capital account as a capital account deficit exactly matching the current account surplus. The capital account deficit shows the outflow of money as domestic residents add to their holding of foreign assets. The balance of payments, the sum of the current and capital accounts of the balance of payments, must be zero when there is a freely floating exchange rate.

Fixed exchange rates

With a fixed exchange rate, the balance of payments need not be zero. When there is a deficit, total outflows exceed total inflows on the combined current and capital accounts. How is the deficit financed?

Since there is a deficit, the supply of pounds to the foreign exchange market, corresponding to the wish to import or acquire foreign assets, exceeds the demand for pounds, corresponding to the wish to export or the desire of foreigners to acquire domestic assets. Hence the balance of payments deficit is exactly the same as the excess supply of pounds in the forex market.

To maintain the fixed exchange rate, the central bank has to offset this excess supply of pounds by demanding an equivalent quantity of pounds. The central bank runs down the foreign exchange reserves, selling dollars to buy pounds. In the balance of payments accounts this shows up as 'official financing'. In 1998 the UK needed no reserve transactions since the payments were anyway in balance in Table 29-1. However, when there is a balance of payments surplus, the government intervenes in the forex market to buy foreign exchange reserves. When there is a balance of payments deficit, reserves must be sold.

Summary

Inclusive of official financing, the balance of payments accounts must sum to zero, just as the forex market must clear inclusive of central bank intervention using the foreign exchange reserves. A current account surplus must be met either by a capital account deficit or by allowing the foreign exchange reserves to increase. A current account deficit must be met either by a capital account surplus or by running down the foreign exchange reserves. Either way, a current account surplus is matched by an increase in foreign assets held and a current account deficit is matched by a reduction in foreign assets held.

From these consolidated accounts, the balance of payments is the part of the accounts dealing with individual, company, and government transactions before official financing and changes in the foreign exchange reserves are taken into account. When the exchange rate is freely floating, intervention is zero, the foreign exchange reserves are constant, and official financing is zero. Since the consolidated accounts inclusive of official financing always sum to zero, the balance of payments must be zero when the exchange rate floats freely.

29-3 Components of the balance of payments

In this section we discuss the determinants of the items on the current and capital accounts of the balance of payments.

Then we briefly consider the relative importance of the two accounts in the short run and the long-run. First, we introduce the concept of the real exchange rate.

The real exchange rate and competitiveness

In 1975, the dollar–sterling exchange rate was \$2.22/£; in 1999 it was only \$1.60/£. Similarly, sterling's effective exchange rate measuring the international value of sterling against all other currencies – an index in which the \$/£ and DM/£ are the most important exchange rates, reflecting the pattern of Britain's international trade – fell from 100 in 1975 to 72 in 1996.

Since a fall in the international value of sterling makes British goods cheaper in foreign currencies and foreign goods more expensive in pounds, this change in the sterling exchange rate tended to increase the quantity of British exports and reduce the quantity of goods imported to Britain. Right?

Not necessarily. Britain had a higher inflation rate during these years than most of its trading partners. Whether British goods became more or less competitive in world markets depends on whether the increase in Britain's competitiveness arising from a fall in the nominal or actual exchange rate was larger than the reduction in Britain's competitiveness because the domestic price of British goods rose more than prices in other countries. Once again, we must distinguish nominal and real variables.

International competitiveness is measured by the real exchange rate.

The **real exchange rate** measures the relative price of goods from different countries when measured in a common currency.

Suppose a shirt can be produced for \$10 in the United States and for £6 in the UK. At the nominal exchange rate of \$2/£, the relative price of UK to US shirts, when measured in a common currency, is 6/5, whether we compare the relative dollar price of shirts (\$12/\$10) or the relative price in pounds (£6/£5). Two things can make UK shirts more competitive with US shirts. An exchange rate depreciation, say from £2/£ to £1.50/£, would change the relative price of UK to US shirts from 6/5 to 9/10, making UK shirts relatively cheaper. Equally, however, at the original nominal exchange rate of \$2/£ a reduction in the domestic price of UK shirts from £6 to £4.50 would also change the relative price of shirts in a common currency from 6/5 to 9/\$10.

Suppose we measure the real exchange rate by comparing dollar prices of goods produced in the two countries. The shirt example shows that we can define the UK's real exchange rate as

$$\text{Real exchange rate} = \frac{\text{£ price of UK goods}}{\text{\$ price of US goods}} \times (\$/\text{£}) \qquad (1)$$

An increase in the real exchange rate, by increasing the price of UK goods relative to US goods when measured in the same currency, makes the UK less competitive relative to the United States. Conversely, a fall in the UK's real exchange rate makes the UK more competitive in international markets.

Table 29-2 shows how this works out in practice. The first row shows the nominal dollar–sterling exchange rate in 1976, 1981, and 1999. Looking at this rate, we might be tempted to conclude that UK competitiveness relative to the United States had increased between 1981 and 1999. The second and third rows show what happened to the price level in each country over the period. The fourth row calculates an index of the real exchange rate, using the formula of equation (1). For example, to calculate the 1976 value we multiply the price index of UK goods, 32, by the nominal exchange rate, 1.81, and then divide by the US price index, 44. Table 29-2 shows that the real exchange rate hardly changed between 1981 and 1999, despite the depreciation of the nominal exchange rate. During 1976–99 the real exchange rate did appreciate. UK goods became less competitive because in a common currency their price increased relative to the price of US goods. The fall in the nominal exchange rate from \$1.81/£ to \$1.60/£ was not sufficient to offset the increase in the domestic price of UK goods relative to the domestic price of US goods over the period.

How much would the nominal exchange rate have had to change to maintain a constant real exchange rate and level of international competitiveness over the period?

Table 29-2	Nominal and real exchange rates		
	1976	1981	1999
\$/£	1.81	2.03	1.60
Prices (1990 = 100)			
UK	32	54	131
US	44	70	129
Real \$/£ rate	1.32	1.57	1.62
PPP exchange rate	1.81	1.71	1.31

Source: IMF *International Financial Statistics*.

The **purchasing power parity** (PPP) exchange rate path is the path of the nominal exchange rate that would keep the real exchange rate constant over a given period.

Table 29-2 shows that in 1999 UK prices were 4.09 times their 1976 level, whereas US prices were only 2.93 times their 1976 level. Using equation (1), we see that the nominal exchange rate would have to fall to 2.693/4.09 (= 0.72) of its 1976 level to offset the change in relative domestic prices and maintain a constant real exchange rate. Hence in the last row of Table 29-2 we show that the nominal exchange rate would have had to fall to \$1.31/£ (= 0.72 × \$1.81/£) in 1999 if the real exchange rate were to remain at its 1976 level.

Similarly, in 1981 the PPP exchange rate was \$1.71/£.

The current account

Exports   In Chapter 22 we made the simple assumption that export demand for domestic goods and services was given. We now recognize that the demand for UK exports will be influenced chiefly by two things. First, the higher the level of income in the rest of the world, the higher will be the demand for UK exports. Second, the lower the UK's real exchange rate and the higher the level of UK competitiveness in world markets, the higher will be the demand for UK exports. Although actual exports usually respond quickly to changes in the level of world income or world trade, a reduction in competitiveness is likely to reduce exports only gradually. Why? Because exporters may be unsure whether the decline in competitiveness is temporary or permanent. If they believe it to be temporary, British exporters may cut their prices to remain competitive in world markets. Even though this may mean losses in the short run, it may be cheaper in the long-run than temporarily withdrawing from those markets and having to spend large sums on advertising and marketing to win back market shares when competitiveness improves again. But if competitiveness fails to improve and the real exchange rate remains high, firms will gradually conclude that the long-run prospects are bleak, and some firms will permanently quit the exporting business.

Imports   For imports we simply tell the same story in reverse. Import demand will be larger the higher is the level of domestic income, the relationship we recognized in Chapter 22 through the marginal propensity to import. But import demand will also be larger the higher is the real exchange rate and the cheaper are foreign goods relative to domestic goods when both are measured in the domestic currency. Again, in practice, imports respond more quickly

BOX 29-1

'Exporters should start their prayers before sterling soars' (The Times, 11 October 1996)

This headline was from an article, by *The Times* economics editor, Anatole Kaletsky. His argument was simple. At a time when continental Europe was tightening fiscal policy in preparation for EMU and President Clinton was coming close to balancing the US budget, the UK's competitors all had tight fiscal policy. Whoever won the 1997 UK election, predicted Kaletsky, the UK would have looser fiscal policy than its main partners. Since the UK was committed to low inflation, it would need tighter monetary policy than its partners. Speculators, starting to figure this out, were piling into sterling anticipating higher interest rates in the UK than abroad. But a sharp rise in sterling's nominal exchange rate was likely, in the short run, to imply a sharp appreciation of the real exchange rate as well. This would hit exports, output, and tax revenue. What should exporters be praying for?

That before sterling went too high, the Chancellor would wake up to the danger and take politically unpopular steps to tighten fiscal policy, if not by tax increases then by spending reductions. The figures below show the rapid rise in sterling in 1996.

Kaletsky's forecast was completely vindicated. By 1998, sterling had risen, to 3 DM/£. And Gordon Brown had embarked on a policy of raising the not-so-visible taxes (not VAT or income tax!) in the hope of making space for the Bank to cut interest rates without jeopardizing the inflation target.

One final point. This dilemma for the Chancellor arises even though the UK is floating the exchange rate. When rapid capital flows make economies very open, much of monetary sovereignty is gone whatever exchange rate policy is pursued. Or as Kaletsky put it: '... the place that is the burial ground for the reputation of British Chancellors – the foreign exchange market. Mr Clarke is only the second Chancellor since 1964 not to have his policies ruined by a currency crisis (the other was Roy Jenkins)'.

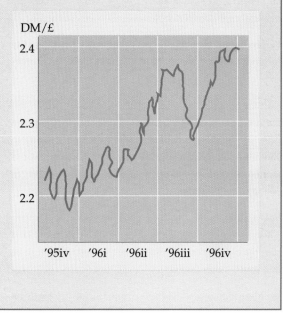

to changes in domestic income than to changes in the real exchange rate. However, if sustained, a change in the real exchange rate will eventually have significant effects on the level of imports as well as exports.

Other items on the current account   Other items include foreign aid and spending on military bases abroad, matters of government policy. Also on the current account we include the net flow of interest, dividend, and profit income between countries, which arises because residents of one country hold assets in another. The size of this net flow of income depends on the pattern of international asset-holding and on the level of interest rates, profits, and dividends at home and abroad.

Capital account items

These arise through international purchases and sales of assets, and have become increasingly important since 1945 for two reasons. First, computers and telecommunications have made it almost as easy for a British resident to transact in the financial markets of New York, Frankfurt, Zurich, Tokyo, and Hong Kong as it is in London. Second, the elaborate system of controls, restricting international transactions on the capital account, have gradually been dismantled.

Since a current account deficit must be matched by a capital account surplus (purchases of domestic assets by foreigners) or by official financing (running down foreign exchange reserves), in practice the West had little option but to meet huge current account deficits by encouraging OPEC to purchase large quantities of assets in the West, thereby providing the capital account inflow to meet the West's current account outflow.

The world's financial markets now have two crucial features. First, capital account restrictions have been almost entirely abolished. Funds can be freely moved from one country to another in search of the highest rate of return. Second, there are billions and billions of pounds that are internationally footloose and capable of being switched between countries and currencies when assets in one currency seem to offer a higher rate of return than assets elsewhere. If the owners of these funds are prepared to transfer them entirely to the currency in which assets seem to offer the highest rate of return, and if there are no obstacles to such transfers, we say that international financial capital is 'perfectly mobile' between countries.

Perfect capital mobility means that an enormous quantity of funds will be transferred from one currency to another whenever the rate of return on assets in one country is higher than in another.

Since the stock of international funds is now so large, in principle the movement of these funds from one country to another could lead to capital account flows that would swamp the typical flows of imports and exports we observe on the current account.

Speculation is the purchase of an asset for subsequent resale, in the belief that the total return – interest or dividend plus the capital gain will exceed the total return that can be obtained in other assets.

In international asset markets, capital gains arising from changes in exchange rates form an important part of the expected rate of return on an asset. You have £100 to invest for a year. Suppose UK interest rates are 10 per cent a year but interest rates in the United States are zero. Keeping your funds in pounds, you will have £110 at the end of the year. But what if you convert them into dollars at the beginning of the year, lend in dollars for a year, and then convert the money back into pounds at the end?

Suppose initially the exchange rate is $2/£. Your £100 will buy $200. At a zero interest rate you will still have $200 at the end of the year. But suppose that sterling has depreciated by 10 per cent during the year. At the end of the year the exchange rate is $1.80/£, a fall of $0.20/£ on the original rate of $2/£. Your $200 will convert back to £110 at an exchange rate of $1.80 at the end of the year. Although you get no interest by investing in dollars for a year, you make a

capital gain of 10 per cent on holding dollars, whose value relative to pounds increases by 10 per cent during the year.

In this example you end up with £110 whether you lend in dollars or pounds during the year. If the pound had depreciated by more than 10 per cent (the excess of the UK interest rate over the US interest rate), the capital gain on holding dollars would have outweighed the loss of interest, and the total return on lending in dollars rather than pounds would have been larger. Conversely, if the pound had depreciated against the dollar by less than the interest rate differential, you would have earned a higher total return by keeping your money in pounds. Equation (2) summarizes this important result. It reminds us that the total return on temporarily lending in a foreign currency is the interest rate paid on assets in that currency plus any capital gain (or minus any capital loss) arising from depreciation (appreciation) of the domestic currency during the period.

$$\begin{array}{l} \text{Return on} \\ \text{foreign} \\ \text{lending} \end{array} = \begin{array}{l} \text{foreign} \\ \text{interest} \\ \text{rate} \end{array} + \begin{array}{l} \text{domestic} \\ \text{currency} \\ \text{depreciation} \end{array} \quad (2)$$

In a world of almost perfect international capital mobility, there will be an enormous capital outflow whenever the total return on foreign lending exceeds the total return on domestic lending, the domestic interest rate. There will be a huge capital inflow when the return on domestic lending exceeds the return on lending abroad. And net flows on the capital account of the balance of payments will be small only when the total return on foreign lending is broadly in line with the return on lending in the domestic currency.

Perfect capital mobility means that there are no barriers to capital flows, and investors equate expected total returns on assets in different currencies.

Equation (2) highlights the importance of current expectations about the level of future exchange rates, for it is these that determine the capital gains or losses that people expect to make through changes in the exchange rate. It also tells us that there will be a crucial difference between a fixed exchange rate regime, in which the government commits itself to intervene to prevent exchange rate changes, and floating exchange rate regimes where changes in the exchange rate can become the most important element on total asset returns.

29-4 Internal and external balance

We now discuss the relation between the state of the economy – boom or recession – and the external balance or current account on the balance of payments.

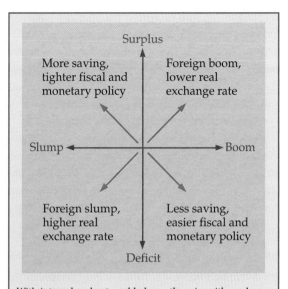

With internal and external balance there is neither a boom nor a slump, and the current account just balances. Each quadrant of the diagram identifies shocks that cause departures from internal and external balance. For example, tight fiscal and monetary policy reduce aggregate demand, creating a domestic slump but a current account surplus since import demand is reduced. however, by increasing export demand, a foreign boom leads to both a domestic boom and a current account surplus. Other possible shocks and their consequences are shown.

Figure 29-3　Internal and external balance

Figure 29-3 shows the different combinations of boom and recessions and current account surpluses and deficits. We begin by thinking about demand and supply for domestic output. Equation (3) reminds us of the basic equation for the goods market.

$$Y = C + I + G + (X - Z) \qquad (3)$$

Domestic output Y equals aggregate demand, which arises from spending on consumption; investment; goods and services purchased by the government; and net exports, that is the excess of exports X over imports Z. If aggregate demand for domestic output equals the level of potential output, firms produce the full-employment output level and in the labour market demand as much employment as workers wish to supply.

A country is in **internal balance** when aggregate demand is at the full-employment level.

With sluggish wage and price adjustment, a lower level of aggregate demand will lead firms to cut back output and sack workers, creating involuntary unemployment. Only

when wages and prices have fallen sufficiently to restore aggregate demand to its full-employment level will internal balance be re-established.

A country is in **external balance** when the current account of the balance of payments just balances.

In the absence of government intervention in the forex market, the capital account of the balance of payments must also be in balance at this point. In Figure 29-3 the point of internal *and* external balance is the intersection of the two axes, where there is neither a boom nor a slump, and neither a current account surplus nor a deficit.

The combination of internal and external balance is the long-run equilibrium of the economy. Wage and price adjustment have restored output to its potential level and there is full employment in the labour market. With external balance, not only is the current account in balance, but there is no long-term pressure to change the stock of foreign exchange reserves, nor any permanent flows on the capital account. Foreigners are not acquiring domestic assets without limit, nor are domestic residents acquiring ever-larger holdings of foreign assets.

Figure 29-3 shows the shocks that in the short run can move the economy away from internal and external balance. For example, the top left-hand quadrant shows a combination of domestic slump and current account surplus. This can be caused by an increase in desired savings (a downward shift in the consumption function) or by the adoption of tight fiscal and monetary policy. These tend to reduce aggregate demand, which causes both a domestic slump and a reduction in imports. Similarly, an increase in the real exchange rate, a decline in international competitiveness, will reduce export demand and increase import demand. The fall in net exports will cause both a current account deficit and a reduction in aggregate demand, leading to a domestic slump in output and employment, as shown in the bottom left-hand quadrant. The figure explains the shocks that move the economy into other quadrants, causing departures from both internal and external balance.

Indeed, one of the main lessons of Figure 29-3 is that most shocks in an open economy will simultaneously move the economy away from *both* internal and external balance. In studying a closed economy, we examined whether the economy could return to internal balance on its own. We concluded that it could, through price and wage adjustment, which affect the level of the real money stock and aggregate demand; but we saw that when adjustment is sluggish it is possible to use monetary and fiscal policy to speed up the process of adjustment. When the economy is in a slump, expansionary monetary and fiscal policy will hasten the return to full employment.

We now study the same questions in an open economy. Without any policy change, will the economy be able to adjust to any shock and get back to the point of both internal and external balance? And can macroeconomic policy be used to make this transition easier? Since the economy behaves very differently under fixed and floating exchange rate regimes, we shall have to analyse the two regimes separately.

29-5 Monetary and fiscal policy under fixed exchange rates

It is useful first to discuss in greater detail the long-run equilibrium position of internal and external balance, using equation (3). Domestic output Y must be at its full-employment level. Given external balance, net exports $X - Z$ must be zero.[3] Hence monetary and fiscal policy must ensure that domestic demand – sometimes called domestic absorption – that is, the desired level of spending on $C + I + G$, must just equal full employment output Y. Given this output level, and given the level of real income in the rest of the world, there is a unique real exchange rate that equates the demand for exports and imports. At a higher real exchange rate, or lower level of international competitiveness, import demand will exceed export demand. At a lower real exchange rate net export demand will be positive. Hence there is only one real exchange rate compatible with internal and external balance.

Under a fixed exchange rate regime, governments are committed to intervention in the forex market to maintain a given nominal exchange rate. Immediately, we reach one important conclusion: under a fixed exchange rate regime, internal and external balance is possible only if the domestic and foreign inflation rates are equal. Otherwise the real exchange rate would be changing in the long run and exports would be changing relative to imports.

The balance of payments and the money supply

We now highlight a key mechanism through which external balance is restored when the economy is not in long-run

equilibrium. Suppose the economy is running a balance of payments deficit. Two things are happening.

First, on average, private individuals are withdrawing money from circulation. They need this money to acquire the foreign exchange with which to purchase foreign goods and assets. The domestic money supply is being reduced by exactly the amount of the balance of payments deficit.

Second, the government is intervening in the forex market. The balance of payments deficit is exactly matched by official financing, as we saw earlier in the chapter. The government is selling foreign exchange reserves, thereby supplying foreign currency to the market. In exchange, the central bank is obtaining pounds sterling which effectively have been withdrawn from circulation.

Thus, under fixed exchange rates, the money supply is not determined exclusively by the original decision of the government about how much money to print. When the economy has a balance of payments deficit, the monetary outflow will be reducing the domestic money supply below the value it would otherwise have attained. Conversely, with a surplus on the balance of payments, the domestic money in circulation will be augmented by the inflow of money from abroad. Exporters will be converting their earnings from foreign currency into pounds and paying this money into the domestic banking system.

Suppose the government does not wish the domestic money supply to be reduced when there is a balance of payments deficit. Can anything be done? The government can try to sterilize the domestic money supply.

Sterilization is an open market operation between domestic money and domestic bonds the sole purpose of which is to neutralize the tendency of balance of payments surpluses and deficits to change the domestic money supply.

Thus, if a balance of payments deficit is causing a reduction in the domestic money supply, the central bank can buy domestic bonds in exchange for money, thereby replenishing the domestic money supply. Although the money supply is unchanged, the government now has fewer outstanding bonds and fewer foreign exchange reserves, which were used for official financing of the payments deficit. Thus perfect sterilization essentially involves swapping domestic bonds for foreign exchange reserves.

Adjustment under fixed policies

In this section we consider how the economy adjusts to a shock when the government takes no monetary or fiscal action to accommodate the shock. Initially we examine a

---

[3] For most countries, the trade balance and the current account are very similar. However, there are exceptions. Japan has built up a large stock of foreign assets, on which it earns income. And countries that are part of the international debt crisis have large interest flows on the current account.

domestic shock. What happens when there is an increase in the desire to save, and a reduction in desired consumption spending at each output level? With an unchanged money supply and fiscal policy, in a closed economy an initial recession would gradually lead to falls in wages and prices which would increase the real money supply, reduce interest rates, and restore aggregate demand to its full-employment level.

How does the adjustment process differ in an open economy, when the government maintains a fixed nominal exchange rate and when there is almost perfect international capital mobility?

When desired consumption demand falls, there is a domestic slump. Income falls, and hence import demand falls. There is a current account surplus. However, this is swamped by what happens on the capital account. At the original money supply and price level, the fall in income reduces the demand for money and tends to reduce interest rates. This immediately induces a capital account outflow. Together, the current and capital accounts are in deficit until monetary outflow reduces the domestic money supply sufficiently to restore interest rates to the level of foreign interest rates, at which point there is no further pressure for outflows on the capital account of the balance of payments.

Gradually, the domestic slump puts downward pressure on wages and prices at home, thereby increasing international competitiveness and net exports $(X - Z)$. Unlike the situation in the closed economy, where falling prices and wages increase aggregate demand by reducing interest rates, in the open economy, with perfect international capital mobility, interest rates are pegged at world levels and falling domestic prices increase aggregate demand by increasing international competitiveness and net exports.

Thus an initial fall in domestic absorption $(C + I + G)$ eventually leads to a sufficient price fall to increase net exports $(X - Z)$ to the point at which domestic absorption plus net exports equals potential output. Internal balance has been re-established. However, there is now a current account surplus. Induced price changes alone cannot restore both internal and external balance.

In the long run, external balance requires that net exports are zero. Hence full equilibrium can be restored only if domestic absorption returns to its full-employment level. But perfect capital mobility pegs interest rates at world levels. Moreover, the real money supply M/P must equal real money demand $L(Y, r)$, which is fixed by the full employment income level Y and the level of world interest rates r. Monetary policy cannot affect the real money supply in the long run. Hence the only way that the economy can

return to internal and external balance is if fiscal policy is used to increase $(C + I + G)$ to offset the reduction in desired consumption. Either government spending must be increased, or tax cuts must be used to boost consumption and investment spending. Unlike the situation in a closed economy, there is no *automatic* mechanism to restore full equilibrium in the long-run.

A shock from abroad   When the shock comes from abroad, the conclusion is rather different. Suppose that higher foreign income increases the demand for our exports. The current account $(X - Z)$ moves into surplus. By increasing aggregate demand and output, the demand for money is increased and domestic interest rates must rise. This leads to an immediate inflow on the capital account as international investors move in funds to take advantage of higher interest rates. The inflow continues until the balance of payments surplus has sufficiently increased the domestic money supply to restore interest rates to world levels.

With sluggish price adjustment, the monetary inflow increases the domestic real money supply in line with the higher demand for real money balances. Rising interest rates do not choke off the increase in aggregate demand caused by the increase in export demand. In the longer run, higher aggregate demand gradually bids up prices and wages, reducing international competitiveness since the nominal exchange rate is fixed. When international competitiveness has been sufficiently eroded to reduce exports and increase imports to the point at which net exports are zero, both internal and external balance are restored. Induced adjustment of wages and prices *can* eventually cope with shocks from abroad.

Thus far, we have assumed that the government does not respond to shocks by adjusting monetary and fiscal policy. We now examine the effects of changes in these policies under fixed exchange rates and when there is perfect or almost perfect international capital mobility.

Monetary policy under fixed exchange rates

When price adjustment is sluggish, an increase in the nominal money supply increases the real money supply in the short run, and tends to reduce domestic interest rates. With perfect capital mobility, this leads to a capital account outflow until the domestic money supply has been reduced to its original level and interest rates have returned to world levels. Hence domestic policy is powerless in a fixed exchange rate regime when capital mobility is perfect.

Perfect capital mobility means that the government cannot fix independent targets for both the money supply

BOX 29-2   EMU's grandfather

In 1999, Bob Mundell won the Nobel prize for inventing much of modern open economy macroeconomics. He was the first to realize that openness in product and factor markets might create powerful pressures for monetary union. He also showed what it would be like for a small country to try to hang on to sovereignty when international capital mobility is very high.

The diagram below uses the *IS–LM* framework to illustrate the case of pegged exchange rates. The UK pegged the pound during its short membership of the ERM in 1990–92. *IS* shows the usual relationship between interest rates and output consistent with goods market equilibrium. A small country can peg its exchange rate only by matching the foreign interest rate r^*. We show this as a horizontal line. The money supply must be adjusted to make sure this is always the domestic interest rate. Initial equilibrium is at *A*.

Any attempt to change the money supply, and hence interest rates, causes an immediate speculative inflow or outflow until the money supply and interest rates are restored to the level needed to peg the exchange rate. Monetary policy is powerless.

A fiscal expansion shifts the *IS* curve to *IS'*. There is a big short-run effect on output, from *Y* to *Y'*, since interest rates cannot increase to dampen the expansion. Monetary policy is forced to create additional money supply to accommodate the extra money demand when output rises. We can think of the horizontal line for interest rates as being achieved by a shift in the implicit *LM* curve from *LM* to *LM'*.

Suppose *Y* denotes full-capacity output. If a decline in thrift boosts consumption and shifts the *IS* curve to *IS'*, how is full capacity output eventually restored? Not by the mechanism of Chapters 25 and 26! Although the boom at *Y'* still causes an increase in the price level, this no longer reduces the real money supply and bids up interest rates. Instead, extra money is created to keep interest rates at r^*.

However, higher prices do reduce competitiveness and hence shift the *IS'* curve leftwards. Under a pegged exchange rate, endogenous changes in the *IS* curve are the fallback mechanism for restoring output to full capacity. If the government does not like these changes in competitiveness, it must use fiscal policy to shift the *IS* curve in response to other shocks.

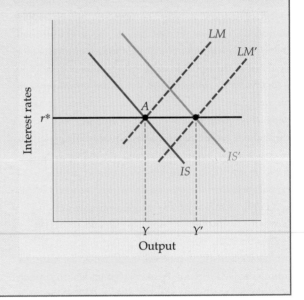

and the exchange rate. Under fixed exchange rates, the government has to accept the domestic money supply that makes domestic and foreign interest rates equal. Later, we shall see that the government can fix the domestic money supply provided it allows the exchange rate to adjust freely. But it cannot fix both.

This is equivalent to the assertion that sterilization will not work. When attempts to increase the domestic money supply are frustrated by a capital account deficit and a monetary outflow, the government can try to pump yet more money into the economy. With interest rates

again below world levels, owners of international funds withdraw yet more money. Since these monetary outflows, and deficits on the balance of payments, require corresponding official financing through reduction in the foreign exchange reserves, the question is who runs out of funds first. The assertion that sterilization won't work requires that the volume of international funds that could be withdrawn if interest rates fall below world levels exceeds the government's foreign exchange reserves. The government will have to give up before the speculators.

Fiscal policy under fixed exchange rates

In a closed economy with sluggish price adjustment, monetary policy can change the real money supply in the short run but not in the long run. In an open economy, we have just seen that capital mobility removes even the short-run power of monetary policy to affect real variables. In contrast, in an open economy fiscal policy is *more* powerful in the short run than in a closed economy.

In a closed economy, fiscal policy leads to two kinds of crowding out. In the short run, a fiscal expansion increases output but bids up interest rates, moderating the output increase. And in the long run, higher demand bids up prices and reduces the real money stock, raising interest rates until consumption and investment demand fall to restore aggregate demand to its full-employment level. In an open economy, capital account flows peg interest rates at world levels and prevent induced changes in interest rates.

Hence, in the short run a fiscal expansion has a larger effect in an open economy with a fixed exchange rate. In the longer run, higher aggregate demand bids up prices and wages, reducing competitiveness and net exports. This process will continue until internal balance or full employment is restored. However, as we noted earlier, this will not be a point of external balance. In this example, there will be a current account deficit in the long run. In fact, at a given exchange rate, a given level of world income, and a given level of world interest rates, there is a unique fiscal policy compatible with both internal and external balance in the long run. The domestic price level can adjust to secure the level of competitiveness that makes imports equal exports when the domestic economy is at full employment. Internal balance then requires that potential output Y equals domestic absorption $(C + I + G)$ when interest rates are at world levels. Given private sector demands for consumption and investment, this determines the fiscal policy that the government will have to implement if the economy is to attain both internal and external balance.

Thus far, we have considered how the economy behaves at a *given* exchange rate. Now we investigate the consequences of changing the exchange rate.

29-6 Devaluation

The fixed exchange rate system in operation in the 25 years after 1945 was sometimes called the *adjustable peg* system. Although exchange rates were pegged at fixed values, occasional adjustments in these values were allowed. For example, the pound sterling was devalued in 1949 and 1967. But the general idea was to keep exchange rates fixed for long periods if possible. We discuss different types of exchange rate regime more fully in Chapter 34.

In this section we assess the consequences of a devaluation. We distinguish its effects in the short run, the medium run, and the long run. Initially, we assume that the domestic country begins from internal and external balance. This allows us to highlight the effect of the devaluation itself. Then we consider whether devaluation may be the appropriate policy response to a shock that has already moved the economy from its long-run equilibrium position.

The short-run effect

When prices and wages adjust slowly, the immediate effect of a devaluation is to increase the domestic price of imports and to reduce the foreign price of the country's exports. Both effects improve international competitiveness. Resources will be drawn into domestic industries such as car production, which can now compete more effectively with imported cars, and will be drawn into export industries, which can now compete more effectively in foreign markets. However, there are two points to note about this short-run impact of devaluation.

First, although devaluation tends to increase the quantity of net exports $(X - Z)$, the initial response may be quite slow. Overnight, there may be a lot of contracts outstanding that were struck at the old exchange rate. Moreover, it may take purchasers some time to adjust to the new prices they face. Similarly, it may take time to build up production capacity in the domestic industries making goods for export or to substitute for goods formerly imported.

Second devaluation may not improve the trade balance in the short run. The trade balance refers to the value of exports minus imports. Suppose we measure the current account in pounds. If domestic prices of export goods are unchanged and the quantity of exports has not yet increased very much, export revenues will be only a little higher in the short run. And if import quantities have not yet fallen very much, but import prices in pounds have risen by the amount of the devaluation, the value of imports in pounds may have risen substantially. In *value* terms, the current account may move into deficit in the short run.[4] However, in the longer run, as purchasers and suppliers adjust the

---

[4] The famous Marshall–Lerner condition says that a devaluation will improve the current account only if the sum of the price elasticities of demand for imports and exports is more negative than -1. Recall from Chapter 5 that, when demand is elastic, the revenue effect of changes in quantity more than offset the effect of a change in price. In the short run, inelastic demand can make a devaluation worsen the current account.

quantities of exports and imports, higher export quantities and lower import quantities are likely both to increase the contribution of net exports $(X - Z)$ to aggregate demand and to move the current account of the balance of payments into surplus.[5]

The medium-run effect

For convenience, we re-write equation (3)

$$Y = (C + I + G) + (X - Z) \qquad (4)$$

The supply of domestic goods Y equals aggregate demand, which comprises domestic absorption $(C + I + G)$ plus net export demand $(X - Z)$. A devaluation increases net export demand $(X - Z)$. What happens next depends crucially on aggregate supply.

If the economy begins with Keynesian unemployment, the economy has the spare resources to produce extra goods and can meet this increase in aggregate demand. Output will increase and unemployment will fall. But if the economy begins at full employment, the economy as a whole cannot produce more goods. The higher aggregate demand will quickly bid up prices and wages. The economy's international competitiveness is reduced, and net exports start to fall again. When domestic prices and wages have risen by the same percentage as that by which the exchange rate was initially devalued, the real exchange rate and competitiveness have returned to their original levels. If the economy began from internal and external balance, net exports have now returned to zero, and aggregate demand has been restored to the full-employment level.

If for some reason the government intended the devaluation to improve the current account balance permanently, the devaluation should be accompanied by fiscal policy to reduce domestic absorption. Thus, beginning at full employment, a devaluation accompanied by higher taxes will increase the demand for net exports without increasing total aggregate demand. Since there is now no upward pressure on domestic prices, the higher international competitiveness and lower exchange rate can be sustained in the medium run.

The long-run effect

One of the themes of modern economics is that it is real variables, not nominal variables, that matter. Can altering the nominal exchange rate permanently change the value of real variables?

Suppose a devaluation has been accompanied by tighter fiscal policy in order to reduce domestic absorption and allow the economy to meet the higher demand for net exports without any direct upward pressure on prices. Although this takes care of demand side effects on prices, we must also think about supply side effects. Domestic firms that import raw materials will want to pass on these cost increases in higher prices. Workers who buy imported consumer goods, from food to TV sets, will conclude that the cost of living has increased, and they will demand nominal wage increases to maintain the value of their real wages. These price and wage increases lead other firms and other workers to react in similar fashion.

Thus, in the absence of any real change in the economy, the eventual effect of a devaluation will be an increase in all other nominal wages and prices in line with the higher import prices, leaving all real variables unchanged. Eventually, a devaluation will have no effect. Most of the leading computer models of the UK economy, models that try to quantify the forces at work by using econometric techniques to analyse past data, conclude that the effects of a sterling devaluation are almost completely offset by a rise in domestic prices and wages by the end of five years.

In September 1992, sterling left the Exchange Rate Mechanism and quickly fell about 15 per cent against other currencies. The UK has had big devaluations before, in 1949 and 1967. What evidence did they contain for the 1992 depreciation?

Table 29-3 shows the effect of the sterling devaluation by 15 per cent in 1967. The first row shows that it took two years before the current account moved from deficit into

---

[5] Thus we have established that a devaluation may lead first to a deterioration of the current account of the balance of payments but then to an improvement in the current account. Economists sometimes describe this response as the *J-curve*. As time elapses after the devaluation, the current account falls down to the bottom of the J but then improves and rises above its initial position.

Table 29-3 The 1967 sterling devaluation

	1967	1968	1969	1970
Current account (£b)	−0.3	−0.2	0.5	0.8
Balance of payments (£b)	−0.7	−1.4	0.7	1.4
PSBR as % of GDP	5.3	3.4	−1.2	0
$/£	2.8	2.4	2.4	2.4
Real exchange rate (1975 = 100)	109	102	102	103

Source: ONS, *Economic Trends*.

surplus. As we explained, a devaluation will not improve the value of the current account until quantities of imports and exports have time to respond. In the third row we show the PSBR as a percentage of GDP, as an indicator of fiscal policy. In 1967 UK unemployment was low and the economy was close to full employment. The economy had few spare resources with which to produce extra goods for export or import substitution. In 1969, fiscal policy was tightened substantially, reducing domestic absorption and allowing an improvement in net exports. The government (including the nationalized industries) actually ran a surplus in 1969.

The final row of the table shows the real exchange rate, the relative price of UK goods to foreign goods when measured in a common currency. It shows two things. First, instead of using the 15 per cent devaluation to reduce export prices in foreign currencies, UK exporters responded in part by raising prices and profit margins. Only about half the competitive advantage was passed on to foreign purchasers as lower foreign prices for UK goods. Second, even by 1970 we can see competitiveness being eroded. Domestic wages had started to rise as workers asked for cost of living wage increases to meet higher import prices. By 1970 the real exchange rate had begun to rise again.

Devaluation and adjustment We have argued that a devaluation is likely to lead to a temporary but not a permanent increase in competitiveness relative to the position that would have been attained without the devaluation. In the long run, real variables are determined by real forces and changes in one nominal variable merely induce offsetting changes in other nominal variables to restore real variables to their equilibrium values. But devaluation may be the simplest way to change competitiveness quickly. It may be a useful policy when the alternative adjustment mechanism is a domestic slump and a protracted period of gradual wage and price reduction until competitiveness is increased.

Suppose the economy begins at internal and external balance. Suppose there is a real shock, a reduction in foreign demand for our exports. In the short run, this leads both to a domestic slump, since the net export component of aggregate demand has fallen, and to a current account deficit, since exports have fallen below the level of imports. Before we think about adjustment, think about what will happen to the economy once long-run equilibrium has been re-established.

If internal and external balance are to be restored, competitiveness must increase. This will boost net exports,

eliminate the current account imbalance, and restore aggregate demand to its full employment level. A higher level of competitiveness essentially means a reduction in domestic real wages. Hence we conclude that, when long-run equilibrium is restored, domestic real wages must be lower than in the long-run equilibrium from which we began. The real shock – a reduction in the demand for our exports – has real consequences, as we should expect.

Now we can think about the adjustment mechanism that secures this real wage reduction and increase in competitiveness to restore long-run equilibrium. In the absence of a devaluation, the fall in net exports leads to a domestic slump which gradually reduces nominal wages and *domestic* prices. The fall in domestic prices increases competitiveness since the nominal exchange rate is fixed. The induced increase in net exports helps eliminate the current account deficit and also boosts domestic aggregate demand. You may be thinking that lower domestic prices also stimulate aggregate demand by boosting the real money supply, but it must be remembered that, with a balance of payments deficit in the short run, there is a net monetary outflow which is reducing the nominal money supply at the same time as prices are falling.

Where does the real wage reduction come in? Even if domestic prices and wages are falling in proportion, we must remember that households spend some of their incomes on imported goods whose prices are *not* being reduced. Imports are becoming relatively more expensive in comparison with domestic prices and wages. That, after all, is what we mean by an increase in domestic competitiveness. And that is why real wages are falling during the adjustment process.

The more slowly domestic nominal wages adjust, the longer will be the adjustment period. Suppose instead the government responds to the fall in export demand by devaluing the exchange rate. Competitiveness improves overnight. And real wages are immediately reduced. At unchanged nominal wages and domestic prices, import prices have risen since the price of foreign goods in foreign currency is unchanged, but these now convert into a larger number of pounds sterling for each imported good.

If workers accept this real wage cut, which will in any case be required if long-run equilibrium is eventually to be restored, then the adjustment process can be completed quickly. However, workers may resist this reduction in their real wages. They may press for 'cost-of-living' wage claims to cover the increase in price of imported goods they consume. If so, competitiveness will deteriorate again and a domestic slump will be required to persuade workers to accept the real wage cuts required to restore long-run equilibrium.

29-7 The determination of floating exchange rates

We now turn to freely floating exchange rates in the absence of any government intervention in the forex market. In this section we explain how the level of the exchange rate is determined. In the next section we use this analysis to investigate the consequences of monetary and fiscal policy in an open economy with floating exchange rates.

Purchasing power parity

Our definition of long-run equilibrium requires that the economy is both in internal balance (full employment) and external balance (zero net exports and current account balance). Import demand depends on domestic output and on the real exchange rate. Export demand depends on foreign output and on the real exchange rate. Hence when both the domestic economy and the rest of the world are at internal balance or potential output, there is only one real exchange rate compatible with external balance at the same time. At any higher real exchange rate the domestic economy will be less competitive. Imports will be higher and exports lower. It will have a current account deficit. Conversely, at any lower real exchange rate, the domestic economy will have a current account surplus. Only one real exchange rate is compatible with internal and external balance.

For given prices in the rest of the world, one country's real exchange rate can be altered either by a change in its nominal exchange rate or by a change in domestic prices. Under fixed exchange rates, since the nominal exchange rate is fixed, the eventual adjustment of the real exchange rate to its long-run equilibrium level must be achieved entirely through a change in domestic prices relative to prices abroad. But under floating exchange rates the nominal exchange rate can also help the adjustment.

Our theory of floating exchange rates in the long run can be summarized very simply. When exchange rates float freely, there is no official intervention in the forex market and no net monetary transfer between countries since the balance of payments is always zero. Just as in a closed economy, the domestic money supply is determined by the quantity of high-powered money issued by the government and by the extent to which the domestic banking system creates domestic bank deposits against this monetary base. In the long run the domestic money supply will determine the domestic price level just as in a closed economy. And in the long run the nominal exchange rate must adjust to achieve the unique real exchange rate required for external and internal balance in long-run equilibrium.

Suppose first that we live in a world without inflation in the long run. We begin in long-run equilibrium with internal and external balance. Suppose there is a once and for all doubling of the domestic money supply and, eventually, a doubling of the domestic price level. Thereafter it remains constant. A once and for all halving of the nominal exchange rate will restore the economy to external balance once all adjustment has been completed. Suppose the exchange rate has fallen from $2/£ to $1/£. Although domestic prices have doubled, the dollar price of British exports is unaffected in the long run. A £10 shirt used to sell for $20 when the exchange rate was $2/£. Now it costs £20 to make the shirt but it still sells for $20 since the exchange rate has fallen to $1/£. Similarly, an American calculator produced for $40 used to sell for £20 in the UK. When the exchange rate has fallen to $1/£ it still costs $40 to produce but now sells for £40 in the UK. The price of imports has doubled because the exchange rate has fallen by 50 per cent. Import prices have risen in line with domestic prices in the UK. Whether we compare the relative price of British and American goods in dollars or in pounds, we conclude that their relative price has not changed in the long run. Competitiveness is unaltered.

How about a world with continuous inflation? Suppose there is no inflation in the United States but that in the UK all nominal variables are increasing at 10 per cent a year. A continuous depreciation of the dollar–sterling exchange rate at 10 per cent a year will preserve the dollar price of British exports (in line with the constant dollar price of American goods) and ensure that the price in pounds of British imports from America rises at 10 per cent a year in line with the price of goods produced in the UK. Again, competitiveness is unaffected.

Earlier in the chapter we defined the *purchasing power parity* (PPP) path of the nominal exchange rate as the path that offsets differential inflation rates across countries and maintains at a constant level the real exchange rate and the level of competitiveness. We can now sum up our theory of how floating exchange rates must be determined in the long run. Since there is only one real exchange rate compatible with internal and external balance, and hence with full long-run equilibrium, in the long run the nominal exchange rate must follow whatever path is required to maintain real competitiveness at this level. In the absence of any real shocks (such as the discovery of large oil reserves, which affect the incentive to import and export even in the long run), the equilibrium level of real competitiveness will remain constant in the long run and the nominal exchange rate will be changing to prevent differences in domestic and foreign inflation rates from altering real competitiveness. The nominal exchange rate will follow the PPP path.

However, in the short run the real exchange rate need not be constant. Goods prices adjust only sluggishly, but floating exchange rates can change by a large magnitude in a short time. The stock of internationally mobile funds is now enormous. If those funds were all to move between currencies on the same day, this massive flow on the capital account could not possibly be offset by the (relatively) small net flows that occur on the current account. And under freely floating exchange rates there is no government intervention and no official financing. The forex market simply could not clear. But clear it does, day by day. Hence, short-run equilibrium in the forex market is achieved because the exchange rate is capable of jumping at any instant to the level necessary to prevent owners of inter-national funds wishing to make massive transfers between currencies.

To understand this process in greater detail, we must now look at the theory of exchange rate speculation.

Speculation

In discussing the capital account we noted that holders of funds in sterling will compare the interest rate obtained by lending on sterling assets with the expected total return that can be obtained by temporarily lending abroad instead. There are two points to note. First, it is the *total* return that counts. The total return from lending in a foreign currency (dollars) is the interest rate on dollar assets such as US government bonds plus the capital gain (loss) from a depreciation (appreciation) of the dollar–sterling exchange rate while the money is lent abroad. Someone who converts £1 into $2 and then converts it back into sterling after the exchange rate has fallen from $2/£ to $1/£ will be able to get £2 for their $2. They will have made a capital gain of 100 per cent (from £1 to £2) by holding their funds in dollars, while the dollar–sterling exchange rate fell.

Second, since speculators cannot be certain how exchange rates are going to change over time, it is the *expected* exchange rate changes, and hence the expected capital gains or losses from temporarily lending abroad, that influence decisions today about which currency looks the most attractive currency in which to lend.

Suppose UK interest rates are 2 per cent higher than US interest rates. Why don't holders of funds move all their funds into sterling? What would make them indifferent about which country they lent in? Suppose speculators expect the pound to depreciate by 2 per cent a year against the dollar. People investing in pounds will get 2 per cent extra interest but make a 2 per cent capital loss on the exchange rate change relative to the alternative strategy of lending in dollars. The extra interest just compensates for the expected loss and most speculators won't mind where they hold their funds. Since there are no massive flows between currencies, the forex market can be in equilibrium. The dollar–sterling exchange rate falls at 2 per cent a year as everyone expected, and investors get the same return on their money in either currency

What would happen if UK interest rates suddenly rose and were now 4 per cent higher than interest rates in the United States? If people still think that the exchange rate will fall at 2 per cent a year, the capital gain earned by holding dollars rather than pounds is no longer sufficient to compensate for the 4 per cent extra interest that can be earned by lending in pounds. Everyone will try to move into pounds. Almost instantaneously, this will bid up the dollar–sterling exchange rate. How high will it rise? Until it has reached such a high level that most people expect the pound then to fall at 4 per cent a year thereafter. Only then will the capital losses expected on funds lent in pounds be sufficient to offset the 4 per cent interest differential, and only then will people stop wanting to get their money into pounds.

Why do speculators believe that a higher value of the pound today makes it more likely that the exchange rate will fall in the future? Because smart speculators figure out that eventually the exchange rate has to return to its PPP path, the only path compatible with external balance in the long run. If the exchange rate does not seem to be moving in that direction, eventually the government is going to have to take some drastic action to restore external balance.

Thus we can sum up the complete theory of exchange rate determination as follows. In the long run the exchange rate will have to follow the purchasing power parity path which offsets differential inflation rates across countries and allows long-run equilibrium at the unique real exchange rate compatible with external balance. But in the short run the nominal exchange rate can depart significantly from this path and competitiveness can change by a large amount.

In the long run, countries with high inflation rates also have higher nominal interest rates. That is the Fisher relation we discussed in Chapter 28. Hence in the long-run equilibrium when the exchange rate is falling along the PPP path, the speculators are quite happy too. The capital losses on the depreciating exchange rate are just offsetting the high nominal interest rates earned by lending in that currency.

But when a country has higher interest rates in the short run than it is expected to have in the long run, the currency will temporarily be attractive to owners of international funds. To stop them all moving their funds into the currency to take advantage of these high interest rates in the short run, the currency will have to appreciate, perhaps significantly, above its purchasing power parity path. Only then are speculators likely to believe that the exchange rate will fall sufficiently in the near future to provide capital losses that offset the high interest rates that are temporarily on offer. In the short run large movements in the exchange rate may be required to prevent the massive flows on the capital account which would be incompatible with day-to-day equilibrium in the forex market.

We now show how this model of exchange rate determination can be used to analyse monetary and fiscal policy under freely floating exchange rates.

29-8 Monetary and fiscal policy under floating exchange rates

In a closed economy with sluggish wage and price adjustment, both monetary and fiscal policy have real effects in the short run, although the economy eventually returns to full employment or internal balance. In an open economy with fixed exchange rates, highly mobile international funds make monetary policy almost powerless in the short run but increase the power of fiscal policy. Under floating exchange rates the converse is true: monetary policy is powerful in the short run, but the effectiveness of fiscal policy is reduced.

Monetary policy

Suppose that the foreign price level and the foreign money supply are fixed. The rest of the world has no inflation. Its nominal and real interest rates are constant and equal, perhaps at 3 per cent per annum. The domestic economy begins in internal and external balance, also with a constant money supply and constant wages and prices. Since there is no domestic inflation, domestic nominal and real interest rates are also 3 per cent.

In this long-run equilibrium, domestic and foreign interest rates are equal. Unless international speculators expect the exchange rate to remain constant, they will wish to transfer all their funds to the currency they expect to appreciate. But with neither domestic nor foreign inflation, speculators recognize that the nominal exchange rate can remain unchanged for ever. It is at the level that secures the

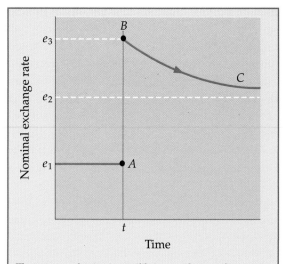

The economy begins in equilibrium with an exchange rate e_1. When the nominal money supply is halved at time t, speculators realize the exchange rate must eventually double from e_1 to e_2 in order to restore competitiveness once prices have fallen by 50 per cent. Since prices do not change immediately, the effect at t is to reduce the real money supply and increase domestic interest rates above world levels. Only by jumping from A to B, and thereby convincing speculators that subsequent capital losses from exchange rate depreciation will offset higher interest rates, can the exchange rate adjust to maintain equilibrium in the forex market. As domestic prices fall, the real money supply increases and interest rates fall back to world levels. When full adjustment is complete, the exchange rate has reached e_2. Thus the initial jump from A to B overshoots the long-run change required in the nominal exchange rate.

Figure 29-4   Exchange rate overshooting

level of competitiveness appropriate to external balance in long-run equilibrium. Hence speculators have no wish to transfer funds between currencies. It is a full long-run equilibrium.

Figure 29-4 shows this nominal exchange rate as e_1. Suppose that at time t there is a once-and-for-all reduction in the nominal money supply by 50 per cent. Eventually domestic prices and wages will fall by 50 per cent. Thus in the long run it will require an appreciation of the nominal exchange rate, a doubling from e_1 to e_2, to restore the real exchange rate to its long-run equilibrium level.

However, domestic prices adjust sluggishly. In the short run, a reduction in the nominal money supply will also reduce the real money supply. Thus the immediate effect is to raise domestic interest rates in order to reduce the demand for money and maintain equilibrium in the domestic money market. Now speculators are keen to invest large amounts in pounds. To choke off a massive inflow of funds on the capital account, the sterling exchange rate must rise *above* its new long-run equilibrium position e_1. We say that the exchange rate must overshoot the change eventually required.

When the exchange rate jumps from e_1 to e_3, speculators realize that it will have to fall to get back to its new long-run equilibrium e_2. The anticipated falls in the exchange rate mean anticipated capital losses for those holding sterling rather than dollars, and these offset the higher sterling interest rate. The exchange rate converges on its new equilibrium by moving along the path BC as time elapses.

The path gets steadily flatter over time. Initially the fall in the nominal money supply caused a large reduction in the real money supply and a big increase in domestic interest rates. But gradually domestic prices and wages start to fall, increasing the real money supply and reducing sterling interest rates. As the interest differential falls, it requires a slower and slower exchange rate depreciation to prevent massive international flows of funds. And, of course, the smart speculators had already figured that out in deciding that an initial jump in the exchange rate to e_3 was exactly what was required to keep them happy with the currency in which their funds were held.

So monetary policy can have a powerful effect in the short run. Changes in the real money supply and domestic interest rates not only influence domestic absorption, as in a closed economy, but also induce large changes in the nominal exchange rate and the level of competitiveness, which are only slowly eroded as domestic wages and prices adjust.

Again we emphasize that the government cannot choose independent targets for both the money supply and the exchange rate. Under a *fixed* exchange rate, there will be a net monetary flow on the balance of payments until, given domestic prices, the domestic real money supply equals the demand for real balances at the domestic level of real income and world interest rates. Domestic interest rates must match foreign interest rates in order to prevent massive capital flows when interest rates are known to be fixed.

In contrast, under a *floating* exchange rate the balance of payments is exactly zero. Combining currency and capital accounts, there are no international monetary flows. Thus the government can determine the domestic money supply at any level it chooses. But, as Figure 29-4 illustrates, the government must then accept the path for the exchange rate that clears the forex market and keep the speculators happy. Equally, even without any official financing, the government can peg the exchange rate simply by announcing

that it will match foreign interest rates for ever. As foreign interest rates change, the government simply alters the domestic money supply to maintain domestic money market equilibrium at the required interest rate. However we consider the problem, we always reach the same conclusion: the government must always allow market forces to determine either the money supply *or* the exchange rate.

Fiscal policy

Whereas the effect of interest rate changes on the exchange rate and competitiveness makes monetary policy a more powerful tool with which to influence aggregate demand under floating exchange rates, the effect of interest rate changes on the exchange rate reduces the short-term effectiveness of fiscal policy.

Suppose the government undertakes a fiscal expansion, say by increasing the level of government spending. This increases aggregate demand and bids up interest rates. The higher interest rate leads to an immediate appreciation of the nominal exchange rate to choke off an inflow of funds, just as in Figure 29-4. In a closed economy, higher interest rates partially crowd out private expenditure by reducing consumption and investment demand. But in an open economy with floating exchange rates, the induced reduction in the demand for net exports further reduces the power of a fiscal expansion to stimulate aggregate demand in the short run.

The pound since 1980

Figure 29-5 shows the behaviour of the nominal and real sterling exchange rates since 1980. We show the exchange rate against a basket of the currencies most important for the UK's international trade.

The UK's real exchange rate had appreciated substantially during 1977–80. First, a tight monetary policy had been introduced to fight inflation. Until domestic prices and wages adjusted, the squeeze in real money meant high interest rates and a sharp appreciation in the nominal exchange rate. Second, the UK found oil. We discuss its effects in the next section.

After 1981, competitiveness gradually improved as the real exchange rate fell. In part, this can be explained by the overshooting story we discussed earlier. The period 1979–81 was a time of sharp appreciation, and subsequently this was gradually reversed.

The UK boom of the mid-1980s was partly built on falls in the real exchange rate and greater international competitiveness. However, domestic tax cuts and monetary

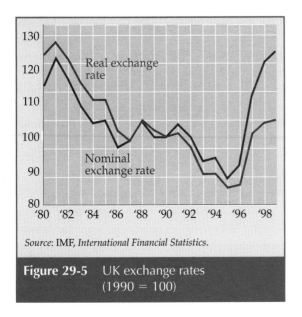

Source: IMF, *International Financial Statistics*.

Figure 29-5   UK exchange rates
(1990 = 100)

growth eventually caused the economy to overheat. A government still committed to low tax rates responded with very sharp increases in UK interest rates. Figure 29-5 confirms that these led to a sharp exchange rate appreciation to stave off a speculative inflow. The late 1980s were partly a rerun of the late 1970s.

In 1990 the UK joined the Exchange Rate Mechanism of the EMS and pegged its nominal exchange rate against other EU countries. Inflation had risen to 10 per cent and the government wanted a rapid improvement before the next election. When eventually the squeeze proved tougher than the economy could stand, speculators foresaw an inevitable easing of monetary policy, lower interest rates, and a devaluation of sterling. On Black Wednesday in September 1992 they bailed out of the pound in such numbers that the UK government abandoned the attempt to hold the exchange rate and suspended membership of the EMS.

Figure 29-5 shows the sharp depreciation of both nominal and real exchange rates in late 1992. Increased competiveness gave the UK an export boom during 1993–95 that helped pull the country out of recession. However, one theme of this chapter has been that nominal devaluation is unlikely to achieve permanent increases in competitiveness. Figure 29-5 shows that by the end of 1996 the real exchange rate had returned to its level of 1992. The UK's European partners tightened their fiscal policy in efforts to meet the Maastricht criteria for EMU, whereas the UK relied on high interest rates to control inflation. This bid up sterling,

very sharply, in real terms. Britain's temporary period of export-led growth quickly petered out.

29-9 North Sea oil

By the late 1970s the UK was beginning to exploit the large reserves of oil discovered in the North Sea. The doubling of oil prices in 1979–80 increased the importance of these reserves. What effect did this have on the exchange rate?

Let's think first about long-run equilibrium with internal and external balance. External balance means that imports equal exports. The UK was formerly a large oil-importer. This trade deficit was offset by a surplus on other trade, primarily trade in manufactured goods. Suppose, for simplicity, that the oil discovery made the UK self-sufficient in oil. To preserve external balance, the UK had to give up its trade surplus in manufactured goods. The monetary mechanism that brought this about was a rise in the real exchange rate and a reduction in competitiveness.

For a given domestic money supply and given domestic prices, there was an appreciation of the exchange rate required for external balance in the long run. Recognizing this, speculators realized that, unless the exchange rate rose immediately, there would be foreseen capital gains as it gradually climbed to its higher long-run value. Since this made holding funds in pounds more attractive than before, the exchange rate had to rise immediately to choke off the potential inflow of funds.

Thus, sterling's real exchange rate rose especially sharply in the period 1979–81 because there was simultaneously a move to tighter monetary policy and a sharp increase in the real value of the UK's oil reserves. And in the period 1981–87 there was an improvement in competitiveness, both because of the gradual recovery from overshooting, equivalent to a movement down the path *BC* in Figure 29-4, and because a world slump had reduced the world demand for oil and the real price of oil.

By the mid-1980s, a considerable part of North Sea oil reserves had been extracted. The importance of oil extraction to the UK economy rapidly diminished. This had two implications. First, the sterling exchange rate was no longer so sensitive to fluctuations in oil prices. Second, on average sterling's real exchange rate was lower in the 1990s than it was in the 1980s. As oil disappeared, greater competitiveness 'crowded in' other types of export. Renewed appreciation since 1996 has eroded this advantage.

SUMMARY

● The exchange rate is the number of units of foreign currency that exchange for a unit of the domestic currency. A fall (rise) in the exchange rate is called a depreciation (appreciation).

● The demand for domestic currency arises from exports, and purchases of domestic assets by foreigners; the supply of domestic currency arises from imports and purchases of foreign assets. Floating exchange rates equate supply and demand in the absence of government intervention in the forex market.

● Under fixed exchange rates, the government meets an excess supply of pounds by running down foreign currency reserves in order to demand pounds. Conversely, any excess demand for pounds at the fixed exchange rate is met by increasing the foreign exchange reserves and supplying pounds to the market.

● In the balance of payments accounts, monetary inflows are recorded as credits and monetary outflows are recorded as debits. The current account shows the balance on trade in goods and services plus net income earned from assets owned in other currencies. The capital account shows net purchases and sales of assets. The balance of payments is the sum of the current and capital account balances.

● Under floating exchange rates, a current surplus must be offset by a capital deficit or vice versa. Under fixed exchange rates, a balance of payments surplus or deficit must be matched by an offsetting quantity of official financing. Official financing is government intervention in the forex market.

● The real exchange rate adjusts the nominal exchange rate for prices at home and abroad, and is the relative price of domestic to foreign goods when measured in a common currency. A rise in the real exchange rate reduces the competitiveness of the domestic economy.

● An increase in domestic (foreign) income increases the demand for imports (exports). An increase in the real exchange rate reduces the demand for exports, increases the demand for imports, and reduces the demand for net exports.

● Holders of international funds compare the domestic interest rate with the total return from temporarily lending abroad. This return is the foreign interest rate plus the depreciation of the international value of the domestic currency over the period of the loan. Perfect international capital mobility means that an enormous quantity of funds will shift between currencies when the perceived rate of return differs across currencies.

● Internal balance occurs when aggregate demand is at the full-employment level. External balance occurs when imports equal exports. Both are necessary for long-run equilibrium.

● A balance of payments deficit leads to an equivalent reduction of the domestic money supply. A balance of payments surplus increases the domestic money supply by an equal amount.

● Under fixed exchange rates and perfect capital mobility, monetary policy is almost powerless. Domestic interest rates are pegged at world levels. An increase in the domestic money supply leads to an equivalent balance of payments deficit until the money supply is restored to the level people wish to demand at the given level of world interest rates.

● In the short run, fiscal policy is a powerful tool under fixed exchange rates. Fiscal expansion no longer bids up domestic interest rates in the short run. Any tendency for interest rates to rise leads to an immediate inflow on the capital account until the money supply is increased enough to maintain interest rates at the world level.

● A devaluation is a reduction in the fixed exchange rate maintained by the government. With sluggish price adjustment, its immediate effect is to increase competitiveness and aggregate demand. With spare resources, output increases. But at full employment, net exports can increase only if domestic absorption is reduced by tighter fiscal policy.

● In the long run, devaluation is unlikely to have much effect. Changing one nominal variable merely leads to offsetting changes in other nominal variables. In passing on higher import prices and seeking cost-of-living wage increases, firms and workers will increase domestic prices and wages to offset the competitive advantage of devaluation. But devaluation could speed up the adjustment process when a shock requires an adjustment in competitiveness to restore internal and external balance.

● Under floating exchange rates, the long-run value of the nominal exchange rate will be determined to secure external balance, given prices at home and abroad. But in the short run it is determined by speculative considerations, and must change to prevent massive flows on the capital account.

● The exchange rate must begin at a level from which the anticipated convergent path to its long-run equilibrium continuously provides capital gains or losses to offset prevailing interest rate differentials, thus equating the rate of return on lending at home and abroad.

● Under floating exchange rates, monetary policy is a powerful short-term tool. A reduction in the money supply increases domestic interest rates and leads to a sharp appreciation of the exchange rate, which overshoots its long-run level. The fall in competitiveness, until domestic prices and wages adjust, sharply reduces aggregate demand in the short run.

● Fiscal policy is now a weaker tool in the short run. Fiscal expansion increases interest rates and the exchange rate, crowding out not merely domestic consumption and investment but also net exports.

● A deterioration in the oil-related part of the current account eventually requires an equivalent improvement in other items on the current account to preserve overall external balance. This is achieved through a fall in the real exchange rate.

KEY TERMS

REVIEW QUESTIONS

1 If $1 exchanges for 2 Deutschmarks (DM) and $2 exchange for £1, what is the exchange rate between DM and £? Can the dollar appreciate against the DM but not against the £?

2 A country has a current account surplus of £6 billion but a capital account deficit of £4 billion. (a) Is its balance of payments in deficit or surplus? (b) Are the country's foreign exchange reserves rising or falling? (c) Is the central bank buying or selling domestic currency? Explain.

3 For over 20 years, Japan has run a persistent trade surplus. How is this compatible with the statement that countries must eventually get back to external balance? Does this mean that there is more pressure on deficit countries to restore external balance than there is pressure on the corresponding surplus countries?

4 Rank the following three situations according to the ability of monetary policy to affect real output and employment in the short run: (a) a closed economy; (b) an open economy with fixed exchange rates; (c) an open economy with floating exchange rates. Explain. Assume the same speed of wage and price adjustment in each case.

5 Newsreaders say that 'the pound had a good day' whenever the sterling exchange rate rises on the forex market. (a) Under what circumstances might an appreciation of the exchange rate be desirable? (b) Undesirable?

6 *Common fallacies* Show why each of the following statements is incorrect. (a) Countries with low inflation must be more competitive in the long run. (b) Under floating exchange rates the current and capital accounts have equal magnitude but opposite sign. Hence both must be equally important in determining day-to-day exchange rate changes. (c) UK interest rates are high. This means the pound will appreciate for the next few months.

30 Economic growth

LEARNING OUTCOMES

When you have finished this chapter, you should be able to:

- Study determinants of the growth of potential output and living standards
- Explain how economics became called the dismal science because Malthus forecast that living standards would fall to starvation levels
- Discuss how, together, technical progress and the accumulation of physical and human capital made Malthus's forecast incorrect
- Study the neoclassical model of economic growth
- Consider how departures from its assumptions can undermine its optimistic conclusion that poor countries enjoy faster growth for a while
- Investigate the growth performance of advanced and less advanced countries
- Analyse whether growth rates could be affected by economic behaviour and economic policy
- Discuss the costs of growth and assess whether growth must be halted in order to preserve the environment

In 1999 real GDP in the UK was 10 times its level of 1870. Real income per person quintupled over that period. On average, we are richer than our grandparents but less rich than our grandchildren will be. Table 30-1 shows that these long-term trends were even more pronounced in other countries. Over the same period 1870–1999, real GDP in Japan increased 100-fold and real income per person 27-fold.

We begin by asking three questions about the long-run growth records shown in Table 30-1: What do we mean by long-run economic growth? What factors are responsible for this growth? And what economic policies can be used to change an economy's rate of growth in the long run? We discuss mainly the experience of industrialized countries. In Chapter 36 we discuss the growth performance of other nations in the world economy.

We also consider whether growth is a good thing. Might it be better to grow more slowly? Can the costs of growth outweigh its benefits?

Economists have always been fascinated by the theory of economic growth. In 1798 Thomas Malthus's *First Essay on Population* predicted that output growth would be far outstripped by population growth until starvation and death brought the latter into line with the former, the origin of the notion of economics as 'the dismal science'. Some countries still seem stuck in a Malthusian trap, but others have clearly broken through into sustained growth and prosperity. We examine how they did it.

As Table 30-1 shows, adding even 0.5 per cent to the annual growth rate makes an enormous difference to potential output after a few decades. By the end of the 1960s, economists had a fully worked out theory of economic growth. It yielded many insights but had one central failing. It could not find any role for government policy in the long run: the long-run growth rate was whatever it was, and policy made no difference.

Since the mid-1980s, there has been a new surge of interest in the theory of economic growth. One simple insight has allowed a whole new approach in which the equilibrium growth rate is affected by the behaviour of government, firms, and households. We outline the new approaches to economic growth.

30-1 Economic growth

The growth rate of a variable is its percentage increase per annum. To define economic growth we must specify both the variable we wish to measure and the period over which we wish to measure its rate of change. Table 30-1 is based on real GDP, but we would obtain very similar results if we looked instead at real GNP or national income.

Economic growth is the rate of change of real income or real output.

GDP and GNP measure the total output and total income of an economy. We begin by reminding you of some of the problems we raised in Chapter 20 when discussing whether such measures are useful indicators of economic performance. In particular, GDP (and GNP) are very incomplete measures of *economic* output; it is difficult to account for

the introduction of new products; and there is no direct relationship between GDP and happiness.

GDP as a measure of economic output

GDP measures the net output or value added of an economy by measuring goods and services purchased with money. It omits output which is not bought and sold and therefore is unmeasured. The two most important omissions are leisure and externalities such as pollution and congestion.

In most industrial countries, the length of an average work week has fallen by at least ten hours a week since 1900. In choosing to work fewer hours per week, people reveal that the extra leisure is worth at least as much as the extra goods that could have been produced by working harder. But when people decide to swap washing machines for extra leisure, recorded GDP is reduced; hence, GDP understates the true economic output of the economy. Conversely, the output of pollution reduces the net economic welfare that the economy is producing and ideally should be subtracted from GDP. For example, sulphur dioxide emissions from coal-fired power stations lead to 'acid rain', destroying vast acres of German and Scandinavian forests. With comprehensive national income accounting, this output of acid rain would have been deducted from GDP.

Including leisure in GDP would have increased recorded GDP in both 1870 and 1999. Since the value of leisure has probably increased less quickly than measured output, which increased 10-fold in the UK and 100-fold in Japan over the same period, this would tend to reduce the rate of growth of a more comprehensive output measure. Similarly, pollution may actually have increased at a faster rate. Hence it is possible that the growth rates for GDP in Table 30-1 overstate the rate at which economies have been increasing their net output of goods and services with an economic value.

Table 30-1	Real GDP and per capita real GDP, 1870–1999				
	Real GDP			Per capital real GDP	
	Ratio of 1999 to 1870	Annual growth (%)		Ratio of 1999 to 1870	Annual growth (%)
Japan	100	3.7		27	2.7
USA	66	3.4		10	1.8
Australia	45	3.1		4	1.2
Sweden	33	2.8		14	2.2
France	15	2.2		10	1.9
UK	10	1.9		5	1.3

Source: Angus Maddison, 'Phases of Capitalist Development', in R. C. O. Matthews (ed.), *Economic Growth and Resources*, vol. 2, Macmillan, 1979; updated from IMF, *International Financial Statistics.*

New products

In 1870 people did not have televisions, cars or computers. Although statisticians do their best to compare the value of real GDP in different years, the introduction of new products creates a genuine difficulty in trying to make comparisons over time. As each new good is introduced, it is usually possible to figure out roughly what it is worth compared with the good it replaces, because both goods are sold in the market at the same time. We can estimate how much people's real income has been increased by the introduction of a new product that accomplishes the same task more cheaply. But this calculation is more difficult when the new product allows an activity that had never been possible before.

GDP as a measure of happiness

Even with an accurate and comprehensive measure of GDP, two problems remain. First, should we be interested in total GDP or in GDP per capita? In part, this depends on the question we wish to ask. Total GDP indicates the size of an economy, which may tell us something about its clout in the world. However, if we care about the happiness of a typical individual in an economy, it makes more sense to look at GDP per capita. Table 30-1 tells us that, although real GDP grew more quickly in Australia than in France or Sweden between 1870 and 1996, in part this was due to very fast population growth, largely through immigration. Sweden and France actually had faster growth in GDP per person over the period.

Even so, real GDP per person is a very imperfect indicator of the happiness of the typical individual within a country. When income is shared equally between its citizens, a country's per capita real GDP does tell us what each and every person is getting. But countries such as Brazil have very unequal income distributions. A few people earn a lot and a lot of people earn only a little. It is possible for such countries to have fairly high per capita real income while many of their citizens are really quite badly off.

Finally, we note that, even when GDP is adjusted to measure leisure, pollution, and so on, higher per capita GDP does not necessarily lead to greater happiness. Material goods are not everything. But they do help. Movements in which people return to 'the simple life' have not had much success, and most of the less industrialized countries are trying to increase their GDP as quickly as possible.

A recent phenomenon?

Table 30-1 makes one final point. A very small increase in the annual growth rate has substantial results when its impact is cumulated over a long period. Even an annual growth rate of only 1.3 per cent in per capita GDP led to a quintupling of UK per capita real GDP between 1870 and 1999. In 1870, UK per capita income was about £1900 in 1999 prices. If the growth rate had always been 1.3 per cent a year, per capita real income would have had to be about £370 in 1750, £75 in 1630 and only about £16 in 1510. Clearly, this is implausible. In fact, it is only in the last two and a half centuries that per capita levels of real income have been persistently increasing.

In the short run, an economy with Keynesian unemployment and spare resources can increase output by increasing demand and employment. But if potential output is constant, the economy will quickly reach full employment and further growth will cease. In the long run, changes in output caused by fluctuations around potential output are swamped by the effect of persistent growth in potential output itself. If potential output increases at 2 per cent a year, it will increase sevenfold in less than a century. In the long run it is in changes in the level of potential output that we must seek the explanation of economic growth.

30-2 Growth: an overview

To organize our ideas, we start from the production function.

The **production function** shows the maximum output that can be produced using specified quantities of inputs, given the existing technical knowledge.

In what follows we assume that the economy is always at potential output, the output level produced when there is full employment and all markets clear. The production function tells us that increases in potential output can be traced to increases in inputs of the factors of production – land, labour, capital, raw materials – or to technical advances allowing the existing factors to produce a higher level of output.

In the very long run we cannot assume that population growth is independent of per capita output, which will influence both the number of children people wish to have or feel able to afford and the quantity of nutrition and medical care that people on average receive. Nevertheless, we simplify by assuming that the rate of population growth is independent of economic factors over some slightly shorter period. Thus we assume that anything that increases total output will also increase per capita output.

Capital

Productive capital is the stock of machinery, buildings, and inventories with which other factors of production combine to produce output. For a given labour force, an increase in total capital and capital per worker will increase output. However, capital depreciates over time. Some new investment is required merely to maintain the existing capital stock intact. And with a growing labour force, an even higher quantity of investment is required if capital per worker is to be maintained. With yet faster investment, capital per worker will increase over time, thereby increasing the output each worker can produce. An increase in capital per worker is one of the principal ways in which output per worker and per capita income is increased.

Labour

Employment may increase for two reasons. First, there may be population growth. Second, a larger fraction of a given population may be in employment. However, labour input depends on the hours worked as well as the number of people working. Even for a given level of employment, an increase in hours worked will increase effective labour input to the production function, and hence increase output.

Since the average work week has fallen substantially over the last 100 years, the increases in per capita real output in Table 30-1 cannot be attributed to increased hours of work. Since 1945, the most significant aspect of the growth of labour input has been the steady increase in the number of women choosing to participate in the labour force. By increasing the labour input obtained from a given population, this tends to increase total and per capita output.

Human capital Human capital is the skill and knowledge embodied in the minds and hands of the population. Increasing education, training, and experience allows workers to produce more output from the same level of physical capital. For example, much of West Germany's physical capital was devastated during the Second World War; but the human capital of its surviving labour force had not evaporated between 1939 and 1945. Given these skills, Germany was able to recover rapidly after 1945 and rebuild its physical capital, aided by large loans from the United States through the Marshall Plan. But without the inherited stock of human capital, it is doubtful whether we should ever have heard of the postwar German economic miracle.

Land

Land is especially important in an agricultural economy. If each worker has more land it will be possible to increase agricultural output. Land is less important in highly industrialized economies. For example, Hong Kong has been able

to grow rapidly even though it is very overcrowded and land is scarce. Even so, more of a production input is unlikely to reduce the quantity of output that other factors can produce. Increasing the supply of land will allow the economy to produce more output.

Increases in the supply of land are relatively unimportant as a source of growth in modern economies. Indeed, in simple theoretical models we define land as the factor of production whose total supply to the economy is fixed. But in practice the distinction between land and capital is rather blurred. By applying more fertilizer per acre, an input of agricultural capital, the effective quantity of farming land can be increased. With investment in drainage or irrigation, marshes and deserts can be converted into productive land.

Raw materials

Given the quantity of other inputs, an increase in the input of raw materials will increase the quantity of output that can be produced. When raw materials are scarce and expensive, workers will take time and care not to waste them. With a more abundant supply of raw materials, workers can work more quickly.

It is important to distinguish two kinds of raw material. *Depletable* materials are those that can be used only once. When a barrel of oil has been extracted from the ground and used to fuel a machine, the world has one less barrel of oil reserves in the ground. If the world begins with a finite stock of oil reserves, it will eventually run out of oil though this may not happen for many centuries.

In contrast, *renewable* resources can be replaced. Timber and fish are obvious examples. If harvested in moderation, they will be replaced by nature and can be used as production inputs for ever. However, if over-harvested they may become extinct. When there are only a few whales left in the ocean, they may find it impossible to locate partners with which to breed and the stock of whales will gradually disappear.

Factor contributions and scale economies

The marginal product of a factor tells us how much output will increase when the factor input is increased by one unit but all other inputs are held constant. Microeconomics tells us that marginal products eventually decline as factor input is increased. With two workers already on each machine, another worker does very little to increase total output.

Economies of scale Suppose that, instead of increasing one input in isolation, all factor inputs are doubled together. If output exactly doubles, we say there are *constant returns to scale*; if output more (less) than doubles, we say that there are *increasing (decreasing) returns to scale*.

Economies of scale reinforce the growth process. Anything that increases inputs leads to an extra bonus in higher output. And there are sometimes sound engineering reasons to believe that economies of scale will exist. For example, it requires only simple mathematics to show that it takes less than twice the steel input to build an oil tanker of twice the capacity. On the other hand, many developing countries regret the resources they have tied up in huge steel mills which do not produce very efficiently. Bigger is not always better. In practice, economists frequently assume constant returns to scale.

Having briefly discussed the different factor inputs, we turn now to the role of technical knowledge.

30-3 Technical knowledge

At any given time, a society has a stock of **technical knowledge** about ways in which goods can be produced.

Some of this knowledge is written down in books and blueprints, but much is reflected in working practices learned by hard experience.

Technical advances come through **invention**, the discovery of new knowledge, and **innovation**, the incorporation of new knowledge into actual production techniques.

Inventions

Major inventions can lead to spectacular increases in technical knowledge. The wheel, the steam engine, and the modern computer are obvious examples. Although we tend to think of industrial processes, technical progress in agriculture has also been dramatic. Industrialized societies began only when productivity improvements in agriculture allowed some of the workforce to be freed to produce industrial goods. Before then, almost everyone had to work the land merely to get enough food for survival. The replacement of animal power by machines, the development of fertilizer, drainage and irrigation, and new hybrid seeds, have all played a large part in improving agricultural production and enabling economic growth.

Embodiment of knowledge in capital   To introduce new ideas to actual production, innovation frequently requires investment in new machines. Without investment, bullocks cannot be transformed into tractors even once the knowhow for building tractors has been made available. Major new inventions may thus lead to waves of investment and

innovation as these ideas are put into practice. Just as the mid-nineteenth century was the age of the train, and the interwar years the age of the car, we are now seeing the age of the microchip.

Learning by doing   Human capital can matter as much as physical capital. Workers get better at doing a particular job as they have more practice. The most famous example is known as the Horndal effect, after a Swedish steelworks built during 1835–36, and kept in the same condition for the next 15 years. Without changes in the machinery or the size of the labour force, output per worker-hour nevertheless rose by 2 per cent a year. Eventually, however, as skills become mastered, further productivity increases become harder and harder to attain.

Research and development

What determines the amount of invention and innovation? Some new ideas are simply the product of intellectual curiosity or frustration ('There must be a better way to do this!'). But like most activities, the output of new ideas depends to a large extent on the resources devoted to looking for them, which in turn depends on the cost of tying up resources in this way and the prospective benefits from success. Some research activities take place in university departments, usually funded at least in part by the government, but a good deal of research is privately funded through the money firms devote to their research and development (R&D) departments.

The outcome of research is risky. Research workers never know whether or not they will find anything useful. Research is like a risky investment project, since the funds must be committed before the benefits (if any) start to accrue, but there is one important difference. Suppose you spend a lot of money developing a better mousetrap. When you succeed, everyone else copies your new mousetrap; the price is bid down, and you never recoup your initial investment. In such a world, there would be little incentive to undertake R&D.

If the invention becomes widely available when it is discovered, society gets the benefit but the original developer does not: there is an *externality*. Private and social gains do not coincide and the price mechanism does not provide the correct incentives. Society tries to get round this *market failure* in two ways. First, it grants *patents* to private inventors and innovators, legal monopolies for a fixed period of time which allow successful research projects to repay investments in R&D by temporarily charging higher prices than the cost of production alone. Second, the

<table>
<tr><td colspan="2">BOX 30-1</td><td>Technology diffusion in the fast lane</td></tr>
</table>

How are technical breakthroughs in one country gradually diffused throughout the world? Occasionally by industrial espionage. More frequently, by the lure of profits. New processes may be pioneered in the laboratories of rich countries, but frequently the subsequent production line is sited in a less advanced country where wages are lower. Gradually, those in the poorer country learn the technology and begin to adapt it to other purposes. One recent example is the rapid expansion of car makers into Central and Eastern Europe. By moving production a few miles across the border, from Germany to Poland or the Czech Republic, labour costs fall by seven eighths. One day, of course, wages in the east will catch up. Low pay is not the only reason for technology diffusion through foreign investment: car sales are booming in Latin America and Eastern Europe. Poland is now Europe's eighth largest car market.

Foreign direct investment in Central Europe

Company	Country	Billions	Activity
VW	Eastern Germany	DM 3.20	New engine and car plants
Opel	Eastern Germany	DM 1.00	New car plant
VW	Czech Republic	DM 3.70	70% stake in Skoda
VW	Hungary	DM 1.00	New Audi engine and car plant
Opel	Hungary	DM 0.70	New engine and car plant
Suzuki	Hungary	?	80% stake in new car plant
VW	Slovakia	DM 0.22	Assembly and gearbox plant
Ford	Poland	$ 0.05	Car and van assembly
Opel	Poland	DM 0.03	Car assembly
Daewoo	Poland	$ 1.34	Purchase of FSO and FS Lubin Investment in new plant and models
VW	Poland	DM 0.05	Car and van assembly plant
Opel	Poland	DM 0.50	New car plant
Fiat	Poland	$ 1.80	78% stake in FSO Investment in new plant and models

Source: Financial Times, 13 February 1997.

government subsidizes a good deal of basic research in universities, in its own laboratories, and in private industry.

30-4 Growth and accumulation

In this section we explore more fully the links between output growth, factor accumulation, and technical progress. We shall organize our discussion around a simple production function

$$Y = A \times f(K, L) \tag{1}$$

Variable inputs capital K and labour L combine to produce a given output $f(K, L)$. The function f tells us how much we get out when we use specified quantities of the inputs K and L. This function f never changes. We capture technical progress separately through A, which measures the extent of technical knowledge at any date. As technical progress takes place, we get more output from given inputs. A increases in value. In this simple framework, we assume that land is fixed. It is one of the other-things-equal assumptions, and need not feature explicitly in the analysis.

Malthus, land, and population

One of the earliest doomsters was the Reverend Thomas Malthus, writing in 1798. Living in a largely agricultural society, Malthus worried about the fixed supply of land. As a growing population tried to work a fixed supply of land, the marginal product of labour would diminish and agricultural output would fail to increase in line with population. The per capita food supply would fall until starvation started to reduce population to the level that could be fed from the given supply of agricultural land.

In terms of equation (1), when people are starving they have to consume all their income. Without savings, society cannot invest in capital, so K is zero. The production function then has diminishing returns to labour: adding more workers to fixed land drives down productivity.

Some of the poorer developing countries today face this *Malthusian trap*. Agricultural productivity is so low that almost everyone must work on the land if enough food is to be produced. As population grows and agricultural output fails to keep pace, famine sets in and people die. If better fertilizers or irrigation manage to improve agricultural output, population quickly expands as nutrition improves, and people are driven back to starvation levels again.

Yet Malthus's prediction did not prove correct for all countries. Today's rich countries managed to break out of the Malthusian trap. How was this achieved? First, they managed to improve agricultural productivity (without an immediate population increase) so that some workers could be transferred to industrial production. The capital goods thus produced included better ploughs, machinery to pump water and drain fields, and transport to distribute food more effectively. As capital was applied in agriculture, output per worker increased further, allowing yet more workers to be released to industry while maintaining sufficient food production to feed the growing population. Second, the rapid technical progress in agricultural production led to large and persistent productivity increases, reinforcing the effect of moving to more capital-intensive agricultural production. In terms of equation (1), increases in A and in K allowed output to grow faster than labour, causing a *rise* in living standards.

Thus we conclude that even the existence of a factor whose supply is largely fixed need not make sustained growth impossible. If capital can be accumulated, more and more capital can be substituted for fixed land, allowing output to grow at least as rapidly as population, and it is possible that continuing technical progress will allow continuing output growth even when one factor is not increasing. Moreover, the price mechanism provides the correct incentives for these processes to occur. With a given supply of land, increasing agricultural production will increase the price of land and the rental that must be paid for land. This provides both an incentive to switch to production methods that are less land-intensive (heavy fertilizer usage, battery chickens), and an incentive to concentrate on technical progress which will allow the economy either to get by with less land or, effectively, to increase the supply of land. A similar argument applies to any natural resource in finite supply.

Capital accumulation

Postwar theories of economic growth date back to work in the 1940s by Roy Harrod in England and Evsey Domar in the United States. In the late 1950s Bob Solow of MIT assembled the nuts and bolts of the neoclassical growth theory that has formed the basis of empirical work ever since.[1]

It is a theory of growth because it asks why potential output grows in the long run. It is *neoclassical* because it does not ask how actual output gets to potential output. Over a long enough period, the only question of interest is what is happening to potential output itself. So neoclassical growth theory simply assumes that actual and potential output are equal.

Over this horizon, output, labour, and capital are growing. What about equilibrium in the long run? Usually, equilibrium means that things are not changing. Hence we apply equilibrium not to levels but to growth rates and ratios.

Along the **steady-state path**, output, capital and labour are all growing at the same rate. Hence output per worker and capital per worker are constant.

The steady state is the long-run equilibrium in growth theory.

We assume that labour grows at a constant rate n. To keep things simple, we also assume that some constant fraction s of income is saved; the rest is consumed. Aggregate capital formation (public and private) is the part of output not consumed (by both public and private sectors). Investment first widens and then perhaps deepens capital.

In a growing economy, **capital-widening** extends the existing capital per worker to new extra workers. **Capital-deepening** raises capital per worker for all workers.

Keeping capital per person constant requires more investment per person (1) the faster is population growth n (extra workers for whom capital must be provided) and (2) the more capital per person k that has to be provided. In Figure 30-1 we plot the link nk along which capital per person is constant.

Adding more and more capital per worker k increases output per worker y, but with diminishing returns: hence the curve y in Figure 30-1. Since a constant amount of output is saved, sy shows the saving per person. Since saving

---

[1] Solow won a Nobel Prize for his work on long-run growth. He is also famous for his one-liners. Since, in short-run analysis, he is an unrepentant Keynesian, many of his famous remarks are aimed at those who believe that prices clear markets quickly: 'If you take your hands off the wheel, do you believe the car will find the middle of the road before it finds the verge?', or 'Will the olive, unassisted, always settle exactly half way up the martini?'

and investment are equal, it also shows investment per person.

In the steady state, capital per person is constant. Hence investment per person sy must equal nk, the investment per person needed to keep k constant by making capital grow as fast as labour. k^* is the steady-state capital per person, and y^* the steady-state output per person. Capital and output grow at the same rate n as labour along this steady-state path.

Figure 30-1 also shows what happens away from the steady state. If capital per worker is low, the economy begins to the left of the steady state. Per capita saving and investment sy exceeds nk, the per capital investment required to keep capital in line with growing labour. So capital per person rises. Conversely, to the right of the steady state, sy lies below nk and capital per person falls. Figure 30-1 says that, from whatever level of capital the economy begins, it gradually converges on the (unique) steady state.

A higher saving rate

Suppose people permanently increase the fraction of income saved, from s to s'. We get more saving, more investment, and hence a faster rate of output growth. Oh no we don't! Figure 30-2 explains why not.

There is no change in the production function, which relates output to inputs. At the original savings rate s, the steady state is at E as before. At the higher savings rate, $s'y$ shows savings and investment per person. At F it equals nk, the per capita investment needed to stop k rising or falling. Thus F is the new steady state.

F has more capital per worker than does E. Productivity and output per worker are higher. That is the permanent effect of a higher saving rate. It is an effect on levels, not on growth rates. In *any* steady state, L, K, and Y all grow at the same rate, and that rate is determined 'outside the model': it is the rate of growth of labour and population. We return to this issue shortly.

In Figure 30-2, the higher savings rate raises the permanent level of output and capital per worker. To make the transition from E to F, there must be a temporary period in which capital grows faster than labour; only then can capital per worker rise as required. A higher savings rate, if successfully translated into higher investment to keep the economy at full employment, will lead to faster output growth for a while but not for ever. Once capital per worker rises sufficiently, higher rates of saving and investment go entirely in capital widening, which is now more demanding than before. Further capital deepening, the basis of productivity growth, cannot continue without bound.

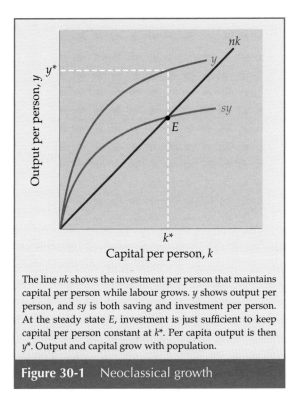

The line nk shows the investment per person that maintains capital per person while labour grows. y shows output per person, and sy is both saving and investment per person. At the steady state E, investment is just sufficient to keep capital per person constant at k^*. Per capita output is then y^*. Output and capital grow with population.

Figure 30-1 Neoclassical growth

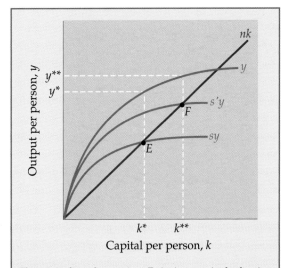

The original steady state is at E. An increase in the fraction of income saved, from s to s', leads to a steady state at F. This raises capital and output per worker, but eventually has no effect on the growth rate. Since y^{**} is constant, output and labour still grow at rate n.

Figure 30-2 A higher savings rate

30-5 Growth through technical progress

We have made a lot of progress, but we still have some problems. First, the theory does not fit *all* the facts. So far, the theory says that output, labour, and capital all grow at rate *n*. Although it is true that capital and output do grow at the same rate, in practice both grow more rapidly than labour. That is why we are better off than our great grandparents.

The answer may lie in technical progress, which we ignored in trying to explain output growth entirely through growth in factor supplies (population growth and the accumulation of capital). It turns out that *labour-augmenting technical progress* would do the trick.

Population growth might eventually double the number of workers. Imagine instead that the number of workers is constant but that new knowledge allows the same workers to do the work of twice as many as before, as if the population had grown.

Labour-augmenting technical progress increases the effective labour supply.

Suppose this progress occurs at rate *t*. Effective labour input grows at rate $(t + n)$ because of technical progress and population growth. Now go back to Figure 30-1, and simply put $(t + n)k$ instead of nk. To make this valid, we have to measure capital and output not per worker but per worker-equivalent. Worker-equivalents are created by population growth or technical progress. Otherwise the diagram is identical.

E remains the steady state. Output per worker-equivalent and capital per worker-equivalent are constant. Since worker-equivalents grow at rate $t + n$, so must capital and output. Since actual workers increase at rate *n*, output and capital per actual worker each increase at rate *t*. Now our growth theory fits all the facts.

It remains uncomfortable that the two key growth rates, *n* and *t*, remain determined outside the model. For that reason, for the next 30 years the main use of this growth theory was in growth accounting: showing how to decompose actual output behaviour into the parts explained by changes in various inputs and the part residually explained by technical progress. We next examine the results of accounting for growth.

30-6 Growth in the OECD

The Organization for Economic Cooperation and Development [OECD (www.oecd.org)] is a club of the world's richest countries, ranging from industrial giants like the United States and Japan to smaller economies like New Zealand, Ireland, and Turkey. Table 30-2 shows the growth of OECD countries since 1950.

The table shows the sharp productivity slowdown after 1973 in all OECD countries. Several explanations have been put forward to explain this slowdown. Some economists have emphasized the role of increasing pollution control and other regulation of 'economic bads' which, though socially desirable, had the consequence of raising production costs and reducing *measured* output and hence *measured* productivity. Other economists stressed the increasing power of trade unions and the increasing legal protection they enjoyed in the 1970s. If this explanation is correct, the supply-side reforms of the late 1980s might have allowed higher productivity growth in the 1990s. There is little evidence that this took place.

1973 was also the year of the first OPEC oil price shock, when real oil prices quadrupled. This had two effects. First, it diverted R&D towards very long-term efforts to find alternative energy-saving technologies. These efforts may take decades to pay off and show up in improvements in actual productivity. Second, the higher energy prices made much of the capital stock economically obsolete overnight. Energy-guzzling factories were simply too expensive to operate and had to be closed down. The world effectively lost a considerable part of its capital stock, and this inevitably reduced output per head. Of course, for a time

Table 30-2	Average annual growth in real output per person employed (%)							
	OECD	Japan	Germany	Italy	France	Sweden	UK	USA
1950–73	3.6	8.0	5.6	5.8	4.5	3.4	3.6	2.2
1973–79	1.4	2.9	3.1	2.9	3.0	1.5	1.6	0
1979–90	1.5	3.0	1.6	1.9	2.6	1.7	2.1	0.7
1990–99	1.3	0.9	3.4	1.3	1.4	1.9	1.5	1.3

Sources: S. Dowrick and D. Nguyen, 'OECD Comparative Economic Growth 1950–85', *American Economic Review*, 1989; OECD, *Economic Outlook*.

BOX 30-2

Failures to take off down the growth runway

So far we have assumed that people save a constant fraction s of their income. Even poor people earning only y save sy and consume $(1 - s)y$. But if y is low enough, $(1 - s)y$ may not be enough to stop starvation. So they will consume all their income and save none. This suggests that below some critical income level y_0, saving drops to zero. What does the Solow diagram look like now? Suppose k_0 is the level of capital per person that just generates the critical income y_0. Higher levels of capital generate savings as in previous diagrams, and nk still shows the level of gross investment needed to maintain a given capital–labour ratio in the face of growing population. There are now three steady states!

When the capital begins above k_1 the economy converges to the steady state at E. Between k_1 and k_2 saving and investment exceed the amount needed just for capital widening: capital-deepening also occurs and the economy grows. Above k_2, saving and investment are insufficient to maintain the capital–labour ratio, and the economy shrinks. Either way it ends at E. This is like the case we have already analysed in Figures 30-1 and 30-2. Suppose, next, the economy begins at exactly k_1. Saving and investment just maintain the capital–labour ratio. So this is a steady state. But it is an unstable one. Beginning just a little above k_1 the economy immediately begins converging on E. And beginning just below k_1, there is now insufficient saving and investment to provide for the growing population, so capital per person now shrinks and keeps shrinking till the economy reaches $k = 0$.

What is interesting about this model, is that countries beginning with capital less than k_1 are stuck in a poverty trap. They can't break out. All output must be consumed to prevent starvation and there is never any surplus to begin accumulation and growth. This model can also explain why convergence seems to occur within the OECD (countries already above k_1), but why simultaneously a (large) group of countries are stuck in poverty. It also suggests that modern growth in the last two centuries began when some key events first generated the surplus to allow saving and accumulation to begin.

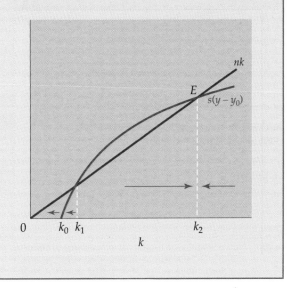

firms tried to struggle on with their existing factories. In practice, scrapping took a long time, though it was given renewed impetus by the second sharp rise in oil prices in 1980–81. That is why its effects were drawn out over such a long period.

Having discussed differences in growth across sub-periods, we now discuss differences across countries. The one sheds light on the other. The fact that all the OECD countries move together across sub-periods shows that many aspects of growth may not be within a country's own control. Technical progress is diffused across countries quite quickly, wherever it originated. Countries are increasingly dependent on the same global economy.

Even so, growth rates differ markedly across countries. Can growth theory explain why? First, it suggests that, if countries enjoy access to the same technology, differences in output growth should reflect differences in labour force growth. Table 30-1 provides some degree of corroborating evidence: differences in per capita output growth are less marked than differences in output growth.

Second, we need to know how long it takes to get to the steady state, a question to which Figures 30-1 and 30-2 provide no direct answer. Is output growth over two or three decades an adjustment *towards* the steady state, or can we assume that an economy has reached it within that time?

Table 30-3 Effect of catch-up and estimate of residual growth (% per year)

	1950–60		1960–73		1979–88	
	Catch-up	Residual	Catch-up	Residual	Catch-up	Residual
Austria	2.8	1.0	1.3	0.0	0.5	−0.9
Belgium	2.1	−0.7	1.1	0.3	0.4	0.8
Denmark	1.9	−1.4	1.1	0.1	0.6	−0.9
France	2.1	0.2	1.0	0.6	0.3	1.1
Germany	2.9	2.0	1.0	−0.3	0.3	1.1
Italy	2.4	0.2	1.2	0.8	0.4	0.1
Netherlands	1.9	−0.2	0.8	−0.3	0.2	0.6
Norway	1.8	−1.3	0.9	−0.9	0.4	0.0
Sweden	1.3	0.1	0.8	0.3	0.3	−0.3
Switzerland	1.1	0.1	0.7	−1.0	0.5	−0.6
UK	1.6	−0.8	0.8	−0.6	0.5	0.8
USA	0.0	0.7	0.0	0.1	0.0	0.3
Japan	4.0	0.4	2.2	2.2	0.9	0.0

Source: N. Crafts, 'Reversing Relative Decline', *Oxford Review of Economic Policy*, 1991.

The convergence hypothesis

Figure 30-1 has a unique steady state at E, and, whatever the level of capital per worker with which an economy begins, the figure implies that it will eventually converge to E. Poor countries with a low inheritance of capital grow extra rapidly until they reach the steady-state growth rate of output and capital; rich countries with a very high inheritance of capital grow at below-average rates until capital per worker falls back to its steady-state level k^*.

When capital per worker is low, it doesn't take much investment to equip new workers with capital (capital-widening), so the rest of investment can go on raising capital per worker (capital-deepening). When capital per worker is already high, it takes a lot of saving and investment just to maintain capital-widening, let alone to deepen capital. This is one reason for the convergence hypothesis.

The **convergence hypothesis** asserts that poor countries grow more quickly than average, but rich countries grow more slowly than average.

This explanation for convergence relies purely on the effect of capital accumulation. A second explanation for convergence or 'catch-up' operates through a different channel. Technical progress no longer falls out of the sky at a fixed rate. Suppose instead we have to invest real resources (universities, research labs, R&D) in trying to make technical improvements. It is rich countries that have the human and physical capital to undertake these activities, and it is in rich countries that technical progress is made. However, once discovered, new ideas are soon disseminated to other countries.

Since poorer countries do not have to use their own resources to make technical break-throughs, they can devote their scarce investment resources to other uses such as building machines. By slipstreaming the richer countries, they can temporarily grow faster.

Using a standard production function and data on the growth of capital and labour inputs, we can see how much of output growth would be explained in each country by the growth of its factor inputs.

That part of output growth not explained by the growth of measured inputs is known as the **Solow residual**.

Solow naturally attributed it to technical progress. The residual is quite large and varies quite a lot across countries.

Table 30-3 sheds some light on this issue. Professor Nick Crafts of the London School of Economics took the Solow residuals and tried to see how much of them could be explained by catch-up. The lower a country's per capita GDP relative to the United States (the assumed technical leader), the larger should be the potential for catch-up. Table 30-3 shows catch-up in each sub-period, and the 'residual', i.e. that part of growth unexplained by inputs or catch-up.

The table makes several interesting points. First, on average there does seem to be a role for catch-up: countries with below-average productivity do enjoy on average a faster rate of technical progress as they make use of ideas already in operation in richer countries.

Second, some countries seem much more able to make use of catch-up opportunities than others. Once we allow for 'average catch-up', big differences remain across countries (the residuals in the table). These may reflect the social and political framework in which the economy must operate. Change usually helps the majority but has very adverse

BOX 30-3 — Standards of living and the convergence hypothesis

The table below shows World Bank estimates of per capita income in 1997 and of its annual real growth during 1980–97. Three points stand out. First, the east Asian economies – China, Korea, Hong Kong, Thailand, Singapore – grew very quickly. Even India is now growing steadily. Second, convergence cannot be a powerful force in the world or the very poorest countries would be growing very rapidly. In reality, poor countries stay poor, and sometimes even decline in absolute terms. Third, within the rich OECD countries, convergence is much more reliable. The richest OECD countries tend to grow less quickly than the poorer OECD countries. These conclusions apply not just in the particular data shown below – they are widely replicated in all empirical studies.

Why did the East Asian 'tigers' grow so quickly in the post-war period? What was their secret? Not perhaps what you think. Professor Alwyn Young of MIT has shown that there is little mystery about their rapid growth, even though they did sustain dramatic rates. These economies managed rapid growth in measured inputs – labour (via increases in participation rates), capital (via high saving and investment rates) and human capital (via substantial expenditure on education). Once we allow for the rapid growth of these inputs, Young showed that the growth of output in the tigers was not very different from what standard estimates, based on OECD and Latin American countries, would have led us to expect. (*See*: A. Young: 'The tyranny of numbers: Confronting the statistics realities of the East Asian growth experience', *Quarterly Journal of Economics*, 1995.)

Per capita GNP (000s of 1997 US $) and annual % growth 1980–97

	97 level	1980–97 growth (%)		97 level	1980–97 growth (%)
Poor & middle income			**OECD**		
Mozambique	0.1	−1.2	Portugal	10.5	2.9
Bangladesh	0.3	2.3	Spain	14.5	2.0
Nigeria	0.3	−1.2	Ireland	18.3	4.2
China	0.8	11.0	Italy	20.1	1.4
Indonesia	1.1	5.5	UK	20.7	2.0
Philippines	1.2	1.1	France	26.5	2.0
Turkey	3.1	1.7	USA	28.7	1.7
Korea	10.5	7.8	Switzerland	44.3	1.6

Source: World Bank, *World Development Report*.

effects on a few people whose skills are made obsolete or whose power is suddenly removed. The large number of winners should club together to buy off the few big losers, allowing change to proceed.

Professor Craft's interpretation of the differences shown in Table 30-3 is that some societies are much better than others in organizing the deals that allow catch-up to be achieved more rapidly.

An example: evaluating Thatcherism

Mrs Thatcher was elected in 1979 to breathe new efficiency and dynamism into the British economy, a long-run task which properly should be evaluated against the long-run criteria measured by growth accounting. A rise in the long-run path of potential output requires either the achievement of higher inputs or greater productivity from those inputs.

In our discussion of labour markets in earlier chapters we noted that, although tax cuts were intended to provide a big boost to labour supply, in fact they had little effect. Any incentive to work longer was neutralized by an equally powerful incentive to have more leisure. Nor was the 1980s a decade of high investment in the UK. Investment rates were much lower than during 1950–70.

So the success of Thatcherism ultimately hinges on improvements in efficiency and productivity. Table 30-3 shows that during 1950–70 the UK had negative residuals: allowing for input growth and 'normal catch-up', UK output grew less quickly than we would expect. In contrast, the final column of Table 30-3 shows that during 1979–88 the residual increased substantially: the UK did better than the framework expects on average.

Supporters of Thatcherism will take this as powerful evidence of an improvement in the UK's ability to take advantage of change rather than to defend the status quo. Professor Crafts notes that another interpretation is possible. Thatcherism may simply have achieved a once-off increase in the level of output by 'get-tough policies' that squeezed out inefficiencies that had survived from earlier decades. In growth accounting, we have to wait for decades of evidence before determining the differences between a change in levels and a permanent change in the growth rate.

30-7 Endogenous growth

Solow's theory makes economic growth depend on population growth and technical progress. Both proceed at given rates. The subsequent literature on catch-up makes technical progress respond to economic and political factors. But it would be nice to have an even stronger link with economic behaviour and the consequent rate of economic growth. We want to make growth *endogenous*, or determined within our theory.

Endogenous growth occurs in models in which the steady-state growth rate can be affected by economic behaviour and economic policy.

One insight is due to Professor Paul Romer of Chicago University. It goes as follows. Saving, investment, and capital accumulation lie at the heart of growth. In Solow's theory, applying more and more capital to a given path for population runs into the diminishing marginal product of capital. It cannot be the source of permanent growth in productivity.

We know there must be diminishing returns to capital alone at the level of individual firms; otherwise one firm would get more and more capital, become more productive at a constant or increasing rate, and gradually take over the entire world! Because we know that this holds at the level of the firm, economists had always assumed that it held also at the level of the economy.

Romer's insight was the possibility (and, once we think about it, the likelihood) that there are significant externalities to capital. Higher capital in one firm increases productivity in *other* firms. When British Telecom invests in better equipment, other firms immediately can do things that were impossible before. The insight also applies to human capital. Training by one firm has beneficial externalities for others.

Thus the production function of each individual firm exhibits diminishing returns to its own capital input, but also depends on the capital of other firms. No firm, acting in isolation, would wish to raise its capital without limit. But when all firms expand together the economy as a whole may face constant returns to aggregate capital.

Consider the following simple example of the aggregate economy. Per capital output y is proportional to capital per person k. To isolate the role of accumulation, suppose there is no technical progress. Thus $y = Ak$ where A is constant. Given a constant saving rate s and population growth at rate n, consider whether there exists a steady state in which capital per person grows at rate g. If so, investment for capital-deepening is gk and investment for capital-widening, to keep up with population growth, is nk. Hence in per capita terms

$$\text{Gross investment} = (g + n)k = sy = sAk = \text{saving}$$

from which the steady-state growth rate g is

$$g = (sA - n) \tag{2}$$

Why does this confirm the possibility of *endogenous* growth? Because it depends on parameters that could be influenced by private behaviour or public policy. In the Solow model, without technical progress, steady-state growth is always n, whatever the savings rate s or the level of productivity A. Equation (2) says that any policy that succeeded in raising the saving rate s would *permanently* increase the growth rate g. Similarly, any policy that achieved a once and for all increase in the *level* of A, for example greater workplace efficiency, would permanently increase the growth rate of k. And since $y = Ak$, this would translate into permanently faster output growth.

Not only is it possible for government policy to affect growth within this framework, there is also some presumption that government intervention may increase efficiency. In the simple Romer model outlined above, there are externalities in capital accumulation: individual firms neglect the fact that, in raising their own capital, they also increase the productivity of *other* firms' capital. Government subsidies to investment might offset this externality.

Since Romer's original work, there has been huge interest in endogenous growth. After all, Table 30-1 and Box 30-2 on page 519 show vividly that sustaining small additions to annual growth rates eventually make huge differences to living standards. As a result of this research we now have many potential channels of endogenous growth. For example, instead of assuming technical progress occurs exogenously, we can model the industry that undertakes

R&D with the objective of producing technical progress. Constant returns in this industry will generate endogenous growth. In fact, constant returns to aggregate production of any *accumulatible* factor (knowledge, capital, etc.) will suffice.

Note, too, that endogenous growth models explain why growth rates in different countries might permanently be different. This might explain why convergence does not take place and why some countries remain poor indefinitely.

While endogenous growth theory has been an exciting development, it also has its critics. Most of these criticisms boil down to one key point. Whatever the relevant accumulatible factor, why should there be *exactly* constant returns in the aggregate? With diminishing returns, we are back in the Solow model where long-run growth is exogenous. With increasing returns, the economy would settle not on steady growth but on ever more rapid expansion of output and capital. We know historically that this is not occurring. So for endogenous growth only constant returns to accumulation will do. Some people think this seems just too good to be true.

30-8 The costs of growth

Some people believe that the benefits of economic growth are outweighed by the costs. Pollution, congestion, and a hectic life-style are too high a price to pay for a rising output of cars, washing machines, and video games.

Since GNP is a very imperfect measure of the net economic value of the goods and services produced by the economy, there is no presumption that our objective should be to maximize the growth of measured GNP. We discussed issues such as pollution in Chapter 16. In the absence of any government intervention, a free market economy is likely to produce too much pollution. However, complete elimination of pollution is also wasteful. Society should undertake activities accompanied by pollution up to the point at which the marginal benefit of the goods produced equals the marginal pollution cost imposed on society. We explained how government intervention through pollution taxes or regulation of environmental standards can be used to move the economy towards an efficient allocation of resources in which marginal social costs and benefits are equalized.

The full implementation of such a policy would probably reduce the growth of measured GNP below the rate that is achieved when there is no restriction on activities such as pollution and congestion. And this is the most sensible way in which to approach the problem. It tackles the issue directly. In contrast, the 'zero-growth' solution tackles the problem only indirectly.

The **zero-growth proposal** argues that, because increases in measured GNP are accompanied by additional costs of pollution, congestion, and so on, the best solution is to aim for zero growth of measured GNP.

The problem with the zero-growth approach is that it does not distinguish between measured outputs that are accompanied by activities with social costs and measured outputs that give rise to no pollution or congestion. It does not provide the correct incentives. The principle of targeting, one of the important insights of the welfare economics we discussed in Part 3, suggests that it is always more efficient to tackle a problem directly than to adopt an indirect approach which also distorts other aspects of production or consumption. Hence we conclude that, when society believes that there is too much pollution, congestion, environmental damage, or stress, the best solution is to provide incentives that directly reduce these phenomena. Simply restricting overall growth in measured output is a terribly crude alternative which is distinctly second best.

Of course, some of these difficulties might be removed if economists and statisticians could devise a more comprehensive measure of GNP which included all the 'quality of life' activities (clean air, environmental beauty, etc.) that yield genuine consumption benefits but at present are not captured in measured GNP. Inevitably voters and commentators tend to judge government performance according to how well the economy is doing on some international league table of published and measurable statistics. A more comprehensive measure of GNP might remove some of the conflicts that governments feel between fostering growth of output as currently measured and encouraging measures to improve the quality of life.

Even so, no matter how complete the statistics, the assessment of the desirable growth rate will always remain a normative question which ultimately hinges on the value judgements of the assessor. Switching resources from consumption, however defined, to investment will nearly always reduce the welfare of people today but allow greater welfare for people tomorrow. The priority attached to satisfying wants of people at different points in time must always remain a value judgement.

SUMMARY

● Economic growth is the percentage annual increase in real GNP or per capita real GNP in the long run. It is a very imperfect measure of the rate of increase of economic well-being.

● Measured GNP omits the value of leisure and the untraded goods and bads which nevertheless may have an important impact on the quality of life. Differences in income distribution make per capita real GNP a very shaky foundation for international comparisons of the welfare of the typical individual in different countries.

● However measured, significant rates of growth of per capita GNP have been observed only during the last two centuries in what are now called the advanced economies. In other countries persistent growth is even more recent.

● Aggregate output can be increased either by increasing the inputs of land, labour, capital and raw materials, or by increasing the output obtained from given input quantities. Technical advances are an important source of productivity gains.

● An apparently fixed supply of a production input, such as a particular raw material, need not make growth impossible in the long run. As the input becomes more scarce, its price will rise. This leads producers to substitute towards other inputs, increases incentives to discover new supplies, and encourages inventions that economize on the use of that resource.

● The simplest theory of growth has a steady state in which capital, output, and labour all grow at the same rate. Whatever its initial level of capital, the economy tends to converge on this steady-state path. This theory can explain output growth but not productivity growth.

● Labour-augmenting technical progress allows permanent growth of labour productivity, and enables even the simplest growth theory to fit many of the facts.

● There is a tendency of economies to converge, both because capital-deepening is easier when capital per worker is low and because of catch-up in technology. Implementing technical change may depend on how well society is organized to buy off (or defeat) the losers.

● Thatcherism did induce an identifiable rise in the UK productivity growth, even after controlling for factor accumulation and catch-up opportunities. It is difficult to be sure whether Thatcherism changed the growth rate for ever.

● Theories of endogenous growth are built on constant returns to accumulation. If aggregate investment does not encounter diminishing returns to capital, choices about saving and investment can affect the long-run growth rate of productivity. An externality on a giant scale provides a powerful rationale for government intervention to encourage education, training, and physical capital formation.

● Nevertheless, endogenous growth rests on the presence of constant returns to accumulation. Nobody has yet explained why this should hold.

KEY TERMS

◆ Economic growth   511
◆ Production function   512
◆ Technical knowledge   514
◆ Invention and innovation   514
◆ Steady-state path   516
◆ Capital-widening, capital-deepening   516
◆ Labour-augmenting technical progress   518
◆ Convergence hypothesis   520
◆ Solow residual   520
◆ Endogenous growth   522
◆ Zero-growth proposal   523

REVIEW QUESTIONS

1 Explain the distinction between total output and per capita output. Which grows more rapidly? Why? Always?

2 'Britain produces too many scientists but too few engineers.' What kind of evidence might help you decide if this is true? Will a free market lead people to choose the career that most benefits society?

3 Name two economic bads. Suggest feasible ways in which they might be measured. Should they be included in GNP? *Could* they be?

4 What evidence would you look for in the 1990s to see whether Thatcherism had changed the underlying UK growth rate?

5 'If the convergence hypothesis is correct, the poor African countries should have grown long ago!' Is this correct? Do any of the newer approaches to economic growth help explain why some countries remain so poor?

6 'It is because we know Malthus got it wrong that we take a more relaxed view about the fact that some minerals are in finite supply.' Is there a connection? Explain.

7 Is economic growth confined to recent centuries? If so, why?

8 *Common fallacies* Show why each of the following statements is incorrect. (a) High government spending must be good for growth. (b) High government spending must be bad for growth. (c) Since the earth's resources are limited, growth cannot continue for ever. (d) If we save more, we'd definitely grow faster.

31 The business cycle

LEARNING OUTCOMES

When you have finished this chapter, you should be able to:

- Distinguish trend growth and economic cycles around this path
- Study theories of why business cycles occur
- Consider whether fluctuations are departures of output from the path of potential output or could also reflect swings in potential output itself
- Investigate whether national business cycles are becoming more correlated as economies become more integrated with each other
- Apply these principles to recent UK business cycles

After a deep recession during 1990–92, the UK left the Exchange Rate Machanism in 1992, reduced interest rates, and allowed the pound to depreciate substantially. The new Chancellor, Kenneth Clarke, presided over a steady recovery. Prime Minister Major delayed the General Election until May 1997, the last possible date, in the hope that an increasing 'feel-good factor' would win the election for the Conservatives.

This episode illustrates many of the issues that we examine in this chapter. First, is there a business cycle? We know output fluctuates a lot in the short run, but a cycle does not mean merely temporary departures from trend: it also requires a degree of regularity. Can we see it in the data? If we can, how do we explain it? If we can explain it, why did economic recovery after 1992 not boost the feel-good factor and government popularity as it had done in the past.

We also explore the international dimension. Can a single country display cycles that are out of phase with those in its trading partners? In Part 5 we shall see that this is one of the relevant issues in considering which countries might find it

advantageous to have a common policy (e.g. monetary union).

31-1 Trend and cycle: statistics or economics

In practice, aggregate output and productivity do not grow smoothly. In some years they grow very rapidly but in other years they actually fall.

The **trend path of output** is the smooth path it follows in the long run once the short-term fluctuations are averaged out.

Actual output fluctuates around this hypothetical trend path. British economists used to refer to these short-term fluctuations as the *trade cycle*, but nowadays the American term *business cycle* is generally used.[1]

---

[1] The trade cycle did not refer exclusively to international trade; the Victorians used 'trade' to mean industry in general and manufacturing in particular.

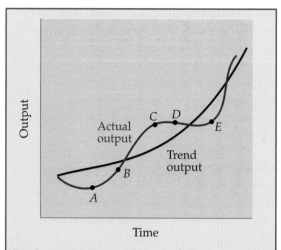

Trend output grows steadily over time as productive potential increases. Actual output fluctuates around this trend. Point *A* slows a slump, the trough of a cycle. At *B* recovery has begun and it continues until the peak of the cycle is reached at *C*. At *C* there is a boom. Then a period of recession follows until the next slump is reached at *E*. It takes roughly five years to move from one point in the cycle to an equivalent point in the next cycle, for example from *A* to *E*.

Figure 31-1   The business cycle

The **business cycle** is the short-term fluctuation of total output around its trend path.

Figure 31-1 presents a stylized description of the business cycle. The black curve shows the steady growth in trend output over time. But actual output follows the coloured curve. Point *A* represents a *slump*, the bottom of a business cycle. At *B* the economy has entered the *recovery* phase of the cycle. As recovery proceeds, output climbs above its trend path, reaching point *C*, which we call a *boom*. Then the economy enters a *recession* in which output is growing less quickly than trend output, and is possibly even falling. Point *E* shows a *slump*, after which recovery begins and the cycle starts again. Output grows most quickly during a recovery and grows least quickly (and possibly actually falls) during a recession.

Figure 31-2 shows the annual percentage growth of real GDP and of real output per employed worker in the UK during the period 1970–99. Output and productivity were growing most rapidly in 1964, 1968, 1973, and 1986–88 and growing least rapidly in 1966, 1974–75, 1980–81, and 1990–92. The figure makes three basic points. First, the growth of output and productivity is far from smooth in the short run. Second, although the economy is not subject to perfectly regular cycles, there does seem to be evidence of a

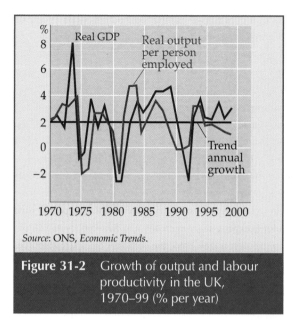

Source: ONS, *Economic Trends*.

Figure 31-2   Growth of output and labour productivity in the UK, 1970–99 (% per year)

pattern of slump, recovery, boom, and recession, with each complete cycle lasting around four or five years. Finally, in the short run there is a close relation between changes in output and changes in output per person. These are the facts that we seek to explain in the rest of this chapter.

Any series of points may be decomposed statistically into an average trend and fluctuations around that trend. We begin by assuming that potential output grows smoothly. Later we shall consider whether potential output itself can fluctuate significantly in the short run. For the moment, we assume that deviations of actual output from trend reflect departures of aggregate demand and actual output from their full-employment level. Although Figure 31-2 shows that cycles are not perfectly regular, either in the extent of the output change between boom and slump or in the time it takes to move from one cycle to the next, nevertheless the data show a pattern that is too regular to be explained away as a pure fluke. What causes business cycles?

We have studied at length the influences on aggregate demand. An increase in the demand for exports, an increase in government spending, or a reduction in interest rates are examples of changes that will increase aggregate demand in the short run. Conversely, an increase in tax rates, a reduction in export demand, or a reduction in firms' expectations about future profits can all lead to reductions in aggregate demand in the short run. It is possible to argue that the factors on which aggregate demand depends just happen to fluctuate in the short run and that the observed fluctuations in output merely reflect this. However, we should not wish to call this an *explanation* of the business cycle: it does not tell us why these influences on aggregate demand happen to fluctuate in quite a regular way.

One version of this approach does at least claim to be a theory. It is known as the *political business cycle*. The argument is simple. Suppose voters have short memories and are heavily influenced by how the economy is doing immediately prior to the election. Suppose, too, that the government understands how to use monetary and fiscal policy to manipulate aggregate demand in the short run. To maximize its chances of re-election, the government adopts a tight monetary and fiscal policy just after it has been elected, manipulates the economy into a slump, and then adopts expansionary monetary and fiscal policy just before the election is due. Since the economy has spare resources during the slump, it is possible to make output grow considerably faster than its trend growth rate during the period immediately before the election. The voters think that the government has got things under control and votes them in for another term of office.

The **political business cycle** arises from cycles in policy between general elections.

This theory provides a reason for fluctuations and also suggests why business cycles tend to last about five years – that is the period between elections in countries such as the UK. And it probably does contain a grain of truth. On the other hand, it supposes that voters are pretty naive and do not see what the government is up to. Voters are not always so short-sighted. For example, in 1997 the Major government lost the election even though output was growing strongly. Voters thought Labour could do even better.

31-2 Theories of the business cycle

If government policy is not the source of the business cycle, in which components of aggregate demand can the cycle originate? Fluctuations in net exports can be important in practice. However, imports fluctuate primarily because of fluctuations in domestic output, and exports fluctuate primarily because of business cycles abroad. International trade helps explain how cycles get transmitted from one country to another, but we really require a theory of domestic business cycle to initiate the process.

The very notion of a cycle suggests sluggish adjustment. If the economy responded immediately to any shock we should expect to see sharp rises and falls in economic activity but not sustained periods of recession or recovery. Since a theory of a domestic cycle must be based on consumption or investment spending, it seems plausible

that investment spending is the most likely candidate. Whereas households can in principle adjust their consumption spending relatively quickly, changes in investment spending are likely to take more time. Firms are unlikely to rush into major and irreversible investment projects and new factories cannot be built overnight. Hence we concentrate on investment as the most likely source of the business cycle.

The multiplier–accelerator model of the business cycle

The multiplier–accelerator model distinguishes the consequences and the causes of a change in investment spending. The consequence is straightforward. In the simplest Keynesian model, an increase in investment leads to a larger increase in income and output in the short run. Higher investment not only adds directly to aggregate demand, but by increasing incomes adds indirectly to consumption demand. In Chapters 21 and 22 we referred to this process as the multiplier.

What about the cause of a change in investment spending? Firms invest when their existing capital stock is smaller than the capital stock they would like to hold. When firms are holding the optimal capital stock, the marginal cost of another unit of capital just equals its marginal benefit, the present-value of future operating profits to which it is expected to give rise over its lifetime. This present value can be increased either by a fall in the interest rate at which the stream of expected future profits is discounted or by an increase in the future profits expected.

In previous chapters we have focused on the role of changing interest rates in changes in investment demand. However, in Chapter 28 we learned how to analyse an economy when inflation is present, and we saw that changes in inflation are the main source of changes in nominal interest rates. In fact, real interest rates don't change very much. The simplest way to calculate the present value of a new capital good is to assess the likely stream of *real* operating profits (by valuing future profits at *constant prices*) and then discount them at the *real* interest rate.[2] Hence in practice changes in interest rates may *not* be the most important source of changes in investment spending. Almost certainly, changes in expectations about future profits are more important. If real interest rates and real

---

[2] In Chapter 14 we showed that it was wrong to discount at the nominal interest rate, which is high when the market expects inflation in the future, without simultaneously recognizing that inflation will increase the *nominal value* of future profits.

wages change only slowly, the most important source of short-term changes in beliefs about future profits is likely to be beliefs about future levels of sales and real output. Other things equal, higher expected future output is likely to raise expected future operating profits and increase the benefit from a marginal addition to the current capital stock. This is the insight of the accelerator model of investment.

The **accelerator model of investment** assumes that firms guess future output and profits by extrapolating past output growth. Constant output growth leads to a constant level of investment and a constant rate of growth of the desired capital stock. It takes *accelerating* output growth to *increase* the desired level of investment.

Of course, the accelerator is only a useful simplification. A complete model of investment would allow both for the effect of changing output (and other forces) in changing expected future profits and the desired capital stock, and the role of changes in interest rates in altering the present value of these expected future profits, and hence the incentive to invest today. Nevertheless, many empirical studies confirm that the accelerator is a useful simplification.

Precisely how firms respond to changes in output will depend on two things: first, the extent to which firms believe that current output growth will be sustained in the future; second, the cost of quickly adjusting investment plans, capital installation, and the production techniques thus embodied. The more costly it is to adjust *quickly*, the more firms are likely to spread investment over a longer period.

We now show how a simple version of the multiplier–accelerator model can lead to a business cycle. In Table 31-1 we make two specific assumptions, although the argument holds much more generally. First, we assume that the value of the multiplier is 2. Each unit of extra investment increases

income and output by 2 units. Second, we assume that current investment responds to the growth in output *last* period. If last period's income grew by 2 units, we assume that firms will increase current investment by 1 unit. The economy begins in equilibrium with output Y_t equal to 100. Since output is constant, last period's output change was zero. Investment I_t is 10, which we can think of as the amount of investment required to offset depreciation and maintain the capital stock intact.

Suppose in period 2 that some component of aggregate demand increases by 20 units. Output increases from 100 to 120. Since we have assumed that a growth of 2 units in the previous period's output leads to a unit increase in current investment, the table shows that in period 3 there is a 10-unit increase in investment in response to the 20-unit output increase during the previous period. Since the assumed value of the multiplier is 2, the 10-unit *increase* in investment in period 3 leads to a further increase of 20 units in output, which increases from 120 to 140.

In period 4 investment remains at 20 since the output growth in the previous period was 20. Thus output in period 4 remains at 140. But in period 5 investment reverts to its original level of 10, since there was no output growth in the previous period. This fall of 10 units in investment leads to a multiplied fall of 20 units in output in period 5. In turn this induces a further fall of 10 units of investment in period 6 and a further fall of 20 units in output. But since the rate of output change is not accelerating, investment in period 7 remains at its level of period 6. Hence output is stabilized at the level of 100 in period 7. With no output change in the previous period, investment in period 8 returns to 10 units again and the multiplier implies that output increases to 120. In period 9 the 20 unit increase in output in the previous period increases investment from 10 to 20 units and the cycle begins all over again.

The **multiplier–accelerator model** explains business cycles by the dynamic interaction of consumption and investment demand.

The insight of the multiplier–accelerator model is that it takes an *accelerating* output growth to keep increasing investment. But this does not happen in Table 31-1. Once output growth settles down to a constant level of 20, investment settles down to a constant rate of 20 per period. Then in the following period, the level of investment must *fall*, since output growth has been reduced. The economy moves into a period of recession, but once the rate of output fall stops accelerating, investment starts to pick up again.

This simple model should not be regarded as the

Period t	Change in last period's output $(Y_{t-1} - Y_{t-2})$	Investment I_t	Output Y_t
$t = 1$	0	10	100
$t = 2$	0	10	120
$t = 3$	20	20	140
$t = 4$	20	20	140
$t = 5$	0	10	120
$t = 6$	−20	0	100
$t = 7$	−20	0	100
$t = 8$	0	10	120
$t = 9$	20	20	140

Table 31-1   The multiplier–accelerator model of the business cycle

definitive model of the business cycle. If output keeps cycling, surely firms will stop extrapolating past output growth to form assessments of future profits? Firms, like economists, will begin to recognize that there is a business cycle. The less firms' investment decisions respond to the most recent change in past output, the less pronounced will be the cycle. Even so, this simple model drives home a simple result which can be derived in more realistic models. When the economy reacts sluggishly, its behaviour is likely to resemble that of a large oil tanker at sea: it takes a long time to get it moving and a long time to slow it down again. Unless the brakes are applied well before the desired level of the capital stock is reached, it is quite likely that the economy will overshoot its desired position. It will have to turn round and come back again.

Ceilings and floors   The multiplier–accelerator model can generate cycles even without any physical limits on the extent of fluctuations. Cycles are even more likely when we recognize the limits imposed by supply and demand. Aggregate supply provides a *ceiling* in practice. Although it is possible temporarily to meet high aggregate demand by working overtime and running down stocks of finished goods, output cannot expand indefinitely. In itself this tends to slow down growth as the economy reaches a boom. Having overstretched itself, the economy is likely to bounce back off the ceiling and begin a downturn. Conversely, there is a *floor*, or a limit to the extent to which aggregate demand is likely to fall. Gross investment (including replacement investment) cannot actually become negative unless, for the economy as a whole, machines are being unbolted and sold to foreigners. Thus although falling investment may be an important component of a downswing, investment cannot fall indefinitely, whatever our model of investment behaviour.

Fluctuations in stockbuilding

Thus far we have emphasized investment in fixed capital. Now we consider inventory investment in working capital. Firms hold stocks of goods even though these have a cost, namely the interest payments on the funds tied up in producing the goods for which no revenue from sales has yet been received. What is the corresponding benefit of holding stocks? If output could be instantly and costlessly varied it would always be possible to meet sales and demand by varying current production. Holding stocks makes sense because it is expensive to adjust production *quickly*. Output expansion may involve heavy overtime payments and costs of recruiting new workers. Cutting

output may involve expensive redundancy payments. Holding stocks allows firms to meet short-term fluctuations in demand without incurring the expense of short-run fluctuations in output.

Consider how firms respond to a fall in aggregate demand. We have argued that wages will not respond fully and immediately to allow firms to cut prices and boost aggregate demand to eliminate the short-term fluctuation in the quantity of output demanded. Nor, since output adjustment on a large scale is expensive, do firms immediately react by reducing output substantially and laying off large numbers of workers. In the short run, firms undertake the adjustments that can be made most cheaply. They reduce hours of overtime and possibly even move on to short-time working. If demand has fallen substantially, this still leaves firms producing a larger output than they can sell. Firms build up stocks of unsold finished output.

If aggregate demand remains low, firms gradually reduce their workforce, partly through natural wastage and partly because it becomes cheaper to sack some workers than to meet the interest payments on ever larger volumes of stocks. And as wages gradually fall in response to higher unemployment, prices can be reduced, the real money supply increases, interest rates fall, and aggregate demand picks up again. However, firms are still holding all the extra stocks which they built up when the recession began. Only by increasing output *more slowly* than the increase in aggregate demand can firms eventually sell off these stocks and get back to their long-run equilibrium position.

Hence a fall in aggregate demand will be accompanied by a gradual process of output reduction. And once aggregate demand starts to pick up again, output will increase more slowly until stocks have been sold off and output can return to its full-employment level. Thus changes in stocks help explain why output adjustment is so sluggish; they explain why the economy is likely to spend several years during the phase of recovery or recession.

Now we can make sense of the behaviour of productivity shown in Figure 31-2. The figure shows that output per worker tends to rise during the boom and fall during the slump. In other words, output adjusts more quickly than employment. This is what we would expect, given the adjustment story we have developed. A fall in demand is met initially by cutting hours and increasing stocks. With a shorter work week, output per worker falls. Only as the recession intensifies do firms undertake the costlier process of sacking workers and restoring hours to their normal level. Conversely, a boom is the time when output and overtime are high and productivity per worker peaks.

31-3 Real business cycles

Thus far we have argued that the business cycle reflects fluctuations in aggregate demand when output, employment, and wage adjustment are sluggish in the short run. In particular, our account of the business cycle is completely compatible with the earlier analysis of the sluggishness of wage adjustment in the short run. The view that output fluctuates around the trend level of potential output fits nicely with our account of adjustment in Chapters 25 and 26, which might be succinctly described as Keynesian in the short run but classical or monetarist in the long run.

Nevertheless, not all economists share our assessment of how the economy works. In particular, there is an influential school known as the New Classical economists whose intellectual leader is Professor Robert Lucas of the University of Chicago. Although we discuss competing views of macroeconomics more fully in the next chapter, one implication of the New Classical view should be discussed immediately.

One of the key assumptions of the New Classical school, is that all markets clear almost instantaneously. Effectively, output is almost always at its full-employment level.[3]

Real business cycle theories explain cycles as fluctuations in potential output itself.

Proponents of the theory argue that macroeconomics is intrinsically about dynamics over time, and that simplifications such as the consumption function, or even IS–LM analysis, are too simple to be useful.

Rather, we need firmly to base theories of firms and households in a microeconomic analysis of choice between the present and the future. For example, this approach would view each household as making a plan to supply labour and demand goods both now and in the future in such a way that lifetime spending was financed out of lifetime income plus any initial assets. Such plans would then be aggregated to get total consumption spending and total labour supply. An equivalently complex story would apply to firms and investment.

One implication of this approach is that it is no longer helpful to distinguish between supply and demand. If labour supply and consumption demand are part of the same household decision, things that induce the house-

hold to change its demand also induce it to change its supply.

For this reason, real business cycle theorists simply discuss what happens to actual output, which reflects both supply and demand and, by assumption, equates the two at potential output. In this view, the economy is then bombarded with shocks (e.g. breakthroughs in technology, changes in government policy) which alter these complicated plans and give rise to equilibrium behaviour that looks like a business cycle.

Before giving an example, we should explain why this approach is called the *real* business cycle approach. In Chapter 26 we saw that in the classical model changes in nominal money only affect other nominal variables, such as prices and wages (and, from Chapter 29, the nominal exchange rate too), but monetary policy does not affect real variables in the classical model.

Since real business cycle theorists believe in the classical model, they take it for granted that the source of business cycles must be in real shocks. In contrast, a Keynesian would argue that sluggish adjustment of nominal wages and prices give ample time for nominal shocks (e.g. money) to have significant real effects. We now give an example of real business cycle analysis in action.

Intertemporal substitution: a key to persistence

Real business cycle theories need to combine rapid market adjustment to equilibrium with the smooth or sluggish behaviour of aggregate output over the business cycle. Intertemporal substitution means making trade-offs over time, postponing or bringing forward actions in the sophisticated long-run plans of households and firms. This behaviour can cause effects to persist and look like part of a business cycle.

Suppose the Nintendo genie visits while we are all asleep. When we wake up, our productivity has doubled. But the game lasts only a year. We know that by next year our productivity will have returned to normal. We will face a temporary productivity shock, a blip in our technology. What should we do?

We are definitely wealthier after the genie's visit. We are pleased it happened. We could simply behave as before, working just as hard and investing just as much. In that case, our extra productivity would make extra output this year, but it is output that we would blow entirely on consumption this year. We would get little extra utility out of the hundredth bottle of champagne, and we would be making no provision for the future. There must be a better way.

---

[3] For an accessible introduction to these issues, see the lively exchange between Charles Plosser and Greg Mankiw in the *Journal of Economic Perspectives*, Summer 1989.

BOX 31-1 — The real-wage puzzle

In a recession, firms employ fewer workers. Imagine a competitive firm that pays workers the real value of their marginal product. The marginal product of labour can be determined from a production function. Since there is a diminishing marginal product of labour, cutting back on workers should raise labour's marginal product. So real wages should rise in a slump. But they don't. If anything, they fall. This is the *real-wage puzzle* over the business cycle.

Real business cycle theorists have offered a particular solution to this puzzle. A temporarily adverse shock may make it advisable to engage in some intertemporal labour substitution. When times are tough, you don't sacrifice much by taking time off; lifetime earnings can be rebuilt when conditions are easier. So recessions, caused by temporarily low productivity, make firms offer temporarily low wages, and households temporarily reduce their labour supply. We get low employment *and* low wages.

The Keynesian response is that recessions and unusually high unemployment reflect more than an intertemporarily optimal decision to catch up on sleep and leisure until wages improve. But how do they explain the real-wage puzzle?

One possibility is that, during a recession, utilization of capital capacity is severely cut back. There may be fewer workers, but with machines also idle, the effective input of capital has fallen. If the latter is sufficiently large, labour's marginal product will fall even though there are fewer workers than before; temporarily, there is even less capital.

We could put in a temporary spurt of extra work while we are superproductive, but in itself that would only exacerbate the problem: even more champagne today, still nothing extra for tomorrow. In fact, because leisure is a luxury and because we are better off than before, we may feel like taking it easy and doing less work.

We need a way of transferring some of our windfall benefit into future consumption. The solution is investment. A sharp rise in the share of output going to investment will provide more capital for the future, thereby allowing higher future consumption even after our productivity bonus has evaporated. Once we get to the future, being then richer than we would have been without the genie, we may in consequence work less hard than we would have done, since leisure is a luxury.

The point of this example is to show that even a temporary shock can have effects that persist well into the future. Persistence occurs both through investment (in human as well as physical capital) and through intertemporal labour substitution – deciding when in one's life to put the effort in.

Real business cycle theories still need to be worked out fully. To date, they seem vulnerable to two possible criticisms. First, they are usually theories of persistence rather than of cycles. Shocks have long drawn out effects, but rarely are these cyclical effects. Thus, to 'explain' business cycles, so far real business cycle theorists have had to assume a cyclical pattern to the shocks themselves. The theory is therefore incomplete.

Second, and related, since the most widely research example involves shocks to technology, a cyclical pattern of shocks implies that in some years technical knowledge actually diminishes: we forget how to do things. Not just once, but regularly every few years. This may be a bit hard to swallow.

Policy implications

Even if research on real business cycles has much still to accomplish, it does have one vital message for macro-economic policy. If the theory is right, it destroys the case for trying to stabilize output over the business cycle. Fluctuations in output are fluctuations in an equilibrium output that efficiently reconciles people's desires.

For example, in the parable of the Nintendo genie, the induced effects on investment, labour supply, output, and consumption implement people's preferred way to take advantage of the beneficial opportunity. Trying to prevent these ripples is misguided policy.

While this caveat is important, it undermines the case for stabilization policy only if we buy totally the assumptions of complete and instant market-clearing and the absence of any externalities. For most economists these assumptions are too extreme to reflect the real world, and so valid reasons for stabilization policy remain.

Even so, real business cycles contain an insight that every economist should acknowledge: there is no reason why potential output should grow as smoothly as trend output. The latter is a statistical artefact whose construction, averaging, forces it to be smooth.

Our discussion of supply-side economics in Chapter 27 suggested that there are forces that can change full employment and potential output even in the short run. The most sophisticated theory of the business cycle might involve short-term Keynesian fluctuations in aggregate demand around a path of potential output which itself was fluctuating. Nevertheless, we believe that the Keynesian component is likely to be important in the short run.

31-4 An international business cycle?

National politicians want all the credit when output is high but produce a cast-iron alibi when the economy turns sour. They say domestic difficulties were caused by the world recession. How good is their alibi?

Figure 31-3 plots data during 1980–99 for the three major players in the world economy: the United States, Japan, and the EU. Although output fluctuations are by no means identical, they have some similarities. The 1982–83 period was one of recession, followed by rapid recovery; 1987–89 was a boom, from which there was a large crash in 1991–92. However, Japan alone failed to recover in the late 1990s.

Figure 31-4 shows business cycles in the four largest countries of the EU. It confirms that countries of the EU move more closely with one another than with Japan or the USA, and suggests European integration may also be increasing over time. We discuss European integration in Chapter 35.

Although national circumstances play some role, these patterns warn us how interdependent the leading countries have become in the modern world. Economies are becoming more open. In product markets, protectionist policies are being removed, through global institutions like the World Trade Organization and through regional integration as in the creation of a Single European Market. We discuss such developments in Part 5.

Improvements in transport and telecommunications also favour greater integration of product markets; and when R&D costs are large, producers need a global market if they are to recover their overheads. Product market integration provides an international transmission mechanism through exports and imports.

This is not the only channel through which one country affects another. Increasingly, we have a global financial market. Closer financial integration increases the likelihood that different countries pursue similar monetary policies. As we explain in Part 5, it is correct to say that high UK interest rates in the early 1990s had 'made in Frankfurt' written underneath them.

Thus, the business cycle is transmitted from one country to another not just through private sector decisions about imports and exports (and their induced effects on labour supply, investment, and consumption), but also, sometimes,

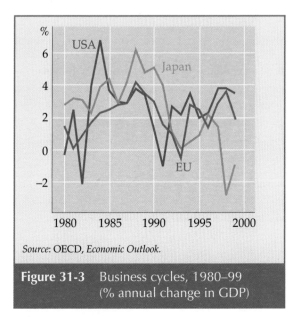

Source: OECD, *Economic Outlook*.

Figure 31-3   Business cycles, 1980–99 (% annual change in GDP)

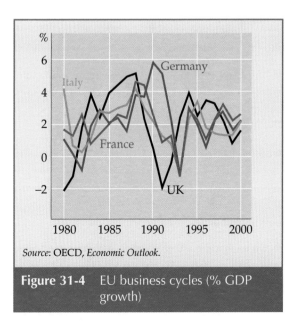

Source: OECD, *Economic Outlook*.

Figure 31-4   EU business cycles (% GDP growth)

through induced changes in the economic policy of other governments.

31-5 Recovery after 1992

As we remarked in earlier chapters, the 1980s saw financial reform in most countries. Deregulation of credit, and greater competition in its supply, was particularly marked in the United States and the UK. The recession of the early 1990s was the first world recession since the financial revolution. Should this make any difference?

Imagine you had been a consumer in the boom of 1986–88. Life looked rosy, and for the first time in modern history financial institutions were competing vigorously to lend you money. So of course you borrowed. The boom surely wouldn't end just yet, would it? Table 31-2 shows the collapse of the saving rate. There was a consequent rise in UK household debt.

Perhaps if you had seen charts such as Figures 31-2 and 31-3, you would have been a bit more realistic. In any case, when the crash came, you got very badly hurt. Around the world, interest rates were suddenly very high as governments tried to stop economies overheating at the end of the 1980s. The interest cost of your huge debt soared.

Worse still, the collateral you had offered when you borrowed – your house or your portfolio on the stock market – was suddenly much less valuable. Higher interest rates lower asset prices by reducing the present value of the future income that the assets provide. In the UK, Japan, and

Table 31-2	UK household saving (% of disposable income)			
1982	1988	1992	1996	1999
10	4	12	10	5

Source: ONS, *Economic Trends*.

the United States, the three countries where consumer debt had risen most in the 1980s, asset prices had fallen 25 per cent by 1992.

Table 31-2 shows clearly how consumers responded. Having acquired too much debt in the 1980s, they tried to put things right at the start of the 1990s. They saved a larger fraction of their incomes in order to try to repay some of the debt and bring it back to manageable proportions.

However, it can be a slow process. When debt is nearly as large as income, and only a small fraction of income is saved, debt cannot be paid off very quickly. This continuing 'debt overhang' explains why the feel-good factor was slow to return after 1992. It helps explain why consumer spending recovered only slowly and why the Major government lost the 1997 election.

Paradoxically, the success of the Major government in defeating inflation after 1992 (see Chapter 28) paved the way for reductions in nominal interest rates and a recovery in the housing market. Table 31-2 shows that by 1999, the saving rate had collapsed again as consumers went on another spending spree.

SUMMARY

● The trend path of output is the long-run path after short-run fluctuations are ironed out. The business cycle describes fluctuations in output around this trend. Cycles last about five years but are not perfectly regular.

● The political business cycle argues that the government manipulates the economy to make things look good just before an election. Government may also inadvertently induce cycles by well-meaning but ill-judged attempts at stabilization policy.

● Cycles require either sluggish adjustment or intertemporal substitution. We also have to explain why cycles are fairly regular.

● The multiplier–accelerator model highlights the dependence of investment on expected future profits, and assumes that expectations reflect past output growth. This model delivers a cycle but assumes that firms are pretty stupid, that their expectations neglect the cycle implied by their own behaviour.

● Full capacity and the impossibility of negative gross investment provide ceilings and floors that limit the extent to which output can fluctuate.

● Fluctuations in stockbuilding are important in the business cycle. Only planned fluctuations can cause cycles. Unplanned changes are a symptom, not a cause. The need to restore stocks, however they were accumulated, to a normal level can explain why cycles are necessary.

● Real business cycles assume that output is always at potential and that fluctuations are in potential output itself. A desire for some intertemporal smoothing can generate persisting reactions to changes. Generating cycles is more difficult.

● Some swings in potential output do occur, but many short-run fluctuations probably reflect Keynesian departures from potential output. Aggregate demand and aggregate supply both contribute to the business cycle.

● Increasing integration of world financial and product markets has made most countries heavily dependent on the wider world. Business cycles in the rich countries are closely correlated.

● Recovery from the recession of 1990–92 was slow and weak. One key difference from previous cycles was the large burden of household debt accumulated during financial deregulation in the 1980s. Continued saving to meet interest payments and repay some of the debt meant lower consumption for a long time. By the late 1990s, consumer confidence had returned.

KEY TERMS

◆ Trend output path   526

◆ Business cycle   527

◆ Political business cycle   528

◆ Accelerator model of investment   529

◆ Multiplier–accelerator model   529

◆ Real business cycle   531

REVIEW QUESTIONS

1 Look again at Figure 31-2. Can you say which fluctuations in output were caused by changes to aggregate supply and which by changes to aggregate demand? Does the cyclical behaviour of productivity help to answer this question?

2 'If firms could forecast future output and profits accurately, there could not be a business cycle.' Is this true?

3 The one country in Western Europe with a business cycle out of line with all the others is Norway. Norway is heavily dependent on oil production and fishing. (a) Why might Norway be different? (b) Does this help us think about the relative importance of Keynesian and real business cycles?

4 Empirical researchers have found that the economic variable most correlated with election success is the rate of economic growth in the period immediately before the election. Why might voters care more about the direction in which the economy is heading than about the absolute level of its position at election time?

5 In spite of all this, the previous government messed up and you are suddenly in power. How should you run the economy to maximize your chances of re-election in about five years' time? Is this what governments seem to do?

6 Would it be more helpful for the world economy if all the largest countries elected governments on the same day? Why, or why not?

7 What is real about a business cycle?

8 *Common fallacies* Show why each of the following statements is incorrect. (a) Closer integration of national economies will gradually abolish business cycles. (b) Only Keynesians can explain business cycles. (c) The more we expect cycles, the more we will get them. (d) Because output and labour productivity are closely correlated, this proves that fluctuations in productivity are the main cause of business cycles.

32 Macroeconomics: where do we stand?

LEARNING OUTCOMES

When you have finished this chapter, you should be able to:

● Relate different assertions about how the macroeconomy works to differing interpretations of key assumptions behind the analysis
● Discuss the significance of different judgements about how quickly market forces, unassisted by policy, can restore output to full capacity
● Explain how different assumptions about how expectations are formed has an important effect on the speed of adjustment
● Examine the role of the assumption about the speed with which wages adjust to labour market developments
● Consider the potential for hysteresis and more than one long-run equilibrium
● Outline how the major schools of macroeconomic thought differ in their assessments
● Relate these differences to differing recommendations for demand management policy, and for differing judgements about the importance of supply-side policy

We have come a long way since we began our discussion of macroeconomics in Chapter 20. In the last 12 chapters we have slowly built up an analysis of how the economy works. Within this model we have studied the effects of government policy in both the short run and the long run. In this concluding chapter on macroeconomics we describe the main competing views of macroeconomics and their implications for government policy.

We begin by highlighting the major issues on which there is important disagreement. By major issues we mean issues on which a different view will lead almost inevitably to very different conclusions, whatever the details of the model in which the general approach is applied. We organize our discussion around attitudes to four major

issues: the speed with which markets clear, whether or not equilibrium is unique, the way in which expectations are formed and the relative importance of the short run and the long run.

Against this background we then describe and evaluate the four most prominent schools of macroeconomics thought today. We encourage you to view these competing positions not as unrelated and contradictory beliefs, but as the outcome of adopting slightly different positions within the spectrum of possible views.

The purpose of the chapter is to define the spectrum and indicate where different macroeconomists lie along that range of possible beliefs. In so doing, we pull together many of the themes of Part 4.

BOX 32-1　　Adjustment speeds in different markets

Our macroeconomic model now has four markets – goods, labour, money, and foreign exchange – and four variables – the price of goods, the nominal wage, the interest rate, and the nominal exchange rate – which can respond to excess supply or excess demand in these markets. Which market can adjust most quickly?

Under floating exchange rates, the exchange rate can adjust very quickly. Foreign exchange dealers sit facing banks of computers on which they transact billions of pounds the minute they think the exchange rate is out of line. A similar story is relevant in the money market. These markets clear almost instantly.

Goods markets adjust more slowly. The prices of goods are not usually set in a daily auction. In practice, most firms quote a price and adjust it only when they perceive significant excess supply or excess demand for their product. A decision to change the price takes time and effort. Moreover, some firms have long-term understandings with regular customers and are reluctant to bombard these customers with frequent price changes.

In the labour market, long-term understandings between a firm and its workforce are even more important. Loyalty and trust can be valuable commodities. At best, wage negotiations can take time. At worst they may involve expensive strikes and interruption of production. Wages are likely to be the slowest of the four variables to adjust, and the labour market is likely to be the slowest of the four markets to clear.

Few economists dispute this ordering of the relative adjustment speeds of the four markets. Where economists disagree is how long it takes for equilibrium to be re-established even in the market that is slowest to adjust, the labour market. Some economists think even the labour market adjusts quickly. Others believe it takes a very long time.

32-1 Areas of disagreement

We begin by asking why economists disagree at all. Surely, by looking carefully at the evidence we can say which views are correct and which must be rejected as inconsistent with the facts?

In Chapter 1 we introduced the distinction between positive and normative economics. Positive economics relates to how the world actually works. Normative economics relates to different value judgements about what is desirable. Some disagreements between macroeconomists arise from differing value judgements. Suppose for example everyone agreed that more unemployment today would allow greater output in five years' time. Some people alive today will be dead in five years' time and some people then alive have not yet been born. Choosing between higher unemployment today with more output in the future and lower future output but lower unemployment today involves a choice between the welfare of different groups of people. It is a value judgement on which different people might quite reasonably make different choices. Some disagreements between economists fall into this category. Since they do not arise from differing beliefs about how the world works, they cannot be settled by looking at the facts.

However, many important disagreements are disagreements in the positive economics of how the world actually works. Unlike some of the physical sciences, economists can rarely undertake controlled laboratory experiments. In practice, we have to try to unscramble historical data to make judgements about how the economy works. In Chapter 2 we indicated how econometricians attempt to undertake this task.

Even so, empirical research in economics does not always offer clear-cut answers. Suppose for example we wish to study how the economy works when exchange rates are floating. Since many relevant data, such as GDP, are available only quarterly, we have only 100 separate pieces of data since freely floating exchange rates were adopted in 1973. For some purposes we simply do not have sufficient data to offer more than tentative conclusions. Economists who don't like these tentative conclusions argue that as yet the case against them remains unproved.

Moreover, we live in a world that is constantly evolving. Even if we had a good estimate of the empirical magnitudes in the demand for money equation during 1950–80, should we expect these to be relevant in the 1990s, when credit cards have been adopted on a wide scale? The truthful answer may be that as yet it is simply too early to say. Only when credit cards have been in widespread use for a long time shall we be able to measure their impact with more confidence. And, of course, by then we will be worrying about the effect of the internet on the demand for money.

Taking a different example, much current behaviour is heavily influenced by expectations of the future. The spending decisions of firms and households depend critically on today's expectations of future incomes and profits. But whereas purchases and sales allow us to measure actual spending, we collect no equivalent data on current expectations. Suppose a sharp increase in income and output is *not* preceded by a sharp increase in consumption and investment spending: are we to conclude that nobody had previously expected income and output to rise, or should we conclude that the rise was foreseen but that expected income and profits in fact have little effect on consumption and investment decisions? Different schools of economists can look at the same data and give it different interpretations.

Empirical economists do the best they can. In some cases their research is rather persuasive and their conclusions are widely accepted. Few people dispute that current consumption and the current demand for money are influenced by what is happening to current income. But in other cases empirical research is much less conclusive. Although economists agree about many aspects of positive economics, some disagreements will inevitably remain. We now pick out key disagreements that are not mere quibbles about points of detail. They fundamentally affect one's view of the world and the policy decisions one is likely to support.

Market clearing

A market clears and is in equilibrium when the quantity sellers wish to supply equals the quantity purchasers wish to demand. Whether, and if so how quickly, all markets clear remains the most important issue in macroeconomics. At the one extreme we have the classical analysis which assumes that all markets clear. The economy is then at full employment and potential output. In these circumstances a monetary expansion will increase prices but not output, and a fiscal expansion will crowd out private consumption and investment until aggregate demand is restored to its full-employment level. At the other extreme, Keynesian analysis assumes that markets, especially the labour market, do not clear. With imperfect wage flexibility, a reduction in the

aggregate demand for goods and the demand for labour leads to lower output and employment. In such a situation, expansionary fiscal and monetary policy can increase real output.

Do markets clear or not? It is interesting how the onus of proof changes over time. Before Keynes's *General Theory*, most economists took it for granted that markets cleared and tried to explain periods of high unemployment within this framework. In the immediate postwar period, most economists took it for granted that markets did not clear continuously and sought to interpret macroeconomics within the Keynesian paradigm.

In the 1970s the pendulum swung back again. Many economists argued that, if wage stickiness leads to involuntary unemployment, surely workers will find a way to make wages more flexible, thus avoiding the cost of involuntary unemployment. It became fashionable to say that the Keynesian assumption of wage stickiness could not be given any plausible microeconomic foundation. Since the 1980s the pendulum has been in motion again. New Keynesian economists began to articulate microeconomic foundations for wage stickiness, and fewer economists believe there is a presumption that markets automatically clear. It is for historians of economic thought to decide whether fluctuations in the mood of the economics profession reflect the persuasiveness of new theories or the accumulation of evidence.

The attempt by some economists to explain even short-run fluctuations with market clearing models has, of course, spawned a rich new literature on what determines potential output and equilibrium unemployment, topics that tended to be neglected when the main focus of analysis was simply movements in aggregate demand. It is now generally accepted that movements in potential output might be significant, even in the short run. Whether they are the *only* source of short-run output fluctuations is essentially the same question as whether market clearing can be assumed, even in the short run.

Is long-run equilibrium unique?

Suppose an economy begins in long-run equilibrium but then experiences a *temporary* shock which drives it to a different position in the short run. What happens when the shock has disappeared? Does the economy, sooner or later, go back to the original equilibrium, or does it settle down in a new, *permanently different*, long-run equilibrium?

The latter case is called *hysteresis*. We introduced it in Chapter 27 when discussing unemployment, but the same argument applies to aggregate supply and potential output.

Hysteresis exists when the path an economy follows in the short run affects which long-run equilibrium it eventually reaches. In Chapter 27 we mentioned several possible mechanisms that could give rise to hysteresis.

Suppose an economy faces a temporary fall in aggregate demand. This could lead to the following effects. First, when workers initially lost their jobs, the number of remaining workers still in employment goes down. When demand picks up again, there are fewer insiders than there used to be in long-run equilibrium, and they use their increased scarcity to bid up their own wages, rather than to allow their firms to rehire workers sacked in the slump. For this to work, insiders must have a lot of power in the wage bargaining process. In the new long-run equilibrium, potential output is lower and unemployment higher than in the original long-run equilibrium.

Second, during a recession some unemployed workers may get permanently discouraged from looking for work. A culture of unemployment develops, and labour supply is permanently reduced. Third, firms may scrap capital in a slump, and no longer have the factories when demand picks up again. The new long-run equilibrium has lower potential output, both because there is less capital input and because this in turn will reduce productivity, real wages, and the quantity of labour supplied.

Finally, at low levels of activity, the matching process between firms and workers may break down. Not only is it not worth unemployed workers looking for work, it is not worth firms trying to find workers. This may become self-sustaining even when demand picks up again.

Whether or not hysteresis is quantitatively an important phenomenon is one of the most controversial issues of the last ten years. The more economists believe that hysteresis matters, the more they argue that the easiest way to prevent its damaging effects is to prevent the economy from entering a recession in the first place. In contrast, economists who believe that hysteresis is not very important can take a more relaxed attitude to temporary recessions since they believe that these have no long-term consequences.

Expectations formation

Most economists accept that beliefs about the future are an important determinant of behaviour today. For example, consumer spending will depend both on how much today's households wish to spend out of their expected future incomes *and* on how today's households decide what future incomes to expect.

Some important disagreements between economists can be traced to different beliefs about how expectations are formed. For simplicity, we divide the possible approaches to this question into three categories.

Exogenous expectations   Some economists remain almost completely agnostic on the vital question of how expectations are formed. When analysing the behaviour of the economy, they simply treat expectations as exogenous or given. Expectations are one of the inputs to the analysis. The analysis can display the *consequences* of a change in expectations – for example, an increase in expected future profits might increase firms' investment spending at each level of interest rates – but the analysis does not investigate the *cause* of the change in expectations. In particular, it is unrelated to other parts of the analysis. With given expectations, there is no automatic feedback from rising output to expectations of higher profits in the future.

Exogenous expectations are not explained within the model.

Thus, at best, economists using exogenous expectations in their analysis give an incomplete account of how the economy works. At worst, they completely neglect some inevitable feedbacks from the variables they are analysing to the expectations that were an input to this analysis. On the other hand, since modelling expectations remains a contentious issue, proponents of this approach might argue that the various types of possible feedback on expectations can be explored in an *ad hoc* manner.

Extrapolative expectations   One simple way to make expectations endogenous, or determined by what is going on elsewhere in the analysis, is to assume that people forecast future profits by extrapolating the behaviour of profits in the recent past, or extrapolate past inflation in order to form expectations of inflation in the near future.

Extrapolative expectations assume that the future will be similar to the recent past.

Proponents of this approach suggest that it offers a simple rule of thumb and corresponds to what many people seem to do in the real world.

Rational expectations   Suppose the rate of money growth is steadily increasing and inflation is steadily accelerating. Extrapolating past inflation rates will persistently under-forecast future inflation. Many economists believe that it is implausible that people will continue to use a forecasting rule that makes the same mistake (underforecasting of future inflation, say) period after period.

BOX 32-2   The government's policy options and constraints

The following checklist may be useful in working through this chapter.

Aggregate demand The demand for domestic output. The sum of consumer spending, investment spending by firms, government spending on goods (and services), and net exports.

Demand management Policies to stabilize aggregate demand close to its full-employment level. The government tries to influence aggregate demand either directly, by changing the government component of aggregate demand, or indirectly. Indirect policies include changes in taxation, which affect private expenditure, and monetary policy. Changes in the money supply and the interest rate affect domestic spending but also influence net exports via their effect on the exchange rate.

Potential output The level of output that firms wish to supply when there is full employment. It depends both on the level of full employment and on the capital stock with which labour combines to produce output.

Full employment The level of employment when the labour market is in equilibrium. At the equilibrium real wage, the only people unemployed are the people who do not wish to work at this real wage but are nevertheless part of the labour force.

Supply-side policies Policies aimed at increasing potential output. These include tax cuts to increase business investment and the capital stock; personal tax cuts; union reform or retraining grants aimed at increasing the effective labour supply at each real wage rate; and less government involvement in the economy in the hope that market forces stimulate effort and enterprise. Reducing inflation is also a kind of supply-side policy if high inflation has real economic costs.

Hysteresis The view that temporary shocks have permanent effects on long-run equilibrium.

The hypothesis of **rational expectations** assumes that, on average, people guess the future correctly.

They do not use forecasting rules that systematically give too low a forecast or too high a forecast. Any tendency for expectations to be systematically in error will quickly be detected and put right.

This in no way says that everybody gets everything exactly right all the time. We live in a risky world where unforeseeable things are always happening. Expectations will be fulfilled only rarely. Rational expectations says that people make good use of the information that is available today and do not make forecasts that are already knowably incorrect. Only genuinely unforeseeable things cause present forecasts to go wrong. Sometimes people will underpredict and sometimes they will overpredict. But any systematic tendency to do one or other will be noticed and the basis of expectations formation will be amended until guesses are on average correct.

Short tun and long run

Where it is agreed that certain policies have short-run benefits but long-run costs, or vice versa, different groups of economists may adopt differing value judgements about how these gains and losses should be traded off. In part, the differing policy prescriptions offered by different groups of economists can be seen as reflecting differing judgements about the relative importance of the short run and the long run.

In practice, these judgements are closely connected with the three issues on which we have already focused. The more quickly one believes markets clear, the less scope there will be for demand management in the short run and the greater will be the importance attached to supply-side policy aimed at increasing potential output over the longer run. Conversely, the more one believes in the possibility of high levels of Keynesian unemployment in the short run, the more likely one is to judge that the short-run benefits of getting back to full employment are more important than any tendency thus induced to reduce the level of potential output in the long run. Similarly, the more one wishes to focus on very short-run analysis, the more plausible it becomes that expectations can somehow be treated as given in the short run; and the more one wishes to discuss what is happening in the long run, the more important it is likely to be to take account of how expectations are changing over time. And the more one believes in hysteresis, the more one must look after the short run in order to look after the long run.

Having picked out four major areas of disagreement, we now examine the major schools of contemporary macroeconomic thought.

32-2 New Classical macroeconomics

The **New Classical macroeconomics** is based on the twin principles of almost instantaneous market clearing and rational expectations.

The analysis is *classical* because it assumes that wage and price flexibility restore the economy to its position of full employment and potential output. The analysis is *new* because it assumes that wage and price flexibility is almost instantaneous. At best, monetary and fiscal policy can affect the *composition* of full-employment aggregate demand. Its *level* is necessarily the full-employment level. And this being so, hysteresis is unimportant.

Whereas the classical analysis was sometimes rather vague about the period being analysed – it was whatever period was necessary to allow complete wage and price adjustment and hence the restoration of full employment – the New Classical macroeconomics confronts this question explicitly. Wage and price adjustment is almost instantaneous. Whatever level of unemployment is observed must therefore be the natural rate of unemployment. Unemployment changes over time because microeconomic incentives alter the natural rate itself.

Much of the flavour of this analysis can be understood using the following simple example. Money wages are set at the beginning of each period and are then fixed for the period, since firms and workers cannot forever be arguing about the wage to be paid today. On what basis are wages set? At the level expected to clear the market for labour. Since workers and firms both care about *real* wages this requires that, after forming expectations about the likely level of prices during the period, firms and workers agree on a money wage that is expected to provide the equilibrium level of real wages during the period.

Suppose prices turn out to be unexpectedly high. Firms will have made a good deal. With money wage, fixed for the period, real wages are unexpectedly low. Firms are likely to expand output temporarily while real wages are low. But at the beginning of the following period, wages are renegotiated in the light of the price expectations then prevailing for the next period, and money wages are then

set once again at the level that is expected to produce the equilibrium real wage.

Thus, in each period unexpectedly high prices are accompanied by unexpectedly high output. Conversely, if prices are unexpectedly low, workers will have made a good wage bargain. Real wages will be unexpectedly high and firms will temporarily cut back output. But because of the assumption that, at the start of each period, wages are set at the level expected to clear the market, there is no tendency for deviations of output and employment from their full-employment levels to persist from one period to the next.

One of the *new* things about the New Classical macroeconomics is its explicit assumption of rational expectations. Why does the assumption of rational expectations play an important role in the analysis? Because it implies that the government cannot use fiscal and monetary policy systematically to fool people. Suppose the government switches to a more expansionary monetary policy. This tends to make prices rise, since the economy begins close to full employment. If the initial policy change was not foreseeable, workers will not have foreseen that prices will rise. They will have settled for too low a money wage. Firms will temporarily have cheap labour and will expand output. The unanticipated monetary expansion will have caused an unanticipated rise in output and employment above their full employment or natural rates.

But if everyone has rational expectations they will quickly catch on to what the government is up to. When wages are renegotiated, everyone will know that the money supply is expanding and prices are rising. The money wage settlement will suitably reflect this and, in the absence of any further surprises, real wages will now be at their equilibrium level again.

The New Classical macroeconomics can thus be summed up as follows. It is only the fact that some variables, particularly money wages, must be set in advance that prevents continuous attainment of full employment and potential output. Variables that must be set in advance are set at the levels expected to produce full employment. Only unexpected developments make them temporarily inappropriate and allow output and employment to depart temporarily from their natural rates. But the government cannot use fiscal and monetary policy to make prices unexpectedly high period after period, and thus it cannot hold output systematically above its natural rate. If the government attempted to undertake such a policy, people would quickly see through the policy intentions and start to anticipate the expansion. Thus expansionary policy would already be incorporated in the previous wage claims. It would stop being a surprise. But the combination of expected market clearing and rational expectations means that it is only surprises that can move the economy away from full employment. Essentially, demand management through monetary and fiscal policy is completely impotent.

What remains for the government to do? Only to control the price level and to worry about the supply-side policies aimed at increasing the level of potential output. Supply-side policies include income tax cuts to increase the incentive to work. Tight monetary policy will keep inflation under control. It will increase potential output by reducing shoe-leather and menu costs. It will also reduce the distortions that arise when the tax system is not completely inflation-neutral. Low government spending will prevent large government borrowing from bidding up interest rates and crowding out private investment.

Nor will tight fiscal and monetary policy cause Keynesian unemployment. Wages and prices will quickly fall to boost the real money supply and restore aggregate demand to its full-employment level. If a switch to tighter policy takes people by surprise, at worst it will have only temporary effects on output and unemployment. As soon as wages can be renegotiated they will be reduced to the level now compatible with full employment. The consequent fall in prices will then boost the real money supply and aggregate demand.

Indeed, this principle can be extended. Since it is only unforeseen surprises that move the economy away from full employment in the short run, the aim of demand management should be to minimize surprises and keep the economy as close to full employment as possible. Policies should be pre-announced precisely so that private individuals can anticipate them and set wages and prices at the full-employment level.

Is it true that the New Classical economists believe the dramatic rise in European unemployment has almost nothing to do with a fall in aggregate demand? Yes it is. It must all be explained by a rise in the natural rate of unemployment, caused by factors such as those we explored in Chapter 27.

Real business cycle theorists

In the previous chapter we introduced the theory of real business cycles, made popular in the United States by economists such as Robert Lucas and Edward Prescott. This approach belongs to the same family as the New Classical macroeconomics, although its emphasis is a little different. Both emphasize near-continuous market clearing and rational expectations.

The New Classicals place emphasis on the effects of temporary surprises until expectations quickly catch up, thus developing a theory of fluctuations around potential output. Real business theorists take this a stage further and seek to explain all fluctuations as fluctuations in potential output itself.

Thus, the real business cycle approach is both more extreme and more general than the New Classical macroeconomics. It is more extreme because its analysis neglects deviations from potential output even for a short time. Since changes in nominal money have no real effects in such a context, the cause of changes must be sought in shocks to real variables such as technical knowledge.

The approach is more general than the New Classical macroeconomics because it concentrates all its powers of analysis on making explicit the microeconomic foundations for the intertemporal decisions of firms, households, and governments. It is in decisions to amend intertemporal plans and reallocate them over time that real business cycle theorists believe they can explain how large movements in actual output and employment could be movements in equilibrium output and employment.

32-3 Gradualist monetarists

This school is associated with Milton Friedman. We use the term 'monetarist' to mean those economists espousing the classical doctrine that an increase in the money supply leads essentially to an increase in prices rather than to an increase in output. Thus, the New Classical economists believe in almost instant monetarism. Whereas the New Classical economists believe in only temporary departures from full employment as a result of unforeseeable shocks which cannot immediately be reflected in wages, the Gradualist monetarists accept that restoration of full employment may take a little longer. Even so, they believe that within a *few* years wage and price adjustment *will* restore full employment. Like the New Classical economists, Gradualist monetarists do not believe that hysteresis is important. When the economy gets gack to full employment after a temporary shock, they believe it is the *same* long-run equilibrium (in real terms) to which it returns.

Gradualist monetarists believe that full employment is restored within a few years, so the main effect of higher money is simply higher prices.

Thus, this school believes there is some force in the arguments for wage rigidity that we presented in Chapter 27, but only for a short time. Different members of this school adopt different assumptions about expectations formation. Sluggish adjustment in expectations formation may provide an additional reason for slower adjustment back to full employment.

For the New Classical macroeconomists there is no important distinction between the short run and the long run in the design of fiscal and monetary policy for demand management: the classical long run is relevant almost instantaneously. In contrast, the Gradualist monetarists believe that in the short run a fiscal or monetary stimulus would alter aggregate demand, output, and employment, but that it is neither sensible nor desirable to undertake such policies. The short run must be subordinated to the interests of the long run. Let us examine this argument in more detail.

Since wage and price adjustment takes a few years to complete, it follows from the analysis of Chapters 25 and 26 that expansionary monetary or fiscal policy can increase aggregate demand, output, and employment in the short run. However, the Gradualists offer two reasons why policy should not be used in this way. First, the economy will automatically return to full employment within a few years anyway. In the long run, persistent attempts to expand output beyond its full-employment level will lead simply to inflation. Second, if the objective of policy is not to raise the average level of output and employment (which in any case will be the full-employment level) but rather to react quickly to offset other shocks and reduce fluctuations around full employment, there is a real danger that policy will be counterproductive. By the time the government has diagnosed a downward shock and taken the necessary expansionary action, the economy may already be expanding on its own as wage and price adjustments begin to lead it back towards full employment. Stabilization policy may exacerbate cycles rather than dampen them.

Thus Milton Friedman has frequently recommended that the government should adopt a low but fixed rate of money growth, and reject the 'interest rate activism' followed by the Bank of England's Monetary Policy Committee. Because money growth is low, it will tend to keep inflation down in the long run. Because its rate of growth is constant, the government will not be exacerbating the business cycle by intervening too late when corrective action is no longer required.

The term Gradualist derives from the implication of this analysis for a government that inherits a high rate of money growth and inflation and wishes to reduce inflation considerably in the long run. Under the New Classical analysis, immediately slashing the rate of money growth

might lead to a very temporary increase in unemployment until existing wages could be renegotiated, but that is all. Since the Gradualists believe that wage adjustment is more sluggish, they believe that a very large reduction in the money supply might lead to quite a large Keynesian slump because a large adjustment in wages and prices would be required. Thus, even though the economy would return to full employment within two or three years, it would make sense to obtain the eventual benefits of lower inflation without incurring the worst of the severe recession in the short run. By reducing the rate of money growth more slowly, the problems of wages and price adjustment could be eased and the recession would be much less severe. Hence the term Gradualist.

Even so, since departures from full employment last a relatively short time, it is on the long-run classical analysis that the Gradualists place the most emphasis. The government's chief responsibility is to increase potential output and full employment by supply-side policies and the reduction of inflation.

32-4 Moderate Keynesians

Broadly speaking, this group of economists might be summarized as short-run Keynesians and long-run monetarists.

Moderate Keynesians believe that the economy will eventually return to full employment, but they believe that wage and price adjustment is fairly sluggish so the process could take many years.

In the short run, a fall in aggregate demand can generate a significant recession. Although many economists in this group believe that expectations adjustment is also sluggish, some of them believe in rational expectations and hold that it is not systematic mistakes in expectations formation, but rather the forces for wage rigidity discussed in Chapter 27, that prevent rapid restoration of full employment.

Moderate Keynesians believe that recessions last a bit longer than the couple of years or so at which a Gradualist monetarist would estimate the time required to restore full employment. And this leads them to draw a different judgement about the relative importance of the short run and the long run. On the one hand, it reduces the danger that attempts at stabilization policy are going to end up making things fluctuate more rather than less. And on the other hand, it increases the need for stabilization policy since recessions can be more severe and more persistent than the Gradualist monetarists believe possible. Thus Moderate

Keynesians believe that the government should accept responsibility for stabilization policy in the short run.

Since Moderate Keynesians believe the economy will *eventually* return to full employment, they accept that persistent rapid monetary growth must eventually lead to inflation once the full employment position has been reached. And in the very long run, it is only supply-side policies that will generate sustained economic growth by increasing the level of potential output. Thus many economists in this group would argue that the government should not neglect two of the policy prescriptions of the monetarists. Supply-side policies will be important in the long run; and, if high inflation reduces potential output, in the long run the average level of fiscal and monetary policy should be chosen to be compatible with a low inflation rate. Moderate Keynesians see no conflict between this stance of policy in the long run and the recommendation that in the short run active stabilization policies should be undertaken.

New Keynesians

The Keynesian approach fell out of fashion in the 1970s for two reasons. The first was empirical and practical. Unemployment increased, and the Keynesian policy response, stimulating aggregate demand, caused only inflation. Many people concluded that the Keynesian approach was wrong. And so it was, in part: it had paid too little attention to the supply side. The rise in unemployment primarily reflected a deterioration in aggregate supply. It was an increase in the natural rate of unemployment. Moderate Keynesians now recognize the necessity of keeping track of aggregate demand as well as aggregate supply. But they continue to believe that many shocks have their origins (and solutions) in shifts in aggregate demand.

The second reason why Keynesianism fell out of favour was that its followers appeared to neglect microeconomics. Key relationships, such as the consumption function, seemed to appear out of thin air. As New Classical and real business cycle theorists developed theories with elegant microfoundations for the dynamics of choice over time, they became increasingly critical of the absence of micro-foundations for Keynesian analysis. Like the boy brave enough to say that the emperor had no clothes, they had a big impact.

The task the New Keynesians set for themselves is therefore to provide the microfoundations for Keynesian analysis. Instead of asserting that markets do not work well, they aim to deduce that markets *will* not work well. Market failures follow from problems with information, from externalities, from costs of decision-making and change. Since these are all tough to analyse, it has taken a while to produce the rejoinder to the New Classical criticism.

Broadly, this rejoinder falls into three headings. First, economists such as Greg Mankiw of Harvard and David Romer of Berkeley have tried to analyse sluggish price and wage adjustment in greater detail. They have shown that, with one proviso, even a small amount of nominal rigidity – say, the menu costs of deciding to change prices, negotiating changes in wages, and then implementing these changes – may be sufficient to produce all the standard Keynesian features described in earlier chapters. The one proviso is that we need some real rigidity in the labour market as well. Let's see why.

An adverse shock to aggregate demand, given a little price sluggishness, makes firms want to cut back output and employment. But why don't workers then take wage cuts? While prices are fixed, workers will think they are taking a real wage cut, so it is in real rigidities that we must seek the answer.

In Chapters 12 and 27 we set out some of the New Keynesian answers. The efficiency wage theory says that firms choose to set wages too high to clear the labour market, for example because this means a worker caught shirking on the job then faces a big penalty in being sacked. Another justification is provided by the insider–outsider approach, which emphasizes that the senior workers who retain their jobs place little weight on their less fortunate colleagues.

A second type of New Keynesian response is particularly associated with Joseph Stiglitz, formerly Chief Economist of the World Bank. Although agreeing that these real rigidities in the labour market are an essential feature of Keynesian economics, he emphasizes that near-instant price flexibility in product markets is little help, and may actually exacerbate Keynesian problems.

Suppose there is an adverse shock to aggregate demand. For only a tiny period, prices are sluggish to adjust. During that time, real aggregate demand falls. If firms are very risk-averse, they may quickly react to this more difficult world by contracting supply: getting overextended is simply too dangerous, especially since banks get tough quickly in a recession. So, quite quickly, we reach a position in which the goods market clears. Supply and demand curves have both shifted left. From now on, price flexibility is not enough to fix things up: supply and demand clear, but at a lower level. The shift in demand has caused a shift in supply.

The New Keynesians who believe in hysteresis (see Box 27-4 on page 458) go further. This shift in supply may have permanent repercussions. If so, active stabilization is desirable because it prevents short-run difficulties from becoming long-run problems which can then be broken down only by slow-working supply-side remedies.

32-5 Extreme Keynesians

Extreme Keynesians not only insist that markets fail to clear in the short run; they also believe that markets do not clear in the long run.

Keynesian unemployment may persist indefinitely unless the government intervenes to boost aggregate demand.

Extreme Keynesians reject the view that slumps can eventually restore full employment via downward pressure on wages and prices. In this they agree with those New Keynesians who believe in hysteresis. But they disagree too. Whereas hysteresis suggests that, once a recession has done its damage, supply has then gone so boosting demand no longer works, Extreme Keynesians believe that boosting aggregate demand through government policy will do the trick.

Their case must therefore rest primarily on labour market rigidity. Real-wage rigidity causes excess supply in the labour market, and this pool of involuntarily unemployed workers remains available at any time to be mopped up through a demand expansion. Extreme Keynesians refer to this assumption of labour market inflexibility as the *real-wage hypothesis*.

Even if, for reasons we have discussed at length, a degree of real-wage rigidity is plausible, why can't all nominal variables fall to boost the real money supply, reduce interest rates, and thereby eventually move the economy to full employment through market forces alone? Extreme Keynesians have several answers.

First, it is impossible to co-ordinate the changes in nominal wages and prices. If all could be cut together, no real wage need change. But in practice, some workers have to go first. Unless and until all other wages and prices come down, the first workers to cut nominal wages also cut real wages. This may be sufficient to prevent the cut taking place, especially if each group of workers is very sensitive about its wages relative to other groups.

Second, even if some general reduction in nominal variables could be engineered, its effect may be minimal when the economy is deep in recession. When times are tough and firms are losing money, they do not wish to invest, even if interest rates are driven down to zero (as happened recently in Japan). Implicitly, this means that the

IS curve may be near vertical at very low levels of output: demand does not respond to lower interest rates. Notice that, while this destroys nominal wage and price reductions as an adjustment mechanism during a slump, it also means that monetary expansion would be equally ineffective in such circumstances. In a boom, when everyone wants to invest, there is no problem raising interest rates, and sufficiently high interest rates will reduce aggregate demand. But in a slump monetary expansion may fail. Old Keynesians used to compare monetary policy to a string: you can pull tight on it, but pushing on it may have no effect. Thus, Extreme Keynesians tend to emphasize the significance of fiscal policy in getting the economy out of a serious recession.

Finally, a word about expectations. Just as New Classical economists are optimists about both the speed of market clearing and the ability of people intelligently to form, and rapidly to adjust, expectations about the future, Extreme Keynesians are nearly as pessimistic about expectations as they are about market clearing. Keynes himself compared expectations to a beauty contest. The modern equivalent would be a TV game show where the competitor has to guess the answer most frequently chosen by the TV audience.

In such situations, what matters is not getting the right answer (which is how economists try to evaluate rational expectations): what matters is guessing what other people guess. Multiple equilibria may be very common, which rather undermines the ease with which we can assume that people quickly adjust expectations to *the* right answer. Through Extreme Keynesian spectacles, co-ordination failures (i.e. externalities) occur as much in expectations as in wage-setting.

32-6 A summing up

We have set out the views of the competing schools of modern macroeconomics. In each case, we have sought to interpret their views against the four basic criteria that we set out in Section 32-1: the assumption about market clearing, the assumption about expectations formation, the assumption about hysteresis, and the relative priority given to short run and long run when making policy prescriptions. Table 32-1 summarizes our discussion.

By now it should be evident that the competing views of *macroeconomics* rest on differing views about *microeconomics* as well. The economists who are optimistic about market clearing believe that markets work fairly well. Some of these economists – Milton Friedman is a notable example –

Table 32-1   A stylized picture of the competing views

	New Classical	Gradualist monetarist	Moderate Keynesian	Extreme Keynesian
Market clearing	Very fast	Quite fast	Quite slow	Very slow
Expectations	Rational – adjust quickly	Adjust more slowly	Could be fast or slow to adjust	Adjust slowly
Long run/ short run	Not much difference since fast adjustment	Long run more important	Don't neglect short run	Short run very important
Full employment	Always close	Never too far away	Could be far away	Could stay away
Hysteresis	No problem	No problem	Might be big problem	Not a big problem
Policy conclusion	Demand management useless; supply side needed	Supply side more important; avoid wild swings in demand	Demand management important too	Demand management what counts

champion free markets in general and hold that free competition is a good thing. Government should break up monopolies where they exist, and use supply-side policies to help markets function even more efficiently.

In contrast, the economists who are pessimistic about market clearing tend to stress all the things that can inhibit markets from working efficiently. They emphasize the difficulties in acquiring the relevant information to make sensible choices, and the fact that many markets for goods and labour are far from competitive. They do not believe that free unregulated markets are necessarily a good thing. Governments should intervene to help markets function in the social interest.

We discussed these issues at length in our examination of positive and normative microeconomics in Parts 2 and 3. Fortunately, it is not necessary to divide economics arbitrarily into unconnected areas of analysis. Many of the recent developments in macroeconomics to which we have referred in Part 4 reflect the growing conviction that macro-economists must pay close attention to what is going on at the micro-level. In Chapter 20 we introduced macro-economics by saying that sometimes we get a clearer idea of the big picture by surveying the whole scene with the naked eye. But it can be useful to have the occasional squint through binoculars to check that our interpretation of the big picture makes sense.

It is not our intention here to adjudicate between the competing views of macroeconomics, though in fact we should probably place ourselves in the Moderate Keynesian group of economists. Rather, our intention in the preceding chapters has been to develop a framework in which the differing positions can be interpreted. In this chapter we have explained how alterations in the basic assumptions, especially the assumption about the speed of adjustment, the time required for restoration of full employment, and the possibility of hysteresis, allow this framework to be used to represent the views of the different schools of modern macroeconomics and to show why they reach differing policy recommendations.

SUMMARY

● Although there is much about which all economists agree, there remain some important differences of opinion, both in the positive economics of how the world actually works and in the normative economics of how the government should behave. Although some differences in policy recommendations stem from different positive assessments of how the world works, some differences in policy recommendations are based purely on value judgements.

● It is desirable that economic theories should be tested against the facts. However, in some cases such tests are unlikely to yield conclusive answers. Some key variables such as expectations are not observable. The world is constantly changing, and it may be impossible to obtain a sufficiently long period of data on the world as it is today to allow definitive empirical tests of the competing theoretical models.

● In seeking to understand the major schools of macroeconomic thought, it is helpful to bear in mind their attitude to four key issues: the speed with which the labour market clears, the way in which expectations are formed, the possibility of hysteresis, and the relative importance of the short run compared with the long run.

● The New Classical macroeconomics assumes that market clearing is almost instantaneous. Only predetermined contracts prevent continuous full employment. The additional assumption of rational expectations implies that predetermined variables will have been set at the level reflecting the best guess about their required equilibrium value. Any change that could have been foreseen will already have been reflected in the process that set these variables. Only pure surprises lead to temporary departures from full employment until preset variables can be altered and full employment restored. Since the economy is close to full employment, demand management policies simply induce offsetting price and wage changes to restore aggregate demand to its full-employment level. Government policy should minimize surprises. Movements in actual output and unemployment are largely explained as movements in the full employment or natural rates. The government should concentrate on keeping inflation down and on promoting supply-side policies to increase the level of full employment and potential output.

● Real business cycle theorists neglect even temporary departures from full market clearing. They argue that a detailed analysis of the intertemporal decisions of households, firms, and government can explain even short-term fluctuations as movements in potential output.

● Gradualist monetarists believe that the restoration of full employment is not immediate but will take only a few years. A violent reduction in the money supply could induce quite a deep albeit temporary recession and should be avoided. Moreover, attempts at demand management might be counterproductive if the economy is already recovering strongly by the time a recession is diagnosed. Hence the government should abandon attempts to 'fine-tune' aggregate demand and concentrate on long-run policies to keep inflation down and promote supply-side policies which increase full employment and potential output.

● Moderate Keynesians believe that the automatic restoration of full employment could take many years but that it may happen eventually. Although demand management policies cannot increase output and employment without limit, active stabilization policy is worth undertaking to prevent booms and slumps that could last several years and therefore could be diagnosed relatively easily. In the long run, supply-side policies are still important, but the elimination of large slumps may be important if hysteresis leads to permanent effects on long-run equilibrium.

● New Keynesians try to provide microeconomic foundations for Keynesian macroeconomics. Menu costs may explain nominal rigidities. In turn, these are compounded by real rigidities in the labour market. Several channels for hysteresis have now been developed.

● Extreme Keynesians believe that departures from full employment could be even more protracted. Keynesian unemployment will not lead to real-wage reductions and may not lead to lower money wages and prices. Even if it does, aggregate demand may not respond to lower interest rates: pessimistic expectations may be sufficient to prevent a significant improvement in aggregate demand. In these circumstances the first responsibility of the government is not supply-side policies aimed at increasing a level of potential output that is not being attained, but restoration of the economy to potential output by expansionary fiscal and monetary policy, especially the former.

KEY TERMS

◆ Exogenous expectations 539

◆ Extrapolative expectations 539

◆ Rational expectations 540

◆ New Classical macroeconomics 541

◆ Gradualist monetarists 542

◆ Moderate Keynesians 543

◆ Extreme Keynesians 545

 REVIEW QUESTIONS

1 Beginning from full employment, the government reduces the level of the money supply. Explain carefully the predictions of the four schools of macroeconomics about what happens (a) in the short run and (b) in the long run. Does it matter whether the contraction of the money supply had previously been anticipated?

2 How might the four schools of macroeconomics explain why European unemployment increased in the 1980s? Since fiscal and monetary policy remained tight during the 1990s, what forecast for unemployment would the four schools have offered?

3 As compared with a closed economy, how is the speed of adjustment likely to differ (a) in an open economy with a fixed exchange rate? (b) in an open economy with a floating exchange rate?

4 Identify each of the following statements with one of the four schools: (a) Reducing inflation is easy and will not be accompanied by an increase in unemployment. (b) Expansionary monetary and fiscal policy will always increase output unless there is a sudden surge of imports. (c) It is always worth incurring a temporary increase in unemployment to obtain a permanent inflation reduction. (d) The government can always generate a domestic slump and reduce inflation, but the cost in output forgone could be quite high in the short run.

5 *Common fallacies* Show why each of the following statements is incorrect. (a) The assumption of rational expectations implies that the economy is always at full employment. (b) There is never a trade-off between inflation and unemployment. (c) There is always a trade-off between inflation and unemployment. (d) Keynesians are people who believe that microeconomics is irrelevant. (e) Monetarists believe that the level of the nominal money supply is the main determinant of the level of real output and employment.

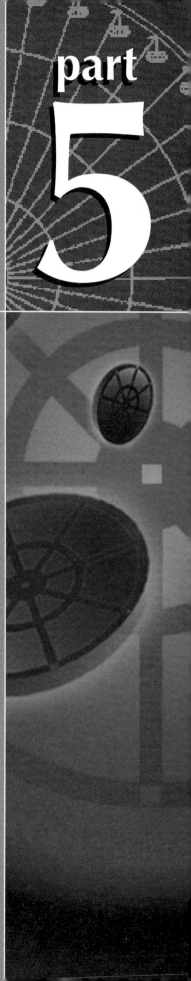

part

5

The World Economy

Part 5 focuses on the world as a whole. What determines the pattern of international trade, and the tariff policies pursued by individual countries? Can free trade benefit everyone? What difference does the international monetary system make? Can the IMF prevent financial crises? Part 5 also discusses how small European economies have become sufficiently interdependent that they have been driven to much greater policy co-operation, both in regulatory policy and in seeking exchange rate stability through monetary union. Part 5 concludes with a wider examination of trends in Central and Eastern Europe and, more generally, in the poorer countries of the world.

Chapter 33 analyses why international trade takes place, studies the gains from trade, and considers what this implies for trade policy of nation states. Chapter 34 examines the international monetary system through which countries finance international trade flows, and discusses arguments for different kinds of exchange rate regime. Chapter 35 studies European integration, the single market, the EMU, and progress in Eastern Europe. Chapter 36 looks at the problems of developing countries.

33 International trade and commercial policy

LEARNING OUTCOMES

When you have finished this chapter, you should be able to:

● Study patterns of international trade
● Explain comparative advantage and the gains from trade
● Analyse how differences in technology or relative factor endowment create comparative advantage
● Examine how scale economies and a demand for diversity lead to two-way trade in the same product
● Discuss the welfare economics of levying tariffs, quotas, and export subsidies
● Introduce the principle of targeting and explore first-best and second-best motives for tariffs

International trade is a part of daily life. Britons drink French wine, Americans drive Japanese cars, and Russians eat American wheat. If this is unremarkable, why is there a separate branch of economics devoted to international trade? Why is trade between the UK and Japan different from trade between London and Birmingham?

There are two reasons. First, because international trade crosses national frontiers, governments can monitor this trade and treat it differently. It is hard to tax or regulate goods moving from London to Birmingham but much easier to impose taxes or quota restrictions on goods imported from Taiwan or Japan. Governments have to decide whether or not such policies are desirable.

Second, international trade may involve the use of different national currencies. A British buyer of American wine pays in sterling but the American vineyard worker is paid in dollars. International trade involves international payments. We examine the system of international payments more fully in the next chapter.

In this chapter we concentrate on trade flows and trade policy. Who trades with whom and in what commodities? We then examine why international trade takes place. Countries trade with one another because they can buy foreign goods at a lower price than it costs to make the same goods at home.

How can this be possible for all countries? The basis of international trade is *exchange* and *specialization*. International differences in the availability of raw materials and other factors of production lead to international differences in production costs and goods prices. Through international exchange, countries supply the world economy with the commodities that they produce relatively cheaply and demand from the world economy the goods made relatively cheaply elsewhere.

These benefits from trade are reinforced if there are economies of scale in production. Instead of each country having a lot of small producers, different countries concentrate on different things and everyone can benefit from the cost reductions that ensue.

We discuss in detail the benefits from international trade and examine whether our analysis can explain the trade flows that actually take place. Although there are many circumstances in which international trade can make countries better off, trade can also carry costs, especially in the short run. Cheap foreign cars are great for British consumers but not so good for unemployed car workers in the Midlands.

Because foreign competition may make life difficult for some voters, governments are frequently under pressure to restrict imports. We conclude the chapter by discussing trade or commercial policy and whether it is ever a good idea to restrict imports.

33-1 Trade patterns

Since every international transaction has both a buyer and a seller, one country's imports must be another country's exports. To get an idea of how much trade takes place, we can count the total value of exports by all countries or the total value of imports. To count both imports and exports would be to count every transaction twice.

Table 33-1 shows the value of world exports and, as a benchmark, the value relative to GNP in the world's largest single economy, the United States.

Two facts stand out. First, in real terms world trade has grown rapidly since 1950, at an average annual rate of 7.5 per cent. International trade has been playing an increasingly important part in national economies. Between 1960 and 1995, UK exports as a fraction of GNP rose from 18 per cent to 27 per cent. Details for selected countries are shown in Table 33-2. By 1998, world exports were nearly 20 per cent of world GNP.

Second, the Great Depression of the 1930s and the Second

World War virtually destroyed international trade. It was not until the 1960s that world trade again reached its level of 1928.

As trade has grown, both in absolute terms and relative to the size of national economies, the interdependence of national economies has increased. Like many of the countries shown in Table 33-2, Britain is now a very open economy. Smaller countries are of course more open. When New York trades with California it does not count as *international* trade. Events in other countries affect our daily lives much more than they did 20 years ago. We now look at the facts about who trades with whom.

World trade patterns

In Table 33-3 we show the pattern of trade. The industrial or developed countries include Western Europe, North America, Japan, Australia, and New Zealand, the rich countries with the largest share of world trade and world income. The remaining countries are the *less developed countries* (LDCs) – ranging from the very poor, such as China and India, to the nearly rich, such as Brazil and Mexico. We study these in greater detail in Chapter 36.

Thus 50 per cent of world trade is between different industrial countries, and only 14 per cent does not involve industrial countries at all. Table 33-3 tells us that world trade and world income are organized around the rich industrial countries.

Table 33-2 Exports as % of GDP

	1967	1998
Belgium	36	75
Netherlands	43	55
UK	18	27
France	14	26
Italy	17	26
USA	5	11
Japan	10	11

Source: IMF, *International Financial Statistics*.

Table 33-1 The value of world exports

	1928	1935	1950	1973	1998
World exports (billions of 1990 £)	277	117	176	931	5460
(% of US GNP)	57	27	20	40	64

Sources: League of Nations, *Europe's Trade*, Geneva, 1941; IMF, *International Financial Statistics*; *National Income Accounts of the United States*, 1928–49.

Table 33-3 Trade patterns, 1996

	Industrial countries	LDCs
% of world trade from industrial countries	50	18
LDCs	18	14
% of world income	80	20

Sources: GATT, *Directions of Trade*; World Bank, *World Development Report*.

Table 33-4	The composition of world exports	
% share of	1955	1995
Primary commodities:	50.5	22.5
Food, agricultural goods	22.3	11.8
Fuels	11.2	7.4
Other minerals	3.8	3.3
Manufactures	49.5	74.7

Sources: GATT, *Networks of World Trade 1955–76*, Geneva; UNCTAD, *Handbook of International Trade and Development Statistics*.

Table 33-5	Trade patterns, mid-1990s		
	EU	N. America	Asia
% of exports			
Primary	19	21	16
Manufactures	79	73	83
% of imports			
Primary	25	18	28
Manufactures	73	79	69

Source: GATT, *International Trade*.

The commodity composition of trade

Services account for most of the GDP of rich countries and are a rapidly growing part of international trade, but from a small baseline. The reason trade in goods – or merchandise trade – remains important is that many countries import goods, add a little value and then re-export them. The value added makes a small contribution to GDP but gross flows of imports and exports of goods are large.

Table 33-4 shows which goods are being internationally traded. It distinguishes between *primary commodities* (agricultural commodities, minerals, and fuels) and manufactured or processed commodities (chemicals, steel, cars, etc.). Note in particular the sharp declining share of *non-fuel* primary commodities, which fell from 39.3 per cent of world trade in 1955 to only 15.1 per cent in 1995.[1] In contrast, the share of manufactures in world trade rose by over 25 per cent.

Examples of trade patterns

Table 33-5 completes our introduction to the basic facts about world trade. We show the breakdown of exports and imports for selected countries. Although the EU is chiefly an exporter of manufactures, primary commodities account for one-fifth of exports. And although the EU has to import many raw materials, imports of wholly or partly finished manufactures account for three-quarters of EU imports. US trade exhibits the same general pattern.

Asian countries have similar trade patterns but typically export fewer primary products and import more primary products than the EU or North America. Asia concentrates heavily on exports of manufactures: in Europe we buy lots of products from Nissan, Sony, Pentax, Proton and Daewoo.

World trade: the facts and the issues

Tables 33-1 to 33-5 set out the basic facts about world trade. First, world trade has been growing more quickly than world income, and is increasingly important. Second, world trade centres on the industrialized countries. Half of all international trade takes place between these countries and they are also the most important export markets for LDCs. Third, about a fifth of world trade is in primary products, the remainder in manufactures.

These facts help explain some of the key issues in world trade that we discuss in Part 5. We introduce three issues at once.

Raw materials prices LDCs worry that the industrial countries are exploiting them by buying raw materials at a low price and sending them back, in the form of manufactures, at a much higher price. Producers of coffee, sugar, copper, and many other products would like to be able to copy OPEC and triple the price of their primary products without suffering a significant reduction in the quantities demanded.

Manufactured exports from LDCs The LDCs want to make their own manufactured goods and export them to the industrial countries. Brazil, Mexico, and Korea already have major manufacturing industries. But exports to industrial countries have led to complaints in industrial countries that jobs are being threatened by competition from cheap foreign labour.

Trade disputes between the industrial countries In some industries, such as motor cars and steel, established producers in the UK, the United States, and the EU are being undercut by efficient modern producers, especially from Japan and East Asia. Should Asian exports be restricted to prevent massive job losses in Western Europe and North America, or should these countries take advantage of low costs in Asia?

---

[1] Calculated by subtracting the share of fuels from the share of primary commodities in Table 33-4.

These are the kind of issues that we shall be examining. First we need to analyse why international trade takes place at all.

33-2 Comparative advantage

We start by showing the benefits of trade when there are international differences in the opportunity cost of goods.

The **opportunity cost** of a good is the quantity of other goods sacrificed to make one more unit of that good.

Suppose a closed economy with given resources can make video recorders or shirts. The more resources are used to make videos, the less resources can be used to make shirts. The opportunity cost of videos is the quantity of shirt output sacrificed by using resources to make videos instead of shirts.

Opportunity costs tell us about the *relative* costs of producing different goods. We now develop a model in which international differences in relative production costs determine the pattern of international trade. The model demonstrates the law of comparative advantage.

The **law of comparative advantage** states that countries specialize in producing and exporting the goods that they produce at a lower *relative cost* than other countries.[2]

There are many reasons why opportunity costs or relative costs may differ in different countries. We begin with a very simple model in which technology or productivity is the source of the difference. Suppose there are two countries, the United States and the UK, producing two goods, video recorders and shirts. We pretend that labour is the only factor of production and there are constant returns to scale. Table 33-6 shows the assumptions about production costs. It takes 30 hours of American labour to produce one video and 5 hours to produce one shirt. UK labour is less productive. It takes 60 hours of British labour to produce one video and 6 hours to produce one shirt.

Costs and prices

For simplicity, we assume that there is perfect competition. Hence the price of each good equals its marginal cost. Since there are constant returns to scale, marginal costs equal

Table 33-6 Production techniques and costs

	USA	UK
Unit labour requirement (hours/output unit)		
Videos	30	60
Shirts	5	6
Wage per hour	$6	£2
Unit labour cost		
Videos	$180	£120
Shirts	$30	£12

average costs. Hence prices equal average costs of production. Because labour is the only factor of production in our example, average costs are given by the value of labour input per unit of output, the unit labour cost.

We assume that American workers earn $6 an hour and British workers £2 an hour. The last two rows of Table 33-6 show the unit labour costs of the two goods in each country. In the absence of international trade, each country produces both goods and these unit labour costs are the domestic prices for which the goods are sold.

American unit labour requirements are *absolutely* lower for *both* goods than those in the UK. But American labour is *relatively* more productive in videos than in shirts. It takes twice as many labour hours to produce a video in the UK as it does in the United States but only 6/5 times as many hours to produce a shirt. These relative productivity differences are the basis for international trade.

Allowing international trade

Suppose the countries can now trade with each other. In this section we make two key points. First, if each country concentrates on producing the good that it makes relatively cheaply, the two countries together can make more of *both* goods. Trade leads to a pure gain, additional output to be shared between the two countries. Second, the free market will provide the right incentives for this beneficial trade to occur.

The countries trade. Since they use different currencies, a foreign exchange market must be set up and an equilibrium exchange rate established. In Chapter 29 we saw that a country's balance of payments accounts include financial flows on the capital account as well as trade flows on the current account. A current account surplus must be offset by a capital account deficit (including any government transactions using foreign exchange reserves), or vice versa. However, the current account must be zero in long-run equilibrium. For simplicity we ignore the capital account

---

[2] This law was first formulated by the great English economist David Ricardo (1772–1823), who was a successful stockbroker before retiring at the age of 40 to become a member of Parliament and an economist. Ricardo's arguments have a modern ring to them because he used models, clearly stating their assumptions and implications.

Table 33-7   Costs, prices, and the range of equilibrium exchange rates

| | Domestic price | | Cost in £ at an exchange rate of: | | | | | |
| | | | $2.50/£ | | $2/£ | | $1.50/£ | |
	Videos	Shirts	Videos	Shirts	Videos	Shirts	Videos	Shirts
US goods	$180	$30	£72	£12	£90	£15	£120	£20
UK goods	£120	£12	£120	£12	£120	£12	£120	£12

and assume that the equilibrium exchange rate is determined to make the value of imports equal to the value of exports, thus balancing the trade account.

Table 33-7 shows the unit labour cost and price of videos and shirts in different currencies and then shows their price in pounds at three possible exchange rates: $2.50/£, $2/£, and $1.50/£. The domestic prices are based on the unit cost data shown in Table 33-6. The price in pounds of UK goods is unaffected by the exchange rate. The more dollars to the pound, the cheaper are both US goods when valued in pounds. At the exchange rate of $2.50 the price in pounds of both US goods is exactly three-fifths their price in pounds when the exchange rate is $1.50/£.

At the exchange rate of $2.50, US videos are cheaper in pounds than British videos but the prices of British and American shirts are exactly the same. If the exchange rate offers more than $2.50 per pound, even US shirts will cost less in pounds. The equilibrium exchange rate *cannot* lie above $2.50, for then everyone would want to buy US goods and nobody would want to buy UK goods.[3] A one-way flow in trade and foreign exchange cannot be an equilibrium.

Conversely, at $1.50/£ US shirts are now more expensive than UK shirts but video prices are the same. If the exchange rate is any lower than $1.50/£ both US goods will be more expensive than UK goods when valued in the same currency. For example, at $1/£, US videos cost £180 and US shirts cost £30. Hence at any exchange rate below £1.50/£ there will be a one-way flow of trade and foreign exchange, though it will now be UK not US goods that everyone wants to buy.

The foreign exchange market can be in equilibrium only if the value of UK imports, and hence the demand for dollars with which to purchase them, is equal to the value of UK exports, and hence the supply of dollars as UK exporters convert their revenues back into pounds. Hence the highest

possible equilibrium exchange rate is $2.50/£, the exchange rate at which one UK good (shirts) is still just competitive with US shirts; and the lowest possible equilibrium exchange rate is $1.50/£, the exchange rate at which one US good (videos) is still just competitive with UK goods.

Table 33-7 shows one intermediate exchange rate, $2/£. The exact position of the equilibrium exchange rate will depend on the demand for videos and shirts. If the United States is large relative to the UK, US demand for imports of UK shirts will tend to be larger than UK demand for US videos. To balance trade, the equilibrium exchange rate must be close to $2.50/£, the top of the feasible range, to make the pound price of US videos low and the dollar price of UK shirts high, encouraging the UK to import videos and discouraging the United States from importing shirts. We can draw this conclusion from our analysis.

Regardless of a country's domestic production costs or **absolute advantage** in producing goods more cheaply, there always exists an exchange rate that will allow that country to produce at least one good more cheaply than other countries when all goods are valued in a common currency. At the equilibrium exchange rate, the country must have at least one good it can export to pay for its imports.

Production and trade patterns

Consider again the range of feasible exchange rates shown in Table 33-7. At $2.50/£ the UK is importing cheaper US videos. In return, the UK must be exporting shirts to the United States. At $2.50/£, the UK can just compete with US shirt producers.

At $2/£, UK producers have a competitive edge over US shirt producers. The UK still exports shirts and, although the pound price of US videos has risen, the UK still imports US videos, which remain cheaper than videos produced in the UK. And even at $1.50/£ the UK must be importing US videos, although they cost just the same in pounds as UK videos. Otherwise the United States would be unable to pay for the shirts it is importing from the UK at a price that now undercuts US producers by a considerable margin.

---

[3] If both US goods are cheaper than British goods when valued in pounds, they must also be cheaper when valued in dollars. We simply multiply all prices in pounds by the *same* exchange rate to get the corresponding dollar prices.

BOX 33-1 — Comparative advantage and the gains from trade

The table summarizes earlier data on unit labour requirements (ULR) in labour hours per unit output, unit labour cost (ULC) in domestic prices, and opportunity cost (OC) in domestic goods forgone. With lower unit labour requirements, the United States has an *absolute advantage* in both goods. One way to calculate *comparative advantage* is to compare ULRs across countries. Relative to the UK, the United States needs relatively less labour to produce videos than to produce shirts. The United States has a comparative advantage in videos, the UK in shirts.

Alternatively, we can compare opportunity costs, OC. By sacrificing 6 shirts, the United States gets 30 labour hours which make an extra video. More simply, 6 shirts cost $180, the price of 1 video. The opportunity cost of a video is 6 shirts in the United States and 10 shirts in the UK. But the opportunity cost of a shirt in the UK (1/10 of a video) is less than in the United States (1/6 of a video). Hence, again, the United States has a comparative advantage in videos and the UK in shirts. When there are many factor inputs, this method of calculating comparative advantage is simpler. We look at domestic relative prices reflecting opportunity costs.

The gains from trade

To produce 60 shirts, the UK gives up production of 6 videos. To produce 6 videos, the United States gives up only 36 shirts. Trade and international specialization allow the world economy to have an extra 24 shirts with no loss of videos. Or if the United States produces another 10 videos, giving up 60 shirts, the world economy has an extra 4 videos with no loss of shirts. These are the *gains from trade*. Only when opportunity costs are the *same* in both countries are there no gains to exploit. Suppose it now takes 10 hours of UK labour to produce a shirt. In both countries videos and shirts exchange in the ratio of 6 shirts per video. No country has a comparative advantage in either good, and there is no gain from trade. We reach the same conclusion using the first method of calculating comparative advantage. The United States uses half as much labour as the UK in producing each good and has no *comparative* advantage.

	ULR	ULC	OC
USA			
Videos	30	$180	6 shirts
Shirts	5	$30	1/6 video
UK			
Videos	60	£120	10 shirts
Shirts	6	£12	1/10 video

Thus, for any exchange rate in the feasible range that could balance trade between the United States and the UK, the UK always exports shirts and the United States always exports videos. Trade leads the UK to produce more shirts than it needs for domestic consumption and leads the United States to produce more videos than it needs for domestic consumption. The UK specializes in producing shirts and the United States specializes in producing videos. We now explain why.

Comparative advantage

This pattern of trade and production illustrates the law of comparative advantage. Countries specialize in producing the goods they make *relatively* cheaply. Although the United States has a lower absolute labour requirement for both goods, the relative cost of videos is lower in the United States, and the relative cost of shirts higher, than in the UK.

In the United States, where videos cost $180 and shirts $30, videos are 6 times the price of shirts. In the UK, where shirts cost £12 and videos £120, videos are 10 times the price of shirts. Making videos costs less relative to shirts in the United States than it does in the UK. The *opportunity cost* of videos is lower in the United States, which must give up 6 shirts to make another video. Conversely, the opportunity cost of shirts is lower in the UK than in the United States. The UK must give up only 1/10 of a video to make another shirt but the United States must give up 1/6 of a video to make another shirt. The law of comparative advantage says that the UK will specialize in shirts, which have a low opportunity cost for UK producers, and the United States will specialize in videos, which have a low opportunity cost for US producers. We discuss comparative advantage further in Box 33-1 opposite.

The reason that production and trade patterns depend on *comparative* advantage and *relative* costs is that the level of the equilibrium exchange rate will take care of differences in absolute advantage. Even though US producers have lower unit labour requirements for both goods, a sufficiently low dollar–sterling exchange rate will make US goods exorbitantly expensive in the UK and UK goods outrageously cheap in the United States. Beginning from a high $/£ exchange rate at which no UK goods can compete with US goods, which of the UK goods first becomes competitive as the exchange rate falls? The answer is, the good in which the UK has a comparative advantage or lower opportunity costs.

The principle of comparative advantage has many applications in everyday life. Suppose two students share a flat. One is faster both at making the dinner and at vacuuming the carpet. But if tasks are allocated according to absolute advantage, the other student is not helping at all. The jobs will get done most quickly if each student does the task at which he or she is relatively faster.

Many goods

The principle of comparative advantage continues to hold when there are more than two goods. Table 33-8 shows a range of commodities. The first two rows show the unit labour requirements for production of each good in the United States and in the UK. In the third row we show the unit labour requirement in the United States relative to the UK.

We have ranked the commodities in order. Beginning at the left, the United States has the largest comparative advantage in computers, where its relative unit labour requirement is only 1/6 that of the UK. Next comes cars, where the US relative labour requirement is one-half that in the UK; then TVs, textiles, glass, and finally shoes. The comparative advantage of the United States declines as we move to the right in the table.

Conversely, the UK has the largest comparative advantage in producing shoes. This is the good in which UK producers are most efficient relative to those in the United States. As we move to the left in the table, the comparative advantage of the UK declines. Producers in the United States become increasingly efficient relative to producers in the UK.

The United States has an absolute advantage in producing computers, cars, TVs, and textiles, but the UK has an absolute advantage in producing glass and shoes. Nevertheless, absolute advantage plays no direct part in the analysis. It is comparative advantage that counts.

Differences in capital–labour ratios

Consider the UK and Hong Kong. The UK has more capital (machinery and buildings) and more labour than Hong Kong, partly because the UK is a bigger country. But it also has *relatively* more capital than Hong Kong. The UK has more capital per worker than Hong Kong.

What is this likely to imply about the relative price of hiring labour and capital in the two countries? With more capital per worker, the marginal product of labour will be higher in the UK than in Hong Kong. This tends to make real wages higher in the UK than in Hong Kong. Conversely, the number of workers per unit of capital is lower in the UK than in Hong Kong. The marginal product of capital and the rental of capital will tend to be lower in the UK, where machinery is relatively plentiful, than in Hong Kong, where machinery is relatively scarce. Because the UK is supplied or endowed with more capital relative to labour than Hong Kong, the cost of using labour relative to capital is likely to be higher in the UK than in Hong Kong.

What does this international difference in the cost of renting factors imply for the relative prices of goods in the two domestic economies? Goods made by labour-intensive methods are likely to cost more relative to goods produced by capital-intensive methods in the UK than in Hong Kong. Suppose car production is capital-intensive with sophisticated assembly lines, but textile production is

Table 33-8	Unit labour requirements and comparative advantage: many goods (hours of labour input per unit output)					
	Computers	Cars	TVs	Textiles	Glass	Shoes
US goods	200	300	50	5	7	15
UK goods	1200	600	90	8	6	10
US/UK relative unit labour requirement	1/6	1/2	5/9	5/8	7/6	3/2

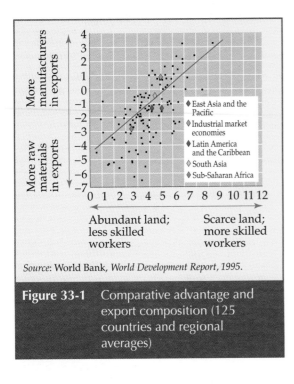

Source: World Bank, *World Development Report*, 1995.

Figure 33-1 Comparative advantage and export composition (125 countries and regional averages)

labour-intensive with a lot of fiddly jobs that can only be done by hand. The price of cars relative to textiles is likely to be lower in the UK than in Hong Kong.

We thus reach the following conclusion. A *relatively* abundant supply or endowment of one factor of production tends to make the cost of renting that factor relatively cheap. Goods that use that factor relatively intensively will therefore be relatively cheap. They will be the goods in which the country has a comparative advantage. Thus the UK, which is relatively generously supplied with capital relative to labour, should export capital-intensive cars to Hong Kong. Hong Kong, which is relatively well endowed with labour, should export labour-intensive textiles to the UK. Differences in relative factor supply are an important explanation for comparative advantage and the pattern of international trade.

Figure 33-1 offers some evidence in favour of this analysis. It emphasizes skills, or human capital, rather than physical capital, although, of course, the two are usually correlated. Countries with scarce land but abundant skills tend to have the high shares of manufactures in their exports; countries with lots of land but few skills typically export raw materials. The figure also shows regional averages. Africa lies at one end, the industrial countries at the other.

We now have two explanations for comparative advantage or international differences in relative production costs.

First, there is the Ricardian explanation of international differences in technology: differences in relatively physical productivity and relative unit labour requirements. Second, even if countries have access to the same technology and there are no physical differences in productivity, the domestic relative price of goods may differ across countries because the relative cost of renting factor inputs differs across countries. Where a factor is in relatively abundant supply, goods that use that factor relatively intensively are likely to be relatively cheaper than in other countries.

33-3 Intra-industry trade

The theory suggests that different countries have a comparative advantage in different goods and specialize in producing these goods for the world economy. It explains why the UK exports cars to Hong Kong and imports textiles from Hong Kong. It does not explain why the UK exports cars (Rovers, Jaguars, etc.) to Germany while simultaneously importing cars (Mercedes, Audis, etc.) from Germany.

Intra-industry trade is two-way trade in goods made within the same industry.

Of course, a Jaguar is not exactly the same commodity as a Mercedes, nor is Danish Carlsberg exactly the same commodity as Fosters lager. We are now discussing industries each making a wide range of different, and highly substitutable, products which enjoy some brand allegiance.

In analysing intra-industry trade, we must take account of three factors. First, consumers like a wide choice of brands. They don't want exactly the same car or radio as everyone else. Second, there are important economies of scale. Instead of each country trying to make small quantities of each brand in each industry, it makes sense for the UK to make Jaguars, Germany to make Mercedes, and Sweden to make Volvos, and then swap them around through international trade. Third, the tendency to specialize in a particular brand, to which the demand for diversity and the possibility of scale economies gives rise, is limited by transport costs. Intra-industry trade between Germany and Sweden is likely to be larger than intra-industry trade between Germany and Japan.

To measure the importance of intra-industry trade we define an index as zero when trade in a particular commodity is entirely one-way: a country either exports or imports the good, but not both. At the opposite extreme, the index equals 1 when there is a complete two-way trade in a

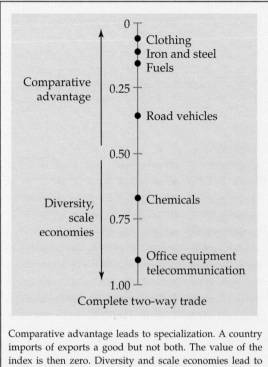

Comparative advantage leads to specialization. A country imports of exports a good but not both. The value of the index is then zero. Diversity and scale economies lead to different countries specializing in different brands within the same industry. When a country imports as much of a good as it exports, the value of the index is unity. Actual values of the index of US trade in selected commodities are shown.

Figure 33-2 US trade patterns

Table 33-9 Index of intra-industry trade

	EC	Japan
Primary commodities	0.58	0.05
All manufactures	0.80	0.20
Road vehicles	0.70	0.02
Household appliances	0.80	0.04
Textiles	0.91	0.36
Other consumer goods	0.80	0.44
Weighted average	0.83	0.23

Source: GATT, *International Trade.*

tariffs – the larger is the extent of intra-industry trade we expect. Table 33-9 compares intra-industry trade indices for the European Union and Japan.

Japan's trade is substantially one-way. Primary commodities are imported and manufactures are exported. There are very few industries in which Japan is simultaneously importing and exporting. Hence the index of intra-industry trade is low for most goods.

In contrast, the EU has a more diversified resource endowment and is a more integrated market, in which distance, information barriers, and tariffs are relatively unimportant. Intra-industry trade is extensive and the value of the index is high for most commodities. The gain from trade arises less from the exploitation of differences in relative prices across countries than from the increase in diversity and specialization in brands, with the consequent reductions in unit costs through the economies of scale that a larger international market allows.

33-4 Gainers and losers

Countries trade because they have a comparative advantage based either on a relative advantage in technology or on relative factor abundance, or because different countries specialize in producing different brands when economies of scale exist. In the latter case the gain from trade is the reduction in average costs that economies of scale allow. Since it takes less factor input to make each output unit, the world economy can produce more goods from its given stock of factor inputs. In the former case, where trade is based on cross-country differences in opportunity costs, Box 33-1 on page 558 shows that trade again allows the world economy to produce more output from any given stock of factor inputs.

These results tell us that the world economy gains when countries first begin international trade: some trade is better than no trade. But they do not tell us that everything that

commodity: a country imports as much of the commodity as it exports. Figure 33-2 shows the index for trade by the world's largest trading nation, the United States.

At one extreme we have clothing, in which there is little two-way trade. The United States imports clothing but exports very little. Its trade in fuels is also explained by the principles of comparative advantage. At the other extreme we have office equipment (including telecommunications). Here trade is almost completely two-way. As a general principle, the more commodities are undifferentiated goods (fuel, steel), the more we expect comparative advantage based on relative resource abundance to dictate trade patterns. As we move towards finished manufactures, product differentiation becomes dominant and comparative advantage loses some of its overriding role. Intra-industry trade becomes more significant in cars and office equipment.

The more closely markets are integrated, and the lower are the obstacles to trade – in terms both of distance and

happens in the world economy makes everyone better off. We now give two examples of the conflicts to which international trade gives rise.

Refrigeration

At the end of the nineteenth century, the invention of refrigeration enabled Argentina to become a supplier of frozen meat to the world market. Argentina's exports of meat, non-existent in 1900, had risen to 400 000 tons a year by 1913. The United States, with exports of 150 000 tons in 1900, had virtually stopped exporting beef by 1913.

Who gained and who lost? In Argentina the entire economy was transformed. Cattle grazers and meat exporters attracted resources. Owners of cattle and land gained; other land users lost out because, with higher demand, land rents increased. Argentine consumers found their steaks becoming more expensive as meat was shipped abroad. Although Argentina's GNP increased significantly, the benefits of trade were not equally distributed. Some people in Argentina were worse off.

In Europe and the United States, cheaper beef made consumers better off. But beef producers lost out because beef prices fell.

Refrigeration opened up the world economy to Argentinian beef producers. As a whole, the world economy gained. In principle, it would have been possible for the gainers to compensate the losers and still have something left over. But, in practice, gainers do not often offer compensation to losers. So some people lost out. In this example the major losers were beef producers elsewhere in the world, and other users of land in Argentina.

The UK car industry

The second example is the UK car industry. Table 33-10 shows that, as recently as 1971, imports of cars were only 15 per cent of the domestic market while exports were 35 per cent of the sales of UK car producers. Since 1971 UK car manufacturers have been losing their share of the domestic market to foreign imports. By 1996 imports were 59 per cent of the UK market. Exports recovered in the 1990s, in part

Table 33-10	The UK car industry		
	1971	1990	1996
Ratio of:			
Imports to home sales	0.15	0.51	0.59
Exports to UK car output	0.35	0.33	0.51
Source: ONS, *Annual Abstracts of Statistics*.			

because Nissan and Toyota established major UK plants to produce not just for the UK market but for export within the EU.

UK car buyers and producers of foreign cars benefited from the increase in UK imports of cheaper foreign cars. But Rover, the major UK car producer, had a tough time and there were redundancies among its workforce. The UK government faced pressure to restrict UK imports of cars to prevent further job losses in the car industry.

Restricting car imports to the UK would help the UK car industry but raise car prices to UK consumers of cars. Should the government heed the wishes of producers or consumers? More generally, how should we decide whether to restrict imports or have free unrestricted trade in all goods? We now develop the general theory of how to analyse the costs and benefits of tariffs or other types of trade restriction. In so doing, we move from *positive economics*, the analysis of the reasons for, and the pattern of, world trade, to *normative economics*, the study of how the government should choose its commercial policy.

Commercial policy is government policy that influences international trade through taxes or subsidies or through direct restrictions on imports and exports.

33-5 The economics of tariffs

The most common type of trade restriction is a tariff or import duty.

An **import tariff** requires the importer of a good to pay a specified fraction of the world price to the government.

If t is the tariff rate, expressed as a decimal fraction (e.g. 0.2), the domestic price of imported goods will be $(1 + t)$ times the world price of the imported good. By raising the domestic price of imports, a tariff helps domestic producers but hurts domestic consumers.

The free trade equilibrium

In Figure 33-3 we study the domestic market for cars. Suppose the UK faces a given world price of cars, say £10 000 per car, shown by the solid horizontal line. Schedules DD and SS represent the demand for cars by UK consumers and the supply of cars by UK producers. We assume that domestic and foreign cars are perfect substitutes. Consumers will buy whichever is cheaper.

At a price of £10 000, UK consumers wish to purchase Q_d cars. They want to be at the point G on the demand curve. Domestic firms wish to produce only Q_s cars at this price.

The difference between domestic supply Q_s and domestic demand Q_d comes from imports.

Equilibrium with a tariff

Now the government levies a 20 per cent tariff on imported cars. Car importers have to charge £12 000 to cover their costs inclusive of the tariff. The broken horizontal line at this price shows that importers are willing to sell any number of cars in the domestic market at a price of £12 000. The tariff raises the domestic tariff-inclusive price above the world price.

What is the effect of the tariff on domestic consumption and production of cars? By raising domestic car prices, the tariff encourages domestic car production. Firms increase production from Q_s to Q_s'. The tariff provides protection for domestic producers by raising the domestic price at which imports becomes competitive. In moving up the supply curve from point C to point E, domestic producers whose marginal costs lie between £10 000 and £12 000 find that they can now survive because the domestic price of imports has been raised by the tariff.

On the demand side, the price increase moves consumers up their demand curve from point G to point F. The quantity

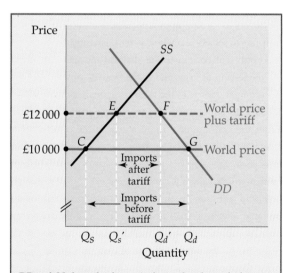

DD and SS show the domestic demand and supply for cars. In the absence of a tariff, consumers can import cars at a price of £10 000. In free trade equilibrium, domestic producers produce at C and domestic consumers consume at G. The quantity of imported cars is CG. Q_d is the total quantity demanded. Domestic production Q_s is supplemented by imports ($Q_d - Q_s$). A 20 per cent tariff raises the domestic price of imports to £12 000. Domestic output is now at E and consumers consume at F. Imports fall from CG to EF.

Figure 33-3 The effect of a tariff

of cars demanded falls from Q_d to Q_d'. From the consumers' viewpoint, the tariff is like a tax. Consumers have to pay more for cars.

Figure 33-3 shows the combined effect of the increase in domestic production and the reduction in domestic consumption: namely a fall in imports. Imports fall both because domestic production increases *and* because domestic consumption is reduced. For any given tariff, the extent of the reduction in imports will depend on the slopes of the domestic supply and demand schedules. The more elastic these schedules are, the more a given increase in the domestic tariff-inclusive price will reduce imports. When both schedules are very steep, the tariff-induced rise in the domestic price will have little effect on the quantity of imports.

Costs and benefits of a tariff

Figure 33-4 provides a detailed accounting of the costs and benefits of imposing a tariff. We have to be careful to distinguish *net costs to society* from *transfers* between one part of the economy and another.

We start by noting that, after the tariff has been imposed, consumers purchase the quantity Q_d'. Since the price to the consumer has risen by £2000, consumers are spending (£2000 × Q_d') *more* than it would previously have cost them to buy the same quantity Q_d' at the world price. We begin by discussing who gets these extra payments, which in total are given by the area *LFHJ* in Figure 33-4.

Some of the extra consumer payments go to the government, whose revenue from the tariff is the rectangle *EIHF*, being the tariff of £2000 per imported car times ($Q_d' - Q_s'$) the number of imported cars. This transfer, *EIHF*, from consumers to the government is *not* a net cost to society. For example, the government may use the tariff revenue to reduce income tax rates.

Increased consumer payments also go in part to firms as extra profits. Firms receive a higher domestic price for their output. The supply curve shows how much firms need to cover the extra cost of producing Q_s' rather than Q_s. Hence the area *ECJL* shows the increase in firms' profits. It measures the extra revenue from higher prices not required to meet increased production costs. Thus *ECJL* represents a transfer from consumers to the pure profits or economic rent earned by firms. It is not a net cost to society as a whole.

What about the shaded area A? This is part of the area *LFHJ* showing extra consumer payments, but it is neither revenue for the government nor extra profits for firms. It *is* a net cost to society: the cost of supporting inefficient domestic firms.

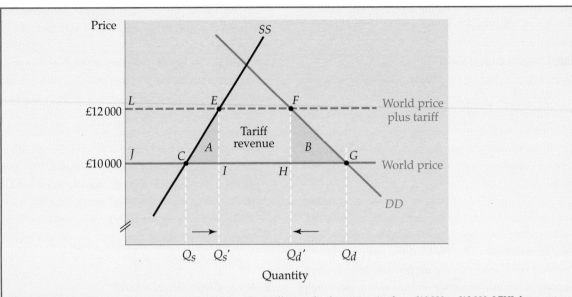

The tariff leads both to transfers and to net social losses. The tariff raises the domestic price from £10 000 to £12 000. *LFHJ* shows extra consumer payments of the Q_d' cars they now buy. But *EFHI* is a transfer to the government and *ECJL* is a transfer to extra profits of producers. Areas *A* and *B* are pure waste and net social losses. Triangle *A* is the extra that society spends by producing cars domestically instead of importing them at the world price. Triangle *B* is the excess of consumer benefits over social marginal cost that society sacrifices by reducing its consumption of cars from Q_d to Q_d'.

Figure 33-4   The welfare costs of a tariff

The supply curve *SS* shows the marginal cost of making the last car in the home economy. But society *could* import cars from the rest of the world in unlimited quantities at the world price £2000. This world price is the true marginal cost of cars to the domestic economy. The triangle *A* shows the resources that society is wasting by producing the quantity $(Q_s' - Q_s)$ domestically when it could have been imported at a lower cost. The resources drawn into domestic car production could be used more efficiently elsewhere in the economy.

There is a second net loss to society, the triangle labelled *B*. Suppose the tariff was abolished and free trade restored. The quantity of cars demanded would increase to Q_d. The triangle *B* shows the excess of consumer benefits, as measured by the height of the demand curve showing how much consumers are prepared to pay for the last unit demanded, over the marginal costs of expanding from Q_d' to Q_d, the world price at which imports could be purchased. Conversely, by imposing the tariff, society incurs a net loss equal to the shaded triangle *B*. It shows the net benefit society has given up by reducing the quantity of cars purchased by consumers.

To sum up, when we begin from free trade equilibrium and then impose a tariff, the subsequent rise in the domestic price leads both to transfers and to pure waste. Money

is transferred from consumers to the government and to producers. As a first approximation, the net cost of these transfers to society as a whole is zero. This approximation is exact only if all consumers are identical and share equally in the ownership of firms and in the benefits of whatever the government does with the tariff revenue. In practice this is unlikely to be the case, and we shall also have to worry about the distributional implications of the transfers. For example, if the government uses the tariff revenue on car imports to subsidize city buses, rural car users will be hurt by the tariff but city bus users will benefit.

But in addition to the transfers and potential distributional effects, a tariff involves pure waste. Society can always import cars at the world price. In the post-tariff equilibrium, the domestic price of cars exceeds the world price. Since consumers buy cars until the marginal benefits of the last car equals the price they have to pay, the last car purchased is worth more to consumers than the world price at which the country as a whole could get another car. Consumers are consuming too little. Conversely, domestic producers are producing too many cars. Domestic producers will expand car production until the domestic price just covers the cost of making the last car. Since this exceeds the world price, society is paying domestic producers more for the last car than it would have to pay foreigners for a

---

BOX 33-2   Twentieth century falls

Tariff reduction is only part of the story behind booming international trade. The diagram shows how costs of doing international business plummeted after 1920.

Source: World Bank, *World Development Report*, 1995

- Sea transport
- Air transport
- Telephone call
- Freight
- Satellite use

Table 33-11   Arguments for tariffs

Type	Example
First-best	Foreign trade monopoly
Second-best	Way of life, Anti-luxury, Infant industry, Defence, Revenue
Strategic	Games against foreigners
Non-argument	Cheap foreign labour

similar car. Society would do better to use less resources in the car industry and to transfer these resources to an export industry which could earn enough foreign exchange to import cars at the cheaper world price. In Figure 33-4 the two triangles *A* and *B* show the waste arising from domestic overproduction and domestic underconsumption of cars. They are a *deadweight burden* or pure waste. This is the *case for free trade*.

Does this mean that tariffs should never be imposed? We now examine some of the most frequently heard arguments in favour of tariffs.

33-6 Good and bad arguments for tariffs

Table 33-11 lists some of these arguments. We group them under several headings. The *first-best* argument is a case where a tariff is *the* best way to achieve a given objective. *Second-best* arguments are cases where the policy would indeed be beneficial but where there is another policy that would be even better if only it could be implemented. Non-arguments are cases in which the claimed benefits are partly or completely fallacious.

The optimal tariff: the first-best argument for tariffs

In presenting the case for free trade, we were careful to assume that the domestic economy could import as many cars as it wished without bidding up the world price of cars. For a small economy this may be a reasonable assumption. However, when a country's imports form a significant share of the world market for a commodity, a higher level of imports is likely to bid up the world price.

In this case, the world price of the last unit imported is *lower* than the true cost of the last import to the domestic economy. The domestic economy should recognize that, in demanding another unit of imports, it raises the price it has to pay on the quantity already being imported. But in a free trade world without tariffs, each individual will think only about the price that he or she pays. Although no single individual bids up the price, collectively the individuals of the domestic economy bid up the price of imports.

Under free trade, each individual buys imports up to the point at which the benefit to that individual equals the world price the individual must pay. Since the collective cost of the last import exceeds its world price, the cost of that import to society exceeds its benefit. There are too many imports. Society will gain by restricting imports until the benefit of the last import equals its cost to society as a whole.

When a country has monopoly power in international trade, the **optimal tariff** can restore imports to the level at which social marginal cost and social marginal benefit are equal.

Only when a country does not bid up the world price of its imports is the cost to society of the last unit imported equal to the world price. Then and only then is the optimal tariff zero. There is no longer any reason to discourage imports. That is the case for free trade under those circumstances.

The optimal tariff is a straightforward application of the principles of efficient resource allocation which we discussed in Part 3. There is another way to see how the optimal tariff works. When a country faces an upward-sloping supply curve for its imports, levying a tariff will reduce the world price of the good by moving foreign suppliers down their supply curve as their output falls. Effectively this is a transfer from foreign suppliers, who lose out, to the importing country, which gains.

Second-best arguments for tariffs

We now introduce the principle of targeting.

The **principle of targeting** says that the most efficient way to attain a given objective is to use a policy that influences that activity directly. Policies that attain the objective but also influence other activities are **second best** because they distort these other activities.

The optimal tariff is a first-best application of the principle of targeting precisely because the source of the problem is a divergence between social and private marginal costs in trade itself. That is why a tariff on trade is the most efficient solution. The arguments for tariffs that we now examine are all second-best arguments because the original source of the problem does not directly lie in trade. The principle of targeting assures us that there are ways to solve these problems at a lower net social cost.

Way of life Suppose society wishes to help inefficient farmers or craft industries. It believes that the old way of life, or sense of community, should be preserved. It levies tariffs to protect such groups from foreign competition.

But there is a cheaper way to attain this objective. A tariff helps domestic producers but also hurts domestic consumers through higher prices. A production subsidy would still keep farmers in business and, by tackling the problem directly, would avoid hurting consumers. In terms of Figure 33-4, triangle A shows the net social cost of subsidizing domestic producers so they can produce Q_s' rather than Q_s. But a tariff, the second-best solution, also involves the social cost given by the triangle B.

Suppressing luxuries Some poor countries believe it is wrong to allow their few rich citizens to buy Rolls-Royces or luxury yachts when society needs its resources to stop people starving. A tariff on imports of luxuries will reduce their consumption but, by raising the domestic price, may also provide an incentive for domestic producers to use scarce resources to produce them. A consumption tax tackles the problem directly, and is more efficient.

Defence Some countries believe that, in case there is a war, it is important to preserve domestic industries that produce food or jet fighters. Again, a production subsidy rather than an import tariff is the most efficient way to meet this objective.

Infant industries One of the most common arguments for a tariff is that it allows infant industries to get started. Suppose there is *learning by doing*. Only by actually being in business will firms learn how to reduce costs and become as efficient as foreign competitors. A tariff provides protection to new or infant industries until they master the business and can compete on equal terms with more experienced foreign suppliers.

Society should invest in new industries only if they are socially profitable in the long run. The long-run benefits must outweigh the initial losses during the period when the infant industry is producing at a higher cost than the goods could have been obtained through imports. But in the absence of any divergence between private and social costs or benefits, an industry will be socially profitable only if it is privately profitable.

If the industry is such a good idea in the long run, society should begin by asking why private firms can't borrow the money to see them through the early period when they are losing out to more efficient foreign firms. If the problem is that banks or other lenders are not prepared to risk their money, society should ask whether the industry is such a good idea after all. And if the industry does make sense but there is a problem in the market for lending, the principle of targeting says that the government should intervene by lending money to private firms.

Failing this, a production subsidy during the initial years is still better than a tariff, which also penalizes consumers. And the worst outcome of all is the imposition of a *permanent* tariff, which allows the industry to remain sheltered and less efficient than its foreign competitors long after the benefits of learning-by-doing are supposed to have been achieved. We return shortly to the question of why so many tariffs exist that are justified by the infant industry argument.

Revenue In the eighteenth century, most government revenue came from tariffs. Administratively, it was the simplest tax to collect. Today this remains true in some developing countries. But in modern economies with sophisticated systems of accounting and administration, the administrative costs of raising revenue through tariffs are not lower than the costs of raising revenue through income taxes or taxes on expenditure. The balance of tax collection should be determined chiefly by the considerations examined in Chapter 17: the extent to which taxes induce distortions, inefficiency, and waste, and the extent to which they bring about the distribution of income and wealth desired by the government. The need to raise revenue is not a justification for tariffs themselves.

Strategic trade policy

In Chapter 10 we argued that game theory is a useful tool in analysing strategic conflict between oligopolists. In international trade, strategic rivalry may exist directly, between the giant firms or 'national champions' of different countries, or indirectly, between governments acting on their behalf.

In Chapter 18 we argued that strategic international competition might provide one rationale for domestic industrial policy. We used the example of commercial aircraft. The British government initially subsidized British Aerospace in its participation in Airbus Industrie not only as a pre-commitment to deter Boeing from trying to force Airbus out of the industry, but perhaps also to try to induce the third producer, McDonnell-Douglas, to quit.

Similar considerations arise in trade policy. Levying a tariff on imports, thereby protecting domestic producers, may deter foreigners from attempting a price war to force the domestic producers out of the industry, and may prevent foreign producers from entering the industry.

This sounds like a very general and robust argument for tariffs, but it should be viewed with considerable caution. If

it is attractive for one country to impose tariffs for this purpose, it may be equally attractive for foreigners to retaliate with tariffs of their own. We then reach an equilibrium in which little trade takes place, domestic giants have huge monopoly power since they no longer face effective competition from foreigners, and all countries suffer.

In fact, this game has the structure of the prisoners' dilemma game we introduced in Chapter 10. All countries may be led to impose tariffs even though all would be better off if they were abolished. This suggests there is a role for international co-operation to agree on, and subsequently enforce, low tariff levels. We take up this theme shortly.

Dumping Although the preceding discussion relates to tariffs, it can also be applied to trade subsidies.

Dumping occurs when foreign producers sell at prices below their marginal production cost, either by making losses or with the assistance of government subsidies.

Domestic producers say this is unfair and demand a tariff to protect them from this foreign competition.

If we could be assured the foreigner would supply cheap goods indefinitely, we should say thank you, close down our more expensive industry, and put our resources to work elsewhere. To this extent, dumping is a non-argument for a tariff.

Much more likely, however, the foreign producers, with or without the assistance of their government, are engaged in predatory pricing intended to drive our producers out of the industry. Once the foreigners achieve monopoly power in world markets, they intend to raise prices and cash up.

If so, it may be wise for our government to resist. Even so, for reasons we explained earlier, a production subsidy is the efficient way to insulate our producers from this threat. A tariff has the undesirable side effect of distorting consumer prices.

Non-arguments for tariffs

Cheap foreign labour Home producers frequently argue that tariffs are needed to protect them from cheap foreign labour. However, the whole point of trade is to exploit international differences in the relative prices of different goods. If the domestic economy is relatively well endowed with capital, it benefits from trade precisely because its exports of capital-intensive goods allow it to purchase *more* labour-intensive goods from abroad than would have been obtained by diverting domestic resources to production of labour-intensive goods.

As technology and relative factor endowments change

over time, countries' comparative advantage alters. In the nineteenth century Britain exported Lancashire textiles all over the world. But textile production is relatively labour-intensive. Once the countries of Southeast Asia acquired the technology, it was inevitable that their relatively abundant labour endowment would give them a comparative advantage in producing textiles.

New technology frequently gives a country a temporary comparative advantage in particular products. As time elapses, other countries acquire the technology, and relative factor endowments and relative factor costs become a more important determinant of comparative advantage. Inevitably, the domestic producers who have lost their comparative advantage start complaining about competition from imports using cheap foreign labour.

The basic proof of the gains from trade tells us that in the long run the country as a whole will benefit by facing facts, recognizing that its comparative advantage has changed, and transferring production to the industries in which it now has a comparative advantage. And our analysis of comparative advantage promises us that there *must* be some industry in which each country has a comparative advantage. In the long run, trying to use tariffs to prop up industries that have lost their comparative advantage is both futile and expensive.

Of course, in the short run the adjustment may be painful and costly. Workers lose their jobs and must start afresh in industries where they don't have years of experience and acquired skills. But the principle of targeting tells us that, if society wants to smooth this transition, some kind of retraining or relocation sudsidy is more efficient than a tariff.

Why do we have tariffs?

Aside from the optimal tariff argument, there is almost nothing to be said in favour of tariffs. Economists have been arguing against them for well over a century. Why are tariffs still so popular?

Concentrated benefits, diffuse costs A tariff on a particular commodity helps a particular industry. It is relatively easy for firms and workers in an industry to organize effective political pressure, for they can all agree that this single issue is central to their livelihood, at least in the short run. But if the tariff is imposed, the cost in higher consumer prices is borne by a much larger and more diverse group of people whom it is much harder to organize politically. Hence the politicians are more likely to heed the vociferous, well organized group lobbying *for* tariffs, especially if they are

geographically concentrated in an area where, by voting together, they could have a significant effect on the outcome of the next selection.

Tariffs versus subsidies Even so, why does government assistance frequently take the form of tariffs rather than production subsidies, which are frequently more appropriate? First, because if domestic industry is suffering from imports of Japanese goods, the solution seems to be to do something which will hurt Japan directly. Second, because the government would have to raise taxes to finance a subsidy. A tariff is politically easier in many cases, not merely because it seems to hurt foreign producers, but because it seems to augment government revenues (raising hopes of an income tax cut), whereas a subsidy seems to deplete government revenues (raising fears of a rise in income tax rates). Although we now know that a tariff hits consumers directly by raising the domestic price of the good, the government may be able to invoke impersonal 'market forces'. Tariffs cause the government less political hassle.

33-7 Tariff levels: not so bad?

In the nineteenth century world trade grew rapidly in part because the leading country, the UK, pursued a vigorous policy of free trade. In contrast, US tariffs averaged about 50 per cent, although they had fallen to around 30 per cent by the early 1920s. As the industrial economies went into the Great Depression of the late 1920s and 1930s, there was increasing pressure to protect domestic jobs by keeping out imports. Tariffs in the United States returned to around 50 per cent, and the UK abandoned the policy of free trade that had been pursued for nearly a century.

Table 33-1 showed that the combination of world recession and increasing tariffs led to a disastrous slump in the volume of world trade, further exacerbated by the Second World War.

GATT (now WTO)

After the war there was a collective determination to see world trade restored. Bodies such as the International Monetary Fund and the World Bank were set up and many countries signed the General Agreement on Tariffs and Trade (GATT), a commitment to reduce tariffs successively and dismantle trade restrictions.

Under successive rounds of GATT, tariffs fell steadily. By 1960 US tariffs were only about one-fifth their level at the outbreak of the Second World War. In the UK the system of wartime quotas on imports had been dismantled by the mid-1950s, after which tariffs were reduced by nearly half in the ensuing 25 years. Europe as a whole has moved towards an enlarged European Union in which tariffs between member countries have been abolished.

The GATT Secretariat, now called the World Trade Organization, began the latest round of negotiations – the Seattle round – in 2000, and late in 1999 the USA and China announced an agreement paving the way for Chinese membership of the WTO.

Thus, tariff levels throughout the world are probably as low as they have ever been. And world trade has seen four decades of rapid growth, arising at least in part from the success of GATT in removing trade restrictions.

33-8 Other commercial policies

Tariffs are not the only form of commercial policy. In this section we examine three other policy instruments: quotas, non-tariff barriers, and export subsidies.

Quotas

Quotas are restrictions on the maximum quantity of imports.

For example, the EU now has a ceiling on imports of steel from Eastern Europe. Although quotas restrict the *quantity* of imports, this does not mean they have no effect on domestic prices of the restricted goods. With a lower supply, the equilibrium price will be higher than under free trade.

Thus quotas are rather like tariffs. The domestic price to the consumer is increased, and it is this higher price that allows inefficient domestic producers to produce a higher output than under free trade. Quotas lead to social waste for exactly the same reasons as tariffs.

Because quotas raise the domestic price of the restricted good, the lucky foreign suppliers who succeed in getting some of their goods sold will make large profits on these sales. In terms of Figure 33-4, the rectangle *EFHI*, which would have accrued to the government as revenue from a tariff, now accrues to foreign suppliers or domestic importers. It represents the difference between domestic and world prices on the goods that are imported, multiplied by the quantity of imports allowed.

If these profits accrue to foreigners they represent a net social cost of quotas over and above the costs of imposing an equivalent tariff. However, the government could always auction off licences to import and so recoup this revenue.

Private importers or foreign suppliers would be prepared to bid up to this amount to get their hands on an important licence.

Non-tariff barriers

Non-tariff barriers are administrative regulations that discriminate against foreign goods and in favour of home goods.

They may take the form of delaying imports at the frontier, ordering civil servants to use goods made at home, or merely a publicity campaign to 'buy British'. Non-tariff barriers may also be more subtle. Contracts can specify standards with which domestic producers are familiar but foreign producers are not. The 1992 programme aimed to end non-tariff barriers inside the EU. We study it in detail in Chapter 35.

Export subsidies

So far, we have looked only at restrictions on imports. But countries also use commercial policy to boost exports. This can vary from outright subsidy to cheap credit or exemption from certain domestic taxes.

Export subsidies protect domestic firms by offering government help in competing with foreign firms.

Figure 33-5 shows the economics of an export subsidy. Suppose the world price of a computer is £5000. Under free trade, domestic consumers would purchase a quantity Q_d at point G on their demand curve, producers would make a quantity Q_s at point E on their supply curve, and a quantity GE would be exported.

To boost the computer industry, the government now imposes a 20 per cent *export subsidy* applying only to computers that are exported. On such goods, domestic producers now earn a total of £6000. No firm will sell at home for £5000 when it can sell abroad and get £6000. The supply to the domestic market will be curtailed to Q_d' so that consumers are prepared to pay this price. Total domestic production increases to Q_s' and exports are AB.

Although the subsidy increases exports, it does so at the net social cost given by the shaded triangles H and K. Triangle H measures the net social cost of reducing domestic consumption from Q_d to Q_d'. The consumer benefits from the extra consumption would have exceeded the world price or social marginal cost at which the economy would always have obtained computers. Triangle K measures the social cost of increasing output from Q_s to Q_s' even though the marginal domestic cost of using these

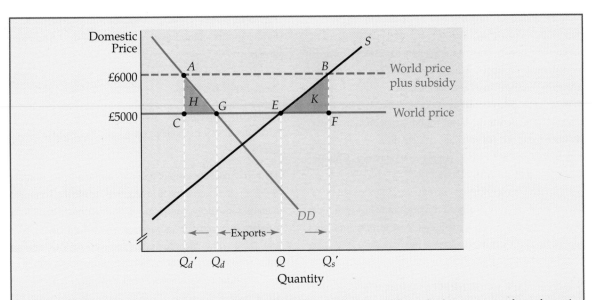

Under free trade, consumers demand Q_d, production is Q_s, and exports are GE. With a subsidy on exports alone, domestic producers will restrict supply to the home market to Q_d' so that home consumers pay £6000, the same as producers can earn by exporting. Total output is Q_s' and exports AB. K shows the social cost of producing goods whose marginal cost exceeds the world price for which they are sold. H shows the social cost of restricting consumption when marginal benefits exceed the world price of the good.

Figure 33-5   An export subsidy

extra resources exceeds the price being received from the foreigners who buy computers.

Just as with a tariff, an export subsidy is usually a second-best policy. Even if the country did wish to increase its output of computers, it would be cheaper to use a production subsidy, incurring the cost of the triangle K, but avoiding the rise in the domestic price and the cost of the triangle H.

SUMMARY

● World trade has grown rapidly over the previous 40 years, and is dominated by the developed industrial countries. Primary commodities make up about 25 per cent of world trade; the rest is trade in manufactures.

● Countries trade because they can buy goods more cheaply from other countries. Differences in international production costs arise from differences in technology and factor endowments. Economies of scale also lead to international specialization.

● Countries produce the goods in which they have a comparative advantage, or produce relatively cheaply. By exploiting international differences in opportunity costs, trade leads to a pure gain.

● The extension of trade theory to more than one factor of production emphasizes *relative* factor endowments. Countries tend to produce and export goods that use intensively the factors with which the country is *relatively* well endowed.

● Intra-industry trade occurs because of scale economies and consumer demand for diversity. The gain from trade is now a larger market and the lower costs that this enables.

● If trade is to balance, and the foreign exchange market is to be in equilibrium, each country must have a comparative advantage in at least one good. The level of the equilibrium exchange rate copes with international differences in absolute advantage.

● Although international trade can benefit the world as a whole, some people will lose out unless the gainers compensate the losers.

● By raising the domestic price, a tariff reduces consumption but increases domestic production. Hence imports fall.

● A tariff leads to two deadweight losses that are net social costs: overproduction by domestic firms whose marginal cost exceeds the world price, and underconsumption by consumers whose marginal benefit exceeds the world price.

● When a country affects the price of its imports, the world price is less than the social marginal cost of importing. This is the case for the optimal tariff. Otherwise, arguments for tariffs are usually second-best solutions. A production subsidy or consumption tax would achieve the objective at lower social cost.

● Export subsidies raise domestic prices, reducing consumption but increasing output and exports. As with a tariff, they involve waste. Goods are exported for less than society's marginal production cost and for less than the marginal benefit to domestic consumers.

● Tariffs have fallen substantially since the Second World War, partly in response to the disastrous collapse of world trade under tariff restrictions of the 1930s. But high unemployment in the 1980s led to new pressure for tariffs and protection.

● Trade protection is usually harmful to society. Yet governments frequently adopt it because it is an easy option politically.

 KEY TERMS

 **REVIEW QUESTIONS**

1 (a) Why does the composition of North American and Asian trade differ in Table 33-5? (b) Which of those patterns do you expect Brazil to resemble more closely? Why?

2 'A country with uniformly low productivity can only lose by allowing foreign competition.' Discuss this assertion in detail.

3 'Large countries gain less from world trade than small countries.' True or False? Why?

4 Suppose in Table 33-8 that the United States produces computers, cars, and TVs and the UK produces the other goods. Now a lot of UK labour goes to live in the United States. What will happen to the pattern of trade and specialization?

5 Stereos, wine, transistor radios, steel sheeting: which of these do you think will have a high index of intra-industry trade? Why?

6 Making TVs has economies of scale. Is this a good argument for imposing a tariff on TV imports?

7 To preserve its national heritage, society bans exports of works of art. (a) Is this better than an export tax? (b) Who gains and who loses from the export ban? (c) Will this measure encourage young domestic artists?

8 *Common fallacies* Show why the following statements are incorrect. (a) British producers are rapidly becoming uncompetitive in every commodity. (b) Free trade is always the best policy. (c) Buy British and help Britain. (d) Tariffs simply transfer money from consumers to producers and the government.

34 The international monetary system

LEARNING OUTCOMES

When you have finished this chapter, you should be able to:

- Consider alternative exchange rate regimes
- Examine the gold standard
- Discuss the adjustable peg Bretton Woods system
- Analyse the determination and behaviour of floating exchange rates
- Examine the rise of capital mobility and the reasons for speculative attacks within adjustable peg systems
- Consider ways in which international linkages give rise to motives for co-ordination of national macroeconomic policies
- Study the European Monetary System as an example of monetary policy co-ordination

Few areas of economics seem as mysterious to the outsider as the economics of exchange rates and international finance. Indeed they are sometimes mysterious even to insiders. It is said that, in speculating on exchange rate changes, Keynes made three fortunes but lost two.

In the previous chapter we studied the pure theory of international trade. It is known as the 'pure theory' because it discusses questions such as comparative advantage by examining the real resources – physical quantities of land, labour, and capital – used to make different goods in different countries. But it does not highlight the monetary mechanism through which international payments are made.

In a closed economy, we distinguish between a barter economy, where goods and services are swapped directly for one another, and a monetary economy, in which people sell goods, services, and assets in exchange for money which is then used to make further purchases of goods, services,

and assets. Money serves as a medium of exchange to reduce transaction costs. In the same way, the international monetary system provides a medium of exchange for international transactions. We now study international payments in more detail.

The exchange rate measures the price at which the two national currencies can be exchanged in the foreign exchange market. Chapter 29 pointed out that several systems of international payments or *exchange rate regimes* are possible. We discussed a fixed exchange rate regime and a regime of freely floating exchange rates.

In Chapter 29 we were chiefly interested in how the adoption of a particular exchange rate regime would affect the operation of domestic monetary and fiscal policies in a particular country. Now we are interested in a different question. What is the implication of a particular exchange rate regime for the world economy as a whole?

We begin the chapter by briefly reviewing the possible

exchange rate regimes. Then we discuss the relative merits of the different regimes. We conclude the chapter by looking at some of the questions raised by the possibility of international economic co-operation and *policy co-ordination*. In Part 4 we discussed only the policy options for a single country acting in isolation. Would the member countries of the world economy be better off if they took deliberate steps to co-ordinate their domestic monetary and fiscal policies? Could this help reduce the world's business cycle? We try to answer these questions. We also examine steps towards international policy co-ordination in Europe.

34-1 Exchange rate regimes

In Chapter 29 we explained that the exchange rate is the price at which two national currencies are traded in the foreign exchange (forex) market. The demand for pounds arises from the desire of foreigners to purchase British goods, services, and assets. Conversely, the supply of pounds to the forex market arises from the British desire to buy foreign goods, services, and assets.

In the absence of government intervention in the forex market, the equilibrium exchange rate will be determined by these supplies and demands. However, the government may *intervene* in the forex market. If you have forgotten the details of how this works, we suggest you go back and read the first part of Chapter 29 before continuing.

An **exchange rate regime** is the policy rule for intervening in the forex market.

Table 34-1 summarizes the regimes that we shall be discussing: the gold standard, a currency board, the adjustable peg, managed floating, and freely floating exchange rates.

The nineteenth-century gold standard is an example of an automatic system with fixed exchange rates. A totally free floating exchange rate is an automatic system with flexible exchange rates. The adjustable peg and managed floating systems allow governments some discretion about how to

intervene using their foreign exchange reserves. We now consider these regimes in more detail.

34-2 The gold standard

There are three distinguishing characteristics of the gold standard. First, the government of each country fixes the price of gold in terms of its domestic currency.

The **par value** of gold is the price of gold in terms of domestic currency.

Second, the government maintains the *convertibility* of domestic currency into gold. The government will buy or sell as much gold as people wish to transact at the par value. Third, the government follows a rule that links domestic money creation to the government's holdings of gold. The government can issue pounds only by buying gold from the general public. If the public converts its paper money back into gold, the stock of outstanding pounds is automatically reduced again. This is called *100 per cent gold backing* for the money supply. Each pound in circulation must be backed by an equivalent value of gold in the vaults of the central bank.

Suppose there are two countries following the three rules of the gold standard: a par value, convertibility, and 100 per cent cover. Suppose the United States has a par value of $20.67 per ounce of gold and the UK a par value of £4.25 per ounce. The dollar–pound exchange rate *must* always be $4.86/£, the ratio of the relative price of gold in the two countries ($20.67/£4.25). At any other exchange rate it would be possible to sell gold in one country and buy gold in the other country, making a profit with certainty. Everyone would be doing it. In the forex market, the flow between currencies would be entirely one way. It could not be an equilibrium. The equilibrium exchange rate *must* equal the relative gold prices in the two currencies.

The **gold standard** was a monetary union based on fixed gold prices, convertible currencies, and complete gold backing for the money supply.

Balance of payments adjustment under the Gold Standard
Suppose we begin from full long-run equilibrium. In each country there is *internal balance* or full employment and there is also *external balance*, neither a balance of payments surplus nor a balance of payments deficit. Each country also has a constant money supply, a given level of gold in the government vaults, and a given price level.

Suppose Americans now decide to spend more on

Table 34-1	Exchange rate regimes		
	Exchange rate		
Forex intervention	Fixed		Flexible
None			Free float
Automatic	Gold standard, Currency board		
Some discretion	Adjustable peg		Managed float

BOX 34-1

The gold standard and international capital flows

In the text we ignored international flows on the capital account of the balance of payments. We treated the balance of trade and the balance of payments as the same thing. This simplification makes the automatic adjustment mechanism of the gold standard seem more successful than it really was in practice. International flows on the capital account allowed the adjustment mechanism to be frustrated in two ways.

First, countries with a trade deficit sometimes raised domestic interest rates to encourage an inflow on the capital account of the balance of payments. If the overall balance of payments was thus in balance, there was no net monetary flow between countries, no change in countries' gold stocks, and no pressure on domestic wages and prices to adjust. Thus a trade deficit could persist longer than the idealized account of automatic adjustment suggests.

Second, capital flows are crucial to understanding Britain's role in the world economy during the nineteenth century. In the first half of the century, Britain's early start during the Industrial Revolution and its worldwide empire allowed Britain to run a huge trade surplus. To maintain an overall payments balance, Britain had a huge outflow on the capital account of the balance of payments, partly because of heavy investment in its colonies. However, investment gradually earns interest and profits. Eventually, Britain's stock of foreign assets became so large that the inflow from interest, profits, and dividends exceeded the rate at which Britain could find new opportunities for foreign investment.

The net inflow of money started to raise domestic prices and wages and make UK producers uncompetitive. Overall payments balance was maintained by a move from surplus to deficit on the trade account to offset the net inflow from financial transactions. The monetary adjustment mechanism of the gold standard suggests that it was probably inevitable that Britain would have a trade deficit in the late nineteenth century. It was not necessarily the result of laziness or decadence, as some Victorians believed at the time.

imports of goods produced in the UK. Britain now has a trade surplus. If domestic prices and wages are sluggish to adjust, the UK will enjoy an export-led Keynesian boom in the short run since aggregate demand for British output has increased. Conversely, the United States faces a recession and a balance of payments deficit.

This provides an automatic international adjustment mechanism. Initially the UK has a balance of payments surplus. This leads to an increase in the stock of pounds in circulation and the stock of gold at the Bank of England. Gradually, the higher domestic money supply puts further upward pressure on domestic prices through the standard mechanism of reducing interest rates and increasing aggregate demand for goods.

As prices rise, the UK gradually becomes less competitive since the nominal exchange rate remains fixed. In turn this gradually eliminates the balance of payments surplus as export demand falls and import demand increases. When UK prices have risen, and UK competitiveness fallen, to the extent required to restore balance of payments equilibrium, international flows of money and gold cease. With the domestic money supply unchanging, there is no further pressure on domestic prices. Internal and external balances have been restored.

Of course, exactly the opposite effects are happening in the United States. With an initial deficit, the American stock of gold and money is falling, thus increasing American interest rates and putting downward pressure on aggregate demand. Gradually American prices and wages fall and American competitiveness starts to increase. When this has restored the American balance of payments to equilibrium, the process comes to a halt.

Thus the gold standard does provide an automatic mechanism for adjusting imbalances in the trade and payments of different countries in the world economy. However, adjustment is far from instantaneous. Since it occurs because the changes in domestic wages and price change international competitiveness, the speed of adjustment depends on the speed with which domestic prices and wages adjust to the pressures of excess supply or excess demand.

The gold standard in action   The gold standard was in operation through most of the nineteenth and early twentieth centuries. In Britain there was an established par value of gold in sterling from the end of the Napoleonic wars in 1816 until 1931, though there were occasional periods, such as the period during and immediately after the First World War, when convertibility was suspended and the system allowed to lapse temporarily.

The gold standard in action was not quite the same as the idealized version described here. Since the money supply was not usually 100 per cent backed by gold, the changes in official gold reserves incurred while defending the parity value of the exchange rate did not necessarily lead to identical changes in domestic money supplies.

The gold standard had one big benefit and one large drawback. By tying the domestic money supply closely, if not perfectly, to the stock of gold, it effectively ruled out persistent money creation of a large scale and ruled out persistently high inflation rates. However, since the major mechanism by which full employment could be restored was a fall in domestic prices and wages, which might take many years to adjust fully to a large fall in aggregate demand, the period of the gold standard was a period in which individual economies were vulnerable to long and deep recessions.

34-3 The adjustable peg and the dollar standard

Under the gold standard, nominal exchange rates are fixed indefinitely.

In an **adjustable peg regime**, exchange rates are normally fixed but countries are occasionally allowed to alter their exchange rate.

This system, in operation for a quarter of a century after the Second World War, became known as the Bretton Woods system after the small American town where the details of the system were first hammered out. The principal architects of the final plan were Harry White, for the Americans, and John Maynard Keynes, for the British.

Because other countries agreed to fix their exchange rates against the dollar (and hence against each other), this system also became known as the **dollar standard**.

Each country announced a par value for its currency against the dollar, just as under the gold standard each country had announced par value against gold.

The second rule of the gold standard was convertibility. Under the dollar standard, currencies were convertible against dollars rather than gold. At the fixed exchange rate,

central banks were committed to buy or sell dollars from their stock of foreign exchange reserves or dollar holdings. They were committed to intervene in the foreign exchange market to defend the exchange rate against the dollar.

The crucial difference between the gold standard and the dollar standard was that there was no longer 100 per cent backing for the domestic currency. Britain's domestic money supply did not have to bear any relation to the stock of dollars held by the Bank of England as foreign exchange reserves. Governments in Britain and other countries could print as much money as they wished.

Why does this matter? Because it inhibits the adjustment mechanism built into the gold standard. Countries with a balance of payments deficit lost gold and their domestic money supply fell. Eventually this put downward pressure on the price level and began to increase competitiveness. Under the dollar standard, countries with a balance of payments deficit lost money, but there was nothing to stop the domestic government printing more money to restore the domestic money supply to its original level. Thus governments of deficit countries that wished to avoid deflationary pressure from monetary contraction could simply print extra money. Although this might prevent higher unemployment in the short run, it also prevented the long-run adjustment mechanism from operating through a fall in domestic money and prices, and a rise in competitiveness.

Such policies were unlikely to be feasible for ever. As the balance of payments deficit persisted, the government eventually ran out of foreign exchange reserves. Then the country had to devalue its exchange rate, moving to a lower par value against the dollar, to attempt permanently to increase competitiveness and remove the underlying imbalance in international payments.

Thus the first problem with an adjustable peg system is that it does not necessarily provide an *automatic* mechanism for resolving imbalances in international payments. Rather, deficit countries tended to stave off the required adjustment until a major crisis had built up, and then undertake a significant exchange rate devaluation.

In such circumstances, speculators had a field day. If a country was in balance of payments difficulties there was no danger that its exchange rate would be *raised*. Either the exchange rate would stay the same or there would be a devaluation. Speculators couldn't lose. For example, in 1967 the UK devalued from $2.80 to $2.40. People who converted £1 into $2.80 just before the devaluation could convert it back into £1.17 (= 2.80/2.40) as soon as the exchange rate had changed, making 17 per cent immediately. The big loser was the Bank of England, which gave people $2.80 for each

£1 one day, and bought the same dollars back the next day at $2.40/£.

The dollar standard had a second drawback. Since dollars had become the world's medium of exchange, the United States could never run out of foreign exchange reserves. The US government could always finance an American balance of payments deficit by printing more dollars.

In the mid-1960s the United States began to run much larger payments deficits, partly because of heavy military spending in Vietnam. In consequence the world's supply of outstanding dollars increased rapidly. By increasing the world's money supply, this process began to increase the inflation rate throughout the trading world.

In contrast, under the gold standard national and international money supplies could increase only as quickly as new gold could be supplied. On the one hand this system wasted real resources. Why use scarce workers to dig up gold for use as money when money can be printed at a fraction of the opportunity cost in real resources? But on the other hand, the very difficulty of increasing the gold supply quickly ensured that the world's rate of monetary growth was restricted in the long run. It was a pre-commitment to low inflation.

34-4 Floating exchange rates

As explained in Chapter 29, *pure* or *clean* floating implies that forex markets are in continuous equilibrium in the absence of any government intervention via the foreign exchange reserves. The reserves remain constant and there is no external mechanism changing the domestic money supply. Since receipts from foreigners equal payments to foreigners, money is neither flowing into nor out of the country. The balance of payments is exactly in balance.

Before we can evaluate floating exchange rates as a mechanism for international adjustment, we need a theory of how floating exchange rates are determined. It is convenient to review the analysis of Chapter 29.

Purchasing power parity
Taking 1974 as 100, by 1999 the price of US goods had risen to 326 but the price of UK goods had risen to 470. If the nominal exchange rate between US dollars and sterling had remained constant, UK competitiveness would have fallen dramatically compared with that of the United States.

International competitiveness is measured by comparing the relative prices of the goods from different countries when these are measured in a common currency.

Thus, if the nominal $/£ exchange rate had remained constant during 1974–99, the UK would have become 44 per cent less competitive against the United States because UK prices rose 1.44 times as much as those in the United States. Suppose, however, that the $/£ exchange rate had fallen 44 per cent over the same period. The $ price of UK exports would then have risen at the same rate as US prices, and the £ price of US exports would have risen at the same rate as UK prices. Competitiveness would have been unaltered.

The **purchasing power parity** path for the nominal exchange rates is the path that would keep competitiveness constant over time. Countries with higher domestic inflation than their competitors would face a depreciating nominal exchange rate and countries with lower inflation than their competitors would face an appreciating exchange rate.

Under a regime of fixed nominal exchange rates, a single country cannot have higher domestic inflation than its competitors for ever. Gradually it becomes less and less competitive in international trade, and is likely to face an increasing trade deficit and a lower level of aggregate demand since net exports are negative. However, under flexible exchange rates it is *possible* that different countries can maintain different domestic inflation rates indefinitely. If countries with high inflation rates simultaneously face depreciating exchange rates, purchasing power parity may be maintained and competitiveness unaltered.

Do exchange rates adjust to maintain purchasing power parity? This question has been the subject of a great deal of research. The short answer seems to be they do in the long run but not in the short run. We picked the example of the UK and the United States to illustrate this point. Between 1974 and 1999 the nominal exchange rate changed by 32 per cent, from $2.34/£ to $1.60/£. Thus, international competitiveness changed only about 10 per cent between the beginning and end of the period. Thus the first feature to note about a floating exchange rate regime is that it *can* cope with enormous international discrepancies in domestic rates of inflation and money growth in the long run.

Speculation and interest rate differentials
However, in Chapter 29 we made a second point of equal importance. Floating exchange rates do *not* follow the purchasing power parity path in the short run. Floating exchange rates clear the forex market day by day. Demand and supplies of currency arise both from transactions on the current account of the balance of payments – international

BOX 34-2

A random walk through the forex market

In mathematical statistics, a random walk is a variable whose expected value tomorrow is its value of today. For example, if an asset price today is £10, your best guess about its price tomorrow is £10. But this is only your best guess: its actual price tomorrow may be £9, £10, or £11.

In this chapter, as in Chapter 29, we have argued that speculators, who equate expected total returns in different currencies, would lead to equilibrium in the forex market where the interest differential between assets in two currencies would have to be compensated by anticipated changes in the exchange rate, offering expected capital gains or losses to offset these interest differentials. Except when interest rate differentials are zero, exchange rates should *not* be random walks. Today's interest rate differential should, on average, be associated with exchange rate changes between today and tomorrow.

In a famous study in 1983, Richard Meese and Ken Rogoff[1] found that floating exchange rates seemed to be surprisingly close to random walks. This puzzled economists most of whom liked the model of speculation based on interest rate differentials. So there has

been a stream of research trying to overturn the finding of Meese and Rogoff, whose conclusion keeps being confirmed by subsequent research. Now economists are abandoning the idea of a 'single' set of expectations. Instead, they are modelling different groups with different expectations.

For example, some 'technical analysts' look at patterns in past movements of the exchange rate and try to extrapolate these, without much use of economics directly. If almost everybody does this, it will determine the equilibrium and you should do it too whether or not you think it makes sense. Or you might try to be even smarter. Knowing how the others behave, you could plug this into an economic model to figure out when these extrapolations would go wrong and the forex market would change its mind. You could try to be one step ahead. Modern research is based on increasingly complicated models of dynamics within the forex market.

---

[1] R. A. Meese and K. Rogoff, 'Empirical models of the seventies: Do they fit out of sample?' *Journal of International Economics*, 1983.

---

trade in goods and services – and from transactions on the capital account – international asset transactions.

There is now a huge outstanding stock of footloose investment funds which can rapidly be switched from one currency to another in search for the highest expected rate of return in the short run. The rate of return depends both on a comparison of interest rates offered on assets denominated in different currencies *and* on the expected capital gain or loss arising from exchange rate changes while the currency is held.

The stock of outstanding funds is now so large that if even one-tenth of it were to move between currencies it would *swamp* supplies and demand for currencies arising that day from trade on the current account. Hence the forex market would not clear. So the minute funds start to move, *or even threaten to start moving*, the exchange rate is likely to change. For example, a rise in sterling interest rates is likely to lead to an immediate rise in the sterling exchange rate. If the exchange rate rises enough, speculators are likely to conclude that it will have to fall back in the immediate

future. The threat of this capital loss on a falling exchange rate will deter some of the speculators who were about to be tempted by higher sterling interest rates to hold more of their funds in London. This keeps the *actual* transactions on the capital account down to manageable proportions and allows the forex market to clear day by day.

Suppose a government is elected with a commitment to reduce the money supply and cut the inflation rate. What happens? If domestic prices and wages are slow to adjust, the initial impact of a reduction in the nominal money supply is a reduction in the real money stock. Interest rates are pushed up and the exchange rate must rise to choke off a potentially massive inflow of funds on the capital account of the balance of payments. Since domestic prices and wages have still not adjusted, competitiveness is eroded overnight. Over time, high interest rates and the slump in net imports lead first to a domestic slump, and then to downward pressure on domestic prices and wages. When adjustment is complete, the domestic economy will have a lower nominal money supply, lower prices and wages, and a higher nominal exchange rate. However, the fall in domestic prices will offset the rise in the nominal exchange rate and competitiveness will have been restored. The purchasing power parity path of the nominal exchange rate is re-established.

We now see that speculation can lead to large departures from the purchasing power parity path in the short run. Interest rates and the exchange rate can change much more quickly than domestic prices and wages. UK international competitiveness fell by between 50 and 60 per cent between 1976 and January 1981 before it significantly improved again. We have picked these particular dates deliberately. Neither of the end-points may have been a very representative or sustainable value of the exchange rate, but they do show how much competitiveness can change in the short run. Deviations from the purchasing power parity path can be large in the short run and can persist for a long time, even though there is a long-run tendency for the exchange rate to return to its purchasing power parity path and for competitiveness to be restored.

Hence a floating exchange rate regime does not provide continuous short-run insulation from large changes in international competitiveness. A government switching to a tight monetary policy to fight inflation may find that there is a severe Keynesian slump in the short run. Until prices fall and the real money supply expands again, temporarily high interest rates don't just hit domestic consumption and investment spending; they are also likely to lead to a rapid exchange rate appreciation which reduces competitiveness in the short run, further reducing aggregate demand through the effect on net exports.

A managed float

Under a free float there is no central bank intervention in the forex market. The foreign exchange reserves remain constant, the balance of payments is exactly zero, and the net monetary inflow from abroad is also zero.

In practice, exchange rates have rarely been allowed to float absolute freely during the period since 1973 when the Bretton Woods system of the adjustable peg was replaced by a floating exchange rate regime.

In a **managed float**, central banks intervene in the forex market both in an attempt to smooth out fluctuations in the exchange rate and to nudge the exchange rate in the desired direction.

Such intervention may smooth day-to-day exchange rate fluctuations, but in the long run it probably makes little difference to the path the exchange rate follows. Central banks have large stocks of foreign exchange reserves which they could dump on the foreign exchange market in an effort to alter the equilibrium exchange rate. But the speculators have even larger funds at their disposal.

34-5 Speculative attacks on pegged exchange rates

National policy-makers are always reluctant to admit that national sovereignty is being eroded. Capital mobility increased in the last two decades of the twentieth century. Under floating exchange rates, the influence of capital flows and speculative opinion was immediately evident. Under fixed exchange rates, policy-makers sometimes deluded themselves that their sovereignty was unaffected. Often, it took a crisis to convince them otherwise.

Later in this chapter, we discuss the European Monetary System (EMS). Most people still remember Black Wednesday when the UK was forced to depreciate and abandon the EMS. More recently, supposedly pegged exchange rates were successfully attacked in Mexico (1994), many Asian countries (1997), and Brazil (1999). When the speculators have more money than the central bank, the foreign exchange reserves can't always hold the line.

Raising interest rates may also be unconvincing if the domestic economy obviously can't stand the pain. Politically, it may be impossible to sustain the tough policy. Speculators understand that if they push hard enough, the government will have to cave in.

A **speculative attack** occurs when a country faces a sharp loss of reserves, a sharp depreciation, or both.

There are several interpretations of such a speculative attack. One is that it is correcting a policy mistake. Where a country has such a large budget deficit that it needs to print money, it is bound to have inflation, and promising to peg the nominal exchange rate makes little sense. However, many of the Asian economies, such as Korea and the Philippines, attacked in 1997, appeared to have no such problem.

A second interpretation is that there are two possible equilibrium exchange rates. Without any attack, the original peg is fine. For example, the exchange rate may be a little overvalued, but the cost of devaluing (raising inflation expectations) may outweigh the cost of having a small amount of uncompetitiveness. However, once attacked, the cost of repelling the attack must be added to the scales. It may tip the balance, making it optimal now to accept defeat, and take the (temporary) advantage of higher competitiveness that the devaluation achieves. Whether the peg survives or not depends entirely on whether speculators decide to attack.

Attacks can, however, be very costly. When domestic banks have borrowed in foreign currency, these debts increase when the exchange rate falls and may bankrupt the banks and cause a widespread loss of confidence. Suppose a country wants to be less vulnerable to attack, what can it do?

Repelling boarders

Three types of response have been adopted. First, the one can try to reduce capital mobility making it easier to defend these fixed but adjustable exchange rate pegs. This was the solution adopted by those designing the Bretton Woods system after the Second World War. Private capital flows were outlawed by capital controls.

Capital controls prohibit, restrict, or tax the flow of private capital across currencies.

Capital controls made it easy to defend pegged exchange rates. However, from the 1970s onwards, controls were progressively dismantled as a global financial system was created. It also became harder and harder to enforce controls – smart bankers found offshore ways of doing the same business.

One form of control that might stand a chance in the modern world is a tiny tax on financial transactions, first proposed many years ago by Nobel prize winner James Tobin. Paying a tiny tax on a 10-year investment would be almost trivial, the same tax on holding a foreign asset for two hours would take away all the profits. Hence a Tobin tax would mainly hit short-term 'hot money'.

Capital controls have been used quite successfully in Chile, and were introduced by Malaysia in 1997 after its currency was attacked. Whether the global economy is consistent with widespread controls remains a contentious issue. Small emerging markets can probably use them. The more highly integrated a country is with the world's financial markets, the harder it will be.

If capital controls are not to be the answer, the exchange rate regime has to become more robust. Pegged exchange rates are an uncomfortable halfway house: usually pegged but sometimes adjustable. While they are pegged the central bank is obliged to try to defend them, even when a one way bet is emerging. But because they are not completely pegged, the speculators can win in the end.

If this is the diagnosis, the solution may be to retreat to one of the safer extremes: float or peg completely. Thus, a second solution for repelling boarders and avoiding spectacular exchange rate crashes is simply to float. Let the speculators punch thin air. They can take the currency down, but, if it was for no good reason, the currency will probably come up again. As we show in Chapter 36, most Asian exchange rates have now recovered from 1997.

The alternative is to make the peg much more credible, akin to the old gold standard. One popular device is a currency board.

A **currency board** is a constitutional commitment to peg the exchange rate by giving up monetary independence.

A currency board removes the ability of the central bank to change the monetary base. Balance of payments surpluses (deficits) become the only source of expansion (contraction) of the monetary base. Suppose a country has a deficit because it imports too much. Importers take domestic money to the currency board to get the foreign exchange they need; the board simply keeps the domestic money which is retired from circulation. Countries with currency boards in 1999 include Estonia, Bulgaria, and Argentina.

Like all pre-commitments, it hurts when it has to take the strain. Since the country loses monetary independence, it cannot use interest rates for domestic reasons. If it has any trouble doing the right thing with fiscal policy, it can get into trouble. If its banks face bankruptcy, it is difficult to ease credit conditions to help them. If it is possible a country may have to give up even a currency board, speculators may still attack.

Thus no solution is ideal. If any single solution was perfect, everyone would have been doing it long ago. We now consider some other issues that arise in choosing between fixed and floating exchange rates.

34-6 Fixed versus floating

In this section, we look at robustness, volatility, and financial discipline.

Robustness

How do different regimes cope with major strains? Nominal strains arise when different countries have very different domestic inflation rates. Real strains occur when the world economy suffers a major real shock such as a quadrupling of real oil prices.

Countries whose domestic inflation rate is higher than that of their international competitors will gradually become less competitive in international markets. Either they must undertake tight domestic monetary and fiscal policy to get their inflation rate back in line with that in the rest of the world, or they must seek a devaluation of their currency to restore the exchange rate to its purchasing power parity level. And if they persist in having higher domestic inflation than the rest of the world, they will need a series of devaluations at regular intervals to maintain their international competitiveness. In short, unless countries pursue domestic monetary policies that lead to roughly equal inflation rates, a fixed exchange rate system simply cannot cope.

How about strains caused by real shocks to the world economy? Just imagine how the OPEC oil price shocks would have hit a fixed exchange rate regime. Overnight, countries that were heavy oil importers would have faced enormous balance of payments deficits and speculative pressure would have built up as speculators started to bet that these currencies would have to be devalued. The OPEC oil price shock would have led to round after round of consultations, tentative exchange rate adjustments, and further consultations to determine whether the adjustments already undertaken had been of the correct magnitude to achieve the adjustments required.

History tells us two things. First, the Bretton Woods system of the adjustable peg had to be abandoned in the early 1970s because it could *not* cope with the nominal and real strains in the world economy. Even a series of exchange rate realignments in the early 1970s, such as the revaluation of the Deutschmark, did not remove either current account imbalances or speculative pressures on the capital account. Second, whatever else we may say about floating exchange rates, the system *was* able to cope with the dramatic shocks experienced by the world economy in the 1970s. Believers in floating exchange rates count this a point in their favour.

Volatility

Critics of floating exchange rates point to their extreme volatility. Between 1949 and 1967 the dollar–sterling exchange rate was rarely more than 1 cent either side of $2.80/£, and between 1967 and 1972 rarely more than 1 cent either side of $2.40/£. The job of the central banks was to intervene in the forex market to hold exchange rates close to their par values. In contrast, Figure 34-1 shows the volatility of the dollar–sterling exchange rates during the period of floating exchange rates since 1973. Not only has the rate been as high as $2.50 and as low as $1.30, but it has sometimes moved *very* rapidly. Between the first and third quarters of 1981 the dollar–sterling exchange rate fell from $2.32/£ to $1.83/£ in less than six months. Such volatility, it is argued, leads to great uncertainty and is likely to

reduce the level of international trade and the amount of investment undertaken by firms competing in world markets.

The assertion of volatility cannot be disputed. But is volatility necessarily a bad thing? First, it is the real, or inflation-adjusted, exchange rate that affects competitiveness. For example, the fall in the dollar–sterling exchange rate in the mid-1970s was largely offsetting higher UK inflation. Under a fixed exchange rate, competitiveness would have been changing even more quickly. When inflation discrepancies between countries are large and uncertain, pegging the nominal exchange rate throws all the inflation uncertainty on to the level of real competitiveness. The real exchange rate is not necessarily constant or predictable just because the nominal exchange rate has been fixed.

Second, it is not obvious that a system with usually fixed nominal exchange rates but occasionally large changes leads to less uncertainty than a system in which nominal exchange rates change every day. Living in a world where the exchange rate *may* change by 17 per cent in a single day can be just as hair-raising as living in a world where the exchange rate often changes by 1 per cent five days running.

Finally, what would have happened if the exchange rate had not adjusted so much? If high inflation leads to a large exchange rate depreciation under floating exchange rates, what would have been the government's response if it had been trying to defend a fixed exchange rate? Would it have adopted a tight domestic policy, jacking up interest rates and raising taxes, to try to get domestic inflation back in

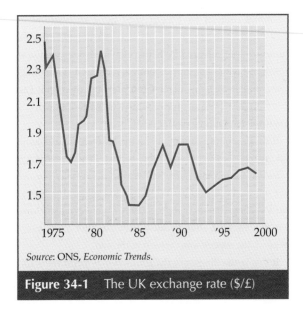

Source: ONS, *Economic Trends*.

Figure 34-1   The UK exchange rate ($/£)

BOX 34-3   A yen for a stable currency?

Japan stagnated for much of the 1990s and in 1995 the government began trying to talk the yen down in order to make Japanese industry more competitive. By now, of course, you understand that 'talking a currency down' is shorthand for 'leading the market to believe that, unless the currency falls quickly, the government will take steps to reduce interest rates, thereby encouraging speculators to bid the currency down'. And in the 18 months after April 1995 the yen fell dramatically, by 40 per cent against the US $.

So was this good news for the Japanese electronics firms whose goods are on sale in every European high street? It would have been if all their productions had been based in Japan. But Japan had spent the previous 10 years learning to live with a strong yen by transferring more and more of its manufacturing capacity to lower-wage economies overseas. It used to be the largest producer of pocket calculators. Now it *imports*

90 per cent of its calculators, mainly from Japanese off-shore plants. Since 1994 it has been a net importer of televisions!

Establishing plants abroad has helped famous Japanese manufacturers diversify exchange rate risks. The dip in the yen after 1995 also helped break the belief that the yen would rise and rise without bound. Some companies such as Aiwa quickly reverted to domestic Japanese suppliers as the yen came down. A yen depreciation increases competitiveness of factories in Japan, but, when multinationals are quick to switch suppliers, suppliers based in Japan are not always those producing the brandname goods on sale in Europe and the United States.

Source: Adapted from 'Japanese industry: learning to live with a strong yen', *Financial Times*, 12 November 1996.

---

line with inflation rates abroad? Is uncertainty about competitiveness under floating exchange rates necessarily worse than uncertainty about interest rates and tax rates under a fixed exchange rate regime? British business was pleased when the pound fell out of the Exchange Rate Mechanism on Black Wednesday in 1992.

One of the things we learn from figures such as Figure 34-1 was that the world has been an uncertain place since the 1970s. Because everyone has adopted a floating exchange rate regime, much of this uncertainty showed up in volatile exchange rates, but it would have shown up somewhere else if the world had been on a fixed exchange rate regime. And there would surely have been some large exchange rate changes in any case.

Hence it is hard to conclude that the volatility argument goes decisively against floating exchange rates. However, this argument also comes in a more sophisticated form. It is argued that the shocks with which the world international monetary system has to deal are not independent of the exchange rate regime in force. In short, by their very flexibility and robustness, floating exchange rates make shocks more likely. We now turn to the most important version of this argument, which relates to financial discipline.

Financial discipline

Floating exchange rates allow different countries to pursue different inflation rates indefinitely. In the long run the exchange rates of high-inflation countries will depreciate to maintain purchasing power parity or constant international competitiveness. By the same token, floating exchange rates do nothing to *prevent* individual countries from adopting fast domestic monetary growth and high domestic inflation. Thus, critics of floating exchange rates argue that they do not provide any *financial discipline*.

In contrast, under a fixed exchange rate system countries become uncompetitive if they have above-average inflation. Unless they are allowed to devalue, they eventually have no choice but to adopt more restrictive domestic policies to get their inflation rates back in line with the rest of the world.

Shortly, we examine the EMS as an instrument of financial discipline within Western Europe. In the next chapter we discuss the even tighter discipline that the European Monetary Union imposes. Here we note that membership of an exchange rate regime is neither the only route to financial discipline nor a route guaranteed to succeed.

It is not the only route because the government can make domestic pre-commitments instead.

In 1992 the UK government announced greater independence for the Bank of England and published a tough target range (0–4 per cent) for annual growth of M0. Since then UK inflation has remained in this range, and the Bank of England's quarterly *Inflation Report* has helped monitor inflation conditions. In 1997 the Bank of England was given operational independence in setting interest rates, and an explicit target of 2.5 per cent inflation.

Domestic pre-commitments are not always foolproof. But exchange rate commitments are no certainty either, as the weaker EMS currencies (sterling, the lira, the peseta, and the escudo) all found out in September 1992. More recently, exchange rate pegs had to be abandoned in Mexico (1994), Korea (1997), and Brazil (1999).

Where the government is weak at home, invoking external pressures may be a useful tactic. This helps us understand the EMS as a vehicle for disinflation in continental Europe in the 1980s. But a tough government may be able to institute domestic forms of pre-commitment (appointing a tough governor of the central bank; or giving that bank greater independence from government control) which still leave the choice of exchange rate regime determined by other factors.

34-7 International policy co-ordination

By policy co-ordination, we mean a concerted attempt by a group of countries to formulate policy collectively. At one extreme, this might eventually imply a supranational body to which national sovereignty is subordinated. Clearly, the world economy is a long way from any such arrangement, but much of Europe has a monetary union with a single European central bank. At the other extreme, we might mean agreements to brief other governments about one's own policy, and to exchange information. In between lie a spectrum of arrangements which specify some 'rules of the game' subject to which national governments still have a measure of discretion. For example, under Bretton Woods, governments agreed that exchange rates would usually be fixed, but they retained sovereignty over their domestic monetary and fiscal policies subject only to this constraint. On the other hand, even when floating, sterling has sometimes been driven to uncompetitive levels.

What do governments stand to gain by co-ordinating macroeconomic policy to some extent? Like oligopolists, governments are essentially interdependent, the outcome for each depending on the policies pursued by others. Like oligopolists, they face a tension between the incentive to collude and the incentive to compete. Collusion allows them

to 'internalize' the externalities they otherwise impose on one another when each sets policy without regard for its impact on the welfare of others. But there is also an incentive to compete by cheating on collective agreements.

How do these ideas apply in international policy co-ordination?

The externality argument for co-ordination

The most obvious externality imposed by non-cooperative behaviour is the externality acting through the exchange rate. Suppose a government wants to get inflation down. Essentially, it has two weapons. Demand management can be used to generate a domestic recession, which will put downward pressure on wages and prices. An exchange rate appreciation, in addition to these effects, will reduce prices directly by making imports cheaper. A smart government will wish to use both policy weapons, as for example the UK government did in 1989–90 when trying to combat inflation that had built up under the Lawson boom of 1987–88.

But what works for a country in isolation cannot work for the world as a whole. We cannot all appreciate our exchange rates. A rise in the $/£ rate is necessarily a fall in the £/$ rate. Countries that use exchange rate appreciation to reduce their own inflation effectively export inflation abroad. That is the externality they fail to take into account.

In principle, policy co-ordination can solve this market failure: countries can agree not to use exchange rate policy in this manner. As with other collusive or co-operative agreements, an effective punishment threat is required to prevent individual countries from subsequently cheating on the agreement. If this can be devised, the agreement will be credible, and all countries may benefit.

The reputation argument for co-ordination

Earlier, we discussed the issue of financial discipline. It is of course possible that a government would like to keep inflation under control by tight policies but is unable to resist reflating the economy as the next election draws near. Because everyone knows this will happen, inflation expectations remain high and inflation is hard to control even at the start of the government's period of office.

Such a government might be glad if it could make a binding pre-commitment which ruled out the option to reflate as the next election drew near. We have already portrayed the creation of an independent Bank of England as an attempt to devise such a pre-commitment, but policy co-ordination may offer an alternative.

Why do people go to Weightwatchers or Alcoholics Anonymous? Because, alone, they are too weak to stick to

BOX 34-4 — Exchange rate regimes and inflation

The commitment by a country to restrict its exchange rate flexibility *might* act as a useful pre-commitment that allows the private sector to reduce its inflation expectations because it trusts the government not to print money and make inflation. Exchange rate commitments *might* also reduce the volatility of inflation, essentially by ruling out wild swings in domestic monetary policy. For example, incoming governments may be more constrained to follow the same policies as their predecessors. Since exchange rates are between the currencies of two different counties, it takes two governments, and hence international co-ordination, to restrict exchange rate flexibility; loss of national sovereignty is the other side of the same coin. However, if exchange rate restrictions *do in practice* act as commitments that reduce both expected inflation and inflation uncertainty, governments of nation states may choose to adopt such arrangements.

The table shows evidence assembled by the IMF in a study of 136 countries inflation behaviour over three decades (1960–90). A hard peg is adjusted only rarely; a soft peg is frequently realigned (usually devaluations!).

The table confirms that countries that have pursued more stringent exchange rate regimes have typically had inflation below the world average, and also had more stable inflation rates than the rest of the world. Countries with looser exchange rate arrangements, including those pegging but frequently realigning, typically had higher and more variable inflation. These results are surprisingly robust across different levels of economic development.

The IMF rightly concludes that ability to sustain a tough exchange rate policy may be a symptom of sound macroeconomic policy as well as a cause of it: 'Viewed together with the recent decline in inflation in many flexible exchange rate countries to their lowest level since the 1950s, this evidence supports the argument that simply pegging the exchange rate does not necessarily deliver low inflation. Rather, it is the pursuit of appropriate macroeconomic policies that is important, whether in enabling an exchange rate peg to be maintained, or, in the case of flexible exchange rates, in ensuring adherence to a domestic nominal anchor.'

% deviation from annual average in all 136 countries	Exchange rate regime			
	Hard peg	Soft peg	Intermediate	Float
Average inflation:				
All countries	−1.1	3.3	5.5	7.2
Rich and upper-middle-income	−2.3	−0.6	7.6	8.0
Poor and lower-middle-income	−0.4	5.2	4.0	6.6
Volatility of inflation				
All countries	−1.5	0.2	2.6	1.4
Rich and upper-middle income	−3.1	0.6	1.2	−1.2
Poor and lower-middle-income	2.2	−0.1	4.4	6.8

Source: IMF, *World Economic Outlook 1996*.

their resolutions. Joining a club provides peer discipline. Even in everyday language, it shows commitment. You look silly if you subsequently pull out.

Policy co-ordination may act in a similar way. Hence it may allow national governments to make credible the promises that would otherwise be incredible. That is the second argument for policy co-ordination.

We now turn to a closer examination of one of the most studied recent examples of co-ordination, the European Monetary System.

34-8 The European Monetary System

In March 1979 the members of the European Community (*including* the UK) founded and joined the European Monetary System (EMS).

Table 34-2		ECU composition (% share of each currency)		
Deutschmark	(DM)	30.1	Spanish peseta	(SP)	5.3
French franc	(FF)	19.0	Danish krone	(DK)	2.4
Pound sterling	(£)	13.0	Irish punt	(IP)	1.1
Italian lira	(IL)	10.2	Greek drachma	(GD)	0.8
Dutch guilder	(DG)	9.4	Portuguese escudo	(PE)	0.8
Belgian franc	(BF)	7.6	Luxembourg franc	(LF)	0.3

The **EMS** was a system of monetary and exchange rate co-operation in Western Europe.

The most important features of the agreement were as follows.

First, the European Currency Unit (ECU) was used as a unit of account for certain transactions between EC governments. Table 34-2 shows the shares of the different currencies in this currency bundle.

Second, member governments each deposited 20 per cent of their foreign exchange reserves with the European Monetary Co-operation Fund, and received ECUs in exchange. These funds were to be available for short-term central bank intervention in foreign exchange markets.

It was only the third but key provision, the Exchange Rate Mechanism (ERM), in which the UK did not initially participate.

Under the **ERM**, each country fixed a nominal exchange rate against each other ERM participant, though collectively the group floated against the rest of the world.

Each country participating in the ERM could allow its exchange rate to fluctuate within a band of ±2¼ per cent of the parities it has agreed to defend.[1] When the currency hit the edge of a band, *all* central banks in the ERM countries were obliged to intervene to try to defend the parity.

The ERM had two other features. Realignments were allowed but had to be unanimously agreed by participants of the ERM. In practice, finance ministers had to sneak off in secret to some schloss or chateau and get the agreement hammered out before the forex markets reopened! Otherwise, speculative pressures on a one-way option for anticipated exchange rate changes were almost impossible to resist. And this speculative pressure arose as soon a realignment was suspected, as Italy, the UK, and Spain discovered during September 1992.

---

[1] Italy, an especially high-inflation country in 1979, was allowed a band of ±6 per cent. By the mid-1980s, it was a matter of honour for Italy not to use this wider band. Spain and the UK also joined the ERM with a wider band.

The EMS up to 1992

Table 34-3 shows the realignments of the major ERM currencies during 1979–91. (Recall that the UK did not join until 1990 and left again in 1992.) Two facts stand out. First, realignments largely followed the strategy of restoring purchasing power parity. The relatively high-inflation countries (initially Italy and France) were allowed nominal exchange rate devaluations. Second, whereas there was a realignment almost every six months between 1979 and 1983, after 1983 realignments were much less frequent. Between 1987 and 1991 there was no realignment.

Did the EMS exert financial discipline? Were France and Italy forced to live with tight German policies and low German inflation? Not initially. When they became uncompetitive at fixed nominal exchange rates, they were soon allowed to devalue to improve competitiveness. Typically, realignments did not *fully* restore purchasing power parity, so some discipline was being exerted. After 1983 discipline was much stricter.

Thus, the EMS was founded when its members had very different inflation rates, but these were gradually brought into line. The EMS played some role in this. It did not reflect a political will to do this quickly, nor did it instantly force countries to harmonize policies. But over time, it did have an effect.

One final aspect of the EMS experience should be mentioned. It reduced nominal exchange rate volatility in the short run. Nor did its members experience the dramatic swings in real competitiveness to which the floating sterling and dollar were subject over the same period.

Why did it work up to 1992?

Only part of the success of the EMS should be attributed to policy convergence. Could other reasons explain the success of the EMS up till 1992? Two stand out. First, with a band of ±2¼ per cent, there were long periods when countries were effectively floating. High-inflation countries had exchange rates that started off near the top of the band and gradually depreciated, just as they would have done under floating. When they got near the bottom of the band, people started to talk about the need for a realignment. In part, the early EMS was cosmetic.

Second, most countries initially had foreign exchange controls which prevented large capital account flows. This allowed fixed bilateral parities to survive even when interest rates were out of line. Only occasionally was the prospect of a realignment so imminent that exchange controls had trouble stemming the speculative tide. As part of the 1992 programme of reforms, the major EMS countries

Table 34-3   EMS realignments, 1979–91 (date and percentage realignment)

Date	DM	FF	DG	IL	BF	DK	LF	IP
Sept. 79	+2.0					−2.9		
Nov. 80						−4.8		
Mar. 81				−6.0				
Oct. 81	+5.5	−3.0	+5.5	−3.0				
Feb. 82					−8.5	−3.0	−8.5	
June 83	+4.3	−5.8	+4.3	−2.8				
Mar. 83	+5.5	−2.5	+3.5	−2.5	+1.5	+2.5	+1.5	−3.5
July 85	+2.0	+2.0	+2.0	−6.0	+2.0	+2.0	+2.0	+2.0
Apr. 86								−8.0
Jan. 87	+3.0		+3.0		+2.0			
Cumulative	+23.7	−9.1	+19.1	−18.7	−3.3	−6.2	−5.3	−9.5

DM (Deutschmark), etc. refer to currencies listed in Table 34.2.

committed themselves to remove all foreign exchange controls by June 1990. Greece, Spain, and Portugal were allowed until 1992.

The UK finally joined the ERM in 1990. In the next chapter we discuss the ERM in the 1990s and look more generally at the process of increasing European integration.

BOX 34-5 Capital controls and the EMS

By the late 1990s, the EMS had been operating nearly 20 years. Initially, it had allowed high inflation countries regular devaluations that did little more than mimic the nominal exchange rate depreciation they would have had if they had floated. After 1983 discipline increased, and realignments became less frequent. During 1983–85 inflation rates converged substantially on the low German inflation rate.

In 1986 members signed the Single European Act, paving the way for the 1992 programme. This needed an end to capital controls to create a single financial market in western Europe. Yet capital controls had underpinned the early EMS.

For a high inflation country, Figure (a) shows the path *ABDE* of nominal exchange rate depreciation to maintain real competitiveness. Initially, the exchange rate is pegged within a band around central parity e_0. When the exchange rate hits the bottom of the band at B, central banks intervene to try to defend the band. As time elapses, the exchange rate moves along BC. With continuing inflation, competitiveness is now being eroded. Eventually this prompts a devaluation of the central parity from e_0 to e_1, so the whole band shifts down. The actual exchange rate jumps from C to D on the day of the realignment.

This is a one-way bet. As the exchange rate moves along BC nobody is expecting a sharp appreciation! Only the presence of controls on international capital movements prevents massive speculation against the central banks trying to defend the original parity. Had capital controls been removed in the early 1980s, there would have been an immediate crisis. Figure (b) explains why this did not occur after 1986.

By the mid-1980s, inflation convergence within the EMS meant even Italian inflation was only a little above that in Germany. The depreciation rate of the lira required to offset inflation was much lower than before. The line is flatter in Figure (b) than in Figure (a). In Figure (b) when the parity is devalued from e_0 to e_1, the *actual* exchange rate at B is inside *both* the old band and the new band. No jump is required in the exchange rate, and there is no one-way bet for speculators. A small interest differential will compensate them for the gradual depreciation.

Success in inflation convergence convinced European policy-makers that the EMS could survive the end of capital controls.

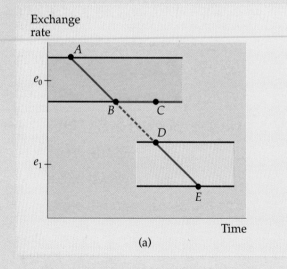

Exchange rate

e_0

e_1

Time

(a)

(b)

SUMMARY

● Under the gold standard, each country fixed the par value of its currency against gold, maintained the convertibility of its currency into gold at this price, and linked the domestic money supply to gold stocks at the central bank. It was a fixed exchange rate regime.

● In the absence of capital flows, countries with a trade deficit faced a payments deficit, a monetary outflow, and a reduction in gold stocks. By inducing a domestic recession which put downward pressure on wages and prices and increased competitiveness, this provided an automatic adjustment mechanism. Similarly, trade surplus countries faced a monetary inflow, higher prices, and an erosion of competitiveness. In practice, this adjustment mechanism was hampered by capital flows. Trade imbalance did not necessarily lead to the required monetary flows.

● The postwar Bretton Woods system was an adjustable peg in which fixed exchange rates could occasionally be adjusted. Effectively, it was a dollar standard. But the domestic money supply was no longer linked to the stock of foreign exchange reserves, so much of the adjustment mechanism of the gold standard was lost.

● The purchasing power parity path of the exchange rate is the path that maintains constant competitiveness by offsetting differential inflation across countries. In the long run, floating exchange rates return to the PPP path.

● In the short run, the level of floating exchange rates is determined largely by speculation. Speculators like high interest rates but dislike expected depreciation of the exchange rate. Exchange rates adjust in the short run to choke off large speculative flows. A sharp exchange rate appreciation increases the chance of a future depreciation. In the short run, exchange rates can depart significantly from their PPP path. Short-run changes in competitiveness can be large if domestic prices change only slowly.

● Unlike fixed exchange rates, floating exchange rates can cope with permanent differences in domestic inflation rates. High-inflation countries simply face a depreciating exchange rate in the long run. In practice, floating exchange rates also coped with the severe real shocks of the 1970s. This suggests floating exchange rate regimes are more robust than fixed exchange rate regimes.

● Critics of floating exchange rates claim they are very volatile in the short run, which discourages international trade and investment. However, they are volatile because the world is uncertain. Under fixed exchange rates the uncertainty would show up somewhere else, possibly in volatile domestic monetary policy to maintain the fixed exchange rate.

● Fixed exchange rates impose financial discipline by preventing one country from having a permanently higher domestic inflation than the rest of the world. However, there are other ways to prevent governments from adopting rapid rates of domestic money growth. And fixed exchange rates do not always survive!

● Floating exchange rates are less likely to lead to pressures for restrictions on international trade and capital flows for balance of payments reasons. Under floating exchange rates the balance of payments is always in balance.

● Under floating exchange rates, the adoption of a tighter monetary policy in one country alone will lead to a sharp appreciation of its currency. This sharp loss of competitiveness will exacerbate the domestic slump. The staggered adoption of tighter monetary policy in different countries may lead to wild fluctuations in their competitiveness in the short run. A concerted move to tighter monetary policies would mean that they all had high interest rates. Exchange rates would not fluctuate so much in the short run.

● If countries can agree to adopt the same rate of monetary growth, they will tend to have similar domestic inflation rates and it might be possible to move back to a fixed exchange rate regime.

● There are two general arguments in favour of international policy co-ordination. First, it allows policymakers to take account of the externalities they impose on each other. Second, it may allow individual governments to commit themselves to policies that would otherwise not be credible.

● The UK was always a member of the European Monetary System but did not join its most important feature, the Exchange Rate Mechanism, until 1990 and left again in 1992. The early survival of the ERM and its success in reducing exchange rate volatility arose only partly from greater co-ordination of monetary policy by ERM participants. Foreign exchange controls and exchange rate bands were also important.

 KEY TERMS

◆ Exchange rate regime   573

◆ Par value of gold   573

◆ Gold standard   573

◆ Adjustable peg regime   575

◆ Dollar standard   575

◆ International competitiveness   576

◆ Purchasing power parity (PPP)   576

◆ Managed float   578

◆ Speculative attack   578

◆ Capital controls   579

◆ Currency board   579

◆ European Monetary System (EMS)   585

◆ Exchange Rate Mechanism (ERM)   585

 REVIEW QUESTIONS

1 Reread Box 34-1 on page 574. During the First World War the gold standard was suspended. Britain also sold off most of its foreign assets to pay for the war. What do you think happened in 1925 when Britain tried to rejoin the gold standard at the old par value of gold?

2 How did the dollar standard differ from the gold standard? Explain the differences in (a) the automatic adjustment mechanism, (b) financial discipline.

3 What would happen in the long run if floating exchange rates did not return to their PPP path? How can speculators make use of the knowledge that PPP will eventually be restored?

4 What are the advantages and disadvantages of a currency board?

5 'There is no more reason to peg exchange rates than to peg the price of motor cars.' Do you agree?

6 When the UK left the ERM in September 1992 the news had different effects on the UK stock market and the UK bond market. Which market rose strongly? What was worrying the other market?

7 *Common fallacies* Show why each of the following statements is incorrect. (a) Floating exchange rates make sure that exports and imports always balance. (b) Since one country's surplus is another country's deficit, it makes no difference to the world economy whether individual countries have a balance of payments equal to zero. (c) Fixed exchange rate regimes prevent world inflation.

35 European integration

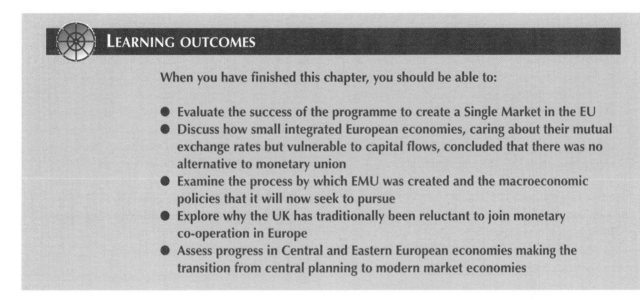

LEARNING OUTCOMES

When you have finished this chapter, you should be able to:

- Evaluate the success of the programme to create a Single Market in the EU
- Discuss how small integrated European economies, caring about their mutual exchange rates but vulnerable to capital flows, concluded that there was no alternative to monetary union
- Examine the process by which EMU was created and the macroeconomic policies that it will now seek to pursue
- Explore why the UK has traditionally been reluctant to join monetary co-operation in Europe
- Assess progress in Central and Eastern European economies making the transition from central planning to modern market economies

The European economy of the new millennium looks very different from the Europe of 30 years ago. Some of these developments were political. But others were economic, and the economics we have learned in this book is directly useful in thinking about them. In this chapter we describe the forces at work, and set out a checklist of what to watch for as the future unfolds.

This chapter is about three things. First, the Single European Act of 1987 committed members of the EC to a single market in goods, services, assets, and people by 31 December 1992. What difference did the Single Market make?

Second, for 11 countries Economic and Monetary Union (EMU) began in January 1999. Why did EMU happen and what difference will it make?

The third development was the dramatic reforms, both political and economic, in Eastern Europe after 1989. How are these countries doing in their transition from central planning to market economies?

35-1 The Single Market

The European Community was established by the original six members in 1957. Its chief features were a free trade area inside the Community, and Community-wide programmes financed by fiscal contributions from member governments. The largest programme was the Common Agricultural Policy (CAP), a system of administered high prices for agricultural commodities which has led to the famous wine 'lakes' and butter 'mountains'. A more modest programme was the Structural Funds, designed to provide subsidies for social infrastructure, especially in poorer areas of the Community.

Over the following 40 years, the Community was enlarged. The original six – West Germany, France, Italy, Netherlands, Belgium and Luxembourg – were joined by Denmark, Ireland and the UK in the 1970s, by Spain, Portugal and Greece in the 1980s, and by Austria, Finland and Sweden in the 1990s. The European Community (EC) then became the European Union (EU). Those already pressing for inclusion in an enlarged EU include countries from Central Europe, the Baltics, and the Balkans.

The enlargement of the EU was not accompanied by any change in its fundamental structure. Member states continued to set national policies. The dreamers and the Eurocrats were always pressing for closer integration, for example by harmonizing industrial standards or national tax rates, but this was usually thwarted for two reasons. First, since each country had a different way of doing things, it was impossibly cumbersome to negotiate the single set of regulations which would apply to all member states. Second, it was political dynamite. Nobody wanted to adopt somebody else's procedures and policy.

In the mid-1980s there was a breakthrough, and it is important to understand why it occurred. Instead of trying to agree on a single set of comprehensive rules, hammered out in Brussels and then rigidly enforced in all member states, the logic of competition led to a different approach. Member states agreed on some broad outlines for harmonizing policy. Each country was then responsible for deciding how these should be implemented. And each country recognized the validity of the regulations imposed by other member states.

Let's look at an example. Each country has regulations determining which institutions may register as a bank or an insurance company, and what conditions they must fulfil. Previously, the differences in national regulations were so great that a bank registered in the UK under UK law did not comply with standards laid down for banks in France, Germany, or Italy. So banks in one country found it almost impossible to compete in other countries. National markets were segmented. Since there are economies of scale in banking, each small national market had only a few banks enjoying significant market power.

Under the new approach, member states agreed on some general principles governing the regulation of banks – minimum standards for capital adequacy (the amount of financial backing needed to undertake particular types of risky business), for external monitoring (to check up that managers are doing their job properly), and so on. Then each government decided how to apply these general criteria and to licence banks in its country. Finally, and crucially, a bank registered in Germany under German law was allowed to operate throughout the EU.

This new approach had two major advantages. First, it provided a politically acceptable way of moving towards European integration. Individual governments no longer looked like they are yielding all political control. Second, it

brought competition more directly into the process. Instead of having to 'pick a winner' or make an all-or-nothing guess about which system of regulation to adopt for everyone, different countries adopt different ways of implementing general principles, *and then the market decided*. Countries that adopted regulatory structures which turn out to be good for business found their firms getting a bigger share of EU trade. Countries with unfavourable systems (which might have too much regulation but might have too little: business is frightened of anarchy, legal ambiguity, and possible fraud) lost business. Thus, *competition between forms of regulation* took place.

Once negotiations had moved to this new basis, progress became rapid. In 1987 the member states of the EC ratified the Single European Act. The Act set December 1992 as the target for achieving completion of the internal market by harmonizing regulations in the manner described above. Among its main objectives were: (*a*) abolition of all remaining foreign exchange controls on capital flows; (*b*) removal of all non-tariff barriers to trade within the EU (differences in trade-marks, patent laws, and safety standards, which act to segment national markets); (*c*) elimination of the bias in public sector purchasing (defence, etc.) favouring domestic producers; (*d*) removal of frontier controls (delays), subject to retaining necessary safeguards for security, social and health reasons; and (*e*) progress towards harmonization of tax rates.

A **single market** is not segmented by national regulations, taxes, or informal practices.

35-2 Benefits of the Single Market

Table 35-1 shows that the completion of the Single Market created an economic area larger than the United States or Japan. The potential benefits accruing to member states can be divided into three categories: more efficient resource allocation, fuller exploitation of scale economies, and gains from intensified competition.

Table 35-1 The size of the single market

	EC	USA	Japan
Population (million)	349	261	125
GDP (billion ECU*)	5248	5114	3531

*1 ECU is about $1.3 or £0.8.
Source: World Bank, *World Development Report 1996*.

Gains from improved resource allocation

In Chapter 33 we introduced the principle of comparative advantage and discussed how free trade could lead to a more efficient resource allocation. Opening up trade allows each country to specialize more in the commodities that it makes *relatively* cheaply. Although the EC had for many years operated as a free trade zone without tariffs on trade between member states, the rationale for 1992 was that there still remained non-tariff barriers which continued to segment national markets.

Non-tariff barriers are differences in national regulations or practices which prevent free movement of goods, services, and factors across countries.

Thus, the Single Market (SM) aimed to break down non-tariff barriers and allow countries to exploit their true comparative advantage more fully.

Gains from scale economies

When national markets are small and segmented from one another, firms may not be able fully to exploit economies of scale. Scale economies are important. In Chapter 33 we explained how these give rise to two-way trade between countries in the same industry. The SM intensified this trade in goods, and initiated such trade in some services (such as financial services) where differences in national regulation effectively precluded EC trade in the past.

Gains from intensified competition

The SM intensified competition for two different reasons. First, on average, the degree of regulation around which harmonization taking place was lower for most countries than in the past. For many continental countries, the SM programme embodied a substantial amount of deregulation.

Second, a larger market enabled individual firms to enjoy scale economies *without* necessarily having the large market share they would enjoy in a small, segmented national economy. This is a force for competition, which may stimulate greater cost efficiency. In Part 3 we showed how imperfect competition leads to allocative distortions. These should be smaller, the larger the market and the greater the competition.

This argument needs to be qualified in one important regard. For competition to increase, it is important that the size of firms does not increase in proportion to the increase in the size of the market; then the market shares would be unaltered. The late 1980s saw a wave of mergers between European firms as they were getting ready for 1992. The within-Europe share of world mergers and acquisitions activity increased from 10 per cent during 1985–87 to 29 per cent during 1991–93. Similarly, the share of manufacturing sales of the four largest firms in each industry increased from 20 per cent to 23 per cent between 1987 and 1993 (*source*: as in Table 35-2). There was also a sharp rise in mergers between EC firms and firms from outside the EC. The latter frequently involved US and Japanese firms ensuring a European foothold in case a single Europe became a fortified Europe.

This merger wave reflected company restructuring to get in better shape to exploit comparative advantage and scale economies after 1992. It was the market mechanism at work.

We should think not just about the market for goods and services but also the market for factors. Free capital mobility allowed firms to locate in areas in which the rate of return was highest, an important mechanism for increasing efficiency. Labour mobility was also enhanced, although most of the evidence is that labour mobility within the EU still remains small.

35-3 Quantifying the effects of the SM

How large were the gains in practice? A study by the European Commission in 1997 found clear evidence of efficiency gains both from greater trade within the EU and from the pro-competitive effect of lower profit margins. Table 35-2 shows estimates by Professor Alasdair Smith (now Vice Chancellor of Sussex University) and two colleagues, computing the welfare gain country by country.

The welfare gain should be viewed as the pure extra consumption available as a result of permanent supply-side improvements that enhance potential output. Answers depend partly on the assumptions of the analysis. For example, it is unclear whether we should assume a truly

Table 35-2	Gains from the SM (extra consumption, as % of initial GDP)
2–3	France, Germany, Italy, UK
2–5	Denmark
3–4	Netherlands, Spain
4–5	Belgium, Luxembourg
4–10	Ireland
5–16	Greece
19–20	Portugal

Source: C. Allen, M. Gasiorek, A. Smith, 'The competition effects of the single market in Europe', *Economic Policy 1998*.

BOX 35-1

The EMS and the Bundesbank

To understand the 1990s, we need a history lesson.

1 Without hyperinflation in 1923, German history might have been very different. More than any other nation, Germans now hate inflation and are determined to prevent it. The Bundesbank (Buba) has a constitution mandating it to achieve price stability as its overriding objective.

2 When capital mobility is high, to peg the exchange rate between two countries, both countries need to have the same interest rate. The key issue is who chooses the common interest rate.

3 When the EMS began in 1979, countries still had the exchange controls on capital flows that had survived from the earlier Bretton Woods system. Countries could run different monetary policies. There was a dispute between countries (e.g. France) that wanted a symmetric system and countries (e.g. Germany, and in particular the Buba) that wanted asymmetry.

4 Symmetry meant countries with exchange rates near the bottom of the band had to tighten monetary policy; those near the top of the band to loosen it. Germany would not sign up for a system in which it could be forced to print money and increase its inflation rate: symmetry would have meant converging on average inflation, much higher than the rate acceptable in Germany. Without Germany, the ERM would have been a dead duck.

5 The compromise reached in 1979 was that there would be a *presumption*, but no *requirement*, that countries would respond to signals from the exchange rate and change domestic policy accordingly. In fact, Germany rarely did. As the 1980s wore on, and German inflation remained low, the Deutschmark became a *nominal anchor* for the ERM. Germany set German interest rates for purely German reasons, and other countries moved interest rates in line with Germany.

6 This solution gave Germany the assurances it needed. It gave other countries, such as Italy and France, a means of borrowing the Buba's reputation. Previously, when Italian governments said they would be tough, nobody believed them. Wage-setters, anticipating monetary growth, put in for large nominal wage increases. Inflation expectations were self-fulfilling. For many countries the ERM became a pre-commitment to tougher monetary policy. Since Germany could veto the devaluations needed to reconcile high Italian inflation and Italian competitiveness, wage-setters in Italy could safely put in for lower rates of increase in nominal wages.

7 Speculators knew that the Buba at best would be uncomfortable about meeting any open-ended commitment to print money in order to help weaker currencies.

8 In fact, in 1978 during the negotiations to establish the EMS, the Buba had foreseen that such a situation might eventually arise, and had obtained its own 'opt out' deal. The German government privately assured the Bundesbank that the Buba had the option not to intervene if in its own opinion this threatened German price stability.

9 In mid-1992 several exchange rates appeared over-valued. Germany proposed a general EMS realignment in August, but this was declined by other countries. As speculative pressure continued, the Buba did in fact intervene massively, as did others such as the Bank of England and Banca

Realignments during 1992–97

Date	Punt	Peseta	Escudo	Lira
9/92		−5		−7 (left ERM)
11/92		−6	−6	
2/93	−10			
5/93		−8	−6.5	
3/95		−7		
12/96				(rejoin ERM)

D'Italia. But massively is not infinitely. Sterling and the lira were forced out of the ERM and depreciated substantially. The peseta and escudo, and the Irish punt, were devalued but remained within the system.

10 A new attack on the franc in August 1993 led to a face-saving 'redesign' of the ERM to allow the franc to survive within the ERM. Previous narrow bands (2¼ per cent each side of the parity) were replaced by very wide bands (15 per cent each side of the parity). Although everyone had expected a large movement of the franc within this wider band, in fact this never happened.

The table shows ERM realignments during 1992–97.

---

single market has yet been achieved. The range of estimates reflects the different possible assumptions.

Essentially, small countries gained more than large countries, but gains also depended on the pattern of commodities that a particular country traded. The largest gains came as the most protected activities were opened up. Not only was the SM programme good for the EU, it turned out to boost trade with the outside world. Fears of fortress Europe were unfounded.

Finally, it should be stressed that these estimates allow for adjustment to the new situation but not for any permanent effects on growth itself. The endogenous growth models we discussed in Chapter 30 would allow an additional role. For example, Professor Dick Baldwin of Geneva University has argued that higher potential output may enable more saving, more investment, and yet more output, which could increase the estimate of Table 33-2 even further.[1]

35-4 From EMS to EMU

By 1988, capital controls had been abolished as part of the SM programme. Some policy-makers realized that it was only a matter of time before speculators attacked the pegged exchange rates of the ERM. One possible solution was to go forward rapidly to completely fixed exchange rates.

A **monetary union** has permanently fixed exchange rates within the union, an integrated financial market, and a single central bank setting the single interest rate for the union.

A monetary union need not have a single currency. English and Scottish currencies circulate side by side in Edinburgh. What matters is that the exchange rate is certain and that a single authority (the Bank of England) sets the interest rate for both.

In 1988, the European heads of state established the Delors Committee to recommend how to get to European monetary union. Interestingly, the Committee was not asked to discuss whether EMU was a good idea. The Delors Committee recommendations became the basis of the Treaty of Maastricht in 1991.

European Monetary Union was to be attempted in three stages. Stage 1, which began in 1990, saw any remaining capital controls abolished, and the UK encouraged to join the ERM (it did that autumn). Realignments within the ERM were to be frowned on but were not impossible. In Stage 2, which eventually began in January 1994, a new European Monetary Institute was to begin preparing the ground for EMU, realignments were to be even harder to obtain, and excessive budget deficits were to be discouraged though not outlawed.

Stage 3, in which exchange rates were irreversibly fixed and the single monetary policy would begin, would start in 1997 provided a majority of potential entrants fulfilled the 'Maastricht criteria' (this deadline was not in fact achieved). Otherwise, EMU would begin in January 1999 with whatever number of countries then met the criteria. Monetary policy in EMU would be set by an independent central bank, mandated to achieve price stability as its principal goal.

What were the Maastricht criteria and what was their purpose? There were two sets of criteria, one for monetary policy and nominal variables, one for fiscal policy.

The **Maastricht criteria** for joining EMU said that a country must already have achieved low inflation and sound fiscal policy.

The monetary criteria said that to be eligible, a potential entrant had to have low inflation, low nominal interest rates (market confirmation of low inflation expectations), and two prior years in the ERM without any devaluation. This

---

[1] See R. Baldwin, 'The growth effects of 1992', *Economic Policy, 1990*. Note that since saving means forgoing consumption, the extra consumption benefit from the induced effect is smaller than the induced extra output.

last requirement was to prevent competitive devaluations or 'last realignments' as EMU approached.

The fiscal criteria said budget deficits must not be excessive, interpreted to mean that budget deficits should be less than 3 per cent of GDP; and that the debt/GDP ratio should not be over 60 per cent. Tight fiscal policy would mean there was little pressure on the central bank to bail out fiscal authorities.

Many economists complained that the Maastricht criteria were caution taken to extremes. An independent central bank with a tough constitution was an adequate pre-commitment to low inflation. It was unnecessary to constrain fiscal policy as well. Indeed, since national governments would no longer have a national interest rate or national exchange rate policy to deal with purely national circumstances, leaving them fiscal room for manoeuvre might be a good idea.

The Maastricht deal reflected the balance of power in the negotiations. At the time, Germany ran the EMS and trusted itself to do so in its own interests. Why would Germany give up such a good position? Only if EMU was going to be super safe. The Maastricht criteria were the price of getting Germany on board.

Sterling and UK membership

What arguments were advanced against UK membership of the ERM and EMU? First, until the late 1980s, North Sea oil made sterling behave differently from other European currencies. As UK oil production wound down, this objection evaporated.

Second, whereas the core countries of Europe are now very integrated with one another, offshore UK is less integrated with the rest of Europe. A common policy may be less suitable. Table 35-3 shows the composition of UK trade and how it has changed since the UK joined the EU in 1973. The trend is clear. The UK is getting more integrated with continental Europe all the time, even if from a lower base-line than some other European countries. If this trend continues, the issue is not whether the UK should join but when.

Table 35-3 UK trade patterns (%)			
	EU	N. America	Rest of world
1972	34	17	49
1998	57	15	28

Source: UN, *International Trade Statistics*.

Third, the UK has a greater tradition of macroeconomic sovereignty: it seems to have more to lose. Whereas ERM countries had been in a fixed exchange rate arrangement since 1979, and in an ERM in which the 'single' interest rate was increasingly set by Germany alone, sterling floated during the entire period except for the two years of its ERM membership in 1990–92.

However, the absence of capital controls and the power of the speculators limit monetary sovereignty whatever the exchange rate regime. The Bank of England has often wished to raise interest rates for domestic reasons, to cool down a housing boom, but been unprepared to do so because higher interest rates would bid up further the value of the floating pound, exacerbating the woes of UK exporters. The Bank has often found itself hoping for interest rate rises in Frankfurt and Washington that would allow it to raise sterling interest rates without causing a further appreciation of sterling.

Finally, Black Wednesday (16 September 1992) makes it hard for UK politicians to appear too in favour of EMU. Then Chancellor John Major had taken the UK into the ERM in 1990 to combat rising inflation at the end of the Lawson boom. Unfortunately, this coincided with German reunification. Big subsidies to East Germany caused German overheating. When Chancellor Kohl refused to raise taxes, the Buba raised interest rates to cool down the German economy. Interest rates high enough to do this job were far too high for Germany's partners in the ERM. This provoked the crisis of 1992–93. The UK and Italy left the ERM, slashed interest rates, and depreciated their currencies. Other countries struggled on inside the ERM though many had devaluations (Box 35-1, page 592).

German unification was the biggest country-specific economic shock in postwar Europe. It may not be a good guide to how EMU will fare. Indeed, the mandate of the European Central Bank to take an EU-wide view will prevent it reacting in such extreme fashion to the needs of one country. But UK voters remember the UK flirtation with a single European interest rate as an unhappy experience.

During 1996–98 EU countries scrambled frantically to get their budget deficits below the 3 per cent Maastricht limit to be eligible for EMU. There was fiscal tightening in continental Europe. Since the UK was enjoying the effects of looser policy after 1992 – the whole point of leaving the ERM had been to reduce interest rates and stimulate the economy – the UK business cycle got out of phase with the rest of Europe. This had little to do with any structural difference. It simply reflected the fact that while the UK had its foot on the accelerator its EU partners still had the brakes on

Table 35-4	European business cycles – UK and Euroland (%)			
	96	97	98	99
Euroland				
Real growth	2	2	3	2
Output gap	−2	−2	−1	−1
Unemployment	12	12	12	11
Interest rate	5	4	4	3
UK				
Real growth	3	4	2	1
Output gap	0	1	1	0
Unemployment	8	7	6	6
Interest rate	6	7	7	5

Source: OECD, *Economic Outlook*.

tight. By the end of the decade, the UK was having to start worrying about overheating at a time when the rest of the EU was finally coming out of its policy-induced recession and looking forward to a period of steady growth.

Eleven countries (all of those that wished to go ahead) were deemed in spring of 1998 to be fit and ready for EMU at the start of 1999. Table 35-4 contrasts the healthy UK performance during the late 1990s with the recession that EMU countries endured while they tightened fiscal policy to meet the Maastricht criteria.

With looser fiscal policy but as strong a commitment to low inflation, the UK inevitably had higher interest rates than its EU partners. Even if the UK wanted to join EMU, it would require tighter fiscal policy to make EMU interest rates appropriate for the UK. Announcing a 'tax for Europe' would have been political suicide in the UK, even though the Treasury did manage to raise tax revenue quite substantially by a host of less visible measures.

35-5 The economics of EMU

In 1999, Professor Robert Mundell won the Nobel Prize for Economics, in part for his pioneering work on optimal currency areas.

An **optimal currency area** is a group of countries better off with a common currency than keeping separate national currencies.

Mundell and the economists who came after him identified three attributes that might make countries suitable for a currency area. First, countries that trade a lot with each other may have little ability to affect their equilibrium real exchange rate against their partners in the long run; but they may face temptations to devalue to gain a temporary advantage. A fixed exchange rate rules out such behaviour and allows gains from trade to be enjoyed.

Second, the more similar the economic and industrial structure of potential partners, the more likely it is they face common shocks, which can be dealt with by a common monetary policy. It is country-specific shocks that pose difficulties for a single monetary policy.

Third, the more flexible are the labour markets within the currency area, the more easily any necessary changes in competitiveness and real exchange rates can be accomplished by (different) changes in the price level in different member countries.

Conversely, countries gain most by keeping their monetary sovereignty when they are not that integrated with potential partners, have a different structure, and hence are likely to face different shocks, and cannot rely on domestic wage and price flexibility as a substitute for exchange rate changes.

To these purely economic arguments, we should add an important political argument. Currency areas are more likely to work when countries within the area are prepared to make at least some fiscal transfers to partner countries. In practice, this cultural and political identity may be at least as important as any narrow economic criteria for success.

Is Europe an optimal currency area?

Those who have studied the structure of national economies, and the correlation of shocks across countries, generally reach the following conclusions.[2] First, Europe is quite, but not very, integrated. Second, there is a clear inner core of countries – the usual suspects – who are more closely integrated than the rest.

However, the act of joining EMU is likely to change the degree of integration, possibly quite substantially. The Single Market will be underpinned by EMU, enhancing integration of product markets and removing the need for national legislation that is partly responsible for existing segmentation of markets. There is also independent evidence that countries which trade a lot have more correlated business cycles. Moreover, countries which belong to currency unions tend historically to trade much

[2] See T. Bayoumi and B. Eichengreen, 'Shocking aspects of European monetary unification', in F. Giavazzi and F. Torres (eds.), *Adjustment and Growth in the European Monetary Union*, Cambridge University Press, Cambridge, 1994; and T. Bayoumi and B. Eichengreen, 'Operationalizing the theory of optimum currency areas', Discussion Paper 1484, Centre for Economic Policy Research, London, 1996.

more with each other than can be explained simply by the fact that their exchange rates are fixed.[3]

These pieces of evidence imply that it may be possible successfully to start a currency union before all the microeconomic pre-conditions are fully in place. The act of starting may speed up the process.

The Stability Pact

The Stability Pact, ratified by the Treaty of Amsterdam in 1997, confirmed that the Maastricht fiscal criteria would not merely be entry conditions for EMU but would continue to apply after countries joined the monetary union. Some EMU members have debt/GDP ratios of close to 100 per cent. Reducing these towards 60 per cent may take decades. The real focus has been on the 3 per cent ceiling for budget deficits.

In principle, countries exceeding the limit may have to pay fines unless their economy is in evident recession (automatic stabilizers mean tax revenues fall in a slump). To avoid this, and to retain the ability to use fiscal expansion as a last resort in a slump, countries may aim for something more like budget balance in normal times. Note that if budgets are roughly in balance over the business cycle, but output grows for ever, debt/GDP ratios should exhibit trend decline, whatever their cyclical behaviour. This may eventually lead to the tough conditions of the Stability Pact being eased.

The European Central Bank

The single monetary policy is now set in Frankfurt by the **European Central Bank** (ECB). National central banks have not been abolished, but the board of the ECB sets the interest rate on the euro.

The ECB mandate says its first duty is to ensure price stability, but it can take other aims into account provided price stability is not in doubt. In 1999, the ECB cut interest rates when Germany and Italy were stagnating and there was little sign of inflation.

Whereas the Bank of England is very transparent, revealing its inflation forecast and publishing minutes of meetings of its Monetary Policy Committee, the ECB has had a more difficult job. On the one hand, it wished to appear transparent. On the other hand, it needed to emphasize continuity with the Bundesbank, whose tradition had been not to publish the minutes and to give monetary growth forecasts pride of place as a leading indicator of inflation. Moreover, it may be easier for ECB board members to take a truly European interest, even if against the direct interest of the country from which they come, if voting records are not revealed.

One issue yet to be fully resolved is how the ECB will interact with the 11 national fiscal authorities. Since no procedure exists for co-ordinating fiscal policy, fiscal authorities may sometimes face temptations to free-ride on others: when Euroland is overheating, let other countries take the unpopular measures to tighten fiscal policy. Proponents of the Stability Pact point out that it helps redress this balance, keeping fiscal free-riding in check.

Fiscal federalism?

One reason for the survival of the monetary union that we call the United States is its federal fiscal structure. When a particular state has a slump, it pays less income tax revenue to Washington, and gets more social security money from Washington, without any decisions having to be taken. This is automatic stabilizers at work, courtesy of federal tax rates and federal rates of social security payments. Conversely, a booming state pays more tax revenue to Washington, and gets less social security money back.

A **federal fiscal system** has a central government setting taxes and expenditure rules that apply in its constituent states or countries.

When state income increased $1, the state paid an extra 30 cents in income tax and got an extra 10 cents in social security. Originally, economists thought that this meant each state was effectively insured up to about 40 cents in the dollar. Euroland has no federal fiscal structure on anything like this scale. The pessimists concluded that EMU would come under pressure from country-specific shocks.

The idea was correct but the sums were wrong. The original US calculations would have been correct if they described a world in which state incomes were completely uncorrelated. In practice, of course, the correlation is quite high. Hence, when one state slumps and gets help from Washington, many other states are slumping and also getting help. But this increases US government debt and means *every* state has to pay higher future taxes.

But an individual state could have done that on its own, without membership of the federal 'mutual insurance' club. It could have borrowed in the slump to boost its own fiscal spending, and paid it back later when times were better. Making allowance for this, US states are probably insured more like 10 cents in the dollar than 40 cents. However, the Stability Pact might *prevent* individual EMU countries

---

[3] A Rose, 'One money, one market', *Economic Policy*, 2000.

behaving in this way, by restricting their ability to borrow in bad times.

Macroeconomic policy in an EMU member

Figure 35-1 shows what life is like for an EMU member. Interest rates are set by the ECB in Frankfurt. From an individual country's viewpoint, it is as if the LM curve is horizontal at r_0. Suppose the initial level of the IS curve allows equilibrium at A. Aggregate demand equals potential output.

Now the country faces a shock that shifts the IS curve down to IS_1. With full monetary sovereignty, the country might have reduced its own interest rate to restore full employment output at C. This might still happen in EMU if the country is very correlated with other EMU countries. Then the ECB will react to what is happening throughout Euroland and cut interest rates for everybody.

At the opposite extreme, if no other countries face the IS curve shock and the country is too small to influence Euroland data to which the ECB reacts, then interest rates will remain at r_0. The country now faces two choices. Provided it does not infringe the Stability Pact, it can use fiscal policy to shift IS_1 to the right, or it can wait for its labour market to do the same thing.

How does this work? At B the country is facing a slump. This gradually bids down wages and prices. At the fixed

nominal exchange rate against its partners, this makes the country more competitive. Higher exports and lower imports shift the IS_1 curve to the right. If wage and price flexibility is high enough, there may be no need for fiscal policy. However, given that many European labour markets are quite sluggish, sensible use of fiscal policy may speed up the process.

35-7 Central and Eastern Europe

For 40 years after 1945, Central and Eastern Europe (CEE) was under rigid political and economic control from Moscow, a planned economy with only a small role for market forces. The inefficiency of planning cumulated as any market history receded. Capital was old, incentives were poor, and productivity was low.

Table 35-5 confirms two points about CEE on the eve of reform. It shows the low level of living standards compared with most Western neighbours. In affluent Northern Europe, per capita incomes in 1988–89 averaged about $20 000 a year. Table 35-5 also shows the failure of attempts in the 1970s to prop up planning by borrowing from the West to rebuild capital in the East. Countries such as Hungary and Poland were left with the debts but without corresponding benefits: inefficiencies in planning often left investment projects unfinished and hence wasted.

Some countries, such as Poland, had a portion of past debts written off by Western creditors. And the European Bank for Reconstruction and Development was set up in London to finance investment by the West in projects in the reforming economies.

Supply-side reforms

In the past, production, investment, and employment decisions were made largely by bureaucrats. A larger scale of operation meant greater prestige, even if it used more

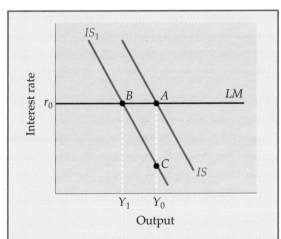

A small EMU member faces a horizontal LM curve at the interest rate set by the ECB. If the IS curve shifts to IS_1, interest rates will be reduced only if the whole of EMU is affected by the shock. Otherwise, the country faces a slump that gradually reduces its prices and wages, boosting competitiveness and shifting IS_1 to the right. A fiscal expansion could induce this shift more quickly.

Figure 35-1   A member of Euroland

Table 35-5	CEE in 1988–89	
	Per capita $ of	
	GDP	Foreign debt
East Germany	9300	1300
Czechoslovakia	7600	400
Hungary	6500	1900
Bulgaria	5600	1000
Poland	5600	1100
Romania	4100	0

Sources: American Express, *Amex Bank Review*, November 1989; HM Treasury, *Economic Progress Report*, 1990.

inputs than it produced outputs. Supply-side reform meant allowing the price mechanism to take over the role of allocating resources. This had several aspects.

First, prices needed to reflect true scarcity. Previously, prices were held artificially low. This made inflation look good, but such data were meaningless. Consumers couldn't get goods, and factories couldn't buy inputs at these artificial prices. There was chronic excess demand.

Freeing-up prices inevitably means that prices rise sharply. During January 1990, the first month of the Polish reform, measured inflation was 70 per cent in a month, an annual rate of almost 1000 per cent. But this was a one-off phenomenon. And it was precisely these high prices that were the market mechanism telling suppliers it was now time to increase production.

Success does not depend merely on freeing-up prices. A supply response to higher prices must take place. Incentives have to work. Bureaucrats who ran state enterprises may not be the best people to rise to this challenge. Many enterprises have since been privatized. The aim of privatization was less the need to raise revenue for the government – consumers had little wealth with which to pay – than to put the profit motive up front for those managing the new enterprises.

Several strategies of privatization were tried. Hungary tried to find foreign buyers willing to contribute hard cash and management expertise. The Czech Republic gave citizens vouchers with which to bid for shares in firms being privatized. Although appearing to achieve rapid privatization, many of these shares were eventually bought by state-owned banks! In Russia, the emphasis on privatization to existing managers led to accusations that organized crime had become too involved.

Trade and foreign investment

CEE needed markets for its output if it was to grow quickly. And the pressure of external competition was a powerful force for rapid productivity improvement, even if it meant unemployment in the short run while painful adjustment took place. The most obvious market for their goods was the EU.

In 1992, Poland, Hungary, and the then Czechoslovakia (subsequently two separate states) signed the Europe Agreements for the associate membership of the EC. Other CEE countries have subsequently made similar deals. These agreements promised rapid moves to free trade in many commodities, but not in the ones that really mattered. Declining or problem industries in the West were deemed too sensitive to be subject to competition from cheap imports from CEE. This applied to textiles, steel, and, of course, agriculture – three of the most obvious areas for exports westwards.

EU policy may have been excessively protectionist in this regard. Accepting imports from CEE has three big benefits for the EU. First, there is the benefit for EU consumers of cheap imports. Second, there is the consequent creation of economic growth in CEE as a natural export market for EU producers. Together, these two reasons put the classic case for exploiting comparative advantage. Third, if the experiment in CEE fails, the EU will face either massive immigration or a renewed political and military threat on its doorstep, and probably both. Liberal trade agreements are the most effective investment the EU can make in Eastern Europe's success. The 'Trade not Aid' slogan also applies in general to the third world, as we discuss in the final chapter.

CEE has an educated workforce. Besides market access, what it needs is physical investment and the management expertise to run market-oriented businesses. Here too the West can help, and in some cases has done so with success. Box 30-1 on page 515 gave details of extensive western investment in car plants in CEE.

Macroeconomic conditions for success

If reform programmes were to succeed, they had to prevent initial price increases spilling over into hyperinflation. Basically, what was needed is a fairly austere macro policy until the supply side can adjust. Subsidized credit and artificial exchange rates had to be abolished; interest rates and exchange rates had to find their own level. Then monetary policy had to be sound, and those countries with large fiscal deficits had to tackle their fiscal problems.

Every country was different, and no automatic formula could be applied. But it is easy to describe the form of package that seems to have worked most often in developing countries tackling similar difficulties. The currency should become convertible – an end to exchange rate rationing for importers and exporters – and it should be substantially devalued, since domestic prices are about to rise sharply, once and for all. The new lower exchange rate should then be rigidly enforced by macroeconomic policy, thereby providing a nominal anchor.

Initially, foreign exchange controls should be maintained on the capital account (just as in postwar Western Europe) in case residents panic and try to get all their money out of the country. As confidence builds up, these controls can be relaxed.

If unemployment rises during the initial period of immense restructuring, aggregate demand management should *not* be increased to take care of unemployment. That would prevent the adjustment from taking place, and would make inflation more of a danger in an already fragile situation.

In short, macroeconomic policy needed to be firm and to be believed to be so. Many economists believed that there was no point in half measures when attempting the biggest change in 50 years: 'If you are going to chop off a cat's tail, do it in one stroke, not bit by bit', remarked Gonzalo Sanchez de Losada, the minister responsible for Bolivia's similar reform package during 1986–89.[4]

If planning was so bad, why did things get worse?

Transition economics are those making the adjustment from central planning to a market economy.

Box 35-2 that follows shows that the reforming economies faced falls of at least 25 per cent in measured real GDP during 1990–92 before growth resumed in 1993 or 1994. How can we explain this?

First, we emphasize that there remains quite wide disagreement about the reliability of statistics such as those in Box 35-2. Before prices were freed, how did we measure real GDP (say in 1989)? If prices did not reflect scarcity, why value quantities at silly prices? One solution to this is to use *world prices*: simply measure quantities and then use dollar or DM prices. Economists who have done this find that some of the old industries were producing with *negative* value added: they used more inputs than they produced output.

Second, as explained earlier, a period of macroeconomic restraint was important to stop once-off price rises becoming embedded in permanent inflation expectations. For example, after price liberalization in Czechoslovakia, prices rose 25 per cent in January 1991; by July 1991, monthly inflation was down to zero.

But the deep recession cannot just be attributed to statistical quirks or a temporary period of disinflation. Three other factors played significant roles. First, as the former Soviet Union imploded, most countries in CEE lost their major export market. Reorientation of exports to the West was not easily accomplished overnight. Even in Western Europe,

Finland faced a severe recession as Russian markets collapsed.

Second, the lynchpin role of banks must be understood. Freeing prices does not introduce a market economy unless budget constraints bite. In the West, useless firms go bankrupt and physical resources get reallocated elsewhere. In Eastern Europe, state banks had previously been passive in lending. They made loans to state-owned enterprises (SOEs) to allow them to meet the output and investment targets laid down by the planners.

When prices were liberalized, many SOEs quickly lost money (as they should have). But nobody closed them down! State banks simply lent them new money to meet old debts and finance ongoing losses. When a giant SOE was the only employer in town, it was sometimes 'too big to fail'. Banks behaved in this way partly because they too were state-owned and still felt a responsibility to employment, but also because most of their assets – old loans to SOEs – were themselves worthless. Making a fuss might have revealed the extent of the trouble in the banks.

Governments, wisely, began tackling bad debts in the banks, and aimed to make banks early candidates for privatization. Without banks to enforce bankruptcy (in the West it is creditors who close down companies), we cannot expect prices to allocate resources more efficiently. Inefficient old firms continue, and new entrepreneurs find it hard to get loans.

Finally, there has been a major failure of corporate control. Even in the West we have trouble providing good incentives for managers (see Chapter 7). In reforming economies the problem has been acute. The watchful eye of the state was removed from SOEs as governments try to dissociate themselves from the old ways of planning. But until SOEs were privatized and monitored by informed shareholders, there was a vacuum of control. Managers could do what they like. What they liked may have been the easy life (concede unjustified wage claims to the workers banging on the door) or worse. Many countries faced outbreaks of 'spontaneous privatization'. In the West we call it theft.

The sharp contraction of output in the early 1990s owed a lot to the end of the COMECON system of trading and the implosion of the former USSR, to deep problems in banking and both the allocation and enforcement of credit, and to problems of corporate control.

Transition in CEE, and in other parts of the former Soviet bloc including Russia itself, reminds us that adoption of markets, while perhaps necessary, is by no means sufficient to enjoy the high living standards enjoyed in OECD countries. Well-functioning markets, like icebergs, have a lot

---

[4] Reported in J. Sachs and D. Lipton, 'Creating a Market Economy in Eastern Europe: The Case of Poland', Brookings Papers on Economic Activity, 1990. Professor Jeff Sachs of Harvard University, who advised both the Bolivian and the Polish governments on how to design their reform package, is also fond of saying 'You can't jump a chasm in two steps.'

BOX 35-2   CEE transition: a progress report

The two tables below show inflation and real output growth in the first eight years of transition. It is generally a picture of improvement, both in disinflation and in output growth, after severe initial recession. Although many countries seem launched on success, there were setbacks in Romania, Bulgaria, and Albania in 1997.

Inflation 1991–98, end year (% per annum)

	91	92	93	94	95	96	97	98
Central Europe								
Czech Republic	52	13	18	10	8	9	10	9
Hungary	32	22	21	21	28	22	18	14
Poland	60	44	38	29	22	19	13	10
Slovakia	58	9	25	12	7	6	6	9
South East Europe								
Albania	104	237	31	16	6	20	42	10
Bulgaria	339	79	64	122	33	165	578	10
Croatia	249	937	1150	−3	4	5	4	6
FYR Macedonia	115	1935	230	55	9	2	3	1
Romania	223	199	296	62	28	60	6	9
Slovenia	247	93	23	18	9	10	9	7
Baltics								
Estonia	304	954	36	42	29	24	12	8
Latvia	262	958	35	26	23	19	7	5
Lithuania	345	1161	189	45	36	26	9	4

Real output 1990–98

	% change per annum									1998 output level
	90	91	92	93	94	95	96	97	98	(1989 = 100)
Central Europe										
Czech Republic	0	−14	−6	−1	3	5	5	1	−1	97
Hungary	−4	−12	−3	−1	3	2	2	4	5	95
Poland	−12	−7	3	4	5	7	5	7	5	118
Slovakia	−3	−15	−7	−4	5	7	6	7	5	100
South East Europe										
Albania	−10	−28	−10	11	9	9	5	−7	9	87
Bulgaria	−9	−12	−7	−2	2	3	−4	−7	4	66
Croatia	−9	−20	−10	−4	1	2	5	7	4	79
FYR Macedonia	−10	−12	−21	−8	−4	−2	3	2	5	59
Romania	−6	−13	−9	1	4	7	5	−7	−5	78
Slovenia	−5	−8	−5	1	5	4	3	4	4	103
Baltics										
Estonia	−8	−11	−14	−9	−3	3	3	11	5	77
Latvia	3	−8	−35	−16	1	−2	1	7	4	58
Lithuania	−5	−13	−38	−24	1	3	2	6	3	63

Source: EBRD Transition Report.

below the waterline: invisible but important. They have legal contracts whose impartial enforcement in courts of law has a track record that inspires confidence and trust. They have regulations intended to mitigate market power and administered by public officials without endemic corruption. They have tax collection agencies that are fair and an attitude of tax compliance among citizens that keeps tax evasion within tolerable bounds. They have sophisticated systems of social insurance and protection designed to prevent the emergence of an underclass which first loses hope then takes revenge.

The list could be longer. Merely setting it out shows that many of its key items require expensive infrastructure and necessarily take time in which to build trust and reputation. This had two implications. First, transition will take time to succeed, especially where the social fabric is under threat.

Second, establishing markets is not something to be done on the cheap. Essential market infrastructure needs installing.

Despite these caveats, Box 35-2 shows that many economies, especially those in Central Europe closest to EU markets, are now growing steadily. Our discussion of convergence and catch-up in Chapter 30 suggests that there are grounds for expecting these economies to grow more rapidly than Western Europe over the next decade.

 SUMMARY

● The Single European Act committed EC governments to completion of the Single Market by 1992. The framework was a common set of broad outlines for regulation, national implementation, and mutual recognition of firms licensed in other member states.

● For many countries this meant substantial deregulation. Together with enlarged market size, this increased competition.

● The main winners were the small southern countries of the EU, who could exploit their relatively cheap labour and still had scope for scale economies. However, even the large, rich EU countries benefited.

● A monetary union means permanently fixed exchange controls, free capital movements, and a common monetary policy.

● In abolishing capital controls for 1992, the EMS was already committed to almost complete harmonization of monetary policy. The UK became a full EMS member in 1990, but withdrew in 1992.

● The Delors Report recommended progress to EMU in three stages. Stage 1 began on 1 July 1990 and envisaged exchange rate stability gradually increasing. In 1994 in Stage 2, the new institutions began rehearsing their eventual role, though as yet without formal power. In 1999, Stage 3 established the European Central Bank to run monetary policy. Exchange rates between EMU members were fixed for ever.

● The Maastricht criteria say that EMU entrants, including future ones, must have shown low inflation, low interest rates, and stable nominal exchange rates before entry;

and must have budget deficits and government debt under control.

● EMU members must continue to obey the Stability Pact, which fines countries for excessive budget deficits, except when they are in recession.

● In EMU, countries can change their competitiveness through the slow process of domestic wage and price adjustment. In the absence of any federal fiscal system, individual member states are likely to want to retain control of fiscal policy as a last resort for dealing with crises.

● Central and Eastern Europe has begun economic reform. It began with high foreign debt. Western countries offered aid but only limited access to Western markets.

● Supply-side reform means introducing the profit motive and deregulation, and allowing the price system to work. Because prices had been artificially low, initially there were sharp increases in prices. One challenge for policy was to stop this turning into hyperinflation. Macroeconomic policy needed to be firm during this dangerous phase.

● Output fell sharply in CEE during 1990–92. The principal causes were the collapse of COMECON and the Soviet market, the inability and unwillingness of banks to monitor and enforce credit agreements, a vacuum of corporate control, and other necessary infrastructure for a market economy.

● Most CEE countries resumed growth during 1993–94 and may now be expected to grow quickly provided sensible policies are maintained.

KEY TERMS

♦ The single market   590

♦ Non-tariff barriers   591

♦ Monetary union   592

♦ Maastricht criteria   593

♦ Optimal currency area   595

♦ European Central Bank   596

♦ Federal fiscal system   596

♦ Transition economies   599

REVIEW QUESTIONS

1 'Workers have power in the labour market only because their own firms have power in the goods market. In a perfectly competitive firm, attempts to raise wages just drive the firm out of business.' (a) Do you agree? (b) If 1992 increased competition in product markets, what effect would this have had on the labour market within the EU?

2 Name three EU countries you think have a comparative advantage in goods that use human capital intensively. Name three countries for which this is not the case.

3 You have been commissioned to write a report on whether London will remain Europe's leading financial centre after 2000. What arguments can you think of? What evidence would you want to collect?

4 Suppose two countries fix their exchange rate for ever, but they have foreign exchange controls preventing private sector capital account flows between them. Is this a monetary union? If not, why not?

5 In the light of your answer to problem 4, are the currencies of different members of a monetary union perfect substitutes? What does this tell you about their interest rates? What does that tell you about the possibility of conducting separate monetary policies?

6 Why might a government trying to pursue an economic programme of liberalization and reform be unable to carry it out?

7 What would be the consequences of free trade between the EU and CEE?

8 *Common fallacies* Show why the following statements are incorrect. (a) 1992 was a recipe for the rest of Europe to enjoy West German living standards. (b) European Monetary Union will severely reduce the monetary sovereignty of individual members of the EMS. (c) The European Central Bank must be accountable to politicians, and individual member-states. That is the recipe for guaranteeing democracy and low inflation.

36 Problems of developing countries

LEARNING OUTCOMES

When you have finished this chapter, you should be able to:

- Analyse why poor countries are poor and explore ways in which they may do better in the future
- Identify the handicaps with which developing countries begin
- Examine whether reliance on comparative advantage, usually the export of primary products, is a secure route to prosperity
- Discuss the role of industrialization and the export of manufactures
- Study the problems that have arisen in seeking development through foreign borrowing
- Explore the role that structural adjustment can now play in future development
- Assess the importance of aid from rich countries

In Europe or the United States a drought is bad for the garden; in poor countries it kills people. In this chapter we pay special attention to the poorer countries in the world economy.

We begin by showing how unequally the world's income is divided between the rich industrial countries and the poor, less developed countries (LDCs).

Less developed countries (LDCs) are those with low levels of per capita output.

We then briefly review the major problems that low-income countries face in trying to develop their economies. However, the theme of Part 5 is the world economy as a whole, not a description of its constituent parts. Therefore two major issues that we discuss are the best way for LDCs to take advantage of the world economy as it currently exists, and the extent to which LDCs actually benefit from participating in the world economy.

In May 1974, the General Assembly of the United Nations passed a resolution calling for a New International Economic Order (NIEO). It called for international co-operation to reduce the widening gap between the developed and the developing countries. The resolution reflected the feeling of many LDCs that the world economy is arranged to benefit the industrial countries and exploit the poorer countries. Since 1974 we have had a quarter of a century of talk about restructuring the world economy – but not much action.

We look at the facts behind the movement for an NIEO and the proposals that have been made. Economics cannot give all the answers, but it can be used to analyse the proposed solutions. We begin with the enormous inequality between the countries of the world.

36-1 World income distribution

In 1997, 35 per cent of the world's people lived in low-income countries, with an average annual income of about £220 per person. In the rich countries, people enjoyed an average annual income of about £16000 per person. *Most of the world's people live in poverty beyond the imagination of people in rich Western countries*. And, of course, not everyone in a country gets exactly the average income. Even in some middle-income countries, many people live in great poverty.

Table 36-1 shows data on per capita income, life expectancy at birth, and adult illiteracy. The low-income countries are very badly off on every measure.

Progress 1965–97 Nevertheless, the situation of low-income countries has improved since 1965. Table 36-2 shows a marked increase in life expectancy in low-income countries, a clear indication that the quality of life has improved since 1965.

Table 36-2 shows that per capita income grew in all groups of countries. Although low-income countries achieved real growth, in absolute terms they fell even further behind the rest of the world.

Thus there has been some progress in the past three decades, but the gap between low-income and other countries is wide and in most cases widening.

The north and the south

The north–south distinction sees the world divided into the rich north and the poor south. Those in the south claim the right to a larger share of the world's income, and their claims are on the rich countries of the north. The north–south division is essentially the same as the division between the industrialized countries and the LDCs. The LDCs are the countries of the Third World, ranging from the very poor countries of Africa and Asia to the middle-income countries such as Argentina and Mexico.

People living in the industrial north may be interested in the problems of LDCs not merely out of a concern for fairness and an abhorrence of poverty wherever it occurs. In Chapter 33, we argued that an increase in world trade will usually benefit everyone concerned. Even from a purely selfish standpoint, the north has many reasons to be interested in the economic development of the LDCs.

36-2 Economic development in low-income countries

Why do so many countries have such low per capita real GNP? To get to this position, they must have grown slowly for a long time. In this section we examine the special problems faced by countries with very low incomes.

Population growth The growth of per capita real income depends on the growth of total real income relative to the growth of population. In rich countries birth control is widespread; in poor countries much less so. In the absence of state pensions and other benefits, having children is one way people can try to provide security against their old age when they are no longer able to work. In recent decades the population of low-income countries has been growing at about 2.5 per cent per annum; in rich countries annual population growth is less than 1 per cent per annum. Merely to maintain per capita living standards, poor countries have to increase total output much faster than rich countries.

A rapidly expanding labour force can allow rapid GNP growth if other factor inputs are expanding at an equal rate. The problem for poor countries is that they cannot expand supplies of land, capital, and natural resources at the same rate as the labour force. Decreasing returns to labour set in.

Resource scarcity Dubai is generously endowed with oil and has a per capita GNP in excess of the United States or Germany. Most of the world's low-income countries have not been blessed with natural resources that can profitably

Table 36-1	World welfare indicators, by country group, late 1990s		
	Low income	Middle income	Rich industrial
Per capita GNP (£)	220	1180	16060
Life expectancy at birth (years)	59	68	78
Adult illiteracy (%)	47	18	<5

Source: World Bank, *Development Report* (various issues).

Table 36-2	World development, 1965–97		
Country income group	Per capita real growth (% p.a.)	Life expectancy at birth	
		1965	1997
Low	2.1	50	59
Middle	1.6	52	68
Rich	2.6	71	78

Source: World Bank, *Development Report* (various issues).

BOX 36-1

'70s dream world with no hunger destroyed by conflict' (*The Times*, 14 November 1996)

Henry Kissinger, the Harvard Professor who went on to be Richard Nixon's Secretary of State, was famous for his 'shuttle diplomacy' in trying to solve the Middle East crisis. Less well known is the fact that at the UN Food Summit in 1974 he forecast that world hunger would be eradicated within ten years. Reporting the next UN Food Summit in 1996, at which vows were made to halve the number of hungry and mal-nourished people within 20 years, *The Times* wryly noted that the announcement 'was overshadowed by the more immediate crisis in Zaire'. The UN Secretary-General 'issued an emotional plea for "collective help" for more than a million refugees "facing certain death" in eastern Zaire'. Civil wars have been a major impediment to economic development.

Chronically undernourished (million people)	1970	1980	1990	2010
N. Africa and Near East	60	40	50	60
Latin America	60	50	70	40
East Asia	470	380	280	120
South Asia	250	300	260	200
Sub-Saharan Africa	90	150	220	260

Adapted from *The Times*, 14 November 1996.

be exploited. And having resource deposits is not enough: it takes scarce capital resources to extract mineral deposits.

Capital   The rich countries have built up large stocks of physical capital which make their labour forces productive. Poor countries have few spare domestic resources to devote to physical investment. Most domestic resources are required to provide even minimal consumption. Financial loans and aid allow poor countries to buy in machinery and pay foreign construction firms. However, LDCs frequently complain both that financial assistance is inadequate[1] and that multinational firms brought in to assist in economic development actually prevent sustained economic growth by LDCs: they use foreign workers, thus preventing domestic workers from acquiring valuable skills and experience, and they repatriate the profits to their own countries, thus preventing the accumulation of financial capital within LDCs to finance further development.

Social investment in infrastructure   Developed countries achieve economies of scale and high productivity through specialization, which is assisted by sophisticated networks of transport and communications. Without expensive investment power generation, roads, telephone systems, and urban housing, poor countries have to operate in smaller communities which are unable fully to exploit the possibility of scale economies and specialization.

Human capital   Without resources to devote to investment in health, education, and industrial training, workers in poor countries are often less productive than workers using the same technology in rich countries. Yet without higher productivity, it is hard to generate enough output (surplus to consumption requirements) to increase investment in people as well as in machinery.

Customs   It is easy for people from the north to claim that in LDCs tribal customs and communal living inhibit the development of enterprise and initiative. This argument may have some force. Yet it is easy to forget that the business traditions of the industrial countries and the acceptance of factory working took decades or even centuries to develop. Some LDCs are explicitly searching for alternative develop-ment strategies which recognize the culture from which they begin.

Low productivity agriculture   If agricultural productivity is low, most people must work on the land to produce enough food for the population. Few workers are available for work in other activities. Yet increased agricultural production requires better drainage, irrigation, modern fertilizers and seeds, or better equipment. Until workers can be released from the land, poor countries cannot devote resources to investment to improve agricultural productivity. It is all part of the same vicious circle.

---

[1] At the 1996 Food Summit, Jacques Diouf, Director of the Food and Agriculture Organization said his annual budget was 'less than what nine developed countries spend on dog and cat food in six days, and less than 5 per cent of what inhabitants of just one developed country spend on slimming products every year'. *The Times*, 14 November 1996.

Conflict In addition to these narrow economic reasons, some people believe that the poorest regions have been those where colonially imposed boundaries made little sense and where colonial rule did not sufficiently prepare the indigenous people for administration. The end of empire then left governments without wide domestic support, and both internal and international conflict followed.

In the rest of this chapter, we discuss the extent to which the world economy can help. However, we do not focus exclusively on the very poorest countries. The group of countries classified as LDCs also includes the newly industrialized countries – countries such as Mexico and Brazil which are well on their way to becoming rich countries. In some cases these middle-income countries have developed in the way the poorest countries hope to develop. But together, the LDCs share many grievances about the way the world economy operates. In their view it is stacked in favour of the rich industrial countries.

36-3 Development through trade in primary products

In Chapter 33 we analysed the gains from trade when countries specialize in the commodities in which they have a comparative advantage. We saw that relative factor abundance is an important determinant of comparative advantage. In many LDCs, the factor with which they are relatively most abundantly supplied is land. This suggests that LDCs can best take advantage of the world economy by exporting goods that use land relatively intensively.

Primary products are agricultural goods and minerals. Their production relies heavily on the input of land.

In this section we study LDC exports of primary commodities, both the 'soft' commodities – agricultural products such as coffee, cotton, and sugar – and the 'hard' commodities or minerals, such as copper or aluminium.

Traditionally, the LDCs have indeed sought to secure the gains from trade by exporting primary products to the rest of the world and using the revenue to obtain badly needed machinery and other manufactured imports. As late as 1960, exports of primary commodities accounted for 84 per cent of all LDC exports. Nevertheless, many LDCs have become sceptical of the route to development through specialization in production of primary products. Today, less than half of all LDC exports are primary products. We now explain why.

Table 36-3 Real price of primary products 1955–99 (1995 = 100)

	55	75	85	95	99
Petroleum	57	180	229	100	125
Gold	43	120	118	100	62
8 other metals	152	200	128	100	71
28 soft products	186	217	129	100	70

Source: IMF, *International Financial Statistics*.

Trends in primary commodity prices

Table 36-3 shows that, with the exceptions of petroleum, where supply was effectively curtailed by OPEC, and gold, where the price used to be artificially controlled, the trend in real prices of primary products has been downwards for the last two decades. This can be attributed both to increased supply and to reduced demand. On the demand side, technical advances such as artificial rubber and plastics have reduced the price for which many raw materials can be sold in industrial markets.

On the supply side, the problem has been the success of the LDCs in increasing productivity and output. In going for growth through exports of primary products, LDCs invested in better drainage and irrigation, better seeds, and more fertilizers. Asian agriculture was transformed by the 'green revolution'. Mineral producers developed more capital-intensive mining methods, which again increased productivity and output. The concerted effort of LDCs to increase output and obtain more export earnings contributed to the fall in the real price of the commodities that they were trying to sell.

Will these trends in primary product prices continue? Not necessarily. With finite world supplies of some minerals, real prices will eventually have to rise to ration increasingly scarce supplies. But the real price of reproducible commodities such as natural rubber will probably continue to fall as more artificial substitutes are developed. Land currently used for rubber trees may eventually be diverted to more profitable uses.

Price volatility

A second disadvantage of concentrating on the production of primary products is that their real prices tend to be very volatile. For both soft and hard commodities, a change of more than 40 per cent in the *real* price within a single year is not uncommon. In any particular year, LDCs are uncertain how many imports their exports revenue is going to finance.

Equilibrium prices for primary products tend to be volatile because both the supply and the demand are price-inelastic. On the demand side, people need food and industrial raw materials. On the supply side, crops have already been planted and perishable output has to be marketed whatever the price. Similarly, the supply of metals and minerals tends to be inelastic because it takes many years to develop a new copper mine or aluminium plant. Output cannot be quickly changed.

Because both supply and demand curves are very steep, a small shift in one curve will lead to a large change in the equilibrium price. Demand curves shift because the industrial economies move through periods of boom and slump. Harvest failures are the most important source of supply shifts.

Export concentration

Fluctuations in the real price of primary products lead to volatile export earnings and fluctuations in GNP in those LDCs that concentrate on producing primary products for the world economy. Table 36-4 shows that a single commodity can account for a large share of total exports of some LDCs.

The real price of, say, cocoa is volatile. Suppose Ghana faces a 50 per cent drop in cocoa prices: its export earnings fall 11 per cent, which is catastrophic. Of course, Ghana does very well when cocoa prices soar. But Ghana's entire economy will be buffeted by changes in the world cocoa market.

The combination of a downward long-run trend in real prices and large short-term fluctuations around this trend has made LDCs reluctant to persist with the route of development through exports of primary products if this means excessive concentration on a single commodity. Each of the countries in Table 36-4 has managed to reduce the export share of its dominant commodity by over 10 per cent since 1974. Diversifying production and exporting into other commodities helps to stabilize export revenue and general macroeconomic performance.

Commodity stabilization schemes

By acquiring more economic power, it is possible that primary producers could continue to pursue their natural

comparative advantage but within a world economy from which they could more easily benefit. Suppose they got together to organize a stabilization scheme for a particular primary product. By stabilizing the price of the commodity, the scheme would stabilize the export earnings of countries heavily dependent on exports of that commodity.

Figure 36-1 shows how the scheme would work. *DD* shows the inelastic demand curve for the commodity. The total supply curve of competitive producers fluctuates between SS_1 and SS_2 depending on the state of the harvest. In a free market, equilibrium will oscillate between points A_1 and A_2 on the demand curve. Since demand is inelastic, these oscillations imply major changes in the equilibrium commodity price.

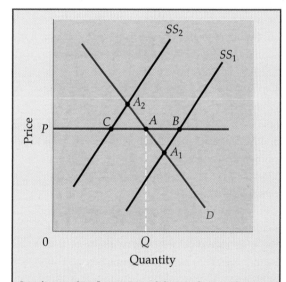

In a free market, fluctuations of the supply curve between SS_1 and SS_2 lead to movements along the demand curve between A_1 and A_2. When the supply curve is SS_1 the buffer stock scheme purchases a quantity AB. The quantity OQ is exported at a price P. When the supply curve is SS_2 the buffer stock scheme sells the quantity CA. Again a total quantity OQ is exported at a price P. Thus commodity prices and export earnings are stabilized.

Figure 36-1 Commodity price stabilization

Table 36-4 Export concentration and real price variability 1966–98				
	Zambia (copper)	Mauritius (sugar)	Mali (cotton)	Ghana (cocoa)
% of total exports (1995)	81	15	40	22
Real price (min & max)	86 & 323	19 & 46	61 & 207	65 & 432

Note: Real prices in 1995 US cents/lb.
Source: IMF, *International Financial Statistics*.

Now suppose a buffer stock is established.

A **buffer stock** is an organization aiming to stabilize a commodity market. It buys when the price is low, sells when the price is high.

Suppose a bumper harvest means the supply curve is SS_1. In the absence of intervention, equilibrium would be at A_1. The buffer stock organization can buy a quantity AB, leaving a quantity OQ to be purchased by other buyers at a price P. If the government runs the buffer stock, the country's exports will be Q at the price P.

The buffer stock stores the commodity in warehouses. When there is a harvest failure, the producers' supply curve will be SS_2. Rather than allow free market equilibrium at the point A_2, the buffer stock sells off a quantity CA from the warehouse. Together with new production PC, this implies that again the total quantity exported is Q and the price is P. Thus the activities of the buffer stock organization not only stabilize the commodity price at P but, by stabilizing the quantity of exports at Q, stabilize export earnings.

Although Figure 36-1 illustrates fluctuations in supply, fluctuations in the demand may also provide a reason for establishing a buffer stock. The demand schedule for copper tends to fluctuate in line with the business cycle in Europe and North America where copper is a major input to production. Try drawing for yourself a figure like Figure 36-1 to illustrate how a buffer stock might work when demand schedule fluctuates.

At which price should the buffer stock aim to stabilize the market? If the only aim is the elimination of price volatility, the price should be stabilized at the level that implies neither accumulation nor decumulation of buffer stock holdings in the long run. Suppose in Figure 36-1 that the producers' supply curve fluctuates regularly between SS_1 and SS_2. At the price P shown in the figure, there are as many years in which the buffer stock is purchasing the quantity AB as there are years in which it is selling the equal quantity CA. Stabilizing at a higher price would make AB larger than CA and imply that buffer stocks in the warehouses were growing in the long run.

Such a policy may also make sense. It is simply the policy of restricting supply to the market, the policy so successfully undertaken by OPEC. OPEC did not even need a warehouse. The separate producing countries formed a cartel and agreed to leave the quantity AB in the ground. Since the demand for oil and other primary products is inelastic, restricting the quantity supplied not only raises the price but also raises export earnings of commodity producers. Thus, in principle, effective cartels of producers could not only stabilize the prices of primary products; they could follow the OPEC example and combat the trend of declining real prices by restricting supply.

In recent years there have been attempts by LDCs to organize commodity price stabilization schemes in coffee, cocoa, and tin. Sometimes these take a simple form. For example, when there has been a bumper coffee crop in Brazil, the world's largest coffee producer, the Brazilian government has purchased coffee from Brazilian farmers and simply burned it. But none of the LDCs has managed to copy OPEC's example with much success. For many primary commodities, governments have to deal not with a few large oil fields but with a large number of small producers who are much harder to organize.

We discussed cartels in detail in Chapter 10. One problem with the strategy of supply restriction to force up the price is that there is an incentive for individual producers to cheat on the collective agreement. When price is forced above marginal cost, each producer has an incentive to produce more than the agreed output. Yet if all producers cheat, the price will come tumbling down or the buffer stock will be forced to acquire enormous warehouse stocks to keep this production off the market. Even the rich countries of the EU complain about the cost of warehouse stocks of the famous 'butter mountain'. LDCs simply cannot afford to tie up money in this way.

Since LDCs have been unsuccessful in policing their own attempts to restrict primary commodity supply, and since they cannot afford to stockpile vast quantities when individual producers refuse to cut back output, LDCs would like assistance from the rest of the world in establishing effective commodity stabilization schemes. By maintaining higher real prices for primary commodities, these schemes would effectively transfer purchasing power from rich industrial users and consumers to poorer producers. But, by also stabilizing real prices, LDCs argue that benefits would also accrue to industrial nations that are heavily dependent on exporting these commodities.

36-4 Development through industrialization

Many countries have concluded that the route to development lies not through increased specialization in production of primary products but in the expansion of industries that produce manufactures. In this section we discuss the two very different forms that industrial development has taken.

Table 36-5   Growth and trade by South East Asian economies 1965–97

	Annual real growth of per capita GDP (%)		.	Share of manufactures in merchandise exports	
	1965–80	1980–97		1965	1997
Indonesia	9	6		2	51
Hong Kong	9	5		90	92
Malaysia	7	5		6	76
Singapore	10	7		34	84
South Korea	10	7		59	92
Thailand	7	6		4	73
China (since 1980)	—	9		47	84

Source: World Bank, *World Development Report*.

Import substitution

When world trade collapsed in the 1930s, many LDCs found their export revenues reduced by more than 50 per cent. Not unnaturally, some LDCs resolved never again to be so dependent on the world economy. After the war, they began a policy of import substitution.

Import substitution is a policy of replacing imports by domestic production under the protection of high tariffs or import quotas.

Import substitution reduces world trade and involves suppressing the principle of comparative advantage. LDCs used tariffs and quotas to direct domestic resources away from the primary products in which they had a comparative advantage, into industrial manufacturing where they had a comparative disadvantage.

International trade theory suggests that this policy is likely to be wasteful. Countries are using more domestic resources to make manufactured products than would have been required to make the exports to finance imports of the same quantity of manufactures.[2]

Import substitution was pursued partly because LDCs wanted to reduce their specialization in particular primary commodities for the reasons we discussed in the previous section, and partly because these countries associated a developed industrial sector with the high productivity levels observed in the rich industrial countries. Embarking on a strategy of import substitution has one great danger and one possible merit.

The danger is that import substitution may prove a dead end. In the short run, the policy is costly because domestic manufactures are being produced using more resources and at a higher cost than the country's social marginal cost of

these goods, namely the world price at which they could be imported. And, although domestic industry may expand quite rapidly behind tariff barriers while imports are being replaced, once import substitution has been completed economic growth may come to an abrupt halt. The country is now specialized in industries in which it has a comparative *disadvantage*, and further expansion can come only from expanding *domestic* demand. That is the danger.

The possible merit is that comparative advantage is a dynamic, not a static, concept. In Chapter 33 we saw that a tariff may help an infant industry even though production subsidies would achieve the same outcome at lower social cost. By developing an industrial sector and learning to use the technology, LDCs may eventually come to have a comparative advantage in some industrial products. Although high-tech projects will continue to be pioneered in the rich countries, which can afford large expenditure on research and development, subsequently many of these production technologies become relatively routine. LDCs may be able to exploit their relative abundance of labour to produce manufactures that are labour-intensive.

Thus import substitution may not be an end in itself. It may be a preliminary phase in which industry gets started, as a prelude to export-led growth.

Export-led growth stresses production and income growth through exports rather than the displacement of imports.

Exports of manufactures

The real success stories of the last three decades are the countries that have made this transition and are no longer high-tariff countries but rather are successful exporters of manufactures. Instead of withdrawing from the world economy, they are turning it to their advantage. This has been particularly true in the countries of South East Asia, including China. Table 36-5 shows their rapid growth and the key role of exports of manufactured goods.

---

[2] By closing itself off from the world economy, the communist bloc also pursued import substitution on a grand scale. It was not an economic success.

BOX 36-2　　　　　　　Fickle capital flows hurt LDCs

During the 1990s, capital mobility increased. Many LDCs attracted foreign capital in large amounts. Some inflows reflected long-term investment in factories and production, but many inflows were lured by high domestic returns in 'emerging market' economies steadily dismantling previous controls. Frequently, these economies pegged their exchange rate to the US dollar. Foreign investors thought they could take advantage of high returns yet get their money out before any devaluation materialized.

In 1997 East Asia caught a cold. Country after country faced a speculative attack on its exchange rate peg. Even countries with healthy 'fundamentals' were attacked. Since Asian banks had borrowed in foreign currency, drastic falls in exchange rates led to large increases in the real value of bank liabilities, making the banking system bankrupt and inducing further panic.

The table below shows the dramatic depreciation of real exchange rates. The IMF found itself organizing large rescue packages. Where these helped restore solvency, the depreciated 'super-competitive' exchange rate then allowed recovery in 1998. As confidence returned, exchange rates climbed to more reasonable levels, as the table shows.

Lessons of the crisis? First, allowing massive capital inflows is dangerous: what flows in can also flow out. Increasingly, LDCs are encouraged to float the exchange rate as a way of limiting the capital inflow. Second, retaining some restrictions on capital flows may not be such a bad idea, at least until the domestic banking system is well regulated and more robust. Third, LDCs should not borrow too much in foreign currency, whose domestic value increases when the exchange rate plunges. Fourth, the IMF success came at a price, and not only for the rich countries who paid its bills. Bailing out foreign investors raises expectations of future bail-outs. Some critics said that if the IMF had not bailed out Mexico in 1995, the Asian crisis of 1997 would not have been so bad.

	Indonesia	Korea	Malaysia	Thailand	Philippines
Real exchange rates (1990–96 = 100)					
June 1997	105	95	111	107	115
Dec. 1997	62	66	80	72	89
June 1998	33	76	79	87	92
Dec. 1998	71	85	77	98	91

Source: World Bank, *Global Development Finance 1999*.

Should producers of manufactures in the rich countries worry about competition from Asian producers of manufactures? High-tech industries aside, will the 'tigers' wipe out producers of labour-intensive manufactures in Europe, North America, and even Japan?

Although we tend to think of LDCs exporting very labour-intensive low-quality manufactures such as cheap textiles, this stereotype is outdated. It remains true that textiles are the largest single manufactured commodity exported by LDCs, but exports of machinery and consumer durables are growing the most rapidly. LDCs are now major producers of everything from cars to transistors and television sets. How will the industrial countries react?

The principle of comparative advantage suggests that in the long run the industrial countries and the world as a whole should exploit the gains from this new trade in manufactures. The established industrial economies should reallocate factors to industries in which their comparative advantage now lies, industries such as genetics and telecommunications, which use relatively intensively the capital and technical expertise with which the rich countries are relatively well endowed.

However, the adjustment process is costly. Factories have to be closed, outdated plant written off, and workers retrained. In Chapter 33 we explained why politicians may give in to pressure from declining industries to protect them through tariffs and quotas rather than insist that new industries be established. In a world where tariffs among industrial countries have been largely abolished, there is now a re-emergence of protection through quotas, voluntary export restrictions, and non-tariff barriers. Restrictions of trade in textiles and clothing date back to the 1960s. New restrictions have subsequently appeared in cars, steel, and video recorders.

In Chapter 33 we showed how tariffs lead society to waste resources. They also lead to substantial transfers from consumers to producers. Although the new protectionism in the industrial countries is by no means universal; it can be significant in some industries:

For every $20 000 job in the Swedish shipyards, Swedish taxpayers pay an estimated $50 000 annual subsidy. Protection costs Canadian consumers $500 million a year to provide an additional $135 million of wages in the clothing industry. And when Japanese consumers pay eight times the world price for beef, Japanese farmers are not made eight times better off. It costs them that much more to produce it.[3]

Compared with these costs, subsidized retraining, redundancy benefits, and the closing of plants that are no longer efficient make much more sense. In the long run, protection costs more than subsidizing adjustment as comparative advantage changes.

Nevertheless, the LDCs are justifiably frightened that their strategy of economic development through industrialization and export-led growth through manufactures will be frustrated by protection in their industrial markets. The movement for an NIEO does not want merely an assurance that the rich countries will not impose tariffs and other restrictions on imports from LDCs. It would like the industrial countries to go further: to accelerate imports of manufactures from LDCs by actually imposing tariffs on imports from other industrial countries. At present, the prospects for such discrimination in favour of LDCs seem small.

36-5 Development through borrowing

A third route to economic development is by external borrowing, and a third complaint of LDCs about the way the world economy works is that borrowing terms are too tough. LDCs have traditionally borrowed in world markets to finance an excess of imports over exports. By importing capital goods, LDCs were able to supplement domestic investment financed by domestic savings.

---

[3] World Bank, *World Development Report*.

The international debt crisis

We remind ourselves of the basic balance of payments arithmetic:

$$\text{Current account deficit} = \text{trade deficit} + \text{debt interest}$$
$$= \text{increase in net foreign debt}$$

(1)

The first line shows the sources of the current account deficit; the second reminds us that it has to be paid for by selling domestic assets to foreigners or by new foreign borrowing.

Table 36-6 shows the dramatic build-up in debt for almost every type of LDC in the 1980s.

The **international debt crisis** arose when many poor countries were no longer able to pay interest on their foreign debts.

But the *burden* of the debt is not measured simply by the debt/GNP ratio. Debt hurts only when the real interest rate is positive: only then does a country have to sacrifice real resources to repay the debt in the future. A crucial reason why a debt crisis emerged after 1980 was the rise in real interest rates. Indeed, for many of the previous decades real interest rates were actually negative, and debtor countries were being subsidized in real terms by creditors.

It is also arguable that the right measure of a country's ability to pay is not its GNP but its export earnings. Hence

Table 36-6 LDC debt (% of GNP)		
	1980	1996
All LDCs	26	34
Sub-Saharan Africa	29	77
East Asia, Pacific	17	30
South Asia	17	32
Middle East, N. Africa	31	38
Latin America, Caribbean	35	36
E. Europe, Central Asia	24	34

Source: World Bank, *World Development Report*.

Table 36-7 Debt service (% of net exports)			
	1970	1980	1997
Argentina	22	37	64
Columbia	12	16	29
Brazil	12	63	62
Mexico	24	50	37
Venezuela	3	27	33
Burundi	2	10	29
Kenya	6	21	21

Source: World Bank, *World Development Report*.

BOX 36-3   The Brady Plan and the debt crisis

It is the mid-1980s, you have just become president of one of the LDCs, and life is tough. Your predecessors thought OPEC would quickly fall to bits, so they borrowed abroad to pay for oil imports. They also thought that, since real interest rates had been low foreign borrowing was essentially free. So they borrowed a lot abroad. You inherit massive foreign debts, but think higher oil prices and higher real interest rates may be around for a while.

Your country owes foreign banks $100 billion, in dollars. You can't reduce it by devaluing or by creating inflation at home. You are supposed to pay $10 billion a year in interest. Since world interest rates are also 10 per cent, if you could pay in full the market would trade your bonds at their par value of $100 per bond for the outstanding 1 billion bonds. $100 is the present value of $10 a year for ever when the interest rate is 10 per cent a year.

Unfortunately, your country can't now pay what it owes. By imposing very tough domestic policies, you have cut back consumption and imports, creating a trade surplus of $2 billion a year; but you owe $10 billion a year. You can't squeeze the domestic economy any more: people are starving. Nor will the bankers lend you any more: they think you are going bankrupt. In fact, the secondary (or second-hand) market for your outstanding bonds shows exactly what the market thinks of your chances. If people think that the most you can pay for ever is $2 billion, not $10 billion, a year, each bond will trade for $20. It trades for one-fifth of its par value because the market only expects to receive one-fifth of what it should.

Who lost out? The person to whom you originally issued the bond at par for $100. As soon as the market figured out you were in trouble, the secondary price fell immediately to the level then considered realistic. Your bonds are trading *at a discount*, or below par. You are less than fully creditworthy, and hence find it hard to borrow any more money.

Creditors will never get more than 20 per cent of what they are owed: that is the most you can pay. Why don't creditors simply let you off 80 per cent of your debts?

If banks let you off today, they'll have every other debtor government coming to them tomorrow with a similar plea. Perhaps for banks it is better simply to make a dreadful fuss and hope that governments in *rich* countries put up some of the money. Provided you keep paying almost $2 billion a year, any extra money from northern governments goes not to making your life easier but rather to reducing the losses of northern shareholders in northern banks!

This was the basis of the *Brady Plan*, a proposal in 1989 by the US Treasury Secretary to start organizing debt write-offs of the kind described above. Debtors committed themselves to sound economic policies and to trying to pay what they could. Governments kicked in a bit of money: some went to allow debtors to pay less than previously, some to reducing the losses of northern banks.

Two questions to see if you are budding banker material. First, after the write-off, what happens to bond prices in the secondary market? Second, why is it necessary for *all* creditors to agree the write-off at the same instant? Don't read on. Think.

First, if the secondary market thinks the country can now meet in full its obligations as newly defined, bonds will no longer trade at a discount in the secondary market. They should trade at par. The figure shows, for three of the big Latin American debtors, how secondary market prices recovered as a combination of austerity and organized write-offs restored creditworthiness. The figure confirms that creditworthiness improved not with the austerity of 1987, but with the announcement of the Brady Plan in 1989.

Second, suppose there were two creditors, a UK and a German bank, each owed half the money. Initially, bonds trade at only 20 per cent of par value. The UK bank alone writes off all the bonds *it* has bought. Now all the borrower's trade surplus can go towards paying off the German bank. The bonds *it* holds jump in second-hand value from, say, 20 to 40 per cent of par value. Since it is less than 100 per cent, the LDC is still not paying in full, and the bank is still insisting that it pay as much as it can. Thus, the effect of the generosity of the UK bank (perhaps assisted by well-meaning UK taxpayers who supported the write-off) is *entirely to benefit the German bank, not the LDC borrower!*

Thus, there is a free-rider problem. Every creditor wants every other creditor to be the first to offer write-offs. Left to themselves, no write-offs ever occur. The success of the Brady Plan was to orchestrate world

agencies (IMF, World Bank, etc.) to shepherd the different creditors into the same fold at the same time. Together, they were able to internalize the externality and co-operate on a solution.

Source: *The Economist*, 12 September 1992.

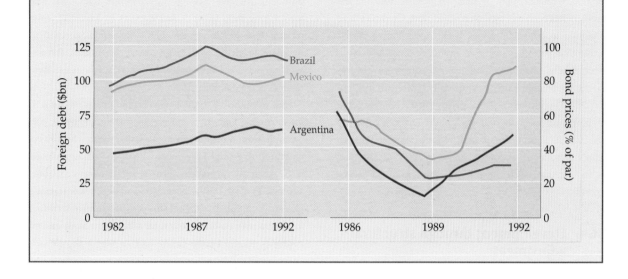

in Table 36-7 we look not at the debt/GNP ratio but the ratio of debt service to exports. Debt service is the flow of interest payments on the existing debt. Table 36-7 shows that for many countries the increase in the ratio of debt service to exports has increased much more sharply than the simple debt/GNP ratio. It explains why debtor countries were hurting so much.

Default and debt rescheduling   Suppose you are the government of a big debtor country, and the only way to meet the burden of debt interest (and repayment of the original loan) is to plunge your economy into a deep and long recession. This will slash imports and allow export revenue to go to servicing the debt. Politically, you are in big trouble. Voters won't put up with austerity for long.

Do you have any other options? First, you can call in the IMF and the World Bank. Under their *adjustment programmes* you can probably get a short-term loan to pay your other creditors. But these international agencies will insist that you take tough action to get the long-run position under control.

Second, you can go to your creditors – in this case mainly the large private banks of the world's richest economies – and seek a debt rescheduling.

Debt rescheduling is an agreement with creditors to pay back over a longer payback period with a lower repayment per period.

If you think your economy will expand in the future this may be a good strategy, and you can grow your way out of trouble without too much short-run pain.

If things are even more desperate, you may consider outright default or refusal to repay what you owe. Obviously, this deals with the immediate burden of the debt, but what are the costs? In the most extreme case, governments of the creditors may think about sending in their armies, though this has almost never happened. But governments of creditors might attempt to exert what leverage they could through international negotiations, trade embargoes, and so on. Economists are more interested in a direct market mechanism which might have the same deterrent effect.

When countries borrow in world financial markets, they do not all face the same interest rate. Like individuals, riskier countries face higher interest rates, which build in a *risk premium* to cover the possibility of default. Hence it is possible that countries that default face prohibitive risk premia when they try to borrow in the future. The knowledge that this will happen may be sufficient to deter them from defaulting in the first place.

What has happened in practice? First, there have been very few outright defaults. Second, and somewhat surprisingly, there is very little evidence that, as a country's debt position becomes more risky, the financial markets substantially raise the interest rate on new borrowing. So the deterrent effect may be small. In practice, much of the problem has been met by debt rescheduling. Creditors have preferred to get some money back over a longer period rather than provoke debtors to announce outright default. And, finally, under international pressure from governments, the creditor banks have actually written off much of the debt. This means they acknowledge that it is never going to be repaid even though the debtor has not explicitly announced a complete default. Many famous Western banks announced operating losses as they set off bad debts against their healthy profits from domestic operations.

36-6 Development through structural adjustment

Poor countries are poor not because they have massive unused capacity but because their level of potential output is so low. Investment may be necessary to improve human and physical infrastructure, but investment is not sufficient. We only have to recall that the Soviet bloc spent decades restraining consumption in order to create resources for high levels of investment. By the 1970s and 1980s, the rate of return on this investment was close to zero. Their economies stagnated.

Productivity growth need not come from additions to capital: it can also come from using more efficiently the resources already available. In Section 36-4 we noted that countries that had been exposed to the world economy had grown more rapidly than those which had cut themselves off behind protective tariffs. One theme of advice to LDCs in the 1990s was an emphasis on structural adjustment.

Structural adjustment is the pursuit of supply-side policies aimed at increasing potential output by increasing efficiency.

Examples of such policies are reductions in government subsidies to industry, privatization, lower levels of protection against imports, broader and less distortionary tax rates, less government intervention to ration and allocate credit by quota rather than by price. This pursuit of microeconomic efficiency has usually been underpinned by a recommendation to abolish large budget deficits, financed by money creation and causing endemic inflation.

Structural adjustment policies were already being encouraged in LDCs before the Soviet bloc abandoned central planning after 1989, but the former communist 'transition economies' were encouraged to make structural adjustment the centrepiece of reform. Even in OECD economies, greater stress on supply-side policies after 1980 took a long time to work and appears to have had only modest measurable success. LDCs sometimes claim that unpalatable medicine is being forced down their throats as the price for loans and aid from rich countries. Two rejoinders are possible.

First what the doctor dispenses is rarely pleasant but it is often useful. Second, we have increasing evidence, for example from transition economies, that those which have embraced structural adjustment with more enthusiam have also generally achieved greater subsequent economic success. In part this is a chicken-and-egg phenomenon. Countries confident of their future prospects and committed to reform may embrace structural adjustment more easily; countries fearful of the future and in which the debate still rages about which economic system is appropriate are countries more likely to find reasons to go slow on structural adjustment. Nevertheless, in economics as in medicine, we have little evidence that delaying the treatment is usually good for the patient.

36-7 Aid

Many of the complaints of the poor south come down to the view that the rich north should provide them with more aid.

Aid is an international transfer payment from rich countries to poor countries.

Such aid can take many forms: subsidized loans, outright gifts of food or machinery, or technical help and the free provision of expert advisers.

The basic issue is a moral or value judgement about equality. Within a country the government usually makes transfer payments to the poor, financed by taxes on the rich, thereby implementing a view of society as a whole that the income distribution thrown up by market forces is unfair and inequitable.

The same value judgement lies at the heart of aid or transfer payments between countries. However, it is complicated by two additional factors. First, within a country with a sense of national identity and social cohesion, it may seem right that the government should be concerned with *all* its citizens. But there is no single government of the world that can accept worldwide responsibility for welfare. Governments of individual countries, and the citizens they represent, may feel much less responsibility for the welfare of people of a different nationality in a distant country, of which they have little knowledge or experience. Second, the issue is complicated by history. Many people of the south feel that the prosperity of the north was first established during a colonial period when the resources of the south were exploited. Aid seems at least partial compensation. The northern countries do not share this interpretation of history.

Aid and the recipient countries

If aid is to be given, does it matter in what form it is given? Many LDCs believe the single most important contribution the rich countries can make is to provide free access for the LDCs to the markets of the developed countries. 'Trade, not aid' is the slogan. Just as the best service a domestic government can render a 30-year-old redundant steel worker may be to provide retraining to allow a useful working life for another 30 years, LDCs believe that trade rather than handouts is a more effective and more lasting form of assistance and encouragement.

Critics of existing aid programmes also argue that the donor countries should do more to check up on who is actually benefiting from their transfers. It is argued that too much aid finds its way into the hands of the ruling elite in the recipient countries rather than the poorest people for whom it was intended.

Of course, some people in rich countries like to exaggerate the extent of government corruption in poorer countries. More practically, recipient governments dislike donors telling them what to do, and it is usually necessary to channel aid through recipient governments.

Whenever aid and redistribution are discussed, it is useful to recall the analogy of a leaking bucket. When transfers are made, it is like transferring water in a leaky bucket. Some of the water leaks out (it disappears along the way), but some makes it to the other end and is used for the purpose that was intended. Whether the process is worthwhile depends on how fast the water leaks and how urgently the water is needed at the other end. And in the meantime, we should be looking for buckets with fewer holes.

Aid and migration

The quickest way to equalize world income distribution would be to permit free migration between countries. Residents of poor countries could go elsewhere in search of higher incomes. And in emigrating, they would increase the capital and land per worker for those who stayed behind.

Nor is this idea entirely fanciful. The massive movements of population from Europe to the Americas and the colonies in the nineteenth and early twentieth centuries represented an income-equalizing movement of this sort. Since the Second World War the major migrations have been temporary, although the steady flow of Mexicans (illegally) across the US border is one major exception. More common has been the EU's use of temporary migrant labour from Turkey, the Balkans, and North Africa, which countries have all benefited from payments sent home to their families by workers temporarily abroad. Similarly, Egypt, India, and Pakistan receive significant transfer payments from workers temporarily abroad. And in 1989–90 we saw substantial westward migration from Eastern Europe as the barriers came tumbling down.

None the less, there is no free and unrestricted immigration to the rich countries today. Indeed, even migrant workers are frequently outlawed. One difference between conditions today and conditions during the massive migrations of the nineteenth century is that there are now extensive systems of welfare and public health in rich countries. Quite apart from any racial or religious arguments, opponents of immigration say that existing residents would end up subsidizing unskilled immigrants who would spend most of their lives receiving public handouts.

The United States grew extremely quickly during the period of large-scale immigration. With economies of scale, it is not clear that existing residents inevitably lose out by admitting immigrants. Although fascinating, the question is largely academic. At present there is little prospect of the rich countries allowing immigration on a significant scale, least of all from the poorest countries of the world economy.

SUMMARY

● The call for a New International Economic Order (NIEO) was an attempt by LDCs to get a larger share of the world's income and wealth. It reflected the extreme inequality between the rich north and the poor south. Half the world's population had an annual income of scarcely more than £220 per person in 1996.

● The south complains that (*a*) markets for their primary products are controlled by the north; (*b*) northern protectionism is hampering their prospects for industrial development; (*c*) borrowing is too expensive; (*d*) austere and unpopular domestic policies are being forced upon them; and (*e*) simple justice dictates that the north should take practical steps to close the north–south gap.

● In the world's poorest countries, population growth is faster than the rate at which supplies of other factors can be increased. Hence labour productivity is low and, after provision for consumption, there are few spare resources to increase human and physical capital. It is hard to break out of this vicious circle.

● The downward trend in real prices, price volatility, and danger of extreme concentration in a single commodity have made LDCs reluctant to pursue development by exploiting a comparative advantage in primary products. Buffer stocks and cartel supply restrictions have proved difficult to organize, with the conspicuous exception of OPEC.

● LDCs are increasing their export of labour-intensive manufactures. Although the LDCs are beginning from a small base, their market share could quickly become much more significant.

● Industrial countries are tempted to protect their declining manufacturing industries. Yet they would probably do better by encouraging adjustment towards the industries in which their comparative advantage now lies.

● Structural adjustment policies aim to improve incentives and the efficiency with which existing resources are used.

● LDCs ran large deficits, financed by external borrowing. Larger debts and high interest rates led to threats of default and an international debt crisis.

● Increasing financial market integration in the 1990s led to large capital inflows to LDCs. When investors got scared, many LDCs faced drastic crises.

● Trade may help the LDCs more effectively than aid. Migration would help equalize world incomes but there is little prospect of rich countries allowing significant immigration.

KEY TERMS

◆ **Less developed countries (LDCs)**   603

◆ **Primary products**   606

◆ **Buffer stocks**   608

◆ **Import substitution**   609

◆ **Export-led growth**   609

◆ **International debt crisis**   611

◆ **Debt rescheduling**   613

◆ **Structural adjustment**   614

◆ **Aid**   614

REVIEW QUESTIONS

1 Discuss two forces tending to reduce the real price of agricultural produce in the long run.

2 How would a world boom affect a country specializing in producing copper?

3 Why have LDCs been particularly successful in exporting textiles, clothing, and leather footwear?

4 (a) Describe how a buffer stock scheme works. (b) What could go wrong? (c) Why don't private speculators smooth out prices of primary products in any case? (d) Does your answer to (c) help you answer (b)?

5 Can a small LDC gain by a policy of import substitution?

6 How could rich countries best help the poor countries?

7 Why might a floating exchange rate insulate an LDC from capital flows more effectively than a pegged exchange rate?

8 What are the complaints of the LDCs that have led to their call for an NIEO? Do you think this call will be heeded?

9 *Common fallacies* Show why the following statements are incorrect. (a) Aid is all the help LDCs need. (b) Europe's problem is competition from cheap labour in LDCs. (c) LDCs do best by sticking to production of raw materials for the world economy.

Index

Key terms appear in **bold** type; *n* following a page number indicates a footnote